MICROECONOMICS

MICROECONOMICS

Theory and Applications

Fifth Edition

DOMINICK SALVATORE

Fordham University

New York   Oxford
OXFORD UNIVERSITY PRESS
2009

Oxford University Press, Inc., publishes works that further Oxford University's
objective of excellence in research, scholarship, and education.

Oxford   New York
Auckland   Cape Town   Dar es Salaam   Hong Kong   Karachi
Kuala Lumpur   Madrid   Melbourne   Mexico City   Nairobi
New Delhi   Shanghai   Taipei   Toronto

With offices in
Argentina   Austria   Brazil   Chile   Czech Republic   France   Greece
Guatemala   Hungary   Italy   Japan   Poland   Portugal   Singapore
South Korea   Switzerland   Thailand   Turkey   Ukraine   Vietnam

Published by Oxford University Press, Inc.
198 Madison Avenue, New York, New York 10016
http://www.oup.com

Oxford is a registered trademark of Oxford University Press

Library of Congress Cataloging-in-Publication Data

Salvatore, Dominick.
   Microeconomics: theory and applications/Dominick Salvatore.—5th ed.
     p. cm.
   Includes bibliographical references and index.
   ISBN 978-0-19-533610-8 (cloth: alk. paper) 1. Microeconomics. I. Title.
   HB172.S139 2009
   338.5—dc22   2008032928

Printing number: 9 8 7 6 5 4 3 2 1

Printed in the United States of America
on acid-free paper

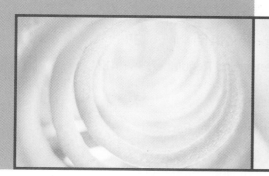

BRIEF CONTENTS

* Core Chapter

v

_____

* Core Chapter

CONTENTS

LIST OF EXAMPLES AND AT THE FRONTIER

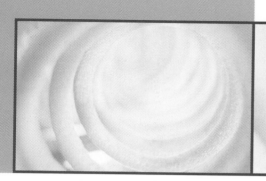

PREFACE

This is the fifth edition of a text that has enjoyed enviable market success in an increasingly crowded field and that has been adopted at hundreds of colleges throughout the United States and the English-speaking world. The text has also been translated into several languages.

I had three principal aims in writing this text: to present a judicious blend of the standard topics of traditional microeconomic theory and the many exciting recent developments in the field; to bring important but neglected international aspects into the course; and to devise a number of fresh, realistic, and truly useful examples that could vividly demonstrate modern microeconomic theory at work.

This is a text for modern undergraduate courses in intermediate microeconomics in economics and business programs. A prior course in principles of economics is required, and only simple geometry is used. There is an optional mathematical appendix at the end of the text for students who have had calculus.

THE MODERN APPROACH TO MICROECONOMICS

A unique feature of this text is that it presents a judicious blend of all the standard topics of traditional microeconomic theory as well as the many exciting recent developments in the field. *Some of the exciting new theoretical developments covered in this text are:* behavioral economics, learning curves, open innovation maker, new pricing practices, contestable markets, experimental economics, new advances in game theory, financial microeconomics, the theory of public choice, industrial policies and firm competitiveness, and the economics of information.

Each chapter has a section called "At the Frontier," which presents recent and exciting applications or more advanced theoretical developments in microeconomics today. Some of these are Nonclearing Markets Theory; New Markets and New Competition on the Internet; The New Computer-Aided Production Revolution and the International Competitiveness of U.S. Firms; Minimizing Costs Internationally—The New Economies of Scale; Auctioning Airwaves; Near-Monopoly Lands Microsoft in the Courts; The Art of Devising Airfares; The Virtual Corporation; Derivatives: Useful but Dangerous; and The Internet and the Information Revolution.

INTERNATIONAL DIMENSION OF MICROECONOMICS

Another unique feature of this text is the introduction of an international dimension into microeconomics to reflect the globalization of production and distribution in today's world. Other microeconomics texts approach microeconomics as if the international economy did not exist. However, many of the commodities we consume are imported, and firms today purchase many inputs abroad and sell an increasing share of their outputs overseas. Even more importantly, domestic firms face more and more competition from foreign producers. None of these issues are reflected in current microeconomic texts, and I feel it is time to rectify such deficiencies by incorporating international ramifications throughout the intermediate course.

Modern microeconomics should deal with the effect of imports on domestic prices, the international convergence of tastes, technological progress and international competitiveness, minimizing costs internationally, the new economies of scale, dumping, immigration and domestic wages, domestic production and strategic trade policies, and other such topics.

PUTTING THE THEORY TO WORK

To introduce more realism than most other microeconomics texts offer, this text includes five to eight demarked examples in each chapter—not the usual tired examples but truly relevant and modern ones. These examples (including At the Frontier 146 in all—more than in any other text) show how theory can be used to analyze and yield possible solutions to important present-day economic problems. My intention is to demonstrate that only by "putting theory to work" does theory truly come alive. Examples deepen understanding of the theory and enhance motivation by displaying the usefulness of theory in specific modern contexts.

Some of the exciting new examples are: Fighting the Drug War by Reducing Demand and Supply; Equilibrium Price by Auction; Giffen Behavior Found!; Gillette Introduces the Sensor and Mach3 Razors—Two Truly Global Products; Behavioral Economics in Finance; What Is an "American" Car?; America's Gambling Craze; How Do Firms Get New Technology?; The Market-Sharing Ivy League Cartel and Financial-Aid Leveraging; Strategic Moves and Countermoves by Airbus and Boeing; Deregulation and the New Merger Boom; From Welfare to Work—The Success of Welfare Reform in the United States; Congestion Pricing; The Market for Dumping Rights; and Do Golden Parachutes Reward Failure?

OTHER INNOVATIVE FEATURES OF THIS BOOK

I have tried to balance traditional topics with contemporary concerns in the following ways.

The chapter on *Choice Under Uncertainty* (Chapter 6) reflects the fact that most consumer choices in the real world are made under conditions of uncertainty rather than certainty. The chapter includes a discussion of how risk and uncertainty affect demand choices, how to measure risk, utility theory and risk aversion, and insurance and gambling.

The chapter on *Game Theory* (Chapter 12) presents a clear introduction to advances that have been made in this field, and it provides significant insights into modern business behavior in oligopolistic markets. There is a discussion of the prisoners' dilemma, price and nonprice competition, threats, commitments, credibility, entry deterrence, repeated games, and strategic moves.

A chapter on *Market Structure, Efficiency, and Regulation* (Chapter 13) examines the efficiency implications of monopoly, monopolistic competition, and oligopoly. It also evaluates the case for deregulation of economic activities.

Chapter 16 concentrates on *Financial Microeconomics*. Financial microeconomics, in general, and the cost of capital, in particular, are of growing importance in today's world, but they are not covered in most other microeconomics texts.

The Economics of Information (Chapter 19)—another important, modern topic—is covered by a full-length chapter. The chapter deals with the economics of search, asymmetric information and adverse selection, moral hazard, market signaling, the principal-agent problem, the efficiency wage theory, and other topics.

Other important topics covered are: the concept of the margin as the key unifying theme in all of microeconomics, the characteristics approach to consumer demand theory, behavioral economics, the open innovation model, the new economies of scale, two-part tariff, tying, bundling, limit pricing, cost-plus pricing, contestable markets, experimental economics, the theory of public choice, and effluent fees for optimal pollution control.

More advanced optional topics are covered (in chapter appendices): theory of revealed preference, the characteristics approach to consumer demand theory, index numbers and changes in consumer welfare, demand estimation and forecasting, Cobb–Douglas production function, extensions and uses of production and cost analysis, the Cournot and Stackelberg models, and others.

The *At the Frontier* section in each chapter presents very recent applications or more advanced theoretical developments in microeconomics.

NEW OR EXPANDED TREATMENT IN THE FIFTH EDITION

- The number of examples has been increased to 146 in this edition; previous examples were either replaced with more recent ones or updated.
- Nonclearing market theories and auctions are examined in Chapter 2.
- The theory of revealed preference is presented in Chapter 3.
- The characteristics approach to consumer demand theory is introduced in Chapter 4.
- Chapter 6, on choice under uncertainty, has been expanded by the inclusion of behavioral economics
- The new production revolution and the open innovation model are examined in Chapter 7.
- The new international economies of scale are discussed in Chapter 8.
- Chapter 12, on game theory, has been expanded with new real-world examples.
- The functioning of markets and experimental economics is examined in Chapter 13.
- The economics of discrimination is discussed in Chapter 15.
- Measures of income inequalities and rising income inequalities in the United States are examined in Chapter 17.
- Efficiency versus equity in U.S. tax reform is discussed in Chapter 18.
- Internet site addresses for the most important topics are presented in each chapter.

ORGANIZATION OF THE TEXT

The text is organized into six parts.

- *Part One* (Chapters 1 and 2) introduces microeconomic theory and reviews some principles of economics. This part shows clearly the importance and relevance of the international dimension in microeconomic theory and how it will be integrated into this text.

- *Part Two* (Chapters 3–6) presents the theory of consumer behavior and demand. It examines how consumers maximize utility and how an individual's and the market's demand curves are derived. It shows the measurement and usefulness of the various demand elasticities, and it examines choice under uncertainty.
- *Part Three* (Chapters 7–9) examines the theory of production, cost, and pricing in competitive markets. The international aspects of domestic production are shown throughout.
- *Part Four* (Chapters 10–13) focuses on the theory of the firm in imperfectly competitive markets. It brings together the theory of consumer behavior and demand (from Part Two) and the theory of production and costs (from Part Three) to analyze how price and output are determined under various types of imperfectly competitive markets.
- *Part Five* (Chapters 14–16) examines the theory of input pricing and employment (i.e., how input prices and the level of their employment are determined in the market). As in previous parts of the text, the presentation of the theory is reinforced with many real-world examples and important modern applications.
- *Part Six* (Chapters 17–19) presents the theory of general equilibrium and welfare economics, examines the role of the government in the economy, and deals with the economics of information. This part interrelates with material covered in all the previous parts of the text.

The twelve core chapters are 1–5, 7–11, and 13–14. Additional chapters and topics may be emphasized at the discretion of the instructor.

PEDAGOGICAL FEATURES

This text has been carefully planned to facilitate student learning using the following pedagogical features.

- The main sections of each chapter are numbered for easy reference, and longer sections are broken into two or more subsections.
- All of the graphs and diagrams are carefully explained in the text and then summarized briefly in the captions.
- Diagrams are generally drawn on numerical scales to allow the reading of answers in actual numbers rather than simply as distances. Consistent, judicious use of color and shading in the illustrations aid student understanding.
- No calculus is used in the text, but an extensive (and optional) Mathematical Appendix is given at the end of the book.
- A glossary of important terms is given at the end of the text.

Each chapter also contains the following teaching aids:

- All chapters begin with a list of learning objectives.
- A side (margin) glossary of all important terms has been added in this edition.
- Concept Checks have been added in each chapter.
- Key terms are boldfaced when they are first introduced and are listed at the end of each chapter; definitions are given in the margin near their first text use and are provided again, arranged alphabetically, in the Glossary at the end of the text.
- A *Summary* reviews the main points covered in the chapter.

- Twelve *Review Questions* help the student remember the material covered in the chapter.
- Twelve *Problems* ask students to apply and put to use what they learned from the chapter. Answers to selected problems, marked by an asterisk (*), are provided at the end of the book for the type of quick feedback that is so essential to effective learning.

ACCOMPANYING SUPPLEMENTS

The following ancillaries are available for use with this book.

1. A substantial *Instructor's Manual,* written by the text author, is available. It includes chapter objectives, lecture suggestions, detailed answers to all end-of-chapter questions and problems, a set of 25 multiple-choice questions and answers for each chapter that I personally feel cover the most important ideas in each chapter. The *Manual* also includes *additional examples and problems* (with answers) for class discussions and/or examinations. Finally, there is an annotated list of *Supplementary Readings* with references on the various topics covered in each chapter. The *Manual* was prepared with as much care as the text itself.
2. A separate *Test Bank,* prepared by Professor Mary Lesser of Iona College, contains nearly 1,000 multiple-choice questions with answers and is available to adopters of the text. This comprehensive *Test Bank,* more extensive than that of any competing text, is also available in computerized form for custom test-making on IBM PCs, Macintosh, and compatibles.
3. PowerPoint presentations of all figures and tables in the text are available to adopters of the text.
4. A *Study Guide,* prepared by Professor Mary Lesser of Iona College, is available from Oxford University Press to assist students in text content review and practice. It provides, for each text chapter, a review of concepts from previous chapters, an annotated chapter outline, fill in the blanks, and a wealth of multiple-choice questions with answers.
5. A *Website* for the text has been set up that includes at least one other example for each chapter and includes updates of other material.

ACKNOWLEDGMENTS

This text grew out of the undergraduate and graduate courses in microeconomics that I have been teaching at Fordham University during the past 30 years. I was very fortunate to have had many excellent students who, with their questions and comments, have contributed much to the clarity of exposition of this text.

I owe a great intellectual debt to my brilliant former teachers: William Baumol (New York University and Princeton University), Victor Fuchs (Stanford University and National Bureau of Economic Research), Jack Johnston (University of California), and Lawrence Klein (University of Pennsylvania and Wharton School of Business). It is incredible how many of the insights that one gains as a superb economist's student live on for the rest of one's life.

Many of my colleagues in the Department of Economics at Fordham University made numerous comments that significantly improved the final product. Professors Joseph Cammarosano in particular read through the entire manuscript and made invaluable notes for improvements. Many valuable suggestions were also made by Mary Burke, Fred Campano, Clive Daniel, Edward Dowling, Duncan James, Sophie Mitra, Henry Schwalbenberg, Booi Themeli, and Greg Winczewski.

The following professors reviewed the fifth edition of this text and made many valuable suggestions for improvements: John Cochran, Metropolitan State College of Denver; Mehidi Haririan, Bloomsburg University of Pennsylvania; Michael Magura, University of Toledo; Michael Szenberg, Pace University; Robert Whaples, Wake Forest University.

The following professors reviewed the previous editions of this book; their numerous and excellent comments resulted in a much improved text: Mary Acker, Iona College; Richard Ballman, Augustana College; Taeho Bark, Georgetown University; Joseph Barr, Framingham State College; William Beaty, Tarelton State University; Gordon Bennett, University of Southern Florida; Charles Berry, University of Cincinnati; Joseph Brada, Arizona State University; Charles Breeden, Marquette University; Robert Brooker, Gannon University; William Buchanan, University of Texas—Permian Basin; John Cochran, Metropolitan State College; Elizabeth Erikson, University of Akron; G. R. Ghorashi, Stockton State College; James Giordano, Villanova University; Paulette Graziano, University of Illinois; Ralph Gunderson, University of Wisconsin—Oshkosh; Simon Hakim, Temple University; John D. Harford, Cleveland State University; Mehdi Haririan, Bloomsburgh University of Pennsylvania; Andy Harvey, St. Mary's University; Paul M. Hayashi, The University of Texas—Arlington; Roy Hensley, University of Miami; Thomas R. Ireland, University of Missouri—St. Louis; Joseph Jadlow, Oklahoma State University; H. A. Jafri, Tarleton State University; Joseph Kiernin, Fairleigh Dickinson University; Janet Koscianski, Shippensburg University; Vani Kotcherlakota, University of Nebraska—Kerney; W. E. Kuhn, University of Alabama; Louis Lopilato, Mercy College; Mike Magura, University of Toledo; Jessica McGraw, University of Texas at Arlington; Larry Mielnicki, New York University; Stephen Miller, University of Connecticut; Thomas Mitchell., Southern Illinois University—Carbodale; Peter Murrell, University of Maryland; Kathryn Nantz, Fairfield University; Felix Ndukwe, Lafayette College; Patricia Nichol, Texas Tech University; Lee Norman, Idaho State University; Paul Okello, University of Texas—Arlington; Edward O'Rieley, North Dakota State University; Patrick O'Sullivan, State University of New York—Old Westbury; Donal Owen, Texas Tech University; Ray Pepin, Stonehill College; Martin Richardson, Georgetown University; Howard Ross, Baruch College; Timothy P. Roth, University of Texas—El Paso; Siamack Shojai, Manhattan College; Philip Sorensen, Florida State University; Charles Stuart, University of California—Santa Barbara; Michael Szenberg, Pace University; Allen Wilkins, University of Wisconsin—Madison; Anne E. Winkler, University of Missouri—St. Louis; H. A. Zavareei, West Virginia Institute of Technology.

Finally, I would like to express my gratitude to John Challice, Terry Vaughn, Catherine Rae, and the entire staff of Oxford University Press for their truly expert assistance throughout this project. My thanks also go to Mariana Barrientos, Mara Gabor, Jennifer Murray, Yumna Omar, and Russen Trendafilov (my graduate assistants) and to Angela Bates and Josephine Cannariato (the department secretaries at Fordham University) for their efficiency and cheerful dispositions.

Dominick Salvatore

ABOUT THE AUTHOR

Dominick Salvatore is Distinguished Professor of Economics at Fordham University in New York and Honorary Professor at the Shanghai Finance University and Hunan University. He is President of the North American Economic and Finance Association, Past President of the International Trade and Finance Association, Chairperson of the New York Academy of Sciences, and Research Associate at the Vienna University of Economics and Business. He is Chairman of the Society for Policy Modeling and consultant to the United Nations, the World Bank, and the Economic Policy Institute in Washington, D.C.

Professor Salvatore is the author of 48 books, including *Managerial Economics in a Global Economy,* 6th edition (2007), and *International Economics,* 9th edition (2007). He also wrote *Schaum's Outline of Microeconomic Theory,* 4th edition (2006), which has been translated into 10 languages and has sold more than one-half million copies.

Professor Salvatore is coeditor of the *Journal of Policy Modeling* and *Open Economies Review* and associate editor of *The American Economist* (the journal of the International Honor Society in Economics). His research has been published in more than 100 articles in leading scholarly journals and presented at numerous national and international conferences.

MICROECONOMICS

PART ONE

Introduction to Microeconomics

Part One (Chapters 1 and 2) presents an introduction to microeconomic theory and a review of some basic tools of economics. Chapter 1 deals with scarcity as the fundamental economic fact facing every society and examines the function and purpose of microeconomic theory and its methodology. Chapter 1 also discusses the concept of the margin as the central unifying theme in microeconomics and examines the importance of introducing an international dimension, or globalization, in microeconomic analysis. The "At the Frontier" section discusses agreement and disagreement among economists on the most important economic questions of the day. Chapter 2 is a brief review of the concepts of demand, supply, and equilibrium. In addition, the chapter examines the benefits and costs resulting from the growing interdependence of the United States in the world economy, while the "At the Frontier" section discusses nonclearing market theories.

Introduction

After Studying This Chapter, You Should Be Able to:

- Explain why scarcity is the fundamental economic fact of every society
- Identify the functions of any economic system
- Describe the circular flow of economic activity, the determination and function of prices, and the role of the government in the economic system
- Explain why the concept of the margin is the unifying theme in microeconomics
- Understand the importance of globalization in the study of microeconomics

Microeconomic theory is perhaps the most important course in all economics and business programs. Microeconomic theory can help us answer such questions as why there is a trade-off between spending on health care and spending on other goods and services; why the price of housing has risen sharply in recent years; why the price of beef is higher than the price of chicken; why the price of gasoline rose sharply during the 1970s and declined in the 1980s; why textiles are produced with much machinery and few workers in the United States but with many workers and a small amount of machinery in India; why there are only a handful of automakers but many wheat farmers in the United States; why the courts ordered the breakup of AT&T in 1982; why physicians earn more than cab drivers and college professors; why raising the minimum wage leads to increased youth unemployment; why environmental pollution arises and how it can be regulated; and why the government provides some goods and services such as national defense. Microeconomic theory provides the tools for understanding how the U.S. economy and most other economies operate.

Microeconomic theory is also the basis for most "applied" fields of economics such as industrial economics, labor economics, natural resources and environmental economics, agricultural economics, regional economics, public finance, development economics, and international economics.

In this introductory chapter, we define the subject matter and the methodology of microeconomics. We begin by examining the meaning of scarcity as the fundamental economic fact facing every society. We then discuss the basic functions that all economic systems must somehow perform and the way they are performed in a free-enterprise economic system, such as that of the United States. We also examine why the concept of the margin is the central unifying theme in microeconomics and the importance of introducing an international dimension into microeconomic analysis. Subsequently, we examine the role of theory or models in microeconomics, discuss the basic methodology of economics, and distinguish between positive and normative analysis. The "At the Frontier" section discusses agreement and disagreement among economists on the most important economic issues of the day.

1.1   WANTS AND SCARCITY

Economics The study of the allocation of scarce resources among alternative uses.

Economics deals with the allocation of scarce resources among alternative uses to satisfy human wants. The essence of this definition rests on the meaning of human wants and resources, and on the scarcity of economic resources in relation to insatiable human wants.

Can Human Wants Ever Be Fully Satisfied?

Human wants All the goods and services that individuals desire.

Human wants refer to all the goods, services, and conditions of life that individuals desire. These wants vary among different people, over different periods of time, and in different locations. However, human wants always seem to be greater than the goods and services available to satisfy them. Although we may be able to get all the hamburgers, beer, pencils, and magazines we desire, there are always more and better things that we are unable to obtain. In short, the sum total of all human wants can never be fully satisfied.

Economic resources Resources that are limited in supply or scarce and thus command a price.

Economic resources are the inputs, the factors, or the means of producing the goods and services we want. They can be classified broadly into *land* (or natural resources), *labor* (or human resources), and *capital.* These are the resources that firms must pay to hire. Land refers to the fertility of the soil, the climate, the forests, and the mineral deposits present in the soil. Labor refers to all human effort, both physical and mental, that can be directed toward producing desired goods and services. It includes entrepreneurial talent that combines other labor, capital, and natural resources to produce new, better, or cheaper products. Finally, capital refers to the machinery, factories, equipment, tools, inventories, irrigation, and transportation and communications networks. All of these "produced" resources facilitate the production of other goods and services. In the economist's sense, money is not capital because it does not produce anything. Money simply facilitates the exchange of goods and services.

Scarcity: The Pervasive Economic Problem

Resources have alternative uses. For example, a particular piece of land could be used for a factory, housing, roads, or a park. A laborer could provide cleaning services, be a porter, construct bridges, or provide other manual services. A student could be trained to become an accountant, a lawyer, or an economist. A tractor could be used to construct a road or a dam. Steel could be used to build a car or a bridge. Because economic resources are limited, they command a price. While air may be unlimited and free for the purpose of operating an internal-combustion engine, *clean* air to breathe is not free if it requires the installation and operation of antipollution equipment.

Because resources are generally limited, the amount of goods and services that any society can produce is also limited. Thus, the society must choose which commodities to produce and which to sacrifice. In short, society can only satisfy some of its wants. If human wants were limited or resources unlimited, there would be no scarcity and there would be no need to study economics.

✓ **Concept Check**
Why is scarcity the pervasive economic problem of every society?

Over time, the size and skills of the labor force rise, new resources are discovered and new uses are found for available land and natural resources, the nation's stock of capital is increased, and technology improves. Through these advances, the nation's ability to produce goods and services increases. But human wants always seem to move well ahead of society's ability to satisfy them. Thus, scarcity remains. Scarcity is the fundamental economic fact of every society (see Example 1–1).

EXAMPLE 1–1

More Health Care Means Less of Other Goods and Services

One of the most serious concerns of individuals, businesses, and governments in the United States and in most other countries today is the explosion of health-care costs. Nearly $1.9 trillion, or 16% of national income, was spent for health care in 2004 in the United States, up from 4% in 1940 and 7% in 1970. Health-care costs have thus risen much faster than income and now exceed $6,200 per person living in the United States. There is, of course, nothing wrong with spending more on health care if that is what society wants. But a higher proportion of income spent on health care means that proportionately less is available for all other goods and services. Resources are scarce and incomes are limited, and so we cannot have more of everything.

Despite spending more on health care than any other country, both in absolute amount and as a proportion of national income, millions of Americans have no medical insurance (most other advanced nations have universal health care), infant mortality is higher, and life expectancy is lower. What is even more serious is that large cost increases are built into the U.S. health-care system because of an aging population, the development of new and more expensive medical technologies and medicines, and the move to third-party (private and government-sponsored health insurance plans), which reduced the incentive to contain medical expenses.

In the attempt to contain costs, the United States rapidly moved to a system of managed care, or HMOs (health-maintenance organizations, the term commonly used for managed-care providers) during the past decade, and these now cover over 170 million people. The government picks up the tab for 40 million elderly and disabled Americans (through Medicare) and about 38 million poor (through the state–federal Medicaid scheme). This leaves nearly 46 million people, or 16% of Americans, uninsured.

HMOs try to contain health-care costs by providing a flat fee per person to health-care providers (physicians, hospitals, etc.) and limiting patients' access to specialists. This made physicians angry at their loss of income and made patients furious at the restrictions on the treatment that they can receive, and it prompted Congress to introduce a "Patients Bill of Rights" in order to overcome some of these restrictions. The upshot of all of this is that exploding health-care costs are likely to remain one of the most serious economic problems facing Americans (and people in other nations).

Sources: M. Feldstein, "The Economics of Health Care: What Have We Learned? What Have I Learned?," *American Economic Review,* May 1995, pp. 28–49; U. E. Reinhardt, "Health Care for the Aging Baby Boom: Lessons from Abroad," *Journal of Economic Perspectives,* Spring 2000, pp. 71–84; "Organizational Innovations to Contain Health Costs," *Economic Report of the President,* 2001, pp. 225–229; "Propelled by Drugs and Hospital Costs, Health Spending Surged in 2000," *New York Times,* January 8, 2002, p. 14; "Desperate Measures," *The Economist,* January 28, 2006, pp. 24–26; and "World's Best Medical Care?" *New York Times,* August 12, 2007, p. 9.

1.2   FUNCTIONS OF AN ECONOMIC SYSTEM

Price system The system in which economic activity is determined by commodity and resource prices.

Free-enterprise system The market organization where economic decisions are made by individuals and firms.

What to produce The goods and services a society chooses to produce and in what quantities.

How to produce The way resources or inputs are combined to produce goods and services.

Faced with the pervasiveness of scarcity, all societies, from the most primitive to the most advanced, must somehow determine (1) what to produce, (2) how to produce, (3) for whom to produce, (4) how to provide for the growth of the system, and (5) how to ration a given quantity of a commodity over time. Let us see how the **price system** performs each of these functions under a free-enterprise system (such as our own). In a **free-enterprise system** individuals own property and individuals and firms make private economic decisions.

What to produce refers to which goods and services a society chooses to produce and in what quantities to produce them. No society can produce all the goods and services it wants, so it must choose which to produce and which to forgo. Over time, only those goods and services for which consumers are willing and able to pay a price sufficiently high to cover at least the costs of production will generally be produced. Automobile manufacturers will not produce cars costing $1 million if no one is there to purchase them. Consumers can generally induce firms to produce more of a commodity by paying a higher price for it. On the other hand, a reduction in the price that consumers are willing to pay for a commodity will usually result in a decline in the output of the commodity. For example, an increase in the price of milk and a reduction in the price of eggs are signals to farmers to raise more cows and fewer chickens.

How to produce refers to the way in which resources or inputs are organized to produce the goods and services that consumers want. Should textiles be produced with a great deal of labor and little capital or with little labor and a great deal of capital? Since the prices of resources reflect their relative scarcity, firms will combine them in such a way as to minimize costs of production. By doing so, they will use resources in the most efficient and productive way to produce those commodities that society wants and values the most. When the price of a resource rises, firms will attempt to economize on the use of that resource and substitute cheaper resources so as to minimize their production costs. For example, a rise in the minimum wage leads firms to substitute machinery for some unskilled labor.

For whom to produce
The way that output is distributed among members of society.

Economic growth The increase in resources, technology, commodities, and incomes over time.

✓ Concept Check
What are the functions of any economic system?

Rationing over time
The allocation of a commodity over time.

For whom to produce deals with the way that the output is distributed among the members of society. Those individuals who possess the most valued skills or own a greater amount of other resources will receive higher incomes and will be able to pay and coax firms to produce more of the commodities they want. Their greater monetary "votes" enable them to satisfy more of their wants. For example, society produces more goods and services for the average physician than for the average clerk because the former has a much greater income than the latter.

In all but the most primitive societies there is still another function that the economic system must perform: It must provide for the growth of the nation. Although governments can affect the rate of **economic growth** with tax incentives and with incentives for research, education, and training, the price system is also important. For example, interest payments provide the savers an incentive to postpone present consumption, thereby releasing resources to increase society's stock of capital goods. Capital accumulation and technological improvements are stimulated by the expectations of profits. Similarly, the incentive of higher wages (the price of labor services) induces people to acquire more training and education, which increases their productivity. Through capital accumulation, technological improvements, and increases in the quantity and quality (productivity) of labor, a nation grows over time.

Finally, an economic system must allocate a given quantity of a commodity over time. **Rationing over time** is also accomplished by the price system. For example, the price of wheat is not so low immediately after harvest that all the wheat is consumed very quickly, thus leaving no wheat for the rest of the year. Instead, some people (speculators) will buy some wheat soon after harvest (when the price is low) and sell it later (before the next harvest) when the price is higher; the available wheat is thus rationed throughout the year.

1.3 MICROECONOMIC THEORY AND THE PRICE SYSTEM

In this section, we define the subject matter of microeconomic theory, briefly examine the determination and function of prices in a system of free enterprise, and show how governments affect the operation of the economic system. We will see that prices play such an important role that microeconomic theory is often referred to as "price theory."

The Circular Flow of Economic Activity

Microeconomic theory
The study of the economic behavior of *individual* decision-making units in a free-enterprise economy.

Macroeconomic theory The study of *aggregate* levels and variables of economic activity for the economy *as a whole.*

Microeconomic theory studies the economic behavior of *individual* decision-making units such as individual consumers, resource owners, and business firms, and the operation of individual markets in a free-enterprise economy. This is to be contrasted with **macroeconomic theory,** which studies (a) the total or *aggregate* level of output and national income and (b) the level of national employment, consumption, investment, and prices for the economy *viewed as a whole.* Both microeconomics and macroeconomics provide very useful tools of analysis and both are important. While macroeconomics often makes the headlines, microeconomics attempts to explain some of the most important economic and social problems of the day. These range from the high cost of energy, to welfare programs, environmental pollution, rent control, minimum wages, safety regulations, rising medical costs, monopoly, discrimination, labor unions, wages and leisure, crime and punishment, taxation and subsidies, and so on.

Microeconomics focuses attention on two broad categories of economic units: households and business firms, and it examines the operation of two types of markets: the market for goods and services, and the market for economic resources. The interaction of households and business firms in the markets for goods and services and in the markets for economic resources represents the core of the free-enterprise economic system. Specifically, households own the labor, the capital, the land, and the natural resources that business firms require to produce the goods and services households want. Business firms pay to households wages, salaries, interest, rents, and so on, for the services and resources that households provide. Households then use the income that they receive from business firms to purchase the goods and services produced by business firms. The income of households are the production costs of business firms. The expenditures of households are the receipts of business firms. The so-called **circular flow of economic activity** is complete.

Circular flow of economic activity The flow of resources from households to firms and the opposite flow of money incomes from firms to households.

The circular flow of economic activity can be visualized in Figure 1.1. The inner loop shows the flow of economic resources from households to business firms and the flow of goods and services from business firms to households. The outer loop shows the flow of money incomes from business firms to households and the flow of consumption expenditures from households to business firms. Thus, the inner loop represents production flows while the outer loop represents financial flows.

Looking at it from a different perspective, we see that the top part of Figure 1.1 shows the flow of goods and services from business firms to households and the opposite flow of consumption expenditures from households to business firms. Here are the markets where goods and services are bought and sold. The bottom part of Figure 1.1 shows the flow of resources from households to business firms and the opposite flow of money incomes to households. Here are the markets where resources or their services are bought and sold.

Specifically, the top loop shows consumers' purchases of foods, clothing, housing, health care, education, transportation, recreation, vacations, and so on, and the expenditures that consumers incur to pay for them. The bottom loop shows the labor time, the capital, the land, and the entrepreneurship that individuals provide to firms in return for

✓ Concept Check

What is the flow of economic activity in terms of resources and incomes?

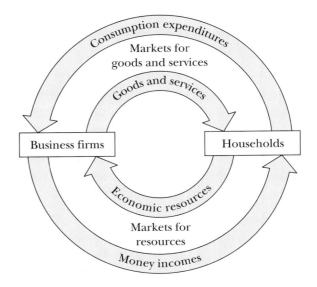

FIGURE 1.1   The Circular Flow of Economic Activity
The inner loop shows the flow of resources from households to business firms and shows the flow of goods and services from business firms to households. The outer loop shows the flow of money incomes from business firms to households and shows the flow of consumption expenditures from households to business firms. The prices of goods and services are determined in the top half of the figure, and the prices of resources are determined in the bottom half of the figure.

wages, interest, rent, and profits, which represent the incomes with which consumers purchase the goods and services they want.

Determination and Function of Prices

The prices of goods and services are determined in the markets for goods and services (the top half of Figure 1.1), while the prices of resources and their services are determined in the markets for resources (the bottom half of Figure 1.1). If households want to purchase more of a commodity than is placed on the market by business firms, the price of the commodity will be bid up until the *shortage* of the commodity is eliminated. This occurs because at a higher price, households will want to *purchase less* of the commodity while business firms will want to *produce more* of the commodity. For example, if automobile prices rise, consumers will want to purchase fewer automobiles while automakers will want to produce more automobiles. Automakers can produce more automobiles at higher prices because they are able to bid resources (labor, capital, and land) away from other uses.

On the other hand, if households want to purchase less of a commodity than business firms place on the market, the price of the commodity will fall until the *surplus* of the commodity disappears. This occurs because at a lower price, households will want to *purchase more* of the commodity while business firms will want to *produce less* of the commodity. For example, if consumers want to purchase less beef than farmers send to market, the price of beef falls until the quantity demanded of beef matches the quantity supplied. In the process, farmers will hire fewer resources so that some resources will be freed to produce more of other commodities that consumers value more highly. Thus, it is the system of commodity prices that determines which commodities are produced and in what quantities (the "what to produce" question of the previous section) and how resources are used.

Turning to factor markets, if households provide less of a resource or service than business firms want to hire at a given price, the price of the resource will be bid up until the shortage of the resource is eliminated. This occurs because at higher resource prices, households will usually provide more of the resource or service while business firms will economize on the use of the resource (so as to minimize production costs). For example, if hospitals want to hire more nurses than are available, nurses' salaries rise. This results in more people entering nursing schools and in hospitals economizing on the use of nurses (for example, by employing more orderlies at lower salaries to perform some of the tasks previously performed by nurses). The process continues until the adjustment (i.e., the shortage of nurses) is eliminated.[1]

On the other hand, if too much of a resource is made available at a given price, the price falls until the surplus is eliminated. This occurs because at lower resource prices, households will usually provide less of the resource or service while business firms will substitute in production the cheaper resource for the more expensive one (so as to minimize production costs). Thus, in a free-enterprise economy it is the system of resource prices that determines how production is organized and how the income of resource owners is established (the "how to produce" and the "for whom to produce" questions of the previous section).

✓ Concept Check
How are prices determined and what is their function?

---

[1] The shortage of nurses may last many years if the demand for hospital care and for nurses outstrips the increasing number of nurses being trained or if market imperfections and government involvement prevents wages from rising to the equilibrium level. This is what seems to have happened in fact in many areas of the United States.

Price theory
Another name for microeconomic theory that stresses the importance of prices.

It is because of the crucial function of prices in determining what goods are produced and in what quantities, how production is organized, and how output or income is distributed that microeconomic theory is often referred to as **price theory.**[2] Example 1–2 shows how changes in supply and demand affect the price of agricultural commodities in the United States and abroad.

EXAMPLE 1–2

Bad Weather and High Demand Send Wheat Prices Soaring

During 1988 and 1989, Kansas suffered the worst drought since the "dust bowl" days of the early 1930s. Kansas normally produces more than one-third of the nation's crop of hard red winter wheat (the wheat used for making bread), and with about 40% of this crop destroyed by the drought, wheat prices shot up from about $2.50 per bushel in 1987 to over $4.25 in spring 1989. American wheat stocks were heavily depleted, and American wheat exports fell sharply. The drought in the United States also encouraged Canada, Argentina, and Australia to plant more wheat and replace U.S. wheat exports to other nations such as Russia. The wheat market is actually one big global market.

Consumer prices in the United States did not increase very much, however, because a $1 loaf of bread contains only 4 cents' worth of wheat (the rest reflects manufacturing and marketing costs) and because food prices represent only one-sixth of the consumer price index. Most wheat farmers' income also increased because wheat prices rose proportionately more than the reduction in crops and because the U.S. government provided a subsidy ranging from $3.17 to $3.80 for each bushel of wheat lost to drought. The rains came back in 1990, however, and wheat output increased and wheat prices declined. The cycle of drought, reduced output, and rising prices followed by good weather, large outputs, and lower prices (and higher government subsidies) was repeated a number of times since the 1990s.

The weather affected the output of wheat not only in the United States but also in other large producing countries, such as Canada, Australia and Argentina—thus, influencing the world price, trade, and the consumption of wheat around the world. In February 2008, the price of wheat in the United States exceeded $10 per bushel (two-and-half times its price in 2006 and four times that in 2000) because of the combination of disappointing production levels due to bad weather and increased demand.

This example vividly portrays the workings of the price system, the effect of government intervention, and the large interdependence that exists in the world economy today.

Sources: T. Tregarthen, "Drought Sends Farm Prices Soaring," *The Margin,* January/February 1989, pp. 22–23; "Farmers Are Back in the Green," *Business Week,* June 11, 1990, pp. 18–19; "Strong Harvests Set to Restrain Wheat Price Rise," *Financial Times,* January 27, 2000, p. 34, and "In Price and Supply, wheat is the Unstable Staple," *New York Times,* February 13, 2008, p. 1.

---

[2] In imperfectly competitive markets (monopoly, monopolistic competition, and oligopoly) the price system does not function as smoothly as indicated above and the determination of commodity and resource prices and quantities is more complex.

What Role for the Government?

So far our discussion has deliberately excluded government. Bringing government into the picture will modify somewhat the operation of the system, but it will not, in a free-enterprise system such as that of the United States, replace the operation of markets. Governments affect the circular flow of economic activity by purchasing goods and services for public consumption (education, defense, police, and so on) that compete with privately consumed goods and services. Governments may themselves produce some goods and services, thereby leaving fewer resources for business firms to use. Most importantly, governments, through taxes and subsidies, usually redistribute income from the rich to the poor. By doing so, they can greatly affect the circular flow of economic activity. Governments also use taxes to discourage the consumption of certain commodities such as alcohol and tobacco and provide incentives for the consumption of others such as housing and education. Thus, the United States operates under a **mixed economy** comprising private enterprise and government actions and policies.

Although government policies certainly affect the circular flow of economic activity in a free-enterprise system, they do not replace the price system.[3] This can be contrasted with a centrally planned economy such as that of the former Soviet Union, where most economic decisions were made almost exclusively by government officials or planning committees. In that type of economy, the government rather than the market sets prices. The result is usually persistent shortages of certain commodities and excess production of others. Thus, central planning is usually less efficient than a free-enterprise system (see Example 1–3).

In the United States and other free-enterprise or mixed economies, the price system operates so smoothly that people are not even aware of it. Only on rare occasions (usually as a result of government interference) do we become aware that something is wrong. The long lines at most gas stations during the petroleum crisis in 1979 were the result of the U.S. government's attempt to keep gasoline prices below the market or equilibrium level. When price controls were eliminated and the price of gasoline was allowed to rise to the market level, gasoline lines disappeared. When bad weather sharply reduced the output of Florida oranges in 1977 and 1981 and that of fresh fruits and vegetables in 1984, no waiting lines were seen outside food stores in the United States. The prices of oranges and vegetables simply rose, and this rationed available supplies to match the amounts that consumers wanted to purchase at the higher prices.

Mixed economy An economy characterized by private enterprise and government actions and regulations.

✓ Concept Check
What is the role of the government in a mixed economy?

EXAMPLE 1–3

Economic Inefficiencies Cause Collapse of Communist Regimes

In 1957, Communist Party Chair Nikita Khrushchev proudly asserted that the Soviet Union would "bury" the United States—not with atomic warheads but with superior productive power. Instead, in 1989 the Soviet Union and former Eastern European

[3] Government sometimes does replace the price system in some markets by imposing price controls such as rent ceilings and minimum wages. In general, however, in a free-enterprise economy such as that of the United States, government works through the market (with taxes, subsidies, and state-owned enterprises) rather than supplanting it. See "How We Got Here," *Wall Street Journal*, September 27, 1999, pp. R6 and R8; and Mehdi Haririan, *State Owned Enterprises in a Mixed Economy* (Boulder: Westview Press, 1989).

communist regimes collapsed as a result of massive economic failures. Consumer goods were shabby, assortment was very limited, and shortages of even basic food-stuffs were common. Automobiles, refrigerators, TV sets, and other durable goods were primitive by world standards. In computers and machine tools, the former Soviet Union was a decade behind the United States and its standard of living was less than one-third that of the United States. These massive economic failures were the direct result of the command economy that operated throughout the communist world. Economic decisions were centralized, capital goods or the means of production were owned by the state, and incentives were lacking or grossly distorted.

The collapse of communism brought severe economic dislocations in the form of sharply reduced outputs, rising unemployment, rapid inflation, huge budget deficits, unsustainable international debts, and disrupted trade relations. Poland, Hungary, the Czech Republic, and the other countries in central and eastern Europe, as well as Russia and the other republics of the former Soviet Union have been struggling for the past two decades to set up working market economies. This is a monumental task after decades of central planning and gross inefficiencies.

The establishment of a market economy requires (1) freeing prices and wages from government control (so that goods and resources can be efficiently allocated by markets); (2) transferring productive resources from the state to private ownership (i.e., privatizing the economy); (3) opening the economy to competition and liberalizing international trade (i.e., replacing state trading with trade based on market principles); and (4) establishing the legal and institutional framework necessary for the functioning of a market economy (such as property rights, a Western-style banking system, a capital market, cost accounting, business law, etc.). The problems of transition to a market economy are enormous, and market economies are not yet fully operational in the former communist nations after nearly two decades of reforms. Despite communism's spectacular failure, some of Marx's ideas persist in the world to this day—and not only in Castro's Cuba and Chavez's Venezuela.

Sources: W. Easterly and Stanley Fischer, "What We Can Learn from the Soviet Collapse," *Finance and Development,* December 1994, pp. 2–5; "Assessing the Reform Record in the Transition Economies," *International Monetary Fund Survey,* January 9, 1995, pp. 1–6; D. Salvatore, "The Problems of Transition, EU Enlargement, and Globalization," *Empirica,* July 2001, pp. 1–21; and "Behold Marx's Twitch," *New York Times,* December 28, 2006, p. 9.

1.4   THE MARGIN: THE KEY UNIFYING CONCEPT IN MICROECONOMICS

In this section, we provide an overview of the crucial importance of the margin as the central unifying theme in all of microeconomics and examine some clarifications on its use.

The Crucial Importance of the Concept of the Margin

Because of scarcity, all economic activities give rise to some benefits but also involve some costs. The aim of economic decisions is to maximize net benefits. Net benefits increase as long as the marginal or extra benefit from an action exceeds the marginal or

Marginal benefit The change in the total benefit resulting from an economic action.

Marginal cost The change in the total cost resulting from an economic action.

Concept of the margin The central unifying theme in all of microeconomics

Marginal analysis The analysis whereby any activity should be pursued until the marginal benefit equals the marginal cost.

extra cost resulting from the action. Net benefits are maximized when the **marginal benefit** is equal to the **marginal cost** (see Example 1–4). This concept applies to all economic decisions and market transactions. It applies to consumers in spending their income, to firms in organizing production, to workers in choosing how many hours to work, to students in deciding how much to study each subject and how many hours to work after classes, and to individuals in determining how much to save out of their income. It also applies in deciding how much pollution society should allow, in choosing the optimal amount of information to gather, in choosing the optimal amount of government regulation of the economy, and so on. Indeed, the **concept of the margin** and **marginal analysis** represent the key unifying concepts in all of microeconomics.

Specifically, the aim of consumers is to maximize the satisfaction or net benefit that they receive from spending their limited income. The net benefit or satisfaction of a consumer increases as long as the marginal or extra benefit that he or she receives from consuming one additional unit of a commodity exceeds the marginal or opportunity cost of forgoing or giving up the consumption of another commodity. A consumer maximizes satisfaction when the marginal benefit that he or she receives per dollar spent on every commodity is equal. More concretely, if the satisfaction or benefit that an individual gets from consuming one extra hamburger with a price of $2 is more than twice as large as the satisfaction of consuming a hot dog with a price of $1, then the individual would increase net benefits or satisfaction by consuming more hamburgers and fewer hot dogs. As the individual does this, the marginal benefit of consuming each additional hamburger declines, while the marginal loss in giving up each additional hot dog increases. The individual maximizes net benefits when the marginal benefit per dollar spent on each becomes equal. This central unifying theme of the margin in consumer behavior and demand is examined in Part Two (Chapters 3–6) of the text.

EXAMPLE 1–4

Marginal Analysis in TV Advertising

Table 1.1 shows a firm's total and marginal benefits and costs of increasing the number of TV spots per week. With each additional TV spot, the firm's total benefits (sales or revenues) increase, but the extra or marginal benefit declines. The reason is that each additional TV spot reaches fewer and fewer additional people and becomes less effective in inducing more consumers to buy the product. At the same time, the extra

TABLE 1.1   Benefits and Costs of TV Spots

Number of TV Spots	Total Benefits	Marginal Benefits	Total Costs	Marginal Cost	Net Benefit
1	$20,000	—	$4,000	—	$16,000
2	34,000	$14,000	8,000	$4,000	26,000
3	42,000	8,000	12,000	4,000	30,000
4	**46,000**	**4,000**	**16,000**	**4,000**	**30,000**
5	48,000	2,000	20,000	4,000	28,000
6	49,000	1,000	24,000	4,000	25,000

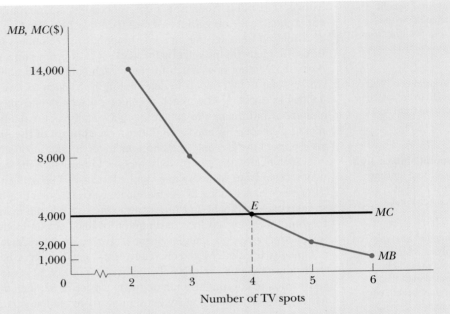

FIGURE 1.2   Marginal Benefit and Marginal Cost of TV Advertising   The marginal benefit (*MB*) of each additional TV spot declines while the marginal cost (*MC*) is constant at $4,000. The net benefit is maximized at point *E* at which *MB* = *MC*.

or marginal cost of each TV spot remains at $4,000. The last column of the table shows that the net benefit (total benefits or revenues minus total costs) is maximized at $30,000 when the firm airs four TV spots per week, at which the marginal benefit equals the marginal cost. Note that in cases like this where we deal with whole units (i.e., where we cannot buy a fraction of a TV spot), the net benefit of $30,000 also results when the firm airs three TV spots per week, but only with four TV spots is the marginal benefit equal to the marginal cost, and this is the general rule that we follow to maximize net benefits (see point *E* in Figure 1.2).

To be noted is that the very high cost TV advertising today is a far cry from the first TV ad (a 20-second spot for a Bulova clock that was broadcast on July 1, 1941) that cost $9. Today the same TV ad would cost about $900. As the cost of reaching mass audiences rises and direct marketing to individuals becomes more effective (see "At the Frontier" for Chapter 5), advertisers are shifting some of their advertising expenditures to these other channels (the ability to measure the effectiveness of advertising on sales remains, however, elusive).

Sources: "Ad Industry Benefits of a Recovery," *Wall Street Journal,* February 8, 1993, p. B1; "Target Micromarkets Is Way to Success," *Wall Street Journal,* May 31, 1995; p. A1; "Commercial Breakdown," *Financial Times,* August 1999, p. 11; and "Internet Advertising—The Ultimate Marketing Machine," *The Economist,* July 6, 2006, Special Report.

Similarly, it pays for a firm to expand output as long as the marginal or extra revenue that it receives from selling each additional unit of the commodity exceeds the marginal or extra cost of producing it. But as the firm produces and sells more units of the commodity, the marginal revenue may decline while its marginal cost rises. The firm maximizes total profits when the marginal revenue is equal to the marginal cost. The application of the marginal concept in firms' production decisions is examined in detail in Part Three (Chapters 7–9) of the text. The same general concept applies to an individual's decision on how many hours to work. The individual will maximize welfare when the marginal benefit he or she receives from the wages of an extra hour of work just matches the marginal cost in terms of the leisure or earnings and consumption foregone by not working the extra hour. The optimal amount of savings by an individual is the amount at which the marginal benefit from the interest earned from saving an extra dollar just matches the marginal cost of postponing spending the dollar on present consumption. These applications of marginal analysis are examined in Part Five (Chapters 14–16).

✓ Concept Check
What is marginal analysis?

Similarly, the optimal amount of government regulation of the economic system is the amount at which the marginal benefit of such intervention just matches its marginal cost. The same concept applies to the gathering of information. Gathering information provides some benefits but involves some costs. Thus, the optimal amount of information gathering is the amount at which the marginal benefit equals the marginal cost. These uses of the marginal concept are examined in Part Six (Chapters 17–19) of the text.

Some Clarifications on the Use of the Margin

Several clarifications are in order on the application of the concept of the margin and marginal analysis in microeconomics. First, the maximization of net benefits by marginal analysis does not imply that individuals are entirely selfish and does not preclude a certain degree of altruistic behavior. A more selfish person will maximize satisfaction in terms of material goods and services that the individual himself or herself consumes. A less selfish person will maximize satisfaction by using part of his or her income or resources in helping others. Similarly, a firm may contribute part of its profits to some "worthy causes" or choose to maximize sales rather than profits. Second, individuals, firms, and governments seldom have all the information required to maximize net benefits at the margin precisely. The concept of optimization at the margin is nevertheless an invaluable tool of analysis because it provides the motivation or driving force for most economic actions. Even when individuals and firms are not explicitly trying to maximize net benefits, they often behave as if they are. In fact, the assumption has very good predictive power. Third, marginal analysis leads to the maximization of individual benefits but not to the maximization of the welfare of society as a whole when private benefits and costs differ from social benefits and costs. One situation that leads to this arises in the presence of imperfect competition and justifies government intervention in the economic system to overcome the problem, or at least to minimize its harmful impact. Indeed, whenever some individuals in society can be made better off without making someone else worse off, there is a case for government intervention at the margin to improve society's welfare. When production and consumption can no longer be reorganized so as to improve the welfare of some without at the same time reducing the welfare of others, society is said to be at **Pareto optimum.** These applications of marginal analysis are examined in Part Four (Chapters 10–13) and Part Six (Chapters 17–19) of the text.

Pareto criterion
Postulates that a change increases social welfare if it benefits some members of society without harming anyone.

Despite these clarifications and qualifications, we can clearly see that the concept of the margin and marginal analysis provide the central unifying theme in all of microeconomics.

| 1.5 | SPECIALIZATION, EXCHANGE, AND THE INTERNATIONAL FRAMEWORK OF MICROECONOMICS |

In this section we discuss specialization and exchange and the need to provide an international framework for the study of microeconomics.

Specialization and Exchange

Specialization The use of resources where most efficient.

Two important characteristics that greatly increase the efficiency of market economies are specialization in production and exchange. **Specialization** refers to the use of labor and other resources in performing those tasks in which each resource is most efficient. Efficiency and output are then maximized. For example, by concentrating in the production of food, farmers produce a much greater output than if they tried to be self-sufficient and make their own clothing and manufacture all the utensils and equipment they need. By avoiding being "the jack of all trades" and specializing instead in the production of food, where they are most efficient, the farmers' output becomes much greater. Farmers can then exchange some of their excess food for the clothes, utensils, and equipment that they need and, as a result, be able to consume more of every good.

Division of labor The assignment of each production task to different workers.

But there is an even more important aspect of specialization that increases the efficiency of labor still more. This is division of labor. **Division of labor** refers to the breaking up of a task into a number of smaller, more *specialized* tasks and assigning each of these tasks to different workers. Such a division of labor is likely to greatly increase workers' efficiency by allowing each of them to become more proficient at performing one task, developing shortcuts in the performance of the task, and avoiding the time lost from shifting from one task to another.

Exchange The trade of one commodity for another.

Specialization and division of labor, however, create the need for **exchange.** When individuals perform only one task in the production of a single commodity, there is a need for them to exchange part of their output for all the other things that they want. This exchange is greatly facilitated by the use of money. That is, in a monetized economy, individuals are paid in money for their work and can use this income to purchase in the market desired goods and services.

Comparative advantage The greater *relative* efficiency in the production of a good or service.

Specialization in production occurs not only at the individual level but also at the regional and national levels. A region or nation can specialize in the production of those goods and services in which it has a **comparative advantage** or is relatively more efficient, and then exchange part of its output for the output of other regions or nations. By doing so, each region or nation will end up consuming more than it could if it tried to be self-sufficient. Trade or exchange makes possible specialization in production and provides benefits to all parties to the exchange. This is discussed in detail in Part Three (Chapters 7–9) of the text.

The International Framework of Microeconomics

As consumers, we purchase Japanese Toyotas and German Mercedes, Italian handbags and French perfumes, Hong Kong clothes and Taiwanese calculators, Scotch whiskey and Swiss chocolates, Canadian fish and Mexican tomatoes, Costa Rican bananas and Brazilian coffee. Often, we are not even aware that the products we consume, or parts of them, are made abroad. For example, imported cloth is used in American-made suits, many American brand-name shoes are entirely manufactured abroad, and a great deal of the orange juice that we drink is imported. American multinational corporations produce and import many parts and components from abroad and export an increasing share of their output. Most of the parts and components of the Dell PC are in fact manufactured abroad (see Example 1–5), and more than one-third of Dell revenues and profits are generated abroad. General Motors and Ford face stiff competition from Toyota, Nissan, and Honda, and many U.S. steel companies are today near bankruptcy as a result of foreign competition and rising steel imports.

Internationalization of economic activity The trend toward producing and distributing goods throughout the world.

In view of the **internationalization of economic activity** and the international repercussions of domestic competitiveness policies, we cannot study microeconomics in

EXAMPLE 1-5

Dell and Other PCs Sold in the United States Are Everything but American!

Dell, headquartered in Round Rock, Texas, coordinates a global production network in 34 countries in the Americas, Europe, and Asia. For most of the PCs sold in the United States, Dell performs only the final assembly domestically, relying on outside suppliers and contract manufacturers for components, peripherals, printed circuit board (PCB) assemblies, and subassemblies (box builds). The reason is that most parts and components are cheaper to produce in other parts of the world and are thus imported (see Table 1.2). Neither high-value components nor very low-value components (such as power supplies and keyboards) have to be made close to Dell's assembly plants. Only some mid-level components (such as motherboards and other PCB assemblies) that are too expensive to ship by air to meet volatility in demand, as well as to risk holding in inventory, are produced locally, but even that is not always the case. In 2004, more than 90% of all the parts and components going into Dell's and HP's PCs were made outside the United States, and IBM sold its PC business to Lenovo of China.

TABLE 1.2 Locations and Companies That Supply Specific Parts and Components for Dell's PCs

Part/Component	Location	Company
Monitors	Europe and Asia	Phillips, Nokia, Samsung, Sony, Acer
PCBs	Asia, Scotland, and eastern Europe	SCI, Celestica
Drives	Asia, mainly Singapore	Seagate, Maxtor, W. Digital
Printers	Europe (Barcelona)	Acer
Box builds	Asia and eastern Europe	HonHai/Foxteq
Chassis	Asia and Ireland	HonHai/Foxteq

Source: J. Dedrick and K. L. Kraemer, "Dell Computer: Organization of a Global Production Network" and "Globalization of the Personal Computer Industry: Trends and Implications," *Working Paper*, Irvine, CA; Center for Research on Information Technology and Organizations CRITO), University of California, Irvine, 2002; "Lenovo Buys IBM's PC Unit for $1.75 Billion," *Financial Times*, December 9, 2004, p. 16; and "The Laptop Trail," *Wall Street Journal*, June 9, 2005, p. 31.

an international vacuum. The large and growing degree of interdependence of the United States in the world economy today makes a closed-economy approach to the study of microeconomics unrealistic. This text will explicitly introduce and integrate the international dimension into the body of traditional microeconomics to reflect the globalization of most economic activities in the world today.[4]

| 1.6 | MODELS, METHODOLOGY, AND VALUE JUDGMENTS |

✓ Concept Check
Why is an international framework essential in studying microeconomics?

Model Another name for theory.

We will now discuss the meaning and function of theory or models, examine the methodology of economics and distinguish between positive and normative analysis.

Models and Methodology

In microeconomic theory, we seek to predict and explain the economic behavior of individual consumers, resource owners, and business firms and the operation of individual markets. For this purpose we use models. A **model** abstracts from the many details surrounding an event and identifies a few of the most important determinants of the event. For example, the amount of a commodity that an individual demands over a given period of time depends on the price of the commodity, the individual's income, and the price of related commodities (i.e., substitute and complementary commodities). It also depends on the individual's age, gender, education, background, whether the individual is single or married, whether he or she owns a house or rents, the amount of money he or she has in the bank, the stocks the individual owns, the individual's expectations of future income and prices, geographic location, climate, and many other considerations.

However, given the consumer's tastes and preferences, demand theory identifies the price of the commodity, the individual's income, and the price of related commodities as the most important determinants of the amount of a commodity demanded by an individual. Although it may be *unrealistic* to focus only on these three considerations, demand theory postulates that these are generally capable of predicting accurately and explaining consumer behavior and demand. One could, of course, include additional considerations or variables to gain a fuller or more complete explanation of consumer demand, but that would defeat the main purpose of the theory or model, which is to simplify and generalize.

A theory or model usually results from casual observation of the real world. For example, we may observe that consumers generally purchase less of a commodity when its price rises. Before such a theory of demand can be accepted, however, we must go back to the real world to test it. We must make sure that individuals in different places and over different periods of time do indeed, as a group, purchase less of a commodity when its price rises. Only after many such successful tests and the absence of contradictory results can we accept the theory and make use of it in subsequent analysis to predict and explain consumer behavior. If, on the other hand, test results contradict the model, then the model must be discarded and a new one formulated.

To summarize, a theory or model is usually developed by casual observation of the real world, but we must then go back to the real world to determine whether the implications or predictions of the theory are indeed correct. Only then can we accept the theory

---

[4] See D. Salvatore, "Globalization and International Competitiveness," in S. Shojai, ed., *Globalization: Virtue or Vice?* (New York: Praeger, 2001), pp. 7–21.

or model. According to the Nobel Laureate economist Milton Friedman, a model is not tested by the realism or lack of realism of its assumptions, but rather by its ability to predict accurately and explain. The assumptions of the model are usually unrealistic in that they must necessarily represent a simplification and generalization of reality. However, if the model predicts accurately and explains the event, it is tentatively accepted. For example, demand theory, as originally developed, was based on the assumption that utility (i.e., the satisfaction that a consumer receives from the consumption of a commodity) is cardinally measurable (i.e., we can attach specific numerical values to it). This assumption is clearly unrealistic. Nevertheless, we accept the theory of demand because it leads to the correct prediction that a consumer will purchase less of a commodity when its price rises (other things, such as the consumer's income and the price of related commodities, remaining equal).

While most assumptions represent simplifications of reality, and to that extent are unrealistic, most economists take a broader position. According to these economists, the appropriate **methodology of economics** (and science in general) is to test a theory not only by its ability to predict accurately, but also by whether the predictions follow logically from the assumptions and by the internal consistency of those assumptions. For example, the theory of perfect competition postulates that the economy operates most efficiently when consumers and producers are too small individually to affect prices and output. But this theory cannot be tested for the economy as a whole. It can only be tested by tracing the loss of welfare of individual consumers when the atomistic assumptions of the theory do not hold. Thus, an adequate test of the theory requires not only confirming that the predictions are accurate but also showing how the outcome follows logically or results directly from the assumptions.

Throughout this text we will look at many economic theories or models that seek to predict and explain the economic behavior of consumers, resource owners, and business firms as they interact in the markets for goods, services, and resources. The models presented are generally those that have already been successfully tested. In a microeconomic theory course, we are not concerned with the actual testing of these theories or models, but rather with their presentation, usefulness, and applications.

Positive and Normative Analysis

In discussing the methodology of economic analysis, an important distinction is also made between positive and normative analysis. **Positive analysis** studies what *is*. It is concerned with how the economic system performs the basic functions of what to produce, how to produce, for whom to produce, how it provides for growth, and how it rations the available supply of a good over time. In other words, how is the price of a commodity, service, or resource actually determined in the market? How do producers combine resources to minimize costs of production? How does the number of firms in a market and the type of product they produce affect the determination of the price and quantity sold of the commodity? How do the number and type of owners and users of a resource affect the price and quantity of the resource placed on the market? How do specific taxes and subsidies affect the production and consumption of various commodities and the use of various resources? What are the effects of minimum wages on employment and incomes? The level of real wages on work and leisure? Rent control on the availability of housing? Deregulation of gas on gas prices and consumption? How does the economic system provide for the growth of the nation? How does it ration the available supply of a commodity over time? All of these and many more topics fall within the realm of positive analysis. For the most part, positive

Methodology of economics The proposition that a model is tested by its predictive ability.

Concept Check
Is the methodology of economics scientific?

Positive analysis The study of *what is* or how the economic system performs the basic economic functions.

analysis is factual or hypothetically testable and objective in nature, and it is devoid of ethical or value judgments.

Normative analysis
The study of *what ought to be* or how the basic economic functions *should* be performed.

Normative analysis, on the other hand, studies what *ought* to be. It is concerned with how the basic economic functions *should* be performed. Normative analysis is thus based on value judgments and, as such, is subjective and controversial. Whereas positive analysis is independent of normative analysis, normative analysis is based on positive analysis and the value judgments of society. Controversies in positive analysis can be (and are) usually resolved by the collection of more or better market data. On the other hand, controversies in normative analysis usually are not, and cannot, be resolved. Take, for example, the case of providing national health insurance for everybody. Many people favor it, but others are opposed, and no amount of economic analysis can resolve the controversy. Economists can provide an analysis of the *economic* costs and benefits of national health insurance. Such an analysis can be useful in clarifying the economic issues involved, but it is not likely to lead to general agreement on the proposition that national health insurance should or should not be provided for everybody. The economists' tools of analysis and logic can be applied to determine the economic benefits and costs of normative questions, but it is society as a whole (through elected representatives) that must make normative decisions.

✔ Concept Check
What is the distinction between positive and normative economics?

It is extremely important in economics to specify exactly when we are leaving the real world of positive analysis and entering that of normative analysis—that is, when disagreements can be resolved by the collection of more or better data (facts) and when ethical or value judgments are involved. This book is primarily concerned with positive analysis. A statement such as "universal national health insurance should be established" is a proposition of normative analysis because it is based on value judgments. Normative analysis are discussed in detail in Chapters 17 and 18.

AT THE FRONTIER
Do Economists Ever Agree on Anything?

You have probably heard some of the many jokes about economists disagreeing on almost everything. "How many opinions on the same subject do you expect to find in a room with three economists?" Answer: "four." In response to an economist's answer framed as "on the one hand . . . and on the other . . . ," President Truman is supposed to have snapped: "Give me a one-handed economist." Such jokes do not seem justified according to the results of a recent study.

Table 1.3 reports the responses to 10 of 40 propositions form 464 respondents to a questionnaire sent to a random sample of 1,350 economists in 1992. Table 1.3 shows that the vast majority of economists agreed on the first three propositions (that a ceiling on rents reduces the quantity and quality of housing, that tariffs and import quotas usually reduce general economic welfare, and that fiscal policy has a significant stimulative effect on a less than fully employed economy), but strongly disagreed on the last two propositions. In general, there was much more agreement on questions of microeconomics (which are overrepresented in the propositions reported in Table 1.3)

TABLE 1.3   Responses of Economists of Various Propositions

Proposition	Percentage of Respondents Who	
	Agreed	Disagreed*
1. A ceiling on rents reduces the quantity and quality of housing available.	92.9	6.5
2. Tariffs and import quotas usually reduce general economic welfare.	92.6	6.5
3. Fiscal policy (e.g., tax cuts and/or expenditure increase) has a significant stimulative impact on a less than fully employed economy.	89.9	9.1
4. Cash payments increase the welfare of recipients to a greater degree than do transfers-in-kind of equal cash value.	83.9	15.1
5. A large federal budget deficit has an adverse effect on the economy.	82.7	15.7
6. The redistribution of income distribution within the U.S. is a legitimate role for government.	81.9	16.8
7. A minimum wage increases unemployment among young and unskilled workers.	78.9	20.5
8. Antitrust laws should be enforced vigorously to reduce monopoly power from its current level.	71.8	27.6
9. Reducing the regulatory power of the Environmental Protection Agency (EPA) would improve the efficiency of the U.S. economy.	36.0	62.3
10. The U.S. government should retaliate against (foreign) dumping and subsidies in international trade.	50.2	47.6

*The sum of the percentages of those who agree and disagree does not add to 100 because of nonrespondents to the particular question.

than on questions of macroeconomics. More recently, however, behavioral and heterodox economists—still a small minority of economists to be sure—have been questioning even the most generally accepted propositions of economics.

But even on the questions that elicit widespread agreement among economists, the gap between the public's (especially non–college graduates) and economists' views are very wide. There is, however, a great deal of agreement on what are the major issues that society faces today (i.e., the state of the economy, education, health care, taxes, crime, globalization, and income inequalities).

Sources: R. M. Alston, J. R. Kearl, and M. B. Vaughan, "Is There a Consensus Among Economists in the 1990s?," *American Economic Review,* May 1992, pp. 203–209; R. J. Blendon et al., "Bridging the Gap Between the Public's and Economists' Views of the Economy," *Journal of Economic Perspectives,* summer 1997, pp. 105–118; "What Does the Public Know About Economic Policy?" *IMF Survey,* January 9, 2006, p. 16; "In Economics Departments, A Growing Will to Debate Fundamental Assumptions," *New York Times,* July 11, 2007, p. B6; and D. Rodrik, "Why Do Economists Disagree?," August 5, 2007, http://rodrik.typepad.com/dani_rodriks_weblog/2007/08/why-do-economis.html.

SUMMARY

1. Economics deals with the allocation of scarce resources among alternative uses to satisfy human wants. Scarcity of resources and commodities is the fundamental economic fact of every society.

2. All societies must decide what to produce, how to produce, for whom to produce, how to provide for the growth of the system, and how to ration a given amount of a commodity over time. Under a free-enterprise or mixed economic system such as that in the United States, it is the price system that performs these functions, for the most part.

3. Microeconomic theory studies the economic behavior of individual decision-making units such as individual consumers, resource owners, and business firms and the operation of individual markets in a free-enterprise economy. This is contrasted with macroeconomic theory, which studies the economy viewed as a whole. Microeconomic theory focuses attention on households and business firms as they interact in the markets for goods and services and resources.

4. Because of scarcity, all economic activities give rise to some benefits but also involve some costs. The aim of economic decisions is to maximize net benefits. Net benefits increase as long as the marginal or extra benefit from an action exceeds the marginal or extra cost resulting from the action. Net benefits are maximized when the marginal benefit is equal to the marginal cost. This concept applies to all economic decisions and market transactions. It applies as much to the consumption decisions of individuals as to the production decisions of firms, the supply choices of input owners, and government decisions. Indeed, the concepts of the margin and marginal analysis represent the key unifying concepts in all of microeconomics.

5. Specialization and exchange are two important characteristics that greatly increase the efficiency of individuals and firms in market economies. Many of the commodities we consume today are imported, and American firms purchase many inputs abroad, sell an increasing share of their products to other nations, and face increasing competition from foreign firms in the U.S. market and around the world. The international flow of capital, technology, and skilled labor has also reached unprecedented dimensions. In view of such internationalization of economic activity in the world today, it is essential to introduce an international dimension into the body of traditional microeconomics.

6. Theories make use of models. A model abstracts from the details surrounding an event and seeks to identify a few of the most important determinants of an event. A model is tested by its predictive ability, the consistency of its assumptions, and the logic with which the predictions follow from the assumptions. There is more agreement among economists than is commonly believed.

KEY TERMS

Economics
Human wants
Economic resources
Price system
Free-enterprise system
What to produce
How to produce
For whom to produce
Economic growth
Rationing over time

Microeconomic theory
Macroeconomic theory
Circular flow of economic activity
Price theory
Mixed economy
Marginal benefit
Marginal cost
Concept of the margin
Marginal analysis
Pareto optimum

Specialization
Division of labor
Exchange
Comparative advantage
Internationalization of economic
    activity
Model
Methodology of economics
Positive analysis
Normative analysis

REVIEW QUESTIONS

1. Will the problem of scarcity disappear over time as standards of living increase?

2. Distinguish between the real and the financial flows that link product and factor markets.

3. Explain in terms of the circular flow of economic activity why some individuals are richer while others are poorer.

4. Explain why some football players earn more than others. Why would a team sign a superstar for millions of dollars when it could sign a good player for much less?

5. Does a firm maximize its total revenue when it maximizes its total profits?

6. It has been proven that a speed limit of 55 MPH, rather than 65 MPH, on the nation's highways saves lives and fuel. Is there any cost in keeping the speed limit at 55 MPH?

7. Why is it that imports and exports as a percentage of gross national product (GNP) are much smaller in the United States than in Switzerland?

8. What is the relationship between import prices and domestic prices?

9. What happens to the dollar price of Japanese exports to the United States and to the yen price of U.S. exports to Japan if the Japanese yen increases in value with respect to the U.S. dollar?

10. Two models predict equally well, but one is based on a larger number of assumptions and the logic with which the predictions follow from the assumptions is more intricate than for another model. Why is the second model better?

11. A model using three variables explains 85% of an event (say, a price increase), while another model, using ten variables, explains 95% of the event. Which of the two models is better? Why?

12. The government should pass more stringent pollution control laws. Do you agree? What can economists contribute to the discussion?

PROBLEMS

*1. Why do we study microeconomics?

2. Explain why an increasing proportion of income spent on health care does not necessarily involve a reduction in the quantity of all other goods and services that can be purchased overtime. In what way is exploding health care costs related to the problem of scarcity?

3. Briefly explain how the sharp increase in petroleum prices since the fall of 1973 affected driving habits and the production of cars in the United States since then.

4. Explain why India produces textiles with much more labor relative to capital than does the United States.

5. Explain how the introduction of government affects the circular flow of economic activity.

*6. Explain the effect of government setting the price of a commodity

  a. below equilibrium with a price ceiling;

  b. above equilibrium with a price floor.

7. How does the concept of the margin provide a key unifying concept in microeconomics?

8. Using some data obtained from a publication such as *The Survey of Current Business, The U.S. Statistical Abstract,* or *International Financial Statistics* available in your library, show that the interdependence of the U.S. economy with the rest of the world has increased sharply during the past three decades.

9. a. If two models predict equally well but one is more complicated than the other, indicate which one you would use and why.

  b. Indicate how you would determine which of the two models is more complex.

10. a. Explain how you would go about constructing a model to predict total sales of American-made cars in the United States next year.

  b. Indicate how you would test your model.

11. Economists often disagree on economic matters, so economics is not a science. True or false? Explain.

*12. Briefly indicate which aspects of the redistribution of income from higher- to lower-income people involve

  a. positive analysis;

  b. normative analysis.

---

* = Answer provided at end of book.

INTERNET SITE ADDRESSES

For the state of the U.S. economy, see the *Economic Report of the President* at:

> http://www.access.gpo.gov.eop

General directories and indexes of economic information are:

> YAHOO—Economics:
> http://www.yahoo.com/Social_Science/Economics/
>
> Infoseek—Economics:
> http://www.infoseek.com/Business/Economics

For U.S. economic data, indicators and statistics, see:

> Bureau of Economic Analysis: http://www.bea.doc.gov/
>
> Bureau of Labor Statistics: http://stats.bls.gov/
>
> Census Bureau: http://www.census.gov/
>
> Department of Commerce: http://www.doc.gov/
>
> Department of the Treasury: http://www.ustreas.gov/
>
> Economic Indicators Monthly:
> http://www.gpo.ucop.edu/catalog/econind.html
>
> Economic History Services: http://www.eh.net/hmit
>
> National Bureau of Economic Analysis:
> http://www.nber.org

The gateway to all the major federal statistical sites:
http://www.fedstats.gov

For international economic data, indicators and statistics, see:

> International Monetary Fund: http://IMF.org
>
> Organization for Economic Cooperation and Development: http://oecd.org
>
> World Bank: http://worldbank.org
>
> World Trade Organization: http://www.wto.org

For current national and international economics and business news, see:

> Bloomberg business news: http://www.bloomberg.com/
>
> *Financial Times:* http://news.ft.com/home/us
>
> *The Wall Street Journal* interactive edition:
> http:/online.wsj.com/public/us
>
> *Business Week:* http://www.businessweek.com/
>
> *Forbes:* http://www.forbes.com/
>
> *Fortune:* http://www.fortune.com
>
> *The Economist:* http://www.economist.com/

CHAPTER 2

Basic Demand and Supply Analysis

After Studying This Chapter, You Should Be Able to:

- Know the meaning of demand and the law of demand
- Describe how the market demand and supply of a commodity determine its price
- Explain how changes in demand and supply affect the equilibrium price and quantity of a commodity
- Understand how imports affect product prices
- Describe the meaning of "working through the market" as opposed to "interfering with the market"

Have you ever stopped to think about how the price of a commodity (say, the price of your favorite music compact disc) is determined and why it often changes over time? In this chapter we seek to answer these questions by providing an overview of how markets function. We begin by defining the concept of a market. Next we discuss the meaning of demand and a change in demand. After reviewing supply, we examine how the interaction of the forces of market demand and supply determine the equilibrium price and quantity of a commodity. Then we examine how the equilibrium price and quantity of a commodity are affected by changes in demand and supply and by imports. Finally, we examine the effect of modifications and interferences in the operation of markets. So widespread is the applicability of the market model, that one could safely start answering any question of microeconomics by saying that it depends on demand and supply. Note, however, the "At the Frontier" discussion of nonclearing market theories.

Market An institutional arrangement for economic transactions.

Most of microeconomic analysis is devoted to the study of how individual markets operate. A **market** is an institutional arrangement under which buyers and sellers can exchange some quantity of a good or service at a mutually agreeable price. Markets provide the framework for the analysis of the forces of demand and supply that, together, determine commodity and resource prices. As explained in Chapter 1, prices play the central role in microeconomic analysis.

A market can, but need not, be a specific place or location where buyers and sellers actually come face to face for the purpose of transacting their business. For example, the New York Stock Exchange is located in a building at 11 Wall Street in New York City. On the other hand, the market for college professors has no specific location; rather, it refers to all the formal and informal information networks on teaching opportunities throughout the nation. There is a market for each good, service, or resource bought and sold in the economy. Some of these markets are local, some are regional, and others are national or international in character.

Perfectly competitive market A market where no buyer or seller can affect the price of the product.

Throughout this chapter, we assume that markets are perfectly competitive. A **perfectly competitive market** is one in which there are so many buyers and sellers of a product that each of them cannot affect the price of the product, all units of the product are homogeneous or identical, resources are mobile, and knowledge of the market is perfect. For the purpose of the present chapter, this definition of a perfectly competitive market suffices. A more detailed definition and analysis of this and other types of markets is given in Chapter 9 and in Part Three of the text.

The concept of demand is one of the most crucial in microeconomic theory and in all of economics. In this section, we review the concepts of the market demand schedule and the market demand curve, and examine the meaning of a change in demand.

Demand Schedule and Demand Curve

Market demand schedule A table showing the quantity of a commodity that consumers are willing and able to purchase at each price.

A **market demand schedule** is a table showing the quantity of a commodity that consumers are willing and able to purchase over a given period of time at each price of the commodity, while holding constant all other relevant economic variables on which demand depends (the *ceteris paribus* assumption). Among the variables held constant are consumers' incomes, their tastes, the prices of related commodities (substitutes and complements), and the number of consumers in the market.

For example, Table 2.1 provides a hypothetical daily demand schedule for hamburgers in a large market (say, New York City, Chicago, or Los Angeles). At the price of $2.00 per hamburger, the quantity demanded is 2 million hamburgers per day. At the lower price of $1.50, the quantity demanded is 4 million hamburgers per day. At the price of $1.00, the quantity demanded is 6 million hamburgers, and at the prices of $0.75 and $0.50, the quantity demanded is 7 and 8 million hamburgers, respectively.

TABLE 2.1	Market Demand Schedule for Hamburgers	
Price per Hamburger	Quantity Demanded per Day (million hamburgers)	
$2.00	2	
1.50	4	
1.00	6	
0.75	7	
0.50	8	

At lower prices, greater quantities of hamburgers are demanded. Each additional hamburger consumed per day provides declining marginal or extra benefit, and so consumers would only purchase greater quantities at lower prices. This is practically always true for all commodities. Lower commodity prices will also bring more consumers into the market. The inverse price-quantity relationship (indicating that a greater quantity of the commodity is demanded at lower prices and a smaller quantity at higher prices) is called the **law of demand.**

By plotting on a graph the various price-quantity combinations given by the market demand schedule, we obtain the **market demand curve** for the commodity. The price per unit of the commodity is usually measured along the vertical axis, while the quantity demanded of the commodity per unit of time is measured along the horizontal axis. For example, Figure 2.1 shows the market demand curve for hamburgers corresponding to the market demand schedule of Table 2.1. The demand curve has a *negative slope;* that is, it slopes downward to the right. This negative slope is a reflection of the law of demand or inverse price-quantity relationship.

The various points on the demand curve represent *alternative* price-quantity combinations. For example, at the price of $2.00 per hamburger, the quantity demanded is 2 million hamburgers (point *B* in Figure 2.1). If the price is $1.50, the quantity demanded is 4 million hamburgers (point *C*), and so on. A demand curve also shows the maximum price consumers are willing to pay to purchase each quantity of a commodity per unit of time. For example, the demand curve of Figure 2.1 shows that the *demand price* (i.e., the maximum price that consumers are willing to pay) for 2 million hamburgers is $2.00 per hamburger (point *B*); for 4 million hamburgers, the demand price is $1.50, and so on. Finally, a particular demand curve refers to a specific period of time. The demand curve of Figure 2.1 is for one day. The demand curve for hamburgers for a month is correspondingly higher.[1]

Law of demand The inverse price–quantity relationship of the demand for a commodity.

Market demand curve The graphic representation of a demand curve.

✔ Concept Check
Why do you think we have the "law" rather than the "hypothesis" of demand?

Changes in Demand

A demand curve can shift so that more or less of the commodity would be demanded at any commodity price. The entire demand curve for a commodity would shift with a change in (1) consumers' incomes, (2) consumers' tastes, (3) the price of related commodities, (4) the number of consumers in the market, or in any other variable held constant in drawing a market demand curve. For example, with a rise in consumer income

---
[1] The demand curve can, but need not, be a straight line.

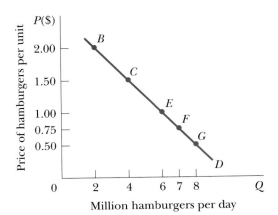

FIGURE 2.1   Market Demand Curve for Hamburgers   Market demand curve *D* shows that at lower hamburger prices, greater quantities are demanded. This is reflected in the negative slope of the demand curve and is referred to as the "law of demand."

the demand curve for most commodities (normal goods) shifts to the right, because consumers can then afford to purchase more of each commodity at each price. The same is true if consumers' tastes change (or if the quality of the product improves) so that they demand more of the commodity at each price, or if the number of consumers in the market increases.

A demand curve also shifts to the right if the price of a substitute commodity rises or if the price of a complementary commodity falls. For example, if the price of hot dogs (a substitute for hamburgers) *rises*, people will switch some of their purchases away from hot dogs and demand more hamburgers at each and every price of hamburgers (a rightward shift in the demand for hamburgers). Similarly, if the price of the bun (a complement of hamburgers) *falls*, the demand for hamburgers also shifts to the right (since the price of a hamburger with the bun is then lower).

On the other hand, the demand curve for a commodity usually shifts to the left (so that less of it is demanded at each price) with a decline in consumer income, a decrease in the price of substitute commodities, or a decrease in the number of consumers in the market. The demand curve also shifts to the left if the price of complementary commodities rises or if consumer tastes change so that they demand less of the commodity at each price.

Figure 2.2 shows *D*, the original demand curve for hamburgers (from Figure 2.1) and *D'*, a higher demand curve for hamburgers. With *D'*, consumers demand more hamburgers at each price. For example, at the price of $1.00, consumers demand 12 million hamburgers per day (point *E'*) as compared with 6 million demanded (point *E*) on curve *D*. The shift from *D* to *D'* leads consumers to demand 6 million *additional* hamburgers per day at each price.

A shift in demand is referred to as a *change in demand* and must be clearly distinguished from a *change in the quantity demanded,* which refers instead to a movement along a given demand curve as a result of a change in the commodity price. Thus, the shift in demand from *D* to *D'* is an increase in demand, while the movement along *D*, say, from point *E* to point *F*, is a change in the quantity demanded. The change in demand is caused by the change in the economic variables that are held constant in drawing a given demand curve (the *ceteris paribus* assumption), whereas a change in the quantity demanded is a movement along a given demand curve as a result of a change in the price of the commodity (with all the other economic variables on which demand depends remaining constant).

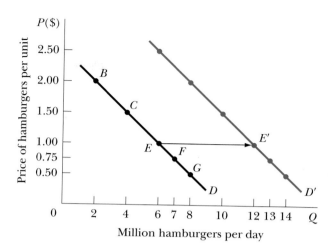

FIGURE 2.2   Change in Demand for Hamburgers
Consumers demand more hamburgers at each price when
the demand curve shifts to the right from *D* to *D'*. Thus, at
P = $1.00, consumers purchase 12 million hamburgers with
D' instead of only 6 million with *D*.

2.3	

MARKET SUPPLY

We have examined the market demand, now it is time to turn to the supply side.

Supply Schedule and Supply Curve

Market supply schedule A table showing the quantity supplied of a commodity at each commodity price.

A **market supply schedule** is a table showing the quantity supplied of a commodity at each price for a given period of time. It assumes that technology, resource prices, and, for agricultural commodities, weather conditions, are held constant (the *ceteris paribus* assumption). Table 2.2 gives a hypothetical daily supply schedule for hamburgers. Starting at the bottom, the table shows that at the price of $0.50 per hamburger, the quantity supplied is 2 million hamburgers per day. At the higher price of $0.75 per hamburger, the quantity supplied is 4 million hamburgers per day. At the price of $1.00, the quantity supplied is 6 million hamburgers per day, and so on. Higher hamburger prices allow producers to bid resources away from other uses and supply greater quantities of hamburgers.

The various price-quantity combinations of a supply schedule can be plotted on a graph to obtain the **market supply curve** for the commodity. For example, Figure 2.3 shows the market supply curve for hamburgers corresponding to the market supply schedule of Table 2.2. The *positive slope* of the supply curve (i.e., its upward-to-the-right inclination) reflects the fact that higher prices must be paid to producers to cover rising marginal, or extra, costs and thus induce them to supply greater quantities of the commodity.

Market supply curve The graphic representation of the market supply schedule.

As with the demand curve, the various points on the supply curve represent *alternative* price–quantity combinations. For example, at the price of $0.50 per hamburger, the quantity supplied is 2 million hamburgers per day (point *R* in Figure 2.3). If instead the price is $0.75, the quantity supplied is 4 million hamburgers (point *N*), and so on. A supply curve also shows the *minimum* price that producers must receive to cover their rising marginal costs and supply each quantity of the commodity. For example, the supply curve of Figure 2.3 shows that the *supply price* (i.e., the minimum price that suppliers must receive) in order to supply 2 million hamburgers per day is $0.50 (point *R*); for 4 million hamburgers, the supply price is $0.75 (point *N*), and so on. A particular supply curve is drawn for a specific

TABLE 2.2	Market Supply Schedule for Hamburgers

Price per Hamburger	Quantity Supplied per Day (million hamburgers)
$2.00	14
1.50	10
1.00	6
0.75	4
0.50	2

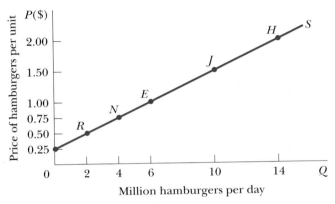

FIGURE 2.3   Market Supply Curve for Hamburgers   Market supply curve S shows that higher hamburger prices induce producers to supply greater quantities.

period of time. The supply curve of Figure 2.3 is for one day. The supply curve of hamburgers for a month is correspondingly larger or farther out.[2]

Changes in Supply

An improvement in technology, a reduction in the price of resources used in the production of the commodity, and, for agricultural commodities, more favorable weather conditions (i.e., a change in the *ceteris paribus* assumption) would cause the entire supply curve of the commodity to shift to the right. Producers would then supply more of the commodity at each price. For example, Figure 2.4 shows that at the price of $1.00, producers supply 12 million hamburgers per day (point E′) with S′ as opposed to only 6 million hamburgers with S.

The shift to the right from S to S′ is referred to as *an increase in supply*. This must be clearly distinguished from *an increase in the quantity supplied,* which is instead a movement on a given supply curve in the upward direction (as, for example, from point E to point J, in Figure 2.4) resulting from an increase in the commodity price (from $1.00 to

---

[2] As in the case of demand, the supply curve can, but need not, be a straight line.

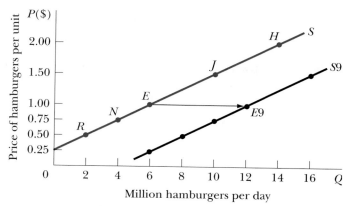

FIGURE 2.4   Change in the Supply of Hamburgers When the supply curve shifts to the right from S to S', producers supply more hamburgers at each price. Thus, at P = $1.00, producers supply 12 million hamburgers with S' instead of only 6 million with S.

$1.50). On the other hand, a decrease in supply refers to a leftward shift in the supply curve and must be clearly distinguished from a decrease in the quantity supplied of the commodity (which is a movement down a supply curve and results from a decline in the commodity price).

| 2.4 |

WHEN IS A MARKET IN EQUILIBRIUM?[3]

We now examine how the interaction of the forces of demand and supply determines the equilibrium price and quantity of a commodity in a perfectly competitive market. A market is in equilibrium when no buyer or seller has any incentive to change the quantity of the commodity that he or she buys or sells at the given price. The **equilibrium price** of a commodity is the price at which the quantity demanded of the commodity equals the quantity supplied and the market clears. The process by which equilibrium is reached in the marketplace can be shown with a table and illustrated graphically.

Equilibrium price
The price at which the quantity demanded of a commodity equals the quantity supplied.

Table 2.3 brings together the market demand and supply schedules for hamburgers from Tables 2.1 and 2.2. From Table 2.3, we see that only at P = $1.00 is the quantity supplied of hamburgers equal to the quantity demanded and the market clears. Thus, P = $1.00 is the equilibrium price and Q = 6 million hamburgers per day is the equilibrium quantity.

Surplus The excess quantity supplied of a commodity at higher-than-equilibrium prices.

At prices above the equilibrium price, the quantity supplied exceeds the quantity demanded and there is a **surplus** of the commodity, which drives the price down. For example, at P = $2.00, the quantity supplied (QS) is 14 million hamburgers, the quantity demanded (QD) is 2 million hamburgers, so there is a surplus of 12 million hamburgers per day (see the first line of Table 2.3). Sellers must reduce prices to get rid of their unwanted inventory accumulations of hamburgers. At lower prices, producers supply

---
[3] An algebraic analysis of how equilibrium is determined for this case is given in the appendix to this chapter. A more general analysis is provided in section A1.11 of the Mathematical Appendix at the end of the book.

TABLE 2.3	Market Supply Schedule, Market Demand Schedule, and Equilibrium			
Price per Hamburger	Quantity Supplied per Day (million hamburgers)	Quantity Demanded per Day (million hamburgers)	Surplus (+) or Shortage (−)	Pressure on Price
$2.00	14	2	12	Downward
1.50	10	4	6	Downward
1.00	6	6	0	Equilibrium
0.75	4	7	−3	Upward
0.50	2	8	−6	Upward

smaller quantities and consumers demand larger quantities until the equilibrium price of $1.00 is reached, at which the quantity supplied of 6 million hamburgers per day equals the quantity demanded and the market clears.

On the other hand, at prices below the equilibrium price, the quantity supplied falls short of the quantity demanded and there is a **shortage** of the commodity, which drives the price up. For example, at $P = \$0.50$, $QS = 2$ million hamburgers while $QD = 8$ million hamburgers, so that there is a shortage of 6 million hamburgers per day (see the last line of Table 2.3). The price of hamburgers is then bid up by consumers who want more hamburgers than are available at the low price of $0.50. As the price of hamburgers is bid up, producers supply greater quantities while consumers demand smaller quantities until the equilibrium price of $P = \$1.00$ is reached, at which $QS = QD = 6$ million hamburgers per day and the market clears. Thus, bidding drives price and quantity to their equilibrium level.

The determination of the equilibrium price can also be shown graphically by bringing together on the same graph the market demand curve of Figure 2.1 and the market supply curve of Figure 2.3. In Figure 2.5 the intersection of the market demand curve and the market supply curve of hamburgers at point E defines the equilibrium price of $1.00 per hamburger and the equilibrium quantity of 6 million hamburgers per day.

At higher prices, there is an excess supply or surplus of the commodity (the top shaded area in Figure 2.5). Suppliers then lower prices to sell their excess supplies. The surplus is eliminated only when suppliers have lowered their price to the equilibrium level. On the other hand, at below equilibrium prices, the excess demand or shortage (the bottom shaded area in the figure) drives the price up to the equilibrium level. This occurs because consumers are unable to purchase all of the commodity they want at below-equilibrium prices and they bid up the price. The shortage is eliminated only when consumers have bid up the price to the equilibrium level, that is, only at $P = \$1.00$, $QS = QD = 6$ million hamburgers per day, and the market is in equilibrium (clears). So, both demand and supply play a role in determining price.

Equilibrium is the condition which, once achieved, tends to persist in time. That is, as long as buyers and sellers do not change their behavior and D and S do not change, the equilibrium point remains the same.

At a particular point in time, the observed price may or may not be the equilibrium price. However, we know that market forces generally push the market price toward

Shortage The excess quantity demanded of a commodity at lower-than-equilibrium prices.

✓ Concept Check
How is the equilibrium price determined?

Equilibrium The market condition that, once achieved, tends to persist.

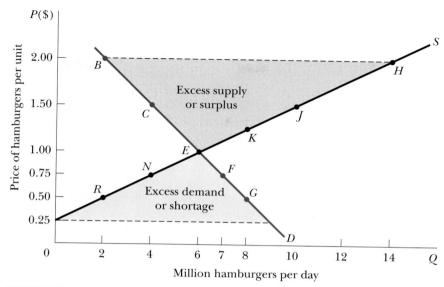

FIGURE 2.5   Demand, Supply, and Equilibrium   The intersection of *D* and *S* at point *E* defines the equilibrium price of $1.00 per hamburger and the equilibrium quantity of 6 million hamburgers per day. At *P* larger than $1.00, the resulting surplus will drive *P* down toward equilibrium. At *P* smaller than $1.00, the resulting shortage will drive *P* up toward equilibrium.

Auction The bidding process in the purchase of commodities.

equilibrium. This may occur very rapidly or very slowly. Before the market price reaches a particular equilibrium price, demand and supply may change (shift), defining a new equilibrium price. For now we will assume that, in the absence of price controls, the market price *is* the equilibrium price. Example 2–1 shows how the market-clearing, or equilibrium, price is actually approximated in the real world by **auction** or similar mechanisms.

EXAMPLE 2–1

Equilibrium Price by Auction

One way equilibrium prices are actually reached in the real world is by auction. Over the centuries, auctions have been used to approximate the market-clearing, or equilibrium, price of everything from tulips to fine art and government bonds. How do auctions work? Suppose that a seller of a product or service faces a group of potential buyers. The seller knows what his or her minimum acceptable (reservation) price, and each buyer knows more or less the maximum price he or she is willing to pay for the good or service. The seller and the buyers, however, do not reveal this information unless and until it is in their interest to do so.

The actual market, or equilibrium, price for the good or service will settle between the price that the buyer who is willing to pay the most for the good or service (call him

✓ Concept Check
How is price determined
in an auction?

or her Buyer 1) and the price that the buyer who is willing to pay the second-highest price (call him or her Buyer 2)—provided that this price is higher than the seller's reservation price. Buyer 1 will then be the one who actually purchases the good or service.

But how would the seller find Buyer 1? One way to do this is by auction. In ascending-price auctions, a low price is announced and buyers are given the opportunity to bid. The price is then increased until only Buyer 1 is left. This is the market-clearing, or equilibrium, price. In descending-price, or Dutch, auctions, on the other hand, a high price is announced and then lowered until the first buyer accepts the price ("hits the panic button"). This will again be our Buyer 1.

Another mechanism for matching buyers and sellers is bilateral bargaining, or "haggling." Here, a buyer and seller, each with some knowledge of the market, enter into unstructured negotiation to find a mutually acceptable price. If that is not reached, both try again with another party until a sale is made and the market clears. A related mechanism, familiar to consumers, is the fixed-price list. Here sellers announce a price list at which they are willing to sell. Potential buyers examine the list and decide whether or not to buy, from whom to buy, and when. Sellers adjust the price, and buyers decide to purchase until, again, the market clears.

In general, all of the foregoing mechanisms uncover roughly the price at which buyers and sellers are more or less matched and the market clears. Note that the process of determining the equilibrium price in the real world is often not as smooth or clear-cut as might be implied by theory. But that is precisely the function of theory—that is, to abstract from all details, simplify, and generalize, which is precisely what *price theory* does.

Sources: "The Brave New World of Pricing," *Financial Times*, August 2, 2001, pp. 2–4; and "Auction," *Wikipedia*, July, 2007, http://en.wikipedia.org/wiki/Auction.

2.5 ADJUSTMENT TO CHANGES IN DEMAND AND SUPPLY: COMPARATIVE STATIC ANALYSIS

What is the effect of a change in the behavior of buyers and sellers, and hence in demand and supply, on the equilibrium price and quantity of a commodity? Because the behavior of buyers and sellers often does change, causing demand and supply curves to shift over time, it is important to analyze how these shifts affect equilibrium. This analysis is called **comparative static analysis.**

Adjustment to Changes in Demand

Comparative static analysis The analysis of the effect of a change in demand and/or supply price and quantity.

We have seen that the market demand curve for a commodity shifts as a result of a change in consumers' income, their tastes, the price of substitutes and complements, and the number of consumers in the market (i.e., a change in the *ceteris paribus* assumption). Given the market supply curve of a commodity, an increase in demand (a rightward shift of the entire demand curve) results both in a higher equilibrium price and a higher equilibrium quantity. A reduction in demand has the opposite effect.

Figure 2.6 shows a shift from *D* to *D'* resulting, for example, from an increase in consumers' income. The shift results in a temporary shortage of 6 million hamburgers

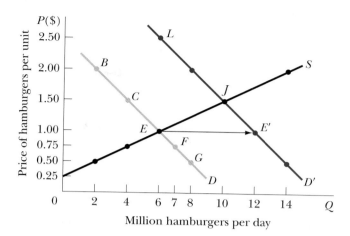

FIGURE 2.6   Adjustment to an Increase in Demand
D and *S* are the original demand and supply curves (as in Figure 2.5). The shift from *D* to *D'* results in a temporary shortage of hamburgers, which drives the price up to *P* = $1.50 at which *QS* = *QD* = 10 million hamburgers.

(*EE'* in the figure) at the original equilibrium price of *P* = $1.00 (point *E*). As a result, the price of hamburgers is bid up to *P* = $1.50 at which *QS* = *QD* = 10 million hamburgers. As the price of hamburgers rises to *P* = $1.50, the quantity demanded declines (from point *E'* to point *J* along *D'*) while the quantity supplied increases (from point *E* to point *J* along *S*) until the new equilibrium point *J* is reached. At the new equilibrium point *J*, both *P* and *Q* are higher than at the old equilibrium point *E* and the market, once again, clears.

Adjustment to Changes in Supply

The market supply curve of a commodity can shift as a result of a change in technology, resource prices, or weather conditions (for agricultural commodities). Given the market demand curve for the commodity, an increase in supply (a rightward shift of the entire supply curve) results in a lower equilibrium price but a larger equilibrium quantity. A reduction in supply has the opposite effect.

Figure 2.7 shows a shift from *S* to *S'* resulting, for example, from a reduction in the price of beef. The shift results in a temporary surplus of 6 million hamburgers (*EE'* in the figure) at the original equilibrium price of *P* = $1.00 (point *E*). To get rid of their surplus, sellers reduce their price to *P* = $0.50, at which *QS* = *QD* = 8 million hamburgers. As the price of hamburgers falls to *P* = $0.50, the quantity demanded increases (from point *E* to point *G* along *D*) while the quantity supplied decreases (from point *E'* to point *G* along *S'*) until the new equilibrium point *G* is reached. At new equilibrium point *G*, *P* is lower and *Q* is higher than at old equilibrium point *E* and the market, once again, clears.

Starting from Figure 2.5, you should be able to show what happens to the equilibrium price and quantity if both the demand and supply of hamburgers increase, if both decrease, or if one increases and the other decreases. We can similarly examine the effect of changes in demand and supply on the equilibrium price and quantity of any other commodity or service (see Example 2–2).

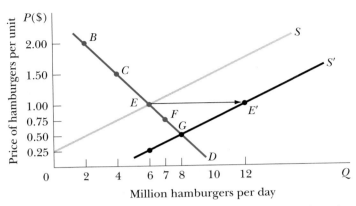

FIGURE 2.7   Adjustment to an Increase in Supply   *D* and *S* are the original demand and supply curves. The shift from *S* to *S'* results in a temporary surplus of hamburgers, which drives the price down to *P* = \$0.50 at which *QS* = *QD* = 8 million hamburgers.

EXAMPLE 2-2

Changes in Demand and Supply and Coffee Prices

Changes in the demand and the supply of coffee explain why world wholesale coffee prices fell by nearly half from 1998 to 2004, reaching their lowest level in three decades. The sharp decline in coffee price threw millions of small coffee farmers and their families in developing countries into extreme poverty, while multinational food companies (such as Nestlé) and coffee shops (such as Starbucks) posted very high profits from coffee sales.

The problem in the coffee market arose from the fact that the supply of coffee increased faster than its demand, causing coffee prices to fall. Since coffee prices fell faster than quantities increased, the earnings of coffee farmers also declined. This can be shown with Figure 2.8, where *D* represents the world's demand curve for coffee and *S* represents the world's supply curve. Curves *D* and *S* intersect at the equilibrium world price of coffee of \$1 per pound and the equilibrium quantity of 10 billion pounds per year (point *E* in the figure), giving coffee farmers a total revenue (income) of \$10 billion per year. If, over time, *D* shifts to *D'* and *S* shifts to *S'*, the world price of coffee falls to \$0.50 per pound and the quantity rises to 15 billion pounds per year (shown by new equilibrium point *E''* in the figure). This, however, produces a total revenue (income) for coffee farmers of only \$7.5 billion per year. If only *D* shifted to *D'*, the price of coffee would be \$1.25 (point *E'* in the figure); while if only *S* shifted to *S'*, the price of coffee would be \$0.25 (point *E**).

During the past few years, the supply of coffee has been increasing at twice the rate of the increase in demand as a result of new countries (such as Vietnam) starting to produce and export coffee on a large scale and others (such as Indonesia and Brazil) sharply increasing exports. This caused the price of coffee that growers received to fall from \$1.40 per pound in 1998 to as low as \$0.48 in June 2002, which was lower than the production costs of many poor small farmers. As more efficient larger farmers increased their production to make up for the reduction in price, the market supply curve for coffee shifted to the right, causing coffee prices to fall even lower.

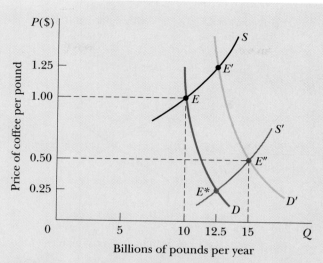

FIGURE 2.8   Demand, Supply and Coffee Prices   Curves D and S refer, respectively, to the world's demand and supply curve for coffee. Curves D and S intersect at point E, giving the equilibrium price of coffee of $1.00 and the equilibrium quantity of 10 billion pounds per year. If D and S shifted, respectively, to D' to S', the new equilibrium point would be E'', giving the price of $0.50 and the quantity of 15 million pounds per year.

A plan drawn up in May 2000 by the 28-member Association of Coffee Producing Countries (ACPC) sponsored by Brazil and Colombia (respectively, the world's largest and third largest coffee exporter) failed to reduce coffee exports and stabilize prices. But then bad weather in producing nations and higher demand in consuming nations came to the rescue, resulting in coffee prices rising above $1.30 per pound in fall 2007 and $1.58 in February 2008.

Sources: "Drowning in Cheap Coffee," *The Economist*, September 29, 2001, pp. 43–44; "Crisis Call to Coffee Growers," *Financial Times*, April 16, 2002, p. 23; "Coffee Reaches Five-Year Highs on Signs of Smaller Brazil Crop," *Wall Street Journal*, February 24, 2005, p. 4; and "Price of Coffee Jumps to 10-Year High," *Financial Times*, October 15, 2007, p. 18.

2.6   DOMESTIC DEMAND AND SUPPLY, IMPORTS, AND PRICES

When the domestic price of a commodity is higher than the commodity price abroad, the nation will import the commodity until domestic and foreign prices are equalized, in the absence of trade restrictions and assuming no transportation costs. This is shown in Figure 2.9. Curves D_T and S_T in Panels A and C refer to the demand and supply curves for textiles in the United States and in the rest of the world per year, respectively. Panel A shows that in the absence of trade, the United States would produce and consume 200 million yards of textiles at the price of $3 per yard (point F). Panel C shows that the rest of the world produces and consumes 300 million yards at the price of $1

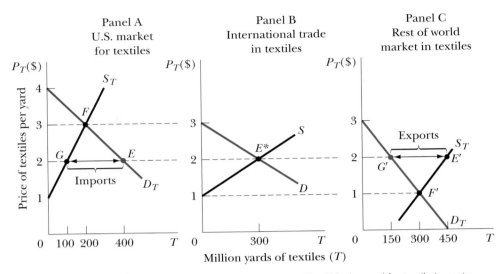

FIGURE 2.9   Equilibrium Commodity Price with Trade   The U.S. demand for textile imports (*D*) in Panel B is derived from the excess demand at below–equilibrium prices in the absence of trade in Panel A. On the other hand, the foreign supply of textile exports to the United States (*S*) in Panel B is derived from the foreign excess supply at above–equilibrium prices in the absence of trade in Panel C. The *D* and *S* curves intersect at point *E** in Panel B, establishing the equilibrium price of $2 per yard and the equilibrium quantity of textiles traded of 300 million yards.

Excess demand The excess in the quantity demanded over the quantity supplied of a commodity.

Excess supply The excess in the quantity supplied over the quantity demanded of a commodity.

per yard (point *F′*). With free trade in textiles, and assuming (for simplicity) zero transportation costs, the price of textiles will be $2 per yard both in the United States and abroad. The United States will import 300 million yards of textiles (*EG* in Panel A), which is equal to the textile exports of the rest of the world (*E′G′* in Panel C). This result, which is easily visualized by examining Panels A and C only, is formally derived in Panel B.

Panel B shows the U.S. demand for textile imports (*D*) and the foreign supply curve of textile exports (*S*). The U.S. demand for textile imports in Panel B is derived from the U.S. **excess demand** for textiles at each price below the U.S. equilibrium price in Panel A. Specifically, at the equilibrium price of $3 per yard, the United States produces and consumes 200 million yards of textiles (point *F* in Panel A). This corresponds to the vertical intercept of the U.S. demand curve for textile imports (*D*) in Panel B. At $P_T = 2, the United States produces 100 million yards domestically (point *G* in Panel A), consumes 400 million yards (point *E* in Panel A), and thus imports 300 million yards (*EG* in Panel A). This corresponds to point *E** on the U.S. demand curve for textile imports (*D*) in Panel B.

The foreign supply curve of textile exports to the United States (*S* in Panel B) is derived from the **excess supply** of textiles in the rest of the world at prices above the equilibrium price in Panel C. Specifically, at the equilibrium price of $1 per yard, the rest of the world produces and consumes 300 million yards of textiles (point *F′* in Panel C). This corresponds to the vertical intercept of the supply curve of textile exports of the rest of the world (*S*) in Panel B. At $P_T = 2, the rest of the world produces 450 million yards (point *E′* in Panel C), consumes 150 million yards (point *G′* in Panel C), and exports 300 million yards (*E′G′* in Panel C). This corresponds to point *E** on the supply curve of textile exports of the rest of the world (*S*) in Panel B.

The U.S. demand curve for textile imports (*D* in Panel B) intersects the foreign supply curve of textile exports from the rest of the world (*S* in Panel B) at point *E**, resulting in the equilibrium quantity of textiles traded of 300 million yards at the equilibrium price of $2 per yard. Just as for any other commodity, the equilibrium price and quantity of textiles traded is given at the intersection of the demand and supply curves. Note that in the absence of any obstruction to trade in textiles and assuming no transportation costs, the price of textiles is equal in the United States and abroad. Thus, the price of textiles with trade is lower in the United States and higher in the rest of the world than in the absence of trade. With transportation costs, the price of textiles in the United States would exceed the price of textiles in the rest of the world by the cost of transportation.

This analysis clearly shows that in today's interdependent world, the tendency for the domestic price of a commodity to rise is moderated by the inflow of imports of the commodity. This is certainly the case for automobiles in the United States (see Example 2–3).

EXAMPLE 2–3

The Large U.S. Automotive Trade Deficit Keeps U.S. Auto Prices Down

Table 2.4 shows that even though automobiles were by far the largest U.S. exports, the United States had an automotive trade deficit of nearly $150 billion in 2006. This represented nearly one fifth of the total U.S. trade deficit for that year. Without such automobile imports, automobile prices in the United States would have been more than $1,000 higher than they were. Table 2.4 also shows that the other major imports of the United States in 2006 were petroleum, household appliances, and computers, while the other main exports were chemicals, aircraft, food and beverages, and semiconductors. Since the price of all traded goods are affected (sometimes a lot) by imports and exports, it would not make much sense to study microeconomic theory, in general, and the process whereby equilibrium prices are determined, in particular, without considering imports and exports in our highly globalized and interdependent world.

TABLE 2.4	Major Goods Exports and Imports of the United States in 2006 (billions of dollars)			
Imports	**Value**		**Exports**	**Value**
Petroleum	302.4		Automobiles	107.2
Automobiles	256.7		Chemicals	83.0
Household appliances	105.8		Aircraft	75.2
Computers	101.3		Food and beverages	66.0
Textiles	83.4		Semiconductors	52.4
Food and beverages	74.9		Computers	47.3
Chemicals	53.8		Electrical generating machinery	39.3
Electrical generating machinery	49.8		Scientific and medical equipment	30.0
Telecommunication equipment	40.3		Telecommunication equipment	28.3
Semiconductors	27.4		Household appliances	26.2

Source: U.S. Department of Commerce, *Survey of Current Business* (Washington, DC: U.S. Government Printing Office, July 2007), pp. 84–86.

| 2.7 | INTERFERING WITH VERSUS WORKING THROUGH THE MARKET |

In the analysis presented so far in this chapter, we have implicitly assumed that the market is allowed to operate without government or other interferences. In that case, demand and supply determine the equilibrium price and quantity for each commodity or service. If, on the other hand, the government interfered with the operation of the market by imposing effective price controls (say, in the form of rent control or an agricultural price-support program), the market would not be allowed to operate and a persistent shortage or surplus of the commodity or service would result. Contrast this situation with *working through or within the market* (as, for example, with the imposition of an excise tax or the federal antidrug program). Working through the market would result in a shift in demand or supply, but the equilibrium price and quantity of the commodity or service would still be determined by demand and supply, and no persistent shortage or surplus would arise.

Current, real-world examples can illustrate the differences. Example 2–4 shows the detrimental effect of rent control in New York City. Example 2–5 shows the waste that results from U.S. agricultural price-support programs and why many people want to do away with them. On the other hand, Example 2–6 examines the economic effects of working through the market with the imposition of an excise tax, while Example 2–7 shows how the federal antidrug program seeks to reduce drug use in the United States by reducing the demand and supply of illegal drugs.

By interfering with the working of markets, rent control, price ceilings on gasoline, and agricultural price-support programs create huge waste and inefficiencies in the economy. These arise because markets communicate crucial information to consumers about the relative availability of goods and services, and to suppliers about the relative value that consumers place on various goods and services. Without the free flow of information transmitted through market prices, persistent shortages and surpluses—and waste—arise. Working through the market (see Examples 2–6 and 2–7) leads to different (and better) results.

EXAMPLE 2–4

Rent Control Harms the Housing Market

"There is probably nothing that distorts a city worse than rent regulation. It accelerates the abandonment of marginal buildings, deters the improvement of good ones, and creates wondrous windfalls for the middle class—all the while harming those it was meant to help, the poor."[4] More than 90% of economists would agree (see Table 1.3). Rent control was adopted in New York City as an emergency measure during World War II, but it has been kept ever since. Although rent control is most stringent in New York City, today more than 200 cities (including Washington, D.C., Boston, Los Angeles, and San Francisco) have some form of rent control. More than 10% of rental housing in the United States is under rent control.

Price ceiling The maximum price allowed for a commodity.

Rent controls are **price ceilings** or maximum rents set below equilibrium rents. Although designed to keep housing affordable, the effect has been just the opposite—a shortage of apartments. For example, Figure 2.10 might refer to the market for

---

[4] "End Rent Control," *New York Times,* May 12, 1987, p. 30.

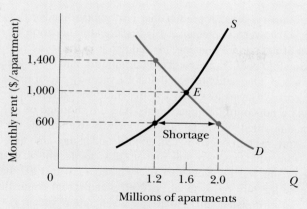

FIGURE 2.10   Rent Control   At the controlled rent of $600 per month, 2.0 million apartments could be rented. Only 1.2 million apartments are available at that rent, so there is a shortage of 800,000 million apartments. Apartment seekers would be willing to pay a rent of $1,400 per month when only 1.2 million apartments are available.

apartment rentals in New York City. Without rent control (and assuming, for simplicity, that all apartments are identical), the equilibrium rent is $1,000 and the equilibrium number of apartments rented is 1.6 million. At the controlled rent of $600 per month, 2 million apartments could be rented. Only 1.2 million apartments are available at that rent, so there is a shortage of 800,000 apartments. Indeed, apartment seekers would be willing to pay a rent of $1,400 per month rather than go without an apartment when only 1.2 million apartments are available.[5]

Rent control introduces many predictable distortions into the housing market. First, as we have seen, rent control results in a shortage of apartments for rent. This is evidenced by the great difficulty and time required to find a vacant, rent-controlled apartment to rent. Second, owners of rent-controlled apartments usually cut maintenance and repairs to reduce costs, and so the quality of housing deteriorates. Because of the shortages to which rent control gives rise, however, apartments vacated as a result of inadequate maintenance can be filled easily and quickly. Third, rent control reduces the return on investment in rental housing, and so fewer rental apartments will be constructed.[6] Fourth, rent control encourages conversion into cooperatives (since their *price* is not controlled), which further reduces the supply of rent-controlled apartments.[7] Finally, with rent control, there must be a substitute for market price allocation; that is, nonprice rationing is likely to take place as landlords favor families with few or no children or pets and families with higher incomes.

---

[5] A price ceiling at or above the equilibrium price has no effect. For example, rent is $1,000 and the number of apartments rented is equal to 1.6 million in Figure 2.10 regardless of whether a rent ceiling of $1,000 or higher is imposed. Only if rent control or the maximum rent allowed by law is below the equilibrium rent of $1,000 does a shortage of apartments for rent result.

[6] To overcome this, rent control laws usually exempt new apartments.

[7] Many localities have passed laws restricting this practice.

✓ Concept Check
What is the effect of a price ceiling?

In summary, we can predict that rent control leads to (1) a shortage of rental housing, (2) lower maintenance, (3) inadequate allocation of resources to the construction of new rental housing, (4) reduction in the stock of rental housing through conversion into cooperatives and condominiums, and (5) nonprice rationing of apartments for rent. One study revealed that the vacancy rate of rent-controlled apartments in New York City was less than 1%, expenditures on repairs were only about half as much as on noncontrolled apartments, and the shortage of new rental housing construction amounted to over $3 billion. One way to eliminate the housing shortage and other distortions introduced by rent control, and at the same time protect tenants in residence from sudden sharp rent increases, is to decontrol apartments only as they become vacant. Indeed, New York City passed a law in 1997 that permitted landlords to increase the rent by as much as 20% when a rent-controlled apartment became vacant and eliminated all regulations when, upon vacancy, the rent rose beyond $2,000.

Similar distortions result from the imposition of price ceilings on other commodities and services. For example, it was estimated that the price ceiling on gasoline in the United States in the summer of 1979 (at the height of the petroleum crisis) resulted in $200 million in lost time and 100 million gallons of gas wasted per month from waiting in long lines to obtain gasoline. Black markets also sprung up as some consumers were willing to pay a higher price for gasoline rather than stand in lines, and some suppliers were willing to accommodate them at higher prices. When price control was abolished, gasoline prices rose to the equilibrium level and long lines at the pumps and other market distortions soon disappeared. Similarly, the cap placed on doctor reimbursements by third parties (see Example 1–1) led to a shortage of doctor services, which is reflected in delays that patients experience when trying to see a doctor. Another example is given by the wait that users experience before the requested information appears on their computer screens when "surfing the Net." This results from the government's resistance to levying charges based on Internet usage.

Sources: "End Rent Control," *New York Times,* May 12, 1987, p. 30; "A Model for Destroying a City," *Wall Street Journal,* March 12, 1993, p. A8; "Rent Deregulation Has Risen Sharply Under 1997 Law," *New York Times,* August 8, 1997, p. B1; and "The Great Manhattan Rip-off," *The Economist,* June 7, 2003, pp. 25–26.

EXAMPLE 2–5

The Economics of U.S. Farm Support Programs

For more than 70 years, American agriculture has been the nation's largest recipient of political intervention and economic aid. Demand and supply analysis can again enlighten us on how the U.S. farm-support program worked and on the gross inefficiencies to which it led.

The federal government has used the following three basic methods to prop up farm incomes: (1) From the 1930s until 1973, the federal government operated a price-support program (i.e., it established a **price floor** or a minimum price above the equilibrium price) for several agricultural commodities to increase farm incomes. This resulted in a surplus of agricultural commodities, which was then purchased by the

Price floor A minimum price for a commodity.

government. The government used part of the surplus to assist low-income people, to subsidize school lunch programs, and for foreign aid. But a great deal of the surplus had to be stored and some spoiled. (2) From the early 1930s, the government also provided incentives for farmers to keep part of their land idle to avoid ever-increasing surpluses. (3) Starting in 1973, the government also gave farmers a direct subsidy if the market price of certain commodities fell below a target price.

We can analyze the effect of these three farm-support programs with the aid of Figure 2.11 which refers to the wheat market. In the absence of any support program, wheat farmers produce the equilibrium quantity of 2 billion bushels per year, sell it at the equilibrium price of $3 per bushel, and realize a total income of $6 billion. If the government establishes a price floor of $4 per bushel for wheat, farmers supply 2.2 billion bushels per year, consumers purchase only 1.8 billion bushels, and the government must purchase the surplus of 0.4 billion bushels at the support price of $4 per bushel, for a total cost of $1.6 billion. This does not include the cost of storing the surplus. The price floor has no effect if the market price rises above it.

If, through acreage restriction, output falls from 2.2 to 2.1 billion bushels at the supported price of $4 per bushel, the surplus declines to 0.3 billion bushels, and the cost of the price-support program falls to $1.2 billion. With direct subsidies, farmers sell the equilibrium quantity of 2 billion bushels at the equilibrium price of $3 per bushel, and the government then provides farmers a direct subsidy of $1 per bushel at a total cost of $2 billion (if the government sets the target price for wheat at $4 per bushel). With a direct subsidy, however, there is no storage problem, and consumers obtain wheat at the lower market price of $3 per bushel.

The Fair Act of 1996 (more often called the "Freedom to Farm Act") freed U.S. farmers from government production controls but was supposed to gradually phase out farm subsidies. When commodity prices plummeted in 1998, however, U.S. farmers lobbied Congress and received nearly $3 billion in emergency assistance

✓ **Concept Check**
What is the effect of a price floor?

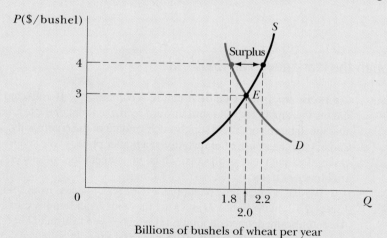

FIGURE 2.11   **Agricultural Support Programs**   At the price floor of $4 per bushel, farmers supply 2.2 billion bushels, consumers purchase 1.8 billion bushels, and the government purchases the surplus of 0.4 billion bushels at a total cost of $1.6 billion.

payments on top of the huge payments they were still receiving under the other farm programs (that were supposed to be phased out). Emergency assistance payments increased to $7.5 billion in 1999, $9 billion in 2000, and $20 billion in 2001. Furthermore, most of the assistance went to very large growers rather than to small family farms. Thus, instead of liberalizing agriculture, as agreed at the World Trade Organization (the Geneva-based international institution that regulates international trade), the U.S. farming sector was as protected in 2001 as it was in 1996.

The farm bill signed into law by President Bush in May 2002 that runs from 2003 to 2008 increased subsidies to U.S. farmers even more. This represented a reversal of course from what the president had proposed in 2001 (i.e., to shift U.S. farm policy away from subsidies and toward freer markets and more open international trade in agricultural products) and created even more trade friction with the European Union and developing countries. The European Union and Japan are, of course, just as guilty. Indeed, they provide even more aid to their farmers than the United States. The total amount of farm aid provided in the year 2005 was $47 billion in the United States, $49 billion in Japan, and $133 billion in the European Union. This comes to over $350 dollars per person living in the United States, Japan, and the European Union, and more than half of the price that farmers receive for some crops represents government subsidies. In spring 2008, a new $307 billion farm bill was passed that for the most part preserves the extensive program of subsidies to U.S. farmers over the subsequent five years.

Sources: "Farmers Harvest a Bumper Crop of Subsidies," *Wall Street Journal,* August 10, 1999, p. A24; "Administration Seeks to Shift Farm Policy from Subsidies," *New York Times,* September 20, 2001, p. 12; "Reversing Course, Bush Signs Bill Raising Farm Subsidies," *New York Times,* May 14, 2002, p. 16; OECD, *Agricultural Policies in OECD Countries* (Paris: OECD, 2006); "Senate Approval of Farm Bill Threatens Clash on Tax," *Financial Times,* December 16, 2007, p. 5; and "Farm Bill Goes to Bush," *New York Times,* May 16, 2008, p. 21.

EXAMPLE 2−6

Working Through the Market with an Excise Tax

Excise tax A tax on each unit of a commodity.

An **excise tax** is a tax on each unit of a commodity.[8] If collected from sellers, the tax causes the supply curve to shift upward by the amount of the tax, because sellers require that much more per unit to supply each amount of the commodity. The result is that consumers purchase a smaller quantity at a higher price, while sellers receive a smaller *net* price after payment of the tax. Thus, consumers and producers share the burden or **incidence of a tax.**

Incidence of tax The relative burden of a tax on buyers and sellers.

We can analyze the effect of an excise tax collected from sellers through the use of Figure 2.12. In the figure, D and S are the demand and supply curves of hamburgers with the equilibrium defined at point E (at which $P = \$1.00$ and $Q = 6$ million hamburgers, as in Figure 2.5). If a tax of $0.75 per hamburger is collected from sellers, S shifts up

---

[8] An excise tax can be of a given dollar amount *per unit* of the commodity or of a given percentage of the price of the commodity (ad valorem). If all units of the commodity are of equal quality and price (as we assume here), the per-unit and the ad valorem excise tax are equal and the distinction is unnecessary.

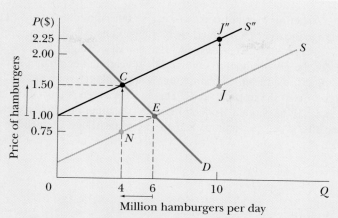

FIGURE 2.12   Effect of an Excise Tax   With D and S, $P = \$1.00$ and $Q = 6$ million hamburgers (point E), as in Figure 2.5. If the tax of $\$0.75$ per hamburger is collected from sellers, S shifts up by $\$0.75$ to S''. With D and S'', $Q = 4$ million hamburgers and $P = \$1.50$ for consumers (point C), but sellers receive a net price of only $\$0.75$ after paying the $\$0.75$ tax per unit.

by the amount of the tax to S'', since sellers now require a price $\$0.75$ higher than before to realize the same net after-tax price. Now D and S'' define equilibrium point C with $Q = 4$ million hamburgers and $P = \$1.50$, or $\$0.50$ higher than before the imposition of the tax. Thus, at the new equilibrium point, consumers purchase a smaller quantity and pay a higher price. Sellers also receive the smaller net price of $\$0.75$ (the price of $\$1.50$ paid by consumers minus the $\$0.75$ collected by the government on each hamburger sold).

In the case shown in Figure 2.12, two-thirds of the burden of the tax falls on consumers and one-third on sellers. That is, consumers pay $\$0.50$ more and sellers receive a net price that is $\$0.25$ less than before the imposition of the excise tax. Thus, even though the tax is collected from sellers, the forces of demand and supply are such that sellers are able to pass on or shift part of the burden of the tax to consumers in the form of a higher price for hamburgers. Given the supply of a commodity, the less sensitive the quantity demanded is to price (i.e., the steeper the demand curve), the greater is the share of the tax paid by consumers in the form of higher prices. On the other hand, given the demand for a commodity, the less sensitive the quantity supplied is to price (i.e., the steeper the supply curve), the smaller is the share of the tax paid by consumers and the larger is the share left to be paid by sellers (see Problem 12 at the end of the chapter).

If the government collected the tax of $\$0.75$ per hamburger from buyers or consumers rather than from sellers, D would shift down by $\$0.75$ to D'' (pencil D'' in Figure 2.12 through point N, parallel to D). With D'' and S, $Q = 4$ million hamburgers, $P = \$0.75$ (that buyers pay to sellers) and then buyers have to pay the tax of $\$0.75$ per hamburger to the government. Again, consumers pay $\$1.50$, which is $\$0.50$ more than the previous equilibrium price, and sellers receive $\$0.25$ less. Therefore, the net result is the same whether the tax is collected from sellers or from buyers.

✓ Concept Check
How much of an excise tax falls on consumers as compared to sellers?

Sometimes governments use excise taxes not only to raise money but also to discourage the use of a product, such as cigarettes, which is harmful to health. An excise tax on cigarettes increases their price and discourages their use. An alternative would be for the government to conduct an educational campaign explaining, especially to teenagers, the harm from smoking. In general, governments do both. Another type of excise tax is the **import tariff.** This is a tax on each unit of the imported commodity. As such, it has both a production and a consumption effects; these, as well as the welfare effects of a per-unit tax and an import tariff, are analyzed in Section 9.8.

Import tariff
A per-unit tax on the imported commodity.

EXAMPLE 2–7

Fighting the Drug War by Reducing Demand and Supply

The battle against illegal drug use in the United States is being fought by trying to reduce their demand and supply. The federal government is trying to shift the demand curve for illegal drugs down and to the left through an educational campaign to explain the destructive effect of illegal drugs. By itself, this campaign would reduce sales and the price for illegal drugs (compare equilibrium point E in Figure 2.13) before the government campaign, with equilibrium point E' after a successful government campaign to reduce demand. The government is also trying to reduce the supply of illegal drugs by providing payments (subsidies) to Bolivian, Colombian, and Peruvian farmers (who raise most of the coca crop from which a majority of the cocaine entering the United States is extracted) to shift to other crops and by increasing border surveillance and interdiction (seizures) of illegal drugs entering the United States. By itself, this would shift the supply curve for illegal drugs upward and to the left and lead to reduced sales and higher drug prices (compare equilibrium point E with E^* in Figure 2.13).

Thus, both a reduced demand and a reduced supply would lower sales of illegal drugs, but the former would also reduce the price of illegal drugs while the latter would increase drug prices. If both the demand and the supply of drugs were reduced, drug sales would fall, but drug prices would remain unchanged (compare equilibrium point E'' to E), increase, or decrease, respectively, depending on whether the downward shift in the demand curve is equal, smaller, or greater than the upward or leftward shift in the supply curve.

Therefore, we cannot determine by looking only at drug prices whether the government campaign is successful. Specifically, if the reduction in drug prices is due to a reduction in demand, the campaign can be said to be successful because it is accompanied by reduced sales. But the reduction in drug prices could also result from an increased drug supply. In that case, the campaign against illegal drugs would not be successful. It all depends on whether the price reduction is accompanied by a reduction or an increase in drug sales. On the other hand, if at the same time that the demand for illegal drugs declines their supply increases, drug prices will definitely fall, but sales can remain the same, decrease, or increase depending, respectively, on whether the leftward shift in the demand curve is equal, greater, or smaller than the rightward shift in the supply curve (you can clearly see this by penciling in these changes in Figure 2.13). Despite

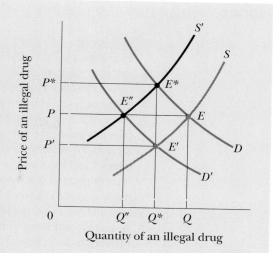

Figure 2.13   Reducing the Demand and Supply for Illegal Drugs   *D* and *S* refer to the demand and supply curves for illegal drugs before the government campaign to reduce demand and supply. With *D* and *S*, the equilibrium price of drugs is *P* and the equilibrium quantity is *Q*. With a reduction in demand from *D* to *D′*, the equilibrium price of drugs falls to *P′* and the sales to *Q**. With a reduction (leftward shift) in supply from *S* to *S′*, the price rises to *P** and sales fall to *Q**. With *D′* and *S′*, the price is *P* and sales *Q″*

some recent dramatic successes in apprehending and jailing of some powerful Colombian drug lords, the flow of cocaine and other illegal drugs to American cities and their price remain high.

Sources: United Nations, *World Drug Report 2006*, New York, UN, 2006; and "At War with the Law of Demand and Supply," *Financial Times*, January 14, 2008, p. 7.

AT THE FRONTIER
Nonclearing Markets Theory

Nonclearing markets theory Theory that seeks to explain the persistence of surpluses and shortages.

In this chapter we have seen how an excess demand for a commodity is automatically eliminated by a price rise and an excess supply is eliminated by a price decline. Markets clear by quantity responses to price changes resulting from a disequilibrium. Some real-world markets, however, do not clear and do not seem to move toward clearing. For example, financial markets (especially credit markets) often do not clear. That is, we often observe excessive demand or excessive supply of credit that persists over time. Sometimes nonclearing markets also arise in labor, commodity, and other markets. To explain these situations, economists have developed **nonclearing markets theory.**

The new theory of nonclearing markets postulates that sometimes markets do not clear, because economic agents react to both price signals (as in traditional theory) and to quantity signals. In particular, economic agents sometimes deliberately create a disequilibrium situation because of the advantages that they can extract from the persistence of a surplus or a shortage of the commodity or service that they sell or buy. One of the main insights of nonclearing markets theory is that a disequilibrium in one market can actually create desirable *spillover effects* in a related market.

Continued . . .

Nonclearing Markets Theory   *Continued*

For example, ticket prices for concerts by a superstar, such as Billy Joel or Madonna, are often deliberately set below the equilibrium price so as to create a shortage (i.e., excess demand) for tickets. Long lines form in front of ticket booths long before tickets go on sale and all available tickets are quickly sold out as soon as they do go on sale. The news media report on the long lines to get tickets and interview some of the people camped outside ticket booths days before the tickets go on sale, fans talk about the hot concert coming up, and an aura of anticipation and success is created. Promoters play this price game in the expectation that all the "hype" about the concert and the free publicity that it gets will lead to much greater sales of the star's recordings, and that these spillovers will more than make up for the loss of revenue by pricing concert tickets below the equilibrium level. The same occurs in pricing admission tickets to Disneyland or meals at a chic restaurant. Lines in front of the new restaurant and word of mouth are the best and cheapest forms of advertising that the restaurant could have. Most people believe that if it is difficult to get into the restaurant, it must be great.

These and other examples of nonclearing markets do not mean that the traditional theory of clearing markets examined in this chapter is wrong, but only that the traditional theory is not applicable in some cases where shortages or surpluses are deliberately created and tend to persist over time. The theory of nonclearing markets acknowledges this fact and tries to explain it. In the ticket example above, it is clear that excess demand for tickets is fully and voluntarily planned by the price-maker or promoter as a way to increase overall or combined revenues from the concert and the sales of the star's recordings.

✓ **Concept Check**
Does nonclearing markets theory invalidate the demand and supply model?

Sources: "Nonclearing Markets: Microeconomic Concepts and Macroeconomic Applications," *Journal of Economic Literature,* June 1993, pp. 732–761 and "So Long, Supply and Demand," *Wall Street Journal,* January 1, 2000, p. R31.

SUMMARY

1. Most of microeconomic analysis is devoted to the study of how individual markets operate. A market is in equilibrium when no buyer or seller has any incentive to change the quantity of the good, service, or resource that he or she buys or sells at the given price. Markets provide the framework for the analysis of the forces of demand and supply that determine commodity and resource prices. A market can, but need not, be a specific place or location. A perfectly competitive market is a market in which no buyer or seller can affect the price of the product, all units of the products are homogeneous, resources are mobile, and knowledge of the market is perfect.

2. A market demand schedule is a table showing the quantity demanded of a commodity at each price over a given time period while holding constant all other relevant economic variables on which demand depends. The market demand curve is the graphic representation of the demand schedule. It is negatively sloped, which reflects the inverse price-quantity relationship or the law of demand. A change in consumers' incomes, tastes for the commodity, the number of consumers in the market, or the price of substitutes or complements shifts the demand curve.

3. A market supply schedule is a table showing the quantity supplied of a commodity at each price over a given time period. The market supply curve is the graphic representation of the

supply schedule. Because of rising marginal costs, the supply curve is usually positively sloped, which indicates that producers supply more of the commodity at higher prices. A change in technology, resource prices, and, for agricultural commodities, weather conditions, shifts the supply curve.

4. The equilibrium price and quantity of a commodity are defined at the intersection of the market demand and supply curves of the commodity. At higher than equilibrium prices, there is a surplus of the commodity, which leads sellers to lower their prices to the equilibrium level. At lower than equilibrium prices, there is a shortage of the commodity, which leads consumers to bid prices up to the equilibrium level. Equilibrium is the condition that, once achieved, tends to persist. In the real world, the approximate equilibrium price is often reached by auction.

5. An increase in demand (a rightward shift in the demand curve) results in an increase in both the equilibrium price and quantity of the commodity. A decrease in demand has the opposite effect. On the other hand, an increase in supply (a rightward shift in the supply curve) results in a lower equilibrium price but a higher equilibrium quantity. A decrease in supply has the opposite effect.

6. A nation's demand for imports is derived from the nation's excess demand for the importable commodity at below-equilibrium prices in the absence of trade. On the other hand, the foreign supply of exports of the commodity is derived from the foreign excess supply of the commodity at above-equilibrium prices in the absence of trade. The equilibrium price and quantity of the traded commodity are given at the intersection of the demand and supply curves of imports of the commodity. In today's interdependent world, the tendency for the domestic price of a commodity to rise is moderated by the inflow of imports of the commodity.

7. A price ceiling below the equilibrium price (such as rent control) leads to a shortage of the commodity and possibly black markets. A price floor above the equilibrium price (as for some agricultural commodities) leads to a surplus of the commodity. Given the supply of a commodity, the steeper the demand for the commodity, the greater the burden or incidence of a per-unit tax on consumers. The federal antidrug program relies on reducing the demand and supply of illegal drugs. Some real-world markets do not clear, and this fact gave rise to a new nonclearing market theory.

KEY TERMS

Market	Equilibrium price	Excess supply
Perfectly competitive market	Surplus	Price ceiling
Market demand schedule	Shortage	Price floor
Law of demand	Equilibrium	Excise tax
Market demand curve	Auction	Incidence of a tax
Market supply schedule	Comparative static analysis	Import tariff
Market supply curve	Excess demand	Nonclearing markets theory

REVIEW QUESTIONS

1. Which of the following cause demand to increase? An increase in consumers' income, an increase in the price of substitutes, an increase in the price of complements, an increase in the number of consumers in the market.

2. Will the supply curve shift to the right or to the left if (a) technology improves or (b) input prices increase? (c) What happens if both (a) and (b) occur?

3. Explain why Q D 4 is not the equilibrium quantity in Figure 2.5 and how equilibrium is reached.

4. Explain why Q D 8 is not the equilibrium quantity in Figure 2.5 and how equilibrium is reached.

5. Using comparative static analysis, explain how a wheat shortage was avoided in the United States after the drought in Kansas in 1988 and 1989 (described in Example 1–2).

6. Was the increase in the demand for large automobiles in the United States since the collapse of petroleum prices in 1986 rational? Do you foresee any difficulty for the United States if this trend continues?

7. Why is the textile price of $1.50 in Figure 2.9 not the equilibrium price?

8. What would be the difference in textile prices between the United States and the rest of the world if textiles were freely traded but the cost of transporting each yard of textiles between the United States and the rest of the world was $1? What would be the quantity of textiles traded?

9. a. When is the price ceiling or price floor ineffective?

   b. What is an example of an effective price ceiling? What is its effect?

   c. What is an example of an effective price floor? What is its effect?

10. Does it make any difference whether an excise tax is collected from sellers or from buyers? Why?

11. Determine the minimum size of a prohibitive tariff in Figure 2.9 in the absence of transportation costs.

12. How does nonclearing markets theory explain why markets sometimes do not clear?

PROBLEMS

1. Given the following demand schedule of a commodity

P($)	6	5	4	3	2	1	0
QD	0	10	20	30	40	50	60

show that by substituting the prices given in the table into the following demand equation or function, you obtain the corresponding quantities demanded given in the table:

$$QD = 60 - 10P$$

*2. a. Derive the demand schedule from the following demand function:

$$QD' = 80 - 10P$$

   b. On the same graph, plot the demand schedule of Problem 1 and label it D and the demand curve of part (a) of this problem and label it D'.

   c. Does D' represent an increase in demand or an increase in the quantity demanded? Why?

3. a. Derive the supply schedule from the following supply function:

$$QS = 10P$$

   b. Derive the supply schedule from the following supply function:

$$QS' = 20 + 10P$$

   c. On the same graph, plot the supply schedule of part (a) and label it S and the supply curve of part (b) and label it S'.

   d. What may have caused S to shift to S'?

*4. a. Construct a table similar to Table 2.3 giving the supply schedule of Problem 3(a), and the demand schedule of Problem 1. In the same table identify the equilibrium price and quantity of the commodity, the surplus or shortage at prices other than the equilibrium price, and the pressure on price with a surplus or a shortage.

   b. Show your results of part (a) graphically.

5. Using the demand function of Problem 1 and the supply function of Problem 3(a), determine the equilibrium price and quantity algebraically.

6. a. Repeat the procedure in Problem 4(a) for the supply schedule of Problem 3(b) and the demand schedule of Problem 2(a).

   b. Show your results of part (a) graphically.

   c. On the same graph, draw D and S from Problem 4(b) and D' and S' from Problem 6(b). What general conclusion can you reach as to the effect of an increase in the demand and supply of a commodity on the equilibrium price and quantity of the commodity?

7. On separate sets of axes, show that

   a. a decrease in demand reduces the equilibrium price and quantity of the commodity.

   b. a decrease in supply increases price but reduces quantity.

_____

* = Answer provided at end of book.

c. a decrease in both demand and supply will reduce quantity but may increase, reduce, or leave price unchanged.

8. On separate sets of axes, show that

a. an increase in both demand and supply will increase quantity and may increase, reduce, or leave price unchanged.

b. a decrease in demand and an increase in supply will reduce price but may increase, decrease, or leave quantity unchanged.

c. an increase in demand and a decrease in supply will increase price but may increase, decrease, or leave quantity unchanged.

*9. Indicate what happens in the market for hamburgers if

a. the price of hot dogs increases.

b. a disease develops that kills a large proportion of cattle.

c. a new breed of cattle is developed with much faster growth.

d. medical research proves that this new breed results in hamburgers with less cholesterol.

e. a direct subsidy on each head of cattle is given to farmers raising cattle.

10. Using Panels A and C of Figure 2.9, show the price of textiles in the United States and in the rest of the world.

Also show the quantity of textiles traded if the cost of transportation for each yard of cloth is $1 and if this cost falls equally on the United States and the rest of the world.

11. With reference to your answer to Problem 4(a), indicate the effect of the government imposing on the commodity a

a. price ceiling of $P = \$2$.

b. price ceiling of $P = \$3$.

c. price ceiling higher than $P = \$3$.

d. price floor of $P = \$5$.

e. price floor of $P = \$4$.

f. price floor equal to or smaller than $P = \$3$.

*12. Draw a figure showing that

a. given the supply of a commodity, the less sensitive the quantity demanded is to price (i.e., the steeper the demand curve), the greater is the share of the tax paid by consumers in the form of higher prices.

b. given the demand for a commodity, the less sensitive the quantity supplied is to price (i.e., the steeper the supply curve), the smaller is the share of the tax paid by consumers and the larger is the share paid by sellers.

APPENDIX THE ALGEBRA OF DEMAND, SUPPLY, AND EQUILIBRIUM

In this appendix, we show the algebraic analysis corresponding to the graphical analysis of equilibrium, surplus and shortages, shifts in the demand and supply functions, and the effect of an excise tax shown in this chapter.

Market Equilibrium Algebraically

To show the algebraic determination of equilibrium, we begin by expressing the market demand curve of Figure 2.1 and the supply curve of Figure 2.3 algebraically, as follows:

$$QD = 10 - 4P \qquad [1]$$

$$QS = -2 + 8P \qquad [2]$$

From equation [1], we see that if $P = \$2$, $QD = 2$; if $P = \$1$, $QD = 6$, and if $P = \$0.50$, $QD = 8$, as shown by demand curve D in Figure 2.1. Similarly, from equation [2], we see that if $P = \$0.50$, $QS = 2$; if $P = \$1$, $QS = 6$, and if $P = \$2$, $QS = 14$, as shown by supply curve S in Figure 2.3.

To find the equilibrium price $(\overline{P})$ we set

$$QD = QS \qquad [3]$$

and get

$$10 - 4P = -2 + 8P$$
$$12 = 12P$$

Thus,

$$\overline{P} = \$1 \qquad\qquad [4]$$

Substituting the equilibrium price of $\overline{P} = \$1$ either into demand equation [1] or supply equation [2], we get the equilibrium quantity $(\overline{Q})$ of

$$QD = 10 - 4(\$1) = 6 = \overline{Q} \qquad\qquad [1A]$$

or

$$QS = -2 + 8(\$1) = 6 = \overline{Q} \qquad\qquad [2A]$$

as shown by point E in Figure 2.5.
    At the nonequilibrium price of $P = \$1.50$,

$$QD = 10 - 4(\$1.50) = 4$$

while

$$QS = -2 + 8(\$1.50) = 10$$

Thus, we would have a surplus of 6 units, as shown in Figure 2.5.
    On the other hand, at $P = \$0.50$,

$$QD = 10 - 4(\$0.50) = 8$$

while

$$QS = -2 + 8(\$0.50) = 2$$

Thus, we would have a shortage of 6 units, as shown in Figure 2.5.

Shifts in Demand and Supply and in Equilibrium

The shift in the demand curve from D to D' in Figure 2.2 can be represented algebraically by

$$QD' = 16 - 4P \qquad\qquad [5]$$

The new equilibrium price is determined by setting QD' equal to QS. That is,

$$16 - 4P = -2 + 8P \qquad\qquad [6]$$
$$18 = 12P$$

Thus,

$$\overline{P} = \$1.50 \qquad [7]$$

and

$$QD' = 16 - 4(\$1.50) = 10 = \overline{Q} \qquad [5A]$$

or

$$QS = -2 + 8(\$1.50) = 10 = \overline{Q} \qquad [2B]$$

as shown by equilibrium point J in Figure 2.6.

On the other hand, the shift in the supply curve from S to S' in Figure 2.4 can be represented algebraically by

$$QS' = 4 + 8P \qquad [8]$$

The new equilibrium price is determined by setting QD equal to QS'. That is,

$$10 - 4P = 4 + 8P \qquad [9]$$
$$10 - 4P = 4 + 8P$$
$$6 = 12P$$

Thus,

$$\overline{P} = \$0.50 \qquad [10]$$

and

$$QD = 10 - 4(\$0.50) = 8 = \overline{Q} \qquad [1B]$$

or

$$QS' = 4 + 8(\$0.50) = 8 = \overline{Q} \qquad [8A]$$

as shown by equilibrium point G in Figure 2.6.

The Effect of an Excise Tax

The effect of the excise tax shown by the shift of S to S' in Figure 2.12 can be represented algebraically by

$$QS'' = -8 + 8P \qquad [11]$$

Setting QD equal to QS'', we get the equilibrium price of

$$10 - 4P = -8 + 8P \qquad [12]$$
$$18 = 12P$$

Thus,

$$\overline{P} = \$1.50 \tag{13}$$

and

$$QD = 10 - 4(\$1.50) = 4 = \overline{Q} \tag{1C}$$

or

$$QS'' = -8 + 8(\$1.50) = 4 = \overline{Q} \tag{11A}$$

as shown by equilibrium point C in Figure 2.12.
    At $Q = 4$, sellers get a net price of

$$
\begin{aligned}
QS &= -2 + 8P \\
4 &= -2 + 8P \tag{2C} \\
6 &= 8P \\
P &= \$0.75 \tag{12}
\end{aligned}
$$

as shown by point N in Figure 2.12.
    For a more general and advanced algebraic analysis of demand, supply, and equilibrium, see Section A.11 of the Mathematical Appendix at the end of the book.

INTERNET SITE ADDRESSES

General directories and indexes of economic information are:

YAHOO—Economics: http://www.yahoo.com/
Social_Science/Economics/

Market conditions and prices for coffee are found in:

http://www.ico.org/coffee_prices.asp
http://www.ico.org/prices/pr.htm

For agricultural policies in OECD countries, see:

http://www.oecd.org/publications/e-book/51011.pdf

Information on tax rates in the various States of the United States is found in:

http://www.taxadmin.org/fta/rate/sales.html
http://www.taxadmin.org/fta/rate/tax_stru.html

Data on the International transactions of the United States are found in the Bureau of Economic Analysis web site:

http://bea.gov and clicking "international data."

PART TWO

Theory of Consumer Behavior and Demand

Part Two (Chapters 3–6) presents the theory of consumer behavior and demand. Chapter 3 examines the tastes of the consumer and how the consumer maximizes utility or satisfaction in spending his or her income. These concepts are used and extended in Chapter 4 to derive the consumer's demand curve for a commodity. Chapter 5 shows how, by aggregating or summing up individual consumers' demand curves, we get the market demand curve for the commodity. Chapter 5 also examines in detail the measurement and usefulness of various demand elasticities. Chapter 6 discusses consumer choices in the face of uncertainty. Each chapter in Part Two includes an "At the Frontier" section with some new theories or applications of consumer behavior and demand, and Chapters 4 and 5 also have an optional appendix presenting some more advanced topics in consumer demand theory.

CHAPTER 3

Consumer Preferences and Choice

After Studying This Chapter, You Should Be Able to:

- Know how consumer tastes are measured or represented
- Describe the relationship between money and happiness
- Know how the consumer's constraints are represented
- Understand how the consumer maximizes satisfaction or reaches equilibrium
- Describe how consumer tastes or preferences can be inferred without asking the consumer

In this chapter, we begin the formal study of microeconomics by examining the economic behavior of the consumer. A consumer is an individual or a household composed of one or more individuals. The consumer is the basic economic unit that determines which commodities are purchased and in what quantities. Millions of such decisions are made each day on the more than $13 trillion worth of goods and services produced by the American economy each year.

What guides these individual consumer decisions? Why do consumers purchase some commodities and not others? How do they decide how much to purchase of each commodity? What is the aim of a rational consumer in spending income? These are some of the important questions to which we seek answers in this chapter. The theory of consumer behavior and choice is the first step in the derivation of the market demand curve, the importance of which was clearly demonstrated in Chapter 2.

We begin the study of the economic behavior of the consumer by examining tastes. Consumers' tastes can be related to utility concepts or indifference curves. These are discussed in the first two sections of the chapter. In Section 3.3, we examine the convergence of tastes internationally. We then introduce the budget line, which gives the constraints or limitations consumer's face in purchasing goods and services. Constraints arise because the commodities that the consumer wants command a price in the marketplace (i.e., they are not free) and the consumer has limited income. Thus, the budget line reflects the familiar and pervasive economic fact of scarcity as it pertains to the individual consumer.

Because the consumer's wants are unlimited or, in any event, exceed his or her ability to satisfy them all, it is important that the consumer spend income so as to maximize satisfaction. Thus, a model is provided to illustrate and predict how a rational consumer maximizes satisfaction, given his or her tastes (indifference curves) and the constraints that the consumer faces (the budget line). The "At the Frontier" section presents a different way to examine consumer tastes and derive a consumer's indifference curves.

The several real-world examples and important applications presented in the chapter demonstrate the relevance and usefulness of the theory of consumer behavior and choice.

3.1　UTILITY ANALYSIS

In this section, we discuss the meaning of utility, distinguish between total utility and marginal utility, and examine the important difference between cardinal and ordinal utility. The concept of utility is used here to introduce the consumer's tastes. The analysis of consumer tastes is a crucial step in determining how a consumer maximizes satisfaction in spending income.

Total and Marginal Utility

Utility The ability of a good to satisfy a want.

Total utility (TU) The total satisfaction received from consuming a good or service.

Marginal utility (MU) The extra utility received from consuming one additional unit of a good.

Util The arbitrary unit of measure of utility.

Goods are desired because of their ability to satisfy human wants. The property of a good that enables it to satisfy human wants is called **utility.** As individuals consume more of a good per time period, their **total utility (TU)** or satisfaction increases, but their marginal utility diminishes. **Marginal utility (MU)** is the extra utility received from consuming one additional unit of the good per unit of time while holding constant the quantity consumed of all other commodities.

For example, Table 3.1 indicates that one hamburger per day (or, more generally, one unit of good X per period of time) gives the consumer a total utility (TU) of 10 utils, where a **util** is an arbitrary unit of utility. Total utility increases with each additional hamburger consumed until the fifth one, which leaves total utility unchanged. This is the *saturation point.* Consuming the sixth hamburger then leads to a decline in total utility because of storage or disposal problems.[1] The third column of Table 3.1 gives the extra or marginal utility resulting from the consumption of each *additional* hamburger. Marginal utility is positive but declines until the fifth hamburger, for which it is zero, and becomes negative for the sixth hamburger.

---

[1] That is, some effort (disutility), no matter how small, is required to get rid of the sixth hamburger. Assuming that the individual cannot sell the sixth hamburger, he or she would not want it even for free.

TABLE 3.1	Total and Marginal Utility	
Q_X	TU_X	MU_X
0	0	. . .
1	10	10
2	16	6
3	20	4
4	22	2
5	22	0
6	20	−2

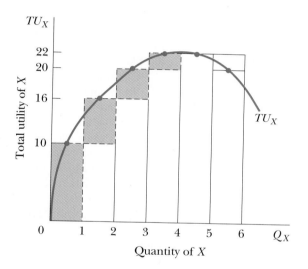

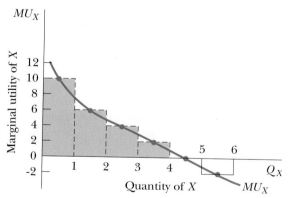

FIGURE 3.1   Total and Marginal Utility   In the top panel, total utility (*TU*) increases by smaller and smaller amounts (the shaded areas) and so the marginal utility (*MU*) in the bottom panel declines. *TU* remains unchanged with the consumption of the fifth hamburger, and so *MU* is zero. After the fifth hamburger per day, *TU* declines and *MU* is negative.

Plotting the values given in Table 3.1, we obtain Figure 3.1, with the top panel showing total utility and the bottom panel showing marginal utility. The total and marginal utility curves are obtained by joining the midpoints of the bars measuring *TU* and *MU* at each level of consumption. Note that the *TU* rises by smaller and smaller amounts (the shaded areas) and so the *MU* declines. The consumer reaches saturation after consuming

Law of diminishing marginal utility Each additional unit of a good eventually gives less and less extra utility.

✓ Concept Check

What is the relationship between diminishing marginal utility and the law of demand?

Cardinal utility An actual measure of utility, in util.

Ordinal utility The rankings of the utility received from consuming various amounts of a good.

the fourth hamburger. Thus, *TU* remains unchanged with the consumption of the fifth hamburger and *MU* is zero. After the fifth hamburger, *TU* declines and so *MU* is negative. The negative slope or downward-to-the-right inclination of the *MU* curve reflects the **law of diminishing marginal utility.**

Utility schedules reflect tastes of a particular individual; that is, they are unique to the individual and reflect his or her own particular subjective preferences and perceptions. Different individuals may have different tastes and different utility schedules. Utility schedules remain unchanged so long as the individual's tastes remain the same.

Cardinal or Ordinal Utility?

The concept of utility discussed in the previous section was introduced at about the same time, in the early 1870s, by William Stanley Jevons of Great Britain, Carl Menger of Austria, and Léon Walras of France. They believed that the utility an individual receives from consuming each quantity of a good or basket of goods could be measured cardinally just like weight, height, or temperature.[2]

Cardinal utility means that an individual can attach specific values or numbers of utils from consuming each quantity of a good or basket of goods. In Table 3.1 we saw that the individual received 10 utils from consuming one hamburger. He received 16 utils, or 6 additional utils, from consuming two hamburgers. The consumption of the third hamburger gave this individual 4 extra utils, or two-thirds as many extra utils, as the second hamburger. Thus, Table 3.1 and Figure 3.1 reflect cardinal utility. They actually provide an index of satisfaction for the individual.

In contrast, **ordinal utility** only *ranks* the utility received from consuming various amounts of a good or baskets of goods. Ordinal utility specifies that consuming two hamburgers gives the individual more utility than when consuming one hamburger, but it does not specify exactly how much additional utility the second hamburger provides. Similarly, ordinal utility would say only that three hamburgers give this individual more utility than two hamburgers, but *not* how many more utils.[3]

Ordinal utility is a much weaker notion than cardinal utility because it only requires that the consumer be able to rank baskets of goods in the order of his or her preference. That is, when presented with a choice between any two baskets of goods, ordinal utility requires only that the individual indicate if he or she prefers the first basket, the second basket, or is indifferent between the two. It does not require that the individual specify how many more utils he or she receives from the preferred basket. *In short, ordinal utility only ranks various consumption bundles, whereas cardinal utility provides an actual index or measure of satisfaction.*

---

[2] A market basket of goods can be defined as containing specific quantities of various goods and services. For example, one basket may contain one hamburger, one soft drink, and a ticket to a ball game, while another basket may contain two soft drinks and two movie tickets.

[3] To be sure, numerical values could be attached to the utility received by the individual from consuming various hamburgers, even with ordinal utility. However, with ordinal utility, higher utility values only indicate higher rankings of utility, and no importance can be attached to actual numerical differences in utility. For example, 20 utils can only be interpreted as giving more utility than 10 utils, but not twice as much. Thus, to indicate rising utility rankings, numbers such as 5, 10, 20; 8, 15, 17; or I (lowest), II, and III are equivalent.

The distinction between cardinal and ordinal utility is important because a theory of consumer behavior can be developed on the weaker assumption of ordinal utility without the need for a cardinal measure. And a theory that reaches the same conclusion as another on weaker assumptions is a superior theory.[4] Utility theory provides a convenient introduction to the analysis of consumer tastes and to the more rigorous indifference curve approach. It is also useful for the analysis of consumer choices in the face of uncertainty, which is presented in Chapter 6. Example 3–1 examines the relationship between money income and happiness.

EXAMPLE 3–1

Does Money Buy Happiness?

Does money buy happiness? Philosophers have long pondered this question. Economists have now gotten involved in trying to answer this age-old question. They calculated the "mean happiness rating" (based on a score of "very happy" = 4, "pretty happy" = 2, and "not too happy" = 0) for individuals at different levels of personal income at a given point in time and for different nations over time. What they found was that up to an income per capita of about $20,000, higher incomes in the United States were positively correlated with happiness responses, but that after that, higher incomes had little, if any, effect on observed happiness. Furthermore, average individual happiness in the United States remained remarkably flat since the 1950s in the face of a considerable increase in average income. Similar results were found for other advanced nations, such as the United Kingdom, France, Germany, and Japan. These results seem to go counter to the basic economic assumption that higher personal income leads to higher utility.

Two explanations are given for these remarkable and puzzling results: (1) that happiness is based on relative rather than absolute income and (2) that happiness quickly adapts to changes in the level of income. Specifically, higher incomes make individuals happier for a while, but their effect fades very quickly as individuals adjust to the higher income and soon take it for granted. For example, a generation ago, central heating was regarded as a luxury, while today it is viewed as essential. Furthermore, as individuals become richer, they become happier, but when society as a whole grows richer, nobody seems happier. In other words, people are often more concerned about their income relative to others' than about their absolute income. Pleasure at your own pay rise can vanish when you learn that a colleague has been given a similar pay increase.

The implication of all of this is that people's effort to work more in order to earn and spend more in advanced (rich) societies does not make people any happier because others do the same. (In poor countries, higher incomes do make people happier). Lower taxes in the United States encourage people to work more and the nation to grow faster than in Europe, but this does not necessarily make Americans happier than

[4] This is like producing a given output with fewer or cheaper inputs, or achieving the same medical result (such as control of high blood pressure) with less or weaker medication.

Europeans. The consensus among happiness researchers is that after earning enough to satisfy basic wants (a per capita income of about $20,000), family, friends, and community tend to be the most important things in life.

Sources: R. A. Easterlin, "Income and Happiness," *Economic Journal,* July 2000; B. S. Frey and A. Stutzer, "What Can Economists Learn from Happiness Research?," *Journal of Economic Literature,* June 2002; R. Layard, *Happiness: Lessons from a New Science* (London: Penguin, 2005); R. Di Tella and R. MacCulloch, "Some Uses of Happiness Data, *Journal of Economic Perspectives,* Winter 2006, pp. 25–46; and A. E. Clark, P. Frijters, and M. A. Shields, "Relative Income, Happiness, and Utility: An Explanation for the Easterlin Paradox and Other Puzzles," **Journal of Economic Literature**, March 2008, pp. 95–144.

3.2 | CONSUMER'S TASTES: INDIFFERENCE CURVES

In this section, we define indifference curves and examine their characteristics. Indifference curves were first introduced by the English economist F. Y. Edgeworth in the 1880s. The concept was refined and used extensively by the Italian economist Vilfredo Pareto in the early 1900s. Indifference curves were popularized and greatly extended in application in the 1930s by two other English economists: R. G. D. Allen and John R. Hicks. Indifference curves are a crucial tool of analysis because they are used to represent an ordinal measure of the tastes and preferences of the consumer and to show how the consumer maximizes utility in spending income.

Indifference Curves—What Do They Show?[5]

Consumers' tastes can be examined with ordinal utility. An ordinal measure of utility is based on three assumptions. First, we assume that when faced with any two baskets of goods, the consumer can determine whether he or she prefers basket *A* to basket *B*, *B* to *A*, or whether he or she is indifferent between the two. Second, we assume that the tastes of the consumer are *consistent* or *transitive.* That is, if the consumer states that he or she prefers basket *A* to basket *B* and also that he or she prefers basket *B* to basket *C*, then that consumer will prefer *A* to *C*. Third, we assume that more of a commodity is preferred to less; that is, we assume that the commodity is a **good** rather than a **bad,** and the consumer is never satiated with the commodity.[6] The three assumptions can be used to represent an individual's tastes with indifference curves. In order to conduct the analysis by plane geometry, we will assume throughout that there are only two goods, *X* and *Y*.

An **indifference curve** shows the various combinations of two goods that give the consumer equal utility or satisfaction. A higher indifference curve refers to a higher level of satisfaction, and a lower indifference curve refers to less satisfaction. However, we have no indication as to how much additional satisfaction or utility a higher indifference curve indicates. That is, different indifference curves simply provide an ordering or ranking of the individual's preference.

Good A commodity of which more is preferred to less.

Bad An item of which less is preferred to more.

Indifference curve The curve showing the various combinations of two commodities that give the consumer equal satisfaction.

---
[5] For a mathematical presentation of indifference curves and their characteristics using rudimentary calculus, see Section A.1 of the Mathematical Appendix at the end of the book.
[6] Examples of bads are pollution, garbage, and disease, of which less is preferred to more.

For example, Table 3.2 gives an indifference schedule showing the various combinations of hamburgers (good X) and soft drinks (good Y) that give the consumer equal satisfaction. This information is plotted as indifference curve U_1 in the left panel of Figure 3.2. The right panel repeats indifference curve U_1 along with a higher indifference curve (U_2) and a lower one (U_0).

Indifference curve U_1 shows that one hamburger and ten soft drinks per unit of time (combination A) give the consumer the same level of satisfaction as two hamburgers and six soft drinks (combination B), four hamburgers and three soft drinks (combination C), or seven hamburgers and one soft drink (combination F). On the other hand, combination R (four hamburgers and seven soft drinks) has both more hamburgers and more soft drinks than combination B (see the right panel of Figure 3.2), and so it refers to a higher level of satisfaction. Thus, combination R and all the other combinations that give the same level of satisfaction as combination R define higher indifference curve U_2. Finally, all combinations

✓ Concept Check
Are the indifference curves of various individuals the same?

TABLE 3.2 Indifference Schedule

Hamburgers (X)	Soft Drinks (Y)	Combinations
1	10	A
2	6	B
4	3	C
7	1	F

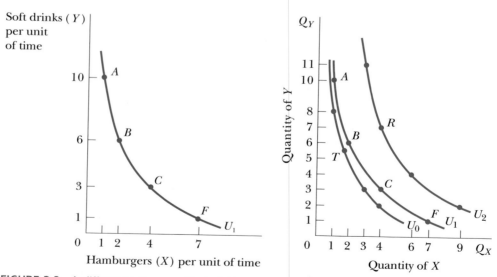

FIGURE 3.2 Indifference Curves   The individual is indifferent among combinations A, B, C, and F since they all lie on indifference curve U_1. U_1 refers to a higher level of satisfaction than U_0, but to a lower level than U_2.

on U_0 give the same satisfaction as combination T, and combination T refers to both fewer hamburgers and fewer soft drinks than (and therefore is inferior to) combination B on U_1.

Although in Figure 3.2 we have drawn only three indifference curves, there is an indifference curve going through each point in the XY plane (i.e., referring to each possible combination of good X and good Y). That is, between any two indifference curves, an additional curve can always be drawn. The entire set of indifference curves is called an **indifference map** and reflects the entire set of tastes and preferences of the consumer.

Indifference map
The entire set of indifference curves reflecting the consumer's tastes and preferences.

Characteristics of Indifference Curves

Indifference curves are usually negatively sloped, cannot intersect, and are convex to the origin (see Figure 3.2). Indifference curves are negatively sloped because if one basket of goods X and Y contains more of X, it will have to contain less of Y than another basket in order for the two baskets to give the same level of satisfaction and be on the same indifference curve. For example, since basket B on indifference curve U_1 in Figure 3.2 contains more hamburgers (good X) than basket A, basket B must contain fewer soft drinks (good Y) for the consumer to be on indifference curve U_1.

✓ Concept Check

Why are indifference curves negatively sloped?

A positively sloped curve would indicate that one basket containing more of both commodities gives the same utility or satisfaction to the consumer as another basket containing less of both commodities (and no other commodity). Because we are dealing with goods rather than bads, such a curve could not possibly be an indifference curve. For example, in the left panel of Figure 3.3, combination B' contains more of X and more of Y than combination A', and so the positively sloped curve on which B' and A' lie cannot be an indifference curve. That is, B' must be on a higher indifference curve than A' if X and Y are both goods.[7]

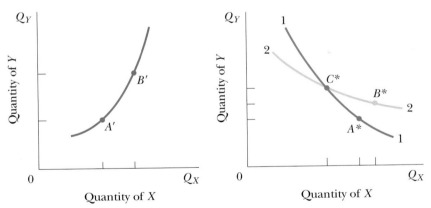

FIGURE 3.3   Indifference Curves Cannot Be Positively Sloped or Intersect
In the left panel, the positively sloped curve cannot be an indifference curve because it shows that combination B'', which contains more of X and Y than combination A', gives equal satisfaction to the consumer as A'. In the right panel, since C^* is on curves 1 and 2, it should give the same satisfaction as A^* and B^*, but this is impossible because B^* has more of X and Y than A^*. Thus, indifference curves cannot intersect.

---

[7] Only if either X or Y were a bad would the indifference curve be positively sloped as in the left panel of Figure 3.3.

Indifference curves also cannot intersect. Intersecting curves are inconsistent with the definition of indifference curves. For example, if curve 1 and curve 2 in the right panel of Figure 3.3 were indifference curves, they would indicate that basket $A*$ is equivalent to basket $C*$ since both $A*$ and $C*$ are on curve 1, and also that basket $B*$ is equivalent to basket $C*$ since both $B*$ and $C*$ are on curve 2. By transitivity, $B*$ should then be equivalent to $A*$. However, this is impossible because basket $B*$ contains more of both good X and good Y than basket $A*$. Thus, indifference curves cannot intersect.

Indifference curves are usually convex to the origin; that is, they lie above any tangent to the curve. Convexity results from or is a reflection of a decreasing marginal rate of substitution, which is discussed next.

The Marginal Rate of Substitution

Marginal rate of substitution (MRS)
The amount of a good that a consumer is willing to give up for an additional unit of another good while remaining on the same indifference curve.

The **marginal rate of substitution (MRS)** refers to the amount of one good that an individual is willing to give up for an additional unit of another good while maintaining the same level of satisfaction or remaining on the same indifference curve. For example, the marginal rate of substitution of good X for good Y (MRS_{XY}) refers to the amount of Y that the individual is willing to exchange per unit of X and maintain the same level of satisfaction. Note that MRS_{XY} measures the downward vertical distance (the amount of Y that the individual is willing to give up) per unit of horizontal distance (i.e., per additional unit of X required) to remain on the same indifference curve. That is, $MRS_{XY} = -\Delta Y/\Delta X$. Because of the reduction in Y, MRS_{XY} is negative. However, we multiply by -1 and express MRS_{XY} as a positive value.

For example, starting at point A on U_1 in Figure 3.4, the individual is willing to give up four units of Y for one additional unit of X and reach point B on U_1. Thus, $MRS_{XY} = -(-4/1) = 4$. This is the absolute (or positive value of the) slope of the chord from point A to point B on U_1. Between point B and point C on U_1, $MRS_{XY} = 3/2 = 1.5$ (the absolute slope of chord BC). Between points C and F, $MRS_{XY} = 2/3 = 0.67$. At a particular point on the indifference curve, MRS_{XY} is given by the absolute slope of the tangent to the indifference curve at that point. Different individuals usually have different indifference curves and different MRS_{XY} (at points where their indifference curves have different slopes).

We can relate indifference curves to the preceding utility analysis by pointing out that all combinations of goods X and Y on a given indifference curve refer to the same level of total utility for the individual. Thus, for a movement down a given indifference curve, the gain in utility in consuming more of good X must be equal to the loss in utility in consuming less of good Y. Specifically, the increase in consumption of good X (ΔX) times the marginal utility that the individual receives from consuming each additional unit of X (MU_X) must be equal to the reduction in Y ($-\Delta Y$) times the marginal utility of Y (MU_Y). That is,

$$(\Delta X)(MU_X) = -(\Delta Y)(MU_Y) \qquad [3.1]$$

so that

$$MU_X/MU_Y = -\Delta Y/\Delta X = MRS_{XY} \qquad [3.2]$$

Thus, MRS_{XY} is equal to the absolute slope of the indifference curve and to the ratio of the marginal utilities.

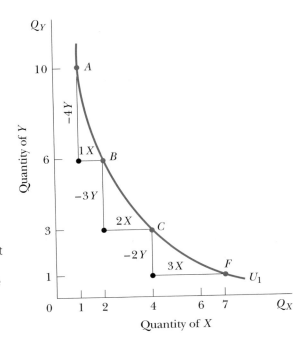

FIGURE 3.4   Marginal Rate of Substitution (*MRS*)   Starting at point *A*, the individual is willing to give up 4 units of *Y* for one additional unit of *X* and reach point *B* on U_1. Thus, $MRS_{XY} = 4$ (the absolute slope of chord *AB*). Between points *B* and *C*, $MRS_{XY} = 3/2$. Between *C* and *F*, $MRS_{XY} = 2/3$. MRS_{XY} declines as the individual moves down the indifference curve.

Note that MRS_{XY} (i.e., the absolute slope of the indifference curve) declines as we move down the indifference curve. This follows from, or is a reflection of, the convexity of the indifference curve. That is, as the individual moves down an indifference curve and is left with less and less *Y* (say, soft drinks) and more and more *X* (say, hamburgers), each remaining unit of *Y* becomes more valuable to the individual and each additional unit of *X* becomes less valuable. Thus, the individual is willing to give up less and less of *Y* to obtain each additional unit of *X*. It is this property that makes MRS_{XY} diminish and indifference curves convex to the origin. We will see in Section 3.5 the crucial role that convexity plays in consumer utility maximization.[8]

Some Special Types of Indifference Curves

Although indifference curves are usually negatively sloped and convex to the origin, they may sometimes assume other shapes, as shown in Figure 3.5. Horizontal indifference curves, as in the top left panel of Figure 3.5, would indicate that commodity *X* is a **neuter;** that is, the consumer is indifferent between having more or less of the commodity. Vertical indifference curves, as in the top right panel of Figure 3.5, would indicate instead that commodity *Y* is a neuter.

The bottom left panel of figure 3.5 shows indifference curves that are negatively sloped straight lines. Here, MRS_{XY} or the absolute slope of the indifference curves is constant. This means that an individual is always willing to give up the same amount of good *Y* (say, two cups of tea) for each additional unit of good *X* (one cup of coffee). Therefore, good *X* and two units of good *Y* are *perfect substitutes* for this individual.

---

[8] A movement along an indifference curve in the upward direction measures MRS_{YX}, which also diminishes.

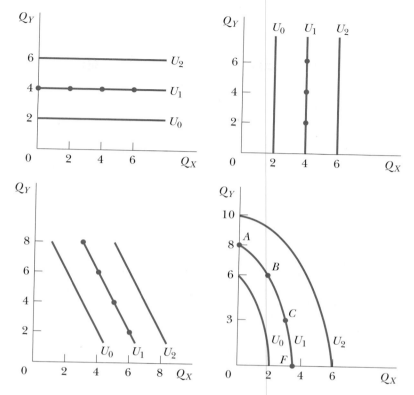

FIGURE 3.5   Some Unusual Indifference Curves   Horizontal indifference curves, as in the top left panel, indicate that X is a neuter; that is, the consumer is indifferent between having more or less of it. Vertical indifference curves, as in the top right panel, would indicate instead that commodity Y is a neuter. Indifference curves that are negatively sloped straight lines, as in the bottom left panel, indicate that MRS_{XY} is constant, and so X and Y are perfect substitutes for the individual. The bottom right panel shows indifference curves that are concave to the origin (i.e., MRS_{XY} increases).

Finally, the bottom right panel shows indifference curves that are concave rather than convex to the origin. This means that the individual is willing to give up more and more units of good Y for each additional unit of X (i.e., MRS_{XY} increases). For example, between points A and B on U_1, $MRS_{XY} = 2/2 = 1$; between B and C, $MRS_{XY} = 3/1 = 3$; and between C and F, $MRS_{XY} = 3/0.5 = 6$. In Section 3.5, we will see that in this unusual case, the individual would end up consuming only good X or only good Y.

Even though indifference curves can assume any of the shapes shown in Figure 3.5, they are usually negatively sloped, nonintersecting, and convex to the origin. These characteristics have been confirmed experimentally.[9] Because it is difficult to derive indifference curves experimentally, however, firms try to determine consumers' preferences by marketing studies, as explained in Example 3–2.

---

[9] See, for example, K. R. MacCrimmon and M. Toda, "The Experimental Determination of Indifference Curves," *Review of Economic Studies,* October 1969.

EXAMPLE 3-2

How Ford Decided on the Characteristics of Its Taurus

Firms can learn about consumers' preferences by conducting or commissioning marketing studies to identify the most important characteristics of a product, say, styling and performance for automobiles, and to determine how much more consumers would be willing to pay to have more of each attribute, or how they would trade off more of one attribute for less of another. This approach to consumer demand theory, which focuses on the characteristics or attributes of goods and on their worth or *hedonic prices* rather than on the goods themselves, was pioneered by Kelvin Lancaster (see "At the Frontier" in Chapter 4). This is in fact how the Ford Motor Company decided on the characteristics of its 1986 Taurus.

Specifically, Ford determined by marketing research that the two most important characteristics of an automobile for the majority of consumers were styling (i.e., design and interior features) and performance (i.e., acceleration and handling) and then produced its Taurus in 1986 that incorporated those characteristics. The rest is history (the Taurus regained in 1992 its status of the best-selling car in America—a position that it had lost to the Honda Accord in 1989). Ford also used this approach to decide on the characteristics of the all-new 1996 Taurus, the first major overhaul since its 1986 launch, at a cost of $2.8 billion, as well as in deciding the characteristics of its world cars, Focus, launched in 1998, the Mondeo introduced in 2000, and the new Fiesta in Europe in 2008 and in the United States in 2010. Other automakers, such as General Motors, followed similar procedures in determining the characteristics of their automobiles. Since then U.S. automakers have shifted somewhat toward producing "sports wagons," which are a cross between sedans and sport-utility vehicles (SUVs) to reflect recent changes in consumer tastes, and toward more fuel-efficient and "green" automobiles as a result of the sharp increase in gasoline prices and heightened environmental concerns.

Market studies can also be used to determine how consumers' tastes have changed over time. In terms of indifference curves, a reduction in the consumer's taste for commodity X (hamburgers) in relation to commodity Y (soft drinks) would be reflected in a flattening of the indifference curve of Figure 3.4, indicating that the consumer would now be willing to give up less of Y for each additional unit of X. The different tastes of different consumers are also reflected in the shapes of their indifference curves. The consumer who prefers soft drinks to hamburgers will have a flatter indifferences curve than a consumer who does not.

Sources: "Ford Puts Its Future on the Line," *New York Times Magazine,* December 4, 1985, pp. 94–110; V. Bajic, "Automobiles and Implicit Markets: An Estimate of a Structural Demand Model for Automobile Characteristics," *Applied Economics,* April 1993, pp. 541–551; "Ford Hopes Its New Focus Will Be a Global Best Seller," *Wall Street Journal,* October 8, 1998, p. B10; S. Berry, J. Levinsohn, and A. Pakes, "Differentiated Products Demand Systems from a Combination of Macro and Micro Data: The New Car Market," National Bureau of Economic Research, *Working Paper 6481,* March 1998; and "Ford's Taurus Loses Favor to New-Age Sport Wagon," *New York Times,* February 7, 2002, p. B1; "Once Frumpy, Green Cars Start Showing Some Flash," *New York Times,* July 15, 2007, p. 13; "Ford Eyes More Cuts, as Recovery Advances," *Wall Street Journal*, April 23, 2008, p. A1; and "One World, One Car, One Name," *Business Week*, March 24, 2008, p. 63.

3.3	INTERNATIONAL CONVERGENCE OF TASTES

A rapid convergence of tastes is taking place in the world today. Tastes in the United States affect tastes around the world and tastes abroad strongly influence tastes in the United States. Coca-Cola and jeans are only two of the most obvious U.S. products that have become household items around the world. One can see Adidas sneakers and Walkman personal stereos on joggers from Central Park in New York City to Tivoli Gardens in Copenhagen. You can eat Big Macs in Piazza di Spagna in Rome or Pushkin Square in Moscow. We find Japanese cars and VCRs in New York and in New Delhi, French perfumes in Paris and in Cairo, and Perrier in practically every major (and not so major) city around the world. Texas Instruments and Canon calculators, Dell and Hitachi portable PCs, and Xerox and Minolta copiers are found in offices and homes more or less everywhere. With more rapid communications and more frequent travel, the worldwide convergence of tastes has even accelerated. This has greatly expanded our range of consumer choices and forced producers to think in terms of global production and marketing to remain competitive in today's rapidly shrinking world.

In his 1983 article "The Globalization of Markets" in the *Harvard Business Review*, Theodore Levitt asserted that consumers from New York to Frankfurt to Tokyo want similar products and that success for producers in the future would require more and more standardized products and pricing around the world. In fact, in country after country, we are seeing the emergence of a middle-class consumer lifestyle based on a taste for comfort, convenience, and speed. In the food business, this means packaged, fast-to-prepare, and ready-to-eat products. Market researchers have discovered that similarities in living styles among middle-class people all over the world are much greater than we once thought and are growing with rising incomes and education levels. Of course, some differences in tastes will always remain among people of different nations, but with the tremendous improvement in telecommunications, transportation, and travel, the cross-fertilization of cultures and convergence of tastes can only be expected to accelerate. This trend has important implications for consumers, producers, and sellers of an increasing number and types of products and services.

EXAMPLE 3–3

Gillette Introduces the Sensor and Mach3 Razors—Two Truly Global Products

As tastes become global, firms are responding more and more with truly global products. These are introduced more or less simultaneously in most countries of the world with little or no local variation. This is leading to what has been aptly called the "global supermarket." For example, in 1990, Gillette introduced its new Sensor Razor at the same time in most nations of the world and advertised it with virtually the same TV spots (ad campaign) in 19 countries in Europe and North America. In 1994, Gillette introduced an upgrade of the Sensor Razor called SensorExcell with a high-tech edge. By 1998, Gillette had sold over 400 million of Sensor and SensorExcell razors and more than 8 billion twin-blade cartridges, and it had captured an incredible 71% of the global blade market. Then in April 1998, Gillette unveiled the Mach3, the company's most important new product since the Sensor. It has three blades with a new revolutionary edge produced with chipmaking technology that took five years to develop. Gillette developed its new razor in stealth secrecy at the astounding cost of over $750 million, and spent another $300 million to advertise it. Since it went on sale in July 1998, the Mach3 has proven to be an even greater success than the Sensor Razor. Gillette introduced the Mach3 Turbo Razor worldwide in April 2002, in June 2004 its M3Power Razor, as an evolution of its Mach 3, and its five-blade Fusion in early 2006. With the merger of Gillette and Procter & Gamble, the global reach of the M3Power and Fusion are likely to be even greater than for its predecessors.

Concept Check

Why are tastes converging internationally?

The trend toward the global supermarket is rapidly spreading in Europe as borders fade and as Europe's single currency (the euro) brings prices closer across the continent. A growing number of companies are creating "Euro-brands"—a single product for most countries of Europe—and advertising them with "Euro-ads," which are identical or nearly identical across countries, except for language. Many national differences in taste will, of course, remain; for example, Nestlé markets more than 200 blends of Nescafé to cater to differences in tastes in different markets. But the converging trend in tastes around the world is unmistakable and is likely to lead to more and more global products. This is true not only in foods and inexpensive consumer products but also in automobiles, tires, portable computers, phones, and many other durable products.

Sources: "Building the Global Supermarket," *New York Times,* November 18, 1988, p. D1; "Gillette's World View: One Blade Fits All," *Wall Street Journal,* January 3, 1994, p. C3; "Gillette Finally Reveals Its Vision of the Future, and it Has 3 Blades," *Wall Street Journal,* April 4, 1998, p. A1; "Gillette, Defying Economy, Introduces a $9 Razor Set," *New York Times,* October 31, 2001, p. C4; "Selling in Europe: Borders Fade," *New York Times,* May 31, 1990, p. D1; "Converging Prices Mean Trouble for European Retailers," *Financial Times,* June 18, 1999, p. 27; "Can Nestlé Be the Very Best?," *Fortune,* November 13, 2001, pp. 353–360; "For Cutting-Edge Dads," *US News & World Report,* June 14, 2004, pp. 80–81; "P&G's $57 Billion Bargain," *BusinessWeek,* July 25, 2005, p. 26; and "How Many Blades Is Enough?" *Fortune,* October 31, 2005, p. 40; and "Gillette New Edge," *Business Week,* February 6, 2006, p. 44.

3.4   THE CONSUMER'S INCOME AND PRICE CONSTRAINTS: THE BUDGET LINE

In this section, we introduce the constraints or limitations faced by a consumer in satisfying his or her wants. In order to conduct the analysis by plane geometry, we assume that the consumer spends all of his or her income on only two goods, *X* and *Y*. We will see that the constraints of the consumer can then be represented by a line called the budget line. The position of the budget line and changes in it can best be understood by looking at its endpoints.

Definition of the Budget Line

Budget constraint
The limitation on the amount of goods that a consumer can purchase imposed by his or her limited income and the prices of the goods.

In Section 3.2, we saw that we can represent a consumer's tastes with an indifference map. We now introduce the constraints or limitations that a consumer faces in attempting to satisfy his or her wants. The amount of goods that a consumer can purchase over a given period of time is limited by the consumer's income and by the prices of the goods that he or she must pay. In what follows we assume (realistically) that the consumer cannot affect the price of the goods he or she purchases. In economics jargon, we say that the consumer faces a **budget constraint** due to his or her limited income and the given prices of goods.

By assuming that a consumer spends all of his or her income on good X (hamburgers) and on good Y (soft drinks), we can express the budget constraint as

$$P_X Q_X + P_Y Q_Y = I \qquad [3.3]$$

where P_X is the price of good X, Q_X is the quantity of good X, P_Y is the price of good Y, Q_Y is the quantity of good Y, and I is the consumer's money income. Equation [3.3] postulates that the price of X times the quantity of X plus the price of Y times the quantity of Y equals the consumer's money income. That is, the amount of money spent on X plus the amount spent on Y equals the consumer's income.[10]

Suppose that $P_X = \$2$, $P_Y = \$1$, and $I = \$10$ per unit of time. This could, for example, be the situation of a student who has $10 per day to spend on snacks of hamburgers (good X) priced at $2 each and on soft drinks (good Y) priced at $1 each. By spending all income on Y, the consumer could purchase $10Y$ and $0X$. This defines endpoint J on the vertical axis of Figure 3.6. Alternatively, by spending all income on X, the consumer could purchase $5X$ and $0Y$. This defines endpoint K on the horizontal axis. By joining endpoints J and K with a straight line we get the consumer's **budget line.** This line shows the various combinations of X and Y that the consumer can purchase by spending all income at the given prices of the two goods. For example, starting at endpoint J, the consumer could give up two units of Y and use the $2 not spent on Y to purchase the first unit of X and reach point L. By giving up another $2Y$, he or she could purchase the second unit of X. The slope of -2 of budget line JK shows that for each $2Y$ the consumer gives up, he or she can purchase $1X$ more.

Budget line A line showing the various combinations of two goods that a consumer can purchase by spending all income.

By rearranging equation [3.3], we can express the consumer's budget constraint in a different and more useful form, as follows. By subtracting the term $P_X Q_X$ from both sides of equation [3.3] we get

$$P_Y Q_Y = I - P_X Q_X \qquad [3.3A]$$

By then dividing both sides of equation [3.3A] by P_Y, we isolate Q_Y on the left-hand side and define equation [3.4]:

$$Q_Y = I/P_Y - (P_X/P_Y)Q_X \qquad [3.4]$$

---

[10] Equation [3.3] could be generalized to deal with any number of goods. However, as pointed out, we deal with only two goods for purposes of diagrammatic analysis.

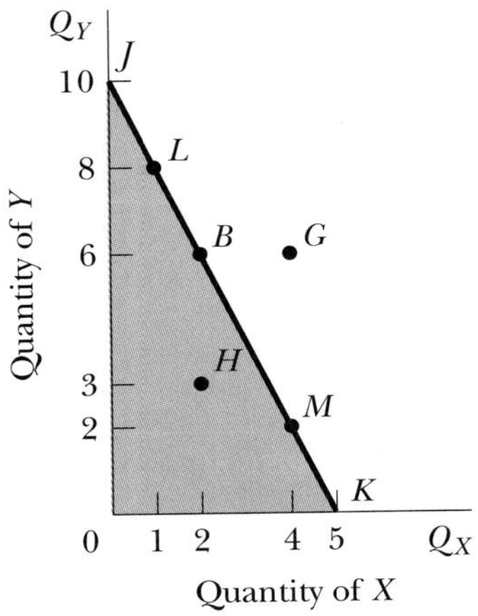

FIGURE 3.6   The Budget Line   With an income of $I = $10, and $P_Y = $1 and $P_X = $2, we get budget line JK. This shows that the consumer can purchase $10Y$ and $0X$ (endpoint J), $8Y$ and $1X$ (point L), $6Y$ and $2X$ (point B), or ... $0Y$ and $5X$ (endpoint K). $I/P_Y = $10/$1 = 10$ is the vertical or Y-intercept of the budget line and $-P_X/P_Y = -$2/$1 = -2$ is the slope.

The first term on the right-hand side of equation [3.4] is the vertical or Y-intercept of the budget line and $-P_X/P_Y$ is the slope of the budget line. For example, continuing to use $P_X = $2, $P_Y = 1, and $I = 10, we get $I/P_Y = 10$ for the Y-intercept (endpoint J in Figure 3.6) and $-P_X/P_Y = -2$ for the slope of the budget line. The slope of the budget line refers to the rate at which the two goods can be exchanged for one another in the market (i.e., $2Y$ for $1X$).

The consumer can purchase any combination of X and Y on the budget line or in the shaded area below the budget line (called *budget space*). For example, at point B the individual would spend $4 to purchase $2X$ and the remaining $6 to purchase $6Y$. At point M, he or she would spend $8 to purchase $4X$ and the remaining $2 to purchase $2Y$. On the other hand, at a point such as H in the shaded area below the budget line (i.e., in the budget space), the individual would spend $4 to purchase $2X$ and $3 to purchase $3Y$ and be left with $3 of unspent income. In what follows, we assume that the consumer *does* spend all of his or her income and is on the budget line. Because of the income and price constraints, the consumer cannot reach combinations of X and Y above the budget line. For example, the individual cannot purchase combination G ($4X$, $6Y$) because it requires an expenditure of $14 ($8 to purchase $4X$ plus $6 to purchase $6Y$).

Changes in Income and Prices and the Budget Line

A particular budget line refers to a specific level of the consumer's income and specific prices of the two goods. If the consumer's income and/or the price of good X or good Y change, the budget line will also change. When only the consumer's income changes, the budget line will shift up if income (I) rises and down if I falls, but the slope of the budget line remains unchanged. For example, the left panel of Figure 3.7 shows budget line JK (the same as in Figure 3.6 with $I = $10), higher budget line $J'K'$ with $I = $15, and still higher budget line $J''K''$ with $I = $20 per day. P_X and P_Y do not change, so the three budget lines are parallel and their slopes are equal. If the consumer's income falls, the budget line shifts down but remains parallel.

If only the price of good X changes, the vertical or Y-intercept remains unchanged, and the budget line rotates upward or counterclockwise if P_X falls and downward or clockwise if P_X rises. For example, the right panel of Figure 3.7 shows budget line JK (the same as in Figure 3.6 at $P_X = \$2$), budget line JK'' with $P_X = \$1$, and budget line JN' with $P_X = \$0.50$. The vertical intercept (endpoint J) remains the same because I and P_Y do not change. The slope of budget line JK'' is $-P_X/P_Y = -\$1=\$1 = -1$. The slope of budget line JN' is $-1/2$. With an increase in P_X, the budget line rotates clockwise and becomes steeper.

On the other hand, if only the price of Y changes, the horizontal or X-intercept will be the same, but the budget line will rotate upward if P_Y falls and downward if P_Y rises. For example, with $I = \$10$, $P_X = \$2$, and $P_Y = \$0.50$ (rather than $P_Y = \$1$), the new vertical or Y-intercept is $Q_Y = 20$ and the slope of the new budget line is $-P_X/P_Y = -4$. With $P_Y = \$2$, the new Y-intercept is $Q_Y = 5$ and $-P_X=P_Y = -1$ (you should be able to sketch these lines). Finally, with a proportionate reduction in P_X and P_Y and constant I, there will be a parallel upward shift in the budget line; with a proportionate increase in P_X and P_Y and constant I, there will be a parallel downward shift in the budget line. Example 3–4 shows that time, instead of the consumer's income, can be a constraint.

✓ **Concept Check**

What happens to the budget line if the price of Y falls more than the price of X?

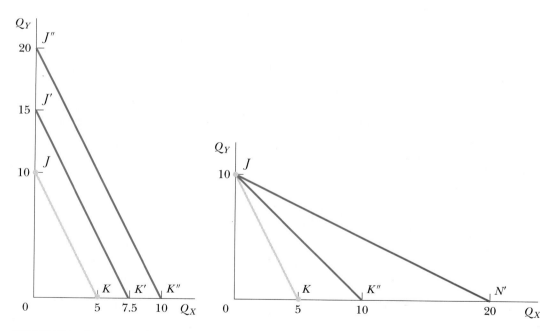

FIGURE 3.7   Changes in the Budget Line   The left panel shows budget line JK (the same as in Figure 3.6 with $I = \$10$), higher budget line $J'K'$ with $I = \$15$, and still higher budget line $J''K''$ with $I = \$20$ per day. P_X and P_Y do not change, so the three budget lines are parallel and their slopes are equal. The right panel shows budget line JK with $P_X = \$2$, budget line JK'' with $P_X = \$1$, and budget line JN'' with $P_X = \$0.50$. The vertical or Y-intercept (endpoint J) remains the same because income and P_Y do not change. The slope of budget line JK'' is $-P_X/P_Y = -\$1/\$1 = -1$, while the slope of budget line JN' is $-1/2$.

EXAMPLE 3–4

Time as a Constraint

In the preceding discussion of the budget line, we assumed only two constraints: the consumers' income and the given prices of the two goods. In the real world, consumers are also likely to face a time constraint. That is, since the consumption of goods requires time, which is also limited, time often represents another constraint faced by consumers. This explains the increasing popularity of precooked or ready-to-eat foods, restaurant meals delivered at home, and the use of many other time-saving goods and services. But the cost of saving time can be very expensive—thus proving the truth of the old saying that "time is money."

For example, the food industry is introducing more and more foods that are easy and quick to prepare, but these foods carry with them a much higher price. A meal that could be prepared from scratch for a few dollars might cost instead more than $10 in its ready-to-serve variety which requires only a few minutes to heat up. More and more people are also eating out and incurring much higher costs in order to save the time it takes to prepare home meals. McDonald's, Burger King, Taco Bell, and other fast-food companies are not just selling food, but fast food, and for that customers are willing to pay more than for the same kind of food at traditional food outlets, which require more waiting time. Better still, many suburbanites are increasingly reaching for the phone, not the frying pan, at dinner time to arrange for the home delivery of restaurant meals, adding even more to the price or cost of a meal.

Time is also a factor in considering transportation costs and access to the Internet. You could travel from New York to Washington, D.C., by train or, in less time but at a higher cost, by plane. Similarly, you can access the Internet with a regular but slow telephone line or much faster, but at a higher cost, by DSL or fiber optics.

Sources: "Suburban Life in the Hectic 1990s: Dinner Delivered," *New York Times,* November 20, 1992, p. B1; "How Much Will People Pay to Save a Few Minutes of Cooking? Plenty," *Wall Street Journal,* July 25, 1985, p. B1; "Riding the Rails at What Price," *New York Times,* June 18, 2001, p. 12; and "Shining Future for Fiber Optics," *New York Times,* November 19, 1995, p. B10.

3.5   CONSUMER'S CHOICE

We will now bring together the tastes and preferences of the consumer (given by his or her indifference map) and the income and price constraints faced by the consumer (given by his or her budget line) to examine how the consumer determines which goods to purchase and in what quantities to maximize utility or satisfaction. As we will see in the next chapter, utility maximization is essential for the derivation of the consumer's demand curve for a commodity (which is a major objective of this part of the text).

Utility Maximization

Rational consumer An individual who seeks to maximize utility or satisfaction in spending his or her income.

Given the tastes of the consumer (reflected in his or her indifference map), the **rational consumer** seeks to maximize the utility or satisfaction received in spending his or her income. A rational consumer maximizes utility by trying to attain the highest indifference

Constrained utility maximization The process by which the consumer reaches the highest level of satisfaction given his or her income and the prices of goods.

curve possible, given his or her budget line. This occurs where an indifference curve is tangent to the budget line so that the slope of the indifference curve (the MRS_{XY}) is equal to the slope of the budget line (P_X/P_Y). Thus, the condition for **constrained utility maximization, consumer optimization,** or **consumer equilibrium** occurs where the consumer spends all income (i.e., he or she is on the budget line) and

$$MRS_{XY} = P_X/P_Y \qquad\qquad [3.5]$$

Figure 3.8 brings together on the same set of axes the consumer indifference curves of Figure 3.2 and the budget line of Figure 3.6 to determine the point of utility maximization. Figure 3.8 shows that the consumer maximizes utility at point B where indifference curve U_1 is tangent to budget line JK. At point B, the consumer is on the budget line and $MRS_{XY} = P_X/P_Y = 2$. Indifference curve U_1 is the highest that the consumer can reach with his or her budget line. Thus, to maximize utility the consumer should spend \$4 to purchase $2X$ and the remaining \$6 to purchase $6Y$. Any other combination of goods X and Y that the consumer could purchase (those on or below the budget line) provides less utility. For example, the consumer could spend all income to purchase combination L, but this would be on lower indifference curve U_0.

At point L the consumer is willing to give up more of Y than he or she has to in the market to obtain one additional unit of X. That is, MRS_{XY} (the absolute slope of indifference curve U_0 at point L) exceeds the value of P_X/P_Y (the absolute slope of budget line JK). Thus, starting from point L, the consumer can increase his or her satisfaction by purchasing less of Y and more of X until he or she reaches point B on U_1, where the slopes of U_1 and the budget line are equal (i.e., $MRS_{XY} = P_X/P_Y = 2$). On the other hand, starting from point M, where $MRS_{XY} < P_X/P_Y$, the consumer can increase his or her satisfaction by purchasing less of X and more of Y until he or she reaches point B on U_1, where $MRS_{XY} = P_X/P_Y$. One tangency point such as B is assured by the fact that there is an indifference curve going through each point in the XY commodity space. The consumer

✓ **Concept Check**

Why is utility not maximized if the indifference curve crosses the budget line twice?

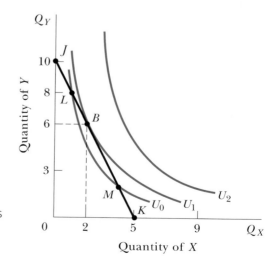

FIGURE 3.8   Constrained Utility Maximization   The consumer maximizes utility at point B, where indifference curve U_1 is tangent to budget line JK. At point B, $MRS_{XY} = P_X/P_Y = 2$. Indifference curve U_1 is the highest that the consumer can reach with his or her budget line. Thus, the consumer should purchase $2X$ and $6Y$.

cannot reach indifference curve U_2 with the present income and the given prices of goods X and Y.[11]

Utility maximization is more prevalent (as a general aim of individuals) than it may at first seem. It is observed not only in consumers as they attempt to maximize utility in spending income but also in many other individuals—including criminals. For example, a study found that the rate of robberies and burglaries was positively related to the gains and inversely related to the costs of (i.e., punishment for) criminal activity.[12] Utility maximization can also be used to analyze the effect of government warnings on consumption, as Example 3–5 shows.

EXAMPLE 3–5

Utility Maximization and Government Warnings on Junk Food

Suppose that in Figure 3.9, good X refers to milk and good Y refers to soda, $P_X = \$1$, $P_Y = \$1$, and the consumer spends his or her entire weekly allowance of $10 on milk and sodas. Suppose also that the consumer maximizes utility by spending $3 to purchase three containers of milk and $7 to purchase seven sodas (point B on indifference curve U_1) before any government warning on the danger of dental cavities and obesity from sodas. After the warning, the consumer's tastes may change away from sodas and toward milk. It may be argued that government warnings change the information available to consumers rather than tastes; that is, the warning affects consumers' perception

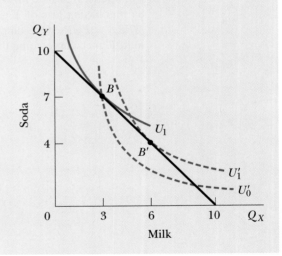

FIGURE 3.9   Effect of Government Warnings   The consumer maximizes utility by purchasing 3 containers of milk and 7 sodas (point B on indifference curve U_1) before the government warning on the consumption of sodas. After the warning, the consumer's tastes change and are shown by dashed indifference curves U'_0 and U'_1. The consumer now maximizes utility by purchasing 6 containers of milk and only 4 sodas (point B', where U'_1 is tangent to the budget line).

---

[11] For a mathematical presentation of utility maximization using rudimentary calculus, see Section A.2 of the Mathematical Appendix.

[12] See I. Ehrlich, "Participation in Illegitimate Activities: A Theoretical and Empirical Investigation," *Journal of Political Economy,* May/June 1973; W. T. Dickens, "Crime and Punishment Again: The Economic Approach with a Psychological Twist," National Bureau of Economic Research, *Working Paper No. 1884,* April 1986; and A. Gaviria, "Increasing Returns and the Evolution of Violent Crimes: The Case of Colombia," *Journal of Development Economics,* February 2000.

as to the ability of various goods to satisfy their wants—see M. Shodell, "Risky Business," *Science,* October 1985.

The effect of the government warning can be shown with dashed indifference curves U'_0 and U'_1. Note that U'_0 is steeper than U_1 at than original optimization point B, indicating that after the warning the individual is willing to give up more sodas for an additional container of milk (i.e., MRS_{XY} is higher for U'_0 than for U_1 at point B). Now U'_0 can intersect U_1 because of the change in tastes. Note also that U'_0 involves less utility than U_1 at point B because the seven sodas (and the three containers of milk) provide less utility after the warning. After the warning, the consumer maximizes utility by consuming six containers of milk and only four sodas (point B', where U'_1 is tangent to the budget line).

The above analysis clearly shows how indifference curve analysis can be used to examine the effect of any government warning on consumption patterns, such as the 1965 law requiring manufacturers to print on each pack of cigarettes sold in the United States the warning that cigarette smoking is dangerous to health. Indeed, the World Health Organization is now stepping up efforts to promote a global treaty to curb cigarette smoking. We can analyze the effect on consumption of any new information by examining the effect it has on the consumer's indifference map. Similarly, indifference curve analysis can be used to analyze the effect on consumer purchases of any regulation such as the one requiring drivers to wear seat belts.

Sources: "Some States Fight Junk Food Sales in School," *New York Times,* September 9, 2001, p. 1; and "Companies Agree to Ban on Sale of Fizzy Drinks in Schools," *Financial Times,* May 4, 2006, p. 6.

Corner Solutions

Corner solution
Constrained utility maximization with the consumer spending all of his or her income on only one or some goods.

If indifference curves are everywhere either flatter or steeper than the budget line, or if they are concave rather than convex to the origin, then the consumer maximizes utility by spending all income on either good Y or good X. These are called **corner solutions.**

In the left panel of Figure 3.10, indifference curves U_0, U_1, and U_2 are everywhere flatter than budget line JK, and U_1 is the highest indifference curve that the consumer can reach by purchasing $10Y$ and $0X$ (endpoint J). Point J is closest to the tangency point, which cannot be achieved. The individual could purchase $2X$ and $6Y$ and reach point B, but point B is on lower indifference curve U_0. Since point J is on the Y-axis (and involves the consumer spending all his or her income on good Y), it is called a corner solution.

The middle panel shows indifference curves that are everywhere steeper than the budget line, and U_1 is the highest indifference curve that the consumer can reach by spending all income to purchase $5X$ and $0Y$ (endpoint K). The individual could purchase $1X$ and $8Y$ at point L, but this is on lower indifference curve U_0. Point K is on the horizontal axis and involves the consumer spending all his or her income on good X, so point K is also a corner solution.

In the right panel, *concave* indifference curve U_1 is tangent to the budget line at point B, but this is not optimum because the consumer can reach higher indifference curve U_2 by spending all income to purchase $10Y$ and $0X$ (endpoint J). This is also a corner solution. Thus, the condition that an indifference curve must be tangent to the budget line for

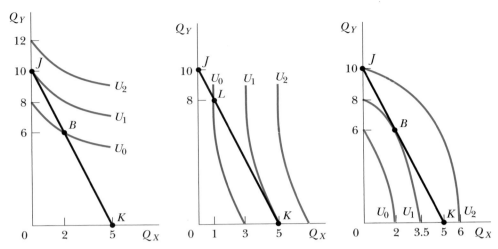

FIGURE 3.10   Corner Solutions   In the left panel, indifference curves are everywhere flatter than the budget line, and U_1 is the highest indifference curve that the consumer can reach by purchasing $10Y$ only (point J). The middle panel shows indifference curves everywhere steeper than the budget line, and U_1 is the highest indifference curve that the consumer can reach by spending all income to purchase $5X$ (point K). In the right panel, concave indifference curve U_1 is tangent to the budget line at point B, but this is not the optimum point because the consumer can reach higher indifference curve U_2 by consuming only good Y (point J).

optimization is true only when indifference curves assume their usual convex shape and are neither everywhere flatter nor steeper than the budget line.

Finally, although a consumer in the real world does not spend all of his or her income on one or a few goods, there are many more goods that he or she does not purchase because they are too expensive for the utility they provide. For example, few people purchase a $2,000 watch because the utility that most people get from the watch does not justify its $2,000 price. The nonconsumption of many goods in the real world can be explained by indifference curves which, though convex to the origin, are everywhere either flatter or steeper than the budget line, yielding corner rather than interior solutions. Corner solutions can also arise with rationing, as Example 3–6 shows.

EXAMPLE 3–6

Water Rationing in the West

Rationing
Quantitative
restrictions.

Because goods are scarce, some method of allocating them among individuals is required. In a free-enterprise economy such as our own, the price system accomplishes this for the most part. Sometimes, however, the government rations goods, such as water in the West of the United States (as a result of recurrent droughts) and gasoline in 1974 and 1979 (at the height of the petroleum crisis). If the maximum amount of the good that the government allows is less than the individual would have purchased or used, the **rationing** will reduce the individual's level of satisfaction.

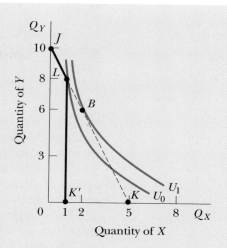

FIGURE 3.11 **Rationing** In the absence of rationing, the individual maximizes satisfaction at point B, where indifference curve U_1 is tangent to budget line JK, and consumes $2X$ and $6Y$ (as in Figure 3.8). If the government did not allow the individual to purchase more than $1X$ per week, the budget line becomes JLK', with a kink at point L. The highest indifference curve that the individual can reach with budget line JLK', is now U_0 at point L, by consuming $1X$ and $8Y$.

The effect of rationing on utility maximization and consumption can be examined with Figure 3.11. In the absence of rationing, the individual maximizes satisfaction at point B, where indifference curve U_1 is tangent to budget line JK, by consuming $2X$ and $6Y$ (as in Figure 3.8). Good X could refer to hours per week of lawn watering (in absence of an automatic water sprinkler system), while good Y could refer to hours per week of TV viewing. If the government did not allow the individual to use more than $1X$ per week, the budget line becomes JLK', with a kink at point L. Thus, rationing changes the constraints under which utility maximization occurs. The highest indifference curve that the individual can reach with budget line JLK' is now U_0 at point L, by consuming $1X$ and $8Y$. In our water rationing case, this refers to one hour of lawn watering and eight hours of TV viewing per week. With water rationing, the incentive arises to illegally water lawns at night under the cover of darkness. On the other hand, gasoline rationing during 1974 and 1979 led to long lines at the gas pump and to black markets where gasoline could be purchased illegally at a higher price without waiting. Thus, rationing leads to price distortions and inefficiencies.

If rations were $2X$ or more per week, the rationing system would not affect this consumer since he or she maximizes utility by purchasing $2X$ and $6Y$ (point B in the figure). Rationing is more likely to be binding or restrictive on high-income people than on low-income people (who may not have sufficient income to purchase even the allowed quantity of the rationed commodity). Thus, our model predicts that high-income people are more likely to make black-market purchases than low-income people. Effective rationing leads not only to black markets but also to "spillover" of consumer purchases on other goods not subject to rationing (or into savings). Both occurred in the United States during the 1974 and 1979 gasoline rationing periods. As pointed out in Section 2.7, allowing the market to operate (i.e., letting the price of the commodity reach its equilibrium level) eliminates the inefficiency of price controls and leads to much better results.

☑ Concept Check
Can rationing lead to a black market?

Sources: "Trickle-Down Economics," *Wall Street Journal,* August 23, 1999, p. A14; "Water Rights May Become More Liquid," *Wall Street Journal,* February 15, 1996, p. A2; W. C. Lee, "The Welfare Cost of Rationing-by-Queuing Across Markets," *Quarterly Journal of Economics,* July 1987; J. Brewer, et al., "Water Markets in the West: Prices, Trading, and Contractual Forms," *NBER Working Paper No. 13002,* March 2007, and M. Greenstone, "Tradable Water Rights," *Democracy Journal,* No. 8, Spring 2008, pp. 1–2.

Marginal Utility Approach to Utility Maximization

Until now we have examined constrained utility maximization with ordinal utility (i.e., with indifference curves). If utility were cardinally measurable, the condition for constrained utility maximization would be for the consumer to spend all income on X and Y in such a way that

$$\frac{MU_X}{P_X} = \frac{MU_Y}{P_Y} \qquad [3.6]$$

Equation [3.6] reads, the marginal utility of good X divided by the price of good X equals the marginal utility of good Y divided by the price of good Y. MU_X/P_X is the extra or marginal utility per dollar spent on X. Likewise, MU_Y/P_Y is the marginal utility per dollar spent on Y. Thus, for constrained utility maximization or optimization, the marginal utility of the last dollar spent on X and Y should be the same.[13]

For example, Table 3.3 shows a portion of the declining marginal utility schedule for good X and good Y (from Table 3.1), on the assumption that MU_X is independent of MU_Y (i.e., that MU_X is not affected by how much Y the individual consumes, and MU_Y is not affected by the amount of X consumed). If the consumer's income is $I = \$10$, $P_X = \$2$, and $P_Y = \$1$, the consumer should spend $4 to purchase $2X$ and the remaining $6 to purchase $6Y$ so that equation [3.6] is satisfied. That is,

$$\frac{6 \text{ utils}}{\$2} = \frac{3 \text{ utils}}{\$1} \qquad [3.6A]$$

If the consumer spent only $2 to purchase $1X$ and the remaining $8 to purchase $8Y$, $MU_X/P_X = 10/2 = 5$ and $MU_Y/P_Y = 1/1 = 1$. The last (second) dollar spent on X thus gives the consumer five times as much utility as the last (eighth) dollar spent on Y and the consumer would not be maximizing utility. To be at an optimum, the consumer should purchase more of X (MU_X falls) and less of Y (MU_Y rises) until he or she purchases $2X$ and $6Y$, where equation [3.6] is satisfied.[14] This is the same result obtained with the indifference curve approach in Section 3.5. Note that even when the consumer purchases $1X$ and $4Y$ equation [3.6] is satisfied ($MU_X/P_X = 10/2 = MU_Y/P_Y = 5/1$), but the consumer would not be at an optimum because he or she would be spending only $6 of the $10 income.

TABLE 3.3   Marginal Utility of X and Y

Q_X	MU_X	Q_Y	MU_Y
1	10	4	5
2	6	5	4
3	4	6	3
4	2	7	2
5	0	8	1

[13] We will see in footnote 14 that equation [3.6] also holds for the indifference curve approach.

[14] By giving up the eighth and the seventh units of Y, the individual loses 3 utils. By using the $2 not spent on Y to purchase the second unit of X, the individual receives 6 utils, for a net gain of 3 utils. Once the individual consumes $6Y$ and $2X$, equation [3.6] holds and he or she maximizes utility.

The fact that the marginal utility approach gives the same result as the indifference curve approach (i.e., $2X$ and $6Y$) should not be surprising. In fact, we can easily show why this is so. By cross multiplication in equation [3.6], we get

$$\frac{MU_X}{MU_Y} = \frac{P_X}{P_Y}$$

[3.7]

But we have shown in Section 3.2 that $MRS_{XY} = MU_X/MU_Y$ (see equation [3.2]) and in Section 3.5 that $MRS_{XY} = P_X/P_Y$ when the consumer maximizes utility (see equation [3.5]). Therefore, combining equations [3.2], [3.5], and [3.7], we can express the condition for consumer utility maximization as

$$MRS_{XY} = \frac{MU_X}{MU_Y} = \frac{P_X}{P_Y}$$

[3.8]

Thus, the condition for consumer utility maximization with the marginal utility approach (i.e., equation [3.6]) is equivalent to that with the indifference curve approach (equation [3.5]), except for corner solutions. With both approaches, the value of equation [3.8] is 2.

AT THE FRONTIER
The Theory of Revealed Preference

Theory of revealed preference The theory that postulates that a consumer's indifference curve can be derived from the consumer's market behavior.

U ntil now we have assumed that indifference curves are derived by asking the consumer to choose between various market baskets or combinations of commodities. Not only is this difficult and time consuming to do, but we also cannot be sure that consumers can or will provide trustworthy answers to direct questions about their preferences. According to the **theory of revealed preference** (developed by Paul Samuelson and John Hicks), a consumer's indifference curves can be derived from observing the actual market behavior of the consumer and without any need to inquire directly about preferences. For example, if a consumer purchases basket A rather than basket B, even though A is not cheaper than B, we can infer that the consumer prefers A to B.

The theory of revealed preference rests on the following assumptions:

1. The tastes of the consumer do not change over the period of the analysis.
2. The consumer's tastes are *consistent,* so that if the consumer purchases basket A rather than basket B, the consumer will never prefer B to A.
3. The consumer's tastes are *transitive,* so that if the consumer prefers A to B and B to C, the consumer will prefer A to C.
4. The consumer can be induced to purchase any basket of commodities if its price is lowered sufficiently.

Figure 3.12 shows how a consumer's indifference curve can be derived by revealed preference. Suppose that the consumer is observed to be at point *A* on budget line *NN* in the left panel. In this case, the consumer prefers *A* to any point on or below *NN*. On the other hand, points above and to the right of *A* are superior to *A* since they involve more of commodity *X* and commodity *Y*. Thus, the consumer's indifference curve must be tangent to budget line *NN* at point *A* and be above *NN* everywhere else.

Continued . . .

The Theory of Revealed Preference   *Continued*

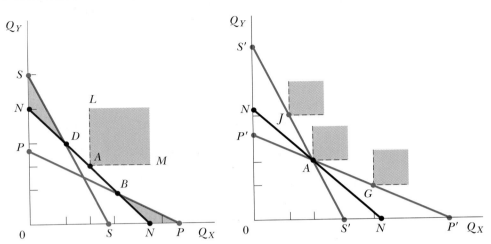

FIGURE 3.12   Derivation of an Indifference Curve by Revealed Preference   In the left panel, the consumer is originally at optimum at point *A* on *NN*. Thus, the indifference curve must be tangent to *NN* at point *A* and above *NN* everywhere else. It must also be to the left and below shaded area *LAM*. If the consumer is induced to purchase combination *B* (which is inferior to *A*) with budget line *PP*, we can eliminate shaded area *BPN*. Similarly, with combination *D* on budget line *SS*, shaded area *DSN* can be eliminated. Thus, the indifference curve must be above *SDBP*. In the right panel, the consumer prefers *G* to *A* with budget line *P'P'* and prefers *J* to *A* with budget line *S'S'*. Thus, the indifference curve must be below points *G* and *J*.

The indifference curve must also be to the left and below shaded area *LAM*. Such an indifference curve would be of the usual shape (i.e., negatively sloped and convex to the origin).

To locate more precisely the indifference curve in the *zone of ignorance* (i.e., in the area between *LAM* and *NN*), consider point *B* on *NN*. Point *B* is inferior to *A* since the consumer preferred *A* to *B*. However, the consumer could be induced to purchase *B* with budget line *PP* (i.e., with P_X/P_Y sufficiently lower than with *NN*). Since *A* is preferred to *B* and *B* is preferred to any point on *BP*, the indifference curve must be above *BP*. We have thus eliminated shaded area *BPN* from the zone of ignorance. Similarly, by choosing another point, such as *D*, we can, by following the same reasoning as for *B*, eliminate shaded area *DSN*. Thus, the indifference curve must lie above *SDBP* and be tangent to *NN* at point *A*.

The right panel of Figure 3.12 shows that we can chip away from the zone of ignorance immediately to the left of *LA* and below *AM*. Suppose that with budget line *P'P'* (which goes through point *A* and thus refers to the same real income as at *A*), the consumer chooses combination *G* (with more of *X* and less of *Y* than at *A*) because P_X/P_Y is lower than on *NN*. Points in the shaded area above and to the right of *G* are preferred to *G*, which is preferred to *A*. Thus, we have eliminated some of the upper zone of ignorance. Similarly, choosing another budget line, such as *S'S'*, we can eliminate the area above and to the right of a point such as *J*, which the consumer prefers to A at the higher P_X/P_Y given by $S'S'$. It follows that the indifference curve on which A falls must lie below points G and J. The process can be repeated any number of times to further reduce the upper and lower zones of ignorance, thereby locating the indifference curve more precisely. Note that the indifference curve derived is the one we need to show consumer equilibrium because it is the indifference curve that is tangent to the consumer's budget line.

Although somewhat impractical as a method for actually deriving indifference curves, the theory of revealed preference (particularly the idea that a consumer's tastes can be inferred or revealed by observing actual choices in the market place) has been very useful in many applied fields of economics such as public finance and international economics. The appendix to Chapter 4 applies the theory of revealed preference to measure changes in standards of living and consumer welfare during inflationary periods.

SUMMARY

1. The want-satisfying quality of a good is called utility. More units of a good increase total utility (TU) but the extra or marginal utility (MU) declines. The saturation point is reached when TU is maximum and MU is zero. Afterwards, TU declines and MU is negative. The decline in MU is known as the law of diminishing marginal utility. Cardinal utility actually provides an index of satisfaction for a consumer, whereas ordinal utility only ranks various consumption bundles.

2. The tastes of a consumer can be represented by indifference curves. These are based on the assumptions that the consumer can rank baskets of goods according to individual preferences, tastes are consistent and transitive, and the consumer prefers more of a good to less. An indifference curve shows the various combinations of two goods that give the consumer equal satisfaction. Higher indifference curves refer to more satisfaction and lower indifference curves to less. Indifference curves are negatively sloped, cannot intersect, and are convex to the origin. The marginal rate of substitution (MRS) measures how much of a good the consumer is willing to give up for one additional unit of the other good and remain on the same indifference curve. Indifference curves also generally exhibit diminishing MRS.

3. A rapid convergence of tastes is taking place in the world today. Tastes in the United States affect tastes around the world, and tastes abroad strongly influence tastes in the United States. With the tremendous improvement in telecommunications, transportation, and travel, the convergence of tastes can only be expected to accelerate—with important implications for us as consumers, for firms as producers, and for the study of microeconomics.

4. The budget line shows the various combinations of two goods (say, X and Y) that a consumer can purchase by spending all income (I) on the two goods at the given prices (P_X and P_Y). The vertical or Y-intercept of the budget line is given by I/P_Y and $-P_X/P_Y$ is the slope. The budget line shifts up if I increases and down if I decreases, but the slope remains unchanged. The budget line rotates upward if P_X falls and downward if P_X rises.

5. A rational consumer maximizes utility when reaching the highest indifference curve possible with the budget line. This occurs where an indifference curve is tangent to the budget line so that their slopes are equal (i.e., $MRS_{XY} = P_X/P_Y$). Government warnings or new information may change the shape and location of a consumer's indifference curves and the consumption pattern. If indifference curves are everywhere either flatter or steeper than the budget line or

if they are concave, utility maximization requires the consumer to spend all income on either good Y or good X. These are called corner solutions. Corner solutions can also arise with rationing. The marginal utility approach postulates that the consumer maximizes utility when he or she spends all income and the marginal utility of the last dollar spent on X and Y are the same. Since $MRS_{XY} = MU_X/MU_Y = P_X/P_Y$, the marginal utility and the indifference curve approaches are equivalent. Indifference curves can also be derived by the theory of revealed preference.

KEY TERMS

Utility
Total Utility (*TU*)
Marginal Utility (*MU*)
Util
Law of diminishing
    marginal utility
Cardinal utility
Ordinal utility

Good
Bad
Indifference curve
Indifference map
Marginal rate of
    substitution (*MRS*)
Neuter
Budget constraint

Budget line
Rational consumer
Constrained utility maximization
Consumer optimization
Consumer equilibrium
Corner solution
Rationing
Theory of revealed preference

REVIEW QUESTIONS

1. The utility approach to consumer demand theory is based on the assumption of cardinal utility, while the indifference curve approach is based on ordinal utility. Which approach is better? Why?

2. If Alan is indifferent between Coke and Pepsi, what would Alan's indifference curves look like?

3. The indifference curve between a good and garbage is positively sloped. True or false? Explain.

4. What is the relationship between two goods if the marginal rate of substitution between them is zero or infinite? Explain.

5. What is the marginal rate of substitution between two complementary goods?

6. Are indifference curves useless because it is difficult to derive them experimentally?

7. Why is there a convergence of tastes internationally?

8. If Jennifer's budget line has intercepts 20X and 30Y and $P_Y = \$10$, what is Jennifer's income? What is P_X? What is the slope of the budget line?

9. Must a consumer purchase some quantity of each commodity to be in equilibrium?

10. Janice spends her entire weekly food allowance of $42 on hamburgers and soft drinks. The price of a hamburger is $2, and the price of a soft drink is $1. Janice purchases 12 hamburgers and 18 soft drinks, and her marginal rate of substitution between hamburgers and soft drinks is 1. Is Janice in equilibrium? Explain.

11. Why is a consumer likely to be worse off when a product that he or she consumes is rationed?

12. In what way is the theory of revealed preference related to traditional consumer theory? What is its usefulness?

PROBLEMS

1. From the following total utility schedule

Q_X	0	1	2	3	4	5	6	7
TU_X	0	4	14	20	24	26	26	24

a. derive the marginal utility schedule.
b. plot the total and the marginal utility schedules.
c. determine where the law of diminishing marginal utility begins to operate.
d. find the saturation point.

2. The following table gives four indifference schedules of an individual.

    a. Using graph paper, plot the four indifference curves on the same set of axes.

    b. Calculate the marginal rate of substitution of X for Y between the various points on U_1.

    c. What is MRS_{XY} at point C on U_1?

    d. Can we tell how much better off the individual is on U_2 than on U_1?

*3. a. Starting with a given *equal* endowment of good X and good Y by individual A and individual B, draw A's and B's indifference curves on the same set of axes, showing that individual A has a preference for good X over good Y with respect to individual B.

    b. Explain why you drew individual A's and individual B's indifference curves as you did in Problem 3(a).

4. Draw an indifference curve for an individual showing that

    a. good X and good Y are perfect complements.

    b. item X becomes a bad after 4 units.

    c. item Y becomes a bad after 3 units.

    d. *MRS* is increasing for both X and Y.

5. Suppose an individual has an income of $15 per time period, the price of good X is $1 and the price of good Y is also $1. That is, $I = \$15$, $P_X = \$1$, and $P_Y = \$1$.

6. This problem involves drawing three graphs, one for each part of the problem. On the same set of axes, draw the budget line of Problem 5 (label it 2) and two other budget lines:

    a. One with $I = \$10$ (call it 1), and another with $I = \$20$ (label it 3), and with prices unchanged at $P_X = P_Y = \$1$.

    b. One with $P_X = \$0.50$, $P_Y = \$1$, and $I = \$15$ (label it 2A), and another with $P_X = \$2$ and the same P_Y and I (label it 2B).

    c. One with $P_Y = \$2$, $P_X = \$1$, and $I = \$15$ (label it 2C), and another with $P_X = P_Y = \$2$ and $I = \$15$ (label it 2F).

*7. a. On the same set of axes, draw the indifference curves of Problem 2 and the budget line of Problem 5(c).

    b. Where is the individual maximizing utility? How much of X and Y should he or she purchase to be at optimum? What is the general condition for constrained utility maximization?

    c. Why is the individual not maximizing utility at point A? At point G?

    d. Why can't the individual reach U_3 or U_4?

8. On the same set of axes (on graph paper), draw the indifference curves of problem 2 and budget lines

Combination	U_1		U_2		U_3		U_4	
	Q_X	Q_Y	Q_X	Q_Y	Q_X	Q_Y	Q_X	Q_Y
A	3	12	6	12	8	15	10	13
B	4	7	7	9	9	12	12	10
C	6	4	9	6	11	9	14	8
F	9	2	12	4	15	6	18	6.4
G	14	1	15	3	19	5	20	6

a. Write the equation of the budget line of this individual in the form that indicates that the amount spent on good X plus the amount spent on good Y equals the individual's income.

b. Write the equation of the budget line in the form that you can read off directly the vertical intercept and the slope of the line.

c. Plot the budget line.

a. 1, 2, and 3 from Problem 6(a); label the points at which the individual maximizes utility with the various alternative budget lines.

b. 2 and 2A from Problem 6(b); label the points at which the individual maximizes utility on the various alternative budget lines: E and L.

*9. Given the following marginal utility schedule for good X and good Y for the individual, and given that the price of X

---

* = Answer provided at end of book.

and the price of *Y* are both $1, and that the individual spends all income of $7 on *X* and *Y*,

Q	1	2	3	4	5	6	7
MU_X	15	11	9	6	4	3	1
MU_Y	12	9	6	5	3	2	1

   a. indicate how much of *X* and *Y* the individual should purchase to maximize utility.

   b. show that the condition for constrained utility maximization is satisfied when the individual is at his or her optimum.

   c. determine how much total utility the individual receives when he or she maximizes utility? How much utility would the individual get if he or she spent all income on *X* or *Y*?

10. Show on the same figure the effect of (1) an increase in cigarette prices, (2) an increase in consumers' incomes, and (3) a government warning that cigarette smoking is dangerous to health, all in such a way that the net effect of all three forces together leads to a net decline in cigarette smoking.

11. a. Draw a figure showing indifference curve U_2 tangent to the budget line at point *B* (8*X*), and a lower indifference curve (U_1) intersecting the budget line at point *A* (4*X*) and at point *G* (12*X*).

   b. What happens if the government rations good *X* and allows the individual to purchase no more than 4*X*? No more than 8*X*? No more than 12*X*?

   c. What would happen if the government instead mandated (as in the case of requiring auto insurance, seat belts, and so on) that the individual purchase at least 4*X*? 8*X*? 12*X*?

*12. Show by indifference curve analysis the choice of one couple not to have children and of another couple, with the same income and facing the same costs of having and raising children, to have one child.

INTERNET SITE ADDRESSES

The relationship between income and happiness is analyzed by David G. Blanchflower in:

   http://www.dartmouth.edu/~blanchflower/papers/Wellbeingnew.pdf

   http://cep.lse.ac.uk/events/lectures/layard/RL040303.pdf

   http://www.princeton.edu/main/news/archive/S15/15/09S18/index.xml?section=topstories

   http://ideas.repec.org/a/ecj/econjl/v111y2001i473p465-84.html

For the competition between the Ford Taurus and the Honda Accord, see:

   http://www.theautochannel.com/vehicles/new/reviews/2001/heilig_ford_taurus.html

   http://www.edmunds.com/insideline/do/Features/articleId=46007

   http://www.epinions.com/content_81797287556

For water rationing in the U.S. West, see the website for the Political Economy Research Center at:

   http://www.perc.org and

   http://www.cleartheair.org/waterinthewest/chapter6.vtml

The harmful effects of junk food and the need for government regulation are examined at:

   http://faculty.db.erau.edu/stratect/sf320/ARTICLE10.htm

   http://www.commercialfreechildhood.org/pressreleases/iomlacksobjectivity.htm

   http://llr.lls.edu/volumes/v39-issue1/docs/yosifon.pdf

CHAPTER 4

Consumer Behavior and Individual Demand

After Studying This Chapter, You Should Be Able to:

- Know how to derive an individual consumer's demand curve for a commodity
- Know what a Giffen good is, how it can arise theoretically, and where it has been found
- Understand why a cash subsidy is better than food stamps
- Know the meaning and importance of consumer surplus
- Describe how to measure the benefits of exchange

I n Chapter 3 we saw how a consumer maximized utility by reaching the highest possible indifference curve with the given budget line. In this chapter, we examine how the consumer responds to changes in income and prices while holding tastes constant. Incomes and prices change frequently in the real world, so it is important to examine their individual effects on consumer behavior.

We begin by examining how the consumer responds to changes in his or her income when prices and tastes remain constant. This will allow us to derive a so-called Engel curve and to distinguish between normal and inferior goods. Then we examine the consumer's response to a change in the price of the good and derive the individual's demand curve for the good. This is the basic building block for the market demand curve of the good (to be derived in Chapter 5), the importance of which was outlined in Chapter 2.

After deriving an individual's demand curve, we discuss how to separate the substitution from the income effect of a price change for normal and inferior goods. The ability to separate graphically the income from the substitution effect of a price change is one of the most powerful tools of analysis of microeconomic theory, with many important applications. Subsequently, we examine the degree by which domestic and foreign goods and services are substitutable and the great relevance of this substitution in the study of microeconomics. We then consider some important applications of the theory presented in this chapter. These applications, together with the real-world examples included in the theory sections, highlight the importance of the theory of consumer behavior and demand. Finally, the "At the Frontier" section presents the characteristics approach to consumer theory, which provides some additional insights and uses of consumer theory. The optional appendix to this chapter deals with index numbers and how they are used to measure changes in consumer welfare.

4.1	CHANGES IN INCOME AND THE ENGEL CURVE

A change in the consumer's income shifts his or her budget line, and this shift affects consumer purchases. In this section we examine how a consumer reaches a new optimum position when income changes but prices and tastes do not.

Income–Consumption Curve and Engel Curve

Income–consumption curve The locus of consumer optimum points resulting when only the consumer's income varies.

By changing the consumer's money income while holding prices and tastes constant, we can derive the consumer's income–consumption curve. The **income–consumption curve** is the locus of (i.e., joins) consumer optimum points resulting when only the consumer's income varies. From the income–consumption curve we can then derive the consumer's Engel curve (discussed below).

For example, the top panel of Figure 4.1 shows that with budget line JK the consumer maximizes utility or is at an optimum at point B, where indifference curve U_1 is tangent to budget line JK and the consumer purchases $2X$ and $6Y$ (the same as in Figure 3.8). That is (continuing with the example from Chapter 3), the best way for the student to spend a daily income allowance of $10 on snacks of hamburgers (good X) and soft drinks (good Y) is to purchase two hamburgers and six soft drinks per day. If the prices of hamburgers and soft drinks remain unchanged at $P_X = \$2$ and $P_Y = \$1$ but the daily income allowance rises from $10 to $15 and then to $20, budget line JK shifts up to $J'K'$ and then to $J''K''$ (the same as in the left panel of Figure 3.7). The three budget lines are parallel because the prices of X and Y do not change.

With an income of $15 and budget line $J'K'$, the consumer maximizes utility at point R, where indifference curve U_2 is tangent to budget line $J'K'$ and the consumer purchases $4X$ and $7Y$ (see the top panel of Figure 4.1). Indifference curve U_2 is the same as in the right panel of Figure 3.2 because tastes have not changed. Finally, with an income of $20

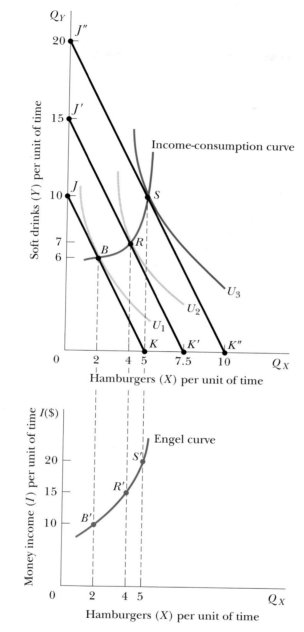

FIGURE 4.1   Income–Consumption Curve and Engel Curve   With
budget lines *JK, J'K', J"K"* and indifference curves U_1, U_2, and U_3 in the top
panel, the individual maximizes utility at points *B, R,* and *S,* respectively. By
joining optimum points *B, R,* and *S* we get the income–consumption curve
(top panel). By then plotting income on the vertical axis and the various
optimum quantities purchased of good *X* along the horizontal axis, we can
derive the corresponding Engel curve *B'R'S'* in the bottom panel.

and budget line $J''K''$, the consumer maximizes utility or is at an optimum at point S on U_3 by purchasing 5X and 10Y per unit of time (per day). By joining optimum points B, R, and S we get (a portion of) the income–consumption curve for this consumer (student). Thus, the income–consumption curve is the locus of consumer optimum points resulting when only the consumer's income varies.[1]

From the income–consumption curve in the top panel of Figure 4.1, we can derive the Engel curve in the bottom panel. The **Engel curve** shows the amount of a good that the consumer would purchase per unit of time at various income levels. To derive the Engel curve we keep the same horizontal scale as in the top panel but measure money income on the vertical axis.

The derivation of the Engel curve proceeds as follows. With a daily income allowance of $10, the student maximizes utility by purchasing two hamburgers per day (point B) in the top panel. This gives point B' (directly below point B) in the bottom panel. With an income allowance of $15, the student is at an optimum by purchasing four hamburgers (point R) in the top panel. This gives point R' in the bottom panel. Finally, with a daily income allowance of $20, the student maximizes utility by purchasing five hamburgers (point S in the top panel and S' in the bottom panel). By joining points B', R', and S' we get (a portion of) the Engel curve in the bottom panel. Thus, the Engel curve is derived from the income–consumption curve and shows the quantity of hamburgers per day (Q_X) that the student would purchase at various income levels (i.e., with various income allowances). Since the Engel curve is derived from points of consumer (student) utility maximization, $MRS_{XY} = P_X/P_Y$ at every point on the curve.

Engel curves are named after Ernst Engel, the German statistician of the second half of the nineteenth century who pioneered studies of family budgets and expenditure patterns. Sometimes Engel curves show the relationship between income and *expenditures* on various goods rather than the *quantity* purchased of various goods. However, because prices are held constant, we get the same result (i.e., the same Engel curve).

For some goods, the Engel curve may rise only gently. This indicates that a given increase in income leads to a proportionately larger increase in the quantity purchased of the good. These goods are sometimes referred to as "luxuries." Examples of luxuries may be education, recreation, and steaks and lobsters (for some people). On the other hand, the Engel curve for other goods may rise rather rapidly, indicating that a given increase in income leads to a proportionately smaller increase in the quantity purchased of these goods. These goods are called "necessities." Basic foodstuffs are usually regarded as necessities. A more precise definition of luxuries and necessities is given in Chapter 5.

Engel curve Shows the amount of a good that a consumer would purchase at various income levels.

EXAMPLE 4–1

Engel's Law After a Century

Table 4.1 gives the percentages of total consumption expenditures on various items for U.S. families in selected income classes in 2005. The table shows that higher-income families generally spend a smaller percentage of their income than lower-income families on food but spend a larger percentage on personal insurance and

[1] At each point along the income–consumption curve the value of the MRS_{XY} is the same. This is because $-P_X/P_Y$ is the same for each of the budget lines (i.e., parallel lines have identical slopes).

TABLE 4.1 Percentage of Total Consumption by Income Class for U.S. Families in 2005

Consumption Item	Annual Income						
	0–$9,999	$10,000–$19,999	$20,000–$29,999	$30,000–$39,999	$40,000–49,000	$50,000–$69,000	$70,000 and over
Food	16.3%	15.2%	13.9%	13.3%	13.0%	13.4%	11.4
Housing	39.7	38.9	35.1	34.8	33.6	31.5	31.0
Apparel and services	5.0	4.1	3.9	4.3	3.6	4.0	4.0
Transportation	14.2	14.5	19.9	18.1	19.4	20.1	17.6
Health care	6.2	6.5	7.9	6.9	6.9	5.6	4.7
Entertainment	4.6	3.9	4.2	4.9	4.8	4.9	5.6
Education	4.6	2.0	1.1	1.1	1.2	1.3	2.6
Insurance and pensions	1.8	3.3	5.4	7.8	9.3	11.1	14.8
Other	7.6	11.6	8.6	8.8	8.2	8.1	8.3
Total	100.0	100.0	100.0	100.0	100.0	100.0	100.0

Source: U.S. Department of Labor, Bureau of Labor Statistics, *Consumer Expenditures in 2005,* Report 998 (Washington, D.C.: May 2001), Table 2.

✓ **Concept Check**
Is Engel's law always true?

Engel's law The proportion of total expenditures on food declines as family incomes rise.

pensions. Less regularity is found in the proportion of expenditures on other goods and services.

The decline in the proportion of total expenditures on food as income rises has been found to be true not only for the United States in the period of the survey, but also at other times and in other nations. Thus, food in general is a necessity rather than a luxury. This regularity is sometimes referred to as *Engel's law*. Indeed, the higher the proportion of income spent on food in a nation, the poorer the nation is taken to be. For example, in India almost 50% of income is spent on food on the average.

Normal and Inferior Goods

Normal good A good of which the consumer purchases more with an increase in income.

Inferior good A good of which a consumer purchases less with an increase in income.

A **normal good** is one of which the consumer purchases more with an increase in income. An **inferior good** is one of which the consumer purchases less with an increase in income. Good X in Figure 4.1 is a normal good because the consumer purchases more of it with an increase in income. For example, an increase in the student's income allowance from $10 to $15 leads to an increase in the purchase of hamburgers from two to four per day. Thus, for a normal good, the income–consumption curve and the Engel curve are both positively sloped, as in Figure 4.1.

Figure 4.2 shows the income–consumption curve and the Engel curve for an inferior good. This results from supposing that the student, instead of spending the daily income allowance on soft drinks (good Y) and hamburgers (good X), spends it on soft drinks and candy bars (good Z), and supposing the student views candy bars as an inferior

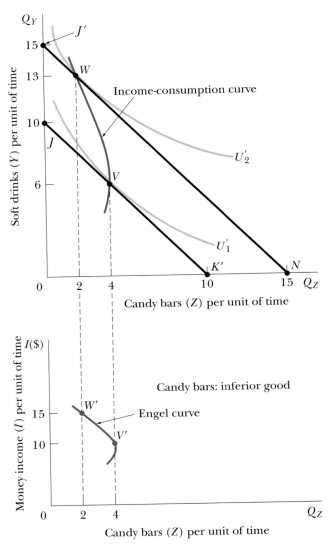

FIGURE 4.2   Income–Consumption Curve and Engel Curve
for an Inferior Good   With budget lines *JK'* and *J'N* and
indifference curves U_1' and U_2' in the top panel, the individual
maximizes utility at points *V* and *W*, respectively. By joining points
V and *W* we get the income–consumption curve (top panel). By
then plotting income on the vertical axis and the optimum
quantities purchased of good *Z* along the horizontal axis, we
derive corresponding Engel curve *V'W'* in the bottom panel. Since
the income–consumption curve and Engel curve are negatively
sloped, good *Z* is an inferior good.

good.[2] With the price of soft drinks at $1 and the price of candy bars also at $1, the budget line of the student is JK' with a daily income allowance of $10 and $J'N$ with an income of $15 (see the top panel of Figure 4.2).

If indifference curves between soft drinks and candy bars are U_1' and U_2' the student maximizes satisfaction at point V, where indifference curve U_1' is tangent to budget line JK' with a daily income allowance of $10. The student maximizes utility at point W, where indifference curve U_2' is tangent to budget line $J'N$ with an income of $15 (see the top panel of Figure 4.2). Thus, the consumer purchases four candy bars with an income of $10 and only two candy bars with an income of $15. Candy bars are, therefore, inferior goods for this student. The income–consumption curve for candy bars (VW in the top panel of Figure 4.2) and the corresponding Engel curve ($V'W'$ in the bottom panel) are both negatively sloped, indicating that the student purchases fewer candy bars as his or her income allowance increases.

The classification of a good as normal or inferior depends only on how a specific consumer views the particular good. Thus, the same candy bar can be regarded as a normal good by another student. Furthermore, a good can be regarded as a normal good by a consumer at a particular level of income and as an inferior good by the same consumer at a higher level of income. For example, with an allowance of $40 dollars per day, the student in the previous section may begin to regard hamburgers as an inferior good, because he or she now can afford steaks and lobsters. Also note that an inferior good is not a "bad" because more is preferred to less, and indifference curves remain negatively sloped (refer back to Section 3.2).

In the real world, most broadly defined goods such as food, clothing, housing, health care, education, and recreation are normal goods. Inferior goods are usually narrowly defined cheap goods, such as bologna, for which good substitutes are available. As pointed out earlier, a normal good can be further classified as a luxury or a necessity, depending on whether the quantity purchased increases proportionately more or less than the increase in income.

EXAMPLE 4–2

Many People Are Blowing Their Pension Money Long Before Retirement

There is a retirement crisis brewing in America today, not because people are not putting enough money into their retirement plans, but because they are taking billions of dollars out long before old age. Today, workers have many chances to take out their retirement money in the form of a lump sum before the usual retirement age. They can do so when they change jobs, when they work for a company that is sold and are thus ejected from their retirement plan, or by taking early retirement. But instead of putting

[2] Other commodities that are, perhaps, even more readily recognized as inferior goods in the United States today might be bologna and cheaper cuts of meats.

their money into sound investments on which to live when they retire, many workers are blowing their lump-sum retirement-plan payouts on new cars, appliances, furniture, and boats, as well as in casinos.

A 1993 Labor Department study of how 60,000 households handled a retirement-plan lump sum showed that only 21% of the recipients rolled their money into Individual Retirement Accounts (IRAs), as recommended by financial planners. Almost 30% spent their lump sums on consumer products or used them to pay medical or educational expenses for themselves and their children, and another 23% put the money into a business or house or repaid debts. Younger people were more likely to spend rather than invest their retirement money into IRAs, but so did more than one-fifth of those in the 55–64 age group. Experts predict that by the end of the decade about half of the pension money in traditional firm-sponsored and firm-administered pension plans will have been distributed to the contributors. Employers prefer distributing pension money in a lump sum to employees because it saves them the cost of administering a string of retirement checks and other expenses. The problem is that many people treat their lump-sum pension money as a win at the lottery and go on spending spree, leaving little on which to live in their retirement years. Humans, it seems (and contrary to the usual assumption of rationality made by traditional economic theory), often behave quite irrationally! (Choices under uncertainty are examined in detail in Chapter 6.)

Sources: "Offered a Lump Sum, Many Retirees Blow It and Risk Their Future," *Wall Street Journal,* July 31, 1995, p. A1; "Borrowing on a 401k? Better Think Twice," *Wall Street Journal,* October 12, 2001, p. C1; and L. A. Muller, "Does Retirement Education Teach People to Save Pension Distribution?" *Social Security Bullettin,* No. 4, 2001/2002, pp. 48–65.

4.2   CHANGES IN PRICE AND THE INDIVIDUAL DEMAND CURVE

Commodity prices frequently change in the real world, and it is important to examine their effect on consumer behavior. A change in commodity prices changes the consumer budget line, and this affects consumer purchases. In this section we examine how the consumer reaches a new optimum position when the price of a good changes but the price of the other good, income, and tastes remain unchanged.

By changing the price of good X while holding constant the price of good Y, income, and tastes, we can derive the consumer's price–consumption curve for good X. The **price–consumption curve** for good X is the locus of (i.e., joins) consumer optimum points resulting when only the price of good X varies. From the price–consumption curve we can then derive the consumer's demand curve for good X.

For example, the top panel of Figure 4.3 shows once again that with budget line JK, the consumer maximizes utility or is at an optimum at point B, where indifference curve U_1 is tangent to budget line JK and the consumer purchases $2X$ and $6Y$ (the same as in Figure 3.8). Suppose that the consumer's income (i.e., the student allowance) remains unchanged at $I = \$10$ per day and the price of good Y (soft drinks) also remains constant at $P_Y = \$1$. A reduction in the price of good X (hamburgers) from $P_X = \$2$ to $P_X = \$1$ and then to $P_X = \$0.50$ would cause the consumer's budget line to become flatter or

Price–consumption curve The locus of consumer optimum points resulting when only the price of a good varies.

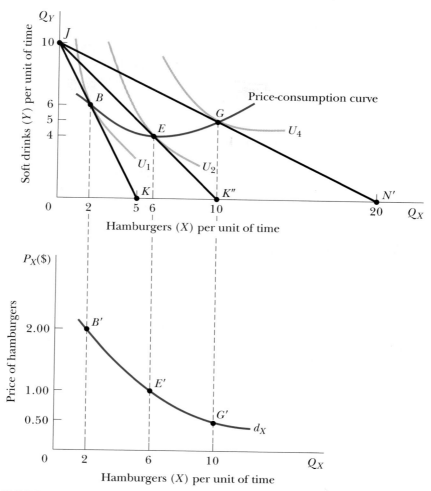

FIGURE 4.3   Price–Consumption Curve and the Individual's Demand Curve
The top panel shows that with $I = \$10$ and $P_Y = \$1$, the consumer is at an optimum at point B by purchasing $2X$ with $P_X = \$2$, at point E by purchasing $6X$ with $P_X = \$1$, and at point G by purchasing $10X$ with $P_X = \$0.50$. By joining points BEG, we get the price-consumption curve for good X. In the bottom panel, by plotting the optimum quantities of good X on the horizontal axis and the corresponding prices of good X on the vertical axis, we derive the individual's negatively sloped demand curve for good X, d_X.

to rotate counterclockwise from JK to JK'' and then to JN' (the same as in the right panel of Figure 3.7).[3]

With $P_X = \$1$ and budget line JK'', the consumer maximizes utility at point E, where indifference curve U_2 is tangent to budget line JK'' and the consumer purchases $6X$ and $4Y$ (see the top panel of Figure 4.3). Indifference curve U_2 is the same as in the right

---

[3] Remember that the X-intercepts of the budget lines are obtained by I/P_X. Thus, with $I = \$10$ and $P_X = \$2$, we get endpoint K and budget line JK. With $P_X = \$1$, we get endpoint K'' and budget line JK'', and with $P_X = \$0.50$, we get endpoint N' and budget line JN'.

panel of Figure 3.2 because tastes have not changed. Finally, with $P_X = \$0.50$ and budget line JN', the consumer maximizes utility or is at an optimum at point G on U_4 by purchasing $10X$ and $5Y$ per unit of time (per day). By joining optimum points B, E, and G we get (a portion of) the price–consumption curve for this consumer (student). Thus, the price–consumption curve for good X is the locus of consumer optimum points resulting when only the price of X changes.[4]

From the price–consumption curve in the top panel of Figure 4.3, we can derive the individual consumer's (student's) demand curve for good X in the bottom panel. The **individual's demand curve** for good X shows the amount of good X that the consumer would purchase per unit of time at various alternative prices of good X while holding everything else constant. It is derived by keeping the same horizontal scale as in the top panel but measuring the price of good X on the vertical axis.

The derivation of the individual's demand curve proceeds as follows. With $I = \$10$, $P_Y = \$1$, and $P_X = \$2$, the student maximizes utility by purchasing $2X$ (two hamburgers) per day (point B) in the top panel. This gives point B' (directly below point B) in the bottom panel. With $P_X = \$1$, the consumer is at optimum by purchasing $6X$ (point E) in the top panel. This gives point E' in the bottom panel. Finally, with $P_X = \$0.50$, the consumer maximizes utility by purchasing $10X$ (point G in the top panel and G' in the bottom panel). Other points could be similarly obtained. By joining points B', E', and G' we get the individual consumer's demand curve for good X, d_X, in the bottom panel. Thus, the demand curve is derived from the price–consumption curve and shows the quantity of the good that the consumer would purchase per unit of time at various alternative prices of the good while holding everything else constant (the *ceteris paribus* assumption).

We will see in Chapter 5 that the market demand curve for a good (our ultimate aim in Part Two of the text) is obtained from the addition or the horizontal summation of all individual consumers' demand curves for the good. Note that the individual consumer's demand curve for a good (d_x in the bottom panel of Figure 4.3) is negatively sloped. This reflects the *law of demand,* which postulates that the quantity purchased of a good per unit of time is inversely related to its price. Thus, the individual purchases more hamburgers per unit of time when their price falls and less of them when their price rises. Also note that an individual consumer's demand curve for a good is derived by holding constant the individual's tastes, his or her income, and the prices of other goods. If any of these change, the entire demand curve will shift. This is referred to as a change in demand as opposed to a change in the quantity demanded, which is a movement along a given demand curve as a result of a change in the price of the good while holding everything else constant (refer back to Section 2.2).

Individual's demand curve Shows the quantity that the individual would purchase of a good per unit of time at various alternative prices of the good while keeping everything else constant.

✓ Concept Check

Does the individual's demand curve reflect both the substitution and income effects?

EXAMPLE 4–3

Higher Alcohol Prices Would Sharply Reduce Youth Alcohol Use and Traffic Deaths

Road accidents are the single largest cause of deaths among young people in America, and about half of the road fatalities are caused by young people driving while intoxicated. Efforts to reduce alcohol use by youths have centered on increasing the minimum legal age for purchasing and drinking alcohol, which is now 21 in

---

[4] At each point along the price–consumption curve, $MRS_{XY} = P_X/P_Y$. However, unlike the case of the income–consumption curve, these ratios will vary because the budget lines are no longer parallel.

all 50 states. The hope is that this will shift the demand curve for alcohol use by young people to the left (despite the fact that some forge identity cards to get around the rule). Surprisingly, little use has been made in the United States of an even more powerful deterrent to youth alcohol use—higher alcohol prices through higher federal alcohol taxes. In fact, the real price (i.e., the nominal price divided by the price index to adjust for inflation) of alcoholic beverages has declined by about 40% for beer and wine and 70% for hard liquor in the United States since 1951. Taxes are currently only about $2 per quart for beer and $3.60 for hard liquor in the United States, compared with $18.20 and $34.50 in England.

Using simulations for a sample of high school students, Douglas Coate and Michael Grossman found that by indexing the tax on beer to the rate of inflation (so as to keep the real price of beer constant at the 1951 level) would have cut the number of frequent young beer drinkers by about 20% and that this would have saved 1,660 lives from traffic accidents per year (twice as many as resulting from increasing the minimum legal drinking age from 18 to 21). Of course, raising taxes even higher so as to increase the real price of alcoholic beverages would have reduced drinking and road fatalities even more. This is not surprising, since most teenagers have much less disposable income than adults. Thus, increasing the price of alcoholic beverages would have a more powerful deterring effect on them than on older drinkers. What is surprising is that despite the predictions of economic theory and the confirmation of empirical studies, the government has chosen thus far not to use price as a powerful deterrent to youth alcohol use.

Sources: "Efforts to Reduce Teen Drinking May Provide Lessons," *Wall Street Journal,* August 10, 1995, p. B1; "Beer, Taxes and Death," *The Economist,* September 18, 1993, p. 33; Douglas Coate and Michael Grossman, "Effects of Alcoholic Beverage Prices and Legal Drinking Ages on Youth Alcohol Use," *Journal of Law and Economics,* April 1988, pp. 145–172; "Traffic Death Rose in 2001, But Rates for Miles Fell," *New York Times,* August 8, 2002, p. 21; and Center for Disease Control and Prevention, "Teen Drivers: Fact Sheets," April 20, 2007, http://www.cdc.gov/ncipc/factsheets/teenmvh.htm.

4.3 SUBSTITUTION EFFECT AND INCOME EFFECT

In this section, we separate the substitution effect from the income effect of a price change for both normal and inferior goods. This separation will give us an important analytical tool with wide applicability and will also allow us to examine the exception to the law of downward sloping demand.

How Are the Substitution Effect and the Income Effect Separated?[5]

We have seen in the previous section that when the price of a good falls the consumer buys more of it. This is the combined result of two separate forces at work called the substitution effect and the income effect. We now want to separate the total effect of a price change into these two components. We begin by first reviewing how the total effect of a price change (discussed in Section 4.2) operates.

---

[5] The separation of the substitution effect from the income effect of a price change using rudimentary calculus is shown in section A.4 of the Mathematical Appendix at the end of the book.

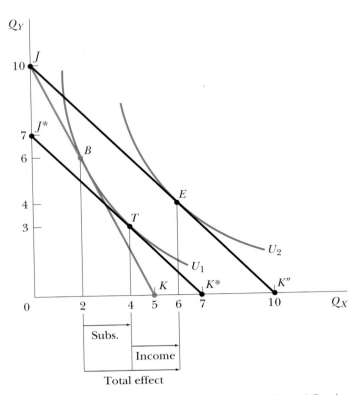

FIGURE 4.4   Income and Substitution Effects for a Normal Good
Starting from optimum point B (as in the top panel of Figure 4.3),
we can isolate the substitution effect by drawing imaginary budget
line J^*K^* tangent to U_1 at T. The movement along U_1 from point B to
point T is the substitution effect and results from the relative
reduction in P_X only (with real income constant). The shift from point
T on U_1 to point E on U_2 is then the income effect. The total effect
($BE = 4X$) equals the substitution effect ($BT = 2X$) plus the income
effect ($TE = 2X$).

In Figure 4.4, $I = \$10$ and $P_Y = \$1$, and these remain constant. With $P_X = \$2$, we
have budget line JK and the consumer maximizes utility at point B on indifference curve
U_1 by purchasing $2X$. When the price of good X falls to $P_X = \$1$, the budget line becomes
JK'' and the consumer maximizes utility at point E on indifference curve U_2 by purchasing $6X$ (so far this is the same as in Figure 4.3). The increase in the quantity purchased
from $2X$ to $6X$ is the total effect or the sum of the substitution and income effects. We are
now ready to separate this total effect into its two components: the substitution effect and
the income effect. *The substitution effect measures the increase in the quantity
demanded of a good when its price falls resulting only from the relative price decline
and independent of the change in real income.* On the other hand, *the income effect measures the increase in the quantity purchased of a good resulting only from the increase
in real income that accompanies a price decline.*

Substitution effect
The increase in the quantity demanded of a good when its price falls, resulting only from the relative price decline and independent of the change in real income.

First, consider the **substitution effect.** In Figure 4.4, we see that when the price of X falls from $P_X = \$2$ to $P_X = \$1$, the individual moves from point B on U_1 to point E on U_2 so that his or her level of satisfaction increases. Suppose that as P_X falls we could reduce the individual's money income sufficiently to keep him or her on original indifference curve U_1. We can show this by drawing hypothetical or imaginary budget line J^*K^* in Figure 4.4. Imaginary budget line J^*K^* is parallel to budget line JK'' so as to reflect the *new* set of relative prices (i.e., $P_X/P_Y = \$1/\$1 = 1$) and is below budget line JK'' in order to keep the individual at the original level of satisfaction (i.e., on indifference curve U_1).[6] The individual would then maximize satisfaction at point T, where indifference curve U_1 is tangent to imaginary budget line J^*K^* (so that $MRS_{XY} = P_X/P_Y = \$1/\$1 = 1$).

The movement along indifference curve U_1 from original point B to imaginary point T measures the substitution effect only (since the individual remains on the same indifference curve or level of satisfaction). From Figure 4.4, we see that the substitution effect, by itself, leads the individual to increase the quantity purchased of good X from two to four units when P_X falls from $\$2$ to $\$1$. That is, the individual substitutes hamburgers for, say, hot dogs and purchases two additional hamburgers and fewer hot dogs per unit of time. The substitution effect results exclusively from the reduction in the **relative price** of X (from $P_X/P_Y = \$2/\$1 = 2$ to $P_X/P_Y = \$1/\$1 = 1$) with the level of satisfaction held constant. Because indifference curves are convex, the substitution effect always involves an increase in the quantity demanded of a good when its price falls.

Relative price The price of one good in terms of that of another.

Income effect The increase in the quantity purchased of a good resulting only from the increase in real income that accompanies a price decline.

Next, consider the **income effect.** The shift from the imaginary point T on U_1 to the actual new point E on U_2 can be taken as a measure of the income effect. The shift from point T to point E does not involve any price change. That is, since the imaginary budget line J^*K^* and the actual new budget line JK'' are parallel, relative prices are the same (i.e., $P_X/P_Y = 1$ in both). The shift from indifference curve U_1 to U_2 can thus be taken as a measure of the increase in the individual's real income or purchasing power.[7] Because good X is a normal good, an increase in the consumer's purchasing power or real income leads him or her to purchase more of X (and other normal goods). In Figure 4.4, the income effect, by itself, leads the consumer to purchase two additional hamburgers (i.e., to go from $4X$ to $6X$).[8]

Thus, the total effect of the reduction in P_X ($BE = 4X$) equals the substitution effect ($BT = 2X$) plus the income effect ($TE = 2X$). The substitution effect reflects the increase in Q_X resulting only from the reduction in P_X and is independent of any change in the consumer's level of satisfaction or real income. On the other hand, the income effect reflects the increase in Q_X resulting only from the increase in satisfaction or real income. Only the total effect of the price change is actually observable in the real world, but we have been able, at least conceptually or experimentally, to separate this total effect into a substitution effect and an income effect.

---

[6] Budget line J^*K^* is imaginary in the sense that we do not actually observe it, unless the reduction in P_X is in fact accompanied by a lump-sum tax that removes $\$3$ ($JJ^* = K''K^*$) from the money income of the individual.

[7] The shift from point T to point E could be observed by giving back to the consumer the hypothetical lump-sum tax of $\$3$ collected earlier. Only with such an increase in real income or purchasing power can the consumer move from point T on U_1 to point E on U_2.

[8] It also leads the individual to purchase one additional soft drink (i.e., to go from $3Y$ to $4Y$). See Figure 4.4.

In Figure 4.4, the substitution effect and the income effect are of equal size. In the real world, the substitution effect is likely to be much larger than the income effect. The reason is that most goods have suitable substitutes, and when the price of a good falls, the quantity of the good purchased is likely to increase very much as consumers substitute the now-cheaper good for others. On the other hand, with the consumer purchasing many goods and spending only a small fraction of his or her income on any one good, the income effect of a price decline of any one good is likely to be small. There are, however, exceptional cases in which the income effect exceeds the substitution effect. Also note that although the substitution effect of a price reduction is always positive (i.e., it always leads to an increase in the quantity demanded of a good), the income effect can be positive if the good is normal or negative if the good is inferior.[9]

✓ Concept Check

Why is the substitution effect usually larger than the income effect?

EXAMPLE 4–4

Substitution Effect and Income Effect of a Gasoline Tax

One of the biggest political battles being fought in Congress centers on energy policy in general and the size of the federal gasoline tax in particular. This is not a new battle. It is a battle that has been fought periodically every five years or so during the past three decades, every time the price of petroleum and American dependence on imported petroleum increased. It is surely a battle that will be fought again before the end of this decade because of the need for an energy policy in the United States.

Overall, gasoline taxes are now about 47 cents per gallon in the United States, as compared with more than $2 per gallon in Europe and Japan. Ever since the first petroleum crisis in 1973–1974, many in Congress have sought a gasoline tax of 50 cents per gallon. The tax would increase gasoline prices for American motorists and lead to a reduction in gasoline consumption and American dependence on foreign oil (which now stands at more than 60%, up from 35% in 1973). To avoid the deflationary impact (i.e., the reduction in purchasing power) of the tax on the economy, it has been proposed to either (a) return to consumers the amount of the tax collected on gasoline in the form of a *general* tax rebate unrelated to gasoline consumption or (b) reduce other taxes.

The gasoline tax, coupled with a general tax rebate to avoid the deflationary impact of a gasoline tax, relies on the distinction between the substitution effect and the income effect of an increase in gasoline prices. The substitution effect would result as people switch to cheaper means of transportation (trains, buses, subways), car pools, and more

---

[9] We could derive a demand curve along which real, rather than nominal, income is kept constant (i.e., showing or reflecting only the substitution effect). Such a demand curve would be steeper than the usual demand curve (which shows both the substitution and the income effects) if the good is normal (because in that case the income effect reinforces the substitution) and flatter than the usual demand curve if the good is inferior (because in that case part of the substitution effect would be neutralized by the opposite income effect).

fuel-efficient cars and economize on the use of automobiles in general. The general income subsidy would then neutralize the reduction in real income associated with the increase in the price of gasoline. Thus, while the reduction in purchasing power would be neutralized by the general income subsidy, the increase in the gasoline price would reduce its consumption. Despite strong opposition to a large increase in the gasoline tax from road builders, tourist interests, farm groups, the oil industry, and truckers, a large increase in the gasoline tax seems likely. It has been estimated that the optimal gasoline tax in the United States is $1.00 per gallon. Americans strongly prefer (and have relied on) tougher fuel-efficiency rules on automakers to reduce the growth of gasoline consumption. The sharp increase in gasoline prices since 2007 is leading Americans to drive less and reduce gasoline consumption.

Sources: A. A. Taheri, "Oil Shocks and the Dynamics of Substitution Adjustments in Industrial Fuels in the U.S.," *Applied Economics,* August 1994, pp. 751–756; "Oil Prices Generate Political Heat," *Wall Street Journal,* August 30, 2000, p. A18; "Looking for Ways to Save Gasoline," *Wall Street Journal,* July 12, 2001, p. A1; "Want to Cut Gasoline Use? Raise Taxes," *Business Week,* May 27, 2002, p. 26; "The Gasoline Tax: Should It Rise?" *Wall Street Journal*, August 18, 2007, p. A4; and "Drinking Less, Americans Finally React to Sting of Gas Prices," *New York Times,* June 19, 2008, p. C3.

Substitution Effect and Income Effect for Inferior Goods

For a normal good, the substitution effect and the income effect of a price decline are both positive and reinforce each other in leading to a greater quantity purchased of the good. On the other hand, when the good is inferior, the income effect moves in the opposite direction from the substitution effect. That is, when the price of an inferior good falls, the substitution effect continues to operate as before to *increase* the quantity purchased of the good. This results from the convex shape of indifference curves. However, the increase in purchasing power or real income resulting from the price decline leads the consumer to purchase *less* of an inferior good. But, because the substitution effect is usually larger than the income effect, the quantity demanded of the inferior good increases when its price falls and the demand curve is still negatively sloped.

We can separate the substitution effect from the income effect of a price decline for an inferior good by returning to the candy bar (inferior good Z) example of the previous section. In the top panel of Figure 4.5, the consumer is originally at optimum at point V, where indifference curve U'_1 is tangent to budget line JK' and the consumer purchases four candy bars (as in the top panel of Figure 4.2). If the price of candy bars declines from $P_Z = \$1$ to $P_Z = \$0.50$, the consumer moves to optimum point S, where indifference curve U'_2 is tangent to budget line JN' and the consumer purchases 6Z. The movement from point V to point S (+2Z) is the sum or net effect of the substitution and income effects.

To separate the substitution effect from the income effect, we now draw the imaginary budget line J^*N^*, which is lower than, but parallel to, budget line JN' and tangent to U'_1 at point T. The movement along U'_1 from the original point V to imaginary point T is the *substitution effect.* It results exclusively from the reduction in P_Z relative to P_Y and is independent of any increase in real income. Thus, the substitution effect, by itself, leads the individual to purchase four additional units of good Z per unit of time (from 4Z to 8Z).

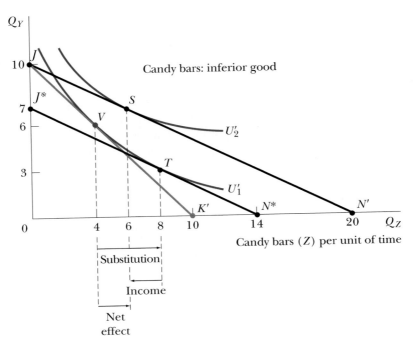

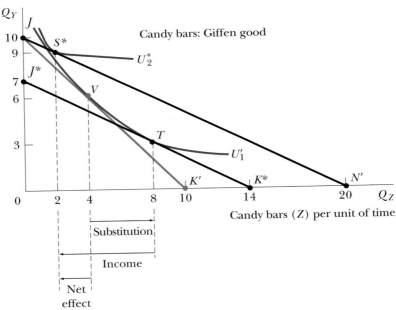

FIGURE 4.5   Income and Substitution Effects for Inferior Goods   Starting from optimum point
V in the top panel, we can isolate the substitution effect by drawing J^*N^* parallel to JN' and tangent to
U_1' at point T. The movement along U_1' from point V to point T is the substitution effect. The movement
from point T on U_1' to point S on U_2' is the income effect. Since the income effect is negative, good Z is
inferior. However, since the positive substitution effect exceeds the negative income effect, Q_Z increases
when P_Z falls. In the bottom panel, the positive substitution effect ($VT = 4Z$) is smaller than the negative
income effect ($TS^* = -6Z$), so that Q_Z declines by $2Z$ when P_Z falls. Good Z is then a Giffen good.

On the other hand, the movement from imaginary point T on U_1' to the new point S on U_2' can be taken as a measure of the *income effect.* It results exclusively from the increase in the level of satisfaction of the consumer with relative prices constant ($P_Z/P_Y = \$0.50/\$1 = 1/2$ for imaginary budget line J^*N^* and for new budget line JN'). The income effect, by itself, leads the consumer to purchase two *fewer* units of good Z per unit of time (from $8Z$ to $6Z$) because good Z is an inferior good.

Thus, the total effect ($VS = 2Z$ given by the movement from point V on U_1' to point S on U_2') equals the positive substitution effect ($VT = 4Z$ given by the movement from point V to T on U_1') plus the negative income effect ($TS = -2Z$ given by the movement from point T on U_1' to point S on U_2'). However, since the positive substitution effect exceeds the negative income effect, the consumer purchases two additional units of good Z when its price declines. Thus, the demand curve for good Z is negatively sloped, even though good Z is an inferior good. That is, the consumer purchases $4Z$ at $P_Z = \$1$ and $6Z$ at $P_Z = \$0.50$.

On the other hand, if the positive substitution effect is smaller than the negative income effect when the price of an inferior good falls, then the demand curve for the inferior good is positively sloped. This very rarely, if ever, occurs in the real world, and is referred to as the **Giffen good,** after the nineteenth-century British economist, Robert Giffen, who supposedly first discussed it. Note that a Giffen good is an inferior good, but not all inferior goods are Giffen goods. If it existed, a Giffen good would lead to a positively sloped demand curve for the individual and would represent an exception to the law of negatively sloped demand.[10]

The bottom panel of Figure 4.5 is drawn on the assumption that good Z is now a Giffen good. In this panel, the consumer is originally at optimum point V and hypothetically moves to point T because of the substitution effect (as in the top panel). However, with *alternative* indifference curve U_2^* in the bottom panel (as opposed to U_2' in the top panel), the income effect is given by the movement from point T to point S^*. Point S^* is to the left of point T because good Z is an inferior good, so that an increase in real income leads to less of it being purchased. The total effect is now $VS^*(-2Z)$ and is equal to substitution effect $VT(4Z)$ plus income effect $TS^*(-6Z)$. Because the positive substitution effect is smaller than the negative income effect, the quantity demanded of good Z *declines* when its price falls, and d_Z would be positively sloped over this range. That is, the individual would purchase $4Z$ at $P_Z = \$1$ but only $2Z$ at $P_Z = \$0.50$.

Although theoretically interesting, the Giffen paradox rarely, if ever, occurs in the real world. The reason is that inferior goods are usually narrowly defined goods for which suitable substitutes are available (so that the substitution effect usually exceeds the opposite income effect). Giffen thought that potatoes in nineteenth-century Ireland provided an example of the paradox, but subsequent research did not support his belief.[11] Example 4–5 presents the first, rigorous empirical evidence of Giffen behavior.

The separation of the substitution effect from the income effect (and all of the analysis in this chapter) could easily be shown for a price increase rather than for a price decline. These alternatives are assigned as end-of-chapter problems.

Giffen good An inferior good for which the positive substitution effect is smaller than the negative income effect, so less of the good is purchased when its price falls.

✓ Concept Check
What two conditions are necessary to have a Giffen good?

✓ Concept Check
Why does a Giffen good represent an exception to the law of demand?

---

[10] If we kept real rather than nominal income constant in deriving the demand curve (i.e., if the demand curve showed or reflected only the substitution effect), there would be no Giffen exception to the law of negatively sloped demand.

[11] See S. Rosen, "Potatoes Paradoxes," *Journal of Political Economy*, December 1999.

EXAMPLE 4–5

Giffen Behavior Found!

Jensen and Miller (2007) provided the first, rigorous empirical evidence of the existence of Giffen behavior among extremely poor households in two provinces of China in 2006. The authors conducted a field experiment in which they provided randomly selected poor households with price subsidies for the primary dietary staple food (rice in Hunan province in southern China and wheat flour in Gansu province in northern China).

The sample consisted of 100–150 households in each of 11 county seats in Hunan and Gansu provinces, for a total of 1,300 households (650 in each province) with 3,661 individuals. Within each county, households were chosen at random from the list of the urban poor obtained from the office of the Ministry of Civil Affairs. Households on the list typically had incomes of between 100 and 200 yuan per person per month, or $0.41 to $0.82 per person per day (which is below even the World Bank's "extreme" poverty line of $1 per person per day). Data were gathered at three different times: April, September, and December 2006. After completing the first (April) survey to choose the sample, the sample households were informed that they would receive subsidies from June through October to purchase their staple food; the change in the quantity purchased of the staple food was recorded.

The authors found strong and clear evidence of the Giffen behavior with respect to rice in Hunan province. The evidence with respect to wheat flour in Gansu province was less robust, because some of the theoretical conditions necessary for the Giffen behavior were not met. By restricting the Gansu sample to households that met those conditions, the authors were able to find strong evidence of the Giffen behavior in Gansu province also. Note that Giffen behavior was found precisely where theory would predict: among very poor consumers, heavily dependent on a staple food, with limited substitution possibilities.

Source: Robert T. Jensen and Nola H. Miller, "Giffen Behavior: Theory and Evidence," *NBER Working Paper No. 13243*, July 2007.

4.4   SUBSTITUTION BETWEEN DOMESTIC AND FOREIGN GOODS

The substitution between domestic and foreign goods and services has reached an all-time high in the world today and is expected to continue to increase sharply in the future. This increase has been the result of (1) transportation costs having fallen to very low levels for most products, (2) increased knowledge of foreign products due to an international information revolution, (3) global advertising campaigns by multinational corporations, (4) the explosion of international travel, and (5) the rapid convergence of tastes internationally. For homogeneous products such as a particular grade of wheat or steel, and for many industrial products with precise specifications such as computer chips, fiber optics, and specialized machinery, substitutability between domestic and foreign products is almost perfect. Here, a small price difference can lead quickly to large shifts in sales from domestic to foreign sources and vice versa. Indeed, so fluid is the market for such products that governments often step in to protect these industries from foreign competition.

Even for differentiated products, such as automobiles and motorcycles, computers and copiers, watches and cameras, TV films and TV programs, soft drinks and cigarettes, soaps and detergents, commercial and military aircraft, and most other products that are similar but not identical, substitutability between domestic and foreign products is very high and continues to rise. Despite the quality problems of the past, U.S.-made automobiles today are highly substitutable for Japanese and European automobiles, and so are most other products. Indeed, intraindustry trade in such differentiated products now represents over 60% of total U.S. trade and an even larger percentage of the trade of most other industrial countries.[12] With many parts and components imported from many nations, and with production facilities and sales around the world often exceeding sales at home, even the distinction between domestic and foreign products is fast becoming obsolete.

EXAMPLE 4–6

What Is an "American" Car?

Strange as it may seem, the question of what is an American car may be difficult to answer. Should a Honda Accord produced in Ohio be considered American? What about a Chrysler minivan produced in Canada (especially after Chrysler was acquired by Germany's Mercedes-Benz)? Is a Kentucky Toyota or Mazda that uses nearly 50% of imported Japanese parts American? It is clearly becoming more and more difficult to define what is American, and opinions differ widely.

For some, any vehicle assembled in North America (the United States, Canada, and Mexico) should be considered American because these vehicles use U.S.-made parts. But the United Auto Workers union views cars built in Canada and Mexico as taking away U.S. jobs. Some regard automobiles produced by Japanese-owned plants in the United States as American because they provide jobs for Americans. Others regard production by these Japanese "transplants" as foreign, because the jobs they create were taken from the U.S. automakers, because they use nearly 40% of imported Japanese parts, and because they remit profits to Japan. What if Japanese transplants increased their use of American parts to 75% or 90%? Was the Ford Probe, built for Ford by Mazda in Mazda's Flat Rock Michigan plant, American?

It is difficult to decide exactly what is an American car—even after the American Automobile Labeling Act of 1992, which requires all automobiles sold in the United States to indicate what percentage of the car's parts are domestic or foreign. One could even ask if this question is relevant at all in a world growing more and more interdependent and globalized. In fact, rapid consolidation in the industry has left only five truly global automakers—General Motors, Ford, Toyota, Daimler

---

[12] D. Salvatore, *International Economics*, 9th ed. (Hoboken, N.J.: John Wiley & Sons, 2007), Section 6.4.

Chrysler, and Volkswagen—and each has developed or is developing a truly world car (essentially the same basic type of automobile sold everywhere) and using parts from all over the world.

Sources: "Honda's Nationality Proves Troublesome for Free-Trade Pact," *The New York Times,* October 9, 1992, p. 1; "Want a U.S. Car? Read the Label," *The New York Times,* September 18, 1994, Section 3, p. 6; "Made in America? Not Exactly: Transplants Use Japanese Car Parts," *Wall Street Journal,* September 1, 1995, p. A3B; "And Then There Were Five," *U.S. News & World Report,* March 4, 2000, p. 46; and "Defining an American Car," August 2007, http://autos.msn.com/advice/article.aspx?contentid=4021986.

4.5	SOME APPLICATIONS OF INDIFFERENCE CURVE ANALYSIS

We now can apply the tools developed in this chapter to analyze the economics of the food stamp program, consumer surplus, and exchange. These applications deal only with the demand for goods and services, but the tools developed in this chapter have many other applications (examined in other parts of the text). For example, the distinction between the substitution and income effects is useful in analyzing the effect of overtime pay on the number of hours worked and on leisure time. Because this topic deals with the supply of labor, however, it is appropriately postponed until Chapter 14, which deals with input price and employment. Indifference curve analysis is also useful in analyzing the choice between borrowing or lending from present income (examined in Chapter 16), in general equilibrium and welfare economics (examined in Chapter 17), and in the analysis of time as an economic good (discussed more extensively in Chapter 19).

Is a Cash Subsidy Better Than Food Stamps?

Food stamp program
A federal program under which eligible low-income families receive free food stamps to purchase food.

Under the federal **food stamp program,** low-income families receive free food stamps, which they can use only to purchase food. At its peak in 1988, more than 4.8 million eligible low-income families received free food stamps at a cost of $12.4 billion to the federal government. The important question is whether it would have been better (i.e., provided more satisfaction) to have given an equal amount of subsidy in cash to these families.

We can examine this question using Figure 4.6. Suppose that, initially, a typical poor family has a weekly income of $100. If the poor family spent its entire weekly income on nonfood items, it could purchase $100 worth of nonfood items per week (point *A* on the vertical axis). On the other hand, if the poor family spent the entire $100 on food, it could purchase 100 units of food per week if the unit price of food were $1 (point *C* on the horizontal axis). The initial budget line of the family would be *AC.*

With free food stamps that allow the family to purchase $50 worth of food per week, the budget line of the family becomes *AB′C′,* where *AB′ = CC′ = 50.* Combinations on dashed segment *A′B′* are not available with the food stamp program because the family would have to spend more than its $100 money income on nonfood items and less than the $50 of food stamps on food (and this is not possible if it cannot sell its food stamps). Were the government to provide $50 in cash rather than in food stamps, the budget line would then be *A′C′.* Thus, we have three alternative budget lines for the family: budget line *AC* without any aid, budget line *AB′C′* with $50 in food stamps, and budget line *A′C′* with $50 cash aid instead.

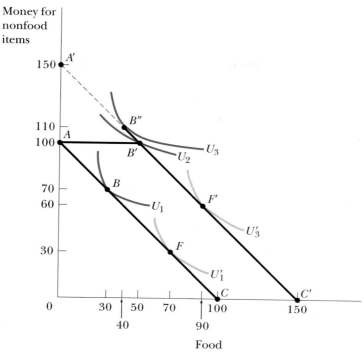

FIGURE 4.6   Food Stamps Versus Cash Aid   A poor family's budget line, *AC*, becomes *AB'C'* with $50 worth of free food stamps per week, and *A'C'* with a $50 cash subsidy instead. The family maximizes utility at point *B* on U_1 without any aid, at point *B'* on U_2 with food stamps, and at point *B''* on U_3 with the cash subsidy. However, another family with the same original income and budget line *AC* but with a stronger preference for food may go instead from point *F* on U_1' to point *F'* on U_3' either with the cash subsidy or with food stamps.

✓ Concept Check

Why is a cash subsidy generally better than a subsidy in kind?

If the family's indifference curves are U_1, U_2, and U_3, the family maximizes utility at point *B* where U_1 is tangent to *AC* before receiving any aid, at point *B'* on U_2 with food stamps, and at point *B''* (preferred to *B'*) on U_3 with the cash subsidy. In this case, the cash subsidy allows the family to reach a higher indifference curve than do food stamps.[13] However, *another family* with the same initial income of $100 (and budget line *AC*) but stronger preference for food and facing indifference curves U_1' and U_3' will move instead from point *F* on U_1' to point *F'* on U_3' either with the cash subsidy or with food stamps. Thus, depending on the family's tastes, *a cash subsidy will not be worse than food stamps and may be better* (i.e., provide more satisfaction). Why then does the federal government continue to use food stamps? One reason is to improve nutrition.[14]

---

[13] Both cost the government $50.

[14] Note that the indifference curves of the two *different* families shown in Figure 4.6 would cross if extended. It is only the individual indifference curves of each family that cannot cross.

Consumer Surplus Measures Unpaid Benefits

Consumer surplus
The difference between what the consumer is willing to pay for a given quantity of a good and what he or she actually pays for it.

Consumer surplus is the difference between what a consumer is willing to pay for a good and what he or she actually pays. It results because the consumer pays for *each* unit of the good only as much as he or she is willing to pay for the *last* unit of the good (which gives less utility than earlier units). We can see how consumer surplus arises and how it can be measured with the aid of Figure 4.7.

The figure shows that $5 is the maximum amount that the consumer is willing to pay for the first unit of good X (say, hamburgers) rather than go without it. Thus, the area of the first rectangle (with height of $5 and width of 1) measures the marginal value or benefit that the consumer gets from the first hamburger. After all, by being willing to purchase the first hamburger for $5, the consumer indicates that he or she prefers paying $5 for the first hamburger rather than keeping the $5 in cash or spending the $5 on other goods. The second unit of good X (hamburger) gives the consumer less utility than the first, and the consumer would be willing to pay $4 for it rather than go without it. Thus, $4 (the area of the second rectangle) can be taken as a measure of the marginal value or benefit of the second hamburger to the consumer. The third hamburger gives the consumer less utility than either the first or the second and so the consumer is willing to pay only $3 for it. Thus, the marginal value or benefit of the third hamburger is $3 and is given by the area of the third rectangle. For the fourth hamburger, the consumer would be willing to pay $2 (the area of the fourth rectangle), and this is a measure of the marginal value or benefit of the fourth hamburger, and so on.

To summarize, the consumer would be willing to pay $5 for the first hamburger, $4 for the second, $3 for the third, and $2 for the fourth, for a total of $14 for all four hamburgers. Thus, $14 is the total benefit that the consumer receives from purchasing four hamburgers. However, if the market price is $2 per hamburger, the consumer can purchase all four hamburgers at a total cost of (i.e., by actually spending) only $8. Because the consumer would be willing to pay $14 for the first four hamburgers rather than go entirely

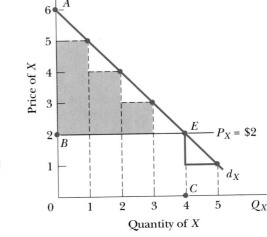

FIGURE 4.7   Consumer Surplus   The difference between what the consumer is willing to pay for 4X ($5 + $4 + $3 + $2 = $14) and what he or she actually pays ($8) is the consumer surplus (the shaded area that equals $6). If good X could be purchased in infinitesimally small units, the consumer surplus would equal the area under d_X and above $P_X = 2 (area AEB = $8).

without them, but actually pays only $8, he or she enjoys a net benefit or *consumer surplus* equal to the difference ($6).

To put it another way, the consumer is willing to pay $5 for the first hamburger, but since he or she can purchase it for only $2, he or she receives a surplus of $3 for the first hamburger. Since the consumer is willing to pay $4 for the second hamburger but pays only $2, there is a surplus of $2 on the second hamburger. For the third hamburger, the consumer is willing to pay $3, but since he or she pays only $2, the surplus is $1. For the fourth hamburger, the consumer is willing to pay $2, and since he or she has to pay $2 for it, there is no surplus on the fourth hamburger. The consumer would not purchase the fifth hamburger because he or she is not willing to pay the $2 market price for it.

By adding the consumer surplus of $3 on the first hamburger, $2 on the second, $1 on the third, and $0 on the fourth, we get the consumer surplus of $6 obtained earlier. This is given by the sum of the shaded areas in the figure. The same result would have been obtained if the consumer had been asked for the maximum amount of money that he or she would have been willing to pay for four hamburgers rather than do entirely without them—*all or nothing.*

If hamburgers could have been purchased in smaller and smaller fractions of a whole hamburger, then the consumer surplus would have been given by the entire area under demand curve d_X above the market price of $2. That is, the consumer surplus would have been the area of triangle *AEB,* which is $(1/2)(4)(4) = \$8$. This exceeds the consumer surplus of $6 that we found by adding only the shaded areas in the figure. Specifically, the consumer would have been willing to pay $16 (the area of *OAEC*) for four hamburgers. Note that *OAEC* is composed of triangle *AEB* plus rectangle *OBEC.* Since the consumer only pays $8 (*OBEC*), the consumer surplus is $8 (*AEB*). If P_X fell to $1, the consumer would purchase five hamburgers and the consumer's surplus would be $12.50 (the area under d_X and above $P_X = \$1$ in the figure) if hamburgers could be purchased by infinitely small fractions of a whole hamburger.[15]

The concept of consumer surplus was first used by Jules Dupuit in 1844 and was subsequently refined and popularized by Alfred Marshall. The concept helped resolve the so-called **water–diamond paradox,** which plagued classical economists until 1870. Why is water, which is essential for life, so cheap, whereas diamonds, which are not essential, are so expensive? The explanation is that because water is so plentiful (relatively cheap) and we use so much of it, the utility of the last unit is very little (washing the car), and we pay as little for all units of water as we are willing to pay for the last *nonessential* unit of it. On the other hand, diamonds are scarce in relation to demand, and because we use very little of them, the utility and price of the *last unit* are very great. The *total* utility and the consumer surplus from all the water used are far greater than the total utility and the consumer surplus from all the diamonds purchased. However, demand depends on marginal utility, not on total utility. In a desert, the first glass of water would be worth much more than any glassful of diamonds.

The above analysis referred to an individual's demand curve, but a similar analysis would also apply to a market demand curve. In subsequent chapters we will use the concept of consumer surplus to measure the benefits and costs of excise taxes, import tariffs,

---

[15] Measuring consumer surplus by the area under the demand curve and above the prevailing market price is only an approximation (it is based on the assumption that a consumer's indifference curves are parallel), but for most purposes it is sufficiently accurate to be a useful tool of analysis. See, R. D. Willig, "Consumer Surplus without Apology," *American Economic Review,* September 1976. See, however, K. S. Lyon and Ming Yan, "Compensating Variation Consumer's Surplus Via Successive Approximations," *Applied Economics,* June 1995, pp. 547–554.

Concept Check
In what way does consumer surplus benefit the consumer?

Water–diamond paradox The question of why water, which is essential to life, is so cheap, whereas diamonds, which are not essential, are so expensive.

Concept Check
Why is water so cheap whereas diamonds are so expensive?

pollution control, government projects, and other microeconomic policies, as well as to measure the benefits and costs of alternative market structures.

Benefits from Exchange

Suppose that two individuals, A and B, have a given amount of good X and good Y and decide to trade some of these goods with each other. If the exchange is voluntary, the strong presumption is that both individuals gain from the exchange (otherwise, the individual who loses would simply refuse to trade). We can examine the process of voluntary exchange by indifference curve analysis.

Suppose that individual A's tastes and preferences for good X and good Y are shown by indifference curves U_1, U_2, and U_3 in the top left panel of Figure 4.8. Individual B's tastes and preferences are given by indifference curves U'_1, U'_2, and U'_3 (with origin $0'$) in the top right panel. Initially, individual A has an allocation of $3X$ and $6Y$ (point C in the top left panel) and individual B has $7X$ and $2Y$ (point C' in the top right panel).

We now rotate individual B's indifference diagram by 180 degrees (so that origin $0'$ appears in the top right corner) and superimpose it on individual A's indifference diagram in such a way that the axes of the two diagrams form the so-called **Edgeworth box diagram,** shown in the bottom panel of Figure 4.8. The length of the box ($10X$) measures the combined amount of X initially owned by individual A ($3X$) and individual B ($7X$). The height of the box ($8Y$) measures the amount of Y initially owned by individual A ($6Y$) and individual B ($2Y$). A's indifference curves are convex to origin 0 (as usual), while B's indifference curves are convex to origin $0'$.

Any point inside the box indicates how the total amount of X and Y may be distributed between the two individuals. For example, the initial distribution of X and Y given by point C indicates that individual A has $3X$ and $6Y$ (viewed from origin 0) and individual B has the remainder of $7X$ and $2Y$ (when viewed from origin $0'$) for a total of $10X$ and $8Y$ (the dimensions of the box). Individual A is on indifference curve U_1 and individual B is on indifference curve U'_1.

Since at point C (where U_1 and U'_1 intersect) the marginal rate of substitution of good X for good Y (MRS_{XY}) for individual A exceeds MRS_{XY} for individual B, there is a basis for mutually beneficial exchange between the two individuals. Starting at point C, individual A would be willing to give up $4Y$ to get one additional unit of X (and move to point D on U_1). On the other hand, individual B would be willing to give up $1X$ for about 0.2 additional units of Y (and move to point H on U'_1). Because A is willing to give up more of Y than necessary to induce B to give up $1X$, there is a basis for trade in which individual A gives up some of Y in exchange for some of X from individual B.

Whenever the MRS_{XY} for the two individuals differs at the initial distribution of X and Y, either or both may gain from exchange. For example, starting from point C, if individual A exchanges $4Y$ for $1X$ with individual B, A would move from point C to point D along indifference curve U_1, while B would move from point C on U'_1 to point D on U'_3. By moving from indifference curve U'_1 to indifference curve U'_3, individual B receives all of the gains from the exchange while individual A gains or loses nothing (since A remains on U_1). At point D, U_1 and U'_3 are tangent, and so their slopes (MRS_{XY}) are equal. Thus, there is no basis for further exchange (at point D, the amount of Y that A is willing to give up for $1X$ is exactly equal to what B requires to give up $1X$). Any further exchange would make either one or both individuals worse off than they are at point D.

Edgeworth box diagram A diagram constructed from the indifference map diagrams of two individuals, which can be used to analyze voluntary exchange.

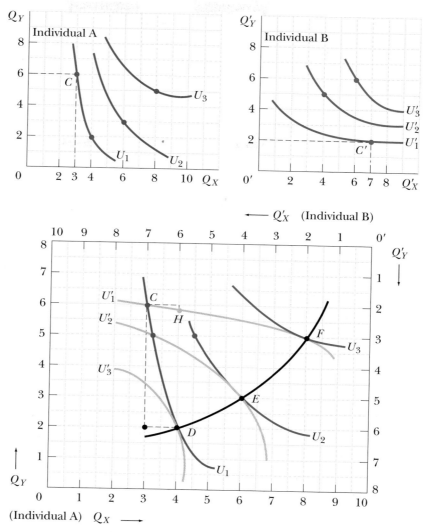

FIGURE 4.8   Edgeworth Box Diagram   The top left panel shows individual A's indifference curves, and the top right panel shows B's indifference curves. The box in the bottom panel is obtained by rotating B's indifference map diagram 180 degrees and superimposing it on A's diagram in such a way that the dimensions of the box equal the initial combined amounts of goods X and Y owned by A and B. Any point in the box refers to a particular distribution of X and Y between A and B. At point C, MRS_{XY} for the two individuals differs (U_1 and U_1' cross) and there is a basis for mutually beneficial exchange until a point between D and F on curve DEF is reached (where MRS_{XY} for A and B are equal).

Alternatively, if individual A exchanged $1Y$ for $5X$ with individual B, individual A would move from point C on U_1 to point F on U_3, while individual B would move from point C to point F along U_1'. In this case, A would reap all the benefits from exchange while B would neither gain nor lose. At point F, MRS_{XY} for A equals MRS_{XY} for B and there is no further basis for exchange. Finally, starting again from point C on U_1 and U_1', if A exchanges $3Y$ for $3X$ with B and gets to point E, both individuals gain from the exchange since point E is on U_2 and U'_2.

Starting from any point within $CDEF$ but not on curve DEF, both individuals can gain from exchange by moving to a point on curve DEF between points D and F. The closer individual A gets to point F (i.e., the more shrewd A is as a bargainer), the greater is the proportion of the total gain from the exchange accruing to A and the less is left for B. The Edgeworth box is named after the English economist F. Y. Edgeworth, who in 1881 first outlined its construction. (We will return to exchange in greater detail in Chapter 17.)

✔ Concept Check

Until what point does mutual beneficial exchange take place?

AT THE FRONTIER
The Characteristics Approach to Consumer Theory

Characteristics approach to consumer theory The theory that postulates that a consumer demands a good because of the characteristics, properties, or attributes of the good.

The **characteristics approach to consumer theory,** pioneered by Kelvin Lancaster, postulates that consumers demand a good because of the characteristics, properties, and attributes of the good, and it is these characteristics that give rise to utility.[16] For example, a consumer does not demand beef, as such, but rather the characteristics of protein and calories, which are the direct source of utility. But protein and calories are also provided (though in different proportions) by pork and chicken. Thus, a good usually possesses more than one characteristic, and any given characteristic is present in more than one good.

The characteristics approach to consumer theory can be shown graphically. In the top panel of Figure 4.9, the horizontal axis measures the characteristic of protein and the vertical axis measures calories. Suppose that the consumer's income is $10 and that $10 worth of pork provides the combination of protein and calories given by point A, while $10 worth of beef gives the combination at point B.[17] The budget line is then AB. Area $0AB$ is called the *feasible region* and budget line AB is the *efficiency frontier*. That is, the consumer can purchase any combination of protein and calories in area $A0B$, but he or she will maximize utility or satisfaction by choosing combinations on line AB.

If U_1 is a consumer's indifference curve in characteristics space (i.e., with characteristics protein and calories measured along the axes), the consumer maximizes utility at point C, where indifference curve U_1 is tangent to budget line AB. The consumer reaches point C by obtaining $0F$ characteristics from spending $5 on beef and FC characteristics from spending the remaining $5 on pork. $0F = 1/2\ 0B$ and $0G = 1/2\ 0A$. Note that FC equals $0G$, both in length and direction.[18]

In the bottom panel, a new good is introduced, chicken, which has half as many calories per unit of protein as beef. If $10 worth of chicken provides the combination of protein and calories given by point H, the budget line or efficiency frontier becomes

---

[16] Kelvin Lancaster, *Consumer Demand: A New Approach* (New York: Columbia University Press, 1971).

[17] Note that the characteristics ray for pork has a slope four times larger than the characteristics ray for beef. Thus, pork provides four times as many calories per unit of protein as beef.

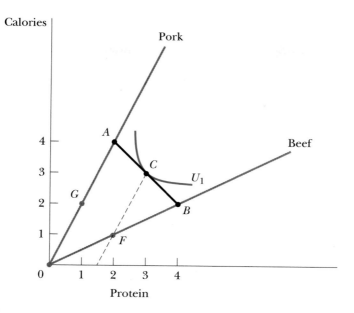

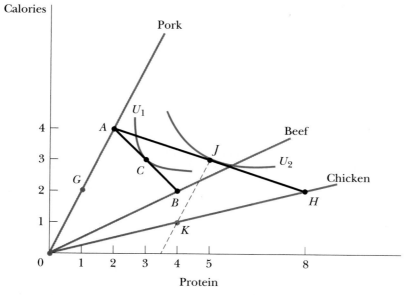

FIGURE 4.9 The Characteristics Approach to Consumer Demand Theory In the top panel, $10 worth of pork gives the combination of protein and calories indicated by point *A* and $10 worth of beef gives the combination at point *B*. Thus, *AB* is the budget line. The consumer maximizes utility at point *C*, where U_1 is tangent to *AB*, by spending $5 on pork and $5 on beef, and receiving *OF* characteristics from beef and *FC* (equals *OG*) from pork. In the bottom panel, $10 worth of chicken gives point *H*, so that the budget line is *AH*. The consumer maximizes utility at point *J* on U_2 by spending $5 on pork and $5 on chicken, and obtaining *OK* characteristics from chicken and *KJ* (equals *OG*) characteristics from pork, with no beef purchased.

Continued . . .

The Characteristics Approach to Consumer Theory   *Continued*

AH. The consumer now maximizes utility at point *J*, where indifference curve U_2 is tangent to budget line *AH*. The consumer reaches point *J* by obtaining 0*K* characteristics from spending $5 on chicken and *KJ* (equals 0*G*) characteristics from spending the remaining $5 on pork. No beef is now purchased.

The reduction in the price of a good can be shown by a proportionate outward movement along the characteristics ray of the good, while an increase in income can be shown by a proportionate outward shift of the entire budget line. These shifts will allow the consumer to reach a higher indifference curve as in traditional consumer theory.

The characteristics approach to consumer theory has several important advantages over traditional demand theory. First, substitution among goods can be easily explained in terms of some common characteristics of the goods. For example, according to this theory coffee and tea are substitutes because they both have the characteristic of being stimulants.

Second, the introduction of a new good can easily be taken care of by drawing a new ray from the origin reflecting the combination of the two characteristics of the new good. This was shown by the introduction of chicken in the bottom panel of Figure 4.9. However, the new good will only be purchased if its price is sufficiently low (e.g., chicken in the bottom panel of Figure 4.9). Had $10 worth of chicken provided only the combination of protein and calories given by point *K* on the characteristics ray for chicken, the budget line would become *ABK* and the consumer would maximize utility by remaining at point *C* and purchasing no chicken.

Third, a quality change can be shown by rotating the characteristics ray for the good. For example, the introduction of a new breed of leaner hogs resulting in pork with less calories per unit of protein can be shown by a clockwise rotation of the characteristics ray for pork. Finally, by comparing the price of two goods that are identical except for a particular characteristic, this approach permits the estimation of the implicit or *hedonic* price of the characteristic. For example, by comparing the price of houses that are otherwise identical except for some other characteristic, such as lower noise pollution, proximity to good schools, parks, and a good transportation network, we can estimate the implicit or hedonic price of each of these characteristics. Thus, if the price of a house that is near a park is $10,000 more than the price of another identical house that is not near a park, the characteristic of being closer to a park is worth $10,000.

✓ **Concept Check**

How does the characteristics approach to consumer demand theory differ from the traditional approach?

One disadvantage of the theory is that some characteristics, such as taste and style, are subjective and cannot be measured explicitly. The problem is even more serious in dealing with the characteristics of services. Nevertheless, the hedonic approach is very useful because it allows at least an *implicit* measure of the various characteristics of each good.

---

[18] *FC* and 0*G* are called vectors. Thus, the above is an example of vector analysis, whereby vector 0*C* (not shown in the top panel of Figure 4.9) is equal to the sum of vectors 0*F* and 0*G*.

SUMMARY

1. The income–consumption curve joins consumer optimum points resulting when only the consumer's income is varied. The Engel curve is derived from the income–consumption curve and shows the amount of a good that the consumer would purchase per unit of time at various income levels. A normal good is one of which the consumer purchases more with an increase in income. An inferior good is one of which the consumer purchases less with an increase in income. The income–consumption curve and the Engel curve are positively sloped for normal goods and negatively sloped for inferior goods.

2. The price–consumption curve for a good joins consumer optimum points resulting when only the price of the good varies. This curve shows the amount of the good that the consumer would purchase per unit of time at various prices of the good while holding everything else constant. The individual consumer's demand curve for a good is negatively sloped, reflecting the law of demand.

3. When the price of a good falls, consumers substitute this good for other goods and their real income rises. If the good is normal, the income effect reinforces the substitution effect in increasing the quantity purchased of the good. If the good is inferior, the substitution effect tends to increase while the income effect tends to reduce the quantity demanded of the good. Because the former usually exceeds the latter, the quantity demanded of the good increases and the demand curve is negatively sloped. Only if the income effect overwhelms the opposite substitution effect for an inferior good will the quantity demanded of the good decrease when its price falls, and the demand curve will slope upward. This is called a Giffen good. Only recently, however, has an example of true Giffen behavior been found.

4. With the substitutability between domestic and foreign goods and services having reached an all-time high in the world today, and with the expectation that it will rise even more in the future, the need to introduce an important international dimension in the study of microeconomics becomes even clearer.

5. A cash subsidy leads to an equal or greater increase in utility than a subsidy in kind (such as the food stamp program) that costs the same. The consumer surplus is given by the difference between what the consumer is willing to pay for a good and what the consumer actually pays for it. Its value can be approximated by the area under the demand curve and above the market price of the good. An Edgeworth box diagram is constructed by rotating an individual's indifference map diagram by 180 degrees and superimposing it on another's, so that the dimensions of the box equal the combined initial distribution of the two goods between the two individuals. The Edgeworth box diagram can be used to analyze voluntary exchange. The characteristics approach to consumer theory can be used to measure the implicit or hedonic price of a particular characteristic of a good or service.

KEY TERMS

Income–consumption curve
Engel curve
Normal good
Inferior good
Price–consumption curve
Individual's demand curve
Substitution effect

Relative price
Income effect
Giffen good
Food stamp program
Consumer surplus
Water–diamond paradox
Edgeworth box diagram

Characteristics approach to
    consumer theory
Income or expenditure
    index (E)
Laspeyres price index (L)
Paasche price index (P)

REVIEW QUESTIONS

1. A consumer buys an Oldsmobile for $20,000 instead of a Toyota for $22,000. Does this mean that the consumer prefers the Oldsmobile to a Toyota?

2. How would indifference curves between money and automobiles differ between two individuals with the same money income but with one having a stronger preference for automobiles than the other?

3. Why would the use of gasoline decline if its price rose as a result of a gasoline tax but the effect of the price rise was compensated by a tax rebate?

4. The income effect of a 20% increase in housing rents is larger than the effect of a 20% increase in the price of salt. True or false? Explain.

5. A demand curve showing only the substitution effect can never be positively sloped, not even theoretically. True or false? Explain.

6. Is a demand curve showing both the substitution and income effects flatter or steeper than the

demand curve showing only the substitution effect? Explain.

7. Will a consumer purchase more or less of an inferior good when its price declines? Explain.

8. Can all goods purchased by a consumer be inferior?

9. In 2003, the Men's Hair Company increased the price of its shampoo and subsequently sold more shampoo than in 2002. Is the demand curve for this company's shampoo positively sloped? Explain.

10. Why is the gift of any good likely to provide less satisfaction to the recipient than an equal cash gift?

11. When would the gift of a good provide the recipient as much satisfaction as an equal cash gift?

12. How can a black market in food stamps be explained?

13. What are the advantages and disadvantages of the characteristics approach to consumer theory?

PROBLEMS

1. a. Derive the income-consumption curve and Engel curve from the indifference curves of Problem 2 in Chapter 3 and the budget lines from Problem 6(a) in Chapter 3. Is good X a normal or an inferior good? Why?

  b. Derive the Engel curve for good Y. Is good Y a normal or an inferior good? Why?

2. a. For the budget lines of Problem 6(a) in Chapter 3, draw indifference curves that show that good X is inferior; derive the income-consumption curve and the Engel curve for good X.

  b. Draw the Engel curve for good Y. Must good Y be normal?

*3. a. Derive the price-consumption curve and demand curve for good X from the indifference curves of Problem 2 in Chapter 3 and the budget lines from Problem 6(b) in Chapter 3 when the price of X falls from $P_X = \$2$ to $P_X = \$1$ and then to $P_X = \$0.50$.

  b. Use the figure for your answer to 3(a) to explain how you would derive the price-consumption curve and demand curve for good X when the price of X rises from $P_X = \$0.50$ to $P_X = \$1$ and then to $P_X = \$2$.

4. Using the indifference curves of Problem 2 in Chapter 3 and the budget lines of problem 6(b) in Chapter 3, separate the substitution effect from the income effect when the price of X falls from $P_X = \$2$ to $P_X = \$1$ and then from $P_X = \$1$ to $P_X = \$0.50$.

*5. Separate the substitution effect from the income effect for an *increase* in the price of an inferior good.

6. Separate the substitution effect from the income effect for an increase in price of a Giffen good.

*7. It is sometimes asserted that rice in very poor Asian countries might be an inferior good. Even though there is no evidence that this is indeed the case, explain the reasoning behind this assertion.

8. The average number of children per family has declined in the face of rapidly rising family incomes, so children must be an inferior good. True or false? Explain.

*9. Use indifference curve analysis to show that a poor family can be made to reach a given higher indifference curve with a smaller cash subsidy than with a subsidy in kind (such as, for example, by the government paying half of the market price of food for the family). Why might the government still prefer a subsidy in kind?

_____
* = Answer provided at end of book.

10. With reference to Figure 4.7 in the text, indicate the size of the consumer surplus when $P_X = \$3$ if
    a. good X can only be purchased in whole units.
    b. good X can be purchased in infinitesimally small fractional units.
11. With reference to Figure 4.8 in the text, indicate how exchange could take place starting from the initial

distribution of good X and good Y between individual B given by the intersection of U_1 and U'_2.

12. Starting with the top panel of Figure 4.9, show
    a. a 50% reduction in the price of pork and its effect on consumer utility maximization.
    b. a 50% increase in the consumer's income and its effect on consumer utility maximization.

APPENDIX   INDEX NUMBERS AND CHANGES IN CONSUMER WELFARE

In this appendix, we discuss index numbers and their use in measuring changes in standards of living or welfare, especially during inflationary periods. For example, workers and their unions are keen to know if money wages are keeping up with rising prices. Cost-of-living indices are often used for inflation adjustment in wage contracts, for pensions and welfare payments and, since 1984, even for tax payments. In this appendix, we will define three indices and, by comparing the values of these indices in two different time periods, determine if the standard of living has increased, decreased, or remained unchanged. For simplicity, we will assume that the consumer spends all income on only two commodities, X and Y.

Expenditure, Laspeyres, and Paasche Indices

To measure changes in the standard of living or welfare from one time period to another, we begin by defining three indices: the income or expenditure index, the Laspeyres price index, and the Paasche price index.

Income or expenditure index (E) The ratio of period-1 to base-period money income or expenditures.

The **income or expenditure index** (E) is the ratio of period 1 to base period money income or expenditures. That is,

$$E = \frac{x_1 P_{x1} + y_1 P_{y1}}{x_0 P_{x0} + y_0 P_{y0}} \qquad [4.1]$$

where x and y refer to the quantities of commodities X and Y purchased, respectively; P refers to price, and the subscripts "1" and "0" refer to period 1 and the base period, respectively.

Thus, the income and expenditure index is the sum of the product of period 1 quantities and their respective period 1 prices divided by the sum of the product of base period quantities and their respective base period prices. In short, E measures the ratio of the consumer's period 1 expenditures or income to the base period expenditures or income. If E is greater than 1, the individual's *money* income or expenditures have increased from the base period to period 1. However, since prices usually also rise, we cannot determine simply from the value of E whether the individual's *real* income or standard of living has also increased. To do that, we need to define the Laspeyres and the Paasche price indices and compare their values with that of the income or expenditure index.

Laspeyres price index (L) The ratio of the cost of purchasing base-period quantities at period-1 prices relative to base-period prices.

The **Laspeyres price index (L)** is the ratio of the cost of *base period quantities* at period 1 prices relative to base period prices. That is,

$$L = \frac{x_0 P_{x1} + y_0 P_{y1}}{x_0 P_{x0} + y_0 P_{y0}} \qquad [4.2]$$

In the Laspeyres price index, we use the base period quantities as the weights and measure the cost of purchasing these base period quantities at period 1 prices relative to base period prices.

Paasche price index (P)
The ratio of the cost of purchasing period-1 quantities at period-1 prices relative to base-period prices.

The **Paasche price index (P)** is the ratio of the cost of *period 1 quantities* at period 1 prices relative to base period prices. That is,

$$P = \frac{x_1 P_{x1} + y_1 P_{y1}}{x_1 P_{x0} + y_1 P_{y0}}$$ [4.3]

In the Paasche price index, we use period 1 quantities as the weights and measure the cost of purchasing period 1 quantities at period 1 prices relative to base period prices. Thus, the difference between the Laspeyres and the Paasche price indices is that the former uses the base period quantities as the weights while the latter uses the period 1 quantities.

For example, using the hypothetical data in Table 4.2, we can calculate

$$E = \frac{x_1 P_{x1} + y_1 P_{y1}}{x_0 P_{x0} + y_0 P_{y0}} = \frac{(3)(\$2) + (6)(\$1)}{(4)(\$1) + (3)(\$2)} = \frac{\$12}{\$10} = 1.2, \text{ or } 120\%$$

$$L = \frac{x_0 P_{x1} + y_0 P_{y1}}{x_0 P_{x0} + y_0 P_{y0}} = \frac{(4)(\$2) + (3)(\$1)}{\$10} = \frac{\$11}{\$10} = 1.1, \text{ or } 110\%$$

$$P = \frac{x_1 P_{x1} + y_1 P_{y1}}{x_1 P_{x0} + y_1 P_{y0}} = \frac{\$12}{(3)(\$1) + (6)(\$2)} = \frac{\$12}{\$15} = 0.8, \text{ or } 80\%$$

How Are Changes in Consumer Welfare Measured?

Because some quantities and prices rise over time and others fall, it is often impossible to determine by simple inspection of the quantity-price data whether an individual's standard of living or welfare has increased, decreased, or remained unchanged from one time period to the next. To measure changes in the standard of living, we compare the value of the income or expenditure index to the values of the Laspeyres and the Paasche price indices.

An individual's standard of living is higher in period 1 than in the base period if E is greater than L. That is, the individual is better off in period 1 than in the base period if the increase in his or her money income (E) exceeds the increase in the cost of living using base-period quantities as weights (L). For example, since we calculated from Table 4.2 that E = 1.2, or 120%, while L = 1.1, or 110%, the individual's standard of living

TABLE 4.2	Hypothetical Quantity Price Data in a Base Period and in Period 1			
Period	x	Px	y	Py
0 (base)	4	$1	3	$2
1	3	2	6	1

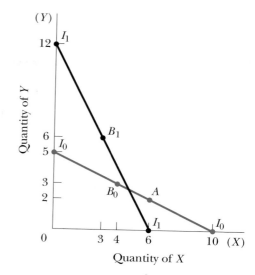

FIGURE 4.10   Changes in Consumer Welfare   An individual is better off at B_1 in period 1 than at B_0 in the base period because B_0 was available in period 1 (i.e., B_0 is below period 1 budget line I_1I_1) but was not chosen. Had the individual been at point A in the base period, we would need the individual's indifference curves to determine if B_1 is superior, inferior, or equal to A.

increased from the base period to period 1 because his or her income has risen more than his or her costs or prices.

On the other hand, *the individual's standard of living is higher in the base period than in period 1 if E is smaller than P*. That is, the individual is better off in the base period than in period 1 if the increase in his or her money income (E) is smaller than the increase in the cost of living using period 1 quantities as the weights (P). If E is not smaller than P, the individual's standard of living is not higher in the base period. For example, since $E = 120\%$ and $P = 80\%$ from Table 4.2, the individual is not better off in the base period than in period 1. Thus, with E greater than L and E not smaller than P, the individual of the above numerical example is definitely better off in period 1 than in the base period.

Figure 4.10 presents a graphic interpretation of the numerical example of Table 4.2. In the figure, $I_0 I_0$ is the individual's budget line in the base period. That is, with $X = 4$, $P_X = \$1$, $Y = 3$, and $P_y = \$2$, the individual's total income (I) and expenditure in the base period is $10 (obtained from $4X$ times $1 plus $3Y$ times $2). If the individual had spent the entire base-period income of $10 on commodity X, he or she could have purchased $10X$. If instead the individual had spent his or her entire base-period income of $10 on commodity Y, he or she could have purchased $5Y$. This defines $I_0 I_0$ as the individual's budget line in the base period. The individual's purchase of $4X$ and $3Y$ in the base period (see the first row of Table 4.2) is indicated by point B_0 on budget line $I_0 I_0$. We can similarly determine from the second row of Table 4.2 that in period 1 the individual's income is $12 (obtained from $3X$ times $2 plus $6Y$ times $1), so that his or her budget line is I_1I_1. The individual's purchase of $3X$ and $6Y$ in period 1 is indicated by point B_1 on budget line I_1I_1.

From Figure 4.10 we can conclude that since point B_0 is below budget line I_1I_1, the individual must be better off in period 1 than in the base period. That is, since B_0 was available to the individual in period 1 but was not chosen, the individual must be better off in period 1. Specifically, in period 1 the individual could have purchased the base period bundle (B_0) at period 1 prices by spending only $11 (4$X$ times $2 plus 3$Y$ times $1) of his or her period 1 income of $12. On the other hand, in the base period the individual could not have purchased period 1 quantities at base period prices since that would have required an expenditure of $15 (3$X$ times $1 plus 6$Y$ times $2), which would have exceeded his or her base period income of $10. Thus, the individual must be better off with B_1 in period 1 than with B_0 in the base period.

Had the individual been at a point such as A rather than at point B_0 on budget line I_0I_0 in the base period (see Figure 4.10), we could no longer determine without the individual's indifference curves whether the individual was better off in period 1, in the base period, or was equally well off in period 1 as in the base period. This would depend on whether point B_1 was on a higher, lower, or the same indifference curve as point A, respectively. You should be able to calculate from comparing point A on I_0I_0 in the base period to point B_1 on I_1I_1 in period 1 that $E = 120\%$, $L = 140\%$, and $P = 80\%$. Since E is not larger than L (so that the individual is not necessarily better off in period 1) but E is not smaller than P (so that the individual is not necessarily better off in the base period), we have conflicting results and we cannot tell whether the standard of living is higher, lower, or equal in period 1 as compared with the base period. This confirms the inconclusive results of the graphic analysis (in the absence of the individual's indifference curves) in Figure 4.10.

Because the Laspeyres price index (L) uses base period quantities as the weights, L becomes available sooner than the Paasche price index (P).[19] The most common of the price indices is the Consumer Price Index (CPI), which has been published monthly by the Bureau of Labor Statistics for more than sixty years. The CPI is a Laspeyres index for a "typical" urban family of four. It is the weighted average of the price of 400 goods and services purchased by consumers in the United States. The weights of the various commodities in the basket are periodically changed to reflect variations in consumption patterns. Other important (Laspeyres) price indices are the wholesale price index (WPI) and the GNP deflator. The latter is used to calculate GNP in real terms.

EXAMPLE 4–7

The Consumer Price Index, Inflation, and Changes in the Standard of Living

One application of index numbers is in measuring changes in real earnings and standards of living over time. According to the Bureau of Labor Statistics, total private nonagricultural weekly money earnings in the United States was $345.35 in 1990 and $472.73 in 2000. The CPI rose from 100 in 1990 to 131.8 in 2000. Dividing the weekly money earnings by the corresponding CPI, we find that weekly *real* earnings increased only slightly from $345.35 in 1990 to $358.67 in 2000. Since the CPI is known to have an upward bias, however, the true increase in real earnings may in fact have been somewhat greater.

According to the CPI Commission (set up by the Senate Finance Committee in 1995 and reporting in 1996), the consumer price index or CPI overstates the rate of inflation by about 1.1 percentage points, making the true rate of inflation in the United

[19] The Laspeyres price index also uses period 1 prices. However, period 1 prices become available much sooner than period 1 quantities.

States in recent years closer to 2% rather than the reported 3%. According to the Commission's final report, of the 1.1 percentage point overstatement in the CPI, 0.6 percentage points were due to the failure of the CPI to take into account new products and quality changes, 0.4 percentage points were due to the failure to consider the substitution of goods in consumption as a result of changes in relative prices, and the remaining 0.1 percentage points resulted from not taking into consideration the availability of new outlets (stores) with cheaper prices. Some of these revisions in the calculation of the CPI have already been made and the others are in the process of being implemented.

These revisions in the CPI will save the U.S. government billions of dollars in lower cost-of-living adjustments to social security recipients; they will also lead to higher income tax collection (because of the slower increases in standard deductions); they will result in about $95 billion higher national savings (and lower national debt) per year, and they eliminate the underestimation in the growth of the real GDP of the nation. The CPI revisions will also affect the three million private-sector workers with union contracts tied to the CPI (and are likely to influence how much other employers pay as well).

Sources: M. J. Boskin et al., *Toward a More Accurate Measure of the Cost of Living* (Washington, D.C.: Senate Finance Committee, 1996); M. J. Boskin et al., "The CPI Commission: Findings and Recommendations," *American Economic Review,* May 1997; M. J. Boskin and D. W. Jorgenson, "Implications of Overstating Inflation for Indexing Government Programs and Understating Economic Progress," *American Economic Review,* May 1997; D. L. Costa, "Estimating Real Income in the U.S. from 1888 to 1994: Correcting CPI Bias Using Engle Curves," *Journal of Political Economy,* December 2001; B. W. Hamilton, "Using Engel's Law to Estimate CPI Bias," American Economic Review, June 2001; and Congressional Budget Office, *Explaining the Consumer Price Index*, Washington, D.C., CBO, June 20, 2007.

EXAMPLE 4–8

Comparing the Standard of Living of Various Countries

One of the most commonly used measures of the standard of living or well-being of a nation is its per capita income. Using per capita income to compare standard of livings around the world presents some difficulties, however. First, some services provided by individuals for personal use (such as mowing the lawn) affect well-being but are not included in the measure of per capita income because the service is not purchased through the market. Only if the person hires a lawn service will the cost of the service be included in the GDP measure. Per capita incomes that do not include the imputed (estimated) value of these nonmarket services underestimate the standard of living in the nation. The underestimation is larger in poor than in rich countries because in poor countries more goods and services are produced for personal use rather than being sold in the market.

A second difficulty in making international comparisons arises because the per capita GDP of other nations must be converted into dollars. Conversion is troublesome because the exchange rate between the dollar and other currencies may not correctly reflect the purchasing power of the dollar in different nations. For example, if the real exchange rate between the dollar and the Philippines' pesos (P) is $1 = P2 when measured in dollars of equivalent purchasing power, a per capita GDP of P6,000 in the Philippines refers to a per capita income of $3,000. But if the actual exchange rate is $1 = P3, the same per capita income of P6,000 gives a per capita income of only $2,000. Thus, it is necessary to use dollars of equivalent purchasing power to convert the GDP per capita in dollars of different countries for purposes of international comparison.

Table 4.3 presents data on the per capita income of the United States and the six other leading industrial nations in the world (Japan, Germany, France, the United Kingdom, Italy, and Canada), five large developing countries (South Korea, Mexico, Brazil, China, and India), and Russia for the year 2005. The second column of Table 4.3 gives the per capita income for each of the 13 nations in terms of U.S. dollars adjusted to include nonmarket goods and services and the true purchasing power of the dollar in different nations. Although not perfect, the adjusted GDP per capita is a more acceptable measure of the standard of living of a nation because it measures the true ability of the people of a nation to purchase goods and services in the market place.

According to this measure, the United States has the highest standard of living in the world, exceeding the United Kingdom's standard of living (the second richest nation shown in the table) by about 28%, and exceeding the standard of living of Canada (the nations with the third highest standard of living) by about 30% and that of other countries by still higher percentages. The third column of Table 4.3 gives the GDP per capita using the actual or unadjusted rather than adjusted exchange rates. With unadjusted per capita incomes, the ranking and the differences among the various

TABLE 4.3	Measures of Standard of Living in the United States and Abroad in 2005	
Country	Adjusted per capita Income	Unadjusted per capita Income
1. United States	$41,950	$43,740
2. United Kingdom	32,690	37,600
3. Canada	32,220	32,600
4. Japan	31,410	38,980
5. France	30,540	34,810
6. Germany	29,210	34,580
7. Italy	28,840	30,010
8. S. Korea	21,850	15,830
9. Russia	10,640	4,460
10. Mexico	10,030	7,310
11. Brazil	8,230	3,460
12. China	6,600	1,740
13. India	3,460	720

Source: World Bank, *World Development Report* (Washington, D.C.: World Bank, 2007, pp. 288–289).

countries are much greater, especially between developed and developing countries. While media sources often present these data, comparisons using the actual or unadjusted exchange data are obviously not appropriate.

Even the adjusted per capita income figures leave a great deal to be desired as measures of a nation's standard of living because the standard of living depends not only on the quantity of goods and services that individuals consume but also on many other considerations, such as the level of education, health, leisure, crime, and so on, of the population. The United Nations is trying to address this problem by devising a measure of the standard of living that includes some of these other considerations with its "human development index."

Sources: The World Bank, *World Development Report* (Washington, D.C.: World Bank, 2007) and United Nations Development Program, *Human Development Report* (New York: United Nations, 2007).

INTERNET SITE ADDRESSES

For data on total consumption by income classes for U.S. families to demonstrate Engel's law and derive Engel's curves, see:

> http://www.bls.gov/cex/csxann05.pdf

On teenage drinking and driving, and on what to do about it, see:

> http://www.cdc.gov/ncipc/factsheets/teenmvh.htm.
> http://www.firsteagle.com/tdd.htm
> http://www.iihs.org/research/qanda/underage.html
> http://www.alcoholalert.com/teenage-drinking-and-driving.html

The level of and the debate on gasoline tax is examined at:

> http://www.aei.org/publications/pubID.26625,filter.all/pub_detail.asp
> http://www.econbrowser.com/archives/2006/02/just_how_implau.html

For a discussion of the sources of bias in measuring the consumer price index (CPI) as well as the use of the CPI to measure changes in the standard of living, see:

> http://www.bls.gov/
> http://www.cbo.gov/ftpdocs/82xx/doc8253/06-22-CPI.pdf
> http://www.bls.gov/cpi/cpifaq.htm
> http://www.investopedia.com/articles/07/consumerpriceindex.asp
> http://www.shadowstats.com/cgi-bin/sgs/article/id=343

For the *World Development Report 2007* and the UN *Human Development Report*, see:

> http://web.worldbank.org/WBSITE/EXTERNAL/EXTDEC/EXTRESEARCH/EXTWDRS/EXTWDR2007/0,contentMDK:21055591~menuPK:1489854~pagePK:64167689~piPK:64167673~theSitePK:1489834,00.html
> http://hdr.undp.org/hdr2006/pdfs/report/HDR06-complete.pdf

CHAPTER 5

Market Demand and Elasticities

After Studying This Chapter, You Should Be Able to:

- Know how to derive the market demand curve for a commodity
- Remember that each elasticity of demand measures the percentage change in the quantity demanded, or the change in demand, with respect to each of the variables that affect demand.
- Describe the factors that determine the price elasticity of demand
- Know the relationship between price, marginal revenue, and elasticity
- Describe some of the important applications (examples) of the various elasticities of demand

I n this chapter, we begin by examining how the *market* demand curve for a commodity is obtained by summing up individual's demand curves for the commodity. As shown in Chapter 2, the market demand curve for a commodity, together with the market supply curve, determine the equilibrium price of the commodity. After deriving the market demand curve for a commodity, we discuss the various elasticities of demand, including price and income elasticities in international trade. Finally, since consumers' expenditures on a commodity represent the revenues of the producers or sellers of the commodity, we consider the producer's side of the market. This is done by examining total and marginal revenues from the sale of the commodity and their relationship to the price elasticity of demand.

An important dose of realism is introduced into the discussion by actual real-world estimates of the various elasticities for many commodities and the way they are used in the analysis of many current economic issues. The "At the Frontier" section then examines some new revolutionary marketing research approaches to demand estimation, while the optional appendix shows how demand is estimated and forecasted by regression analysis.

5.1   THE MARKET DEMAND FOR A COMMODITY

Market demand curve Shows the quantity demanded of a commodity in the market per time period at various alternative prices while holding everything else constant.

In this section, we examine how the market demand curve for a commodity is derived from the individuals' demand curves. The **market demand curve** for a commodity is simply the horizontal summation of the demand curves of all the consumers in the market. Thus, the market quantity demanded at each price is the sum of the individual quantities demanded at that price. For example, in the top of Figure 5.1, the market demand

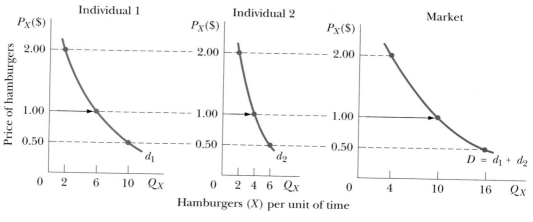

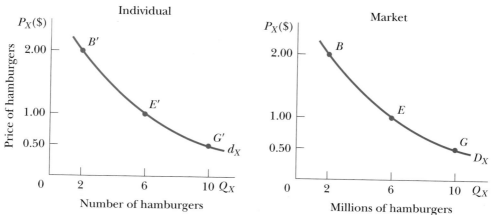

FIGURE 5.1   From Individual to Market Demand   The top part of the figure shows that the market demand curve for hamburgers, D, is obtained from the horizontal summation of the demand curve for hamburgers of individual 1 (d_1) and individual 2 (d_2). The bottom part of the figure shows an individual's demand curve, d_X, and the market demand curve, D_X, on the assumption that there are 1 million individuals in the market with demand curves for hamburgers identical to d_X.

curve for hamburgers (commodity X) is obtained by the horizontal summation of the demand curve of individual 1 (d_1) and individual 2 (d_2), on the assumption that they are the only two consumers in the market. Thus, at the price of $1, the market quantity demanded of 10 hamburgers is the sum of the 6 hamburgers demanded by individual 1 and the 4 hamburgers demanded by individual 2.

If instead there were 1 million individuals in the market, each with demand curve d_X the market demand curve for hamburgers would be D_X (see the bottom part of Figure 5.1). Both D_X and d_X have the same shape, but the horizontal scale for D_X refers to millions of hamburgers. Note that d_X is the individual's demand curve for hamburgers derived in Chapter 4 (see Figure 4.3).

The market demand curve for a commodity shows the various quantities of the commodity demanded in the market per unit of time at various alternative prices of the commodity while holding everything else constant. The market demand curve for a commodity is negatively sloped (just as an individual's demand curve), indicating that price and quantity are inversely related. That is, the quantity demanded of the commodity increases when its price falls and decreases when its price rises. The variables held constant in drawing the market demand curve for a commodity are incomes, the prices of substitute and complementary commodities, tastes, and the number of consumers in the market. A change in any of these will cause the market demand curve for the commodity to shift (see Section 2.2).[1]

Finally, it must be pointed out that a market demand curve is simply the horizontal summation of the individual demand curves *only if* the consumption decisions of individual consumers are independent (i.e., in the absence of so-called *network externalities*). This is not always the case. For example, people sometimes demand a commodity because others are purchasing it, either to be "fashionable" and to "keep up with the Joneses" or because it makes the commodity more useful (as in the case of e-mail, which becomes more useful as more people use it). The result is a **bandwagon effect** or *positive network externality* and this makes the market demand curve for the commodity flatter or more elastic than otherwise.

At other times, the opposite or **snob effect** (a *negative network externality*) occurs as many consumers seek to be different and exclusive by demanding less of a commodity, as more people consume it. That is, as the price of a commodity falls and more people purchase the commodity, some people will stop buying it in order to stand out and be different. This tends to make the market demand curve steeper or less elastic than otherwise. There are then some individuals who, to impress other people, demand more of certain commodities (such as diamonds, mink coats, Rolls Royces, etc.) the more expensive these goods are. This form of "conspicuous consumption" is called the **Veblen effect** (after Thorstein Veblen, who introduced it). For example, some high-income people may be less willing to purchase a $4,000 mink coat than a $10,000 one when the latter clearly looks much more expensive. A Rolex does not keep time better than a Timex, but, ah, what it says about the wearer! This also results in a steeper, or less elastic, demand curve for the commodity than otherwise.[2]

Bandwagon effect The situation where some people demand a commodity because other people purchase it.

Snob effect The situation where some people demand a smaller quantity of a commodity as more people consume it in order to be different and exclusive.

Veblen effect The situation in which some people purchase more of certain commodities the more expensive they are; also called *conspicuous consumption.*

---

[1] A change in expectations about the future price of the commodity will also affect its demand curve. For example, the expectation that the price of the commodity will be lower in the future will shift the market demand curve to the left (so that less is demanded at each price in the current period) as consumers postpone some of their purchases of the commodity in anticipation of a lower price in the future.

[2] Conceivably, in some cases, the snob and Veblen effects could even make the market demand curve for the commodity positively sloped, though no such cases have yet been found in the real world.

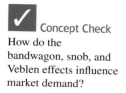

Concept Check
How do the
bandwagon, snob, and
Veblen effects influence
market demand?

In what follows, we assume that the bandwagon, snob, and Veblen effects are not significant, so that the market demand curve for the commodity can be obtained simply by the horizontal summation of the individual demand curves. Example 5–1 examines the market demand for Big Macs, Example 5–6 presents the various elasticities of the demand for alcoholic beverages, while Example 5–7 in the appendix to this chapter discusses the actual estimation and forecast of the demand for electricity in the United States.

EXAMPLE 5–1

Demand for Big Macs

The market demand curve for hamburgers faced by McDonald's is the sum of the individuals' demand curves for hamburgers. What follows shows how the market demand curve for hamburgers changed over time as a result of competitive pressures and changes in consumers' tastes and how McDonald's responded to these changes.

With more than 30,000 restaurants serving nearly 50 million people in 119 countries around the world every day in 2007, McDonald's dwarfed the competition in the fast-food burger market (its closest competitor, Burger King, had 11,200 restaurants in 61 countries). In the United States, McDonald's has 13,700 outlets, compared with Burger King's 8,400, and its burger market share is 46%, as compared with Burger King's 14% and Wendy's 13%. After nearly three decades of double-digit gains, however, domestic sales at McDonald's grew slowly from the mid-1980s through the 1990s as a result of higher prices, changing tastes, demographic changes, increased competition from other fast-food chains and other forms of delivering fast foods, the mad-cow disease in Europe, and, more recently, obesity concerns in the United States.

Price increases at McDonald's exceeded inflation in each year since 1986. The average check at McDonald's now exceeds $4—a far cry from the 15-cent hamburger on which McDonald's got rich—and this sent customers streaming to lower-priced competitors. Concern over cholesterol and calories has also reduced growth. In addition, the proportion of the 15- to 29-year-olds (the primary fast-food customers) in the total population has shrunk from 27.5% to 22.5% during the past decade. Increased competition from other fast-food chains (especially Burger King and Wendy's), other fast-food options (pizza, chicken, tacos, and so on), frozen fast foods, mobile units, and the vending machines have also slowed down the growth of demand for Big Macs. In 2002, McDonald's was even hit by a highly publicized multimillion dollar suit for allegedly misleading young consumers about the healthfulness of its products (which inspired the 2004 movie *Super Size Me*).

McDonald's did not sit idle but tried to meet its challenges head on by introducing new menu items and by cutting prices. For example, in 1990 McDonald's introduced a value menu, with small hamburgers selling for as little as 59 cents (down from 89 cents) and a combination of a burger, french fries, and a soft drink for as much as half off. In response to increased public concern about cholesterol and calories, McDonald's substituted vegetable oils for beef tallow in frying its french fries, replaced ice cream with lowfat yogurt, introduced bran muffins and cereals to its breakfast menu, and in 1991 it introduced the McLean Deluxe—a new, reduced-fat, quarter-pound hamburger, which McDonald's spent from $50 million to $70 million to develop and promote. Then McDonald's introduced McPizza in 1995, its Arch Deluxe, in 1996, and the "Made for You" freshly cooked meals in 1999. McDonald's also set up a drive-through in an increasing number of its franchises.

All of these efforts failed to stimulate sales, and McDonald's abandoned most of these initiatives. McDonald's just seemed to have lost its golden touch at home, and that is why it rapidly expanded abroad, where it faced much less competition and where there was much more room for growth. By 2007 there were more McDonald's restaurants abroad (16,200) than in the United States (13,800). In recent years, McDonald's has been opening restaurants abroad at a rate four to five times as fast as in the United States, and it is now earning more than 60% of its profits in other countries. McDonald's now predicts that it will have more than 50,000 restaurants around the world (two-thirds of them outside the United States) by the year 2010.

Since 2003, however, McDonald's seems to have reinvented itself and once again sales have experienced rapid growth. It phased out the "super-sized" fries and drinks, and it introduced several new menu items, such as chicken wraps, premium coffee, apple slices, and premium salads. In 2006, McDonald's became the first fast-food company to put nutritional labels on its products, and in 2007 it started to replace artery-clogging trans fats with new cooking oils to make its foods healthier.

Sources: "An American Icon Wrestles with a Troubled Future," *New York Times,* May 12, 1991, Section 3, p. 1; "Too Skinny a Burger Is a Mighty Hard Sell, McDonald's Learns," *Wall Street Journal,* April 15, 1994, p. A1; "Fallen Arches," *Fortune,* April 29, 2002, pp. 74–76; "Big Mac Trims Portions as Worry on Waistline Grow," *Financial Times,* March 3, 2004, p. 8; "McDonald's to Introduce Nutrition Labels," *Financial Times,* October 26, 2005, p. 15; "McDonald's Selects Oil to Avoid Trans Fat Risk, *Financial Times,* January 30, 2007; "McDonald's Says Latest Results Are Strongest in 30 Years, *New York Times,* January 25, 2007, p. C2; and "How Wendy's Faltered, Opening Way to Buyout," *Wall Street Journal,* August 28, 2007, p. A1.

5.2   PRICE ELASTICITY OF MARKET DEMAND

In this section, we show how to measure the price elasticity of demand, both algebraically and graphically. We also examine the important relationship between the price elasticity of demand and the total expenditures of consumers on the commodity. That is, when the price of a commodity changes, will consumers' expenditures on the commodity increase, decrease, or remain unchanged? Finally, we examine the determinants or the factors that affect the value of the price elasticity of demand.

Measuring the Price Elasticity of Demand[3]

The price elasticity of demand measures the responsiveness in the quantity demanded of a commodity to a change in its price. This could be measured by the inverse of the slope of the demand curve (i.e., by $\Delta Q/\Delta P$).[4] The disadvantage is that the inverse of

---

[3] For a discussion of the price elasticity of demand using calculus, see Section A.5 of the Mathematical Appendix at the end of the book.

[4] Since the turn of the century, the convention in economics (started by Alfred Marshall) is to plot price on the vertical axis and quantity on the horizontal axis. Therefore, the quantity response to a change in price could be measured by $\Delta Q/\Delta P$, which is the inverse of the slope of the demand curve.

the slope is expressed in terms of the units of measurement. A change of 100,000 units in the quantity demanded of a commodity is very large if the commodity is new housing units, but it is not very large if the commodity is hamburgers. Similarly, a price change of one dollar is insignificant for houses, but very large for hamburgers. Thus, measuring the responsiveness in the quantity demanded of a commodity to a change in price by the inverse of the slope of the demand curve is not very useful. Furthermore, comparison of changes in quantity to changes in price across commodities is meaningless. These problems can be resolved by using percentage rather than absolute changes in quantity and prices.

In order to have a measure of the responsiveness in the quantity demanded of a commodity to a change in its price that is independent of the units of measurement, Alfred Marshall, the great English economist of the beginning of the twentieth century, refined and popularized the concept of the price elasticity of demand. This measure is defined in terms of *relative* or *percentage* changes in quantity demanded and price. As such, price elasticity of demand is a pure number (i.e., it has no units attached to it), and its value is not affected by changes in the units of measurement. This also allows meaningful comparisons in the price elasticity of demand of different commodities.

Price elasticity of demand (η) The percentage change in the quantity demanded of a commodity during a specific period of time divided by the percentage change in its price.

The **price elasticity of demand** is given by the percentage change in the quantity demanded of a commodity divided by the percentage change in its price. Letting η (the Greek letter eta) stand for the coefficient of price elasticity of demand, ΔQ for the change in quantity demanded, and ΔP for the change in price, we have the formula for the price elasticity of demand:

$$\eta = \frac{\Delta Q/Q}{\Delta P/P} = \frac{\Delta Q}{\Delta P} \cdot \frac{P}{Q} \qquad [5.1]$$

Since quantity and price move in opposite directions, the value of η is negative. To compare price elasticities, however, we use their absolute value (i.e., their value without the negative sign). Thus, we say that a demand curve with a price elasticity of -2 is more elastic than a demand curve with a price elasticity of -1 (even though -2 is algebraically smaller than -1). Note that the inverse of the slope of the demand curve (i.e., $\Delta Q/\Delta P$) is a component, but only a component, of the price elasticity formula.

Point elasticity of demand The price elasticity of demand at a specific point on the demand curve.

Formula [5.1] measures **point elasticity of demand** or the elasticity at a particular point on the demand curve. More frequently, we are interested in the price elasticity between two points on the demand curve. We then calculate the **arc elasticity of demand.** If we used formula [5.1] to measure arc elasticity, however, we would get different results depending on whether the price rises or falls.[5] To avoid this, we use the *average* of the two prices and the *average* of the two quantities in the calculations. Letting P_1 refer to the higher of the two prices (with Q_1 the quantity at P_1) and P_2 refer to the lower of the two prices (with Q_2 the corresponding quantity), we have the formula for arc elasticity of demand[6]:

Arc elasticity of demand The price elasticity of demand between two points on the demand curve.

$$\eta = \frac{\Delta Q}{\Delta P} \cdot \frac{(P_1 + P_2)/2}{(Q_1 + Q_2)/2} = \frac{\Delta Q}{\Delta P} \cdot \frac{(P_1 + P_2)}{(Q_1 + Q_2)} \qquad [5.2]$$

---

[5] As we will see below, this results because a different base is used in calculating percentage changes for a price increase than for a price decrease.

[6] For the second ratio in the formula, we could use $\overline{P}/\overline{Q}$, where the bar on P and Q refers to their average value.

Using formula [5.1] to measure the elasticity for a *price decline* from point B ($Q = 2$, $P = \$2.00$) to point G ($Q = 10$, $P = \$0.50$) on the market demand curve in Figure 5.1, we get

$$\eta = \frac{8}{(-1.50)} \frac{2}{(2)} = -\frac{16}{3} = -5.33$$

On the other hand, measuring elasticity for a *price increase* from point G to point B on the same demand curve, we get

$$\eta = -\frac{8}{(1.50)} \frac{0.50}{(10)} = -\frac{4}{15} = -0.27$$

Using formula [5.2] for arc elasticity, we get

$$\eta = -\frac{8}{(1.50)} \frac{2.50}{(12)} = -\frac{20}{18} = -1.11$$

✔ Concept Check

Why is price elasticity only an approximation to the true elasticity?

The price elasticity of demand is usually different at and between different points on the demand curve, and it can range anywhere from zero to very large or infinite. Demand is said to be *elastic* if the absolute value of η is larger than 1, *unitary elastic* if the absolute value of η equals 1, and *inelastic* if the absolute value of η is smaller than 1.

Price Elasticity Graphically

We can also measure graphically the price elasticity at any point on a linear or nonlinear demand curve. To measure the price elasticity at point E on D_X in the left panel of Figure 5.2 (the same as in the right bottom panel in Figure 5.1), we proceed as follows. We draw tangent AEH to point E on D_X and drop perpendicular EJ to the quantity axis. The slope of tangent line AEH is negative and constant throughout and can be measured by

$$\frac{\Delta P}{\Delta Q} = -\frac{JE}{JH}$$

The first component of the price elasticity formula is the inverse of the slope of the demand curve or

$$\frac{\Delta Q}{\Delta P} = -\frac{JH}{JE}$$

The second component of the price elasticity formula is

$$\frac{P}{Q} = \frac{JE}{0J}$$

Reassembling the two components of the elasticity formula, we have

$$\eta = \frac{\Delta Q}{\Delta P} \cdot \frac{P}{Q} = -\frac{JH}{JE} \cdot \frac{JE}{0J} = -\frac{JH}{0J} = -\frac{6}{6} = -1$$

That is, the price elasticity of D_X at point E in the left panel of Figure 5.2 is equal to 1. Since EJH, AKE, and AOH are similar triangles (see the left panel of Figure 5.2), the

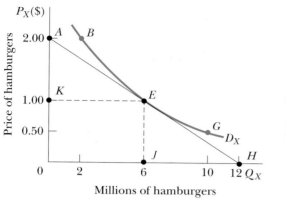 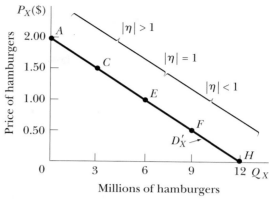

FIGURE 5.2   Measurement of Price Elasticity of Demand Graphically   In the left panel, the price elasticity at point E on D_X is measured by drawing tangent AEH to point E on D_X and dropping perpendicular EJ to the horizontal axis. At point E, $\eta = -JH/OJ = -6/6 = -1$. In the right panel, the absolute value of $\eta = 1$ at point E (the midpoint of D_X'), $\eta > 1$ above the midpoint, and $\eta < 1$ below the midpoint.

✓ Concept Check

How can the price elasticity be measured at a point?

price elasticity of D_X at point E can be measured by any of the following ratios of distances:

$$\eta = -\frac{JH}{OJ} = -\frac{KO}{AK} = -\frac{EH}{AE} \qquad [5.3]$$

The price elasticity of demand at any other point on D_X can be found in a similar way by drawing a tangent to D_X at that point and then proceeding as indicated above (see Problem 2). This provides a convenient and easy way to measure the price elasticity of demand at any point on a nonlinear demand curve.

The same procedure can be used to measure the price elasticity at any point on a straight-line demand curve. For example, by inspecting the right panel of Figure 5.2, we can find that $\eta = -9/3 = -3$ at point C on D_X', $\eta = -3/9 = -1/3$ at point F, and $\eta = -6/6 = -1$ at point E (the midpoint of D_X'). Furthermore, $\eta \to \infty$ at point A and $\eta = 0$ at point H (see Problem 3). Thus, while the slope of a straight-line demand curve is constant throughout, its price elasticity varies between each point on (and its absolute value declines as we move down) the demand curve. As a general rule, a straight-line demand curve is unitary elastic at its geometric midpoint, price elastic above its midpoint, and inelastic below its midpoint (see the right panel of Figure 5.2).

Two other simple rules are useful in considering the price elasticity of demand. The first is that of two parallel demand curves (linear or nonlinear), the one further to the right has a smaller price elasticity at each price (see Problem 4(a), with answer at the end of the text). Second, when two demand curves intersect, the flatter of the two is more price elastic at the point of intersection (see Problem 4(b), with the answer also provided at the end of the text).

Price Elasticity and Total Expenditures

An important relationship exists between the price elasticity of demand and the total expenditures of consumers on the commodity. This relationship is often used in economics. It postulates that a decline in the commodity price results in an increase in total expenditures if demand is elastic, leaves total expenditures unchanged if demand is unitary elastic, and results in a decline in total expenditures if demand is inelastic.

TABLE 5.1   Total Expenditures and Price Elasticity of Demand

Point	P_X ($)	Q_X (million units)	Total Expenditures (million $)	Absolute Value of η
A	2.00	0	0	∞
C	1.50	3	4.5	3
E	1.00	6	6.0	1
F	0.50	9	4.5	1/3
H	0	12	0	0

Specifically, when the price of a commodity falls, total expenditures (price times quantity) increase if demand is elastic because the percentage increase in quantity (which by itself tends to increase total expenditures) exceeds the percentage decline in price (which by itself tends to reduce total expenditures). Total expenditures are maximum when $|\eta| = 1$ and decline thereafter. That is, when $|\eta| < 1$, a reduction in the commodity price leads to a percentage increase in the quantity demanded of the commodity that is smaller than the percentage reduction in price, and so total expenditures on the commodity decline. This is shown in Table 5.1, which refers to D_X' in Figure 5.2.

From Table 5.1 we see that between points A and E, $|\eta| > 1$ and total expenditures on the commodity increase as the commodity price declines. The opposite is true between points E and F over which $|\eta| < 1$. Total expenditures are maximum at point E (the geometric midpoint of D_X' in Figure 5.2). The general rule summarizing the relationship among total expenditures, price, and the price elasticity of demand is that *total expenditures and price move in opposite directions if demand is elastic and in the same direction if demand is inelastic* (see Table 5.1).

Figure 5.3 shows a demand curve that is unitary elastic throughout. Thus, $\eta = -JH/J0 = -6/6 = -1$ at point E on D^*, $\eta = -LJ/0L = -3/3 = -1$ at point B', and $\eta = -HN/0H = -12/12 = -1$ at point G'. Note that total expenditures (price times quantity) are constant ($6 million) at every point on D^*. This type of demand curve is a rectangular hyperbola. Its general equation is

$$Q = \frac{C}{P} \qquad [5.4]$$

where Q is the quantity demanded, P is its price, and C is a constant (total expenditures). Thus, $P \cdot Q = C$. For example, at point B', $(P)(Q) = (\$2)(3) = \$6$. At point E, $(\$1)(6) = \$6$, and at point G', $(\$0.50)(12) = \$6$ also.

What Determines Price Elasticity?

Because the price elasticity of demand is so useful (i.e., it tells us, among other things, what happens to the level of total expenditures on the commodity when its price changes), it is important to identify the forces that determine its value. The size of the price elasticity of demand depends primarily on two factors. First and foremost, *the price elasticity of demand for a commodity is larger the closer and the greater are the number of available substitutes.* For example, the demand for coffee is more elastic than the demand for salt because coffee has better and more substitutes (tea and cocoa) than salt. Thus, the same percentage increase in the price of coffee and salt elicits a larger percentage reduction in the quantity demanded of coffee than of salt.

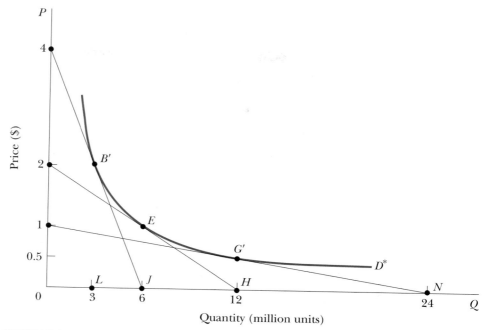

FIGURE 5.3   Unitary Elastic Demand Curve   Demand curve D^* has unitary elasticity throughout. Thus, $\eta = -JH/OJ = -6/6 = -1$ at point E, $\eta = -LJ/OL = -3/3 = -1$ at point B', and $\eta = -HN/OH = -12/12 = -1$ at point G'. Total expenditures ($P \cdot Q$) are the same ($6 million) at every point on D^*. This demand curve is a rectangular hyperbola.

In general, a commodity has closer substitutes and thus a higher price elasticity of demand the more narrowly the commodity is defined. For example, the price elasticity for Marlboro cigarettes is much larger than for cigarettes in general, and still larger than for all tobacco products. If a commodity is defined so that it has perfect substitutes, its price elasticity of demand is infinite. For example, if a wheat farmer attempted to increase his or her price above the market price, the farmer would lose all sales as buyers would switch all their wheat purchases to other farmers (who produce identical wheat).

Second, *price elasticity is larger, the longer is the period of time allowed for consumers to adjust to a change in the commodity price*. The reason for this is that it usually takes time for consumers to learn of a price change and to fully respond or adjust their purchases. For example, consumers may not be able to reduce much the quantity demanded of electricity soon after learning of an increase in the price of electricity. Over a period of several years, however, households can replace electric heaters with gas heaters, purchase appliances that consume less electricity, and so on. Thus, for a given price change, the quantity response *per unit of time* is usually much greater in the long run than in the short run, and so the absolute value of η is larger in the former than in the latter time period. This is clearly shown in Example 5–2.[7]

✓ Concept Check
What factors determine the price elasticity of demand?

[7] Sometimes it is stated that the price elasticity of demand is larger the greater is the number of uses of the commodity. However, no satisfactory reason has been advanced as to why this should be so. It is also sometimes said that price elasticity is lower the smaller is the importance of the commodity in consumers' budgets (i.e., the smaller is the proportion of the consumers' incomes spent on the commodity). However, empirical estimates often contradict this.

EXAMPLE 5-2

Price Elasticity for Clothing Increases with Time

The first row of Table 5.2 shows that the price elasticity of demand for clothing in the United States is −0.90 in the short run but rises to −2.90 in the long run. This means that a 1% increase in price leads to a reduction in the quantity demanded of clothing of only 0.90% in the short run but 2.90% in the long run. Although the price elasticity of demand for gasoline (the last row of Table 5.2) is three times higher in the long run than in the short run, both elasticities are very small. It seems that people cannot find suitable substitutes for gasoline even in the long run. The table also shows the short-run and long-run price elasticities of demand for a selected list of other commodities. The estimated price elasticity of demand for any commodity is likely to vary (sometimes widely), depending on the nation under consideration, the time period examined, and the estimation technique used. Thus, estimated price elasticity values should be used with caution.

TABLE 5.2 Selected Price Elasticities of Demand

Commodity	Short Run	Long Run
Clothing (U.S.)[a]	−0.90	−2.90
Tobacco products (U.S.)[b]	−0.46	−1.89
Jewelry and watches (U.S.)[b]	−0.41	−0.67
Beer (U.S.)[c]	−1.72	−2.17
Wine (Canada)[d]	−0.88	−1.17
Household natural gas (U.S.)[e]	−1.40	−2.10
Electricity (household—U.S.)[b]	−0.13	−1.89
Public Transport (England)[f]	−0.51	−0.69
Public Transport (France)[f]	−0.32	−0.61
Gasoline (U.S.)[f]	−0.25	−0.92
Gasoline (Canada)[f]	−0.15	−0.60
Gasoline (Australia)[f]	−0.12	−0.58

Sources:
[a]M. R. Baye, D. W. Jansen, and T. W. Lee, "Advertising in Complete Demand Systems," *Applied Economics,* vol. 24, 1992.
[b]H. S. Houthakker and L. S. Taylor, *Consumer Demand in the United States: Analyses and Projections* (Cambridge, MA: Harvard University Press, 1970).
[c]C. A. Gallet and J. A. List, "Elasticity of Beer Demand Revisited," *Economic Letters,* October 1998.
[d]J. A. Johnson, E. H. Oksanen, M. R. Veall, and D. Fretz, "Short-Run and Long-Run Elasticities for Canadian Consumption of Alcoholic Beverages," *Review of Economics and Statistics,* February 1992.
[e]G. R. Lakshmanan and W. Anderson, "Residential Energy Demand in the United States," *Regional Science and Urban Economics,* August 1980.
[f]B. Hagler, "Transportation Elasticities," *TDM Encyclopedia* (Victoria BC, Canada: Victoria Transport Policy Institute, 2005), found at http://www.vtpi.org/tdm/tdm11.htm; and J. E. Hughes, "Evidence of a Shift in the Short-Run Price Elasticity of Gasoline," *NBER Working Paper No. 12530,* September 2006.

Many economic policies (such as reducing American dependence on imported petroleum) rely crucially on price elasticities. For example, with the U.S. price of gasoline of about $3.50 per gallon in 2007 and a short-run price elasticity of 0.25 (see Table 5.2), a $1.00 tax per gallon would increase the price of gasoline from about $3.50 to $4.50 per gallon, or by about 29%, and reduce the quantity demanded of gasoline by 7.3% $[(\eta)(\%\Delta P) = (-0.25)(0.29) = -7.3\% = \%\Delta Q]$ in the short run. With the price elasticity equal to 0.92 in the long run, the reduction in the quantity demanded of gasoline in the long run would be about 27%. In fact, there is evidence (Hughes, 2006) that the price elasticity of demand for gasoline in the United States has sharply fallen since the beginning of the decade. This would result in a much smaller response in the quantity of gasoline demanded in the United States as a result of a $1.00 tax on gasoline.

| 5.3 | INCOME ELASTICITY OF DEMAND[8] |

Engel curve Shows the amount of a good that a consumer would purchase at various income levels.

In Section 4.1 we defined the **Engel curve** as showing the amount of a commodity that a consumer would purchase per unit of time at various income levels, while holding prices and tastes constant. We can measure the responsiveness or sensitivity in the quantity demanded of a commodity at any point on the Engel curve by the **income elasticity of demand.** This is defined as

Income elasticity of demand (η_I) The percentage change in the quantity purchased of a commodity over a specific period of time divided by the percentage change in consumers' income.

$$\eta = \frac{\Delta Q/Q}{\Delta I/I} = \frac{\Delta Q}{\Delta I} \cdot \frac{I}{Q} \qquad [5.5]$$

where ΔQ is the change in the quantity purchased, ΔI is the change in income, Q is the original quantity, and I is the original money income of the consumer.

A commodity is normal if η_I is positive and inferior if η_I is negative. A normal good can be further classified as a **necessity** if η_I is less than 1 and as a **luxury** if η_I is greater than 1. In the real world, most broadly defined commodities such as food, clothing, housing, health care, education, and recreation are normal goods. Inferior goods are usually narrowly defined inexpensive goods, such as bologna, for which good substitutes are available. Among normal goods, food and clothing are necessities while education and recreation are luxuries.

Necessity A commodity with income elasticity of demand between 0 and 1.

Luxury A commodity with income elasticity of demand greater than 1.

This classification of goods into inferior and normal, and necessity and luxury, cannot be taken too seriously, however, because the same commodity can be regarded as a luxury by some individuals or at some income levels, and as a necessity or even as an inferior good by other individuals or at other income levels.[9] A simple geometric method can determine if a commodity is a luxury, a necessity, or an inferior good at each income level. If the tangent to the Engel curve is positively sloped and crosses the income axis, η_I exceeds 1 and the good is a luxury at that income level. If the tangent crosses the origin, $\eta_I = 1$. If the tangent crosses the horizontal axis, η_I is less than 1 and the commodity is a necessity at that income level. Finally, if the tangent to the Engel curve is negatively sloped, the commodity is an inferior good.

---

[8] For a discussion of the income elasticity of demand using calculus, see Section A.5 of the Mathematical Appendix at the end of the book.

[9] Indeed, some economists feel that the necessity-luxury classification of goods is entirely spurious and meaningless.

For example, Table 5.3 and Figure 5.4 show that the student in Chapters 3 and 4 would regard hamburgers as a luxury at income levels (allowances) of up to $15 per day. Hamburgers would become a necessity for daily allowances of between $15 and $30 and would be regarded as an inferior good at higher incomes (where the student could afford steaks and lobsters).

TABLE 5.3	Income Elasticity and Classification of Hamburgers (X) at Various Daily Income Allowances				
I	Q_X	$\%\Delta Q_X$	$\%\Delta I$	η_I	Classification
10	2	. . .	. . .	. . .	. . .
15	4	100	50	2.00	Luxury
20	5	25	33	0.76	Necessity
30	6	20	50	0.40	Necessity
40	4	−33	33	−1.00	Inferior

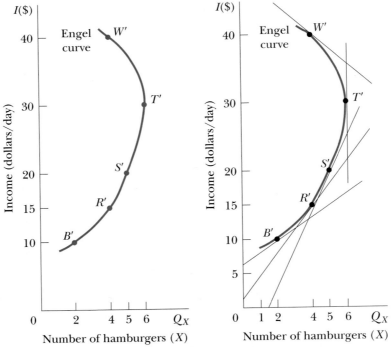

✓ Concept Check
How is Engel's law reflected in the shape of the Engel curve?

FIGURE 5.4   Engel Curve and Income Elasticity   Because the tangent to the Engel curve is positively sloped and crosses the income axis up to the daily income allowance of $15, hamburgers are a luxury for this individual. The tangent goes through the origin at $I = \$15$ and $\eta_I = 1$ at that income level. Since the tangent is positively sloped and crosses the quantity axis from $I = \$15$ to $\$30$, hamburgers are a necessity between these income levels. For I higher than $30, the Engel curve is negatively sloped and hamburgers become an inferior good for this individual.

The concept and measurement of the income elasticity of demand and Engel curve can refer to a single customer or to the entire market. When referring to the entire market, Q and ΔQ are the total or the market quantity purchased and its change, while I and ΔI are the total or aggregate money income of all consumers in the market and its change.[10]

As pointed out in Section 4.1, the proportion of total expenditures on food declines as family incomes rise. This is referred to as **Engel's law.** Indeed, the higher the proportion of income spent on food, the poorer a family or nation is taken to be. For example, in the United States less than 20% of total family incomes is spent on food as compared with over 50% for India (a much poorer nation). As Example 5–3 shows, the income elasticity of demand can be very different for different products.

Engel's law Postulates that the proportion of total expenditures on food declines as family income rises.

EXAMPLE 5–3

European Cars Are Luxuries, Flour Is an Inferior Good

The second and last rows of Table 5.4 show, respectively, that the income elasticity of demand is 1.93 for European cars and –0.36 for flour in the United States. This means that a 1% increase in consumers' income leads to a 1.93% increase in expenditures on European cars but to a 0.36% *reduction* in expenditures on flour in the United States. Thus, European cars are (strong) luxury goods, whereas flour is a (weak) inferior good in the United States. The table shows that Asian and domestic cars as well as household electricity are also a luxury, whereas cigarettes and chicken are necessities; beef is on the borderline.

TABLE 5.4 Selected Income Elasticity of Demand

Commodity	Income Elasticity
Electricity (household)[a]	1.94
European cars[b]	1.93
Asian cars[b]	1.65
Domestic cars[b]	1.63
Beef[c]	1.06
Cigarettes[d]	0.50
Chicken[c]	0.28
Flour[a]	−0.36

Sources:
[a]H. S. Houthakker and L. S. Taylor, *Consumer Demand in the United States: Analyses and Projections* (Cambridge, MA: Harvard University Press, 1970).
[b]P. S. McCarthy, "Market Price and Elasticities of New Vehicle Demands," *Review of Economics and Statistics*, August 1996, pp. 543–547.
[c]D. B. Suits, "Agriculture," in W. Adams and J. Brock, eds., *Structure of American Industry* (Englewood Cliffs, NJ: Prentice-Hall, 2000).
[d]F. Calemaker, "Rational Addictive Behavior and Cigarette Smoking," *Journal of Political Economy*, August 1991.

---

[10] Remember, however, that the income elasticity of market demand is not well defined unless it is also specified on which commodities income increments are spent.

Note that the income elasticities given in Table 5.4 are measured as the percentage change in expenditures on the various commodities (rather than the percentage change in the *quantity* purchased of the various commodities). To the extent that prices are held constant, however, we get the same results as if the percentage change in quantities were used.

5.4   CROSS ELASTICITY OF DEMAND [11]

Substitutes Two commodities are substitutes if an increase in the price of one of them leads to more of the other being purchased.

Complements Two commodities are complements if an increase in the price of one of them leads to less of the other being purchased.

Cross elasticity of demand (η_{XY}) The percentage change in the quantity purchased of a commodity divided by the percentage change in the price of another commodity.

We have seen in Section 2.2 that one of the things held constant in drawing the market demand curve for a commodity is the price of substitute and complementary commodities. Commodities X and Y are **substitutes** if more of X is purchased when the price of Y goes up. For example, consumers usually purchase more coffee when the price of tea rises. Thus, coffee and tea are substitutes. Other examples of substitutes include butter and margarine, hamburgers and hot dogs, Coca-Cola and Pepsi, electricity and gas, and so on.

On the other hand, commodities X and Y are **complements** if less of X is purchased when the price of Y goes up. For example, consumers usually purchase fewer lemons when the price of tea goes up. Thus, lemons and tea are complements. Other examples of commodities that are complements are coffee and cream, hamburgers and buns, hot dogs and mustard, cars and gasoline, and so on.

An increase in the price of a commodity leads to a reduction in the quantity demanded of the commodity (a movement along the demand curve for the commodity) but causes the demand curve for a substitute to shift to the right and the demand curve for a complement to shift to the left. For example, an increase in the price of tea will cause the demand for coffee (a substitute of tea) to shift to the right (so that more coffee is demanded at each coffee price) and the demand for lemons (a complement of tea) to shift to the left (so that fewer lemons are demanded at each lemon price).

We can measure the responsiveness or sensitivity in the quantity purchased of commodity X as a result of a change in the price of commodity Y by the **cross elasticity of demand** (η_{XY}). This is given by:

$$\eta_{XY} = \frac{\Delta Q_X / Q_X}{\Delta P_Y / P_Y} = \frac{\Delta Q_X}{\Delta P_Y} \cdot \frac{P_Y}{Q_X} \qquad [5.6]$$

where ΔQ_X is the change in the quantity purchased of X, ΔP_Y is the change in the price of Y, P_Y is the original price of Y, and Q_X is the original quantity of X. Note that in measuring η_{XY}, we hold constant P_X, consumers' incomes, their tastes, and the number of consumers in the market.

If η_{XY} is greater than zero, X and Y are substitutes because an increase in P_Y leads to an increase in Q_X as X is substituted for Y in consumption. On the other hand, if η_{XY} is less than zero, X and Y are complements because an increase in P_Y leads to a reduction in (Q_Y and) Q_X. The absolute value (i.e., the value without the sign) of the cross elasticity of

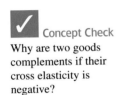 Concept Check

Why are two goods complements if their cross elasticity is negative?

---
[11] For a discussion of the cross elasticity of demand using calculus, see Section A.5 of the Mathematical Appendix at the end of the book.

demand measures the degree of substitution or complementarity. For example, if η_{XY} between coffee and tea is found to be larger than that between coffee and hot chocolate, this means that coffee and tea are better substitutes than coffee and hot chocolate. If η_{XY} is close to zero, X and Y are independent commodities. This may be the case with cars and pencils, telephones and chewing gum, pocket calculators and beer, and so on.

Several additional things must be kept in mind with respect to the cross elasticity of demand. First, the value of η_{XY} need not equal the value of η_{YX} because the responsiveness of Q_X to a change in P_Y need not equal the responsiveness of Q_Y to a change in P_X. For example, a change in the price of coffee is likely to have a greater effect on the quantity of sugar (a complement of coffee) demanded than the other way around, since coffee is the more important of the two in terms of total expenditures.

Second, a high positive cross elasticity of demand is often used to define an industry since it indicates that the various commodities are very similar. For example, the cross elasticity of demand between Chevrolets and Oldsmobiles is very high, and so they belong to the same (auto) industry. This can lead to some difficulty, however. For example, how high must the positive cross elasticity between two commodities be for them to be in the same industry? Also, if the cross elasticity between cars and station wagons and between station wagons and trucks is "high," but the cross elasticity of demand between cars and trucks is "low," are cars and trucks in the same industry? In these cases the definition of the industry usually depends on the problem to be studied.

Third, the above definition of substitutes and complements is sometimes referred to as a "gross" definition; as such, it refers to the entire market response and reflects both the income and the substitution effects. For an individual consumer, there is a more rigorous definition (in terms of the substitution effect only) discussed in more advanced treaties.[12] Example 5–4 gives the estimated gross elasticity of demand between a number of products and shows its usefulness in the analysis of important economic issues.

EXAMPLE 5–4

Margarine and Butter Are Substitutes, Entertainment and Food Are Complements

The first row of Table 5.5 shows that the cross elasticity of demand of margarine with respect to the price of butter is 1.53%. This means that a 1% increase in the price of butter leads to a 1.53% increase in the demand for margarine. Thus, margarine and butter are substitutes in the United States. On the other hand, row 6 of Table 5.5 shows that the cross elasticity of demand of entertainment with respect to food is –0.72. This means that a 1% increase in the price of entertainment leads to a *reduction* in the demand for food by 0.72%. Thus, entertainment and food are complements in the United States. The table also shows the cross elasticity of demand of other selected commodities.

Cross-price elasticities of demand have important economic applications—even in the courtroom, as the celebrated Cellophane Case shows (see *U.S. Reports,* Vol. 351, Washington, DC: U.S. Government Printing Office, 1956, p. 400). In that case, the court decided that DuPont had not monopolized the market for cellophane even though

---

[12] See J. R. Hicks, *Value and Capital* (New York: Oxford University Press, 1946), p. 44.

TABLE 5.5	Selected Cross Elasticities of Demand	
Commodity	With Respect to Price of	Cross-Price Elasticity
Margarine	Butter	1.53^a
Pork	Beef	0.40^a
Chicken	Pork	0.29^a
Natural gas	Electricity	0.80^b
Clothing	Food	-0.18^c
Entertainment	Food	-0.72^d
European cars	U.S. domestic and Asian cars	0.76^e
Asian cars	U.S. domestic and European cars	0.61^e
U.S. domestic cars	European and Asian cars	0.28^e

Sources:
[a]D. M. Heien, "The Structure of Food Demand: Interrelatedness and Duality," *American Journal of Agricultural Economics,* May 1982.
[b]G. R. Lakshmanan and W. Anderson, "Residential Energy Demand in the United States," *Regional Science and Urban Economics*, August 1990.
[c]M. R. Baye, D. W. Jansen, and T. W. Lee, "Advertising in Complete Demand Systems," *Applied Economics*, vol. 24, 1992.
[d]E. T. Fujii et al., "An Almost Ideal Demand System for Visitor Expenditures," *Journal of Transport Economics and Policy,* May 1985.
[e]P. S. McCarthy, "Market Price and Elasticities of New Vehicle Demands," *Review of Economics and Statistics*, August 1996, pp. 543–547.

it had 75% of the market. The reason? The cross-price elasticity of demand between cellophane and other flexible packaging materials (waxed paper, aluminum foil, and others) was sufficiently high to indicate that the relevant market was not cellophane as such, but flexible packaging materials, and DuPont, with only a 20% market share, had not monopolized that market.

PRICE ELASTICITY AND INCOME ELASTICITY OF IMPORTS AND EXPORTS

5.5

Price elasticity of demand for imports
The percentage change in the quantity purchased of imports by a nation divided by the percentage change in their prices.

Price elasticity of demand for exports
The percentage change in the quantity purchased of a nation's exports divided by the percentage change in the price of the nation's exports.

We have seen that when the price of a commodity falls, consumers purchase more of the commodity. The increase in the quantity purchased of the commodity resulting from a decline in its price (while holding everything else constant) is measured by the price elasticity of demand. The same is true for U.S. imports and exports. When import prices fall, domestic consumers import more from abroad. When the price of U.S. exports fall, foreigners purchase more American goods and U.S. exports rise. The increase in the quantity of U.S. imports and exports resulting from a price decline is measured, respectively, by the **price elasticity of demand for imports** and the **price elasticity of demand for exports.**

One complication arises, however, when we deal with imports and exports. The price of imports to U.S. consumers depends not only on prices in exporting nations

Exchange rate The price of a unit of a foreign currency in terms of the domestic currency.

![checkmark] **Concept Check**
What is the relationship between the exchange rate and the price elasticity of demand for imports and exports?

Income elasticity of demand for imports The percentage change in the demand for imports by a nation over a specific period of time divided by the percentage change in the income of the nation.

Income elasticity of demand for exports The percentage change in the demand for the exports of a nation over a specific period of time divided by the percentage change in the income of other nations.

(expressed in foreign currencies) but also on the rate of exchange between the dollar and foreign currencies. The rate of exchange between the dollar and a foreign currency is called the **exchange rate.** For example, the exchange rate (R) between the U.S. dollar and the euro (€), the currency of the 16-nation European Monetary Union (Austria, Belgium, Cyprus, Finland, France, Germany, Greece, Ireland, Italy, Luxembourg, Malta, Netherlands, Portugal, Slovakia, Slovenia, and Spain), was about 1.36 in July 2007. This meant that U.S. consumers had pay $1.36 to get €1. Thus, the price of a music record that costs €1 in the European Monetary Union (EMU) was $1.36 to U.S. consumers. If the price of the record fell to €0.50 in the EMU, U.S. consumers had to pay only $0.68 for the record. The price of an EMU record to U.S. consumers would also fall to $1.00, even if the price remained at €1 in the EMU, if the exchange rate between the dollar and the euro fell from $1.36 to €1 to $1.00 to €1.[13]

Exchange rates change very frequently in the real world. How exchange rates are determined and the reasons that they change are not important at this point (they are explained in the appendix to Chapter 9). What is important is that the *dollar* price of U.S. imports can change because of a change in foreign-currency prices abroad or because of a change in exchange rates. Regardless of the reason for the change in the price of U.S. imports, we can measure the increase in quantity of U.S. imports resulting from a fall in their *dollar* price by the price elasticity of demand for imports. Similarly, regardless of the reason for the change in the price of U.S. exports, we can measure the increase in quantity of U.S. exports resulting from a fall in their *dollar* price by the price elasticity of demand for U.S. exports. On the other hand, an increase in U.S. income leads to an increase in U.S. imports, while an increase in income in foreign countries leads to an increase in U.S. exports. These can be measured, respectively, by the **income elasticity of demand of imports** and the **income elasticity of demand for exports.**

EXAMPLE 5–5

Price Elasticity and Income Elasticity for Imports and Exports in the Real World

The short-run price elasticity of demand for U.S. imports has been estimated to be about 0.6. Thus, a 1% decline in the dollar price of U.S. imports was expected to lead to a 0.6% increase in the quantity demanded of imports (and thus to a decline of about 0.4% in U.S. expenditures on imports). On the other hand, the price elasticity of demand for U.S. exports was estimated to be 0.5 in the short run. This means that a 1% decline in the price of U.S. exports can be expected to lead to a 0.5% increase in the quantity of U.S. exports within a year or two of the price change (and to a decline of 0.5% in U.S. export earnings). The price elasticity of demand for imports and exports for the six other largest advanced economies (Japan, Germany, the United Kingdom, France, Italy, and Canada) are generally lower than those for the United States.

---
[13] This is only the immediate outcome. Over time, the dollar price of U.S. imports is likely to fall by less than that just indicated because of other forces at work (which need not be examined here).

Turning to income elasticity, we find that the income elasticity of demand for imports was estimated to be 2.3 in the United States. This means that a 1% increase in U.S. income or GNP can be expected to lead to an increase of about 2.3% in U.S. imports. Thus, U.S. imports are normal goods and can be regarded as luxuries. The income elasticity of imports for the six other largest industrial countries are 1.7 for France, 1.3 for Canada, and 1.0 for Japan, Germany, the United Kingdom, and Italy.

Source: D. Salvatore, *International Economics*, 9th ed. (Hoboken, NJ: John Wiley and Sons, 2007), Chapters 16 and 17.

5.6 — MARGINAL REVENUE AND ELASTICITY[14]

Up to this point, we have examined demand from the consumers' side only. However, consumers' expenditures on a commodity are the receipts or the total revenues of the sellers of the commodity. In this section, we look at the sellers' side of the market. We begin by defining marginal revenue and showing how the marginal revenue curve can be derived geometrically from the demand curve. Then we examine the relationship between marginal revenue, price, and the price elasticity of demand. Thus, the material in this section represents the link or bridge between the theory of demand (Part Two of the text) and the theory of the firm (Chapters 9–13).

Demand, Total Revenue, and Marginal Revenue

Total revenue (TR) The price of a commodity times the quantity sold of the commodity.

Marginal revenue (MR) The change in total revenue per unit change in the quantity sold.

The total amount earned by sellers of a commodity is called **total revenue (TR)**; it is equal to the price per unit of the commodity times the quantity of the commodity sold. **Marginal revenue (MR)** is then the change in total revenue per unit change in the quantity sold; MR is calculated by dividing the change in total revenue (ΔTR) by the change in the quantity sold (ΔQ):

$$MR = \frac{\Delta TR}{\Delta Q}$$ [5.7]

We can also show that the sum of the marginal revenues on all units of the commodity sold equals total revenue.

In Table 5.6, price (column 1) and quantity (column 2) give the demand schedule of the commodity. Price times quantity gives total revenue (column 3). The change in total revenue resulting from each additional unit of the commodity sold gives the marginal revenue (column 4). As a check on the calculations, we see that the sum of the marginal revenues equals total revenues (column 5). Note that TR/Q equals **average revenue (AR)**, and $AR = P$ (the height of the demand curve).

Average revenue (AR) Total revenue divided by the quantity sold.

[14] For the definition of marginal revenue in terms of calculus, see Section A.7 of the Mathematical Appendix at the end of the book.

TABLE 5.6 Demand, Total Revenue, and Marginal Revenue

P (1)	Q (2)	TR (3)	MR (4)	Sum of MR's (5)
$11	0	$0	. . .	. . .
10	1	10	$10	$10
9	2	18	8	18
8	3	24	6	24
7	4	28	4	28
6	5	30	2	30
5	6	30	0	30
4	7	28	−2	28
3	8	24	−4	24

The information given in Table 5.6 is plotted in Figure 5.5. The top panel gives the total revenue curve. The bottom panel gives the corresponding demand (D) and marginal revenue curves. Since MR is defined as the change in TR per unit change in Q, the MR values are plotted at the midpoint of each quantity interval in the bottom panel of Figure 5.5. On the other hand, points on the TR and D curves are plotted *at* each level of output. For example, at $P = \$11$, $Q = 0$, and so TR (which equals P times Q) is zero and is plotted at the origin in the top panel of Figure 5.5. At $P = \$10$, $Q = 1$, and so $TR = \$10$ and MR $(\Delta TR/\Delta Q)$ is also $10. This TR value is plotted at $Q = 1$ in the top panel, while the corresponding MR is plotted between $Q = 0$ and $Q = 1$ (i.e., at $Q = 0.5$) in the bottom panel.

The MR curve starts at the same point on the vertical axis as the D curve and is everywhere else below the D curve. This is because to sell one more unit of the commodity, price must be lowered not only for the additional unit sold but also on all previous units. For example, we see in Table 5.6 that to sell the second unit of the commodity, price must be lowered from $10 to $9 on both units. Therefore, the MR on the second unit is given by $P = \$9$ (a point on D) minus the $1 reduction on the price of the first unit. That is, $MR = \$8$, which is lower than P, so the MR curve is below the D curve (see the bottom panel of Figure 5.5). When D is elastic, MR is positive because an increase in Q increases TR. When D is unitary elastic, $MR = 0$ because an increase in Q leaves TR unchanged (at its maximum level). When D is inelastic, MR is negative because an increase in Q reduces TR (see the bottom panel of Figure 5.5). We will make a great deal of use of the relationship between the demand curve and the marginal revenue curve in Chapters 9–13, where we deal with the theory of the firm and market structure.

✓ Concept Check
Why is demand elastic if marginal revenue is positive?

Geometry of Marginal Revenue Determination

The marginal revenue curve for a straight-line and for a nonlinear demand curve can easily be found geometrically. This is shown in Figure 5.6. In the left panel, we can find the marginal revenue corresponding to point C on D'_X by dropping perpendicular CJ to the vertical axis and CW to the horizontal axis, and then subtracting distance AJ from CW. This identifies point C'. Thus, at $Q = 3$, $P = WC = \$1.50$, and $MR = WC' = \$1.00$. Similarly, by dropping perpendiculars EK and EE' from point E on D'_X and subtracting distance AK from EE', we get point E'. Thus, at $Q = 6$, $P = E'E = \$1$, and $MR = 0$. By joining points C' and E' we derive the MR'_X curve shown in the left panel of Figure 5.6. Note that the MR'_X curve starts at point A (as the D'_X curve) and every

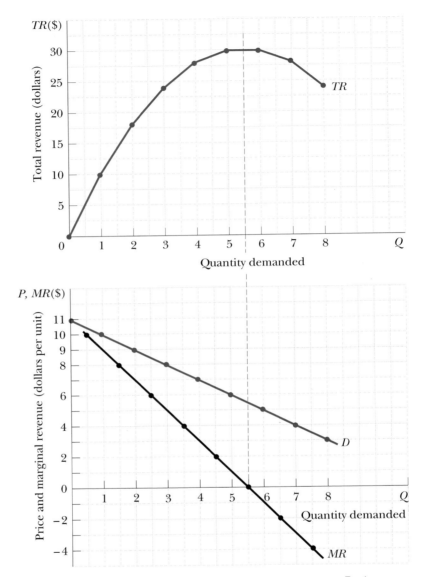

FIGURE 5.5   Total Revenue, Demand, and Marginal Revenue   Total revenue rises up to 5 units of the commodity sold, remains constant between 5 and 6 units, and declines thereafter. When D is elastic, MR is positive because TR increases. When D is unitary elastic, $MR = 0$ because TR is constant (at its maximum). When D is inelastic, MR is negative because TR declines (as Q increases).

point on it bisects (i.e., cuts in half) the distance from the D_X' curve to the vertical or price axis. (Indeed, this provides an alternative but equivalent method of deriving the MR curve geometrically for a straight-line demand curve.) Thus, $JV = 1/2JC$, $KC' = 1/2KE$, and $0E' = 1/20H$ (see the figure).

To find the marginal revenue curve corresponding to any point on a nonlinear demand curve, we draw a tangent to the demand curve at that point and then proceed

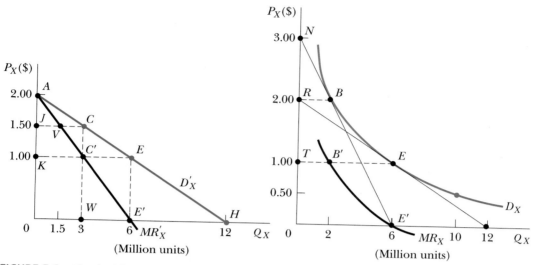

FIGURE 5.6   Marginal Revenue Determination   In the left panel, for point C on the D_X' curve, $MR = C'W$ and is obtained by subtracting distance AJ from price CW. For point E, $MR = 0$ and was obtained by subtracting distance $AK = EE'$ from P_X. In the right panel, to find the MR at point B we draw a tangent to the D_X curve at point B, and then we move down distance NR from point B. This identifies point B' on the MR_X curve. By moving down distance RT from point E on the D_X curve, we define point E' ($MR = 0$) on the MR_X curve.

as described above. Thus, to find the marginal revenue corresponding to point B on D_X in the right panel of Figure 5.6, we draw the tangent to demand curve D_X at point B and move distance NR downward from point B. This identifies point B' on the MR_X curve. Another point on the MR_X curve is obtained by moving distance RT down from point E. This identifies point E'. Other points on the MR_X curve can be similarly obtained. By joining these points we get the MR_X curve for the D_X curve (see the right panel of Figure 5.6). Note that when the demand curve is nonlinear, the marginal revenue curve is also nonlinear.

Marginal Revenue, Price, and Elasticity[15]

There is an important and often-used relationship among marginal revenue, price, and the price elasticity of demand given by

$$MR = P(1 + 1/\eta)$$

[5.8]

For example, at point C on D_X' in the left panel of Figure 5.6, $\eta = -WH/0W = -9/3 = -3$, and

$$MR = \$1.50(1 - 1/3) = \$1.00$$

---

[15] For a more straightforward derivation of expression [5.8] using simple calculus, see Section A.7 of the Mathematical Appendix at the end of the book.

(the same as WC' found earlier geometrically). At point E, $\eta = -E'H/0E' = -6/6 = -1$ and $MR = \$1.00(1 - 1/1) = \$1.00(0) = 0$. At point A, $\eta = -0H/0 = -12/0 = -\infty$, and $MR = \$2.00(1 - 1/\infty) = \$2.00(1 - 0) = \$2.00$.

Formula [5.8] also applies to nonlinear demand curves. For example, at point B on D_X in the right panel of Figure 5.6, $\eta = -4/2 = -2$ and

$$MR = \$2(1 - 1/2) = \$1.00$$

(the same as found earlier geometrically). Similarly, at point E, $\eta = -6/6 = -1$ and $MR = \$1.00(1 - 1/1) = 0$.

Formula [5.8] can be derived with reference to the straight-line demand curve in the left panel of Figure 5.6. Take, for example, point C on D_X'. At point C,

$$\eta = -\frac{WH}{0W} = -\frac{CH}{AC} = -\frac{J0}{AJ}$$

But $J0 = CW$ and, by congruent triangles, $AJ = CC'$. Hence,

$$\eta = -\frac{J0}{AJ} = -\frac{CW}{CC'} = -CW/(CW - C'W) = -\frac{P}{(P - C'W)} = -\frac{P}{(P - MR)}$$

With this result, we manipulate the equation algebraically, to isolate MR on the left-hand side:

$$\eta(P - MR) = -P$$
$$P - MR = -\frac{P}{\eta}$$
$$-MR = -\frac{P}{\eta} - P$$
$$MR = P + \frac{P}{\eta}$$
$$MR = P(1 + 1/\eta) \text{ (expression (5.8))}$$

So far, we have discussed the market demand curve for a commodity (D_X' or D_X in Figure 5.6). If there is only one producer or seller in the market (a monopolist), the firm faces the market demand curve for the commodity. When there is more than one producer or seller of the commodity, each firm will face a demand curve that is more elastic than the market demand curve because of the possible substitution among the products of the different firms. With a very large number of sellers of a homogeneous or identical product, the demand curve for the output of each firm might be horizontal or infinitely elastic (perfect competition). In this case the change in total revenue in selling one additional unit of the commodity (i.e., the marginal revenue) equals price. This is confirmed by using formula [5.8]; that is,

$$MR = P(1 - 1/\infty) = P$$

For example, in Figure 5.7, if the firm sells $5X$, its $TR = \$5$. If it sells $6X$, $TR = \$6$. Thus, $MR = P = \$1$, and the demand curve and the marginal revenue curves coincide. (The perfectly competitive model will be examined in Chapter 9.)

Example 5–6 gives the price, cross, and income elasticities of demand for beer, wine, and spirits in the United States and examines the relationship among the various elasticities as well as between price elasticities and total revenue. The "At the Frontier" section then examines some new revolutionizing approaches to consumer demand estimation and marketing.

✓ Concept Check
Is demand elastic if an increase in price leads to an increase in total expenditures? Why or why not?

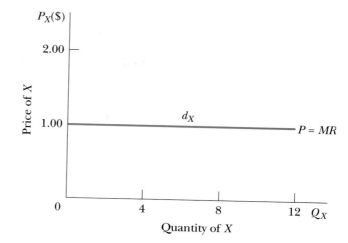

FIGURE 5.7   Demand Curve for the Output of a Perfectly Competitive Firm   The demand curve for the output of a perfectly competitive firm is horizontal or infinitely elastic. Thus, $P = MR$ and the demand curve and the marginal revenue curve coincide.

EXAMPLE 5–6

U.S. Consumer Demand for Alcoholic Beverages

Table 5.7 gives the price, cross, and income (expenditures) elasticities of the U.S. demand for alcoholic beverages (beer, wine, and spirits) estimated from U.S. Department of Agriculture individual and household food-consumption survey data for 1987–1988.

From Table 5.7, we see that the price elasticity of demand for beer (η_{XX}) is -0.23. This means that a 10% *increase* in the price of beer results in a 2.3% *reduction* in the quantity of beer demanded by U.S. consumers and thus to an *increase* in consumer expenditures on beer. The price elasticity of wine (η_{YY}) is -0.40 and that of spirits (η_{ZZ}) is -0.25, so that an increase in their price also leads consumers to demand a smaller quantity of wine and spirits, but also to spend more on these alcoholic beverages.

TABLE 5.7   Price, Cross, and Income Elasticities of Demand for Beer, Wine, and Spirits in the United States

Beer	Wine	Spirits
$\eta_{XX} = -0.23$	$\eta_{YY} = -0.40$	$\eta_{ZZ} = -0.25$
$\eta_{XY} = 0.31$	$\eta_{YX} = 0.16$	$\eta_{ZX} = 0.07$
$\eta_{XZ} = 0.15$	$\eta_{YZ} = 0.10$	$\eta_{ZY} = 0.09$
$\eta_{XI} = -0.09$	$\eta_{YI} = 5.03$	$\eta_{ZI} = 1.21$

Legend: X = beer, Y = wine, Z = spirits, I = Income

Table 5.7 also shows that the cross-price elasticity of demand for beer with respect to wine (η_{XY}) is 0.31 and with respect to spirits (η_{XZ}) is 0.15. This means that wine and spirits are substitutes for beer, with wine being a better substitute. Thus, a 10% increase in the price of wine will lead to a 3.1% increase in the demand for beer, while a 10% increase in the price of spirits leads to a 1.5% increase in the demand for beer. Note that the cross price elasticity of wine and spirits with respect to beer (i.e., η_{YX} and η_{ZX} in columns two and three of the table) are somewhat different from the cross price elasticity of demand for beer with respect to wine and spirits (η_{XY} and η_{XZ} in column one).

Finally, Table 5.7 shows that with $\eta_{XI} = -0.09$, $\eta_{YI} = 5.03$, and $\eta_{ZI} = 1.21$, a 10% increase in consumer income (expenditure) leads to a 0.9% *reduction* in the demand for beer, but to a 50.3% *increase* in the demand for wine, and a 12.1% *increase* in the demand for spirits. Thus, beer can be considered an inferior good, while wine and spirits can be regarded as luxuries (with wine being a much stronger luxury than spirits).

Source: X. M. Gao, E. J. Wiles, and G. L. Kramer, "A Microeconometric Model of the U.S. Consumer Demand for Alcoholic Beverages," *Applied Economics,* January 1995, pp. 59–69.

AT THE FRONTIER
The Marketing Revolution with Micromarketing

Marketing research approaches to demand estimation
The estimation of consumer demand for a product or service by consumer surveys, consumer clinics, or market experiments.

While regression analysis (discussed in the appendix to this chapter) is by far the most useful and used method of estimating demand, **marketing research approaches to demand estimation** are being revolutionized and becoming increasingly important as a result of new technological developments that permit micromarketing.

There are several traditional marketing approaches to estimate market demand curves and elasticities. One involves *consumer surveys* using interviews or questionnaires in which consumers are asked how much of a commodity they would purchase at various prices. It is, however, generally agreed that this procedure yields very biased results, because consumers either cannot or will not give trustworthy answers. Another traditional marketing approach to demand estimation is *consumer clinics,* in which consumers are given a sum of money and asked to spend it in a simulated store to see how they react to price changes. However, the sample of consumers must necessarily be small because this procedure is expensive. Also, the results are questionable because consumers are aware that they are in an artificial situation. Still another traditional marketing approach to demand estimation is a *market experiment,* whereby the seller increases the price of the commodity in one market or store and lowers it in another and then records the different quantities purchased in the two markets or stores. This procedure is questionable because a small sample is involved, the seller can permanently lose customers in the high-priced market or store, and only the immediate or short-run response to the price change is obtained.

Recent technological developments in telecommunications, however, have greatly changed and completely revitalized marketing research approaches to consumer demand estimation to the point where they have become crucial marketing tools and are bound to become even more important in the future. One such tool is micromarketing.

Today, more and more consumer-product companies are narrowing their marketing strategy from the region and city to the individual neighborhood and single store. The aim of such a detailed point-of-sale information, or **micromarketing,** is to identify on a store-by-store basis the types of products with the greatest potential appeal for the specific customers in the area. Using census data and checkout scanners, Market Metrics, a marketing research firm, now collects consumer information at more than 30,000 supermarkets around the country. For example, for a particular grocery store in Georgia, Pennsylvania, Market Metrics found that potential customers were predominantly white, blue collars, owned two cars, lived in households of three or four people, and had an average income of $54,421, and 26% of the people were below the age of 15. Based on these demographic and economic characteristics, Market Metrics determined that the strongest sellers in this market would be baby foods and grooming items, baking mixes, desserts, dry dinner mixes, cigarettes, laundry supplies, first aid products, and milk. Less strong would be sales of artificial sweeteners, tea, books, film, prepared food, yogurt, wine, and liquor. Such store-specific micromarketing is likely to become more and more common and necessary for successful retailing in the future.

As marketers refine their tools, they are increasingly taking aim at the ultimate narrow target: the individual consumer. Indeed, many companies, led by banks, are assembling customer profiles and employing sophisticated technology called *neural networks* in order to set up *one-to-one marketing* (also called relationship marketing or customer–relationship management). This seeks to reach the individual consumer and establish a learning relationship with each customer, starting from the most valuable ones. This is exactly what Amazon.com (the internet book seller) does when it reminds a customer that a book that might interest her has just come in. One-to-one marketing requires identifying the company's customers, differentiating among them, interacting with them, and customizing the product or service to fit each individual customer's needs.

For example, the Quaker Oats Company tracks how your household redeems coupons and uses the information to refine the coupons it will offer you in the future, and Merrill Lynch & Co. provides detailed financial information about its customers to its brokers in order to help them promote the company's financial products. Depositing a $10,000 check may thus eliminate the customer as a likely candidate for a car loan, but not for a home mortgage loan. It may even determine whether your telephone call gets answered first (if your profile, which comes up immediately on the bank's computer screen, identifies you as a valued customer) or last. Although it is not easy to set up one-to-one marketing and most companies may not yet be capable or ready for it, it is almost certain that marketing will be getting more and more personalized in the future.

Many firms already claim to be "customer driven" or "consumer-centric." Their claims are now tested as never before. Trading on shoppers' ignorance is no longer possible. Today, window shopping takes place online. Shoppers compare products, prices, and reputations by finding out what previous buyers of the product have to say.

Continued . . .

Micromarketing
Narrowing a marketing strategy to the individual store or consumer.

✓ Concept Check
In what way is micromarketing a revolution?

The Marketing Revolution with Micromarketing   *Continued*

Although most purchases still take place in brick-and-mortar stores, more than 90% of shoppers between the ages of 18 and 54 turn to the Internet first for product information.

Sources: "Know Your Customer," *Wall Street Journal,* June 21, 1999, p. R18; "Is Your Company Ready for One-to-One Marketing?," *Harvard Business Review,* January–February 1999, pp. 151–160; "Winning in Smart Markets," *Sloan Management Review,* Summer 1999, pp. 59–69; "The Vanishing Mass Market," *Business Week,* July 12, 2004; and "Power at Last," *The Economist,* April 2, 2005, p. 11.

SUMMARY

1. The market demand curve for a commodity is obtained from the horizontal summation of the demand curves of all the individual consumers in the market and shows the total quantity demanded at various prices. It is negatively sloped; and, in drawing it, we must hold constant the consumers' incomes, the price of substitutes and complementary commodities, tastes, and the number of consumers in the market. The market demand curve is flatter or more elastic than otherwise with a bandwagon effect (a positive network externality), and steeper and less elastic when a snob effect (a negative network externality) is present, or with conspicuous expenditures or Veblen effect.

2. The price elasticity of demand is measured by the percentage change in the quantity demanded of a commodity divided by the percentage change in its price. By drawing a tangent to a point on a nonlinear demand curve and dropping a perpendicular to either axis, we can measure price elasticity at that point by the ratio of two distances. A straight-line demand curve is unitary elastic at its midpoint, elastic above the midpoint, and inelastic below the midpoint. Total expenditures and price move in opposite directions if demand is elastic and in the same direction if demand is inelastic. A rectangular hyperbola demand curve has unitary elasticity and constant total expenditures throughout. A demand curve is more elastic (a) the closer and the better are the available substitutes, and (b) the longer the adjustment period to the price change.

3. The income elasticity of demand (η_I) measures the percentage change in the quantity purchased of a commodity divided by the percentage change in consumers' incomes. A commodity is usually considered to be a necessity if η_I is between 0 and 1 and a luxury if η_I exceeds 1. η_I exceeds 1 if the tangent to the Engel curve is positively sloped and crosses the income axis. η_I is between 0 and 1 if the tangent to the Engel curve is positively sloped and crosses the quantity axis. If η_I is negative, the commodity is an inferior good and the Engel curve is negatively sloped. According to Engel's law, the proportion of total expenditures on food declines as family incomes rise.

4. Commodities X and Y are substitutes if more of X is purchased when the price of Y goes up, and complements if less of X is purchased when the price of Y goes up. The cross elasticity of demand between commodities X and Y (η_{XY}) measures the percentage change in the quantity purchased of X divided by the percentage change in the price of Y. If η_{XY} is positive, X and Y are substitutes. If η_{XY} is negative, X and Y are complements, and if $\eta_{XY} = 0$, X and Y are independent commodities.

5. We can measure the increase in U.S. imports and exports as a result of a decline in their prices by their respective price elasticities of demand. The only complication is that the price of U.S. imports and exports is also affected by changes in the exchange rate. The exchange rate gives the number of units of the domestic currency required to purchase one unit of the foreign currency. We can also measure the income elasticity of demand for U.S. imports and for the imports of other nations.

6. The total revenue (*TR*) of sellers equals price times quantity. Marginal revenue (*MR*) is the change in *TR* per unit change in the quantity of the commodity sold. *MR* is positive when demand (*D*) is elastic because a reduction in price increases *TR*. When *D* is unitary elastic, $MR = 0$ because *TR* is constant (at its maximum). When *D* is inelastic, *MR* is negative because a reduction in price reduces *TR*. The *MR* curve for a straight-line *D* curve bisects the quantity axis. The *MR* at a point on a nonlinear *D* curve is found geometrically by drawing a tangent to the demand curve at that point. Marginal revenue, price, and price elasticity of demand are related by $MR = P(1 + 1/\eta)$. The demand curve facing a perfectly competitive firm is horizontal and $P = MR$ because η is infinite. Today, marketing research approaches to demand estimation are being revolutionized by new technological developments that permit micromarketing.

KEY TERMS

Market demand curve
Bandwagon effect
Snob effect
Veblen effect
Price elasticity of demand (η)
Point elasticity of demand
Arc elasticity of demand
Engel curve
Income elasticity of demand (η_I)
Necessity

Luxury
Engel's law
Substitutes
Complements
Cross elasticity of demand (η_{XY})
Price elasticity of demand for imports
Price elasticity of demand for exports
Exchange rate
Income elasticity of demand for imports

Income elasticity of demand for exports
Total revenue (*TR*)
Marginal revenue (*MR*)
Average revenue (*AR*)
Marketing research approaches to consumer demand
Micromarketing
Identification problem
Multiple regression

REVIEW QUESTIONS

1. Which is more elastic, an individual's demand curve for a commodity or the market demand curve for a commodity? Why? Is this always true? Explain.

2. Will a decrease in a commodity price increase expenditures on that commodity? Why?

3. If the price of household natural gas increases by 10%, by how much can we expect the quantity demanded of household natural gas and total expenditures on household natural gas to change in the short run and in the long run according to the elasticity values in Table 5.2?

4. Is the price elasticity of demand for Marlboro cigarettes more or less elastic than the demand for all tobacco products? Why? By how much would the quantity demanded of Marlboro cigarettes change in the long run if the price rose by 5% and the long-run price elasticity of demand is 3.56? If the price of all tobacco products also increased by 5%, would the quantity demanded of Marlboro cigarettes change by more or less as compared to the case when only the price of Marlboro cigarettes changed?

5. Suppose that a study has found that the price elasticity of demand for subway rides is 0.7 in Washington, D.C., and the mayor wants to cut the operating deficit of the subway system. Should the mayor contemplate increasing or decreasing the price of a subway ride? Why?

6. Can you say with reference to Table 5.4 whether producers and sellers of beef or pork, products would be affected more adversely from a recession?

7. Which of the following are more likely to have a positive cross elasticity of demand: pencils and paper, an IBM PC and a Dell PC, or automobiles and gasoline?

8. What other demand elasticities, besides those examined in this chapter, are likely to be important for beachwear? How would you measure such elasticities?

9. If the price of books in England falls by 10%, but at the same time the dollar appreciates (i.e., increases in value with respect to the British pound) by 10%, how is the U.S. demand for imported books from the United Kingdom likely to be affected?

10. If prices and exchange rates remain unchanged, but income rises by 4% in the United States and 3% in the rest of the world during a given year, by how much would U.S. imports from and exports to the rest of the world change if the income elasticity of demand for U.S. imports is 1.94 while the income elasticity of demand for U.S. exports is 0.80? How would the U.S. trade balance (exports minus imports) change over the year if it was balanced at the beginning of the year?

11. If the price of a product is $10 and the marginal revenue is $5, what is the price elasticity of demand for the product at that point?

12. If the demand curve faced by a firm is $d_X = P_X = \$10$, what is the price elasticity of demand at $Q_X = 10$? Between $Q_X = 10$ and $Q_X = 12$?

13. What are the marketing research approaches to demand estimation? What is meant by micromarketing?

PROBLEMS

1. Measure the price elasticity of the market demand curve in the left panel of Figure 5.2
   a. from point B to point E.
   b. from point E to point B.
   c. as an average over arc BE.

2. Measure graphically the price elasticity of demand curve D_X in the left panel of Figure 5.2
   a. at point B.
   b. at point G.

3. Using the general formula for the price elasticity of demand (i.e., equation [5.1]), prove that
   a. $\eta = \infty$ at point A on D'_X in the right panel of Figure 5.2.
   b. $\eta = 0$ at point H in the same diagram.

*4. Explain the following.
   a. Of two parallel demand curves, the one further to the right has a smaller price elasticity at each price.
   b. When two demand curves intersect, the flatter of the two is more elastic at the point of intersection.

5. Using only the total expenditures criterion, determine if the demand schedules given in the following table are elastic, inelastic, or unitary elastic.

$P(\$)$	5	4	3	2	1
Q_X	100	130	180	275	560
Q_Y	100	120	150	220	430
Q_Z	100	125	167	250	500

6. If the price elasticity of demand for Marlboro cigarettes is -6 and its price rose by 10%

   a. by how much would the quantity demanded decrease?
   b. would the consumers' total expenditures on Marlboro cigarettes increase, decrease or remain unchanged?
   c. If the price of all other brands of cigarettes also increased by 10%, what would happen to the quantity demanded of Marlboro? To consumers' expenditures on Marlboro?

7. From the following table

Q_X	100	250	350	400	300
I	$10,000	15,000	20,000	25,000	30,000

   a. calculate the income elasticity of demand for commodity X between various income levels and determine what type of good is commodity X;
   b. plot the Engel curve; how can you tell from the shape of the Engel curve what type of good is commodity X?

*8. a. Explain why in a two-commodity world both commodities cannot be luxuries.
   b. What would be the effect on the quantity of cars purchased if consumers' incomes rose by 10% and the income elasticity of demand is 2.5?

9. Which of the following sets of commodities are likely to have positive cross elasticity of demand?
   a. aluminum and plastics
   b. wheat and corn
   c. pencils and paper
   d. private and public education
   e. gin and tonic
   f. ham and cheese
   g. men's and women's shoes

---

* = Answer provided at end of book.

*10. Using the values for the price and income elasticity of demand for electricity and for the cross elasticity of demand between electricity and natural gas given in Tables 5.2, 5.4, and 5.5, answer the following questions:

a. Is the demand for electricity elastic or inelastic in the short run? In the long run? How much would the quantity demanded of electricity change as a result of a 10% increase in its price in the short run? In the long run?

b. Is electricity a necessity or a luxury? How much would electricity consumption change with a 10% increase in consumers' incomes?

c. Is natural gas a substitute or complement of electricity? By how much would electricity consumption change with a 10% increase in the price of natural gas?

11. Given the following demand schedule

P($)	8	7	6	5	4	3	2	1	0
Qx	0	1	2	3	4	5	6	7	8

a. find the total revenue and the marginal revenue.

b. plot the total revenue curve, the demand curve, and the marginal revenue curve.

c. Using the formula relating marginal revenue, price, and elasticity, confirm the values of the marginal revenue found geometrically for $P = \$8$, for $P = \$4$, and for $P = \$2$.

12. Explain why a firm should never operate in the inelastic range of its demand curve.

*13. The following proposition (proved in Section A.6 of the Mathematical Appendix at the end of the text) is given:

$$K_X \eta_{XI} + K_Y \eta_{YI} = 1$$

where K_X is the proportion of the consumer's income I spent on commodity X (i.e., $K_X = P_X Q_X / I$, η_{XI} is the income elasticity of demand for commodity X, K_Y is the proportion of income spent on Y (i.e., $K_Y = P_Y Q_Y / I$), and η_{YI} is the income elasticity of demand for Y. Also, suppose that a consumer spends 75% of his or her income on commodity X and the income elasticity of demand for commodity X is 0.9. Assume that the individual consumes only commodities X and Y.

a. Find the income elasticity of demand for commodity Y.

b. What kind of commodity is Y? X? How high would the income elasticity of demand for X have to be before commodity Y becomes inferior?

APPENDIX EMPIRICAL ESTIMATION OF DEMAND BY REGRESSION ANALYSIS

The most useful and used method of estimating market demand curves today is regression analysis. This method uses actual market data of the quantities purchased of the commodity at various prices over time (i.e., time series data) or for various consuming units or areas at one point in time (i.e., cross-sectional data). Indeed, all of the actual demand elasticities presented in the examples in this chapter were estimated by regression analysis. However, only if the scatter of quantity–price observations (points) fall as in the left panel of Figure 5.8 can we estimate a demand curve from the data. If the points fall as in the right panel, we face an **identification problem** and may be able to estimate neither a reliable demand curve nor a supply curve for the commodity from the data.[16]

When quantity–price observations (points) fall as in the left panel of Figure 5.8, we can estimate the average demand curve for the good by correcting for the forces that

Identification problem
The difficulty sometimes encountered in estimating the market demand or supply curve of a commodity from quantity–price observations.

---

[16] Each quantity–price observation (point) is usually given by the intersection of a different (and unknown) demand and supply curve for the commodity. The reason for this is that demand and supply curves usually shift over time and are usually different for different consumers and in different places. When the points fall as in the left panel, we can correct for the forces that cause the demand curve to shift and derive an average demand curve from the data. When the points fall as in the right panel and the shifts in demand and supply are not independent, we are unable to do so.

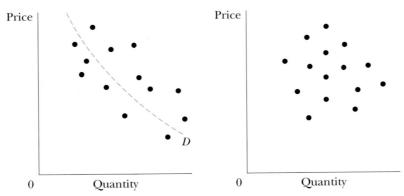

FIGURE 5.8   Scatter Diagram of Quantity–Price Observations When the scatter points of quantity–price observations fall as in the left panel, we can estimate an average demand curve from the data using regression analysis, such as dashed line *D*. However, when the points fall as in the right panel, we may be unable to estimate or identify either a reliable demand or supply curve.

Multiple regression A statistical technique that allows the economist to disentangle the independent effects of the various determinants of a dependent variable, such as demand.

cause the demand curve to shift (i.e., by correcting for the changes or differences in incomes and in the prices of related commodities). This is accomplished by the **multiple regression** statistical technique.[17] Regression analysis allows the economist to disentangle the independent effect of the various determinants of demand so as to identify from the data the average market demand curve for the commodity (such as dashed line *D* in the left panel).

To conduct the regression analysis, the researcher collects data on the quantity purchased of the good in question, its price, the income of consumers, and the price of one or more related commodities (substitutes and complements). Regression analysis allows the researcher to correct for the effect of changes or differences in consumers' incomes and in the prices of related commodities and permits the estimation of the average demand function that best fits the data (as, for example, *D* in the left panel of Figure 5.8). The values of all the collected variables are usually first transformed into logarithms because by doing so the estimated coefficients of the demand function are the various elasticities of demand.[18]

By regression analysis we estimate a demand function of the following form:

$$Q_X = a + bP_X + cI + eP_Y \qquad [5.9]$$

where Q_X, P_X, I, and P_Y usually refer to the logarithm of the quantity purchased of commodity X per unit of time, its price, the consumers' income, and the price of related

---

[17] Regression analysis is explained in a course in statistics. For an introduction to regression analysis, see D. Salvatore and D. Reagle, *Statistics and Econometrics*, 2nd ed. (New York: McGraw-Hill, 2002, Chapters 6 and 7).

[18] In order for the estimated coefficients to be elasticities, the value of each variable collected must first be transformed into the natural logarithm. Natural logs are those to the base 2.718 (as opposed to common logs, which are to the base 10). For example, the natural log of 100, written ln 100, is 4.61 (i.e., ln 100 = 4.61). This is obtained by looking up the number 100 in a table of natural logs or more simply using a pocket calculator. The time series or the cross-section data of each variable transformed into natural logs are then used to run the regression and obtain the various coefficients of the demand function. These estimated coefficients are the elasticities. Why this is so is explained in a course of mathematics for economists.

commodity Y, respectively. $Q_X = a$ (the constant) when P_X, I, and P_Y are all zero. The estimated coefficient of P_X, b, is the price elasticity of demand (when the regression is performed on the data transformed into logarithms). On the other hand, c is the estimated income elasticity of demand, while e is the estimated cross elasticity of demand of good X for good Y.

For the demand curve of good X to obey the law of demand, the estimated b coefficient (η_X) must be negative (so that quantity demanded and price are inversely related). Good X is a necessity if the estimated c coefficient (η_I) is positive but smaller than 1. On the other hand, good X is a luxury if $c > 1$ and an inferior good if $c < 0$. If the estimated e coefficient (η_{XY}) is positive, good Y is a substitute for good X. If $e < 0$, good Y is a complement of good X. Regression analysis is also used to forecast future demand, as Example 5–7 illustrates.

EXAMPLE 5–7
Estimating and Forecasting U.S. Demand for Electricity

Estimating and forecasting the demand for electricity is very important because it takes many years to build new capacity to meet future needs. One such an estimate was provided by Halvorsen, who used multiple regression analysis to estimate the market demand equation for electricity with cross-sectional data transformed into natural logarithms for the 48 contiguous states in the United States for the year 1969.

Table 5.8 reports the estimated elasticity of demand for electricity for residential use in the United States with respect to the price of electricity, per capita income, the price of gas, and the number of customers in the market. Although the results of various studies differ somewhat, the results reported below indicate that the amount of electricity for residential use consumed in the United States would fall by 9.74% as a result of a 10% increase in the price of electricity, would increase by 7.14% with a 10% increase in per capita income, would increase by 1.59% with a 10% increase in the price of gas, and is proportional to the number of customers in the market. Thus, the market demand curve for electricity is negatively sloped, electricity is a normal good and a necessity, and gas is a substitute for electricity.

Using the above estimated demand elasticities and projecting the growth in per capita income, in the price of gas, in the number of customers in the market, and in the price of electricity, public utilities could forecast the growth in the demand for

TABLE 5.8   Elasticities of Demand for Electricity for Residential Use in the United States

Variable	Value
Price	−0.974
Per capita income	0.714
Price of gas	0.159
Number of customers	1.000

Sources: R. Halvorsen, "Demand for Electric Energy in the United States," *Southern Economic Journal*, April 1976.

electricity in the United States so as to adequately plan new capacities to meet future needs. For example, if we assume that per capita income grows at 3% per year, the price of gas at 20% per year, the number of customers at 1% per year, and the price of electricity at 4% per year, we can forecast that the demand for electricity for residential use in the United States will expand at a rate of 2.43% per year. This rate is obtained by adding the products of the value of each elasticity to the projected growth of the corresponding variable, as indicated in the following equation:

$$Q = (0.714)(3\%) + (0.159)(20\%) + (1.000)(1\%) - (0.974)(4\%)$$
$$= 2.142 + 3.180 + 1.000 - 3.896$$
$$= 6.322 - 3.896$$
$$= 2.426$$

With different projections of the yearly growth in per capita income, the price of gas, the number of customers in the market, and the price of electricity, we will get correspondingly different results.

The above results are shown in Figure 5.9, where P_0 and Q_0 are the original price and quantity of electricity demanded in the United States on hypothetical demand

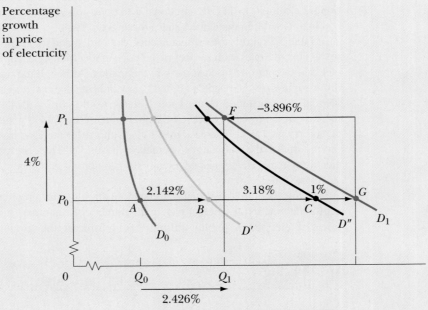

Percentage growth in quantity of electricity

FIGURE 5.9   Forecast of Electricity in the United States P_0 and Q_0 are the original price and quantity of electricity demanded in the United States on hypothetical demand curve D_0. Demand curve D' results from projecting a 3% increase in per capita incomes, D'' by also projecting a 20% increase in the price of gas, and D_1 from a 1% increase in the number of customers in the market as well. If the price elasticity is also assumed to increase by 4% (from P_0 to P_1), the demand for electricity increases from 2.426% per year (the movement from point A on D_0 to point F on D_1).

curve D_0 in the base period (say, the current year). Demand curve D' results from the projected increase in per capita income, D'' results from the increase in the price of gas also, and D_1 results from the increase in the number of customers in the market as well. Thus, D_1 takes into account or reflects the cumulative effect of all the growth factors considered.

Were the price of electricity to remain constant, the demand for electricity would rise by 6.322% per year (given by the movement from point A on D_0 to point G on D_1 in the figure). The projected increase in the price of electricity by 4% per year (from P_0 to P_1), by itself, will result in a decline in the quantity demanded of electricity by 3.896% (the movement from point G to point F on D_1). The net result of all forces at work gives rise to a net increase in Q of 2.426% per year (the movement from point A on D_0 to point F on D_1).

Until the mid-1990s when the deregulation of the electricity market started in the United States, the nation's regulatory commissions set low electricity rates and this discouraged the building of new power plants. Electrical power companies simply preferred charging higher electricity rates at times of peak demand rather than building the new plants. All this began to change during the past decade as the electricity market started to be deregulated. Botched-up deregulation, however, led to widespread electricity shortages, blackouts or brownouts, and sharply higher electricity prices in California and other western states during 2000 and 2001, and this slowed down, put on hold, or even reversed the deregulation process. The United States does need to build from 1,300 to 1,900 new power plants to meet future demand, which is expected to grow by 45% by the year 2020. Since it takes from 6 to 12 years to build a new plant, electrical power companies have no time to waste.

Sources: "R. Halvorsen, "Demand for Electric Energy in the United States," *Southern Economic Journal,* April 1976; "Value Networks—The Future of the U.S. Electric Utility Industry," *Sloan Management Review,* Summer 1997, pp. 21–34; "The Challenge for Utilities: Increase Capacity and Efficiency," *Wall Street Journal,* December 18, 2000, p. C6; "The Trouble with Energy Markets: Understanding California's Restructuring Disaster," *Journal of Economic Perspectives,* Winter 2002, pp. 191–212; Enron's Lessons for the Energy Market," *New York Times,* May 11, 2002, p. 17; Electricity Demand Is Far Outpacing New Supply Sources," *Wall Street Journal,* October 17, 2007, p. A17; and Energy Information Administration, *Annual Energy Outlook,* Washington, DC: EIA, 2007.

INTERNET SITE ADDRESSES

Information about McDonalds can be found at:
   http://www.mcdonalds.com

Some income and cross elasticities are found at:
   http://www.vtpi.org/tdm/tdm11.htm

For the elasticity of demand for alcoholic beverages, see:
   http://links.jstor.org/sici?sici=1058-7195(199609)18%
   3A3%3C477%3AUCDFAB%3E2.0.CO%3B2-K

http://papers.ssrn.com/sol3/papers.cfm?abstract_
id=612704

http://www.cide.info/conf_old/papers/1115.pdf

The demand for electricity, deregulation, and shortages are examined at:

   http://www.eia.doe.gov/cneaf/electricity/dsm/dsm_sum.html
   http://www.opensecrets.org/news/electricity.htm

CHAPTER 6

Choice Under Uncertainty

After Studying This Chapter, You Should Be Able to:

- Know how choice in the face of risk differs from choice in the absence of risk
- Describe how risk is measured
- Understand why some individuals buy insurance and also gamble
- Know how risk and uncertainty can be reduced
- Describe how behavioral economics seeks to improve traditional economic theory

---

Traditional demand theory—as examined until now—implicitly assumed a riskless world. It assumed that consumers face complete certainty as to the results of the choices they make. Clearly, this is not the case in most instances. For example, when we purchase an automobile we cannot be certain as to how good it will turn out to be and how long it will last. Similarly, when we choose an occupation, we cannot be certain as to how rewarding it will be in relation to alternative occupations. Thus, the applicability of traditional economic theory is limited by the fact that it is based on the assumption of a riskless world, while most economic decisions are made in the face of risk or uncertainty.

In this chapter we extend traditional demand theory to deal with choices subject to risk or uncertainty. We begin the chapter by distinguishing between risk and uncertainty and introducing some of the concepts essential for risk analysis. Then we examine methods for measuring risk and for analyzing an individual's attitude toward risk. We go on to discuss gambling and insurance, risk–return indifference curves and their use in analyzing choices subject to risk. Subsequently, we summarize ways by which an individual or other economic agent can reduce risk. Finally, we discuss behavioral economics. A large dose of realism is introduced into the analysis by the many real-world examples included in the chapter. The "At the Frontier" section deals with foreign-exchange risk and hedging.

6.1	

RISK AND UNCERTAINTY IN DEMAND CHOICES

Certainty The situation where there is only one possible outcome to a decision and this outcome is known precisely; risk-free.

Risk The situation where there is more than one possible outcome to a decision and the probability of each possible outcome is known or can be estimated.

Uncertainty The situation where there is more than one possible outcome to a decision and the probability of each specific outcome is not known or even meaningful.

✓ Concept Check

What is the difference between risk and uncertainty?

Consumer choices are made under conditions of certainty, risk, or uncertainty. **Certainty** refers to the situation where there is only one possible outcome to a decision, and this outcome is known precisely. For example, investing in Treasury bills leads to only one outcome (the amount of the yield), and this is known with certainty. The reason is that there is virtually no chance that the federal government will fail to redeem these securities at maturity or that it will default on interest payments. On the other hand, when there is more than one possible outcome to a decision, risk or uncertainty is present.

   Risk refers to a situation where there is more than one possible outcome to a decision and the probability of each specific outcome is known or can be estimated. Thus, risk requires that the decision maker know all the possible outcomes of the decision and have some idea of the probability of each outcome's occurrence. For example, in tossing a coin, we can get either a head or a tail, and each has an equal (i.e., a 50–50) chance of occurring (if the coin is balanced). Similarly, investing in a stock can lead to a set of possible outcomes, and the probability of each possible outcome can be estimated from past experience. In general, the greater the variability (i.e., the greater the number and range) of possible outcomes, the greater the risk associated with the decision or action.

   Uncertainty is the case when there is more than one possible outcome to a decision and where the probability of each specific outcome occurring is not known or even meaningful. This may be due to insufficient past information or instability in the structure of the variables. In extreme forms of uncertainty, not even the outcomes themselves are known. For example, drilling for oil in an unproven field carries with it uncertainty if the investor does not know either the possible oil outputs or their probability of occurrence.[1]

   In the analysis of choices involving risk or uncertainty, we will utilize such concepts as strategy, states of nature, and payoff matrix. A *strategy* refers to one of several alternative courses of action that a decision maker can take to achieve a goal. For example, an individual may have to decide on how much of its savings to put in stocks (which can offer high returns but are subject to high volatility and risk) and how much in government bonds (which offer lower returns but are also subject to low volatility and risk). *States of nature* refer to conditions in the future that will have a significant effect on the degree of success or failure of any strategy, but over which the decision maker has little or no control. For example, the economy may be booming, normal, or in a recession in the future. The decision maker has no control over the states of nature that will prevail in the future, but the future states of nature can affect the outcome of any strategy that he or she may adopt. The particular decision made will depend, therefore, on the decision-maker's knowledge or estimation of how the particular future state of nature will affect the outcome or result of each particular strategy (such as the return on stocks and bonds). Finally, a *payoff matrix* is a table that shows the possible outcomes or results of each strategy under each state of nature. For example, a payoff matrix may show the return that

---

[1] Although the distinction between risk and uncertainty is theoretically important, in this chapter we follow the usual convention (when introducing this topic) of using these two terms interchangeably.

the individual would obtain from an investment if the economy will be booming, normal, or in a recession in the future.

EXAMPLE 6–1

The Risk Faced by Coca-Cola in Changing Its Secret Formula

On April 23, 1985, the Coca-Cola Company announced that it was changing its 99-year-old recipe for Coke. Coke is the leading soft drink in the world, and the company took an unusual risk in tampering with its highly successful product. The Coca-Cola Company felt that changing its recipe was a necessary strategy to ward off the challenge from Pepsi-Cola, which had been chipping away at Coke's market lead over the years. The new Coke, with its sweeter and less fizzy taste, was clearly aimed at reversing Pepsi's market gains. Coca-Cola spent over $4 million to develop its new Coke and conducted taste tests on more than 190,000 consumers over a three-year period. These tests seemed to indicate that consumers preferred the new Coke over the old Coke by 61% to 39%. Coca-Cola then spent over $10 million on advertising its new product.

When the new Coke was finally introduced in May 1985, there was nothing short of a consumers' revolt against the new Coke, and in what is certainly one of the most stunning multimillion dollar about-faces in the history of marketing, the company felt compelled to bring back the old Coke under the brand name Coca-Cola Classic. The irony is that with the Classic and new Cokes sold side by side, Coca-Cola regained some of the market share that it had lost to Pepsi. While some people believed that Coca-Cola intended all along to reintroduce the old Coke and that the whole thing was part of a shrewd marketing strategy, most marketing experts are convinced that Coca-Cola had underestimated consumers' loyalty to the old Coke. This did not come up in the extensive taste tests conducted by Coca-Cola because the consumers tested were never informed that the company intended to *replace* the old Coke with the new Coke rather than sell them side by side. This example clearly shows that even a well-conceived strategy is risky and can lead to results estimated to have a small probability of occurrence. While Coca-Cola recuperated from the fiasco, most companies are not so lucky! In the meantime, the perennial cola battle for market supremacy between Coke and Pepsi rages on.

Sources: "Coca-Cola Changes Its Secret Formula in Use for 99 Years," *New York Times,* April 24, 1985, p. 1; " 'Old' Coke Coming Back After Outcry by Faithful," *New York Times,* July 11, 1985, p. 13; "Flops," *Business Week,* August 16, 1993, pp. 76–82; "Facing Slow Sales, Coke and Pepsi Gear Up for New Battle," *Wall Street Journal,* April 16, 2001; "A Better Model? Diversified Pepsi Steals Some of Coke's Sparkle," *Financial Times,* February 28, 2005, p. 15; and "Coke Gets Real: The World's Most Valuable Brand Wakes up to a Waning Thirst for Cola," *Financial Times,* September 22, 2005, p. 11.

6.2   MEASURING RISK

In the previous section we defined risk as the situation where there is more than one possible outcome to a decision and the probability of each possible outcome is known or can be estimated. In this section we examine the meaning and characteristics of probability distributions, and then we use these concepts to develop a precise measure of risk.

TABLE 6.1	Probability Distribution of States of the Economy
State of the Economy	Probability of Occurrence
Boom	0.25
Normal	0.50
Recession	0.25
Total	1.00

Probability Distributions

Probability The chance or odds that an event will occur.

The **probability** of an event is the chance or odds that the event will occur. For example, if we say that the probability of booming conditions in the economy next year is 0.25, or 25%, this means that there is 1 chance in 4 for this condition to occur. By listing all the possible outcomes of an event and the probability attached to each, we get a **probability distribution.** For example, if only three states of the economy are possible (boom, normal, or recession) and the probability of each occurring is specified, we have a probability distribution such as the one shown in Table 6.1. Note that the sum of the probabilities is 1, or 100%, since one of the three possible states of the economy must occur with certainty.

Probability distribution The list of all possible outcomes of a decision or strategy and the probability attached to each.

The concept of probability distribution is essential in evaluating and comparing different outcomes or investments. In general, the outcome or payoff from an investment (e.g., from the purchase of a stock) is generally highest when the economy is booming and smallest when the economy is in a recession (when the value of the stock is likely to fall). If we multiply each possible outcome or payoff of an investment by its probability of occurrence and add these products, we get the expected value of the investment. For example, if there are two possible outcomes for investment or event X with payoffs X_1 and X_2 and probabilities Pr_1 and Pr_2, then the expected value of X or $E(X)$ is

$$\text{Expected value of } X = E(X) = Pr_1 X_1 + Pr_1 X_1 \qquad [6.1]$$

If there are n possible outcomes, the expected value becomes

$$E(X) = Pr_1X_1 + Pr_2X_2 + \cdots + Pr_nX_n \qquad [6.2]$$

Expected value The sum of the products of each possible outcome of a decision or strategy and the probability of its occurrence.

Thus, the **expected value** of an investment is the weighted average of all possible payoffs that can result from the investment under the various states of the economy, with the probability of those payoffs used as weights. The expected value of an investment is a very important consideration in deciding whether or not to make an investment and which of two or more investments is preferable.

For example, Table 6.2 presents the payoff matrix of investment A and investment B and shows how the expected value or mean of each investment is determined. In this case the expected value of each of the two investments is $500, but the range of outcomes or payoffs for investment A (from $400 in recession to $600 in boom) is much smaller than for investment B (from $200 in recession to $800 in boom).

The expected profit and the variability in the outcomes of investment A and investment B are shown in Figure 6.1, where the height of each bar measures the probability that a particular outcome (measured along the horizontal axis) will occur. Note that the

Investment	(1) State of Economy	(2) Probability of Occurrence	(3) Outcome of Investment	(4) Expected Value (2) × (3)
TABLE 6.2 Calculation of the Expected Profits of the Two Investments				
A	Boom	0.25	$600	$150
	Normal	0.50	500	250
	Recession	0.25	400	100
		Expected earnings from investment A		$500
B	Boom	0.25	$800	$200
	Normal	0.50	500	250
	Recession	0.25	200	50
		Expected earnings from investment B		$500

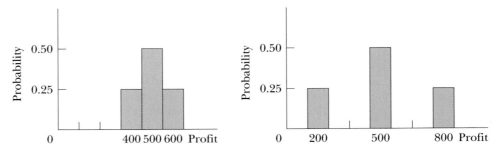

FIGURE 6.1   Probability Distribution of Profits from Investment A and Investment B   The expected profit is $500 for both projects A and B, but the range of profits (and therefore the risk) is much smaller for project A than for project B. For project A the range of profits is from $400 in a recession to $600 in a boom. For project B, the range of profits is from $200 in a recession to $800 in a boom.

relationship between the state of the economy and profits is much tighter (i.e., less dispersed) for investment A than for investment B. Thus, investment A is less risky than investment B. Since both investments have the same expected profit, investment A is preferable to investment B if the individual is risk averse (the usual case). Had the expected value of investment A been lower than for investment B, the individual would have to decide whether the lower risk from investment A compensates him or her for its lower expected value. In Section 6.3 we will show how an individual makes such decisions. Before doing that, however, we want to show how to measure risk more precisely.

The Standard Deviation

Standard deviation (*sd*) A measure of the dispersion of possible outcomes from the expected value of a distribution.

We have seen above that the tighter or the less dispersed a probability distribution, the smaller the risk of a particular strategy or decision. The reason is that there is a smaller probability that the actual outcome will deviate significantly from the expected value. We can measure the tightness or the degree of dispersion of a probability distribution by the standard deviation. Thus, the **standard deviation (*sd*)** measures the dispersion of possible outcomes from the expected value. The smaller the value of *sd*, the tighter or less dispersed the distribution—and the lower the risk attached to it.

TABLE 6.3	Calculation of the Standard Deviation of Profits for Investments A and B		

Deviation from Expected Value	Deviation Squared	Probability	Deviation Squares Times Probability
		Project A	
$600 - $500 = $100	$10,000	0.25	$2,500
500 - 500 = 0	0	0.50	0
400 - 500 = -100	10,000	0.25	2,500
		Sum of deviations squared = Variance = $5,000	
		Standard deviation = Square root of variance = $70.71	
		Project B	
$800 - $500 = $300	$90,000	0.25	$22,500
500 - 500 = 0	0	0.50	0
200 - 500 = -300	90,000	0.25	22,500
		Sum of deviations squared = Variance = $45,000	
		Standard deviation = Square root of variance = $212.13	

To find the value of the standard deviation (*sd*) of a particular probability distribution, we follow the three steps outlined below.

1. Subtract the expected value or the mean of the distribution from each possible outcome or payoff to obtain a set of deviations from the expected value.
2. Square each deviation, multiply the squared deviation by the probability of its expected outcome, and then sum these products. This weighted average of squared deviations from the mean is the *variance* of the distribution.
3. Take the square root of the variance to find the standard deviation (*sd*).[2]

Concept Check
How is risk measured?

Table 6.3 shows how to calculate the standard deviation of the probability distribution of payoffs or profits for investment A and investment B given in Table 6.2. The expected value was found earlier to be $500 for each investment. From Table 6.3, we see that the standard deviation of the probability distribution of payoffs for investment A is $70.71, while that for investment B is $212.13. These values provide a numerical measure of the absolute dispersion of payoffs from the expected value of each investment and confirm the greater dispersion of payoffs and risk for investment B than for investment A, shown earlier graphically in Figure 6.1. Note that risk analysis is useful not only in analyzing investments but also in examining any activity involving risk, as Example 6–2 demonstrates.

---

[2] The actual formula for the standard deviation (*sd*) is

$$sd = \sqrt{\sum_{i=1}^{n}(X_i - \overline{X})^2 \cdot \mathrm{Pr}_i}$$

where $\sum$ is the "sum of," X_i is payoff or outcome i (of n payoffs or outcomes), $\overline{X}$ is the mean or expected value of the distribution of X [i.e., $E(X)$], and Pr_i is the probability of occurrence of payoff or outcome i.

EXAMPLE 6–2

Risk and Crime Deterrence

Risk analysis can be used to analyze crime deterrence. A 1973 study found that criminals often respond to incentives in much the same way as people engaged in legitimate economic activities. For example, the rate of robberies and burglaries was found to be positively related to the gains and inversely related to the costs of (i.e., punishment for) criminal activity. It was found that for each 1% increase in the probability of being caught and sent to jail, the rate of robberies declined by 0.85% and for each 1% increase in the duration of imprisonment, the rate of burglaries declined by 0.9%. Thus, it seems that increasing the efficiency of the police in apprehending criminals and the imposition of stiffer sentences discourages crime.

Other studies, however, did not confirm this relationship but found that reducing the opportunity to commit crimes is a more effective way to reduce criminal activity. For example, a survey conducted by the *New York Times* in September 2000 found homicide rates to be higher in states with the death penalty than in states without it. Furthermore, homicide rates showed similar up-and-down trends over the years, thus offering little support to the contention that capital punishment is a deterrent. Some economists do not accept the results of these studies, however. They point out that when variations in other factors, such as the rate of unemployment, income inequality, and the likelihood of apprehension, as well as the existence of the death penalty, are considered in the analysis, then the death penalty is a significant deterrent.

Obviously, more empirical studies are needed to resolve this controversy, but risk analysis will necessarily have to be part of any such study. Indeed, risk analysis has already shown its usefulness in the analysis of crime. For example, it has been shown that the greater the probability of apprehension for a crime (and hence the lower the cost of law enforcement), the lighter the sentence. Thus, lovers' quarrels and brawls involving alcohol have the highest probability of being caught and also the lightest sentences. On the other hand, the crime of arson has an exceptionally low probability of apprehension and consequently the highest average sentence. Furthermore, risk analysis indicates that by increasing the penalty, law enforcement agencies can reduce the cost of enforcement. For example, imposing a fine of, say, $100 for a small crime and catching one violator in ten leads to an expected cost of apprehension for the violator of $10 ($100 times 0.1). But this has the same deterring effect as imposing a fine of $1,000 for the same crime and catching only one in 100 violators (which is much cheaper to do) since the expected cost of apprehension for the criminal is the same (i.e., $1,000 times 0.01 = $10).

Sources: I. Ehrlich, "Participation in Illegitimate Activities: A Theoretical and Empirical Investigation," *Journal of Political Economy,*" May/June 1973; W. T. Dickens, "Crime and Punishment Again: The Economic Approach with a Psychological Twist," National Bureau of Economic Research, *Working Paper No. 1884,* April 1986; E. Glaeser and B. Sacerdote, "The Determinants of Punishment: Deterrence, Incapacitation and Vengeance," National Bureau of Economic Research, *Working Paper No. 1884,* August 2000; "States with no Death Penalty Share Lower Homicide Rates," *New York Times,* September 22, 2001, p. 1; Learning to Live with Uncertainty," *The Economist,* January 4, 2004, pp. 15–16; "In Murder City," *The Economist,* February 3, 2007, p. 30; and "Does Death Penalty Save Lives? A New Debate," *New York Times,* November 18, 2007, p. 1.

6.3 | UTILITY THEORY AND RISK AVERSION

In this section we first examine the different views or preferences toward risk of different individuals and then use this information to examine consumers' choices in the face of risk. We will see that in making choices under risk or certainty the consumer maximizes utility or satisfaction. When risk or uncertainty is present, the consumer maximizes *expected* utility.

Different Preferences Toward Risk

Risk averter An individual for whom the marginal utility of money diminishes.

Most individuals, faced with two alternative investments of equal expected value or profit, but different standard deviation or risk, will generally prefer the less risky investment (i.e., the one with the smaller standard deviation). That is, most individuals seek to minimize risks or are **risk averters.** Some individuals, however, may very well choose the more risky investment (i.e., are **risk seekers or lovers**), while still others may be indifferent to risk (i.e., are **risk neutral**). The reason is that different individuals have different preferences toward risk. Most individuals are risk averters because they face **diminishing marginal utility of money.** The meaning of diminishing, constant, and increasing marginal utility of money can be explained with the aid of Figure 6.2.

Risk seeker or lover An individual for whom the marginal utility of money increases.

In Figure 6.2, money income or wealth is measured along the horizontal axis while the utility or satisfaction of money (measured in utils) is plotted along the vertical axis.[3]

Risk neutral An individual for whom the marginal utility of money is constant.

Diminishing marginal utility of money The decline in the extra utility received from each dollar increase in income.

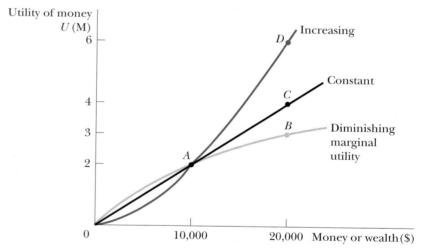

FIGURE 6.2   Diminishing, Constant, and Increasing Marginal Utility of Money
A $10,000 money income or wealth provides 2 utils of utility to a particular individual (point *A*), while $20,000 provides 3 utils (point *B*) if the total utility of money curve of the individual is concave or faces down (so that the marginal utility of money declines), 4 utils (point *C*) if the total utility curve is a straight line (so that the marginal utility is constant), and 6 utils (point *D*) if the total utility curve is convex or faces up (so that marginal utility increases). The individual would then be, respectively, a risk averter, risk neutral, or a risk seeker.

---

[3] As pointed out in Section 3.1, a *util* is a fictitious unit of utility. Here, we assume that the utility or satisfaction that a particular individual receives from various amounts of money income or wealth can be measured in terms of utils.

From the figure, we can see that $10,000 in money or wealth provides 2 utils of utility to a particular individual (point *A*), while $20,000 provides 3 utils (point *B*), 4 utils (point *C*), or 6 utils (point *D*), respectively, depending on the *total* utility of money curve for this individual being concave or facing down, a straight line, or convex (facing up).

If the *total* utility curve is concave or faces down, doubling the individual's income or wealth from $10,000 to $20,000 only increases his or her utility from 2 to 3 utils, so that the *marginal* utility of money (the slope of the total utility curve) diminishes for this individual. If the total utility of money curve is a straight line, doubling income also doubles utility, so that the marginal utility of money is constant. Finally, if the total utility of money curve is convex or faces up, doubling income more than doubles utility, so that the marginal utility of money income increases.

Most individuals are risk averters and face diminishing marginal utility of money (i.e., their total utility curve is concave or faces down—see Figure 6.2). To see why this is so, consider an offer to engage in a bet to win $10,000 if "head" turns up in the tossing of a coin or to lose $10,000 if "tail" comes up. Since the probability of a head or a tail is 0.5 or 50% and the amount of the win or loss is $10,000, the expected value of the money won or lost from the gamble is

$$0.5(\$10,000) + 0.5(-\$10,000) = 0 \qquad [6.3]$$

Even though the expected value of such a *fair game* is zero, a risk averter (an individual facing diminishing marginal utility of money) would gain less utility by winning $10,000 than he or she would lose by losing $10,000. Starting from point *A* in Figure 6.2, we see that by losing $10,000, the risk-averting individual loses 2 utils of utility if he or she loses $10,000 but gains only 1 util of utility if he or she wins $10,000. Even though the bet is fair (i.e., there is a 50–50 chance of winning or losing $10,000), the **expected utility** of the bet is negative. That is,

$$\text{Expected utility} = E(U) = 0.5(1 \text{ util}) + 0.5(-2 \text{ utils}) = -0.5 \qquad [6.4]$$

In such a case, the individual will refuse a fair bet.[4] From this, we can conclude that a risk-averting individual will not necessarily accept an investment with positive expected monetary value. To determine whether or not the individual would undertake the investment, we need to know his or her utility function of money or income. ˉ

Maximizing Expected Utility

To determine whether or not an individual should undertake an investment, he or she needs to determine the expected utility of the investment. For example, suppose that an investment has a 40% probability of providing profit of $20,000 and a 60% probability of resulting in a loss of $10,000. Since the *expected monetary return* of such a project is positive (see Table 6.4), a risk-neutral or a risk-seeking individual would undertake the project. However, if the individual is risk averse (the usual case) and his or her utility function is as indicated in Figure 6.3, the individual would not make the investment because the *expected utility* from the investment is negative (see Table 6.5).

---

[4] With constant utility, $E(U) = 0.5(2 \text{ utils}) + 0.5(-2 \text{ utils}) = 0$ and the individual is risk neutral and indifferent to the bet. With increasing marginal utility, $E(U) = 0.5(4 \text{ utils}) + 0.5(-2 \text{ utils}) = 1$ and the individual is a risk seeker and would accept the bet.

✓ Concept Check
How is a risk-averse individual defined?

Expected utility The sum of the product of the utility of each possible outcome of a decision or strategy and the probability of its occurrence.

✓ Concept Check
Why would a risk-averse individual not accept a fair gamble?

TABLE 6.4	Expected Return from the Investment		
States of Nature	**(1)** Probability	**(2)** Monetary Outcome	**(3)** Expected Return (1) × (2)
Success	0.40	$20,000	$8,000
Failure	0.60	−$10,000	−6,000
			Expected return = $2,000

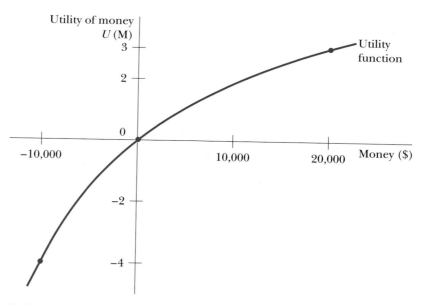

FIGURE 6.3   The Utility Function of a Risk-Averse Individual   An investment with a 40% probability of providing a return of $20,000 (3 utils of utility) and a 60% probability of resulting in a loss of $10,000 (−4 utils of utility) has an expected utility of (0.4)(3 utils) + (0.6)(−4 utils) = −1.2 utils, and it would not be made by the individual.

TABLE 6.5	Expected Utility from the Investment			
States of Nature	**(1)** Probability	**(2)** Monetary Outcome	**(3)** Associated Utility	**(4)** Expected Return (1) × (3)
Success	0.40	$20,000	3	1.2
Failure	0.60	−$10,000	−4	−2.4
				Expected utility = −1.2

✓ Concept Check

How does a choice made in the face of risk differ from choices made in the absence of risk?

Thus, even if the expected *monetary* return is positive, a risk-averse manager will not make the investment if the expected *utility* of the investment is negative. The general rule is that the individual seeks to maximize utility in a world of no risk or uncertainty, but maximizes *expected* utility in the face of risk.[5] Needless to say, even different risk-averse individuals have different utility functions and face different marginal utilities of money, and so even they can reach different conclusions with regard to the same investment. Being risk averse, it would seem irrational for most individuals to engage in gambling. Yet, America seems to be in the grip of a gambling craze (see Example 6–3).

EXAMPLE 6–3

America's Gambling Craze

There was a time, not too many years ago, when gambling was considered morally wrong and was illegal in most parts of the United States. The lust to get something for nothing, which gambling represents, was considered a weakness of character, and bookies and number racketeers were regarded not much better than drug dealers. All of that has changed and gambling has become America's favorite pastime. Today, gambling casinos can brag more than 70 million visitors per year—more than Major League Ballparks. Americans now spend more than $80 billion per year on all sorts of gambling, from casinos to state lotteries, racetrack and off-track betting, sports betting, bingo, and so on—more than on movie theaters, books, amusement attractions, and recorded music *combined*. Gambling expenditures have been rising at more than 10% per year; there are now more than 41 state lotteries and casinos operating in 13 states. In fact, gambling flourishes in every state but Utah and Hawaii. Many go on vacation only where there is a casino, gambling is rampant in the nation's colleges, and electronics is even bringing gambling into homes, restaurants, and planes. In short, we have become a nation of gamblers, and gambling has become America's craze.

Why the change in America's tastes in favor of gambling? The boom in legal gambling can be largely attributed to state and local governments' desire to raise more money without increasing taxes. If many people would gamble anyway, why not legalize gambling and tax gambling profits to finance education and other social programs? But in doing so, state and local governments have encouraged gambling and increased its social costs. Many poor people spend a great deal of their meager incomes on gambling in the hope of a big win that would lift them out of their poverty. But for the vast majority of them, there is no big win and gambling represents a very regressive tax. With gambling legalized and even encouraged, more and more people can be expected to become compulsive or problem gamblers. As a cash business, gambling also lures criminals and organized crime and it corrupts public officials.

✓ Concept Check

Is gambling good for the economy?

Gambling is also not as much as a net stimulus to the economy as it is often made out to be because it takes away from other forms of entertainment and other expenditures in general. For example, more than three decades ago, Atlantic City in New Jersey

---

[5] Only for a risk-neutral individual does maximizing the expected monetary value or return correspond to maximizing expected utility.

allowed casino gambling in order to revitalize the city. At the time, Atlantic City's unemployment rate was twice the state's unemployment rate. Today, more than 30 years and many casinos later, Atlantic City's unemployment rate is still twice the state's unemployment rate and many other of the city's ills remain. Why does America have such a craze for gambling if gambling seems irrational for risk averters? Because of the exaggerated hope of winning that many people have, because of the entertainment that gambling provides, and because many individuals may be risk averters for small gambles but risk lovers for big gambles.

Source: "Electronics Is Bringing Gambling into Homes, Restaurants and Planes," *Wall Street Journal,* August 16, 1995, p. A1; "America's Gambling Fever," *U.S. News & World Report,* January 15, 1996, pp. 51–53; "The Economics of Casino Gambling," *The Journal of Economic Perspectives,* Summer 1999, pp. 173–192; National Gambling Impact Study Commission, *Final Report* (Washington, D.C.: U.S. Government Printing Office, August 3, 1999; "Against the Odds," *U.S. News & World Report,* May 23, 2005, pp. 47–53; "The Wheel of Fortune," *The Economist,* September 24, 2005, p. 74; and "Bad Bet," *New York Times Magazine,* April 13, 2008, pp. 13–14.

6.4   INSURANCE AND GAMBLING

In this section we take a closer look at insurance and gambling. Specifically, we examine why some individuals insure themselves while others gamble, and, what seems entirely contradictory, why the same individual sometimes does both, buy insurance and gamble.

Why Do Some Individuals Buy Insurance?

We have seen in the previous section that a risk averter faces a total utility function of money that is concave or faces down, so that the marginal utility of money for the individual declines. This means that the individual prefers a given sum of money with certainty to any risky asset of equal expected value. It also means that an individual is willing to pay a small amount of money to avoid the small risk of incurring a large loss (i.e., to buy insurance).

For example, suppose that, as shown in Figure 6.4, an individual owns a small business that generates a daily income of $200 (point *A*) without a fire and $20 after a fire (point *B*), and the probability of no fire is $p = 0.899$ (i.e., 89.9%), so that the probability of a fire is $1 - p = 0.111$ (11.1%). Then the **expected income** from the business is

Expected income The probability of one level of income (p) times that income level plus the probability of an alternative income times that alternative income level.

$$\text{Expected income} = (0.889)(\$200) + (0.111)(\$20) = \$2.22 + \$178.8 = \$180.02$$

The income of $180.02 or $180 (rounded to the nearest dollar) is not actually available to the individual. That is, the individual faces only two alternatives: (1) an income of $200 with probability of 89.90% or (2) an income of $20 with probability of 11.1%. The expected income of $180 is a weighted average of these two alternatives using the probabilities as weights. However, the individual would never actually have the income of $180. Different probabilities of occurrence attached to the incomes of $200 and $20 would result in a different expected daily income. For example, with $p = 0.8$, the expected income from the business would be

$$\text{Expected income} = (0.8)(\$200) + (0.2)(\$20) = \$164$$

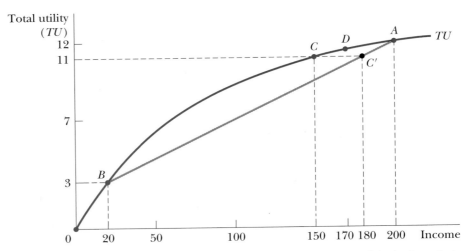

FIGURE 6.4   The Utility Function for an Insurer   The expected value of the business that provides a daily income of $200 (point A) with no fire and $20 with a fire (point B), and with the probability of 0.989 of no fire and 0.111 of a fire, is: (0.889)($200) + (0.111)($20) = $180 (point C′). The certain daily income of $150 (point C) gives the same utility to the individual as owning the business. Insuring against the loss resulting from a fire at a daily cost $30 leaves the individual with a higher level of utility (point D) than would owning the business without insurance (point C′). Thus, the individual will buy the insurance.

Insurer An individual who is willing to pay a small sum of money in order to ensure against the small probability of a large loss; a risk averter.

The utility of the expected income is given by the height of straight-line line (chord) BA at the point directly above the level of the expected income in Figure 6.4. For example, the utility of expected income of $180 is 11 utils (point $C′$ on chord AB). This convenient geometric property results directly from the definition of the expected income (i.e., as the weighted average of the two alternative incomes using objective probabilities as the weights). The utility of the expected income does not fall on the total utility curve because the expected income is not an income that the individual can actually achieve (such as the income shown by point A or B).

From Figure 6.4 we can see that an income of $150 with certainty (point C on the individual's utility function) provides the individual with the same 11 utils of utility as a business that provides an expected (risky) income of $180 (point $C′$ on chord AB). The distance $CC′ = \$30$ is called the **risk premium.** This is the maximum amount that the individual would be willing to pay to avoid the risk. Specifically, since a daily income of $150 with certainty provides the same utility to the individual as a risky business with an expected daily income of $180, the individual would be willing to pay up to $30 per day to insure himself or herself against a large loss from a fire.

Risk premium The maximum amount that a risk-averse individual would be willing to pay to avoid a risk.

Since, in our case, the individual already owns the business (rather than having to decide whether or not to enter it) and after a fire the business would still generate an income of $20 per day, he or she would actually be willing to pay up to $50 per day ($AC$ in Figure 6.4) to insure against the loss of the entire business. If the owner of the business could insure the business for $30 per day, he or she would definitely do so since that would put him or her at point D on the utility curve, and point D provides more utility (11.5 utils) than owning the business without insurance, which provides 11 utils of utility (point C'). Point D is on the utility curve because it is a daily income that the individual can actually achieve with insurance.[6]

Why Do Some Individuals Gamble?

Next we turn to the analysis of gambling. To do so, suppose that the individual of Figure 6.4, after having purchased the fire insurance for $30 (thus ending up with the certain daily income of $170 shown by point D in Figure 6.4), faces a total utility function that is convex or faces up (so that the marginal utility of money increases) *for higher incomes*—as shown in Figure 6.5. The individual now contemplates purchasing a lottery ticket costing $20 with a 20% probability of winning and receiving an extra daily income of $250.[7] After purchasing the ticket for $20, the individual's daily income would then either be $150 (shown by point C in Figure 6.5) if the individual does not win or $400 (the $150 from the business and the $250 from the win, as shown by point G in Figure 6.5) if

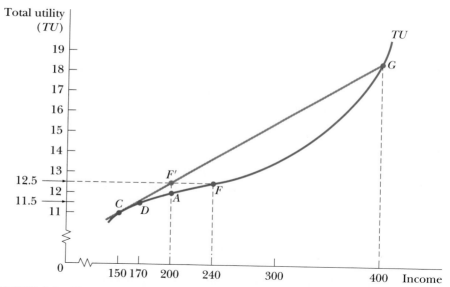

Gambler An individual who is willing to pay a small sum of money in order to have the small probability of a large gain or win; a risk seeker or lover.

FIGURE 6.5   The Utility Function for a Gambler   With the purchase of a lottery ticket that costs $20, the individual's income is either $150 with 80% probability of not winning or $400 with a 20% probability of winning, resulting in the expected income of ($150)(0.2) + $400(0.2) = $200 (point F' on chord CG). This provides a higher utility for the individual than the certain sum of $200 (point A on the total utility curve). Indeed, buying the ticket gives the individual the same utility as the certain income of $240 (point F). Thus, the individual is a gambler for increases in income.

---

[6] In Section 6.6 we will see why an insurance company would be willing to sell an insurance policy to the individual for a premium payment of $30 per day.

[7] Although lotteries usually provide one or two large prizes, people usually convert a lump-sum win into an annuity that provides a certain flow income over time in order to pay a lower tax rate.

he or she wins. Since the probability of winning is 0.2 or 20%, the expected value of the individual's income by purchasing the ticket is

$$\text{Expected value} = (\$150)(0.8) + (\$400)(0.2) = \$120 + \$80 = \$200$$

From Figure 6.5 we see that the individual's utility with purchasing the ticket that provides an expected income of $200 (point F' on chord CG) exceeds the individual's utility of the certain income of $170 without purchasing the ticket (point D on the total utility function of the individual). In fact, the utility that the individual receives by buying the lottery ticket (and continuing to hold on to his or her business) is equal to the certain daily income of $240 dollars (point F on the total utility function). Another way of looking at it is to realize that the individual prefers to purchase the lottery ticket and hold on to his or her business with an expected value of $200 (point F' on chord CG) than having $200 of certain income (point A on the total utility curve in Figure 6.5). This makes the individual a risk seeker or risk lover for increases in income. Example 6–4 explains why some individuals gamble and buy insurance.

EXAMPLE 6–4

Gambling and Insuring by the Same Individual—A Seeming Contradiction

✓ Concept Check

Why do some individuals buy insurance and also gamble?

In the real world, we often observe individuals purchasing insurance and also gambling. For example, many people insure their homes against fire and also purchase lottery tickets. This behavior may seem contradictory. Why should the same individual act as a risk avoider (purchase insurance) and at the same time as a risk seeker (gamble)? One possible explanation for this seemingly contradictory behavior is provided by Milton Friedman and Leonard Savage, who postulate that the total utility of money curve may look like that in Figure 6.6. This total utility curve is concave or faces down (so that the marginal utility of money diminishes) at low levels of money income, and it is convex or faces up (so that the marginal utility of money increases) at higher levels of income. An individual with an income at or near the point of inflection on the total utility curve (point A) will find it advantageous both to spend a small amount of money to insure himself or herself against the small chance of a large loss (say, through a fire that destroys his or her home) and to purchase a lottery ticket providing a small chance of a large win. Starting with an income level at or near A, the individual would act as a risk avoider for declines in income and as a risk seeker for increases in income. Indeed, Figure 6.6 was obtained by bringing together Figure 6.4 and Figure 6.5.

One shortcoming of the above analysis is that it rationalizes more than explains economic behavior in the face of risk. In fact, Kenneth Arrow has found that many people do not take out flood insurance even at favorable government-subsidized rates, whereas flight insurance and lotteries offer examples of people accepting extremely unfavorable odds. A recent study by Garrett and Sobel, however, did find that the utility curve of people who buy lottery ticket have the shape predicted by

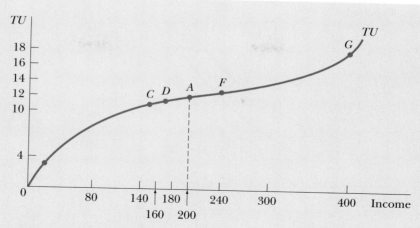

FIGURE 6.6   The Utility Function of an Individual Who Buys Insurance and Gambles   An individual whose income is $200 (point *A*), which is at or near the point of inflection of the total utility curve, will act as a risk averter and will spend a small amount of money to purchase insurance against the small chance of a large loss of income and at the same time will act as a risk seeker and gamble a small amount of money (say, to purchase a lottery ticket) that gives a small chance of a large win.

Friedman and Savage. Furthermore, financial planners and brokers do make a great deal of use of the concepts discussed above in trying to assess their clients' tolerance for risk in providing financial advice.

Sources: M. Friedman and L. J. Savage, "The Utility Analysis of Choices Involving Risk," *Journal of Political Economy,* August 1948; K. Arrow, "Risk Perception in Psychology and Economics," *Economic Inquiry,* January, 1982. T. A. Garrett and R. S. Sobel, "Gamblers Favor Skewness, Not Risks: Further Evidence from U.S. Lottery Games," *Economic Letters,* April 1999; and "Dealing with Risk," *Business Week,* January 17, 2000, pp. 102–112; "Against the Odds," *U.S. News & World Report,* May 23, 2005, pp. 47–53; "The Wheel of Fortune," *The Economist,* September 24, 2005, p. 74; and "Bad Odds," *Wall Street Journal,* June 11, 2007, p. R5.

6.5   RISK AVERSION AND INDIFFERENCE CURVES

The extent of an individual's risk aversion can also be shown by indifference curves that relate expected income (measured along the vertical axis) to the variability of expected income (measured by the standard deviation along the horizontal axis). Each indifference curve shows all the combinations of standard deviation and expected income that give the individual the same level of utility or satisfaction. Since a higher variability of income (risk) must be compensated by a higher expected income, these indifference curves are positively sloped. Figure 6.7 shows two sets of such indifference curves. The indifference curves in the left panel are steep and refer to an individual who has a strong aversion to risk, while those in the right panel are flatter for a less risk-averse individual.

Specifically, indifference curve U_1 in the left panel shows that the individual is indifferent among the standard deviation of 0.5 and the expected income of $80 (point *A*), the

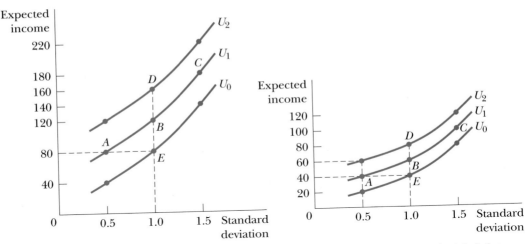

FIGURE 6.7   Indifference Curves for Risk-Averse Individuals   An increase in the standard deviation from 0.5 to 1.0 requires an increase in the expected income of $40 to keep the highly risk-averse individual shown in the left panel on indifference U_1 (compare point B with point A), while it requires an increase in the expected income of only $20 for the less risk-averse individual in the right panel.

standard deviation of 1.0 and the expected income of $120 (point B), and the standard deviation of 1.5 and the expected income of $180 (point C). Thus, indifference curve U_1 shows that, starting at point A, the individual requires an additional $40 in expected income to just compensate him or her for an increase in the standard deviation from 0.5 to 1.0 (and reach point B) and the individual requires an additional $60 in expected income to compensate him or her for an increase in the standard deviation from 1.0 to 1.5 (and reach point C). On the other hand, starting at point B on U_1, and the standard deviation of 1.0, the higher expected income of $160 puts the individual at point D on higher indifference curve U_2, while the lower expected income of $80 puts the individual at point E on lower indifference curve U_0. Finally, an increase in the standard deviation from 0.5 to 1.0 at the expected income of $80 shifts the individual from point A on U_1 to point E on lower indifference curve U_0.

The right panel of Figure 6.7 shows the indifference curves for an individual who is less risk averse than the individual in the left panel. For example, indifference curve U_1 in the right panel shows that the individual is indifferent among the expected income of $40 and standard deviation of 0.5 (point A), the expected income of $60 and standard deviation of 1.0 (point B), and the expected income of $100 and standard deviation of 1.5 (point C). On the other hand, for the standard deviation of 1.0, the higher expected income of $80 puts the individual at point D on higher indifference curve U_2 (from point B on U_1), while the lower expected income of $40 puts the individual at point E on a lower indifference curve U_0. Finally, an increase in the standard deviation from 0.5 to 1.0 at the expected income of $40 shifts the individual from point A on U_1 to point E on lower indifference curve U_0. The return-risk indifference curves discussed above can be used to determine the choice of the best investment portfolio for an individual (see Example 6–5).

EXAMPLE 6–5

Spreading Risks in the Choice of a Portfolio

Since investors are risk averse, on the average, they will hold a more risky portfolio of stocks and bonds only if it provides a higher return. The way by which an individual chooses an optimum investment portfolio can be shown by Figure 6.8.

In the figure, curve *ABCD* is the individual's risk–return trade-off function or indifference curve. It shows that the individual is indifferent among a 10% rate of return on the investment with zero standard deviation (point *A*), a 14% rate of return with standard deviation of 0.5 (point *B*), a 20% rate of return with a standard deviation of 1.0 (point *C*), and a rate of return of 32% with a standard deviation of 1.5 (point *D*).

Suppose also that there exist only two assets, with risk and return given by points *E* and *F* in Figure 6.8. If the risk of assets *E* and *F* are independent of each other, the investor can choose any mixed portfolio of assets *E* and *F* shown on the frontier or curve *ECF*. To understand the shape of frontier *ECF*, note that the return on a mixed portfolio will be between the return on asset *E* and on asset *F* alone, depending on the particular combination of the two assets in the portfolio. As far as risk is concerned, there are portfolios (such as that indicated by point *C*) on frontier *ECF* that have lower risks than those composed exclusively of either asset *E* or asset *F*. The reason for this can be gathered by assuming that the probability of a low return is 1/2 on asset *E* and 1/4 on asset *F* and that, for the moment, we take the probability of a low return as a

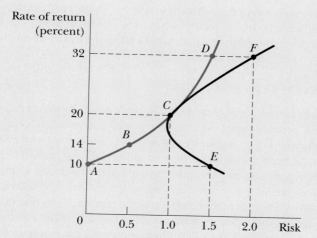

FIGURE 6.8   Choosing an Investment Portfolio   The risk–return trade-off function or indifference curve *ABCD* shows the various risk–return trade-off combinations among which the investor is indifferent. On the other hand, frontier *ECF* represents the combinations of risk and return that are obtainable with mixed portfolios of asset *E* and asset *F*, with independent risk. The optimum portfolio for the investor is represented by point *C*, where the risk–return trade-off function or indifference curve *ABCD* is tangent to frontier *ECF*.

measure of risk. If these probabilities are independent of each other, the probability of a low return on both assets E and F at the same time is $(1/2)(1/4) = 1/8$, which is smaller than for either asset E or F separately.

Given the risk–return trade-off function or indifference curve $ABCD$ shown in Figure 6.8, we can see that the optimum portfolio for this investor is the mixed portfolio indicated by point C, where risk–return indifference curve $ABCD$ is tangent to frontier ECF. Indeed, market evidence shows that a well-diversified portfolio containing various mixes of stocks, bonds, Treasury bills, real estate, and foreign securities can even-out a lot of the ups and downs of investing without sacrificing much in the way of returns. Of course, the type of portfolio that an investor actually chooses depends on his/her tolerance for risk, as shown by his or her risk–return trade-off functions or indifference curves.

Sources: H. M. Markowitz, "Portfolio Selection," *Journal of Finance,* March 1952, pp. 77–91; "For Volatile Times, the Psychology of Risk," *New York Times,* November 23, 1997, p. 3; "What's Your Risk Tolerance?," *Wall Street Journal,* January 23, 1998, p. C1W; "Dealing with Risk," *Business Week,* January 17, 2000, pp. 102–112; "Gauging Investors' Appetite for Risk," *Wall Street Journal,* September 18, 2001, p. C14; "Just How Risky is Your Portfolio? *Fortune,* November 26, 2001, pp. 219–224; and "Why Do Stocks Pay So Much More than Bonds?" *New York Times,* February 26, 2006, p. 4.

6.6   REDUCING RISK AND UNCERTAINTY

We have seen above that, although some individuals are risk seekers or risk lovers, most are risk averters. In this section we examine three basic ways by which an individual can reduce risk or uncertainty. These are (1) gathering more information, (2) diversification or risk spreading, and (3) insurance.

Gathering More Information

Individuals and decision makers can often make better predictions and sharply reduce the risk or uncertainty surrounding a particular strategy or event by collecting more information. For example, by consulting *Consumer Reports,* consumers can determine how frequently a particular type of automobile or brand of refrigerators are likely to require repairs and take this information into consideration in their purchases. Similarly, investors can obtain information about the riskiness of a bond by checking Moody's, Standard & Poor, or other rating agencies' reports. Gathering information is costly, however, and the individual or manager should treat it as any other investment. That is, he or she should continue to gather information until the marginal benefit (return) from it is equal to the marginal cost. The *value of complete information* is the difference between the expected income or value of a choice with complete information and the expected value without complete information. The economics of information is examined in detail in Chapter 19.

Diversification

Diversification The spreading of risks.

Another very important method of reducing risk or uncertainty is **diversification**, or spreading the risks. Diversification involves investing a given amount of resources in a number of independent projects instead of investing them in a single one. This is an example of the old saying "Don't put all of your eggs in one basket." As long as the projects are not closely related, investing in a number of them can reduce the risk. If there is a *perfect negative correlation* between two activities (so that when one occurs, the other definitely will not), the risk can be entirely eliminated by engaging in both activities at the same time. Only if there is a perfect positive correlation between two events will engaging in both not reduce the risk at all. Under any other circumstance (i.e., when events are imperfectly correlated or entirely unrelated), diversification can reduce risks.

✔ **Concept Check**
How does diversification reduce risk?

For example, a person can reduce risk by investing his or her money in a number of stocks instead of investing it in a single stock because the stocks of different companies do not exhibit perfect positive correlation. This can be accomplished more simply by buying shares of mutual funds. These are shares of companies that buy a large number of different stocks. Even doing so, however, does not eliminate all risks because in case of a recession the stocks of all companies tend more or less to fall. That is, while diversification can go a long way toward reducing risk, it cannot eliminate all of them. Systemic risks are nondiversifiable and remain.

Insurance

We have seen in Section 6.4 that risk averters can avoid risk by purchasing insurance. This involves paying a small sum to avoid the small risk of a big loss. The maximum price that an individual is willing to pay for insurance is equal to the risk premium. This is the difference between the expected value of a loss and a certain sum that provides the individual with the same utility.

For example, suppose that an individual owns a house worth $100,000 and faces a probability of 1 in 100, or 1%, that the house will burn down during any given year. The expected value of the loss from a fire during any year is then $(0.01)(\$100,000) = \$1,000$. If a fire insurance policy were offered to home owner for $1,000, a risk-averse home owner will definitely buy it. Such an insurance would be *fairly priced* or be *actuarially fair* because it is equal to the expected loss that it covers. In fact, a risk-averse home owner would be willing to pay much more for it, depending on his or her degree of risk aversion (as measured by the risk premium).

Would an insurance company be willing to sell such an insurance policy to home owners? To answer this question, suppose that the insurance company can sell the fire insurance to 100 homeowners. By insuring 100 homeowners, each paying an insurance premium of $1,000, and with the risk of 1% that one of the 100 insured homes will burn down during a year, the insurance company collects $100,000 in insurance premiums during the year and expects to pay out $100,000 for the one house that it expects to actually burn down during the year. Since the insurance company must also cover its operating expenses (i.e., the costs of administering the policy), however, it will actually have to charge a premium in excess of $1,000 for the insurance policy. With competition among insurance companies, the *insurance premium* will tend to exceed $1,000 only by the operating expenses of the insurance company. This will usually be much smaller than the *risk premium* that an individual home owner is willing to pay to avoid the risk of a fire, thus making the insurance policy still very advantageous to the average home owner. Example 6–6 explains why some disasters are nondiversifiable risks.

EXAMPLE 6–6

Some Disasters as Nondiversifiable Risks

Some risks, such as those arising from a war, affect everyone. Such risks are nondiversifiable, and so insurance companies do not offer insurance against them because they cannot spread their risks. In recent years, some insurance companies have started viewing major natural disasters (hurricanes, flooding, earthquakes) as nondiversifiable risks. In the wake of the terrorist attack against the World Trade Center (WTC) in New York City on September 11, 2001, insurance companies would probably add losses from future terrorist attacks to the list on nondiversifiable (and hence noninsurable) risks in the absence of government help. Most insurance companies are reluctant to offer coverage for terrorist acts because they cannot calculate the risk and thus cannot set appropriate premiums.

It has been estimated that the insurance claims from the terrorist attack on the WTC will exceed $50 billion dollars to cover everything from the cost of rebuilding the WTC to reimbursing businesses for lost sales and paying workers' compensation claims. Losses to just 13 insurance companies that provided coverage at the WTC were estimated to exceed $7 billion. The terrorist attack against the WTC is surely the worst insurance disaster in history. It would result in some insurance companies actually going bankrupt and others refusing to sell insurance against acts of terrorism in the future or sharply increasing the cost of coverage without help from Washington. Lawmakers in Washington are now working on a proposal under which insurers would cover initial terrorism claims but their losses would be limited, with the government picking up the remainder.

Even before the attack on the WTC, however, many insurance companies refused to offer hurricane and earthquake insurance in many parts of the country that face a relatively high probability of occurrence of these catastrophic events in order to limit payment claims on them. For example, in terms of 1995 prices, insurers paid about $18 billion for losses resulting from the 1994 Los Angeles earthquake, $20 billion for the September 11, 2001, World Trade Center and Pentagon terrorist attacks, $21 billion for 1992's Hurricane Andrew, and more than $28 billion for 2005's Hurricane Katrina. As an alternative, state-run insurance policies have been offered to households against these disasters in Florida and California, but they provide less protection and charge rates about three times higher than previously available commercial rates.

Sources: "For Insurers, Some Failures and Rate Jumps," *New York Times*, September 15, 2001, p. C1; "Under U.S. Plan, Taxpayers Would Cover Terror Claims," *New York Times,* October 7, 2001, p. B1; "Calculating Tragedy," *The Economist*, June 26, 2004, pp. 76–77; "Assessing the Damage," *The Economist*, November 17, 2005, pp. 73–74; and "The Price of Sunshine," *The Economist*, June 6, 2006, pp. 76–77.

6.7   BEHAVIORAL ECONOMICS

Traditional economic theory assumes that individuals and other economic agents always behave and act rationally. That is, it assumes they make logical, rational, and self-interested decisions that weigh benefits against costs so as to maximize utility, value, or profit. The "economic man" is analytic, calculating, unemotional, and selfish. This is often contradicted by reality, where actual human beings often act illogically or irrationally, make inconsistent and even self-sabotaging choices, fail to learn from experience, exhibit reluctance to trade, retreat to unscientific "rules of thumb" in making choices in the face of uncertainty, and behave in other ways that depart from the standard model of unbounded (i.e., unrestricted) rationality.

Behavioral economics is the study of how people actually make choices in the real world by drawing on insights from psychology and economics. It is a combination of psychology and economics that studies what happens when some economic agents exhibit human limitations and complications in making economic decisions. It explains why we often procrastinate, adopt rules of thumb in making complex decisions, make choices that are not in our long-term interest, behave altruistically, or otherwise display bounded rationality. By looking at people's complex psychological reactions to economic events, behavioral economics thus enriches traditional economic analysis by offering a fuller picture of how individuals or other economic agents actually behave or operate in the marketplace.[8]

> **Behavioral economics** is the study of how people actually make choices in the real world by drawing on insights from psychology and economics.

Here are some illustrative examples: People state (and mean it) that they intend to eat better, start exercising, stop smoking, and save enough for retirement—but in reality they often do no such things; gamblers keep betting even though they expect to lose; people often keep buying a stock well past the point where rational valuation justifies it; teachers often put their professional reputation ahead of attempts to maximize their pay; many people give to charity and do volunteer work.

Furthermore, New York City's taxi drivers choose to work shorter shifts on good days (days when earnings are higher) than on bad days, so as to reach a target earning per day, rather than doing the opposite and maximizing weekly earnings; a change in income has been found to change a worker's expenditures and saving rate permanently, despite standard theory (the life-cycle model) postulating that it should not; most people do not bother to sign up for a voluntary (saving) 401(k) plan even though it is most beneficial to them, but they do pull out of such a plan if the employer signs them on automatically; workers resist a reduction in wages even when unemployment is rising, despite traditional theory postulating that workers would accept less pay to save their jobs.

In a famous experiment, *Daniel Kahneman*, a Princeton University psychologist and 2002 Nobel Prize recipient in economics for his work in behavioral economics, gave a coffee mug to some students volunteer and asked another group of student volunteers to make bids on the mugs. The buyers bid on average $2.87 for the mugs; the sellers, on average, would not sell the mugs for less than $7.12. Traditional economics says that the right price is what people are willing to pay. Kahneman's theory, instead, is that people tend to overvalue money when they are buying but overvalue goods when they are selling. His theory also explains why investors hold on much too long to losing stocks and why shoppers are willing to pay exorbitant fees for service contracts on inexpensive appliances.

Behavioral economics also has shown that the effectiveness of a policy may depend a great deal on how it is formulated, presented, and introduced. For example, traditional economics postulates that to sell more soap, a company should strive to make soap more to

✓ Concept Check
How does behavioral economics seek to improve on traditional economic theory?

---

[8] The seminal works in behavioral economics are: H. A. Simon "A Behavioral Model of Rational Choice," *Quarterly Journal of Economics*, February 1955, pp. 99–118; and D. Kahneman and A. Tversky, "Prospect Theory: An Analysis of Decision under Risk," *Econometrica*, March 1979, pp. 263–291. An important, more recent work is P. Diamond and H. Vartiainen, *Behavioral Economics and Its Applications* (Princeton, NJ: Princeton University Press, 2007).

consumers' likings and to sell it at a lower price, whereas behavioral economics might suggest getting supermarkets to display the company's soap at eye level so that customers see the company's brand first and buy it.[9] To conclude, behavioral economics does not replace traditional (neoclassical) economics but tries to enrich it by basing it on more realistic assumptions and on showing how real people actually make choices in the real world. Example 6–7 presents an important application of behavioral economics to financial economics.

EXAMPLE 6–7
Behavioral Economics in Finance

Until the late 1980s, the "efficient market hypothesis" was regarded as one of the best established facts of traditional economics. The efficient market hypothesis postulates that (1) stock prices are correct in the sense that asset prices reflect the true or rational value of the security and (2) it is not possible to predict future stock price movements based on publicly available market information.

Behavioral economics has shown that both of these basic principles of traditional economics are often violated! Thus, in the late 1980s shares of Royal Dutch were selling at a different price in Amsterdam than were shares of Shell in London, even though they were shares of the same company (Royal Dutch/Shell). This represents a violation of one of the most basic principles of traditional economics: the law of one price. It meant that irrational forces limited arbitrage (buying in the low-price market and reselling in the high-price market at a profit until price differences were entirely eliminated), even in the long run.

Other research showed that the second postulate of the efficient market hypothesis was also sometimes refuted, as indicated by the fact that small firms and firms with low price–earning ratios earned higher returns than other stocks with the same risk. Stocks that performed well in the past also tended to be priced too high, whereas stock that performed badly in the past tended to be priced too low (i.e., some investors overreact), and some other investors and stocks underreacted. Psychological evidence indicated that underreaction occurs at short horizons, whereas overreaction takes place at longer horizons. Shifting to investors, it was found that they were less willing to sell a loser stock than a winner stock, even though tax laws encourage just the opposite behavior.

Sources: "A Victory for Economists Who Want Investors to Change Their Behavior," *Wall Street Journal,* September 27, 2006, p. D1; K. Froot, and E. M. Dabora, "How Are Stock Prices Affected by the Location of Trade?," *Journal of Financial Economics,* August 1999, pp. 189–216; W. F. M. De Bondt and R. Thaler, "Does the Stock Market Overreact?," *Journal of Finance,* July 1985, pp. 793–805; A. Shleifer, *Inefficient Markets: An Introduction to Behavioral Finance* (New York: Oxford University Press, 2000); and T. Odean, "Are Investors Reluctant to Realize Their Losses," *Journal of Finance,* December 1998, pp. 1775–1798.

---

[9] See, J. Conlisk, "Why Bounded Rationality," *Journal of Economic Literature,* June 1996, pp. 669–700; C. Camerer et al., "Labor Supply of New York City Cab Drivers: One Day at a Time," *The Quarterly Journal of Economics,* May 1997, pp. 407–441; J. Banks, R. Blundell, and S. Tanner, "Is There a Retirement-Savings Puzzle?" *American Economic Review,* September 1998, pp. 769–788; and D. Laibson, "Golden Eggs and Hyperbolic Discounting," *The Quarterly Journal of Economics,* May 1997, pp. 443–477.

AT THE FRONTIER
Foreign-Exchange Risks and Hedging

Foreign-exchange rate The price of a unit of a foreign currency in terms of the domestic currency.

Hedging The covering of risks arising from changes in future commodity and currency prices.

Forward contract An agreement to purchase or sell a specific amount of a foreign currency at a rate specified today for delivery at a specified future date.

✓ Concept Check
How is a foreign-exchange risk covered by hedging?

Futures contract A standardized forward contract for predetermined quantities of the currency and selected calendar dates.

Portfolios with domestic and foreign securities usually enjoy lower overall volatility and higher dollar returns than portfolios with U.S. securities only. Many experts have traditionally recommended as much as 40% of a portfolio to be in foreign securities. Investing in foreign securities, however, gives rise to a foreign-exchange risk because the foreign currency can depreciate or decrease in value during the time of the investment.

For example, suppose that the return on European Monetary Union (EMU) securities is 15%, compared with 10% at home. As a U.S. investor, you might then want to invest part of your portfolio in the EMU. To do so, however, you must first exchange dollars for euros (€), the currency of the EMU, in order to make the investment. If the **foreign-exchange rate** is $1 to the euro (that is, $1/€1), you can, for example, purchase €10,000 of EMU securities for $10,000. In a year, however, the exchange rate might be $0.90/€1, indicating a 10% depreciation of the euro (i.e., each euro now buys 10% fewer dollars). In that case, you will earn 15% on your investment in terms of euros, but lose 10% on the foreign-exchange transaction, for a net *dollar* gain of only 5% (as compared with 10% on U.S. securities). Of course, the exchange rate at the end of the year might be $1.10/€1, which means that the euro appreciated by 10%, or that you would get 10% more dollars per euro. In that case, you would earn 15% on the euro investment *plus* another 10% on the foreign-exchange transaction. As an investor (rather than a speculator), however, you will probably want to avoid the risk of a large foreign-exchange loss and would not invest in the EMU unless you can hedge or cover the foreign-exchange risk.

Hedging refers to the covering of a foreign-exchange risk. Hedging is usually accomplished with a **forward contract.** This is an agreement to purchase or sell a specific amount of a foreign currency at a rate specified today for delivery at a specific future date. For example, suppose that an American exporter expects to receive €1 million in 3 months. At today's exchange rate of $1/€1, the exporter expects to receive $1 million in three months. To avoid the risk of a large euro depreciation by the time the exporter is to receive payment (and thus receive much fewer dollars than anticipated), the exporter hedges his foreign-exchange risk. He does so by selling €1 million forward at today's forward rate for delivery in three months, so as to coincide with the receipt of the €1 million from his exports. Even if today's forward rate is $0.99/€1, the exporter willingly "pays" 1 cent per euro to avoid the foreign-exchange risk. In 3 months, when the U.S. exporter receives the €1 million, he will be able to immediately exchange it for $990,000 by fulfilling the forward contract (and thus avoid a possible large foreign-exchange loss). An importer avoids the foreign-exchange risk by doing the opposite (see Problem 12).

Hedging can also be accomplished with a **futures contract.** This is a standardized forward contract for *predetermined quantities* of the currency and *selected calendar dates* (for example, for €25,000 for March 15 delivery). As such, futures contracts are more liquid than forward contracts. There is a forward market in many currencies and a futures market in the world's most important currencies (the U.S.

Continued . . .

Foreign-Exchange Risks and Hedging   *Continued*

dollar, the euro, Japanese yen, British pound, Swiss franc, and Canadian dollar). Futures markets exist not only in currencies but also in many other financial instruments or derivatives (a broad class of transactions whose value is based on, or derived from, a financial market such as stocks, interest rates, or currencies) and commodities (corn, oats, soybeans, wheat, cotton; cocoa, coffee, orange juice; cattle, hogs, pork bellies; copper, gold, silver, platinum). Hedging in forward or futures markets reduces transaction costs and risks and increases the volume of domestic and foreign trade in the commodity, currency, or other financial instrument. Of course, forward and futures contracts can also be used for speculation, where they can lead to very large wins or huge losses.

Source: D. Salvatore, *International Economics*, 9th ed. (Hoboken, NJ: John Wiley & Sons, 2007), Chapter 14.

SUMMARY

1. Most consumer choices are made in the face of risk or uncertainty. Risk refers to the situation where there is more than one possible outcome to a decision and the probability of each specific outcome is known or can be estimated. Under uncertainty, on the other hand, the probability of each specific outcome is not known or even meaningful. Choices involving risk utilize the concepts of strategy, states of nature, and payoff matrix.

2. The probability of an event is the chance or odds that the event will occur. A probability distribution lists all the possible outcomes of a decision and the probability attached to each. The expected value of an event is obtained by multiplying each possible outcome of the event by its probability of occurrence and then adding these products. The standard deviation (sd) measures the dispersion of possible outcomes from the expected value and is used as a measure of risk.

3. While some individuals are risk neutral or risk seekers, most are risk averters. Risk aversion is based on the principle of diminishing marginal utility of money, which is reflected in a total utility of money curve that is concave or faces down. A risk averter would not accept a fair bet, a risk-neutral individual would be indifferent to it, and a risk seeker would accept even some unfair bets. In investment decisions subject to risk, a risk-averse individual seeks to maximize expected utility rather than monetary returns. The expected utility of a decision or strategy is the sum of the product of the utility of each possible outcome and the probability of its occurrence.

4. A total utility curve that is concave or faces down (so that the marginal utility of money diminishes) for decreases in income and is convex or faces up (so that the marginal utility of money increases) for increases in income can be used to rationalize the seeming contradicting behavior of an individual buying insurance and gambling at the same time. The risk premium is the maximum amount that a risk-averse individual would be willing to pay to avoid a risk.

5. The extent of an individual's risk aversion can be shown by indifference curves. Each indifference curve shows all the combinations of standard deviation and expected income that give the individual the same level of utility or satisfaction. Since a higher variability of income (risk) must be compensated by a higher expected income, these indifference curves are positively sloped. The stronger the risk aversion of an individual, the steeper are his or her indifference curves. Risk–return indifference curves can be used to determine the choice of the best portfolio.

6. Individuals and decision makers can often make better predictions and sharply reduce the risk or uncertainty surrounding a particular strategy or event by collecting more information. They can also do so by diversification or risk spreading. Individuals can also reduce risks by buying insurance. Insurance premiums are usually higher than those actuarially fair to allow insurance companies to cover their operating expenses. But they are usually still much lower than the risk premium that risk-averting individuals are willing to pay. Some risks, such as those arising from wars, are nondiversifiable and insurance companies refuse to ensure them. The same is true for major natural disasters and terrorist attacks.

7. Behavioral economics is the study of how people actually make choices in the real world by drawing on insights from psychology and economics. Behavioral economics seeks to enrich traditional economic analysis by offering a fuller picture of how individuals or other economic agents actually behave or operate in the marketplace.

8. Including foreign securities in an investment portfolio can reduce risk (through diversification) and increase the rate of return, but also gives rise to a foreign-exchange risk because the foreign currency can depreciate during the time of the investment. Such foreign-exchange risk can be covered by hedging. This is usually accomplished with a forward or a futures contract. A forward contract is an agreement to purchase or sell a specific amount of a foreign currency at a rate specified today for delivery at a specific future date. A futures contract is a standardized forward contract for predetermined quantities of the currency and selected calendar dates.

KEY TERMS

Certainty	Risk neutral	Gambler
Risk	Risk averter	Diversification
Uncertainty	Diminishing marginal utility of	Behavioral economics
Probability	money	Foreign-exchange rate
Probability distribution	Expected utility	Hedging
Expected value	Expected income	Forward contract
Standard deviation (sd)	Insurer	Futures contract
Risk seeker or lover	Risk premium	

REVIEW QUESTIONS

1. What is the meaning of risk, uncertainty? Why are these concepts important in the theory of consumer choice or demand?

2. What is meant by probability distribution, expected value, variance, standard deviation?

3. What is the value of the standard deviation if all the outcomes of a probability distribution are identical? Why is this so? What does this mean?

4. How does the process of consumer utility maximization differ in the case of certainty and risk?

5. What is the meaning of diminishing, constant, and increasing marginal utility of money?

6. Why is maximization of the expected value not a valid criterion in decision making subject to risk? Under what conditions would that criterion be valid?

7. What is the meaning of risk aversion, risk seeking or loving and risk neutrality?

8. Who is an insurer? A gambler? How can we measure the degree risk aversion or risk loving?

9. What is a risk premium? How is it measured?

10. What does a risk–return indifference curve show? What is its use?

11. How are risks and returns balanced in choosing a portfolio?

12. Why is decision making under uncertainty necessarily subjective?

13. What can an individual do to reduce risk?

14. What is behavioral economics? What is its relationship with traditional economic theory?

15. Why does investing abroad involve a foreign-exchange risk? How can such a risk be covered?

PROBLEMS

1. An individual has two investment opportunities, each involving an outlay of $10,000. The possible earnings from each investment and their respective probabilities are given in the following table.

	Investment I		Investment II		
Earnings	$4,000	$6,000	$3,000	$5,000	$7,000
Probability	0.6	0.4	0.4	0.3	0.3

a. Calculate the expected earnings of each investment.

b. Calculate the standard deviation of each investment.

c. Determine which of the two investments the individual should choose.

2. An individual has to choose between investment A and investment B. The individual estimates that the income and probability of the income from each investment are given in the following table.

Investment A		Investment B	
Income	Probability	Income	Probability
$4,000	0.2	$4,000	0.3
5,000	0.3	6,000	0.4
6,000	0.3	8,000	0.3
7,000	0.2		

a. Calculate the standard deviation of the distribution of each investment.

b. Which of the two investments is more risky?

c. Which investment should the individual choose?

3. An individual is considering two investment projects. Project A will return a loss of $45 if conditions are poor, a profit of $35 if conditions are good, and a profit of $155 if conditions are excellent. Project B will return a loss of $100 if conditions are poor, a profit of $60 if conditions are good, and a profit of $300 if conditions

are excellent. The probability distribution of conditions are as follows:

Conditions:	Poor	Good	Excellent
Probability:	40%	50%	10%

a. Calculate the expected value of each project and identify the preferred project according to this criterion.

b. Calculate the standard deviation of the expected value of each project and identify the project with the highest risk.

*4. An individual is considering two investment projects. Project A will return a loss of $5 if conditions are poor, a profit of $35 if conditions are good, and a profit of $95 if conditions are excellent. Project B will return a loss of $15 if conditions are poor, a profit of $45 if conditions are good, and a profit of $135 if conditions are excellent. The probability distribution of conditions are as follows:

Conditions:	Poor	Good	Excellent
Probability:	40%	50%	10%

a. Calculate the expected value of each project and identify the preferred project according to this criterion.

b. Calculate the standard deviation of the expected value of each project and identify the project with the highest risk.

c. Which of the two projects should a risk-averse individual prefer?

5. a. What is the expected utility of an investment with a 40% probability of gaining 3 utils and a 60% probability of losing 1 util? Should a risk-averse individual undertake this project? (b) What if the payoff of the project were the same as above, except that the utility lost with a loss was 3 utils?

6. a. An investment has a 40% probability of providing a profit of $20,000, which would give an individual 4 utils of utility, and a 60% probability of losing

$10,000, which would result in a loss of 3 utils for the individual. (a) What is the expected value of the investment? (b) What is the expected utility of the investment? (c) Should a risk-averse individual undertake this investment? Why?

*7. An individual is considering two investment projects. Project A will return a zero profit if conditions are poor, a profit of $16 if conditions are good, and a profit of $49 if conditions are excellent. Project B will return a profit of $4 if conditions are poor, a profit of $9 if conditions are good, and a profit of $49 if conditions are excellent. The probability distribution of conditions are as follows:

Conditions:	Poor	Good	Excellent
Probability:	40%	50%	10%

a. Calculate the expected value of each project and identify the preferred project according to this criterion.

b. The individual's utility function for profit is equal to the square root of the profit. Calculate the expected utility of each project and identify the preferred project according to this criterion.

c. Is this individual risk averse, risk neutral, or risk seeking? Why?

8. An individual is considering two investment projects. Project A will return a zero profit if conditions are poor, a profit of $4 if conditions are good, and a profit of $8 if conditions are excellent. Project B will return a profit of $2 if conditions are poor, a profit of $3 if conditions are good, and a profit of $4 if conditions are excellent. The probability distribution of conditions are as follows:

Conditions:	Poor	Good	Excellent
Probability:	40%	50%	10%

a. Calculate the expected value of each project and identify the preferred project according to this criterion.

b. Assume that the individual's utility function for profit is $U(X) = X - 0.05X^2$. Calculate the expected utility of each project and identify the preferred project according to this criterion.

c. Is this individual risk averse, risk neutral, or risk seeking? Why?

9. Suppose that a risk averse individual's income is $80 per day in Figure 6.6. Explain why this individual would not buy a lottery ticket that would increase his or her income to $200 per day with a win.

10. Suppose that a risk–return indifference curve of individual A starts on the vertical axis at a rate of return of 10% and is positively sloped, while an indifference curve of individual B starts on the vertical axis at a rate of return of 6% and is also positively sloped but less steep than the indifference curve of individual A. Finally, assume that an indifference curve of individual C starts on the vertical axis at a rate of 5% and is horizontal. (a) Which individual is risk neutral? And who is risk averse? Why? (b) Of the two risk-averse individuals, which is the least risk averse? Why? (c) What does the fact that individual A's indifference curve starts on the vertical axis at the rate of return of 10% mean?

11. An individual owns a house worth $100,000 with a probability of 1% that it will burn down in any year, which would result in a total loss. The individual's risk premium is $1,200, and he can purchase fire insurance on the house for $100 above fair or actuarial value of the loss. (a) Would the individual purchase the insurance? Why? (b) Why would an insurance company be willing to provide such insurance?

*12. A U.S. firm imports $200,000 worth of EMU goods and agrees to pay in three months. The exchange rate is $1.00/€1 today and the three-month forward rate is $1.01/€1. Explain how the importer can hedge his foreign-exchange risk.

INTERNET SITE ADDRESSES

For a discussion of risk analysis, see:

http://en.wikipedia.org/wiki/Risk_analysis

http://www.sra.org/

http://www.palisade.com/risk/default.asp

http://www.blackwellpublishing.com/journal.asp?ref=0272-4332

For a discussion of the introduction of the new Coke as well as an analysis of what Coca-Cola is doing to meet its competition, see:

http://en.wikipedia.org/wiki/New_Coke

http://www.geocities.com/colacentury/

http://en.wikipedia.org/wiki/Coca-Cola

http://www.hoovers.com/the-coca-cola-company/—ID__10359—/free-co-factsheet.xhtml

The *Final Report of the National Gambling Impact Commission*, examining gambling in America, as well as other information on gambling are found at:

http://govinfo.library.unt.edu/ngisc/

http://en.wikipedia.org/wiki/Gambling

http://www.gambling.co.uk/

For reducing risks and uncertainty, see:

http://www.husdal.com/gis/flexibility.htm

http://web.mit.edu/rvalerdi/www/97.pdf

http://greenbook.treasury.gov.uk/annex04.htm

http://opim.wharton.upenn.edu/risk/downloads/01-15-HK.pdf

For behavioral economics, see:

http://en.wikipedia.org/wiki/Behavioral_economics

http://www.sfb504.uni-mannheim.de/glossary/behave.htm

http://www.harvardmagazine.com/on-line/030640.html

http://www.iies.su.se/nobel/papers/Encyclopedia%202.0.pdf

http://arielrubinstein.tau.ac.il/papers/behavioral-economics.pdf

For futures trading and hedging, see the Commodity Futures Trading Commission and the Chicago Mercantile Exchange Websites at:

http://www.cftc.gov

http://www.cme.com/

http://en.wikipedia.org/wiki/Chicago_Mercantile_Exchange

http://www.associatedcontent.com/article/323409/coping_with_risk_and_uncertainty_of.html

PART THREE

Production, Costs, and Competitive Markets

P art Three (Chapters 7–9) presents the theory of production, cost, and pricing in competitive markets. Chapter 7 examines production theory, or how firms combine resources or inputs to produce final commodities. These concepts are then utilized and extended in Chapter 8 to examine costs of production and to derive the short-run and the long-run cost curves of the firm. Finally, Chapter 9 brings together the theory of consumer behavior and demand (from Part Two) with the theory of production and costs (from Chapters 7 and 8) to analyze how price and output are determined under perfect competition. The chapter appendices present more advanced topics in the theory of production, cost, and pricing. The presentation of the theory is reinforced throughout with many real-world examples, while the "At the Frontier" sections present some new and important developments in production and cost theory and in the operation of perfectly competitive markets.

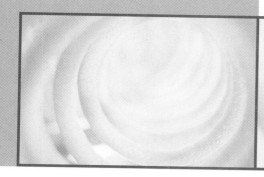

CHAPTER 7

Production Theory

After Studying This Chapter, You Should Be Able to:

- Know the reason for the existence of firms
- Describe how production takes place in the short run with only one variable input
- Describe the production process in the long run
- Know the meaning and reasons for constant, increasing, and decreasing returns to scale
- Know the meaning of technological progress, how it takes place, and its importance

---

In Part Two, we examined the theory of consumer behavior and demand. Our focus of attention was the consumer. In Part Three, we examine the theory of production, cost, and pricing in competitive markets. Here the focus is on the firm. This chapter examines the theory of production or how firms organize production; that is, we examine how firms combine resources or inputs to produce final commodities. Chapter 8 builds on the discussion and analyzes the costs of production of the firm. Then Chapter 9 brings together the theory of consumer behavior and demand with the theory of production and costs to analyze how price and output are determined under perfect competition.

This chapter begins with a discussion of the organization of production. We define the meaning of production, examine why firms exist, consider their aims, classify resources or inputs into various categories, and define the meaning of short-run and long-run production. From this, we go on to the theory of production when only one input is variable. This is accomplished by defining the total, the average, and the marginal product curve of the variable input. Production theory is subsequently extended to deal with two variable inputs by the introduction of isoquants.

From the theory of production where only one or two inputs are variable, we proceed to examine cases in which all inputs are variable. Here, we define the meaning of constant, increasing, and decreasing returns to scale, the conditions under which they arise, and their importance. Finally, we examine technological progress and international competitiveness.

The real-world examples included in this chapter highlight the importance and relevance of the theory of production, while the "At the Frontier" section discusses the new computer-aided revolution that is now sweeping America. The optional appendix examines the most used production function (the Cobb–Douglas) and its empirical estimation.

| 7.1 | **RELATING OUTPUTS TO INPUTS** |

In this section, we examine the organization of production and classify inputs into various categories. We begin by focusing on the meaning and organization of production, why firms exist, and the aim of firms. Then we classify inputs into various broad categories. This section serves as a general background for the theory of production presented in subsequent sections.

Organization of Production

Production The transformation of resources or inputs into outputs of goods and services.

Production refers to the transformation of resources into outputs of goods and services. For example, General Motors hires workers who use machinery in factories to transform steel, plastic, glass, rubber, and so on into automobiles. The output of a firm can either be a final commodity such as automobiles or an intermediate product such as steel (which is used in the production of automobiles and other goods). The output can also be a service rather than a good. Examples of services are education, medicine, banking, legal counsel, accounting work, communications, transportation, storage, wholesaling, and retailing. Production is a flow concept or has a time dimension. In other words, production refers to the rate of output over a given period of time. This is to be distinguished from the stock of a commodity or input, which refers to the quantity of the commodity (such as the number of automobiles) or input (such as the tons of steel) at hand or available at a particular point in time.

More than 80% of all goods and services consumed in the United States are produced by firms. The remainder is produced by the government and such nonprofit organizations as the Red Cross, private colleges, foundations, and so on. A **firm** is an organization that combines and organizes resources for the purpose of producing goods and services for sale at a profit. There are millions of firms in the United States. These include proprietorships (firms owned by one individual), partnerships (owned by two or more individuals), and corporations (owned by stockholders). The way the firm is organized is not of primary concern in the study of microeconomic theory; what the firm does is. Firms arise because it would be inefficient and costly for workers and for the owners of capital and

Firm An organization that combines and organizes resources for the purpose of producing goods and services for sale at a profit.

Concept Check
Why do firms exist?

Inputs The resources or factors of production used to produce goods and services.

Labor or human resources The different types of skilled and unskilled workers that can be used in the production of goods and services.

Capital or investment goods The machinery, factories, equipment, tools, inventories, irrigation, transportation, and communications networks that can be used to produce goods and services.

Land or natural resources The land, its fertility, mineral deposits, and forests that can be used to produce goods and services.

Entrepreneurship The introduction of new technologies and products to exploit perceived profit opportunities.

land to enter into and enforce contracts with one another to pool their resources for the purpose of producing goods and services.

Just as consumers seek to maximize utility or satisfaction, firms generally seek to maximize profits. Both consumers and firms can be regarded as maximizing entities. Profits refer to the revenue of the firm from the sale of the output after all costs have been deducted. Included in costs are not only the actual wages paid to hired workers and payments for purchasing other inputs, but also the income that the owner of the firm would earn by working for someone else and the return that he or she would receive from investing his or her capital in the best *alternative* use. For example, the owner of a delicatessen must include in his or her costs not only payments for the rental of the store, hired help, and for the purchase of the hams, cheeses, beers, milk, crackers, and so on in the store. He or she must also include as part of costs the foregone earnings of the money invested in the store as well as the earnings that he or she would receive by working for someone else in a similar capacity (e.g., as the manager of another delicatessen). The owner earns (economic) profits only if total revenue exceeds total costs (which include actual expenses and the alternatives foregone).

The profit-maximizing assumption provides the framework for analyzing the behavior of the firm in microeconomic theory. It is from this assumption that the behavior of the firm can be studied most fruitfully. This assumption has recently been challenged by the so-called "managerial theories of the firm," which postulate multiple goals for the firm. That is, after attaining "satisfactory" rather than maximum profits, the large modern corporation is said to seek to maintain or increase its market share, maximize sales or growth, maintain a large staff of executives and lavish offices, minimize uncertainty, create and maintain a good public image as a desirable member of the community and a good employer, and so on. However, because many of these goals can be regarded as indirect ways to earn and increase profits in the long run, we will retain the profit-maximizing assumption.

Classification of Inputs

Firms transform inputs into outputs. **Inputs,** resources, or factors of production are the means of producing the goods and services demanded by society. Inputs can be classified broadly into **labor or human resources** (including entrepreneurial talent), **capital or investment goods,** and **land or natural resources.** This threefold classification of inputs is only a convenient way to organize the discussion, however, and it does not convey the enormous variety of specific resources in each category. For example, labor includes clerks and assembly-line workers as well as accountants, teachers, engineers, doctors, and scientists. And we must consider the specific types of labor and other inputs required for the analysis of production of a particular firm or industry.[1]

Particularly important among inputs is **entrepreneurship,** which refers to the ability of some individuals to see opportunities to combine resources in new and more efficient ways to produce a particular commodity or to produce entirely new commodities. The motivation is the great profit possibilities that an entrepreneur may believe to exist. The entrepreneur either uses his or her resources to exploit these profit opportunities or,

---

[1] The reason is that different skills require varying training costs and wages to be supplied. Thus, to analyze the production process of a particular firm or industry, we must consider the *specific* types of labor and other inputs that are required. Yet, for general theoretical work, it is often convenient to deal with the broad input categories of labor, capital, and land.

more likely, attempts to convince other people with large sums of money to put some of that money at his or her disposal to introduce new production techniques or new products and share in the potential profits. There are many examples of entrepreneurship during the late 1970s and early 1980s in the field of microcomputers. This was a time when some young engineers and computer experts sought to combine new and more powerful chips (the basic memory component of computers) to produce cheaper or better microcomputers. Some of these entrepreneurs were successful and became rich overnight (e.g., the developers of the Apple Computers). Most, however, had to abandon their dreams after huge losses. In any event, entrepreneurs play a crucial role in modern economies. They are responsible for the introduction of new technology and new products, and for most of the growth of the economy as a whole.

Inputs can be further classified into fixed and variable. **Fixed inputs** are those that cannot be varied or can be varied only with excessive cost during the time period under consideration. Examples of fixed inputs are the firm's plant and specialized equipment. For example, it takes many years for General Motors to build a new automobile plant and introduce robots to perform many repetitive assembly-line tasks. **Variable inputs,** on the other hand, are those that can be varied easily and on short notice during the time period under consideration. Examples of these are raw materials and many types of workers, particularly those with low levels of skills. Thus, whether an input is fixed or variable depends on the time horizon being considered. The time period during which at least one input is fixed is called the **short run,** and the time period during which all inputs are variable is called the **long run.** Obviously, the length of time it takes to vary all inputs (i.e., to be in the long run), varies for firms in different industries. For a street vendor of apples, the long run may be a day. For an apple farmer, it is at least five years (this is how long it takes for newly planted trees to begin bearing fruit).

Fixed inputs The resources that cannot be varied or can be varied only with excessive cost during the time period under consideration.

Variable inputs The resources that can be varied easily and on short notice during the time period under consideration.

Short run The time period when at least one input is fixed.

Long run The time period when all inputs can be varied.

| 7.2 |

PRODUCTION WITH ONE VARIABLE INPUT

In this section, we present the theory of production when only one input is variable. Thus, we are dealing with the short run. We begin by defining the total, the average, and the marginal product of the variable input and examining their relationship graphically, and then we discuss the important law of diminishing returns. Production theory with more than one variable input is taken up in subsequent sections.

Production function
The unique relationship between inputs and outputs represented by a table, graph, or equation showing the maximum output of a commodity that can be produced per period of time with each set of inputs.

Total product (TP)
Total output.

Total, Average, and Marginal Product

A production function is a unique relationship between inputs and outputs. It can be represented by a table, a graph, or an equation and shows the maximum output of a commodity that can be produced per period of time with each set of inputs. Both output and inputs are measured in physical rather than monetary units. Technology is assumed to remain constant. A simple short-run production function is obtained by applying various amounts of labor to farm one acre of land and recording the resulting output or **total product (TP)** per period of time. This is illustrated by the first two columns of Table 7.1.

The first two columns of Table 7.1 provide a hypothetical production function for a farm using various quantities of labor (i.e., number of workers per year) to cultivate wheat on one acre of land (and using no other input). When no labor is used, total output

TABLE 7.1	Total, Average, and Marginal Product of Labor in the Cultivation of Wheat on One Acre of Land (Bushels Per Year)			
Labor (Workers per Year) (1)	Output or Total Product (2)	Average Product of Labor (3)	Marginal Product of Labor (4)
0	0	. . .	. . .
1	3	3	3
2	8	4	5
3	12	4	4
4	14	3.5	2
5	14	2.8	0
6	12	2	−2

or product is zero. With one unit of labor (1L), total product (TP) is 3 bushels of wheat per year. With 2L, TP = 8 bushels. With 3L, TP = 12 bushels, and so on.[2]

From the output or total product schedule we can derive the (per-unit) average and marginal product schedules for the input. Specifically, the total (physical) output or total product (TP) divided by the quantity of labor employed (L) equals the **average product** of labor (AP_L). On the other hand, the change in output or total product per-unit change in the quantity of labor employed is equal to the **marginal product** of labor (MP_L).[3]

Average product (AP) The total product divided by the quantity of the variable input used.

Marginal product (MP) The change in total product per unit change in the variable input used.

$$AP_L = \frac{TP}{L} \qquad [7.1]$$

and

$$MP_L = \frac{\Delta TP}{\Delta L} \qquad [7.2]$$

Column 3 in Table 7.1 gives the average product of labor (AP_L). This equals TP (column 2) divided by the quantity of labor used (column 1). Thus, with one unit of labor (1L), the AP_L equals 3/1 or 3 bushels. With 2L, AP_L is 8/2 or 4 bushels, and so on. Finally, column 4 reports the marginal product of labor (MP_L). This measures the change in total product per-unit change in labor. Since labor increases by one unit at a time in column 1, the MP_L in column 4 is obtained by subtracting successive quantities of the TP in column 2. For example, TP increases from 0 to 3 bushels when we add the first unit of labor. Thus, the MP_L is 3 bushels. For an increase in labor from 1L to 2L, TP increases from 3 to 8 bushels. Thus, the MP_L is 5 bushels. For an increase in labor from 2L to 3L, the MP_L is 4 bushels (12 − 8), and so on.

Plotting the total, average, and marginal product quantities of Table 7.1 gives the corresponding product curves shown in Figure 7.1. Note that TP grows to 14 bushels with 4L. It stays at 14 bushels with 5L and then declines to 12 bushels with 6L (see the top panel of Figure 7.1). The reason for this is that laborers get into each other's way and actually

---

[2] The reason for the decline in TP when six units of labor are used will be discussed shortly.

[3] In subsequent chapters, when the possibility arises of confusing the AP and the MP with their monetary values, they will be referred to as the average *physical* product and the marginal *physical* product.

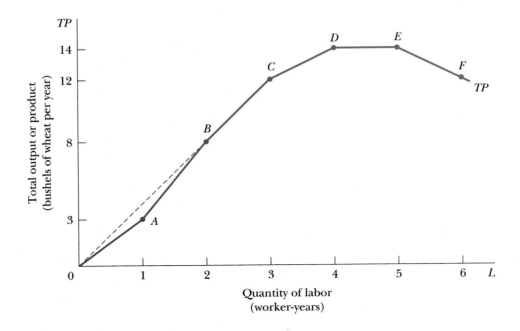

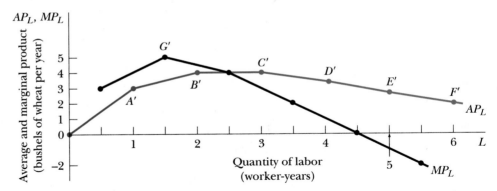

FIGURE 7.1 Total, Average, and Marginal Product Curves   The top panel shows the total output or total product (*TP*) curve. The AP_L at point *A* on the *TP* curve is 3 bushels (the slope of *OA*) and is plotted as *A'* in the bottom panel. The AP_L curve is the highest between 2*L* and 3*L*. The MP_L between *A* and *B* on the *TP* curve is 5 bushels (the slope of *AB*) and is plotted between 1 and 2 in the bottom panel. The MP_L is highest at 1.5*L*, $MP_L = AP_L$ at 2.5*L*, $MP_L = 0$ at 4.5*L*, and it is negative thereafter.

trample the wheat when the sixth worker is employed. In the bottom panel, we see that the AP_L curve rises to 4 bushels and then declines. Since the marginal product of labor refers to the change in total product per-unit change in labor used, each value of the MP_L is plotted halfway between the quantities of labor used. Thus, the MP_L of 3 bushels, which results from increasing labor from 0*L* to 1*L*, is plotted at 0.5*L*; the MP_L of 5 bushels, which results from increasing labor from 1*L* to 2*L*, is plotted at 1.5*L*, and so on. The MP_L curve rises to 5 bushels at 1.5*L* and then declines. Past 4.5*L*, the MP_L becomes negative.

The Geometry of Average and Marginal Product Curves

The shape of the average and marginal product of labor curves is determined by the shape of the corresponding total product curve. The AP_L at any point on the TP curve is equal to the slope of the straight line drawn from the origin to that point on the TP curve. Thus, the AP_L at point A on the TP curve in the top panel of Figure 7.1 is equal to the slope of $0A$. This equals 3/1 or 3 bushels and is plotted directly below A, as point A', in the bottom panel of Figure 7.1. Similarly, the AP_L at point B on the TP curve is equal to the slope of dashed line $0B$. This equals 8/2 or 4 bushels and is plotted as point B' in the bottom panel. At point C, the AP_L is again equal to 4. This is the highest AP_L. Past point C, the AP_L declines but remains positive as long as the TP is positive.

The MP_L between any two points on the TP curve is equal to the slope of the TP between the two points. Thus, the MP_L between the origin and point A on the TP curve in the top panel of Figure 7.1 is equal to the slope of $0A$. This is equal to 3 bushels and is plotted halfway between $0L$ and $1L$ (i.e., at 0.5L) in the bottom panel of Figure 7.1. Similarly, the MP_L between points A and B on the TP curve is equal to the slope of AB. This is equal to 5 (the highest MP_L) and is plotted as point G' at 1.5L in the bottom panel. The MP_L between B and C on the TP curve is equal to the slope of BC. This equals 4 and is the same as the highest AP_L (the slope of $0B$ and $0C$). Between points D and E, TP remains unchanged and the $MP_L = 0$. Past point E, TP falls and MP_L becomes negative.

We have drawn the curves in Figure 7.1 under the assumption that labor is used in whole units. If this were not the case and labor time were infinitesimally divisible, we would have the smooth TP, AP_L, and MP_L curves shown in Figure 7.2. In this figure, the AP_L (given, as before, by the slope of a ray from the origin to the TP curve) rises up to point H on the TP curve in the top panel and then declines. Thus, the AP_L curve in the bottom panel rises up to point H' and declines thereafter (but remains positive as long as TP is positive). On the other hand, the MP_L at any point on the TP curve is equal to the slope of the tangent to the TP curve at that point. The slope of the TP curve rises up to point G (the point of inflection) and then declines. Thus, the MP_L curve in the bottom panel rises up to point G' and declines thereafter. The MP_L is zero at point I' directly below point I, where the TP is highest or has zero slope, and it becomes negative when TP begins to decline.[4]

Note that the MP_L curve reaches its maximum point before the AP_L curve. Furthermore, as long as the AP_L curve is rising, the MP_L curve is above it. When the AP_L curve is falling, the MP_L curve is below it, and when the AP_L curve is highest, the MP_L intersects the AP_L curve. The reason for this is that for the AP_L to rise, the MP_L must be greater than the average to pull the average up. For the AP_L to fall, the MP_L must be lower than the average to pull the average down. For the average product to be at a maximum (i.e., neither rising nor falling), the marginal product must be equal to the average (the slope of line $0H$). For example, for a student to increase his or her cumulative average test score, he or she must receive a grade on the next (marginal) test that exceeds his or her average. With a lower grade on the next test, the student's cumulative average will fall. If the grade on the next test equals the previous average, the cumulative average will remain unchanged.

✓ Concept Check
Does the AP curve rise only as long as the MP curve rises?

---

[4] Note that the TP curve in Figure 7.2 has an initial portion over which it faces up (so that the MP_L increases). That is, up to point G, labor is used so sparsely on one acre of land that the MP_L increases as more labor is employed. This is usual but not always true. That is, in some cases, the TP curve faces down from the origin (so that MP_L falls from the very start). An example of this is discussed in the appendix to this chapter.

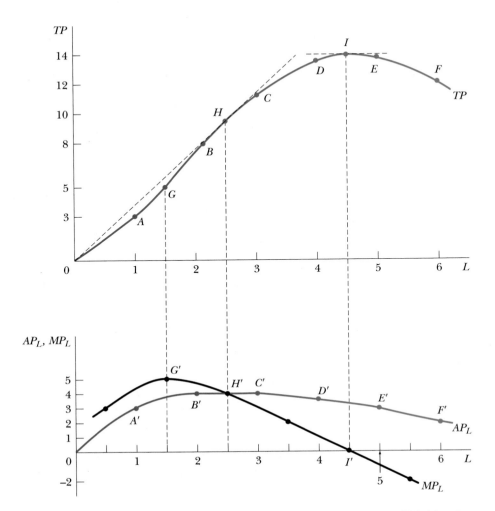

FIGURE 7.2   Geometry of Total, Average, and Marginal Product Curves   With labor time infinitesimally divisible, we have smooth TP, AP_L, and MP_L curves. The AP_L (given by the slope of the line from the origin to a point on the TP curve) rises up to point H' and declines thereafter (but remains positive as long as TP is positive). The MP_L (given by the slope of the tangent to the TP curve) rises up to point G', becomes zero at I', and is negative thereafter. When the AP_L curve rises, the MP_L is above it; when the AP_L falls, the MP_L is below it; and when AP_L is highest, $MP_L = AP_L$.

The Law of Diminishing Returns

Law of diminishing returns After a point, the marginal product of the variable input declines.

The decline in the MP_L curve in Figures 7.1 and 7.2 is a reflection of the **law of diminishing returns.** This is an empirical generalization or a physical law, not a proposition of economics. It postulates that as more units of a variable input are used with a fixed amount of other inputs, after a point, a smaller and smaller return will accrue to each additional unit of the variable input. In other words, the marginal (physical) product of the variable input eventually declines. This occurs because each additional unit of the variable input has less and less of the fixed inputs with which to work.

In Figure 7.2, the law of diminishing returns for labor begins to operate past point G' (i.e., when more than $1.5L$ is applied to one acre of land). Further additions of labor will eventually lead to zero and then to negative MP_L. Note that to observe the law of diminishing returns, at least one input (here, land) must be held constant. Technology is also assumed to remain unchanged. It should also be noted that when less than $1.5L$ is employed, labor is used too sparsely in the cultivation of one acre of land and the MP_L rises. Had land been kept constant at two acres instead of one, the TP, AP_L, and MP_L curves would retain their general shape but would all be higher, since each unit of labor would have more land to work with (see Section 7.3). Example 7–1 discusses the most famous historical application of the law of diminishing returns.

EXAMPLE 7–1

Economics—The Dismal Science Because of Diminishing Returns

✓ Concept Check
Has Malthus's prediction been correct? Why?

In the early nineteenth century, Thomas Malthus (in his *Essay on the Principles of Population,* 1798) and other classical economists predicted that population growth in the face of fixed stocks of land and other nonhuman resources could doom humanity to a subsistence standard of living. That is, rapid population growth could reduce the average and the marginal product of labor sufficiently to keep people always near starvation. This gloomy prediction earned for economics the label of the "dismal science."

These predictions have not proved correct, especially for the United States and other industrial nations of the world where standards of living are much higher than they were a century or two ago. The reasons for the sharply increased standard of living are as follows: (1) The quantities of capital, land, and minerals used in production have vastly increased since the beginning of the nineteenth century; (2) population growth has slowed down considerably in the industrial nations; and (3) most importantly, very significant improvements in technology have greatly increased productivity.

Contrary to Malthus's dismal predictions, standards of living have in fact increased over the past century throughout most of the world. Malthus inappropriately applied a short-run law (the law of diminishing returns) to the long run (when technology can improve dramatically) and came up with a spectacularly wrong prediction! As Table 7.2 shows, food production per capita has increased during the 1980s and

TABLE 7.2	Index of Food Production per Capita in Major Developing-Country Groups in 1990 and in 2000 (1978–1981 = 100)	
Developing-Country Groups	Index in 1990	Index in 2000
East Asia and the Pacific (China)	127(133)	160(215)
South Asia (India)	116(119)	146(124)
Latin America (Brazil)	106(115)	118(149)
Middle East and North Africa (Egypt)	101(118)	107(151)
Sub-Saharan Africa (Ethiopia)	94(84)	94(74)

Source: World Bank and Food and Agriculture Organization, 2002.

1990s in all major developing-country groups (with the exception of sub-Saharan Africa) as a result of new high-yielding and disease-resistant grains, better fertilizer, more irrigation, and so on. The reduction in food production per capita in sub-Saharan Africa was due to internal strife, wars, and droughts. Concern with climate change and the recent rapid increase in the world demand and price of food and raw materials, however, is once again raising the specter of Malthus.

Sources: "Food and the Specter of Malthus," *Financial Times*, February 27, 2008, p. 11; "New Limits to Growth Revive Malthusian Fears, *Wall Street Journal*, March 24, 2008, p. A1; and "Malthus Redux: Is Doomsday upon Us, Again," *New York Times*, June 15, 2008, p. 3.

7.3 PRODUCTION WITH TWO VARIABLE INPUTS

In this section we examine production theory with two variable inputs by introducing isoquants. We also show how to derive total product curves from an isoquant map, thereby highlighting the relationship between production with one and two variable inputs. We then examine the shape of isoquants in Section 7.4.

What Do Isoquants Show?

Isoquant A curve showing the various combinations of two inputs that can be used to produce a specific level of output.

An **isoquant** shows the various combinations of two inputs (say, labor and capital) that can be used to produce a specific level of output. A higher isoquant refers to a larger output, whereas a lower isoquant refers to a smaller output. If the two variable inputs (labor and capital) are the only inputs used in production, we are in the long run. If the two variable inputs are used with other fixed inputs (say, land), we would still be in the short run.

Figure 7.3 gives a hypothetical production function, which shows the outputs (the $Q's$) that can be produced with various combinations of labor (L) and capital (K) per time period. For example, the left panel of the figure shows that 12 units of output (i.e., $12Q$) can be produced with 1 unit of labor (i.e., $1L$) and 5 units of capital (i.e., $5K$) or with $1L$ and $4K$.[5] The left panel also shows that $12Q$ can also be produced with $3L$ and $1K$ or with $6L$ and $1K$ per time period. On the other hand, the figure indicates that 26 units of output ($26Q$) could be produced with $2L$ and $5K$, $2L$ and $4K$, $3L$ and $2K$, and $6L$ and $2K$. From the figure, we can also determine the various combinations of L and K to produce $34Q$ and $38Q$. Note that to produce a greater output per time period, more labor, more capital, or both more labor and more capital are required. For visual aid, equal levels of output are joined together by a curve in the body of the left panel of Figure 7.3

Plotting the various combinations of labor and capital that can be used to produce 12, 26, 34, and 38 units of output per time period gives the isoquant for each of these levels of output shown in the right panel of Figure 7.3. The figure shows that 12 units of output (the lowest isoquant shown) can be produced with 1 unit of labor ($1L$) and 5 units of capital ($5K$). This defines point J. Twelve units of output can also be produced with $1L$ and

---
[5] Of course, since inputs are not free, a firm would prefer to produce $12Q$ with $1L$ and $4K$ rather than with $1L$ and $5K$.

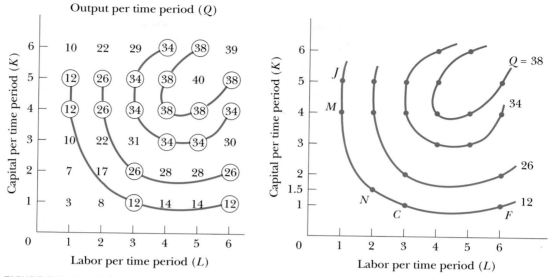

FIGURE 7.3 **Production Function with Two Variable Inputs: Isoquants** The isoquants in the right panel are obtained from the data in the left panel. The lowest isoquant shows that 12 units of output can be produced with 1L and 5K (point J), 1L and 4K (point M), 2L and 1.5K (point N), 3L and 1K (point C), or 6L and 1K (point F). Higher isoquants refer to higher levels of output.

4K (point M), 3L and 1K (point C), and 6L and 1K (point F). Joining these points with a smooth curve, we obtain the isoquant for 12 units of output. Similarly, by plotting the various combinations of labor and capital that can be used to produce 26 units of output (2L and 5K, 2L and 4K, 3L and 2K, and 6L and 2K) and joining the resulting points by a smooth curve we get the isoquant for 26Q in the right panel of Figure 7.3. The isoquants for 34Q and 38Q in the figure can be similarly derived from the data in Figure 7.3.

Derivation of Total Product Curves from the Isoquant Map

By drawing a horizontal line across an isoquant map at the level at which the input measured along the vertical axis is fixed, we can generate the total product curve for the variable input measured along the horizontal axis. For example, by starting with the isoquant map in the right panel of Figure 7.3 and keeping capital constant at $K = 4$, we can derive the total product curve of labor for $K = 4$. This corresponds to the higher of the two TP curves in the bottom panel of Figure 7.4. Thus, from point M (1L and 4K) on the isoquant for 12Q in the top panel, we obtain point M' on the TP curve for $K = 4$ in the bottom panel. From point V (2L and 4K) on the isoquant for 26Q in the top panel, we derive point V' on the TP curve for $K = 4$ in the bottom panel, and so on. This is equivalent to reading across the row for $K = 4$ in the left panel of Figure 7.3.

With capital held constant at the lower level of $K = 1$, we generate the lower total product curve in the bottom panel of Figure 7.4. This is equivalent to reading across the row for $K = 1$ in the left panel of Figure 7.3. Note that when capital is held constant at a smaller level, the TP curve for labor is lower because each unit of labor has less capital with which to work.

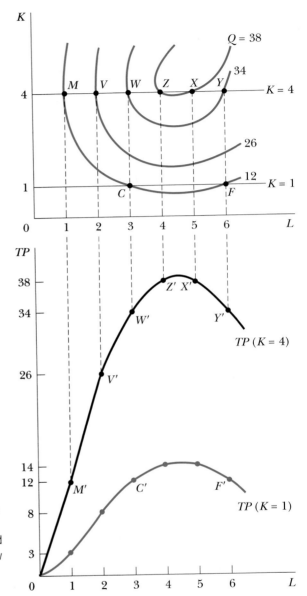

FIGURE 7.4   Derivation of Total Product Curves from the Isoquant Map   By keeping capital constant at $K = 4$ in the top panel, we can derive the higher of the two total product curves in the bottom panel. Thus, from point M (1L and 4K) on the isoquant for 12Q in the top panel, we obtain point M' on the TP curve for $K = 4$ in the bottom panel. From point V (2L and 4K) in the top panel we derive point V' in the bottom panel, and so on. With capital constant at $K = 1$ (i.e., reading across the row for $K = 1$ in the left panel of Figure 7.3), we get the lower total product curve in the bottom panel.

✓ Concept Check

Can we derive the total product curve of an input from the isoquant map if one input is held fixed?

If, instead, we held the quantity of labor constant and changed the quantity of capital used, we would derive the TP curve for capital. This can be obtained by drawing a vertical line on the isoquant map at the level at which labor is held constant. This is equivalent to reading up to the appropriate column in the left panel of Figure 7.3. The higher the level at which labor is held constant, the higher is the total product curve of capital. From a given total product curve, we could then derive the corresponding average and marginal product curves, as shown in the bottom panel of Figure 7.2. Thus, Figure 7.3 could provide information about the long run as well as the short run, depending on whether labor and capital are the only two inputs and both are variable (the long run), or whether labor and capital are used with other fixed inputs (such as land), or either labor or capital is fixed (the short run).

THE SHAPE OF ISOQUANTS

In this section we examine the characteristics of isoquants, define the economic region of production, and consider the special cases where commodities can only be produced with fixed input combinations. We will see that the shape of isoquants plays as important a role in production theory as the shape of indifference curves plays in consumption theory.

Characteristics of Isoquants[6]

The characteristics of isoquants are crucial for understanding production theory with two variable inputs. Isoquants are similar to indifference curves. However, whereas an indifference curve shows the various combinations of two commodities that provide the consumer equal satisfaction (measured ordinally), an isoquant shows the various combinations of two inputs that give the same level of output (measured cardinally, or in actual units of the commodity).[7]

Isoquants have the same general characteristics of indifference curves. That is, they are negatively sloped in the economically relevant range, are convex to the origin, and do not intersect. These properties are shown in Figure 7.5.[8] The nonintersecting property of isoquants can easily be explained. Intersecting isoquants would mean that two different levels of output of the same commodity could be produced with the identical input combination (i.e., at the point where the isoquants intersect). This is impossible under our assumption that the most efficient production techniques are always used.

Isoquants are negatively sloped in the economically relevant range. This means that if the firm wants to reduce the quantity of capital used in production, it must increase the quantity of labor in order to continue to produce the same level of output (i.e., remain on

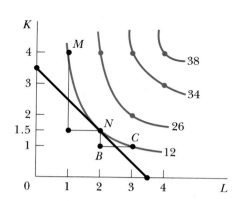

FIGURE 7.5   Marginal Rate of Technical Substitution (*MRTS*)   Between point *M* and point *N* on the isoquant for 12 units of output (12*Q*), the marginal rate of technical substitution of labor for capital (*MRTS_{LK}*) equals 2.5. Between point *N* and point *C*, $MRTS_{LK} = 1/2$. At point *N*, $MRTS_{LK} = 1$ (the absolute slope of the tangent to the isoquant at point *N*).

---

[6] Compare Figure 7.5 with Figure 3.2.

[7] The positively sloped portions of the isoquants have been omitted in Figure 7.5 because they are irrelevant. The reason for this is discussed in the next subsection.

[8] The reasoning is exactly the opposite as for the decline in MP_L.

the same isoquant). For example, starting at point M (1L and 4K) on the isoquant for 12 units of output (12Q), the firm could reduce the quantity of capital by 2.5K by adding 1L in production and reach point N on the same isoquant (see Figure 7.5). Thus, the average slope of the isoquant between points M and N is $-2.5K/1L$. The average slope between N and C is $-1/2$.

The absolute value of the slope of the isoquant is called the **marginal rate of technical substitution (MRTS)**. This is analogous to the marginal rate of substitution of one good for another in consumption, which is given by the absolute value of the slope of an indifference curve. For a downward movement along an isoquant, the marginal rate of technical substitution of labor for capital ($MRTS_{LK}$) is given by $-\Delta K/\Delta L$. It measures the amount of capital that the firm can give up by using one additional unit of labor and still remain on the same isoquant. Because of the reduction in K, $MRTS_{LK}$ is negative. However, we multiply by -1 and express $MRTS_{LK}$ as a positive value. Thus, the average $MRTS_{LK}$ between points M and N on the isoquant for 12Q is 2.5. Similarly, the average $MRTS_{LK}$ between points N and C is $1/2$. The $MRTS_{LK}$ at any point on an isoquant is given by the absolute value of the slope of the isoquant at that point. Thus, the $MRTS_{LK}$ at point N is 1 (the absolute value of the slope of the tangent to the isoquant at point N; see Figure 7.5).

The $MRTS_{LK}$ is also equal to MP_L/MP_K. To prove this, we begin by remembering that all points on an isoquant refer to the same level of output. Thus, for a movement down a given isoquant, the gain in output from using more labor must be equal to the loss in output from using less capital. Specifically, the increase in the quantity of labor used (ΔL) times the marginal product of labor (MP_L) must equal the reduction in the amount of capital used (ΔK) times the marginal product of capital (MP_K). That is,

$$(\Delta L)(MP_L) = -(\Delta K)(MP_K) \qquad [7.3]$$

✔ Concept Check

Is the $MRTS$ of L for K equal to the $MRTS$ of K for L?

so that

$$\frac{MP_L}{MP_K} = -\frac{\Delta K}{\Delta L} = MRTS_{LK} \qquad [7.4]$$

Thus, $MRTS_{LK}$ is equal to the absolute value of the slope of the isoquant and to the ratio of the marginal productivities.

Although we know that the absolute value of the slope of the isoquant or $MRTS_{LK}$ equals the ratio of MP_L to MP_K, we cannot infer from that the actual value of MP_L and MP_K. For example, at point N on the isoquant for 12Q in Figure 7.5, we know that $MRTS_{LK} = -\Delta K/\Delta L = MP_L/MP_K = 1$ (so that $MP_L = MP_K$), but we do not know what the individual values of MP_L and MP_K are. Similarly, we know that between points N and C on the isoquant for 12Q, $MRTS_{LK} = -\Delta K/\Delta L = MP_L/MP_K = 1/2$ (so that $MP_L = 1/2MP_K$), but we do not know what the actual value of either marginal product is. These values can, however, be calculated from Figure 7.5.

For example, we can find the value of MP_L and MP_K between points N and C on the isoquant for 12Q in Figure 7.5 by comparing point N (2L, 1.5K) and point C (3L, 1K) referring to 12Q, to point B (2L, 1K) referring to 8Q (see the left panel of Figure 7.3). The rightward movement from point B to point C keeps capital constant at 1K and increases labor by 1L, and it results in an increase of output of 4Q (from 8Q to 12Q). Thus, $MP_L = 4$. On the other hand, the upward movement from point B to point N keeps labor constant at 2L and increases capital by $1/2K$, and it also results in an increase in output of 4Q. Thus, the $MP_K = 8$. With $MP_L = 4$ and $MP_K = 8$, $MP_L/MP_K = 4/8 = 1/2 = MRTS_{LK}$, as found earlier.

Within the economically relevant range, isoquants are not only negatively sloped but also convex to the origin. That is, as we move down along an isoquant, the absolute value of its slope or $MRTS_{LK}$ declines and the isoquant is convex (see Figure 7.5). The reason for this can best be explained by separating the movement down along an isoquant (say, from point N to point C along the isoquant for $12Q$ in Figure 7.5) into its two components: the movement to the right (from point B to point C) and the movement downward (from point N to point B). The increase in L with constant K (the movement from point B to point C) will lead to a decline in the MP_L because of diminishing returns. In addition, the reduction in K (the movement from point N to point B), by itself, will cause the entire MP_L curve to shift down. Thus, MP_L declines for both reasons. On the other hand, by using less K and more L, the MP_K rises.[9] With the MP_L declining and the MP_K rising as we move down along an isoquant, the $MRTS_{LK} = MP_L/MP_K$ will fall and the isoquant is convex to the origin.

Economic Region of Production

The firm would not operate on the positively sloped portion of an isoquant because it could produce the same level of output with less capital and less labor. For example, the firm would not produce $34Q$ at point P in Figure 7.6 because it could produce $34Q$ by using the smaller quantity of labor and capital indicated by point R. Similarly, the firm would not produce $34Q$ at point S because it could produce $34Q$ at point T with less L and K. Since inputs are not free, the firm would not want to produce in the positively sloped range of isoquants.

Ridge lines separate the relevant (i.e., the negatively sloped) from the irrelevant (or the positively sloped) portions of the isoquants. In Figure 7.6, ridge line $0RU$ joins points on the various isoquants where the isoquants have zero slope (and thus zero $MRTS_{LK}$).

Concept Check Why is an isoquant convex in its relevant range?

Ridge lines The lines that separate the relevant (i.e., the negatively sloped) from the irrelevant (or the positively sloped) portions of the isoquants.

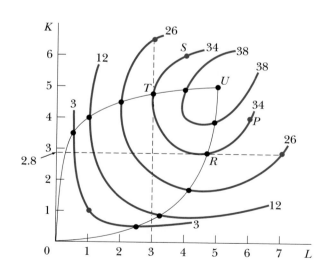

FIGURE 7.6 Economic Region of Production Isoquants are positively sloped to the right of ridge line $0RU$ and to the left of or above ridge line $0TU$. The firm would never produce at a point such as P or S in the positively sloped portion of the isoquant because it could produce the same output with less of both inputs.

[9] For a mathematical presentation of isoquants and their characteristics, see Section A.8 of the Mathematical Appendix at the end of the book.

The isoquants are negatively sloped to the left of this ridge line and positively sloped to the right. This means that starting, for example, at point R on the isoquant for $34Q$, if the firm used more labor it would also have to use more capital to remain on the same isoquant (compare point P to point R on the isoquant for $34Q$). Starting from point R, if the firm used more labor with the same amount of capital, the level of output would fall (i.e., the firm would fall back to a lower isoquant; see the dashed horizontal line at $K = 2.8$ in Figure 7.6). The same is true at all other points on ridge line $0RU$. Therefore, the MP_L must be negative to the right of this ridge line. Note that points on ridge line $0RU$ specify the minimum quantity of capital required to produce the levels of output indicated by the various isoquants. Note also that at all points on this ridge line, $MRTS_{LK} = MP_L/MP_K = 0/MP_K = 0$.

On the other hand, ridge line $0TU$ joins points where the isoquants have infinite slope (and thus infinite $MRTS_{LK}$). The isoquants are negatively sloped to the right of this ridge line and positively sloped to the left. This means that starting, for example, at point T on the isoquant for $34Q$, if the firm used more capital it would also have to use more labor to remain on the same isoquant (compare point S to point T on the isoquant for $34Q$). Starting at point T, if the firm used more capital with the same quantity of labor, the level of output would fall (i.e., the firm would fall back to a lower isoquant; see the dashed vertical line at $L = 3$ in Figure 7.6). The same is true at all other points on ridge line $0TU$. Therefore, the MP_K must be negative to the left of or above this ridge line. Note that points on ridge line $0TU$ indicate the minimum quantity of labor required to produce the levels of output indicated by the various isoquants. Note also that at all points on this ridge line, $MRTS_{LK} = MP_L/MP_K = MP_L/0 = $ infinity.

Thus, we conclude that the negatively sloped portion of the isoquants within the ridge lines represents the economic region of production, where the MP_L and the MP_K are both positive but declining. Producers will never want to operate outside this region. As a result, from this point on, whenever we will draw isoquants, we will usually show only their negatively sloped portion. Indeed, some special types of production functions have isoquants without positively sloped portions.

Fixed-Proportions Production Functions

So far, we have drawn isoquants as smooth curves, indicating that there are many different (really, an infinite number of) input combinations that can be used to produce any output level. There are cases, however, where inputs can only be combined in fixed proportions in production. In such cases, there would be no possibility of input substitution in production and the isoquants would be at a right angle, or L-shaped.

For example, Figure 7.7 shows that 10 units of output ($10Q$) can only be produced at point A with $2L$ and $1K$. Employing more labor will not change output since $MP_L = 0$ (the horizontal portion of the isoquant). Similarly, using more capital will not change output since $MP_K = 0$ (the vertical portion of the isoquant). Here, there is no possibility of substituting L for K in production and the $MRTS_{LK} = 0$. Production would only take place at the constant capital-labor ratio of $K/L = 1/2$. A larger output can only be produced by increasing both labor and capital in the same proportion. For example, $20Q$ can be produced at point B by using $4L$ and $2K$ at the constant K/L ratio of $1/2$. Similarly, $30Q$ can only be produced at point C with $6L$ and $3K$ and $K/L = 1/2$.

In the real world, some substitution of inputs in production is usually possible. The degree to which this is possible can be gathered from the curvature of the isoquants.

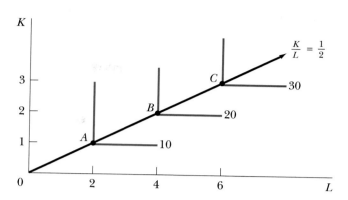

FIGURE 7.7   Fixed-Proportions Production Function
When isoquants are at right angles, or L-shaped, inputs must be used in fixed proportions in production. Thus, 10 units of output (10Q) can only be produced at point A with 2L and 1K. Using more labor or capital would not change output; 20Q can only be produced with 4L and 2K (point B), and 30Q only with 6L and 3K (point C). Thus, output can only be produced at the constant or fixed capital–labor ratio or proportion of $K/L = 1/2$.

In general, the smaller the curvature of the isoquants, the more easily inputs can be substituted for each other in production. On the other hand, the greater the curvature (i.e., the closer are isoquants to right angles, or L-shape), the more difficult is substitution. Being able to easily substitute inputs in production is extremely important in the real world. For example, if petroleum had good substitutes, users could easily have switched to alternative energy sources when petroleum prices rose sharply in the fall of 1973. Their energy bill would then not have risen very much. As it was, good substitutes were not readily available (certainly not in the short run), and so most energy users faced sharply higher energy costs. As Example 7–2 shows, gasoline and driving time can also be substituted for each other, and this can be shown by isoquants.

EXAMPLE 7–2

Trading Traveling Time for Gasoline Consumption on the Nation's Highways

Higher automobile speed reduces the driving time needed to cover a given distance but reduces gas mileage and thus increases gasoline consumption. It has been estimated that reducing the speed limit on the nation's highways from 65 to 55 mph reduced gasoline consumption by about 3%. The trade-off between traveling time and gasoline consumption for a 600-mile trip can be represented by the isoquant shown in Figure 7.8. In the figure, the vertical axis measures hours of traveling time, while the horizontal axis measures gallons of gasoline consumed. Gasoline and travel time are thus the inputs into the production of automobile transportation.

The isoquant in Figure 7.8 shows that at 50 mph, the 600 miles can be covered in 12 hours and with 16 gallons of gasoline, at 37.5 miles per gallon (point A). At 60 mph, the 600 miles can be covered in 10 hours and with 20 gallons of gasoline, at 30 miles per gallon (point B). Driving at 60 mph saves 2 hours of travel time (one scarce resource) but increases gasoline consumption by 4 gallons (another scarce resource). Thus, the trade-off or marginal rate of technical substitution (MRTS) of gasoline for travel time between point A and point B on the isoquant in Figure 7.8 is 1/2. At 66.7 mph (assuming that the speed limit is above it), the 600 miles can be covered in 9 hours with 30 gallons of gasoline, at 20 miles per gallon (point C). Thus, the MRTS of gasoline for travel time between points B and C is 1/10.

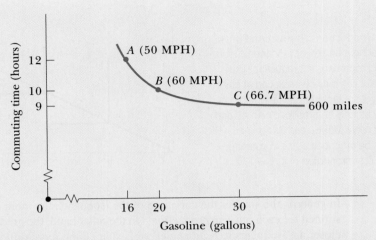

FIGURE 7.8   Speed Limit and Gasoline Consumption   Isoquant *ABC* shows the trade-off between traveling time and gasoline consumption. At 50 MPH, 600 miles can be covered in 12 hours and with 16 gallons of gasoline (point *A*). At 60 MPH, the 600 miles can be covered in 10 hours and with 20 gallons of gasoline (point *B*). At 66.7 MPH, 600 miles can be covered in 9 hours with 30 gallons (point *C*).

In order to determine the most economical (i.e., the least cost) combination of gasoline and travel time to cover the 600 miles, we need to know the price of gasoline and the value of time to the individual. This is addressed in the next chapter, where we take up costs of production. If the price of gasoline were to increase, the individual would want to substitute traveling time for gasoline (i.e., drive at a lower speed so as to increase gas mileage and save gasoline) to minimize the cost of traveling the 600 miles (see Example 8–3). Note that there is also a trade-off between travel speed and safety (i.e., lower speeds increase travel time but save lives).

Sources: Charles A. Lave, "Speeding, Coordination, and the 55-mph Limit," *American Economic Review,* December 1985, pp. 1159–1164; "Death Rate on U.S. Roads Reported at a Record Low," *New York Times,* October 27, 1998, p. 16; "How Much Is Your Times Worth?" *New York Times,* February 26, 2003, p. D1; "At $2 a Gallon, Gas Is Still Worth Guzzling," *New York Times,* May 16, 2004, Sect. 4, p. 14; "Politics Is Forcing Detroit to Support New Rules on Fuel," *New York Times,* June 20, 2007, p. A1; and "Can U.S. Adopt Europe's Fuel-Efficient Cars?" *Wall Street Journal,* June 26, 2007, p. B1.

| **7.5** | CONSTANT, INCREASING, AND DECREASING RETURNS TO SCALE |

Constant returns to scale Output changes in the same proportion as inputs.

Increasing returns to scale Output changes by a larger proportion than inputs.

The word "scale" refers to the long-run situation where all inputs are changed in the same proportion. The result might be constant, increasing, or decreasing returns. **Constant returns to scale** refers to the situation where output changes by the *same* proportion as inputs. For example, if all inputs are increased by 10%, output also rises by 10%. If all inputs are doubled, output also doubles. **Increasing returns to scale** refers to the case where output changes by a *larger* proportion than inputs. For example, if all inputs are

Decreasing returns to scale Output changes by a smaller proportion than inputs.

increased by 10%, output increases by more than 10%. If all inputs are doubled, output more than doubles. Finally, with **decreasing returns to scale,** output changes by a *smaller* proportion than inputs. Thus, increasing all inputs by 10% increases output by less than 10%, and doubling all inputs, less than doubles output.

Constant, increasing, and decreasing returns to scale can be shown by the spacing of the isoquants in Figure 7.9. The left panel shows constant returns to scale. Here, doubling inputs from $3L$ and $3K$ to $6L$ and $6K$ doubles output from 100 (point A along ray $0D$) to 200 (point B). Tripling inputs from $3L$ and $3K$ to $9L$ and $9K$ triples output from 100 (point A) to 300 (point C). Thus, $0A = AB = BC$ along ray $0D$ and we have constant returns to scale. The middle panel shows increasing returns to scale. Here, output can be doubled or tripled by less than doubling or tripling the quantity of inputs. Thus, $0A > AB > BC$ along ray $0D$ and the isoquants are compressed closer together. Finally, the right panel shows decreasing returns to scale. In this case, in order to double and triple output we must more than double and triple the quantity of inputs. Thus, $0A < AB < BC$ and the isoquants move farther and farther apart. Note that in all three panels, the capital–labor ratio remains constant at $K/L = 1$ along ray $0D$.

Constant returns to scale make sense. We would expect two similar workers using identical machines to produce twice as much output as one worker using one machine. Similarly, we would expect the output of two identical plants employing an equal number of workers of equal skill to produce double the output of a single plant. Nevertheless, increasing and decreasing returns to scale are also possible.

Increasing returns to scale arise because, as the scale of operation increases, a greater division of labor and specialization can take place and more specialized and productive machinery can be used. With a large scale of operation, each worker can be assigned to perform only one repetitive task rather than numerous ones. Workers become more proficient in the performance of the single task and avoid the time lost in moving from one machine to another. The result is higher productivity and increasing returns to scale. At higher scales of operation, more specialized and productive machinery can also be used. For example, using a conveyor belt to unload a small truck may not be justified, but it greatly increases efficiency in unloading a whole train or ship. In addition, some physical properties of equipment and machinery also lead to increasing returns to scale. Thus, doubling the diameter of a pipeline more than doubles the flow, doubling the weight of a ship more than doubles its capacity to transport cargo, and so on. Firms also need fewer supervisors, fewer spare parts, and smaller inventories per unit of output as the scale of operation increases.

✓ **Concept Check**

Why do decreasing returns to scale occur?

Decreasing returns to scale arise primarily because, as the scale of operation increases, it becomes ever more difficult to manage the firm effectively and coordinate the various operations and divisions of the firm. The channels of communication become more complex, and the number of meetings, the paper work, and telephone bills increase more than proportionately to the increase in the scale of operation. All of this makes it increasingly difficult to ensure that the managers' directives and guidelines are properly carried out. Thus, efficiency decreases (this is sometimes referred to as "managerial diseconomies"). Decreasing returns to scale must be clearly distinguished from diminishing returns. *Decreasing returns to scale* refers to the long-run situation when all inputs are variable. On the other hand, *diminishing returns* refers to the short-run situation where at least one input is fixed. Diminishing returns in the short run is consistent with constant, increasing, or decreasing returns to scale in the long run.

In the real world, the forces for increasing and decreasing returns to scale often operate side by side. The forces for increasing returns to scale usually prevail at small scales

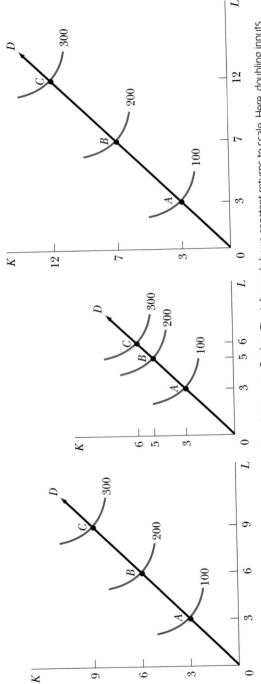

FIGURE 7.9 Constant, Increasing, and Decreasing Returns to Scale The left panel shows constant returns to scale. Here, doubling inputs from 3L and 3K to 6L and 6K doubles output from 100 (point A along ray OD) to 200 (point B). Tripling inputs to 9L and 9K triples output to 300 (point C). Thus, OA = AB = BC along ray OD. The middle panel shows increasing returns to scale. Here, output can be doubled or tripled by less than doubling or tripling the quantity of inputs. Thus, OA > AB > BC and the isoquants become closer together. The right panel shows decreasing returns to scale. Here, output changes proportionately less than labor and capital and OA < AB < BC.

of operation. The tendency for increasing returns to scale may be balanced by the tendency for decreasing returns to scale at intermediate scales of operation. Eventually, the forces for increasing returns to scale may be overcome by the forces for decreasing returns to scale at very large scales of operation. Whether this is true for a particular firm can only be determined empirically. In the real world, most firms seem to exhibit near constant returns to scale (see Table 7.7 in the appendix to this chapter). As Example 7–3 shows, however, General Motors believes that it faces decreasing returns to scale and wants to shrink.

EXAMPLE 7–3

General Motors Decides Smaller Is Better

General Motors (GM), the largest carmaker in the world, has had a turbulent two decades. It started by incurring huge losses of $2 billion in 1990 and $4.5 billion in 1991 as the result of a bloated workforce and management, low capacity utilization, too many divisions and models, and high-cost suppliers. For a corporation that had been extolled in 1946 as the epitome of a successful company, this was a dramatic decline indeed! As the data on sales per employee in Table 7-3 seem to indicate, GM was too large and faced strong diseconomies of scale, Chrysler was too small, and Ford was just about right.

Since the early 1990s, GM went through a number of reorganizations that cut more than half of its capacity, shed more than half of its labor force, and lost more than half of its market share in North America. In 2007, GM's North American capacity was about 5 million automobiles, its labor force less than 150,000, and its market share about 22%. Just closing plants and reducing GM's size, however, were not sufficient. Although these increased efficiency, its competitors did not stand still, and GM productivity still lagged in relation to that of its domestic competitors. For example, in 1998 GM required 34 worker-days to produce its average car, as compared with Chrysler's 32 and Ford's 30.

To close this productivity gap, GM consolidated its North American and international operations; reduced further the number of models it produced; cut average manufacturing time per vehicle; centralized its sales, service, and marketing system; spun

TABLE 7.3	Total Sales, Employees and Sales per Employee at GM, Ford and Chrysler		
	Sales (in billion dollars)	Employees (in thousands)	Sales per Employee (in thousand dollars)
General Motors	123.1	756	162.7
Ford	88.3	333	265.4
Chrysler	29.4	123	238.8

Source: The Economist, May 2, 1992, p. 78.

off its auto-components group (Delphi Automotive Systems); and outsourced more of the assembly task. Nevertheless, GM continued to lose market share. The year 2005 was also GM's worst since 1992, with losses of almost $15 billion, which necessitated still another restructuring plan to eliminate another 30,000 jobs by 2008. In 2006, GM finally made a profit of about $2 billion (as compared with a loss of $12.7 billion for Ford and with the loss-making Chrysler sold by Daimler-Benz at an almost complete loss from its acquisition price of $37 billion in 1998). In 2008, GM and Toyota were neck and neck for the title as the largest automotive company in the world.

Source: "Automobiles: GM Decides Smaller Is Better," *The Margin,* November/December 1988, p. 29; "GM Posts Record '91 Loss of $4.45 Billion, Sends Tough Message to UAW on Closings," *New York Times,* February 25, 1992, p. 3; "GM Plans to Close Assembly Plants in North America," *Financial Times,* August 31, 2005, p. 13; "GM Posts Worst Loss since 1992," *New York Times,* January 17, 2006, p. C1; "Big Three Face New Obstacles in Restructuring," *Wall Street Journal,* January 26, 2007, p. A1; and "Toyota and GM Are Neck and Neck in the Race to Be Number One," *Financial Times,* January 24, 2008, p. 16.

7.6   TECHNOLOGICAL PROGRESS AND INTERNATIONAL COMPETITIVENESS

In this section, we examine the meaning and importance of technological progress, discuss the process by which firms get new technology, and examine the crucial role that technological progress plays in the international competitiveness of firms.

Meaning and Importance of Innovations

Technological progress The development of new and better production techniques to make a given, improved, or entirely new product.

Product innovation The introduction of new or improved products.

Process innovation The introduction of new or improved production processes.

In our analyses so far, we have assumed a given technology. Over time, however, technological progress takes place. **Technological progress** refers to the development of new and better production techniques to make a given, improved, or an entirely new product. The introduction of innovations is the single most important determinant of a firm's long-term competitiveness at home and abroad. Innovations are basically of two types: **product innovation,** which refers to the introduction of new or improved products, and **process innovation,** the introduction of new or improved production processes. Contrary to popular belief, most innovations are incremental; that is, they involve more or less continuous small improvements in products or processes rather than a single, major technological breakthrough. Furthermore, most innovations involve the commercial utilization of ideas that may have been around for years. For example, it took a quarter of a century before firms (primarily Japanese ones) were able to perfect the flat video screen (invented in the mid-1960s by George Heilmeier of RCA) and introduce the screens commercially in portable personal computers (PCs).

Innovations can be examined with isoquants. A new or improved product requires an entirely new isoquant map showing the various combinations of inputs to produce each level of output of the new or improved product. On the other hand, a process innovation can be shown by a shift toward the origin of the firm's given product isoquants, showing that each level of output can be produced with fewer inputs after the innovation than before. Unless a firm aggressively and continuously improves its product or production process, it will inevitably be overtaken by other more innovative firms. To be successful in today's world, firms must adopt a global competitive strategy, which means that they must continuously scout the world for new product ideas and processes. It is also crucial for firms to have a presence, first through exports and then by local production, in the world's major markets. Larger sales mean increasing returns to scale in production and distribution, and they allow the firm to spend more on research and development and thus stay ahead of the competition.

The introduction of innovations is stimulated by strong domestic rivalry and geographic concentration—the former because it forces firms to constantly innovate or else lose market share (and even risk being driven entirely out of the market), the latter because it leads to the rapid spread of new ideas and the development of specialized machinery and other inputs for the industry. Sharp domestic rivalry and great geographic concentration make Japanese firms in many high-tech industries fierce competitors in the world economy today.[10]

The risk in introducing innovations is usually high. For example, eight of ten new products fail within a short time of their introduction. Even the most carefully introduced innovations can fail, as evidenced by the failure of RJR Nabisco's "smokeless cigarette" and Coca-Cola's change in 1985 of its 99-year-old recipe. In general, the introduction of a new product or concept (such as McDonald's hamburgers and Sony Walkmans) is more likely to succeed than changing an existing product (such as launching a new soup, cheese, or biscuit globally). Product innovations can also die because of poor planning and unexpected production problems. This happened, for example, to Weyerhauser. Encouraged by market testing that showed its diaper product was better than competitors' products and could be produced more cheaply, Weyerhauser introduced its UltraSoft diapers in 1990, but the product failed within a year because of unexpected production problems.[11]

EXAMPLE 7–4

How Do Firms Get New Technology?

Table 7.4 provides the results of a survey of 650 executives in 130 industries on the methods that U.S. firms use to acquire new technology. From the table, we see that the most important method of acquiring product and process innovations is by independent research and development (R&D) by the firm. The other methods of acquiring process innovations, arranged in order of decreasing importance, are: licensing technology by the firms that originally developed the technology, publications or technical meetings, reverse engineering (i.e., taking the competitive product apart and devising a method of producing a similar product), hiring employees of innovating firms, patent disclosures (i.e., from the detailed information available from the patent office which can be used to develop a similar technology or product in such a way as not to infringe on the patent), and information from conversations with employees of innovating firms (who may inadvertently provide secret information in the course of general conversations). For product innovations, reverse engineering

---

[10] See M. Porter, *The Competitive Advantage of Nations* (New York: Free Press, 1990); "Competition: How American Industry Stacks Up Now," *Fortune*, April 18, 1994, pp. 52–64; and "The Five Stages of Successful Innovation," *Sloan Management Review*, Spring 2007, pp. 8–9.

[11] See "Diaper's Failure Shows How Poor Plans, Unexpected Woes Can Kill NewProducts," *Wall Street Journal*, October 9, 1990, p. B1.

TABLE 7.4	Methods of Acquiring New Technology by American Firms	
	Rank	
Method of Acquisition	Process Innovation	Product Innovation
Independent R&D	1	1
Licensing	2	3
Publications or technical meetings	3	5
Reverse engineering	4	2
Hiring employees of innovating firms	5	4
Patent disclosures	6	6
Conversations with employees of innovating firms	7	7

Sources: R. E. Levin, "Appropriability, R&D Spending, and Technological Performance," *American Economic Review,* May 1988, pp. 424–428; "Spy vs. Spy: Are Your Company Secrets Safe?" *Fortune,* February 17, 1997, p. 136; "P&G Admits Spying on Unilever," *Financial Times,* August 31, 2001, p. 17; and "Speed Demons," *Business Week,* March 27, 2007, pp. 69–76.

becomes more important than licensing, and hiring employees from innovating firms is more important than publications or technical meetings. Last but not least (and something that firms would hardly admit—except when caught), firms try to obtain new technology by industrial espionage.

| 7.7 | OPEN INNOVATION MODEL

Closed innovation model The situation where companies generate, develop, and commercialize their own ideas, innovations, or technological breakthroughs.

Open innovation model The situation where companies commercialize both their own ideas and innovations as well as the innovations of other firms and deploy external as well as internal, or in-house, pathways to market.

Companies are today increasingly rethinking the ways in which they get new technology and bring products to market. In the past, in what we may call the **closed innovation model**, companies generated, developed and commercialized for the most part their own ideas, innovations, or technological breakthroughs. Today, many leading companies are moving toward an **open innovation model**, which involves the commercialization of both its own ideas and innovations as well as the innovations of other firms and deploying external as well as internal, or in-house, pathways to market.

Specifically, a firm today seeks to explore ways in which it can utilize external technologies to fill gaps in its businesses and encourage other firms to use its own technology through licensing agreements, joint ventures, and other arrangements. By doing so, the firm is not constrained by the technologies it develops through its R&D, but it can use any technology available to develop and introduce new and innovative products on the market. Similarly, the firm can profit greatly by licensing its own technology to others.

Concept Check
What are the
advantages of a firm's
operating under an
open innovation model?

The old closed innovation model is not dead, but it is increasingly being integrated into the open model by redirecting the scope of the in-house lab R&D toward utilizing external technologies and finding ways by which firms in other sectors can profitably utilize the firm's own technological breakthroughs.[12]

EXAMPLE 7–5

Open Innovations at Procter & Gamble

P&G has recently changed its approach to innovation from the closed to the open model and has since become one of the most aggressive adopters of the latter with the slogan "Connect & Develop." One of the first steps that P&G undertook was to create the position of director of external innovation, with the goal of sourcing 50% of its innovations from outside the company by 2007, up from an estimated 10% in 2002. Recently, P&G introduced the SpinBrush, an electric toothbrush that runs on batteries and sells for about $5, which quickly became the best-selling toothbrush in the United States and was developed not in its own labs but by four Cleveland entrepreneurs. P&G also encourages other firms to use its innovations by instituting the policy that any new idea or innovation not used by the firm within three years can be offered to others, even competitors, through a licensing agreement, a joint venture, or a fee, so as not to kill a promising project but to benefit from them.

The ability to rescue "false negatives," or projects that initially do not seem promising by the firm or that fall outside the firm's main line of business, is an important advantage of the open innovation model over the closed one. The classic example is Xerox Corporation and its Palo Alto Research center (PARC), which developed many computer hardware and software technologies (such as Ethernet and the graphical user interface, or GUI) that were not directly applicable to copiers and printers, in which the company focused, but that were subsequently put to brilliant use by Apple Computer and Microsoft, without any benefit to Xerox. On the other hand, IBM has created a patent "commons" that allows open-source software developers to use the innovations and build on IBM patents without risk of infringement.

Source: L. Huston and N. Sakkab, "Connect and Develop," *Harvard Business Review*, March 2006, pp. 58–66; and "An Open Secret," *The Economist*, October 22, 2005, pp. 12–14.

Innovations and the International Competitiveness of U.S. Firms

Product cycle model
The introduction of new products by firms in an advanced nation, which are then copied and produced by firms in lower-wage countries.

There has hardly been a technological breakthrough during the past four decades, from TVs to robots, from copiers to fax machines, from semiconductors to flat video screens, that was not made by an American firm or laboratory. According to the **product cycle model**, however, firms that first introduce an innovation eventually lose their export market and even their domestic market to foreign imitators who pay lower wages and

[12] H. W. Chesbrough, "The Era of Open Innovation," *Sloan Management Review*, Spring 2003, pp. 35–41; "Floodgates Open to a Sea of Ideas," *Financial Times*—Special Report on Innovation, June 8, 2005, p. 1; "At 3M, a Struggle Between Efficiency and Creativity," *IN*, June 207, pp. 8–22; and "Thinking Outside the Company's Box," *New York Times*, March 30, 2008, p. 4.

generally face lower costs. In the meantime, however, technologically leading firms introduce even more advanced products and technologies.

The problem is that the period during which firms can exploit the benefits of successful innovations is becoming shorter and shorter before foreign imitators take the market away. In fact, in many cases American discoveries such as the fax machine and the flat video screen were first introduced and exploited commercially by foreign (Japanese) firms. Although many American firms remain world leaders in their industries (e.g., Boeing in commercial aircraft, IBM in mainframe computers, Hewlett-Packard in laser printers, Gillette in razors, Coca-Cola in soft drinks, and McDonald's in fast food—to mention only a few), firms in many other industries such as steel, automobiles, consumer electronics, and semiconductors lost international competitiveness to foreign competitors, especially the Japanese, during the 1970s and 1980s. One important reason for this was that American firms generally stressed product innovation, whereas Japanese firms stressed process innovations. Thus, even when American firms were the first to introduce a new product, Japanese firms were soon able to produce it better and more cheaply and in a few years were able to outsell American competitors both at home and abroad.[13]

Under the Japanese competitive threat, American firms, especially the high-tech ones, underwent a fundamental and painful restructuring during the 1980s that returned them to a position of leadership in their industries during the late 1980s. Xerox was one of the first U.S. companies to regain its lost competitiveness (see Example 7–6). The "At the Frontier" section shows how U.S. industry regained the ground lost to the Japanese during the 1970s and 1980s in a wide range of high-tech products as a result of the new revolution in computer-aided production that swept America. In any event, most of the trade taking place among industrial nations is now **intraindustry trade** in differentiated manufactured products.

✅ **Concept Check**
How is innovation related to international competitiveness?

Intraindustry trade
International trade in the differentiated products of the same industry or broad product group.

EXAMPLE 7–6
How Xerox Lost and Regained Market Share but Is Now Struggling to Remain Internationally Competitive

The Xerox Corporation was the first to introduce the copying machine in 1959, based on its patented xerographic technology. Until 1970, Xerox had no competition and thus had little incentive to reduce manufacturing costs, improve quality, and increase customers' satisfaction. Even when Japanese firms entered the low end of the market with better and cheaper copiers in 1970 and began to take over this segment of the market, Xerox did not respond, concentrating instead on the mid and high ends of the market, where profit margins were much higher. Xerox also used the profits from its copier business to expand into computers and office systems during the second half of the 1990s. It was not until 1979 that Xerox finally awakened to the seriousness of the Japanese threat. From so-called *competitive benchmarking* missions to Japan to compare relative production efficiency and product quality, Xerox was startled to find that Japanese competitors were producing copiers of higher quality at far lower costs and were positioning themselves to move up into the more profitable mid- and high-end segments of the market.

---

[13] "In the Realm of Technology, Japan Seizes a Greater Role," *New York Time,* May 28, 1991, p. C1.

Faced with this life-threatening situation, Xerox, with the help of its Japanese subsidiary (Fuji Xerox), mounted a strong response that involved reorganization and integration of development and production, as well as ambitious companywide quality-control efforts. Employee involvement was greatly increased, suppliers were brought into the early stages of product design, and inventories and the number of suppliers were greatly reduced. Constant benchmarking was then used to test progress in the companywide quality-control program and customer satisfaction. By taking these drastic actions, Xerox was able to reverse the trend toward loss of market share to Japanese competitors, even at the low segment of the market during the second half of the 1990s.

History seemed to repeat itself, however, at the beginning of the new decade when Xerox once again found itself battling Japan's Canon for supremacy in the new digital world of office information technology. This, despite the fact that during the second half of the 1990s Xerox had recast itself as a digital document and solutions company that combines hardware, software, and services into a service and consulting package, industry by industry. It is clear that to remain competitive in today's globalized environment requires constant alertness to the competition and continuous innovations on the part of the firm.

Sources: The MIT Commission on Industrial Productivity, *Made in America* (Cambridge, MA: MIT Press, 1989), pp. 270–277; "Japan Is Tough, but Xerox Prevails," *New York Times,* September 3, 1992, p. D1; "Xerox Recasts Itself as a Formidable Force in Digital Revolution," *Wall Street Journal,* February 2, 1999, p. A1; "Downfall of Xerox," *Business Week,* March 5, 2001, pp. 82–92; "Canon Takes Aim at Xerox," *Fortune,* October 14, 2002, pp. 215–220; and "Xerox's Inventor-in-Chief," *Fortune,* July 9, 2007, pp. 65–72.

AT THE FRONTIER
The New Computer-Aided Production Revolution and the International Competitiveness of U.S. Firms

Computer-aided design (CAD) The process that allows research and development engineers to design a new product or component on a computer screen.

Computer-aided manufacturing (CAM) The computer instructions to a network of integrated machine tools to produce a product.

Since the early 1990s, a veritable revolution in production has been taking place in the United States, based on computer-aided design and computer-aided manufacturing, which has greatly increased the productivity and international competitiveness of U.S. firms. **Computer-aided design (CAD)** allows research and development engineers to design a new product or component on a computer screen, quickly experiment with different alternative designs, and test the strength and reliability of different materials—all on the screen! Then, **computer-aided manufacturing (CAM)** issues instructions to a network of integrated machine tools to produce a prototype of the new or changed product. These developments allow firms to avoid many possible production problems, greatly speed up the time required to develop and introduce new or improved products, and reduce the optimal lot size or the production runs to achieve maximum production efficiency. This revolution has been taking place mostly in the United States, based primarily on its world leadership and superiority in computer software and computer networks.

Continued . . .

The New Computer-Aided Production Revolution and the International Competitiveness of U.S. Firms   *Continued*

These new developments have led to a new digital factory—an information-age marvel that is responsible for a quantum leap in the speed, flexibility, and productivity of U.S. firms resulting from the ingenious marriage of computer software and computer networks in industries as diverse as construction equipment, automobiles, PCs, and electronic pagers. This new digital factory has unheard of agility that allows it to customize products down to one unit while achieving mass-production speed and efficiency. For example, as a Dell salesperson specifies an order for a PC for a particular consumer, the digitized data flow to the assembly line where production begins immediately and is completed in a very short time, so that the customer can have his or her customized PC in a day or two. This is sometimes called software-controlled continuous flow manufacturing—a process that is basically merging manufacturing and retailing. This much faster time-to-market and customizing capability is beginning to provide American firms with tremendous advantage over foreign competitors. As a result, after losing the competitive war during the 1980s and early 1990s, the United States regained all of its lost ground, and then some, since the mid-1990s.

Computer-aided design (CAD) is dramatically increasing the pace of innovations. For example, a designer can call up on the screen a car door she may be working on, test opening and closing the door, run the window up and down, experiment with lighter materials, and direct machinery to make a prototype door. Such CAD allowed Chrysler to design and build its highly successful NEON subcompact car in 33 months instead of the usual 45 months. Even more exotically, scientists at Caterpillar, the largest earth-moving equipment builder in the world, test drive huge machinery that they are developing in virtual reality long before they are built. The Boeing 777 jetliner was developed entirely in this way. CAD is even used to design and simulate entire assembly lines, and it can be used to send production orders to suppliers' machinery so that, in a sense, they become an extension of the firm's plant. In short, we are likely to be at the dawn of the biggest revolution in manufacturing since the perfection of the industrial lathe in the year 1800. And with the U.S. undisputed superiority in software, it is unlikely that foreign competitors can easily copy and match the new American manufacturing genius anytime soon.

✔ **Concept Check**
What is the relationship between CAD and CAM and the digital factory?

Sources: "The Digital Factory," *Fortune,* November 14, 1994, pp. 92–110; "The Totally Digital Factory May Not Be So Far Away," *Financial Times,* November 1, 2000, p. XII; "Incredible Shrinking Plants," *The Economist,* February 23, 2002, pp. 71–73; "The Way to the Future," *Business Week,* October 11, 2004; and "Speed Demons, *Business Week,* March 27, 2006, pp. 69–76.

SUMMARY

1. Production refers to the transformation of resources or inputs into outputs of goods and services. A firm is an organization that combines and organizes resources for the purpose of producing goods and services for sale at a profit. In general, the aim of firms is to maximize profits. Profits refer to the revenue of the firm from the sale of the output after all costs have been deducted. Inputs can be broadly classified into labor, capital, and land, and into fixed and variable. Entrepreneurship refers to the introduction of new technologies and products to exploit perceived profit opportunities. The time period during which at least one input is fixed is called the short run. In the long run, all inputs are variable.

2. The production function is a unique relationship between inputs and output. It can be represented by a table, graph, or equation showing the maximum output or total product (*TP*) of a commodity that can be produced per time period with each set of inputs. Average product (*AP*) is total product divided by the quantity of the variable input used. Marginal product (*MP*) is the change in total output per-unit change in the variable input. The *MP* is above the *AP* when *AP* is rising, *MP* is below *AP* when *AP* is falling, and *MP* = *AP* when *AP* is at a maximum. The declining portion of the *MP* curve reflects the law of diminishing returns.

3. An isoquant shows the various combinations of two inputs that can be used to produce a specific level of output. From the isoquant map, we can generate the total product curve of each input by holding the quantity of the other input constant.

4. Isoquants are negatively sloped in the economically relevant range, convex to the origin, and do not intersect. The absolute value of the slope of the isoquant is called the marginal rate of technical substitution (*MRTS*). This equals the ratio of the marginal product of the two inputs. As we move down along an isoquant the absolute value of its slope, or *MRTS,* declines and the isoquant is convex. Ridge lines separate the relevant (i.e., the negatively sloped) from the irrelevant (or positively sloped) portions of the isoquants. With right-angled, or L-shaped, isoquants, inputs can only be combined in fixed proportions in production.

5. Constant, increasing, and decreasing returns to scale refer to the situation where output changes, respectively, by the same, by a larger, and by a smaller proportion than do inputs. Returns to scale can be shown by the spacing of isoquants. Increasing returns to scale arise because of specialization and division of labor and from using specialized machinery. Decreasing returns to scale arise primarily because as the scale of operation increases, it becomes more and more difficult to manage the firm and coordinate its operations and divisions effectively. In the real world, most industries seem to exhibit near-constant returns to scale.

6. The introduction of innovations is the single most important determinant of a firm's long-term competitiveness. Product innovations refer to the introduction of new or improved products, while process innovations refer to the introduction of new or improved production processes. More and more firms are adopting an open, as opposed to a closed, innovation model, whereby they commercialize both their own ideas and innovations as well as the innovations of other firms. Since the early 1990s, a veritable revolution in production has been taking place in the United States based on computer-aided design and computer-aided manufacturing, which has greatly increased productivity and international competitiveness of U.S. firms.

KEY TERMS

Production	Total product (*TP*)	Product innovation
Firm	Average product (*AP*)	Process innovation
Inputs	Marginal product (*MP*)	Closed innovation model
Labor or human resources	Law of diminishing returns	Open innovation model
Capital or investment goods	Isoquant	Product cycle model
Land or natural resources	Marginal rate of technical substitution	Intraindustry trade
Entrepreneurship	(*MRTS*)	Computer-aided design
Fixed inputs	Ridge lines	Computer-aided manufacturing
Variable inputs	Constant returns to scale	Cobb–Douglas production function
Short run	Increasing returns to scale	Output elasticity of labor
Long run	Decreasing returns to scale	Output elasticity of capital
Production function	Technological progress	Homogeneous of degree 1

REVIEW QUESTIONS

1. Where on the total product and on the marginal product of labor curves of Figure 7.2 does the law of diminishing returns begin to operate? What gives rise to the law of diminishing returns?

2. What does the total product curve look like if diminishing returns set in after the first unit of labor is employed?

3. Would a rational producer be concerned with the average or the marginal product of an input in deciding whether or not to hire the input?

4. Which of the following points ($5L$ and $7K$, $3L$ and $9K$, $4L$ and $5K$, and $6L$ and $6K$) cannot be on the same isoquant? Why?

5. If the marginal product of labor is 6 and the marginal rate of technical substitution between labor and capital is 1.5, what is the marginal product of capital?

6. Is the firm facing increasing, constant, or decreasing returns to scale if it expands the quantity of labor and capital used in production from $10L$ and $10K$ to $13L$ and $13K$, and output increases from 256 units to 300 units? Why?

7. Can a firm have a production function that exhibits increasing, constant, and decreasing returns to scale at different levels of output? Explain.

8. Is technical efficiency sufficient to determine at what point on an isoquant a firm operates? Why?

9. Is diminishing returns to a single factor of production consistent with constant or nonconstant returns to scale?

10. What is meant by an innovation? What are the different types of innovations?

11. What is the difference between technological progress and increasing returns to scale?

12. What is the difference between an open innovation model and a closed innovation model?

13. What is meant by the "digital factory"?

PROBLEMS

1. From the following production function, showing the bushels of corn raised on one acre of land by varying the amount of labor employed (in worker-years),

Labor	1	2	3	4	5	6
Output	8	20	30	34	34	30

   a. derive the average and the marginal product of labor.

   b. plot the total, the average, and the marginal product curves.

2. Plot again the total product curve of Problem 1 on the assumption that labor time is infinitesimally divisible, and derive graphically the corresponding average and marginal product curves.

3. From the production function given in Table 7.6.

   a. derive the isoquants for 8 units of output, $8Q$, $20Q$, $25Q$, $30Q$, and $34Q$.

   b. what is the relationship between Table 7.6 and the table in Problem 1?

4. From the isoquant map of Problem 3(a), derive

   a. the total product curve for labor when the quantity of capital is held fixed at $K = 4$.

   b. the average and the marginal product curves for labor from the total product curve of 4(a) above.

5. a. From Problem 3, redraw the isoquant for 20 units of output ($20Q$) and show how to measure the marginal rate of technical substitution of labor for capital (i.e., $MRTS_{LK}$) between the point where 2 units of labor and 4 units of capital (i.e., $2L$ and $4K$) are used (call this point M) and the point where ($3L$, $2K$) are used (call this point N). What is the $MRTS_{LK}$ at point N? At point C ($4L$, $1.5K$)?

   b. Find the value of the MP_L and MP_K for a movement from point N on the isoquant for $20Q$ and point N' ($4L$, $2K$) and N'' ($3L$, $3K$) on the isoquant for $25Q$, and show that $MRTS_{LK} = MP_L/MP_K$.

   c. Explain why the $MRTS_{LK}$ falls as we move down along the isoquant.

6. a. On the isoquant map of Problem 3, draw the ridge lines.

   b. Explain why a firm would never produce below the lower ridge line or above the top ridge line.

*7. On the same set of axes draw two isoquants, one indicating that the two inputs must be combined in fixed proportions in production, and the other showing that inputs are perfect substitutes for each other.

TABLE 7.6 Production Function with Two Variable Inputs

Capital	(K)								
		6	6	18	25	30	30	25	
		5	8	20	30	34	34	30	
		4	8	20	30	34	34	30	Q
		3	6	18	25	30	30	25	
		2	4	13	20	25	25	20	
↑ K		1	1	5	7	8	8	7	
		0	1	2	3	4	5	6	
		L →				Labor		(L)	

*8. If the price of gasoline is $1.50 per gallon and travel time is worth $6.00 per hour to the individual, determine at which speed the cost of traveling the 600 miles is minimum in Figure 7.8.

9. Does the production function of Problem 3 exhibit constant, increasing, or decreasing returns to scale? Explain.

*10. Suppose that the production function for a commodity is given by

$$Q = 10\sqrt{LK}$$

where Q is the quantity of output, L is the quantity of labor, and K is the quantity of capital:

a. Indicate whether this production function exhibits constant, increasing, or decreasing returns to scale.

b. Does the production function exhibit diminishing returns? If so, when does the law of diminishing returns begin to operate? Could we ever get negative returns?

*11. Indicate whether each of the following statements is true or false and give the reason.

a. A student preparing for an examination should not study after reaching diminishing returns.

b. If large and small firms operate in the same industry, we must have constant returns to scale.

12. Explain the importance of the new production revolution for the international competitiveness of American firms.

APPENDIX   THE COBB–DOUGLAS PRODUCTION FUNCTION

In this appendix, we present the Cobb–Douglas production function. This is the simplest and most widely used production function in empirical work today. We begin with the formula, which is followed by a simple illustration. Next we consider the methods available to empirically estimate the Cobb–Douglas production function and some of the difficulties involved. We conclude with some empirical results.

The Formula

Cobb-Douglas production function The relationship between inputs and output expressed by $Q = AL^\alpha K^\beta$, where Q is output, L is labor, and K is capital.

The formula for the **Cobb–Douglas production function** is

$$Q = AL^\alpha K^\beta \qquad [7.5]$$

where Q = output in physical units, L = quantity of labor, K = quantity of capital, and A, α (alpha), and β (beta) are positive parameters estimated in each case from the data. The

---

* = Answer provided at end of book.

Output elasticity of labor The percentage increase in output resulting from a 1% increase in the quantity of labor used.

Output elasticity of capital The percentage increase in output resulting from a 1% increase in the quantity of capital used.

Homogeneous of degree 1 In production, it refers to constant returns to scale.

parameter A refers to technology. The more advanced the technology, the greater the value of A. The parameter α refers to the percentage increase in Q for a 1% increase in L, while holding K constant. Thus, α is the **output elasticity of labor.** For example, if $\alpha = 0.7$, this means that a 1% increase in the quantity of labor used (while holding the quantity of capital constant) leads to a 0.7% increase in output. Thus, the output elasticity of labor (α) is 0.7. Similarly, the parameter β refers to the percentage increase in Q for a 1% increase in K, while holding L constant. Thus, β is the **output elasticity of capital.** For example, if $\beta = 0.3$, this means that a 1% increase in K, while holding L constant, leads to a 0.3% increase in Q. Thus, the output elasticity of K (β) is 0.3.

In the above example, $\alpha + \beta = 0.7 + 0.3 = 1$. Thus, we have constant returns to scale. That is, a 1% increase in both L and K leads to a 1% increase in Q. Specifically, a 1% increase in L, by itself, leads to a 0.7% increase in Q; a 1% increase in K, by itself, leads to a 0.3% increase in Q. Thus, with an increase of both L and K by 1%, Q increases by a total of 1% also and we have constant returns to scale. Another name for constant returns to scale is **homogeneous of degree 1.**

On the other hand, if $\alpha + \beta > 1$, we have increasing returns to scale. That is, a 1% increase in L and K leads to a greater than 1% increase in Q. For example, if $\alpha = 0.8$ and $\beta = 0.3$, a 1% increase in L and K leads to a $0.8 + 0.3 = 1.1\%$ increase in Q. Finally, if $\alpha + \beta < 1$, we have decreasing returns to scale (i.e., an increase in L and K by 1% leads to an increase in Q of less than 1%).

Illustration

Suppose $A = 10$, $\alpha = \beta = 1/2$, and $\overline{K} = 4$ and is held constant (so that we are dealing with the short run). By substituting these values into equation [7.5], we get

$$Q = 10L^{1/2}4^{1/2} = 10\sqrt{4}\sqrt{L} = 20\sqrt{L} \qquad \text{[7.5A]}$$

By then substituting alternative quantities of L used in production into equation [7.5A], we derive the total product (TP) schedule, and from it, the average product of labor (AP_L) and the marginal product of labor (MP_L) schedules. The results are given in Table 7.7.

Plotting the TP, the AP_L, and the MP_L schedules of Table 7.7 as Figure 7.10, we see that the Cobb–Douglas production function exhibits diminishing AP_L and MP_L from the very start or with the first unit of L used, and that the MP_L never becomes negative. Note that the MP_L is plotted between the various quantities of labor used. The AP_L and the MP_L are functions of or depend only on the K/L ratio. That is, they remain the same regardless of how much L and K are used in production as long as the K/L ratio remains the same (as along any given ray from the origin).[14]

In the long run, both L and K are variable. Thus,

$$Q = 10L^{1/2}K^{1/2} = 10\sqrt{L}\sqrt{K} = 10\sqrt{LK} \qquad \text{[7.5B]}$$

Since $\alpha + \beta = 0.5 + 0.5 = 1$ in this case, we have constant returns to scale. This is shown in Table 7.8. Here, output grows at the same rate as the rate of increase in both inputs. For example, doubling the quantity of labor and capital used, from 1 to 2 units, doubles

---

[14] This is proved in more advanced texts.

TABLE 7.7	Total, Average, and Marginal Product of Labor		
L	TP	AP_L	MP_L
0	0	. . .	. . .
1	20.00	20.00	20.00
2	28.28	14.14	8.28
3	34.64	11.55	6.36
4	40.00	10.00	5.36
5	44.72	8.94	4.72

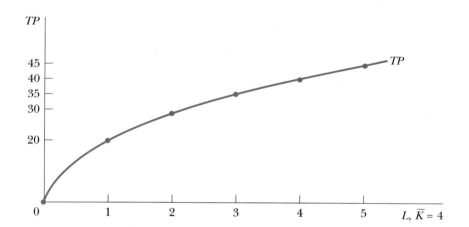

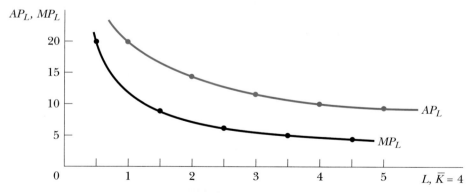

FIGURE 7.10   Total, Average, and Marginal Product of Labor for the Cobb-Douglas Production Function   This figure shows the TP, the AP_L, and the MP_L schedules given in Table 7.7. From the figure, we see that the AP_L and the MP_L decline from the very start and the MP_L never becomes negative for the Cobb-Douglas production function. Note that the MP_L is plotted between the various quantities of labor used and capital is held constant at $\bar{K} = 4$.

TABLE 7.8	Production in the Long Run		
L	K	$10\sqrt{(L)(M)}$	Q
0	0	$10\sqrt{(0)(0)}$	0
1	1	$10\sqrt{(1)(1)}$	10
2	2	$10\sqrt{(2)(2)}$	20
3	3	$10\sqrt{(3)(3)}$	30
4	4	$10\sqrt{(4)(4)}$	40
5	5	$10\sqrt{(5)(5)}$	50

output from 10 to 20 units. Increasing L and K by 50%, from 2 to 3 units, increases Q by 50% from 20 to 30 units, and so on.

We can also define the isoquants for this Cobb–Douglas production function. For example, the isoquant for $50Q$ can be defined by substituting 50 for Q in equation [7.5B]. By then substituting various quantities of labor into the resulting equation, we get the corresponding quantities of capital required to produce the $50Q$:

$$50 = 10\sqrt{LK}$$
$$5 = \sqrt{LK}$$
$$25 = LK \qquad\qquad [7.5C]$$
$$\frac{25}{L} = K$$

Thus, if $L = 10$, $K = 2.5$; if $L = 5$, $K = 5$; if $L = 2.5$, $K = 10$, and so on. Other isoquants can be similarly derived. Isoquants are parallel along any ray from the origin and are equally spaced to reflect constant returns to scale (as in the left panel of Figure 7.9).

Empirical Estimation

One method of estimating the parameters of the Cobb–Douglas production function (i.e., A, α, and β) is to apply statistical (i.e., regression) analysis to time series data on the inputs used and the output produced.[15] For example, the researcher may collect data on the number of automobiles produced by an automaker in each year from 1951 to 1997 and on the quantity of labor and capital used in each year to produce the automobiles. The data are usually transformed into natural logarithms (indicated by the symbol ln) and the regression analysis is conducted on the transformed data. The form of the estimated Cobb–Douglas production function is then

$$\ln Q = \ln A + \alpha \ln L + \beta \ln K \qquad\qquad [7.5D]$$

The researcher thus obtains an estimate of the value of $\ln A$, α, and β.[16] Of primary interest to the researcher is the value of α and β.[17]

Another method of estimating the value of A, α, and β is by regression analysis using cross-section data. In this case, the researcher collects data for a given year (or other time

---

[15] For a general discussion of regression analysis, see the appendix to Chapter 5.

[16] The value of parameter A can then be obtained by finding the antilog of ln A.

[17] In Cobb–Douglas time series estimates, technological progress must also be accounted for. This is usually accomplished by including time (t) as an additional explanatory variable in equation [7.5D].

unit) for each of many producers or firms in a particular industry on the quantity of labor and capital used and the output produced. That is, instead of collecting data for one firm over many years (time series), the researcher now collects data for a given year for many firms in the same industry (cross section). As in the previous case, the researcher usually first transforms the data into natural logarithms and then estimates equation [7.5D] by regression analysis to obtain the values of parameters A, α, and β. Once again the researcher is primarily interested in the values of α and β. Table 7.9 in Example 7–7 presents the values of α and β estimated for various U.S. manufacturing industries.[18]

Input–output relationships can also be obtained from engineering studies. All of these methods (i.e., regression analysis using time series or cross-section data and engineering studies) face difficulties. One of these is that we must assume that the best production techniques are used by all firms at all times. Due to a lack of information or erroneous decisions, this may not be the case. Another difficulty arises in the measurement of the capital input, since machinery and equipment are of different types, ages (vintage), and productivities. A further shortcoming characteristic of engineering studies is that they typically cover only some production activities of the firm. Despite these and other problems, numerous studies have been conducted over the years using these different approaches. They have provided very useful information on production for the entire economy and for various industries.

EXAMPLE 7–7

Output Elasticity of Labor and Capital and Returns to Scale in U.S. and Canadian Manufacturing

Table 7.9 reports the estimated output elasticities of labor (α) and capital (β) for various U.S. manufacturing industries. The value of $\alpha = 0.90$ for furniture means that a 1% increase in the quantity of labor used (holding K constant) results in a 0.90% increase in the quantity produced of furniture. The value of $\beta = 0.21$ means that a 1% increase in K (holding L constant) increases Q by 0.21%. Increasing both L and K by 1% increases Q by $0.90 + 0.21 = 1.11\%$. This means that the production of furniture is subject to increasing returns to scale.

The values of α and β reported in Table 7.9 were estimated by regression analysis using cross-section data for many firms in each industry for the year 1957. The value of α ranges from 0.51 for food and beverages to 0.96 for leather. This is the output elasticity of production and nonproduction workers combined. The value of β ranges from 0.08 for leather to 0.56 for food and beverages. Note that most industries exhibit close-to-constant returns to scale (i.e., the value of $\alpha + \beta$ is close to 1).

A similar study for 107 Canadian industries found that in 1979 the value of α ranged from 0.04 for watches and clocks to 1.26 for distilleries, the value of β ranged from 0.02 for flour and breakfast cereal products to 1.36 for glass manufacturers, while the values of $\alpha + \beta$ ranged from 2.20 (very strong economies of scale) for the feed industry to 0.82 (relatively strong diseconomies of scale) for tread mill.

---

[18] Data for many firms in each of the various U.S. manufacturing industries for the year 1957 were used to estimate the values of α and β for each industry. Thus, these are cross-section estimates.

TABLE 7.9	Estimated Output Elasticity of Labor (α) and Capital (β) in U.S. Manufacturing		
Industry	α	β	$\alpha + \beta$
Furniture	0.90	0.21	1.11
Chemicals	0.89	0.20	1.09
Printing	0.62	0.46	1.08
Food, beverages	0.51	0.56	1.07
Rubber, plastics	0.58	0.48	1.06
Instruments	0.84	0.20	1.04
Lumber	0.65	0.39	1.04
Apparel	0.91	0.13	1.04
Leather	0.96	0.08	1.04
Electrical machinery	0.66	0.37	1.03
Nonelectrical machinery	0.62	0.40	1.02
Transport equipment	0.79	0.23	1.02
Textiles	0.88	0.12	1.00
Paper pulp	0.56	0.42	0.98
Primary metals	0.59	0.37	0.96
Petroleum	0.64	0.31	0.95

Sources: J. Moroney, "Cobb–Douglas Production Functions and Returns to Scale in U.S. Manufacturing Industry," *Western Economic Journal,* December 1967; and J. R. Baldwin and P. K. Goreki, *The Role of Scale in Canada/U.S. Productivity Differences in the Manufacturing Sector, 1970–1979* (Toronto: Toronto University Press, 1986).

Thus, Canadian manufacturing industries seemed to exhibit a wider range of output elasticities of labor and capital as well as a wider range of economies and diseconomies of scale than U.S. firms.

INTERNET SITE ADDRESSES

For world's food production and consumption, see:

http://en.wikipedia.org/wiki/Thomas_Malthus

http://www.fao.org/DOCREP/005/Y4252E/y4252e05.htm

For gasoline consumption and substitution, see:

http://www.techstandards.co.uk/system/index.html

http://sciway.net/statistics/scsa98/en/en17.html

For production, employment, and earnings information on General Motors, see:

http://www.npr.org/templates/story/story.php?storyId=9814470

http://seekingalpha.com/article/29614

http://money.cnn.com/2005/06/07/news/fortune500/gm_closings/

General Motors: http://www.gm.com

For information on Ford, Chrysler, and Toyota, see:

Ford: http://www.ford.com

Chrysler: http://www.chrysler.com

Toyota: http://www.Toyota.com

For the open innovation model, see:

http://en.wikipedia.org/wiki/Open_Innovation

http://www.pdma.org/visions/apr06/open-innovation-primer.php

For competition between Xerox and Canon, see:

Canon: http://www.usa.canon.com

Xerox: http://www.xerox.com

For computer-aided design (CAD) and computer-aided manufacturing (CAM), see:

Microsoft: http://www.microsoft.com

Motorola: http://www.mot.com

Dell: http://www.dell.com

Caterpillar: http://www.caterpillar.com

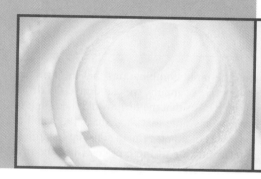

CHAPTER 8

Costs of Production

After Studying This Chapter, You Should Be Able to:

- Know the meaning of explicit, implicit, and opportunity costs
- Describe how to derive the short-run and the long-run cost curves of a firm
- Know the meaning and importance of economies of scope and learning curves
- Know the meaning and importance of the new international economies of scale
- Descibe the effect of a change in input prices on production and costs

In this chapter, we consider the costs of production of the firm and their relationship to production theory (presented in Chapter 7). After examining the nature of costs, we derive short-run and long-run cost curves for the firm. These curves will be used to determine the profit-maximizing level of output for a perfectly competitive firm in Chapter 9 and for imperfectly competitive firms in Chapters 10–11. This chapter also introduces economies of scope and learning curves. The many real-world examples highlight the importance and relevance of the analysis, while the "At the Frontier" section examines the growing importance of international economies of scale. In the optional appendix, we examine in a more technical way the relationship between production and costs and the effect of input-price changes on production and costs.

| 8.1 | THE NATURE OF PRODUCTION COSTS |

From the firm's production function (showing the input combinations that the firm can use to produce various levels of output) and the price of inputs, we can derive the firm's cost functions. These functions show the minimum costs that the firm would incur in producing various levels of output. For simplicity, we assume that the firm is too small to affect the prices of the inputs it uses. Thus, the prices of inputs remain constant regardless of the quantity demanded by the firm. (The determination of input prices when the firm does and does not affect input prices is discussed in Part Five, Chapters 14–16.)

Explicit costs The actual expenditures of the firm to purchase or hire inputs.

In economics, costs include explicit and implicit costs. **Explicit costs** are the actual out-of-pocket expenditures of the firm to purchase or hire the inputs it requires in production. These expenditures include the wages to hire labor, interest on borrowed capital, rent on land and buildings, and the expenditures on raw and semifinished materials. **Implicit costs** refer to the value of the inputs owned and used by the firm in its own production processes. The value of these owned inputs must be imputed or estimated from what these inputs could earn in their best alternative use.

Implicit costs The value of the inputs owned and used by the firm.

Implicit costs include the maximum wages that the entrepreneur could earn in working for someone else in a similar capacity (say, as the manager of another firm), and the highest return that the firm could obtain from investing its capital elsewhere and renting out its land and other inputs to others. The inputs owned and used by the firm in its own production processes are not free to the firm, even though the firm can use them without any actual or explicit expenditures. Accountants traditionally include only actual expenditures in costs, whereas economists always include both explicit and implicit costs, or opportunity costs.[1]

Opportunity cost What an input could earn in its best alternative use.

The **opportunity cost** to a firm in using any input is what the input could earn in its best alternative use (outside the firm). This is true for inputs purchased or hired by the firm as well as for inputs owned and used by the firm in its own production. For example, a firm must pay wages of $20,000 per year to one of its employees if that is the amount the worker would earn in his or her best alternative occupation in another firm. If this firm attempted to pay less, the worker would simply seek employment in the other firm. Similarly, if the entrepreneur could earn more in managing another firm than in directing his or her own firm, it would not make much economic sense to continue to be self-employed.[2] Thus, for a firm to retain any input for its own use, it must include as a cost the opportunity cost that the input could earn in its best alternative use or employment. This is the **alternative** or **opportunity cost doctrine.** Similarly, the opportunity cost of attending college includes not only the explicit cost of tuition, books, and so on, but also the foregone earnings of not working (see Example 8–1).

Alternative or opportunity cost doctrine The doctrine that postulates that the cost to a firm in using any input is what the input could earn in its best alternative use.

Private costs The costs incurred by individuals and firms.

Costs are also classified into private and social. **Private costs** are the opportunity costs incurred by *individuals and firms* in the process of producing goods and services. **Social costs** are the costs incurred by *society* as a whole. Social costs are higher than private costs when firms are able to escape some of the economic costs of production. For example, a firm dumping untreated waste into the air imposes a cost on society (in the form of higher cleaning bills, more breathing ailments, and so on) that is not reflected in

Social costs The costs incurred by society as a whole.

---

[1] For tax purposes, the accountant's definition of costs, which includes only explicit costs, is usually used. However, in economics, we must always consider both explicit and implicit, or opportunity costs.
[2] This is true unless the individual valued the freedom associated with being self-employed more than the extra income in managing a similar firm for someone else.

✓ Concept Check
Why must implicit costs be taken into consideration in reaching correct economic decisions?

the costs of the firm. Private costs can be made equal to social costs by public regulation requiring the firm to install antipollution equipment. In this and subsequent chapters, we will be primarily concerned with private costs. Social costs will be examined in detail in Chapter 18.

EXAMPLE 8–1
Cost of Attending College

Table 8.1 reports the average annual explicit and implicit or opportunity costs of attending a four-year public or private college for residents, commuters, and out-of-state students in the United States during the 2007–2008 academic year.

Explicit costs include tuition and fees, books and supplies, room and board, transportation, and other expenses. The data show that the explicit costs of attending a private college are much higher than for state residents attending a public college and marginally higher for out-of-state residents attending a public college.

The implicit costs of attending college are the student's earnings foregone by attending college rather than entering the labor force. The average entering wage for a high school graduate without any training or work experience is about $15,080. This represents, respectively, 87% of the explicit costs of attending a four-year public college for state residents, 84% for commuters, and 54% for out-of-state residents. The implicit costs of attending a four-year private college are about 43% of the explicit costs for residents and commuters.

TABLE 8.1 Annual Cost of Attending College

	Four-Year Public			Four-Year Private	
	In-State Resident	Commuter	Out-of-State Resident	Resident	Commuter
Explicit costs					
Tuition and fees	$6,185	$6,185	$16,640	$23,712	$23,712
Books and supplies	988	988	988	988	988
Room and board	7,404	7,419	7,404	8,595	7,499
Transportation	911	1,284	911	768	1,138
Other expenses	1,848	2,138	1,848	1,311	1,664
Total expenses	$17,336	$18,014	$27,791	$35,374	$35,001
Implicit costs					
Foregone earnings	$15,080	$15,080	$15,080	$15,080	$15,080
Total opportunity costs	$31,437	$32,047	$41,384	$48,381	$48,165
Implicit costs as a % of explicit costs	87%	84%	54%	43%	43%

Source: College Board, *Trends in College Pricing* (Washington, DC: 2007), p. 7.

| 8.2 | COST IN THE SHORT RUN |

In this section, we examine the theory of cost in the short run. We first define fixed, variable, and total costs and draw these total cost curves. We then define average fixed cost, average variable cost, average total cost, and marginal cost and draw these per-unit cost curves. Finally, we show how per-unit cost curves can be derived graphically from the corresponding total cost curves.

Total Costs

Total fixed costs (TFC) The total obligations of a firm per time period for all fixed inputs.

Total variable costs (TVC) The total obligations of a firm per time period for all the variable inputs the firm uses.

Total costs (TC) TFC plus TVC.

In the short run, some inputs are fixed and some are variable; this leads to fixed and variable costs. **Total fixed costs (*TFC*)** are the total obligations of the firm per time period for all fixed inputs. These fixed or sunk costs include payments for renting the plant and equipment (or the depreciation on plant and equipment if the firm owns them), most kinds of insurance, property taxes, and some salaries (such as those of top management, which are fixed by contract and must be paid over the life of the contract whether the firm produces or not). Fixed costs are sometimes referred to as *sunk costs* by economists and *overhead costs* by business people. **Total variable costs (*TVC*)** are the total obligations of the firm per time period for all the variable inputs of the firm. These include payments for raw materials, fuels, most types of labor, excise taxes, and so on. **Total costs (*TC*)** equal *TFC* plus *TVC*.

Within the limits imposed by the given plant, the firm can vary its output in the short run by varying the quantity of the variable inputs used per period of time. This gives rise to *TFC*, *TVC*, and *TC* schedules and curves. These show, respectively, the *minimum* fixed, variable, and total costs of producing the various levels of output in the short run. In defining these cost schedules and curves, all inputs are valued at their opportunity cost, which includes both explicit and implicit costs.

Table 8.2 presents hypothetical *TFC*, *TVC*, and *TC* schedules. These schedules are then plotted in Figure 8.1. From Table 8.2, we see that *TFC* are $30 regardless of the level of output. This is reflected in Figure 8.1 in the horizontal *TFC* curve at the level of $30. *TVC* are zero when output is zero and rise as output rises. The shape of the *TVC* curve follows directly from the law of diminishing returns. Up to point *W'* (the point of inflection), the firm uses so little of the variable inputs with the fixed inputs that the law of diminishing returns is not yet operating. As a result, the *TVC* curve faces downward or rises at a decreasing rate. Past point *W'* (i.e., for output levels greater than 1.5), the law of diminishing returns operates and the *TVC* curve faces upward or rises at an increasing rate. Since

TABLE 8.2   Fixed, Variable, and Total Costs

Quantity of Output	Total Fixed Costs	Total Variable Costs	Total Costs
0	$30	$0	$30
1	30	20	50
2	30	30	60
3	30	45	75
4	30	80	110
5	30	145	175

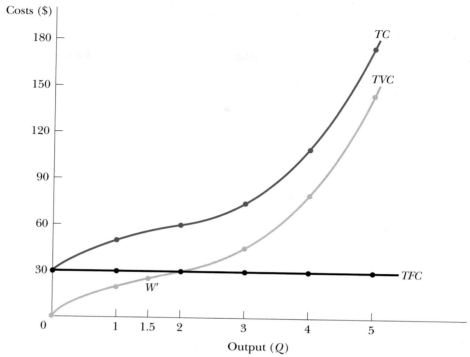

FIGURE 8.1   Total Cost Curves   The total fixed cost (*TFC*) curve is horizontal at the level of $30, regardless of the level of output. The total variable costs (*TVC*) are zero when output is zero and rise as output rises. Past point *W'*, the law of diminishing returns operates and the *TVC* curve faces upward or rises at an increasing rate. Total costs (*TC*) equal *TFC* plus *TVC*. Thus, the *TC* curve has the same shape as the *TVC* curve but is $30 above it at each output level.

$TC = TFC + TVC$, the *TC* curve has the same shape as the *TVC* curve but is $30 (the *TFC*) above it at each output level.

Per–Unit Costs

Average fixed cost (*AFC*) Total fixed costs divided by output.

Average variable cost (*AVC*) Total variable costs divided by output.

Average total cost (*ATC*) Total costs divided by output. Also equals *AFC* + *AVC*.

Marginal Cost (*MC*) The change in total costs.

From total costs we can derive per-unit costs. These are even more important in the short-run analysis of the firm. **Average fixed cost (*AFC*)** equals total fixed costs divided by output. **Average variable cost (*AVC*)** equals total variable costs divided by output. **Average total cost (*ATC*)** equals total costs divided by output. *ATC* also equals *AFC* plus *AVC*. **Marginal cost (*MC*)** equals the change in *TC* or in *TVC* per unit change in output.

Table 8.3 presents the per-unit cost schedules derived from the corresponding total cost schedules of Table 8.2. The *AFC* values given in column 5 are obtained by dividing the *TFC* values in column 2 by the quantity of output in column 1. *AVC* (column 6) equals *TVC* (column 3) divided by output (column 1). *ATC* (column 7) equals *TC* (column 4) divided by output (column 1). *ATC* also equals *AFC* plus *AVC*. *MC* (column 8) is given by the change in *TVC* (column 3) or in *TC* (column 4) per unit change in output (column 1). Thus, *MC* does not depend on *TFC*.

The per-unit cost schedules given in Table 8.3 are plotted in Figure 8.2. Note that *MC* is plotted *between* the various levels of output. From Table 8.3 and Figure 8.2, we see that

TABLE 8.3 Total and Per-Unit Costs

Quantity of Output (1)	Total Fixed Costs (2)	Total Variable Costs (3)	Total Costs (4)	Average Fixed Cost (5)	Average Variable Cost (6)	Average Total Cost (7)	Marginal Cost (8)
1	$30	$20	$50	$30	$20	$50	$20
2	30	30	60	15	15	30	10
3	30	45	75	10	15	25	15
4	30	80	110	7.50	20	27.50	35
5	30	145	175	6	29	35	65

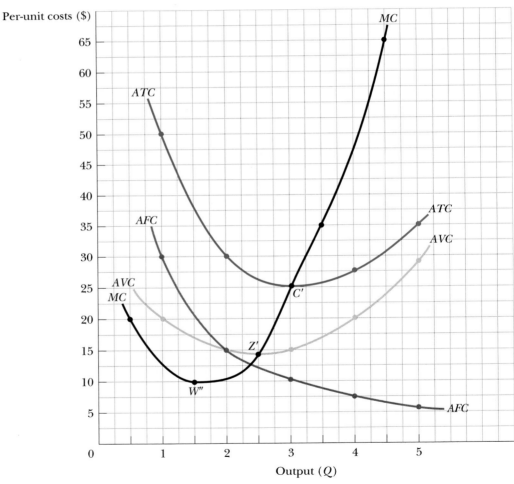

FIGURE 8.2   Per-Unit Cost Curves   The average fixed cost (*AFC*) curve falls continuously, while the average variable cost (*AVC*), average total cost (*ATC*), and marginal cost (*MC*) curves are U-shaped. The *MC* is plotted between the various output levels. The *ATC* curve falls as long as the decline in *AFC* exceeds the rise in *AVC*. The rising portion of the *MC* curve intersects from below the *AVC* and the *ATC* curves at their lowest point.

the *AFC* curve falls continuously, while the *AVC*, *ATC*, and *MC* curves first fall and then rise (i.e., they are U-shaped). Since the vertical distance between the *ATC* and the *AVC* curve equals *AFC*, a separate *AFC* curve is superfluous and can be omitted from the figure.

The reason the *AVC* curve is U-shaped can be explained as follows. With labor as the only variable input in the short run, *TVC* for any output level (*Q*) equals the given wage rate ($\overline{w}$) times the quantity of labor (*L*) used. Then,

$$AVC = \frac{TVC}{Q} = \frac{\overline{w}L}{Q} = \frac{\overline{w}}{Q/L} = \frac{\overline{w}}{AP_L} = \overline{w}\left(\frac{1}{AP_L}\right) \qquad [8.1]$$

With $\overline{w}$ constant and from our knowledge (from Section 7.2) that the average physical product of labor (AP_L or Q/L) usually rises first, reaches a maximum, and then falls, it follows that the *AVC* curve first falls, reaches a minimum, and then rises. Thus, the *AVC* curve is the monetized mirror image, reciprocal, or "dual" of the AP_L curve. Since the *AVC* curve is U-shaped, the *ATC* curve is also U-shaped. The *ATC* curve continues to fall after the *AVC* curve begins to rise because, for a while, the decline in *AFC* exceeds the rise in *AVC* (see Figure 8.2).

The U-shape of the *MC* curve can similarly be explained as follows:

$$MC = \frac{\Delta TVC}{\Delta Q} = \frac{\Delta(\overline{w}L)}{\Delta Q} = \frac{\overline{w}(\Delta L)}{\Delta Q} = \frac{\overline{w}}{\Delta Q/\Delta L} = \frac{\overline{w}}{MP_L} = \overline{w}\left(\frac{1}{MP_L}\right) \qquad [8.2]$$

Since the marginal product of labor (MP_L or $\Delta Q/\Delta L$) first rises, reaches a maximum, and then falls, it follows that the *MC* curve first falls, reaches a minimum, and then rises. Thus, the rising portion of the *MC* curve reflects the operation of the law of diminishing returns.[3]

The *MC* curve reaches its minimum point at a smaller level of output than the *AVC* and the *ATC* curves, and it intersects from below the *AVC* and the *ATC* curves at their lowest points (see Figure 8.2). The reason is that for average costs to fall, the marginal cost must be lower. For average costs to rise, the marginal cost must be higher. Also, for average costs neither to fall nor rise (i.e., to be at their lowest point), the marginal cost must be equal to them. Although the *AVC*, *ATC*, and *MC* curves are U-shaped, they sometimes have a fairly flat bottom (see Example 8–2).

Geometry of Per-Unit Cost Curves

The shapes of the per-unit cost curves are determined by the shapes of the corresponding total cost curves. The *AVC* and *ATC* are given, respectively, by the slope of a line (ray) from the origin to the *TVC* and *TC* curves, while the *MC* is given by the slope of the *TC* and the *TVC* curves. This is similar to the derivation of the average and marginal product curves from the total product curve in Section 7.2.

Figure 8.3 shows that the *AVC* at 1 and 4 units of output (*Q*) is given by the slope of ray 0*Y*, which is $20. Note that the slope of a ray from the origin to the *TVC* curve in the

Concept Check
Why is the shape of the marginal cost curve the opposite of that of the marginal product curve?

Concept Check
Why does the marginal cost curve intersect the average variable curve and the average total costs curves at their lowest point?

---

[3] If factor prices increased, the *MC* and the other cost curves would shift up, as shown in the appendix to this chapter.

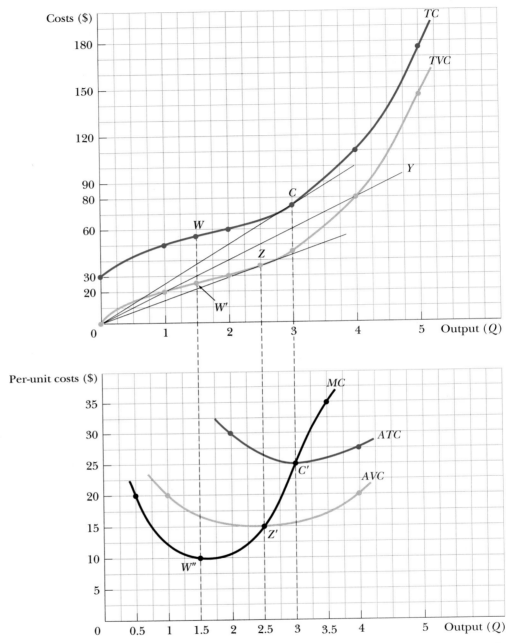

FIGURE 8.3   Graphic Derivation of Per-Unit Cost Curves   The *AVC* and *ATC* are given, respectively, by the slope of a line from the origin to the *TVC* and *TC* curves, while the *MC* curve is given by the slope of the *TC* or *TVC* curves. The slope of a ray from the origin to the *TVC* curve (the *AVC*) falls up to point *Z* and rises thereafter. The slope of a ray from the origin to the *TC* curve (the *ATC*) falls up to point *C* and rises thereafter. The slope of the *TC* and *TVC* curves (the *MC*) falls up to point *W* and *W'*, respectively, and then rises and intersects from below the *AVC* and the *ATC* curves at their lowest points.

top panel falls up to point Z (where the ray from the origin is tangent to the TVC curve) and then rises. Thus, the AVC curve in the bottom panel falls up to point Z' (i.e., up to $Q = 2.5$) and rises thereafter. The bottom panel of Figure 8.3 also shows that the ATC at $Q = 3$ is $25 (the slope of ray $0C$ in the top panel). Note that the slope of a ray from the origin to the TC curve falls up to point C (where the ray from the origin is tangent to the TC curve) and then rises. Thus, the ATC curve falls up to point C' (i.e., up to $Q = 3$) and rises thereafter.

The top panel of Figure 8.3 also shows that the slope of the TC and TVC curves falls up to point W and W' (the points of inflection) on the TC and TVC curves, respectively, and then rises. Thus, the MC curve in the bottom panel falls up to W'' and rises thereafter. At point Z, the MC and AVC are both equal to the slope of ray $0Z$. This is $35/2.5$, or $14, and equals the lowest AVC. At point C, the MC and ATC are both equal to the slope of ray $0C$. This is $75/3$, or $25, and equals the lowest ATC. Note that the AVC, ATC, and MC curves derived geometrically in Figure 8.3 are identical to those in Figure 8.2 and correspond to the values in Table 8.3.

Not shown in Figure 8.3 (in order not to complicate the figure unnecessarily) is the geometrical derivation of the AFC curve. This, however, is very simple. For example, turning back for a moment to Figure 8.1, we can see that the AFC for one unit of output is equal to the slope of the ray from the origin to $Q = 1$ on the $TFC = 30$ curve. This is $30/1$, or $30. At $Q = 2$, $AFC = 30/2 = 15$. At $Q = 3$, $AFC = 30/3 = 10$, and so on. Note that because TFC are constant, AFC falls continuously as output rises. Thus, the AFC curve is a rectangular hyperbola (see Figure 8.2). As pointed out earlier, AFC is equal to the vertical distance between the ATC curve and the AVC curve, and so a separate AFC curve is not really necessary.

EXAMPLE 8–2

Per-Unit Cost Curves in Corn Production and in Traveling

Figure 8.4 shows the actual estimated AVC, ATC, and MC per bushel of corn raised on central Iowa farms. The per-unit cost curves in the figure have the same general shape as the typical curves examined earlier, but with flatter bottoms. Once MC starts rising, it does so very rapidly. This is true not only in raising corn but also in many other cases. For example, traveling costs (in terms of travel time) rise very steeply during peak hours on highways. Similarly, landing costs (in terms of landing time) at airports also rise rapidly during peak hours (3–5 P.M.).

Sources: D. Suits, "Agriculture," in W. Adams and J. Brock (eds.), *The Structure of the American Economy* (Englewood Cliffs, NJ: Prentice-Hall, 1995), p. 12; A. Carlin and R. Park, "Marginal Cost Pricing of Airport Runway Capacity," *American Economic Review,* June 1970; M. Samuel, "Traffic Congestion: A Solvable Problem," *Issues in Technology,* Spring 1999; and "What's the Toll? It Depends on the Time of Day," *New York Times,* Business Review, February 11, 2007, p. 7.

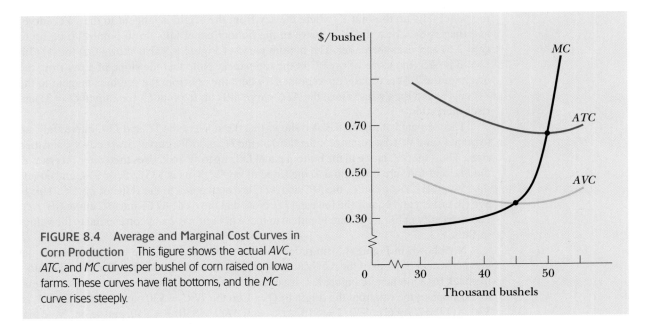

FIGURE 8.4   Average and Marginal Cost Curves in Corn Production   This figure shows the actual *AVC*, *ATC*, and *MC* curves per bushel of corn raised on Iowa farms. These curves have flat bottoms, and the *MC* curve rises steeply.

8.3   COST IN THE LONG RUN

In the long run, all inputs and costs are variable; that is, there are no fixed inputs and no fixed costs. In this section, we define isocost lines and examine how a firm chooses the combination of inputs to minimize the cost of producing a given level of output when all factors are variable.

Isocost Lines

Suppose that a firm uses only labor and capital in production. Then the total cost (*TC*) of the firm for the use of a specific quantity of labor and capital is equal to the price of labor (*w* or the wage rate) times the quantity of labor hired (*L*), plus the price of capital (*r* or the rental price of capital) times the quantity of capital rented (*K*). If the firm owns the capital, *r* is the rent foregone from not renting out the capital (such as machinery) to others. The total cost of the firm can thus be expressed as

$$TC = wL + rK \qquad [8.3]$$

That is, the total cost (*TC*) is equal to the amount that the firm spends on labor (*wL*) plus the amount that the firm spends on capital (*rK*).

Isocost line Shows the various combinations of two inputs that the firm can hire with a given total cost outlay.

Given the wage rate of labor (*w*), the rental price of capital (*r*), and a particular total cost (*TC*), we can define an **isocost line** or equal-cost line. This shows the various combinations of labor and capital that the firm can hire or rent for the given total cost. For example, for $TC_1 = \$80$, $w = \$10$, and $r = \$10$, the firm could either hire $8L$ or rent $8K$, or any combination of *L* and *K* shown on isocost line *RS* in the left panel of Figure 8.5. For each unit of capital the firm gives up, it can hire one more unit of labor. Thus, the slope of isocost line *RS* is −1.

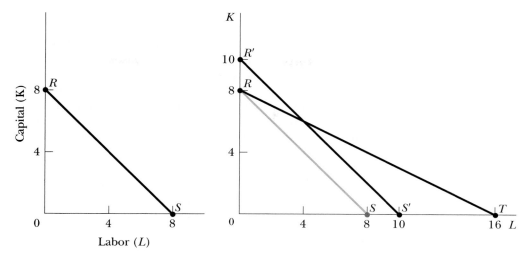

FIGURE 8.5   Isocost Lines   With capital measured along the vertical axis, for $TC_1 = \$80$ and $w = r = \$10$, the Y-intercept of the isocost line is $TC_1/r = \$80/\$10 = 8K$ and the slope is $-w/r = -\$10/\$10 = -1$. This gives budget line RS in the left and right panels. With $TC_2 = \$100$ and unchanged $w = r = \$10$, we have isocost line $R'S'$, with Y-intercept of $TC_2/r = \$100/\$10 = 10K$ and slope of $-w/r = -\$10/\$10 = -1$ in the right panel. With $TC_1 = \$80$ and $r = \$10$ but $w = \$5$, we have isocost line RT with slope of $-1/2$.

By subtracting wL from both sides of equation [8.3] and then dividing by r, we get the general equation of an isocost line in the following more useful form:

$$K = TC/r - (w/r)L \qquad\qquad [8.4]$$

The first term on the right-hand side of equation [8.4] is the vertical or Y-intercept of the isocost line, and $-w/r$ is the slope. Thus, for $TC_1 = \$80$ and $w = r = \$10$, the vertical or Y-intercept is $TC_1/r = \$80/\$10 = 8K$, and the slope is $-w/r = -\$10/\$10 = -1$ (see isocost line RS in the left panel of Figure 8.5).

A different total cost will define a different but parallel isocost line, while a different relative price of an input will define an isocost line with a different slope. For example, an increase in total expenditures to $TC_2 = \$100$ with unchanged $w = r = \$10$ will generate isocost line $R'S'$ in the right panel of Figure 8.5. The vertical or Y-intercept of isocost line $R'S'$ is equal to $TC_2/r = \$100/\$10 = 10K$ and its slope is $-w/r = -\$10/\$10 = -1$. With $TC_1 = \$80$ and $r = \$10$ but $w = \$5$, we have isocost line RT with slope of $-1/2$.

Note the symmetry between the isocost line and the budget line. In Section 3.4 we defined the *budget line* as showing the various combinations of two commodities that a consumer could purchase with a given money income. The *isocost line* shows the various combinations of two inputs that a firm can hire at a given total cost. However, whereas an individual's income is usually given and fixed over a specific period of time (so that we usually deal with only one budget line), a firm's total costs of production vary with output (so that we have a whole family of isocost lines).[4]

---

[4] A consumer's budget line can also change over a given period of time because consumers can save or borrow as well as vary the hours worked and type of job. However, these possibilities are usually not considered in order to keep the analysis simple.

Least-Cost Input Combination[5]

Least-cost input combination The condition where the marginal product per dollar spent on each input is equal.

To minimize the cost of producing a given level of output, the firm must produce at the point where an isocost line is tangent to the isoquant. For example, the left panel of Figure 8.6 shows that the minimum cost of producing four units of output ($4Q$) is $80 (isocost line RS). This is the lowest isocost line that will allow the firm to reach the isoquant for $4Q$. The firm must produce at point D and use $4L$ (at the cost of $wL = \$40$) and $4K$ (at the cost of $rK = \$40$). This is the least-cost input combination. Any other input combination results in higher total costs for the firm to produce four units of output (i.e., to reach isoquant $4Q$).

Minimizing the cost of producing a given level of output is equivalent to maximizing the output for a given cost outlay. The right panel of Figure 8.6 shows that the maximum output or highest isoquant that the firm could reach at the total cost of $80 (i.e., with isocost line RS) is the isoquant for $4Q$. Thus, the condition for cost minimization is equivalent to the condition for output maximization. For both, the firm must produce where an isoquant and an isocost are tangent (point D in both panels of Figure 8.6). The concept of output maximization for a given cost outlay for a producer is completely analogous to the concept of consumer utility maximization for a given budget constraint, which was discussed in Section 3.5.

At the point of tangency, the absolute value of the slope of the isoquant or marginal rate of technical substitution of labor for capital is equal to the absolute value of the slope of the isocost line. That is,

$$MRTS_{LK} = w/r \qquad\qquad [8.5]$$

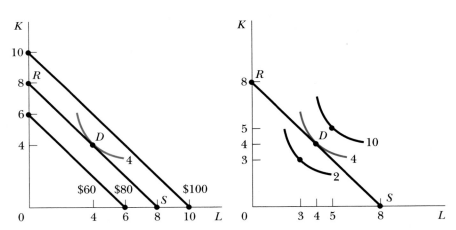

FIGURE 8.6   Optimal Input Combination   The left panel shows that RS is the lowest isocost with which the firm can reach isoquant $4Q$. The firm minimized the cost of producing 4 units of output at point D by using $4L$ and $4K$ at a total cost of $80. The right panel shows that isoquant $4Q$ is the highest isoquant the firm can reach with isocost line RS. Thus, the firm maximizes output with a total cost of $80 by producing at point D and using $4L$ and $4K$.

---

[5] For a mathematical presentation of cost minimization using rudimentary calculus, see Section A.9 of the Mathematical Appendix at the end of the book.

Since the $MRTS_{LK} = MP_L/MP_K$, we can rewrite the **least-cost input combination** as

$$MP_L/MP_K = w/r \qquad\qquad [8.6]$$

Cross multiplying, we get

$$MP_L/w = MP_K/r \qquad\qquad [8.6B]$$

✓ Concept Check

If the price of labor is double the price of capital, why must the marginal product of labor also be double for the least-cost input combination?

Equation [8.6B] indicates that to minimize production costs (or maximize output for a given total cost), the extra output or marginal product per dollar spent on labor must be equal to the marginal product per dollar spent on capital. If $MP_L = 5$, $MP_K = 4$, and $w = r$, the firm would not be maximizing output or minimizing costs since it is getting more extra output for a dollar spent on labor than on capital. To maximize output or minimize costs, the firm would have to hire more labor and rent less capital. As the firm does this, the MP_L declines and the MP_K increases (because of diminishing returns). The process would have to continue until condition [8.6B] held. If w were higher than r, the MP_L would have to be proportionately higher than the MP_K for condition [8.6B] to hold.

The same general condition would have to hold to minimize production costs, no matter how many inputs the firm uses. That is, the MP per dollar spent on each input would have to be the same for all inputs. Another way of stating this is that, for costs to be minimized, an additional or marginal unit of output should cost the same whether it is produced with more labor or more capital.

Cost Minimization in the Long Run and in the Short Run

We have seen in the left panel of Figure 8.6 that the minimum cost of producing four units of output ($4Q$) is $80 when the firm uses four units of labor ($4L$) at $10 per unit and four units of capital ($4K$) at $10 per unit (point D, where the isoquant for $4Q$ is tangent to the isocost for $80). This is repeated in Figure 8.7. Figure 8.7 also shows that in the long run (when both L and K can be varied), the firm can produce $10Q$ with $5L$ and $5K$ at the *minimum* total cost of $100 (point H, where the isoquant for $10Q$ is tangent to the isocost for $100). Points D and H can also be interpreted as the points of maximum output for cost outlays of $80 and $100, respectively. Note that this production function exhibits strong economies of scale (i.e., $4L$ and $4K$ produce $4Q$, while $5L$ and $5K$ produce $10Q$).

✓ Concept Check

Why are costs lower in the long run than in the short run even if factor prices remain constant?

If capital were fixed at $4K$ (in the short run), the *minimum cost* of producing $10Q$ would be higher, or $110, because the firm would have to use $7L$ and $4K$ (point V, where the isoquant for $10Q$ *crosses* the isocost for $110). Thus, the minimum cost of producing a given level of output is lower in the long run when both L and K are variable than in the short run when only L is variable. Note that at point V, the $MRTS_{LK} < w/r$. This means that the rate at which L can be substituted for K *in production* is smaller than the rate at which L can be substituted for K *in the market*. Thus, total costs can be reduced in the long run by using less labor and more capital in production. But this is impossible in the short run. As Example 8–3 shows, total costs would also be higher if government regulation prevented the attainment of the long-run cost minimization point.

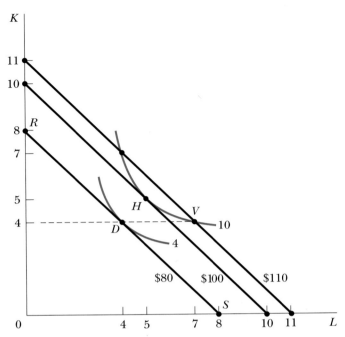

FIGURE 8.7 Long-Run and Short-Run Cost Minimization
Starting from point D, the firm minimizes the long-run cost of
producing 10Q at point H, where isoquant 10Q is tangent to the isocost
line for $100 and the firm uses 5L and 5K. If capital is fixed at 4K, the
firm minimizes the short-run cost of producing 10Q by using 7L and 4K
(point V, where the isoquant for 10Q crosses the isocost line for $110).

EXAMPLE 8–3
Least-Cost Combination of Gasoline and Driving Time

Figure 8.8 repeats the isoquant of Figure 7.8, showing the various combinations of gasoline consumption and driving time required to cover 600 miles. If the price of gasoline is $1.50 per gallon and the opportunity cost of driving time is $6.00 per hour, the minimum total cost for the trip would be $90. This is given by point B, where the isocost line (with absolute slope of $1.50/$6.00 = 1/4) is tangent to the isoquant. Thus, to minimize traveling cost, the individual would have to drive 10 hours at 60 mph and use 20 gallons of gasoline. The individual would spend $30 on gasoline (20 gallons at $1.50 per gallon) and incur an opportunity cost of $60 for travel time (10 hours of driving at $6.00 per hour), for a total cost of $90 for the trip.

If the government set the speed limit at 50 mph, the trip would require 16 gallons of gasoline and 12 hours of driving time (point A). The total cost of the trip would then be $24 for gasoline (16 gallons at $1.50 per gallon) plus $72 for the driving time (12 hours at $6.00 per hour), or $96. Thus, enforcing a 50 mph speed limit saves gasoline but increases driving time and the total cost of the trip.

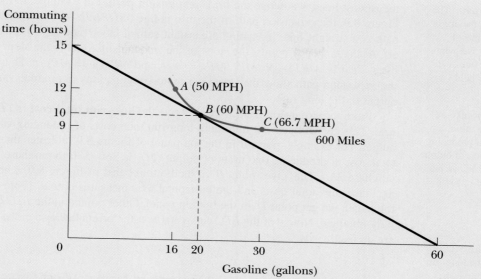

FIGURE 8.8   The Minimum Cost of a Trip   The minimum cost for the trip is $90 and is given at point *B*, where the isoquant is tangent to the isocost. The individual spends $30 on gasoline (20 gallons at $1.50 per gallon) and $60 in driving time (10 hours at $6.00 per hour).

Thus, the final repeal of the 55-mile-an-hour law in 1995 (which had been imposed in 1974 at the start of the petroleum crisis to save gasoline) seems a rational response to the decline in gasoline prices (in relation to other prices) and the increase in real wages that has taken place since 1981. Opposition to the repeal of the 55-mile-an-hour law came primarily from those who believe that lower speed limits save lives. The reduction in gasoline price did, however, bring to a halt progress in energy efficiency.

Sources: C. A. Lave, "Speeding, Coordination, and the 55-mph Limit," *American Economic Review,* December 1985, pp. 1159–1164; "How Much Is Your Time Worth?" *New York Times,* February 26, 2003, p. D1; "At $2 a Gallon, Gas Is Still Worth Guzzling," *New York Times,* May 16, 2004, Sect. 4, p. 14; "Politics Is Forcing Detroit to Support New Rules on Fuel," *New York Times,* June 20, 2007, p. A1; and "Can U.S. Adopt Europe's Fuel-Efficient Cars?" *Wall Street Journal,* June 26, 2007, p. B1.

8.4   EXPANSION PATH AND LONG-RUN COST CURVES

In this section, we first define the firm's expansion path and, from it, derive the firm's long-run total cost curve. From the firm's long-run total cost curve, we then derive the firm's long-run average and marginal cost curves. Finally, we show the relationship between the firm's short-run and long-run average cost curves.

Expansion Path and the Long-Run Total Cost Curve

With constant input prices and higher total cost outlays by the firm, isocost lines will be higher and parallel. By joining the origin with the points of tangency of isoquants and

Expansion path The line joining the origin with the points of tangency of isoquants and isocost lines with input prices held constant.

Long-run total cost (LTC) The minimum total cost of producing various levels of output when the firm can build any desired scale of plant.

✓ Concept Check
How can the long-run total cost curves be derived from the firm's expansion path?

Long-run average cost (LAC) The minimum per-unit cost of producing any level of output when the firm can build any desired scale of plant.

Long-run marginal cost (LMC) The change in long-run total costs per unit change in output.

the isocost lines, we derive the firm's **expansion path.** For example, in the top panel of Figure 8.9, the expansion path of the firm is line $0BDFHJN$. In this case, the expansion path is a straight line, indicating a constant capital-labor ratio (K/L) for all output levels. At the tangency points, the slope of the isoquants is equal to the slope of the isocost lines. That is, $MRTS_{LK} = MP_L/MP_K = w/r$, and $MP_L/w = MP_K/r$. Thus, points along the expansion path show the least-cost input combinations to produce various levels of output in the long run.

From the expansion path, we can derive the **long-run total cost (LTC)** curve of the firm. This curve shows the minimum long-run total costs of producing various levels of output. For example, point B in the top panel of Figure 8.9 indicates that the minimum total cost of producing two units of output $(2Q)$ is \$60 (\$30 to purchase $3L$ and \$30 to purchase $3K$). This gives point B' in the bottom panel of Figure 8.9, where the vertical axis measures total costs and the horizontal axis measures output. From point D in the top panel, we get point D' in the bottom panel. Other points on the LTC curve are similarly obtained. Note that the LTC curve starts at the origin because in the long run there are no fixed costs.

Derivation of the Long-Run Average and Marginal Cost Curves

The **long-run average cost (LAC)** curve is derived from the LTC curve in the same way as the short-run average total cost $(SATC)$ curve is derived from the short-run total cost (STC) curve. For example, in Figure 8.10, the $LAC = \$30$ for two units of output $(2Q)$ is obtained by dividing the LTC of \$60 (point B' on the LTC curve in the top panel) by 2. This is the slope of the ray from the origin to point B' on the LTC curve and is plotted as point B in the bottom panel. Other points on the LAC curve are similarly obtained. Note that the slope of a line from the origin to the LTC curve falls up to point H' (in the top panel of Figure 8.10) and then rises. Thus, the LAC curve in the bottom panel falls up to point H $(10Q)$ and rises thereafter. However, whereas the U-shape of the $SATC$ curve is explained by the law of diminishing returns, the U-shape of the LAC curve depends on the operation of increasing, constant, and decreasing returns to scale, respectively, as explained in Section 7.5.

The relationship between the *long-run* total and per-unit cost curves is generally the same as between the *short-run* total and per-unit cost curves and is also shown in Figure 8.10. The **long-run marginal cost (LMC)** curve is given by the slope of the LTC curve. From the top panel of Figure 8.10, we see that the slope of the LTC curve (the LMC) falls up to $Q = 7$ (the point of inflection) and rises thereafter. Also, the slope of the LTC curve (the LMC) is smaller than the slope of a ray from the origin to the LTC curve (the LAC) up to point H' and larger thereafter. At point H, $LMC = LAC$. Note that the LMC curve intersects from below the LAC curve at the lowest point of the latter. The LMC is \$30 at $Q = 1$ because LTC increases from 0 to \$60 when output rises from zero (the origin) to two units. Thus, the change in LTC per unit change in output (the LMC) is \$60/2 = \$30. The LMC is \$10 at $Q = 3$ because LTC increases from \$60 to \$80 for a two-unit increase in output (from $Q = 2$ to $Q = 4$). The other LMC values shown in Figure 8.10 are obtained in the same way.

The Relationship Between Short- and Long-Run Average Cost Curves

There is an important relationship between the firm's $SATC$ and LAC curves. Figure 8.11 shows that the LAC curve is tangent to various $SATC$ curves. Each $SATC$ curve represents

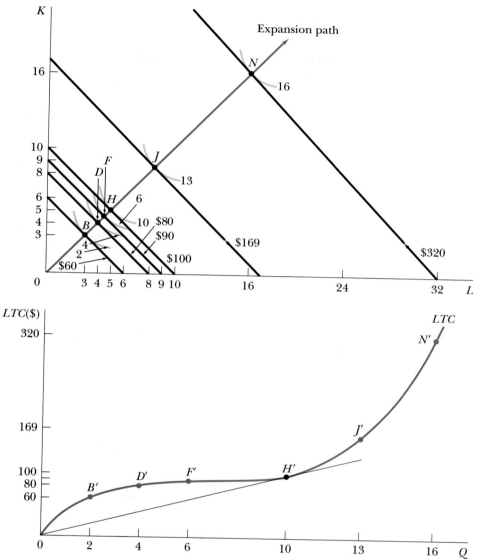

FIGURE 8.9   Derivation of the Expansion Path and the Long-Run Total Cost Curve   The expansion path of the firm is line *OBDFHJN* in the top panel. It is obtained by joining the origin with the points of tangency of isoquants with the isocost lines holding input prices constant. Points along the expansion path show the least-cost input combinations to produce various output levels in the long run. The long-run total cost curve in the bottom panel is derived from the expansion path. For example, point *B′* on the *LTC* curve is derived from point *B* on the expansion path. The *LTC* curve shows the minimum long-run total costs of producing various levels of output when the firm can build any desired scale of plant.

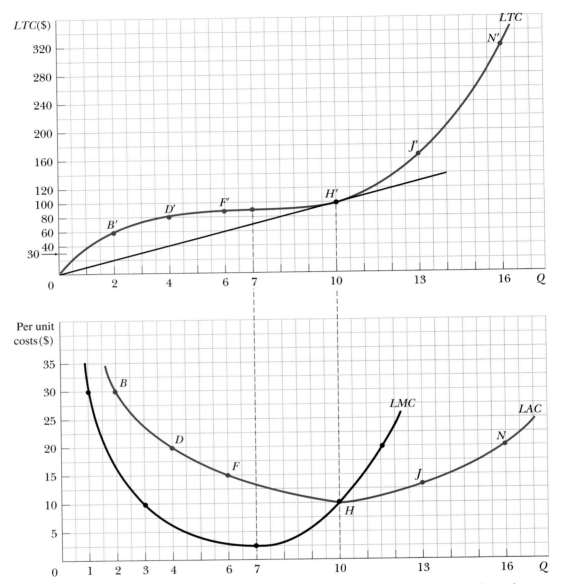

FIGURE 8.10   Derivation of the Long-Run Average and Marginal Cost Curves   The slope of a ray from the origin to the *LTC* curve in the top panel falls up to point *H′* and rises thereafter. Thus, the *LAC* curve in the bottom panel falls up to point *H* and rises thereafter. On the other hand, the slope of the *LTC* in the top panel (the *LMC* in the bottom panel) falls up to the point of inflection (at $Q = 7$) and then rises.

the plant to be used to produce a particular level of output at minimum cost. The *LAC* curve is then the tangent to these *SATC* curves and shows the minimum cost of producing each level of output. For example, the lowest *LAC* (of $30) to produce two units of output results when the firm operates plant 1 at point *B* on its $SATC_1$ curve. The lowest *LAC* (of $20) to produce four units of output results when the firm operates plant 2 at point *D* on its $SATC_2$ curve. Four units of output could also be produced by the firm operating

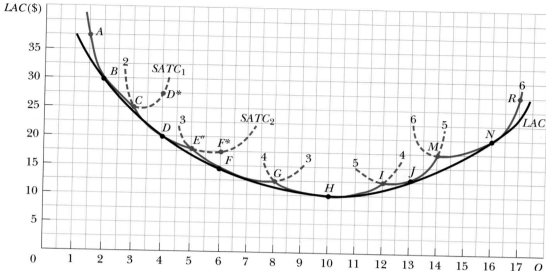

Figure 8.11 **Relationship Between Short- and Long-Run Average Cost Curves** The *LAC* curve is tangent to the *SATC* curves, each representing the plant size to produce a particular level of output at minimum cost. With only six plants, the *LAC* curve would be *ABCDE″FGHIJMNR* (the solid portion of the *SATC* curves). With the infinite or very large number of plant sizes that the firm could build in the long run, the *LAC* curve would be the smooth curve passing through points *BDFHJN*.

✓ Concept Check

Why is the long-run average cost curve the "envelope" of the firm's short-run curve curves?

Planning horizon

The time period when a firm can build any desired scale of plant; the long run.

plant 1 at point $D*$ on its $SATC_1$ curve (see the figure). However, this would not represent the lowest cost of producing $4Q$ in the long run. Other points on the *LAC* curve are similarly obtained. Thus, the *LAC* curve shows the minimum per-unit cost of producing any level of output *when the firm can build any desired scale of plant.* Note that the *LAC* to produce $3Q$ is the same for plant 1 and plant 2 (point C).

With only six plant sizes, the *LAC* curve would be *ABCDE″FGHIJMNR* (the solid portion of the *SATC* curves). With the infinite or very large number of plant sizes that the firm could build in the long run, the *LAC* curve would be the smooth curve passing through points *BDFHJN* (that is, the "kink" at points C, $E″$, G, I, and M would be eliminated by having many plant sizes). Mathematically, the *LAC* curve is the "envelope" to the *SATC* curves.

The long run is often referred to as the **planning horizon.** In the long run, the firm has the time to build the plant that minimizes the cost of producing any anticipated level of output. Once the plant has been built, the firm operates in the short run. Thus, the firm plans in the long run and operates in the short run. Example 8–4 shows the long run average cost curve in the generation of electricity.

EXAMPLE 8–4

Long-Run Average Cost Curve in Electricity Generation

Figure 8.12 shows the actual estimated *LAC* curve for a sample of 114 firms generating electricity in the United States in 1970. The figure shows that the *LAC* is lowest at

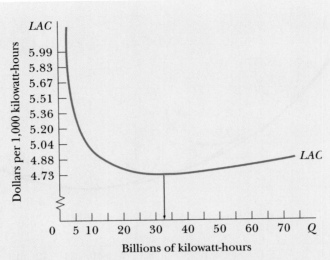

FIGURE 8.12 Long-Run Average Cost Curve in Electricity Generation This figure shows the actual estimated *LAC* curve for a sample of 114 firms generating electricity in the United States in 1970. The lowest point on the *LAC* curve is at the output level of about 32 billion kilowatt-hours. However, the *LAC* curve is nearly L-shaped.

the output level of about 32 billion kilowatt-hours. The *LAC*, however, is nearly L-shaped, indicating that *LAC* do not increase much for outputs greater than 32 billion kilowatt-hours. Electrical companies were able to avoid the increasing costs that they would have incurred in producing more power themselves to satisfy increasing consumer demand by buying more and more power from independent power producers. But all of this is changing very rapidly in the face of deregulation and the end of monopoly power by electrical companies (see Chapters 9 and 12). Furthermore, recent technological advances have greatly reduced the average cost of producing electricity with micro-turbine generators, and this may soon provide even small businesses with the choice of generating their own electricity efficiently.

Sources: L. Christensen and H. Green, "Economies of Scale in U.S. Electric Power Generation," *Journal of Political Economy,* August 1976, p. 674; and "Electric Utilities Brace for an End to Monopolies," *New York Times,* August 18, 1994, p. 1; "Energy: Power Unbound," *Wall Street Journal,* September 14, 1998, pp. R4, R10; The Royal Academy of Engineering, *The Cost of Generating Electricity* (London: Royal Academy of Engineering, 2004); and OECD, *Projected Costs of Generating Electricity* (Paris: OECD, 2005).

8.5	

SHAPE OF THE LONG-RUN AVERAGE COST CURVE

In Figures 8.10 and 8.11, the *LAC* curve has been drawn as U-shaped, just like the *SATC* curve. The reason for this similarity, however, is entirely different. The *SATC* curve turns upward when the rise in *AVC* (resulting from the operation of the law of diminishing returns) exceeds the decline in *AFC* (see Figure 8.2 and the discussion relating to it). However, in the long run, all inputs are variable (i.e., there are no fixed inputs) and so the law of diminishing returns is not applicable. The U-shape of the *LAC* curve depends instead on increasing and decreasing returns to scale. That is, as output expands from very low levels, increasing returns to scale prevail and cause the *LAC* curve to fall. As output continues to expand, the forces for decreasing returns to scale eventually begin to overtake the forces for increasing returns to scale and the *LAC* curve begins to rise.

As seen in Section 7.5, increasing returns to scale means that output rises proportionately more than inputs, and so the cost per unit of output falls if input prices remain constant. On the other hand, decreasing returns to scale means that output rises proportionately less than inputs, and so the cost per unit of output rises if input prices remain constant. Therefore, decreasing *LAC* and increasing returns to scale are two sides of the same coin.[6] Similarly, increasing *LAC* and decreasing returns to scale are equivalent. When the forces for increasing returns to scale are just balanced by the forces for decreasing returns to scale, we have constant returns to scale and the *LAC* curve is horizontal.

Empirical studies seem to indicate that in many industries the *LAC* curve has a very shallow bottom or is nearly L-shaped, as in Figure 8.12. This means that economies of scale are rather quickly exhausted, and constant or near-constant returns to scale prevail over a considerable range of output. This permits relatively small and large firms to coexist in the same industry (see Example 8–5). The smallest quantity at which the *LAC* curve reaches its minimum is called the **minimum efficient scale (MES).** The smaller the MES, the smaller the prevalence of economies of scale and the larger the number of firms that can operate efficiently in the industry (see Example 8–6).

Were increasing returns to scale to prevail over a very large range of output, large (and more efficient) firms would drive smaller firms out of business. In an extreme case, only one firm could most efficiently satisfy the entire market demand for the commodity. This is usually referred to as a "natural monopoly." In such cases, the government allows only one firm to operate in the market, but the firm is subject to regulation. Examples are provided by public utilities (such local electrical water and gas companies). Natural monopolies are discussed in detail in Chapter 13. On the other hand, the reason we do not often observe steeply rising *LAC* in the real world is that firms may generally know when their *LAC* would begin to rise rapidly and avoid expanding output in that range.

Minimum efficient scale (MES) The smallest quantity at which the *LAC* curve reaches its minimum.

EXAMPLE 8–5

Shape of the Long-Run Average Cost Curves in Various Industries

Table 8.4 gives the long-run average cost for small firms as a percentage of the long-run average cost of large firms in seven U.S. industries or sectors. The table shows that the *LAC* of small hospitals is 29% higher than for large hospitals. This implies that small hospitals operate in the declining portion of the *LAC* curve. For Ph.D.-granting institutions, the *LAC* for small universities is about 19% higher than for large ones. For most other industries, the *LAC* of small firms is not much different from the *LAC* for large firms in the same industry. These results are consistent with the widespread

[6] Increasing returns to scale and decreasing costs and economies of scale are synonymous only if the firm keeps the capital-labor ratio unchanged as it expands its scale of operation.

TABLE 8.4	Long-Run Average Cost (LAC) of Small Firms as a Percentage of LAC of Large Firms	
Industry		**Percentage**
Hospitals		129
Higher education		119
Commercial Banking		
Demand deposits		116
Installment loans		102
Electric power		112
Airline (local service)		100
Railroads		100
Trucking		95

near-constant returns to scale reported in Table 7.9 and with L-shaped or at least flat-bottomed *LAC* curves. Only in trucking does the *LAC* curve seem mildly U-shaped (since small firms have lower *LAC* costs than large ones).

These above results are also consistent with those of a more extensive study conducted in India and in Canada. Of the 29 industries examined in India, 18 were found to have L- or nearly L-shaped *LAC* curves, 6 were found to have horizontal *LAC* curves or nearly so, and only 5 were found to be U-shaped. Of 94 manufacturing industries studied in Canada, 31 had a *LAC* curve that was L-shaped, 23 had a *LAC* that was horizontal, 18 had a *LAC* curve falling throughout, 14 had rising *LAC*, and only for 8 was the *LAC* curve U-shaped.

Sources: H. E. Frech and L. R. Mobley, "Resolving the Impasse on Hospital Scale Economies: A New Approach," *Applied Economics,* March 1995; H. Cohen, "Hospital Cost Curves with Emphasis on Measuring Patient Care Output," in H. Klarman (ed.), *Empirical Studies in Health Economics* (Baltimore: Johns Hopkins Press, 1979); R. K. Koshal and M. Koshal, "Quality and Economies of Scale in Higher Education," *Applied Economics,* Vol. 27, 1995; F. Bell and N. Murphy, *Costs in Commercial Banking* (Boston: Federal Reserve Bank of Boston, Research Report No. 41, 1968); L. Christensen and W. Greene, "Economies of Scale in U.S. Electric Power Generation," *Journal of Political Economy,* August 1976; G. Eads, M. Nerlove, and W. Raduchel, "A Long-Run Cost Function for the Local Service Airline Industry," *The Review of Economics and Statistics,* August 1969; Z. Griliches, "Cost Allocation in Railroad Regulation," *The Bell Journal of Economics and Management Science,* Spring 1972; R. Koenker, "Optimal Scale and the Size Distribution of American Trucking Firms," *Journal of Transport Economics and Policy,* January 1977; V. K. Gupta, "Cost Functions, Concentration, and Barriers to Entry in Twenty-Nine Manufacturing Industries in India," *Journal of Industrial Economics,* November 1968; B. Robidoux and J. Lester, "Econometric Estimates of Scale Economies in Canadian Manufacturing," *Applied Economics,* January 1992.

EXAMPLE 8–6

Minimum Efficient Scale in Various U.S. Food Industries

Table 8.5 shows the minimum efficient scale (MES) as a percentage of output in various U.S. food industries in 1986. The table shows that the MES was 12.01% of the total cane sugar industry output. Thus, economies of scale seem to be very important in this

	MES as Percentage of Output		MES as Percentage of Output
TABLE 8.5 Minimum Efficient Scale (MES) as a Percentage of Output in Various U.S. Food Industries			
Industry	MES as Percentage of Output	Industry	MES as Percentage of Output
Cane sugar	12.01	Beer	1.37
Breakfast cereals	9.47	Frozen food	0.92
Roasted coffee	5.82	Processed meat	0.26
Canned soup	2.59	Canned vegetables	0.17
Biscuits	2.04	Bread	0.12
Margarine	1.75	Mineral water	0.08

Source: J. Sutton, *Sunk Costs and Market Structure* (Cambridge, MA: MIT Press, 1991), pp. 106–105.

industry. One way to interpret this is to say that if all firms in the industry were identical in size and were just large enough to produce at the smallest output at which their *LAC* curve was minimum, only eight firms could exist in this industry. This is to be contrasted with the mineral water industry, where the MES was 0.08% of the total industry output, so that economies of scale seem to be very small indeed and a very large number of firms could exist in the industry. For all the other industries studied, the MES is between these two extremes.

8.6   MULTIPRODUCT FIRMS AND DYNAMIC CHANGES IN COSTS

Until now, we have assumed that a firm produced a single product. In this section, we examine how a firm producing more than one product may face lower costs for each product than if it produced only one or fewer products. We also examine the reduction in costs that often occur as a firm gains experience or "learns" in the production of a given product.

Economies of Scope

Economies of scope The lowering of costs that a firm often experiences when it produces two or more products jointly rather than separate firms producing the products independently.

In the real world, we often observe firms producing more than one product rather than a single product. For example, automobile companies produce cars and trucks, computer firms produce desktops and portables, universities produce teaching and research, and chicken farms produce poultry and eggs. **Economies of scope** are present if it is cheaper for a single firm to produce various products jointly than for separate single-product firms to produce the products independently.[7] For example, economies of scope exist if the total cost (*TC*) of jointly producing cars (*C*) and trucks (*T*) is smaller than if cars and trucks were produced independently by different firms. That is, economies of scope exist if

$$TC(C,T) < [TC(C,0) + TC(0,T)] \qquad [8.7]$$

[7] See J. C. Panzar and R. D. Willig, "Economies of Scope," *American Economic Review,* May 1981; and E. E. Bailey and A. F. Friedlaender, "Market Structure and Multiproduct Industries: A Review Article," *Journal of Economic Literature,* September 1982.

Diseconomies of scope
The higher costs that a firm can experience when it produces two or more products jointly rather than separate firms producing the products independently.

✓ Concept Check
What is the difference between economies of scale and economies of scope?

In other words, economies of scope are present if it is more expensive to produce cars and trucks independently rather than jointly. If the opposite is the case (i.e., it is less expensive to produce cars and trucks independently than jointly), so that the direction of the above inequality sign is reversed, we would have **diseconomies of scope.**

Economies of scope may arise when products can be produced with common production facilities or other inputs, thus lowering costs. For example, automobiles and trucks can be produced with the same metal sheet and engine assembly facilities, and their joint production leads to a better utilization of those production facilities and lower costs than when automobiles and trucks are produced independently by different firms. Similarly, a small commuter airline may face lower costs if it also provides cargo services than if it provided only commuter service. Economies of scope also arise when a firm produces a second product in order to utilize the by-products (which before, the firm had to dispose at a cost) arising from the production of the first product. In addition, economies of scope can result from better marketing strategies and the better utilization of a common administration. Firms must constantly be alert to the possibility of profitably extending their product lines to exploit such economies of scope. Indeed, one reason for the existence of multiproduct conglomerates is the synergy or the increase in efficiency and lower costs arising from economies of scope.

Economies of scope must be clearly distinguished from economies of scale. There is simply no direct relationship between the two. For example, full-service banking arose because of the economies of scope in providing savings and checking deposits, loans, currency exchange, and data processing to customers by the same bank, and not because of economies of scale (which have been found to be fully exhausted for banks as small as with $25 million in deposits).[8] Sometimes, however, expected synergies and economies of scope fail to materialize and the conglomerate either fails or deliberately splits into separate entities. This is exactly what happened to ITT in 1995 when it decided to split into three different companies: an insurance company, an industrial product manufacturing business, and a casino, hotel, and sports company.[9] In 2000, AT&T announced its intention of splitting itself into four separate companies (business services, consumer products, wireless, and broadband).[10]

The Learning Curve

Learning curve The curve showing the decline in average costs with rising cumulative total outputs over time.

As a firm gains experience in the production of a commodity or service, its average cost of production usually declines. In other words, *for a given level of output per time period,* the increasing *cumulative total output* over many time periods often provides the manufacturing experience that enables the firm to significantly lower its average cost of production. The **learning curve** shows the decline in the average input cost of production with rising cumulative total outputs of the firm over time. For example, it might take 1,000 hours for an aircraft manufacturer to assemble the 100th aircraft, but only 700 hours to assemble the 200th aircraft because as managers and workers gain production experience they usually become more efficient, especially when the production process is relatively new. Contrast this with economies of scale, which refers to declining long-run average cost as the firm's output *per time period* increases.

[8] T. G. Gilligan, M. Smirlock, and W. Marshall, "Scale and Scope Economies in the Multiproduct Banking Firm," *Journal of Monetary Economics,* October 1984.
[9] "ITT, The Quintessential Conglomerate, Plans to Split Up," *New York Times,* June 14, 1995, p. D1.
[10] "AT&T Gives Details of Pending Breakup," *New York Times,* May 12, 2001, p. C3.

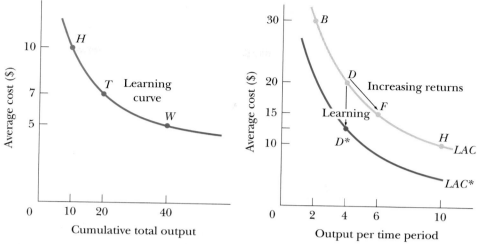

FIGURE 8.13   Learning and Increasing Returns Compared   The left panel shows that as the total cumulative output of the firm doubles from 10 to 20 units over time, the average cost declines from $10 to $7 (the movement from point *H* to point *T* on the learning curve). The right panel shows that *LAC* declines from $20 to $15 as output increases from 4 to 6 units per time period (the movement from point *D* to point *F* along the *LAC* curve) due to increasing returns to scale. But *LAC* falls from $20 to $12.50 to produce 4 units of output per time period as the firm learns from larger cumulative total outputs (the downward shift of the *LAC* curve from point *D* to point *D**).

✓ Concept Check

What is the difference between learning curves and economies of scale?

The left panel of Figure 8.13 shows a learning curve that indicates that the average cost declines from $10 for producing the 10th unit of the product (point *H*), to $7 for producing the 20th unit (point *T*), and to $5 for producing the 40th unit of the product (point *W*). Average cost declines at a decreasing rate so that the learning curve is convex to the origin. This is the usual shape of learning curves; that is, firms usually achieve the largest decline in average input costs when the production process is relatively new and smaller declines as the firm matures.

The difference between the reduction in average costs due to learning and to increasing returns to scale is clarified by examining the right panel of Figure 8.13. In the figure, the reduction in long-run average cost (*LAC*) due to increasing returns to scale is shown by a movement, say from point *D* to point *F*, along the *LAC* curve (the same as in Figure 8.11) as output *per time period* increases. The reduction in *LAC* due to learning is instead shown by the downward shift in the *LAC* curve, say from point *D* to point *D**, for a given level of output per time period, but as the firm learns from a larger total cumulative output over many periods.

Learning curves have been documented in many manufacturing and service sectors including manufacturing of airplanes, appliances, ships, computer chips, refined petroleum products, and the operation of power plants. Learning curves have also been used to forecast the need for personnel, machinery, and raw materials and for scheduling production, determining the price at which to sell output, and even to evaluate suppliers' price quotations. For example, in its early days as a producer of computer chips, Texas Instruments adopted an aggressive price strategy based on the learning curve. Believing that the learning curve in chip production was steep, the firm kept unit prices very low to increase its total cumulative output rapidly, thereby learning by doing. The strategy was successful and the rest is history (Texas Instruments became one of the world's major players in this market).

How rapidly the learning curve (i.e., average input cost) declines can differ widely among firms and is greater the smaller the rate of employee turnover, the fewer production interruptions (which would lead to "forgetting"), and the greater the ability of the firm to transfer knowledge from the production of other similar products. The average cost typically declines by 20% to 30% for each doubling of cumulative output for many firms (see Example 8–7).[11]

EXAMPLE 8–7

Learning Curve for the Lockheed L-1011 Aircraft and for Semiconductors

Figure 8.14 shows the learning curve for the L-1011 aircraft that Lockheed produced between 1970 and 1984 in the United States. The figure shows that the number of

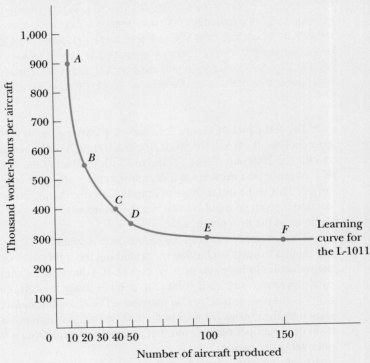

FIGURE 8.14   Learning Curve for the Lockheed 1011 Aircraft   The figure shows that the number of worker-hours (in thousands) that Lockheed used to produce its L-1011 aircraft declined at a about the rate of 20% and essentially came to an end when cumulative production reached about 100 aircraft.

[11] The classic paper on learning curves is K. Arrow, "The Economic Implication of Learning by Doing," *Review of Economic Studies,* June 1962. See also L. Argote and D. Epple, "Learning Curves in Manufacturing," *Science,* February 23, 1990, and D. A. Irwin and P. J. Klenow, "Learning-by-Doing Spillovers in the Semiconductor Industry," *Journal of Political Economy,* December 1994.

worker-hours (in thousands) that Lockheed used was 900 to produce the 10th aircraft, 550 for the 20th, 400 for the 40th, 350 for the 50th, 300 for the 100th, and slightly lower than 300 to produce the 150th aircraft. This implies a learning rate of about 20%. Thus, a 10% increase in cumulative production would lead to a 2% reduction in cost. Learning essentially came to an end with the production of the 100th aircraft. After producing 150 of the L-1011, the rate of production slowed down considerably and the worker-hours required to produce each aircraft went back up to about 500,000 (not shown in the figure). This implies organizational forgetting when the rate of production slows down significantly (Lockheed stopped producing the L-1011 in 1984 after producing 250 aircraft).

Learning has also been important in the production of semiconductors (the memory chips that are used in personal computers, cellular telephones, electronic games, etc.). The semiconductor industry introduced seven generations of dynamic random access memory chips (DRAM) between 1974 and 1992. A study found that the learning rate in the production of each generation of DRAMs also averaged about 20%, so that a doubling of cumulative output reduced the average cost of production by about 20%. The study also found that there was no discernible difference in the speed of learning of U.S. and Japanese firms, but that intergenerational learning was low. That is, having a lower cost in the production of one generation of DRAMs was no guarantee of continued success cess in the production of the next generation. Related to the learning curve is *Moore's Law*, which accurately predicted in 1965 that semiconductors (chip) performance would double roughly every 18 months!

Sources: C. L. Benkard, "Learning and Forgetting: The Dynamics of Aircraft Production," *American Economic Review,* September 2000; D. A. Irwin and P. J. Klenow, "Learning-by-Doing Spillovers in the Semiconductor Industry," *Journal of Political Economy*, December 1994; "Moore's Law at 40: Happy Birthday," *The Economist*, March 26, 2005, p. 65; "More Life for Moore's Law," *Business Week*, June 20, 2005, pp. 108–109; and "Moore's Law Triumphant," *Forbes*, February 26, 2007, p. 33.

AT THE FRONTIER
Minimizing Costs Internationally—The New Economies of Scale

During the past decade, there has been a sharp increase in international trade in parts and components. Today, more and more products manufactured by international corporations have parts and components made in many different nations. The reason is to minimize production costs. For example, the motors of some Ford Fiestas are produced in the United Kingdom, the transmissions in France, the clutches in Spain, and the parts are assembled in Germany for sales throughout Europe. Similarly, Japanese and German cameras are often assembled in Singapore to take advantage of the cheaper labor there.

Foreign "sourcing" of inputs is often not a matter of choice to earn higher profits, but simply a requirement to remain competitive. Firms that do not look abroad for cheaper inputs face loss of competitiveness in world markets and even in the domestic

Continued ...

Minimizing Costs Internationally   *Continued*

market. This is the reason that $625 of the $860 total cost of producing an IBM PC was outsourced from abroad and most of the major components going into the production of a Boeing 777 are made abroad. Of 162 major multinationals surveyed, 139 outsourced some activities in 2005. U.S. firms now spend more than $100 billion on outsourcing and by doing so they cut costs by 10–15%. Outsourcing now accounts for more than one-third of total manufacturing costs by Japanese firms and this saves them more than 20% of production costs. Such low-cost offshore purchase of inputs is likely to continue to expand rapidly in the future and is being fostered by joint ventures, licensing arrangements, and other nonequity collaborative arrangements. Indeed, this represents one of the most dynamic aspects of the global business environment of today.

Not only are more and more inputs imported, but more and more firms are opening production facilities in more and more nations. For example, Nestlé, the largest Swiss company and the world's second largest food company, has production facilities in 59 countries, America's Gillette has facilities in 22 countries. In 2006, Ford had major manufacturing operations in Canada, Mexico, the United Kingdom, Germany, Brazil, Argentina, China, and South Africa and component factories in 26 other countries and employed more people abroad than in the United States (respectively 150,000 and 130,000). Bertelsman AG, the $7 billion German media empire, owns printing plants around the world and the Literary Guild Book Club, and it also prints books at competitors' plants and sells them through Time-owned Book-of-the-Month Club.

So widespread and growing is international trade in inputs and the opening of production facilities abroad that we are rapidly moving toward truly multinational firms with roots in many nations rather than in only one country, as in the past. This change affects not only the multinational companies. Indeed, more and more firms that, until a few years ago, operated exclusively in the domestic market are now purchasing increasing quantities of inputs and components and shifting some of their production to foreign nations. For example, Malachi Mixon, the American medical equipment company, now buys parts and components in half a dozen countries, from China to Colombia, when ten years ago it did all of its shopping at home. The popular Mazda Miata automobile, which is manufactured in Japan, was conceived in Mazda's California design lab by an American engineer at the same time that Mazda opened production facilities for other models in the United States.

International economies of scale The lower costs resulting from a firm's integration of its entire system of manufacturing operations around the world.

Firms must constantly explore sources of cheaper inputs and overseas production to remain competitive in our rapidly shrinking world. Indeed, this process can be regarded as manufacturing's new (international) economies of scale in today's global economy. Just as companies were forced to rationalize operations within each country in the 1980s, they now face the challenge of integrating their operations for their entire system of manufacturing around the world to take advantage of the new **international economies of scale.** What is important is for the firm to focus on those components that are indispensable to the company's competitive position over subsequent product generations and "outsource" other components for which outside suppliers have a distinctive production advantage.

The new international economies of scale can be achieved in five basic areas: product development, purchasing, production, demand management, and order fulfillment.

Concept Check

What is the difference between traditional and the international economies of scale?

In product development, the firm can design a core product for the entire world economy by building into the product the possibility of variations and derivatives to meet the needs of local markets. Firms can achieve new economies of scale by purchasing raw materials, parts, and components on a global rather than on a local basis—no matter where their operations are located. Firms can also coordinate production in low-cost manufacturing centers with final assembly in high-cost locations near markets. They can forecast the demand for their products and undertake demand management on a world rather than on a national basis. Firms can achieve important economies of scale by shipping products from the plants closest to customers more quickly and with smaller inventory on a global basis. International economies of scale are likely to become even more important in the future as we move closer and closer to a truly global economy.

Manufacturing Site Location," *MIT Sloan Management Review*, Summer 1994; R. J. Trent and R. M. Monczka, "Achieving Excellence in "Global Sourcing," *MIT Sloan Management Review*, Fall 2005, pp. 24–32; and W. M. Becker and V. M. Freeman, "Going from Global Trends to Global Strategy, *McKinsey Quarterly*, No. 3, 2006, pp. 17–27.

SUMMARY

1. In economics, costs include explicit and implicit costs. Explicit costs are the actual expenditures of the firm to purchase or hire inputs. Implicit costs refer to the value (imputed from their best alternative use) of the inputs owned and used by the firm in its own production process. The opportunity cost to a firm in using any input (whether owned or hired) is what the input could earn in its best alternative use. Costs are also classified into private and social. Private costs are those incurred by individuals and firms, while social costs are those incurred by society as a whole.

2. In the short run we have fixed, variable, and total costs. Total fixed costs (TFC) plus total variable costs (TVC) equal total costs (TC). The shape of the TVC curve follows directly from the law of diminishing returns. Average fixed cost (AFC) equals TFC/Q, where Q is output. Average variable cost (AVC) equals TVC/Q. Average total cost (ATC) equals TC/Q. $ATC = AFC$ plus AVC also. Marginal cost (MC) equals the change in TC or in TVC per-unit change in output. The AVC, ATC, and MC curves first fall and then rise (i.e., they are U-shaped). AVC and MC move inversely to the AP_L and the MP_L, respectively. The AVC and the ATC are given, respectively, by the slope of a line from the origin to the TVC and to the TC curves, while the MC is given by the slope of the TC and the TVC curves.

3. Given the wage rate of labor (w), the rental price of capital (r), and a particular total cost (TC), we can define the isocost line. This line shows the various combinations of L and K that the firm can hire in the long run. With K plotted along the vertical axis, the Y-intercept of the isocost line is TC/r and its slope is $-w/r$. To minimize production costs or maximize output, the firm must produce where an isoquant is tangent to an isocost line. At this point, $MRTS_{LK} = w/r$, and $MP_L/w = MP_K/r$. This means the MP per dollar spent on L must be equal to the MP per dollar spent on K. The minimum cost of producing a given level of output is usually lower in the long run than in the short run.

4. The expansion path joins the origin with the points of tangency of isoquants and isocost lines with input prices held constant. It shows the least-cost input combination to produce various output levels. From the expansion path, we can derive the long-run total cost (LTC) curve. This shows the minimum long-run total costs of producing various levels of output when the

firm can build any desired plant. From the long-run total cost curve, we can then derive the long-run average and marginal cost curves. The long-run average cost (LAC) equals LTC/Q, while the long-run marginal cost (LMC) equals $\Delta LTC/\Delta Q$. The LAC curve is tangent to the short-run average total cost curves. The firm plans in the long run and operates in the short run.

5. The U-shape of the long-run average cost curve of the firm results from the operation of increasing, constant, and decreasing returns to scale, respectively. Empirical studies seem to indicate that in many industries the LAC curve has a very shallow bottom or is nearly L-shaped. This means that economies of scale are quickly exhausted, and constant or near-constant returns to scale prevail over a considerable range of output. This permits relatively small and large firms to coexist in the same industry. The smallest quantity at which the LAC curve reaches its minimum is called the minimum efficient scale (MES).

6. Economies of scope are present if it is cheaper for a firm to produce various products jointly than for separate firms to produce the same products independently. The opposite situation refers to diseconomies of scope. The learning curve shows the decline in the average cost of production with rising cumulative total outputs over time by the firm. During the past decade, there has been a sharp increase in international trade in parts and components, and more and more firms have opened production facilities abroad to keep production costs as low as possible and thus be able to meet the growing international competition. This process can be regarded as manufacturing's new (international) economies of scale in today's global economy.

KEY TERMS

Explicit costs	Total costs (TC)	Long-run average cost (LAC)
Implicit costs	Average fixed cost (AFC)	Long-run marginal cost (LMC)
Opportunity cost	Average variable cost (AVC)	Planning horizon
Alternative or opportunity cost	Average total cost (ATC)	Minimum efficient scale (MES)
doctrine	Marginal cost (MC)	Economies of scope
Private costs	Isocost line	Diseconomies of scope
Social costs	Least-cost input combination	Learning curve
Total fixed costs (TFC)	Expansion path	International economies
Total variable costs (TVC)	Long-run total cost (LTC)	of scale

REVIEW QUESTIONS

1. An individual quits his job as a manager of a small photocopying business in which he was earning $30,000 per year and opens his own shop by renting a store for $5,000 per year, using $10,000 of his own money to rent the photocopying machines, and hiring a helper for $10,000 per year. What are the individual's accounting costs? What are his economic costs?

2. State colleges are more efficient than independent colleges in providing college education because they charge lower tuition. True or false? Explain.

3. Is the annual retainer paid by a firm to a lawyer a fixed or a variable cost?

4. How should a firm utilize each of two plants to minimize production costs for the firm as a whole?

5. If the marginal cost of a firm is rising, does this mean that its average cost is also rising?

6. Is it always better to hire a more qualified and productive worker than a less qualified and productive worker? Explain.

7. Is a firm minimizing costs if the marginal product of labor is six, the marginal product of capital is five, the wage rate is $2, and the interest on capital is $1? If not, what must the firm do to minimize costs?

8. Must a firm's long-run average cost curve be U-shaped if its long-run marginal cost curve is U-shaped?

9. What does the long-run marginal cost curve of a firm look like if its long-run average cost curve is L-shaped?

10. What is the difference between economies of scale, economies of scope, and the reduction in average costs as a result of learning?

11. Should a firm purchase abroad some parts and components needed to produce its product, even if that creates employment opportunities abroad instead of at home?

12. What is meant by "international economies of scale"?

PROBLEMS

*1. A woman working in a large duplicating (photocopying) establishment for $15,000 per year decides to open a small duplicating business of her own. She runs the operation by herself without hired help and invests no money of her own. She rents the premises for $10,000 per year and the machines for $30,000 per year. She spends $15,000 per year on supplies (paper, ink, envelopes), electricity, telephone, and so on. During the year her gross earnings are $65,000.

a. How much are the explicit costs of this business?

b. How much are the implicit costs?

c. Should this woman remain in business after the year if she is indifferent between working for herself or for others in a similar capacity?

2. a. Plot the total fixed costs (*TFC*) curve, the total variable costs (*TVC*) curve, and the total costs (*TC*) curve given in the following table.

Quantity of Output	Total Variable Costs	Total Costs
0	$0	$30
1	20	50
2	30	60
3	48	78
4	90	120
5	170	200

b. Explain the reason for the shape of the cost curves in 2(a) above.

3. a. Derive the average fixed costs (*AFC*), the average variable costs (*AVC*), the average total costs (*ATC*), and the marginal costs (MC) from the total cost schedules given in the table of Problem 2.

b. Plot the *AVC*, *ATC*, and *MC* curves of 3(a) on a graph and explain the reason for their shape. How are *AFC* reflected in the figure?

c. How can the *AFC*, *AVC*, *ATC*, and *MC* curves be derived geometrically?

*4. Electrical utility companies usually operate their most modern and efficient equipment around the clock and use their older and less efficient equipment only to meet periods of peak electricity demand.

a. What does this imply for the short-run marginal cost of these firms?

b. Why do these firms not replace all of their older equipment with newer equipment in the long run?

5. Suppose that the marginal product of the last worker employed by a firm is 30 units of output per day and the daily wage that the firm must pay is $20, while the marginal product of the last machine rented by the firm is 80 units of output per day and the daily rental price of the machine is $40.

a. Why is this firm not maximizing output or minimizing costs in the long run?

b. How can the firm maximize output or minimize costs?

6. With reference to Figure 8.7, answer the following questions.

a. If capital were fixed at 5 units, what would be the minimum cost of producing 10 units of output in the short run?

b. If capital were variable but labor fixed at 4 units, what would be the minimum cost of producing 10 units of output?

7. a. Suppose that $w = 10 and $r = 10 and the least-cost input combination is $3L$ and $3K$ to produce 2 units of output ($2Q$), $4L$ and $4K$ to produce $4Q$, $4.5L$ and $4.5K$ to produce $6Q$, $5L$ and $5K$ to produce $8Q$, $7.5L$ and $7.5K$ for $10Q$, and $12L$ and $12K$ for $12Q$. Draw the isocost lines, the isoquants, and the expansion path of the firm.

b. From the expansion path of 7(a), derive the long-run total cost curve of the firm.

c. Redraw your figure of 7(b) and on it draw the *STC* curve from the data given for Problem 2(a), the *STC*

*= Answer provided at end of book.

curve tangent to the *LTC* curve at $Q = 8$, and the *STC* curve tangent to the *LTC* curve at $Q = 12$.

8. a. From the *LTC* curve of the firm of Problem 7(b), derive the *LAC* and the *LMC* curves of the firm.

   b. Redraw the figure of 8(a), and on the same figure draw the *ATC* and the *MC* curves of Problem 3(b). Also draw the *ATC* curve that forms the lowest point of the LAC curve at $Q = 8$ and the corresponding *SMC* curve. On the same figure, draw the *ATC curve* that is tangent to the *LAC* curve at $Q = 12$ and the corresponding *SMC* curve.

*9. a. Under what condition would the *LTC* curve be a positively sloped straight line through the origin?

   b. What would then be the shape of the *LAC* and the *LMC* curves?

   c. Would this be consistent with U-shaped *STC* curves?

   d. Draw a figure showing your answer to 9(a), 9(b), and 9(c).

10. Suppose that in Figure 8.8 the opportunity cost of driving time remained at $6.00 per hour but the price of gasoline increased to $4.50 per gallon.

   a. Approximately how much gasoline and driving time would the individual use for the trip of 600 miles?

   b. What would be the minimum total cost of the trip?

11. a. Draw a figure showing that the best plant for a range of outputs may not be the best plant to produce a given level of output.

    b. Why might the firm build the first rather than the second type of plant?

*12. Given the following learning curve equation,

$$AC - 1,000 \ Q^{-0.3}$$

where *AC* refers to the average cost of production and *Q* to the total cumulative output of the firm over time, find the *AC* of the firm for producing the

   a. 100th unit of the product.

   b. 200th unit of the product.

   c. 400th unit of the product.

   d. Draw the learning curve from the results obtained from parts (a) to (c).

APPENDIX   EXTENSIONS AND USES OF PRODUCTION AND COST ANALYSIS

This appendix shows how the total variable cost curve can be derived from the total product curve, examines input substitution in production to minimize costs, and shows the effect of an increase in input prices on the firm's cost curves.

Derivation of the Total Variable Cost Curve from the Total Product Curve

The top panel of Figure 8.15 reproduces the total product (*TP*) curve of Figure 7.2. With labor (*L*) as the only variable input and with the constant wage rate of $10, the total variable cost (*TVC*) of producing various quantities of output is given by $TVC = \$10L$ (the lower horizontal scale in the top panel). If we now transpose the axes and plot *TVC* on the vertical axis and output on the horizontal axis, we obtain the *TVC* curve shown in the bottom panel of Figure 8.15. Thus, the shape of the *TVC* curve is determined by the shape of the *TP* curve.

Note that the slope of the *TP* curve (or MP_L) rises up to point *G* (the point of inflection) in the top panel and then declines. On the other hand, the slope of the *TVC* curve (the *MC*) falls up to point *G'* (the point of inflection) in the bottom panel and then rises. At points *G* and *G'*, the law of diminishing returns begins to operate. The *MC* is the monetized mirror image or dual of the MP_L. That is, *MC* falls when MP_L rises, *MC* is minimum when MP_L is highest, and *MC* rises when MP_L falls. The same inverse relationship exists between the *AVC* and the AP_L. Note also that the *TVC* curve is dashed above point *I'* in the bottom panel because no firm would want to incur higher *TVC* to produce smaller outputs.

Input Substitution in Production to Minimize Costs

We now examine how a firm minimizes the cost of producing any given level of output by substituting a cheaper for a more expensive input in production. Figure 8.16 shows that with

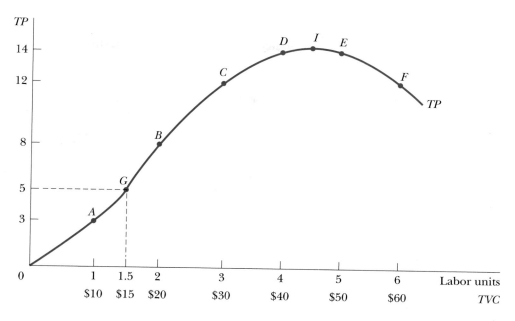

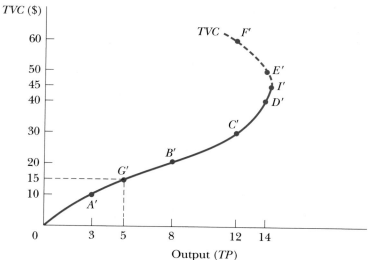

FIGURE 8.15   Derivation of the *TVC* Curve from the *TP* Curve   The top panel reproduces the *TP* curve of Figure 6.2. With labor (*L*) as the only variable input and with the constant wage rate of $10, *TVC* = $10*L* (the lower horizontal scale in the top panel). If we now transpose the axes and plot *TVC* on the vertical axis and output on the horizontal axis, we obtain the *TVC* curve shown in the bottom panel. At points *G* and *G'*, the law of diminishing returns begins to operate.

$TC = \$140$ and $w = r = \$10$, the firm minimizes the cost of producing 10*Q* by using 7*K* and 7*L* (point *A*, where isocost line *FG* is tangent to isoquant 10*Q*). At point *A*, $K/L = 1$.

If *r* remains at $10 but *w* falls to $5, the isocost line becomes *FH* and the firm can reach an isoquant higher than 10*Q* with $TC = \$140$. The firm can now reach isoquant 10*Q* with $TC = \$100$. This is given by isocost *F'H'*, which is parallel to *FH* (i.e., $w/r = 1/2$ for

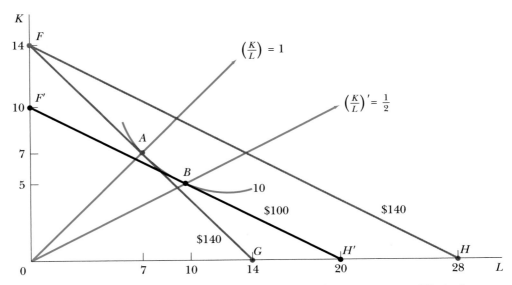

FIGURE 8.16   Input Substitution in Production   With $TC = \$140$ and $w = r = \$10$, the firm minimizes the cost of producing $10Q$ by using $7K$ and $7L$ (point A, where isocost FG is tangent to isoquant $10Q$). At point A, $K/L = 1$. If r remains at $\$10$ but w falls to $\$5$, the firm can reach isoquant $10Q$ with $TC = \$100$. The least-cost combination of L and K is then given by point B, where isocost $F'H'$ is tangent to isoquant $10Q$. At point B, $K/L = 1/2$.

both) and is tangent to isoquant $10Q$ at point B. At point B, $K/L = 1/2$. Thus, with a reduction in w (and constant r), a lower TC is required to produce a given level of output. To minimize production costs, the firm will have to substitute L for K in production, so that K/L declines.

The ease with which the firm can substitute L for K in production depends on the shape of the isoquant and can be measured by the elasticity of substitution (see Example 8–8). The flatter the isoquant, the easier it is to substitute L for K in production. On the other hand, if the isoquant is at a right angle, or L-shaped (as in Figure 7.7), no input substitution is possible (i.e., $MRTS_{LK} = 0$). In such a case, K/L will then always be constant regardless of input prices.

EXAMPLE 8-8

Elasticity of Substitution in Japanese Manufacturing Industries

A more precise method of measuring the ease with which a firm can substitute one input for another in production than looking at the curvature of the isoquant is with the *elasticity of substitution*. This is given by the percentage change in K/L with respect to the percentage change in P_L/P_K. The larger the value of this elasticity, the easier it is for the firm to substitute L for K in production. Table 8.6 gives the value of the elasticity of substitution of nonskilled labor for capital (σ_{NK}), skilled labor for capital (σ_{SK}), and nonskilled

TABLE 8.6 Elasticity of Substitution in Japanese Manufacturing Industries			
Industry	σ_{NK}	σ_{SK}	σ_{NS}
Food	0.14	0.62	0.38
Pulp and paper	0.76	0.75	1.32
Metal products	0.99	0.86	1.72
Non-electrical machinery	0.31	0.56	1.44
Electrical machinery	0.52	0.60	0.96
Precision instruments	0.67	0.62	1.15

labor for skilled labor (σ_{NS}), in a number of Japanese manufacturing industries from 1970 to 1988.

The table shows that for the food industry, a 1% reduction in the wages of unskilled labor relative to the price of capital would lead to a 0.14% reduction in the capital-to-unskilled-labor ratio (while holding the wages of skilled labor constant), as firms substitute nonskilled labor for capital in production. This means that the isoquant between nonskilled labor and capital is almost L-shaped, offering little possibility of factor substitution in production. On the other hand, the elasticity of substitution between nonskilled and skilled workers of 1.72 for metal products implies a fairly flat isoquant and a strong possibility of substituting nonskilled for skilled workers. The table also shows that, except for the food industry, it is easier to substitute nonskilled for skilled labor than to substitute nonskilled or skilled labor for capital.

Source: K. Hashimoto and J.A. Heath, "Estimating Elasticities of Substitution by the CDE Production Function: An Application to Japanese Manufacturing Industries," Applied Economic, February 1995, p. 170.

Input Prices and the Firm's Cost Curves

In deriving the firm's cost curves, input prices are kept constant. Per-unit costs differ at different levels of output because the physical productivity of inputs varies as output varies. If input prices do change, the AC and the MC curves of the firm will shift—up if input prices rise and down if input prices fall. These shifts are called external diseconomies and economies, respectively, and are examined in detail in Chapter 9.

For example, point B in Figure 8.16 shows that $10Q$ is produced at $TC = \$100$ when $w = \$5$, so that $AC = \$10$. With $w = \$10$, the production of $10Q$ requires $TC = \$140$ (point A in Figure 8.16), so that $AC' = \$14$. This is shown in Figure 8.17 by point B' and A' on average cost curves AC and AC', respectively. Note that the marginal cost curve will also shift up from MC to MC' when w rises.

For simplicity, we assumed in Figure 8.17 that the firm produces at the lowest point on its average cost curve before and after the increase in w. Be that as it may, the minimum cost of producing a given level of output is always achieved by substituting the cheaper input (in this case, capital) for the input that has become more expensive (labor) until the tangency of the given isoquant with the new (steeper) isocost is reached (point A in Figure 8.16, at which, once again, $MRTS_{LK} = w/r$).

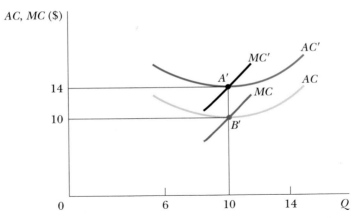

FIGURE 8.17   Input Prices and the *AC* and *MC* Curves   Point *B'* on curve *AC* shows that with *w* = $5, *AC* = $10 for *Q* = 10 (from point *B* in Figure 8.16). Point *A'* on curve *AC'* shows that with *w* = $10, *AC* = $14 for *Q* = 10 (from point *A* in Figure 8.16). Thus, an increase in *w* from $5 to $10 shifts *AC* and *MC* up to *AC'* and *MC'* .

INTERNET SITE ADDRESSES

For the cost of a college education, see:

http://www.collegeboard.com/prod_downloads/press/cost06/trends_college_pricing_06.pdf

For gasoline consumption and substitution, see:

http://www.techstandards.co.uk/system/index.html

http://sciway.net/statistics/scsa98/en/en17.html

For economies of scale and economies of scope, see:

http://en.wikipedia.org/wiki/Economies_of_scale

http://en.wikipedia.org/wiki/Economies_of_scope

http://www.tutor2u.net/economics/content/essentials/economies_scale_scope.htm

Estimates of scale economies in electricity generation are found at:

http://www.springerlink.com/content/ q8t1364727721892/

http://ideas.repec.org/a/eee/ecolet/v11y1983i3p285-289.html

For economies or diseconomies of scale at General Motors, Ford, and Chrysler, see:

http://www.gm.com

http://www.ford.com

http://www.chrysler.com

For how far afield companies go to reduce costs, see:

Southwest Airlines: http://www.southwest.com

Domino's Pizza: http://www.dominos.com

Federal Express: http://www.fedex.com

GE Information Services: http://www.geis.com

Learning curves are discussed at National Bureau of Economic Research:

http://www.nber.org/papers/w7127

For Moore's Law, see:

http://blogs.forbes.com/digitalrules

For competition in industry for commercial aircraft, see:

Lockheed: http://www.lockheedmartin.com

Boeing: http://www.boeing.com

More information on outsourcing is found at:

http://en.wikipedia.org/wiki/Outsourcing

http://www.networkworld.com/topics/outsourcing.html

http://www.outsourcing.org/Directory/Business_Process/

http://www.businessweek.com/magazine/content/06_05/b3969401.htm

http://www.cio.com/topic/1513/Outsourcing

CHAPTER 9

Price and Output Under Perfect Competition

Chapter Outline

List of Examples

After Studying This Chapter, You Should Be Able to:

- Know the meaning and importance of perfect competition
- Describe how perfectly competitive firms determine their best level of output in the short run
- Know how to derive the short-run supply curve of a perfectly firm
- Describe the long-run equilibrium of the perfectly competitive firm and industry
- Know why perfect competition is the most efficient form of market organization

I n this chapter, we bring together the theory of consumer behavior and demand (from Part Two) and the theory of production and costs (from Chapters 7 and 8) to analyze how price and output are determined under perfect competition. As explained in Chapter 1, the analysis of how price and output are determined in the market is a primary aim of microeconomic theory.

The chapter begins by identifying the various types of market structure and defining perfect competition. It then examines price determination in the market period, or the very short run, when the supply of the commodity is fixed. Subsequently, we discuss how the firm determines its best level of output in the short run at various commodity prices. In the process, we derive the short-run supply curve of the firm and industry, and show how the interaction of industry demand and supply curves determines the equilibrium price of the commodity. This was already demonstrated in Chapter 2, but now we know what lies behind the market demand and supply curves and how they are derived.

From the analysis of the market period and the short run, we go on to examine the long-run equilibrium of the firm and define constant-, increasing-, and decreasing-cost industries. Subsequently, we consider the very significant effect of international competition on the domestic economy. The chapter concludes with an analysis of perfectly competitive markets. This analysis, together with the real-world examples presented in the theory sections as well as the "At the Frontier" discussion of the auction of airwaves, highlights the great importance and relevance of the analytical tools developed in the chapter. In the optional appendix, the foreign-exchange market and the dollar exchange rate are examined and their importance to the operation of the firm in today's highly integrated world is discussed.

9.1　MARKET STRUCTURE: PERFECT COMPETITION

In economics, we usually identify four different types of market structure: perfect competition, monopoly, monopolistic competition, and oligopoly. This chapter examines perfect competition. The other three types of market organization are considered in the next three chapters (monopoly in Chapter 10 and monopolistic competition and oligopoly in Chapters 11 and 12). Chapter 13 then analyzes the efficiency implications of market imperfections and regulation.

Perfect competition
The form of market organization where no buyer or seller can affect the price of the product, all units of the product are homogeneous, resources are mobile, and knowledge of the market is perfect.

Perfect competition refers to the type of market organization in which (1) there are many buyers and sellers of a commodity, each too small to affect the price of the commodity; (2) the commodity is homogeneous; (3) there is perfect mobility of resources; and (4) economic agents have perfect knowledge of market conditions (i.e., prices and costs). Let us now examine in detail the meaning of each of the four aspects of the definition.

First, in perfect competition, there are many buyers and sellers of the commodity, each of which is too small (or behaves as if he or she is too small) in relation to the market to have a perceptible effect on the price of the commodity. Under perfect competition, the equilibrium price and quantity of the commodity are determined at the intersection of the market demand and supply curves of the commodity. The equilibrium price will not be affected perceptibly if only one or a few consumers or producers change the quantity demanded or supplied of the commodity.

Second, the commodity is *homogeneous,* identical, or perfectly standardized, so that the output of each producer is indistinguishable from the output of others. An example of this might be grade A winter wheat. Thus, buyers are indifferent as to the output of which producer they purchase.

Third, resources are perfectly mobile. This means that resources or inputs are free to move (i.e., they can move at zero cost) among the various industries and locations within the market in response to monetary incentives. Firms can enter or leave the industry in the long run without much difficulty. That is, there are no artificial barriers (such as patents) or natural barriers (such as huge capital requirements) to entry into and exit from the industry.

Fourth, consumers, firms, and resource owners have perfect knowledge of all relevant prices and costs in the market. This ensures that the same price prevails in each part of the market for the commodity and for the inputs required in the production of the commodity.

Concept Check

What is the importance and use of the perfectly competitive model?

Needless to say, these conditions have seldom if ever existed in any market. The closest we might come today to a perfectly competitive market is the stock market (see Example 9–1) and the foreign exchange market (in the absence of intervention by national monetary authorities) examined in the appendix. Another example might be U.S. agriculture at the turn of the century, when millions of small farmers raised wheat. Despite its rarity, the perfectly competitive model is extremely useful to analyze market situations that approximate perfect competition. More importantly, the perfectly competitive model provides the point of reference or standard against which to measure the economic cost or *inefficiency* of departures from perfect competition. These departures can take the form of monopoly, monopolistic competition, or oligopoly. In the case of monopoly, there is a *single* seller of a commodity for which there are no good substitutes. Under monopolistic competition, there are many sellers of a *differentiated* commodity.[1] In oligopoly, there are *few sellers* of either a homogeneous or a differentiated commodity. Imperfectly competitive markets are examined in Part Four (Chapters 10–13).

The economist's definition of perfect competition is diametrically opposite to the everyday usage of the term. In economics, the term "perfect competition" stresses the *impersonality* of the market. One producer does not care and is not affected by what other producers are doing. The output of all producers is identical, and an individual producer can sell any quantity of the commodity at the given price without any need to advertise. On the other hand, in everyday usage, the term "competition" stresses the notion of *rivalry* among producers or sellers of the commodity. For example, GM managers speak of the fierce competition that their firm faces from other domestic and foreign auto producers with regard to style, mileage per gallon, price, and so on. Because of this, GM mounts elaborate and costly advertising campaigns to convince consumers of the superiority of its vehicles. This is not, however, what the economist means by competition.

Under perfect competition, the firm is a *price taker* and can sell any quantity of the commodity at the given market price. If the firm raised its price by the slightest amount, it would lose all of its consumers. On the other hand, there is no reason for the firm to reduce the commodity price since the firm can sell any quantity of the commodity at the given market price. Thus, the perfectly competitive firm faces a horizontal or infinitely elastic demand curve (as in Figure 5.7) at the price determined at the intersection of the market demand and supply curves for the commodity (as in Figure 2.5).

EXAMPLE 9–1

Competition in the New York Stock Market

The market for stocks traded on the New York and other major stock exchanges is as close as we come today to a perfectly competitive market. In most cases the price of a particular stock is determined by the market forces of demand and supply of the stock, and individual buyers and sellers of the stock have an insignificant effect on price (i.e., they are price takers). All stocks within each category are more or less homogeneous. The fact that a stock is bought and sold frequently is evidence that resources are mobile. Finally, information on prices and quantities traded is readily available.

---

[1] An example of a differentiated commodity is the different brand names of the same commodity.

In general, the price of a stock reflects all the publicly known information about the present and expected future profitability of the stock. This is known as the *efficient market hypothesis.* Funds flow into stocks, and resources flow into uses in which the rate of return, corrected for risk, is highest. Thus, stock prices provide the signals for the efficient allocation of investments in the economy. Despite the fact that the stock market is close to being a perfectly competitive market, imperfections occur even here. For example, the sale of $1 billion worth of stocks by IBM or any other large corporation will certainly affect (depress) the price of its stocks. Furthermore, stock prices can sometimes become grossly overvalued (i.e., we could have a "bubble market") and thus subject to a subsequent steep correction (fall). This is, in fact, what happened in the New York stock market at the end of the 1990s.

Today, more and more Americans trade foreign stocks, and more and more foreigners trade American stocks. This has been the result of a communications revolution that linked stock markets around the world into a huge global capital market and around-the-clock trading. While this provides immense new earning possibilities and sharply increased opportunities for portfolio diversification, it also creates the danger that a crisis in one market will very quickly spread to other markets around the world. This actually happened when the New York Stock Exchange collapse in October 1987 caused sharp declines in stock markets around the world and again 10 years later (in the fall of 1997), when the collapse of stock markets in Southeast Asia led to a sharp decline in the New York stock market and in stock markets in other nations. In 2002, history repeated itself when sharp declines in the New York stock market (as a result of low corporate profits and huge financial scandals) quickly spread to other stock markets around the world. It happened again in August 2007 as a result of the financial crisis triggered by the subprime (high-risk) mortgage problem in the U.S. housing market.

In recent years, the New York Stock Exchange seems to have lost some of its former ability to predict changing economic conditions and its importance as the central source of capital for corporate America, as the latter borrowed increasing amounts from banks for takeovers and mergers. Indeed, global markets for securities, featuring automated, round-the-world, round-the-clock trading could eventually eclipse Wall Street's capital-raising dominance.

Sources: New York Stock Exchange, *You and the Investment World* (New York: The New York Stock Exchange, 1998); "The Future of Wall Street," *Business Week,* November 5, 1990, pp. 119–124; "Luck or Logic? Debate Rages On Over 'Efficient Market Theory'," *The Wall Street Journal,* November 4, 1993, p. C1; "Worrying About World Markets," *Fortune,* July 24, 1995, pp. 43–45; "Unreality Check for the Bull Market," *The Wall Street Journal,* May 25, 1999, p. C1; "Another Scandal, Another Scare," *The Economist,* June 29, 2002, pp. 67–69; "Mortgage Losses Echo in Europe and on Wall Street," *New York Times,* August 10, 2007, p. 1; and "The Capital of Capital No More," *New York Times Magazine*, October 11, 2007, pp. 62–65.

9.2   PRICE DETERMINATION IN THE MARKET PERIOD

Market period The time period during which the market supply of a commodity is fixed.

The **market period,** or the very short run, refers to the time period during which no input can be varied (i.e., all costs are fixed) and so the market supply of a commodity is also fixed. The market period may be a day, a week, a month, or longer, depending on the industry. For example, if milk is delivered every morning to New York City, and no other deliveries can be arranged for the rest of the day, the market period is one day. For wheat,

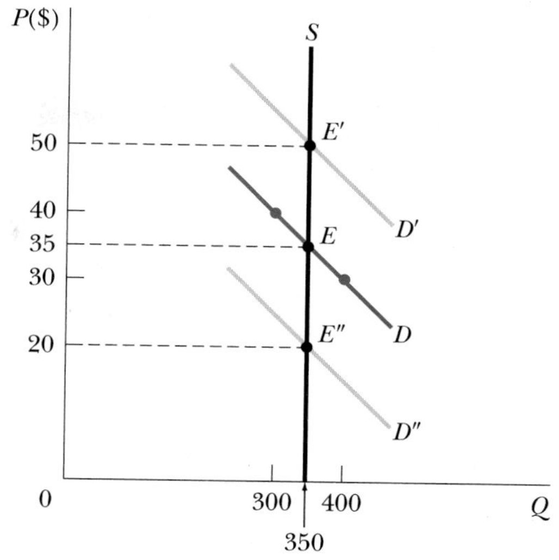

FIGURE 9.1   Price Determination in the Market Period   With the quantity supplied fixed at 350, the market supply curve of the commodity is S. With D as the market demand curve, the equilibrium price is $35. At prices higher than $35, there will be unsold quantities, and this will cause the price to fall to the equilibrium level. At prices below $35, the quantity demanded exceeds the quantity supplied, and the price will be bid up to $35. With D' as the demand curve, $P = $50. With D'', $P = $20.

the market period extends from one harvest to the next. For Michelangelo's paintings, the length of the market period is infinite because the supply is fixed forever.

During the market period, costs of production are irrelevant in the determination of price, and the entire stock of a perishable commodity is put up for sale at whatever price it can fetch. Thus, with perfect competition among buyers and sellers, demand alone determines price, while supply alone determines quantity. This is shown in Figure 9.1.

In the figure, S is the fixed or zero-elastic market supply curve for 350 units of the commodity. With D as the market demand curve, the equilibrium price is $35. Only at this price does the quantity demanded equal the quantity supplied, and the market clears. At higher prices, there will be unsold quantities, and this will cause the price to fall to the equilibrium level. For example, at the price of $40, only 300 units would be demanded (see the figure); hence, the quantity supplied would exceed the quantity demanded and the commodity price would fall. On the other hand, at lower than the equilibrium price, the quantity demanded exceeds the quantity supplied, and the price will be bid up to $35. For example, at the price of $30, 400 units of the commodity would be demanded; hence, the quantity demanded would exceed the quantity supplied and the price would be bid up to $35 (the equilibrium price at which the quantity demanded equals the quantity supplied). With D' as the demand curve, $P = $50. With D'', $P = $20.

✓ Concept Check
How is the commodity price determined in the market period?

9.3   SHORT-RUN EQUILIBRIUM OF THE FIRM

Even though analysis of the market period is interesting, we are primarily interested in the short run and in the long run, when the quantity produced and sold of the commodity can be varied. In this section, we examine the determination of output by the firm in the short run. We first do so with the total approach and then with the marginal approach. Finally, we focus on the process of profit maximization or loss minimization by the firm.

Total Approach: Maximizing the Positive Difference Between Total Revenue and Total Costs

We have seen in Section 7.1 that profit maximization provides the framework for the analysis of the firm. The equilibrium output of the firm is the output that maximizes the total profits of the firm. Total profits equal total revenue minus total costs. Thus, total profits are maximized when the positive difference between total revenue and total costs is largest. This is shown in Figure 9.2.

The short-run total cost (*STC*) curve in the top panel of Figure 9.2 is the one of Figure 8.1. The vertical intercept ($30) gives the fixed costs of the firm. Within the limits imposed by the given plant, the firm can vary its output by varying the quantity of the variable inputs it uses. This generates the *STC* curve of the firm. The *STC* curve shows the minimum total costs of producing the various levels of output in the short run. Past point *W*, the law of diminishing returns begins to operate and the *STC* curve faces upward or rises at an increasing rate (see Section 8.2).

The total revenue curve is a straight line through the origin because the firm can sell any quantity of the commodity at the given price (determined at the intersection of the market demand and supply curves of the commodity). With $P = \$35$, the total revenue (*TR*) of the firm is $35 if the firm sells one unit of output. The $TR = \$70$ if the firm sells two units of output, $TR = \$105$ with $Q = 3$, $TR = \$140$ with $Q = 4$, and so on. Put more succinctly, $TR = (\$35)(Q)$. Thus, the *TR* of the firm is a straight line through the origin with slope equal to the commodity price of $35 (see the top panel of Figure 9.2).

At zero output, $TR = 0$ while $STC = \$30$. Thus, the firm incurs a total loss of $30 equal to its fixed costs. This gives the negative intercept of $(-)\$30$ of the total profit curve in the bottom panel. At $Q = 1$, $TR = \$35$ and $STC = \$50$, so that total profits are $-\$15$. At $Q = 1.5$, $TR = STC = \$52.50$ (point *W* in the top panel), and total profits are zero (point *W'* in the bottom panel). This is called the **break-even point.** Between $Q = 1.5$ and $Q = 5$, *TR* exceeds *STC* and the firm earns a profit. Total profits equal the positive difference between *TR* and *STC*. Total profits are largest at $31.50 when $Q = 3.5$ (i.e., where the *TR* and the *STC* curves are parallel and the total profit curve has zero slope). At *Q* smaller than 3.5, say, $Q = 3$, $TR = \$105$ and $STC = \$75$, so that total profits are $30. At $Q = 4$, $TR = \$140$, $STC = \$110$, and total profits are again $30. At $Q = 5$, $TR = STC = \$175$, so that total profits are zero (points *T* and *T'*, respectively). At *Q* greater than 5, *TR* is smaller than *STC* and the firm incurs a loss. Thus, the level of output at which the firm maximizes total profits is $Q = 3.5$ (point *E* and *E'* in the top and bottom panels, respectively). Figure 9.2 is summarized in Table 9.1.[2]

Break-even point The point where total revenues equal total costs and profits are zero.

Marginal Approach: Equating Marginal Revenue and Marginal Cost[3]

Although the total approach to determine the equilibrium output of the firm is useful, the marginal approach is even more valuable and more widely used. This approach is shown in Figure 9.3. In the figure, the demand curve facing the firm (*d*) is horizontal or infinitely elastic at the given price of $P = \$35$. That is, the perfectly competitive firm is a price taker

---

[2] When the firm has no knowledge of the exact shape of its *STC* curve, it uses a break-even chart to determine the minimum sales volume to avoid losses (see Problem 4, with the answer at the end of the book).
[3] For a mathematical presentation of profit maximization using rudimentary calculus, see Section A.10 of the Mathematical Appendix at the end of the book.

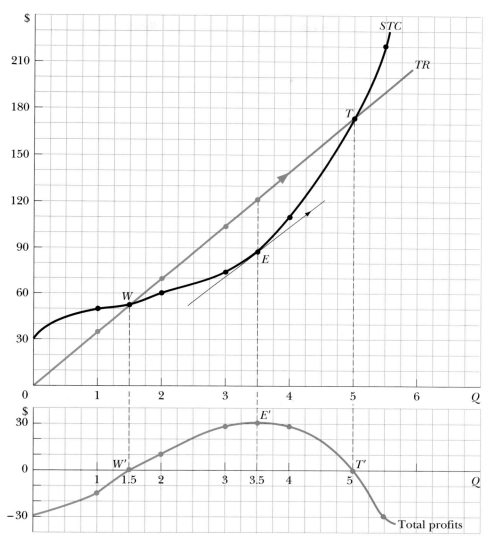

FIGURE 9.2   Short-Run Equilibrium of the Firm: Total Approach   The *STC* curve in the top panel is that of Figure 8.1. The *TR* curve is a straight line through the origin with slope of *P* = $35. At *Q* = 0, *TR* = 0 and *STC* = $30, so that total profits are −$30 and equal the firm's *TFC* (see the bottom panel). At *Q* = 1, *TR* = $35 and *STC* = $50, so that total profits are −$15. At *Q* = 1.5, *TR* = *STC* = $52.50, and total profits are zero. This is the break-even point. Between *Q* = 1.5 and *Q* = 5, *TR* exceeds *STC* and the firm earns (positive) economic profits. Total profits are greatest at $31.50 when *Q* = 3.5 (and the *TR* and the *STC* curves are parallel). At *Q* = 5, *TR* = *STC* = $175 so that total profits are zero (points *T* and *T'*). At *Q* greater than 5, *TR* is smaller than *STC* and the firm incurs a loss.

TABLE 9.1	Total Revenue, Total Costs, and Total Profits			
Quantity of Output	Price	Total Revenue	Total Costs	Total Profits
0	$35	$0	$30	$−30
1	35	35	50	−15
1.5	35	52.50	52.50	0
2	35	70	60	+10
3	35	105	75	+30
*3.5	35	122.50	91	+31.50
4	35	140	110	+30
5	35	175	175	0
5.5	35	192.50	220	−27.50

*Output at which firm maximizes total profits.

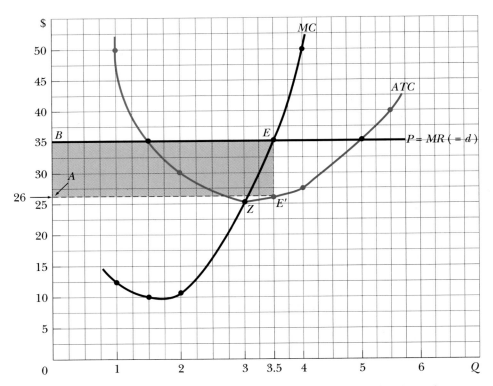

FIGURE 9.3   Short-Run Equilibrium of the Firm: Marginal Approach   The demand curve facing the firm (*d*) is horizontal or infinitely elastic at the given price of $P = \$35$. Since *P* is constant, marginal revenue (*MR*) equals *P*. The firm maximizes total profits where $P = MR = MC$, and *MC* is rising. This occurs at $Q = 3.5$ (point *E*). At $Q = 3.5$, $P = \$35$ and $ATC = \$26$. Therefore, profit per unit is $9 (*EE'*), and total profits are $31.50 (shaded rectangle *EE' AB*).

and can sell any quantity of the commodity at $P = \$35$. Since marginal revenue (MR) is the change in total revenue per-unit change in output, and price (P) is constant, then $P = MR$ (see Section 5.6). For example, with $P = \$35$ and $Q = 1$, $TR = \$35$. With $P = \$35$ and $Q = 2$, $TR = \$70$. Thus, the change in TR per-unit change in output (the slope of the TR curve or marginal revenue) is $MR = P = \$35$ (see Figure 9.3).

The short-run marginal cost (MC) and the average total cost (ATC) curves of the firm in Figure 9.3 are those of Figure 8.2 (and derived from the STC curve of Figures 8.1 and 9.2). The $MC = \Delta STC/\Delta Q$, while $ATC = STC/Q$. As explained earlier, total profits are maximized where the TR and the STC curves are parallel and their slopes are equal. Since the slope of the TR curve is $MR = P$ and the slope of the STC curve is MC, this implies that when total profits are at a maximum, $P = MR = MC$. Furthermore, since the STC curve faces upward where profits are maximum, the MC curve must be rising. Thus, the firm is in short-run equilibrium or maximizes total profits by producing the output where $P = MR = MC$, and MC is rising.

For example, the best level of output for the firm in Figure 9.3 is $Q = 3.5$ (point E), and this is the same result as with the total approach. At $Q = 3.5$, $P = \$35$ and $ATC = \$26$. Therefore, profit per unit is \$9 (EE' in the figure), and total profits are $(\$9)(3.5) = \$31.50$ (shaded rectangle $EE'AB$). Until point E, MR exceeds MC and so the firm earns higher profits by expanding output. On the other hand, past point E, MC exceeds MR and the firm earns higher profits by *reducing* output. This leaves point E as the profit-maximizing level of output. Note that at point E, P or $MR = MC$ and MC is rising so that the conditions for profit maximization are fulfilled.

Also note that profit per unit is largest (\$10) at point Z where $Q = 3$, $P = \$35$, and $ATC = \$25$. The firm, however, seeks to maximize total profits, not profit per unit, and this occurs at $Q = 3.5$, where total profits are \$31.50, as opposed to \$30 at $Q = 3$. The total profits of the firm at various levels of output with $P = \$35$ are summarized in Table 9.2. The MR, MC, and ATC values given in the table are read off Figure 9.3 at various output levels. For example, at $Q = 1$, $MR = \$35$, $MC = \$12.50$, and $ATC = \$50$. At $Q = 2$, $MR = \$35$, $MC = \$11$, and $ATC = \$30$, and so on.

The rule that a firm maximizes profits at the output level at which the marginal revenue to the firm equals its marginal cost is a specific application of the general *marginal*

✓ **Concept Check**
How does a perfectly competitive firm determine the best level of output in the short run?

| TABLE 9.2 | Profit Maximization for the Perfectly Competitive Firm: Per-Unit Approach |

Q	P = MR	MC	ATC	Profit Per Unit	Total Profits	Relationship Between MR and MC
1	$35	$12.50	$50	$-15	$-15	
1.50	35	10	35	0	0	
2	35	11	30	+5	+10	MR > MC
3	35	25	25	+10	+30	
*3.50	35	35	26	+9	+31.50	MR = MC
4	35	50	27.50	+7.50	+30	
5	35		35	0	0	MR < MC
5.5	35		40	-5	-27.50	

*Output at which firm maximizes total profits.

concept that any activity should be pursued until the marginal benefit from the activity equals the marginal cost.

Profit Maximization or Loss Minimization?

We have seen that the best or optimum level of output of the firm is given at the point where P (or MR) equals MC, and MC is rising. At this level of output, however, the firm can either make a profit (as in Figure 9.3), break even, or incur a loss. In Figure 9.3, P was higher than the ATC at the best level of output, and the firm made a profit. If P were smaller than the ATC at the best level of output, the firm would incur a loss. However, as long as P exceeds the average *variable* cost (AVC), it pays for the firm to continue to produce, because by doing so it would *minimize its losses*. That is, the excess of P over the AVC can be used to partially cover the fixed costs of the firm. Were the firm to shut down, it would incur a greater loss equal to its total fixed costs. This is shown in Figure 9.4.

In the figure, the MC and the ATC curves are the same as in Figure 9.3. Figure 9.4 also includes the AVC curve of the firm (from Figure 8.2). In Figure 9.4, we assume that $P = MR = \$20$. The best level of output of the firm is then 2.75 units, given at point F, where $P = MR = MC = \$20$, and MC is rising. At $Q = 2.75$, ATC exceeds P and the firm incurs a loss equal to $F'F$ (about \$5.50) per unit, and a total loss equal to the area of

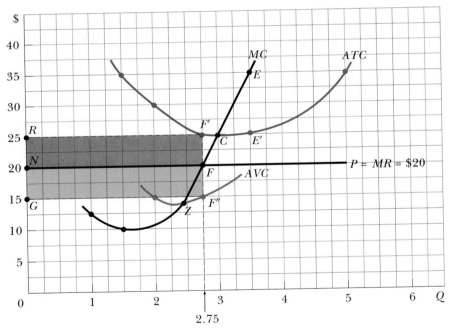

FIGURE 9.4   Profit Maximization or Loss Minimization   At $P = \$20$, the best level of output of the firm is 2.75 units (point F, where $P = MR = MC$, and MC is rising). At $Q = 2.75$, average total cost (ATC) exceeds P and the firm will incur a loss of $F'F$ (about \$5.50) per unit, and a total loss equal to rectangle $F'FNR$ (about \$15). If, however, the firm were to shut down, it would incur the greater loss of \$30 equal to its total fixed costs (the area of the larger rectangle $F'F''GR$). The shutdown point (Z) is at $P = AVC$.

✓ Concept Check

Does a perfectly competitive firm shut down if it incurs a loss in the short run?

Shutdown point The output level at which price equals average variable cost and losses equal total fixed costs, whether the firm produces or not.

rectangle $F'FNR$ (about \$15). Were the firm to shut down, it would incur the greater loss of \$30 (its total fixed costs, given by the area of the larger rectangle $F'F''GR$).

Put another way, by continuing to produce $Q = 2.75$ at $P = \$20$, the firm will cover FF'' (about \$5.50) of its fixed costs per unit and $FF''GN$ (about \$15) of its total fixed costs. Thus, it pays for the firm to stay in business even though it incurs a loss. That is, by remaining in business, the firm will incur losses that are smaller than its total fixed costs (which would be the firm's losses by shutting down). Only if P were smaller than the AVC at the best level of output would the firm minimize losses by shutting down. By doing so, the firm would limit its losses to an amount no larger than its total fixed costs. Finally, if $P = AVC$, the firm would be indifferent between producing or shutting down, because in either case it would incur a loss equal to its total fixed costs. The point where $P = AVC$ (point Z in the figure) is called the **shutdown point.**[4]

9.4   SHORT-RUN SUPPLY CURVE AND EQUILIBRIUM

In this section, we derive the short-run supply curve of a perfectly competitive firm and industry. We also examine how the equilibrium price of the commodity is determined at the intersection of the market demand and supply curves for the commodity. This is the price at which the perfectly competitive firm can sell any quantity of the commodity.

Short-Run Supply Curve of the Firm and the Industry

We have seen so far that a perfectly competitive firm always produces at the point where $P = MC$ and MC is rising, and this is so as long as $P > AVC$. As a result, the rising portion of the firm's MC curve above the AVC curve is the firm's short-run supply curve of the commodity. This is shown in the left panel of Figure 9.5.

✓ Concept Check

How is the short-run supply curve of a perfectly competitive firm determined?

The left panel of Figure 9.5 reproduces the firm's MC curve above point Z (the shutdown point) from Figure 9.4. This is the perfectly competitive firm's short-run supply curve (s) because it shows the quantity of the commodity that the firm would supply in the short run at various prices. For example, the firm supplies 3 units of the commodity at the price of \$25 (point C in the left panel). The reason is that at $P = \$25$, $P = MR = MC = \$25$, and MC is rising. At $P = \$35$, the firm supplies 3.5 units of the commodity (point E), while at $P = \$50$, it supplies 4 units (point T). The firm will supply no output at prices below the shutdown point (point Z in the figure). Thus, the rising portion of the firm's MC curve above the shutdown point is the firm's short-run supply curve of the commodity (s in the left panel of Figure 9.5). It shows the quantity of the commodity that the firm would supply in the short run at various prices. The firm's short-run supply curve is positively sloped because the MC curve is positively sloped, and the MC curve is positively sloped because of diminishing returns.

The horizontal summation of the supply curves of all firms in the industry then gives the industry short-run supply curve for the commodity. This is given by the $\Sigma MC = S$ curve in the right panel of Figure 9.5, where the symbol Σ refers to the "summation of."

[4] Recall that $STC = TVC + TFC$ and total profits equal $TR - STC$. When $P = AVC$, $TR = TVC$, so the firm's total losses would equal its TFC whether it produces or shuts down. Thus, point Z, at which $P = AVC$ (and $TR = TVC$), is the firm's shutdown point.

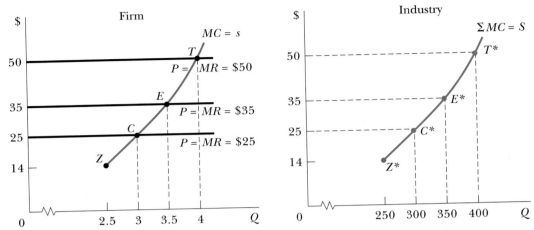

FIGURE 9.5   Short-Run Supply Curve of the Firm and Industry   The left panel reproduces the firm's
MC curve above point Z (the shutdown point) from Figure 8.4. This is the perfectly competitive firm's short-run
supply curve s. For example, at $P = \$25, Q = 3$ (point C); at $P = \$35, Q = 3.5$ (point E); at $P = \$50, Q = 4$
(point T). The right panel shows the industry's short-run supply curve on the assumption that there are 100
identical firms in the industry and input prices are constant. This is given by the $\Sigma MC = S$ curve. Thus, at
$P = \$25, Q = 300$ (point C^*); at $P = \$35, Q = 350$ (point E^*); at $P = \$50, Q = 400$ (point T^*).

The perfectly competitive industry's short-run supply curve in the right panel is based on
the assumption that there are 100 identical firms in the industry (and input prices do not
vary with industry output). For example, at $P = \$25$, each firm supplies 3 units of the
commodity (point C in the left panel) and the entire industry supplies 300 units (point C^*
in the right panel). At $P = \$35$, each firm supplies 3.5 units (point E) and the industry
supplies 350 units (point E^*). At $P = \$50$, $Q = 4$ for the firm (point T) and $Q = 400$ for
the industry (point T^*). Note that no output of the commodity is produced at prices below
$P = \$14$ (points Z and Z^* in the figure).[5]

The derivation of the perfectly competitive industry short-run supply curve of the
commodity as the horizontal summation of each firm's short-run supply curve is based on
the assumption that input prices are constant regardless of the quantity of inputs that each
firm and the industry demand. That is, it is based on the assumption that the firm is able
to hire a greater quantity of the inputs (to produce the larger output) at constant input
prices. If input prices were to rise as firms demanded more of the inputs, the industry
supply curve would be steeper or less elastic than indicated in the right panel of Figure
9.5. An increase in the commodity price will then result in a smaller increase in the quantity supplied of the commodity (see Problem 8, with the answer at the end of the book).

The responsiveness or sensitivity in the quantity supplied of a commodity to a change
in its price can be measured by the **price elasticity of supply.** This is analogous to the
price elasticity of demand and is given by the percentage change in the quantity supplied

**Price elasticity of
supply** The percentage
change in the quantity
supplied of a commodity
during a specific period
of time divided by the
percentage change in its
price.

_____
[5] Point Z in the left panel of Figure 9.5 corresponds to point Z' in Figure 8.2.

of the commodity divided by the percentage change in its price. That is, letting ϵ (the Greek letter epsilon) refer to the price elasticity of supply, we have

$$\epsilon = \frac{\Delta Q/Q}{\Delta P/P} = \frac{\Delta Q}{\Delta P} \cdot \frac{P}{Q} \qquad\qquad [9.1]$$

The only difference between the price elasticity of supply and that of demand is that in the numerator of the elasticity formula we now have the percentage change in the quantity *supplied* of the commodity rather than the percentage change in the quantity demanded. However, since quantity and price are usually directly related along the supply curve the price elasticity of supply is usually positive. Note that in the very short run or market period (when the supply curve is vertical), the price elasticity of supply is zero.[6] Example 9–2 examines the supply curve of petroleum from tar sands, while Example 9–3 shows how to derive the short-run world supply curve for copper.

EXAMPLE 9–2

Supply Curve of Petroleum from Tar Sands

The industry supply curve of petroleum from tar sands (often called "synthetic fuel" or "shale oil") was estimated to be as indicated by curve S in Figure 9.6 in 1978. Large cost overruns, however, made actual production costs much higher, so that the supply curve looked like S' by 1984.

The supply curve estimated in 1978 (S) showed that it would not be economical to produce oil from tar sands at prices below $10 per barrel. The quantity of oil supplied, in millions of barrels per day, would be 2 at the price of $10 per barrel, 6 at the price of $16 per barrel, and 16 at $18 per barrel. The maximum that would be supplied at any price would be about 16 million barrels per day, at a time when the international price of petroleum was $13 per barrel.

In 1980, Congress created the Synthetic Fuel Corporation to stimulate the production of oil from tar sands in Alaska and reduce American dependence on imported petroleum. By the end of 1984, $3 billion of federal subsidies had been spent on four projects. Because of large cost overruns, however, the actual cost of extracting petroleum from tar sands was found to be more than three times higher than anticipated and about double the price of $28 per barrel for imported oil (supply curve S' in Figure 9.6) in 1984. This led Exxon, one of the co-sponsors of the project, to withdraw from the project. The entire synthetic fuel project was abandoned at the end of 1985 when the U.S. government refused to provide further subsidies.

But with the average price of petroleum shooting up from $31 per barrel in 2003 to $56 in 2005, and $72 in 2007 (and reaching $120 in April 2008), it has become profitable to extract increasing amounts of high-cost petroleum form the tar sands in

---

[6] For a discussion of the price elasticity of supply using calculus, see Section A.5 of the Mathematical Appendix at the end of the book.

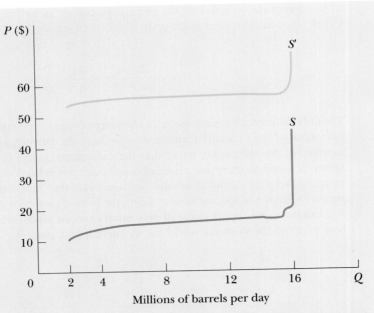

FIGURE 9.6   The Supply Curve of Oil from Tar Sands   The supply curve of oil from tar sands estimated in 1978 (*S*) rises gently up to 16 million barrels per day, where it becomes vertical. The actual supply curve *S'* in 1984 showed much higher costs per barrel.

Canada's provience of Alberta, which has more than 170 billion potential recoverable barrels of petroleum (as compared with 262 billion barrels in Saudi Arabia).

Sources: N. Ericson and P. Morgan, "The Economic Feasibility of Shale Oil: An Activity Analysis," *Bell Journal of Economics,* August 1978; "Exxon Abandons Shale Oil Project," *New York Times,* May 3, 1982, p. 1; "Congressional Conferees End Financing of Synthetic Fuels Program," *New York Times,* December 17, 1985, p. B11; "Unlocking Oil in Canada's Tar Sands," *New York Times,* December 1994, p. D5; "Oils Sands Are Shifting in Alberta," *Wall Street Journal,* February 5 2008, p. A8; and "Record Run Brings Crude Close to $120 a Barrel," *Financial Times,* April 26, 2008, p. 16.

EXAMPLE 9–3

Short-Run World Supply Curve of Copper

Table 9.3 gives the production (in thousand metric tons) and the estimated marginal cost of production (in cents per pound) of the copper producers in the major copper-producing countries of the world. Summing up the production in the various countries at the marginal cost of production in each country gives the short-run world supply curve of copper (*Sc*) shown in Figure 9.7. The supply curve slopes up as countries facing higher marginal costs of production are included.

Note that the short-run world supply curve of copper has a steplike appearance because we assume that all the producers in a country have the same marginal costs.

TABLE 9.3	Copper Production and Costs by Country in 2000 (in thousand metric tons and cents per pound)		
Country	Production	Cumulative Production	Cents Per Pound
1. Chile	4,500	4,500	54
2. Russia	520	5,020	54
3. Indonesia	850	5,870	60
4. China	510	6,380	60
5. Kazakhstan	380	6,760	60
6. Zambia	260	7,020	60
7. Australia	760	7,780	70
8. United States	1,450	9,230	76
9. Peru	530	9,760	76
10. Mexico	390	10,150	76
11. Canada	650	10,800	80
12. Poland	480	11,280	87
13. All Others	1,600	12,880	87

Sources: U.S. Geological Survey, *Mineral Commodity Summaries* and *Mineral Industry Surveys* (Washington, D.C.: U.S. Government Printing Office, 2001), 2001; and Daniel E. Eldstein, "Copper," *U.S. Geological Survey Mineral Yearbook* (Washington, D.C.: U.S. Government Printing Office, 2001), Chapter 10. For the latest data, see http://minerals.usgs.gov/minerals/pubs/commodity/copper/.

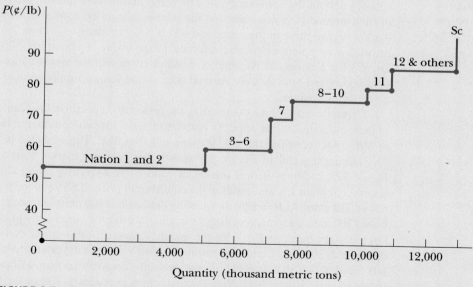

FIGURE 9.7   The Short-Run World Supply Curve of Copper   The short-run world supply curve of copper is obtained by summing up horizontally the marginal cost curve of the various countries. The short-run world supply curve of copper slopes up as countries facing higher marginal costs of production are included.

The *Sc* curve would have a smoother shape if we knew the individual firm's marginal cost curve. The *Sc* curve shows that Chile and Russia are the low-cost producers (at 54 cents per pound), but their combined capacity is limited 5,020 thousand metric tons in the short run. The marginal costs of each producer vary because of differences in the ore content of individual mines and in labor, transportation, and other costs. The marginal cost of production is 60 cents per pound for Indonesia, China, Kazakhstan, and Zambia for a combined short-run output of 2,000 thousand metric tons. The marginal cost of production is 70 cents per pound for Australia, 76 cents for the United States (the world's second largest producer after Chile), Peru and Mexico, 80 cents for Canada, 87 cents for Poland and all other world's smaller producers. The maximum short-run world supply of copper is 12,880 thousand tons at which the *Sc* curve becomes vertical. Note that the *Sc* curve is very elastic at low copper prices and becomes progressively less so at higher prices.

Since the year 2000, the need to greatly increase the production of copper to meet the rapidly increasing demand for the metal (especially by China) has led to rapidly rising marginal costs and prices.

Short-Run Equilibrium of the Industry and the Firm[7]

✓ Concept Check

When is a perfectly competitive firm in long-run equilibrium?

In Section 5.1, we showed how the market demand curve for a commodity was derived from the horizontal summation of the demand curves of all the individual consumers of the commodity in the market. We have now shown how to derive the industry or market supply curve of the commodity. In a perfectly competitive market, the equilibrium price of the commodity is determined at the intersection of the market demand curve and the market supply curve of the commodity. This was explained in Section 2.4. Thus, we have traveled a complete circle and returned to the point of departure. Now, however, we know what lies behind the market demand curve and the market supply curve of the commodity and how they are derived (i.e., we no longer simply assume these curves as given, as in Chapter 2).

Given the price of the commodity, the perfectly competitive firm can sell any quantity of the commodity at that price. As noted earlier, the firm will produce at the point where P or $MR = MC$, provided that MC is rising and $P \geq AVC$. This is shown in Figure 9.8.

The right panel of Figure 9.8 shows the short-run market supply curve S (from Figure 9.5) and hypothetical market demand curve D for the commodity. These curves intersect at point E^*, and result in the equilibrium price of $35 and the equilibrium quantity of 350 units. At $P = 25, the quantity demanded (400 units) exceeds the quantity supplied (300 units), and the resulting shortage will drive the commodity price up to $P = 35. On the other hand, at $P = 50, the quantity supplied (400 units) exceeds the quantity demanded (300 units), and the resulting surplus will drive the price down to $P = 35. The left panel shows that at $P = 35, the perfectly competitive firm will produce 3.5 units (point E, as in Figure 9.3). Note that each firm produces 1/100 of the total industry or market output.

---

[7] For a mathematical presentation of how equilibrium is determined in a perfectly competitive industry using rudimentary calculus, see Section A.11 of the Mathematical Appendix at the end of the book.

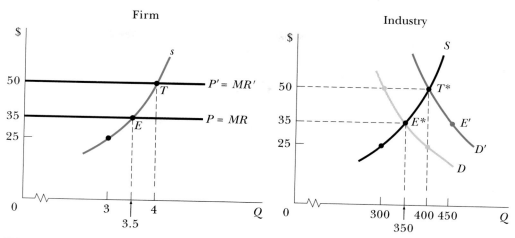

FIGURE 9.8   Short-Run Equilibrium of the Firm and the Industry   With S (from Figure 9.5) and D in the right panel, $P = \$35$ and $Q = 350$ (point E^*), and the perfectly competitive firm would produce 3.5 units (point E in the left panel, as in Figure 9.3). If D shifted up to D', $P = \$50$ and $Q = 400$ (point T^*), and the firm would produce 4 units of output (point T in the left panel).

If the market demand curve then shifted up to D' (for example, as a result of an increase in consumers' incomes), there would be a shortage of 100 units of the commodity at $P = \$35$ (E^*E' in the right panel of Figure 9.8). This would cause the equilibrium price to rise to $50 and the equilibrium quantity to 400 units (point T^*). Then, at $P = \$50$, the perfectly competitive firm maximizes profits at point T by producing 4 units of output (see the left panel). This is based on the assumption that there are 100 identical firms in the perfectly competitive industry and that input prices remain constant.

| 9.5 | |

LONG–RUN EQUILIBRIUM OF THE FIRM AND THE INDUSTRY

Having analyzed how equilibrium is reached in the market period and in the short run, we can now go on to examine how the perfectly competitive firm and industry reach equilibrium in the long run. This will set the stage for the analysis of constant, increasing-, and decreasing-cost industries in Section 9.6.

Long-Run Equilibrium of the Firm

In the long run, all inputs are variable and the firm can build the most efficient plant to produce the best or most profitable level of output. The *best (i.e., the profit-maximizing) level of output* of the firm in the long run is the one at which price or marginal revenue equals long-run marginal cost. The *most efficient plant* is the one that allows the firm to produce the best level of output at the lowest possible cost. This is the plant represented by the *SATC* curve tangent to the *LAC* curve of the firm at the best level of output, as shown in Figure 9.9.[8]

---

[8] Since in the long run all costs are variable, the firm must at least cover all of its costs to remain in business.

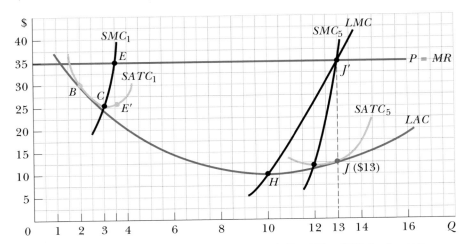

FIGURE 9.9   Long-Run Equilibrium of the Firm   At $P = MR = \$35$, the firm is in short-run equilibrium at point E (as in Figure 9.3). In the long run, the firm can increase its profits by producing at point J', where P or $MR = LMC$ (and LMC is rising), and operating plant $SATC_5$ at point J. In the long run, the firm will make profits of \$22 ($J'J$) per unit and \$286 in total (\$22 times 13 units of output). Since at point J', $P = MR = SMC = LMC$, the firm is also in short-run equilibrium.

The LAC curve in Figure 9.9 is the one of Figure 8.11, and the $SATC_1$ curve is that of Figures 8.2, 8.11, and 9.3. At $P = MR = \$35$ in Figure 9.9, the firm is in *short-run* equilibrium at point E by producing 3.5 units of output. Note that SMC refers to the short-run MC to distinguish it from LMC. The firm makes a profit of \$9 per unit (vertical distance EE') and \$31.50 in total (as in Figure 9.3).

In the long run, the firm can increase its profits significantly by producing at point J', where P or $MR = LMC$ (and LMC is rising). The firm should build plant $SATC_5$ and operate it at point J (at $SATC = \$13$). Plant $SATC_5$ is the best plant (i.e., the one that allows the firm to produce the best level of output at the lowest $SATC$). In the long run, the firm will make profits of \$22 ($J'J$) per unit and \$286 in total (\$22 times 13 units of output). This compares with total profits of \$31.50 in the short run. Note that when the firm is in long-run equilibrium, it will also be in short-run equilibrium since P or $MR = SMC = LMC$ (see point J' in the figure).[9] This analysis assumes that input prices are constant.

Long-Run Equilibrium of the Industry and the Firm

Even though the firm would be in long-run equilibrium at point J' in Figure 9.9, the industry would not. This is because the large profits that this and other firms earn at point J' will attract more firms to the industry. As new firms enter the industry (entry is free and resources are mobile), aggregate output expands. This will shift the short-run industry supply curve to the right until it intersects the market demand curve at the commodity price at which all firms make zero economic profits (i.e., they earn only a normal

---

[9] Note that $SMC_5 = LMC$ at $P = MR = \$35$ because the STC_5 curve is tangent to the LTC curve (neither curves shown in Figure 9.9) at $Q = 13$.

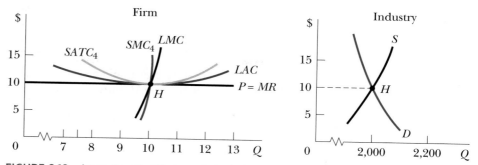

FIGURE 9.10   Long-Run Equilibrium of the Industry and Firm   The industry (in the right panel) and the firm (in the left panel) are in long-run equilibrium at point *H*, where $P = MR = SMC = LMC = SATC = LAC = \$10$. The firm produces at the lowest point on its *LAC* curve (operating optimal plant $SATC_4$ at point *H*) and earns zero profits.

return) in the long run. Then, and only then, will the industry (and the firm) be in equilibrium. In fact, the building of the best plant by the firm and the entrance of new firms into the industry will take place simultaneously in the long run. The final result (equilibrium) is shown in Figure 9.10.

In the figure, the industry (in the right panel) and the firm (in the left panel) are in long-run equilibrium at point *H*, where $P = MR = LMC = SMC = LAC = SATC = \$10$.[10] The firm produces at the lowest point on its *LAC* curve (operating optimal plant $SATC_4$ at point *H*) and earns zero economic profits. Zero economic profit means that the owner of the firm receives only a normal return on investment when the industry and firm are in long-run equilibrium. That is, the owner receives a return on the capital invested in the firm equal only to the amount that he or she would earn by investing the capital in a similarly risky venture. If the owner manages the firm, zero economic profits also includes what he or she would earn in the best *alternative* occupation (i.e., managing a similar firm for someone else). Thus, zero profits in economics means that the total revenues of the firm just cover all costs (explicit and implicit).[11]

Efficiency Implications of Perfect Competition

We have seen that when the perfectly competitive industry is in long-run equilibrium, the firm not only earns zero profits but produces at the lowest point on its *LAC* curve (point *H* in the left panel of Figure 9.10). Thus, resources are used most efficiently to produce the goods and services most desired by society at the minimum cost. Since firms also earn zero profits, consumers purchase the commodity at the lowest possible price ($10 at point *H* in the figure). In this sense, perfect competition is the most efficient form of market organization. This is to be contrasted to the situation under imperfect competition (discussed in the next four chapters), where we will see that firms seldom, if ever, produce at

---

[10] Note that the supply curve labeled *S* in the right panel of Figure 9.10 is much larger than the supply curve *S* in the right panel of Figure 9.8 because more firms have entered the industry in the long run and industry output is larger.

[11] As pointed out in Section 7.1, the meaning of *profit* in economics is to be distinguished clearly from the everyday use of the term (which considers implicit costs as part of profits). In economics, profits always refer only to the excess of total revenue over total costs, and total costs include both explicit and implicit costs (see Section 8.1). In short, in economics, profits mean above-normal returns.

the lowest point on their *LAC* curve, and they charge a price that also usually includes a profit margin.

To summarize, when a perfectly competitive industry is in equilibrium, $P = LAC = LMC$ for each firm in the industry. Since $P = LAC$, the perfectly competitive firm earns zero economic profits, and so there is distributional efficiency. Since $P = LMC$, each firm produces at the lowest point on its *LAC* curve, and so there is production efficiency. Finally, since $P = LMC$, there is allocative efficiency in the sense that the amount of the commodity supplied represents the best use of the economy's resources.

We have seen so far that when a perfectly competitive firm earns (economic) profits, more firms will enter the industry in the long run and this will lower the commodity price until all firms just break even (i.e., earn zero economic profits). On the other hand, if the perfectly competitive firm incurs a loss in the short run and would continue to incur a loss in the long run even by constructing the best plant, some firms would leave the industry. This would shift the industry supply curve to the left until it intersected the industry demand curve at the (higher) commodity price at which the remaining firms made zero economic profits but incurred no losses. The final result would be as shown in Figure 9.10, except that there would now be fewer firms in the industry and the industry output would be smaller. As it is, Figure 9.10 indicates that if all firms had identical cost curves, there would be 200 identical firms in the industry when in long-run equilibrium. Each firm would produce 10 units of output and break even.

Perfectly competitive firms need not have identical cost curves (although we assume so for simplicity), but the *minimum point* on their *LAC* curves must occur at the same cost per unit. If some firms had more productive inputs and, thus, lower average costs than other firms in the industry, the more productive inputs would be able to extract from their employer higher rewards (payments) commensurate to their higher productivity, under the threat of leaving to work for others. As a result, their *LAC* curves would shift upward until the lowest point on the *LAC* curve of all firms is the same. Thus, competition in the input markets as well as in the commodity market will result in all firms having identical (minimum) average costs and zero economic profits when the industry is in the long-run equilibrium. Example 9–4 examines the long-run adjustment in the U.S. cotton textile industry.

✓ Concept Check
Why is perfect competition the best form of market organization?

EXAMPLE 9–4

Long-Run Adjustment in the U.S. Cotton Textile Industry

In a study of U.S. industries between the world wars, Lloyd Reynolds found that the U.S. cotton textile industry was the one that came closest to being perfectly competitive. Cotton textiles were practically homogeneous, there were many buyers and sellers of cotton cloth, each was too small to affect its price, and entry into and exit from the industry was easy. Reynolds found that the rate of return on investments in the cotton textile industry was about 6% in the South and 1% in the North (because of higher costs for raw cotton and labor in the North), as contrasted to an average rate of return of 8% for all other manufacturing industries in the United States over the same period of time.

Because of the lower returns, the perfectly competitive model would predict that firms would leave the textile industry in the long run and enter other industries. The model would also predict that because returns were lower in the North than in the South, a greater contraction of the textile industry would take place in the North than in the South. Reynolds found that both of these predictions were borne out by the facts. Capacity in the U.S. textile industry declined by over 33% between 1925 and 1938, with the decline being larger in the North than in the South. Thus, textile firms, cotton farms, and firms using cloth did seem to make use of this knowledge and did respond to these economic forces in their managerial decisions.

Most U.S. textile firms were able to remain in business after World War II only as a result of U.S. restrictions on cheaper textile imports and, subsequently, as a result of the introduction of labor-saving innovations that sharply cut their labor costs. But with the reduction in trade protection negotiated at the Uruguay Round (1986–1993), U.S. textile firms have come under renewed pressure, especially from China, which is expected to produce half of the world textiles before the end of the decade.

Sources: L. Reynolds, "Competition in the Textile Industry," in W. Adams and T. Traywick, eds., *Readings in Economics* (New York: Macmillan, 1948); "Apparel Makes Last Stand," *New York Times,* September 26, 1990, p. D2; W. McKibbin and D. Salvatore, "The Global Economic Consequences of the Uruguay Round," *Open Economies Review,* April 1995, pp. 111–129; "U.S. Textiles Makers Unravel under Debt, Import Pressure," *Wall Street Journal,* December 27, 2001, p. A2; and "Free of Quota, China Textiles Flood the U.S.," *New York Times,* March 3, 2005, p. 3.

9.6   CONSTANT-, INCREASING-, AND DECREASING-COST INDUSTRIES

In the previous section, we examined how a perfectly competitive industry and firm reach equilibrium in the long run. Starting from a position of long-run equilibrium, we now examine how the perfectly competitive industry and firm adjust in the long run to an increase in the market demand for the commodity. This allows us to define constant-, increasing-, and decreasing-cost industries and to analyze their operation graphically.

Constant-Cost Industries

Constant-cost industry An industry with a horizontal long-run supply curve.

Starting from the long-run equilibrium condition of the industry and the firm (point H) in Figure 9.10, if the market demand curve for the commodity increases, the equilibrium price will rise in the short run and firms earn economic profits (i.e., they receive above-normal returns). This will attract more firms into the industry, and the short-run industry or market supply curve of the commodity increases (shifts to the right). If input prices remain constant (as more inputs are demanded by the expanding industry), the new long-run equilibrium price for the commodity will be the same as before the increase in demand and supply. Then the long-run industry supply curve (*LS*) for the commodity is horizontal at the minimum *LAC*. This is a **constant-cost industry**, which is shown in Figure 9.11.

In Figure 9.11, point H in the right and left panels shows the long-run equilibrium position of the perfectly competitive industry and firm, respectively (as in Figure 9.10), before the increase in demand (*D*) and supply (*S*). The increase in *D* to *D'* results in the short-run equilibrium price of $20 (point H' in the right panel). At $P = \$20$, each of the 200 identical firms in the industry will produce $Q = 10.5$ (given by point H' in the left panel at which $P = SMC_4 = \$20$) for a total industry output of 2,100 units.

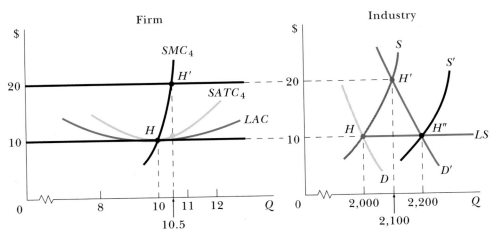

FIGURE 9.11   Constant-Cost Industry   Point *H* is the original long-run equilibrium point of the industry and firm. An increase in *D* to *D'* results in *P* = $20, and all firms earn economic profits. As more firms enter the industry, *S* shifts to *S'* and *P* = $10 if input prices remain constant. By joining points *H* and *H''* in the right panel, we derive horizontal long-run supply curve *LS* for the (constant-cost) industry.

Because each firm earns profits at *P* = $20 (see the left panel), more firms enter the industry in the long run, shifting *S* to the right. If input prices remain constant, *S* shifts to *S'*, reestablishing the original equilibrium price of $10 (point *H''* in the right panel). At *P* = $10, each firm produces at the lowest point on its *LAC* and earns zero economic profit (point *H* in the left panel). By joining points *H* and *H''* in the right panel, we derive the long-run supply curve of the industry (*LS*). Since *LS* is horizontal, this is a constant cost industry (with 220 identical firms producing a total output of 2,200 units).

Constant costs are more likely to result in industries that utilize general rather than specialized inputs and that account for only a small fraction of the total quantity demanded of the inputs in the economy. In these cases, the industry may be able to hire a greater quantity of the general inputs it uses without driving input prices upward.

Increasing-Cost Industries

Increasing-cost industry An industry with a positively sloped long-run supply curve.

If input prices *rise* as more inputs are demanded by an expanding industry, the long-run industry supply curve for the commodity will be positively sloped and we have an **increasing-cost industry.** This means that greater outputs of the commodity per time period will be supplied in the long run only at higher commodity prices (see Figure 9.12).

Starting from point *H* in the right and left panel of Figure 9.12, the increase in *D* to *D'* results in *P* = $20 (point *H'* in the right panel), at which all firms earn economic profits (point *H'* in the left panel). More firms enter the industry in the long run, and more inputs are demanded as industry output expands. *So far, this is identical to Figure 9.11.* If input prices now rise, each firm's per-unit cost curves shift up (as explained in the appendix to Chapter 8), and *S* shifts to the right to *S'* so as to establish equilibrium *P* = minimum *LAC'* = $15 (see point *H''* in both panels of Figure 9.12). All profits are squeezed out as costs rise and price falls. By joining points *H* and *H''* in the right panel, we get the long-run

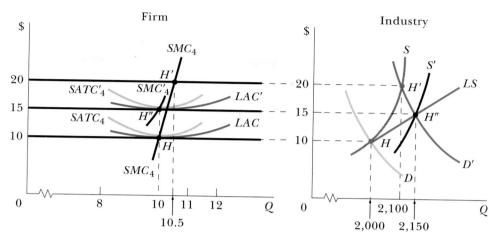

FIGURE 9.12   Increasing-Cost Industry   Point *H* is the original long-run equilibrium point of the industry and firm. An increase in *D* to *D'* results in *P* = $20 and all firms earn economic profits. As more firms enter the industry, *S* shifts to *S'* and *P* = $15 if input prices rise. By joining points *H* and *H''* in the right panel, we derive positively sloped long-run supply curve *LS* for the (increasing–cost) industry.

industry supply curve (*LS*). Since *LS* is positively sloped, the industry is an increasing-cost industry (with 217.5, or 218, identical firms).

Increasing costs are more likely to result in industries that utilize some specialized input, such as labor with unique skills (e.g., highly trained lab technicians to conduct experiments in genetics) or custom-made machinery to perform very special tasks (e.g., oil-drilling platforms). These industries may have to pay higher prices to bring forth a greater supply of the specialized inputs they require, creating an increasing-cost industry.

Decreasing-Cost Industries

Decreasing-cost industry An industry with a negatively sloped long-run supply curve.

If input prices *fall* as more inputs are demanded by an expanding industry, the long-run industry supply curve for the commodity will be negatively sloped and we have a **decreasing-cost industry.** This means that greater outputs of the commodity per time period will be supplied in the long run at lower commodity prices (see Figure 9.13).

The movement from point *H* to point *H'* in both panels of Figure 9.13 is the same as in Figures 9.11 and 9.12. Since at point *H'* firms earn profits, more firms enter the industry in the long run. Industry output expands, and more inputs are demanded. If input prices fall, each firm's per-unit cost curves shift down, and *S* shifts to the right to *S'* so as to establish equilibrium *P* = minimum *LAC'* = $5 (point *H''* in both panels). By joining points *H* and *H''* in the right panel, we derive *LS*, the industry long-run supply curve. Since *LS* is negatively sloped, we have a decreasing-cost industry (with 230 identical firms).

Decreasing costs may result when the expansion of an industry leads to (1) the establishment of technical institutes to train labor for skills required by the industry at a lower cost than firms in the industry do; (2) the setting up of enterprises to supply some equipment used by the industry that was previously constructed by the firms in the industry for themselves at higher cost; (3) the exploitation of some cheaper natural resource that the industry can substitute for more expensive resources but which was not feasible to exploit when the demand for the natural resource was smaller.

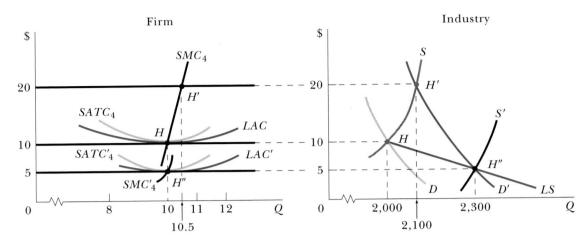

FIGURE 9.13   Decreasing-Cost Industry   Points H and H' are the same as in the preceding two figures. Starting from point H', as more firms enter the industry, S shifts to S' and $P = \$5$ if input prices fall. By joining points H and H'' in the right panel, we derive the negatively sloped long-run supply curve LS for the (decreasing-cost) industry.

✔ Concept Check

What are constant-, increasing-, and decreasing-cost industries?

External economy A downward shift in all firms' per-unit cost curves resulting from a decline in input prices as the industry expands.

External diseconomy An upward shift in all firms' per-unit cost curves resulting from an increase in input prices as the industry expands.

In the real world, we have examples of constant-, increasing-, and decreasing-cost industries. In fact, a particular industry could exhibit constant, increasing, or decreasing costs over different time periods and at various levels of demand.[12] It should also be noted that the shifts in firms' per-unit cost curves in the left panel of Figures 9.12 and 9.13 were vertical (so the lowest point on both the LAC and LAC' curves occurred at $Q = 10$). This is the case if the prices of all inputs change in the same proportion. Otherwise, per-unit cost curves would also shift to the right or to the left.

The *downward shift* in the firm's per-unit cost curves (due to a fall in input prices) as the *industry expands* is called an **external economy,** while the *upward shift* in the firm's per-unit cost curves (due to an increase in input prices) as the *industry expands* is called an **external diseconomy.** These terms are to be clearly distinguished from economies or diseconomies of scale, which are *internal* to the firm and refer instead to a downward or an upward *movement along* a given LAC curve (as the firm expands output and builds larger scales of plants). The assumption here is that as only a single firm expands output, input prices remain constant. External economies and diseconomies are examined in detail in Chapter 18.

9.7   INTERNATIONAL COMPETITION IN THE DOMESTIC ECONOMY

Domestic firms in most industries face a great deal of competition from abroad. Most U.S.-made goods today compete with similar goods from abroad and in turn compete with foreign-made goods in foreign markets. Steel, textiles, cameras, wines, automobiles, television sets, computers, and aircraft are but a few of the domestic

---

[12] Of the three cases, increasing-cost industries may be, perhaps, somewhat more common than the other two cases. Some important examples of decreasing-cost industries are computers, VCRs, and many other consumer electronics products.

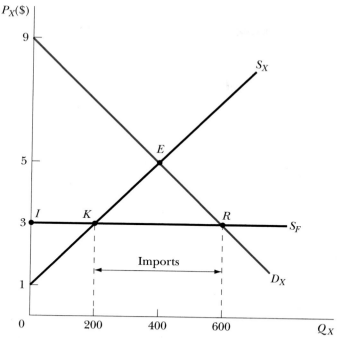

**FIGURE 9.14   Consumption, Production, and Imports Under Free
Trade**   In the absence of trade, equilibrium is at point E, where D_x and
S_x intersect, so that $P_x = \$5$ *and* $Q_x = 400$. With free trade at the world
price of $P_x = \$3$, domestic consumers purchase $IR = 600X$, of which
$IK = 200X$ are produced domestically and $KR = 400X$ are imported.

products that compete with foreign products for consumers' dollars in the U.S.
economy today. Competition from imports allows domestic consumers to purchase
more of a commodity at a lower price than in the absence of imports. This is shown
by Figure 9.14.

In the figure, D_X and S_X refer to the domestic market demand and supply curves of
commodity X. In the absence of trade, the equilibrium price is given by the intersection of
the D_X and S_X at point E, so that domestic consumers purchase $400X$ (all of which is produced domestically) at $P_X = \$5$. With free trade at the world price of $P_X = \$3$, the price
of commodity X to domestic consumers will fall to the world price. The foreign supply
curve of this nation's imports of commodity X, S_F, is horizontal at $P_X = \$3$ *on the
assumption that this nation's demand for imports of commodity X is small in relation to
the foreign supply.* From the figure, we can then see that domestic consumers will purchase IR or $600X$ at $P_X = \$3$ with free trade (and no transportation costs), as compared
with $400X$ at $P_X = \$5$ in the absence of trade (given by point E).

Figure 9.14 also shows that with free trade, domestic firms produce only IK or
$200X$, so that KR or $400X$ are imported at $P_X = \$3$. Resources in the nation will then
shift from the production of commodity X to the production of other commodities that
the nation can produce relatively more efficiently (i.e., in which the nation has a comparative advantage). By doing this, the nation will be able to obtain more of commodity

X through exchange than if it had used the same amount of domestic resources to produce commodity X domestically.[13]

ANALYSIS OF COMPETITIVE MARKETS

In this section, we examine a number of important applications of the tools of analysis
developed in this chapter. These include the definition and measurement of producer surplus, using consumers' and producers' surplus to further demonstrate the efficiency of
perfect competition, and showing the effects of a per-unit tax and an import tariff. These
applications, together with those from Chapter 2 (which presented an introductory
overview of the perfectly competitive model) on rent control, U.S. farm-support programs, and the incidence of (i.e., who pays for) an excise tax, clearly demonstrate the
great usefulness of the perfectly competitive model.

Producer Surplus

Producer surplus is a concept analogous to that of the consumer surplus examined in
Section 4.5. Consumer surplus is the difference between what consumers are willing to
pay for a commodity and what they actually pay, and it is measured by the area under the
demand curve and above the commodity price. **Producer surplus** is defined as the excess
of the commodity price over marginal cost, and it is measured by the area between the
commodity price and the producer's marginal cost curve. This is shown in Figure 9.15.

Producer surplus The
excess of the market
price of a commodity
over the marginal cost
of production.

Figure 9.15 shows that a perfectly competitive firm facing a price of $5 produces $4X$
(given by point E at which $d_X = MR_X = P_X = \$5 = MC_X$). This is derived from the opti-
mization rule that a firm should expand production as long as price or marginal revenue
exceeds marginal cost and until marginal revenue and marginal cost are equal. Since the
firm sells all four units of commodity X at the market price of $5, but faces a marginal cost
(or minimum price at which it will supply the first unit of the commodity) of only $2 on
the first unit produced, the firm receives a surplus of $3 (given by the area of the first
shaded rectangle in the figure) on the first unit sold. With $P_X = \$5$ but a marginal cost of
$3 to produce the second unit of commodity X, the firm receives a surplus of $2 (the area
of the second shaded rectangle) on the second unit sold. With $P_X = \$5$ and $MC = \$4$
on the third unit of commodity X produced, the firm receives a surplus of $1 (the area of
the third shaded rectangle) on the third unit of X sold. Finally, since $P_X = MC_X = \$5$
on the fourth unit, producer surplus is zero on the fourth unit of X. The firm will not produce the fifth unit of commodity X because the marginal cost of producing the fifth unit
($6) exceeds the commodity price of $5 (see the figure).

By adding the producer surplus of $3 on the first unit of commodity X, $2 on the second unit, $1 on the third unit, and $0 on the fourth unit, we get the total producer surplus of
$6 that the firm receives from the sale of $4X$. If commodity X could be produced and sold in
infinitesimally small units, the total producer surplus would be given by the total area
between the price of the commodity and the firm's marginal cost curve. This is the area of

---

[13] If the nation's demand for the imports of commodity X is large in relation to the total world supply of the
exports of commodity X to the nation, then S_F would be positively sloped and intersect D_X at a higher price,
so that the domestic production of commodity X would be higher while domestic consumption and imports
would be smaller than indicated in Figure 9.14. Try to pencil in this change in Figure 9.14.

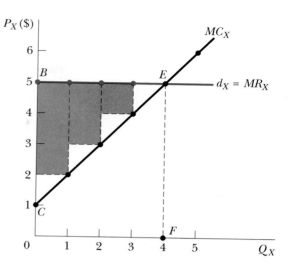

FIGURE 9.15   Producer Surplus   At $P_x = \$5$ the firm produces $4X$ (point E). Since the marginal cost is $2 on the first unit of X produced, the firm receives a surplus of $3 (given by the area of the first shaded rectangle). With $MC_x = \$3$ on the second unit of X, producer surplus is $2 (the area of the second shaded rectangle). With $MC_x = \$4$ on the third unit, producer surplus is $1 (the area of the third shaded rectangle). With $MC_x = \$5$ on the fourth unit, producer surplus is zero. Total producer surplus on $4X$ is $6. If commodity X were infinitesimally divisible, total producer surplus would be $8 (the area of triangle BEC).

triangle BEC, which is equal to $8 (as compared with $6 found above). At the market price of $P_X = \$5$ and with output of $4X$, the total revenue of the firm is $20 (given by the area of rectangle $BEFO$ in the figure). Of this, $CEFO$ or $12 represents the opportunity cost of the variable inputs used or the minimum cost that the producer will incur to produce $4X$. The difference of $8 (the area of triangle BEC) thus represents the producer surplus or the amount that is not necessary for the producer to receive in order to induce him or her to supply $4X$.

If the market price of commodity X fell to $4, we can see from the figure that the best level of output of the firm would be $3X$ and the total producer's surplus would be $4.50 (given by the area of the triangle formed by $P_X = \$4$ and the MC_X curve). On the other hand, if the price of commodity X rose to $6, the best level of output of the firm would be $5X$ and the total producer's surplus would be $12.50 (given by the area of the triangle formed by $P_X = 6$ and the MC_X curve in Figure 9.15). This analysis applies to each producer in a perfectly competitive market. Indeed, the concepts of consumer and producer surplus are used in the next section to further demonstrate the efficiency of a perfectly competitive market and in the last two sections of this chapter to show the welfare effects of an excise tax and an import tariff.

Consumers' and Producers' Surplus, and the Efficiency of Perfect Competition

We have seen in Section 9.4 that in a perfectly competitive market, equilibrium occurs at the intersection of the industry or market demand and supply curves for the commodity. At this point, the marginal benefit to consumers from the last unit of the commodity purchased just matches the marginal cost to producers, and the combined consumers' and producers' surplus is at a maximum. This is another way of proving that perfect competition is the most efficient form of market structure, and is shown in Figure 9.16.

In Figure 9.16, D_X and S_X refer, respectively, to the industry or market demand and supply curves for commodity X. The intersection of D_X and S_X defines equilibrium point E at which $P_X = \$5$ *and* $Q_X = 400$. The total consumers' surplus (the sum of the surpluses of all the consumers of commodity X in the market) is given by triangle AEB (the area under D_X and above P_X), which is equal to $800. The total producers' surplus (the sum of the surpluses of all

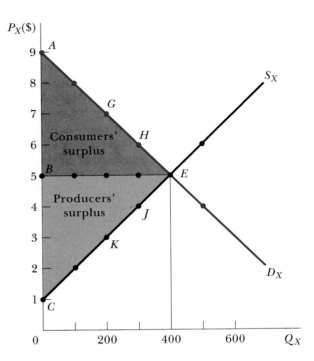

FIGURE 9.16 The Efficiency of Perfect Competition
Expanding output from 300X to 400X increases consumers'
plus producers' surplus by HEJ = $100. Expanding output past
the competitive equilibrium output of 400X reduces the total
surplus, because the marginal benefit to consumers is less than
the marginal cost of producers. Thus, consumers' plus
producers' surplus is maximized when a perfectly competitive
market is in equilibrium.

the producers of commodity X in the market) is given by triangle BEC (the area below P_X and above S_X), which is also $800. Thus, the total combined consumers' and producers' surplus is given by area $AEC = \$1{,}600$.

We can use Figure 9.16 to show that when a perfectly competitive market is in equilibrium, consumers' plus producers' surplus is maximized. For example, expanding output from 200X to 300X leads to a combined increase of consumers' and producers' surplus equal to $GHJK = \$300$. The increase in consumers' and producers' surplus arises because the marginal benefit to consumers exceeds the marginal cost to producers for each additional unit produced and consumed. Expanding output from 300X to 400X leads to a further increase in consumers' plus producers' surplus of $HEJ = \$100$. If output expands past the equilibrium output of 400X, the total surplus declines because consumers value the extra output at less than the marginal cost of producing it. Only at the competitive equilibrium output of 400X does the marginal benefit to consumers equal the marginal cost of producers and is the total combined consumers' and producers' surplus maximized. This can also be regarded as the benefit from exchange or trading (i.e., from buying and selling commodity X).

We will see in Part Four (Chapters 10–13) that imperfect competitors restrict output and charge a higher price so that the total combined consumers' and producers' surplus is smaller than under perfect competition. So important are the benefits of competition that market economies have been reducing the number and size of government regulations during the past decade. Even China has increasingly been relying on markets and less on planning.[14]

---

[14] See "The Global March of Free Markets," *New York Times,* July 19, 1987, Section 3, p. 1; and "Support Is Growing in China for Shift to Free Markets," *New York Times,* June 28, 1992, p. 1.

Welfare Effects of an Excise Tax

We will now use changes in consumers' and producers' surplus to measure the net loss in welfare resulting from an excise tax. The production and consumption effects of an excise tax as well as its incidence (i.e., who pays for the tax) were discussed in Section 2.7. Here, we expand that discussion to include a measurement of the loss in consumers' and producers' surplus resulting from the imposition of the tax. This is shown in Figure 9.17.

In Figure 9.17, D_X and S_X are, respectively, the market demand and supply curves for commodity X. The intersection of D_X and S_X defines the equilibrium price of $5 and the equilibrium quantity of 400X (just as in Figure 9.16). A tax of $2 per unit causes the S_X curve to shift up by $2 to S'_X because producers must now pay the $2 tax in addition to the previous marginal cost of producing each unit of commodity X shown by the S_X curve. This defines the new equilibrium point H at which $P_X = $6 to consumers and $Q_X = 300$. Producers, however, receive a net price of only $4 after paying the tax of $2 per unit. Thus, the tax raises the price to consumers from $5 to $6 and lowers the net price received by producers from $5 to $4, so consumers and producers in this case share equally the burden of the tax. So far, this is the same as in Section 2.7.

We can now go further, however, and measure the welfare effect of the tax by the change in consumers' and producers' surplus resulting from the tax. From Figure 9.17 we

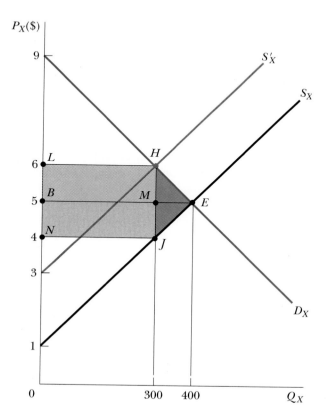

FIGURE 9.17   Welfare Effects of an Excise Tax   With D_X and S_X, equilibrium is at point E at which $P_X = $5 and $Q_X = 400$. A tax of $2 per unit on commodity X shifts S_X up to S_x' and defines new equilibrium point H at which $P_X = $6 to consumers, $Q_X = 300$, and producers receive a net price of $4 per unit. The loss of consumers' surplus is $LHEB = 350, the loss of producers' surplus is $BEJN = 350, for a combined loss of $LHEJN = 700. Since tax revenues are $LHJN = $600 ($2 per unit on 300 units), there is a deadweight loss of $HEJ = 100.

can see that the imposition of the tax leads to a reduction in consumers' surplus equal to
$LHEB = \$350$ and a reduction in producers' surplus equal to $BEJN = \$350$, for an overall combined loss of consumers' and producers' surplus of $700. Since the government
collects $2 per unit on 300 units of the commodity, or a total of $600 (the area of rectangle $LHJN$), the tax results in a *net* loss of $100 (the area of triangle HEJ) in consumers'
and producers' surplus. This **deadweight loss** remains even if the government were to
return the entire amount of tax collected in the form of a general income subsidy to consumers. The loss results because of the distortions resulting from the tax. Specifically,
some of society's resources shift from the production of commodity X to the production
of other commodities that consumers value less. The provision of a per-unit production
subsidy to producers would have the opposite effect of an excise tax (see Problem 11 at
the end of this chapter).

Deadweight loss The
excess of the combined
loss of consumers' and
producers' surplus from
a tax.

✓ Concept Check
How are the welfare
effects of an excise tax
measured?

Effects of an Import Tariff

We can show the effects of an import tariff using Figure 9.18. In Figure 9.18, D_X and S_X
refer, respectively, to the domestic market demand and supply curves of commodity X.
S_F is the foreign supply curve of exports of commodity X to the nation at the world price
of $3 (on the assumption that the quantity demanded of imports of commodity X by the
nation is very small in relation to the total foreign supply of exports of the commodity).
With free trade at the world price of $P_X = \$3$, domestic consumers purchase $IR = 600X$,
of which $IK = 200X$ are produced domestically and $KR = 400X$ are imported (so far this
is the same as in Figure 9.14 in Section 9.7).

Suppose that from the free trade position, the nation imposes a 33% import tariff,
or a tariff of $1 on each unit of commodity X imported. The new foreign supply curve
for the nation's imports now becomes $S_F + T$, where T refers to the tariff. The price of
commodity X to domestic consumers now becomes $4 (see Figure 9.18). At $P_X = \$4$,
domestic consumers purchase $NU = 500X$, of which $NJ = 300X$ are produced domestically and $JU = 200X$ are imported. Thus, the consumption effect of the tariff (i.e., the
reduction in domestic consumption resulting from the tariff) is $RW = -100X$, the
production effect (i.e., the expansion of domestic production resulting from the tariff) is
$KV = 100X$, the trade effect (i.e., the decline in imports) is $RW + KV = -200X$, and the
revenue effect (i.e., the revenue collected by the government) is $JUWV = \$200$ ($JV = \$1$
on each of the 200X imported).

We can also measure the welfare effects of the tariff. From Figure 9.18, we see that
the tariff leads to a reduction in consumers' surplus equal to $NURI = \$550$. Of this,
$NJKI = \$250$ represents a transfer to producers in the form of an increase in producers'
surplus, $JUWV = \$200$ is the tariff revenue collected by the nation's government, and the
sum of triangles $URW = \$50$ and $JKV = \$50$ represents the protection cost or deadweight
loss of the tariff. This results from the production and consumption distortions arising
from the tariff.

Results would be similar if, starting from the free trade position in Figure 9.18, the
nation imposed an import quota that directly restricted the *quantity* of imports of commodity X into the nation to $JU = 200X$. If the nation auctioned off import licenses to the
highest bidder, it would collect the same revenue ($JUWV = \$200$) as with the 33% or $1
tariff on each unit of imports. If the nation does not auction off import licenses (as is often
the case), the nation's importers or the foreign exporters would earn that much greater

✓ Concept Check
How are the effects of
an import tariff
measured?

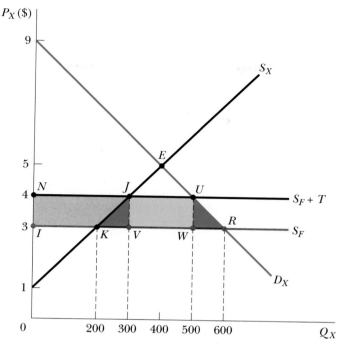

FIGURE 9.18   Effects of an Import Tariff D_X and S_X represent the domestic market demand and supply curves of commodity X. At the free trade price $P_X = \$3$, domestic consumers purchase $IR = 600X$, of which $IK = 200X$ are produced domestically and $KR = 400X$ are imported. With a \$1 import tariff, P_X to domestic consumers rises to \$4. At $P_X = \$4$, domestic consumers purchase $NU = 500X$, of which $NJ = 300X$ are produced domestically and $JU = 200X$ are imported. Thus, the consumption effect of the tariff is $RW = -100X$, the production effect is $KV = 100X$, the trade effect is $RW + KV = -200X$, and the revenue effect is $JUWV = \$200$. Consumers' surplus declines by $NURI = \$550$, of which $NJKI = \$250$ represents an increase in producers' surplus, $JUWV = \$200$ is the tariff revenue, and $URW = \$50$ plus $JKV = \$50$ represents the deadweight loss of the tariff.

profits. This is exactly what happened when the United States negotiated an agreement with Japan during the 1980s under which Japan "voluntarily" reduced its automobile exports to the United States. Japanese automakers were, therefore, able to sell automobiles in the United States at the world price plus the equivalent tariff (i.e., the tariff that would have reduced imports by the same amount as the quota) and earn huge profits. If trade restrictions were necessary to allow domestic automakers to improve quality and meet Japanese competition, then it would have been better for the United States to impose an equivalent import tariff and collect the tariff revenue.[15]

---

[15] See D. Salvatore, *International Economics*, 8th ed. (New York: John Wiley & Sons, 2003), Section 9.3a.

AT THE FRONTIER (1)
New Markets and New Competition on the Internet

The Internet has created new markets and new competition. The three icons of e-commerce are Amazon.com, eBay, and Priceline. Amazon.com sells books, videos, and gifts by traditional methods—only without the bricks and mortar of storefronts. In October 1999, Amazon opened its Website to merchants of all kinds, essentially becoming an Internet shopping bazaar. eBay's auctions originally matched buyers and sellers of collectibles, such as Beanie Babies and baseball cards, but they now include most products; eBay has now more than 150 million customers in over 15 countries around the world, and in the United States it opened 50 regional marketplaces for large items, such as cars, boats, and refrigerators, that are not well suited for its national Website. In 2007, eBay had a market capitalization in excess of $185 billion, which exceeded that of Wal-Mart, Coca-Cola, and IBM.

Priceline allows buyers to name the price they are willing to pay for flights, hotel rooms, mortgages, cars, and groceries. The only condition is that the buyer be flexible as to seller or brand name. For example, in the purchase of an airline ticket to a certain city, the buyer cannot specify the airline or the time of flight but has to take what is offered by the carrier that accepts the bid. This allows airlines to sell empty seats without losing their regular customers. As customers learned to make realistic bids and as Priceline added more airlines and flights, more and more bids have been successful (although they are still less than half). Students at the University of Pennsylvania's Wharton School of Business registering for elective courses have even been able to log on to Wharton's course auction Website and bid on the courses they want.

Several new, smaller sites have also been established that not only led to lower prices than at Priceline but even identify the price of the winning bid and the company that accepted the bid—something that Priceline won't (really cannot) do because it has promised the companies not to do so. Now a new crop of start-ups, such as Become.com, Smarter.com, and BuySafe, is pushing the price-comparison concept even further, offering extra discounts, greater convenience, and protection against fraud. The Internet has certainly been a fertile ground for creating new markets and competition by launching entirely new ways of doing business!

Sources: "Wired for the Bottom Line," *Newsweek*, September 20, 1999, pp. 43–49; "eBay Plans to Open 50 Web Markets for Regional Use," *Wall Street Journal*, October 1, 1999, p. B6; "Business School Puts Courses in the Hands of an On-Line Market," *New York Times*, September 9, 1999, p. G3; "The Brave New World of Pricing," *Financial Times*, August 2, 2001, p. 2; "How to Beat Priceline: New Sites Post Secret Bids," *Wall Street Journal*, April 9, 2002, p. D1; The Next Generation of Price-Comparison Sites," *Wall Street Journal*, September 14, 2005, p. D1; "Collective Bargain Hunting," *New York Times Magazine*, September 18, 2005, p. 32; and "Google Shares Power Past $600 Mark," *Financial Times*, October 9, 2007, p. 23.

AT THE FRONTIER (2)
Auctioning Airwaves

Since the time of its creation in 1927 until December 1994, the Federal Communications Commission (FCC) handed out airwaves (radio frequency) licenses free of charge, through either lotteries or merit-based hearings, favoring local radio and TV stations, on the theory that they would be more attuned to community programming needs. During the 1980s, pressure began to mount to scrap the old system and allow market forces to allocate these scarce resources (airwaves). Between December 5, 1994, and March 1995, the U.S. government auctioned off to the highest bidder thousands of licenses to blanket the nation with new personal communications services (PCS) for the huge sum of $7.7 billion.

Although similar to an art auction—except that all licenses rather than a single one were up for bidding at the same time—auctioning airwaves licenses was unlike anything ever done before. The plan carved the nation into 51 regions and 492 subregions (metropolitan areas) and auctioned two licenses for each of the 51 regions and up to five licenses for each of the 492 subregions. A large company or group of companies could bid for a nationwide license by combining bids for a license for each region. Thus, each metropolitan area could have as many as seven new wireless services (five for the metropolitan area alone and another two from the region of which the metropolitan area is part), and each of these would compete with the one or two already-established cellular telephone companies (which were allowed to bid and did bid for some of the new wireless licenses).

Since March 1995, 14 other auctions of wireless licenses were held, which netted the government an additional $59 billion, and more auctions were planned for the future. It is estimated that during this decade more than 100 million Americans will create a $100 billion-a-year industry for wireless services. Such large revenues are needed in order for the industry to recoup the original investments. These include the nearly $50 billion already paid for the licenses as well as the even larger investments that wireless companies are collectively making in order to set up the new digital transmission systems. Thus, it may take a decade before wireless companies can break even and possibly become profitable. In the end, the difference between a profit and a loss could be the price of the license itself. Wireless companies may simply have paid too much for these licenses. This is called the **winner's curse**.

The winner's curse arises because if the average for all the bids equals the true (but unknown) value of a license (based on the future stream of incomes that it is expected to generate), then the price paid by the highest bidder would exceed the average bid and the true value of the license. This is exactly what happened in the bidding for oil leases in the Gulf of Mexico during the 1950s and 1960s. The winner's curse can also arise when publishers bid for a novel. The most optimistic company is likely to be the highest bidder, and its bid will exceed the average bid and true value of the asset. The only way to avoid the winner's curse is for a company to adopt a prudent bidding approach and not to overbid.

The winner's curse seems to have happened in this instance, as evidenced by the fact that, starting in 1996, several of the less-known large bidders for the licenses

Winner's curse
The overbidding or the paying of a price higher than the true (but unknown) value of an asset by the highest bidder at an auction.

Continued . . .

Auctioning Airwaves   *Continued*

started to default on payments. It seems that many successful bidders overpaid for the licenses, in view of the strong competition that the sale of multiple licenses for each market generates. The government then reauctioned these licenses. Legislation has also been passed requiring TV broadcasters to go all-digital by February 2009 and to relinquish their analog airwaves so that they can also be auctioned off by the government at an estimated price of as much as $20 billion.

Sources: "U.S. Lays Out Rules for a Big Auction of Radio Airwaves," *New York Times*, September 24, 1993, p. 1; "Winners of Wireless Auctions to Pay $7 Billion," *New York Times*, March 14, 1995, p. D1; "Clinton Orders a New Auction of Airwaves," *New York Times*, October 14, 2001, p. 1; "Everybody Wants a Piece of the Air," *Business Week*, July 4, 2005, pp. 38–39; "A Scramble for the Perfect Wave," *Business Week*, June 25, 2007, p. 54; "Auction of Wireless Spectrum Brings U.S. $19 Billion," *New York Times*, March 19, 2008, p. C2; P. Milgrom, "Auctions and Bidding: A Primer," *Journal of Economic Perspectives*, Summer 1989, pp. 3–22; and S. Thiel, "Some Evidence on the Winner's Curse," *American Economic Review*, December 1988, pp. 884–895.

SUMMARY

1. Economists identify four different types of market organization: perfect competition, monopoly, monopolistic competition, and oligopoly. In a perfectly competitive market, no buyer or seller affects (or behaves as if he or she affects) the price of a commodity, all units of the commodity are homogeneous or identical, resources are mobile, and knowledge of the market is perfect.

2. The market period, or the very short run, refers to the period of time during which the market supply of a commodity is fixed. During the market period, costs of production are irrelevant in the determination of the price of a perishable commodity and the entire supply of the commodity is put up for sale at whatever price it can fetch. Thus, demand alone determines price (while supply alone determines quantity).

3. The TR of a perfectly competitive firm is a straight line through the origin with slope of $MR = P$. The best or profit-maximizing level of output occurs where the positive difference between TR and STC is greatest. The same result is obtained where P or $MR = MC$ and MC is rising, provided that $P \geq AVC$. If P is smaller than ATC at the best level of output, the firm will incur a loss. As long as P exceeds AVC, it pays for the firm to continue to produce because it covers all variable costs and part of its fixed costs. If the firm were to shut down, it would incur a loss equal to its total fixed costs. The shut down point is where $P = AVC$.

4. The rising portion of the firm's MC curve above the AVC curve (the shutdown point) is the firm's short-run supply curve for the commodity. The industry short-run supply curve is the horizontal summation of the firms' short-run supply curves. The equilibrium price is at the intersection of the market demand and supply curves of the commodity. The firm will then produce the output at which P or $MR = MC$, and MC is rising (as long as P exceeds AVC). With an increase in demand, the equilibrium price will rise and firms will expand their output. If input prices rise, the MC curve of each firm shifts up, and so the short-run supply curve of each firm and of the industry are less elastic.

5. In the long run, the industry and the firm are in long-run equilibrium where $P = MR = SMC = LMC = SATC = LAC$. Each firm operates at the lowest point on its LAC curve and earns zero profits. Competition in the input markets as well as in the commodity market will result in all firms having identical average costs and zero profits when the industry is in long-run equilibrium.

6. One of three possible cases can result as industry output expands and more inputs are demanded. If input prices remain constant, the industry long-run supply curve is horizontal

and we have a constant-cost industry. If input prices rise (external diseconomy), the industry long-run supply curve is positively sloped and we have an increasing-cost industry. This may be more common than the former two cases. If input prices fall (external economy), the industry long-run supply curve is negatively sloped and we have a decreasing-cost industry.

7. Domestic firms in most industries face a great deal of competition from imports. International trade leads to a decline in the domestic price of the commodity, and larger domestic consumption and lower domestic production of the commodity than in the absence of trade.

8. Producer surplus equals the excess of the commodity price over the producer's marginal cost of production. The combined consumers' and producers' surplus is maximized when a perfectly competitive market is in equilibrium. A tax leads to a deadweight loss. An import tariff increases the domestic price of the importable commodity, reduces domestic consumption and imports, increases domestic production, generates tax revenues, and leads to a deadweight loss.

9. The Internet has created new markets and new competition. Between 1994 and 2007, the U.S. government auctioned off to the highest bidder thousands of licenses to offer new personal communications services (PCS) for nearly $50 billion. Some of the new wireless companies that purchased these licenses may have overpaid (and faced the winner's curse).

KEY TERMS

Perfect competition	Increasing-cost industry	Winner's curse
Market period	Decreasing-cost industry	Foreign-exchange market
Break-even point	External economy	Exchange rate
Shutdown point	External diseconomy	Depreciation
Price elasticity of supply	Producer surplus	Appreciation
Constant-cost industry	Deadweight loss	

REVIEW QUESTIONS

1. If perfect competition is rare in the real world, why do we study it?

2. A firm's total revenue is $100, its total cost is $120, and its total fixed cost is $40. Should the firm stay in business? Why?

3. Why might a firm remain in business in the short run even if incurring a loss but always leave the industry if incurring a loss in the long run?

4. At what level of output is profit per unit maximized for a perfectly competitive firm? Why will the firm not produce this level of output?

5. Why would a firm enter a perfectly competitive industry if it knows that its profits will be zero in the long run?

6. Must a perfectly competitive industry be in long-run equilibrium if a perfectly competitive firm is in long-run equilibrium? Must each perfectly competitive firm be in equilibrium if the industry is in long-run equilibrium? Why?

7. Why should a nation trade if such trade benefits domestic consumers but harms domestic producers?

8. What is the difference between economic profit and producer surplus?

9. What is the combined consumers' and producers' surplus at the output level of 500X in Figure 9.15? Why is this not the best level of output?

10. Is the deadweight loss from an excise tax greater when the market demand and supply curves of the commodity are elastic or inelastic? Why?

11. What is the size of a prohibitive tariff in Figure 9.18? What would be the effects of such a prohibitive tariff?

12. What is meant by the winner's curse in an auction? How can this be avoided?

13. Assuming a two-currency world—the U.S. dollar and the British pound sterling—what does a depreciation of the dollar mean for the pound? Explain.

PROBLEMS

*1. Suppose that the market demand function of a perfectly competitive industry is given by $QD = 4{,}750 - 50P$ and the market supply function is given by $QS = 1{,}750 + 50P$, and P is expressed in dollars.

   a. Find the market equilibrium price.

   b. Find the quantity demanded and supplied in the market at $P = \$50, \$40, \$30, \$20$, and $\$10$.

   c. Draw the market demand curve, the market supply curve, and the demand curve for one of 100 identical perfectly competitive firms in this industry.

   d. Write the equation of the demand curve of the firm.

2. a. If the market supply function of a commodity is $QS = 3{,}250$, are we in the market period, the short run, or the long run?

   b. If the market demand function is $QD = 4{,}750 - 50P$ and P is expressed in dollars, what is the market equilibrium price (P)?

   c. If the market demand increases to $QD' = 5{,}350 - 50P$, what is the equilibrium price?

   d. If the market demand decreases to $QD' = 4{,}150 - 50P$, what is the equilibrium price?

   e. Draw a figure showing parts (b), (c), and (d) of this problem.

3. Using the STC schedule provided in the table for Problem 2(a) in Chapter 8 and $P = \$26$ for a perfectly competitive firm,

   a. draw a figure similar to Figure 9.2 and determine the best level of output for the firm.

   b. construct a table similar to Table 9.1 showing TR, STC, and total profits at each level of output.

*4. Suppose that a perfectly competitive firm has no knowledge of the exact shape of its STC curve. It knows that its total fixed costs are $200, and it assumes that its average variable costs are constant at $5.

   a. If the firm can sell any amount of the commodity at the price of $10 per unit, draw a figure and determine the sales volume at which the firm breaks even.

   b. How can an increase in the price of the commodity, in the total fixed costs of the firm, and in average variable costs, be shown in the figure of part (a) of this problem?

   c. What is an important shortcoming of this analysis?

*5. Using the per-unit cost schedules derived from the table for Problem 2(a) in Chapter 7 and $P = \$26$,

   a. draw a figure similar to Figure 9.3 and show the best level of output of the firm.

   b. construct a table similar to Table 9.2 showing P, MR, ATC, and MC at each level of output.

6. For your figure in Problem 5a, determine the best level of output, the profit or loss per unit, total profit or losses, and whether the firm should continue to produce at

   a. $P = \$42$.

   b. $P = \$18$.

   c. $P = \$12.50$

7. Graph the quantity supplied (Q) at various prices (P) by firms 1, 2, and 3 given below, and derive the industry supply curve on the assumptions that the industry is composed only of these three firms and input prices remain constant.

Price and Quantity Supplied By Firms 1, 2, and 3

P	Q_1	Q_2	Q_3
$1	0	0	0
2	20	0	0
3	40	10	10
4	60	20	2

*8. Starting from Figure 9.5, suppose that as each of the 100 identical firms in the perfectly competitive industry increases output (as a result of an increase in the market price of the commodity), input prices rise, causing the SMC curve of each firm to shift upward by $15. Draw a figure showing the original and the new MC curve and the quantity supplied by each firm and by the industry as a whole at the original price of $P = \$35$ and at $P = \$50$. On the same figure, show the supply curve of each firm and of the industry.

9. a. For the perfectly competitive firm of Problem 5, draw a figure similar to Figure 9.9 showing the short-run and long-run equilibrium on the assumption that the firm, but not the industry, is in long-run equilibrium. Assume $P = \$30$, the lowest $LAC = \$12.50$ at $Q = 8$, the best level of output is $Q = 10$, and $LAC = \$15$ with $SATC_5$ and $SMC_5 = LMC = \$30$ when the firm, but not the industry, is in long-run equilibrium.

   b. Draw a figure similar to Figure 9.10 for the firm of part (a) showing the long-run equilibrium point for the firm and the industry.

*10. Starting from long-run equilibrium in a perfectly competitive increasing-cost industry, show on one diagram the effect on price and quantity of an increase in demand in the market period, in the short run, and in the long run.

---

* = Answer provided at end of book.

11. Starting with D_X and S_X in Figure 9.17, show all the effects of a production subsidy of $2 per unit given by the government to all producers of commodity X.

12. Starting with D_X and S_X in Figure 9.17, determine the effect of a price ceiling of $4 using the concepts of the consumers' and producers' surplus.

13. Starting with D_X and S_X of Figure 9.18, draw a figure similar to Figure 9.18 showing all the effects of a 100% import tariff on commodity X if the free trade price of commodity X is $2.

APPENDIX — ## THE FOREIGN-EXCHANGE MARKET AND THE DOLLAR EXCHANGE RATE

A firm will import a commodity as long as the domestic currency price of the imported commodity is lower than the price of the identical or similar domestically produced commodity and until they are equal (in the absence of transportation costs, tariffs, or other obstructions to the flow of trade). In order to make the payment, the domestic importer will have to exchange the domestic currency for the foreign currency. Since the U.S. dollar is also used as an international currency, however, a U.S. importer could also pay in dollars. In that case, it is the foreign exporter that will have to exchange dollars into the local currency.

Foreign-exchange market The market where national currencies are bought and sold.

The market where one currency is exchanged for another is called the foreign-exchange market. The **foreign-exchange market** for any currency, say the U.S. dollar, is formed by all the locations (such as London, Tokyo, Frankfurt, and New York) where dollars are bought and sold for other currencies. These international monetary centers are connected by telephone and the Internet and are in constant contact with one another. The rate at which one currency is exchanged for another is called the **exchange rate.** This is the price of a unit of the foreign currency in terms of the domestic currency. For example, the exchange rate (R) between the U.S. dollar and the euro (€), the currency of the 16-nation European Monetary Union (Austria, Belgium, Cyprus, Finland, France, Germany, Greece, Ireland, Italy, Luxembourg, Malta, Netherlands, Portugal, Slovakia, Slovenia, and Spain), is the number of dollars required to purchase one euro. That is, $R = \$/\euro$. Thus, if $R = \$/\euro = 1$, this means that one dollar is required to purchase one euro.

Exchange rate The price of a unit of a foreign currency in terms of the domestic currency.

Under a flexible exchange rate system of the type we have today, the dollar price of the euro (R) is determined (just like the price of any other commodity in a competitive market) by the intersection of the market demand and supply curves of euros. This is shown in Figure 9.19, where the vertical axis measures the dollar price of euros, or the exchange rate ($R = \$/\euro$), and the horizontal axis measures the quantity of euros. The market demand and supply curves for euros intersect at point E, defining the equilibrium exchange rate of $R = 1$, at which the quantity of euros demanded and the quantity of euros supplied are equal at €300 million per day. At a higher exchange rate, the quantity of euros supplied exceeds the quantity demanded, and the exchange rate will fall toward the equilibrium rate of $R = 1$. At an exchange rate lower than $R = 1$, the quantity of euros demanded exceeds the quantity supplied, and the exchange rate will be bid up toward the equilibrium rate of $R = 1$.

The U.S. demand for euros is negatively inclined, indicating that the lower the exchange rate (R), the greater the quantity of euros demanded by the United States. The reason is that the lower the exchange rate (i.e., the fewer the number of dollars required to purchase one euro), the cheaper it is for the United States to import from and invest in the European Monetary Union (EMU), and thus the greater the quantity of euros demanded by U.S. residents. On the other hand, the U.S. supply of euros is usually positively inclined, indicating that the higher the exchange rate (R), the greater the quantity of euros earned by or supplied to the United States. The reason is that at higher exchange rates, residents

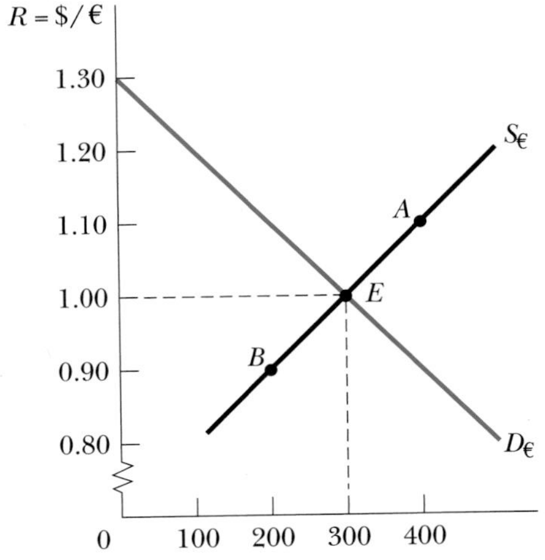

FIGURE 9.19   The Foreign-Exchange Market and the Dollar Exchange Rate   The vertical axis measures the dollar price of euros ($R = \$/€$), and the horizontal axis measures the quantity of euros. Under a flexible exchange rate system, the equilibrium exchange rate is $R = 1$ and the equilibrium quantity of euros bought and sold is €300 million per day. This is given by point E, at which the U.S. demand and supply curves for euros intersect.

of the EMU receive more dollars for each of their euros. As a result, they find U.S. goods and investments cheaper and more attractive and spend more in the United States, thus supplying more euros to the United States.

If the U.S. demand curve for euros shifted up (for example, as a result of increased U.S. tastes for EMU's goods) and intersected the U.S. supply curve for euros at point A (see Figure 9.19), the equilibrium exchange rate would be $R = 1.10$, and the equilibrium quantity would be €400 million per day. The dollar is then said to have depreciated since it now requires $1.10 (instead of the previous $1.00) to purchase one euro. **Depreciation** thus refers to an increase in the domestic price of the foreign currency. On the other hand, if through time the U.S. demand for euros shifted down so as to intersect the U.S. supply curve of euros at point B (see Figure 9.19), the equilibrium exchange rate would fall to $R = 0.90$ and the dollar is said to have appreciated (because fewer dollars are now required to purchase one euro). An **appreciation** thus refers to a decline in the domestic price of the foreign currency. Shifts in the U.S. supply curve of euros through time would similarly affect the equilibrium exchange rate and equilibrium quantity of euros.

In the absence of interferences by national monetary authorities, the foreign-exchange market operates just like any other competitive market, with the equilibrium price and quantity of the foreign currency determined at the intersection of the market demand and supply curves for the foreign currency. Sometimes, monetary authorities attempt to affect exchange rates by a coordinated purchase or sale of a currency on the foreign-exchange market. For example, U.S. and foreign monetary authorities may sell dollars for foreign currencies to induce a dollar depreciation (which makes U.S. goods cheaper to foreigners) in order to reduce the U.S. trade deficit. These official foreign-exchange market interventions are only of limited effectiveness, however, because the foreign-exchange resources at the disposal of national monetary authorities are very small in relation to the size of daily transactions on the foreign-exchange market (now estimated to be over $1 trillion per day!). Such huge volume of transactions has been made possible by sharp improvements in telecommunications and the coming into existence of a 24-hour foreign-exchange market around the world.[16]

Depreciation An increase in the domestic-currency price of a foreign currency.

Appreciation A decrease in the domestic-currency price of a foreign currency.

---

[16] See D. Salvatore, *International Economics*, 9th ed. (Hoboken, NJ: John Wiley & Sons), Chapter 14.

EXAMPLE 9-5

Foreign-Exchange Quotations

Table 9.4 gives the exchange rate for various currencies with respect to the U.S. dollar for Wednesday, April 30, 2008 and for Tuesday April 29, 2008—defined first as the dollar price of the foreign currency (as in the text) and then, alternatively, as the

TABLE 9.4 Foreign Exchange Quotations

Currency	Foreign Currency in Dollars Wed.	Tue.	Dollars in Foreign Currency Wed.	Tue.	Currency	Foreign Currency in Dollars Wed.	Tue.	Dollars in Foreign Currency Wed.	Tue.
NORTH AMERICA/CARIBBEAN					Singapore (Dollar)	.7380	.7344	1.3550	1.3616
Canada (Dollar)	.9954	.9879	1.0046	1.0122	So. Korea (Won)	.000994	.000998	1006.10	1002.50
Dominican Rep (Peso)	.0294	.0294	34.05	34.05	Taiwan (Dollar)	.0328	.0329	30.49	30.40
Mexico (Peso)	.095400	.094900	10.4822	10.5374	Thailand (Baht)	.03150	.03150	31.75	31.75
					Vietnam (Dong)	.000062	.000062	.16120	.16120
CENTRAL AMERICA					**EUROPE**				
Costa Rice (Colon)	.0019	.0019	517.75	517.75	Britain (Pound)	1.9893	1.9681	.5027	.5081
El Salvador (Colon)	.1143	.1143	8.7520	8.7520	Czech Rep (Koruna)	.0619	.0615	16.16	16.26
Guatemala (Quetzal)	.1337	.1337	7.4800	7.4800	Denmark (Krone)	.2095	.2085	4.7733	4.7962
Honduras (Lempira)	.0529	.0529	18.90	18.90	Europe (Euro)	1.5642	1.5564	.6393	.6425
Nicaragua (Cordoba)	.0517	.0516	19.35	19.38	Hungary (Forint)	.0061	.0061	163.93	163.93
Panama (Balboa)	1.00	1.00	1.00	1.00	Norway (Krone)	.1965	.1943	5.0891	5.1467
					Poland (Zloty)	.4531	.4495	2.21	2.22
SOUTH AMERICA					Russia (Ruble)	.0422	.0422	23.6987	23.6967
Argentina (Peso)	.3160	.3160	3.1646	3.1646	Slovak Rep (Koruna)	.0484	.0482	20.66	20.75
Bolivia (Boliviano)	.1360	.1360	7.3529	7.3529	Sweden (Krona)	.1675	.1662	5.9701	6.0168
Brazil (Real)	.5913	.5854	1.6912	1.7082	Switzerland (Franc)	.9673	.9632	1.0338	1.0382
Chile (Peso)	.002100	.002100	476.19	476.19	Turkey (Lira)	.7852	.7743	1.2736	1.2915
Colombia (Peso)	.000565	.000561	1769.50	1783.50	**MIDDLE EAST/AFRICA**				
Paraguay (Guarani)	.000244	.000244	4092.50	4092.50	Bahrain (Dinar)	2.6528	2.6521	.3770	.3771
Peru (New Sol)	.3478	.3500	2.875	2.857	Egypt (Pound)	.1854	.1853	5.3937	5.3955
Uruguay (New Peso)	.0503	.0503	19.8807	19.8807	Iran (Rial)	.000111	.000111	8985.00	8985.00
Venezuela (Bolivar)	.4657	.4657	2.1473	2.1473	Israel (Shekel)	.2926	.2890	3.4176	3.4602
					Jordan (Dinar)	1.4113	1.4112	.7086	.7086
ASIA/PACIFIC					Kenya (Shilling)	.0161	.0160	62.15	62.50
Australia (Dollar)	.9472	.9340	1.0657	1.0707	Kuwait (Dinar)	3.7540	3.7557	.2664	.2663
China (Yuan)	.1430	.1431	6.9930	6.9881	Lebanon (Pound)	.000661	.000661	1512.00	1512.00
Hong Kong (Dollar)	.1283	.1283	7.7942	7.7942	Saudi Arabia (Riyal)	.2666	.2666	3.7509	3.7509
India (Rupee)	.0247	.0247	40.486	40.486	So. Africa (Rand)	.1323	.1315	7.5586	7.6046
Indonesia (Rupiah)	.000108	.000109	9237.50	9213.00	U.A.E. (Dirham)	.2722	.2722	3.6738	3.6738
Japan (Yen)	.009600	.009600	104.17	104.17					
Malaysia (Ringgit)	.3165	.3173	3.1596	3.1516					
New Zealand (Dollar)	.7848	.7738	1.2742	1.2924					
Pakistan (Rupee)	.0154	.0155	64.94	64.52					
Philippines (Peso)	.0236	.0237	42.37	42.19					

a-Russian Central Bank rate.
All prices as of 3:00 p.m. Eastern Time.
Sources: Moneyline Tolerate and other sources

foreign-currency price of the dollar. For example, next to Europe, we find that the exchange rate of the euro (€) was \$1.5642/€1 on Wednesday and \$1.5564 on Tuesday. On the same line, we find that the euro price of the dollar was €0.6393/\$ on Wednesday and €0.6425 on Tuesday.

EXAMPLE 9-6
Depreciation of the U.S. Dollar and Profitability of U.S. Firms

A depreciation of the dollar, by making U.S. goods and services cheaper to foreigners in terms of their currency, allows U.S. firms to sell more abroad without lowering the dollar price of their products, and thus increases their profits and their share of foreign markets. U.S. firms also receive more dollars for their foreign-currency profits earned abroad. Against these benefits are the higher dollar prices that U.S. firms must pay for imported inputs. How much a U.S. firm gains from a depreciation of the dollar, therefore, depends on the amount of its foreign sales as opposed to its expenditures on imported inputs.

For example, the Black & Decker Corporation, a maker of power tools and appliances with about half of its sales abroad, found that the depreciation of the dollar during 1990 led to a 5% increase in its foreign sales and earnings. On the other hand, the Gillette Corporation, which has plants in many countries and uses almost exclusively local inputs to supply each market, benefited mostly through the repatriation of foreign profits. Merck & Company, which has plants in 19 nations and conducts most of its business in local currencies, was in a similar position. In between was Compaq (now part of Hewlett-Packard), which found some of its price advantage abroad resulting from the depreciation of the dollar during 1990 eaten away by the higher cost of its imported disk drives and circuit-board parts.

On the other hand, the 20% appreciation of the dollar vis-à-vis the euro from the time of its launching at the beginning of 1999 until January 2002, meant that U.S. exporters received 20% fewer dollars per euro earned in Europe, while U.S. importers paid 20% less imports from Europe. The opposite occurred in 2008, when the dollar had depreciated (and was undervalued) with respect to the euro by about 20%. Thus, a change in the exchange rate benefits some and harms others but affects all firms with foreign transactions and all individuals (American and foreigners) traveling abroad.

Source: How Dollar's Plunge Aids Some Companies, Does Little for Others," *Wall Street Journal*, October 22, 1990, p. A1; "Exporters in U.S. Confront a New Reality," *Wall Street Journal*, April 28, 1998, p. A2; D. Salvatore, "The Euro: Expectations and Performance," *Eastern Economic Journal*, January 2002, pp. 121–136; "Dollar Dive Helps US Companies," *Wall Street Journal*, April 21, 2003, p. C2; "Bulging Profits in US Often Originate Abroad," *New York Times*, August 4, 2007, p. C3; and "Dollar Doesn't Stretch Far in Buying Global Goods," *New York Times*, March 15, 2008, p. C3.

INTERNET SITE ADDRESSES

For information on the New York Stock Exchange, see:

http://www.nyse.com

Petroleum production from tar sands is examined at:

http://www.fumento.com/environment/oilsands.html

http://www.wired.com/wired/archive/12.07/oil.html

http://en.wikipedia.org/wiki/Tar_sands

Information on the world supply of copper is found at:

http://www.minecost.com/curves.htm

http://minerals.usgs.gov/minerals/pubs/commodity/copper/

http://www.zealllc.com/2005/copper.htm

For a discussion of the economic effects of an import tariff, see:

http://www.usitc.gov/publications/pub3906.pdf

http://en.wikipedia.org/wiki/Tariff

On auctioning of the airwaves, see:

http://www.news.com/2100-1033-251576.html

http://www.msnbc.msn.com/id/20060516/site/newsweek/

http://www.capitaleye.org/inside.asp?ID=294

PART FOUR

Imperfectly Competitive Markets

Part Four (Chapters 10–13) presents the theory of the firm in imperfectly competitive markets. It brings together the theory of consumer behavior and demand (from Part Two) and the theory of production and costs (from Chapters 7 and 8) to analyze how price and output are determined under various types of imperfectly competitive markets. Chapter 10 shows price and output determination under pure monopoly. Chapter 11 does the same for monopolistic competition and oligopoly. Chapter 12 describes how game theory is useful in analyzing oligopolistic behavior. Finally, Chapter 13 examines the efficiency implications of various market structures and regulation. As in previous parts of the text, the presentation of the theory is reinforced with many real-world examples and important applications, while the *At the Frontier* section in each chapter presents some new and important developments in the operation of imperfectly competitive markets.

CHAPTER **10**

Price and Output Under Pure Monopoly

After Studying This Chapter, You Should Be Able to:

- Know the meaning and importance of monopoly
- Describe how a monopolist determines the best level of output in the short run
- Describe the long-run equilibrium of the monopolist
- Know how to measure the social costs of monopoly
- Know how the monopolist can use price discrimination and other pricing practices to increase profits

I n this chapter, we bring together the theory of consumer behavior and demand (from Part Two) and the theory of production and costs (from Chapters 7 and 8) to analyze how price and output are determined under pure monopoly. Monopoly is the opposite extreme from perfect competition in the spectrum or range of market structure or organization. The monopoly model is useful for analyzing cases that approximate monopoly, and it provides insights into the operation of other imperfectly competitive markets (i.e., monopolistic competition and oligopoly).

The chapter begins by defining pure monopoly, describing the sources of monopoly, and explaining why the monopolist faces the market demand curve for the commodity. It then examines the determination of price and output in the short run and in the long run, and it compares the long-run equilibrium of the monopolist with that of a perfectly competitive firm and industry. Subsequently, we extend the monopoly model to examine how a monopolist (1) should allocate production among various plants to minimize production costs, and (2) can increase total profits by charging different prices for different quantities and in different markets at home and abroad. Finally, we discuss some other pricing practices that monopolists often use to increase their profits and present several important applications of the pure monopoly model. As in previous chapters, these applications, together with the real-world examples presented in the chapter, highlight the importance and relevance of the analytical tools developed in the chapter. The *At the Frontier* section examines the operation of one of the most talked-about near monopolies in the American economy today—Microsoft Corporation's Windows operating system.

| 10.1 | PURE MONOPOLY—THE OPPOSITE EXTREME FROM PERFECT COMPETITION |

In this section, we first define pure monopoly and discuss the sources of monopoly power. We then examine the shape of the demand and marginal revenue curves facing the monopolist and compare them with those of a perfectly competitive firm.

Definition and Sources of Monopoly

Pure monopoly The form of market organization in which there is a single seller of a commodity for which there are no close substitutes.

Pure monopoly is the form of market organization in which a *single firm* sells a commodity for which there are *no close substitutes*. Thus, the monopolist represents the industry and faces the industry's negatively sloped demand curve for the commodity. As opposed to a perfectly competitive firm, a monopolist can earn profits in the long run because *entry into the industry is blocked* or very difficult. Monopoly is at the opposite extreme from perfect competition in the spectrum or range of market organizations. Whereas the perfect competitor is a price taker and has no control over the price of the commodity it sells, the monopolist has complete control over price. The monopolist's ability to control or affect price is evidence of its monopoly power.

Monopoly can arise from several causes. First, a firm may own or control the entire supply of a raw material required in the production of a commodity, or the firm may possess some unique managerial talent. For example, until World War II, the Aluminum Company of America (Alcoa) controlled practically the entire supply of bauxite (the basic raw material necessary for the production of aluminum), giving it almost a complete monopoly in the production of aluminum in the United States (see Example 10–1).

Second, a firm may own a patent for the exclusive right to produce a commodity or to use a particular production process. Patents are granted by the government for 17 years as an incentive to inventors.[1] Some argue that if an invention could be copied freely (thus leaving little, if any, reward for the inventor), the flow of inventions and technical progress would be greatly reduced. Examples of monopolies that were originally based on patents are the Xerox Corporation for copying machines and Polaroid for instant cameras. An alternative to patents might be for the government to financially reward the inventor directly and allow inventions to be freely used. However, it is often difficult to determine the value of an invention: government archives are full of patents that found no commercial use.

---

[1] As opposed to copyrights, patents are not renewable. Improvement patents are available, however.

EXAMPLE 10–1

Barriers to Entry and Monopoly by Alcoa

The Aluminum Company of America (Alcoa) is a classic example of how a monopoly was created and maintained for almost 50 years. The monopoly was created in the late nineteenth century when Alcoa acquired a patent on the method to remove oxygen from bauxite to obtain aluminum. This patent expired in 1906, but in 1903, Alcoa had patented another more efficient method to produce aluminum. This patent expired in 1909. By that time, Alcoa had signed long-term contracts with producers of bauxite prohibiting them from selling bauxite to any other American firm. At the same time, Alcoa entered into agreements with foreign producers of aluminum not to export aluminum into each other's market. Alcoa even went as far as purchasing electricity only from those power companies that agreed not to sell energy for the production of aluminum to any other firm.

In 1912, the courts invalidated all of these contracts and agreements. Nevertheless, Alcoa retained monopoly power by always expanding productive capacity in anticipation of any increase in demand and by pricing aluminum in such a way as to discourage new entrants. The monopoly was finally broken after World War II, when Alcoa was not allowed to purchase government-financed aluminum plants built during the war. This is how Reynolds and Kaiser aluminum came into existence. During the 1960s, Reynolds diversified into plastics, gold, and consumer products, while Alcoa stuck to pure aluminum. But in May 2000, Alcoa acquired Reynolds Metals Company, thus remaining the world's largest producer of aluminum. In 2007, Alcoa had revenues of $30 billion, 123,000 employees, operations in 44 countries, and nearly 16% of the world aluminum market, but the merger of Rio Tinto of Britain and Alcan of Canada created the largest aluminum company in the world, and Russia's Rusal became second, leaving Alcoa third.

During the early 1990s, the world price of aluminum declined by almost 50% because of oversupply resulting in part from the sharp increase in aluminum exports by Russia, as internal demand by its military–industrial complex vanished after the collapse of communism. In response to this price collapse, the representatives of 17 nations, including Russia, the European Union countries, the United States, and other major aluminum exporters, agreed in January 1994 to voluntarily cut production for two years, and this led to a partial recovery in aluminum prices. In agreeing to voluntarily cut production, the major exporting nations came very close to behaving like an international monopoly (cartel—cartels are examined in detail in Chapter 11). Despite the relatively high concentration in the aluminum market (e.g., Alcoa and Canadian-European APA, together, have a 27.4% share of the world market), prices rose and fell during the rest of the 1990s and early 2000s primarily because of demand and supply considerations. In 2002, China became the largest producer of primary aluminum, with nearly 60% of world output. Rapidly growing internal demand, however, absorbed all of its increase in supply and contributed to a world aluminum price increase.

Sources: R. Lanzilotti, "The Aluminum Industry," in W. Adams (ed.), *The Structure of American Industry* (New York: Macmillan, 1961); "Reynolds Metals, Alcoa Split on Strategy," *Wall Street Journal,* November 7, 1990, p. A4; "Aluminum Pact Set to Curb World Output," *Wall Street Journal,* January 31, 1994; "Global Merger Could Steady Aluminum Market," *Wall Street Journal,* August 11, 1999, p. A13; "Alcoa's Outlook Is Bright Due to Cost Cuts, Shortages," *Wall Street Journal,* January 1, 2000, p. B4; and "The China Factor: Aluminum Industry Impact," *Journal of Minerals,* September 2004, pp. 1–6; and "Takeovers Recast Fast-Changing Sector," Special Report on Aluminum, *Financial Times,* October 9, 2007, p. 1.

Natural monopoly
The case of declining long-run average costs over a sufficiently large range of outputs so as to leave a single firm supplying the entire market.

✔️ Concept Check
What gives rise to (i.e., what are the sources of) monopoly?

Third, economies of scale may operate (i.e., the long-run average cost curve may fall) over a sufficiently large range of outputs so as to leave a single firm supplying the entire market. Such a firm is called a **natural monopoly.** Examples of natural monopolies are electrical, water, gas, and transportation companies. To have more than one firm supplying electricity, water, gas, and transportation services in a given market would lead to overlapping distribution systems and much higher per-unit costs.

Fourth, some monopolies are created by government franchise itself. For example, licenses are often required by local governments to start a radio or television station, to open a liquor store, to operate a taxi, to be a plumber, a barber, a funeral director, and so on. The purpose of these licenses is to ensure minimum standards of competency. Nevertheless, because the number of licenses issued (e.g., the number of taxi medallions issued in most metropolitan areas) is often restricted by the regulatory agency, licenses also protect present license holders from *new* competition (i.e., confer monopoly power to them as a group). In most cases, local governments turn the regulatory function (such as the issuance of licenses) over to the professional association involved. Examples include the medical and bar associations.

Aside from the few cases just mentioned and for public utilities, pure monopoly is rare in the United States today, and attempts to monopolize the market are forbidden by antitrust laws.[2] Nevertheless, the pure monopoly model is useful for analyzing situations that approach pure monopoly and for other types of imperfectly competitive markets (i.e., monopolistic competition and oligopoly).

A monopolist does not have unlimited market power, however, but faces many forms of direct and indirect competition. On a general level, a monopolist competes for the consumers' dollars with the sellers of all other commodities in the market. Furthermore, while *close* substitutes do not exist for the particular commodity supplied by the monopolist, imperfect substitutes are likely to exist. For example, although DuPont was the only producer of cellophane in the late 1940s, the company faced a great deal of competition from the producers of all other flexible packaging materials (waxed paper, aluminum foil, and so on). In addition, the market power of the monopolist (or the would-be monopolist) is sharply curtailed by fear of government antitrust prosecution, by the threat of potential competitors, and by international competition.

The Monopolist Faces the Market Demand Curve for the Commodity[3]

Because a monopolist is the sole seller of a commodity for which there are no close substitutes, the monopolist faces the negatively sloped industry demand curve for the commodity. In other words, while the perfectly competitive firm is a price taker and faces a demand curve that is horizontal or infinitely elastic at the price determined by the intersection of the industry or market demand and supply curves for the commodity, the monopolist *is* the industry and, thus, it faces the negatively sloped industry demand curve for the commodity. This means that to sell more units of the commodity, the monopolist must lower the commodity price. As a result, marginal revenue (defined as the change in total revenue per-unit change in the quantity sold) is smaller than price, and the monopolist's marginal revenue curve lies below its demand curve (see Section 5.6).[4] This is shown in Table 10.1 and Figure 10.1.

---

[2] It should be noted that "monopoly" per se is not illegal; only "monopolizing" or "attempting to monopolize the market" are illegal under U.S. antitrust laws (Section 2, Sherman Antitrust Act, 1890).

[3] For the relationship between demand and marginal revenue for a monopolist in terms of calculus, see Section A.7 of the Mathematical Appendix at the end of the book.

[4] At this point, a review of the material in Section 5.6 may be helpful.

TABLE 10.1	Hypothetical Demand, Total Revenue, and Marginal Revenue Faced by a Monopolist		
P	Q	TR	MR
$9	0	$0	. . .
8	1	8	$8
7	2	14	6
6	3	18	4
5	4	20	2
4	5	20	0
3	6	18	−2
2	7	14	−4
1	8	8	−6
0	9	0	−8

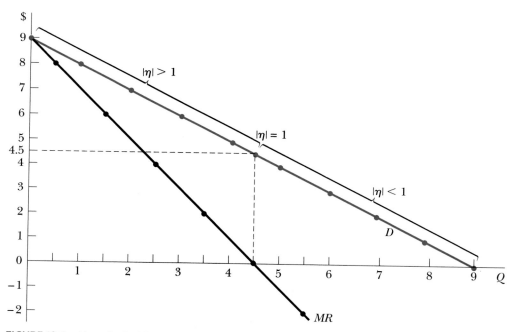

FIGURE 10.1   Hypothetical Demand and Marginal Revenue Curves of a Monopolist   Since D is negatively sloped, MR is lower than P. The MR values are plotted at the midpoint of each quantity interval. The MR curve starts at the same point as the D curve and at every point bisects the distance between D and the vertical axis. MR is positive when D is elastic. $MR = 0$ when D is unitary elastic and TR is at a maximum. MR is negative when D is inelastic.

The first two columns of Table 10.1 give a hypothetical market demand schedule for the commodity faced by a monopolist. In order to sell more of the commodity, the monopolist must lower the commodity price. Price times quantity gives total revenue (the third column of the table). The change in total revenue per-unit change in the quantity of the commodity sold gives the marginal revenue (the fourth column). For example, at $P = \$8$, the monopolist sells one unit of the commodity, so $TR = \$8$. To sell two units of the commodity, the monopolist must lower the price to $7 on both units of the commodity. TR is then $14. The change in TR resulting from selling the additional unit of the commodity is then $MR = \$14 - \$8 = \$6$. This equals the price of $7 for the second unit of the commodity sold minus the $1 reduction in price (from $8 to $7) on the first unit (since to sell two units of the commodity, the monopolist must lower the price of the commodity to $7 for both units).

The information contained in Table 10.1 is plotted in Figure 10.1. Since MR is defined as the change in TR per-unit change in Q, the MR revenue values are plotted at the midpoint of each quantity interval. Note that the MR curve starts at the same point on the vertical axis as the demand curve and at every point bisects (i.e., cuts in half) the distance between D and the vertical or price axis.[5] The MR is positive when D is elastic (i.e., in the top segment of the demand curve) because an increase in Q increases TR. $MR = 0$ when D is unitary elastic (i.e., at the geometric midpoint of D) because an increase in Q leaves TR unchanged (at its maximum level). MR is negative when D is inelastic (i.e., the bottom segment of D) because an increase in Q reduces TR (see Figure 10.1 and Section 5.6).

Contrast this situation with the case of a perfectly competitive firm (examined in Chapter 9), which faced a horizontal or infinitely elastic demand curve for the commodity at the price determined at the intersection of the market demand and supply curves for the commodity. Since the perfect competitor is a price taker and can sell any quantity of the commodity at the given price, price equals marginal revenue, and the demand and marginal revenue curves are horizontal and coincide.

The relationship between price, marginal revenue, and elasticity (η) can be examined with formula [5.8] introduced in Section 5.6:

$$MR = P(1 + 1/\eta) \qquad [5.8]$$

Using the formula, we see that since $\eta = -\infty$ for the perfect competitor, MR always equals P. That is, $MR = P(1 + 1/\infty) = P(1 + 0) = P$. Since $|\eta| < \infty$ (i.e., since the demand curve is not infinitely elastic) for the monopolist, $MR < P$. That is, for any value of $|\eta|$ smaller than infinity, MR will be smaller than P, and the MR curve will be below the market demand curve. Furthermore, we can see from the formula that when $\eta = -1$, $MR = 0$; when $|\eta| > 1$, $MR > 0$; and when $|\eta| < 1$, $MR < 0$. Since $MR < 0$ when $|\eta| < 1$, the monopolist can increase its TR by selling a *smaller* quantity of the commodity. Thus, the monopolist would never operate over the inelastic portion of the demand curve. By reducing output, the monopolist would increase total revenue, reduce total costs, and thus increase total profits. Example 10–2 examines how the De Beers Consolidated Mines diamond monopoly operated for over a century until 2001.

---

[5] This is true only when, as in this case, the demand curve that the monopolist faces is a negatively sloped straight line.

EXAMPLE 10–2

De Beers Abandons Its Diamond Monopoly

In 1887, Cecil Rhodes created the De Beers Consolidated Mines Company, which controlled about 90% of the total world supply of rough uncut diamonds with its South African mines. Until 2001, De Beers produced about half of the world's diamonds in its mines in South Africa, Botswana, and Namibia, and it marketed about 80% of the world's diamonds through its London-based Central Selling Organization (CSO). Producers in Russia, Australia, Botswana, Angola, and other diamond-producing nations sold most of their production to De Beers, which then regulated the supply of cut and polished diamonds to final consumers on the world market so as to keep prices high. When there was a recession in the world's major markets and demand for diamonds was low, De Beers withheld diamonds from the market (i.e., stockpiled them) in order to avoid price declines until demand and prices rose. In short, De Beers acted as a monopolist and earned huge profits for itself and other producers by manipulating the world supply of diamonds. De Beers also advertised diamonds to drum up demand with the famous slogan "diamonds are forever" from the 1971 James Bond movie by the same name. De Beers controls two-thirds of the world's $8 billion market of uncut rough stones, and worldwide retail sales of diamond jewelry by De Beers and other firms exceed $60 billion (half of which is in the United States).

De Beers has had a monopoly in the marketing of diamonds since 1887 through wars, financial crisis, racial strife, hostile governments, and attempts by independent producers to circumvent the monopoly. When the former Soviet Union and Zaire started to sell large quantities of industrial diamonds on the world market outside the CSO in the early 1980s, De Beers immediately flooded the market from its own stockpiles (in excess of $5 billion in 2001), thereby driving prices sharply down and thus convincing the newcomers to join the cartel. And when large quantities of diamonds smuggled from Angola flooded Antwerp in 1992, De Beers purchased up to $400 to $500 million worth of these diamonds to prevent a collapse in prices. But faced with increased production by Russia (which sold only half of its diamonds through CSO) and new suppliers from Australia and Canada, and embarrassed by disclosures that to prop up prices it had bought "blood or conflict diamonds" from rebels in Angola, De Beers abandoned its cartel arrangement in 2001 and began concentrating instead on an advertising-driven strategy through its marketing arm, the Diamond Trading Company (DTC), to increase sales of its diamonds as branded luxuries. In 2001 De Beers also reorganized itself into a private company, with two independent units, one that continued to sell uncut stones and the other (De Beers LV) a retail joint venture with LVMH Moët Hennessy Louis Vuitton.

Sources: "How De Beers Dominates the Diamonds," *The Economist,* February 23, 1980, pp. 101–102; "Can De Beers Hold to Its Own Hammerlock?" *Business Week,* September 21, 1992, pp. 45–46; "Disputes Are Forever," *The Economist,* September 17, 1994, p. 73; "The Rough Trade in Rough Stones," *Forbes,* March 27, 1995, pp. 47–48; "De Beers Halts Its Hoarding of Diamonds," *New York Times,* July 13, 2000, p. C1; "$17.6 Billion Deal to Make De Beers Private Company," *Financial Times,* February 16, 2001, p. W1; "Bumpy Start for De Beers' Retail Diamond Venture," *New York Times*, November 11, 2002, p. W1; and "De Beers Sees More Jewelry Demand," *Financial Times,* April 12, 2005, p. 26.

10.2

SHORT-RUN EQUILIBRIUM PRICE AND OUTPUT

In this section, we examine the determination of price and output by a monopolist in the short run. We will do this first with the total approach and then with the marginal approach. We will also show that a monopolist, like a perfect competitor, can incur losses in the short run. Finally, we demonstrate that, unlike the case of the perfectly competitive firm, the monopolist's short-run supply curve cannot be derived from its short-run marginal cost curve.

Total Approach: Maximizing the Positive Difference Between Total Revenue and Total Costs

As with the perfectly competitive firm, profit maximization provides the framework for the analysis of monopoly. The equilibrium price and output of a monopolist are the ones that maximize total profits. Total profits equal total revenue minus total costs. Total revenue is given by price times quantity. The total costs of the monopolist are similar to those discussed in Chapter 8 and need not differ from those of the perfectly competitive firm (if the monopolist does not affect input prices). Thus, except for the case of natural monopoly, the basic difference between monopoly and perfect competition lies on the demand side rather than on the production or cost side.

Table 10.2 gives the total revenue (TR), the short-run total costs (STC), and the total profits of a monopolist in the short run at various levels of output. The total revenue schedule is that of Table 10.1. As usual, short-run total costs rise slowly at first and then more rapidly (when the law of diminishing returns begins to operate). The best or optimum level of output for the monopolist in the short run is where total profits are maximized. For the monopolist of Table 10.2, this is at three units of output per time period. At this level of output, the monopolist charges the price of $6 and earns the maximum total profit of $4.50 per time period.

The data of Table 10.2 are plotted in Figure 10.2. The top panel shows that, unlike the case of a perfectly competitive firm, the monopolist's TR curve is not a straight line, but has the shape of an inverted U. The reason is that the monopolist must lower the price to sell additional units of the commodity. The monopolist's STC faces upward or increases at an increasing rate past $Q = 2$ because of diminishing returns.

TABLE 10.2 Total Revenue, Short-Run Total Costs, and Total Profits

Q	P	TR	STC	Total Profits
0	$9	$0	$6	$ −6
1	8	8	10	−2
2	7	14	12	2
*3	6	18	13.50	4.50
4	5	20	19	1
5	4	20	30	−10
6	3	18	48	−30

*Output at which firm maximizes total profit.

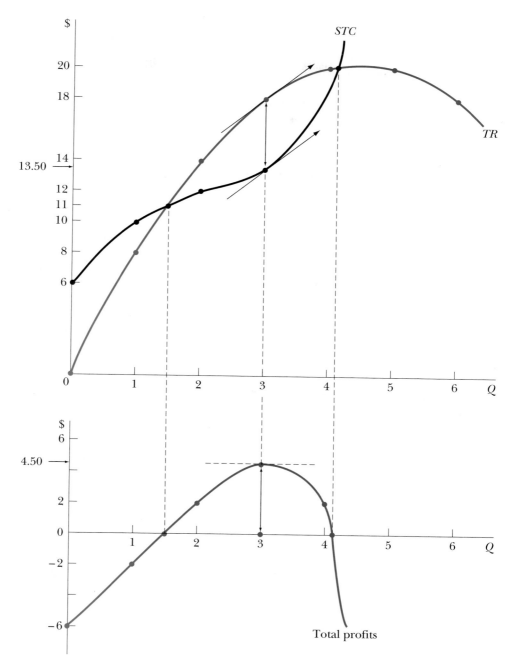

FIGURE 10.2 Short-Run Equilibrium of the Monopolist: Total Approach The monopolist's *TR* curve has the shape of an inverted U because the monopolist must lower the commodity price to sell additional units. The *STC* has the usual shape. Total profits are maximized at $Q = 3$, where the positive difference between *TR* and *STC* is greatest ($4.50). This is the point where the *TR* and the *STC* curves are parallel (see the top panel) and the total profit curve is highest (see the bottom panel). Total profits are positive between $Q = 1.5$ and $Q = 4.1$ and negative at other output levels. At $Q = 0$, total loss is $6 and equals total fixed costs.

Total profits are maximized at $Q = 3$, where the positive difference between the TR and the STC curves is greatest ($4.50). This is the point where the TR and the STC curves are parallel (see the top panel) and the total profits curve reaches its highest point (see the bottom panel). Total profits are positive between $Q = 1.5$ and $Q = 4.1$ and negative at other output levels. At $Q = 0$, $TR = 0$, while $STC = \$6$. Thus, by shutting down, the monopolist would incur the total loss of $6, which equals its total fixed costs. Note that the monopolist maximizes total profits at an output level smaller than the one at which TR is maximum (i.e., at $Q = 3$ rather than at $Q = 4.1$—see Figure 10.2).

Marginal Approach: Equating Marginal Revenue and Marginal Cost[6]

Although the total approach to determine the equilibrium price and output of the monopolist is useful, the marginal approach is even more valuable and widely used. According to the marginal approach, a monopolist maximizes total profits by producing the level of output at which *marginal revenue equals marginal cost*. The difference between the commodity price and the monopolist's average total cost at the best or optimum level of output gives the profit per unit. Profit per unit times output gives total profits. Thus, to be able to use the marginal approach and to determine the level of total profits, we must calculate the marginal cost and the average total cost of the monopolist.[7]

From the monopolist's short-run total cost schedule given in Table 10.2, we can derive the marginal cost and the average total cost schedules given in Table 10.3. Marginal cost equals the change in short-run total costs per-unit change in output. That is, $MC = \Delta STC/\Delta Q$. For example, at $Q = 1$, $STC = \$10$, while at $Q = 2$, $STC = \$12$. Therefore, $MC = (\$12 - \$10)/1 = \$2$. The other MC values in Table 10.3 are similarly obtained. On the other hand, average total costs equal short-run total costs divided by the level of output. That is, $ATC = STC/Q$. For example, at $Q = 1$, $STC = \$10$, and so $ATC = \$10/1 = \$10$. At $Q = 2$, $STC = \$12$, and so $ATC = \$12/2 = \$6$.

TABLE 10.3	Short-Run Total Cost, Marginal Cost, and Average Total Cost		
Q	STC	MC	ATC
0	$6	. . .	. . .
1	10	$4	$10
2	12	2	6
3	13.50	1.50	4.50
4	19	5.50	4.75
5	30	11	6
6	48	18	8

[6] For a mathematical presentation of profit maximization using rudimentary calculus, see Section A.10 of the Mathematical Appendix at the end of the book.
[7] Since we already know the monopolist's MR (see Figure 10.1), all we need to calculate now is the monopolist's marginal cost to determine the best or profit-maximizing level of output. This is given at the point where $MR = MC$. The average total cost is only required to measure the monopolist's profit at the best level of output.

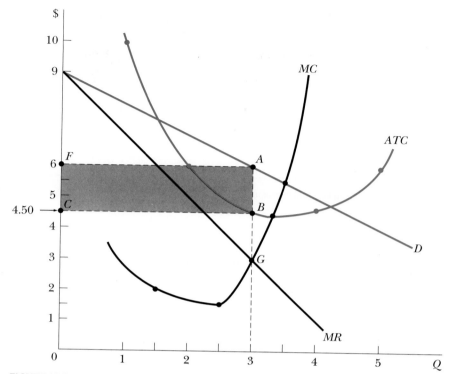

FIGURE 10.3   Short-Run Equilibrium of the Monopolist: Marginal Approach   The best or optimum level of output of the monopolist is three units. This is given by point *G*, where *MR* = *MC* (and the *MC* curve intersects the *MR* curve from below). At *Q* = 3, *P* = $6 (point *A* on the demand curve), *ATC* = $4.50 (point *B* on the *ATC* curve), and the monopolist earns $1.50 (*AB*) per unit of output sold and $4.50 in total (shaded area *ABCF*). At *Q* < 3, *MR* > *MC* and total profits rise by increasing *Q*. At *Q* > 3, *MC* > *MR* and total profits rise by reducing *Q*.

By plotting the monopolist's *D* and *MR* schedules of Table 10.1 and the *MC* and *ATC* schedules of Table 10.3 on the same set of axes, we get Figure 10.3. Note that *MR* and *MC* are plotted *between* the various levels of output, while *D* and *ATC* are plotted *at* the various output levels. In Figure 10.3, the best or optimum level of output of the monopolist is three units. This is given by point *G*, where *MR* = *MC*. At *Q* = 3, *P* = $6 (point *A* on the demand curve), while *ATC* = $4.50 (point *B* on the *ATC* curve). Thus, the monopolist earns $1.50 (*AB*) per unit of output sold and $4.50 in total (shaded area *ABCF* in the figure). Note that at point *G*, the *MC* curve cuts the *MR* curve from below. This is always true for profit maximization, whether the *MC* curve is rising or falling at the point of intersection (see Section 10.8).

At outputs smaller than three units, *MR* exceeds *MC* (see the figure). Therefore, by expanding output, the monopolist would be adding more to *TR* than to *STC*, and total profits would rise. On the other hand, at outputs larger than three units, *MC* exceeds *MR*. A *reduction* in output would reduce *STC* more than *TR* and total profits would also rise. Thus, the monopolist must produce where *MR* = *MC* (in this case three units of output) to maximize total profits. This is the same result obtained earlier by the total approach.

✓ Concept Check
How does a monopolist determine the price and best level of output in the short run?

TABLE 10.4	Profit Maximization for the Monopolist: Marginal Approach						
Q	P	ATC	Profit Per Unit	Total Profits	MR	MC	Relationship of MR to MC
1	$8	$10	$−2	$−2	$7	$3	
2	7	6	1	2	5	1.50	MR > MC
*3	6	4.50	1.50	4.50	3	3	MR = MC
4	5	4.75	0.25	1	1	8	
5	4	6	−2	−10	−1	15	MR < MC

*Output at which firm maximizes total profits.

Table 10.4 summarizes the marginal approach numerically. Note that the *MR* and the *MC* values given in the table are read off Figure 10.3 *at* various output levels, just as *P* and *ATC*. For example, at $Q = 3$, $P = \$6$, $ATC = \$4.50$, and $MR = MC = \$3$. Table 10.4 shows that the monopolist maximizes total profits (equal to \$4.50) at $Q = 3$, where $MR = MC = \$3$ (as shown in Figure 10.3).

Profit Maximization or Loss Minimization?

Like the perfect competitor, the monopolist can earn a profit, break even, or incur a loss in the short run. The monopolist will continue to produce in the short run (minimizing losses) as long as price exceeds the average variable cost at the best or optimum level of output. Were the monopolist to shut down, it would incur the higher loss equal to its total fixed costs (*TFC*).

To show this, assume that, for whatever reason, the monopolist's demand curve shifts down from its level in Figure 10.3 while its cost curves remain unchanged, so that $ATC > P$ at the best level of output. The monopolist will now incur losses at the best level of output. To determine whether the monopolist will minimize losses by continuing to produce, we now need to calculate the monopolist's average variable costs. Average variable costs (*AVC*) equal total variable costs (*TVC*) divided by output (*Q*). We can obtain the monopolist's total variable costs by subtracting its total *fixed* costs from its short-run *total* costs. That is, $TVC = STC − TFC$.

The monopolist's *TVC* and *AVC* are calculated in Table 10.5 from the *STC* of Tables 10.2 and 10.3. Specifically, since $STC = \$6$ at $Q = 0$ in Table 10.5, $TFC = \$6$. The *TVC* schedule is then obtained by subtracting *TFC* from *STC* at various output levels, and *AVC* is calculated by TVC/Q. For example, at $Q = 1$, $TVC = STC − TFC = \$10 − \$6 = \$4$ and $AVC = TVC/Q = \$4/1 = \$4$. At $Q = 2$, $TVC = \$12 − \$6 = \$6$ and $AVC = \$6/2 = \$3$. The other *TVC* and *AVC* values in Table 10.5 are calculated in a similar way.

In Figure 10.4, the *MC* and the *ATC* curves are those of Figure 10.3, and the *AVC* curve is obtained by plotting the *AVC* schedule given in Table 10.5. These per-unit *cost* curves are unchanged from Figure 10.3. The monopolist, however, now faces lower demand curve D' with marginal revenue curve MR'. The best or optimum level of output of the monopolist is now 2.5 units. This is given by point G', where $MR' = MC$ (the *MC* curve intersects the MR' curve from below in Figure 10.4). At $Q = 2.5$, $P = \$4$ (point A' on demand curve D') and

TABLE 10.5	Short-Run Total Cost, Total Fixed Costs, Total Variable Costs, and Average Variable Costs			
Q	STC	TFC	TVC	AVC
0	$6	$6	$0	. . .
1	10	6	4	$4
2	12	6	6	3
3	13.50	6	7.50	2.50
4	19	6	13	3.25

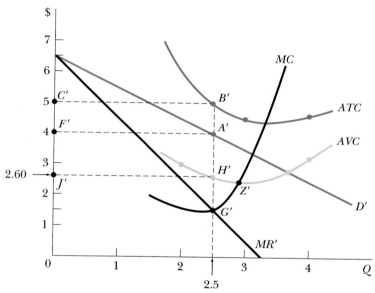

FIGURE 10.4   Profit Maximization vs. Loss Minimization   With D', the best or optimum level of output of the monopolist is $Q = 2.5$ (given by point G', where $MR' = MC$ and the MC curve intersects the MR' curve from below). At $Q = 2.5$, $ATC > P$, and the firm incurs a loss of $1 ($B'A'$) per unit and $2.50 in total (the area of rectangle $B'A'F'C'$). If, however, the firm were to shut down, it would incur the greater loss of $6 equal to its total fixed costs (the area of rectangle $B'H'J'C'$). The shutdown point (Z') is at $P = AVC$.

$ATC = \$5$ (point B' on the ATC curve). Thus, the monopolist incurs a loss of $1 ($B'A'$) per unit of output sold and $2.50 in total (the area of rectangle $B'A'F'C'$).

At $Q = 2.5$, $AVC = \$2.60$ (point H' on the AVC curve). Since price ($4) exceeds average variable costs ($2.60) at the best level of output (2.5 units), the monopolist covers $1.40 ($A'H'$) of its fixed costs per unit and $3.50 (the area of rectangle $A'H'J'F'$) of its total fixed costs. If the monopolist were to shut down, it would incur the greater loss of $6 (its total fixed costs, given by the area of rectangle $B'H'J'C'$). Only if P were smaller than AVC at the best level of output would the monopolist minimize total losses by shutting down (and incurring a loss equal only to its total fixed costs). At $P = AVC$, the monopolist would be indifferent between producing or shutting down because in either case it

Concept Check
How can a monopolist make a loss in the short run?

would incur a loss equal to its total fixed costs. Thus, the point where $P = AVC$ (point Z' in the figure) is the monopolist's shutdown point.

Short-Run Marginal Cost and Supply

While the rising portion of the marginal cost curve over the average variable cost curve (the shutdown point) is a perfect competitor's short-run supply curve (when input prices are constant), this is not the case for the monopolist. The reason is that the monopolist could supply the same quantity of a commodity at different prices depending on the price elasticity of demand. Thus, for the monopolist there is no unique relationship between price and quantity supplied, or no supply curve.

This is shown in Figure 10.5, where D is the original demand curve and D'' is an *alternative* and less elastic demand curve facing the monopolist. In the figure, MR is the marginal revenue curve for demand curve D, while MR'' is the marginal revenue curve for demand curve D''. Since the MC curve intersects the MR and MR'' curves from below

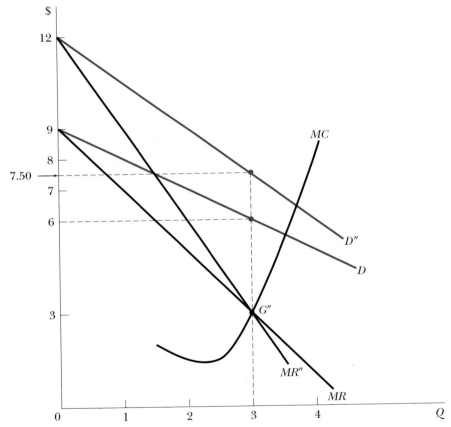

FIGURE 10.5   Short-Run Marginal Cost and Supply D is the original demand curve, and D'' is an alternative and less elastic demand curve facing the monopolist. Since the MC curve intersects the MR and MR'' curves from below at point G'', the best level of output is three units, whether the monopolist faces D or D''. However, with D the monopolist charges $P = \$6$, whereas with D'' it would charge $P = \$7.50$. Thus, under monopoly there is no unique relationship between price and output (i.e., the supply curve is undefined).

at the same point (point G''), the best level of output is three units whether the monopolist faces D or D''. However, with D, the monopolist would sell the three units of output at $P = \$6$ (as in Figure 10.3), whereas with D'', the monopolist would sell the three units of output at $P = \$7.50$ (see Figure 10.5). Thus, the same quantity (i.e., $Q = 3$) can be supplied at two different prices (i.e., at $P = \$6$ or $P = \$7.50$) depending on the price elasticity of demand (i.e., depending on whether the monopolist faced demand curve D or D''). Therefore, under monopoly, costs are related to the quantity supplied of the commodity, but there is no unique relationship between price and output (i.e., we cannot derive the monopolist's supply curve from its MC curve). Note that the monopolist would charge a higher price if it faced the less elastic demand curve (i.e., D'').

✓ Concept Check

Why is it that we cannot derive the short-run supply curve of a monopolist?

<table>
<tr><td>**10.3**</td><td>## Long-Run Equilibrium Price and Output</td></tr>
</table>

In this section, we analyze the behavior of the monopolist in the long run and compare it with the behavior of a perfectly competitive firm and industry. We also measure the welfare costs of monopoly.

Profit Maximization in the Long Run

In the long run, all inputs are variable and the monopolist can build the most efficient plant to produce the best level of output. The best or profit-maximizing level of output is given by the point where the monopolist's *long-run* marginal cost curve intersects the marginal revenue curve from below. The most efficient plant is the one that allows the monopolist to produce the best level of output at the lowest possible cost. This is the plant represented by the $SATC$ curve tangent to the LAC curve at the best level of output. As before, we assume that the monopolist does not affect input prices.

Figure 10.6 shows that the monopolist maximizes profits in the long run by producing $Q = 4$; this is given by point M, where the LMC curve intersects the MR curve from below. The monopolist should build plant $SATC_2$ and operate it at point N with $SATC = \$3.50$. Plant $SATC_2$ is the most efficient plant (i.e., the one that allows the monopolist to produce $Q = 4$ at the lowest $SATC$). In the long run, the monopolist will charge $P = \$5$ (point R), and earn a profit of $\$1.50$ (RN) per unit and $\$6$ in total (as opposed to $\$4.50$ in the short run with $SATC_1$—the same as Figure 10.3).

Even though profits will attract additional firms into the perfectly competitive industry until all firms just break even in the long run, the monopolist can continue to earn profits in the long run because of blocked entry. However, the value of these long-run profits will be capitalized into the market value of the firm. Thus, it is the original owner of the monopoly that directly benefits from the monopoly power. A purchaser of the firm would have to pay a price that reflected the present (discounted) value of the monopoly profits, and so would only break even in the long run. That is, monopoly profits become part of the opportunity costs of the original monopolist (see Example 10–3).

Note also that the monopolist, as opposed to a perfectly competitive firm, does not produce at the lowest point on its LAC curve (see Figure 10.6). Only if the monopolist's MR curve happened to go through the lowest point on its LAC would this be the case (see Problem 7 at the end of the chapter). Furthermore, a monopolist may earn long-run profits. Thus, as compared with a perfectly competitive firm when the industry is in long-run equilibrium (see Section 9.5), monopoly is inefficient because the monopolist is not likely to produce at the lowest point on its LAC curve and consumers are likely to pay a

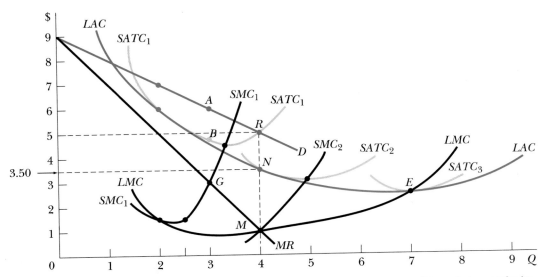

FIGURE 10.6   Long-Run Equilibrium of the Monopolist   In the long run, the monopolist maximizes profits by producing at point $M(Q = 4)$, where the LMC curve intersects the MR curve from below. The monopolist should build plant $SATC_2$, and operate it at point N at $SATC = \$3.50$. The monopolist will earn a profit of $\$1.50$ (RN) per unit and $\$6$ in total (as opposed to $\$4.50$ in the short run).

✓ Concept Check

Why will the monopolist not usually produce at the lowest point on its LAC curve?

price that also usually includes a profit margin. In short, $P > LAC$ implies economic profits, and so there is distributional inefficiency; $LAC \neq LMC$ implies that LAC is not at a minimum, and so there is production inefficiency; and $P > LMC$ means that there is allocative inefficiency in the sense that the quantity of the commodity supplied does not represent the best use of the economy's resources. These social costs of monopoly are measured in the next subsection for a perfectly competitive industry that faces constant returns to scale and is subsequently monopolized.

EXAMPLE 10–3

Monopoly Profits in the New York City Taxi Industry

New York City, as most other municipalities (cities) in the United States, requires a license (medallion) to operate a taxi. Since medallions are limited in number, this confers a monopoly power (i.e., the ability to earn economic profits) to owners of medallions. The value of owning a medallion is equal to the present discounted value of the expected future stream of earnings from the ownership of a medallion—a process called *capitalization*. For example, the number of medallions in New York City remained at 11,787 from 1937 until 1996, when it was increased by 400 to 12,187; it increased to 13,087 by 2007, and the value of a medallion rose from $10 in 1937 to the incredible sum of $600,000 in May 2007 (up from $195,000 in 2001), or by about 18% per year. The price of a medallion is lower (and sometimes much lower) in other cities, reflecting the lower earning power of a medallion in other cities. In 2007, it was estimated to be about \$365,000 in Boston and \$77,000 in Chicago, where taxis are less scarce.

Proposals to increase the number of medallions in New York City have been successfully blocked by a powerful taxi industry lobby. Note that only the original owner benefits from the monopoly rights. A buyer of the rights would now have to pay a price that would fully reflect the future stream of earnings from the monopoly power, and so the buyer would only break even in the long run. The only way to prevent further windfall gains to present owners of the monopoly rights (medallions) is for the government to issue additional medallions. Were the city to freely grant a license to operate a taxi for the asking, the price of the medallion would drop to zero. While not doing that, New York City has allowed a sharp growth during the 1980s in the number of radio cabs, which can only respond to radio calls and cannot cruise the streets for passengers. This has sharply increased competition in the New York City taxi industry and reduced profits to taxi owners from 32% in 1993 to 11% in 2001.

Sources: "Owners Bewail Flood of Cabs in New York," *New York Times,* April 10, 1989, p. B1; "Panel Clears Plan to Enlarge Taxicab Fleet," *New York Times,* January 27, 1996, p. B1; "Medallion Financial Sees Growth in Taxi Tops," *Wall Street Journal,* July 19, 1999, p. B7A; "Yellow Taxis Battle to Keep Livery Cabs off Their Turf," *New York Times*, May 10, 2001, p. 1; "Taken for a Ride?" *The Economist* (April 24, 2004), p. 30; and "Taxi Medallions Fetch a Record \$600,000 Each," http://www.nysun.com/article/55479.

Comparison with Perfect Competition: The Social Cost of Monopoly

To measure the long-run social cost of monopoly, we assume that a perfectly competitive industry operating under constant returns to scale is suddenly monopolized and the market demand and cost curves remain unchanged. We will see that in that case output will be smaller and prices will be higher than under perfect competition. In addition, there will be a redistribution of income from consumers to the monopolist and a welfare loss due to less efficient resource use. These results are shown in Figure 10.7.

In Figure 10.7, D is the perfectly competitive industry market demand curve, and LS is the perfectly competitive industry long-run supply curve under constant costs. The long-run perfectly competitive equilibrium is at point E, where D intersects LS. At point E, $Q = 6$ and $P = \$3$. Consumers collectively would be willing to pay $LEI0$ (\$36) for six units of the commodity, but need only pay $EI0C$ (\$18). Thus, the consumers' surplus is LEC or \$18 (see Section 9.8).

When the perfectly competitive industry is monopolized, the LS curve becomes the monopolist's LAC and LMC curves (the monopolist would simply operate the plants of the previously perfectly competitive firms).[8] The best level of output for the monopolist in the long run is then given by point M, where $MR = LMC$. Thus, with monopoly, $Q = 3$,

---

[8] Specifically, a perfectly competitive, constant-cost industry in long-run equilibrium has a horizontal LS curve at the minimum LAC of the individual firms (see Figure 9.11). A monopolist taking over the industry could change output by changing the number of plants previously operated by the independent firms at minimum LAC (where $LAC = LMC$). Thus, the horizontal LS supply curve of the competitive industry is the LAC and LMC curves of the monopolized industry. These curves show the constant LAC and LMC at which the monopolist can change output.

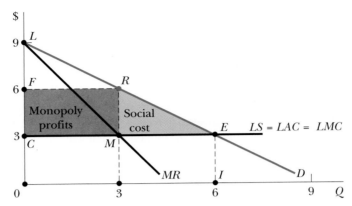

FIGURE 10.7   The Social Cost of Monopoly   With perfect competition, *D* is the market demand curve, and *LS* is the supply curve under constant costs. Equilibrium is at point *E*, where *D* intersects *LS*, and *Q* = 6 and *P* = \$3. When the perfectly competitive industry is monopolized, the *LS* curve becomes the monopolist's *LAC* and *LMC* curve. Equilibrium is at point *M*, where *MR* = *LMC*. At point *M*, *Q* = 3, *P* = \$6, total profits are *RMCF*, and *REM* is the social cost or deadweight loss to society due to the less efficient resource use under monopoly.

P = \$6 (which exceeds *LMC* = \$3), and the monopolist will earn total profits equal to *RMCF* (\$9). The consumers' surplus is now only *LRF* (\$4.50), down from *LEC* (\$18) under perfect competition. Of the *RECF* (\$13.50) reduction in the consumers' surplus, *RMCF* (\$9) represents a redistribution of income from consumers to the monopolist in the form of profits, and *REM* (\$4.50) is the social cost or deadweight loss to society due to the less efficient resource use under monopoly.

Specifically, monopoly profits are not a net loss to society as a whole, because they represent simply a redistribution of income from consumers of the commodity to the monopolist producer. This redistribution is "bad" only to the extent that society "values" the welfare of consumers more than that of the monopolist. As we will see later, all of the monopolist's profits could be taxed away and redistributed to consumers of the commodity. On the other hand, the area of welfare triangle *REM* represents a true welfare or deadweight loss to society as a whole, which is inherent to monopoly and which society cannot avoid under monopoly.

Welfare triangle *REM* arises because the monopolist artificially restricts the output of the commodity so that some resources flow into the production of other commodities that society values less. Specifically, consumers pay *P* = \$6 for the third unit of the commodity produced by the monopolist. This is a measure of the social value or marginal benefit of this unit of the commodity to consumers. The marginal cost (*MC*) to produce this unit of the commodity, however, is only \$3. This means that society forgoes one unit of the monopolized commodity valued at \$6 for a unit of another commodity valued at \$3. Thus, some of society's resources are used to produce less valuable commodities under monopoly. Since under perfect competition, production takes place at point *E*, where *P* = *LMC* (see Figure 10.7), welfare triangle *REM* represents the social cost or welfare (deadweight) loss from the less efficient use of society's resources under monopoly. Example 10–4 gives estimates of the social costs of monopoly in the United States.

✓ Concept Check
How are the social costs of monopoly measured?

EXAMPLE 10–4

Estimates of the Social Cost of Monopoly in the United States

In 1954, Harberger measured the area of the welfare triangle (*REM* in Figure 10.7) in each manufacturing industry in the United States on the assumption that the marginal cost was constant and that the price elasticity of the demand curve was 1. He found that the total social cost of monopoly was only about one-tenth of 1% of GNP. With some refinements of the estimating method, Scherer found that the social welfare loss from monopoly was between 0.5% and 2% of GNP, and most likely about 1%. The reason for these relatively low estimates is that there are few firms in the American economy with a great deal of monopoly power. In fact, Siegfried and Tiemann found that 44% of the total welfare loss due to monopoly power in the United States in 1963 came from the auto industry; the remainder of the loss was mostly due to a few other industries such as petroleum refining, plastics, and drugs.

There are, however, other losses resulting from monopoly power that are not included in the above estimates. One loss is that, in the absence of competition, monopolists do not keep their costs as low as possible, and they prefer the "quiet life" (*X*-inefficiency). For example, when U.S. steel firms started to face increased foreign competition during the 1970s and 1980s, they were able to sharply reduce costs. Another loss is that monopolists waste a lot of resources (from society's point of view) lobbying, engaging in legal battles, and advertising in the attempt to create and retain monopoly power, and to avoid regulation and prosecution under antitrust laws. These losses are sometimes referred to as the social costs of "rent seeking." In fact, some economists believe that these other social costs of monopoly are larger than those measured by the welfare triangle. The method of measurement and actual estimates of the size of these social costs are subject to a great deal of disagreement and controversy.

Sources: A. Harberger, "Monopoly and Resource Allocation," *American Economic Review,* May 1954; F. Scherer, *Industrial Market Structure and Economic Performance* (Chicago: Rand McNally, 1980), pp. 459–464; and J. Siegfried and T. Tiemann, "The Welfare Cost of Monopoly: An Interindustry Analysis," *Economic Inquiry,* June 1974. For the social costs of rent seeking, see W. Rogerson, "The Social Costs of Monopoly and Regulation: A Game-Theoretic Analysis," *Bell Journal of Economics* (now *The Rand Journal of Economics*), Autumn 1982; and F. Fisher, "The Social Costs of Monopoly and Regulation: Posner Reconsidered," *Journal of Political Economy,* April 1985; for more recent estimates of the social or welfare costs of food and tobacco oligopolies, see S. Bhuyan and R. A. Lopez, "What Determines Welfare Losses from Oligopoly Power in the Food and Tobacco Industries?," *Agricultural and Resource Economics Review,* October 1998.

10.4 | PROFIT MAXIMIZATION BY THE MULTIPLANT MONOPOLIST

So far, the discussion has been based on the implicit assumption that the monopolist operated a single plant. This is not always or even usually the case. In this section, we examine how a multiplant monopolist should distribute its best level of output among its various plants, both in the short run and in the long run, to minimize its costs of production and maximize profits.

Short-Run Equilibrium

A multiplant monopolist will minimize the total cost of producing the best level of output in the short run when the marginal cost of the last unit of the commodity produced in each

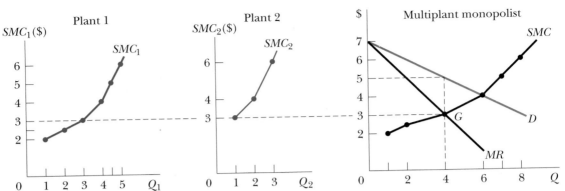

FIGURE 10.8   Short-Run Equilibrium of the Multiplant Monopolist   The *SMC* curves of each of two plants of a monopolist are *SMC*$_1$ and *SMC*$_2$ in the left and center panels, respectively. The horizontal summation of *SMC*$_1$ and *SMC*$_2$ yields *SMC* in the right panel. *SMC* shows the monopolist's minimum *SMC* of producing each additional unit of the commodity. The best level of output is *Q* = 4, given by point *G*, where the *SMC* curve intersects the *MR* curve from below. To minimize *STC*, the monopolist should produce three units of the commodity in plant 1 and one unit in plant 2 so that *SMC*$_1$ = *SMC*$_2$ = *SMC* = *MR* = $3.

plant is equal to the marginal revenue from selling the combined output. This is shown in Figure 10.8, which refers to a two-plant monopolist.

The left and center panels of Figure 10.8 show the *SMC* curve of each of the two plants operated by the monopolist. The *horizontal* summation of *SMC*$_1$ and *SMC*$_2$ yields *SMC* in the right panel. The *SMC* curve shows the monopolist's minimum *SMC* of producing each additional unit of the commodity. Thus, the monopolist should produce the first and second unit of the commodity in plant 1 (at a *SMC* of $2 and $2.50, respectively), the third and fourth unit in plant 1 and plant 2 (one unit in each plant, at *SMC* = $3), and so on.

If the monopolist were to produce all four units of the commodity in plant 1, it would incur a *SMC* = $4 for the fourth unit (instead of a *SMC* = $3 with plant 2). Thus, the monopolist should produce three units of the commodity in plant 1 and one unit in plant 2. By adding the three units of the commodity produced in plant 1 and the one unit produced in plant 2, we get point *G* on the *SMC* curve in the right panel of Figure 10.8. Thus, the *SMC* curve in the right panel is obtained from the horizontal summation of the *SMC*$_1$ and *SMC*$_2$ curves in the left and center panels, respectively. The *SMC* shows the monopolist's minimum *SMC* of producing each additional unit of the commodity.

The best level of output for this monopolist is four units of the commodity and is given by point G, where the *SMC* curve intersects the *MR* curve from below. The monopolist should produce three units of the commodity in plant 1 and one unit of the commodity in plant 2 so that *SMC*$_1$ = *SMC*$_2$ = *SMC* = *MR* = $3 (see the figure). This minimizes the total cost of producing the best level of output of four units at $10.50 ($2 + $2.50 + $3 + $3) in the short run. If the monopolist were to produce all four units in plant 1, it would incur a *STC* = $11.50 ($2 + $2.50 + $3 + $4). The *STC* would be even higher if the monopolist produced all four units in plant 2 (see the center panel of the figure).

Whether the monopolist earns a profit, breaks even, or incurs a loss by producing three units of the commodity in plant 1 and one unit of the commodity in plant 2 depends on the value of the *SATC* at Q = 4. Even if the monopolist were to incur a loss at its best

✓ Concept Check

How does a monopolist utilize each plant in the short run?

level of output, it would pay to continue to produce in the short run as long as $P > AVC$ (see Section 10.2).

Long-Run Equilibrium

In the long run, a monopolist can build as many identical plants of optimal size (i.e., plants whose *SATC* curves form the lowest point of the *LAC* curve) as required to produce the best level of output. This is shown in Figure 10.9. The left panel shows one of the plants of the monopolist. The monopolist will operate this plant at point E', where $SATC_1 = SMC_1 = LAC_1 = LMC_1 = \$1$ and $Q = 3$. To produce larger outputs, the monopolist will build additional identical plants and run them at the optimal rate of output of $Q = 3$. If input prices remain constant, the *LMC* curve of the monopolist is horizontal at $LAC = LMC = \$1$ (see the right panel).

The best level of output of the monopolist in the long run is then given by point E, where $LMC = MR = \$1$ in the right panel. At point E, $Q = 6$, $P = \$4$, $LAC = \$1$, and the monopolist earns a profit of $3 per unit and $18 in total. The monopolist will produce three units of output in each of two identical plants (point E' in the left panel). If the best level of output is not a multiple of three, the monopolist will either have to run some plants at outputs greater than three units or build and run an extra plant at less than three units of output.

If input prices rise when the multiplant monopolist builds additional plants to increase output, then the *LAC* curve of each plant shifts upward (as in Figure 9.12) and the *LMC* curve of the monopolist will be upward sloping.

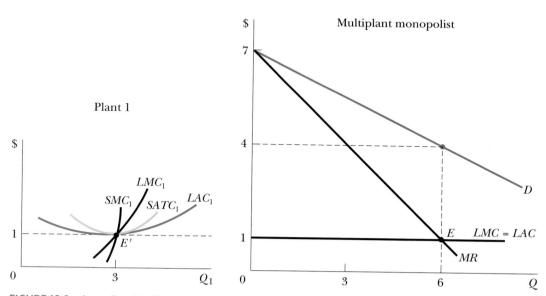

FIGURE 10.9   Long-Run Equilibrium of the Multiplant Monopolist   The left panel shows one of the plants of the monopolist. The monopolist will operate this plant at point E', where $LAC_1 = LMC_1 = \$1$ and $Q_1 = 3$. To produce larger outputs, the monopolist will build additional identical plants and run them at $Q = 3$. If input prices remain constant, the *LMC* curve of the monopolist is horizontal at $LMC = \$1$ (see the right panel). The best level of output is at point E, where the $LMC = MR = \$1$. At point E, $Q = 6$, $P = \$4$, $LAC = \$1$, and the monopolist earns a total profit of $18 and operates two plants.

PRICE DISCRIMINATION—A MONOPOLIST'S METHOD
10.5   OF INCREASING PROFITS

Price discrimination
Charging different
prices (for different
quantities of a
commodity or in
different markets) that
are not justified by cost
differences.

In this section, we examine various types of price discrimination. **Price discrimination** refers to the charging of different prices for different quantities of a commodity or in different markets which are not justified by cost differences. By practicing price discrimination, the monopolist can increase its total revenue and profits. We first examine the charging of different prices by the monopolist for different quantities sold and then the charging of different prices in different markets.

Charging Different Prices for Different Quantities

If a monopolist could sell each unit of the commodity separately and charge the highest price each consumer would be willing to pay for the commodity rather than go without it, the monopolist would be able to extract the entire consumers' surplus from consumers. This is called **first-degree (perfect) price discrimination.**

**First-degree price
discrimination** The
charging of the highest
price for each unit of a
commodity that each
consumer is willing to
pay rather than go
without it.

For example, in Figure 10.10, the consumer would be willing to pay *LRZO* ($22.50) for three units of the commodity. Since he or she only pays *RZOF* ($18), this consumer's surplus is *LRF* ($4.50). If the monopolist, however, charged $8.50 for the first unit (the highest price that this consumer would pay rather than forego entirely the consumption of the commodity), $7.50 for the second unit of the commodity, and $6.50 for the third unit, then the monopolist would receive $22.50 (the sum of the areas of the rectangles above the first three units of the commodity), thereby extracting the entire consumer's

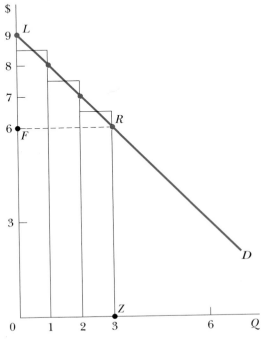

FIGURE 10.10   First- and Second-Degree Price Discrimination
Since the consumer is willing to pay $22.50 for three units of the commodity, but only pays $18, this consumer's surplus is $4.50. If the monopolist charged $8.50 for the first unit, $7.50 for the second, and $6.50 for the third, it would receive $22.50, thus extracting the entire consumer's surplus. This is first-degree price discrimination. If the monopolist set $P = \$7$ for the first two units and $P = \$6$ for additional units, it would sell three units and extract $2 of the consumer's surplus. This is second-degree price discrimination.

surplus from this consumer.[9] The result would be the same if the monopolist made an all-or-nothing offer to the consumer either to purchase all three units of the commodity for $22.50 or none at all.

To be able to practice first-degree price discrimination, however, the monopolist must (1) know the exact shape of each consumer's demand curve and be able to charge the highest price that each and every consumer would pay for each unit of the commodity, and (2) be able to prevent arbitrage, or someone purchasing many units of the commodity at decreasing prices and reselling some of the units to others at higher prices. Even if this were possible, it would probably be prohibitively expensive to carry out. Thus, first-degree price discrimination is not very common in the real world. Something close to first-degree price discrimination is, however, used in making undergraduate financial-aid offers by American colleges (see Example 10–5).

✓ **Concept Check**
Why is first-degree price discrimination not practical?

EXAMPLE 10–5

First–Degree Price Discrimination in Undergraduate Financial Aid at American Colleges

It now costs well over $100,000 for a four-year college education at many private colleges in the United States and more than $50,000 at public colleges. Financial aid is, however, available based on need. The greater the need, the more financial aid received. The way it works (as you may very well know) is as follows. In order to be considered for financial aid, students must provide information on their family's finances on the Free Application for Federal Student Aid (FAFSA) form. Using a government formula, the college then determines the Expected Family Contribution (EFC) toward college expenses. The lower the family's income and the higher the expenses of attending a particular college, the higher the financial aid offered to the student. By basing the amount of financial aid on a family's ability to pay, colleges thus practice something that comes very close to first-degree price discrimination. Many private colleges go well beyond this, however, in determining the aid package offered to each particular student and, in the process, have contributed to skyrocketing tuition costs.

Private colleges all over the country are now making financial-aid offers to prospective students based not only on demonstrated family need but also on the particular student "price sensitivity" to college costs, calculated by statistical models using dozens of factors measuring how eager the student is to attend a particular college. The more eager the student, the less the financial aid offered by the college. By offering less aid to more eager students, given their family's financial situation, the college is in effect charging a higher tuition and thus increasing its tuition revenue. This is referred to as "financial aid leveraging" and is similar to "yield management" used to price and fill airline seats and hotel rooms (discussed in "At the Frontier" section in Chapter 11). Thus, students who apply for early admission, those who go for on-campus interviews, or those who want to major in a very specific field are usually offered less financial aid (i.e., incur more of the college costs themselves). The National Center for Enrollment Management (NCEM), a consulting group that advises many colleges on financial-aid leveraging, estimated that its average college client's tuition revenue increased by about

---

[9] Note that the consumer is willing to pay an amount equal to the area under the demand curve between zero and one on the horizontal axis for the first unit of the commodity. This is equal to the area of the rectangle above the first unit of the commodity in Figure 10.10.

a half-million dollars. About 60% of the nation's 1,500 private four-year colleges now use some form of financial-aid leveraging.

Sources: "Colleges Manipulate Financial-Aid Offers, Shortcoming Many," *Wall Street Journal,* April 1996, p. A1; "Howls of Ivy," Barron's, March 1, 1999, p. 15; "Second Thoughts on Early Admission," *Business Week,* March 11, 2002, p. 96; and "Yale Seeks Shelter for pacts to End Early Admissions," *Wall Street Journal*, May 3, 2002, p. A2; "The New College Try," *New York Times*, September 24, 2007, p. 23; and D. M. Lang, "Financial Aid and Student Bargaining Power," *B.E. Journal of Economic Analysis & Policy*, No. 1, 2007, pp. 1–21.

Second-degree price discrimination
Charging a lower price for each additional batch or block of a commodity.

More practical and common is **second-degree (multipart) price discrimination.** This refers to the charging of a uniform price per unit for a specific quantity of the commodity, a lower price per unit for an additional batch or block of the commodity, and so on. By doing so, the monopolist will be able to extract part, but not all, of the consumer's surplus. For example, in Figure 10.10, the monopolist could set the price of $7 per unit on the first two units of the commodity and a price of $6 on additional units of the commodity. The monopolist would then sell three units of the commodity to this individual for $20 and extract $2 from the total consumer's surplus of $4.50. In general, this is also difficult to do because it requires that the monopolist be able to identify each consumer's demand curve and prevent arbitrage. Second-degree price discrimination is often practiced by public utilities, such as electrical power companies (this is examined in Example 10–6 at the end of the next section).

Charging Different Prices in Different Markets[10]

Third-degree price discrimination
Charging a higher price for a commodity in the one market of two that has the less elastic demand in such a way as to equalize the *MR* of the last unit of the commodity sold in the two markets.

Charging a different price in different markets is called **third degree price discrimination.** For simplicity, we will assume that there are only two markets. To maximize profits, the monopolist must produce the best level of output and sell that output in the two markets in such a way that the marginal revenue of the last unit sold in each market is the same. This will require the monopolist to sell the commodity at a higher price in the market with the less elastic demand. This is shown in Figure 10.11.

The left panel of Figure 10.11 shows D_1 and MR_1, which are, respectively, the market demand and the corresponding marginal revenue curves faced by the monopolist in the first market. The middle panel shows the D_2 and MR_2 for the second market. From the horizontal summation of D_1 and D_2, and from MR_1 and MR_2, we get D and MR for the firm as a whole (monopolist) in the right panel. We sum horizontally D_1 and D_2, and MR_1 and MR_2, because the firm can sell the commodity in and obtain extra revenues from both markets. Note that until $Q = 2.5$, $MR_1 = MR$, and until $Q = 5$, $D_1 = D$.

The best level for output for the monopolist is seven units and is given by the point where the firm's marginal cost curve (*MC*) intersects the firm's total marginal revenue curve (*MR*) from below (point *E* in the right panel). To maximize total profits, the monopolist should then sell four units of the commodity in market 1 (given by point E_1 in the left panel) and the remaining three units in market 2 (given by point E_2 in the middle panel) so that $MR_1 = MR_2 = MR = MC = \$3$ (see the figure). If the *MR* for the last unit of the commodity sold in one market were different from the *MR* of the last unit sold in the other

---

[10] For a mathematical presentation of price discrimination using rudimentary calculus, see Section A.12 of the Mathematical Appendix at the end of the book.

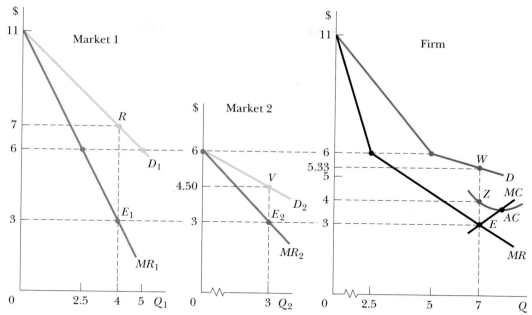

FIGURE 10.11   Third-Degree Price Discrimination D_1 in the left panel is the demand curve faced by the monopolist in market 1 (with MR_1 as the corresponding marginal revenue curve). D_2 and MR_2, in the middle panel refer to market 2. By summing horizontally D_1 and D_2, and MR_1 and MR_2, we get the D and MR curves for the monopolist in the right panel. The best level of output is seven units, given where the MC curve intersects the MR curve from below. To maximize total profits the monopolist should sell $Q = 4$ at $P = \$7$ in market 1 and $Q = 3$ at $P = \$4.50$ in market 2, so that $MR_1 = MR_2 = MR = MC = \$3$. With $AC = \$4$ (point Z in the right panel), the monopolist's total profits are $13.50.

market, the monopolist could increase its total revenue and profits by redistributing sales from the market with the lower MR to the market with the higher MR until $MR_1 = MR_2$.

The monopolist should charge $P = \$7$ for each of the four units of the commodity sold in market 1 (point R on D_1) and $P = \$4.50$ for each of the three units of the commodity in market 2 (point V on D_2). This assumes that resale is not possible. Note that the price is higher in market 1, where demand is less elastic. The total revenue of the monopolist would be $41.50 ($28 from selling four units of the commodity at $P = \$7$ in market 1 plus $13.50 from selling three units of the commodity at $P = \$4.50$ in market 2). With total costs of $28 (seven units at $AC = \$4$, given by point Z in the right panel), the monopolist earns a profit of $13.50 (the total revenue of $41.50 minus the total costs of $28). If the monopolist sold the best level of output of seven units at the price of $5.33 (point W on D in the right panel) in both markets (i.e., if it did not practice third degree price discrimination), the monopolist would earn a profit of $WZ = \$1.33$ per unit (the price of $5.33 minus the average cost of $4) and $9.31 in total (the $1.33 profit per unit times the seven units sold) as compared with $13.50 with third degree price discrimination. Any other output or distribution of sales between the two markets would similarly lead to lower total profits for the monopolist. This type of analysis is valid for the long run as well as for the short run.[11]

✓ **Concept Check**
How can a monopolist increase profits by third-degree price discrimination?

---

[11] If the monopolist knows the price elasticity of demand for the commodity in the two markets, it can determine the price to charge in each market to maximize total profits by utilizing formula [5.8]. See Problem 10, with the answer at the end of the book.

For a firm to be able to practice third-degree price discrimination, three conditions must be met. First, the firm must have some monopoly power (i.e., the firm must not be a price taker). Second, the firm must be able to keep the two markets separate so as to avoid arbitrage. Third, the price elasticity of demand for the commodity or service must be different in the two markets. All three conditions are met in the sale of electricity. For example, electrical power companies can set prices (subject to government regulation). The market for the industrial use of electricity is kept separate from that of household use by meters installed in each production plant and home. The price elasticity of demand for electricity for industrial use is higher than for household use because industrial users have better substitutes and more choices available (such as generating their own electricity) than households. Thus, electrical power companies usually charge lower prices to industrial users than to households (see Example 10–6).

Note that without market power the firm would be a price taker and could not practice any form of price discrimination. If the firm were unable to keep the markets separate, users in the lower-priced market could purchase more of the service than they needed and resell some of it in the higher-priced market (thus underselling the original supplier of the service). Finally, if the price elasticity of demand were the same in both markets, the best that the firm could do would be to charge the same price in both markets.

There are many other examples of third-degree price discrimination: (1) the lower fees doctors usually charge low-income people than high-income people for basically identical services; (2) the lower prices that airlines, trains, and cinemas usually charge children and the elderly than other adults; (3) the lower postal rates for third-class mail than for equally heavy first-class mail; (4) the lower prices that producers usually charge abroad than at home for the same commodity, and so on.

Third-degree price discrimination is more likely to occur in service industries than in manufacturing industries because it is more difficult (often impossible) for a consumer to purchase a service in the low-price market and resell it at a higher price in the other market (thus undermining the monopolist's differential pricing in the two markets). For example, a low-income person could not possibly resell a doctor's visit at a higher fee to a high-income person. On the other hand, if an elderly person were charged a lower price for an automobile, he or she could certainly resell it at a higher price to other people. It is not clear that a supermarket's charging of $0.95 for two bars of soap and $0.50 for one bar is price discrimination, however, because the supermarket saves on clerks' time in marking the merchandise and on cashiers' time in ringing up customers' bills. That is, the charging of different prices to different consumers in different markets is not price discrimination if the different prices are based on different costs.

EXAMPLE 10–6

Price Discrimination by Con Edison

Table 10.6 gives the price per kilowatt-hour (kWh) that Con Edison charged residential users and small and large commercial users for various quantities of electricity consumed in New York City, from June to September and for other months in 2007. Since Con Edison charged different rates for different categories of customers (i.e., residential and commercial) and for different quantities of electricity purchased, it is clear that Con Edison practiced both second- and third-degree price discrimination.

TABLE 10.6	Electricity Rates Charged by Con Edison in 2007 (cents per kilowatt-hour)			
	kWh	Cents/kWh	kWh	Cents/kWh
Residential Rates (Single Residence)				
January	0–250	7.219	Above 250	8.114
Other months	0–250	7.219	Above 250	6.643
Commercial Rates (Small Business)				
January	0–900	9.67	Above 900	8.65
Other months	0–900	8.27	Above 900	7.26
Commercial Rates (Large Business)				
Low tension	0–15,000	2.02	Above 15,000	2.02
High tension	0–15,000	1.87	Above 15,000	1.87

Source: Con Edison, New York City, 2007.

Note that charging higher rates for electricity during peak rather than off-peak hours, or *peak-load pricing,* is different from third-degree price discrimination because higher peak electricity rates are based on or reflect the higher costs of generating electricity at peak hours, when older and less efficient plants and equipment have to be brought into operation to meet demand (peak-load pricing is examined in detail in Section 13.8).

Another way for a seller to practice third-degree price discrimination is by offering coupons to consumers for the purchase of some products (such as a box of breakfast cereal) at a discount. This allows a firm to sell the product at a lower price to only the 20% to 30% of consumers who bother to clip, save, and use coupons (these are the consumers who have a higher price elasticity of demand). In 2007, more than $330 billion in grocery coupons were distributed in the United States, but only a small percentage of them were redeemed. Offering coupons is a form of third-degree price discrimination that the firm can use to increase profits. Firms often also offer rebates and airlines charge many different fares for a given trip for the same reason, and (as we have seen in Example 10-5) colleges offer varying tuition discounts in the form of financial aid.

Sources: Con Edison, *Electric Rates,* New York, 2007; C. Narasimhan, "A Price Discriminatory Theory of Coupons," *Marketing Science,* Spring 1984; "The Art of Devising Airfares," *New York Times,* March 8, 1987, p. D1; and "The New College Try," *New York Times,* September 24, 2007, p. 23.

10.6   INTERNATIONAL PRICE DISCRIMINATION AND DUMPING

Dumping International price discrimination, or the sale of a commodity at a lower price abroad than at home.

Price discrimination can also be practiced between the domestic and the foreign market. International price discrimination is called **dumping.** Dumping refers to the charging of a lower price abroad than at home for the same commodity because of the greater price elasticity of demand in the foreign market. By so doing, the monopolist earns higher profits than by selling the best level of output at the same price in both markets. The price elasticity of demand for the monopolist's product abroad is higher than at home because of the competition from producers from other nations in the foreign market. Foreign competition is usually restricted at home by import tariffs or other trade barriers. These import restrictions serve to segment the market (i.e., keep the domestic market separate from the foreign market) and prevent the reexport of the commodity back to the monopolist's home country (which would undermine the monopolist's ability to sell the commodity at a higher price at home than abroad). International price discrimination can be viewed in Figure 10.11 if D_1 referred to the demand curve faced by the monopolist in the domestic market and D_2 referred to the demand curve that the monopolist faced in the foreign market.

Besides dumping resulting from international price discrimination (often referred to as *persistent dumping* to distinguish it from other types of dumping), there are two other forms of dumping. These are predatory dumping and sporadic dumping. *Predatory dumping* is the *temporary* sale of a commodity at below cost or at a lower price abroad in order to drive foreign producers out of business, after which prices are raised abroad to take advantage of the newly acquired monopoly power. *Sporadic dumping* is the *occasional* sale of the commodity at below cost or at a lower price abroad than domestically in order to unload an unforeseen and temporary surplus of a commodity without having to reduce domestic prices.

Trade restrictions to counteract *predatory* dumping are justified and allowed to protect domestic industries from unfair competition from abroad. These restrictions usually take the form of antidumping duties to offset price differentials. However, it is often difficult to determine the type of dumping, and domestic producers invariably demand protection against any form of dumping. In fact, the very threat of filing a dumping complaint discourages imports and leads to higher domestic production and profits. This is referred to as the "harassment thesis." Persistent and sporadic dumping benefit domestic consumers (by allowing them to purchase the commodity at a lower price), and these benefits may exceed the possible losses of domestic producers.

Over the past decades, Japan was accused of dumping steel, televisions, and computer chips in the United States, and Europeans of dumping cars, steel, and other products. Most industrial nations (especially those of the European Economic Community) have a tendency of persistently dumping surplus agricultural commodities arising from their farm-support programs. Export subsidies are also a form of dumping which, though illegal by international agreement, often occur in disguised forms. When dumping is proved, the violating firm usually chooses to raise its prices (as Volkswagen did in 1976 and Japanese TV exporters did in 1977) rather than face antidumping duties. Example 10–7 examines Kodak's antidumping court victory over Fuji.

EXAMPLE 10–7

Kodak Antidumping Victory over Fuji—But Kodak Still Faces Competitive Problems

In August 1993, the Eastman Kodak Company of Rochester, New York, charged that the Fuji Photo Film Company of Japan had violated U.S. federal law by selling paper and chemicals for color-film processing in the United States at less than one-third of the price that it charged in Japan and that this had materially injured Kodak. Specifically, Kodak charged that Fuji used its excessive profits from its near monopoly in photographic supplies in Japan to dump photographic supplies in the United States in order to undermine the competitive position of Kodak and other U.S. competitors. By 1993, Fuji had captured more than 10% of the U.S. photographic supply market, mostly from Kodak. Kodak asked the U.S. Commerce Department to impose stiff tariffs on Fuji's imports of these products into the United States.

In August 1994, Fuji signed a five-year agreement under which it agreed to sell color paper and chemical components at or above a fair price determined quarterly by the U.S. Department of Commerce from Fuji cost of production figures in Japan and the Netherlands, where Fuji produces the photographic supplies exported to the United States. This "fair" price was about 50% higher than the pre-agreement price that Fuji charged in the United States. The immediate effect of the agreement was higher prices for photographic supplies for U.S. consumers.

In the face of continued loss of U.S. market share, Kodak again accused Fuji in 1995 of unfairly restricting its access to the Japanese market and again demanded the imposition of stiff tariffs on Fuji photographic exports to the United States. The World Trade Organization (the institution created in 1993 to regulate international trade and adjudicate trade disputes among its member nations), however, dismissed the case in 1997.

In the meantime, Fuji spent over $1 billion on new plants to produce photographic supplies in the United States, which made Fuji a domestic supplier and, to a large extent, no longer subject to U.S. antidumping rules. Kodak, on the other hand, has gone through a series of restructurings from 1998 to 2006 that cut costs by nearly $2 billion by eliminating 35,000 jobs, or about 35% of its worldwide labor force and shifting to higher-end products, such as digital cameras. But even here, Kodak dropped from first place in the U.S. market in 2005 to third place in 2006 (after Canon and Sony but ahead of Fuji, which is in seventh place) because of its inability to adapt quickly to new market demands in the face of fast technological changes and increasing Japanese competition.

Sources: "Kodak Asks 25% Tariffs on Some Fuji Imports," *New York Times,* August 31, 1993, p. D1; "Fuji Photo Pact on U.S. Prices," *Wall Street Journal,* August 22, 1994, p. A4; "Kodak Is Loser in Trade Ruling on Fuji Dispute," *New York Times,* December 6, 1997, p. 1; "Kodak Losing U.S. Market Share to Fuji," *Wall Street Journal,* May 28, 1999, p. A3; "Great Pictures, But where are the Profits?" *Financial Times,* September 1, 2005, p. 15; and http://www.macworld.com/news/2007/02/05/cameras/index.php?pf=1.

10.7   TWO-PART TARIFFS, TYING, AND BUNDLING

In this section, we examine some other pricing practices by monopolists: two-part tariffs, tying, and bundling.

Two-Part Tariffs

Two-part tariff
The pricing practice whereby a monopolist maximizes its total profits by charging a usage fee or price equal to its marginal cost and an initial or membership fee equal to the entire consumer surplus.

A two-part tariff is another pricing practice that monopolists sometimes use to extract consumer surplus. It requires consumers to pay an initial fee for the right to purchase a product, as well as a usage fee or price for each unit of the product they purchase. An example of this is amusement parks where visitors are charged an admission fee as well as a fee or price for each ride they take. Other examples are telephone companies that charge a monthly fee plus a message-unit fee; computer companies that charge monthly rentals plus a usage fee for renting their mainframe computers; and golf and tennis clubs that charge an annual membership fee plus a fee for each round or game played. In each case, the monopolist wants to charge the initial fee and the usage fee that extracts as much of consumers' surplus as possible and thus maximizes total profits.

The monopolist maximizes total profits by charging a usage fee or per-unit price equal to its marginal cost and an initial or membership fee equal to the entire consumer surplus. To see this, assume that initially there is a single consumer in the market with demand curve D in the left panel of Figure 10.12. The monopolist should then charge the usage fee or price (P) equal to the marginal cost (MC) of $2 and an initial or membership fee of $8 (area AEB), which equals the entire consumer surplus at P = $2. The monopolist would earn lower profits at any other price. For example, charging P = $3 would

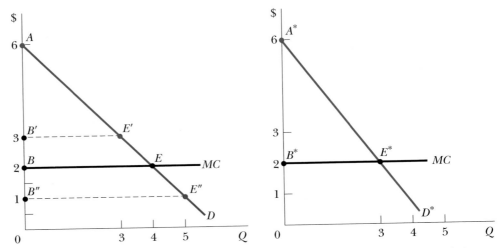

FIGURE 10.12   Two–Part Pricing by a Monopolist   With only one consumer in the market (left panel), the monopolist maximizes its total profits by charging $P = MC = \$2$ and the initial or membership fee of $AEB = \$8$. The monopolist can bring the consumer in the right panel into the market by lowering the initial or membership fee to $6 (equal to the surplus of $A^*E^*B^*$ of the second consumer at $P = MC = \$2$) for each consumer and earn a total profit of $12.

provide the monopolist with a profit of $1 for each of the three units of the product or service that the monopolist would sell at $P = \$3$, but it would allow the monopolist to charge an initial or membership fee of only $4.50 (equal to the consumer surplus of $AE'B'$ for $P = \$3$). Thus, with $P = \$3$, the monopolist's total profit would be $7.50 ($3 from the sale of the three units of the product or service and $4.50 from the initial or membership fee) as compared with a profit of $8 (from the initial or membership fee for $P = MC = \$2$). On the other hand, with a usage fee or price of only $1, the monopolist would incur a loss of $1 on each of the five units of the product or service that it would sell at $P = \$1$, but it could charge an initial or membership fee of $12.50 (equal to the consumer surplus of $AE''B''$). This would leave the monopolist with a net profit of $7.50, which is also less than the total profit of $8 with $P = \$2$.

Suppose now that there was a second customer with demand curve D* in the right panel of Figure 10.12 who could be brought into the market. At $P = MC = \$2$, the consumer surplus for this second customer would be $6 ($A^*E^*B^*$ in the right panel of Figure 10.12), and this is as high an initial fee that the second consumer would be willing to pay. The monopolist would then have to lower the initial fee to $6 for both consumers to bring this second consumer into the market and thus earn the higher total profit of $12 (from the $6 initial fee from each consumer). This leaves $2 of consumer surplus to the first consumer. The monopolist could extract this remaining $2 surplus from the first consumer if it could somehow charge the first consumer a price higher than marginal cost. Another way would be to charge the first consumer an initial fee of $8 and provide a special discount membership of $6 for the second consumer. If both consumers were identical and faced the same demand curve, no such difficulty would arise and the monopolist would set $P = MC$ and charge each consumer an initial fee equal to their (identical) consumer surplus.[12]

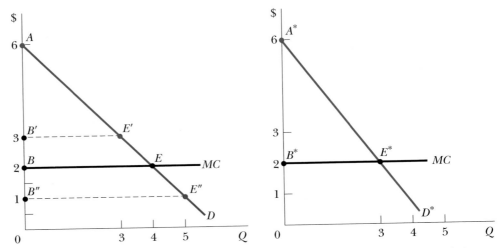

Concept Check
How can a monopolist use a two-part tariff, tying, and bundling to increase profits?

---

[12] For a more in-depth discussion of a two-part tariff, see W. Oi, "A Disneyland Dilemma: Two-Part Tariff for a Mickey Mouse Monopoly," *Quarterly Journal of Economics*, February 1971, pp. 77–96.

Tying and Bundling

Tying The requirement that a consumer who buys or leases a monopolist's product also puchase another product needed in the use of the first.

Tying refers to the requirement that a consumer who buys or leases a monopolist's product also purchase another product needed in the use of the first. For example, when the Xerox Corporation was the only producer of photocopiers in the 1950s, it required those leasing its machines to also purchase paper from Xerox. Similarly, until it was ordered by the court to discontinue the practice, IBM required by contract that the users of its computers purchase IBM punch cards. Sometimes tying of purchases is done to ensure that the correct supplies are used for the equipment to function properly or to ensure quality. More often, tying is used as a form of two-part tariff, whereby the monopolist can charge a price higher than marginal cost for supplies and thus extract more of the consumer surplus from the heavier users of the equipment (those who use more supplies). Often, the courts intervene to forbid these restrictions on competition. For example, McDonald's was forced to allow its franchises to purchase their materials and supplies from any McDonald's-approved supplier rather than only from McDonald's. This increased competition while still ensuring quality and protection of the brand name.[13]

Bundling A common form of tying in which the monopolist requires customers buying or leasing one of its products or services also to buy or lease another product or service when customers have different tastes but the monopolist cannot price discriminate.

Bundling is a common form of tying in which the monopolist requires customers buying or leasing one of its products or services also to buy or lease another product or service *when customers have different tastes* but the monopolist cannot price discriminate (as in tying). By selling or leasing the products or services as a package—a bundle—rather than separately, the monopolist can increase its total profits. A classic example of bundling is in movie leasing (see Example 10–8).

EXAMPLE 10–8

Bundling in the Leasing of Movies

Table 10.7 shows the prices that theater 1 and theater 2 would be willing to pay to lease movie A and movie B. If the film company cannot price discriminate and leases each movie separately to the two theaters, it will have to lease each movie at the lower of the two prices at which each theater is willing to lease each film. Specifically, the film company would have to charge $10,000 for movie A and $3,000 for movie B for a total of $13,000 to lease both movies to each theater (if the film company charged more for either movie, one of the theaters would not lease the movie). But theater 1 would have been willing to pay $15,000 to lease both movies and theater 2 would have been willing to pay

TABLE 10.7 Maximum Price Each Theater Would Pay to Lease Each Film Separately and as a Bundle		
	Theater 1	Theater 2
Movie A	$12,000	$10,000
Movie B	3,000	4,000

---

[13] See B. Klein and L. F. Saft, "The Law and Economics of Franchise Tying Contracts," *Journal of Law and Economics,* May 1985, pp. 345–361.

$14,000 for both movies. The film company can thus lease both movies to both theaters as a package or a bundle for $14,000 (the lowest of the total amounts at which the two theaters are willing to lease the two movies) rather than individually for $13,000. Thus, by leasing the two movies together as a bundle rather than individually, the film company can extract some of the surplus from theater 1 without price discriminating between the two theaters.

Such profitable bundling is possible only when one theater is willing to pay more for leasing one movie but less for leasing the other movie with respect to the other theater (i.e., when the *relative* valuation for the two movies differs between the two theaters or the demand for the two movies by each theater is negatively correlated). If, in our example, both theaters had been willing to pay only $9,000 to lease movie A, then the maximum price that the film company could charge either theater without price discrimination would be $12,000, whether it leased the movies as a bundle or separately. For bundling to be profitable, one theater must be willing to pay more for one movie and less for another movie with respect to the other theater. This occurs only if the two theaters serve different audiences with different tastes and have different relative valuations for the two movies.

Other examples of bundling are complete dinners versus à la carte pricing at restaurants, travel packages (which often include flights, hotel accommodations, and meals) and the sale of wire and wireless telephone services, Internet access and cable TV as a single package by telecommunications companies.

Sources: R. L. Schmalensee, "Commodity Bundling by Single-Product Monopolies," *Journal of Law and Economics,* April 1982, pp. 67–71; A. Lewbel, "Bundling of Substitutes or Complements," *International Journal of Industrial Organization,* No. 3, 1985, pp. 101–107; "The Benefits of Bundling," *Economic Intuition,* Winter 1999, pp. 6–7; and "Product Bundling," *Wikipedia,* October 2007, pp. 1–2, http://en.wikipedia.org/wiki/Product_bundling.

10.8   ANALYSIS OF MONOPOLY MARKETS

Now we consider some analyses of monopoly markets. First, we compare the effect of a per-unit tax on a monopolist and on a perfect competitor, then we show that some commodities could only be supplied with price discrimination, and finally we answer the question of whether monopolists suppress inventions.

Per-Unit Tax: Perfect Competition and Monopoly Compared

One additional way to compare monopoly with perfect competition is with respect to the incidence of a per-unit tax. A per-unit excise tax (such as on cigarettes, gasoline, and liquor) will fall entirely on consumers if the industry is perfectly competitive and will fall only partly on consumers under monopoly, if both the monopolist and the perfectly competitive industry operate under constant costs.[14] For simplicity, we assume that the perfectly competitive industry and the monopolist face the same demand and cost

---

[14] The fact that a per-unit excise tax falls entirely on consumers under perfect competition but falls only partly on consumers with monopoly does not mean, however, that monopoly is "better" than perfect competition. When all inefficiencies associated with monopoly are considered, we would see that perfect competition leads to a higher level of social welfare than monopoly. Furthermore, the incidence of a per-unit tax is entirely on consumers only if the perfectly competitive industry operates under constant costs.

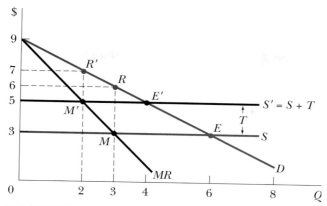

FIGURE 10.13   Per-Unit Tax: Perfect Competition and Monopoly Compared   Before the per-unit tax, the perfectly competitive industry operates at point E, where D and S intersect, so that $Q = 6$ and $P = \$3$. With a $2 per-unit tax, S shifts up to S', and $Q = 4$ and $P = \$5$, so the tax falls entirely on consumers. Before the tax, the monopolist is in equilibrium at point M. $Q = 3$, $P = \$6$, and the monopolist earns a profit of $3 ($RM$) per unit and $9 in total. With a tax of $2 per unit, $Q = 2$, $P = \$7$, and half of the per-unit tax falls on the monopolist.

conditions. Thus, S in Figure 10.13 refers to the long-run supply curve of the perfectly competitive industry and to the $LAC = LMC$ curve of the monopolist under constant costs.

Before the imposition of the per-unit tax, the perfectly competitive industry operates at point E, where D and S intersect, so that $Q = 6$ and $P = \$3$. If a tax of $2 per unit is imposed, S shifts upward by $2 to S'. The perfectly competitive industry would then operate at point E', where D and S' intersect, so that $Q = 4$ and $P = \$5$. Thus, when the industry is perfectly competitive and operates under constant costs, the entire amount of the per-unit tax ($2 in this case) falls on consumers in the form of higher prices (so that $P = \$5$ instead of $3).

The case is different under monopoly. Before the imposition of the tax, the monopolist produces at point M, where MR and S (the $LMC = LAC$ of the monopolist) intersect. $Q = 3$, $P = \$6$ (point R), $LAC = \$3$, and the monopolist earns a profit of $3 ($RM$) per unit and $9 in total. If the same tax of $2 per unit is imposed on the monopolist, S shifts upward to S' ($= LMC' = LMC + 2 = LAC' = LAC + 2$). The monopolist would then operate at point M', where MR and S' intersect. At point M', $Q = 2$, $P = \$7$ (point R'), $LAC' = \$5$, and the monopolist earns $2 per unit ($R'M'$) and $4 in total. Thus, with monopoly, the price to consumers rises by only $1 (one-half of the per-unit tax). The remaining half of the tax falls on the monopolist, so that it now only earns a profit of $2, rather than $3, per unit. Note also that with the tax, the decline in output under monopoly is half that with perfect competition (i.e., output falls from six to four units with perfect competition, but only from three to two units under monopoly).[15]

---

[15] From Figure 10.13, we can also see that the flatter or more elastic the market demand curve faced by the monopolist, the smaller the incidence or proportion of the tax paid by consumers.

Price Discrimination and the Existence of the Industry

Sometimes price discrimination is necessary for an industry to exist. For example, in Figure 10.14, D_1 is the demand curve for the commodity for one group of consumers (i.e., in market 1), while D_2 is the demand curve for another group (market 2). The horizontal summation of D_1 and D_2 yields D (ABC). Since the LAC curve is above D at every level of output, the commodity or service would not be supplied in the long run in the absence of price discrimination or a subsidy.

With third-degree price discrimination (to the extent that the two markets can be kept separate), the firm could sell one unit of the commodity at $P = \$4$ in market 1 and sell three units of the commodity at $P = \$1.50$ in market 2. The total output would then be four units sold at the (weighted) average price of $2.13, which equals the LAC of producing four units in the long run (point F in the figure).[16]

Do Monopolists Suppress Inventions?

A useful invention is one that allows the production of a given-quality product at lower cost or a higher-quality product at the same cost. Many people believe that a monopolist would suppress such inventions. Why, they argue, would a monopolist want to introduce

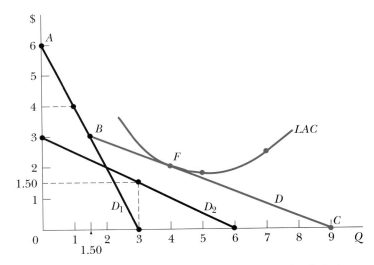

FIGURE 10.14   Price Discrimination and the Existence of an Industry
The demand curve is D_1 in market 1 and D_2 in market 2. The horizontal summation of D_1 and D_2 gives D (ABC). Since the LAC curve is above D at every output level, the commodity or service would not be supplied in the long run without price discrimination or a subsidy. With third–degree price discrimination, the firm could sell $Q = 1$ at $P = \$4$ in market 1 and sell $Q = 3$ at $P = \$1.50$ in market 2 and break even (since at point F, the weighted average $P = \$2.13$ equals LAC).

---

[16] The weighted average price of $2.13 is obtained by $[(1)(\$4) + (3)(\$1.50)]/4 = \$8.50/4$. The sale of $Q = 1$ in market 1 and $Q = 3$ in market 2 was obtained from inspection of the figure. This is the only output and distribution of sales (in whole units of the commodity) between the two markets by which this firm covers all costs.

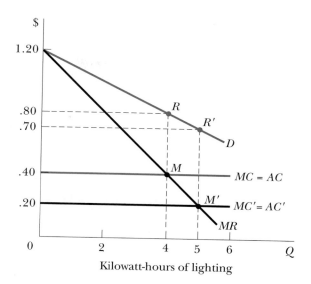

FIGURE 10.15   Monopoly and Inventions   The price per kilowatt-hour (kWh) of light is measured vertically and the quantity of kWhs horizontally. *D* is the market demand curve for kWhs of light. *MC* is the marginal cost of providing kWhs with the original bulbs and *MC'* with new bulbs (which last twice as long but cost the same to produce). With the original bulbs, $Q = 4$ kWhs, $P = \$0.80$ per kWh, $AC = \$0.40$, and profit is $\$0.40$ per kWh and $\$1.60$ in total. If original bulbs last 1/2 kWh, the monopolist sells eight of them at $P = \$0.40$. With new bulbs, $Q = 5$ kWhs, $P = \$0.70$, $AC' = \$0.20$, and profit is $\$0.50$ per kWh and $\$2.50$ in total. The monopolist sells five new bulbs at $\$0.70$ each.

a longer-lasting light bulb that costs the same to produce when that would reduce the number of light bulbs sold, and the total revenue and profits of the monopolist? Such reasoning is wrong. We will see that the introduction of an invention usually increases rather than reduces profits, and so the monopolist has an economic incentive to introduce invention rather than to suppress it. This is shown in Figure 10.15.

The vertical axis of the figure measures the price of a kilowatt-hour (kWh) of electric light, and the horizontal axis measures the quantity (in thousands of hours) of kWhs provided either with original light bulbs or with new and longer-lasting light bulbs.[17] Thus, the axes do not refer to the price and quantity of light bulbs; instead they refer to the main attribute or characteristic of light bulbs, which is to provide light. *D* is the market demand curve for kWhs of light with either the original or new light bulbs, and *MR* is the corresponding marginal revenue curve. The $MC = AC$ curve shows the marginal and average cost of producing kWhs of light with the original light bulbs (produced under conditions of constant cost). The best level of output for the monopolist is 4 kWhs and is given by point *M* where $MC = MR$. At $Q = 4$ kWhs, $P = \$0.80$ per kWh, $AC = \$0.40$ per kWh, and the monopolist earns a profit of $\$0.40$ per kWh and $\$1.60$ in total. If each original light bulb provides or lasts 1/2 kWh, the monopolist sells eight of the original light bulbs at $P = \$0.40$ each.

Suppose that the monopolist considers introducing a new light bulb that costs the same to produce but provides twice as many kWhs (i.e., lasts twice as long) as the original light bulbs. This is shown by the $MC' = AC'$ curve. This curve is half as high as the $MC = AC$ curve, indicating that each kWh of light could now be provided at half the cost. The best level of output for the monopolist is 5 kWhs and is given by point *M'* where $MC' = MR$. At $Q = 5$ kWhs, $P = \$0.70$ per kWh, $AC' = \$0.20$ per kWh, and the monopolist earns a profit of $\$0.50$ per kWh and $\$2.50$ in total (as compared with $\$1.60$ previously). Since each of the new light bulbs provides or lasts for 1 kWh (twice as much as the original light bulbs), the monopolist sells five light bulbs at $P = \$0.70$ each. Even though the monopolist sells fewer of the new light bulbs, it earns larger total profits, and

---

[17] See "Bulb Lighted by Radio Waves May Last for Up to 14 Years," *New York Times*, June 1, 1992, p. 1.

so it has an economic incentive to introduce the invention. Consumers are also better off because after the invention they pay $0.70 instead of $0.80 per kWh of light and consume 5 kWh instead of 4 kWhs.

Thus, the widespread belief that monopolists suppress inventions does not seem to be true.[18] This is a good example of how dispassionate economic analysis based on the marginal principle can dispel some commonly held, yet incorrect, beliefs. Only when the monopolist is unsuccessful in patenting an invention and the introduction of the invention would lead to loss of monopoly power would the monopolist seek to suppress the invention.

AT THE FRONTIER
Near-Monopoly Lands Microsoft in the Courts

Soon after its introduction in 1995, Microsoft's Windows 95 operating system had captured nearly 90% of the U.S. (and world) PC market and faced only weak competition from Apple Macintosh and IBM OS/2 operating systems. Inevitably, the threat from Windows 95 gave rise to predictable cries of monopoly from competitors. The introduction of Windows 95 put at especial risk small software companies that provided specialized programs for such tasks as hooking up to the Internet, retrieving lost files, turning the PC into a fax machine, and allocating memory inside the PC efficiently—since most of these functions were now provided as part of Windows 95. This was good news for computer users but drove many small software companies out of business and represented a serious threat to the others.

In fall 1998, the U.S. Justice Department sued Microsoft, accusing it of illegally using its Windows operating system near-monopoly to overwhelm rivals and hurt consumers. In April 2000, the federal district judge trying the case ruled that Microsoft had violated antitrust laws with predatory behavior, and in June of that year the same judge ordered the breakup of Microsoft. The company, however, appealed. In November 2001, the U.S. Justice Department and Microsoft reached a settlement agreement that not only left Microsoft intact but also continued to permit Microsoft's strategy of "bundling" applications with its Windows operating system. Both represented substantial victories for Microsoft. In 2004, the federal appeals court upheld the 2001 ruling, thus putting an end to Microsoft antitrust problems in the United States. In fact, with the introduction of Windows 98 and in 2001 Windows XP, Microsoft even increased its near-monopoly position in software.

But Microsoft also faced an antitrust suit in Europe. In 2004, the European Commission (the European antitrust regulator) fined Microsoft $600 million, ordered it to offer a version of the Windows operating system without its media player software and to share more technical information with other software makers. Since 2006, the European Commission imposed an additional $2.5 billion in fines on Microsoft for not complying with the 2004 ruling before closing the case in February 2008. Microsoft's legal problems in Europe, however, are not over. In February 2008, Microsoft faced two new suits and fines on the lack of "interoperability" between Microsoft's suite of Office applications, such as Excel, Word, and PowerPoint, and

---

[18] This, however, does not mean that the monopolist innovates as much as competitive firms.

competing products as well as on Microsoft's bundling of other products and functions into its new Vista operating system.

Besides antitrust problems on both sides of the Atlantic, Microsoft faced many private suits. One of the largest was that brought by the Netscape Communications Corporation in 2002. Netscape was the commercial pioneer in Web browsing software, whose fortune faded as a result of the competition from Microsoft and which was acquired by AOL in 1999. Netscape's broad antitrust suit charged that its decline had been the direct result of Microsoft's illegal tactics. This suit was settled in March 2003, with Microsoft paying AOL a $750 million penalty and granting AOL a seven-year royalty-free license to its Internet browsing software and a long-term license to its software for delivering music and video over the Internet. By the end of 2007, Microsoft payouts to settle all antitrust and private suits had reached almost $5 billion; but with over $50 billion in cash at hand, Microsoft was hardly hurt.

Sources: "Windows 95," *Business Week*, July 10, 1995, pp. 94–107; "U.S. Judge Says Microsoft Violated Antitrust Laws with Predatory Behavior," *New York Times*, April 4, 2000, p. 1; "Microsoft Breakup Ordered for Antitrust Law Violations," *New York Times* , June 8, 2000, p. 1; "Settlement or Sellout?," *Business Week,* November 19, 2001, p. 114; "An AOL Unit Sues Microsoft, Saying Tactics Were Illegal," *New York Times,* January 23, 2002, p. C1;"Microsoft to Pay AOL $750 Million to End Long War," *New York Times,* May 30, 2003, p. 1; "Europeans Rule Against Microsoft," *New York Times,* March 25, 2004, p. C1; "Court Lets Settlement Stand in Microsoft Antitrust Case, *New York Times,* July 1, 2004, p. C7; "Microsoft Payouts Set to Top $4.5 Billion," *Financial Times,* April 12, 2005, p. 21; and "Microsoft's Record Fine," **Financial Times**, February 28, 2008, p. 1.

SUMMARY

1. A monopolist is a firm selling a commodity for which there are no close substitutes. Thus, the monopolist faces the industry's negatively sloped demand curve for the commodity, and marginal revenue is smaller than price. Monopoly can be based on control of the entire supply of a required raw material, a patent or government franchise, or declining long-run average costs over a sufficiently large range of outputs so as to leave a single firm supplying the entire market. In the real world, there are usually many forces that limit the monopolist's market power.

2. The best level of output for the monopolist in the short run is the one that maximizes total profits. This occurs where the positive difference between *TR* and *STC* is greatest. The same result is obtained where the *MC* curve intersects the *MR* curve from below. If *P* is smaller than *ATC*, the monopolist will incur a loss in the short run. However, if *P* exceeds *AVC*, it pays for the monopolist to continue to produce because production covers part of the fixed costs. There is no unique relationship between price and output or supply curve for the monopolist.

3. The best, or profit-maximizing, level of output for the monopolist in the long run is given by the point where the *LMC* curve intersects the *MR* curve from below. The best plant is the one whose *SATC* curve is tangent to the *LAC* at the best level of output. The monopolist can make long-run profits because of restricted entry and does not usually produce at the lowest point on the *LAC* curve. The long-run profits of the monopolist will be capitalized into the market value of the firm and benefit only the original owner of the monopoly. As compared with perfect competition, monopoly restricts output, results in a higher price, redistributes income from consumers to the monopolist, and leads to less efficient use of society's resources.

4. A multiplant monopolist minimizes the total cost of producing the best level of output in the short run when the marginal cost of the last unit of the commodity produced in each plant is equal to the marginal revenue from selling the combined output. In the long run, a monopolist

can build as many identical plants of optimal size (i.e., plants whose $SATC$ curves form the lowest point of the LAC curve) as required to produce the best level of output.

5. Under first-degree price discrimination, the monopolist sells each unit of the commodity separately and charges the highest price that each consumer is willing to pay rather than go without the commodity. By doing so, the monopolist extracts the entire consumers' surplus. More practical and common is second-degree price discrimination. This refers to the charging of a lower price per unit of output for each additional batch or block of the commodity. By doing so, the monopolist will be able to extract part of the consumers' surplus. Third-degree price discrimination refers to the charging of a higher price for a commodity in the market with the less elastic demand in such a way as to equalize the MR of the last unit of the commodity sold in the two markets. To do this, the firm must have some control over prices, it must be able to keep the two markets separate, and the price elasticity of demand must be different in the two markets.

6. International price discrimination is called (persistent) dumping. Under this type of dumping, the monopolist sells the commodity at a higher price at home (where the market demand curve is less elastic) than abroad where the monopolist faces competition from other nations and the market demand curve for the monopolist's product is more elastic.

7. A two-part tariff is the pricing practice under which a monopolist maximizes total profits by charging a usage fee or price equal to its marginal cost and an initial or membership fee equal to the entire consumer surplus. Tying refers to the requirement that a consumer who buys or leases a monopolist's product also purchase another product needed in the use of the first. Bundling is a common form of tying in which the monopolist requires customers buying or leasing one of its products or services to also buy or lease another product or service when customers have different tastes but the monopolist cannot price discriminate (as in tying).

8. A per-unit excise tax will fall on consumers in its entirety under perfect competition but only in part under monopoly with constant costs. Price discrimination may be necessary to permit the existence of an industry. The commonly held view that monopolists suppress inventions is not generally true. The introduction of Windows 95 by Microsoft is as close as we come today to a pure monopoly in a major U.S. industry.

KEY TERMS

Pure monopoly
Natural monopoly
Price discrimination
First-degree or (perfect) price discrimination

Second-degree (multipart) price discrimination
Third-degree price discrimination
Dumping

Two-part tariff
Tying
Bundling

REVIEW QUESTIONS

1. a. What forces limit the monopolist's market power in the real world?
   b. Why would a monopolist advertise its product if it has a monopoly power over the product?

2. a. Why would a monopolist never operate in the inelastic range of its demand curve?
   b. What would be the best level of output for a monopolist that faced zero average and marginal costs?

3. a. How does the shape of the monopolist's total revenue curve differ from that of a perfectly competitive firm?
   b. Why doesn't the monopolist produce where total revenue is maximum?

4. Suppose that a monopolist sells a commodity at the price of $10 per unit and that its marginal cost is also $10. Is the monopolist maximizing total profits? Why?

5. If the monopolist's total profits were entirely taxed away and redistributed to consumers, would any social cost of monopoly remain? Why?

6. If $LS = LAC = LMC = \$3$ in Figure 10.7 shifted upward to $5, what would be

   a. the consumers' surplus?

   b. the monopolist's total profits?

   c. the social cost of monopoly?

7. How could the government entirely eliminate the social cost of monopoly in Figure 10.7?

8. Under what condition would a multiplant monopolist keep some of its plants idle?

9. a. Will a monopolist's total revenue be larger with second-degree price discrimination when the

batches on which it charges a uniform price are larger or smaller? Why?

   b. How does a two-part tariff differ from bundling?

10. If the monopolist of Figure 10.11 sold the best level of output at the same price in market 1 and market 2 (i.e., if the monopolist did not practice third-degree price discrimination), how much would it sell in each market?

11. Is persistent dumping good or bad for consumers in the importing country? Against what type of dumping would the nation want to protect itself? Why?

12. Assuming that everything is the same, will a per-unit tax reduce output more under perfect competition or under monopoly? Why?

PROBLEMS

1. Given that the demand function of a monopolist is
$Q = 1/5(55 - P)$

   a. derive the monopolist's demand and marginal revenue schedules from $P = \$55$ to $P = \$20$, at $5 intervals.

   b. On the same set of axes, plot the monopolist's demand and marginal revenue curves, and show the range over which D is elastic and inelastic, and the point where D is unitary elastic.

   c. Using the formula relating marginal revenue, price, and elasticity, find the price elasticity of demand at $P = \$40$.

2. Using the TC schedule of Table 8.2 and the demand schedule of Problem 1

   a. construct a table similar to Table 10.2 showing TR, STC, and total profits at each level of output, and indicate by an asterisk the best level of output for the monopolist.

   b. draw a figure similar to Figure 10.2 and determine the best level of output for the monopolist.

3. Using the per-unit cost curves of Figure 8.2 and the demand and marginal revenue curves from Problem 1(b)

   a. draw a figure similar to Figure 10.3 and show the best level of output for the firm.

   b. From your figure in part (a), construct a table similar to Table 10.4 showing P, ATC, profit per unit, total profits, MR, and MC at each level of output.

*4. Suppose the demand curve facing the monopolist changes to $Q' = 1/5(30 - P)$, while cost curves remain unchanged.

   a. Draw a figure similar to Figure 10.4 showing the best level of output.

   b. Does the monopolist make a profit, break even, or incur a loss at the best level of output? Should the monopolist shut down? Why? Where is the monopolist's shut down point?

5. Suppose that the monopolist has unchanged cost curves but faces two alternative demand functions:

$$Q = 1/5(55 - P) \text{ and } Q'' = 1/5(45 - P)$$

   a. Draw a figure similar to Figure 10.5 showing the best level of output with each demand function.

   b. Which of the two demand functions is more elastic? Where is the monopolist's supply curve?

6. Starting with the cost curves in Figure 8.11 and the demand and marginal revenue curves of problem 1, draw a $SATC$ curve (label it $SATC'_2$ and its associated SMC curve (label it SMC'_2) showing that the monopolist is in long-run equilibrium at $Q = 5$.

*7. Draw two figures and label the best level of output as Q^* and label per-unit profit as AB for a monopolist that

   a. produces at the lowest point on its LAC curve.

   b. overutilizes a plant larger than the one that forms the lowest point on its LAC curve.

---

* = Answer provided at end of book.

8. Given that the market demand function facing a two-plant monopolist is $Q = 20 - 2P$ and the short-run marginal cost for plant 1 and plant 2 *at* various levels of output are

Q		0	1	2	3	4
SMC_1 (\$)	. . .		2	4	6	8
SMC_2 (\$)	. . .		2.50	3.50	4.50	5.50

draw a figure showing D, MR, SMC_1, SMC_2, and MC schedules of this monopolist. What is the best level of output for the monopolist? How much should the monopolist produce in plant 1 and how much in plant 2?

9. Given the following demand curve of a consumer for a monopolist's product

$$Q = 14 - 2P$$

a. find the total revenue of the monopolist when it sells six units of the commodity without practicing any form of price discrimination. What is the value of the consumers' surplus?

b. What would be the total revenue of the monopolist if it practiced first-degree price discrimination? How much would the consumers' surplus be in this case?

c. Answer part (a) if the monopolist charged $P = \$5.50$ for the first three units of the commodity and $P = \$4$ for the next three units. What type of price discrimination is this?

d. With $MC = \$4$, what two-part tariff should the monopolist use to maximize total profits? What if $MC = 0$?

*10. With reference to Figure 10.11, use formula [5-8] to prove that if the monopolist charges $P = \$4.50$ in market 2, it must charge $P = \$7$ in market 1 to maximize total profits with third-degree price discrimination.

11. With reference to Figure 10.13, compare the effect of a \$4 per-unit tax if the industry is perfectly competitive or a monopoly.

*12. Starting from Table 10.3 and Figure 10.3, construct a table and draw a figure showing

a. how a lump-sum tax can be used to eliminate all of the monopolist's profits.

b. what would happen if the government imposed a per-unit tax of \$2.50.

INTERNET SITE ADDRESSES

Information on Alcoa and aluminum prices are found at:

http://www.alcoa.com

http://www.alcoa.com/global/en/news/news_detail.asp?pageID=20070430005939en&newsYear=2007

http://www.world-aluminium.org/About+IAI/Members

http://www.econstats.com/spot/rt_alum.htm

http://www.infomine.com/investment/historicalcharts/showcharts.asp?c=Aluminum

http://www.purchasing.com/article/CA6479841.html

Information on the taxi market and the price of a taxi medallion in New York, Boston, and Chicago is found at:

http://en.wikipedia.org/wiki/Taxicabs_of_the_United_States#New_York_City

http://www.nysun.com/article/55479

http://www.bostonnow.com/news/local/2007/05/07/cab_drive_crazy/

http://hgchicago.org/rn06.html

The operation of the De Beers diamond company is discussed at:

http://en.wikipedia.org/wiki/De_Beers

http://www.debeersgroup.com/debeersweb

Third-degree price discrimination is examined at:

http://www.coned.com

http://media.corporate-ir.net/media_files/irol/61/61493/total.pdf

http://couponing.about.com/b/a/256970.htm

On the antidumping case that Kodak brought against Fuji as well as their present competition, see:

http://www.macworld.com/news/2007/02/05/cameras/index.php?pf=1

http://www.academon.com/lib/essay/kodak.html

An excellent graphical presentation of price discrimination, peak-load pricing, two-part tariff, and bundling is found at:

http://en.wikipedia.org/wiki/Product_bundling

http://en.wikipedia.org/wiki/Two_part_tariff

http://en.wikipedia.org/wiki/Tying_%28commerce%29

The Microsoft antitrust cases are examined at:

http://www.usdoj.gov/atr/cases/ms_index.htm

http://www.eurunion.org/News/press/2005/2005083.htm

http://www.npr.org/templates/story/story.php?storyId=14465160

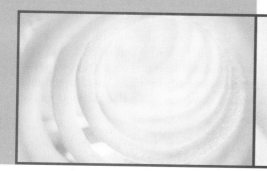

CHAPTER 11

Price and Output Under Monopolistic Competition and Oligopoly

Chapter Outline

11.1 Monopolistic Competition: Many Sellers of a Differentiated Product
11.2 Monopolistic Competition: Short-Run and Long-Run Analysis
11.3 Oligopoly: Interdependence Among the Few Producers in the Industry
11.4 The Cournot and the Kinked–Demand Curve Models
11.5 Collusion: Cartels and Price Leadership Models
11.6 Long-Run Adjustments and Efficiency Implications of Oligopoly
11.7 Other Oligopolistic Pricing Practices
11.8 The March of Global Oligopolists
        Appendix: The Cournot and Stackelberg Models

List of Examples

11–1 Advertisers Are Taking on Competitors by Name ... and Are Being Sued
11–2 Industrial Concentration in the United States
11–3 The Organization of Petroleum Exporting Countries (OPEC) Cartel
11–4 The Market-Sharing Ivy Cartel and Financial-Aid Leveraging
11–5 Firm Size and Profitability
        At the Frontier: The Art of Devising Airfares
11–6 Globalization of the Automobile Industry
11–7 Rising Competition in Global Banking
11–8 Globalization of the Pharmaceutical Industry

After Studying This Chapter, You Should Be Able to:

- Describe the difference between perfect competition and monopolistic competition
- Know how the Cournot model explains duopolists' behavior
- Describe how the kinked–demand curve model explains price rigidity
- Know how the different types of cartels operate
- Know the welfare implications of oligopoly

I n this chapter, we bring together the theory of consumer behavior and demand (from Part Two) and the theory of production and costs (from Chapters 7 and 8) to analyze how price and output are determined under monopolistic competition and oligopoly. These fall between the two extremes of perfect competition and pure monopoly in the spectrum or range of market organizations, and, as such, they contain elements of both.

345

As with perfect competition and monopoly, the best level of output for a monopolistic competitor and oligopolist is where marginal revenue equals marginal cost. But, as in the case of monopoly, price exceeds marginal revenue and marginal cost. This means that monopolistically competitive and oligopolistic firms are able to somewhat restrict output and charge consumers a higher price than perfect competitors would, but their market power is not as great as that of the monopolist.

The chapter begins by examining the meaning and importance of monopolistic competition; it shows how the equilibrium price and quantity are determined in the short run and in the long run, and analyzes product variation and selling expenses. Then, after discussing the meaning and sources of oligopoly, we examine various models of oligopoly pricing and output. We will see that there is no general theory of oligopoly but a number of models of various degrees of realism. Subsequently, we discuss the long-run efficiency implications of oligopoly, review some other oligopolistic pricing practices, and examine the growth in the number and size of international oligopolists. In the next chapter, we consider oligopolistic behavior utilizing game theory. Chapter 13 deals with market structure, efficiency, and regulation.

11.1   MONOPOLISTIC COMPETITION: MANY SELLERS OF A DIFFERENTIATED PRODUCT

Monopolistic competition The market organization where there are many sellers of a differentiated product and entry into the market is easy.

Differentiated products Products that are similar but not identical.

In Chapter 9 we defined perfect competition as the form of market organization in which there are many sellers of a homogeneous product. In Chapter 10 we defined pure monopoly as a single seller of a commodity for which there are no close substitutes. Between these two extreme forms of market organization lies **monopolistic competition.** This refers to the case in which there are many sellers of a heterogeneous or differentiated product and entry into or exit from the industry is rather easy in the long run.

Differentiated products are products that are similar but not identical. The similarity of differentiated products arises from the fact that they satisfy the same basic consumption needs. Examples are the numerous brands of breakfast cereals, toothpaste, cigarettes, detergents, and cold medicines on the market today. The differentiation may be real (as in the case of the various breakfast cereals with various nutritional and sugar contents) or imaginary (as in the case of the different brands of aspirin, all of which contain the same ingredients). Product differentiation may also be based entirely on some sellers being more or less conveniently located or on the kind of service they provide (i.e., more or less friendly).

As the name implies, monopolistic competition is a blend of competition and monopoly. The competitive element arises because there are many sellers of the differentiated product, each of which is too small to affect the other sellers. Firms can also enter and leave a monopolistically competitive industry rather easily in the long run. The monopolistic element arises from product differentiation. That is, since the product of each seller is similar but not identical, each seller has a monopoly power over the *specific* product it sells. This monopoly power, however, is severely limited by the existence of close substitutes. Thus, if a seller of a particular brand of aspirin charged a price more than a few pennies higher than competitive brands, it would lose a great deal of its sales.

Monopolistic competition is most common in the retail and service sectors of the economy. Nationally, clothing, cotton textiles, and food processing are industries that come closest to monopolistic competition. Locally, the best examples of monopolistic competition are the many gasoline stations, barber shops, grocery stores, drug stores, newspaper stands, restaurants, pizzerias, and liquor stores, all located near one another. Each of these businesses has some monopoly power over its competitors due to the uniqueness of its product, better location, slightly lower prices, better service, greater range of products, and so on. Yet, this market power is very limited due to the availability of close substitutes.

Because each firm produces a somewhat different product under monopolistic competition, we cannot define the industry (which refers to the producers of an *identical* product). Chamberlin, who introduced the theory of monopolistic competition in the early 1930s, sought to overcome this difficulty by lumping all the sellers of *similar* products into a **product group.** For simplicity, we will continue to use the term "industry" here, but in this broader sense (i.e., to refer to all the sellers of the differentiated products in a product group). However, because of product differentiation, we cannot derive the industry demand and supply curves as we did under perfect competition, and we do not have a single equilibrium price for the differentiated product, but a cluster of prices. Thus, our graphic analysis will have to be confined to the "typical" or "representative" firm rather than to the industry. Under monopolistic competition, firms can affect the volume of their sales by changing the product price, by changing the characteristics of the product, or by varying their selling expenses (such as advertising). We will deal with each of these choice-related variables next.

Product group
The sellers of a differentiated product.

MONOPOLISTIC COMPETITION: SHORT-RUN AND LONG-RUN ANALYSIS

11.2

In this section, we examine how a monopolistically competitive firm determines its best level of output and price in the short run and in the long run on the assumption that the firm has already decided on the characteristics of the product to produce and on the selling expenses to incur. Later, we examine product variation and selling expenses and evaluate the theory of monopolistic competition.

Price and Output Decisions Under Monopolistic Competition

Because a monopolistically competitive firm produces a differentiated product, the demand curve it faces is negatively sloped; but since there are many close substitutes for the product, the demand curve is highly price elastic. The price elasticity of demand is higher the smaller is the degree of product differentiation. As in the case of monopoly, since the demand curve facing a monopolistic competitor is negatively sloped, the corresponding marginal revenue curve is below it, with the same price intercept and twice the absolute slope. As for firms under any type of market structure, the best level of output for the monopolistically competitive firm in the short run is where marginal revenue equals marginal cost, provided that price exceeds the average variable cost. This is shown in the left panel of Figure 11.1.

The left panel of Figure 11.1 shows that the best level of output for the typical or representative monopolistically competitive firm in the short run is six units and is given by point E, at which $MR = SMC$. At $Q < 6$, $MR > SMC$ and the total profits of the firm increase by expanding output. At $Q > 6$, $SMC > MR$ and the total profits of the firm increase by *reducing* output. To sell the best level of output (i.e., six units) the firm charges

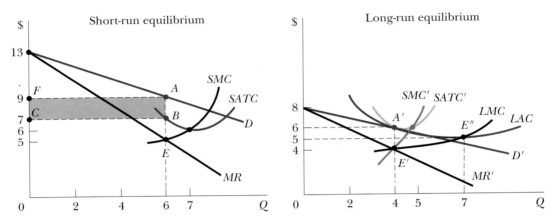

FIGURE 11.1   Short-Run and Long-Run Price and Output Determination Under Monopolistic Competition   The left panel shows that in the short run the firm produces six units, given by point *E*, where *MR* = *SMC*. At *Q* = 6, *P* = $9 (point *A* on the *D* curve) and *SATC* = $7 (point *B*), so that the firm maximizes profits of *AB* = $2 per unit and *ABCF* = $12 in total (the shaded area). The right panel shows that in the long run the firm produces four units, given by point *E'*, where *MR'* = *LMC* = *SMC'*. At *Q* = 4, *P* = *LAC* = *SATC'* = $6 (point *A'*), so that the firm breaks even. This compares to *Q* = 7, where *P* = lowest *LAC* = $5 (point *E''*) under long-run perfectly competitive equilibrium.

a price of $9 per unit (point *A* on the *D* curve). Since at *Q* = 6, *SATC* = $7 (point *B* in the figure), the monopolistic competitor earns a profit of *AB* = $2 per unit and *ABCF* = $12 in total (the shaded area in the figure). As in the case of a perfectly competitive firm and monopolist, the monopolistic competitor can earn profits, break even, or incur losses in the short run. If at the best level of output, *P* > *SATC*, the firm earns a profit; if *P* = *SATC*, the firm breaks even; and if *P* < *SATC*, the firm incurs losses, but it minimizes losses by continuing to produce as long as *P* > *AVC*. Finally, since the demand curve facing a monopolistic competitor is negatively sloped, *MR* = *SMC* < *P* at the best level of output, so that (as in the case of monopoly) the rising portion of the *MC* curve above the *AVC* curve does not represent the short-run supply curve of the monopolistic competitor.

Since the firm in the left panel of Figure 11.1 earns profits in the short run, more firms will enter the market in the long run because entry is easy. With more firms sharing the market, the demand curve facing each monopolistic competitor shifts to the left (as its market share decreases) until it becomes tangent to the firm's *LAC* curve. Thus, in the long run, all monopolistically competitive firms break even and produce on the negatively sloped portion of their *LAC* curve (rather than at the lowest point, as in the case of perfect competition). This is shown in the right panel of Figure 11.1.

In the right panel of Figure 11.1, *D'* is the new demand curve facing the monopolistically competitive firm in the long run. Demand curve *D'* is lower and more price elastic than demand curve *D* that the firm faced in the short run. This is because, as more firms enter the monopolistically competitive market in the long run (attracted by potential profits), the monopolistic competitor is left with a smaller share of the market and faces greater competition from the greater range of (differentiated) products that becomes available in the long run. Demand curve *D'* is tangent to the *LAC* and *SATC'* curves at

✓ Concept Check
Why does a monopolistic competitor break even when in long-run equilibrium?

✓ Concept Check
Why are efficiency and welfare loss not very large under monopolistic competition?

Excess capacity A larger-than-optimal plant.

Product variation
Differences in some of the characteristics of a product.

Selling expenses
Expenditures to induce consumers to purchase more of its product.

point A'—the output at which $MR' = LMC = SMC'$ (point E' in the figure). Thus, the monopolistic competitor sells four units of the product at the price of $6 per unit and breaks even in the long run (as compared to $Q = 6$ and $P = \$9$ and profits of $2 per unit and $12 in total in the short run). At any other price, the monopolistically competitive firm would incur losses in the long run, and with a different number of firms it would not break even.

The fact that the monopolistically competitive firm produces to the left of the lowest point on its LAC curve when in long-run equilibrium means that the average cost of production and price of the product under monopolistic competition are higher than under perfect competition ($6 at point A' as compared with $5 at point E'', respectively, in the right panel of Figure 11.1). This difference, however, is not large, because the demand curve faced by the monopolistic competitor is very elastic. In any event, the slightly higher LAC and P under monopolistic competition than under perfect competition can be regarded as the cost that consumers willingly pay for having a variety of differentiated products appealing to different consumer tastes, rather than a single undifferentiated product.

The difference between the level of output indicated by the lowest point on the LAC curve and the monopolistic competitor's output when in long-run equilibrium measures **excess capacity.** In the right panel of Figure 11.1, excess capacity is three units, given by $Q = 7$ at the lowest point on the LAC curve minus $Q = 4$, indicated by point A' on the LAC curve, at which the firm produces in the long run. Excess capacity permits more firms to exist (i.e., it leads to some overcrowding) in monopolistically competitive markets as compared with perfect competition. Consumers, however, seem to prefer that firms selling some services operate with some unused capacity (i.e., they are willing to pay a slightly higher price for getting a haircut, filling up on gasoline, checking out at a grocery store, and eating at a restaurant) so as to avoid waiting in long lines.

Product Variation and Selling Expenses

Under monopolistic competition, a firm can increase its expenditures on product variation and selling effort to increase the demand for its product and make it more price inelastic. **Product variation** refers to changes in some of the characteristics of the product that a monopolistic competitor undertakes in order to make its product more appealing to consumers. For example, producers may reduce the sugar and increase the fiber content of breakfast cereals. **Selling expenses** are all those expenses that the firm incurs to advertise the product, increase its sales force, provide better service for its product, and so on. Product variation and selling expenses can increase the firm's sales and profits, but they also lead to additional costs. A firm should spend more on product variation and selling effort as long as the MR from these efforts exceeds the MC and until $MR = MC$ (*see Example 1–4*). While spending more on product variation and selling effort (nonprice competition) can increase profits in the short run, monopolistically competitive firms will break even in the long run because of imitation and the entrance of new firms. This is shown in Figure 11.2.

In Figure 11.2, D'' and MR'' are demand and marginal revenue curves that are higher than D' and MR' in the right panel of Figure 11.1 as a result of greater product variation and selling expenses. The LAC curve is that of Figure 11.1, while $LAC*$ and $LMC*$ are the long-run average and marginal cost curves resulting from greater product variation and selling expenses. Note that the vertical distance between $LAC*$ and LAC increases on the (realistic) assumption that to sell greater quantities of the product requires larger expenses

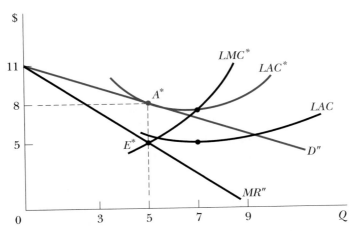

FIGURE 11.2   Long-Run Equilibrium with Product Variation and Selling Expenses   Curves D'' and MR'', as well as LAC^* and LMC^*, are higher than in the right panel of Figure 11.1 because of the firm's greater expenses on product variation and selling effort. While these efforts can increase the firm's profits in the short run, in the long run the firm breaks even. This is shown by point A^*, at which $Q = 5$ units and $P = LAC^* = \$8$, and $MR'' = LMC^*$ (point E^*). At point A^* the firm charges a higher price and sells a greater quantity than at point A' in the right panel of Figure 11.1, but the firm will nevertheless only break even in the long run.

per unit on product variation and selling effort. While these efforts can lead to larger short-run profits, however, our typical or representative firm will break even in the long run because other firms can also increase product variation and selling expenses, and more firms can also enter the market in the long run. The long-run equilibrium of our representative firm is given by point A^* in Figure 11.2, at which $Q = 5$ and $P = LAC^* = \$8$ and $MR'' = LMC^*$ (point E^*). At point A^* the firm charges a higher price and sells a greater quantity than at point A' in the right panel of Figure 11.1, but the firm will nevertheless break even in the long run. If all firms selling similar products increase their expenses on product variation and selling effort, each firm may retain only its share of an expanding market in the long run.

Two important questions arise with respect to selling expenses in general and advertising in particular. First, is advertising manipulative, and does it create false needs? Second, does advertising increase or reduce the degree of competition in a market? The manipulative view that advertising creates false needs has been forcefully advanced by Galbraith.[1] Why, Galbraith asks, would firms keep spending millions on advertising if it didn't work? Recent studies on cigarette and beer consumption in the United States and Canada, however, have shown that although advertising does affect brand choices, it does not seem to be very effective in increasing the overall consumption of a product. With regard to the second question, a recent study has found that industries with higher-than-average advertising expenditures relative to sales had lower rates of price increases and

[1] J. K. Galbraith, *The Affluent Society* (Boston: Houghton Mifflin, 1958).

higher rates of output increases than the average for 150 major U.S. industries studied from 1963 to 1977.[2] Thus, on balance (and as Example 11–1 clearly indicates), advertising seems to enhance, rather than restrict, competition. Even though some advertising is manipulative and can act as a barrier to entry, a great deal of it is informative and increases market competition. More will be said about advertising in Chapter 19, which deals with the economics of information.

EXAMPLE 11–1

Advertisers Are Taking on Competitors by Name ... and Are Being Sued

Since 1981 when the National Association of Broadcasters abolished its guidelines against making disparaging remarks against competitors' products, advertisers have taken their glovess off and begun to praise the superior qualities of their products, not compared to "brand X" as before 1981 but by identifying competitors' products by name. The Federal Trade Commission welcomed the change because it anticipated that this would increase competition and lead to better-quality products at lower prices. Some of these hopes have in fact been realized. For example, the price of eyeglasses was found to be much higher in states that prohibited advertising by optometrists and opticians than in states that allowed such advertising, without any increase in the probability of having the wrong eyeglass prescription. Similarly, the price of an uncontested divorce dropped from $350 to $150 in Phoenix, Arizona, after the Supreme Court allowed advertising for legal services.

Although less sportsmanlike and possibly resulting in legal suits, advertisers have been willing to take on competitors by name because the technique seems very effective. For example, Burger King's sales soared when it began to attack McDonald's by name, when AT&T attacked MCI pricing, and when Unilever named Proctor & Gamble's competitive products specifically. Sectors where comparative advertising are most common include food, retail, automobiles, airlines and, more recently, law. U.S. and European courts have generally allowed comparison advertising, unless dishonest or inaccurate. Thus, the courts threw out the suit and countersuit between Gillette and Wilkinson allowing each to claim superior blades, RBS Bank's to claim its credit cards as superior to Barkleys', and Rayner to claim its tickets were a lot cheaper than British Airway's. A Belgian Court, however, ruled as defamatory Rayner's advertisement with a picture of the Brussels landmark the "Mannequin Pis," a statue of a boy urinating, and the line "Pissed off by Sabene's high fares?"

Sources: "Advertisers Remove the Cover from Brand X," *U.S. News & World Report*, December 19, 1983, pp. 75–76; L. Benham, "The Effect of Advertising on the Price of Eyeglasses," *Journal of Law and Economics*, October 1973, pp. 337–352; "Lawyers Are Facing Surge in Competition as Courts Drop Curbs," *Wall Street Journal*, October 18, 1978, p. 1; "A Comeback May Be Ahead for Brand X," *Business Week*, December 1989, p. 35; "Long-Distance Risks of AT&T MCI War," *Wall Street Journal*, April 14, 1993, p. B9; "Marketeers Increasingly Dispute Health Claims of Rivals' Products," *Wall Street Journal*, April 4, 2002, p. B1; and http://www.bynoother.com/2003/08/comparativ_adv.html

---

[2] E. W. Eckard, "Advertising, Concentration Changes, and Consumer Welfare," *Review of Economics and Statistics,* May 1988, pp. 340–343; and "Cigarette Advertising and Competition," *The Margin,* March/April 1990, p. 22.

How Useful Is the Theory of Monopolistic Competition?

When the theory of monopolistic competition was introduced 70 years ago, it was hailed as a significant theoretical breakthrough. Today, economists have grown somewhat disenchanted with it. There are several reasons for this disenchantment.

First, it may be difficult to define the market and determine the firms and products to include in the theory. For example, should moist paper tissues be included with other paper tissues or with soaps? Are toothpaste, dental floss, toothpicks, and water picks part of the same market or product group?

Second, and more important, in markets where there are many small sellers, product differentiation has been found to be slight. As a result, the demand curve facing the monopolistic competitor is close to being horizontal. Under these circumstances, the perfectly competitive model provides a good approximation to the monopolistically competitive solution, and it is also much easier to use for analysis.[3]

Third, in many markets where there are strong brand preferences, it usually turns out that there are only a few producers, so that the market is oligopolistic rather than monopolistically competitive. For example, while there are numerous brands of breakfast cereals, cigarettes, toothpaste, detergents, soaps, and many other consumer products on the market today (so that the markets may seem to be monopolistically competitive), on closer examination we find that these products are produced by only four or five very large firms (so that the market is in fact oligopolistic). Millions of dollars are likely to be needed to develop and promote a new product in these markets, and this represents a significant barrier to entry into the market. In fact, only a handful of firms have been able to enter these markets during the past two decades.

Fourth (and related to the third point), even in a market where there are many small sellers of a product or service (say, gasoline stations), a change in price by one seller may have little or no effect on most other gasoline stations located far away from it, but the price change will have a significant impact on competitors in the immediate vicinity. These nearby stations are, therefore, likely to react to a reduction in price or to an increased promotional effort on the part of the nearby station. The nearby station is also likely to be aware of this fact and consider it in deciding to change its price or in undertaking a new promotional effort. In cases such as this, the oligopoly model is more appropriate than the model of monopolistic competition.

Despite these serious criticisms, the monopolistically competitive model does provide some important insights, such as the emphasis on product differentiation and selling expenses, which are also applicable to oligopolistic markets, to which we turn next.

OLIGOPOLY: INTERDEPENDENCE AMONG THE FEW PRODUCERS IN THE INDUSTRY

| 11.3 |

Oligopoly The market organization where there are few firms selling a product.

Oligopoly is the form of market organization in which there are few sellers of a homogeneous or differentiated product. If there are only two sellers, we have a **duopoly.** If the

Duopoly An oligopoly of two firms.

---

[3] The short-run and long-run analysis of monopolistic competition presented here is a simplification of the full-fledged monopolistically competitive model introduced by Chamberlin in 1933 (see E. Chamberlin, *The Theory of Monopolistic Competition* (Cambridge, MA: Harvard University Press, 1933).

Pure oligopoly An oligopoly where the product of the firms in the industry is homogeneous.

Differentiated oligopoly An oligopoly where the product is differentiated.

product is homogeneous, we have a **pure oligopoly.** If the product is differentiated, we have a **differentiated oligopoly.** Although entry into an oligopolistic industry is possible, it is not easy (as evidenced by the fact that there are only a few firms in the industry). While there are many firms selling a homogeneous product under perfect competition, many firms selling a differentiated product in monopolistic competition, and only a single firm selling a product with no good substitutes under monopoly, under oligopoly there are few sellers of a homogeneous or differentiated product.

Oligopoly is the most prevalent form of market organization in the manufacturing sector of the United States and other industrial countries. Some oligopolistic industries in the United States are cigarettes, beer, aircraft, breakfast cereals, automobiles, tires, soap and detergents, office machinery, and many others. Some of the products (such as steel and aluminum) are homogeneous, whereas others (such as cigarettes, beer, breakfast cereals, and soaps and detergents) are differentiated. For simplicity, we will deal mostly with pure oligopolies (where products are homogeneous) in this chapter.

Because there are only a few firms selling a homogeneous or differentiated product in oligopolistic markets, the action of each firm affects the other firms in the industry, and vice versa. For example, when GM introduced zero-interest financing or price rebates in the sale of its automobiles, Ford and other car manufacturers selling on the American market immediately followed with zero-interest financing and price rebates of their own. Furthermore, since price competition can lead to ruinous price wars, oligopolists usually prefer to compete on the basis of product differentiation, advertising, and service. Yet, even here, if GM mounts a major advertising campaign, Ford and Chrysler are likely to soon respond in kind. Every time that Coca-Cola or Pepsi mounts a major advertising campaign, the other usually responds with a large advertising campaign of its own.

From what has been said, it is clear that the distinguishing characteristic of oligopoly is the *interdependence* or rivalry among firms in the industry. This interdependence is the natural result of fewness. Since an oligopolist knows that its own actions will have a significant impact on the other oligopolists in the industry, each oligopolist must consider the possible reaction of competitors in deciding its pricing policies, the degree of product differentiation to introduce, the level of advertising to undertake, the amount of service to provide, and so on. Because competitors can react in many different ways (depending on the nature of the industry, the type of product, etc.), we do not have a single oligopoly model but many—each based on the particular behavioral response of competitors to the actions of the first. Because of interdependence, policy decisions on the part of the firm are also much more complex under oligopoly than under other forms of market organization. In this chapter, we present some of the most important oligopoly models. We must keep in mind, however, that each model is usually applicable only to some specific situations, rather than generally, and that most models are more or less unrealistic.

The sources of oligopoly are generally the same as for monopoly: (1) economies of scale may operate over a sufficiently large range of outputs so as to leave only a few firms supplying the entire market; (2) huge capital investments and specialized inputs are usually required to enter an oligopolistic industry (say, automobiles, aluminum, steel, and similar industries), and this acts as an important natural barrier to entry; (3) a few firms may own a patent for the exclusive right to produce a commodity or to use a particular production process; (4) established firms might have a loyal following of customers based on product quality and service that new firms may find very difficult to match; (5) a few firms may own or control the entire supply of a raw material required in the production of the product; and (6) the government may award a franchise to only a few firms to operate in the market. These are not only the sources of oligopoly but also represent the barriers

✔ Concept Check
Why do we have many oligopoly models rather than a single one?

Concentration ratio
The percentage of total
industry sales of the
largest firms in the
industry.

to other firms entering the market in the long run. If entry were not so restricted, the industry would not remain oligopolistic in the long run.

The degree by which an industry is dominated by a few large firms is measured by **concentration ratios,** which give the percentage of total industry sales of the 4, 8, or 12 largest firms in the industry (see Example 11–2). An industry in which the 4-firm concentration ratio is close to 100 is clearly oligopolistic, and industries where this ratio is higher than 50% or 60% are also likely to be oligopolistic. The 4-firm concentration ratio for most manufacturing industries in the United States is between 20% and 80%. As we will see, however, concentration ratios must be used and interpreted with great caution since they may greatly overestimate the market power of the largest firms in an industry.

EXAMPLE 11-2
Industrial Concentration in the United States

Table 11.1 gives the 4-firm and the 8-firm concentration ratios for various industries in the United States from the 2002 Census of Manufacturers (the latest available).

There are several reasons, however, for using these concentration ratios cautiously. First, in industries where imports are significant, concentration ratios may

TABLE 11.1   Concentration Ratios in the United States, 2002

Industry	4-Firm Ratio	8-Firm Ratio
Cigarettes	95	99
Breweries	91	94
Electric lamp bulbs and parts	89	94
Aircraft	81	94
Motor vehicles	81	91
Breakfast cereals	78	91
Office machines	75	86
Tires	73	87
Soap and detergents	61	72
Soft drinks	52	64
Computers	50	65
Men's clothing	49	62
Iron and steel mills	44	58
Petroleum refining	41	64
Cement	39	60
Book printing	38	54
Pharmaceuticals and medicines	34	49
Stationary	29	45
Canned fruits and vegetables	24	38
Women's dresses	22	32

greatly overestimate the relative importance of the largest firms in the industry. For example, since automobile imports represent about 29% of U.S. auto sales, the real 4-firm concentration ratio in the automobile industry (which includes Honda's U.S. output as the fourth-largest U.S. producer) is not 81% (as indicated in the table) but 58% (i.e., 81% times 0.71). Second, concentration ratios refer to the nation as a whole, even though the relevant market may be local. For example, the 4-firm concentration ratio for the cement industry is 39%, but, because of very high transportation costs, only two or three firms may actually compete in many local markets. Third, how broadly or narrowly a product is defined is also very important. For example, the concentration ratio in the office machines industry as a whole is smaller than that in the personal computer segment of the market. Fourth, concentration ratios do not give any indication of potential entrants into the market and of the degree of actual and potential competition in the industry. Indeed, as the *theory of contestable markets* discussed in Chapter 13 shows, vigorous competition can take place even among few sellers. In short, concentration ratios provide only one dimension of the degree of competition in the market, and, although useful, they must be consulted with great caution.

Source: U.S. Bureau of Census, 2002 Census of Manufacturers, *Concentration Ratios in Manufacturing* (Washington, DC: U.S. Government Printing Office, May 2006), Table 2, pp. 2–65.

11.4   THE COURNOT AND THE KINKED–DEMAND CURVE MODELS

✔ Concept Check
Why is the Cournot model unrealistic? Why do we study it then?

Now we examine two of the earliest and best-known oligopoly models: the Cournot model and the kinked–demand curve model. In the Cournot model, oligopolists never recognize their interdependence or rivalry. As such, the Cournot model is quite unrealistic. Nevertheless, the model is useful in highlighting the interdependence that exists among oligopolistic firms (even though they do not actually recognize it). The Cournot model is also the forerunner of more realistic models. In the kinked–demand curve model, oligopolists do recognize their interdependence or rivalry. This model also faces many shortcomings, but it represents a step forward in the direction of greater realism in the analysis of oligopolistic behavior.

The Cournot Model: Interdependence Not Recognized[4]

The first formal oligopoly model was introduced by the French economist Augustin Cournot more than 160 years ago.[5] For simplicity, Cournot assumed that there were only two firms (duopoly) selling identical spring water. Consumers came to the springs with their own containers, so that the marginal cost of production was zero for the two firms. With these assumptions, the analysis is greatly simplified without losing the essence of the model.[6]

---

[4] A more advanced and complete treatment of the Cournot model, as well as an important extension of it (the Stackelberg model), is provided in the appendix to this chapter.

[5] A. Cournot, *Recherches sur les principes mathematiques de la theorie des richess* (Paris: 1838). English translation by N. Bacon, *Researches into the Mathematical Principles of the Theory of Wealth* (New York: Macmillan, 1897).

[6] The model, however, can be extended to deal with more than two firms and nonzero marginal costs.

Cournot model The duopoly model in which each firm assumes that the other keeps output constant.

The basic behavioral assumption made in the **Cournot model** is that each firm, while trying to maximize profits, assumes that the other duopolist holds its *output* constant at the existing level. The result is a cycle of moves and countermoves by the duopolists until each sells one-third of the total industry output. This is shown in Figure 11.3.

In the left panel of Figure 11.3, D is the market demand curve for spring water. Initially, firm A is the only firm in the market, and thus, it faces the total market demand curve. That is, $D = d_A$. The marginal revenue curve of firm A is then mr_A (see the figure). Since the marginal cost is zero, the MC curve coincides with the horizontal axis. Under these circumstances, firm A maximizes total profits where $mr_A = MC = 0$. Firm A sells six units of spring water at $P = \$6$ so that its total revenue (TR) is $36 (point A in the left panel). This is the monopoly solution. Note that point A is the midpoint of demand curve $D = d_A$, at which price elasticity is 1 and TR is maximum (see Section 5.6). With total costs equal to zero, total profits equal $TR = \$36$.

Next, assume that firm B enters the market and believes that firm A will continue to sell six units. The demand curve that firm B faces is then d_B in the left panel, which is obtained by subtracting the six units sold by firm A from market demand curve D (i.e., shifting D six units to the left). The marginal revenue curve of firm B is then mr_B. Firm B maximizes total profits where $mr_B = MC = 0$. Therefore, firm B sells three units at $P = \$3$ (point B, the midpoint of d_B). This is also shown in the right panel of Figure 11.3. Assuming that firm B continues to sell three units, firm A reacts and faces d_A, in the

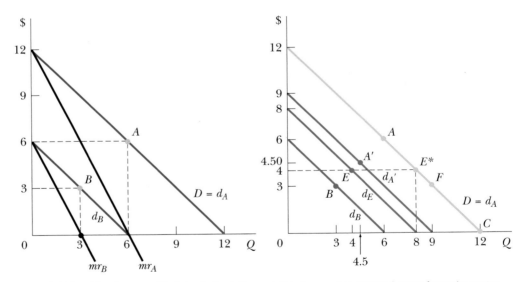

FIGURE 11.3   The Cournot Model   In the left panel, D is the market demand curve for spring water. The marginal cost of production is assumed to be zero. When only firm A is the market, $D = d_A$ and the firm maximizes profits by selling $Q = 6$ at $P = \$6$ (point A, given by $mr_A = MC = 0$). When firm B enters the market, it will face d_B (given by shifting market demand curve D to the left by the six units sold by A). Firm B maximizes profits by selling $Q = 3$ at $P = \$3$ (point B, the midpoint of d_B at which $mr_B = MC = 0$). Duopolist A now faces d'_A (given by D minus 3 in the right panel) and maximizes profits by selling $Q = 4.5$ at $P = \$4.50$ (point A'). The process continues until each duopolist is at point E on d_E and sells $Q = 4$ at $P = \$4$.

right panel of Figure 11.3 (obtained by subtracting the three units supplied by firm B from market demand curve D). Firm A will then maximize profits by selling 4.5 units (point A', at the midpoint of $d_{A'}$ in the right panel). Firm B now reacts once again and maximizes profits on its new demand curve, which is obtained by shifting market demand curve D to the left by the 4.5 units supplied by firm A (not shown in the right panel of Figure 11.3).

The process continues until each duopolist faces demand curve d_E and maximizes profits by selling four units at $P = \$4$ (point E in the right panel of Figure 11.3).[7] This is equilibrium because whichever firm faces demand curve d_E and reaches point E first, the other will also face d_E (obtained by subtracting the 4 units sold by the first duopolist from market demand curve D) and maximize profits at point E. With each duopolist selling four units, a combined total of eight units will be sold in the market at $P = \$4$ (point E^* on D in the right panel of Figure 11.3). If the market had been organized along perfectly competitive lines, sales would have been twelve units, given by point C, where market demand curve D intercepts the horizontal axis. The reason for this is that since we have assumed costs to be zero, price will also have to be zero for each competitive firm to break even, as required, when the perfectly competitive industry is in long-run equilibrium.

Thus, the duopolists supply one-third or four units each (and two-thirds or eight units together) of the total perfectly competitive market quantity of twelve units. Note that the Cournot duopoly outcome of $P = \$4$ and $Q = 8$ lies between the monopoly equilibrium of $P = \$6$ and $Q = 6$ and the competitive equilibrium of $P = \$0$ and $Q = 12$. The final Cournot equilibrium reflects the interdependence between the duopolists, even though they (rather naively) do not recognize it.

In a more advanced treatment, we could show that with three oligopolists, each would supply one-fourth (i.e., three units) of the perfectly competitive market of twelve units and three-fourths (i.e., nine units) in total. Note that when $Q = 9$, $P = \$3$ on market demand curve D (point F in the right panel of Figure 11.3). Thus, as the number of firms increases, the total combined output of all the firms together increases and price falls (compare equilibrium point A with only firm A in the market, with equilibrium point E^* with firms A and B, and equilibrium point F with three firms). Eventually, as more firms enter, the market will no longer be oligopolistic. In the limit, with many firms, total output will approach twelve units and price will approach zero (the perfectly competitive solution—point C in the right panel of Figure 11.3).

The same result (i.e., zero profit) would occur even with only two firms (duopoly), if each firm assumed that the other kept its *price* rather than its quantity constant (as in the Cournot model). In that case, the first firm enters the market and maximizes its profits by producing six units at the price of $6. The second firm, assuming that the first will keep its price constant, will lower its price just a little and captures the entire market (because the product is homogeneous). The first firm will then react by lowering its price even more and recaptures the entire market. If the duopolists do not recognize their interdependence (as in the Cournot model), the process will continue until each firm sells six units at zero price and makes zero profits. This is the **Bertrand model.**[8]

Bertrand model The duopoly model in which each firm assumes that the other will keep its price constant.

---

[7] How this equilibrium is reached is shown in the appendix to this chapter. All that is important at this point is to show that when each duopolist faces demand curve d_E and sells four units at $P = \$4$ (i.e., is at point E), each duopolist and the market as a whole is in equilibrium.

[8] J. Bertrand, "Theorie Mathematique de la Richesse Sociale," *Journal de Savantes,* 1983.

The Kinked–Demand Curve Model: Interdependence Recognized

Kinked–demand curve model The model that seeks to explain price rigidity by postulating a demand curve with a kink at the prevailing price.

The **kinked–demand curve model,** introduced by Paul Sweezy in 1939,[9] attempts to explain the price rigidity that is often observed in some oligopolistic markets. Sweezy postulated that if an oligopolist raised its price, it would lose most of its customers because the other firms in the industry would not match the price increase. On the other hand, an oligopolist could not increase its share of the market by lowering its price, since its competitors would immediately match the price reduction. As a result, according to Sweezy, oligopolists face a demand curve that is highly elastic for price increases and less elastic for price reductions. That is, the demand curve faced by oligopolists has a kink at the established price; and, because of this, oligopolists tend to keep prices constant even in the face of changed costs and demand conditions. This is shown in Figure 11.4.

In Figure 11.4, the demand curve facing the oligopolist is d or HBC and has a "kink" at the prevailing price of $8 and $Q = 4$ (point B). The demand curve is much more elastic above than below the kink on the assumption that competitors will not match price increases but quickly match price cuts.[10] Thus, the oligopolist's marginal revenue curve is mr, or $HJKFG$. Segment HJ of the mr curve corresponds to segment HB of the demand curve, and segment FG of the mr curve corresponds to segment BC of the demand curve (see the figure). The kink at point B on the demand curve results in discontinuity JF in the mr curve.

With SMC as the short-run marginal cost curve, the oligopolist will maximize profits by selling four units of output (given by point K, where the SMC curve intersects the discontinuous segment of the mr curve) at $P = \$8$. Any shift in the oligopolist's SMC curve that falls within the discontinuous segment of the mr curve will leave the oligopolist's price and output unchanged. That is, the oligopolist's best level of output will continue to

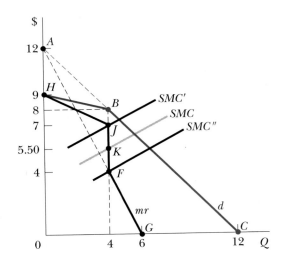

FIGURE 11.4 The Kinked-Demand Curve Model The demand curve facing the oligopolist is d or HBC and has a "kink" at the prevailing price of $8 and $Q = 4$ (point B), on the assumption that competitors match price cuts but not price increases. The marginal revenue curve is mr or $HJKFG$. The oligopolist maximizes profits by selling $Q = 4$ at $P = \$8$ (given by point K, where the SMC curve intersects the discontinuous segment of the mr curve). Any shift between SMC' and SMC'' will leave price and output unchanged.

[9] P. Sweezy, "Demand under Conditions of Oligopoly," *Journal of Political Economy,* August 1939, pp. 568–573.
[10] That is, since competitors do not match price increases, the quantity demanded from the oligopolist that increases price *falls a great deal.* On the other hand, since competitors quickly match price reductions, the quantity demanded from the oligopolist that cuts price *does not increase very much.* This makes the demand curve faced by an oligopolist more elastic for price increases than for price reductions.

be four units and price $8 for any shift in the *SMC* curve up to *SMC'* or down to *SMC"* (see the figure). Only if the *SMC* curve shifts above the *SMC'* curve will the oligopolist raise its price, and only if the *SMC* curve shifts below the *SMC"* curve will the oligopolist lower its price (see Problem 3). Similarly, a rightward or leftward shift in the demand curve will induce the oligopolist to increase or decrease output, respectively, but to keep its price unchanged if the kink remains at the same level (see Problem 4, with the answer at the end of the book). Note that the marginal principle postulating that the best level of output for the firm occurs where $MR = MC$ is still valid, even though the *MR* curve is discontinuous in this case.

When the kinked–demand curve model was first introduced, it was hailed by some economists as a general theory of oligopoly. Yet the model failed to live up to its expectations. For example, Stigler found no evidence that oligopolists were reluctant to match price increases as readily as price reductions, and thus he seriously questioned the existence of the kink.[11] Researchers in other oligopolistic industries found the same thing. Even more serious is the criticism that although the kinked–demand curve model can *rationalize* the existence of rigid prices where they occur, it cannot *explain* at what price the kink occurs in the first place. Since one of the major aims of microeconomic theory is to explain how prices are determined, this theory is, at best, incomplete.

✔ **Concept Check**
Does the kinked–demand curve model really explain price rigidity?

11.5   COLLUSION: CARTELS AND PRICE LEADERSHIP MODELS

Collusion An agreement among the suppliers of a commodity to restrict competition.

In the oligopoly models we have examined so far, oligopolists did not collude. In view of the interdependence in oligopolistic markets, however, there is a natural tendency to collude. With **collusion,** oligopolistic firms can avoid behavior that is detrimental to their general interest (for example, price wars) and adopt policies that increase their profits. Collusion can be overt (i.e., explicit), as in a centralized cartel, or tacit (i.e., implicit), as in price leadership models. In this section we examine oligopolistic models with collusion and provide several real-world examples. (Antitrust laws forbidding collusion in the United States are examined in Chapter 13.)

A Centralized Cartel Operates as a Monopolist

Cartel An organization of suppliers of a commodity aimed at restricting competition and increasing profits.

Centralized cartel A formal agreement of the suppliers of a commodity to operate as a monopoly.

A **cartel** is a formal organization of producers of a commodity. Its purpose is to coordinate the policies of the member firms so as to increase profits. Cartels are illegal in the United States under the provision of the Sherman Antitrust Act passed in 1890 (see Section 13.4) but not in some other nations. Of the many types of cartels, the **centralized cartel** is at one extreme. The centralized cartel sets the monopoly price for the commodity, allocates the monopoly output among the member firms, and determines how the monopoly profits are to be shared. The centralized cartel is shown in Figure 11.5.

In Figure 11.5, *D* is the total market demand curve and *MR* is the corresponding marginal revenue curve for a homogeneous commodity produced by, say, four firms that have formed a centralized cartel. The ΣSMC curve for the cartel is obtained by summing horizontally the *SMC* curve of the four firms on the assumption that input prices remain

[11] G. Stigler, "The Kinky Oligopoly Demand Curve and Rigid Prices," *Journal of Political Economy,* October 1947, pp. 432–449.

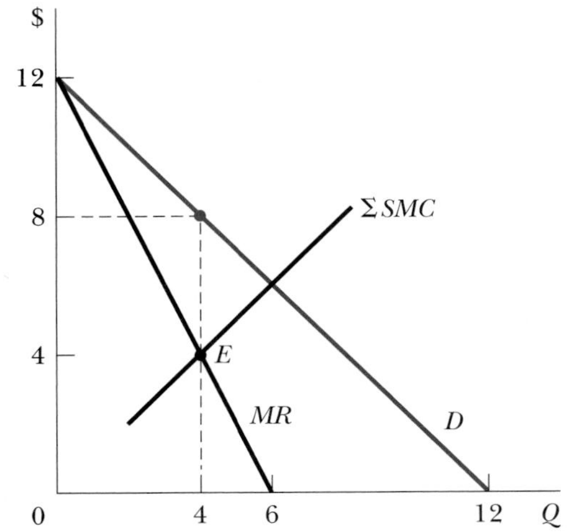

FIGURE 11.5   Centralized Cartel   *D* is the market demand curve and *MR* is the corresponding marginal revenue curve for a homogeneous commodity produced by the four firms in a centralized cartel. The Σ*SMC* curve for the cartel is obtained by summing horizontally the four firms' *SMC* curves on the assumption that input prices are constant. The centralized authority will set *P* = $8 and *Q* = 4 (given by point *E*, where the Σ*SMC* curve intersects the *MR* curve from below). This is the monopoly solution.

✓ Concept Check
In what way is a centralized cartel similar to a monopoly?

constant. The centralized authority will set $P = \$8$ and sell $Q = 4$ (given by point E, where the ΣSMC curve intersects the MR curve from below). This is the monopoly solution. To minimize production costs, the centralized authority will have to allocate output among the four firms in such a way that the SMC of the last unit produced by each firm is equal. If the SMC of one firm is higher than for the other firms, the total costs of the cartel as a whole can be reduced by shifting some production from the firm with higher SMC to the other firms until the SMC of the last unit produced by all firms is equal. The cartel will also have to decide on the distribution of profits.

If all firms are the same size and have identical cost curves, then it is very likely that each firm will be allocated the same output and will share equally in the profits generated by the cartel. In Figure 11.5, each firm would be allocated one unit of output. The result would be the same if a monopolist acquired the four firms and operated them as a multiplant monopolist. If the firms in the cartel are different sizes and have different costs, it will be more difficult to agree on the share of output and profits. Then the allocation of output is likely to be based on past output, present capacity, and bargaining ability of each firm, rather than on the equalization of the SMC of the last unit of output produced by all member firms. Sometimes the market is divided among the firms in the industry as indicated in the next subsection.

Cartels often fail; there are several reasons for this. First, it is very difficult to organize all the producers of a commodity if there are more than a few producers. Second, as pointed out earlier, it is difficult to reach agreement among the member firms on how to allocate output and profits when firms face different cost curves. Third, there is a strong incentive for each firm to remain outside the cartel or cheat on the cartel by selling more than its quota at the high price resulting from the limited output of the other cartel members. Fourth, monopoly profits are likely to attract other firms into the industry and undermine the cartel agreement.

Even though cartels are illegal in the United States, many trade associations and professional associations perform many of the functions usually associated with cartels. Some cartellike associations are actually sanctioned by the government. An example of this was the American Medical Association, which, by rigidly restricting the number of students admitted to medical schools and forbidding advertising by physicians, ensured for many years very high doctors' fees and incomes. Another example is the New York Taxi and Limousine Commission, which restricts the number of taxis licensed, thus conferring monopoly profits to the original owners of the "medallions" (see Example 10–3). The best example of a successful international cartel is OPEC (the Organization of Petroleum Exporting Countries) during the 1970s and early 1980s (see Example 11–3).

EXAMPLE 11–3

The Organization of Petroleum Exporting Countries (OPEC) Cartel

The Organization of Petroleum Exporting Countries (OPEC) is a cartel of petroleum exporters that seeks to increase the petroleum earnings of its members. Thirteen nations are presently members of OPEC: Algeria, Angola, Equador, Indonesia, Iran, Iraq, Kuwait, Libya, Nigeria, Qatar, Saudi Arabia, the United Arab Emirates, and Venezuela (Gabon was also a member but left).

As a result of supply shocks during the Arab–Israeli war in the fall of 1973 and the Iranian revolution during 1979–1980, OPEC was able to increase the price of petroleum from $2.50 per barrel in 1973 to more than $40 per barrel in 1980. This stimulated conservation in developed nations (lowering of thermostats, switching to small, fuel-efficient automobiles, etc.), expanded exploration and production (by the United Kingdom and Norway in the North Sea, by the United States in Alaska, by Mexico in newly discovered fields, and by Canada from the tar sands in Alberta), and switching to other energy sources (such as coal). As a result, from 1974 to 2008, OPEC's share of world oil production fell from 55% to 40% and its share of world petroleum exports declined from more than 90% to 45%. Although OPEC meets regularly for the purpose of setting petroleum prices and production quotas, petroleum prices remained below $20 per barrel under the conditions of excess supply that generally prevailed from 1985 to 1999 (except during Iraq's invasion of Kuwait in 1991). The average price of petroleum was between $20 and $30 from 2000 to 2003, but then it rose to an average of $56 in 2005, $72 in 2007, and reached $120 in April 2008.

✓ Concept Check
Is OPEC a centralized cartel?

There are several reasons for the sharp increase in crude prices since 2003, the most important being the sharp increase in petroleum consumption (especially by China) relative to production, the war in Iraq, the fear of supply disruption from a terrorist attack on production facilities in the Middle East. How high petroleum prices will be in the future depends on how strong world demand grows relative to supply, the political situation in the Middle East and in other petroleum-exporting countries, and how successful and willing OPEC is (with the cooperation of other, non-OPEC oil exporters, such as Russia, Mexico and Norway) to meet the world's growing demand of crude oil.

Sources: "OPEC's Painful Lessons," *New York Times* (December 29, 1985), p. F3; "OPEC Sets New Policy on Quota," *New York Times* (November 29, 1989), p. D1; "OPEC Plan to Lift Oil Prices Goes Awry," *Wall Street Journal* (March 3, 1995), p. A2; "Mid East and Venezuela Turmoil Sends Oil Prices into Wild Swing," *New York Times* (April 9, 2002), p. 1; "Fuel Gold," *The Economist* (March 12, 2005), p. 71; "OPEC" http://en.wikipedia.org/wiki/OPEC, 2008; and "Record Run Brings Guide Close to $1200 Barrell," *Financial Times*, April 26, 2008.

Market-Sharing Cartel

Market-sharing cartel
An organization of suppliers of a commodity that divides the market among its members.

The difficulties encountered by the members of a centralized cartel (such as agreeing on the price to charge, allocating output and profits among members, and avoiding cheating) make a market-sharing cartel more likely to occur. In a **market-sharing cartel** the member firms agree only on how to share the market. Each firm then operates in only one area or region agreed upon without encroaching on the others' territories. An example is the agreement in the early part of this century between Du Pont (American) and Imperial Chemical (English) for the former to have exclusive selling rights for their products in North America (except for British colonies) and the latter in the British Empire. Under certain simplifying assumptions, a market-sharing cartel can also result in the monopoly solution. This is shown in Figure 11.6.

In Figure 11.6, we assume that there are two identical firms selling a homogeneous product and deciding to share the market equally. D is the total market demand for the commodity; d is the half-share demand curve of each firm, and mr is the corresponding marginal revenue curve. If each firm has the same SMC curve as shown in the figure, according to the marginal principle, each will sell two units of output at $P = \$8$ (given by point E', at which $mr = SMC$). Thus, the duopolists together will sell the monopolist output of four units at $P = \$8$ (see the figure). In the real world there may be more than two firms, each may have different cost curves, and the market may not be shared equally. Thus, we are not likely to have the neat monopoly solution shown above. The firm with greater capacity or operating in an inferior territory may demand a greater share of the market. The result will then depend on bargaining, and the possibility of incursions into each other's territory cannot be excluded.

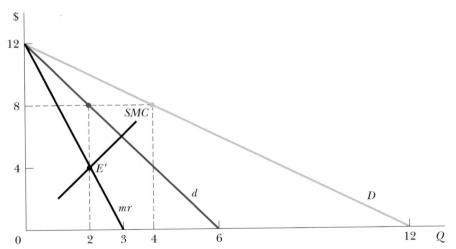

FIGURE 11.6   Market-Sharing Cartel D is the total market demand for a homogeneous commodity, d is the half-share demand curve of each firm, and mr is the corresponding marginal revenue curve. If each duopolist also has the same SMC curve shown in the figure, each will sell two units of output at $P = \$8$ (given by point E', at which $mr = SMC$). Thus, the duopolists together will sell the monopolist output of four units at $P = \$8$.

The firms in a market-sharing cartel can also operate in the same geographic area by deciding which firm is to fill each particular contract. These market-sharing cartels are likely to be unstable due to cheating. Some loose market-sharing cartels are sanctioned by law. For example, local medical and bar associations essentially set the fees that doctors and lawyers are to charge. Similarly, many states had *fair trade laws* (until they became illegal in the mid-1970s), that allowed manufacturers to set the price each retailer was to charge for a product. The market was then shared by means other than price.

EXAMPLE 11–4
The Market Sharing Ivy League Cartel and Financial-Aid Leveraging

For more than three decades prior to 1991, the presidents and top financial officers of the eight Ivy League colleges (Brown, Columbia, Cornell, Dartmouth, Harvard, Princeton, Yale, and the University of Pennsylvania), as well as the Massachusetts Institute of Technology (MIT), held yearly meetings at which they exchanged sensitive information about intended tuition increases, the amount of student financial aid packages, and increases in faculty salaries. The result was tuition increases, student financial aid packages, and faculty salary increases that were closely bunched together. For example, the charge for tuition, room, board, and fees at the eight Ivy League colleges and MIT ranged only from $16,841 to $17,100 for the 1988–1989 academic year. The same was true for increases in faculty salaries and for the amount of student aid packages. Specifically, the colleges agreed not to outbid each other in granting aid to top students who had been accepted to more than one school, thus leaving students and their families no reason to shop around for better financial aid packages. In 1986, this "Ivy League cartel" tried to bring Stanford University into the fold—an attempt that failed because (as court documents later showed) Stanford was worried that the Ivies were colluding illegally. Indeed, this is what the U.S. Justice Department subsequently charged.

In May 1991, the Ivy League colleges (while admitting no wrongdoing) signed a consent decree with the Justice Department to stop colluding on tuition, financial aid, and faculty salaries in order to avoid a costly trial, thereby putting an end to their cartel arrangement. The result was clear and immediate: Average increases in private-college tuition, which had soared fivefold between 1971–1972 and 1989–1990 in the face of only a tripling of consumer prices, subsided and were much smaller after 1990. MIT, however, refused to sign the consent decree and chose instead to fight the case in court, where it argued that antitrust laws did not apply to the noncommercial and charitable activities of universities. But in a ten-day trial in August 1992 that cost MIT $1 million, the court found MIT guilty of price fixing and restricting competition by reducing students' ability to get the best financial aid possible. In September 1993, however, a three-judge U.S. Court of Appeals panel reversed the lower court ruling, setting the stage for a settlement, reached in December 1993, under which the Ivy League Universities could meet to discuss their financial-aid policies, as long as they did not discuss individual grants to specific students and accepted students regardless of need (the so-called need-blind admission). As pointed out in Example 10-5, most private colleges (not just Ivies) today engage in "financial leveraging." Thus, the market-sharing cartel of the Ivies has been replaced with broad first-degree price (tuition) discrimination by most private colleges, which increases their tuition revenues.

Sources: "Ivy League Discussions on Finances Extended to Tuition and Salaries," *Wall Street Journal,* May 8, 1992, p. A1; "M.I.T. Ruled Guilty in Antitrust Case," *New York Times,* September 3, 1992, p. 1; "Antitrust Case Against MIT Dropped Allowing Limited Exchange of Aid Data," *Wall Street Journal,* December 12, 1993, p. A12; "Colleges Manipulate Financial-Aid Offers, Shortchanging Many," *Wall Street Journal,* April 1, 1996, p. A1; D. M. Lang, "Financial Aid and Student Bargaining Power," *B.E. Journal of Economic Analysis & Policy,* No. 1, 2007, pp. 1–21; and College Board, *Trends in College Pricing* and *Trends in Student Aid* (Washington DC: 2007).

Price Leadership

Price leadership The form of market collusion whereby a firm initiates a price change and the other firms in the industry soon match it.

Barometric firm A firm that is recognized as a true interpreter or barometer of the industry.

✔ Concept Check
How does price leadership seek to overcome the charge of illegal collusion?

One way by which firms in an oligopolistic market can make necessary price adjustments without fear of starting a price war and without overt collusion is by **price leadership.** The firm generally recognized as the price leader starts the price change and the other firms in the industry quickly follow. The price leader is usually the dominant or largest firm in the industry. Sometimes, it is the low-cost firm (see Problem 9, with the answer at the end of the book) or any other firm (called the **barometric firm**) recognized as the true interpreter or barometer of changes in demand and cost conditions in the industry warranting a price change. In either case, an orderly price change is accomplished by other firms following the leader.

In the price leadership model by the dominant firm, the dominant firm sets the price for the commodity that maximizes its profits, allows all the other (small) firms in the industry to sell all they want at that price, and then comes in to fill the market. Thus, the small firms in the industry behave as perfect competitors or price takers, and the dominant firm acts as the residual supplier of the commodity. This is shown in Figure 11.7.

In the figure, D (*ABCFG*) is the market demand curve for the homogeneous commodity sold in the oligopolist market. Curve ΣSMC_s is the (horizontal) summation of the marginal cost curves of all the small firms in the industry. Since the small firms in the industry can sell all they want at the industry price set by the dominant firm (i.e., they are price takers), they behave as perfect competitors and always produce at the point where $P = \Sigma SMC_s$. Thus, the ΣSMC_s curve (above the average variable cost of the small firms) represents the short-run supply curve of the commodity for all the small firms in the industry as a group (on the assumption that input prices remain constant).

The horizontal distance between D and ΣSMC_s at each price then gives the (residual) quantity of the commodity demanded from and supplied by the dominant firm at each price. For example, if the dominant firm set $P = \$7$, the small firms in the industry together supply *HB* or five units of the commodity, leaving nothing to be supplied by the dominant firm. This gives the vertical intercept (point H) on the demand curve of the dominant firm (d). If the dominant firm set $P = \$6$, the small firms in the industry supply *JL* or four units of the commodity, leaving two units ($LC = JK$) to be supplied by the dominant firm (point K on the d curve). Finally, if the dominant firm set $P = \$2$, the small firms together supply zero units of the commodity (point M), leaving the entire market quantity demanded of *MF* or ten units to be supplied by the dominant firm. Thus, the demand curve of the dominant firm is d or *HKFG*.

With demand curve d, the marginal revenue curve of the dominant firm is mr_d (which bisects the distance from the vertical axis to the d curve). If the short-run marginal cost

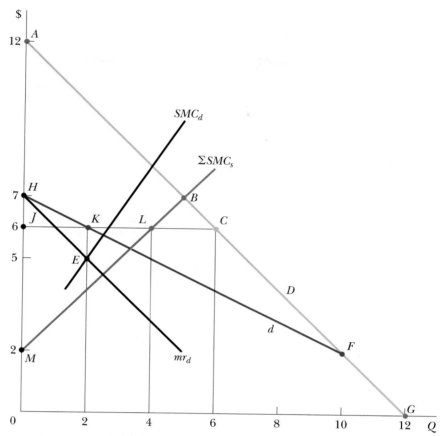

FIGURE 11.7   Price Leadership by the Dominant Firm D (*ABCFG*) is the market demand curve and ΣSMC_s is the marginal cost curve of all the small firms in the industry. Since the small firms can sell all they want at the price set by the dominant firm, they behave as perfect competitors and produce where $P = \Sigma SMC_s$. The horizontal distance between the D and ΣSMC_s curves then gives the (residual) quantity supplied by the dominant firm at each price. Thus, the demand curve of the dominant firm (d) is *HKFG*, and the corresponding marginal revenue curve is mr_d. With SMC_d, the dominant firm will set $P = \$6$ (given by point E, where $mr_d = SMC_d$) to maximize its profits. At $P = \$6$, the small firms will supply four units of the commodity and the dominant firm $JK = LC$ or two units.

curve of the dominant firm is SMC_d, the dominant firm will set $P = \$6$ (given by point E, where $mr_d = SMC_d$) to maximize its profits. Note that the industry price set by the dominant firm is determined on the demand curve of the dominant firm (d), not on the market demand curve (D). At $P = \$6$, the small firms together will supply JL or four units of the commodity (see the figure). The dominant firm will then come in to fill the market by selling $JK = LC$ or two units of the commodity at $P = \$6$ which it set.

Among the firms that have operated as price leaders are Alcoa (in aluminum), American Tobacco, American Can, Chase Manhattan Bank (in setting the prime rate), GM, Goodyear Tire and Rubber, Gulf Oil, Kellogg (in breakfast cereals), U.S. Steel (now USX), and so on. Many of these industries are characterized by more than one large firm, and the role of the price leader has sometimes changed from one large firm to another. For example, Reynolds has also behaved at times as the price leader in tobacco products. Continental Can, Bethlehem and National Steel, and General Mills (in the breakfast cereals market) also behaved as the price leaders in their respective markets during some periods of time. Finally, note that one important advantage of price leadership is that it can be accomplished informally by tacit collusion, which is much more difficult to prove than overt or explicit collusion.

On the international level, Saudi Arabia was the dominant price leader for petroleum during the 1970s. Saudi Arabia set petroleum prices and satisfied only that portion of the world demand that was left unfilled by others. But with other petroleum exporting countries greatly exceeding their export quotas and cheating by selling oil at discount prices, Saudi Arabia's share of the world's export market shrunk considerably. As the holder of the world's largest proven petroleum reserves and largest exporter, Saudi Arabia threatened to flood the market if other petroleum exporting countries continued to exceed their export quotas and sell at a discount. In 1986, Saudi Arabia made good on its threat and sharply increased petroleum production and exports, which caused a collapse in world oil prices to below $10 a barrel. Some degree of price and production discipline was subsequently reestablished, so that the price of petroleum more than doubled (to $22 a barrel) in 1992. As discussed in Example 11–3 above, however, the price of petroleum has exhibited great volatility since then.[12]

11.6   LONG-RUN ADJUSTMENTS AND EFFICIENCY IMPLICATIONS OF OLIGOPOLY

Most of the analysis of oligopoly until this point has referred to the short run. In this section, we analyze the long-run adjustments and efficiency implications of oligopoly. We examine the long-run plant adjustments of existing firms and the entry prospects of other firms into the industry, we discuss nonprice competition, and we examine the long-run welfare effects of oligopoly.

Long-Run Adjustments in Oligopoly

As in other forms of market organization, oligopolistic firms can build the best plant to produce their anticipated best level of output in the long run. However, in view of the uncertainty generally surrounding oligopolistic industries, it is even more difficult than under other forms of market organization for firms to determine their best level of output and plant in the long run. An oligopolist would leave the industry in the long run if it would incur a loss even after building the best scale of plant. On the other hand, if existing firms earn profits, more firms will seek to enter the industry in the long run, and, unless entry is blocked or somehow restricted, industry output will expand until industry profits fall to zero. There may then be so many firms in the industry that the actions of each no longer affect the others. In that case, the industry would no longer be oligopolistic.[13]

---

[12] "Crude Oil Prices Fall Slightly on Traders' Belief that OPEC Again Failed to Set Output Strategy," *Wall Street Journal,* September 22, 1992, p. C14; "OPEC Plan to Lift Oil Prices Goes Awry," *Wall Street Journal,* March 3, 1995, p. A2; "Who's to Blame," *Business Week,* July 3, 2001, pp. 36–37; and "Breaking OPEC," *Fortune,* November 12, 2001, pp. 78–88.

[13] As we will see in the theory of contestable markets discussed in Section 13.2, vigorous competition can take place even among few sellers.

For an industry to remain oligopolistic in the long run, entry must be somewhat restricted. This may result from many reasons, some natural and some artificial. These are generally the same barriers that led to the existence of the oligopoly in the first place. One of the most important natural barriers to entry is the smallness of the market in relation to the optimum size of the firm. For example, only three or four firms can most efficiently supply the entire national market for automobiles. Potential entrants know that by entering this market they would probably face huge losses and possibly also impose losses on the other established auto makers (see Problem 11).

Another important natural barrier to entry in oligopolistic markets are the usually huge investment and specialized inputs required (as, for example, to enter automobile, steel, aluminum, and similar industries). Many artificial barriers to entry may also exist. These include control over the source of an essential raw material (such as bauxite to produce aluminum) by the few firms already in the industry, unwillingness of existing firms to license potential competitors to use an essential industrial process on which they hold a patent, and the inability to obtain a government franchise (for example, to run a bus line or a taxi fleet). Still another artificial barrier to entry is **limit pricing,** whereby existing firms charge a price low enough to discourage entry into the industry.[14] By doing so, they voluntarily sacrifice some short-term profits to maximize their profits in the long run (see Section 11.7).

Limit pricing The charging of a sufficiently low price to discourage entry into the industry.

Nonprice Competition Among Oligopolists

Most oligopoly models presented in this chapter predict infrequent price changes in oligopolistic markets. This conforms to what is often observed in the real world. To be sure, costly price wars do sometimes erupt as a result of miscalculations on the part of one of the oligopolists, but they usually last only short periods. To avoid the possibility of starting a price war, oligopolists prefer to leave price unchanged and compete instead on the basis of **nonprice competition** (advertising, product differentiation, and service). Only when demand and cost conditions make a price change absolutely essential will oligopolists change prices. An orderly price change is then usually accomplished by price leadership.

Nonprice competition Competition based on advertising and product differentiation rather than on price.

As pointed out in Section 11.2, a firm may use advertising to try to increase (i.e., to shift to the right) the demand curve for its product. If successful, the firm will then be able to sell a greater quantity of the product at an unchanged price. The problem is that other firms, upon losing sales, are likely to retaliate and also increase their advertising expenditures. The result may be simply to increase all firms' costs, with each firm retaining more or less its share of the market and earning less profits. For example, when the government banned cigarette advertising on television, all tobacco companies benefitted by spending less on advertising—a step that each firm alone was not willing to take before the ban. Although some advertising provides useful information to consumers on new or improved products and uses, a great deal does not. Examples might be the huge advertising expenditures (running in the hundreds of millions of dollars per year) of beer producers, automakers, and others.

The same is generally true for product differentiation. That is, producers often differentiate their product in order to increase sales, but this usually leads to retaliation and

---

[14] See J. Bain, *Industrial Organization,* rev. ed. (New York: John Wiley & Sons, 1967). Perhaps, more than an artificial barrier to entry, limit pricing is a practice that is designed to exploit barriers that do exist (e.g., economies of scale).

higher costs and prices. Sometimes product changes are simply cosmetic (e.g., the yearly automobile model changes). Other changes may truly improve the product, for example, when a new and longer-lasting razor blade is introduced at the same price. Some product differentiation is introduced to better serve particular segments of the market. Advertising, product differentiation, and market segmentation can be combined in many different ways and used with still other forms of nonprice competition in oligopolistic markets.

Welfare Effects of Oligopoly

We now turn to some of the long-run welfare effects of oligopoly. First, as in the case of monopoly and monopolistic competition, oligopolists usually do not produce at the lowest point on their LAC curve. This would only occur by sheer coincidence if the oligopolist's MR curve intersected the LAC curve at the lowest point of the latter. Only under perfect competition will firms produce at the lowest point on the LAC curve in the long run. Oligopoly, however, often results because of the smallness of the market in relation to the optimum size of the firm, and so it does not make much sense to compare oligopoly to perfect competition. Automobiles, steel, aluminum, and many other products could only be produced at prohibitive costs under perfectly competitive conditions.

Second, as in the case of monopoly, oligopolists can earn long-run profits, and so price can exceed LAC. This is to be contrasted with the case of perfect competition and monopolistic competition where $P = LAC$ in the long run. However, some economists believe that oligopolists utilize a great deal of their profits for research and development (R&D) to produce new and better products and to find cheaper production methods. These are the primary sources of growth in modern economies. These same economists point out that monopolists do not have as much incentive to engage in R&D, and perfect competitors and monopolistic competitors are too small and do not have the resources to do so on a large scale (more will be said on this in Section 13.3).

Third, as in imperfect competition in general, $P > LMC$ under oligopoly, and so there is underallocation of resources to the industry. Specifically, since the demand curve facing oligopolists is negatively sloped, $P > MR$. Thus, at the best level of output (given by the point where the LMC intersects the firm's MR curve from below), $P > LMC$. This means that society values an additional unit of the commodity more than the marginal cost of producing it. But again, $P = LMC$ only under perfect competition, and economies of scale may make perfect competition infeasible.

Fourth, while some advertising and product differentiation are useful because they provide information and satisfy the consumers' tastes for diversity, they are likely to be pushed beyond what is socially desirable in oligopolistic markets. It is difficult, however, to determine exactly how much advertising and product differentiation is socially desirable in the real world. For example, the cost of model changes equals about one-fourth of the price of a new automobile during many years.[15] To the extent that consumers purchase new automobiles and choose to have the options introduced into the new models, we can infer that most of the costs of model changes are wanted by consumers and do not represent a waste of resources. Nevertheless, the demand for some model changes and for some new options is surely created by advertising and may not represent true needs.

Concept Check
How can an oligopolist earn profits in the long run?

Concept Check
Why does an oligopolist tend to invest more in R&D than a perfect competitor does?

---

[15] See F. Fisher, Z. Griliches, and C. Kaysen, "The Cost of Automobile Model Changes Since 1949," *The Journal of Political Economy,* October 1962, pp. 433–451; and V. Bajic, "Automobiles and Implicit Markets: An Estimate of a Structural Demand Model for Automobile Characteristics," *Applied Economics,* April 1993, pp. 541–551.

Turning to oligopoly theory itself, we can now see why we said earlier that there is no general theory of oligopoly. All the oligopoly models that we have examined are somewhat incomplete and unsatisfactory. This is unfortunate because oligopoly is the most prevalent form of market organization in production in all modern economies. Some progress in oligopoly theory is provided by game theory (examined in the next chapter).

EXAMPLE 11-5

Firm Size and Profitability

Do larger firms, because of their size and possible market power, earn larger profits than smaller firms? This question has been of great interest to both business and government and has been hotly debated over the years. To answer this question, we calculated the rank correlation between size (measured by sales) and profits in 2006 for the 20 largest U.S. corporations from the data shown in Table 11.2. The rank correlation, which can range from 0% to 100%, was found to be 49.7% in 2006, but it was only 21% in 2001 and 39.3% in 2005. Thus, the profitability of larger firms seems to have increased from 2001 (a recession year) to 2006 (a year of high growth) in the United States. It should be noted that life at the top is also slippery: 30 to 50 companies are displaced from the *Fortune 500* in a typical year.

TABLE 11.2	Sales and Profits for the 20 Largest U.S. Corporations in 2006 (in millions of dollars)

Company	Sales	Profits
Wal-Mart Stores	351,139	11,284
Exxon Mobil	347,254	39,500
General Motors	207,349	−1,978
Chevron	200,567	17,138
ConocoPhillips	172,451	15,550
General Electric	168,307	20,829
Ford Motor	160,126	−12,613
Citigroup	146,777	21,538
Bank of America Corp.	117,017	21,133
American International Group	113,194	14,048
J.P. Morgan Chase & Co.	99,973	14,444
Berkshire Hathaway	98,539	11,015
Verizon Communications	93,221	6,197
Hewlett-Packard	91,658	6,198
IBM	91,424	9,492
Valero Energy	91,051	5,463
Home Depot	90,837	5,761
McKesson	88,050	751
Cardinal Health	81,895	1,000
Morgan Stanley	76,688	7,472

Source: "Fortune 500 Largest U.S. Corporations," *Fortune,* April 27, 2007, pp. F1–F49.

11.7	OTHER OLIGOPOLISTIC PRICING PRACTICES

In this section, we examine two other pricing practices often used by oligopolists: limit pricing and cost-plus pricing.

Limit Pricing as a Barrier to Entry

Limit pricing was defined earlier as the charging of a price low enough to discourage entry into the industry. By doing so, existing firms voluntarily sacrifice some short-run profits to maximize their profits in the long run. We can show this with Figure 11.8.

In the left panel of Figure 11.8, D is the total market demand curve for the commodity. Suppose that existing firms are already selling four units of the commodity at $P = \$8$ (point A). The entrance of a new firm would increase industry output and cause the price to fall. That is, a potential entrant assumes that it faces the segment of demand curve D to the right of point A. Subtracting the four units of the commodity supplied by existing firms from the market demand curve (D) gives the potential entrant's demand curve (d_2). If, instead, existing firms were selling six units of the commodity at $P = \$6$ (point B), the potential entrant's demand curve would be d_1.

For simplicity, we assume that per-unit costs of existing firms and for the potential entrant are constant. We also assume (quite realistically) that the per-unit costs of the potential entrant are somewhat higher than for the established firms. These costs are shown in the right panel of Figure 11.8, where the horizontal $LAC = LMC$ curve refers to the constant costs of the established firms and the horizontal $LAC^* = LMC^*$ curve refers to the constant and higher costs of the potential entrant.

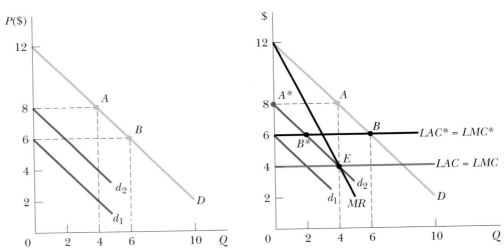

FIGURE 11.8   Limit Pricing   In the left panel, D is the total market demand curve for the commodity. The demand curve of a potential entrant is d_2 if existing firms sell $Q = 4$, and d_1 if they sell $Q = 6$. In the right panel, the $LAC = LMC$ curve refers to the constant costs of the established firms, while $LAC^* = LMC^*$ refers to the constant and higher costs of the potential entrant. Existing firms maximize profits by selling $Q = 4$ at $P = \$8$ (given by point E, at which $MR = LMC$). The demand curve facing the potential entrant is then d_2 and it could earn profits. To discourage entrance, existing firms can set the price at $\$6$ so that d_1 lies everywhere below LAC^*.

Existing firms maximize profits by selling $Q = 4$ at $P = \$8$ (given by point E, at which $LMC = MR$) and earn profits of AE or $\$4$ per unit and $\$16$ in total. The demand curve facing the potential entrant is then d_2. Since over the range A^*B^* of d_2, $P > LAC^*$, the potential entrant would find it profitable to enter the industry. However, this would increase industry output and lower price so that the profits of existing firms would fall. To avoid this, existing firms may choose to sell $Q = 6$ at $P = \$6$ so that the demand curve facing the potential entrant is d_1. Since d_1 lies everywhere below the LAC^* curve, the potential entrant would incur losses at all output levels and would not enter the industry. Therefore, $P = \$6$ is the entry-limit price. This is the highest price that existing firms can charge without inducing entry. By setting the limit price, existing firms sacrifice some profits in the short run (they now make a profit of $\$12$ rather than $\$16$) in order to maximize their profits in the long run.

Note that existing firms may only charge the limit price when they believe entry is imminent and will set their profit-maximizing price of $P = \$8$ at other times. Sometimes existing firms, faced with the entry of another firm, may voluntarily reduce their output to accommodate the new entrant and avoid a price reduction. Finally, note that limit pricing assumes some form of collusion (such as price leadership) on the part of existing firms.[16]

Cost-Plus Pricing: A Common Shortcut Pricing Practice

Cost-plus pricing The setting of a price equal to average cost plus a markup.

Markup The percentage over average cost in cost-plus pricing.

In the real world, firms often lack exact information to set the price that maximizes their profits (given by the point where the firm's MC curve intersects its MR curve from below). In these cases, firms usually use **cost-plus pricing.** Here, the firm estimates the average variable cost for a "normal" output level (usually between 70% and 80% of capacity output) and then adds a certain percentage or **markup** over average variable cost to determine the price of the commodity. The markup is set sufficiently high to cover average variable and fixed costs and also provide a profit margin for the firm. The markup varies depending on the industry and demand conditions. For example, the markup is about 20% in the steel industry in general, but it is higher for products facing less elastic demand or in periods of high demand.

Cost-plus pricing is fairly common in oligopolistic industries, and, under certain conditions, it is not inconsistent with profit maximization. That is, to the extent that the markup is varied inversely with the elasticity of demand of the product, it leads to a price which is approximately the profit-maximizing price. This can be shown as follows:

$$m = \frac{P - AVC}{AVC} \qquad [11.1]$$

where P is price, AVC is average variable cost, and m is the markup over AVC, expressed as a percentage of AVC.

Solving for P, we get

$$m(AVC) = P - AVC$$
$$P = AVC + m(AVC) \qquad [11.2]$$
$$P = AVC(1 + m)$$

---

[16] For more dynamic theories of limit pricing that predict that the limit price will be above existing firms' *LAC*, see R. T. Masson and J. Shaanan, "Stochastic-Dynamic Limiting Pricing: An Empirical Test," *Review of Economics and Statistics,* August 1982, pp. 413–422.

But from Section 5.6 we know that

$$MR = P(1 + 1/\eta) \tag{11.3}$$

where MR is marginal revenue, P is price, and η is the price elasticity of demand.

Solving for P we get

$$P = \frac{MR}{1 + 1/\eta}$$

Since profits are maximized where $MR = MC$, we can substitute MC for MR in the above formula and get

$$P = \frac{MC}{1 + 1/\eta}$$

To the extent that the firm's MC is constant over a wide range of outputs, $MC = AVC$. Substituting AVC for MC in the above formula, we get

$$P = \frac{AVC}{1 + 1/\eta} \tag{11.4}$$

Formula [11.4] for profit maximization equals formula [11.2] for the markup, if $1 + m = 1/(1 + (1/\eta))$ or if $m = -1/(\eta + 1)$. Thus, the firm will maximize profits if its markup is inversely related to the price elasticity of demand for the commodity. For example, when $\eta = -3$, m should be 1/2, or 50%. For $\eta = -5$, $m = 1/4$, or 25%. This means that if $AVC = \$100$, P should equal \$125 (so that the markup is 25% of AVC) for the firm to cover all costs and maximize profits.

Cyert and March found that firms in the retailing sector adjusted prices on the basis of feedback from the market and did reduce the markup and price when the demand for a product declined and became more elastic.[17] Thus, using cost-plus pricing with a markup that varies inversely with the price elasticity of demand is consistent with profit maximization. In any event, those firms that choose a markup and price that is not near the profit-maximizing price are less likely to grow and may go out of business in the long run, as compared to firms that choose the appropriate markup. Cost-plus pricing is one of many *rules of thumb* that firms are forced to use in the real world because of the frequent lack of adequate data.

AT THE FRONTIER
The Art of Devising Airfares

Introductory Comment: The following selection illustrates most of the concepts presented in this chapter as they are actually applied in the real world. It shows the importance of market structure in output and pricing decisions, price leadership, price discrimination, the pricing of multiple products, and how they are all interrelated to marginal analysis in pricing as it is actually conducted in a major oligopolistic industry today.

---

[17] R. M. Cyert and J. G. March, *A Behavioral Theory of the Firm* (Englewood Cliffs, N.J.: Prentice-Hall, 1963).

THE ART OF DEVISING AIRFARES

In the airline business, it is sometimes called the "dark science." The latest round of fare wars, however, has put the spotlight on how carriers use state-of-the-art computer software, complex forecasting techniques, and a little intuition to divine how many seats and at what prices they will offer on any flight.

The aim of this inventory or yield management is to squeeze as many dollars as possible out of each seat and mile flown. This means trying to project just how many tickets to sell at a discount without running out of seats for the business traveler, who usually books at the last minute and therefore pays full fare. Too many wrong projections can lead to huge losses of revenue, or even worse. The inability of People Express (airline) to manage its inventory of seats properly, for example, was one of the major causes of its demise.

"It's a sophisticated guessing game," says Robert E. Martens, vice president of pricing and production planning at American Airlines, the carrier that has the most sophisticated technology for yield management, according to airline analysts and consultants. "You don't sell a seat to a guy for $69 when he is willing to pay $400."

With the industry now adopting very low discount but nonrefundable fares, the complex task of managing seat inventory may become easier because airlines will be better able to predict how many people will show up for a flight. Some airlines have already seen a reduction in their no-shows, which means that they can overbook less and spare more customers from being bumped. The nonrefundable fares could also enable carriers to sell more discount seats weeks before a flight, rather than putting them on sale at the last minute in an effort to fill up the plane.

American's inventory operations illustrate just how complicated the process can be. At the airline's corporate headquarters, 90 yield managers are linked by terminals to five International Business Machines mainframe computers in Tulsa, Oklahoma. The managers monitor and adjust the fare mixes on 1,600 daily flights as well as 528,000 future flights involving nearly 50 million passengers. Their work is hectic: A fare's average life span is two weeks, and industrywide about 2,000 fares change daily.

Few Discounts on Fridays

American and other airlines base their forecasts largely on historical profiles on each flight. Business travelers, for example, book heavily on many Friday afternoon flights, but often not until the day of departure. The airlines reserve blocks of seats for those frequent fliers. Few, if any, discounts are made available. "Good luck on getting a 'Q fare' from New York to Chicago on Fridays afternoon," said James J. Hurtigan, president of United Airlines, using the industry parlance for the low-priced super saver ticket. "It's like winning the New York lottery." The same route on a midday on a Wednesday, however, begs for passengers, so the airline might discount more than 80% of its seats to draw leisure travelers and others with more flexible schedules.

Passengers Angered

Many passengers, attracted by the advertisements trumpeting deep discounts but unaware that fare allocations change from flight to flight, have expressed anger at the carriers and travel agents when the cheap seats were unavailable. To help clear up the confusion, Continental Airlines is now running ads noting the relative demand for

Continued . . .

The Art of Devising Airfares   *Continued*

certain routes, thus giving some sense of the supply of discount seats. Overbooking, too, is based on the computerized history of flights and their no-shows and involves myriad factors that include destination, time of day, and cost of ticket.

The airlines have used inventory management for decades, but its importance in helping carriers to enhance their revenue coincides with new software developed in the past three or four years, analysts and airline executives said. Some of the software has been developed in-house; other systems have been obtained from such companies as the Unis Corporation and the Control Data Corporation. "It's probably the No. 1 management tool required to compete properly in this highly competitive airline environment," said Lee R. Howard, executive vice president of Airline Economics, a Washington-based consulting firm.

Effective inventory management alone can improve an airline's revenues by 5% to 20% annually, analysts estimated. Mr. Martens said American's system was worth "hundreds of millions of dollars" a year to the airline. The airline's total sales exceeded $6 billion last year. "The revenue implications for yield management are enormous," said Julius Maltudis, airline analyst at Salomon Brothers. Inventory management improves a carrier's load factor, or ratio of seats filled. Every 1% increase in the load factor translates into $10 million in revenue for the typical major carrier, analysts said.

"Crystal-Ball Gazing"

As sophisticated as it is, however, yield management is still subject to variables beyond its control. "Yield management is about 70% technology and 30% crystal-ball gazing," said Robert W. Cuggin, assistant vice president of marketing development at Delta Airlines. Bad weather or a last-minute switch to a plane of a different size can wreak havoc with weeks of planning, he said.

At American, inventory management begins 330 days before departure. Yield managers use a profile of a flight's history to parcel out an alphabet soup of fares, rationing full-fare seats first, then moving down the price scale. In the following weeks, the computer alerts managers if sales in a particular fare class picked up unexpectedly. If a travel agent books a large group of passengers in advance, for example, the computer would flag the large order, and yield managers would restrict or expand the number of seats in that category. Otherwise, managers begin checking all fare mixes 180 days before departure, adding or subtracting seats in each according to demand.

The process continues right up to two hours before boarding, according to America's director of yield management, Dennis McKaige. Airlines typically put more discount seats on sale just before an advance purchase requirement expires, he said. Therefore, a new batch of cheap tickets that require a 30-day advance purchase might go on sale 31 days before departure. A cut-rate fare offered on Monday might be sold out by Wednesday, then suddenly reoffered hours before take off on Thursday if passengers projections based on previous flights fail to materialize, Mr. McKaige said.

There are some instances when an airline actually gives preference to discount travelers over customers paying full fare. American has recently developed software to increase the yield on flights through its hubs. American gives preference to a passenger flying on a discount fare from Austin, Texas, to London, through Dallas, over another passenger paying full fare from Austin to Shreveport, Louisiana, through Dallas. The London passenger, who pays $241 each way, is worth more to the airline than the passenger flying to Shreveport, who pays the full fare of $87 each way. For the bargain hunter, finding a discount will increasingly depend on the season, day and time of travel, the destination, and the length of stay.

The New Fare Cuts

Continental, a unit of Texas Air, ignited the latest round of rock-bottom fares in January with "Maxsaver tickets," which require a minimum two-day advance purchase and are nonrefundable. "The spread between our highest and lowest fares is much lower than other airlines," said James O'Donnel, vice president of marketing at Continental. "While our yield management job is no less important than other airlines', it is easier." Mr. O'Donnel said the carrier's system was more automated than those used by some of its competitors.

The two-day purchase requirement has siphoned off some business travelers who would otherwise have paid full fare. (American and several other airlines abandoned plans to raise their lowest discount fares and increase the advance purchase requirement on the cheapest tickets to 30 days, from 2. The airlines backed away from the change when support for the proposal collapsed.) Airline officials said that nonrefundable tickets were here to stay. Mr. Martens said that since the nonrefundable, Maxsaver-type fares were introduced, American's no-show rate has dropped "substantially below" the usual range of 12% to 15%. Passengers who are willing to commit themselves to a particular flight in exchange for lower prices allow yield managers to refine their operations by concentrating on the remaining coach seats.

Concluding Remarks: Yield management (i.e., the idea of selling as many tickets as possible at high fares and fill the rest of the seats at cut rates) is here to stay in the pricing of airline tickets and is constantly being refined with the use of ever more powerful computers and software. Indeed, yield management is considered the single most important technological improvement in airline management in the last decade and is often credited with making the difference between profit and loss for many airlines. For example, *The New York Times* found that on a single flight in 1997, the 33 passengers who held Chicago–Los Angeles tickets paid 27 different fares, ranging from $87 to $728. In 2008, a New York–Los Angeles roundtrip ticket might cost $287 to one flier and $2,247 to another.

The great variety and frequent changes in airfares is, however, creating great confusion and frustration for air travelers as they are routinely unable to book seats at the lowest advertised fares. This led to increasing complaints of false advertisement, which the Transportation Department (the sole authority charged with regulating the airline industry since it was deregulated in 1978) has regularly investigated. Yield management has now come to haunt airlines, as more and more travelers shop around on the Internet for the lowest airfares available and fewer and fewer passengers pay full fare.

Sources: Eric Schmidt, "The Art of Devising Air Fares," *New York Times,* March 4, 1987, pp. D1–D2. Reprinted by permission of the New York Times Corporation. See also "Computers as Price Setters Complicate Travelers' Lives," *New York Times,* January 24, 1994, p. 1; "Special Offers by Airlines Come Under U.S. Review," *New York Times,* January 23, 1995, p. 10; "So, How Much Did You Pay for Your Ticket?," *New York Times,* April 12, 1998, Sect. 4, p. 2; "Airlines Now Offer 'Last Minute' Fare Bargains Weeks Before Flights," *Wall Street Journal,* March 15, 2002, p. B1; "Airline Seats Have Become a Commodity," *Financial Times*, July 13, 2005, p. 5; and S. Borenstein and N. L. Rose, "How Airlines Market Work," NBER, *Working Paper No. 13452,* September 2007.

| 11.8 | THE MARCH OF GLOBAL OLIGOPOLISTS

During the past decade the trend toward the formation of global oligopolies has acceler-ated as the world's largest corporations have been getting bigger and bigger through inter-nal growth and mergers. Indeed, in more and more industries and sectors the pressure to become one of the largest global players seems irresistible. No longer are corporations satisfied to be the largest or the next-to-the-largest national company in their industry or sector. More and more corporations operate on the belief that their very survival requires that they become one of a handful of world corporations or global oligopolists in their sector. Many smaller corporations are merging with larger ones in the belief that either they grow or they become a casualty of the sharply increased global competition. Strong impetus toward globalization has been provided by the revolution in telecommunications and transportation, the movement toward the globalization of tastes, and the reduction of barriers to international trade and investments. Rapid globalization has occurred in prac-tically every sector, including industry, banking, entertainment and telecommunications, consumer products, food, drugs, electronics, and commercial aircraft.

In industry, the total sales in real terms (i.e., after taking inflation into account) of the world's 25 largest *industrial* corporations increased 70% faster than the combined index of real total industrial production in all industrial countries during the past 30 years. Thus, there has been a clear tendency for the largest industrial corporations to become larger.[18] The movement toward globalization is very clear in automobiles, where only a handful of global independent players are likely to survive (see Example 11–6). Globalization has proceeded even more rapidly in tires, where Bridgestone (Japanese), Michelin (French), and Goodyear (American) command more than half of total world's sales and further con-solidation is expected.

The sector in which the size of the largest firms has grown the most during the past decades is international banking. From 1966 to 2007, total deposits of the world's 10 largest banks grew from $87 billion to more than $10,000 billion. Even after accounting for the quadrupling of prices and exchange rate changes (to convert local currency values into dollar values), this means that the size of the world's 10 largest banks increased by more than 16 times during the past three decades. It is often pointed out, however, that after a certain size, stability and profitability are more important than size per se. Nevertheless, the growth in the size of the world's largest banks has been nothing but spectacular (see Example 11-7).

Another sector where corporations have grown sharply in size and gone global has been the entertainment and communication industry. The merger of Time Inc. with Warner Communications and its subsequent acquisition by America Online (AOL) for $110 billion to form Time Warner Inc., Walt Disney's acquisition of Capital Cities/ABC, and Viacom's acquisitions (CBS, MTV, infinity Broadcasting, Simon & Schuster, Blockbuster, and Paramount Pictures) formed, respectively, the world's first-, second-, and third-largest communications company (all three American).[19] Many mergers involved the purchase of American companies by foreigners: Japan's Sony Corporation purchased American CBS

---

[18] See "The Fortune Global 500," in *Fortune* for August 1970, May 1980, July 1990, and July 2007.

[19] In 2005, however, Viacom, reversing direction, decided to split itself into a radio and broadcast TV operations (which includes the CBS network) from its MTV cable network and Paramount film studio in order better to meet the competition from new technologies, which includes the Internet, satellite radio, and digital video recorders. See, "Viacom Board Agrees to Split of Company, *New York Times*, June 15, 2005, p. C4; "Time Warner May Sell AOL," *New York Post*, March 27, 2007, p. 1; and http://www.mediaowners.com/company/waltdisney.html.

Records and MGM; Germany's Bertelsmann acquired RCA Records as well as Doubleday and Bantam Books; Ruppert Murdoch's (from Australia but now residing in the United States) News Corporation owns Harper & Row Publishers, Triangle Publications, Twentieth-Century Fox, and the *Wall Street Journal*; and Vivendi (French) acquired Seagram and US Networks. The industry is now dominated by Time Warner Inc., Walt Disney Company, Viacom, News Corporation, Bertlsmann, and Vivendi. The reason given for most mergers in the entertainment and communications industry is to become more competitive globally. "Competitive," according to the current conventional wisdom, means being equipped to become one of the five to eight giant corporations expected to dominate the industry worldwide. These enterprises, the reasoning goes, will be able to produce and distribute information and entertainment in virtually any medium: books, magazines, news, television, movies, videos, electronic data networks, and so on. This is expected to provide important synergies or cross-benefits from joint operation.[20]

The same type of globalization has been taking place in consumer products, food, drugs, electronics, and commercial aircraft. In 1990, Gillette introduced its new Sensor razor, which took 20 years and $300 million to develop, and it captured an incredible 71% of the world razor market by 1999 when it introduced its Mach3. In 2005, Gillette was acquired by Procter & Gamble. Nestlé, the world's largest food company, has production plants in 59 countries and sells its food products in more than 100 countries. America's Procter & Gamble, Switzerland's Nestlé, and Britain's Unilever are among the world's 100 largest corporations. Coca-Cola has 40% of the U.S. market and an incredible 33% of the world's soft drink market. Despite the need to cater to local food tastes (Nestlé has more than 200 blends of Nescafé to cater to different local tastes), there is a clear trend toward global supermarkets. The same is true in chemicals, electronics, commercial aircraft, petroleum, and drugs (see Example 11–8), for which handful of huge corporations literally controls the world market.

It no longer makes any sense to talk about or be concerned only with national rather than global competition in these sectors. A large corporation can even be a monopolist in the national market and face deadly competition from larger and more efficient global oligopolists. The ideal global corporation is today strongly decentralized, to allow local units to develop products that fit into the local cultures, and yet at its core is very centralized, to coordinate activities around the globe.[21]

EXAMPLE 11–6

Globalization of the Automobile Industry

The automotive industry is rapidly globalizing, with six companies producing more than 65% of the total world sales of automobiles of nearly 60 million units (see Table 11.3). From the more than 40 independent producers during the 1980s, only about 10 or so relatively large automakers remain today. General Motors has acquired

[20] "Media Mergers: An Urge to Get Bigger and More Global," *New York Times*, March 19, 1989, p. 7; "Corporations' Dreams Converge in One Idea: It's Time to Do a Deal," *Wall Street Journal*, February 26, 1997, p. A1; "The New Media Colossus," *Wall Street Journal*, December 15, 2000, p. B1; and "The Urge to Merge," *Fortune* (February 21, 2005), pp. 21–26.

[21] "A View from the Top: Survival Tactics for the Global Business Arena," *Management Review*, October 1992, pp. 49–53; "The Fallout from Merger Mania," *Fortune*, March 2, 1998, pp. 26–27; "If at First," *The Economist* (September 3, 2005), p. 13; and "Europe: Bourses Rise, Gripped by 'Merger Mania,'" *International Herald Tribune*, December 11, 2006, p. 1.

TABLE 11.3   World's Largest Auto Producers in 2006

Company	Vehicles Produced (in millions)
General Motors	8.93
Toyota	8.04
Ford	6.27
Renault/Nissan	5.72
Volkswagen Group	5.69
DaimlerChrysler	4.59
Total	39.24

Source: http://en.wikipedia.org/wiki/Automaker, October 29, 2007.

Saab and Daewoo; Ford acquired Jaguar, Land Rover, Volvo, and Mazda; Renault merged with Nissan; Volkswagen acquired Seat, Skoda and Audi; Daimler-Benz absorbed Chrysler. Only Toyota grew without mergers.

Some of the biggest automobile mergers, however, did not work out and have either been dissolved or are in the process of doing so. In 2008, Ford sold Jaguar and Land Rover to Tata of India, and DaimlerChrysler sold Chrysler to Cerberus, a U.S. private equity fund. Be that as it may, there now remain only a handful of smaller independent automakers in the market today: Honda, PSA, Fiat, Chrysler and Daimler AG (after the split), and BMW. Economies of scale are so pervasive in the automobile industry, however, that more mergers are likely to take place in the near future. There are, of course, some very small but highly luxurious and expensive makes, but even these are owned by some of the larger companies (for example, Rolls Royce is owned by BMW and Ferrari is part of Fiat). Until 2005, Toyota was considered the best automobile company in the world: It made the best-quality cars and earned huge profits. But its growth has slowed down since then, and its reputation was somewhat tarnished because of quality problems. Nevertheless, in 2008 Toyota was about to surpass GM to become the world's largest automaker.

Source: "U.S. Car Makers Lose Market Share," *Wall Street Journal* (January 6, 2004), p. A3; "The Quick and the Dead," *The Economist* (January 29, 2005), pp. 10–11; "GM Slips into Toyota's Rearview Mirror," *Wall Street Journal*, April 25, 2007, p. A7; "Chrysler Deal Heralds New Direction for Detroit," *Wall Street Journal*, May 15, 2007, p. A1; "Back to the Future," *Forbes*, October 15, 2007, pp. 39–40; "Dings and Dents of Toyota," *Wall Street Journal*, November 3, 2007, p. C1; and "Toyota and GM are Neck and Neck in the Race to Be Number One," *Financial Times*, January 1, 2008, p. 16.

EXAMPLE 11–7

Rising Competition in Global Banking

This decade is likely to see aggressively intensified competition in the high-stakes world of international banking, with fewer than 10 of the 40–45 large international banks now aspiring to become global powerhouses actually attaining their goal. From the 1950s through the 1970s, world banking was dominated by U.S. banks; during the 1980s, Japanese banks made a run for the top; but now many of the world's largest banks are European.

American banks were weakened by soured loans on real estate and to developing countries during the 1980s and for highly leveraged takeovers during the 1990s. Japanese banks suffered from years of bad loans, low profits, and antiquated technology during the 1990s, and they were generally less competitive than European banks and much less efficient than American banks. European banks entered the 1990s in better shape than their American counterparts. They were better capitalized and had made much fewer bad loans than American banks to developing countries, especially in Latin America, during the 1980s. They were also not restricted by law, as American Banks were until 1999, from entering the insurance and securities fields. European banks, however, generally lagged in technology and in the introduction of new financial instruments, such as derivatives, when compared with American banks. European banks were also much more exposed, and incurred much higher losses than, American banks from the financial and economic crisis in Southeast Asia during the latter part of the 1990s. The European banking sectors did start to consolidate after the mid-1990s, but mergers generally took place within countries rather than across countries because of persisting nationalism. This changed during the 2000s, when some very large cross-country mergers took place, and more are expected in the next few years.

In 2007, the world's largest bank (with assets of over $2 trillion) was Barclays Bank of England, and the second was Swiss bank UBS. Of the world's top 10 largest banks, three were English, two French, two American (Citi and Bank of America), and one each, Swiss, Japanese, and German. But size is not everything in banking, and once a bank is, say, one of the top 10 largest in the world, efficiency is what then matters the most. Size is important in banking because, with deregulation, each bank must increasingly compete with foreign banks at home and abroad to be successful. Global banks must be able to meet the rising financial needs for lending, underwriting, currency and security trading, insurance, financial advice, and other financial services for customers and investors with increasingly global operations (i.e., they must provide one-stop banking for global corporations). Global banks must also be highly innovative and introduce new financial products and technologies to meet changing customer needs. Overcapacity—too many banks chasing too few customers—will also increase competition. Large U.S. banks are strong on innovations and, with the repeal of the 1933 Glass–Steagal Act (which prevented them from entering the insurance and securities fields) are now able to compete with foreign banks more effectively at home and abroad.

Sources: "Competition Rises in Global Banking," *Wall Street Journal,* March 25, 1991, p. A1; "International Banking Survey," *The Economist,* April 30, 1994, pp. 1–42; "Congress Passes Wide-Ranging Bill Easing Bank Laws," *New York Times,* November 5, 1999, p. 1; "Banking in the 21st Century," *Global Finance,* January 2000, p. 41; and "The World's Biggest Banks," *Global Finance,* October 2007, p. 100.

EXAMPLE 11.8

Globalization of the Pharmaceutical Industry

The past decade has witnessed more than a dozen huge mergers of large pharmaceutical companies—as well as many failed attempts. The largest merger was Pfizer's (the largest drug company in the world—American) acquisition of Warner-Lambert (also American) for $110 billion in 2000. In 2006, Pfizer had annual sales of $45 billion; GlaxoSmithKlein, the second-largest drug company in the world (British) had sales of $37 billion. All of the world's 10 largest pharmaceutical companies have been the result of one or more mergers. The only exception is Merck, the eighth-largest drug company in the world (American), with 2006 sales of $23 billion. Still, the top 10 pharmaceutical companies control less than half of total world drug sales, and so there still seems to be a great deal of room for further mergers in the industry in the future.

There are three major reasons for the urge to merge in the pharmaceutical industry. The first and most important arises from the incredibly high cost (over $1 billion in 2007) of developing and marketing new drugs. Despite average profit rates of about 15% in the industry, these huge development costs are becoming out of reach for even the largest drug companies. Hence the need for further consolidation and globalization in the industry, even by today's largest industry players. The second reason is that management typically expects savings equivalent to 10% of the combined sales of the postmerger company. These can run in the billions of dollars per year for the largest companies. The third reason is that the combined sales force of the merged company can reach that many more doctors and hospitals and thus increase sales. Although making a great deal of sense theoretically, most mergers in the pharmaceutical industry did not deliver the benefits expected. In all cases the merged company lost market share and faced reduced profits after the merger.

Because of price regulation (and thus lower profit margins) and fragmented national markets, European drug companies are losing international competitiveness to U.S. firms. All companies now face very strong competition from generics, as patents (usually granted for 20 years from the date the application is filed) expire on many blockbuster drugs. Generic drugs usually sell for as little as 10–20% of the patented drug. By 2007, more than 60% of all prescriptions were filled by generic drugs (up from 20% in 1984) in the United States (saving consumers more than $10 billion). In recent years several drug companies were also hit by huge lawsuits for the alleged harmful side effects of their drugs. In 2004, Merck was forced to withdraw from the market its painkiller Vioxx (which had brought in $2.5 billion per year in revenues) for causing heart attacks, and in 2007 it agreed to pay $4.85 billion to settle 45,000 lawsuits that had been brought against it. Furthermore, some expected drug successes turned out instead to be huge flops. For example, in 2007 Pfizer withdrew Exubera, an insulin drug for diabetics, which cost $2.8 billion to develop, for lack of sales.

Source: "Drug Makers See 'Branded Generics' Eating into Profits," *Wall Street Journal* (April 18, 2003), p. A1; "Delicate Balance Needed in Uniting of Drug Companies," *New York Times* (April 27, 2004), p. C1; "Merck to Pay $253 Million after Losing Vioxx Suit," *Financial Times* (August 21, 2005), p. 1; "Insulin Flop Cost Pfizer $2.8 Billion" *Wall Street Journal*, October 19, 2007, p. A1; "Drug Drought," *Forbes*, October 29, 2007, pp. 44–47; "More Generics Slow the Surge in Drug Prices," *New York Times*, August 8, 2007, p. 1; and "Merck Is Said to Agree to Pay $4.85 billion for Vioxx Claims," *New York Times*, November 9, 2007, p. 1.

SUMMARY

1. Monopolistic competition is the form of market organization in which there are many sellers of a differentiated product, and entry into and exit from the industry are rather easy in the long run. Differentiated products are those that are similar but not identical and satisfy the same basic need. The competitive element arises from the many firms in the market. The monopoly element results from product differentiation. The monopoly power, however, is severely limited by the availability of many close substitutes. Monopolistic competition is most common in the retail sector of the economy. Because of product differentiation, we cannot derive the market demand curve and we have a cluster of prices. The choice-related variables for a monopolistically competitive firm are product variation, selling expenses, and price.

2. Since a monopolistically competitive firm produces a differentiated product for which there are many close substitutes, the demand curve that the firm faces is negatively sloped but highly price elastic. The best level of output in the short run is given by the point at which $MR = SMC$, provided that $P > AVC$. If firms earn profits in the short run, more firms enter the market in the long run. This shifts the demand curve facing each firm to the left until all firms break even. Because of product differentiation, P and LAC are somewhat higher than if the market had been organized along perfectly competitive lines, there is excess capacity, and this allows more firms to exist in the market. A monopolistically competitive firm can increase the degree of product variation and selling expenses in an effort to increase the demand for its product and make it less elastic. The optimal level of these efforts is given by the point at which $MR = MC$. In the long run, however, the monopolistically competitive firm breaks even. Recently, economists have preferred to use the perfectly competitive and oligopoly models.

3. Oligopoly is the form of market organization in which there are few sellers of either a homogeneous or a differentiated product, and entry into or exit from the industry is possible but difficult. Oligopoly is the most prevalent form of market organization in the manufacturing sector of industrial countries, including the United States. The distinguishing characteristic of oligopoly is the interdependence or rivalry among the firms in the industry. The sources of oligopoly as well as the barriers to entry are economies of scale, the huge investments and specialized inputs required to enter the industry, patents and copyrights, the loyalty of customers to existing firms, control over the supply of a required raw material, and government franchise. The degree by which an industry is dominated by a few large firms is measured by concentration ratios. These ratios, however, can be very misleading as a measure of the degree of competition in the industry and must be used with great caution.

4. Cournot assumed that two firms sell identical spring water produced at zero marginal cost. Each duopolist, in its attempt to maximize profits, assumes the other will keep output constant at the existing level. The result is a sequence of moves and countermoves until each duopolist sells one-third of the total output that would be sold if the market were perfectly competitive. If each duopolist assumes that the other keeps its price (instead of its quantity) constant, then the price will fall to zero. This is the Bertrand model. In the kinked-demand, or Sweezy, model, it is assumed that oligopolists match the price reductions but not the price increases of competitors. Thus, the demand curve has a kink at the prevailing price. Oligopolists maintain the price as long as the SMC curve intersects the discontinuous segment of the MR curve. Some empirical studies do not support the existence of the kink, and the model does not explain how the price is set in the first place.

5. A centralized cartel is a formal organization of suppliers of a commodity that sets the price and allocates output and profits among its members so as to increase their joint profits. A market-sharing cartel is an organization of suppliers of a commodity that overtly or tacitly divides the market among its members. Cartels can result in the monopoly solution but are unstable and often fail. A looser form of collusion is price leadership by the dominant, the low-cost, or the

barometric firm. Under price leadership by the dominant firm, the small firms are allowed to sell all they want at the price set by the dominant firm, and then the dominant firm comes in to fill the market.

6. In the long run, oligopolistic firms can build their best scale of plant and firms can leave the industry. Entry, however, has to be blocked or restricted if the industry is to remain oligopolistic. There can be several natural and artificial barriers to entry. Oligopolists seldom change prices for fear of starting a price war and prefer instead to compete on the basis of advertising, product differentiation, and service. In oligopolistic markets, production does not usually take place at the lowest point on the LAC curve, $P > LAC$, $P > LMC$, and too much may be spent on advertising, product differentiation, and service. Oligopoly, however, may result from the limitation of the market, and it may lead to more research and development.

7. Limit pricing refers to existing firms charging a sufficiently low price to discourage entry into the industry. Cost-plus pricing refers to the setting of a price equal to average variable cost plus a markup. The pricing of airline tickets illustrates most of the concepts presented in this chapter as they are actually applied in a real-world oligopolistic market.

8. During the past decade, the trend toward the formation of global oligopolies has accelerated as the world's largest corporations have been getting even bigger through internal growth and mergers. More and more, corporations operate on the belief that their survival requires that they become one of a handful of world corporations, or global oligopolists, in their sector. This globalization of production and distribution has important implications for the concept of efficiency (to be explored in Section 13.3).

KEY TERMS

Monopolistic competition
Differentiated products
Product group
Excess capacity
Product variation
Selling expenses
Oligopoly
Duopoly
Pure oligopoly
Differentiated oligopoly

Concentration ratios
Cournot model
Bertrand model
Kinked–demand curve model
Collusion
Cartel
Centralized cartel
Market-sharing cartel
Price leadership
Barometric firm

Limit pricing
Nonprice competition
Cost-plus pricing
Markup
Reaction function
Cournot equilibrium
Nash equilibrium
Stackelberg model

REVIEW QUESTIONS

1. a. Why is it that we cannot define the industry in monopolistic competition?
   b. How can cross elasticities of demand help define a product group under monopolistic competition?
2. Can the short-run supply curve of a monopolistically competitive firm be derived? Why?
3. What effect will product variation and selling expenses have on
   a. the firm's demand and cost curves?
   b. short-run and long-run equilibrium?
4. a. What is the usefulness and cost of product variation?

   b. Is advertising good or bad for consumers? Why?
5. Why does excess capacity arise in monopolistic competition? What is its economic significance?
6. What is the distinction between interdependence and rivalry in oligopoly?
7. How much would be produced by each oligopolist and in total in Figure 11.3 if there were
   a. four firms in the market?
   b. five firms in the market?
8. What general conclusion can you draw from the results in the text and from your answer to Question 7 with regard to

the proportion of the perfectly competitive total quantity sold by

  a. each oligopolist?

  b. all oligopolists together?

9. a. What is the usefulness of the kinked–demand curve model?

b. What are its disadvantages?

10. Why do we study cartels and price leadership if they are illegal?

11. Why is there no general theory of oligopoly?

12. What are the advantages and disadvantages of oligopoly?

PROBLEMS

1. Suppose that *SATC* were $10 and *AVC* were $8 at the best level of output for the firm in the left panel of Figure 11.1.

  a. How much profit or loss per unit and in total would the firm have if it continued to produce?

  b. Should the firm continue to produce in the short run? Why?

  c. What would be the total loss of the firm if it stopped producing in the short run and if it didn't stop producing?

*2. Excess capacity is inversely related to the price elasticity of demand faced by a monopolistically competitive firm. True or false? Explain.

3. Starting with the assumptions of the Cournot model, explain what would happen if each duopolist assumed that the other kept its price rather than its output constant (as in the Cournot model).

4. Draw a figure showing the best level of output and price for the oligopolist of Figure 11.4 if its *SMC* curve shifts

  a. upward by $3.50;

  b. downward by $4.

5. Draw a figure showing the best level of output and price for the oligopolist of Figure 11.4 if the government sets a price ceiling of

  a. $8;

  b. $7.

*6. Draw a figure showing the best level of output and price for the oligopolist of Figure 11.4 if the demand curve it faces shifts

  a. upward by $0.50 but the kink remains at $P = \$8$.

  b. downward by $0.50 but the kink remains at $P = \$8$ and the *SMC* curve shifts up to *SMC'*.

7. Assume that (1) the four identical firms in a purely oligopolistic industry form a centralized cartel; (2) the total market demand function facing the cartel is $QD = 20 - 2P$, and *P* is given in dollars;

and (3) each firm's *SMC* function is given by $\$(1/4)Q$, and input prices are constant.

  a. Find the best level of output and price for this centralized cartel.

  b. How much should each firm produce if the cartel wants to minimize production costs?

  c. How much profit will the cartel make if the average total cost of each firm at the best level of output is $4?

8. Redraw Figure 11.6, and show on it the *MR* and the ΣSMC curves for the cartel as a whole. How are the best levels of output and price for the cartel as a whole determined? On the same figure, draw the *SATC* curve of one of the duopolists if $SATC = \$6$ at $Q = 2$ and $Q = 4$. How much profit does each duopolist earn?

*9. Start with Figure 11.6 where the duopolists share equally the market for a homogeneous product.

  a. Draw a figure such that duopolist 1's short-run marginal cost (SMC_1) is as shown in Figure 11.6 and duopolist 2's short-run marginal cost is given by $SMC_2 = 6 + 2Q$. What quantity of the commodity will each duopolist produce? What price would each like to charge? What is the actual result likely to be?

  b. If $SATC_1 = \$5$ at $Q = 2$ and $SATC_2 = \$8$ at $Q = 1$, how much profit will each duopolist earn?

10. Assume that (1) in a purely oligopolistic industry, there is one dominant firm and 10 small identical firms; (2) the market demand curve for the commodity is $Q = 20 - 2P$, where *P* is given in dollars; (3) $SMC_d = 1.5 + Q/2$, while $SMC_s = 1 + Q/4$; and (4) input prices remain constant. Based on the above assumptions

  a. draw a figure similar to Figure 11.7 showing the market demand curve, SMC_d, SMC_s, and the demand curve that the dominant firm faces.

  b. What price will the dominant firm set? How much will the small firms supply together? How much will the dominant firm supply?

---

* = Answer provided at end of book.

11. Draw a figure showing that when two identical firms share the market equally for a homogeneous product they both earn profits, but if a third identical firm entered the industry, they would all face losses. How is this related to the existence of oligopoly?

*12. If an oligopolist knows that the price elasticity of demand of the product it sells (η) is -4 and its $AVC = \$10$, determine
   a. the markup that the oligopolist should use in pricing its product;
   b. the price the oligopolist should charge.

APPENDIX   THE COURNOT AND STACKELBERG MODELS

This appendix is a more advanced and complete treatment of the Cournot model presented in Section 11.4, as well as an important extension of the model known as the Stackelberg model.

The Cournot Model—An Extended Treatment

We begin by writing the equation for market demand curve D shown in both panels of Figure 11.3 as

$$Q = 12 - P \qquad [11.5]$$

where Q is the total quantity of spring water sold in the market per unit of time (say, per week) and P is the market price. For example, applying formula [11.5], $Q = 0$ when $P = \$12$ (the vertical intercept of market demand curve D in the right panel of Figure 11.3, repeated below for ease of reference as the left panel of Figure 11.9). On the other hand, when $P = \$0$, $Q = 12$ (point C on market demand curve D in the left panel of Figure 11.9).

Given the quantity of spring water supplied by duopolist B (Q_B), duopolist A will supply one-half of the difference between 12 (the total that would be supplied to the market at $P = \$0$) and Q_B in order to maximize total profits. That is,

$$Q_A = \frac{12 - Q_B}{2} \qquad [11.6]$$

For example, when $Q_B = 0$, $Q_A = 12/2 = 6$ (point A on d_A in the left panel of Figure 11.9). On the other hand, when $Q_B = 3$, $Q_A = (12 - 3)/2 = 4.5$ (point A' on d_A in the left panel of Figure 11.9). With total costs equal to zero, duopolist A always maximizes total revenue and total profits by producing one-half of 12 minus the amount supplied by duopolist B (formula [11.6]). The reason is that (as shown in the left panel of Figure 11.3) this is the quantity at which $mr = MC = 0$.

Similarly, duopolist B maximizes total revenue and total profits by selling

$$Q_B = \frac{12 - Q_A}{2} \qquad [11.7]$$

For example, when $Q_A = 6$, $Q_B = (12 - 6)/2 = 3$ (point B on d_B in the left panel of Figure 11.9) because (as shown in the left panel of Figure 11.3) this is the quantity at which $mr = MC = 0$.

Reaction function A formula that shows how a duopolist reacts to the other duopolist's action.

Equation [11.6] is duopolist A's **reaction function.** This shows how duopolist A reacts to duopolist B's action and is plotted in the right panel of Figure 11.9. It shows that if $Q_B = 0$, $Q_A = 6$ (given by point A at which duopolist A's reaction function crosses the

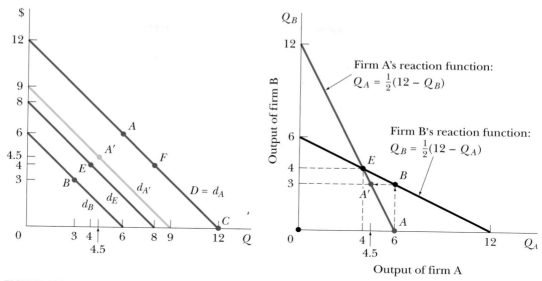

FIGURE 11.9   Duopolists' Demand Curves and Reaction Functions in the Cournot Model   The left panel shows the demand curves faced by duopolists A and B and the quantity sold by each, given the quantity sold by the other (exactly as in the right panel of Figure 11.3). The right panel shows duopolist A's and B's reaction functions. The intersection of the two reaction functions at point E gives the Cournot equilibrium of $Q_A = Q_B = 4$ (in the right panel), so that $Q_A + Q_B = 8$ and $P = \$4$ (point F in the left panel).

horizontal or Q_A axis in the right panel of Figure 11.9) in order for duopolist A to maximize total revenue and total profits. If $Q_B = 3$, $Q_A = 4.5$ (point A' on duopolist A's reaction function).

Similarly, equation [11.7] is duopolist B's reaction function and is also plotted in the right panel of Figure 11.9. It shows that if $Q_A = 6$, $Q_B = 3$ (given by point B on duopolist B's reaction function in the right panel of Figure 11.9) in order for duopolist B to maximize total revenue and total profits. Thus, a duopolist's reaction function shows the quantity that the duopolist should sell to maximize its total profits, given the amount sold by the other duopolist.

Cournot equilibrium
The situation where there is no tendency for each of two duopolists to change the quantity each sells.

The two reaction functions intersect at point E, giving the **Cournot equilibrium** of $Q_A = Q_B = 4$. That is, if $Q_B = 4$, then $Q_A = 4$ (point E on duopolist A's reaction function) for duopolist A to maximize total profits. Similarly, if $Q_A = 4$, then $Q_B = 4$ (point E on duopolist B's reaction function) for duopolist B to maximize total profits. Thus, point E (where the two reaction functions intersect) is the Cournot equilibrium point because there is no tendency for either duopolist to change the quantity it sells. A situation such as the Cournot equilibrium where each player's strategy is optimal, given the strategy chosen by the other player, is called a **Nash equilibrium.**

Nash equilibrium The situation when each player has chosen his or her optimal strategy, given the strategy chosen by the other player.

The right panel of Figure 11.9 can also be used to show the time path or movement toward equilibrium. With $Q_B = 0$, $Q_A = 6$ (point A on duopolist A's reaction function). With $Q_A = 6$, $Q_B = 3$ (point B on duopolist B's reaction function). With $Q_B = 3$, $Q_A = 4.5$ (point A' on duopolist A's reaction function). Note the direction of the arrows from point A to point B and from point B to point A' which move the duopolists toward the final Cournot equilibrium point E at the intersection of the two reaction functions.

The Cournot equilibrium point E can be obtained algebraically by substituting duopolist B's reaction function (i.e., equation [11.7]) into duopolist A's reaction function (equation [11.6]). Doing this, we get

$$Q_A = \frac{12 - (12 - Q_A)/2}{2}$$

$$= \frac{12 - 6 + Q_A/2}{2}$$

$$= 3 + Q_A/4 \qquad [11.8]$$

Multiplying both sides by 4, we get

$$4Q_A = 12 + Q_A$$

so that

$$3Q_A = 12$$

and

$$Q_A = 4 \qquad [11.9]$$

With $Q_A = 4$

$$Q_B = \frac{12 - 4}{2} \qquad [11.10]$$

so that

$$Q_A = 4 = Q_B \text{ (Cournot equilibrium)} \qquad [11.11]$$

and

$$Q = Q_A + Q_B = 4 + 4 = 8 \qquad [11.12]$$

Solving equation [11.5] for P, we get

$$P = 12 - Q \qquad [11.13]$$

With $Q = 8$ at Cournot equilibrium, the price at which each duopolist will sell spring water is

$$P = 12 - 8 = \$4 \qquad [11.14]$$

which is shown by point F in the left panel of Figure 11.9.

The Stackelberg Model

Stackelberg model
The extension of the Cournot model in which one duopolist knows how the other behaves and earns higher profits.

In 1934, the German economist Heinrich von Stackelberg made an important extension to the Cournot model. This became known as the **Stackelberg model.** Stackelberg assumed that one of the duopolists, say duopolist A, knows that duopolist B behaves in the naive Cournot fashion (i.e., A knows B's reaction function) and uses that knowledge in choosing its own output. Duopolist A is then called the *Stackelberg leader,* and duopolist B is referred to as the *Stackelberg follower.* All the other assumptions of the Cournot model hold. The Stackelberg model shows that duopolist A (the Stackelberg leader) will have higher profits than under the Cournot solution at the expense of duopolist B (the Stackelberg follower).

To examine the Stackelberg model, we begin by rewriting equation [11.5] for market demand function D:

$$Q = 12 - P \qquad\qquad [11.5]$$

Since Q refers to the total output of duopolists A and B, we can rewrite equation [11.5] as

$$Q_A + Q_B = 12 - P \qquad\qquad [11.15]$$

Because duopolist A knows duopolist B's reaction function, we can substitute equation [11.7] for Q_B into equation [11.15]. When we do this, we get

$$Q_A + (12 - Q_A)/2 = 12 - P \qquad\qquad [11.16]$$
$$Q_A + 6 - Q_A/2 = 12 - P$$
$$Q_A/2 = 6 - P$$
$$Q_A = 12 - 2P \qquad\qquad [11.17]$$

Equation [11.17] is now the demand function facing duopolist A when duopolist A knows duopolist B's reaction function and behavior. Plotting equation [11.17], we get the (residual) demand curve facing duopolist A, d_A^*, and its corresponding marginal revenue curve, mr_A^* (which, as usual, is twice as steep as the corresponding demand curve), as shown in Figure 11.10. Since marginal cost equals zero, duopolist A maximizes its total revenue and profits by selling six units of output (given by point E^* where $mr_A^* = MC = D$).

With $Q_A = 6$, $Q_B = 3$ (according to B's reaction function given by equation [11.7]). With $Q = Q_A + Q_B = 6 + 3 = 9$, $P = 12 - Q = 12 - 9 = 3$. Thus, duopolist A earns a total revenue and total profit of $18 (six units at $P = \$3$), while duopolist B earns a total revenue and total profit of $9 (three units times $P = \$3$). This compares with the four units of output sold by each duopolist at $P = \$4$ (with each earning a total revenue and profit of $16) under the Cournot model. Thus, duopolist A (the Stackelberg leader) gains at the expense of duopolist B (the Stackelberg follower) with respect to the Cournot solution. Note, however, that what duopolist A gains is less than what duopolist B loses. Of course, if duopolist B were the Stackelberg leader and duopolist A were the Stackelberg follower, duopolist B would earn $18 and duopolist A would earn $9. By allowing one of

FIGURE 11.10   Demand and Marginal Revenue Curves of Stackelberg Duopolist A d_A^* and mr_A^* are, respectively, the demand curve and the marginal revenue curve facing Stackelberg duopolist A. Since $MC = 0$, duopolist A maximizes its total revenue and total profits by selling six units. This is given by point E^* where $mr_A^* = MC = 0$. Duopolist B would then sell three units. With $Q = 9$, $P = \$3$, duopolist A earns $18 and duopolist B earns $9.

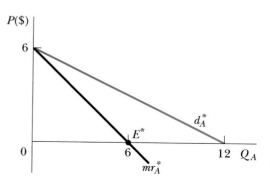

the firms to behave strategically, the Stackelberg model is thus superior to the Cournot model.

When duopolist A is the Stackelberg leader, the solution is the same as point B on duopolist B's reaction function in Figure 11.9. However, while point B is not the Cournot equilibrium, it does represent the Stackelberg solution. Note that under the Stackelberg solution (whether duopolist A or B is the Stackelberg leader), the combined total revenue and profits of both firms would be \$27 (\$18 + \$9). By colluding and operating as a centralized cartel or monopoly (see Section 11.5), the combined output of both firms could be cut from nine units in the Stackelberg solution to six units, which could be sold at $P = \$6$, so that the total combined revenue and profits that both firms could share would be \$36 (rather than \$27). This is sometimes referred to as the *Chamberlin model*.[22]

INTERNET SITE ADDRESSES

For concentration ratios in U.S. manufacturing industries, see:

> http://www.census.gov/prod/ec02/ec0231sr1.pdf

For OPEC, see:

> http://www.opec.org
> http://en.wikipedia.org/wiki/OPEC
> http://www.eia.doe.gov/oiaf/ieo/oil.html

For the Fortune Global 500 companies, see:

> http://fortune.com/global500

For competition in the automobile industry, see:

> http://en.wikipedia.org/wiki/Automaker
> http://www.thetruthaboutcars.com/?p=5928

For competition in international banking, see:

> Bank of America: http://www.bankamerica.com
> Citigroup: http://www.citigroup.com
> Deutsche Bank: http://www.deutschebank.com
> J.P. Morgan Chase: http://www.jpmorganchase.com
> Union Bank of Switzerland: http://www.ubs.com

For competition in the pharmaceutical industry, see:

> http://en.wikipedia.org/wiki/Pharmaceutical_company

Generic drugs: http://www.fda.gov/cder/ogd/

> Pfizer: http://www.pfizer.com
> GlaxoSmithKlein: http://www.gsk.com/
> Sanofi-Aventis: http://sanofi-aventis.com
> Novartis: http://www.novartis.com
> Johnson & Johnson: http://www.jj.com
> Merck: http://www.merck.com
> Procter & Gamble: http://www.pg.com

For the Internet site of other companies discussed in this chapter, see:

> McDonald's: http://www.mcdonalds.com
> AT&T: http://www.att.com
> Coca-Cola: http://www.coca-cola.com
> American Airlines: http://www.aa.com
> Time Warner: http://www.timewarner.com/corp
> Viacom: http://www.viacom.com/default.aspx
> Walt Disney: http://www.webdisney.com

---

[22] See D. Salvatore, "Schaum's Outline," in *Microeconomic Theory*, 4th ed. (New York: McGraw-Hill, 2006), pp. 240, 251–253.

CHAPTER 12

Game Theory and Oligopolistic Behavior

After Studying This Chapter, You Should Be Able to:

- Describe what game theory is and how it is used in economics
- Know the meaning of dominant strategy and Nash equilibrium
- Know the meaning of the prisoners' dilemma and its use in economics
- Describe the tit-for-tat strategy in economic competition
- Describe firms' strategic moves in the form of threats, commitments, and credibility

In this chapter, we extend our analysis of firm behavior in oligopolistic markets using game theory. As we will see, game theory offers many insights into oligopolistic interdependence and strategic behavior that could not be examined with the traditional tools of analysis presented in the previous chapter.

The chapter begins with an explanation of the basic concepts, objectives, and usefulness of game theory. It then defines a dominant strategy and a Nash equilibrium and examines their usefulness in the analysis of oligopolistic behavior. Next, the chapter describes the prisoners' dilemma and its applicability to the analysis of price and nonprice competition and cartel cheating. We conclude our discussion of game theory by analyzing multiple and strategic moves in domestic and international competition, with and without risk. The examples and applications presented in the chapter clearly highlight the importance of game theory to the understanding of many aspects of oligopolistic behavior that could not otherwise be explained. The "At the Frontier" section looks at the virtual corporation—the firm of the future—as the product of strategic alliances.

12.1   GAME THEORY: DEFINITION, OBJECTIVES, AND USEFULNESS

Game theory The theory that examines the choice of optimal strategies in conflict situations.

We have seen that oligopolists must consider the reactions of the other firms in the industry to their own actions. Some have likened the behavior of oligopolists to that of players in a game and to the strategic actions of warring factions. It is this crucial aspect of oligopolistic interdependence that game theory seeks to capture and explain (see Example 12–1).

Game theory was introduced by John von Neumann and Oskar Morgenstern in 1944, and it was soon hailed as a breakthrough in the study of oligopoly.[1] In general, **game theory** is concerned with the choice of an optimal strategy in conflict situations. Specifically, game theory can help an oligopolist choose the course of action (e.g., the best price to charge) that maximizes its benefits or profits after considering all possible reactions of its competitors. For example, game theory can help a firm determine (1) the conditions under which lowering its price would not trigger a ruinous price war; (2) whether the firm should build excess capacity to discourage entry into the industry, even though this lowers the firm's short-run profits; and (3) why cheating in a cartel usually leads to its collapse. Game theory can be of great use in the analysis of such conflict situations. In short, game theory shows how an oligopolistic firm can make strategic decisions to gain a competitive advantage over its rivals or how it can minimize the potential harm from a strategic move by a rival. Before we examine concrete examples, however, let us consider some of the common elements in all game theory.

✓ Concept Check
How does game theory help us understand strategic behavior in oligoplistic markets?

Every game theory model includes players, strategies, and payoffs. The **players** are the decision makers (here, the managers of oligopolist firms) whose behavior we are trying to explain and predict. **Strategies** are the potential choices to change price, to develop new or differentiated products, to introduce a new or a different advertising campaign, to build excess capacity, and all other such actions that affect the sales and profitability of the firm and its rivals. The **payoff** is the outcome or consequence of each strategy. For each strategy adopted by a firm, there is usually a number of strategies (reactions) available to a rival firm. The payoff is the outcome or consequence of each *combination* of strategies by the two firms. The payoff is usually expressed in terms of the profits or losses of the firm that we are examining as a result of the firm's strategies and the rivals' responses. A table that gives the payoffs from all the strategies open to the firm and the rivals' responses is called the **payoff matrix.**

Players The decision makers in the theory of games whose behavior we are trying to explain and predict.

Strategies The potential choices that can be made by the players (firms) in the theory of games.

Payoff The outcome or consequence of each combination of strategies by the players in game theory.

Payoff matrix The table of all the outcomes of the players' strategies.

We must distinguish between zero-sum games and nonzero-sum games. A **zero-sum game** is one in which the gain of one player comes at the expense and is exactly equal to the loss of the other player. An example of this occurs if firm A increases its market share at the expense of firm B by increasing its advertising expenditures (in the face of unchanged advertising by firm B). But if firm B also increases its advertising

Zero-sum game A game where the gains of one player equal the losses of the other.

---

[1] J. von Neumann and O. Morgenstern, *Theory of Games and Economic Behavior* (Princeton, NJ: Princeton University Press, 1944). A more recent and in-depth presentation of game theory with applications to economics is found in M. J. Osborne and A. Rubinstein, *A Course in Game Theory* (Cambridge, MA: MIT Press, 1994).

expenditures, firm A might not gain any market share at all. On the other hand, if firm A increases its price and firm B does not match the price increase, firm A might lose market to firm B. Games of this nature, where the gains of one player equal the losses of the other (so that total gains plus total losses sum to zero) are called zero-sum games. If the gains or losses of one firm do not come at the expense of or provide equal benefit to the other firm, however, we have a **nonzero-sum game.** An example of this might arise if increased advertising leads to higher profits of both firms and we use profits rather than market share as the payoff. In this case we would have a *positive-sum game.* If increased advertising raises costs more than revenues and the profits of both firms decline, we have a *negative-sum game.*

Nonzero-sum game A game where the gains of one player do not come at the expense of or are not equal to the losses of the other player.

EXAMPLE 12–1
Military Strategy and Strategic Business Decisions

According to William E. Peacock, the former president of two St. Louis companies and former assistant secretary of the army under President Carter, decision making in business has much in common with military strategy and can thus be profitably analyzed using game theory. Although business managers' actions are restricted by laws and regulations to prevent unfair practices and the objective of managers, of course, is not to literally destroy the competition, there is much that they can learn from military strategists. Peacock points out that throughout history, military conflicts have produced a set of basic Darwinian principles that can serve as an excellent guideline to business managers about how to compete in the marketplace. Neglecting these principles can make the difference between business success and failure.

In business as in war, it is crucial for the organization to have a clear objective and to explain this objective to all of its employees. The benefits of a simple marketing strategy that all employees can understand are clearly evidenced by the success of McDonald's. Both business and war also require the development of a strategy for attacking. Being aggressive is important because few competitions are ever won by being passive. Furthermore, both business and warfare require unity of command to pinpoint responsibility. Even in decentralized companies with informal lines of command, there are always key individuals who must make important decisions. Finally, in business as in war, the element of surprise and security (keeping your strategy secret) is crucial. For example, Lee Iacocca stunned the competition in 1964 by introducing the immensely successful (high payoff) Mustang. Finally, in business as in war, spying to discover a rival's plans or steal a rival's new technological breakthrough is becoming more common.

More than ever before, today's business leaders must learn how to tap employees' ideas and energy, manage large-scale rapid change, anticipate business conditions five or ten years down the road, and muster the courage to steer the firm in radical new directions when necessary. Above all, firms must think and act strategically in a world of increasing global competition. Game theory can be particularly useful and can offer important insights in the analysis of oligopolistic interdependence. Indeed, more and more firms are making use of war-games simulations in their decision making. At the same time, politicians and military leaders are using advances in game theory made by Robert Aumann and Thomas Schelling, the 2005 economics Nobel Prize winners, in their war games.

Sources: W. E. Peacock, *Corporate Combat* (New York: Facts on File Publication, 1984); "The Valley of Spies," *Forbes,* October 26, 1992, pp. 200–204; "Business War Games Attract Big Warriors," *Wall Street Journal,* December 22, 1994, p. B1; "The Right Game: Use Game Theory to Shape Strategy," *Harvard Business Review,* July–August 1995, pp. 57–71; "From Battlefield to Boardroom," *Financial Times,* February 10, 2003, p . 7; "Global Gamesmanship," *Harvard Business Review,* May 2003, pp. 62–71; "War Games," *The Economist,* October 15, 2005, p. 82; H. Nasheri, *Economic Espionage and Industrial Spying* (New York: Cambridge University Press, 2005); and "Leaders of the Pack," *Wall Street Journal,* March 3–4, 2007, p. R9.

12.2   DOMINANT STRATEGY AND NASH EQUILIBRIUM

In this section, we discuss the meaning of a dominant strategy and the Nash equilibrium, and examine their usefulness in the analysis of oligopolistic interdependence.

Dominant Strategy

Let's begin with the simplest type of game with an industry (duopoly) composed of two firms, firm A and firm B, and a choice of two strategies for each—advertise or don't advertise. Firm A, of course, expects to earn higher profits if it advertises than if it doesn't. But the actual level of profits of firm A depends also on whether firm B advertises. Thus, each strategy by firm A (i.e., advertise or don't advertise) can be associated with each of firm B's strategies (also to advertise or not to advertise). The four possible outcomes from this simple game are illustrated by the payoff matrix in Table 12.1.

In the payoff matrix in Table 12.1, the first number in each of the four cells refers to the payoff (profit) for firm A, while the second is the payoff (profit) for firm B. From Table 12.1, we see that if both firms advertise, firm A will earn a profit of 4, and firm B will earn a profit of 3 (the top left cell of the payoff matrix).[2] The bottom left cell of the payoff matrix shows that if firm A doesn't advertise and firm B does, firm A will have a profit of 2, and firm B will have a profit of 5. The other payoffs in the second column of the table can be interpreted in the same way.

TABLE 12.1   Payoff Matrix for the Advertising Game

		Firm B	
		Advertise	Don't Advertise
Firm A	Advertise	4, 3	5, 1
	Don't Advertise	2, 5	3, 2

---

[2] The profits of 4 and 3 could refer, for example, to $4 million and $3 million, respectively.

What strategy should each firm choose? Let's consider firm A first. If firm B does advertise (i.e., moving down the left column of Table 12.1), we see that firm A will earn a profit of 4 if it also advertises and 2 if it doesn't. Thus, firm A should advertise if firm B advertises. If firm B doesn't advertise (i.e., moving down the right column in Table 12.1), firm A would earn a profit of 5 if it advertises and 3 if it doesn't. Thus, firm A should advertise whether firm B advertises or not. Firm A's profits will always be greater if it advertises than if it doesn't, regardless of what firm B does. We can then say that advertising is the dominant strategy for firm A. The **dominant strategy** is the optimal choice for a player no matter what the opponent does.

The same is true for firm B. Whatever firm A does (i.e., whether firm A advertises or not), it will always pay for firm B to advertise. We can see this by moving across each row of Table 12.1. Specifically, if firm A advertises, firm B's profit would be 3 if it advertises and 1 if it does not. Similarly, if firm A does not advertise, firm B's profit would be 5 if it advertises and 2 if it doesn't. Thus, the dominant strategy for firm B is also to advertise.

In this case, both firm A and firm B have the dominant strategy of advertising and this will, therefore, be the final equilibrium. Both firm A and firm B will advertise regardless of what the other firm does and will earn a profit of 4 and 3, respectively (the top left cell in the payoff matrix in Table 12.1). The advertising solution or final equilibrium for both firms holds whether firm A or firm B chooses its strategy first or if both firms decide on their best strategy simultaneously.

Nash Equilibrium

Not all games have a dominant strategy for each player, however. An example of this is shown in the payoff matrix in Table 12.2. This table is the same as the payoff matrix in Table 12.1, except that the first number in the bottom right cell was changed from 3 to 6. Now firm B has a dominant strategy but firm A does not. The dominant strategy for firm B is to advertise whether firm A advertises or not, because the payoffs for firm B are the same as in Table 12.1. Firm A, however, has no dominant strategy now. If firm B advertises, firm A earns a profit of 4 if it advertises and 2 if it does not. Thus, if firm B advertises, firm A should also advertise. On the other hand, if firm B does not advertise, firm A earns a profit of 5 if it advertises and 6 if it does not.[3] Thus, firm A should advertise if firm B does, and it should not advertise if firm B doesn't. Firm A no longer has a dominant strategy. What firm A should do now depends on what firm B does.

Dominant strategy
The optimal strategy for a player no matter what the other player does.

TABLE 12.2   Payoff Matrix for the Advertising Game

		Firm B	
		Advertise	Don't Advertise
Firm A	Advertise	4, 3	5, 1
	Don't Advertise	2, 5	6, 2

---

[3] This might result, for example, if firm A's advertisement is not effective or if advertising adds more to firm A's costs than to its revenues.

In order for firm A to determine whether to advertise, firm A must first try to determine what firm B will do (and advertise if firm B does and not advertise if firm B does not). If firm A knows the payoff matrix, it can figure out that firm B has the dominant strategy of advertising. Therefore, the optimal strategy for firm A is also to advertise (because firm A will earn a profit of 4 by advertising and 2 by not advertising—see the first column of Table 12.2). This is the Nash equilibrium, named after John Nash, the Princeton University mathematician and 1994 Nobel prize winner who first formalized the notion in 1951.

The **Nash equilibrium** is a situation in which each player chooses an optimal strategy, *given the strategy chosen by the other player.* In our example, the high advertising strategy for firm A and firm B is the Nash equilibrium, because given that firm B chooses its dominant strategy of advertising, the optimal strategy for firm A is also to advertise. Note that when both firms had a dominant strategy, each firm was able to choose its optimal strategy regardless of the strategy adopted by its rival. Here, only firm B has a dominant strategy; firm A does not. As a result, firm A cannot choose its optimal strategy independently of firm B's strategy. Only when each player has chosen its optimal strategy given the strategy of the other player do we have a Nash equilibrium. The Cournot equilibrium examined in Section 11.4 was an example of a Nash equilibrium. Not all games have a Nash equilibrium, and some games can have more than one Nash equilibrium (see Problem 3, with the answer at the end of the book).

Nash equilibrium The situation when each player has chosen his or her optimal strategy, given the strategy chosen by the other player.

✓ Concept Check
What is the relationship between a dominant strategy and Nash equilibrium?

EXAMPLE 12–2
Dell Computers and Nash Equilibrium

Dell Computers of Austin, Texas, a company created by 27-year-old Michael Dell in 1984, ended the 2006 fiscal year with revenues of $57.1 billion, making it the largest PC computer company in the United States and the second largest in the world after Hewlett-Packard (H-P). By offering a 30-day money-back guarantee on next-day, free on-site service through independent contractors for the first year of ownership, and unlimited calls to a toll-free technical support line, Dell established a solid reputation for reliability, thus taking the fear and uncertainty out of mail-order computers. Ordering a computer from Dell by mail is now like ordering a Big Mac at MacDonald's—you know exactly what you will get. By eliminating retailers, Dell was also able to charge lower prices than its larger and more established competitors. Dell ships computers by mail by adding only a 2% shipping charge to the sale price. When receiving a mail order, Dell technicians simply pick up the now-standard components from the shelf to assemble the particular PC ordered. It is simple, quick, and inexpensive. Thus, Dell developed a dominant strategy—one that seemed optimal regardless of what competitors did.

Until the early 1990s, traditional computer firms, such as IBM, H-P, and Apple, always thought that customers were willing to pay a substantial retail markup for the privilege of being able to go to a store and touch the machine before buying it. But by reducing fears and uncertainty from ordering computers through the mail, Dell was able to convince a growing number of customers to bypass the retailers and order directly from Dell by mail at lower prices. Given Dell's dominant and profitable strategy,

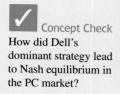

Concept Check

How did Dell's dominant strategy lead to Nash equilibrium in the PC market?

other computer firms in the United States quickly followed and set up their own mail-order departments and 800-phone lines. Their dominant strategy of selling exclusively through retail outlets seemed knocked out by Dell's new market strategy, so the computer industry was in Nash equilibrium. Dell, however, was more adept at selling computers through the mail and retained almost 50% of the mail-order computer business.

By 2005, Dell reached its peak, with 19% of the world PC market and 32% of the U.S. market, and it was growing and earning profits while other PC markers were shrinking and incurring losses. In fact, IBM left the PC market at the end of 2004 when it sold its laptop business to Lenovo of China. Starting in 2006, however, Dell started to lose market share to H-P and other PC firms as consumers in the United States started to gravitate to stores to purchase laptops, and consumers in emerging market never fully embraced Internet shopping for lack of experience and adequate delivery services. By 2007, Dell's share of the world PC market had fallen to 15.2% (as compared to a rise to 19.1% for H-P) and its share of the U.S. market had fallen to 26.8% (while H-P's share increased to 25.5%). This led Dell to rethink its made-to-order, direct-to-customers PC sales model, and in 2007 it began also to sell its laptops at Wal-Mart and other stores in the United States and abroad.

Sources: "The Computer Is in the Mail (Really)," *Business Week*, January 23, 1995, pp. 76–77; "Michael Dell Turns the PC World Inside Out," *Fortune*, September 8, 1997, pp. 76–86; "IBM Plans to Stop Selling Its PC's in Retail Outlets," *New York Times*, October 20, 1999, p. C6; "Dell Domination," *Fortune*, January 21, 2002, pp. 71–75; "IBM Strikes a Deal with Rival Lenovo," *Wall Street Journal*, December 9, 2004, p. A3; "Dell to Rely Less on Direct Sales," *Wall Street Journal*, May 25, 2007, p. A3; and "Profit Fells as Dell Tries to Grow and Limit Costs," *New York Times*, February 29, 2008, p. C3.

12.3 | THE PRISONERS' DILEMMA, PRICE AND NONPRICE COMPETITION, AND CARTEL CHEATING

In this section, we examine the meaning of the prisoners' dilemma and see how it can be applied to explain oligopolistic behavior in the form of price and nonprice competition and cartel cheating.

The Prisoners' Dilemma: Definition and Importance

Prisoners' dilemma
The situation where each player adopts his or her dominant strategy but could do better by cooperating.

Concept Check

What is the prisoners' dilemma?

Oligopolistic firms often face a problem called the **prisoners' dilemma.** This refers to a situation in which each firm adopts its dominant strategy but each could do better (e.g., earn larger profits) by cooperating. Consider the following situation. Two suspects are arrested for armed robbery; if convicted, each could receive a maximum sentence of 10 years imprisonment. Unless one or both suspects confess, however, the evidence is such that they could only be convicted of possessing stolen goods, which carries a maximum sentence of one year in prison. Each suspect is interrogated separately and no communication is allowed between the two suspects. The district attorney promises each suspect that by confessing, he or she will go free while the other suspect (who does not confess) will receive the full 10-year sentence. If both suspects confess, each gets a reduced

TABLE 12.3	Negative Payoff Matrix for Suspect A and Suspect B (years of detention)		
		Suspect B	
		Confess	Don't Confess
Suspect A	Confess	5, 5	0, 10
	Don't Confess	10, 0	1, 1

sentence of five years, imprisonment. The (negative) payoff matrix in terms of detention years is given in Table 12.3.

From Table 12.3, we see that confessing is the best or dominant strategy for suspect A no matter what suspect B does. The reason is that if suspect B confesses, suspect A receives a 5-year jail sentence if he also confesses and a 10-year sentence if he does not. Similarly, if suspect B does not confess, suspect A goes free if he confesses and receives a one-year sentence if he does not. Thus, the dominant strategy for suspect A is to confess. Confessing is also the best (and the dominant) strategy for suspect B. The reason is that if suspect A confesses, suspect B gets a five-year jail sentence if he also confesses and a 10-year jail sentence if he does not. Similarly, if suspect A does not confess, suspect B goes free if he confesses and gets one year if he does not. Thus, the dominant strategy for suspect B is also to confess.

With each suspect adopting his or her dominant strategy of confessing, each ends up receiving a five-year jail sentence. But if each suspect did not confess, each would get only a one-year jail sentence! Each suspect, however, is afraid that if he or she does not confess, the other will confess, and so he or she would end up receiving a 10-year jail sentence. Only if each suspect were sure that the other would not confess, and he or she does not confess, would each get only a one-year sentence. Because it is not possible to reach an agreement not to confess (remember, the suspects are already in jail and cannot communicate), each suspect adopts his or her dominant strategy to confess and receives a five-year jail sentence. Even if an agreement not to confess could be reached, the agreement could not be enforced. Therefore, each suspect will end up confessing and receiving a five-year jail sentence.

Price and Nonprice Competition, Cartel Cheating, and the Prisoners' Dilemma

The concept of the prisoners' dilemma can be used to analyze price and nonprice competition in oligopolistic markets, as well as the incentive to cheat in a cartel (i.e., the tendency to cut prices secretly or to sell more than the allocated quota). Oligopolistic price competition in the presence of the prisoners' dilemma can be examined with the payoff matrix in Table 12.4.

The payoff matrix of Table 12.4 shows that if firm B charged a low price (say, $6), firm A would earn a profit of 2 if it also charged the low price ($6) and 1 if it charged a high price (say, $8). Similarly, if firm B charged a high price ($8), firm A would earn a profit of 5 if it charged the low price and 3 if it charged the high price. Thus, firm A should

TABLE 12.4	Payoff Matrix for Pricing Game		
		Firm B	
		Low Price	High Price
Firm A	Low Price	2, 2	5, 1
	High Price	1, 5	3, 3

adopt its dominant strategy of charging the low price. Turning to firm B, we see that if firm A charged the low price, firm B would earn a profit of 2 if it charged the low price and 1 if it charged the high price. Similarly, if firm A charged the high price, firm B would earn a profit of 5 if it charged the low price and 3 if it charged the high price. Thus, firm B should also adopt its dominant strategy of charging the low price. However, both firms could do better (i.e., earn the higher profit of 3) if they cooperated and both charged the high price (the bottom right cell).

Thus, the firms are in a prisoners' dilemma: Each firm will charge the low price and earn a smaller profit because if it charges the high price, it cannot trust its rival also to charge the high price. Specifically, suppose that firm A charged the high price, with the expectation that firm B would also charge the high price (so that each firm would earn a profit of 3). Given that firm A has charged the high price, however, firm B now has an incentive to charge the low price, because by doing so it can increase its profits to 5 (see the bottom left cell). The same is true if firm B started by charging the high price, with the expectation that firm A would also do so. The net result is that each firm charges the low price and earns a profit of only 2. Only if the two firms cooperate and both charge the high price will they earn the higher profit of 3 (and overcome their dilemma).

Although the payoff matrix of Table 12.4 was used to examine oligopolistic price competition in the presence of the prisoners' dilemma, by simply changing the heading of the columns and rows of the payoff matrix we can use the same payoff matrix to examine nonprice competition and cartel cheating. For example, if we change the heading of "low price" to "advertise" and the heading of "high price" to "don't advertise" in Table 12.4, we can use the same matrix to analyze advertising as a form of nonprice competition in the presence of the prisoners' dilemma. We see that each firm would adopt its dominant strategy of advertising and (as in the case of charging a low price) would earn a profit of 2. Both firms, however, would do better by not advertising because they would then earn (as in the case of charging a high price) the higher profit of 3. The firms then face the prisoners' dilemma. Only by cooperating in not advertising would each increase its profits to 3. For example, when cigarette advertising on television was banned in 1971, all tobacco companies benefitted by spending less on advertising and earning higher profits. While the intended effect of the law was to encourage people not to smoke, the law had the unintended effect of solving the prisoners' dilemma for cigarette producers!

Similarly, if we now change the heading of "low price" or "advertise" to "cheat" and the heading of "high price" or "don't advertise" to "don't cheat" in the columns and rows of the payoff matrix of Table 12.4, we can use the same payoffs in the table to analyze the incentive for cartel members to cheat in the presence of the prisoners' dilemma. In this case, each firm adopts its dominant strategy of cheating and (as in the case of charging the low price or advertising) earns a profit of 2. But by not cheating,

✓ Concept Check

How can the concept of the prisoners' dilemma be used to analyze price competition?

however, each member of the cartel would earn the higher profit of 3. The cartel members then face the prisoners' dilemma. Only if cartel members do not cheat will each share the higher cartel profits of 3. A cartel can prevent or reduce the probability of cheating by monitoring the sales of each member and punishing cheaters. However, the larger the cartel and the more differentiated the product, the more difficult it is for the cartel to do this and prevent cheating.

EXAMPLE 12–3
The Airlines' Fare War and the Prisoners' Dilemma

In April 1992, American Airlines, then the nation's largest carrier, with 20% share of the domestic market, introduced a new, simplified fare structure that included only four kinds of fares instead of 16, and it lowered prices for most business and leisure travelers. Coach fares were cut by an average of 38%, and first-class fares were lowered by 20% to 50%. Other domestic airlines quickly announced similar fare cuts. American and other carriers hoped that the increase in air travel resulting from the fare cuts would more than offset the price reductions and eventually turn losses into badly needed profits (during 1990 and 1991, domestic airlines lost more than $6 billion, Pan Am and Eastern Airlines went out of business, and Continental, TWA, and America West filed for bankruptcy protection).

✓ **Concept Check**
How and why do price wars arise in the U.S. airline industry?

Rather than establishing price discipline, however, American's new fare structure started a process of competitive fare cuts that led to another disastrous price war during the summer of 1992. It started when TWA, operating under protection from creditors and badly needing quick revenues, began to undercut American's fares by 10% to 20% as soon as they were announced. American and other airlines responded by matching TWA price cuts. Then, on May 26, 1992, Northwest, in an effort to stimulate summer leisure travel, announced that an adult and child could travel on the same flight within continental United States for the price of one ticket. The next day, American countered by cutting all fares by 50%. The other big carriers immediately matched American's 50% price cut for all summer travel. Another full-fledged price war had been unleashed.

Even though deep price cuts increased summer travel sharply, all airlines incurred losses (i.e., the low fares failed to cover the industry average cost). Three attempts to increase air fares by 30% above presale levels in the fall of 1992 failed when one or more of the carriers did not go along. Having become used to deep discounts, passengers were simply unwilling to pay higher fares, especially in a weak economy. Similar price wars erupted in summer 1993 and 1994. In short, U.S. airlines seemed to be in a prisoners' dilemma and, unable to cooperate, faced heavy losses. Only with the strong rebound in air travel in 1995 did airlines refrain from engaging in another disastrous price war and thus earned profits.

But tranquility and profits did not last long. The 2001 economic recession and the September 11 terrorist attack on the World Trade Center resulted in a sharp decline in air travel, and the subsequent pressure from low-cost carrier Southwest and the emergence of discount carriers such as Sky West, JetBlue, and AirTran, sparked renewed fare wars, leading to total industry losses of $35.1 billion from 2001 to 2005. This, together with the doubling of jet fuel prices, caused Delta and Northwest to join United and U.S. Airways into Chapter 11 bankruptcy in 2005. Only in 2006 did U.S. airlines return to profitability, by increasing fares, and the load factor (i.e., the percentage of occupied seats), and streamlining their fleet. The further increase in jet fuel prices and fare competition however, plunged American airlines back into the red in 2008.

Sources: "American Air Cuts Most Fares in Simplification of Rate System," *New York Times,* April 10, 1992, p. 1; "The Airlines Are Killing Each Other Again," *Business Week,* June 8, 1992, p. 32; "Airlines Cut Fares by up to 45%," *New York Times,* September 14, 1993, p. D1; "The Age of 'Wal-Mart' Airlines Crunches the Biggest Carriers," *Wall Street* Journal, June 18, 2002, p. A1; "Flying on Empty," *The Economist,* September 17, 2005, pp. 59–60; "Higher Fares Lift US Ailrines, *Financial Times,* October 19, 2007, p. 18; and "Survival of the Biggest," *Business Week,* February 25, 2008, pp. 28–29.

12.4 REPEATED GAMES AND TIT-FOR-TAT STRATEGY

Repeated games
Prisoners' dilemma games of more than one move.

Tit-for-tat The best strategy in repeated prisoners' dilemma games, which postulates "Do to your opponent what he or she has just done to you."

We have seen how two firms facing the prisoners' dilemma can increase their profits by cooperating. Such cooperation, however, is not likely to occur in the single-move prisoners' dilemma games discussed so far. Cooperation is more likely to occur in repeated or many-move games, which are more realistic in the real world. For example, oligopolists do not decide on their pricing strategy only once, but many times over many years. Axelrod found that in such **repeated games** the best strategy is that of tit-for-tat.[4] **Tit-for-tat** behavior can be summarized as follows: Do to your opponent what he or she has just done to you. That is, begin by cooperating and continue to cooperate as long as your opponent cooperates. If he betrays you, the next time you betray him back. If he then cooperates, the next time you also cooperate. This strategy is retaliatory enough to discourage noncooperation but forgiving enough to allow a pattern of mutual cooperation to develop. In fact, Axelrod found through computer simulated experiments that tit-for-tat is the best strategy in repeated prisoners' dilemma games.

For an optimal tit-for-tat strategy, however, certain conditions must be met. First, a reasonably stable set of players is required. If the players change frequently, there is little chance for cooperative behavior to develop. Second, there must be a small number of players (otherwise, it becomes difficult to keep track of what each is doing). Third, it is assumed that each firm can quickly detect (and is willing and able to quickly retaliate for) cheating by other firms. Cheating that goes undetected for a long time encourages cheating. Fourth, demand and cost conditions must be relatively stable (for if they change rapidly, it is difficult to define what is cooperative behavior and what is not). Fifth, it must be assumed that the game is repeated indefinitely, or at least a very large and *uncertain* number of times. If the game is played for a finite number of times, each firm has an incentive not to cooperate in the final period because it cannot be harmed by retaliation. Each firm knows this and thus will not cooperate on the next-to-the-last move. Indeed, in

---

[4] See R. Axelrod, *The Evolution of Cooperation* (New York: Basic Books, 1984).

an effort to gain a competitive advantage by being the first to start cheating, the entire situation will unravel and cheating begins from the first move.[5]

There are, of course, times when a firm finds it advantageous not to cooperate. For example, if a supplier is near bankruptcy, a firm may find every excuse for not paying its bills to the near-bankrupt firm (claiming, for example, that supplies were defective or did not meet specification) in the hope of avoiding payment altogether if the firm does go out of business. It is the necessity to deal with the same suppliers and customers in the future and their ability to retaliate for noncooperative behavior that often forces a firm to cooperate. With a tit-for-tat strategy, however, it is possible for firms to cooperate without actually resorting to collusion. As we will see in the next chapter, this can be a nightmare for antitrust officials.

✔ **Concept Check**
Why is tit-for-tat the best strategy in repeated games?

12.5   STRATEGIC MOVES

In this section, we examine strategic games involving threats, commitments, credibility, and entry deterrence. In the next section, we discuss strategic games and international competitiveness, and in the final section we examine risk in game theory. These concepts greatly enrich game theory and provide an important element of realism and relevance.

Threats, Commitments, and Credibility

Oligopolistic firms often adopt strategies to gain a competitive advantage over their rivals, even if it means constraining their own behavior or temporarily reducing their own profits. For example, an oligopolist may threaten to lower its prices if its rivals lower theirs, even if this means reducing its own profits. This threat can be made credible, for example, by a written commitment to customers to match any lower price by competitors. Schelling defined such a **strategic move** as one that "influences the other person's choice in a manner favorable to one's self by affecting the other person's expectations of how one's self would behave."[6] There must be a *commitment* that the firm making the *threat* is ready to carry it out for the threat to be *credible*.

For example, suppose that the payoff matrix of firms A and B is given by Table 12.5. This payoff matrix indicates that firm A has the dominant strategy of charging a high

Strategic move A player's strategy of constraining his or her own behavior to make a threat credible so as to gain a competitive advantage.

TABLE 12.5   Payoff Matrix for Pricing Game with a Threat

		Firm B	
		Low Price	High Price
Firm A	Low Price	2, 2	2, 1
	High Price	3, 4	5, 3

[5] See D. Kreps, P. Milgron, J. Roberts, and R. Wilson, "Rational Cooperation in the Finitely Repeated Prisoners' Dilemma," *Journal of Economic Theory,* vol. 27, 1982, pp. 245–252.
[6] See T. Schelling, *The Strategy of Conflict* (New York: Oxford University Press, 1960). Another important volume examining strategic moves is M. Porter, *Competitive Strategy* (New York: Free Press, 1980).

price. The reason is that if firm B charged a low price, firm A would earn a profit of 2 if it charged a low price and a profit of 3 if it charged a high price. Similarly, if firm B charged a high price, firm A would earn a profit of 2 if it charged a low price and a profit of 5 if it charged a high price. Therefore, firm A charges a high price regardless of what firm B does. Given that firm A charges a high price, firm B will want to charge a low price because by doing so it will earn a profit of 4 (instead of 3 with a high price). This is shown by the bottom left cell of Table 12.5. Now firm A can threaten to lower its price and also charge a low price. However, firm B does not believe this threat (i.e., the threat is not credible) because by lowering its price firm A would lower its profits from 3 (with a high price) to 2 with the low price (the top left cell in the table).

Concept Check
How can a firm make a credible threat against its competitors?

One way to make its threat credible is for firm A to develop a *reputation* for carrying out its threats, even at the expense of its profits. Although this may seem irrational, if firm A actually carried out its threat several times, it would earn a reputation for making credible threats. This is likely to induce firm B to also charge a high price, which would possibly lead to higher profits for firm A in the long run. In that case, firm A would earn a profit of 5 and firm B a profit of 3 (the bottom right cell) as opposed to a profit of 3 for firm A and 4 for firm B (the bottom left cell). Even if firm B earns a profit of 3 by charging the high price (as compared with a profit of 4 by charging the low price), the profit is still higher than the profit of 2 that it would earn if firm A carries out the threat of charging the low price if firm B does the same (see the top left cell of the table). By showing a commitment to carry out its threats, firm A makes its threats credible and increases its profits over time. The same result would follow if firm A develops a reputation for being irrational and charging a low price to deter entry into the industry—even if this means lower profits in the long run.

Entry Deterrence

One important strategy that an oligopolist can use to deter market entry is to threaten to lower its price and thereby impose a loss on the potential entrant. Such a threat, however, works only if it is credible. *Entry deterrence* can be examined with the payoff matrices of Tables 12.6 and 12.7.

The payoff matrix of Table 12.6 shows that firm A's threat to lower its price is not credible and does not discourage firm B from entering the market. The reason is that firm A earns a profit of 4 if it charges the low price and a profit of 7 if it charges the high price. Unless firm A makes a credible commitment to fight entry even at the expense of profits, it would not deter firm B from entering the market. Firm A could make a credible threat by expanding its capacity before it is needed (i.e., to build excess capacity). The new payoff matrix might then look like the one in Table 12.7.

TABLE 12.6   Payoff Matrix Without Credible Entry Deterrence

		Firm B	
		Enter	Don't Enter
Firm A	Low Price	4, −2	6, 0
	High Price	7, 2	10, 0

TABLE 12.7   Payoff Matrix with Credible Entry Deterrence

		Firm B	
		Enter	Don't Enter
Firm A	Low Price	4, −2	6, 0
	High Price	3, 2	8, 0

The payoff matrix of Table 12.7 is the same as in Table 12.6, except that firm A's profits are now lower when it charges a high price because idle or excess capacity increases firm A's costs without increasing its sales. On the other hand, in the payoff matrix of Table 12.7, we assume that charging a low price would allow firm A to increase sales and utilize its newly built capacity, so that costs and revenues *increase* leaving firm A's profits the same as in Table 12.6 (i.e., the same as before firm A expanded capacity).[7] Building excess capacity in anticipation of future need now becomes a credible threat, because with excess capacity firm A will charge a low price and earn a profit of 4 instead of a profit of 3 if it charged the high price. By charging a low price now, however, firm B would incur a loss of 2 if it entered the market, and so firm B would stay out. Entry deterrence is now credible and effective. An alternative to building excess capacity could be for firm A to cultivate a reputation for irrationality in deterring entry by charging a low price even if this means earning lower profits indefinitely.[8]

EXAMPLE 12–4

Wal-Mart's Preemptive Expansion Marketing Strategy

Rapid expansion during the 1980s (from 153 stores in 1976 to more than 4,000 in 2007) propelled Wal-Mart, the discount retail-store chain started by Sam Walton in 1969, to become the nation's (and the world's) largest and most profitable retailer, at a time when most other retailers were making razor-thin profits or incurring losses as a result of stiff competition. How did Wal-Mart do it? By opening retail discount stores in small towns across America and adopting an everyday low-price strategy. The conventional wisdom had been that a discount retail outlet required a population base of at least 100,000 people to be profitable. Sam Walton showed otherwise: By relying on size, low costs, and high turnover, Wal-Mart earned high profits even in

---

[7] Revenues and profits need not increase exactly by the same amount, so that profits can change even when firm A charges a low price. The conclusion would remain the same, however (i.e., firm B would be deterred from entering the market), as long as firm A earns a higher profit with a low price than with a high price after increasing its capacity.

[8] For a more detailed analysis of the use of excess capacity to deter entry, see J. Tirole, *The Theory of Industrial Organization* (Cambridge, MA: MIT Press, 1988).

✓ Concept Check
What is Wal-Mart's
marketing strategy?

towns of only a few thousand people. Since a small town could support only one large discount store, Wal-Mart did not have to worry about competition from other national chains (which would drive prices and profit margins down). At the same time, Wal-Mart was able to easily undersell small local specialized stores out of existence (Wal-Mart has been labeled the "Merchant of Death" by local retailers), thereby establishing a virtual local retailing monopoly.

The success of Wal-Mart did not go unnoticed by other national discount retailers such as Kmart and Target, and so a frantic race started to open discount stores in rural America ahead of the competition. By adopting such an aggressive expansion or *preemptive investment strategy,* Wal-Mart continued to expand at breathtaking speed and to beat the competition most of the time. Sales at Wal-Mart increased from $80 billion in 1994 to $351 billion in 2006 (thus heading the list of the Fortune 500 companies). Pricier than Wal-Mart and dowdier than Target, Kmart, instead, filed for bankruptcy in January 2002 and merged with Sears Roebuck in 2004 to form Kmart Holdings.

Since 1992, Wal-Mart has also expanded abroad, first in Canada and Mexico (where it is already the largest retailer) and then in Argentina, Brazil, China, Korea, Puerto Rico, Germany, England, and Japan. In 2007, Wal-Mart had 2,980 stores abroad, which generated 20% of its total revenue. Success, however, proved more difficult abroad (in fact Wal-Mart exited Korea and Germany in 2006) after failing to adapt to local tastes and achieve economies of scale. European retailers responded by also consolidating. For example, in fall 1999, French retailers Carrefour and Promedes merged, creating Europe's biggest and the world's second-largest retailer, with annual sales of $99 billion and operating nearly 15,000 stores (of them 5,500 in France) in 30 countries. Rival retailers are also luring customers away from Wal-Mart in the United States by offering greater convenience, more selection, and higher quality or better service. The Wal-Mart era thus seems to be waning amid big shifts in retailing in the United States and abroad.

Sources: "Big Discounters Duel Over Hot Market," *Wall Street Journal*, August 23, 1995, p. A8; "French Retailers Create New Wal-Mart Rival," *Wall Street Journal*, August 31, 1999, p. A14; "Wal-Mart Around the World," *The Economist*, December 8, 2001, pp. 55–57; "Kmart Takeover of Sears Is Set," *New York Times,* November 11, 2004, p. 1; "Wal-Mart," *Forbes*, April 12, 2005, pp. 77–85; "Carrefour at the Crossroad," *The Economist*, October 31, 2005, p. 71; and "Wal-Mart Era Wanes Amid Big Shifts in Retail," *Wall Street Journal*, October 3, 2007, p. A1.

12.6 STRATEGIC MOVES AND INTERNATIONAL COMPETITIVENESS

Game theory can also be used to analyze the strategic trade and industrial policies that a nation could use to gain a competitive advantage over other nations, particularly in the field of high technology. This is best shown through an example.

Suppose that Boeing (the American commercial aircraft company) and Airbus Industrie (a consortium of German, French, English, and Spanish companies) are both deciding whether to produce a new aircraft. Suppose also that because of the huge cost of developing the new aircraft, a single producer would have to have the entire world

TABLE 12.8   Two-Firm Competition and Strategic Trade Policy

		Airbus	
		Produce	Don't Produce
Boeing	Produce	−10, −10	100, 0
	Don't Produce	0, 100	0, 0

market for itself to earn a profit, say of $100 million. If both firms produce the aircraft, each loses $10 million. This information is shown in Table 12.8. The case in which both firms produce the aircraft and each incurs a loss of $10 million is shown in the top left cell of the table. If only Boeing produces the aircraft, Boeing makes a profit of $100 million while Airbus makes a zero profit (the top right cell of the table). On the other hand, if Boeing does not produce the aircraft while Airbus does, Boeing makes zero profit while Airbus makes a profit of $100 million (the bottom left cell). Finally, if neither firm produces the aircraft, each makes a zero profit (the bottom right cell).

Suppose that for whatever reason, Boeing enters the market first and earns a profit of $100 million (we might call this the first-mover advantage). Airbus is now locked out of the market because it could not earn a profit. This is the case shown in the top right cell of the table. If Airbus entered the market, both firms would incur a loss (and we would have the case shown in the top left column of the table). Suppose now that European governments give a subsidy of $15 million per year to Airbus. Airbus would then produce the aircraft even though Boeing is already producing the aircraft, because with the $15 million subsidy, Airbus would turn a loss of $10 million into a profit of $5 million. Without a subsidy, however, Boeing will go from making a profit of $100 million (without Airbus in the market) to incurring a loss of $10 million afterwards (we are still in the top left corner of the table, but with the Airbus entry changed from −10 without the subsidy to +5 with the subsidy). Because of its unsubsidized loss, Boeing will stop producing the aircraft, thereby leaving the entire market to Airbus, which will then make a profit of $100 million without any further subsidy (the bottom left cell of the table).[9]

The U.S. government could, of course, retaliate with a subsidy of its own to keep Boeing producing the aircraft. Except in cases of national defense, however, the U.S. government is much less disposed to grant subsidies to firms than European governments. Although the real world is certainly much more complex than this example, we can see how a nation could overcome a market disadvantage and acquire a strategic comparative advantage in a high-tech field by means of an industrial and strategic trade policy.

One serious shortcoming of the above analysis is that it is usually very difficult to accurately forecast the outcome of government industrial and trade policies (i.e., get the data to fill a table such as Table 12.8). Even a small change in the table could completely change the results. For example, suppose that if both Airbus and Boeing produce the aircraft, Airbus incurs a loss of $10 million (as before) but Boeing makes a profit of $10 million (without any subsidy), say, because of superior technology. Then, even if Airbus

---

[9] This type of analysis was first introduced into international trade by J. Brander and B. Spencer. See their "International R & D Rivalry and Industrial Strategy," *Review of Economic Studies,* October 1983, pp. 707–722. See also M. Porter, *The Competitive Advantage of Nations* (New York: The Free Press, 1990).

produces the aircraft with the subsidy, Boeing will remain in the market because it is able to earn a profit without any subsidy. Then, Airbus would require a subsidy indefinitely, year after year, in order to continue to produce the aircraft. In this case, giving a subsidy to Airbus does not seem to be such a good idea.[10] Thus, it is extremely difficult to carry out this type of analysis in the real world (see Example 12–5). Getting the analysis wrong, however, can be very harmful and may even result in the firm's failure (see Example 12–6). This is the reason that most U.S. economists today are against industrial policy and still regard free trade as the best policy for the United States.[11]

Airbus did decide in 2000 to build its super-jumbo A380 capable of transporting 550 passengers originally scheduled to be ready by 2006 at a cost of over $10 billion, and thus compete head-on with the Boeing 747 (which has been in service since 1969 and can carry up to 475 passengers). Boeing greeted Airbus' decisions to build its A380 by announcing in 2001 plans to build a new "sonic cruiser" jet that can transport, non-stop, up to 300 passengers to any point on earth at close to the speed of sound. Boeing believes that passengers prefer arriving at their destinations sooner and avoid congested hubs and the hassle and delays of intermediate stops. It remains to be seen as to which strategy turns out to be the winning or best one.[12]

EXAMPLE 12–5

Strategic Moves and Countermoves by Airbus and Boeing

In 2000, Airbus decided to build its super-jumbo A380, capable of transporting 550–800 passengers, and to be ready by 2006, at a development cost of nearly $10 billion, and thus compete head-on with the Boeing 747 (which has been in service since 1969 and can carry up to 475 passengers). Boeing greeted Airbus' decisions to build its A380 by announcing in 2001 plans to build the new 787 Dreamliner, which can transport, nonstop, up to 300 passengers to any point on earth at close to the speed of sound. Boeing believes that passengers prefer arriving at their destinations sooner and avoiding congested hubs and the hassle and delays of intermediate stops. Nevertheless, Boeing announced in 2005 a stretched-out version of its 747 (the 747–8) to compete better with the new A380. Airbus responded with the development of the Airbus 350 to compete with the new Boeing 787.

The first delivery of the A380 was made in fall 2007 (with more than one year's delay and at a development cost of nearly $20 billion, or nearly twice what had been originally estimated), while deliveries of the 787 Dreamliner started in 2008. It remains to be seen which strategy turns out to be the winning or best one. The Boeing 787 is already a smashing success (it is likely to be the most successful aircraft ever built), and the A380 is also likely to be a success. Thus it seems that both were winning strategies. The attempt by Boeing to put more life into the 747 by building the

✓ **Concept Check**
What strategic moves has Airbus made in trying to gain a competitive advantage over Boeing?

---

[10] See "A Paper Dart Against Boeing," *The Economist,* June 11, 1994, pp. 61–62.
[11] "Remember Clinton's Industrial Policy? O.K. Now Forget It," *Business Week,* December 12, 1994, p. 53; and P. Krugman, "Is Free Trade Passè?," *Journal of Economic Perspectives,* Fall 1987, pp. 131–144.
[12] "The Birth of Giant," *Business Week,* July 10, 2000, pp. 170–176 and "Boeing Opts to Build New Class of "Sonic Cruiser" Jet," *Financial Times,* March 30, 2001, p. 1.

new 747–8 version will be no match for the A380, and the A350 will not come into service for several years, but they do show the game-theoretic moves and counter-moves in the world's most famous duopoly.

Sources: "The Birth of Giant," *Business Week,* July 10, 2000, pp. 170–176; "Boeing Opts to Build New Class of 'Sonic Cruiser' Jet," *Financial Times,* March 30, 2001, p. 1; D. A. Irwin and N. Pavcnik, "Airbus versus Boeing Revisited: International Competition in the Aircraft Market," *Journal of International Economics*, December 2004, pp. 223–245; "Headway for Boeing with 747 Advanced," *Financial Times,* July 21, 2005, p. 18; "Airbus Offers Up Redesigned A350 in a Challenge to Boeing," *New York Times,* July 18, 2006, p. C1; and "The Giant on the Runway," *The Economist*, October 13, 2007, pp. 79–82.

EXAMPLE 12–6
Companies' Strategic Mistakes and Failures

Nearly 100,000 businesses failed in the United States during 1992 (a recession year) as compared with only about 35,000 in 2000 (the last year of the boom of the 1990s) and nearly 40,000 in 2001 (a recession year). Although the reasons businesses fail are many and the details differ from case to case, several general underlying causes can be identified. *First,* many business failures arise because senior executives do not fully understand the fundamentals of their business or core expertise and business of the firm. Then the company drifts (often through mergers and acquisitions) into lines of business about which it knows little. This, for example, happened to Kodak when it diversified from its core camera and film business into pharmaceuticals and consumer health products during the 1990s.

The *second* basic reason for business failures is lack of vision or the inability of top management to anticipate or foresee serious problems that the business may face down the road. For example, U.S. automakers (General Motors, Ford, and Chrysler) failed to understand early enough the seriousness of the competitive challenge coming from Japan and almost willingly ceded the small-car market to Japan (because of the low profits per car earned in that market) during the 1970s in the erroneous belief that Japan would never be able to compete effectively in the medium-range segment of the market (where profit per automobile was much higher and American automakers were stronger). This resulted in huge losses for American automakers during the second half of the 1980s and early 1990s and almost drove Chrysler out of business (this is examined in Example 13–6). Another example is provided by Sears, which was unable or unwilling to understand the kind of change going on in consumer preferences, and this eventually propelled Wal-Mart to replace it as the nation's top marketeer. Most dangerous are latent or stealthy competitors, who as a result of some major and quick technological or market change can devastate the firm in its very core business. A clear example of this is IBM's inability to recognize early enough the importance and dramatic growth of the PC market in the mid-1980s and subsequent signing of Microsoft to develop the software and Intel to supply the chips for its PCs.

A *third* reason for business failures is the loading of the firm with a heavy debt burden (usually to carry out a program of merger and acquisitions, often at overpriced terms) which then robs the firm of its strength in a market downturn. This is precisely what happened (together with greed, deceit, and financial chicanery) to Enron (one of the world's largest energy traders), which filed the largest U.S. claim for bankruptcy in December 2001 (exceeded by WorldCom bankruptcy in July 2002).

Fourth, business failures arise when firms vainly try to recapture their past glories and become stuck on an obsolete strategy and are unable to respond to new and major competitive challenges. This is, to some extent, what happened to General Motors and IBM during the past decade before the brutal forces of the market shook them out of their complacency. It is often more difficult to keep a business great than to build it in the first place. *Finally,* a company may fail as a result of strikes and hostilities from unhappy workers.

Sources: "Dinosaurs?," *Fortune,* May 3, 1994, pp. 36–42; "Why Companies Fail," *Fortune,* November 14, 1994, pp. 52–68; "How Good Companies Go Bad," *Harvard Business Review,* July–August 1999, pp. 42–52; "Why Enron Went Bust," *Fortune,* December 24, 2001, pp. 58–68; "WorldCom Files for Bankruptcy: Largest U.S. Case," *New York Times,* July 22, 2002, p. 1; "Why Companies Fail," *Business Week,* May 22, 2002, pp. 50–62; and "Mapping Your Competitive Position," *Harvard Business Review,* November 2007, pp. 110–120.

AT THE FRONTIER
The Virtual Corporation

Virtual corporation A temporary network of independent companies coming together, with each contributing its core technology to quickly take advantage of fast-changing opportunities.

Today's joint ventures and strategic alliances provide a glimpse of the virtual corporation—the firm of the future. A **virtual corporation** is a temporary network of independent companies (suppliers, customers, and even rivals) coming together, with each contributing its core competence to quickly take advantage of fast-changing opportunities. In today's world of fierce global competition, this window of opportunity is often so frustratingly brief that it is impossible for a single firm to have all the in-house expertise to quickly launch complex products in diverse markets. By acting strategically and temporarily banding together to take advantage of a specific market opportunity, and with each company bringing its speciality, the virtual firm is a "best-of-everything organization." Informational networks and electronic contracts will permit unusual partners to work together on a particular project and then disband when the opportunity has been fully exploited.

In a virtual firm, one of the partners may have the idea for a new product, another may design the product, another may produce it, and still another market it. For example, IBM, Apple Computer, and Motorola have come together to develop a new operating system and computer chip for a new generation of computers. MCI Communications entered into partnerships with as many as 100 companies to provide a one-stop package of telecommunications hardware and services based on MCI competencies in network integration and software development, with the strength of other companies making all kinds of telecommunications equipment before it was acquired by Verizon in 2005.

Continued . . .

The Virtual Corporation   *Continued*

Although power, flexibility, and quickness are crucial advantages, the virtual corporation model does face two real risks. First, a company joining such a network may lose control of its core technology. Second, by abandoning manufacturing, the company may become "hollow" and become unable to resume the manufacturing of its traditional product in the future when the network dissolves. Some observers point out that IBM's desire to quickly enter the personal computer (PC) market in 1981 by relying on Intel for computer chips and Microsoft for the operating software left IBM without control of the market and encouraged hundreds of clone makers to eventually enter the market with lower prices and better products.

Thus, not everyone is sold on the virtual firm model. In order to work, the virtual firm (1) will have to be formed by partners that are dependable and are the best in their field, (2) the network must serve the interests of all partners in a win-win situation, (3) each company must put its best and brightest people in the network to show its partners that its link with them is important to the company, (4) the objective of the network must be clearly defined as well as what each partner is expected to gain, and (5) the network must build a common telecommunications network and other infrastructures so that each partner can be in constant touch with the other partners to anticipate problems and review progress. Creating and successfully operating a virtual firm is not easy, but it may very well be the strategic way of the future.

Sources: "The Virtual Firm," *Business Week,* February 8, 1993, pp. 98–102; "The Art of Managing Virtual Teams: Eight Key Lessons." *Harvard Business Review,* November 1998, pp. 4–5; H. Hammer, "The Superefficient Company," *Harvard Business Review,* September 2001, pp. 82–91; and J. Hughes and J. Weiss, "Simple Rules for Making Alliances Work," *Harvard Business Review,* November 2007, pp. 122–132.

SUMMARY

1. Game theory is concerned with the choice of an optimal strategy in conflict situations. Every game theory model includes players, strategies, and payoffs. The players are the decision makers (here, the managers of oligopolist firms) whose behavior we are trying to explain and predict. The strategies are the potential choices that can be made by the players (firms). The payoff is the outcome or consequence of each combination of strategies by the two players. The payoff matrix refers to all the outcomes of the players' strategies. A zero-sum game is one in which the gains or losses of one player equal the losses or gains of the other.

2. The dominant strategy is the optimal choice for a player, no matter what the opponent does. The Nash equilibrium occurs when each player has chosen his or her optimal strategy, given the strategy chosen by the other player. The Cournot solution is an example of a Nash equilibrium. Not all games have a Nash equilibrium and some games have more than one.

3. Oligopolistic firms often face a problem called the prisoners' dilemma. This refers to a situation in which each firm adopts its dominant strategy but could do better (i.e., earn larger profit) by cooperating. Oligopolistic firms deciding on their pricing or advertising strategy or on whether to cheat on a cartel face the prisoners' dilemma.

4. The best strategy for repeated or multiple-move prisoners' dilemma games is tit-for-tat. This strategy postulates that each firm should start by cooperating and continue to do so as long as the rival cooperates, but stop cooperating once the rival stops cooperating.

5. Oligopolists often make strategic moves. A strategic move is one in which a player constrains its own behavior in order to make a threat credible so as to gain a competitive advantage over a rival. The firm making the threat must be committed to carrying it out for the threat to be credible. This may involve accepting lower profits or building excess capacity.

6. Just like firms, nations can make strategic moves, such as subsidizing and providing export subsidies to a high-tech industry or adopting an industrial policy for the entire nation, to gain a competitive advantage over other nations. Industrial policies lead to waste if industries that are subsidized or otherwise supported do not become internationally competitive. Similarly, not knowing the exact payoff or outcome of the strategic moves open to it greatly complicates the development and conduct of business strategy by the firm. The virtual corporation is a temporary network of independent companies coming together with each contributing its core technology to quickly take advantage of fast-changing opportunities.

KEY TERMS

Game theory	Zero-sum game	Repeated games
Players	Nonzero-sum game	Tit-for-tat
Strategies	Dominant strategy	Strategic move
Payoff	Nash equilibrium	Virtual corporation
Payoff matrix	Prisoners' dilemma	

REVIEW QUESTIONS

1. In what way does game theory extend the analysis of oligopolistic behavior presented in Chapter 11?

2. a. Can game theory be used only for oligopolistic interdependence?

   b. In what way is game theory similar to playing chess?

3. Do we have a Nash equilibrium when each firm chooses its dominant strategy?

4. a. Why is the Cournot equilibrium a Nash equilibrium?

   b. In what way does the Cournot equilibrium differ from the Nash equilibrium given in Table 12.2?

5. In what way is the prisoners' dilemma related to the choice of dominant strategies by the players in a game and to the concept of Nash equilibrium?

6. How can the concept of the prisoners' dilemma be used to analyze price competition?

7. How can introducing yearly style changes lead to a prisoners' dilemma for automakers?

8. a. What is the incentive for the members of a cartel to cheat on the cartel?

   b. What can the cartel do to prevent cheating?

   c. Under what conditions is a cartel more likely to collapse?

9. Do the duopolists in a Cournot equilibrium face a prisoners' dilemma? Explain.

10. How did the 1971 law banning cigarette advertising on television solve the prisoners' dilemma for cigarette producers?

11. a. What is the meaning of "tit-for-tat" in game theory?

   b. What conditions are usually required for tit-for-tat strategy to be the best strategy?

12. a. How is a strategic move differentiated from a Nash equilibrium?

   b. What is a credible threat? When is a threat not credible?

PROBLEMS

1. From the following payoff matrix, where the payoffs are the profits or losses of the two firms, determine
   a. whether firm A has a dominant strategy.
   b. whether firm B has a dominant strategy.
   c. the optimal strategy for each firm.

		Firm B	
		Low Price	High Price
Firm A	Low Price	1, 1	3, −1
	High Price	−1, 3	2, 2

2. From the following payoff matrix, where the payoffs are the profits or losses of the two firms, determine
   a. whether firm A has a dominant strategy.
   b. whether firm B has a dominant strategy.
   c. the optimal strategy for each firm.
   d. the Nash equilibrium, if there is one.

		Firm B	
		Low Price	High Price
Firm A	Low Price	1, 1	3, −1
	High Price	−1, 3	4, 2

*3. From the following payoff matrix, where the payoffs are the profits or losses of the two firms, determine
   a. whether firm A has a dominant strategy.
   b. whether firm B has a dominant strategy.
   c. the optimal strategy for each firm.
   d. the Nash equilibrium.
   e. Under what conditions is the situation indicated in the payoff matrix likely to occur?

		Firm B	
		Small Cars	Large Cars
Firm A	Small Cars	4, 4	−2, −2
	Large Cars	−2, −2	4, 4

*4. Provide a hypothetical payoff matrix for Example 12.2.

5. From the following payoff matrix, where the payoffs (the negative values) are the years of possible imprisonment for individuals A and B, determine
   a. whether individual A has a dominant strategy.
   b. whether individual B has a dominant strategy.
   c. the optimal strategy for each individual.
   d. Do individuals A and B face a prisoners' dilemma?

		Individual B	
		Confess	Don't Confess
Individual A	Confess	−5, −5	−1, −10
	Don't Confess	−10, −1	−2, −2

6. Explain why the payoff matrix in Problem 1 indicates that firms A and B face the prisoners' dilemma.

7. Do firms A and B in Problem 2 face the prisoners' dilemma? Why?

*8. From the following payoff matrix, where the payoffs refer to the profits that firms A and B earn by cheating and not cheating in a cartel,
   a. determine whether firms A and B face the prisoners' dilemma.
   b. What would happen if we changed the payoff in the bottom left cell to (5, 5)?

		Firm B	
		Cheat	Don't Cheat
Firm A	Cheat	4, 3	8, 1
	Don't Cheat	2, 6	6, 5

*9. Starting with the payoff matrix of Problem 1, show what the tit-for-tat strategy would be for the first five of an infinite number of games if firm A starts by cooperating but firm B does not cooperate in the next period.

10. Given the following payoff matrix
    a. indicate the best strategy for each firm.
    b. Why is the entry-deterrent threat by firm A to lower price not credible to firm B?

---

* = Answer provided at end of book.

c. What could firm A do to make its threat credible without building excess capacity?

		Firm B	
		Enter	Don't Enter
Firm A	Low Price	3, −1	3, 1
	High Price	4, 5	6, 3

11. Show how the payoff matrix in the table of Problem 10 might change for firm A to make a credible threat to lower price by building excess capacity to deter firm B from entering the market.

12. What strategic industrial or trade policy would be required (if any) in the United States and in Europe if the entries in the top left cell of the payoff matrix in Table 12.8 were changed to
   a. 10, 10?
   b. 5, 0?
   c. 5, −10?

INTERNET SITE ADDRESSES

For an excellent presentation of game theory, see:
  http://www.gametheory.net/news/concept.pl
For the Fortune Global 500 companies, see:
  http://fortune.com/global500
For competition in the computer industry, see:
  http://www.iht.com/articles/2007/04/19/news/dell.php
  Apple: http://www.apple.com
  Dell: http://www.dell.com
  Hewlett-Packard: http://www.hp.com
  IBM: http://www.ibm.com
For competition in the airline industry, see:
  http://www.airlines.org/economics/finance/Annual+US+Financial+Results.htm
  http://www.airlines.org/economics/review_and_outlook/annual+reports.htm

  http://www.iht.com/articles/2007/04/02/business/place.php
  http://www.leeham.net/filelib/091007CAR.pdf
For competition in the commercial-aircraft industry, see:
  http://raven.stern.nyu.edu/networks/5.html
  Lockheed Martin: http://www.lockheedmartin.com
  Boeing: http://www.boeing.com
  Airbus: http://www.airbus.com
You can play an interactive online prisoners' dilemma game at:
  http://www.princeton.edu/~mdaniels/PD/PD.html
For competition in retailing by Wal-Mart, see:
  http://investor.walmartstores.com/phoenix.zhtml?c=112761&p=irol-irhome
  http://retailtrafficmag.com/retailing/retail_walmarts_woes/
Data on business failures are found at:
  http://www.BankruptcyData.com

CHAPTER **13**

Market Structure, Efficiency, and Regulation

Chapter Outline

List of Examples

After Studying This Chapter, You Should Be Able to:

- Know why inefficiencies and social costs arise in imperfect markets
- Know how monopoly power is measured
- Describe the aim and effect of antitrust policy
- Know why public utilities are regulated
- Describe the reasons for and the effect of the deregulation movement

"People of the same trade seldom meet together, even for merriment and diversion, but the conversation ends in a conspiracy against the public, or in some contrivance to raise prices."[1] This is one of the most famous quotations in economics, and it is as relevant today as two-and-a-quarter centuries ago when it was written. It explains in a nutshell why we are so interested in market structure, efficiency, antitrust, and regulation. In this chapter, we examine the relationship between these elements.

---

[1] A. Smith, *The Wealth of Nations* (Toronto: Random House, 1937), p. 128.

We begin by reviewing why inefficiency and social costs arise in imperfect markets. We then consider how to measure market imperfections and ways to minimize, prevent, or overcome (through antitrust and regulation) the most serious social costs that arise from these market imperfections. The examples and applications in the chapter show the importance of the theory and its uses, while the "At the Frontier" section examines the relatively new field of experimental economics.

13.1   MARKET STRUCTURE AND EFFICIENCY

Economic efficiency
The situation where the price of a commodity equals the marginal cost of producing it.

The concept and measure of **efficiency,** as well as the need for antitrust and regulation, is based on marginal analysis. Specifically, we have seen in previous chapters that the best level of output for a firm under any form of market organization (be it perfect competition, monopoly, monopolistic competition, or oligopoly) is where marginal revenue equals marginal cost. If marginal revenue exceeds marginal cost, it pays for the firm to expand output because by doing so the firm will add more to its total revenue than to its total costs. On the other hand, if marginal cost exceeds marginal revenue, it pays for the firm to reduce output because by doing so its total costs will decline more than its total revenue. Thus, the best level of output is where marginal revenue equals marginal cost.

Chapter 9 showed that a perfectly competitive firm faces an infinitely elastic demand curve and so price equals marginal revenue. Thus, at the best level of output, $P = MR = MC$. Since price measures the marginal benefit that consumers receive for the last unit of the commodity consumed at the output where $MR = MC$, the marginal benefit to consumers equals the marginal cost to producers under perfect competition. If less of the commodity is produced, $P = MR > MC$, so that consumers' satisfaction would increase if firms produced more of the commodity. On the other hand, if more of the commodity is produced, $P = MR < MC$. This means that consumers would benefit if some inputs were shifted to the production of some other commodity. Thus, application of the $P = MR = MC$ rule by the firm leads to the highest consumer satisfaction when all markets are perfectly competitive. As pointed out in Figure 9.9, in long-run perfectly competitive equilibrium, consumers can purchase the commodity at the lowest possible price (i.e., at $P =$ lowest LAC).

In imperfectly competitive markets (monopoly, monopolistic competition, and oligopoly), however, the firm faces a negatively sloped demand curve, and so price exceeds marginal revenue. Thus, at the best level of output $P > MR = MC$. This means that the marginal benefit to consumers from the last unit of the commodity consumed exceeds the marginal cost that the firm incurs in producing it. Consumers want more of the commodity than is available, but producers have no incentive to produce more. As a result, consumers' satisfaction is not maximized. Furthermore, imperfect competitors do not usually produce at the lowest point on their LAC curve when in long-run equilibrium, and (except for monopolistic competitors) the price that they charge for the commodity may also include a profit margin. The social cost resulting when a constant-cost perfectly competitive industry is suddenly monopolized was shown in Figure 10.7. In the real world, we seldom if ever have (unregulated) monopoly, but firms in various industries have various degrees of monopoly power. Thus, it becomes important to examine ways to measure the degree of monopoly power in order to assess the social costs resulting from it. This topic is explored in Section 13.2. Section 13.3 then compares the social costs with the alleged dynamic benefits of monopoly power.

TABLE 13.1   Comparison of Market Structures

Type of Market	Number of Firms	Type of Product	Conditions of Entry	Firm's Influence Over Price	Interdependence Among Firms	Examples
Perfect competition	Many	Homogeneous	Easy	None	None	Some agricultural products and stock market
Monopolistic competition	Many	Differentiated	Easy	Little	None	Some retail trade and services
Oligopoly	Few	Homogeneous or differentiated	Difficult	Considerable	A great deal	Steel, automobiles
Monopoly	One	No good substitutes	Difficult or impossible	Substantial	No direct competitor	Local telephone service before deregulation

✔ **Concept Check**
Why is perfect competition not feasible in many markets?

In many industries, however, technological conditions require such a large scale of production (to take advantage of economies of scale) that only one firm (natural monopoly) or a handful of firms (oligopoly) arise. For example, it would be inconceivable and highly inefficient to have numerous small producers of automobiles, steel, aircraft, and many other products. In the case of oligopolies, the government usually relies on the enforcement of antitrust laws aimed at attaining some degree of workable competition. This is examined in Section 13.4. In the case of natural monopoly, on the other hand, the single firm is usually allowed to operate, but with the government regulating the price and the quality of service. This is examined in Section 13.5. The rest of the chapter deals with the deregulation movement, the regulation of international competition, and price regulation. Table 13.1 summarizes and compares the various types of market structure that we have examined in previous chapters, from perfect competition to monopoly.

13.2   MEASURING MONOPOLY POWER

In this section, we first define the Lerner index as a measure of the degree of a *firm's* monopoly power and the Herfindahl index as a measure of the degree of monopoly power in an *industry*. We then discuss how effective competition can occur even when there are only a few firms, according to the contestable market theory.

The Lerner Index as a Measure of Monopoly Power

Lerner index A measure of the degree of a firm's monopoly power, which is given by the ratio of the difference between price and marginal cost to price.

We have seen in Chapter 9 that $P = MR = MC$ for a perfectly competitive firm but $P > MR = MC$ for an imperfectly competitive firm (i.e., for a monopolistic competitor, oligopolist, or monopolist). The greater the degree of monopoly power that a firm has, the more inelastic is the demand curve for the product that it faces, and so the larger is the degree by which the commodity price exceeds the firm's marginal revenue and marginal cost. Thus, one way of measuring monopoly power is by the **Lerner index.** This is given by the ratio of the difference between price and marginal cost to price, as shown by formula [13.1]:[2]

$$L = \frac{P - MC}{P} \qquad [13.1]$$

The Lerner index can have a value between zero and 1. For a perfectly competitive firm, $P = MC$ and $L = 0$. On the other hand, the more price exceeds marginal cost (i.e., the greater the degree of monopoly power), the more the value of L approaches the value of 1.

The Lerner index can also be expressed in terms of the price elasticity of the demand curve facing the firm. We can see this as follows. Since at the best level of output $MR = MC$, we can substitute MR for MC in equation [13.1]. But from equation [5.8], we know that $MR = P(1 + 1/\eta)$, where η is the price elasticity of demand. Substituting this value of MR for MC in [13.1], we get

$$L = \frac{P - P(1 + 1/\eta)}{P}$$

Simplifying, we get

$$L = -1/\eta \qquad [13.2]$$

For a perfectly competitive firm, $\eta = \infty$ and $L = 0$. The fewer and the more imperfect are the substitutes available for the firm's product (i.e., the smaller is the absolute value of η), the larger is the value of L. For example, if $\eta = -4$, $L = 0.25$, but if $\eta = -2$, $L = 0.5$.[3] Note that a high value for L (implying a great deal of monopoly power) is not necessarily associated with high profits for the firm, because profits refer to the excess of price over *average* cost, and average costs can be high or low in relation to the commodity price at the output level where $MR = MC$ (see Problem 2, with the answer at the end of the book).

Some difficulties may arise, however, in using the Lerner index. For example, a firm with a great deal of monopoly power may keep its price low to avoid legal scrutiny or to deter entry into the industry (limit pricing). Furthermore, the Lerner index is applicable in a static context, but it is not very useful in a dynamic context when the firm's demand and cost functions shift over time.

Concentration and Monopoly Power: The Herfindahl Index

Herfindahl index A measure of the degree of monopoly power in an industry, which is given by the sum of the squared values of the market sales shares of all the firms in the industry.

One method of estimating the degree of monopoly power *in an industry as a whole* is by the **Herfindahl index** (named after Orris Herfindahl, who introduced it). This is given by the sum of the squared values of the market sales shares of all the firms in the industry, as shown by

$$S = S_1^2 + S_2^2 + \cdots S_N^2 \qquad [13.3]$$

where S_1 is the market sales share of the largest firm in the industry, S_2 is the market sales share of the second largest firm in the industry, and so on, in such a way that the sum of the market sales shares of all firms in the industry totals 1 or 100%. In general, the greater the value of the Herfindahl index, the greater the degree of monopoly power in the industry.

---

[2] A. P. Lerner, "The Concept of Monopoly and the Measurement of Monopoly Power," *Review of Economic Studies,* June 1934, pp. 157–175.

[3] If $\eta = -1$, then $L = 1$. This is the highest value for L because an imperfect competitor never produces in the inelastic portion of its demand curve (where $MR < 0$).

For example, if we have a monopoly or a single firm in the industry, so that its market share is 100%, $H = (100)^2 = 10{,}000$. On the other hand, if there are 1,000 equal-sized firms in the (competitive) industry, each with 0.1% of the market, $H = 1{,}000(0.1)^2 = 10$. If there are 100 equal-sized firms in the (still competitive) industry, each with 1% of the market, $H = 100$. For an industry with 10 equal-sized firms, each with 10% market share, $H = 1{,}000$. But for an industry with 11 firms, one with 50% market share and the other 10 firms with 5% market share each, $H = 2{,}750$. This points to the advantage of the Herfindahl index over the concentration ratios discussed in Section 11.3. The Herfindahl index uses all the information and takes into account the size distribution of firms. Specifically, by squaring the market share of each firm, the Herfindahl index gives much more weight to larger firms in the industry than to smaller firms.

The Herfindahl index has become of great practical importance since 1982 when the Justice Department announced new guidelines (revised in 1984) for evaluating proposed mergers based on this index. According to these guidelines, if the postmerger Herfindahl index is 1,000 or less, the industry is regarded as relatively unconcentrated and a merger is unchallenged. On the other hand, an industry where the postmerger Herfindahl index is greater than 1,800 is regarded as highly concentrated and a merger is likely to be challenged (the full set of guidelines is given in Section 13.4). Table 13.2 shows the Herfindahl index (for the 50 largest firms rather than for all firms) in each of a selected number of industries in the United States in 2002. The table shows that for some industries, such as food and paper, the Herfindahl index is very low; for others, such as motor vehicles, the index is very high.

As with concentration ratios, however, the Herfindahl index must be used with caution. First, in industries where imports are significant (such as automobiles), the Herfindahl index greatly overestimates the relative importance of concentration in the domestic industry. Indeed, Raymond Vernon found that the Herfindahl index for the *world* automobiles, petroleum, aluminum-smelting, and pulp-and-paper industries declined sharply from 1950 to 1970, pointing to sharply increased international competition at

TABLE 13.2	Herfindahl Index for Selected U.S. Industries in 2002	
Industry		**Index***
Food		101.1
Paper		259.3
Footwear		408.9
Pharmaceutical and medicines		506.0
Audio and video equipment		649.9
Sugar		855.5
Computer and peripheral equipment		1,183.3
Telephone apparatus		1,398.5
Tires		1,630.9
Motor vehicles		2,323.5
Breakfast cereals		2,521.3

*Index refers only to the largest 50 firms in each industry.

Source: U.S. Bureau of Census, 2002 Census of manufacturers, *Concentration Ratios in Manufacturing* (Washington, DC: U.S. Government Printing Office, May 2006), Table 2, pp. 2–66.

home.[4] Second, the Herfindahl index for the nation as a whole may not be relevant when the market is local (as in the case of cement where transportation costs are very high). Third, how broadly or narrowly a product is defined is also very important. Fourth, the Herfindahl index does not give any indication of potential entrants into the market and of the degree of actual and potential competition in the industry. Indeed, as the *theory of contestable markets* discussed next shows, vigorous competition can take place even among few sellers.

Contestable Markets: Effective Competition Even with Few Firms

Theory of contestable markets Postulates that even if an industry has only one or a few firms, it would still operate as if it were perfectly competitive if entry into the industry is absolutely free and if exit is entirely costless.

According to the **theory of contestable markets** developed during the 1980s, even if an industry has a single firm (monopoly) or only a few firms (oligopoly), the industry would still operate as if it were perfectly competitive if entry is "absolutely free" (i.e., if other firms can enter the industry and face exactly the same costs as existing firms) and if exit is "entirely costless" (i.e., if there are no sunk costs so that the firm can exit the industry without facing any loss of capital).[5] An example might be an airline that establishes a service between two cities already served by other airlines—*if* the new entrant faces the same costs as existing airlines and could subsequently leave the market by simply reassigning its planes to other routes without incurring any loss of capital.

When entry is absolutely free and exit is entirely costless, the market is contestable. Firms will then operate as if they were perfectly competitive and sell at a price that only covers their average costs (so that they earn zero economic profit) even if there is only one firm or a few firms in the market. In this view, competition within the market is less important than the potential competition for the market. This can be seen in Figure 13.1.

In Figure 13.1, D is the market demand curve, and AC and MC are the average and marginal cost curves, respectively, of each of two identical firms in the market. If the market is contestable (i.e., if entry is absolutely free and exit is entirely costless), each firm will sell 60 units of output at $P = AC = MC = \$6$ (point E in the figure) and behave as a perfect competitor facing horizontal demand curve AEE' and earn zero economic profits. The duopolists will not collude to charge a higher price and earn profits because they know that other firms would quickly enter the market and sell at a slightly lower price. This would lower price to equal marginal cost at the lowest average cost and quickly eliminate all profits. This is true whether the potential entrants are domestic or foreign.

✓ Concept Check

How can we foster effective competition in a market with few firms?

The theory of contestable markets is similar to limit pricing (discussed in Section 11.7). With limit pricing, a firm charges a lower-than-the-profit-maximizing price to discourage potential entrants into the market. But whereas profits can still be earned with limit pricing (even though they are not maximized because the market is not entirely contestable), economic profits are zero in a contestable market because entry is absolutely free and exit is entirely costless. Even purely transitory profits will not be disregarded but result in entry-exit or hit-and-run behavior on the part of potential entrants into the industry until all profit opportunities are entirely exhausted.

The extreme assumptions on which the theory of contestable markets is based have been sharply criticized as unrealistic. That is, entry is seldom if ever absolutely free and exit is seldom if ever entirely costless in the real world, and so the theory is thought to be of limited applicability and usefulness.[6] Nevertheless, we have seen in Section 11.5 that a hypothesis

---

[4] R. Vernon, "Competition Policy Toward Multinational Corporations," *American Economic Review,* May 1974, pp. 276–282.

[5] See W. J. Baumol, "Contestable Markets: An Uprising in the Theory of Industrial Structure," *American Economic Review,* March 1982, pp. 1–5.

[6] W. G. Shepherd, "Contestability vs. Competition," *American Economic Review,* September 1984, pp. 572–587.

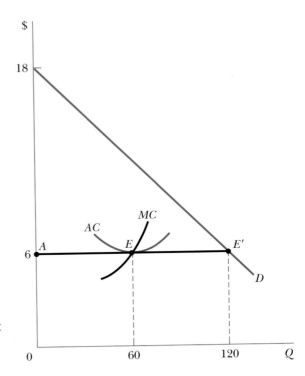

FIGURE 13.1 Two Firms in a Contestable Market *D* is the market demand curve, and *AC* and *MC* are the average and marginal cost curves, respectively, of each of two identical firms in a contestable market. Each firm will sell 60 units of output at *P* = *AC* = *MC* = $6 (point *E* in the figure) and behave as a perfect competitor facing horizontal demand curve *AEE′* and earn zero economic profits. Any higher price invites hit–and–run entrants.

need not be based on entirely realistic assumptions to be acceptable and useful. Thus, the theory of contestable markets can still be useful even if entry into and exit from the industry are only reasonably easy rather than absolutely free and costless. Perhaps the importance of the theory lies in cautioning us against uncritically accepting the view that a market with only one or a few firms must necessarily be noncompetitive and in suggesting that easy entry and exit can severely limit the exercise of monopoly power in contestable markets.

AT THE FRONTIER
Functioning of Markets and Experimental Economics

Experimental economics Seeks to determine how real markets operate by examining how paid volunteers behave within a simple experimental institutional framework.

Experimental economics is a relatively new field of economics that uses laboratory experiments to understand how real-world markets actually work under different institutional settings and levels of information. The field has already provided some interesting and important insights on the functioning of perfectly competitive markets, stock market behavior, monopoly profit maximization, oligopolistic behavior, bilateral monopoly (a monopolist in the product market facing a monopolist in the factor market), auction behavior, consumer response to price changes, and the effect of externalities (divergences between private and social costs and benefits).

According to Vernon Smith, one of the originators of the field (who shared the 2002 economics Nobel Prize in economics with Daniel Kahneman), there are many important reasons for conducting experiments in economics. Some of these reasons include (1) to test a theory or discriminate between theories, (2) to explore the causes of a theory's failure, (3) to establish empirical regularities that can form the basis for a new theory, (4) to compare the effect of operating under different environmental and institutional conditions, (5) to evaluate policy proposals, and (6) to determine the effect of institutional changes.

The experiments are usually conducted with volunteers, often college students, who are given money to buy and sell a fictitious commodity within a simple specified institutional framework. The participants are allowed to keep some of the money that they earn by acting in an economically rational way. For example, participants are allowed to retain the profit from buying the commodity at a lower price from the experimenter or from other participants and reselling it at a higher price to others in the simulated market.

In a simple experiment, it was shown that under certain conditions, the commodity price quickly converges to the equilibrium price even when there are only a few buyers and sellers of the commodity. This would seem to confirm the conclusion of the theory of contestable markets, but from a completely different approach. Whereas the theory of contestable markets reached this conclusion in a purely deductive manner, experimental economics reaches the same conclusion by pure empirical evidence within a simple experimental framework. The results seem to suggest that the perfectly competitive model may have much wider applicability than previously thought. If so, this would go a long way toward overcoming the problems arising from the indeterminacy of oligopoly theory.

In another experiment, Vernon Smith handed out several thousand dollars of his own money to a group of students participating in a simulated stock market study. The study provided some interesting results. One conclusion is that stock market or speculative "bubbles" occur regularly within the experimental framework. Traders seem to be carried away in a rising market and continue to bid stock prices up far past the expected dividend and price-earnings ratio of the stock—inevitably leading to a crash. Despite the very simple setting in which these experiments were conducted, their outcome closely mimics the actual stock market crash of 1987. Only after the participants have been through several boom-bust cycles do bubbles seem to disappear. As time passes, however, and the busts fade in investors' memories, great volatility in stock prices reappears.

In an attempt to eliminate the bubbles, Smith modified the experiment by adding futures trading (i.e., agreements to purchase or sell a stock at a specified price for delivery at a specified future time), margin buying (i.e., requiring a down payment when buying a stock on credit), and rules to stop trading when the market falls by a specified percentage. Smith's experiments showed that imposing limits on price declines only postpones the crash and makes it deeper when it comes. Only the availability of futures trading seemed to reduce the size and duration of speculative bubbles. These experimental results could have important practical implications in devising regulations to make the stock market less volatile in the real world.

Some of the other interesting results obtained by experimental economics are (1) auctions with large numbers of bidders (at least 6 or 7) produce more aggressive

Continued . . .

Functioning of Markets and Experimental Economics   *Continued*

bidding than with small numbers (3 or 4) and result in negative profits (the winner's curse), (2) consumers more readily accept price increases resulting from rising costs of production than those that arise from higher profits, suggesting that firms' voluntary or mandated financial disclosures can influence consumer behavior, (3) providing subjects with complete information retards rather than speeds the convergence of a market to equilibrium, (4) participants come to have common expectations regarding the value of a stock by market experience, not by being given common information, and (5) market efficiency in buying and selling a commodity does not require the complete revelation of buyers' and sellers' preferences.

✓ Concept Check

What is the usefulness of experimental economics?

Despite its promising beginning, we must remember, however, that experimental economics is still in its infancy, and many economists remain skeptical of the usefulness of results obtained in simplistic institutional settings and of their applicability in devising regulatory policies in the real world. The number of converts is growing, however, and the field has boomed in recent years. An important new development that is likely to further stimulate the field is Internet-based experiments, which allow large number of participants in experiments at different sites and over longer periods of time as compared with experiments restricted to classroom laboratories.

Sources: G. W. Harrison and J. A. List, "Naturally Occurring Markets and Exogenous Laboratory Experiments: A Case Study of the Winner's Curse," *NBER Working Paper No. 13072*, April 2007; "A Nobel that Bridges Economics and Psychology," *New York Times*, October 10, 2002, p. C1; "Experimental Economists Try to Fathom Behavior Online," *Wall Street Journal*, October 2, 2000, p. B4; "Research, Teaching, and Practice in Experimental Economics," *Southern Economic Journal*, January 1998, pp. 772–779; V. L. Smith, "Economics in the Laboratory," *Journal of Economic Perspectives*, Winter 1994, pp. 113–131; "Classroom Experimental Economics," Special Issue, *Journal of Economic Education*, Fall 1993; C. R. Plott, "Will Economics Become an Experimental Science?," *Southern Economic Journal*, April 1991, pp. 901–919; V. L. Smith, "Theory, Experiment and Economics," *The Journal of Economic Perspectives*, winter 1989, pp. 151–170, and C. R. Plott, "Industrial Organization and Experimental Economics," *Journal of Economic Literature*, December 1982, pp. 1485–1527.

13.3   SOCIAL COSTS AND DYNAMIC BENEFITS OF MONOPOLY POWER

We have seen that in imperfectly competitive markets the best level of output is where $P > MR = MC$. This means that the marginal benefit to consumers (as measured by the commodity price) from the last unit of the commodity consumed exceeds the marginal cost that the firm incurs in producing it. Consumers want more of the commodity than is available, but producers have no incentive to produce more. The social cost resulting when a constant-cost perfectly competitive industry is suddenly monopolized was shown by triangle *REM* in Figure 10.7. It was also pointed out in Section 10.3 that there are other losses or social costs resulting from monopoly power. The first of these is that monopolists do not have much incentive to keep their costs as low as possible and prefer instead the quiet life (X-inefficiency).[7] Second, monopolists waste a lot of resources lobbying

---

[7] See H. Leibenstein, "Allocative Efficiency vs. X-Inefficiency," *American Economic Review*, June 1966, pp. 392–415.

and engaging in legal battles to avoid or defend themselves against regulation and antitrust prosecution, installing excess capacity to discourage entry into the industry, and advertising in an attempt to create and retain the monopoly power (i.e., engaging in rent-seeking activities). Some economists believe that these other social costs of monopoly are larger than those measured by the welfare triangle *REM* in Figure 10.7, but, as pointed out in Section 10.3, there is disagreement on the exact size of these social costs.[8]

Measuring the social costs of imperfect competition by comparing it with perfect competition begs the question, however, because the need for large-scale production often precludes the existence of perfect competition. We could not, for example, produce steel, automobiles, aluminum, aircraft, and most industrial products with numerous firms under perfect competition—except at exorbitant costs. The benefits that would result if cost conditions made perfect competition possible are thus irrelevant in these cases. Furthermore, there are many alleged benefits that result from large firm size (i.e., with firms with monopoly power) that just would not be possible under perfect competition. These were emphasized by Schumpeter 60 years ago and remain very controversial today.[9]

According to Schumpeter and others, perfect competition is not the market structure most conducive to long-run growth through technological change and innovations. Since long-run profits tend toward zero in perfectly competitive markets, firms will not have the necessary resources to undertake sufficient R&D to maximize growth. Furthermore, with free entry under perfect competition, a firm introducing a cost-reducing innovation or a new product would quickly lose its source of profits through imitation. Thus, Schumpeter argued that large firms with some degree of monopoly power are essential to provide the financial resources required for R&D and to protect the resulting source of profits. Although monopoly leads to some inefficiency at one point in time (static inefficiency), over time, it is likely to lead to much more technological change and innovation (dynamic efficiency) than perfect competition.[10]

In addition, according to Schumpeter, large firms with some monopoly power are not sheltered from competition. On the contrary, they face powerful competition from new products and new production techniques introduced by other large firms. For example, aluminum is replacing steel in many uses, and plastic is replacing aluminum. Such competition is much more dangerous and affects the very existence of the firm. This is the process of "creative destruction" as new products and technologies constantly lead to new investments and the obsolescence of some existing capital stock. In this process, the role of the entrepreneur is crucial. Indeed, the entrepreneur is the star performer in the dynamic process of creative destruction and growth in the economy.

Some economists disagree. They point out that it is not at all clear that monopoly power leads to more R&D and innovations and faster long-run growth than perfectly competitive markets. They also point out that a more decentralized market economy is

✓ Concept Check
What are some of the dynamic benefits of monopoly?

---

[8] The charge often heard that monopolists suppress inventions (e.g., that they would avoid introducing a longer-lasting light bulb) is not correct, however, since consumers would be willing to pay a higher price for such light bulbs and this could lead to higher profits for the monopolist. Only if the monopolist believed that the invention could not be patented and that this would result in loss of monopoly power would the monopolist suppress the invention. See Section 10.8.

[9] See J. Schumpeter, *Capitalism, Socialism, and Democracy* (New York: Harper & Row, 1942), p. 106; and Z. J. Acs and D. B. Audretsch, "Innovation in Large and Small Firms: An Empirical Analysis," *American Economic Review,* September 1988, pp. 678–690.

[10] The question of what is the institutional setting most conducive to technological change and innovations over time is a crucial one, because technological change and innovations are the forces responsible for most of the long-term growth in standards of living in modern societies.

more adaptable and flexible to changes and is much more consistent with individual freedom of choice than an economy characterized by great economic concentration. The challenge, according to these economists, is to devise policies that correct the most serious economic distortions in the economy resulting from monopoly power and encourage a high level of R&D, while retaining and encouraging a large degree of decentralization, equity, and individual freedoms.

After a careful review of the empirical evidence, Scherer and Ross conclude that Schumpeter was right in asserting that perfect competition cannot be the model for dynamic efficiency. But neither can powerful monopolies and tightly knit cartels. What is needed for rapid technical progress is a subtle blend of competition and monopoly, with more emphasis on the former than on the latter, especially in those industries in which technical progress is relatively rapid. In other words, although some monopoly power may be more conducive to innovation than perfect competition when technical progress is relatively slow, a great deal of monopoly power is likely to retard innovations and growth, especially when technical progress is rapid.[11]

13.4   CONTROLLING MONOPOLY POWER: ANTITRUST POLICY

Starting in 1890, a number of *antitrust laws* were passed in the United States which were aimed at preventing monopoly or undue concentration of economic power, protecting the public against the abuses and inefficiencies resulting from monopoly or the concentration of economic power, and maintaining a workable degree of competition in the economy. The two core antitrust laws were the Sherman Antitrust Act and the Clayton Act.

Sherman Antitrust Act Prohibits all contracts and combinations in restraint of trade and all attempts to monopolize the market.

According to Section I of the **Sherman Antitrust Act**, passed in 1890: "Every contract, combination . . . , or conspiracy in restraint of trade or commerce among the several states, or with foreign nations, is hereby declared to be illegal" in the United States. The Sherman Antitrust Act does not make monopoly, as such, illegal. What is illegal is collusion (i.e., formal or informal agreements or arrangements in restraint of trade). These agreements refer to all types of cartels, but also to informal understandings to share the market, price fixing, and price leadership. An illustration of collusion is provided by the market-sharing cartel of the Ivy League colleges in Example 11–4. What the courts did *not* rule as illegal is **conscious parallelism,** or the adoption of similar policies by oligopolists in view of their recognized interdependence. Specifically, the courts have ruled that parallel business behavior does not constitute proof of collusion or an offense under the Sherman Antitrust Act.

Conscious parallelism The adoption of similar policies by oligopolists in view of their recognized interdependence.

The most difficult part of applying Section I of the Sherman Antitrust Act is proving tacit or informal collusion. Sometimes the case is clear-cut. For example, in 1936, the U.S. Department of the Navy received 31 closed bids to supply a batch of steel, all of which quoting a price of $20,727.26. Also in 1936, the U.S. Engineer's Office received 11 closed bids to supply 6,000 barrels of cement, each quoting a price of $3.286854 per barrel! The probability of identical prices, down to the sixth decimal, occurring without some form of collusion is practically zero. Most antitrust cases are seldom so clear-cut, however.

Section II of the Sherman Antitrust Act makes attempts to monopolize the market illegal. The most famous of the recent court cases applying Section II of the Sherman

[11] F. M. Scherer and D. Ross, *Industrial Market Structure and Economic Performance* (Boston: Houghton Mifflin, 1990), pp. 644–660.

Clayton Act
Prohibits mergers that "substantially lessen competition" or tend to lead to monopoly.

Antitrust Act are those brought against AT&T (see Example 13–1) in 1982 and Microsoft in 1998 (see "At the Frontier" in Chapter 10). But monopolization can also occur through merger. Section 7 of the **Clayton Act,** passed in 1914 (and amended by the Celler–Kefauver Act of 1950), prohibits mergers that "substantially lessen competition" or tend to lead to monopoly. According to its 1984 guidelines, the Justice Department would not usually challenge a horizontal merger (i.e., a merger of firms in the same product line) if the postmerger Herfindahl index was less than 1,000. If the postmerger index was between 1,000 and 1,800 and the increase in the index as a result of the merger was less than 100 points, the merger would usually also go unchallenged. But if the postmerger index was between 1,000 and 1,800 and the merger led to an increase in the index of more than 100 points, or if the postmerger index was more than 1,800 and the merger led to an increase in the index of more than 50 points, the Justice Department was likely to challenge the merger. Since the mid-1990s, these guidelines have been relaxed (see Example 13–5).

The Justice Department also considers other factors (besides the Herfindahl index) in horizontal mergers. These include the financial condition of the firm being acquired, the ease of entry into the industry, the degree of foreign competition, and the expected gains in efficiency that the merger would make possible. The Justice Department is more likely approve a horizontal merger if the merger would prevent the failure of the acquired firm, if entry into the industry is easy, if the degree of foreign competition is strong, and if the acquisition would lead to substantial economices of scale.[12] Less clear-cut are the guidelines on vertical and conglomerate mergers. As a result of relaxed guidelines and in the face of sharply increased foreign competition, the number and size of mergers and corporate acquisitions in the United States has increased sharply since the early 1980s.

Since antitrust laws are often broad and general, however, a great deal of judicial interpretation based on economic analysis has often been required in their enforcement. The problems of defining what is meant by "substantially lessening competition," defining the relevant product and geographic markets, and deciding when competition is "unfair" have not been easy to determine and often could not be resolved in a fully satisfactory and uncontroversial way. The fact that many antitrust cases last many years, involve thousands of pages of testimony, and cost millions of dollars to prosecute is ample evidence of their great complexity. Perhaps the most significant effect of the antitrust laws is deterring collusion rather than fighting it after it occurs.

✔️ Concept Check
What is the purpose of antitrust laws and their most significant effect?

EXAMPLE 13–1

Antitrust Policy in Action—The Breakup of AT&T and the Creation of Competition in Long-Distance Telephone Service

In 1974, the U.S. Justice Department filed suit (also under Section II of the Sherman Act) against AT&T for illegal practices aimed at eliminating competitors in the market for telephone equipment and in the market for long-distance telephone service. At the time, AT&T was the largest private firm in the world. After 8 years of litigation

---

[12] See "Symposium on Mergers and Antitrust," *Journal of Economic Perspectives,* Fall 1987, pp. 3–54; and W. E. Kovaric and Carl Shapiro, "Antitrust Policy: A Century of Economic and Legal Thinking," *Journal of Economic Perspectives,* winter 2000, pp. 43–60.

and a cost of $25 million to the government (and $360 million incurred by AT&T to defend itself), the case was settled on January 8, 1982. By consent decree, AT&T agreed to divest itself of the 22 local telephone companies (which represented two-thirds of its total assets) and lose its monopoly on long-distance telephone service. In return, AT&T was allowed to retain Bell Laboratories and its manufacturing arm, Western Electric, and it was allowed to enter the rapidly growing fields of cable TV, electronic data transmission, video-text communications, and computers. The settlement also led to an increase in local telephone charges (which had been subsidized by long-distance telephone service by AT&T) and a reduction in long-distance telephone rates.

By the end of 2001, WorldCom (which had acquired MCI Communications in 1999) and Sprint had captured more than 40% of the long-distance telephone market from AT&T. Furthermore, AT&T, WorldCom, and Sprint entered the local telephone market and the local Bell companies entered the long-distance market. The sharp increase in competition and price wars resulted in much lower prices for local and long-distance telephone services for U.S. consumers. At the end of 2001, AT&T sold its cable-TV business to Comcast for $44 billion, thus ending its frenzied and costly three-year effort to transform itself into a telecommunications powerhouse and returning to being just a long-distance telephone company. Then, in 2005, AT&T itself was acquired by the regional bell SBC, which subsequently adopted the name AT&T, thus putting an end to independent long-distance telephony in the United States. In 2006, a reborn AT&T acquired BellSouth, leaving only two other major telephone companies in the United States (Verizon and Qwest; Sprint Nextel is now primarily a cellular phone company).

Sources: "Ma Bell's Big Breakup," *Newsweek,* January 18, 1982, pp. 58–63; "Congress Votes to Reshape the Communications Industry," *New York Times,* February 2, 1996, p. 1; "Telecoms in Trouble," *The Economist,* December 16, 2000, pp. 77–79; "AT&T Long, Troubled Trip to Its Past," *Wall Street Journal,* December 21, 2001, p. B1; "Justice Department Approves Two Big Telecom Deals," *New York Times,* October 28, 2005, p. C4; and "A Reborn AT&T to Buy BellSouth," *Wall Street Journal*, March 6, 2006, p. A1.

EXAMPLE 13–2

Regulation and the Price of International Telephone Calls in Europe

Until the 1990s, state telephone monopolies ruled everywhere in continental Europe and charged more than twice as much as AT&T charged its American customers for transatlantic telephone calls (and even more for local telephone services). During the 1990s, pressure mounted in Europe to dismantle the legal OPEC-like cartel by which national telecommunications companies cooperated to keep the price of international telephone calls very high and far above actual costs. With AT&T on this side of the Atlantic and British Telecom in Europe creeping into continental European markets with lower rates and with European corporations clamoring for rate reductions, the European Commission decided to open the international telephone market to competition throughout the 15-country European Union in 1998.

As a result, governments privatized their national telephone companies through stock sales, and major European telephone companies rushed to form alliances with other European and American telephone companies. Eventually, this could trigger massive consolidations around four or five telephone superpowers in the world. As these alliances take shape, price wars will be inevitable and are likely to result in sharply lower prices for telephone calls in Europe, just as occurred in the United States. Although still higher than in the United States, the price of local and international telephone calls in Europe has in fact already fallen sharply during the past few years.

Bigger and more frequent during the past few years have been mergers and acquisitions of cellular telephone companies by other wireless operators (such as England's Vodafone's acquisition of German Mannesmann) and by traditional telephone companies (such as France Telecom's acquisition of Orange P.L.C.—Britain's third largest wireless operator for $37 billion—and Deutsche Telekom's acquisition of American VoiceStream Wireless Corporation for $45 billion). With the convergence of telecommunications, information technology, and media services, the European Union's Parliament passed a law in December 2001 aimed at unifying and increasing competition in the entire telecommunication field in the European Union.

Sources: "An Unlikely Trustbuster," *Forbes,* February 18, 1991, pp. 100–104, "Sky-High Overseas Phone Bills May Drop," *Wall Street Journal,* September 20, 1994, p. B2; "European Phone Companies Reach Out for Partners," *Wall Street Journal,* November 30, 1994, p. B4; "Europe Begins Liberalizing Phone Sector," *Wall Street Journal,* December 5, 1994, p. A9F; "Who's on First?" *Wall Street Journal,* September 18, 2000, p. R2; "Telephone Regulation Is Approved," *New York Times,* December 12, 2001, p. W1; and "The War of Wires," *The Economist,* July 30, 2005, pp. 53–54.

13.5   PUBLIC-UTILITY REGULATION

In this section, we consider the need for regulating natural monopolies (such as public utilities) and the dilemma faced by regulatory commissions in determining the appropriate method and degree of regulation.

Public Utilities as Natural Monopolies

Concept Check
Why are public utilities regulated?

As defined in Section 10.1, *natural monopoly* refers to the case in which a single firm can supply a service to the entire market more efficiently than a number of firms could. Natural monopoly arises when the firm's long-run average cost curve is still declining at the point where it intersects the market demand curve. Examples of natural monopolies are *public utilities* (local electrical, gas, water, and transportation companies). To have more than one such firm in a given market would lead to duplication of supply lines and to much higher costs per unit. To avoid this, local governments usually allow a single firm to operate in the market but regulate the price and quantity of the services provided so as to allow the firm only a normal rate of return (say, 10% to 12%) on its investment. This is shown in Figure 13.2.

In Figure 13.2, the *D* and *MR* curves are, respectively, the market demand and marginal revenue curves for the service faced by the public utility, while the *LAC* and *LMC* curves are its long-run average and marginal cost curves. The best level of output for the

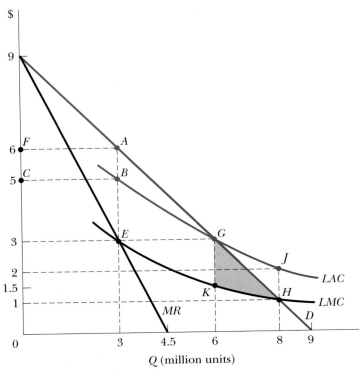

FIGURE 13.2   Natural Monopoly Regulation   A regularity commission usually sets $P = LAC = \$3$ (point G), at which output is 6 million units per time period and the public utility breaks even in the long run. This, however, would result in a welfare loss to society or social cost equal to about $1.50 million (the area of shaded triangle GKH), since only at point H is $P = LMC$. This cost could be avoided if the commission set $P = LMC = \$1$. But this would result in a loss of $1 ($JH$) per unit and $8 million in total for the company, and the public utility would not supply the service in the long run without a subsidy of $1 per unit.

unregulated monopolist in the long run is 3 million units per time period and is given by point E, at which the LMC and MR curves intersect. For $Q = 3$ million units, the monopolist would charge the price of $6 (point A on the D curve) and incur a $LAC = \$5$ (point B on the LAC curve), thereby earning a profit of $1 ($AB$) per unit and $3 million (the area of rectangle $ABCF$) in total. Note that at $Q = 3$ million units, the LAC curve is still declining. Note also that at the output level of 3 million units, $P > LMC$, so that more of the service is desirable from society's point of view. There is, however, no incentive for the unregulated monopolist to expand output beyond $Q = 3$ million units per time period because its profits are maximized at $Q = 3$ million.

To ensure that the monopolist earns only a normal rate of return on its investment, the regulatory commission usually sets $P = LAC$. In Figure 13.2, this is given by point G, at which $P = LAC = \$3$ and output is 6 million units per time period. While the price is lower and the output is greater than at point A, $P > LMC$ at point G. Thus, consumers pay a price for the last unit of the service purchased which exceeds the LMC of producing it (see the figure). The welfare loss to society or social cost of setting $P = LAC = \$3$ is about

$(0.5)(1.50)(2) = \$1.50$ million (the area of shaded triangle GKH). The only way to avoid this social cost is for the regulatory commission to set $P = LMC = \$1$ so that output is 8 million units per time period (point H in the figure). At $Q = 8$ million, however, the $LAC = \$2$ (point J on the LAC curve), and the public utility would incur a loss of $1 ($JH$) per unit and $8 million in total per time period. As a result, the public utility would not supply the service in the long run without a subsidy of $1 per unit. In general, regulatory commissions set $P = LAC$ (point G in Figure 13.2) so that the public utility breaks even in the long run without a subsidy.

Difficulties in Public-Utility Regulation

Although our discussion of public-utility regulation seems fairly simple and straightforward, the actual determination of prices (rates) for public-utility services by regulatory commissions (often called the *rate case*) is complex. For one thing, it is very difficult to determine the value of the plant or fixed assets on which to allow a normal rate of return. Should it be the original cost of the investment or the replacement cost? Usually regulatory commissions decide on the former. Furthermore, since public-utility companies supply the service to different classes of customers, each with different price elasticities of demand, many different rate schedules can be used to allow the public utility to break even. Even more troublesome is the fact that a public utility usually provides many services that are jointly produced, and so it is impossible to allocate costs in any rational way to the various services provided and customers served.

Regulation can also lead to inefficiencies. These result from the fact that, having been guaranteed a normal rate of return on investment, public-utility companies have little incentive to keep costs down. For example, managers may grant salary increases to themselves in excess of what they would get in their best alternative employment, and they may provide luxurious offices and large expense accounts for themselves. Regulatory commissions must, therefore, scrutinize costs to prevent such abuses. Regulated public utilities also have little incentive to introduce cost-saving innovations because they would not be able to keep the increased profits. An example of this is provided by the slowness with which AT&T introduced automatic switching equipment during the 1970s.

Other inefficiencies arise because if rates are set too high, public utilities will overinvest in fixed assets and use excessively capital-intensive production methods to avoid showing above-normal returns (which would lead to rate reductions). On the other hand, if public-utility rates are set too low, public-utility companies will underinvest in fixed assets (i.e., in plant and equipment) and overspend on variable inputs, such as labor and fuel, which tends to reduce the quality of services. Overinvestment or underinvestment in plant and equipment resulting from the wrong public-utility rates being set is known as the **Averch–Johnson (A–J) effect** (from Harvey Averch and Leland Johnson, who first identified this problem) and can lead to large inefficiencies.[13] And yet, it is difficult indeed for regulatory commissions to come up with correct utility rates in view of the difficulty of valuing the fixed assets of public utilities and because of the long planning and gestation period of public-utility investment projects.[14]

Finally, there is usually a lag of 9 to 12 months from the time the need for a rate change is recognized and the time it is granted. This *regulatory lag* results because public

Averch–Johnson (A–J) effect The overinvestments or underinvestments in plant and equipment resulting when public utility rates are set too high or too low, respectively.

[13] H. Averch and L. Johnson, "Behavior of the Firm under Regulatory Constraint," *American Economic Review*, December 1962, pp. 1052–1069.
[14] Recently, regulatory commissions have begun to pay more attention to the structure of rates so as to avoid undue price discrimination against any class of customers.

hearings must be conducted before a regulatory commission can approve a requested rate change. Since the members of the regulatory commissions are either political appointees or elected officials and are thus subject to political pressures from consumer groups, they usually postpone a rate increase as long as possible and tend to grant rate increases that are smaller than necessary. During inflationary periods, this leads to underinvestment in fixed assets and to the inefficiencies discussed above. To avoid these regulatory lags, rates are sometimes tied to fuel costs and are automatically adjusted as variable costs change. However, most public utilities are now in the process of deregulation (see Example 13–3).

✓ **Concept Check**
What are the difficulties in public utility regulation?

EXAMPLE 13–3

Regulated Electricity Rates for Con Edison

In February 1983, after nearly six months of public hearings and deliberations, the New York Public Service Commission approved a 6.5% increase in electricity rates for the 2.7 million New York City customers served by the Consolidated Edison Company. The increase in the monthly electricity charge was about half of the 12.4% that Con Edison had asked and was expected to generate $240 million extra revenue per year for Con Edison, to cover its increasing costs of operation.

Both Con Edison and consumer advocates immediately criticized the rate increase—the former as inadequate and the latter as too high. In fact, the rate increase actually generated $267 million in additional revenues per year for Con Edison, instead of the $240 million expected and approved. In 1986, the city administration threatened to sue Con Edison to have the excess profits returned to customers but dropped its plan when Con Edison agreed not to seek another rate increase until March 1987. Con Edison did not get another rate increase until 1992. The rate increases that it got from 1992 to 1995 were very small, and from 1996 to 1999 rates actually declined slightly. The next rate increase came only in 2004. In 2007, Con Edison asked for an increase in electricity rates that would generate an extra $1.2 billion in revenues to cover increasing costs of energy, but got only $425 million in 2008.

Con Edison and other electric utilities in New York State and in about half of the United States have now been deregulated, thus allowing customers to choose their power company and bargain for rates, just as they do for long-distance telephone services. Furthermore, whereas in the past electric utility companies produced, delivered, metered, and billed for the electricity they sold, with the deregulation these functions are being taken over (for the most part) by separate and more specialized companies. Deregulation increased the efficiency of the electric industry, but it did not lead to lower rates for every type of user. Deregulation also brought blackouts and sharply higher electricity bills in California in 2000 and 2001, and this (together with the collapse of Enron, one of the world's largest energy traders at the end of 2001) convinced many states to delay deregulation until enough generating capacity has been built to ensure ample supply at stable electricity rates.

Source: "Con Edison Wins 6.5% Rise in Rates, Half of its Request," *New York Times,* February 24, 1983, p. B4; "Con Edison Puts Freeze on Its Electricity Rates," *New York Times,* January 13, 1986, p. B1; P. L. Joskow, "Restructuring, Competition and Regulatory Reform in the U.S. Electric Sector," *Journal of Economic Perspectives,* Summer 1997, pp. 119–138; "California Moving Toward Re-regulating Energy," *New York Times,* September 21, 2001, p. 16; and "Con Ed Wins Approval for a Big One-Time Increase in Rates for Electric Service," *New York Times*, March 20, 2008, p. B3.

| **13.6** | **THE DEREGULATION MOVEMENT** |

Regulation in the U.S. economy is not confined to cases of natural monopolies, where there is a single seller of a commodity or service, but extends to many other sectors, especially transportation, banking, and other financial services, where more than one firm operates. For example, airlines needed government approval to enter a market and change fares, railroads needed government approval to abandon a service or a line and change rates, the services that banks can provide and the interest that they can pay on deposits were also regulated, and so were the rates set by insurance companies and other financial institutions. Regulation was justified to ensure that industries operated in a manner consistent with the public interest, ensure a minimum standard of quality of services, and prevent the establishment of monopoly.

Many economists oppose regulation because it restricts competition, contributes to high prices, and reduces economic efficiency. One estimate put the social cost of regulation at more than $100 billion in the year 1979 (of which about 5% were administrative costs and the rest were the costs of compliance) and over $200 billion a year in the 1990s.[15] Even though these estimates were challenged as grossly exaggerated,[16] compliance costs are surely very high, particularly in the area of social regulation (such as job safety), energy and the environment, and consumer safety and health. Regulation often leads to inefficiencies because regulators do not specify the desired result, but only the method of compliance (such as the type of pollution-abatement equipment to use), in the absence of adequate information and expertise. It is now generally agreed that it would be much better if regulators specified the results wanted and left to industry the task of determining the most efficient way to comply. In recent years, there has been a movement in this direction.

Deregulation movement The reduction or elimination of many government regulations since the mid-1970s in order to increase competition and efficiency.

Since the 1970s, a growing **deregulation movement** has sprung up in the United States that led to deregulation of the air travel, trucking, railroads, banking, and telecommunications industries. The *Airline Deregulation Act of 1978* removed all restrictions on entry, scheduling, and pricing in domestic air travel in the United States, and so did the *Motor Carrier Act of 1980* in the trucking industry. The *Depository Institutions Deregulation and Monetary Control Act of 1980* allowed banks to pay interest on checking accounts and increased competition for business loans. The *Railroad Revitalization and Regulatory Reform Act of 1976* greatly increased the flexibility of railroads to set prices and to determine levels of service and areas of operation. The settlement of the *AT&T Antitrust Case in 1982* (see Example 13–1) opened competition in long-distance telephone service and in telecommunications. Natural gas pipelines and oil are now deregulated, and so are the banking and electric power industries (see Example 13–3).

✓ Concept Check

What is the purpose and effect of the deregulation movement?

The general purpose of deregulation is to increase competition and efficiency in the affected industries and lead to lower prices without sacrificing the quality of service. Most observers would probably conclude that, on balance, the net effect has been positive. Competition has generally increased, and prices have fallen in industries that were

---

[15] Murray Weidenbaum, "The High Cost of Government Regulation," *Challenge,* November–December 1979, pp. 32–39 and "A New Project Will Measure the Cost and Effect of Regulation," *New York Times,* March 30, 1998, p. D2.

[16] See William K. Tabb, "Government Regulation: Two Sides of the Story," *Challenge,* November–December 1980, pp. 40–48.

deregulated. As expected, however, deregulation has also resulted in some difficulties and strains in the industries affected, to the point where some consumer groups and some firms in recently deregulated industries are asking Congress to re-regulate them. Nowhere is this more evident than in the airline industry (see Example 13–4). Deregulation has also encouraged and made possible the merger boom that has occurred since the early 1990s (see Example 13–5).

EXAMPLE 13–4

Deregulation of the Airline Industry: An Assessment

By 2007, all of the 16 air carriers that had started following the 1978 deregulation went out of business or merged with established carriers (the last one was the merger of America West Airlines with US Airways in 2005). Several mergers took place among large, established carriers (such as American Airlines' acquisition of TWA in 2001), and Eastern Airlines and Pan Am went out of business. The result was that in 2007 seven carriers handled 91% of all domestic air travel in the United States (as compared with 11 carriers handling 87% of the traffic in 1978). From 1985 to 2007, the market share of the top five carriers jumped from 61% to 72%. Instead of a large number of small and highly competitive airlines envisioned by deregulation, the airline industry has become even more concentrated than it was before deregulation.

Entry into the industry by established airlines was restricted by (1) long-term leasing of the limited number of gates at most airports, (2) frequent flier programs that tie passengers to a given airline, (3) computerized reservations system that give a competitive advantage in attracting customers to the airlines owning the system, (4) the emergence of "hub and spoke" operations, in which airlines funnel passengers through centrally located airports where one or two companies often dominate service, and (5) predatory pricing practices, under which established airlines lower the price and increase flights to drive new entrants out. This, however, did not prevent a number of new discount airlines (such as Skybus, JetBlue, Air Tran and ATA) coming into existence since 2001 and taking away some market share from established airlines with their low-price strategy. Shyrocketing jet fuel prices, however, resulted in most discount airlines shitting down in 2007–2008.

Airfares, after adjusting for inflation, have declined, on average, more than 30% since deregulation, and this greatly stimulated domestic air travel (from about 250 million passengers in 1976 to over 600 million in 2007). However, delays at airports and passenger complaints about lost luggage, canceled flights, overbooking, and general declines in the quality of service have increased significantly since deregulation. Clearly, some restructuring of the airline industry seems required in order to reduce overcapacity, reduce costs, improve service, and avoid price wars. At the end of March 2008, an open-skies agreement between the United States and the European Union went into effect that deregulated transatlantic air travel, and Delta was negotiating a merger with Northwest. Most domestic and foreign airlines are now part of three major international airline alliances (the Star Alliance, the OneWorld Alliance, and SkyTeam Alliance).

Sources: "Airline Deregulation," *Federal Reserve Bank of San Francisco Review,* March 9, 1990; "Airlines and Antitrust: A New World. Or Not," *New York Times,* November 18, 2001, p. 1; "For U.S. Airlines, a Shakeout Runs into Heavy Turbulence," *Wall Street Journal,* September 19, 2005, p. A1; "U.S. and EU Abandon Air-Travel Limitations," *Wall Street Journal,* March 29, 2008, p. A5; "ATA Shutdown Signals Discount-Carrier Woes," *Wall Street Journal,* April 4, 2008; and "Did Ending Regulation Help Fliers?" *New York Times,* April 17, 2008, p. C1.

EXAMPLE 13-5

Antitrust and the New Merger Boom

Since the early 1990s there has been a huge merger boom in the United States and abroad. The year 2000 was the biggest year in history for mergers and acquisitions, with deals valued at more than $1.8 trillion. During the 1990s, mega-deals occurred in telecommunications, defense, railroads, pharmaceuticals, retailing, health care, banking, entertainment, publishing, computers, consulting, and many other industries (see Section 9.5). The biggest merger in history was the America Online (AOL) acquisition of Time Warner for $110 billion in 2000. There were several forces that fueled this urge to merger. The most important were massive technological changes, increased international competition, and deregulation. Firms are under strong pressure to reduce excess capacity, to cut costs, and to become major players in the global marketplace. Only with the U.S. recession in 2001 did the merger boom subside, but it then resumed in 2004 and spread to Europe in 2005.

The new merger wave was also different from that of the 1980s, and so has been the enforcement of antitrust laws. Whereas, in the 1980s many mergers were among firms in unrelated industries (thus creating conglomerates) and raising few antitrust concerns, the merger wave since the early 1990s often involved the merger of competitors, potentially giving the combined companies the power to dominate their industries and, in theory, control prices and the availability of products. Starting from the second half of the 1990s, the enforcement of antitrust laws thus changed its focus from the doctrine that bigness leads to power and unfair behavior to that of protecting consumers and thus refusing to approve mergers that reduced competition and that were likely to increase prices. In short, enforcement has become pro-competition and pro-consumer.

For example, the Federal Trade Commission (FTC) did not approve the proposed merger of Staples and Office Depot, two chains of office-supply superstores, in 1997 because it found that Staples had lower prices in those locations where there was also an Office Depot outlet, thus concluding that their merger would very likely have led to higher consumer prices. Not approved for the same reason were many other proposed mergers, among which were the WorldCom purchase of Sprint in 2000, the United Airlines acquisition of American West, and the General Electric acquisition of Honeywell in 2001 (which was blocked by the European Commission, even though the two companies are American and the merger had been cleared by the U.S. Justice Department).

Whether, in fact, the recent merger boom led companies to reduce costs and increase efficiency and revenue depends on the type of merger taking place. In the defense and the health-care fields, the promise of reduced costs and increased efficiency has been or can be realized. In others sectors, it is not too certain. Often the acquiring company paid a premium over the market price because of synergies that the acquiring company's management saw but the market did not. When such synergies failed to materialize or did not live up to expectations, the acquiring company and its stockholders suffered, especially if the company took on huge debt loads to make the acquisitions. The biggest loss resulted from the 2000 merger of AOL/Time Warner ($200 billion loss in stock market value and $54 billion write-down in the worth of the combined company assets).

Sources: "The New Merger Boom," *Fortune,* November 28, 1994, pp. 95–106; "Aiding Consumers Is Now the Thrust of Antitrust Push," *New York Times,* March 22, 1998, p. 1; "Corporate Governance and Merger Activity in the United States: Making Sense of the 1980s and 1990s," *Journal of Economic Perspectives,* Spring 2001, pp. 121–144; "Volatile Markets and Global Slowdown Cool Corporate Desire to Merge," *Wall Street Journal,* January 2, 2002, p. R10; "Mergers: Why Most Don't Pay Off," *Business Week,* October 14, 2002, pp. 60–80; "What Mergers are Good For," *New York Times Magazine,* June 5, 2005, pp. 56–62; "Europe's M&A Boom Is Set to Hit $930 billion by End of the Year," *Financial Times,* November 7, 2005, p.1; and "The Outlook for Global M&A Activity," *Economic Outlook,* May 2007, pp. 21–27.

13.7 | REGULATING INTERNATIONAL COMPETITION: VOLUNTARY EXPORT RESTRAINTS

Voluntary export restraints (VER) The situation in which an importing country induces another nation to reduce its exports of a commodity "voluntarily" under the threat of higher all-around trade restrictions.

Regulation affects not only domestic companies but also foreign firms. Consider **voluntary export restraints (VER).** These are some of the most important nontariff trade barriers and refer to cases in which an importing country induces another nation to reduce its exports of a commodity "voluntarily," under the threat of higher all-around trade restrictions, when these exports threaten an entire domestic industry.[17] Voluntary export restraints have been negotiated since the 1950s by the United States and other industrial countries to curtail textile exports from Japan, and more recently also to curb exports of automobiles, steel, shoes, and other commodities from Japan and other nations. These are the mature industries that faced sharp declines in employment in the industrial countries during the past three decades. Sometimes called "orderly marketing arrangements," these VER have allowed the United States and other industrial nations making use of them to save at least the appearance of continued support for the principle of free trade.

When voluntary export restraints are successful, they have all the economic effects of equivalent import tariffs, except that they are administered by the exporting country, and so the revenue effect or monopoly profits are captured by foreign exporters. An example of this is provided by the "voluntary" restraint on Japanese automobile exports to the United States negotiated in 1981 (see Example 13–6).

---

[17] The effects of an import tariff were examined in Section 9.7.

Voluntary export restraints are likely to be less effective in limiting imports than import quotas, because the exporting nations agree only reluctantly to curb their exports. Foreign exporters are also likely to fill their quotas with higher-quality and higher-priced units of the product over time. This *product upgrading* was clearly evident in the case of the Japanese voluntary restraint on automobile exports to the United States. Furthermore, as a rule, only major supplier countries are involved, which leaves the door open for other nations to replace part of the exports of the major suppliers and also for trans-shipments through third countries.

✓ Concept Check

What is the purpose and effect of voluntary export restraints?

EXAMPLE 13-6

Voluntary Restraints on Export of Japanese Automobiles to the United States

From 1977 to 1981, U.S. automobile production fell by about one-third, the share of imports rose from 18% to 29%, and nearly 300,000 autoworkers in the United States lost their jobs. In 1980 the Big Three U.S. automakers (GM, Ford, and Chrysler) suffered combined losses of $4 billion. As a result, the United States negotiated an agreement with Japan that limited Japanese automobile exports to the United States to 1.68 million units per year from 1981 to 1983 and to 1.85 million units for 1984 and 1985. Japan "agreed" to restrict its automobile exports out of fear of still more stringent import restrictions by the United States.

U.S. automakers generally used the time from 1981 to 1985 wisely to lower break-even points and improve quality, but the cost improvements were not passed on to consumers, and Detroit reaped profits of nearly $6 billion in 1983, $10 billion in 1984, and $8 billion in 1985. Japan gained by exporting higher-priced autos and earning higher profits. The big loser, of course, was the American public, which had to pay substantially higher prices for domestic and foreign automobiles. The U.S. International Trade Commission (USITC) estimated that the agreement resulted in a price $660 higher for U.S.-made automobiles and $1,300 higher for Japanese cars in 1984. The USITC also estimated that the total cost of the agreement to U.S. consumers was $15.7 billion from 1981 through 1984, and that 44,000 U.S. auto jobs were saved at a cost of more than $100,000 each. This was two to three times the yearly earnings of a U.S. autoworker.

Since 1985, the United States has not asked for a renewal of the VER agreement, but Japan unilaterally limited its auto exports (to 2.3 million from 1986 to 1991 and 1.65 million afterward) to avoid more trade friction with the United States. Since the late 1980s, however, Japan has invested heavily to produce automobiles in the United States in so-called transplant factories, and by 1996 it was producing more than 2 million cars in the United States and had captured 23% of the U.S. auto market. By 2007, Japanese automakers share of the U.S. market had reached 35% (between domestic production and imports) out of a total of 46% for all foreign automakers. Following the U.S. lead, Canada and Germany also negotiated restrictions on Japanese exports (France and Italy already had very stringent quotas). A 1991 agreement to limit the Japanese share of the European Union's auto market to 16% expired at the end of 1999, when the share of Japanese cars (imports and production in Europe) was 11.4%

of the European market. That share exceeded 13% in 2007 and was expected to continue to rise in the future.

Sources: U.S. International Trade Commission, *A Review of Recent Developments in the U.S. Automobile Industry, Including an Assessment of the Japanese Voluntary Restraint Agreements* (Washington, DC: February 1985); "Japanese Car Makers Plan Major Expansion of American Capacity," *Wall Street Journal*, September 12, 1997, p. A1; "Japanese Carmakers Accelerate in Europe," *Financial Times*, September 15, 2003, p. 8; "Foreign Auto Makers Aim to Boost U.S. Market Share," *Wall Street Journal*, January 12, 2005, p. A1; "Japanese Cars Set Europe Sales Record," *Japan Times*, January 16, 2005, p. 1; "Once Again We're Driving What's Not Made Here," *New York Times*, September 30, 2007, p. 3; and U.S. Department of Commerce, *The Road Ahead for the U.S. Auto Market* (Washington, DC: U.S. Printing Office, 2007).

13.8   SOME APPLICATIONS OF MARKET STRUCTURE, EFFICIENCY, AND REGULATION

In this section, we discuss some important applications of the theory presented in this chapter: the regulation of monopoly price, peak-load pricing, and transfer pricing. These applications highlight the importance and relevance of the tools introduced in the chapter.

Regulating Monopoly Price

One way for the government to regulate a monopoly is to set a price below the price that the monopolist would charge in the absence of regulation. This leads to a larger output and lower profits for the monopolist, as shown in Figure 13.3.

The figure shows that, in the absence of regulation, the best level of output of the monopolist is given by point M, where the LMC curve intersects the MR curve (the light blue line) from below. Thus, $Q = 3$, $P = \$6$ (point R), $LAC = \$4$ (point N), and profits are $2 per unit ($RN$) and $6 in total.

If the government now set the maximum price that the monopolist could charge at $P = \$5$, the demand curve facing the monopolist would become CID (see the figure). Thus, the monopolist's demand curve would be horizontal until $Q = 4$ (since the monopolist cannot charge a price higher than $5) and would resume its usual downward shape at $Q > 4$ (since the monopolist can charge prices lower than $5). As a result, the monopolist's MR curve is also horizontal and coincides with the demand curve until point I and resumes its usual downward shape when the demand curve does. That is, the monopolist's MR curve becomes $CIKW$. Note that the MR curve has a discontinuous (vertical) section at point I, where the demand curve has a kink.

With price set at $P = \$5$, the best level of output for the monopolist is given by point J', where $LMC = MR$. Thus, $Q = 4$, $P = \$5$ (point I), $LAC = \$3.60$ (point J), and profits are $1.40 per unit and $5.60 in total. Price is lower, output is larger, and the monopolist's profits are lower than without regulation.

✓ Concept Check
How can the price of a monopolist be regulated?

If the government set the maximum price at point L, where the LMC curve intersects the D curve (so that $P = LMC = \$4$), the best level of output for the monopolist would be 5 units (see the figure). The monopolist would then earn a profit of $0.50 per unit and $2.50 in total. If the government, in an effort to eliminate all monopoly profits, were to set the lower price (about $3.50) given by point H, where the monopolist's LAC curve intersects the D curve, a shortage of the commodity (and a black market) would arise. This is

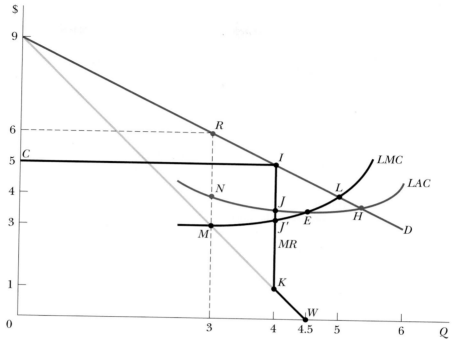

FIGURE 13.3   Regulating Monopoly Price   In the absence of regulation, $Q = 3$, $P = \$6$, $LAC = \$4$, and profits are $2 per unit ($RN$) and $6 in total. If the government set the maximum price at $P = \$5$, the demand curve becomes CID and the MR curve is $CIKW$. Then, $Q = 4$, $P = \$5$, $LAC = \$3.60$, and profits are $1.40 per unit ($IJ$) and $5.60 in total.

because consumers would demand nearly 5.5 units of the commodity while the monopolist would only produce about 4.5 units (given by the point where $P = LMC$ at about $3.50 in the figure).

Regulation and Peak-Load Pricing

The demand for some services (such as electricity) is higher during some periods (such as in the evening and in the summer) than at other times (such as during the day or in the spring). Electricity is also a nonstorable service (i.e., it must be generated when it is needed). In order to satisfy peak demand, electrical power companies must bring into operation older and less efficient equipment and thus incur higher costs. Power companies should, therefore, charge a higher price during peak than during off-peak periods to reflect their higher marginal costs in the former than in the latter periods. Since such price differences would be based on cost differences, they are not technically price discrimination (nevertheless, they have sometimes been referred to as *intertemporal* price discrimination).

Before deregulation, regulatory commissions often did not permit the public utility to charge different prices during peak and off-peak periods, but required it to charge a constant given price that covered the average of the generating costs during both periods together. Such a constant price, in the face of different generating costs, did not represent

Peak-load pricing The charging of a price equal to short-run marginal cost, both in the peak period, when demand and marginal cost are higher, and in the off-peak period, when both are lower.

the best pricing policy. Assuming that the public utility operated in the short run with a given plant and other equipment, the best pricing policy would be to charge the lower price equal to the lower marginal cost during off-peak periods and charge the higher price equal to the higher marginal cost in peak periods. By adopting such **peak-load pricing,** consumer welfare would be higher than by the policy of constant pricing during both off-peak and peak periods, and consumers generally would end up spending less on electricity for the peak and off-peak periods combined. This is shown in Figure 13.4.

In the figure, D_1 is the market demand curve for electricity during the off-peak period, and D_2 is the higher market demand curve for electricity during the peak period. The short-run marginal cost of the firm is given by SMC. The regulatory commission sets the price of 4 cents per kWh at all times to cover average total costs in both periods together. At $P = 4$ cents, the firm would sell 4 million kWh during the off-peak period (point A_1 on D_1) and 8 million kWh during the peak period (point A_2 on D_2). At point A_1, however, the marginal benefit to consumers from one additional kWh (given by the price of 4 cents per kWh) exceeds the marginal cost of generating the last unit of electricity produced (given by point B_1 on the SMC curve). From society's point of view, it would pay if the firm supplied more electricity until $P = SMC = 3$ cents (point E_1 at which D_1 and SMC intersect). The social benefit gained would be equal to the shaded triangle $A_1B_1E_1$.

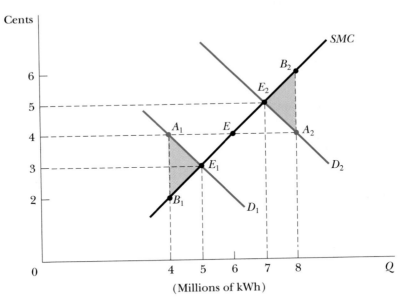

FIGURE 13.4   Peak-Load Pricing   At the constant price of 4 cents per kWh, the public utility sells 4 million kWh of electricity (point A_1) during the off-peak period and 8 million during the peak period (point A_2). But at A_1, $P > SMC$, while at A_2, $P < SMC$. With peak-load pricing, $P = SMC = 3$ cents (point E_1) in the off-peak period and $P = SMC = 5$ cents (point E_2) in the peak period. The gain in consumer welfare with peak-load pricing is thus given by the sum of the two shaded triangles.

On the other hand, at point A_2, the marginal benefit to consumers from one additional kWh (given by the price of 4 cents per kWh) is smaller than the marginal cost of generating the last unit of electricity produced (point B_2 on the *SMC* curve). From society's point of view, it would pay if the firm supplied less electricity until $P = SMC = 5$ cents (point E_2 at which D_2 and *SMC* intersect). The social benefit gained (by using the same resources to produce some other service that society values more) would be equal to the shaded triangle $B_2A_2E_2$. Charging $P = SMC = 3$ cents in the off-peak period (point E_1 in the figure) and $P = SMC = 5$ cents in the peak period (point E_2) would be the most efficient pricing policy.

With deregulation, peak-load or time-of-day pricing is in fact now being used by most electrical companies (telephone companies have been practicing second- and third-degree price discrimination for a long time). For example, in April 2002, Con Edison charged 7.89 cents per kWh for electricity from 10 A.M. to 10 P.M. and 0.70 cents from 10 P.M. to 10 A.M. and on weekends.[18] What is surprising is that it took so long for regulatory commissions to recognize peak-load pricing.

There are other effects from peak-load pricing, which are not shown in Figure 13.4. The first results from the substitution of electricity consumption from peak to off-peak periods to take advantage of the lower price during the off-peak period. This tends to reduce the benefit of peak-load pricing (see Problem 12, with the answer at the end of the book). Another effect also not shown in Figure 13.4 is that with peak-load pricing the scale of plant to meet peak-load demand is smaller (7 million kWh with peak-load pricing as compared with 8 million kWh without peak-load pricing). Thus, in the long run, when the public utility needs to replace the present plant, it can do so with a smaller and more efficient one. One factor that militates against peak-load pricing is that it requires meters to measure consumption at different times of the day, week, or year, and these can be quite expensive to install.

Peak-load pricing is not confined to public utilities. It is equally applicable to such private enterprises as hotels, restaurants, airlines, movie theaters, and so on, which face a demand that fluctuates sharply and in a predictable way during peak and off-peak periods. These enterprises usually charge lower rates during off-season or in periods of naturally low demand (when marginal costs are lower) than during in-season or periods of high demand (when marginal costs are higher).

Regulation and Transfer Pricing

Transfer pricing The determination of the price of intermediate products sold by one semiautonomous division of a firm to another semiautonomous division of the same enterprise.

The rapid rise of modern large-scale enterprises has been accompanied by decentralization and the establishment of semiautonomous profit centers. This occurred because of the need to contain the tendency toward increasing costs for communications and coordination among various divisions. Decentralization and the establishment of semiautonomous profit centers also gave rise to the need for **transfer pricing,** or the need to determine the price of intermediate products sold by one semiautonomous division of a large-scale enterprise and purchased by another semiautonomous division of the same enterprise. The appropriate pricing of intermediate products or transfer pricing is of crucial importance to the efficient operation of the individual divisions as well as the enterprise as a whole. If the wrong transfer prices are set, the various divisions and the firm as a whole will not produce the optimum or profit-maximizing level of output and will not maximize total profits.

---

[18] See "Paying for Electricity by Time of Day," *New York Times,* June 9, 1990, p. 48; and Con Edison, 2002.

Transfer pricing has also been used by multinational corporations to increase their profits. Specifically, by artificially overpricing components shipped *to* an affiliate in a higher-tax nation and underpricing products shipped *from* the affiliate in the high-tax nation, the multinational corporation can minimize its tax bill and increase its profits. To overcome this problem, government regulators usually apply the "arm's length" test, under which the price of parts shipped from one affiliate of a multinational corporation in one country to another affiliate in another country is priced by regulators for taxing purposes according to the price that the same part would be sold to nonaffiliates.

For simplicity, we assume in our analysis that the firm has two divisions, a production division (indicated by the subscript p) and a marketing division (indicated by the subscript m). The production division sells the intermediate product only to the marketing division (i.e., there is no external market for the intermediate product). The marketing division purchases the intermediate product from the production division, completes the production process, and markets the final product for the firm. We further assume that one unit of the intermediate product is required to produce each unit of the final product.

In Figure 13.5, MC_p and MC_m are the marginal cost curves of the production and marketing divisions of the firm, respectively, while MC is the vertical summation of

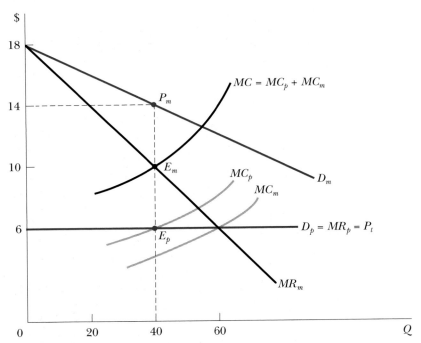

FIGURE 13.5   Transfer Pricing of the Intermediate Product with No External Market   The marginal cost of the firm, MC, is equal to the vertical summation of MC_p and MC_m, the marginal cost curves of the firm's production and marketing divisions. D_m is the external demand for the final product faced by the firm, and MR_m is the corresponding marginal revenue curve. The firm's best level of output is 40 units and is given by point E_m, at which $MR_m = MC$, so that $P_m = \$14$. Since each unit of the final product requires one unit of the intermediate product, the transfer price for the intermediate product, P_t, is set equal to MC_p at $Q_p = 40$ (point E_p). Thus, $P_t = \$6$.

MC_p and MC_m and represents the total marginal cost curve for the firm as a whole. The figure also shows the external demand curve for the final product sold by the marketing division, D_m, and its corresponding marginal revenue curve, MR_m. The firm's best, or profit-maximizing, level of output for the final product is 40 units and is given by point E_m, at which $MR_m = MC$. Therefore, $P_m = \$14$. Since 40 units of the intermediate product are required to produce the 40 units of the final product, the transfer price for the intermediate product, P_t, is set equal to the marginal cost of the intermediate product (MC_p) at $Q_p = 40$. Thus, $P_t = \$6$ and is given by point E_p at which $Q_p = 40$. The demand and marginal revenue curves faced by the production division of the firm are then equal to the transfer price (i.e., $D_p = MR_p = P_t$). Note that $Q_p = 40$ is the best level of output of the intermediate product by the production division of the firm because at $Q_p = 40$, $D_p = MR_p = P_t = MC_p = \$6$. Thus, the correct transfer price for an intermediate product for which there is no external market is the marginal cost of production.[19]

<hr>

SUMMARY

1. In this chapter we have made use of the basic principle that any activity should be carried out until the marginal benefit equals the marginal cost to examine the relationship between market structure and efficiency, public-utility regulation, and antitrust.

2. The Lerner index measures the degree of a *firm's* monopoly power by the ratio of the difference between price and marginal cost to price. The Herfindahl index estimates the degree of monopoly power in an *industry* as a whole by the sum of the squared values of the market sales shares of all the firms in the industry. According to the theory of contestable markets, even if an industry has only one or a few firms, it would still operate as if it were perfectly competitive if entry into the industry is absolutely free and if exit is entirely costless. Experimental economics has been developing during the past two decades. This field seeks to determine how real markets work by using paid volunteers within a simple experimental institutional framework.

3. Static social costs of monopoly power arise because imperfect competitors produce where $P > MR = MC$ and also from rent-seeking activities. These must be balanced with the benefits of economies of scale resulting from large-scale production and the possibility that firms with monopoly power are more innovative than small firms without market power. A great deal of disagreement exists, however, about the alleged dynamic benefits that larger firms have over smaller ones.

4. Section I of the Sherman Antitrust Act, passed in 1890, declared that "Every contract, combination . . . , or conspiracy in restraint of trade or commerce among the several states, or with foreign nations, is hereby declared to be illegal." This does not make monopoly as such, or conscious parallelism, illegal. What is illegal is collusion to restrain trade. Section II of the Sherman Antitrust Act makes attempts to monopolize the market illegal. Section VII of the Clayton Act passed in 1914 (and amended by the Celler–Kefauver Act of 1950), prohibits mergers that "substantially lessen competition" or tend to lead to monopoly.

5. Natural monopolies such as public utilities arise when the firm's LAC curve is still declining at the point where it intersects the market demand curve. The government then usually allows a

<hr>

[19] For a more detailed discussion of transfer pricing, including the case where there is an external market for the intermediate product of the firm, see D. Salvatore, *Managerial Economics in a Global Economy,* 6th ed. (New York: Oxford University Press, 2007).

single firm to operate but sets $P = LAC$ (so that the firm earns only a normal return on investment). Economic efficiency, however, requires that $P = LMC$, but this would result in a loss and the company would not supply the service in the long run without a subsidy. Therefore, P is usually set equal to LAC. Many difficulties arise in public-utility regulation, especially to ensure that the utilities keep costs as low as possible.

6. Since the mid-1970s, the government has deregulated airlines and trucking and reduced the level of regulation for financial institutions, telecommunications, and railroads in order to increase competition and avoid some of the heavy compliance costs of regulation. Even though the full impact of deregulation has yet to be felt, deregulation seems to have led to increased competition and lower prices, but it has also resulted in some problems such as deterioration in the quality of the services provided.

7. Voluntary export restraints (VER) refer to the case in which an importing country induces another nation to reduce its exports of a commodity "voluntarily" under the threat of higher all-around trade restrictions. When successful, the economic impact of voluntary export restraints is the same as that of an equivalent import tariff, except for the revenue effect, which is now captured by foreign suppliers. Voluntary export restraints have been negotiated to curtail exports of textiles, automobiles, steel, shoes, and other commodities to the United States and other industrial countries.

8. By setting price below the monopoly price, a monopolist can be induced to produce a larger output and have lower profits. Peak-load pricing refers to the charging of a price equal to short-run marginal cost, both in the peak period when demand and marginal cost are higher and in the off-peak period when both are lower. The transfer price for an intermediate product for which there is no external market is the marginal cost of production.

KEY TERMS

Efficiency	Sherman Antitrust Act	Voluntary export restraints (VER)
Lerner index	Conscious parallelism	Peak-load pricing
Herfindahl index	Clayton Act	Transfer pricing
Theory of contestable markets	Averch–Johnson (A–J) effect	
Experimental economics	Deregulation movement	

REVIEW QUESTIONS

1. Under what conditions will an economy operate most efficiently? Why?

2. What can be done to increase efficiency if the price of the last unit consumed of a commodity exceeds the marginal cost of producing it?

3. What is the value of the Lerner index if $\eta = -5$? if $\eta = -3$?

4. What is the value of the Lerner index (L) if $P = \$10$ and $MR = \$5$?

5. What is the value of the Herfindahl index
   a. in a duopoly with one firm having 60% of the market?
   b. with 1,000 equal-sized firms?

6. What is the difference between limit pricing and the theory of contestable markets?

7. What are the most important
   a. social costs of monopoly power?
   b. benefits associated with monopoly power?

8. How does the government decide whether to subject a very large firm to antitrust action or regulation?

9. The settlement of the AT&T antitrust case in 1982 involved both good news and bad news for AT&T and its customers. What was
   a. the good news and bad news for AT&T?

b. the good news and bad news for users of telephone services?

10. a. How could a regulatory commission induce a public-utility company to operate as a perfect competitor in the long run?

b. To what difficulty would this lead?

c. What compromise does a regulatory commission usually adopt?

11. Given the difficulties that the regulation of public utilities face, would it not be better to nationalize public utilities, as some European countries have done? Explain your answer.

12. Peak-load pricing can be regarded as an application of the marginal principle. True or false? Explain.

PROBLEMS

1. Explain why the value of the Lerner index can seldom if ever be equal to one (i.e., the value of L usually ranges from zero to smaller than one).

*2. Show with the use of a diagram that a given value of the Lerner index is consistent with different rates of profits for the firm.

3. In measuring the Herfindahl index, the market share of each firm in the industry is sometimes expressed in ratio form rather than in percentages (as in the text). Find the Herfindahl index if the market share of each firm is expressed as a ratio when

a. there is a single firm in the industry.

b. there is a duopoly with one firm having 0.6 of the total industry sales.

c. there is one firm with sales equal to 0.5 of total industry sales and ten other equal-sized firms.

d. there are ten equal-sized firms.

e. there are 100 equal-sized firms in the industry.

f. there are 1,000 equal-sized firms in the industry.

4. Starting with demand curve D in Figure 13.1, draw a figure showing three identical firms in the contestable market.

*5. Draw a figure similar to Figure 10.7 showing the net social losses of monopoly when the firm's marginal cost curve is rising, rather than horizontal as in Figure 10.7.

6. Determine if the Justice Department would challenge a merger between two firms in an industry with ten equal-sized firms, based on its Herfindahl-index guidelines only.

*7. Suppose that the market demand curve for the public-utility service shown in Figure 13.2 shifts to the right by 1 million units at each price level but the LAC and LMC curves remain unchanged. Draw a figure showing

the price of the service that the public-utility commission would set and the quantity of the service that would be supplied to the market at that price.

8. Suppose that the market demand curve for the public-utility service shown in Figure 13.2 shifts to the right by 1 million units at each price level, and, at the same time, the LAC curve of the public-utility company shifts upward by $1 throughout because of production inefficiencies that escape detection by the public-utility commission. Draw a figure showing the price of the service that the public-utility commission would set and the quantity of the service that would be supplied to the market at that price.

9. Compare the effects of a voluntary export restraint that restricts the export of commodity X to the nation to 200 units, with the effects of a $1 import tariff imposed by the nation on commodity X shown in Figure 9.17.

10. Draw a figure showing how a regulatory commission could induce the monopolist of Figure 13.3 to behave as a perfect competitor in the short run by setting the appropriate price.

11. Explain why the problems arising in public-utility regulation do not arise in the case of a monopoly that is not a natural monopoly.

*12. a. Starting from Figure 13.4, draw a figure showing peak-load pricing when substitution in consumption is taken into consideration.

b. Is the benefit of peak-load pricing greater or smaller when substitution in consumption is taken into consideration than when it is not? Why is this so?

INTERNET SITE ADDRESSES

For measures of concentration and Herfindahl index in the United States, see:

http://www.census.gov/prod/ec02/ec0231sr1.pdf

Experimental economics is examined at:

http://en.wikipedia.org/wiki/Experimental_economics

http://www.oswego.edu/~economic/exper.htm

http://eeps.caltech.edu/

Comprehensive antitrust links to the U.S. Department of Justice, the Federal Trade Commission, case summaries, journals, and so on are found at:

http://www.antitrust.org

http://www.usdoj.gov/atr/index.html

http://www.findlaw.com/01topics/01antitrust/index.html

The Internet sites for the Energy Regulatory Commission and for pricing by Con Edison are:

http://www.ferc.ed.us

http://www.conedison.com

For conditions, deregulation, and antitrust cases in the airline industry, see:

http://www.u.arizona.edu/~gowrisan/pdf_papers/airline_competition.pdf

http://www.welcomeurope.com/default.asp?id=1300&idnews=4239&genre=9

http://www.libsci.sc.edu/bob/class/clis748/Studentwebguides/Webguides2007/SnedikerGuide2.html

For information on international trade regulations and rulings of the WTO, see:

http://www.wto.org

PART FIVE

Pricing and Employment of Inputs

Part Five (Chapters 14–16) presents the theory of input pricing and employment. Until this point in the text, we have assumed input prices to be given. In this part, we examine how input prices and the level of their employment are determined in the market. Chapter 14 deals with input pricing and employment under perfect competition in the output and input markets. Chapter 15 examines input pricing and employment under imperfect competition in the output and/or input markets. Chapter 16 deals with financial microeconomics; that is, the allocation of inputs over time and the cost of capital. As in previous parts of the text, the presentation of theory is reinforced with many real-world examples and important applications, while the "At the Frontier" sections present some new and important developments in the analysis of input or factor markets.

CHAPTER 14

Input Price and Employment Under Perfect Competition

After Studying This Chapter, You Should Be Able to:

- Know how a firm determines the amount of each input to use to maximize profits
- Describe how a firm's and the market demand curve for one or more variable inputs are derived
- Describe how the supply curve of labor of one individual is derived and why it could be backward sloping
- Explain how the equilibrium price and employment of an input is determined in a perfectly competitive market
- Describe the effects of increasing the minimum wage

n Chapters 7 and 8 we examined how firms combine inputs to minimize production costs on the assumption of given input prices. In Chapters 9 through 13 we dealt with the product market and examined the pricing and output of consumers' goods, again on the assumption of given input prices. We now turn our attention to the input market and examine how the price and employment of inputs are actually determined.

In many ways the determination of input prices and employment is similar to the pricing and output of commodities. That is, the price and employment of an input is generally determined by the interaction of the forces of market demand and supply for the input.

There are several important qualifications, however. First, whereas consumers demand commodities because of the utility or satisfaction they receive in consuming the commodities, firms demand inputs in order to produce the goods and services demanded by society. That is, the demand for an input is a "derived demand"; it is derived from the demand for the final commodities that the input is used in producing. Second, while consumers demand commodities, firms demand the *services* of inputs. That is, firms demand the *flow* of input services (e.g., labor time), not the stock of the inputs themselves. The same is generally true for the other inputs. Third, the analysis in this chapter and in the next deals with inputs in general; that is, it refers to all types of labor, capital, raw materials, and land inputs. However, since the various types of labor receive nearly three-quarters of the national income, the discussion is couched in terms of labor.

We begin the chapter with a summary discussion of profit maximization and optimal input employment. Then we derive a firm's demand curve for an input. By adding the demand curves for the input of all firms, we get the market demand curve for the input. Next we discuss an individual's decision between work and leisure and the market supply curve of an input in general. The chapter then describes how the interaction of the market demand and supply of an input determines its price and employment under perfect competition (the case of imperfect competition is examined in the next chapter). Subsequently, the chapter shows the process by which input prices tend to be equalized among industries and regions of a country, and internationally among countries. A discussion of rent and quasi-rent follows. This chapter concludes with several important applications and extensions of the theory. The "At the Frontier" section examines the effect of minimum wages on employment.

14.1   PROFIT MAXIMIZATION AND OPTIMAL INPUT EMPLOYMENT

In this section, we bring together and summarize the discussions of Chapters 7, 8, and 9 on the conditions for profit maximization and optimal input employment by firms operating under perfect competition. This is the first step in the derivation of the demand curve for an input by a firm.

In Section 8.3, we saw that the least-cost input combination of a firm was given by equation [8.5B], repeated below as [14.1]:

$$MP_L/w = MP_K/r \qquad [14.1]$$

where *MP* refers to the marginal (physical) product, *L* refers to labor, *K* to capital, *w* to wages or the price of labor time, and *r* to the interest rate or the rental price of capital. Equation [14.1] indicates that to minimize production costs, the extra output or marginal product per dollar spent on labor must be equal to the marginal product per dollar spent on capital. If $MP_L = 5$, $MP_K = 4$, and $w = r$, the firm would not be minimizing costs, because it is getting more extra output for a dollar spent on labor than on capital. To minimize costs, the firm would have to hire more labor and rent less capital. As the firm does this, the MP_L declines and the MP_K increases (because of diminishing returns). The process would have to continue until condition [14.1] held. If w were higher than r, the MP_L would have to be proportionately higher than the MP_K for condition [14.1] to hold. The same general condition would have to hold to minimize production costs, no matter how many inputs the firm uses. That is, the MP per dollar spent on each input would have to be the same for all inputs.

Going one step further, we can show that the reciprocal of each term (ratio) in equation [14.1] equals the marginal cost (MC) of the firm to produce an additional unit of output. That is,

$$w/MP_L = r/MP_K = MC \qquad [14.2]$$

Consider labor first. The wage rate (w) is the addition to the total costs of the firm from hiring one additional unit of labor, while MP_L is the resulting increase in the total output of the commodity of the firm. Thus, w/MP_L gives the change in total costs (in terms of labor) per unit increase in output. This is the definition of marginal cost. That is, $w/MP_L = MC$.[1] For example, if the hourly wage is $10 and the firm produces five additional units of the commodity with an additional hour of labor time, the marginal cost per unit of output is $2 ($w/MP_L = \$10/5 = \$2 = MC$). The same is true for capital. That is, $r/MP_K = MC$.[2]

To maximize profits, the firm must use the optimal or least-cost input combination to produce the *best level of output*. We saw in Section 9.3 that the best level of output for a perfectly competitive firm is the output at which marginal cost (MC) equals marginal revenue (MR) or price (P).[3] Thus, it follows that to maximize profits

$$w/MP_L = r/MP_K = MC = MR = P \qquad [14.3]$$

By cross multiplication and rearrangement of the terms, we get equations [14.4] and [14.5]:

$$MP_L \times MR = w \quad \text{or} \quad MP_L \times P = w \qquad [14.4]$$

$$MP_K \times MR = r \quad \text{or} \quad MP_K \times P = r \qquad [14.5]$$

Thus, the profit-maximizing rule is that the firm should hire labor until the marginal product of labor times the firm's marginal revenue or price of the commodity equals the wage

---

[1] Specifically,

$$\frac{w}{MP_L} = \frac{\Delta TC/\Delta L}{\Delta Q/\Delta L} = \frac{\Delta TC}{\Delta L} \cdot \frac{\Delta L}{\Delta Q} = \frac{\Delta TC}{\Delta Q} = MC$$

[2] Specifically,

$$\frac{r}{MP_K} = \frac{\Delta TC/\Delta K}{\Delta Q/\Delta K} = \frac{\Delta TC}{\Delta K} \cdot \frac{\Delta K}{\Delta Q} = \frac{\Delta TC}{\Delta Q} = MC$$

[3] Remember that with perfect competition in the commodity market, $MR = P$.

rate. Similarly, the firm should rent capital until the marginal product of capital times the firm's marginal revenue or price of the commodity is equal to the interest rate. To maximize profits, the same rule would have to hold for all inputs that the firm uses. In the next section, we will see that this provides the basis for the firm's demand curve for an input.

14.2 THE DEMAND CURVE OF A FIRM FOR AN INPUT

In this section, we build on the discussion of the last section and derive the demand curve of a firm for an input—first, when the input is the only variable input and then, when the input is one of two or more variable inputs.

The Demand Curve of a Firm for One Variable Input

We have stated earlier that a firm demands an input in order to produce a commodity demanded by consumers. Thus, the demand for an input is a **derived demand**—derived, that is, from the demand for the final commodities that the input is used in producing. The demand for an input by a firm shows the quantities of the input that the firm would hire at various alternative input prices. We begin by assuming that only one input is variable (i.e., the amount used of the other inputs is fixed and cannot be changed). This assumption will be relaxed in the next subsection.

According to the marginal concept, a profit-maximizing firm will hire an input as long as the extra income from the sale of the output produced by the input is larger than the extra cost of hiring the input. The extra income is given by the marginal product (MP) of the input times the marginal revenue (MR) of the firm. This is called the **marginal revenue product (MRP)**. That is,

$$MRP = MP \cdot MR \qquad [14.6]$$

When the firm is a perfect competitor in the product market, its marginal revenue is equal to the commodity price (P). In this case, the marginal revenue product is called the **value of the marginal product (VMP)**. That is, when the firm is a perfect competitor in the product market (so that $MR = P$),

$$MRP = MP \cdot MR = MP \cdot P = VMP \qquad [14.6A]$$

If the variable input is labor, we have

$$MRP_L = MP_L \cdot MR = MP_L \cdot P = VMP_L \qquad [14.6B]$$

Thus, the MRP_L or VMP_L is the left-hand side of equation [14.4]. Similarly, the MRP_K or VMP_K is the left-hand side of equation [14.5].

The extra cost of hiring an input, or **marginal expenditure (ME)**, is equal to the price of the input if the firm is a perfect competitor in the input market. Perfect competition in the input market means that the firm demanding the input is too small, by itself, to affect the price of the input. In other words, each firm can hire any amount of the input (service) at the given market price for the input. Thus, the firm faces a horizontal or infinitely elastic *supply* curve for the input. For example, if the input is labor, this means that the firm can hire

TABLE 14.1		Marginal Revenue Product of Labor as the Firm's Demand Schedule for Labor			

L	Q_X	MP_L	P_X	$MRP_L = VMP_L$	$ME_L = w$
0	0	. . .	$10	. . .	$40
1	12	12	10	$120	40
2	22	10	10	100	40
3	30	8	10	80	40
4	36	6	10	60	40
5	40	4	10	40	40
6	42	2	10	20	40

any quantity of labor time at the given wage rate. Thus, a profit-maximizing firm should hire labor as long as the marginal revenue product of labor exceeds the marginal expenditure on labor or wage rate and until $MRP_L = ME_L = w$, as indicated by equation [14.4]. Note that the $MRP = ME$ rule is entirely analogous to the $MR = MC$ profit-maximizing rule employed throughout our discussion of price and output determination in Chapters 9–13.

The actual derivation of a firm's demand schedule for labor, when labor is the only variable input (i.e., when capital and other inputs are fixed), is shown in Table 14.1. In Table 14.1, L refers to the number of workers hired by the firm per day. Q_X is the total output of commodity X produced by the firm by hiring various numbers of workers. The MP_L is the marginal or extra output generated by each additional worker hired. The MP_L is obtained by the change in Q_X per unit change in L. Note that the law of diminishing returns begins to operate with the hiring of the second worker. P_X refers to the price of the final commodity, which is constant (at $10) because the firm is a perfect competitor in the product market. The marginal revenue product of labor (MRP_L) is obtained by multiplying the MP_L by MR_X (the marginal revenue from the sale of commodity X) and is equal to the value of the marginal product of labor (VMP_L) because $P_X = MR_X$.[4] The last column gives the marginal expenditure on labor (ME_L), which is equal to the constant wage rate (w) of $40 per day that the firm must pay to hire each additional worker (since the firm is a perfect competitor in the labor market).

Looking at Table 14.1, we see that the first worker contributes an extra $120 to the firm's revenue (i.e., $MRP_L = \$120$), while the firm incurs an extra expenditure of only $40 to hire this worker (i.e., $ME_L = w = \$40$). Thus, it pays for the firm to hire the first worker. The MRP_L of the second worker falls to $100 (because of diminishing returns), but this still greatly exceeds the daily wage of $40 that the firm must pay the second (and all) worker(s) hired. According to equation [14.4], the profit-maximizing firm should hire workers until the $MRP_L = ME_L = w$. Thus, this firm should hire five workers, at which $VMP_L = w = \$40$. The firm will not hire the sixth worker because he or she will contribute only an extra $20 to the firm's total revenue while adding an extra $40 to its total expenditures.

---

[4] Note also that

$$MRP_L = MP_L \cdot MR = \frac{\Delta Q}{\Delta L} \cdot \frac{\Delta TR}{\Delta Q} = \frac{\Delta TR}{\Delta L}$$

✓ Concept Check
How is a firm's demand curve for one variable input derived?

Thus, the MRP_L schedule gives the firm's demand schedule for labor. It indicates the number of workers that the firm would hire at various wage rates. For example, if $w = \$120$ per day, the firm would hire only one worker per day. If $w = \$100$, the firm would hire two workers. At $w = \$80$, the firm would hire three workers. At $w = \$40$, $L = 5$, and so on. If we plotted the MRP_L values of Table 14.1 on the vertical axis and L on the horizontal axis, we would get the firm's negatively sloped demand *curve* for labor when labor is the only variable input. This is shown next.

The Demand Curve of a Firm for One of Several Variable Inputs

We have seen that the declining MRP_L schedule given in Table 14.1 gives the firm's demand schedule for labor in the short run when labor is the only variable input. This is shown by the negatively sloped MRP_L curve in Figure 14.1 (on the assumption that labor is infinitesimally divisible or that workers can be hired for any part of a day). The MRP_L or demand for labor curve when labor is the only variable input shows that the firm will hire three workers at $w = \$80$ (point A in Figure 14.1) and five workers at $w = \$40$ (point B).

However, when labor is not the only variable input (i.e., when the firm can also change the quantity of capital and other inputs), the firm's demand curve for labor can be derived from the MRP_L curve, but it is not the MRP_L curve itself. Figure 14.1 shows the derivation of the demand curve for labor by a firm when both labor and capital are variable. As a first step, recall that at $w = \$80$, the profit-maximizing firm would hire three workers (point A on the MRP_L curve in Figure 14.1). This gives the first point on the firm's demand curve for labor when only labor is variable and when both labor and capital are variable. When the daily wage rate falls from $w = \$80$ to $w = \$40$, the firm does not move to point B on the given MRP_L curve and hire five workers (as shown before) if labor is not the only variable input.

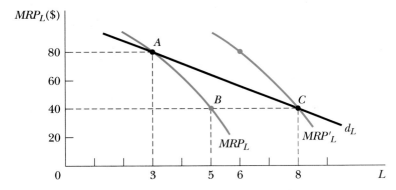

FIGURE 14.1   Demand Curve for Labor of a Firm with Labor and Capital Variable   At $w = \$80$, the firm will employ three workers per day (point A on the MRP_L curve). At $w = \$40$, the firm would employ five workers if labor were the only variable input (point B on the MRP_L curve). However, since capital is also variable and complementary to labor, as the firm hires more labor, the MRP_K shifts to the right and the firm also employs more capital (not shown in the figure). But as the firm employs more capital, the MRP_L curve shifts to the right to MRP'_L and the firm employs eight workers per day at $w = \$40$ (point C on MRP'_L). By joining point A and point C, we derive d_L (the firm's demand curve for labor).

**Complementary
inputs** Inputs related
to one another in such a
way that an increase in
the employment of one
raises the marginal
product of the other.

To get another point on the firm's demand curve for labor when both labor and capital are variable, we should realize that labor and capital are usually **complementary inputs**, in the sense that when the firm hires more labor, it will also employ more capital (e.g., rent more machinery). For example, when the firm hires more computer programmers, it will usually also pay for the firm to rent more computer terminals, and vice versa. Recall also that the MRP_L curve is drawn on the assumption that the quantity of capital used is fixed at a given level. Similarly, the MRP_K curve is drawn on the assumption of a given amount of labor being used. If the quantity of labor used with various amounts of capital increases (because of a reduction in wages), the entire MRP_K curve will shift outward or to the right. The reason for this is that with a greater amount of labor, each unit of capital will produce more output (see Section 7.3). Given the (unchanged) rental price of capital or interest rate, the profit-maximizing firm will then want to expand its use of capital.

But the increase in the quantity of capital used by the firm will, in turn, shift the entire MRP_L curve outward or to the right because each worker will have more capital with which to work (and produce more output). This is shown by the MRP'_L in Figure 14.1. Thus, when the daily wage rate falls to $w = \$40$, the profit-maximizing firm will hire eight workers (point C on the MRP'_L curve) rather than five workers (point B on the MRP_L curve). Thus, point C is another point on the firm's demand curve for labor when labor and capital are both variable. Other points can be similarly obtained. Joining point A and point C gives the firm's demand curve for labor (d_L in Figure 14.1) when labor and capital are both variable and complementary.

To summarize, when $w = \$80$, the firm will hire three workers (point A in Figure 14.1). Point A is a point on the firm's demand curve for labor, whether or not labor is the only variable input. When the wage rate falls to $w = \$40$, the firm will hire five workers (point B on the MRP_L curve) if labor is the only variable input. Thus, the MRP_L curve gives the firm's demand curve for labor when labor is the only variable input. If capital is also variable and complementary to labor, as the firm hires more labor because of the reduction in the wage rate, the MRP_K curve (not shown in Figure 14.1) shifts to the right and the firm uses more capital at the unchanged interest rate. However, as the firm uses more capital, its MRP_L curve shifts outward or to the right to MRP'_L and the firm hires not just five workers (point B on the MRP_L curve), but eight workers (point C on the MRP'_L curve). The reason is that only by hiring eight workers will $MRP'_L = w = \$40$. Joining points A and C gives the demand curve for labor of the firm d_L (see the figure) when labor and capital are both variable and complementary.

If capital or other inputs are substitutes for labor, the increase in the quantity of labor used by the firm as a result of a reduction in the wage rate will cause the MRP curves of these other inputs to shift to the *left* (as the utilization of more labor substitutes for, or replaces, some of these other inputs). This, in turn, will cause the MRP_L curve to shift outward and to the right as in Figure 14.1. Thus, whether other inputs are complements or substitutes for labor, the MRP_L shifts outward and to the right when the wage rate falls (and the price of these other inputs remains unchanged). As a result, the firm will hire more labor than indicated on its original MRP_L curve at the lower wage rate (see Figure 14.1).

Thus, the d_L curve is negatively sloped and generally more elastic than the MRP_L curve in the long run when all inputs are variable (whether the other inputs are complements or substitutes of labor, or both). In general, the better the complement and substitute inputs available for labor, the greater the outward shift of the MRP_L curve as a result of a decline in the wage rate, and the more elastic is d_L. The negative slope of the d_L curve means that when the wage rate falls, the profit-maximizing firm will hire more workers.

✓ Concept Check
How is a firm's demand
curve for one of several
variable inputs derived?

The same is generally true for other inputs. That is, as the price of any input falls, the firm will hire more units of the input (i.e., the demand curve of the input of the firm is negatively sloped). In the process, however, the firm will also make marginal adjustments in the use of all complementary and substitute inputs.

THE MARKET DEMAND CURVE FOR AN INPUT AND ITS ELASTICITY

In this section, we examine how to derive the market demand curve for an input from the individual firms' demand curves for the input. The determination of the market demand curve for an input is important because the equilibrium price of the input is determined at the intersection of the market demand and supply curves of the input under perfect competition. After deriving the market demand curve for an input, we will discuss the determinants of the price elasticity of the demand for the input.

The Market Demand Curve for an Input

The market demand curve for an input is derived from the individual firms' demand curves for the input. Although the process is similar to the derivation of the market demand curve for a commodity from individuals' demand curves for the commodity, the market demand curve for an input is not simply the horizontal summation of the individual firms' demand curves for the input. The reason is that when the price of an input falls, not only this firm but all other firms will employ more of this and other (complementary) inputs, as explained in Section 14.2. Thus, the output of the *commodity* increases and its price falls. Since the *MRP* of an input is equal to the marginal product of the input times the marginal revenue (which is here equal to the commodity price), the reduction in the commodity price will cause each firm's *MRP* and demand curves of the input to shift down or to the left. The market demand curve for an input is then derived by the horizontal summation of the individual firms' demand curves for the input *after the effect of the reduction in the commodity price has been considered.* This is shown in Figure 14.2.

In the left panel of Figure 14.2, d_L is the individual firm's demand curve for labor time derived in Figure 14.1. The d_L curve was derived from the MRP_L of the firm, which itself depended on the marginal product of labor (i.e., MP_L) and the commodity price of $P_x = \$10$. The d_L curve shows that at the wage rate of $w = \$80$ per day the firm would hire three workers per day (point A on d_L). If there were 100 identical firms demanding labor, all firms together would employ 300 workers at $w = \$80$ (point A' in the right panel of Figure 14.2). Point A' is then one point on the market demand curve for labor.

When the wage rate falls to $w = \$40$, the firm would employ eight workers per day (point C on d_L). However, when we consider that all firms will be employing more labor (and capital) when the wage rate falls, they will produce more of the commodity, and the commodity price falls. The reduction in the commodity price will cause a leftward shift in d_L, say to d'_L in the left panel, so that when the wage rate falls to $w = \$40$, the firm will not hire eight workers per day but six workers (point E on d'_L). With 100 identical firms in the market, all firms together will employ 600 workers (point E' in the right panel). By joining points A' and E' in the right panel, we get the market demand curve for labor, D_L. Note that D_L is less elastic than if it were obtained by the simple straightforward horizontal summation of the d_L curves. Example 14–1 examines the increase in the demand for temporary workers.

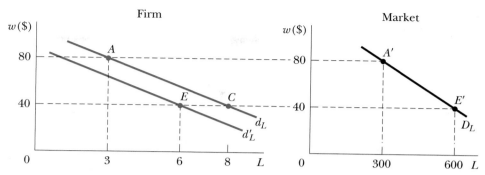

FIGURE 14.2   Derivation of the Market Demand Curve for Labor   In the left panel, d_L is the firm's demand curve for labor derived in Figure 14.1. At $w = \$80$ the firm hires three workers (point A on d_L). One hundred identical firms employ 300 workers (point A' in the right panel). Point A' is one point on the market demand curve for labor. When w falls to $w = \$40$, all firms employ more labor, the output of the commodity rises, and its price falls. Then d_L shifts to the left to d'_L, so that at $w = \$40$ the firm hires $6L$ (point E on d'_L), and all firms together will employ $600L$ (point E' in the right panel). By joining point A' and E', we get D_L.

EXAMPLE 14–1

The Increase in the Demand for Temporary Workers

In recent years there has been a sharp increase in the demand for temporary workers not only for work in offices but also on factory floors around the country. The trend is evident not only in small local firms but also in such large leading multinational corporations as IBM, Microsoft, General Electric, and Johnson & Johnson, and it involves not only low-skilled workers but, increasingly, professionals such as lawyers, doctors, and scientists. With many corporations facing increasing competition from home and abroad, and having already pared their payrolls to the bone, skilled temporary workers are becoming increasingly common in computer labs, operating rooms, and even executive suites.

The tendency to hire temporary workers is strongest during economic downturns, but it persists even in times of strong demand. Some estimates indicate that as many as 30% of new jobs are now temporary, as compared with about 10% a decade ago. In 2007, temporary workers represented 2.2% of the nation's overall work force, double the level in 1991. Temporary workers usually earn significantly less than the permanent employees and can be laid off far more easily than regular employees. They also receive little in the way of nonwage benefits (health insurance, pension benefits, vacations, and so on). Although the lower labor costs make U.S. corporations more flexible and competitive on world markets, hiring temporary workers creates major problems for new entrants into the labor force and for older laid-off workers searching for a new job. Indeed, if the present trend toward hiring temporary workers continues, the traditional American job, with a 40-hour workweek, medical benefits, paid vacations, and a pension at 65, may become more and more rare.

Although some workers like the flexibility and diversity that temporary jobs provide, the vast majority would clearly prefer a more permanent job. This is also true for the many professionals who present themselves as consultants when they fail to secure a regular job. Temporary workers also have less loyalty to the firm than regular workers and can leave suddenly when they find a more permanent job or a better temporary occupation. Furthermore, temporary workers that are kept on a long time are likely to become grumpy and wonder why they are not hired more permanently. Finally, temporary workers create a strong need for society to provide a safety net separate from people's jobs to provide for their health care, pension, and job training.

Sources: "Regulators Probe U.S. Reliance on Temporary Workers," *Wall Street Journal, August* 7, 2000, p. A2; D. Ellwood et al., *A Working Nation: Workers, Work, and Government in the New Economy* (New York: Russell Sage Foundation, 2000); "Temporary Work Is Sidestepping a Slowdown," *New York Times,* July 7, 2001, Section 3, p. 4; http://www.bls.gov/news.release/ empsit.t12.htm.

Determinants of the Price Elasticity of Demand for an Input

In Section 5.2, we defined the price elasticity of demand for a commodity as the percentage change in the quantity demanded of the commodity resulting from a given percentage change in its price. The price elasticity of demand for an input can similarly be defined as the percentage change in the quantity demanded of the input resulting from a given percentage change in its price. The greater the percentage change in quantity resulting from a given percentage change in price, the greater is the price elasticity of demand. For example, if 2% more workers are employed as a result of a 1% reduction in the wage rate, the price (wage) elasticity of the market demand for labor is −2. If the quantity demanded of labor increased by only 1/2%, the wage elasticity of labor would be −1/2.

The determinants of the price elasticity of demand for an input are generally the same as the determinants of the price elasticity of demand for a commodity (discussed in Section 5.2). First, the price elasticity of demand for an input is larger the closer and the greater are the number of available substitutes for the input. For example, the price elasticity of demand for copper is greater than the price elasticity of demand for chromium (a metallic element used in alloys and in electroplating) because copper has better and more substitutes (silver, aluminum, and fiber glass) than chromium. Thus, the same percentage change in the price of copper and chromium elicits a larger percentage change in the quantity demanded of copper than of chromium.

Second, since the demand for an input is derived from the demand for the final commodity produced with the input, the price elasticity of demand for the input is greater, the larger is the price elasticity of demand of the commodity. The reason is that (as we have seen in the previous section) a reduction in the price of an input results in a reduction in the price of the final commodity produced with the input. The more elastic is the demand for the final commodity, the greater is the increase in the quantity demanded of the commodity, and so the greater is the quantity demanded of the input used in the production of the commodity. For example, if the wage rate falls, the price of new homes also declines. If the price elasticity of demand for new homes is very high, then a price reduction for new homes greatly increases the quantity demanded of new homes and greatly increases the demand for labor and other inputs going into the production of new homes.

Third, the price elasticity of demand for an input, say aluminum, is greater the larger is the price elasticity of *supply* of other inputs for which aluminum is a very good substitute in production. The reason is as follows. A reduction in the price of aluminum will lead producers to substitute aluminum for these other inputs. This is the same as the first reason discussed above, but it is not the end of the story. If the supply curves of these other inputs are very elastic, the reduction (i.e., leftward shift) in their demand curves will not result in a large decline in their prices, and so a great deal of the original increase in the quantity demanded of aluminum as a result of a reduction in its price will persist. This makes the demand curve for aluminum price elastic (if aluminum is a good substitute for these other inputs). Had the supply of these other inputs been inelastic, a reduction in their demand would have reduced their price very much, and checked the increase in the quantity demanded (and the price elasticity of demand) for aluminum.

Fourth, the price elasticity of demand for an input is *lower* the smaller is the percentage of the total cost spent on the input. For example, if the percentage of the total cost of the firm spent on an input is only 1%, a doubling of the price of the input will only increase the total costs of the firm by 1%. In that case, a firm is not likely to make great efforts to economize on the use of the input. Therefore, the price elasticity of an input on which the firm spends only a small percentage of its costs is likely to be low. This is usually, but not always, the case.

Finally, the price elasticity of an input is greater the longer the period of time allowed for the adjustment to the change in the input price. For example, an increase in the wage of unskilled labor may not reduce employment very much in the short run because the firm must operate the given plant built to take advantage of the low wage of unskilled labor. In the long run, however, the firm can build a plant using more capital-intensive production techniques to save on the use of the now more expensive unskilled labor. Thus, the reduction in the employment (and the wage elasticity of the demand) of unskilled labor is likely to be greater in the long run than in the short run. In Figure 14.1, the d_L curve (which is the firm's demand curve for labor when labor and other inputs are variable) is more elastic than the MRP_L curve (which is the firm's short-run demand curve for labor when labor is the only variable input). Example 14–2 examines the price elasticity of the demand for inputs in some manufacturing industries.

EXAMPLE 14–2

Price Elasticity of Demand for Inputs in Manufacturing Industries

Table 14.2 presents the price elasticity of the demand for production labor, nonproduction labor, capital, and electricity in the textile, paper, chemicals, and metals industries in Alabama estimated from data on input quantities, input prices, and outputs over the 1971–1991 period. The data show that input demand is price inelastic, except for nonproduction labor in the textile industry, where it is about unitary elastic. This means that an increase in the price of an input reduces the quantity demanded of the input less than proportionately. For example, the table shows that a 10% increase in the

TABLE 14.2	Price Elasticity of Input Demand for Manufacturing Industries			
	Production Labor	Nonproduction Labor	Capital	Energy
Textile	−0.50	−1.04	−0.41	−0.11
Paper	−0.62	−0.97	−0.29	−0.16
Chemicals	−0.75	−0.69	−0.12	−0.25
Metals	−0.41	−0.44	−0.91	−0.69

Source: A. H. Barnett, K. Reutter, and H. Thompson, "Electricity Substitution: Some Local Industrial Evidence," *Energy Economics,* 20, 1998, 411–419.

wage of production workers tends to reduce the quantity demanded of production workers in the textile industry by 5%. A 10% increase in the price of capital reduces the quantity of capital demanded by the paper industry by 2.9%, while a 10% increase in the price of energy reduces the quantity demanded of that input by 1.1% in the textile industry (the lowest price elasticity shown in the table).

14.4   The SUPPLY CURVE OF AN INPUT

In this section, we first derive an individual's supply curve of labor. Then we examine the substitution and the income effects of a wage increase. Finally, we discuss the market supply curve of an input in general, and the market supply of labor in particular. In the following section, we will use the market supply curve examined in this section and the market demand curve derived in Section 14.3 to determine the equilibrium price of an input (the wage rate).

The Supply of Labor by an Individual

The short-run supply curve of an input (like the supply curve of a final commodity) is generally positively sloped, indicating that a greater quantity of the input is supplied per unit of time at higher input prices. For example, if the price of iron ore rises, mining firms will supply more iron ore per time period. The same is true for an **intermediate good** such as steel (produced with iron ore), which is itself used as an input in the production of many final commodities such as automobiles. That is, steel producers will supply more steel at higher steel prices. However, while natural resources (such as iron ore) and intermediate goods (such as steel) are supplied by firms, and their supply curves are generally positively sloped, labor is supplied by individuals and their supply curve may be backward-bending. That is, after some wage rate, higher wage rates may result in individuals demanding more leisure time and supplying fewer *hours* of work per day. This is shown in Figure 14.3.

The left panel of Figure 14.3 is used to derive the backward-bending supply curve of labor of an individual shown in the right panel. The movement from left to right on the horizontal axis of the figure in the left panel measures hours of leisure time for the

Intermediate good
The output of a firm or industry that is the input of another firm or industry producing final commodities.

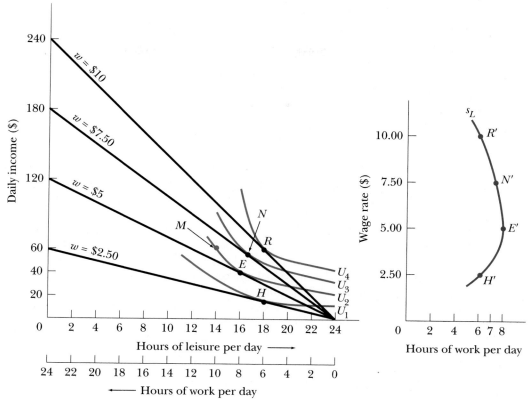

FIGURE 14.3   Derivation of an Individual's Supply Curve of Labor   In the left panel, U_1, U_2, U_3, and U_4 show the trade-off between leisure and income for the individual, while the straight budget lines show the trade-off between leisure and income in the market. The absolute slope of the budget lines gives the wage rates. The individual maximizes satisfaction at point H (with 18 hours of leisure per day and a daily income of $15) on U_1 with $w = \$2.50$, at point E (with 16 hours of leisure and income of $40) on U_2 with $w = \$5$, and so on. By plotting hours of work per day at various wage rates, we get the individual's backward-bending supply curve of labor (S_L) in the right panel.

individual (the top scale at the bottom of the figure). Subtracting hours of leisure from the 24 hours of the day, we get the hours worked by the individual per day (the bottom scale in the left panel). Hours of leisure plus hours of work always equal 24. On the other hand, the vertical axis in the left panel measures money income.

Indifference curves U_1, U_2, U_3, and U_4 in the left panel show the trade-off between leisure and income for the individual. They are similar to the individual's indifference curves between two commodities, discussed in Section 3.2. For example, the individual is indifferent between 14 hours of leisure (10 hours of work) and a daily income of $60 (point M on U_2) on the one hand, and 16 hours of leisure (8 hours of work) and a daily income of $40 (point E on U_2) on the other. Thus, the individual is willing to give up $20 of income to increase leisure time by 2 hours. Indifference curves U_3 and U_4 provide more utility or satisfaction to the individual than U_2, and U_2 provides more utility or satisfaction than U_1.

Given the wage rate, we can easily define the budget line of the individual. When the individual takes all 24 hours in leisure (i.e., works zero hours), the individual's income is zero regardless of the wage rate. Thus, any budget line of the individual starts at this point on the horizontal axis in the left panel. On the other hand, if the individual worked 24 hours per day, his or her income would be $60 if the wage rate were $2.50 (the lowest budget line), his or her income would be $120 if $w = \$5$ (the second budget line), $180 if $w = \$7.50$ (the third budget line), and $240 if $w = \$10$ (the highest budget line). Note that the wage rate is given by the absolute value of the slope of the budget line. Thus, $w = \$60/24$ hours $= \$2.50$/hour for the lowest budget line, $w = \$120/24$ hours $= \$5$ for the second budget line, $w = \$180/24$ hours $= \$7.50$ for the third budget line, and $w = \$240/24$ hours $= \$10$ for the highest budget line. These budget lines are similar to the individual's budget lines derived in Section 3.3.

As shown in Section 3.5, an individual maximizes utility or satisfaction by reaching the highest indifference curve possible with his or her budget line. Thus, if the wage rate is $2.50, the individual will take 18 hours in leisure (i.e., work 6 hours) and earn an income of $15 per day (point H on U_1 in the left panel of Figure 14.3). This gives point H' on the individual's supply curve of labor (s_L) in the right panel. With $w = \$5$, the individual takes 16 hours of leisure (i.e., works 8 hours) and earns an income of $40 per day (point E on U_2 in the left panel). This gives point E' on s_L in the right panel. At $w = \$7.50$, the individual chooses 16.5 hours of leisure (works 7.5 hours) and has an income of $56.25 per day (point N on U_3 and N' on s_L). Finally, at $w = \$10$, the individual chooses 18 hours of leisure (works 6 hours) and has an income of $60 per day (point R on U_4 and R' on s_L).

Note that the individual's supply curve of labor (s_L in the right panel of Figure 14.3) is positively sloped until the wage rate of $5, and it bends backward at higher wage rates. Thus, the individual works *more* hours (i.e., takes less leisure) until the wage rate of $5 per hour and works *fewer* hours (i.e., takes more leisure) at higher wage rates. Example 14-3 shows that, contrary to widespread belief, leisure time per capita seems to have remained practically unchanged in the United States during the past century.

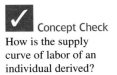

Concept Check
How is the supply curve of labor of an individual derived?

EXAMPLE 14-3

Leisure Time in the United States over the Past Century

Despite rising labor and business productivity and increasing use of labor-saving household appliances, a 2006 study by Ramey and Francis concluded that Americans seem to work as hard today and have no more leisure time than a century ago. Ramey and Francis found that about 70% of the decline in hours worked in the marketplace were offset by an increase in hours spent in school. At the same time, and despite the increasing use of household appliances, Americans actually spend slightly more time cooking, cleaning, caring for children, and in other "home production" activities, leaving leisure per capita approximately the same today as it was in 1900.

These results seem to contradict the conclusions of other studies, which found instead a large increase in leisure time over past decades. These other studies, however, do not take into consideration the large changes that have taken place in labor-force participation rates and in other nonleisure activities. For example in 1910, 25% of male children age 10 to 15 were employed, while child labor laws prevent any from being employed today. Furthermore, the proportion of the population age 65 and over increased from 4% in 1900 to 12% in 2000. The net effect of all these changes, together with changes in other nonleisure activities, is that *leisure per capita* in the United States seems to be no greater today than it was in 1900.

Sources: V. A. Ramey and N. Francis, "A Century of Work and Leisure," *NBER Working Paper No. 12264*, May 2006; M. Aguiar and E. Hurst, "Measuring Trends in Leisure: The Allocation of Time Over Five Decades," *NBER Working Paper No. 12082*, March 2006; and "The Real Reasons You're Working So hard," *Business Week*, October 5, 2005, pp. 60–67.

Substitution and Income Effects of a Wage Increase

The reason that an individual's supply curve of labor may be backward-bending can be explained by separating the substitution effect from the income effect of the wage increase. That is, an increase in wages (just like an increase in a commodity price) gives rise to a substitution effect and an income effect. In the case of an increase in the price of a normal good, the substitution and the income effects work in the same direction (to reduce the quantity demanded of the commodity). On the other hand, in the case of an increase in the wage rate, the substitution and the income effects operate in opposite directions, and (as explained next) this may cause the individual's supply curve of labor to be backward-bending.

According to the substitution effect, an increase in the wage rate leads an individual to work more (i.e., to substitute work for leisure). That is, as the wage rate rises, the price of leisure increases and the individual takes less leisure (i.e., works more). Thus, the substitution effect of the wage increase always operates to make the individual's supply curve of labor *positively* sloped. However, an increase in the wage rate also raises the individual's income, and with a rise in income, the individual demands more of every normal good, including leisure (i.e., supplies fewer hours of work). Thus, the income effect of a wage increase, by itself, always operates to make the individual's supply curve *negatively* sloped.

The substitution and income effects operate over the entire length of the individual's supply curve of labor. Until the wage rate of $w = \$5$ in Figure 14.3, the substitution effect overwhelms the opposite income effect and the individual works more (i.e., his or her supply curve of labor is positively sloped). At $w = \$5$, the substitution effect is balanced by the income effect and S_L is vertical (point E' in the figure). At wage rates higher than $w = \$5$, the (positive) substitution effect is overwhelmed by the (negative) income effect and s_L bends backward. Note that theory does not tell us at what wage rate the bend occurs. It only says that at some sufficiently high wage rate this is likely to occur. Since individuals' tastes differ, the wage rate at which an individual's supply curve of labor bends backward is likely to differ from individual to individual.

Also note that although the substitution effect is usually greater than the income effect for a *commodity*, this is not the case for labor. The reason is that a consumer spends his or her income on many commodities, so that an increase in the price of any one commodity is not going to greatly reduce his or her real income (i.e., the income effect is small in relation to the substitution effect). On the other hand, since most individuals' incomes come primarily from wages, an increase in wages will greatly affect the individuals' incomes (so that the income effect may overwhelm the opposite substitution effect). At the wage rate at which this occurs, s_L will bend backward. The separation of the substitution and the income effects of a wage increase is shown graphically in Section 14.8.

It might be argued that individuals do not have a choice of the number of hours they work per day, and so the above analysis is irrelevant. Yet, this is not entirely true.

✓ Concept Check

Why can the supply curve of an individual slope backward?

For example, an individual may choose to work any number of hours on a part-time basis, may choose an occupation that requires six or seven hours of work per day instead of eight, may choose an occupation that allows more or less vacation time, and may or may not agree to work overtime (see Section 14.8), and so on. All that is required for the analysis to be relevant is for *some* occupations to require different hours of work per day and/or some flexibility in hours of work.

Note that as workers' wages and incomes have risen over time, the average work week (and the length of the average work day) has declined from ten hours per day for six days per week at the turn of the century to eight hours per day for five days per week, or even slightly less, today. However, the trend toward fewer hours of work per day and per week seems to have come to an end or to have considerably slowed down over the past half a century. It may even have been reversed in recent decades. Thus, the substitution and income effects of higher wages must have been more or less in balance in recent decades. Over the same period of time, however, the participation rate (i.e., the percentage of the population in the labor force) has increased, especially for married women (see Example 14–4).

EXAMPLE 14–4

Labor Force Participation Rates

Table 14.3 gives the labor force participation rates for the population as a whole, for males and females, and for married females in the United States in 1960, 1970, 1980, 1990, and 2000. The table shows that from 1960 to 2000 the labor force participation rate increased by about 11% for the population as a whole, declined by about 12% for males, and increased by about 57% for all females and 90% for married females.

Many reasons are responsible for the dramatic increase in the labor force participation rate of married females in the United States over the 1960–2005 period. Some of these are changes in family income, child-rearing practices, rates of unemployment, and female educational levels. What must be true, however, is that the productivity of married women in "market" jobs must have increased much more than for work in the home during the past four-and-a-half decades, and so married females substituted a great deal of work outside the home for work in the home.

TABLE 14.3	Labor Force Participation Rates in the United States (in percentages)			
Year	Total Population	Males	Females	Married Females
1960	59.4	83.3	37.7	31.9
1970	60.4	79.7	43.3	40.5
1980	63.8	77.4	51.5	49.9
1990	66.5	76.4	57.5	58.4
2000	67.1	74.8	59.9	61.1
2005	66.0	73.3	59.3	60.7

Source: Statistical Abstract of the United States (Washington, DC: U.S. Government Printing Office, 2001), pp. 373, 379.

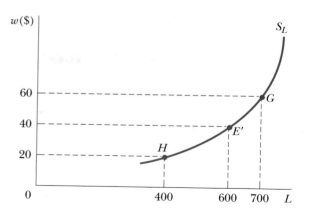

FIGURE 14.4   Market Supply Curve of Labor   Market supply curve of labor S_L shows that at the wage of $20 per day, 400 people are willing to work in this market (point H). At $w = 40 per day, 600 people are willing to work (point E'). At $w = 60, 700 are willing to work (point G), and so on. S_L is positively sloped over the range of daily wages shown but becomes less elastic at high wage rates (and may eventually bend backward at still higher wage rates).

The Market Supply Curve for an Input

The market supply curve for an input is obtained from the straightforward horizontal summation of the supply curve of individual suppliers of the input, just as in the case of the supply curve of a final commodity (see Section 9.4). In the case of inputs of natural resources and intermediate goods, which are supplied by firms, the short-run market supply curve of the input is generally positively sloped (as is the firm's supply curve). The market supply curve of labor is usually also positively sloped, but it may bend backward at very high wages (see Example 14–5).

Figure 14.4 shows a hypothetical market supply curve of labor (S_L) measuring the *number* of workers on the horizontal axis and the *daily* wage rate on the vertical axis. The figure shows that at the wage of $20 per day, 400 people are willing to work in this market (point H). At $w = 40 per day, 600 people are willing to work (point E'). At $w = 60, 700 are willing to work (point G), and so on. Note that S_L is positively sloped over the range of daily wages shown in the figure but becomes less elastic at high wage rates (and may eventually bend backward at still higher wage rates).

The shape of S_L is also the net result of two opposing forces. Higher daily wages will, on one hand, induce some individuals to enter the labor market (to take advantage of the higher wages), but they will also result in some individuals leaving the job market as their spouse's wages and income rise (see Example 14–5). Note that the supply curve of labor is less likely to be backward-bending for a particular industry than for the economy as a whole, because workers can always be attracted to an industry from other industries by raising wages sufficiently.

EXAMPLE 14–5

Backward-Bending Supply Curve of Physicians' Services and Other Labor

The enactment of Medicare (a subsidy for the medical care of the elderly) and Medicaid (a subsidy for the medical care of the poor) in 1965, as well as the increased insurance coverage for physicians' bills, greatly increased the ability of broad segments of the population to pay for medical services and resulted in a sharp rise in medical fees. The rise in medical fees, however, seems to have led to a reduction, rather than to an

TABLE 14.4 Elasticities of Labor Supply (Hours Worked) with Respect to Wages			
	Head's Hours with Respect to Head's Wage	Spouse's Hours with Respect to Spouse's Wage	Head's Hours with Respect to Spouse's Wage
Unmarried males (no children)	0.026		
Unmarried females (no children)	0.011		
Unmarried females (with children)	0.106		
One-earner family (no children)	0.007		
One-earner family (with children)	−0.078		
Two-earner family (no children)	−0.107	−0.028	−0.059
Two-earner family (with children)	−0.002	−0.086	−0.004

Sources: J. H. Kohlhase, "Labor Supply and Housing Demand for One- and Two-Earner Households," *Review of Economics and Statistics,* Vol. 68, No. 1, 1986, pp. 48–57.

increase, in the quantity supplied of physicians' services (i.e., the supply curve for physicians' services seems to be backward-bending).

Martin Feldstein found that the price elasticity of supply of physicians' services in the United States was between −0.67 and −0.91 over the 1948–1966 period. This means that a 10% increase in the price of physicians' services results in a *reduction* in the quantity supplied of services of between 6.7% and 9.1%. Thus, according to Feldstein's results, the sharp increase in the fees for physicians' services in recent years actually resulted in a reduction in the quantity of services supplied. Nurses also seem to have backward-bending supply curves (according to some but not others), and, more generally, so do the head of one-earner families with children and the head and the spouse of two-earner families, with or without children, as Table 14.4 shows.

From Table 14.4, we see that unmarried males and females with or without children as well as one-earner families without children operate on the upward-sloping portion of their labor supply curve, while all the others are on the backward-bending portion of their labor supply curve. The price elasticities of supply of hours worked with respect to wages for all groups, whether positive or negative, are quite small, however (i.e., the labor supply curves are close to being vertical).

Sources: M. Feldstein, "The Rising Price of Physicians' Services," *Review of Economics and Statistics,* May 1970, pp. 121–133; D. Sullivan, "Monopsony Power in the Market for Nurses," *Journal of Law and Economics*, October 1989, pp. S135–S178; and J. Burkett, "The Labor Supply of Nurses and Nursing Assistants in the United States," *Eastern Economic Journal*, Fall 2005, pp. 585–599.

| 14.5 | ## PRICING AND EMPLOYMENT OF AN INPUT |

Just as in the case of a final commodity, the equilibrium price and employment of an input is given at the intersection of the market demand and the market supply curve of the input in a perfectly competitive market. The equilibrium price and level of employment for labor are shown in Figure 14.5.

In Figure 14.5, D_L is the market demand curve for labor (from the right panel of Figure 14.2), and S_L is the market supply curve of labor (from Figure 14.4). The intersection of D_L and S_L at point E' gives the equilibrium (daily) wage of $40 and level of employment of 600 workers per day. At the lower wage rate of $20 per day, firms would like to employ 800 workers per day, but only half that number are willing to work. Thus, there is a shortage of 400 workers per day (HJ in the figure), and the wage rate rises. At the high wage of $60 per day, 700 workers are willing to work, but firms would like to employ only 450. There is a surplus of 250 workers (FG), and the wage rate falls. Only at $w = 40$ is the number of workers who are willing to work equal to the number of workers that firms want to employ (600), and the market is in equilibrium.

Concept Check
How is the equilibrium price and employment of an input determined?

Note that at the equilibrium daily wage of $40, each of the 100 identical firms in the market will employ six workers per day (point E on d'_L in the left panel of Figure 14.2). In a perfectly competitive input market, each firm is too small to perceptibly affect the wage rate (i.e., the firm can employ any number of workers per day at the equilibrium market wage rate of $40 per day). That is, the firm faces a horizontal or infinitely elastic supply curve of labor at the given wage rate. Since the price of an input equals its marginal revenue product (MRP), the theory of input pricing and employment has been called the **marginal productivity theory** (see Example 14–6).

Marginal productivity theory The theory according to which each input is paid a price equal to its marginal productivity.

Finally, note that we have implicitly assumed that all units of the input are identical (have the same productivity) and receive the same price. In the case of labor, the wages of

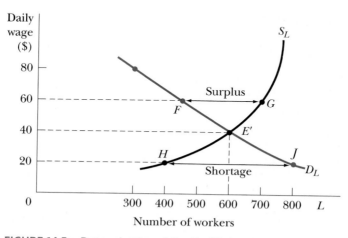

FIGURE 14.5 Determination of the Equilibrium Wage Rate and Level of Employment D_L is the market demand curve for labor (from the right panel of Figure 14.2), and S_L is the market supply curve of labor (from Figure 14.4). The intersection of D_L and S_L at point E' gives the equilibrium (daily) wage rate of $40 and the equilibrium level of employment of 600 workers per day.

all workers would be the same only if all occupations were equally attractive (or unattractive), if all workers had identical qualifications and productivity, and if there was no interference with the operation of the market. These topics are discussed in Section 14.8.

EXAMPLE 14-6
Labor Productivity and Total Compensation in the United States and Abroad

According to the marginal productivity theory, wages equal labor's marginal revenue product, and an increase in labor productivity should be reflected in a similar increase in the real wage. From 1996 to 2006, however, real wages increased by a total of 15% as compared with an increase in the productivity of U.S. labor of 22%. This has prompted a strong debate on whether the long-term link between productivity and wages has been broken. In fact, during the past 150 years, the share of GDP going to labor has remained remarkably stable at between 65% and 69% in all advanced economies. Has this strong regularity now been broken?

According to some economists, the present gap in the growth of real wages and productivity is the beginning of a long-run decline in labor's share of GDP. Others, however, believe that comparing real wages to labor productivity is not appropriate because the proportion of fringe benefits in total compensation has increased over time. In fact, the increase in total real compensation was 21% over the 1996–2006 period—almost identical to the increase in total labor productivity of 22%. Using 1950 as the base, the increase in the real compensation of U.S. labor from 1950 to 2006 was 172% as compared with the increase in U.S. labor productivity of 176% over the same period. Thus, the historical regularity between wages and productivity has not been broken and persists. Furthermore, every time a gap arose between the growth in inflation-adjusted compensation and the growth of labor productivity in the United States, it invariably disappeared after a year or two.

The increase in labor productivity in the United States has been greater than in the other Group of Seven (G-7) leading industrial nations (Japan, Germany, France, Britain, Italy, and Canada) since the second half of the 1990s, but not earlier. Specifically, labor productivity has increased at an annual average of 2.0% in the United States from 1996 to 2006, as compared to 1.1% for the other G-7 nations. From 1981 to 1995, however, labor productivity increased at an average 1.2% per year in the United States and 2.2% in the other G-7 nations. This has led to a great deal of wage convergence to the higher U.S. levels in the G-7 countries (see Example 14–7). The more rapid growth of labor productivity during the second half of the last decade in the United States than in the other G-7 countries has been attributed to a more rapid spread of the "new economy" based on the new information technology and greater flexibility in labor markets and in the economy in general in the United States than abroad.

Sources: "Productivity Is All, But It Doesn't Pay Well," *New York Times*, June 25, 1995, Section E, p. 3; "As Worker's Pay Lags, Causes Spur a Debate," *Wall Street Journal*, July 31, 1995, p. A1; "Productivity Developments Abroad," *Federal Reserve Bulletin*, October 2000; "Salaries Stagnate as Balance of Power Shifts to Employers," *Financial Times*, May 11, 2005, p. 6; OECD, *World Economic Outlook*, December 2007; D. Salvatore, ed. "Growth, Productivity, and Wages in the U.S. Economy," Special Issue, *Journal of Policy Modeling*, June 2008.

INPUT PRICE EQUALIZATION AMONG INDUSTRIES, REGIONS, AND COUNTRIES

In this section, we examine the process whereby input prices tend to be equalized through the movement of inputs among industries and regions, but through trade among countries. We deal specifically with the tendency of wage rates to equalize across industries, regions, and countries on the assumption that all labor is identical. The same price-equalizing process generally tends to operate for each type of labor and capital.

Input Price Equalization Among Industries and Regions of a Country

If the wage rate differs between two industries or regions of a country, some labor will leave the low-wage industry or region for the high-wage industry or region until the wage difference is eliminated. This is shown in Figure 14.6.

In Figure 14.6, the left panel refers to industry or region A, while the right panel refers to industry or region B. The vertical axes measure the daily wage, while the horizontal axes measure the number of workers. In the left panel, the intersection of the industry demand curve (D_A) and supply curve (S_A) at point E gives the equilibrium daily wage of $30 in industry or region A. On the other hand, the right panel shows that the equilibrium daily wage (given by point E at the intersection of D_B and S_B) in industry or

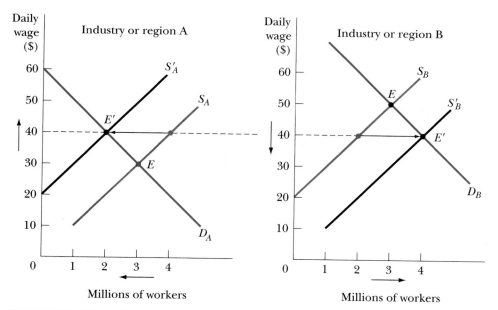

FIGURE 14.6   Wage-Equalizing Shifts in Domestic Supply   The left panel shows that D_A and S_A intersect at point E defining the equilibrium daily wage of $30 in industry or region A, while the right panel shows that D_B and S_B intersect at point E defining the equilibrium daily wage of $50 in industry or region B. As labor leaves industry or region A, attracted by the higher wage in region B, S_A shifts to the left to S_A' in the left panel while S_B shifts simultaneously to the right to S_B' in the right panel, so that the daily wage in the two industries or regions becomes equal at $40 (point E' in both panels).

region B is \$50. Some workers will then leave industry or region A to take advantage of the higher wages in industry or region B. As this occurs, the supply of labor declines (i.e., the supply curve shifts to the left) in industry or region A and simultaneously increases (i.e., shifts to the right) in industry or region B. This continues until S_A has shifted to S'_A in the left panel and S_B has shifted to S'_B in the right panel, so that the wage rate is equal at \$40 per day in both industries (see point E' where D_A and S'_A intersect in the left panel and where D_B and S'_B intersect in the right panel). In total, 1 million workers move from industry or region A to industry or region B (see the direction and the length of the arrows on the quantity axes in both panels).

   If there are obstructions to the movement of labor, or if workers—other things being equal—prefer working in industry or region A rather than in B, then less than 1 million workers will move from industry or region A to industry or region B, and wage differences will only be reduced rather than be entirely eliminated. What is important, however, is the process whereby changes or shifts in input supply in the two industries or regions reduce interindustry or interregional wage differences. The same is true for each particular type of labor and other mobile inputs. They always tend to flow or move to find employment in the industries or regions where returns or earnings are higher. In the process, they reduce interindustry and interregional differences in the returns to homogeneous factors or inputs (i.e., the earnings of inputs of the same quality and productivity). In fact, Bellante has found that when adjustment is made for regional differences in costs of living, North-South real wage differences for the same type of labor have been eliminated for the most part in the United States.[5]

Input Price Equalization Among Countries

The equalizing tendency in the returns or earnings of homogeneous inputs also operates internationally, but it occurs mostly through international trade rather than through the flow or migration of inputs from low- to high-return countries. The reason is that most countries impose serious restrictions on the international flow of some inputs, especially the migration of labor. Figure 14.7 shows how wage equalization occurs internationally through trade. For simplicity, we assume that we have only two homogeneous inputs, labor and capital.

   The left panel shows that D_1 (the demand curve for labor in country 1) intersects S_1 (the supply curve of labor in country 1) at point E, giving the equilibrium daily wage of \$20 in country 1 in the absence of trade. The right panel shows that D_2 and S_2 intersect at point E, giving the equilibrium daily wage of \$40 in country 2 in the absence of trade. We assume that labor cannot migrate from country 1 to country 2. Wages can still tend to be equalized between the two countries through trade, however.

   Because of lower wages, country 1 has a relative or comparative advantage in labor-intensive commodities (i.e., commodities that require a relative abundance of labor in production). Country 2 will then have a comparative advantage in capital-intensive commodities. With trade, country 1 will specialize in the production of and export labor-intensive commodities in exchange for capital-intensive commodities from country 2. The left panel shows that the demand curve for labor will then increase or shift to the right from D_1 to D'_1 in country 1 and defines the new equilibrium daily wage of \$30 at point E'

[5] See D. Bellante, "The North-South Wage Differential and the Migration of Heterogeneous Labor," *American Economic Review*, March 1979.

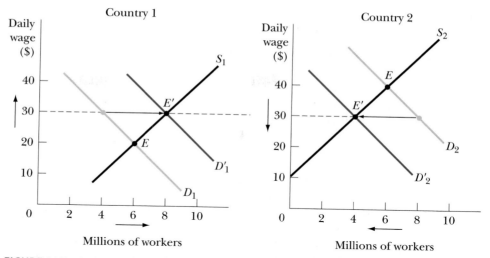

FIGURE 14.7   International Wage-Equalization Through International Trade   The left panel shows that in the absence of trade D_1 and S_1 intersect at point E, defining the equilibrium daily wage of $20 in country 1, while the right panel shows that D_2 and S_2 intersect at point E, defining the equilibrium daily wage of $40 in country 2. As country 1 specializes in the production of and exports labor–intensive commodities, D_1 shifts to the right to D_1' and defines the new equilibrium daily wage of $30 at point E' in the left panel. On the other hand, as country 2 replaces some domestic production of labor–intensive commodities with imports from country 1, D_2 shifts to the left to D_2' and defines the new equilibrium daily wage of $30 at point E' in the right panel.

(where D_1' intersects S_1). On the other hand, the right panel shows that the demand curve for labor will decrease or shift to the left from D_2 to D_2' in country 2 (as country 2 replaces some domestic production of labor-intensive commodities with imports from country 1) and defines the new equilibrium daily wage of $30 at point E' (where D_2' intersects S_2).

Note that now wages have been equalized in the two countries through international trade without any migration of labor from country 1 to country 2. The reason for this is that as long as wages are lower in country 1, labor-intensive commodities will be cheaper in country 1 than in country 2, and country 1 will expand its exports of the labor-intensive commodity. But as trade expands, country 1 will demand more labor until D_1 has shifted all the way to the right to D_1' (see the left panel). The demand for labor in country 2, on the other hand, will simultaneously decline until it reaches D_2' (see the right panel), so that wages are equalized at $30 in both countries. Thus, international trade is a substitute for, or has the same effect on, wages as the international migration of labor (which is often seriously restricted). However, while trade operates on the demand for labor (i.e., shifts the demand curves for labor) in the two countries, international migration operates through the supply (i.e., shifts the supply curves) of labor in the two countries. This is true, however, only in the absence of trade restrictions. If some labor is allowed to migrate from country 1 to country 2, this will reinforce the tendency of international trade to equalize wages in the two countries. Although we have dealt with labor in general, the same process would operate to equalize the wages of each particular type of labor and the price of each other type of input internationally. Example 14–7 shows that a great deal of convergence in real hourly compensation has in fact occurred during the past decades among the G-7 countries.

☑ Concept Check

Why do input prices tend to equalize across regions and countries with perfect mobility?

EXAMPLE 14-7

Convergence in Hourly Compensation in the Leading Industrial Countries

As predicted by theory, Table 14.5 shows that real hourly compensation (wages plus benefits) of production workers in manufacturing have indeed converged among the leading (G-7) industrial countries during the past five decades. It is true that many other forces (including international labor migration and capital flows) have contributed to this convergence, but international trade was certainly a major reason. The existence of transportation costs, trade restrictions, and other market imperfections prevented the complete equalization of hourly compensation internationally, however.

One question remains unanswered. That is, if trade reduces wages in a higher-wage country, why should the higher-wage country trade with a lower-wage country? The reason (not shown in Figure 14.7) is that the higher-wage country will have a comparative advantage in capital-intensive commodities. As it specializes in the production of these commodities for export, the demand and returns on capital increase by more than wages fall. Some of the capital owners' gains from trade could then be taxed away and redistributed to labor in such a way that both labor and capital gain from trade.

TABLE 14.5	Real Hourly Compensation of Production Workers in Manufacturing in the G-7 Countries as a Percentage of U.S. Compensation		
Country	1959	1983	2000
Japan	11	51	99
Italy	23	62	88
France	27	62	93
United Kingdom	29	53	94
Germany	29	84	149
Canada	42	75	91
Unweighted Average	27	65	102
United States	100	100	100

Sources: Calculated from indices from: IMF, *International Financial Statistics;* OECD, *Economic Outlook;* and U.S. Bureau of Labor Statistics, *Bulletin.*

ECONOMIC RENT: AN UNNECESSARY PAYMENT TO BRING FORTH THE SUPPLY OF AN INPUT

14.7

Economic rent That portion of a payment made to the supplier of an input that is in excess of what is necessary to retain the input in its present employment in the long run.

Economic rent differs from the everyday meaning of the term *rent*, which is a payment made to lease an apartment, an automobile, or any other durable asset. Economic rent originally referred only to the payment made to landowners to lease their land (which was assumed to be in fixed supply). Today, **economic rent** is defined as that portion of the payment to the supplier of any input (not just land) that is in excess of the minimum amount necessary to retain the input in its present use. It is the excess payment to an input over its opportunity cost. If the market supply of an input is fixed, demand alone determines

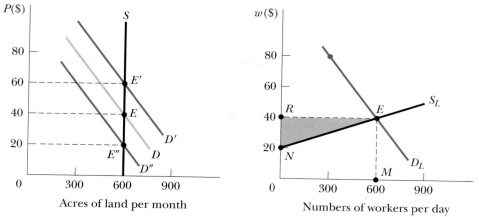

FIGURE 14.8   Measurement of Economic Rent   The left panel shows 600 acres of land supplied per month regardless of the rental price. With D, the price is $40 (point E) and the entire payment of $24,000 ($40 times 600) is rent. With D', P = $60 (point E') and rent is $36,000. With D'', P = $20 and rent is $12,000. In the right panel, S_L is positively sloped. With D_L, w = $40 and 600 workers are employed (point E). Shaded area ENR = $6,000 represents economic rent or a payment that is not needed to retain the 600 workers in the particular industry.

the input price and all of the payment made to the input is rent. If the market supply of an input is positively sloped, only the area above the supply curve and below the price of the input represents rent. This is shown in Figure 14.8.

In the left panel of Figure 14.8, the market supply of the input, say, land, is fixed at 600 acres (i.e., S is vertical). If the market demand curve is D, the (rental) price is $40 per acre (point E), and the entire payment of $24,000 ($40 times 600) per month made to the owners of land is economic rent. If the market demand were D', the rental price would be $60 (point E'), and rent $36,000 per month. If the market demand for the input were D'', the rental price would be $20 (point E''), and rent $12,000 per month. Note that regardless of the level of demand and price, the same quantity of land is supplied per month, even at an infinitesimally small rental price. Thus, all of the payments made to the landowners represent economic rent (since the opportunity cost of land is zero). This is true not only for land but for any input in fixed supply. For example, since the supply of Picasso paintings is fixed, they will be supplied (sold) at whatever price (including the retention or reservation price of present owners) they can fetch. Therefore, all payments made to purchase Picassos represent economic rent.

In the right panel, the supply of the input, say, labor, to an industry is positively sloped. This means that higher daily wages will induce more individuals to work in the industry. The equilibrium wage of $40 is determined at the intersection of D_L and S_L (point E in the figure, at which 600 workers are employed). Each of the 600 (identical) workers receives a wage of $40 per day. Yet, one worker could be found who would work for a wage of only $20, and 300 workers would be willing to work at a daily wage of $30 each (see the S_L curve in the right panel). Thus, the shaded area above the supply curve and below the equilibrium wage of $40 represents economic rent. It is the workers' excess earnings over their next-best employment. That is, the 600 workers receive a total wage of $24,000 (the area of rectangle EMOR), but they only need to be paid EMON to be retained

What is the relationship between the price of an input and economic rent?

in the industry. Therefore, the area of shaded triangle *ENR* ($6,000) represents economic rent or the payment that need not be made by the particular industry to retain 600 workers in the long run.

Note that even land may not be fixed in supply to any industry, because some land could be bid away from other uses. Land may not even be fixed for the economy as a whole, since over time, land can be augmented through reclamation and drainage and depleted through erosion and loss of fertility. Thus, the payment to lease land, too, may be only partly rent. In general, the more inelastic is the supply curve of an input to the industry, the greater is the proportion of economic rent. In the extreme case, the supply curve is vertical and all the payment to the input is rent. The importance of this is that rent could all be taxed away without reducing the quantity supplied of the input. This is an excellent tax since it does not discourage work or reduce the supply of labor (or other inputs) even in the long run. Note that economic rent is analogous to the concept of *producer surplus* (see Section 9.8). Producer surplus was defined as the excess of the commodity price over the *marginal cost of producing a given level of the commodity.* Economic rent is the excess payment that an *input owner* receives over the minimum that he or she requires to continue to keep the input in its present use.

While all or some of the payment made by an industry to the suppliers of an input is rent, all payments made by an *individual firm* to employ an input are a *cost* to the firm, which the firm must pay to retain the use of the input. If the firm tried to pay less than the market price for the input, the firm would be unable to retain any unit of the input. For example, if a firm tried to employ workers at less than the $40 daily wage prevailing in the market, the firm would lose all of its workers to other firms. Finally, note that any payment made to *temporarily* fixed inputs is sometimes called **quasi-rent.** Thus, the returns to fixed inputs in the short run are quasi-rents (see Problem 8). These payments need not be made in order for these fixed inputs to be supplied in the short run. In the long run, however, all inputs are variable, and, unless they receive a price equal to their next-best alternative, they will not be supplied. To the extent that they receive more than this, the inputs receive economic rent. In long-run, perfectly competitive equilibrium, all inputs receive payments equal to their marginal revenue product and the firm breaks even.

Quasi-rent The return or payment to inputs that are fixed in the short run (i.e., $TR - TVC$).

14.8   ANALYSIS OF LABOR MARKETS UNDER PERFECT COMPETITION

In this section, we discuss some important applications of the theory presented in this chapter: separation of the substitution from the income effect of a change in wages, the analysis of overtime pay, the cause of wage differentials, and the effect of minimum wages. These applications clearly indicate the usefulness and applicability of the theory.

Substitution and Income Effects of a Wage Rate Change

We have seen in Section 14.4 that an increase in wages gives rise to a substitution effect and an income effect. That is, when the wage rate rises, on one hand, the individual tends to substitute work for leisure (since the price of leisure has increased). On the other hand, the increase in income resulting from the wage increase leads the individual to demand more of every normal good, including leisure (i.e., to work fewer hours). We can separate the substitution effect from the income effect as in Section 4.3. The separation is shown in Figure 14.9.

The movement from point *E* to point *R* in Figure 14.9 is the combined substitution and income effects of the wage increase from $5 to $10 (as in Figure 14.3). The substitution effect can be isolated by drawing the hypothetical budget line that is tangent to U_2 at

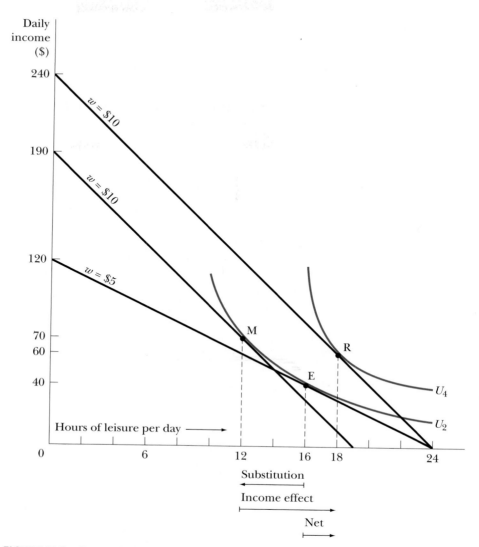

FIGURE 14.9   Separation of the Substitution Effect from the Income Effect of a Wage Increase   The movement from point E to point R is the combined substitution and income effects of the wage increase from $5 to $10 (as in Figure 14.3). We can isolate the substitution effect by shifting the highest budget line down parallel to itself until it is tangent to indifference curve U_2 at point M. The movement along U_2 from point E to point M measures the substitution effect of the wage increase. The shift from point M on U_2 to point R on U_4 is the income effect.

point M with the slope reflecting the higher wage of $10. Since the consumer is on original indifference curve U_2, his or her income is the same as before the wage increase, and the movement along U_2 from point E to point M measures the substitution effect. By itself, the substitution effect shows that when w rises from $5 to $10, the individual reduces leisure time from 16 to 12 hours (i.e., increases hours of work from 8 to 12 per day). The shift from point M on U_2 to point R on U_4 is the income effect of the wage increase. In this case, the increase in wages raises the individual's income by $50 ($240 − $190; see the vertical axis of the figure). By itself, the income effect leads the individual to increase leisure from 12 to 18 hours (i.e., to work 6 hours less). The net result is that the individual increases leisure (works less) by 2 hours per day (*ER*).

Overtime Pay and the Supply of Labor Services

Overtime pay The higher hourly wage of many workers for working additional hours after the regular workday.

The hourly wage of many workers increases after a specific number of hours worked per day. This is called **overtime pay.** Figure 14.10 shows the additional number of hours worked per day by an individual as a result of overtime pay.

Initially, at the wage rate of $5 per hour, the individual demands 16 hours of leisure (works eight hours per day) and earns an income of $40 (point *E* on U_2, as in Figures 14.3 and 14.9). With an overtime pay of $20 per hour (the slope of *ET* in Figure 14.10), the individual can be induced to work two additional hours per day and have a total income of $80 per day (point *T* on higher indifference curve U_3). Thus, the substitution effect (which encourages work) exceeds the income effect (which discourages work), and the individual works more hours with overtime pay.[6] Higher taxes, on the other hand, lead to fewer hours worked (see Example 14–8).

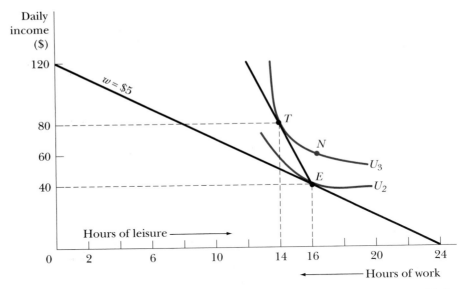

FIGURE 14.10   Overtime Pay and the Supply of Labor Services   Initially, at $w = \$5$, the individual demands 16 hours of leisure (works 8 hours per day) and earns $40 (point *E* on U_2, as in Figures 14.3 and 14.9). With overtime pay of $w = \$20$ per hour (the slope of *ET*), the individual will work 2 additional hours per day and have a total income of $80 (point *T* on U_3).

---

[6] The entire overtime-pay system that was established during the Great Depression and which requires employers to pay a 50% premium to people working over 40 hours per week is under attack, however, and may be relaxed or even abolished. See "Overtime-Pay System May Spark a Battle," *Wall Street Journal,* March 13, 1995.

EXAMPLE 14–8

Higher Tax Rates Reduce Hours of Work

Table 14.6 shows the ratio of hours worked in 2004 relative to hours worked in 1956 in 21 OECD (industrial) countries. For example, the value of 0.97 for Australia means that the average number of hours of work per year in Australia in 2004 was 97% of those in 1956. The table shows that the greatest decline in the number of hours of work between 1956 and 2004 was in Germany and France (two very high-tax nations), while hours of work stayed about the same in the United States (a relatively low-tax country). Other factors, such as unionization, employment protection, and the generosity of unemployment insurance benefits, had only a small effect on hours of work across nations.

TABLE 14.1	Hours Worked in 2004 Relative to 1956 in 21 OECD Countries				
Australia	0.97	Germany	0.60	Norway	0.82
Austria	0.74	Greece	0.99	Portugal	0.84
Belgium	0.70	Ireland	0.70	Spain	0.86
Canada	0.71	Italy	0.74	Sweden	0.80
Denmark	0.71	Japan	0.85	Switzerland	0.83
Finland	0.75	Netherlands	0.81	United Kingdom	0.79
France	0.67	New Zealand	1.05	United States	1.01

Source: L. Ohanian, A. Raffo, and R. Rogerson, "Long-Term Changes in Labor Supply and Taxes: Evidence from OECD Countries, 1956–2004," *NBER Working paper No. 12786*, December 2006; and R. Rogerson and J. Wallenius, "Micro and Macro Elasticities in a Life Cycle Model with Taxes," *NBER Working paper No. 13017*, April 2007.

Wage Differentials

Up to this point, we have generally assumed that all occupations are equally attractive and that all units of an input, say, labor, are homogeneous (i.e., have the same training and productivity), so that the wages of all workers are the same. If all jobs and workers were identical, wage differences could not persist among occupations or regions of a country under perfect competition. As pointed out in Section 14.6, workers would leave lower-wage occupations and regions for higher-wage occupations and regions until all wage differentials disappeared.

In the real world, jobs differ in attractiveness, workers have different qualifications and training, and markets may not be perfectly competitive. All of these factors can result in different wages for different occupations and for workers with different training and abilities. More formally, wages differ among different jobs and categories of workers because of (1) compensating differentials, (2) the existence of noncompeting groups, and (3) imperfect competition. We will now briefly examine each of these factors.

Compensating wage differentials are wage differences that compensate workers for the nonmonetary differences among jobs. Even though some jobs (such as garbage

Compensating wage differentials Wage differences that compensate workers for the nonmonetary differences among jobs.

collection and being a porter in a hotel) may require equal qualifications, one job (garbage collection) may be more unpleasant than another (being a porter). Hence, the more unpleasant job must pay a higher wage to attract and retain workers. These wage differentials equalize or compensate for the nonmonetary differences among jobs and will persist in time. In the real world, many wage differences reflect nonmonetary factors.

For example, police officers' salaries are usually higher than fire fighters' salaries because of the alleged greater risk in being a police officer. Similarly, construction work generally pays more than garbage collection because the former offers less job security. Note that a particular individual may prefer being a police officer or a construction worker even if the salary were the same as (or lower than) that of a fire fighter or garbage collector, respectively. But it is the intersection of the *market* demand and supply curves of labor for each occupation that determines the equilibrium wage in the occupation and the compensating wage differentials among occupations that require the same general level of qualifications and training.

Noncompeting groups

Occupations requiring different capacities, skills, education, and training and, therefore, receiving different wages.

Noncompeting groups are occupations requiring different capacities, skills, education, and training and, therefore, receiving different wages. That is, labor in some occupations does not directly compete with labor in some other occupations. For example, physicians form one noncompeting group not in direct competition with lawyers (which form another noncompeting group). Other noncompeting groups are engineers, accountants, musicians, electricians, and so on. Engineers and electricians belong to different noncompeting groups because, although engineers could probably work easily as electricians, engineers' productivity and wages are so much higher when working as engineers that they form a separate noncompeting group. On the other hand, electricians do not have the training and may not have the ability to be engineers.

Each noncompeting group has a particular wage structure as determined by the intersection of its demand and supply curves. Some mobility among noncompeting groups is possible (as, for example, when an electrician becomes an engineer by attending college at night), and this possibility is greater in the long run than in the short run. However, mobility among noncompeting groups is limited, even in the long run, especially if based on innate ability (e.g., not everyone can be a brain surgeon or an accomplished violinist).

An imperfect labor market can also result in wage differences for identical jobs requiring the same ability and level of training. A labor market is imperfect if workers lack information on wages and job opportunities in other occupations, if they are unwilling to move to other jobs and occupations, or if there are labor unions and large employers able to affect wages. These topics will be explored in detail in the next chapter.

✔ Concept Check
What is the cause of wage differentials?

Effect of Minimum Wages

In 1938, Congress passed the Fair Labor Standard Act, which established a minimum wage of $0.25 per hour. The minimum wage was raised to $3.35 in 1981, to $4.25 in 1991, to $5.15 in 1997, to $5.85 in 2007, and to $6.55 in 2008, and it will be $7.25 from July 2009.[7] Had the minimum wage been adjusted for inflation, it would have been $9.05 in January 2006. In 2006, 21 states had the minimum wage set above the federal level of $5.15. Since skilled workers generally have wages well above the minimum wage, they

---

[7] See "Minimum-Wage Increase to Take Effect," *Wall Street Journal*, July 24, 2007, p. 13.

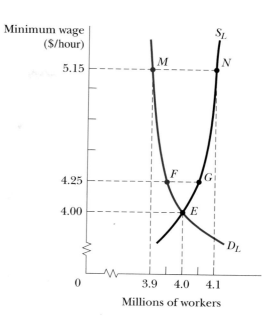

FIGURE 14.11 Effect of Minimum Wages D_L is the market demand curve, and S_L is the market supply curve for unskilled workers. The equilibrium wage is $4.00 per hour at which 4 million workers are employed (point E). A minimum wage of $5.15 results in 3.9 million workers being employed as opposed to 4.1 million willing to work, leaving an unemployment gap of 200,000 workers (MN). The disemployment effect is 100,000 workers (the movement from point E to point M on D_L). The increase in the minimum wage from $4.25 in 1991 to $5.15 in 1997 was estimated to increase the unemployment gap by 100,000 (MN minus FG).

are not affected by it. We can analyze the effect of the minimum wage on unskilled workers (assuming for the moment that all unskilled workers are identical) with the aid of Figure 14.11.

In Figure 14.11, D_L is the market demand curve, and S_L is the market supply curve for unskilled workers. In a perfectly competitive labor market, the equilibrium wage would be $4.00 per hour ($24 per day with an 8-hour workday) and the equilibrium level of employment would be 4 million workers (point E in the figure). The imposition of a federal minimum wage of $5.15 per hour would result in firms hiring only 3.9 million workers (point M on D_L) as opposed to the 4.1 million workers (point N on S_L) willing to work at this minimum wage. Thus, the minimum wage of $5.15 per hour would lead to a total **unemployment gap** of 200,000 workers (MN) from the equilibrium rate of $4.00 per hour. This is composed of the 100,000 additional workers who would like to work at the minimum wage (the movement from point E to point N on the S_L curve) plus the **disemployment effect** of another 100,000 workers as firms employ fewer workers at the above-equilibrium minimum wage (the movement from point E to point M on the D_L curve). On the other hand, the increase in the minimum wage from $4.25 to $5.15 per hour increases the unemployment gap by 100,000 jobs (MN minus FG in Figure 14.11). While an increase of a minimum wage benefits those unskilled workers who remain employed, some unskilled workers would lose their jobs, and still more would like to work but could not find employment.

In 2005, 1.9 million workers, or 2.5% of the 76 million hourly labor force, earned no more than the federal minimum wage (not all workers are covered by the minimum wage), down from 4.4 million in 1998.[8] At the same time about 10% of the labor force was affected by the minimum wage. The U.S. Labor Department estimated that the increase in the minimum wage from $3.35 in 1981 to $4.25 in 1991 led to a loss of 100,000 jobs. Some researchers, however, questioned this estimate and the general

Unemployment gap
The excess in the quantity supplied over the quantity demanded of labor at above-equilibrium wages.

Disemployment effect
The reduction in the number of workers employed as a result of an increase in the wage rate

---

[8] "Revising a Minimum-Wage Axiom," *New York Times*, February 3, 2007, p. 4.

premise that higher minimum wages today would lead to more unemployment of unskilled workers (see the nearby "At the Frontier").

There are other ways by which the imposition or the raising of a minimum wage rate can harm the very people it is supposed to help. An increase in the minimum wage may lead some employers to reduce or cut other fringe benefits (such as some health benefits, free or subsidized meals, free uniforms, and so on). Some employers may suspend apprenticeships and on-the-job training for unskilled workers whom they were hiring at a lower minimum wage. The harmful effect of an increase in the minimum wage is even greater in the long run, when employers have a greater opportunity to substitute more cap-ital-intensive production techniques for unskilled labor. The problem can be addressed by providing more training to improve the skills of minimum-wage workers so that they can qualify for higher-paying jobs.

AT THE FRONTIER
Do Minimum Wages Really Reduce Employment?

As the above analysis shows, economists have traditionally believed that an increase in the minimum wage, by increasing the cost of unskilled labor, leads employers to hire fewer unskilled workers. This ingrained belief was shaken by research by Princeton University's professors David Card and Alan Krueger, who found that increasing minimum wages did not destroy jobs and sometimes even increased them.

In one study (see the first reference at the end of this section), Card found that the reduction in employment after the 1990 and 1991 federal minimum-wage increases was generally not bigger in states with a larger fraction of low-paid workers, such as teenagers (the group expected to be most adversely affected by an increases in the minimum wage) than in high-wage states. Thus, Card concluded that the reduction in employment must have been due to causes other than the increase in the minimum wage. In another study (see the second reference at the end), Card and Krueger found that the additional 19% increase in New Jersey's own minimum wage in April 1992 led to more, not fewer, jobs between February and December 1992 in the state's fast-food restaurants (which paid wages below the new minimum wage), as compared with other New Jersey restaurants that were already paying wages exceeding the new higher minimum wage and with fast-food restaurants in neighboring Pennsylvania, which did not raise its minimum wage in 1992. In short, the new research seemed to show that increasing the minimum wage did not destroy jobs, as previously believed, and may have created them.

Other economists, however, immediately attacked these revisionist studies as being seriously flawed. Donald Deere and Finis Welch of Texas A&M University and Kevin Murphy of the University of Chicago showed that the 27% increase in the fed-eral minimum wage from $3.35 to $4.25 in 1990 and 1991 resulted in a reduction in teenage employment of 12% for males, 18% for females, and 6% for high-school dropouts (the groups expected to be most adversely affected by an increase in the minimum wage). Similarly, David Neumark of Michigan State University and William Wascher of the Federal Reserve, using payroll records (which are more accurate than the telephone poll data used by Card and Krueger in their New Jersey study), found that the 19% increase in New Jersey's minimum wages in April 1992 reduced employment in New Jersey's fast-food restaurants by 4.6% (rather than increased it, as reported by Card and Krueger).

More recent research by David Neuman and William Wascher found that, because of recent welfare reforms that increased work incentives faced by the poor and the near-poor, higher minimum wages did not lead to disemployment and unemployment, except for young minority men and high-school-dropout young women, but even for these the negative effects were rather small. While in previous decades higher minimum wages may have led to higher unemployment of unskilled workers, in this decade the effect has been rather small because of welfare reforms that increased work incentives and was confined only to some groups of unskilled workers.

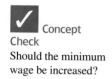

Concept Check
Should the minimum wage be increased?

Sources: D. Card, "Using Regional Variation in Wages to Measure the Effects of the Federal Minimum Wage," *Industrial and Labor Relations Review,* October 1992; D. Card and A. Krueger, "Minimum Wages and Employment: A Case Study of the Fast-Food Industry in New Jersey and Pennsylvania," *American Economic Review,* September 1994; D. Card and A. Krueger, *Myth and Measurement: The New Economics of the Minimum Wage* (Princeton University Press, 1995); D. Deere, K. Murphy, and F. Welch, "Employment and the 1990–1991 Minimum-Wage Hike," *American Economic Review, Papers and Proceedings,* May 1995; D. Neumark and W. Wascher, "The Effect of New Jersey's Minimum Wage Increase on Fast-Food Employment: A Reevaluation Using Payroll Records," *Working Paper 5224,* National Bureau of Economic Research, September 1995; D; and D. Neumark and W. Wascher, "Minimum Wages, the Earned Income Tax Credit, and Employment: Evidence from the Post–Welfare Reform Era," *NBER Working Paper No. 12915,* February 2007.

SUMMARY

1. To maximize profits a firm must produce the best level of output with the least-cost input combination. The optimal or least-cost input combination is the one at which the marginal product per dollar spent on each input is the same. The ratio of the input price to the marginal product of the input gives the marginal cost of the commodity. The best level of output of the commodity for a perfectly competitive firm is the output at which the firm's marginal cost equals its marginal revenue or price.

2. A profit-maximizing firm will employ an input only as long as the input adds more to its total revenue than to its total cost. If only one input is variable, the firm's demand curve for the input (d) is given by the marginal revenue product (*MRP*) curve of the input. The *MRP* equals the marginal product (*MP*) of the input times the marginal revenue (*MR*). If the firm is a perfect competitor in the product market (so that $MR = P$), then $MRP = VMP$ (the value of the marginal product). With more than one variable input, as the input price falls, the demand curve for the input is obtained by points on different *MRP* curves of the input and will be more elastic than the individual *MRP* curves.

3. When the price of an input falls, all firms will hire more of the input and produce more of the final commodity. This will reduce the commodity price and shift the individual firm's demand curves for the input to the left. This must be considered in summing the individual firm's demand curves for the input to obtain the market demand curve. The price elasticity of demand for an input is greater (1) the more and better are the available substitutes for the input, (2) the more elastic is the demand for the final commodity made with the input, (3) the more elastic is the supply of other inputs, and (4) the longer is the period of time under consideration.

4. The market supply curve of an input is obtained by the straightforward horizontal summation of the supply curves of the individual suppliers of the input. While natural resources and intermediate goods are supplied by firms and their supply curves are generally positively sloped, labor is supplied by individuals and their supply curves may be backward-bending. That is, as the wage rate rises, eventually the substitution effect (which, by itself, leads individuals to substitute work for leisure) may be overwhelmed by the opposite income effect, so that the individual's supply curve of labor may bend backward. The market supply curve of labor is usually positively sloped, but it may bend backward at very high wages.

5. Under perfect competition, the equilibrium price and the level of employment of an input are determined at the intersection of the market demand curve and the market supply curve of the input. Each firm can then employ any quantity of the input at the given market price of the input. Since each firm employs an input until the marginal revenue product equals its price, this theory is usually referred to as the marginal productivity theory. If all inputs were identical (and all occupations equally attractive for labor), all units of the same input would have the same price.

6. With perfect mobility of inputs among industries and regions of a country, input prices will be equalized by input flows (supply shifts) from the low-return to the high-return industries and regions. On the other hand, free trade in commodities and services among countries under perfect competition, with no transportation costs, would equalize input prices internationally by shifts in input demands resulting from trade.

7. Economic rent is that portion of the payment made to the supplier of an input that is in excess of the minimum amount necessary (opportunity cost) to retain the input in its present employment. When the supply of an input is fixed, demand alone determines its price and all the payment made to the input is rent. When the market supply curve of an input is positively sloped, the area above the supply curve and below the input price is rent. The return or payment to inputs that are fixed in the short run are sometimes called quasi-rents.

8. By correcting for the income effect of an input-price change, we can graphically isolate the substitution effect as a movement along a consumer leisure-income indifference curve. The same type of analysis can also be used to show the additional number of hours an individual is willing to work per day with overtime pay. Wage differentials can be compensating, and they can be based on the existence of noncompeting groups and imperfect competition. Minimum wages lead to a disemployment effect and to an even greater unemployment gap.

KEY TERMS

Derived demand	Intermediate good	Compensating wage differentials
Marginal revenue product (*MRP*)	Marginal productivity theory	Noncompeting groups
Value of the marginal product (*VMP*)	Economic rent	Unemployment gap
Marginal expense (*ME*)	Quasi-rent	Disemployment effect
Complementary inputs	Overtime pay	

REVIEW QUESTIONS

1. What is the function of input prices in the operation of a free-enterprise system?

2. Why is the marginal revenue product of a firm negatively sloped?

3. What happens to a firm's marginal revenue product of labor curve if the rental price of capital falls and capital is complementary to labor? If capital is a substitute for labor?

4. Why does the market price of a commodity fall with a reduction in the price of an input used in the production of the commodity?

5. What effect will a fall in a commodity price have on the firm's demand curve for an input used in the production of the commodity?

6. How can indifference curve analysis be used to explain an individual's supply curve of labor?

7. Under what condition will an individual's labor supply curve be backward bending?

8. Interregional trade can be a substitute for interregional labor migration in reducing or eliminating interregional wage differences. True or false? Explain.

9. Mexican migrant or seasonal workers to the United States take away jobs from American workers, and so immigration should be stopped. Evaluate this statement.

10. How is a higher interest on capital in industry or region A than in industry or region B eliminated or reduced?

11. Can higher wages persist for technicians in nuclear plants as compared with technicians with the same qualifications and training working in aircraft-engine plants? Explain.

12. Why do we have minimum-wage laws if they increase unemployment among unskilled workers?

PROBLEMS

*1. a. Express in terms of equation [14.1] the condition for a firm utilizing too much labor or too little capital to minimize production costs. What is the graphic interpretation of this?

b. What is the graphic interpretation of a firm utilizing the least-cost input combination but with its marginal cost exceeding its MR?

c. Express in terms of equation [14.3] the condition for a firm minimizing the cost of producing an output that is too small to maximize profits. What is the graphic interpretation of this?

2. You are given the following production function of a firm, where L is the number of workers hired per day (the only variable input) and Q_X is the quantity of the commodity produced per day, and the constant commodity price of $P_X = \$5$ is assumed:

L	0	1	2	3	4	5
Q_X	0	10	18	24	28	30

a. Find the marginal revenue product of labor and plot it.

b. How many workers per day will the firm hire if the wage rate is $50 per day? $40? $30? $20? $10? What is the firm's demand curve for labor?

3. Assume that (1) labor is infinitesimally divisible (i.e., workers can be hired for any part of the day) in the production function of the previous problem; (2) both labor and capital are variable and complementary; and (3) when the wage rate falls from $40 per day to $20 per day, the firm's value of the marginal product curve shifts to the right by two labor units. Derive the demand curve for labor of this firm. How many workers will the firm hire per day at the wage rate of $20 per day?

4. Derive the market demand curve for labor if there are 100 firms identical to the firm of Problem 3 demanding labor, and each individual firm's demand curve for labor shifts to the left by one unit when the wage rate falls from $w = \$40$ to $w = \$20$ per day.

*5. Assume that (1) U_1, U_2, U_3, and U_4 given in the following table are the indifference curves of an individual, where H refers to hours of leisure per day and Y to the daily income, and (2) the wage rate rises from $1 per hour of work to $2, $3, and then to $4.

U_1		U_2		U_3		U_4	
H	Y	H	Y	H	Y	H	Y
10	20	10	32	12	40	14	48
16	8	14	20	15	27	17	28
24	4	24	12	24	16	24	20

a. Derive the individual's supply curve of labor.

b. Why is the individual's supply curve of labor backward bending?

6. Given that the market demand curve is the one derived in Problem 3 and that 400 individuals will work at $w = \$10$, 500 at $w = \$20$, and 600 at $w = \$30$, determine the equilibrium wage rate and the level of employment. What would happen if $w = \$10$? If $w = \$30$?

7. Given the industry demand function for labor, $D_L = 800 - 15w$, where w is given in dollars per day, draw a figure showing the equilibrium wage and find the

*= Answer provided at end of book.

amount of economic rent if the supply function of labor to the industry is $S_L = 500$, $S'_L = 25w$ or $S''_L = 50w - 500$.

8. Draw a figure for a perfectly competitive firm in the product and input markets, and label the price at which quasi-rent is (1) negative as P_1, (2) zero as P_2, (3) smaller than total fixed costs as P_3, (4) equal to total fixed costs as P_4, and (5) exceeds total fixed costs as P_5. (Hint: See Figure 14.4.)

*9. Separate the substitution effect from the income effect of an increase in wages from $w = \$2$ to $w = \$4$ in Problem 5.

10. Starting with your answer to Problem 5 (also provided at the end of the book), draw a figure showing how many additional hours the individual will work and his or her total income (1) starting from $w = \$1$ and overtime $w = \$4$ and (2) starting from $w = \$2$ and overtime $w = \$10$.

*11. Starting from Figure 14.7, draw a figure showing the total demand and supply for labor in both industries or regions, the equilibrium wage rate, and the level of total employment.

12. Starting with Figure 14.7, draw a figure showing that wages will not be equalized when we take transportation costs into consideration.

INTERNET SITE ADDRESSES

A wealth of information on labor markets (employment, unemployment, productivity, earnings, and others) is provided by the Bureau of Labor Statistics at:

http://stats.bls.gov

http://www.bls.gov/news.release/empsit.t12.htm

http://www.bls.gov/news.release/pdf/empsit.pdf

For the backward-bending supply curve of physicians' services, see:

http://lingli.ccer.edu.cn/he2007/ref/1014/extention.pdf

The effect of minimum wages on employment is found at:

http://en.wikipedia.org/wiki/Minimum_wage

http://www.federalreserve.gov/pubs/feds/2003/200323/200323pap.pdf

http://papers.ssrn.com/sol3/papers.cfm?abstract_id=941970

On economic rent, see:

http://www.economics.utoronto.ca/munro5/ECONRENT.pdf

CHAPTER 15

Input Price and Employment Under Imperfect Competition

Chapter Outline

List of Examples

After Studying This Chapter, You Should Be Able to:

- Know how an imperfectly competitive firm determines the amount of each input to use to maximize profits
- Describe how a firm's demand curve and the market demand curve for one or more variable inputs are derived
- Know why the marginal expenditure of labor curve is above the supply curve of labor for a monopsonist
- Explain how the equilibrium price and employment of an input are determined by a monopsonist
- Describe the effects of unions on wages and on discrimination in employment

In the previous chapter, we analyzed the pricing and employment of inputs when the firm is a perfect competitor in both the product and input markets. In this chapter, we extend the discussion to the pricing and employment of inputs when the firm is (1) an imperfect competitor in the product market but a perfect competitor in the input market, and (2) an imperfect competitor in both the product and input markets. As in Chapter 14, the analysis deals with all inputs in general but is geared toward labor because of the greater importance of labor.

The presentation in this chapter proceeds along the same general lines as that of the previous chapter. We begin with a summary discussion of profit maximization and optimal input employment under imperfect competition in the product market. Then we derive the demand curve for an input by a firm and by the market as a whole, and we examine how the interaction of the forces of demand and supply determines the price and employment of the input under imperfect competition in the product market but perfect competition in the input market. We then turn to the case of imperfect competition in input markets and examine the pricing and employment of an input when only that input is variable and then when all inputs are variable. A discussion of international migration and the "brain drain" follows. Finally, the chapter presents several important applications of the theory. The "At the Frontier" section examines the effect of discrimination on gender and race wage differentials.

15.1   PROFIT MAXIMIZATION AND OPTIMAL INPUT EMPLOYMENT

In this section, we extend the discussion of profit maximization and optimal input employment of Section 14.1 to the case where the firm is an imperfect competitor in the product market but is still a perfect competitor in the input markets. A firm that is an imperfect competitor in the product market (a monopolist, an oligopolist, or a monopolistic competitor) faces a negatively sloped demand curve for the commodity it sells, and its marginal revenue is smaller than the commodity price. Such a firm, however, can still be one of many firms hiring inputs. That is, the firm can still be a perfect competitor in the input markets, so that it can hire any quantity of an input at the given market price of the input. This section and the next two sections of this chapter will examine this situation.

We have seen in Section 14.1 that to maximize profits, a firm must use the optimal or least-cost input combination to produce the best level of output. The profit maximizing condition was given by equation [14.3], which is repeated below as [15.1]:

$$w/MP_L = r/MP_K = MC = MR \qquad [15.1]$$

where w is the wage rate, r is the rental price of capital, MP is the marginal (physical) product, L refers to labor time, K refers to capital, MC is the marginal cost of the firm, and MR is its marginal revenue. The only difference between equations [14.3] and [15.1] is that equation [14.3] and the discussion in Section 14.1 referred to the case where the firm was a perfect competitor in both the product and input markets. Thus, the marginal revenue of the firm equaled the product price (P). Since the firm is now an imperfect competitor in the product market, $MR < P$ and equation [15.1] is the relevant condition for profit maximization.

By cross multiplying and rearranging the terms of equation [15.1], we get equations [15.2] and [15.3]:

$$MP_L \times MR = w \qquad [15.2]$$

$$MP_K \times MR = r \qquad [15.3]$$

Thus, the profit-maximizing rule is that the firm should hire labor until the marginal product of labor times the firm's marginal revenue from the sale of the commodity equals the

✓ **Concept Check**
How does a firm that is
imperfectly competitive
in the product but not
in the input market
determine how much
of an input to hire to
maximize profits?

wage rate. Similarly, the firm should rent capital until the marginal product of capital times the firm's marginal revenue equals the rental price of capital. To maximize profits, the same rule would have to hold for all inputs that the firm uses. The condition is the same as when the firm is a perfect competitor in the product market, except that in that case, $MR = P$. In the next section, we will see that equation [15.2] provides the basis for the derivation of the firm's demand curve for labor.

15.2 THE DEMAND CURVE OF A FIRM FOR AN INPUT

We now extend the discussion of the last section and derive the demand curve of a firm for an input, first when the input is the only variable input and then when the input is one of two or more variable inputs.

The Demand Curve of a Firm for One Variable Input

We have seen in Section 14.2 that a profit-maximizing firm will hire more units of a variable input as long as the income from the sale of the extra output produced by the input is larger than the extra cost of hiring the input. When the firm is an imperfect competitor (say, a monopolist) in the product market, the extra income earned by the firm is called the **marginal revenue product (MRP)** and is equal to the marginal product of the input times the marginal revenue of the firm. That is,

$$MRP = MP \times MR \qquad [15.4]$$

Marginal revenue product (MRP) The marginal physical product of the input (MP) multiplied by the marginal revenue of the commodity (MR).

If the variable input is labor, we have

$$MRP_L = MP_L \times MR \qquad [15.4A]$$

Thus, the MRP_L is the left-hand side of equation [15.2]. Similarly, the MRP_K is the left-hand side of equation [15.3]. Note that when the firm is a perfect competitor in the product market, the firm's marginal revenue equals the product price (i.e., $MR = P$) and the marginal revenue product equals the value of the marginal product (i.e., $MRP = VMP$). Since we are now dealing with a firm that is an imperfect competitor in the product market and $MR < P$, $MRP < VMP$.

Because the firm is a perfect competitor in the input market (i.e., faces a horizontal or infinitely elastic supply curve of the input), the extra cost or marginal expenditure (ME) of hiring each additional unit of the variable input is equal to the price of the input. If the variable input is labor, a profit-maximizing firm should hire labor as long as the marginal revenue product of labor exceeds the wage rate and until $MRP_L = w$, as indicated by equation [15.2].

The actual derivation of a firm's demand schedule for labor when labor is the only variable input (i.e., when capital and other inputs are fixed), and when the firm is an imperfect competitor (monopolist) in the product market but a perfect competitor in the labor market is shown with Table 15.1. In Table 15.1, L refers to the number of workers hired by the firm per day. Q_X is the total output of commodity X produced by the firm by hiring various numbers of workers. The MP_L is the marginal or extra output generated by each additional worker hired. The MP_L is obtained by the change in Q_X per unit change in L.

TABLE 15.1		The Marginal Revenue Product of Labor and the Firm's Demand Schedule for Labor				
L	Q_X	MP_L	P_X	TR_X	MRP_L	$ME_L = w$
1	12	12	$13	$156	. . .	$40
2	22	10	12	264	$108	40
3	30	8	11	330	66	40
4	37	7	10	370	40	40
5	43	6	9	387	17	40
6	48	5	8	384	−3	40

Note that the law of diminishing returns begins to operate with the hiring of the second worker. P_X refers to the price for the final commodity, and it declines because the firm is an imperfect competitor (monopolist) in the product market. Total revenue (TR_X) is obtained by multiplying P_X by Q_X. The marginal revenue product of labor (MRP_L) is then given by the change in the firm's total revenue by selling the output of commodity X that results from the hiring of an additional worker. More briefly, $MRP_L = \Delta TR_X / \Delta L$. This is the same as MP_L times MR_X (not given in the table; see Problem 3, with the answer at the end of the text). The MRP_L declines because both the MP_L and MR_X decline. That is, as the firm hires more labor and produces more units of the commodity, the MP_L declines (because of diminishing returns) and MR_X also declines (because the firm must lower the commodity price to sell more units of the commodity). The last column of Table 15.1 gives the daily wage rate (w) that the firm must pay to hire each worker. Since the firm is a perfect competitor in the labor market, w is constant (at $40 per day) and is equal to the increase in the firm's total costs (the marginal expense) of hiring each additional worker.

Looking at Table 15.1, we see that the second worker contributes $108 extra revenue to the firm (i.e., $MRP_L = \$108$), while the firm incurs a cost of only $40 to hire this worker. Thus, it pays for the firm to hire the second worker. (Since the MRP of the first worker is even greater than the MRP of the second worker, the firm should certainly hire the first worker.) The MRP of the third worker falls to $66, but this still exceeds the daily wage of $40 that the firm must pay each worker. Thus, the firm should also hire the third worker. According to equation [15.2], the profit-maximizing firm should hire workers until the $MRP_L = w$. Thus, this firm should hire four workers, at which $MRP_L = w = \$40$. The firm will not hire the fifth worker because he or she will contribute only $17 to the firm's total revenue while adding $40 to its total costs.

The MRP_L schedule gives the firm's demand schedule for labor. It indicates the number of workers that the firm would hire at various wage rates. For example, if $w = \$108$ per day, the firm would hire only two workers per day. If $w = \$66$, the firm would hire three workers. At $w = \$40$, $L = 4$, and so on. If we plotted the MRP_L values of Table 15.1 on the vertical axis and L on the horizontal axis, we would get the firm's negatively sloped demand curve for labor when labor is the only variable input. This is shown in the next section.

Note that since the firm is a monopolist in the product market, the MRP_L is smaller than the VMP_L and the MRP_L curve lies below the VMP_L curve. As a result, the firm hires less labor and produces less of the commodity than if the firm were a perfect competitor in the product market. Joan Robinson called the excess of the VMP_L over the MRP_L at the

FIGURE 15.1   Demand Curve for Labor of a Monopolist with All Inputs Variable   As the wage rate falls and the firm hires more labor (i.e., moves down its MRP_L curve), the MRP curve of inputs that are complements to labor shifts to the right and the MRP curve of inputs that are substitutes for labor shifts to the left. Both of these shifts cause the MRP_L curve to shift to the right to MRP_L'. Thus, when the daily wage falls from $66 to $40, the firm increases the number of workers hired from three (point A on the MRP_L curve) to six (point C on the MRP_L' curve). By joining points A and C, we get the firm's demand curve for labor (d_L).

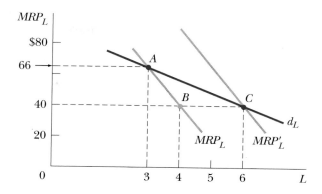

Monopolistic exploitation   The excess of an input's value of marginal product over its marginal revenue product at the level of utilization of the input.

point where $MRP_L = w$ (the level of employment) **monopolistic exploitation.**[1] Yet, this emotionally laden term is somewhat misleading, because the firm does not pocket the difference between the VMP_L and the MRP_L (see Problem 3, with the answer at the end of the text). That is, the last worker hired receives the entire increase in the total revenue of the firm (the MRP) that he or she contributes.

The Demand Curve of a Firm for One of Several Variable Inputs

We have seen that the declining MRP_L schedule given in Table 15.1 gives the firm's demand schedule for labor in the short run when labor is the only variable input. This is shown by the negatively sloped MRP_L curve in Figure 15.1 (on the assumption that labor is infinitesimally divisible or that workers can be hired for any part of a day). The MRP_L or demand for labor curve when labor is the only variable input shows that the firm will hire three workers at $w = $66 (point A in Figure 15.1) and four workers at $w = $40 (point B).

When labor is not the only variable input (i.e., when the firm can also change the quantity of capital and other inputs), the firm's demand curve for labor can be derived from the MRP_L curve, but it is not the MRP_L curve itself. The derivation is basically the same as explained in Section 14.2 and is shown in Figure 15.1. That is, as the wage rate falls and the firm hires more labor (i.e., moves down its MRP_L curve), the MRP curve of inputs that are complements to labor shifts to the right, and the MRP curve of inputs that are substitutes for labor shifts to the left (exactly as explained in Section 14.2). Both of these shifts cause the MRP_L to shift to the right, say, from MRP_L to MRP_L' in Figure 15.1. Thus, when the daily wage falls from $66 to $40, the firm will increase the number of workers hired from three (point A on the MRP_L curve) to six (point C on the MRP_L' curve) rather than to four (point B on the original MRP_L curve). By joining points A and C, we get the firm's demand curve for labor (d_L in Figure 15.1) when other inputs besides labor are variable.

Note that the d_L curve is negatively sloped and generally more elastic than the MRP_L curve in the long run, when all inputs are variable. In general, the better the complementary and substitute inputs available for labor are, the greater is the outward shift of the MRP_L curve as a result of a decline in the wage rate, and the more elastic is d_L.

✓ Concept Check
How is an imperfectly competitive firm's demand curve for one or more variable inputs derived?

---

[1] J. Robinson, *The Economics of Imperfect Competition* (London: Macmillan, 1933), Chapter 25.

| 15.3 | THE MARKET DEMAND CURVE AND INPUT PRICE AND EMPLOYMENT |

The market demand curve for an input is derived from the individual firms' demand curves for the input. If all the firms using the input are monopolists in their respective product markets, the market demand for the input is derived by the straightforward horizontal summation of the individual firms' demand curves for the input. The reason is that the reduction in the commodity price (as each monopolist produces and sells more of its commodity by hiring more inputs) has already been considered or incorporated in full into the calculation of the *MRP* of the input.

The case is different when a commodity market is composed of oligopolists and monopolistic competitors. That is, when all the oligopolists or monopolistic competitors in a product market hire more inputs and produce more of the commodity, the commodity price will decline. This decline in the price of the commodity causes a downward shift in each firm's demand curve for labor, exactly the same as when firms are perfect competitors in the product market (see Section 14.3). The market demand curve is obtained by adding the quantity demanded of each input on these downward shifting demand curves of the input of each firm. The process is identical to that shown in Figure 14.2 in Section 14.3, and it is not repeated here (see Problem 6).

The equilibrium price and employment of an input are then given at the intersection of the market demand and the market supply curves of the input, as described in Section 14.5. When all firms are perfect competitors in the input market, each firm can hire any quantity of the input at the given market price of the input. Each firm will then hire the input until the *MRP* of the input on the firm's demand curve for the input equals the *ME* or input price.

If, for whatever reason, the market demand curve for the input rises (i.e., shifts upward) from the equilibrium position, the market price and employment of the input will also increase until a new equilibrium price is reached at which the *MRP* of the input equals the *MRC* or input price. This usually does not occur instantaneously. During the adjustment period, there will be a temporary shortage of the input (see Example 15–1).

✔ **Concept Check**
How is the marginal expenditure curve of an input of a monopsonist derived?

EXAMPLE 15–1

The Dynamics of the Engineers Shortage

During the late 1950s and early 1960s a shortage of engineers existed in the United States, which might have endangered winning the "space race" with the former Soviet Union. This can be analyzed with the aid of Figure 15.2. The intersection of the hypothetical market demand curve for engineers D_G and the market supply curve of engineers S_G at point E determines the equilibrium daily wage of $40 for engineers. At $w = 40, the 600,000 engineers employed match the number of engineers demanded, and there is no shortage. In the late 1950s and early 1960s, the demand for engineers unexpectedly increased (i.e., shifted up, say, to D'_G) because of the space race. At the original equilibrium wage rate of $w = 40, there is a shortage of 500,000 (EF) engineers and engineers' wages rise. As this occurs, employers economize on the use of engineers, and more students enter engineering studies. Thus, the shortage is somewhat alleviated. For example, at $w = 50, the shortage declines to 250,000 (CM).

FIGURE 15.2 Dynamics of the Engineer Shortage
The intersection of D_G and S_G at point E determines the equilibrium daily wage of $40 for engineers. There are 600,000 engineers employed, and there is no shortage. If D_G shifts upward to D_G', a temporary shortage of 500,000 (EF) results at $w = 40 and wages rise. As this occurs, the shortage is somewhat alleviated. At $w = 50, the shortage declines to 250,000 (CM). Only after the wage rises to $66 and enough new engineers are trained is the temporary shortage eliminated and new equilibrium point E' reached.

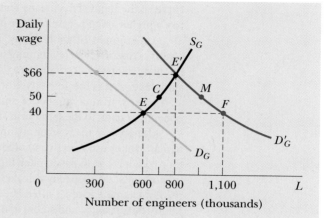

Only after several years, as wages rise to $66 and enough new engineers are trained, is the shortage eliminated and new equilibrium point E' reached with 800,000 engineers employed.

If, over this time, the demand for engineers increases again, a new temporary shortage emerges. On the other hand, if the demand for engineers declines by the time an increasing number of them graduate in response to higher wages, or if the supply response turns out to be excessive, a surplus of engineers develops. This is indeed what occurred during the 1970s and 1980s. Because of the reduced pool of the college-age population and high incomes in other occupations, the National Science Foundation nevertheless predicted that a shortfall of about half a million engineers and scientists would again develop by the end of the twentieth century in the United States. Indeed, a shortage of engineers of about 350,000 was estimated to exist in the United States in 2001. More recent studies, however, have concluded that there is no shortage of engineers in the United States and that any increase in future demand can be met by more engineers being trained in the United States and by immigration.

Sources: K. Arrow and W. Capron, "Dynamic Shortages and Price Rises: The Engineer-Scientist Case," *Quarterly Journal of Economics,* May 1959; C. Holden, "Supply and Demand for Scientists and Engineers: A National Crisis in the Making," *Science*, April 1990; *Duke Outsourcing Study: Industry Trends in Engineering Offshoring* (Duke University, October 2006); and R. A. Freeman, "The Market for Scientists and Engineers," *NBER Reporter*, November 2007, pp. 6–8.

| 15.4 | ## MONOPSONY: A SINGLE FIRM HIRING AN INPUT |

Until this point we have assumed that the firm is a perfect competitor in the input market. This means that the firm faces an infinitely elastic or horizontal supply curve of the input and that the firm can hire any quantity of the input at the given market price of the input. We now examine the case in which the firm is an imperfect competitor in the input market. When there is a single firm hiring an input, we have a **monopsony.** Thus, while *monopoly* refers to the single seller of a commodity, *monopsony* refers to the single buyer of an input. As such, the monopsonist faces the (usually) positively sloped *market* supply

Monopsony A single buyer of an input.

curve of the input. This means that to hire more units of the input, the monopsonist must pay a higher price per unit of the input.

An example of monopsony is provided by the "company towns" in nineteenth-century America, where a mining or textile firm was practically the sole employer of labor in many isolated communities. A present-day example of monopsony might be an automaker that is the sole buyer of some specialized automobile component or part, such as radiators, from a number of small local firms set up exclusively to supply these components or parts to the large firm (the automaker).

Monopsony arises when an input is specialized and thus much more productive to a particular firm or use than to any other firm or use. This allows the firm (in which the input is more productive) to pay a much higher price for the input than other firms and so become a monopsonist. Monopsony can also result from lack of geographic and occupational mobility. For example, people often become emotionally attached to a given locality because of family ties, friends, and so on, and are unwilling to move to other areas. Also, people may lack the information, the money, or the qualifications to move to other areas or occupations. In general, monopsony can be overcome by providing information about job opportunities elsewhere, by helping to pay for moving expenses, and by providing training for other occupations.

We have said that the monopsonist faces the usually positively sloped market supply curve of the input, so that it must pay a higher price to hire more units of the input. However, as all units of the input must be paid the same price, the monopsonist will have to pay a higher price, not only for the last unit hired, but for all units of the input it hires. As a result, the **marginal expenditure (ME)** on the input exceeds the input price. This is shown in Table 15.2 for labor.

In Table 15.2, w is the daily wage rate that a monopsonist must pay to hire various numbers of workers (L). Thus, the first two columns of the table give the market supply schedule of labor faced by the monopsonist. TE_L is the total expenditure incurred by the monopsonist to hire various numbers of workers and is obtained by multiplying L by w. ME_L is the **marginal expenditure on labor** and gives the extra expenditure that the monopsonist faces to hire each additional worker. That is $ME_L = \Delta TC_L / \Delta L$.

Note that $ME_L > w$. For example, the monopsonist can hire one worker at the wage rate of $10 for a total cost of $10. To hire the second worker, the monopsonist must increase the wage rate from $10 to $20 and incur a total expenditure of $40. Thus, the increase in the total expenditure (i.e., the marginal expense) of hiring the second worker is $30 and exceeds the wage rate of $20 that the monopsonist must pay for each of the two workers.

Figure 15.3 gives the positively sloped market supply curve of labor (S_L) faced by the monopsonist (from columns 1 and 2 of Table 15.2) and the marginal expenditure curve

Marginal expenditure (ME) The extra expenditure for or cost of hiring an additional unit of an input.

Marginal expenditure on labor (ME_L) The extra expenditure for or cost of hiring an additional unit of labor.

TABLE 15.2	Marginal Expenditure on Labor		
L	w	TE_L	ME_L
1	$10	$10	—
2	20	40	$30
3	30	90	50
4	40	160	70
5	50	250	90

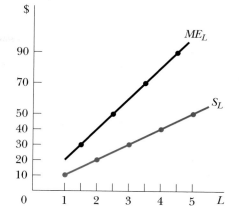

FIGURE 15.3   A Monopsonist's Supply and Marginal Expenditure on Labor Curves S_L is the positively sloped market supply curve of labor faced by the monopsonist (from columns 1 and 2 of Table 15.2) and ME_L is the marginal expenditure on labor curve (from the first and the last columns of Table 15.2). The ME_L values are plotted between the various units of L used, and the ME_L curve is everywhere above the S_L curve.

(ME_L, from the first and the last columns of Table 15.2). Since the ME_L measures the changes in TE_L per unit change in L used, the ME_L values given in Table 15.2 are plotted between the various units of labor hired. Note also that the ME_L curve is everywhere above the S_L curve. Similarly, a firm that is the single renter of a particular type of specialized capital (i.e., a monopsonist in the capital market) faces the positively sloped market supply curve of capital, so that the firm's **marginal expenditure on capital (ME_K)** curve is above the supply curve of capital (S_K).[2]

Marginal expenditure on capital (ME_K) The extra expenditure for or cost of hiring an additional unit of capital.

Although our discussion has been exclusively in terms of monopsony, there are other forms of imperfect competition in input markets. Just as we have monopoly, oligopoly, and monopolistic competition in product markets, so we can have monopsony, oligopsony, and monopsonistic competition in input markets. **Oligopsony** refers to the case where there are only a few firms hiring a homogeneous or differentiated input. **Monopsonistic competition** refers to the case where there are many firms hiring a differentiated input. As for the monopsonist, oligopsonists and monopsonistic competitors must also pay higher prices to hire more units of an input, and so the marginal expenditure on the input exceeds the input price for them also.

Oligopsony The form of market organization in which there are few firms hiring either a homogeneous or a differentiated input.

Monopsonistic competition The situation where there are many firms hiring a differentiated input.

Finally, note that when the firm is a perfect competitor in the input market, the marginal expenditure on the input is equal to the input price, and the marginal expenditure curve is horizontal and coincides with the supply curve of the input that the firm faces. That is, since the firm hires such a small quantity of the input, the supply curve of the input that the firm faces is infinitely elastic, even though the market supply curve of the input is positively sloped. For example, if $w = \$10$ no matter how many workers a firm hires, then $ME_L = w = \$10$ and the ME_L curve is horizontal at $w = \$10$ and coincides with the S_L curve (the supply curve of labor faced by the firm). Example 15–2 examines the effect of occupational licensing on the functioning of labor markets.

---

[2] In Section A.14 of the Mathematical Appendix, we derive an important relationship among input price, marginal expenditure, and the price elasticity of input supply. This is analogous to the relationship among commodity price, marginal revenue, and the price elasticity of commodity demand derived in Section 5.5.

EXAMPLE 15-2

Occupational Licensing, Mobility, and Imperfect Labor Markets

State governments in the United States require a license to engage in certain professional activities. Occupational licensing now affects more than 20% of the U.S. labor force, which is more than the workers affected by the minimum wage (about 10% of the U.S. labor force) or unionization (about 13% of the U.S. labor force), and it is increasing. About 50 occupations are now licensed in all states, and more than 800 occupations are licensed in some states.

Although occupational licensing is imposed to ensure quality of service, it invariably also restricts the flow of labor into the licensed occupations and increases the earnings of licensed labor. Kleiner found that licensing reduced the growth rate of employment by about 20%, increased hourly earnings about 10% to 17%, depending on the occupation, compared to similar unlicensed occupations, and it cost the economy about $38 billion in lost service output per year. At the same time, he did not find that licensing enhanced the quality of the service.

Not only do most states require many occupations to be licensed, but many of them do not recognize the occupational license obtained in other states to pursue the occupation in their own state. This is often the case for dentists and lawyers. Invariably, these nonreciprocity regulations are the result of lobbying on the part of the professions involved as a way of restricting the possible competition that would arise from an inflow of professionals from other states. On theoretical grounds, we would expect that the income of professionals in states without reciprocity agreements would be higher than in states with reciprocity. In fact, Shepard found that the fees and income of dentists in the 35 states that had no reciprocity agreements were 12% to 15% higher than in states with reciprocity. If all states adopted reciprocity agreements, some lawyers and dentists in states with lower fees and incomes would migrate to those states with higher fees and incomes. This would reduce (and in the limit eliminate) all interstate differences in fees and incomes and increase the degree of competition in these labor markets.

Sources: M. M. Kleiner, *Licensing Occupations: Enhancing Quality or Restricting Competition* (Kalamazoo, MI.: Upjohn Institute, 2006); M. M. Kleiner, "Occupational Licensing," *Journal of Economic Perspectives*, Fall 2000; and L. Shepard, "Licensing Restrictions and the Cost of Dental Care," *Journal of Law and Economics*, October 1978.

15.5	MONOPSONY PRICING AND EMPLOYMENT OF ONE VARIABLE INPUT

As pointed out in Section 14.2, a firm using only one variable input maximizes profits by hiring more units of the input until the extra revenue from the sale of the commodity equals the extra expenditure on hiring the input. This is a general marginal condition and applies whether the firm is a perfect or imperfect competitor in the product and/or input markets. If the variable input is labor and the firm is a monopsonist in the labor market, the monopsonist maximizes its total profits by hiring labor until the marginal revenue product of labor equals the marginal expenditure on labor. That is, the monopsonist should hire labor until equation [15.5] or, equivalently, equation [15.5A] holds:

$$MRP_L = ME_L \qquad [15.5]$$

$$MP_L \cdot MR = MRC_L \qquad [15.5A]$$

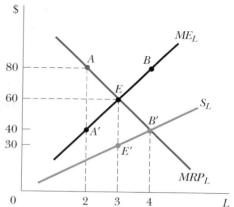

FIGURE 15.4   Optimal Employment of Labor and the Wage Rate Paid by a Monopsonist   The S_L and the ME_L curves are those of Figure 15.3. With MRP_L, the monopsonist maximizes profits by hiring three workers (given by point E, at which the MRP_L curve intersects the ME_L curve and $MRP_L = ME_L = \$60$). The monopsonist then pays $w = \$30$ to each worker (given by point E' on S_L). The excess of MRP_L over w ($EE' = \$30$) at $L = 3$ is called monopsonistic exploitation.

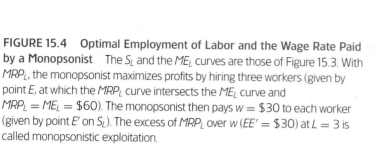

✓ Concept Check

How are the equilibrium price and employment of an input of a monopsonist determined?

The wage rate paid by the monopsonist is then given by the corresponding point on the market supply curve of labor (S_L). This is shown in Figure 15.4.

In Figure 15.4, the S_L and the ME_L curves are those of Figure 15.3. With the firm's MRP_L curve shown in Figure 15.4, the monopsonist maximizes profits by hiring three workers (given by point E, at which the MRP_L curve intersects the ME_L curve and $MRP_L = ME_L = \$60$). To prove this, consider that the second worker adds $80 (point A) to the monopsonist's total revenue but only $40 (point A') to its total expenditure. Thus, the monopsonist's profits rise (by $AA' = \$40$) by hiring the second worker. On the other hand, the monopsonist would not hire the fourth worker because he or she would add more to total expenditure ($80, given by point B) than to total revenue ($40, given by point B'), so that the monopsonist's total profits would fall by $40 ($BB'$ in the figure). Only at $L = 3$, $MRP_L = ME_L = \$60$ (point E) and the monopsonist maximizes total profits.

Figure 15.4 also shows that to hire three workers, the monopsonist must pay the wage of $30. This is given by point E' on the S_L curve at $L = 3$. Thus, the intersection of the MRP_L and ME_L curves gives only the profit-maximizing number of workers that the firm should hire. The wage rate is then given by the amount that the firm must pay each worker, and this is given by the point on the market supply curve of labor at the level of employment. Note that $MRP_L = \$60$ (point E) exceeds $w = \$30$ (point E') at $L = 3$.

Monopsonistic exploitation The excess of the marginal revenue product of an input over the price of the input at the level of utilization of the input.

Joan Robinson called the excess of the marginal revenue product of the variable input over the input price ($EE' = \$30$ at $L = 3$ in Figure 15.4) **monopsonistic exploitation**.[3] It arises because the monopsonist produces where the $MRP_L = ME_L$ in order to maximize profits. Since the S_L curve is positively sloped, the ME_L curve is above it, and $ME_L > w$. The more inelastic the market supply curve that the monopsonist faces, the greater the degree of monopsonistic exploitation. If the firm in Figure 15.4 had been a perfect competitor in the labor market, it would have hired four workers (given by point B', at which $MRP_L = ME_L = w = \$40$). As we have seen, the monopsonist maximizes total profits by restricting output and employment and by hiring only three workers (point E). Example 15–3 examines monopsonistic exploitation in major league baseball. In Section 15.8, we will see how government regulation and/or union power can reduce or eliminate monopsonistic exploitation.

---

[3] J. Robinson, *The Economics of Imperfect Competition* (London: Macmillan, 1933), Chapter 26.

EXAMPLE 15-3

Monopsonistic Exploitation in Major League Baseball

Table 15.3 gives the net marginal revenue product (*MRP*) and the salary of mediocre, average, and star hitters and pitchers in major league baseball calculated by Scully for the year 1969. Scully found that the team's winning record increased attendance and revenues and that a team's performance depended primarily on the "slugging average" for hitters and on the ratio of "strikeouts to walks" for pitchers. Using these data, Scully calculated the net *MRP* or extra gate revenues and broadcast receipts resulting from each type of player's performance after subtracting the player's development cost. In 1969, development costs were as high as $300,000 per player. Table 15.3 shows that for mediocre players, the net *MRP* was negative (−$32,300 for hitters and −$13,400 for pitchers). Of course, the team's scouts and managers could not precisely foresee which players would turn out to be mediocre, average, or stars. The table also shows the average players' salaries in each category.

Mediocre players reduced the team's profits. Average players received salaries far lower than their net *MRP*. Star players received salaries that were more than six times lower than their net *MRP*. Thus, monopsonistic exploitation was large for average players and very large for star players. On the other hand, mediocre players exploited their team! This exploitation was made possible by the "reserve clause," under which the player became the exclusive property of the team that first signed him. Aside from being traded, a player could only play for the team for whatever salary the team offered. Thus, the reserve clause practically eliminated all competition in hiring and remuneration and essentially established a cartel of employers (teams) for major league baseball players. As such, the cartel behaved much like a monopsonist and exploited players.

In 1975, the reserve clause was substantially weakened. After six years of playing for a team, players could declare themselves "free agents" and negotiate their salaries and the team for which they would play. As anticipated, competition resulted in startling increases in players' salaries and sharply reduced the monopsonistic power of baseball clubs. For example, Summers and Quinton found that free-agent star pitchers had an average marginal revenue product of nearly $300,000 and

TABLE 15.3 Net Marginal Revenue Product and Salaries in Major League Baseball, 1969 Average

Type of Player	Quality of Player	Net *MRP*	Salary
Hitters	Mediocre	$−32,300	$15,200
	Average	129,500	28,000
	Star	313,900	47,700
Pitchers	Mediocre	$−13,400	$13,700
	Average	159,900	31,800
	Star	397,000	61,000

Source: G. Scully, "Pay and Performance in Major League Baseball," *American Economic Review,* December 1974, p. 928.

received salaries of nearly $258,000 in 1980. Even after adjusting for inflation, this represented a doubling of the 1969 salary of star pitchers. In an attempt to reduce these huge salaries and restore some of their previous monopsony power, in 1986 club owners did not sign any player that had become a free agent in 1985. The players' union filed a grievance in 1986, charging that the clubs had acted collusively and thus illegally. In fall 1987, an arbitrator for major league baseball ruled that the clubs had indeed conspired to destroy the free-agent market and that the affected players should be awarded financial damages. By 1991, players' salaries had shot up to more than $500,000 per year and were equal, on the average, to their marginal revenue product (thus essentially putting an end to exploitation in major league baseball). Thirty-five players earned $3 million or more per year, with Boston Red Sox pitcher Roger Clemens and New York Mets pitcher Dwight Gooden topping the list with earnings in excess of $5 million per year.

On August 12 1994, players went on strike as a result of the owners' decision to put a salary cap on multimillion dollar star players' salaries. The strike wiped out the last 52 days of the 1994 season as well as the World Series (for the first time in 90 years), and it also led to a three-week delay in the starting of the 1995 season. The strike was ended by a court injunction after the players agreed to some form of "luxury tax" on clubs paying very high star players' salaries (a partial victory for owners). This, however, was regarded as much too modest to equalize differences between the affluent and poor teams.

In December 2000, the nation's sporting establishment was left aghast by the $252 million, 10-year contract—the largest ever in any sport—that shortstop Alex Rodriguez signed with the Texas Rangers. This is more than Tom Hicks had paid for the entire team two years earlier and almost 10 times more than some teams' entire payroll. The Rangers reason: its desire to win (in 1999 the Rangers had the worst record in the league). But experience shows that one player, by himself, cannot turn a team around no matter how great. In 1969, the overall average salary for a baseball player was $34,000; by 2007, it had reached $2.9 million. Only the richest clubs can now pay star salaries, and they almost always win. This takes the competition—and some of the fun—out of baseball!

Sources: G. Scully, "Pay and Performance in Major League Baseball," *American Economic Review,* December 1974; P.M. Summers and N. Quinton, "Pay and Performance in Major League Baseball: The Case of the First Family of Free Agents," *Journal of Human Resources,* Summer 1982; ""Owners: 1, Players: 0," *Business Week,* April 17, 1995, pp. 32–33; "Bring Competition Back to Baseball," *New York Times,* April 5, 1999, p. 22; "Rodriguez Strikes It Rich in Texas," *New York Times,* December 12, 2000, p. D1. For data on salaries in 2007, see: http://sportsline.com/mlb/salaries/avgsalaries; http://sportsline.com/mlb/players; and http://sportsline.com/mlb/salaries.

15.6 MONOPSONY PRICING AND EMPLOYMENT OF SEVERAL VARIABLE INPUTS

We have seen in Section 15.5 that when labor is the only variable input, a monopsonist maximizes profits by hiring labor until the marginal revenue product of labor equals the marginal expenditure on labor. This was given by equations [15.5] and [15.5A]. The same condition holds when there is more than one variable input. That is, the monopsonist maximizes profits by hiring each input until the marginal revenue product of the input equals the marginal expenditure on hiring it. With labor and capital as the variable inputs, the monopsonist should hire labor and capital until equations [15.6A] and [15.6B] hold:

$$MP_L \cdot MR = ME_L \qquad [15.6A]$$

$$MP_K \cdot MR = ME_K \qquad [15.6B]$$

Dividing both sides of equations [15.6A] and [15.6B] by MP_L and MP_K, respectively, and combining the results we get [15.7]

$$ME_L/MP_L = ME_K/MP_K = MC = MR \qquad [15.7]$$

This is identical to equation [15.1], except that w has been replaced by the ME_L and r has been replaced by the ME_K to reflect the fact that the firm is now a monopsonist in the labor and capital markets, and it must pay a higher wage and rental price to hire more labor and rent more capital, respectively. That is, the optimal input combination is now given by equation [15.7] rather than by equation [14.2], and each ratio in equation [15.7] equals the MC of the firm:

$$ME_L/MP_L = ME_K/MP_K = MC \qquad [15.8]$$

For example, if ME_L/MP_L is smaller than ME_K/MP_K, the monopsonist would not be minimizing production costs. The monopsonist can reduce the cost of producing any level of output by substituting labor for capital in production at the margin. As the monopsonist hires more labor, ME_L rises and MP_L declines, so that ME_L/MP_L rises. As the monopsonist rents less capital, ME_K falls and MP_K rises, so that ME_K/MP_K falls. To minimize the cost of producing any level of output, the monopsonist should continue to substitute labor for capital in production until equation [15.8] holds.

Note that the ME_L/MP_L and ME_K/MP_K measure the extra cost (in terms of labor and capital, respectively) to produce an extra unit of the commodity. This is the marginal cost of the firm. For example, if $ME_L = \$10$ and $MP_L = 5$, the marginal cost of the firm is $ME_L/MP_L = \$10/5 = \$2$. This means that it costs the monopsonist $2 extra to hire the additional labor to produce one extra unit of the commodity. The same is true for capital. That is, $ME_K/MP_K = MC$ or the marginal cost of the firm (in terms of capital). The best level of output is then given by the point where $MC = MR$ (see equation [15.7]). Example 15–4 shows the incredibly high compensation of top executives.

EXAMPLE 15–4
Imperfect Competition in Labor Markets and the Pay of Top Executives

Table 15.4 gives the earnings of the 10 highest-paid chief executives in the United States in 2006. The total pay ranged from $71.7 million for Terry Semel of Yahoo to nearly $32 million for Luis Camilleri of Altria Group, for an average compensation of $45.5 million for all 10 executives (as compared with $16.9 million in Europe). A large portion of these incredible incomes resulted from stock options for CEOs (which are less visible to stockholders). While the average remuneration of CEOs was 56 times the average worker's pay in 1940 and 74 times it in 1950, this increased to 122 in 1990 and 350 in 2006. Union leaders have denounced these multimillion-dollar yearly compensations as the "annual executive pig-out."

TABLE 15.4	Earnings of the 10 Highest-Paid CEOs in the United States in 2006 (in millions of dollars)		
Executive/ Company	Salary and Bonus	Stock and Other Options	Total Compensation
1. Terry Semel Yahoo	$0.3	$71.4	$71.7
2. Bob Simpson XTO Energy	32.4	27.1	59.5
3. Ray Irani Occidental Petroleum	7.3	45.5	52.8
4. E. Stanley O'Neil* Merrill Lynch	19.6	26.8	46.4
5. H. Lawrence Culp, Jr. Danaher	5.0	41.2	46.2
6. Angelo Mozilo IBM	24.0	19.0	43.0
7. Alan Mulally Ford	19.5	19.6	39.1
8. Todd Nelson Apollo Group	32.6	0.0	32.6
9. Edward Whitacre AT&T	9.6	22.2	31.8
10. Luis Camilleri Altria Group	21.7	10.0	31.7

Source: Institute for Policy Studies, *Executive Excess* (Washington, DC: IPI, August 29, 2007).

The question is "Are these executives worth to their employer the huge compensation that they are paid?" One answer is that since firms voluntarily make these payments, the marginal revenue product of these top executives must be at least as high. These huge payments, however, also result because of a confluence of interests (collusion) between CEOs and compensation committees and because the latter often have inadequate information or fail to comprehend how rapidly the payments from a complicated, long-term compensation package can escalate if all goes well.

15.7   INTERNATIONAL MIGRATION AND THE BRAIN DRAIN

International migration affects the supply of labor of the nations of emigration and immigration. Migration can take place for economic as well as for noneconomic reasons. Most of the international labor migration into the United States since the end of World War II has been motivated by the prospects of earning higher real wages and incomes in the United States than in the country of origin. Labor migration to the United States, however, is highly restricted (i.e., international labor markets are not perfectly competitive).

We can examine the effect of labor immigration on a nation with Figure 15.5. The figure is based on the assumption that the nation's output is produced under conditions of constant returns to scale with labor and capital inputs only. Before immigration, the nation employs 3 million workers at the daily wage of $60. The total value of output is, therefore, $0FAG = \$270$ million, of which $0HAG = \$180$ million goes to labor and the remainder, or $HFA = \$90$ million, goes to the owners of capital. With 1 million immigrants, the daily wage rate in the nation falls to $40 and the share of total output going to capital owners increases to $JFB = \$160$ million or by $HABJ = \$70$ million. Since the original workers' earnings decline by the area of rectangle $HACJ = \$60$ million, the

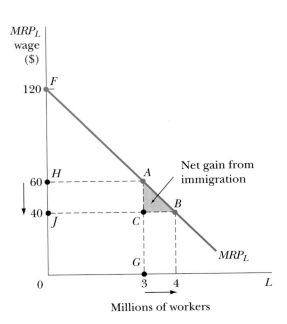

FIGURE 15.5   Effects of Immigration on the Earnings of Labor and Capital   Before immigration, the nation employs 3 million workers at the daily wage of $60. Total output is $OFAG = \$270$ million, of which $OHAG = \$180$ million goes to labor and $HFA = \$90$ million goes to the owners of capital. With 1 million immigrants, the wage falls to $40 and the share of total output going to capital increases to $JFB = \$160$ million, or by $HABJ = \$70$ million. Since the original workers' earnings decline by $HACJ = \$60$ million, the nation receives a net gain equal to the area of triangle $ABC = \$10$ million.

nation as a whole gains a net amount equal to the area of triangle $ABC = \$10$ million. With income redistribution (i.e., with taxes on earnings of capital and subsidies to labor), both workers and owners of capital can gain from immigration.

This analysis is based on the implicit assumption that all labor is homogeneous and of average productivity. This is not the case in the real world. Some labor is much more productive because of better education and training. The immigration laws of the United States and other industrial countries favor the immigration of skilled labor (such as nurses and technicians) and professional people (doctors, engineers, scientists, etc.) and impose serious obstacles to the immigration of unskilled labor, except temporary migrants. The immigration of skilled workers and professionals is likely to provide even greater benefits to the country of immigration because it saves the nation the costs of education and training, but represents a **brain drain** for the nation of emigration (see Examples 15–5 and 15–6).

Brain drain   The migration of highly skilled people from one nation to another.

EXAMPLE 15–5

British and Russian Brain Drain Is U.S. Brain Gain

Concept Check

What is the meaning of a "brain drain," and what is its effects on the countries involved?

From 1983 to 1988 more than 200 well-known scholars in the fields of history, philosophy, political science, and physics left British universities to take positions in some of the top universities in the United States. Their departure resulted from a combination of "push and pull" forces. Among the push forces were the budget cuts that froze professors' salaries and left many vacancies unfilled, the abolishment of tenure and the suspension of promotions, and reductions in funds for libraries and assistants. The pull forces were U.S. salaries that often were more than three times higher than in Britain, as well as the availability of large research funds, assistants, and sophisticated laboratories. There was a time when it was almost impossible to induce a top scholar to leave Oxford or Cambridge University. In the late 1980s, on the other hand, a British scholar who had not received at least one attractive offer from an American university started even to question his reputation outside Britain.

With the collapse of communism in the Soviet Union in the late 1980s and early 1990s, a huge and growing exodus of top Russian scientists headed for the United States either permanently or on temporary work visas. This surpassed the earlier British exodus and became the largest brain drain to (and brain gain of) the United States since the end of World War II. Russia worried a great deal about losing many of its top scientists. Virtually the entire faculty of the University of Minnesota's Theoretical Physics Institute in the mid-1990s was from Russia. Many top Russian scientists flowed into the U.S. computer, biological, and chemical laboratories. As Russia struggled to restructure its economy, few if any funds were available for science. "For science, there is no money, no jobs, and no respect from the public," says one recent emigree. My productivity in America is 10 times more than in Russia," says another. He might have added that in the early 1990s his salary in the United States is also 100 times more than in Russia!

Another form of the brain drain is created when the large number of foreign students getting advanced degrees in the United States chooses to remain. Nearly 600,000 foreign students were studying in the United States in 2004. Almost 50% of the students receiving engineering doctorates in the United States are foreign born, and this percentage is almost as high in mathematics and computer science. (It is nearly 40% in economics.) More than 70% of these students chose to remain in the United States after getting their doctorate.

Finally, in 1990 the H1-B visa program was established. This allowed up to 65,000 educated foreigners a year to fill specialized American jobs, largely in the high-tech industry, for a period of six years (but requiring renewal after the first three years) if an employer petitions the U.S. Immigration and naturalization Service on their behalf. The maximum annual number of H1-B visas was raised to 115,000 in 1998 and to 195,000 in 2001, but it was then scaled back to 65,000 in 2004. Since then, legislation has been under consideration in the U.S. Congress to increase sharply the number of such visas.

Sources: "British Brain Drain Enriches U.S. Colleges," *New York Times*, November 22, 1988, p. 1; "The Soviet Brain Drain Is the U.S. Brain Gain," *Business Week*, November 11, 1991, pp. 94–100; "Foreign Students Spur U.S. Brain Gain," *Wall Street Journal*, August 31, 1994, p. 9A; "Congress Approves a Big Increase in Visas for Specialized Workers," *New York Times*, October 4, 2000, p. 1; R. Freeman, "People Flows in Globalization," *NBER Working Paper No. 12315*, February 2007; and "Skilled-Worker Visa Applicants Expected to Soar," *Wall Street Journal*, April 1, 2008, p. 19.

EXAMPLE 15–6

The Debate Over U.S. Immigration Policy

In 2007, 37.9 million Americans, or 12.6% of the U.S. population, were born elsewhere. This was higher than in any other year since World War II (the all-time high was 14.7% in 1910). Illegal immigrants are 11.3 million, or 29.8%, of the total. The rapid increase in immigration (legal and illegal) in recent years has emerged as a hot issue, especially in California and New York, the states with the highest proportion of foreign born (28% and 22%, respectively). Indeed, an intense national debate is taking place on the nation's immigration policy.

The immigration of highly trained individuals and bright students coming to the United States to get higher degrees and then remaining is clearly of great benefit to the United States. Less clear is the case for immigration of uneducated and unskilled people. U.S. Census data indicate that nearly 21% of recent immigrants over the age of 25 have bachelor's degrees (as compared with about 15% for native Americans), but 31% have no high school diploma (as compared with 8% of the U.S.-born population). Thus, the majority of recent immigrants are either very educated or have little education.

✓ Concept Check
What is the effect of immigration on wages and employment in the United States?

In general, immigration is good for the country. But, at least in the short run, native workers receive lower wages than without immigration, whereas employers gain by being able to pay lower wages. This explains why labor is generally opposed to immigration whereas business favors it. The nation as a whole generally gains from immigration because employers' gains exceed labor's losses. With an appropriate redistribution policy, some of business' gains could be taxed away and used to compensate workers for their loss and also to provide workers with a share of the remaining gains. In a recent study, Borjas estimated that every 10% increase in the supply of foreign workers reduces the wage of competing U.S. workers by 3% or 4%.

Sources: S. A. Camarota, *Immigrants in the United States, 2007* (Washington, DC: Center for Immigration Studies, November 2007); "7-Year Immigration Rate Is Highest in U.S. History," *New York Times*, November 29, 2007, p. 20; G. J. Borjas, "The Labor Market Impact of High-Skill Immigration," *American Economic Review*, May 2005, pp. 56–60; "Higher Migration to U.S. Restrains Wages," *Financial Times*, November 11, 2005, p. 7; and J-C, Dumont and G. Lemaitre, "Counting Immigrants and Expatriates in OECD Countries," *OECD Social, Employment, and Migration, Working Paper No. 25*, 2004.

15.8   ANALYSIS OF IMPERFECT INPUT MARKETS

In this section, we discuss some important applications of the theory presented in the chapter: the regulation of monopsony, bilateral monopoly, the effect of unions on wages, and discrimination in employment. These applications clearly indicate the usefulness and applicability of the theory presented in this chapter.

Regulation of Monopsony

By setting a minimum price for an input at the point where the marginal revenue product curve of the input intersects the market supply curve of the input, the monopsonist can be made to behave as a perfect competitor in the input market, and monopsonistic exploitation is eliminated. If the input is labor, the minimum wage that would eliminate labor exploitation can be set by the government or negotiated by the union. This is shown in Figure 15.6.

In the absence of a minimum wage, the monopsonist of Figure 15.6 hires three workers (given by point E, where the MRP_L curve intersects the ME_L curve) and the daily wage is $30 (point E' on S_L) exactly as explained in Section 15.5 and Figure 15.4. Monopsonistic exploitation of labor is given by the excess of the MRP_L over w at $L = 3$ and is equal to $30 per worker ($EE'$ in the figure). If the daily wage is set at $40 (point B' in the figure, at which the MRP_L curve intersects S_L), $CB'F$ becomes the new supply of labor curve facing the monopsonist. The new ME_L curve is then $CB'BG$, with the vertical or discontinuous portion directly above and caused by the kink (at point B') on the new S_L curve.

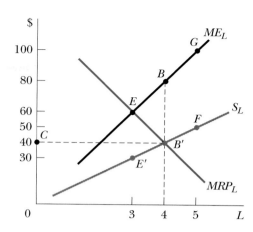

FIGURE 15.6   Regulation of Monopsony   By setting $w = \$40$, $CB'F$ becomes the new supply of labor curve facing the monopsonist. The new ME_L curve is then $CB'BG$, with the vertical or discontinuous portion directly above and caused by the kink (at point B') on the new S_L curve. To maximize total profits, the monopsonist now hires four workers (given by point B', at which the MRP_L curve intersects the new ME_L curve) and $w = MRP_L = \$40$ (so that monopsonistic exploitation is zero).

✔ Concept Check

How can monopsony be regulated?

To maximize total profits when the minimum wage of $40 is imposed, the monopsonist hires four workers (given by point B', at which the MRP_L curve intersects the new ME_L curve) and $w = MRP_L = \$40$. Thus, the monopsonist behaves as a perfect competitor in the input market (operates at point B', where the MRP_L curve intersects S_L), and the monopsonistic exploitation of labor is entirely eliminated. With a daily wage between $30 and $40, the monopsonist will hire three or four workers per day and only part of the labor exploitation will be eliminated. Setting a wage above $40 will eliminate all labor exploitation, but the monopsonist will hire fewer than four workers (see Problem 9, with an answer at the end of the text). This neat result is often unreachable in the real world, however, because of a lack of adequate data on the MRP_L and ME_L.

Bilateral Monopoly: A Monopsonistic Buyer Facing a Monopolistic Seller

Bilateral monopoly

The case where the monopsonist buyer of a product or input faces the monopolist seller of the product or input.

Bilateral monopoly is said to exist when the single buyer of a product or input (the monopsonist) faces the single seller of the product or input (the monopolist). While this is a rare occurrence in the real world, it is approximated by the "one-mill town" of yesteryears facing the union of all of the town's workers; by some military contractors such as Boeing, which is the sole seller of the F-18, and the U.S. Navy, the sole purchaser; and (until 1982) by Western Electric, the sole producer of telephone equipment in the United States, and AT&T, the sole buyer of telephone equipment.

In bilateral monopoly, price and output are indeterminate, in the sense that they cannot be established by the profit-maximizing marginal calculations employed by economists. Rather, they are determined by the relative bargaining strength of the monopsonist buyer and the monopolist seller of the product or input. This is shown in Figure 15.7.

In the figure, D is the monopsonist's demand (MRP) curve for the product or input. Curve D is also the market demand curve faced by the monopolist seller of the product or input. Then MR is the corresponding marginal revenue curve of the monopolist. If the monopolist's marginal cost curve is as shown in the figure, the monopolist will maximize profits by selling five units of the product (given by point B', where its MC curve intersects its MR curve from below) at the price of $15 per unit (point B on its D curve).

To determine the monopsonist's profit-maximizing purchase of the product, we must realize that the monopolist's marginal cost curve is the supply curve of the product that the monopsonist faces. This curve shows the price at which the monopsonist can purchase

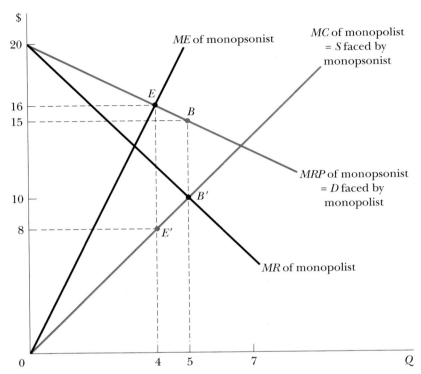

FIGURE 15.7   Bilateral Monopoly   *D* is the monopsonist's demand (*MRP*) curve for the product or input that the monopolist seller faces. *MR* is the monopolist's marginal revenue curve. The monopolist maximizes profits at *Q* = 5 (given by point *B'*, where *MC* = *MR*) at *P* = $15 (point *B* on the *D* curve). The monopolist's *MC* curve is the supply curve of the product that the monopsonist faces, and *ME* is its marginal expenditure curve. The monopsonist maximizes profits at *Q* = 4 (given by point *E*, where *MRP* = *ME*) and *P* = $8 (given by point *E'* on the supply curve that the monopsonist faces). The solution is indeterminate and will be within area *E'B'BE*.

✓ Concept Check

How are the equilibrium price and employment of an input determined under a bilateral monopoly?

various quantities of the product. Thus, the monopsonist's marginal expenditure curve for the product is higher, as indicated by the *ME* curve in the figure. To maximize profits, the monopsonist must buy four units of the product (given by point *E*, at which the monopsonist demand [*D* or *MRP*] curve intersects its *ME* of the product curve) and pay the price of $8 (given by point *E'* on the supply curve of the product that the monopsonist faces).

Thus, to maximize profits, the monopolist seller of the product wants to sell *Q* = 5 at *P* = $15, while the monopsonist buyer of the product wants to purchase *Q* = 4 at *P* = $8. The solution is indeterminate and depends on the relative bargaining strength of the two firms. All we can say is that the level of output and sales of the product will be between four and five units and the price will be between $8 and $16 (i.e., the solution will be within area *E'B'BE*). The greater the relative bargaining strength of the monopolist seller of the product, the closer output will be to five units and price to $15. The greater the relative bargaining strength of the monopsonist buyer of the product, the closer the purchase of the product will be to four units and the price to $8.

Effect of Labor Unions on Wages

Labor union An organization of workers devoted to increasing the wages and welfare of its members through bargaining with employers.

A **labor union** is an organization of workers that seeks to increase the wages and the general welfare of union workers through collective bargaining with employers. The Wagner Act passed in 1935 prohibited firms from interfering with workers' rights to form unions. Union membership as a percentage of the nonagricultural labor force of the United States peaked at 35.5% in 1947, but it had declined to 12% in 2008. Among the reasons for the decline is the increase in the proportion of workers in service industries and women in the labor force, both of whom are less likely to join unions than male production workers. Workers are also less likely to join a union if the union does not have much bargaining clout or if workers lose their jobs when they strike. Furthermore, many workers feel that unions were needed when they started, but with more and more companies setting up work-involvement programs (to avoid unionization), unions are less needed now.

A labor union can try to increase the wages of its members by (1) restricting the supply of union labor that employers must hire, (2) bargaining for an above-equilibrium wage, or (3) increasing the demand for union labor. These strategies are shown in Figure 15.8. In each of the three panels in the figure, the intersection of the market demand curve for labor (D_L) and market supply curve of labor (S_L) at point E determines the equilibrium wage rate of $40 and the equilibrium level of employment of 600 workers in the absence of the union.

The left panel shows that if the union can reduce the supply of union labor that employers must hire from S_L to S_L', the equilibrium daily wage will rise to $66, at which 300 workers are hired (point F, where S_L' intersects D_L). The union can restrict the number of union members by high initiation fees and by long apprenticeship periods. The center panel shows that the union can achieve the wage of $66 through bargaining with employers. The result is the same as if the government set the minimum wage of $66. Note that at $w = $66, 800 workers would like to work, but only 300 find employment. Thus, there is an unemployment gap of 500 workers (FG in the center panel), 300 of whom represent the disemployment effect (see Section 14.8).

Finally, the right panel of Figure 15.8 shows that by shifting D_L upward to D_L', the union can increase wages to $66 and employment to 800 workers (given by point G, where

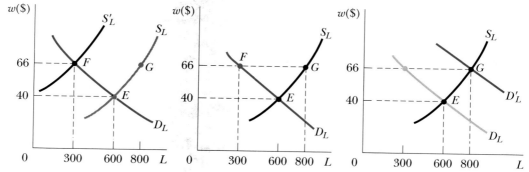

FIGURE 15.8   Methods by Which Labor Unions Can Increase Wages   The union can increase wages from $40 to $66 by reducing the supply of union labor from S_L to S_L' (the left panel), by bargaining with employers for $w = $66 (the center panel), or by increasing the demand for union labor from D_L to D_L' (the right panel). Employment falls from 600 workers to 300 workers with the first two methods (the left and center panels) and increases to 800 workers with the last method (the most difficult to accomplish).

D'_L intersects S_L). The union can increase the demand for union labor by advertising to buy "union labels" and by lobbying to restrict imports. Thus, trying to increase union wages by increasing the demand for union labor is the most advantageous method to raise wages from the point of view of union labor because it also increases employment. This, however, is also the most difficult for unions to accomplish.

There is a great deal of disagreement regarding the amount by which labor unions have increased the wages of their members. To be sure, unionized workers do receive, on the average, higher wages than nonunionized workers. At least to some extent, however, this is because unionized labor has traditionally been more skilled than nonunion labor, is employed in more efficient large-scale industries, and received higher wages even before unionization. On the other hand, wage differences between union and nonunion labor underestimate the effectiveness of labor unions in raising wages because nonunionized firms tend to increase wages when union wages rise in order to retain their workers and avoid unionization. Empirical studies seem to indicate that labor unions, on the average, have been able to increase union wages by 10% to 15% over what they would have been in the absence of unions, but this varies according to occupations, industry, race, and gender. Only during the 1970s and early 1980s were unions able to increase union-nonunion wage differentials to 20% to 30%. By the late 1980s, however, union-nonunion wage differentials returned to the traditional 10% to 15%, but declined in 2008 in the face of a weakening economy.

In their actual negotiations with management, labor unions usually "demand" higher wage increases than they really expect to receive in order to leave room for bargaining. The wage increases in a few major industries, such as the automobile and steel industries, often set the pattern for wage demands in other industries. Union wage demands are also likely to be larger in periods of high profits and employment than in recessionary periods. In the final analysis, the actual wage settlement in a particular industry or firm depends on the relative bargaining strength of the union and the employer, along the lines of the bilateral monopoly model. In making wage demands, unions do take into account the effect of wage increases on employment. Labor unions also seem to have reduced wage differentials among union workers of different skills and among different regions of the country. By bargaining with management for higher wages, unions also tend to reduce monopsonistic exploitation.[4]

Economics of Discrimination in Employment

Discrimination in employment can take many forms, but in this chapter we will consider only discrimination between male and female workers of equal productivity and its effect on their wages and employment. This is shown in Figure 15.9, where S_F and S_M are the supply curves of female and male labor to a particular industry, respectively; S_L is the total supply of female and male labor; and D_L is the total demand for labor by the industry. The figure shows that in the absence of gender discrimination, the equilibrium wage is $40 for males and females (given by point E, at which S_L intersects D_L), and 200 females (point A) and 400 males (point B) are employed.

✓ Concept Check
What is the effect of unions on wages and employment?

Discrimination in employment The (illegal) unwillingness on the part of employers to hire some group of equally productive workers based on gender, color, religion, or national origin under any circumstances or at the same wage rate.

---

[4] For a discussion of labor unions and their effect on wages, see C. J. Parsley, "Labor Unions' Effects on Wage Gains: A Survey of Recent Literature," *Journal of Economic Literature,* March 1980; R. B. Freeman and J. L. Medoff, *What Do Unions Do?* (New York: Basic Books, 1984); R. Edwards and P. Swaim, "Union-Nonunion Earnings Differentials and the Decline of Private Sector Unionism," *American Economic Review,* May 1986; M. W. Reder, "The Rise and Fall of Unions: The Public Sector and the Private," *Journal of Economic Perspectives,* Spring 1988; and Unions Find the Economy is Tough on Bargeining, "*Well Street Journal,* April 4, 2008, p. B4.

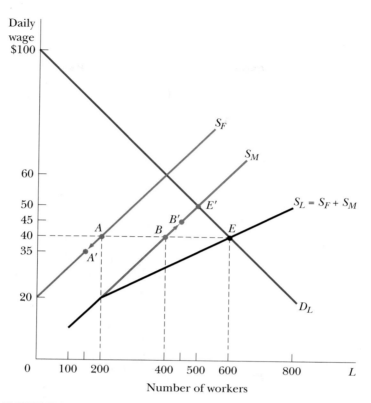

FIGURE 15.9   Effect of Gender Discrimination in Employment
Without discrimination, $w = \$40$ for males and females (given by point E, at which S_L intersects D_L), and 200 females (point A) and 400 males (point B) are employed. If employers refused to hire females, 500 males would be hired at $w = \$50$ (point E', where S_M intersects D_L). Females would have to find employment in other industries, and this would depress wages for all workers in these other industries. With a less extreme form of discrimination, employers may hire females if their wage is, say, $10 less than for males of the same productivity. Employers would then hire 150 females at $w = \$35$ (point A') and 450 males at $w = \$45$ (point B').

However, if employers in the industry refused to hire females, the supply curve of labor to the industry would be only S_M, and 500 male workers would be hired at $w = \$50$ (point E', where S_M intersects D_L). No females would now be hired by the industry. Females would have to find employment in other industries that do not practice gender discrimination, and this would depress wages for all workers in these other industries. Thus, the gains of male workers from gender discrimination in the industry come at the expense of workers (both males and females) in other industries where there is no gender discrimination.

With a less extreme form of gender discrimination against females, employers in the industry may prefer to hire males over females at the same wage rate, but the employers' "taste for discrimination" is not absolute and can be overcome by a sufficiently lower wage for female labor than for male labor. For example, employers may also hire females if the wage of female workers is, say, $10 less than for male workers of the same productivity.

Compared with the no-discrimination case, employers hire more males (and their wages rise) and fewer females (and their wages fall) until the male–female wage difference is $10. In Figure 15.9, employers hire 150 females at $w = \$35$ (point A') and 450 males at $w = \$45$ (point B'), compared with 200 females and 400 males at $40 (points A and B, respectively) without discrimination. Once again, males gain at the expense of females and other employees of this and other industries. The gain is larger the greater is the employers' taste for discrimination in the industry.

If only some employers in the industry discriminated against females, they would employ only male workers while nondiscriminating employers would employ mostly females. If there are enough nondiscriminating employers in the industry to employ all the female workers, no male–female wage differences need arise in the industry. Even if all employers in the industry discriminated against females so that female wages tended to be lower than the wages of male workers, more firms would enter the industry (attracted by the lower female wages), and this, once again, would tend to eliminate gender-based wage differences in the industry. Note that discrimination may also be practiced by employees and by customers. When there is employee discrimination, some workers dislike working with women/minorities. When there is discrimination by customers, some customers dislike buying from women/minorities.

✓ **Concept Check**
What is the effect of discrimination on wages and employment?

AT THE FRONTIER
Discrimination, and Gender and Race Wage Differentials

Table 15.5 shows that in 2005, the median weekly earnings of white females were 80% that of white males (up from 67% in 1985). The median weekly earnings of black males were 75% that of white males (up from 73% in 1985), while the median weekly earnings of black females were 67% that of white males (up from 60% in 1985). Thus, females and blacks earned substantially less than white males in 2007, but the differential diminished over the 1985–2005 period. Male–female wage differentials exist in all occupations indicated and are about of the same order of magnitude as the average difference in overall female–male and black–white differences in earnings.

Empirical studies seem to indicate that most female–male and black–white wage differences are due to differences in productivity based on different levels of education, training, experience, age, hours of work, size of firm, and region of employment. Whether and to what extent the remaining difference is due to discrimination or to other still-unmeasured productivity factors has not yet been settled. The suspicion is that at least part of the unexplained difference is due to discrimination—despite the *Equal Pay Act of 1964,* which prohibits such discrimination.

An empirical study by Francine Blau and Marianne Ferber found that wage discrimination may account for as much as 10–12% of the lower female–male earnings, and occupational discrimination for another 5–9%. Thus, wage and occupational discrimination, together, may account for between 16% and 21% of female–male wage differentials. In addition, Francine Blau and Lawrence Kahn found that if black men had the same productive characteristics of white men, they would receive 89% of white men's earnings. Thus, the upper limit on the effect of race discrimination on black–white earnings differentials is about 11%.

TABLE 15.5	Median Weekly Earnings for Full-Time Workers by Sex and Race in 1985 and 2000 (in dollars)			
	1985	As a Percentage of White Male Earnings	2005	As a Percentage of White Male Earnings
White males	417	100	743	100
White females	281	67	596	80
Black males	304	73	559	75
Black females	252	60	499	67

Source: Department of Commerce, Bureau of Census, *Statistical Abstract of the United States* (Washington, DC: U.S. Government Printing Office, 2007), p. 415.

Comparable worth
The evaluation of jobs in terms of the knowledge and skills required, working conditions, accountability, and the enforcement of equal pay for comparable jobs, or "comparable worth.

To overcome possible discrimination, the **comparable-worth** doctrine proposes the evaluation of jobs in terms of the knowledge and skills required, working conditions, accountability, and the enforcement of equal pay for comparable jobs, or "comparable worth." Many economists, however, consider this too difficult or impossible to do. For example, many of the male–female wage differences are due to fewer work interruptions and longer job tenure for males than for females of equal age and comparable training. Others, however, point out that these work choices themselves are the result of discrimination against females. The major push for comparable worth wages in the United States to date has come from state and local governments, but its effect on female–male wages differences has so far been small.

Sources: G. Becker, *The Economics of Discrimination,* 2nd ed. (Chicago: University of Chicago Press, 1971); F. D. Blau and M. A. Ferber, *The Economics of Men, Women, and Work* (Englewood Cliffs: Prentice-Hall, 1992); F. D. Blau and L. M. Kahn, "Gender Differences in Pay," *Journal of Economic Perspectives,* Fall 2000; F. D. Blau and D. Grutsky, eds., *The Declining Significance & Gender?* (New York: Russell Sage Foundation, 2006); J. L. Hotchkiss and M. Pitts, "The Role of Labor Market Intermittency in Explaining Gender Differentials," *American Economic Review,* May 2007, pp. 417–421; S. Mitra and U. Sambammoorthi, "Disability and the Rural Labor Market in India: Evidence for Males in Tamil Nadu," *World Development,* Vol. 36 (5), 2008, pp. 934–952; F. Welch, "Catching Up: Wages of Black Men," *American Economic Review,* May 2003, pp. 320–325; and P. England, *Comparable Worth: Theory and Evidence* (New York: Aldine DeGruyter, 1993).

SUMMARY

1. A firm that is an imperfect competitor in the product market but a perfect competitor in the input market will maximize profits by hiring any input until the marginal product of the input times the firm's marginal revenue from the commodity equals the price of the input.

2. If only one input is variable and the firm is a monopolist in the product market but a perfect competitor in the input market, the firm's demand curve for the input is given by the marginal revenue product (*MRP*) curve of the input. *MRP* equals the marginal product (*MP*) of the input times the marginal revenue (*MR*) from the commodity. The excess of an input's *VMP*

over *MRP* at the level of utilization of the input is called monopolistic exploitation. When all inputs are variable, the demand curve of an input is obtained by points on different *MRP* curves of the input and will be more elastic than the *MRP* curves. A perfect competitor in an input market will employ the input until the input's *MRP* on its demand curve equals the input price.

3. When all firms hiring an input are monopolists in their respective product markets, the market demand curve of the input is obtained by the straightforward horizontal summation of all the firms' demand curves for the input. On the other hand, when the firms are oligopolists or monopolistic competitors in the product market, the market demand curve of the input is derived as in Section 14.3. The equilibrium price and employment of the input are then determined at the intersection of the market demand and the market supply curve of the input.

4. Monopsony refers to the case where there is a single buyer of an input. The monopsonist faces the positively sloped market supply curve of the input so that its marginal expenditures on the input exceeds the price of the input. Oligopsonists and monopsonistic competitors must also pay higher prices to hire more units of an input. Monopsony arises when an input is much more productive to a particular firm or use than to other firms or uses. It can also result from lack of geographic or occupational mobility.

5. A monopsonist hiring a single variable input maximizes profits by hiring the input until the marginal revenue product (*MRP*) of the input equals the marginal expenditure (*ME*) on the input. The price of the input is then determined by the corresponding point on the market supply curve of the input. A monopsonist hires less of the variable input and pays the input a lower price than would a perfectly competitive firm in the input market. The excess of the *MRP* over the price of the input at the point where *MRP* = *ME* is called monopsonistic exploitation.

6. To maximize profits a firm should hire any variable input until the marginal revenue product of the input equals the marginal expenditure on hiring it. If the firm is a perfect competitor in the product market, the marginal revenue product of the input is identical to the value of the marginal product of the input. If the firm is a perfect competitor in the input market, the marginal expenditure on the input equals the input price.

7. Immigration usually increases the earnings of capital and reduces those of labor. Since the former usually exceeds the latter, however, the nation of immigration as a whole receives a net gain. The emigration of skilled labor and professionals represents a brain drain on the nation of emigration and an even greater gain for the nation of immigration.

8. Monopsonistic exploitation can be eliminated by the government setting the minimum price of an input at the point where the *MRP* curve intersects the market supply curve of the input. Bilateral monopoly occurs when the monopsonist buyer of a product or input faces the monopolist seller of the product or input. Unions seem to have increased wages only slightly. Among the most important goals of unions are higher wages and greater employment of union labor. Discrimination in employment reduces the wages and/or the employment of the discriminated category. The marginal resource cost of an input is related to the price of the input and the price elasticity of the input supply.

KEY TERMS

Marginal revenue product (*MRP*)
Monopolistic exploitation
Monopsony
Marginal expenditure (*ME*)
Marginal expenditure on labor (*ME_L*)

Marginal expenditure on capital (*ME_K*)
Oligopsony
Monopsonistic competition
Monopsonistic exploitation
Brain drain

Bilateral monopoly
Labor union
Discrimination in employment
Comparable worth

REVIEW QUESTIONS

1. Why is the demand curve for an input less elastic when the firm is an imperfect rather than a perfect competitor in the product market?

2. Why are real average wages higher in the United States than in most other countries? Why have real wages in Germany and Japan been catching up with U.S. wages during the period after World War II?

3. Can a demand curve for an input be derived for a monopsonist? Why?

4. Monopsonistic exploitation is true exploitation while monopolistic exploitation is not. True or false? Explain.

5. What is the general rule for a firm to maximize profits in hiring an input? What does the rule become when the firm is a perfect competitor in the product market and/or in the input market?

6. A firm that is a perfect competitor in the product market hires more labor than a firm that is an imperfect competitor in the product market, everything else being equal. True or false? Explain.

7. How does immigration benefit the United States?

8. What trade alternative can the United States use to slow down the inflow of illegal aliens from Mexico?

9. Why are wages and employment indeterminate when a monopsonistic employer faces a monopolistic union?

10. Why might unionization in some industries lead to lower wages in other industries?

11. What are some of the ways by which labor unions can increase and reduce labor productivity?

12. What are the difficulties in establishing the existence and measuring the extent of discrimination in a labor market?

PROBLEMS

1. For a firm that is a monopolist in the product market but a perfect competitor in the input market, express the condition prevailing if the firm

   a. utilizes too much labor or too little capital at the best output level. What is the graphic interpretation of this?

   b. utilizes the least-cost input combination but with its marginal cost exceeding its MR. What is the graphic interpretation of this?

   c. minimizes the cost of producing an output that is too small to maximize profits. What is the graphic interpretation of this?

2. You are given the following data where L is the number of workers hired per day by a firm (the only variable input), Q_X is the quantity of the commodity produced per day, and P_X is the commodity price:

L	1	2	3	4	5
Q_X	10	20	28	34	38
P_X	$5.00	4.50	4.00	3.50	3.00

   a. Find the marginal revenue product of labor and plot it.

   b. How many workers per day will the firm hire if the wage rate is $40 per day? $22? $7? What is the firm's demand curve for labor?

*3. From Table 15.1 in the text

   a. find the MR_X, the MRP_L by multiplying MR_X by MP_L, and the VMP_L.

   b. Plot on the same graph, the VMP_L and the MRP_L on the assumption that labor is infinitesimally divisible. How many workers would the firm employ if it were a perfect competitor in the product market? What is the amount of monopolistic exploitation?

4. Repeat the procedure in Problem 3 for the data in Problem 2 and on the assumption that the daily wage is $22.

5. Assume that (1) labor is infinitesimally divisible (i.e., workers can be hired for any part of the day) in the production function of Problems 2 and 4, (2) all inputs are variable, and (3) when the wage rate falls from $40 to $22 per day, the firm's value of the marginal product curve shifts to the right by two labor units. Derive the demand curve for labor of this firm. How many workers will the firm hire per day at the daily wage rate of $22?

6. a. Derive the market demand curve for labor if there are 100 monopolistically competitive firms identical to the firm of Problem 5 in the labor market and each individual firm's demand curve for labor shifts to the left by one unit when the wage rate falls from $w = $40 to $w = $22 per day.

   b. If 200 workers are willing to work at the daily wage of $10, and 600 are willing to work at the daily wage of $40, what is the equilibrium wage and level of

_____
* = Answer provided at end of book.

employment? How many workers would each firm hire at the equilibrium wage?

7. a. From the following market supply schedule of labor faced by a monopsonist, derive the firm's marginal expenditures on labor schedule.

L	1	2	3	4	5
w	$10	11	16	40	100

b. Plot on the same set of axes the firm's supply and marginal expenditures on labor schedules.

8. On your graph for Problem 7(b), superimpose the monopsonist's value of marginal product and marginal revenue product of labor curves from Problem 4. Assuming that labor is the only variable input, determine the number of workers that the firm hires, the wage rate, and the amount of monopolistic and monopsonistic exploitation if the firm is a monopolist in the product market and a monopsonist in the input market.

*9. Starting with Figure 15.4, explain what happens if the government sets the minimum wage at

a. $35.

b. $50.

*10. Assume that all workers in a town belong to the union and there is a single firm hiring labor in the town. Suppose that the supply for labor function of the firm (a monopsonist) is $S_L = 2w$ (where w refers to wages, measured in dollars per day) and the demand of labor function by the union (the monopolist seller of labor time) is $D_L = 120 - 2w$. Find the wage rate and number of workers that the firm would like to hire and the wage and level of employment that the union would seek if it behaved as a monopolist. What is the likely result?

*11. Draw a figure showing that an increase in union wages usually reduces employment in unionized industries and increases employment and lowers wages in nonunionized industries.

12. Given that (1) $ME_L = w(1 + 1/\epsilon_L)$ where ϵ_L is the price (wage) elasticity of the supply curve of labor (this formula is derived in Section A.15 of the Mathematical Appendix), and (2) S_L is a straight line through the origin, find the value of ME_L if

a. $w = \$40$.

b. $w = \$80$.

INTERNET SITE ADDRESSES

A wealth of information on labor markets (employment, unemployment, productivity, earnings and others) is provided by the Bureau of Labor Statistics at:

http://stats.bls.gov

For the shortage of engineers in the United States, see:

http://www.edn.com/article/CA529820.html

http://www.cato.org/pubs/regulation/regv29n3/v29n3-2.pdf

http://www.physorg.com/news94979949.html

For the licensing of occupations, see:

http://www.upjohninst.org/publications/newsletter/MK_106.pdf

http://www.reason.org/ps361.pdf

For the pay of top executives, see:

http://www.faireconomy.org/reports/2007/ExecutiveExcess2007.pdf

http://www.bls.gov/oco/ocos012.htm

The effect of immigration on labor markets is examined at:

http://www.immigration-usa.com/debate.html

http://borderbattles.ssrc.org/Carter_Sutch/

On the economic effect of labor unions, see:

http://en.wikipedia.org/wiki/Trade_union

http://www.epinet.org/content.cfm/briefingpapers_bp143

http://www.becker-posner-blog.com/archives/2007/10/the_decline_of_1.html

Antidiscrimination laws and the effect of discrimination in labor markets are found at:

http://www.journals.uchicago.edu/JLE/journal/issues/v48n1/480105/480105.web.pdf

http://www.bu.edu/econ/faculty/manove/DiscrimOnlineVersion.pdf

http://www.washingtonpost.com/wp-dyn/content/article/2006/07/07/AR2006070701105.html

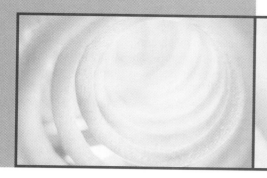

CHAPTER 16

Financial Microeconomics: Interest, Investment, and the Cost of Capital

After Studying This Chapter, You Should Be Able to:

- Know how an individual can maximize satisfaction by borrowing or lending
- Know how the market rate of interest is determined
- Know the meaning of capital budgeting
- Understand how a firm estimates the cost of capital to invest
- Understand the meaning and importance of investment in human capital

I n this chapter, we consider intertemporal choices or the optimal allocation of resources *over time*. We examine the choice between consuming now or saving a portion of this year's income in order to consume more in the future. The alternative is borrowing against future income to increase present consumption. An individual's ability to exchange present income for future income or consumption (by lending or borrowing) enables the individual to maximize the total or joint satisfaction of present and future income and consumption. For example, people save during their working lives to provide for retirement, and by doing so, they maximize the lifetime satisfaction from their earnings. On the other hand, students often borrow against their future income (i.e., they dissave).

Another way by which present income can be exchanged for future income is to free some resources from the production of final commodities for present consumption (i.e., save) to produce more capital goods (i.e., invest in machinery, factories, and so on), which will lead to larger output and consumption in the future. The ability of individuals and firms to trade present for future income and output and vice versa (through lending and borrowing, saving and investing) is crucial in all societies. Indeed, a great deal of the increase in the standards of living in modern societies is the result of investments in physical capital (machinery, factories, etc.) and human capital (education, skills, health, and so on).

An individual usually requires a reward for postponing present consumption (i.e., saving) and lending a portion of this year's income. The reward takes the form of a repayment that exceeds the amount lent. This premium is the interest payment. The alternative would be the borrowing of a given sum today and the repaying of a larger sum in the future (the principal plus the interest). Similarly, individuals and firms will only invest in machinery, factories, or in acquiring or providing skills if they can expect a return on their investment in the form of higher future incomes or outputs than the amounts invested.

In this chapter, we examine the determination of the rate of interest that will balance the quantity of resources lent and borrowed and that equilibrates saving and investment. We also analyze the criteria used by individuals, business firms, and government agencies in their investment decisions. Subsequently, we discuss the reasons for differences in interest rates in the same nation, in different nations, and over time. The chapter also explains how to measure the cost of capital and describes the effects of foreign investments. Since capital is a crucial input, its cost is very important to a firm's production decisions. Finally, several important applications of the theory introduced in the chapter are presented. These range from investment in human capital to the pricing and management of renewable and nonrenewable resources. These applications, together with the numerous examples and the "At the Frontier" section on derivatives, add an important element of realism to the analysis.

16.1   LENDING–BORROWING EQUILIBRIUM

In this section, we examine how an individual maximizes the total or joint satisfaction from spending his or her present and future income by lending or borrowing. We also show how the equilibrium market rate of interest is determined at the level at which the total quantity demanded of loans (borrowings) equals the total quantity supplied of loans (lendings).

Lending

We begin by considering how a consumer can maximize satisfaction over time by lending. For simplicity, we assume that the consumer's income is measured in terms of the quantity of a commodity (say, corn) that he or she has or expects to receive. Also, to simplify matters, we will deal with only two time periods: this year and the next year. (This assumption is relaxed in Section 16.3.) We also begin by assuming that the consumer has an **endowment position,** or receives $Y_0 = 7.5$ units of corn this year and $Y_1 = 3$ units of corn next year (point A in the left panel of Figure 16.1).[1]

Endowment position The quantity of a commodity that the consumer receives in each year.

---
[1] Uncertainty is ruled out here so that the consumer knows exactly how much of the commodity he or she gets this year and next year. This assumption is relaxed in Section 16.4. In what follows, subscripts 0 and 1 denote, respectively, this year (or the present) and next year (or the future).

The consumer, however, is not bound to consume the $Y_0 = 7.5$ units of corn this year and the $Y_1 = 3$ units of corn next year, because he or she can lend part of this year's corn or borrow against next year's corn. The question is how should the consumer distribute consumption between this year and next so as to maximize the total or joint satisfaction over the two periods? This is analogous to the consumer's choice between hamburgers (commodity X) and soft drinks (commodity Y) examined in Section 3.5 and Figure 3.8. The only difference is that here the choice is between the consumption of corn this year or consumption the next.

In the left panel of Figure 16.1, the consumer's tastes between consumption this year and next are given by indifference curves U_1, U_2, and U_3. The consumer also faces budget line FW_0. The latter shows the various combinations of present and future income and consumption available to the consumer. Starting from endowment position A ($Y_0 = 7.5$ and $Y_1 = 3$), the consumer can lend part of this year's corn endowment so that he or she will consume less this year and more next year. This is represented by an upward movement from point A along budget line FW_0. On the other hand, the consumer could increase consumption this year by borrowing against next year's endowment or income by moving downward from point A along FW_0.

The consumer maximizes satisfaction by reaching the highest indifference curve possible with his or her budget line. The optimal choice is given by point E, where budget line FW_0 is tangent to indifference curve U_2. At point E, the individual consumes

✓ Concept Check
How can a consumer maximize satisfaction over time by lending part of this year's income?

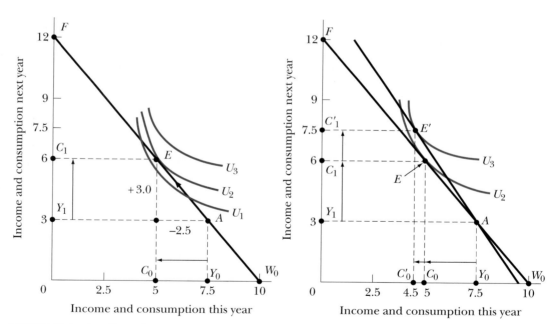

FIGURE 16.1   Lending   Starting from endowment A ($Y_0 = 7.5$ and $Y_1 = 3$), the consumer maximizes satisfaction at point E, where the budget line FW_0 is tangent to indifference curve U_2 in the left panel. The consumer reaches point E by lending $Y_0 - C_0 = 2.5$ units from this year's endowment and receiving 3 additional units next year. Thus, the slope of the budget line is $3/(-2.5) = -1.2$, or $-1(1 + 0.2)$, and the interest rate $r = 0.2$, or 20%. At $r = 50\%$, the optimal point is E' (in the right panel), where the steeper budget line through point A is tangent to indifference curve U_3. Point E' is reached by lending 3 units (instead of 2.5).

$C_0 = 5$ units of corn this year and $C_1 = 6$ units next year (see the left panel of Figure 16.1). The consumer reaches point E by lending $Y_0 - C_0 = 2.5$ units of corn out of this year's endowment or output and by receiving 3 additional units next year.

The slope of the budget line gives the premium or the rate of interest that the lender receives. For example, the movement from point A to point E indicates that the consumer receives 3 units of the commodity next year by lending 2.5 units this year. Thus, the slope of the budget line is $3/(-2.5) = -1.2$, or $-1(1 + 0.2)$, so the interest rate $r = 0.2$, or 20%. That is,

$$\frac{C_1 - Y_1}{C_0 - Y_0} = -(1 + r) = -(1 + 0.2) \qquad [16.1]$$

The negative sign reflects the downward-to-the-right inclination of the budget line. This simply means that for the consumer to be able to consume more next year, he or she will have to consume less this year. In this case, the consumer lends (i.e., reduces consumption by) 2.5 units this year and gets $2.5(1 + 0.2) = 3$ next year. If the consumer lends all of this year's income or endowment of $Y_0 = 7.5$ units at 20% interest, he or she will receive $7.5(1 + 0.2) = 9$ additional units next year (and reach point F on budget line FW_0). The consumer could do this, but does not, because he or she would not be maximizing satisfaction.

Rate of interest
(r) The premium received in one year for lending one dollar this year.

Returning to the slope of the budget line, we can say more generally that the **rate of interest (r)** is the premium received by an individual next year by lending $1.00 today. Another way of stating this is that the rate of interest is the excess in the price next year (P_1) of $1.00 this year (P_0). That is,

$$P_1 = P_0(1 + r) \qquad [16.2]$$

The individual receives $(\$1)(1 + r)$ next year (P_1) by lending $1.00 this year (P_0). If the interest rate r is 0.2, or 20%, the individual receives $(\$1)(1 + 0.2) = \$1.20$ next year by lending $1.00 this year. Of course, the person who borrows $1.00 today must repay $1.20 next year if the rate of interest is 20%. Thus, the interest rate can be viewed as the excess in the price next year of $1.00 lent or borrowed this year.

If the interest rate rises (i.e., if the budget line becomes steeper), lenders will usually lend more. For example, starting with endowment position A in the right panel of Figure 16.1, if the interest rate rises to 50% so that the slope of the budget line becomes $-(1 + 0.5)$, the optimal choice of the consumer is at point E', where the new steeper budget line through point A is tangent to higher indifference curve U_3. The consumer can reach point E' by lending $Y_0 - C_0' = 3$ units (instead of 2.5), for which he or she receives $C_1' - Y_1 = 4.5$ units next year. That is, by lending 3 units at 50% interest, the consumer receives $3(1 + 0.5) = 4.5$ units next year. Thus, the increase in the rate of interest from 20% to 50% leads this individual (the lender) to increase lending from 2.5 to 3 units.[2]

---

[2] The increase in the rate of interest will usually, but not always, increase the amount of lending. The reason is that (as in the case of an increase in the wage rate), an increase in the rate of interest gives rise to a substitution effect and an income effect. According to the substitution effect, the increase in the rate of interest leads the individual to lend more. However, by increasing the future income of the individual, the increase in the rate of interest also gives rise to an income effect, which leads the individual to lend less. At a sufficiently high rate of interest, the negative income effect exceeds the positive substitution effect and the individual's supply curve of loans bends backward. This is examined in Problem 5(a), with the answer at the end of the text.

Borrowing

We will now show that if the endowment position of the consumer in the left panel of Figure 16.1 had been to the left of point E on budget line FW_0 (rather than at point A), the consumer would have been a borrower rather than a lender. This is shown in the left panel of Figure 16.2. Specifically, suppose the endowment position of the consumer had been at point B ($Y_0 = 2.5$ and $Y_1 = 9$) on budget line FW_0. The consumer would maximize satisfaction at point E ($C_0 = 5$ and $C_1 = 6$), where budget line FW_0 is tangent to indifference curve U_2 (the highest the consumer can reach with budget line FW_0). To reach point E, the consumer would have to borrow $C_0 - Y_0 = 2.5$ units of the commodity this year and repay $Y_1 - C_1 = 3$ units next year.

Since $3/2.5 = 1.2$, the rate of interest $r = 0.2$, or 20%, as in the lending example. This means that in order to borrow 2.5 units this year, the individual must repay 3 units next year if the market rate of interest is 20%. That is, $2.5 = 3/(1 + 0.2)$. The reason for this is that 2.5 units this year will grow to 3 units next year at $r = 0.2$, or 20%. More generally, we can say that the price of $1.00 today ($P_0$) is equal to $1.00 next year ($P_1$) divided by $(1 + r)$. That is,

$$P_0 = P_1/(1 + r) \qquad\qquad [16.3]$$

This is obtained by dividing both sides of equation [16.2] by $(1 + r)$. For example, at $r = 20\%$, $1.00 next year is equivalent to $1/(1 + 0.2) = $0.83 this year, because $0.83 lent this year at 20% will grow to $1.00 next year.

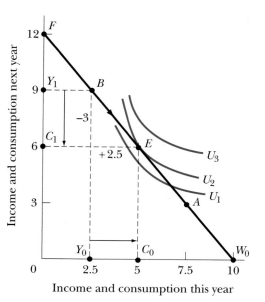
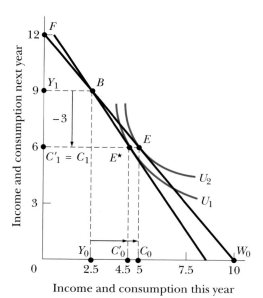

FIGURE 16.2   Borrowing   Starting from endowment B ($Y_0 = 2.5$ and $Y_1 = 9$), the consumer maximizes satisfaction at point E, where budget line FW_0 is tangent to indifference curve U_2 in the left panel. The consumer reaches point E by borrowing $C_0 - Y_0 = 2.5$ and repaying $Y_1 - C_1 = 3$ next year. Thus, the slope of the budget line is $-3/2 = -1.2$, or $-1(1 + 0.2)$, and the interest rate $r = 0.2$, or 20%. At $r = 50\%$, the optimal point is E^* in the right panel, where the steeper budget line through point B is tangent to indifference curve U_1. Point E^* is reached by borrowing 2 units (instead of 2.5).

Wealth The individual's income this year plus the present value of future income.

If the individual borrowed all of next year's income of $Y_1 = 9$, he or she could increase consumption this year by $\$9/(1 + 0.2) = 7.5$ and be at point $W_0 = 10$. Point $W_0 = 10$ gives the **wealth** of the individual. This is equal to the individual's income or endowment this year plus the present value of next year's income or endowment. That is, the consumer's wealth is given by

$$W_0 = Y_0 + [Y_1/(1 + r)] \qquad\qquad [16.4]$$

In our example, the income this year is $Y_0 = 2.5$ and the present value of next year's income is $Y_1/(1 + r) = 9/(1 + 0.2) = 7.5$, resulting in the individual's wealth of 10. Graphically, the wealth of the individual or consumer is given by the intersection of the budget line with the horizontal axis. Thus, wealth plays the same role in intertemporal choice as the consumer's income plays in the consumer's choice between two commodities during the same year. An increase in wealth, like an increase in income, will shift the consumer's budget line outward and allows the consumer to purchase more of every normal good or to consume more, both this year and next.

An increase in the rate of interest leads to a reduction in the amount the individual wants to borrow. Since present consumption becomes more expensive in terms of the future consumption that must be given up, the borrower will borrow less. This is shown in the right panel of Figure 16.2. Starting once again with endowment position B in the right panel of Figure 16.2, an increase in the rate of interest to 50% will result in a new budget line with a slope of $-(1 + 0.5)$. The optimal choice of the consumer is then at point E^*, where the steeper budget line through point B is tangent to lower indifference curve U_1. Indifference curve U_1 is the highest that the consumer can reach with his or her initial endowment position B and $r = 50\%$. To reach point E^* ($C'_0 = 4.5$ and $C'_1 = C_1 = 6$), the consumer will have to borrow $C'_0 - Y_0 = 2$ units (instead of 2.5) this year, and will have to repay $Y_1 - C'_1 = 3$ units next year. That is, $2 = 3/(1 + 0.5)$. Thus, the increase in the rate of interest from 20% to 50% leads this individual to borrow less.[3]

The Market Rate of Interest with Borrowing and Lending

We now examine how the equilibrium rate of interest is determined in the market for borrowing and lending. For simplicity, we assume that we have only two individuals in the market for loans: individual B with endowment position B and individual A with endowment position A on budget line FW_0 (see the left panel of Figure 16.2). That is, instead of assuming as above that an individual has either endowment B (and is a borrower) or endowment A (and is a lender), we now assume that we have two individuals, one with endowment B (the borrower) and the other with endowment A (the lender) on FW_0. We also assume for now that both individuals have the same tastes or time preferences for present (this year) versus future (next year) consumption, as shown by indifference curves U_1, U_2, and U_3 in the left panel of Figure 16.2.

As we can see from the left panel of Figure 16.2, the optimal choice for individual B is to move from point B to point E along budget line FW_0 by borrowing 2.5 units of the commodity this year at the rate of interest of 0.20, or 20% (so he or she will have to repay 3 units

---

[3] As opposed to the supply curve of loans, which could bend backward at a sufficiently high rate of interest, the demand curve for loans is always negatively sloped (see Problem 5(b), with the answer at the end of the text).

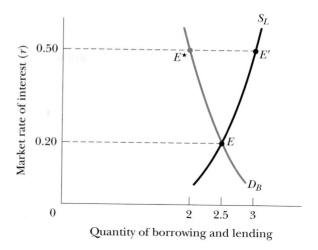

FIGURE 16.3   Borrowing-Lending Equilibrium
Borrowing-lending equilibrium occurs at point E, where the demand curve for borrowing (D_B) intersects the supply curve for lending (S_L). Point E shows that $r = 20\%$ and 2.5 units are borrowed and lent. At $r = 50\%$, the quantity supplied of lending of 3 units (point E') exceeds the quantity demanded of borrowing of 2 units (point E^*) and the interest rate falls to 20% (point E). The opposite is true at r lower than 20%.

next year). Thus, the quantity demanded of loans (borrowing) by individual B is 2.5 units at $r = 20\%$. On the other hand, the optimal choice of individual A is to move from point A to point E along budget line FW_0 by lending 2.5 units of the commodity this year at the rate of interest of 0.20 or 20% (so that he or she will receive an additional 3 units next year). Thus, the quantity supplied of loans (lending) by individual A is 2.5 units at $r = 20\%$.

Since we have assumed that A and B are the only two individuals in the market, the equilibrium market rate of interest is 0.20 or 20%. This is the only market rate of interest at which the desired quantity demanded of loans (borrowing) of 2.5 units equals the desired quantity supplied of loans (lending) of 2.5 units, and the market for loanable funds is in equilibrium. This is shown by point E in Figure 16.3, where the demand curve for borrowing (D_B) intersects the supply curve for lending (S_L). The figure also shows that at $r = 50\%$, individual B wants to borrow only 2 units (point E^* on D_B, from the right panel of Figure 16.2) and individual A wants to lend 3 units (point E' on D_L, from the right panel of Figure 16.1). The resulting excess in the quantity supplied over the quantity demanded of loans of 1 unit (E^*E') at $r = 50\%$ causes the rate of interest to fall to the equilibrium level of $r = 20\%$ (point E).

In the above analysis, we have assumed for simplicity that there are only two individuals, A and B, in the market and that both have identical tastes or time preferences.[4] In the real world, however, there are many individuals with different tastes. Yet, the process by which the equilibrium market rate of interest is determined is basically the same. That is, the equilibrium market rate of interest is the one at which the total or aggregate quantity demanded of borrowing matches the aggregate quantity supplied of lending. At a market rate of interest above the equilibrium rate, the supply of lending exceeds the demand for borrowing and the interest rate falls. On the other hand, at a market rate of interest below the equilibrium rate, the demand for borrowing exceeds the supply of lending and the market rate of interest rises toward equilibrium. Only at the equilibrium market rate of interest does the quantity demanded match the quantity supplied and there is no tendency for the interest rate to change. Example 16–1 gives examines data on personal savings and disposable personal income in the United States.

✓ Concept Check
How is the market rate of interest determined with borrowing and lending only?

───────────────

[4] The determination of the market rate of interest when consumers have different time preferences is examined in Problem 4 (with the answer at the end of the text).

EXAMPLE 16–1

Personal Savings in the United States

Table 16.1 shows the total aggregate amount of personal savings (PS), the level of disposable (i.e., after-tax) personal income (DPI) in 2000 prices, and PS as a percentage of DPI in the United States for selected years from 1960 to 2006. Personal savings was $128.6 billion in 1960; it rose to a high of $386.7 billion in 1980 and fell to a low of $33.8 billion in 2006. As a percentage of GDP, personal savings was 7.3 in 1960, it rose to 10.0 in 1980, and it was 0.4 in 2006. Americans are now dissaving.

TABLE 16.1	Personal Savings and Disposable Personal Income (in billions of 2000 dollars)		
Year	PS	DPI	PS as a % of DPI
1960	$128.6	$1,759.7	7.3
1970	262.8	2,781.7	9.4
1980	386.7	3,857.7	10.0
1990	371.9	5,324.2	7.0
1995	274.0	5,905.7	4.6
2000	168.5	7,194.0	2.3
2002	178.4	7,562.2	2.4
2004	167.6	8,008.9	2.1
2005	40.0	8,147.9	0.5
2006	33.8	8,396.9	0.4

Source: Council of Economic Advisors, *Economic Report of the President* (Washington, DC: U.S. Government Printing Office, 2008), pp. 262–263.

Prior to the establishment of Social Security in 1935, individuals provided for their retirement by voluntarily saving a portion of their earnings during their working years. Social Security provided retirement income through a forced savings (Social Security tax) program, thus reducing the need for personal savings. If the government had saved the Social Security taxes it levied, net savings (personal plus government) would have been more or less unchanged. Because the government chose not to "fund" the system but to use Social Security taxes for current expenditures and pay future Social Security benefits out of future taxes, the nation's level of aggregate savings declined. Michael Darby estimated that the Social Security program reduced the nation's savings by 5% to 20% in the 1970s (and by much more in the 1990s).

Source: Michael R. Darby, *The Effects of Social Security on Income and Capital Stock* (Washington, DC: American Enterprise Institute, 1979).

16.2		## SAVING–INVESTMENT EQUILIBRIUM

In Section 16.1 we analyzed borrowing–lending equilibrium. For simplicity, we assumed that no part of the current endowment or output was invested to increase future productive capacity. In this section, we begin with the opposite situation and examine saving–investment equilibrium without borrowing or lending. That is, we begin by examining the case in which an isolated individual (a Robinson Crusoe) consumes less than he or she produces in this period (saves) in order to have more seeds, or to produce a piece of equipment, to increase production in the next period (invests). Next, we relax the assumption that the individual is isolated and that he or she cannot borrow or lend and examine saving–investment equilibrium with borrowing and lending. Finally, we show how the equilibrium rate of interest is determined with saving and investment and with borrowing and lending.

Saving–Investment Equilibrium Without Borrowing and Lending

Production-possibilities curve
Shows the alternative combinations of commodities that a nation can produce by fully utilizing all of its resources with the best technology available to it.

Saving Refraining from present consumption.

Investment The formation of new capital assets.

Suppose that an individual lives alone on an island and produces and consumes a single commodity. This Robinson Crusoe has no possibility to borrow or lend (or trade) the commodity and can only consume what he produces. Suppose that under present conditions he can count on producing $Y_0 = 7.5$ units of the commodity during this year and $Y_1 = 3$ units next year. This is shown by point A on the production-possibilities curve FQ in Figure 16.4.

Production-possibilities curve FQ shows how much Crusoe can produce and consume next year by saving part of this year's output and investing it to increase next year's output. **Saving** refers to the act of refraining from present consumption. **Investment** refers to the formation of new capital assets. For example, Crusoe may use part of the year to construct a rudimentary net rather than catch fish with a spear. Since he is not catching fish while he is building the net, he is refraining from present consumption (saving). The net is an investment that will allow him to catch more fish in the future. In this case, the saving and the investment are done by the same person, and are one and the same thing.

Disregarding for the moment the indifference curves in Figure 16.4, we see that the FQ curve shows that if the individual consumes $C_0 = 6$ units of the commodity this year, he can produce and consume $C_1 = 6.5$ units of the commodity next year (point G on FQ). Starting from point A, this means that by saving and investing $Y_0 - C_0 = 7.5 - 6 = 1.5$ units of the commodity this year, the individual can increase output by $C_1 - Y_1 = 6.5 - 3 = 3.5$ units next year. Thus, the average yield or return on investment (in terms of next year's output) is $3.5/1.5 = 2.33 = (1 + 1.33)$, or 133%. Should the individual save and invest 3 units of the commodity this year, his output will increase by 6 units next year (the movement from point A to point H on FQ), so that the average yield or rate of return would be $6/3 = 2 = (1 + 1)$, or 100%. Note that the larger the amount invested, the lower the rate of return (because of the operation of the law of diminishing returns).

Starting at point A on production-possibilities curve FQ, the question is, "What is the optimal amount of saving and investment for this individual?" The answer is 1.5 units. The reason is that this will permit the individual to reach point G on indifference curve U_4. Indifference curve U_4 is the highest that Crusoe can reach with his production-possibilities curve. Note that indifference curves here show the trade-off or time preference between consumption this year and next. Thus, starting from point A, Crusoe should

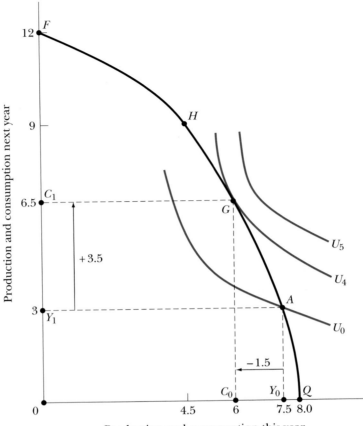

FIGURE 16.4   Saving-Investment Equilibrium Without Borrowing or Lending   Production-possibilities curve *FQ* shows how much an isolated individual can produce and consume next year by saving and investing part of this year's output. Starting at point *A* on *FQ*, the optimal level of saving and investment is 1.5 units. This level allows the individual to reach point *G* on the highest indifference curve possible (U_4). Saving and investing 1.5 units this year allows the individual to produce and consume 3.5 more units next year. Thus, the average yield on investment is 133%.

save and invest 1.5 units of this year's output so as to reach point *G* next year and maximize his total or joint utility or satisfaction over the two years.

Saving–Investment Equilibrium with Borrowing and Lending

Suppose that more people get stranded on Crusoe's island, and they also start producing and consuming the commodity. Now, borrowing and lending become possible. The optimal choice for Crusoe is now to save and invest, borrow or lend, so as to reach the highest indifference curve possible (higher than U_4).

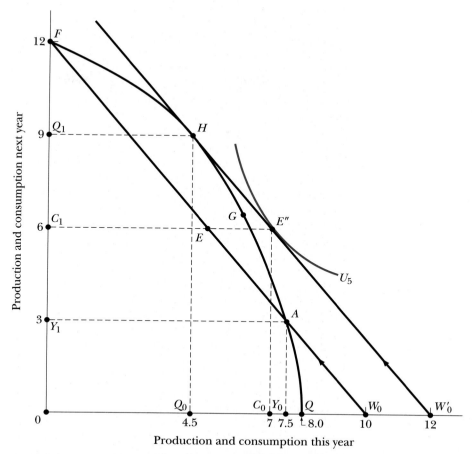

FIGURE 16.5 **Saving-Investment Equilibrium with Borrowing and Lending** Starting from point A, the individual maximizes wealth (at $W_0' = 12$ units) by investing 3 units of the commodity and reaching point H, where market line $HE''W_0'$ (with slope reflecting the market rate of interest) is tangent to production-possibilities curve FQ. The individual then borrows 2.5 units (i.e., moves to the right of point H on market line $HE''W_0'$) and reaches point E'' on U_5 (the highest indifference curve possible). The individual invests 3 units, borrows 2.5, and saves 0.5.

Market line A line from any point on the production-possibilities curve showing the various amounts of a commodity that the individual can consume in each period by borrowing or lending.

To show this, we must realize that from every point of the production-possibilities curve there is a **market line,** the slope of which shows the rate at which the individual (Crusoe) can borrow or lend in the market. For example, starting at point A on the FQ curve in Figure 16.5, the individual can borrow or lend along market line FAW_0 at the rate of interest of $r = 20\%$ (as in the left panel of Figures 16.1 and 16.2). If starting from point A the individual only borrows or lends (or does neither), his wealth is $W_0 = 10$ (given by the intersection of market line FAW_0 with the horizontal axis).

However, with the possibility of saving and investment, and borrowing or lending now open, the optimal choice for Crusoe is to invest first (so as to maximize wealth) and then to borrow (so as to reach the highest indifference curve possible). Wealth is maximized by reaching the highest market line (with slope reflecting the market rate of interest) that is possible with the FQ curve. This is given by market line $HE''W_0'$, which is parallel to market line FAW_0 (so that $r = 20\%$) and tangent to production-possibilities curve FQ at point H. Market line $HE''W_0'$ shows that the maximum attainable wealth is $W_0' = 12$. Starting from point A on the FQ curve, the individual can attain market line $HE''W_0'$ and maximize wealth by investing $Y_0 - Q_0 = 3$ units of this year's output. This allows him to reach point H on this production-possibilities curve and produce $Q_1 = 9$ units of the commodity next year.

Having attained the highest wealth possible by investing 3 units of the commodity (point H on market line $HE''W_0'$), the individual can then borrow $C_0 - Q_0 = 2.5$ units (i.e., move to the right of point H on market line $HE''W_0'$) and reach point E'' on U_5. This is the highest indifference curve that the individual can reach with optimal investment and borrowing. Point E'' on indifference curve U_5 is superior to point A on U_0 (see Figure 16.4) without borrowing or investing, it is superior to borrowing alone (to the right of point A along budget line FEW_0), and it is superior to point G on U_4 (see Figure 16.4) with saving equal to investment and no borrowing.

To summarize, the optimal choice of the individual is to invest $Y_0 - Q_0 = 3$ units (i.e., to move from point A to point H on the FQ curve) in order to maximize wealth (at $W_0' = 12$) and to borrow $C_0 - Q_0 = 2.5$ units (the movement from point H to point E'' on indifference curve U_5) to maximize total or joint satisfaction or utility over both years. Of the total amount of $Y_0 - Q_0 = 3$ invested, the individual borrows $C_0 - Q_0 = 2.5$ and saves $Y_0 - C_0 = 0.5$. That is, the individual is saving a portion of his current output, but not enough to "finance" all of his investment. Therefore, other individuals must be saving 2.5 units of the commodity more than they invest in order to lend this amount to our individual.

If the market rate of interest rises above $r = 20\%$, the market line becomes steeper and tangent to production-possibilities curve FQ to the right of point H, and the individual will invest less (see Figure 16.6 and Problem 6). If the individual borrows more than he invests, he will be dissaving (see Problem 7). If indifference curve U_5 had been tangent to market line HW_0' to the left of point H in Figure 16.5, the individual would have been investing and lending (rather than investing and borrowing) so that his saving would equal the sum of the two (see Problem 8).

The Market Rate of Interest with Saving and Investment, Borrowing and Lending

We now examine how the equilibrium rate of interest is determined in the market with saving and investment and borrowing and lending. For simplicity, we assume that only our individual, borrows and invests while all other individuals collectively only want to lend 2.5 units of the commodity at the rate of interest of $r = 20\%$. The equilibrium rate of interest is then 20% and is shown in Figure 16.6 in two different ways: (1) by point E, where the demand curve of borrowing of our individual (D_B) intersects the supply curve of lending of all other individuals (S_L) as in Figure 16.3, or equivalently, (2) by point E'', where the demand curve for investment of our individual (D_I) intersects the total supply curve of savings of this and other individuals (S_S).

At the equilibrium market rate of interest of $r = 20\%$, the quantity of desired borrowing of 2.5 units (done exclusively by our individual) equals the quantity of desired lending of 2.5 units (supplied by all other individuals). In addition, at $r = 20\%$, the total amount of desired savings of 3 units (2.5 units by other individuals and 0.5 units by our individual) matches the desired level of investment of 3 units (undertaken exclusively by

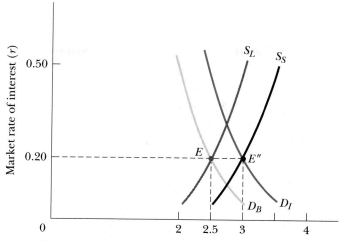

FIGURE 16.6 **Rate of Interest with Borrowing and Lending, Investment and Saving**   The equilibrium rate of interest is 20% and is shown (1) by point E, where the demand curve for borrowing (D_B) intersects the supply curve of lending (S_L), and (2) by point E'', where the demand curve for investment (D_I) intersects the total supply curve of savings (S_S). At $r > 20\%$, desired lending exceeds desired borrowing, and desired savings exceeds desired investments, and r falls. The opposite is true at $r < 20\%$.

✓ Concept Check

How is the market rate of interest determined by saving and investing and by borrowing and lending?

our individual). That is, at equilibrium, desired borrowing equals desired lending (point E) and desired savings equals desired investment (point E''). Note that the excess between the saving-investment equilibrium and the borrowing-lending equilibrium refers to the amount of investment that is self-financed from the investor's own savings rather than from borrowing in the market.[5]

At a rate of interest above equilibrium, there will be (1) an excess in the quantity supplied of lending over the quantity demanded of borrowing, and (2) an excess in the total quantity supplied of savings over the total quantity demanded of investment (see Figure 16.6). As a result, the interest rate will fall to the equilibrium level. The opposite is true at rates of interest below equilibrium. Of course, in the real world, there are many borrowers and many lenders, and many savers and investors, but the principles by which the equilibrium rate of interest is determined are the same (when capital markets are perfectly competitive). That is, at equilibrium, aggregate desired borrowing equals aggregate desired lending, and aggregate desired investment equals aggregate desired saving. Example 16–2 examines data on personal and business savings, and gross and net private domestic investment in the United States.

---

[5] Just as some people can borrow more than they invest so that they dissave, so some individuals can consume more than the sum of what they produce, borrow, and invest. Such individuals would be *disinvesting* or failing to maintain (i.e., not replacing depreciated) capital stock. To some extent, these individuals are "living off their capital." This may also be true for society as a whole during periods of war or natural disaster, or when it borrows abroad to increase present consumption.

EXAMPLE 16-2

Personal and Business Savings and Gross and Net Private Domestic Investment in the United States

Table 16.2 presents the total (aggregate) amount of personal savings (PS), business savings (BS), gross private domestic investment (GPDI), and net private domestic investment (NPDI) in the United States in terms of 2000 prices for selected years from 1960 to 2006. NPDI equals GPDI minus capital consumption allowances or depreciation resulting from the production of the given year's output. Table 16.2 also shows the level of real net national product (NNP) and NPDI as a percentage of NNP during the same years.

From the table, we see that business savings steadily increased (except in 2002) at the same time that personal savings sharply declined. Net private domestic investment is the net addition to society's capital stock and an important contributor to the growth of the economy and standards of living. Personal and business savings are required to provide for the replacement of the capital consumed during the course of producing current output and for the net additions to the capital stock of the country. Not included in the table are government savings and investments and foreign investments. The latter have become increasingly significant over the years.

	Personal and Business Savings and Gross and Net Private Domestic Investment in the United States (in billions of 2000 dollars)					
TABLE 16.2						
Year	PS	BS	GPDI	NPDI	NNP	NPDI as a % of NNP
1960	$128.6	$222.4	$266.6	$159.2	$2,252.4	7.1
1970	262.8	293.0	427.1	257.1	3,407.5	7.5
1980	386.7	365.6	645.3	334.1	4,589.3	7.3
1990	371.9	546.6	895.1	503.8	6,320.5	8.0
1995	274.0	649.2	1,134.0	683.3	7,118.8	9.6
2000	168.5	716.5	1,735.5	1,167.7	8,668.1	13.5
2002	178.4	624.8	1,557.1	939.2	8,840.0	10.6
2004	160.6	804.2	1,770.2	1,141.9	9,438.0	12.1
2005	40.0	831.9	1,869.3	1,212.4	9,640.3	12.6
2006	33.8	870.9	1,919.5	1,256.4	9,985.0	12.6

Source: Council of Economic Advisors, *Economic Report of the President* (Washington, DC: U.S. Government Printing Office, 2008), pp. 244, 256, 262.

16.3   INVESTMENT DECISIONS

The previous discussion has important practical applications and is the basis for very valuable decision rules used by firms and government agencies in determining which investment project to undertake. For example, a bank may have to decide whether to purchase or rent a large computer, a government agency whether to build a dam, and a manufacturing firm whether it should purchase a more expensive machine that lasts longer or a cheaper one that lasts a shorter period of time. The decision rule to answer these questions and to rank various investment projects is called **capital budgeting.** Capital budgeting decisions require consideration of costs and returns that arise not only in the current period but also in the future and so we must find a way to compare future to present costs and returns. Our discussion of capital budgeting begins by considering a simple two-period time frame-work. We then extend and generalize the discussion to a multiperiod time horizon.

Capital budgeting
The ranking of all investment projects from the highest present value to the lowest.

Net Present Value Rule for Investment Decisions: The Two-Period Case

An investment project involves a cost (to purchase the machinery, build the factory, acquire a skill, and so on) and a return in the form of an increase in output or income in the future. In a two-period framework, the cost is usually incurred in the current year and the return or benefit comes the following year. However, since one unit of a commodity or a dollar next year is worth less than a unit of the commodity or a dollar today, costs and benefits occurring at different times cannot simply be added together to determine whether to undertake the project.

For example, for a project that involves the expenditure of $1.00 this year and results in $1.50 return next year, we cannot simply add the $-\$1.00$ of cost this year to the $1.50 return next year and say that the net value of the project is $0.50. The reason is that $1.50 next year is worth less than $1.50 today.[6] Specifically, if the rate of interest is 20%, $1.50 next year is worth $1.50/(1.2) = $1.25 today. The reason is that $1.25 today will grow to $1.50 next year. That is, $1.25(1 + 0.2) = $1.50 if the interest rate or the rate of return is 20%. Thus, to determine the net return of an investment we must compare the cost incurred today with the value of the benefits *today*.

The **net present value (NPV)** of an investment is the value today of all the *net* cash flows of the investment. Expenditures or outflows are subtracted from revenues or inflows in each year to find the net cash flow. For a two-period time horizon, *NPV* is given by

Net present value
(NPV) The value today from the stream of net cash flows (positive and negative) from an investment project.

$$NPV = -C + \frac{R_1}{1+r} \qquad [16.5]$$

where C is the capital investment cost in the current year when the investment is made, R_1 is the net cash flow next year, and r is the rate of interest. For example, suppose that a firm purchases a machine this year for $100, and this increases the firm's net income by $120 next year. Suppose also that the rate of interest is 10%, and the machine has no salvage or scrap value at the end of the next year. The net present value of the machine (*NPV*) is

$$NPV = -\$100 + \frac{\$120}{(1 + 0.1)} = -\$100 + \$109.09 = \$9.09$$

This means that the purchase of the machine will increase the wealth of the firm by $9.09.

Suppose the firm had to decide between the above project (with net present value of $9.09) and another project that costs $150 and generates a net income of $180 next year. The firm should choose the second project because its net present value of $-\$150 + \$180/(1 + 0.1) = \$13.64$ exceeds the net present value of $9.09 for the

---

[6] We assume throughout this discussion that there is no price inflation. This assumption is relaxed in Section 16.4.

previous project. Such a choice arises because firms do not usually have or cannot usually borrow all of the resources required to undertake all of the projects that have a positive net present value.

We will see in the next section that the rule to undertake a project if its net present value is positive or to choose the project with the highest net present value is a general rule and applies to all projects, regardless of the number of periods or years over which the costs and returns of the project are spread. Furthermore, this rule is independent of the tastes or time preference of the investor. That is, regardless of the shape and location of the indifference curves of investors, the general investment or capital budgeting rule is to maximize the wealth of the firm. This is achieved by investing in projects with the highest (positive) net present value. The tastes of investors will then determine whether they will borrow or lend and how they will choose to use their (maximized) wealth. This means that if capital markets are perfect and costless (i.e., if borrowers and lenders are too small individually to affect the rate of interest and can borrow or lend at the same rate), then individuals' production and consumption decisions can be kept completely separate. This is sometimes called the **separation theorem.**

Separation theorem
The independence of the optimum investment decision from the individual's preferences.

Net Present Value Rule for Investment Decisions: The Multiperiod Case

Most investment projects last longer than (i.e., give rise to net cash flows over more than) two periods. Thus, the investment rule given above must be extended to consider many periods (years). This can easily be done by "stretching" equation [16.5] to deal with many (n) years. This is given by

$$NPV = -C + \frac{R_1}{1+r} + \frac{R_2}{(1+r)^2} + \cdots + \frac{R_n}{(1+r)^n} \qquad [16.6]$$

where NPV is the net present value of the investment, C is the capital investment cost incurred this year when the investment is made, R_1 is the net cash flow from the investment next year, R_2 is the net cash flow in two years, R_n is the net cash flow in n years, and r is the rate of interest. Net cash flows refer to the revenue of the firm resulting from the investment during any given year minus the expenses or costs of the project during the same year. Thus, equation [16.5] is a special case of equation [16.6], applicable when there is no net cash flow after the first year.[7]

For example, suppose that a firm purchases a machine this year for $150, and this increases the firm's net income by $100 in each of the next two years. If the rate of interest is 10% and the machine has no salvage value after two years, the net present value of the machine (NPV) is

$$NPV = -C + \frac{R_1}{1+r} + \frac{R_2}{(1+r)^2} = -\$150 + \frac{\$100}{1+0.1} + \frac{\$100}{(1+0.1)^2}$$

$$= -\$150 + \$90.91 + \$82.64 = \$23.55$$

---

[7] If we simply wanted to find the present discounted value (PDV) of a given sum (R) to be received in each of n years, starting with the next year, the equation would simply be

$$PDV = \frac{R}{(1+r)} + \frac{R}{(1+r)^2} + \cdots + \frac{R}{(1+r)^n}$$

If the given sum (R) were to be received in each year indefinitely or in perpetuity (an example of this is the British "consols"), then $PDV = R/r$ (see Section A.15 of the Mathematical Appendix).

This means that the purchase of the machine will increase the wealth of the firm by $23.55. Specifically, $100 received next year is worth $100/(1 + 0.1) = $90.91 this year, because $90.91 this year grows to $100 next year at $r = 10\%$. On the other hand, $100 received two years from now is worth $100/(1 + 0.1)^2 = $82.64 this year, because $82.64 this year grows to $90.91 next year at $r = 10\%$,[8] and the $90.91 next year grows to $100 the year after (i.e., two years from now) at $r = 10\%$. That is, $82.64 today times $(1 + 0.1)^2$, or 1.21, equals $100 two years from now.

If the project generated a net cash flow of $100 in the third year also, this would be "worth" $100/(1 + 0.1)^3 = $100/(1.331) = $75.13 this year because $75.13 this year will grow to $100 (except for rounding errors) in three years at $r = 10\%$. Similarly, $100 in 10 years is worth $100/(1 + 0.1)^{10} = $38.55 this year because $38.55 this year will grow to $100 in 10 years at $r = 10\%$. Finally, $100 in n years (where n is any number of years) is worth $100/(1 + 0.1)^n$ this year because this sum today will grow to $100 in n years at $r = 10\%$.

The *NPV* for any net cash flow is inversely related to r. For example, if r had been 5% in the previous example, the net present value of the investment (*NPV'*) would have been

$$NPV' = -\$150 + \frac{\$100}{(1 + 0.05)^1} + \frac{\$100}{(1 + 0.05)^2}$$

$$= -\$150 + \$95.24 + \$90.70 = \$35.94$$

(as compared with the *NPV* of $23.55 with $r = 10\%$). On the other hand, if r had been 20%,

$$NPV'' = -\$150 + \frac{\$100}{(1 + 0.2)^1} + \frac{\$100}{(1 + 0.2)^2}$$

$$= -\$150 + \$83.33 + \$69.44 = \$2.77$$

The lower *NPV* when r is higher is due to the fact that with a higher r, the *net* cash flows from the project are "discounted" more heavily than the cost, because the net cash flows arise later in time than cost. Also note that the *net* cash flows should include the extra income generated by the machine minus the extra expense (such as maintenance and the higher cost of hiring more skilled workers) to operate the machine during each year. Similarly, the value today of the salvage value of the machine (if any) must also be included.

For example, suppose that the benefits and costs of an investment project (the purchase of a piece of machinery) are those given in Table 16.3. The table shows that the machine costs $1,000 to purchase this year and also gives rise to $200, $300, $300, and $400 maintenance and other expenses in each of the subsequent four years. The revenues from the investment are $600, $800, $800, and $800, and the salvage value of the machine is $200 at the end of the fourth year. The net revenue is the revenue from the investment minus the expenses in each year. The present value coefficient is $1/(1 + 0.1)^n$. For example, for the first year the present value coefficient is $1/(1 + 0.1)^1 = 0.909$.

---

[8] Actually, ($82.64)(1.1) equals $90.904 rather than $90.91 (as indicated) because of rounding errors.

				TABLE 16.3 Benefit–Cost Analysis of an Investment Project	

End of Year	Investment (Year 0) and Cost	Revenue	Net Revenue	Present Value Coefficient $1/(1 + 0.1)^n$	Present Value of Net Revenue
0	$1,000	. . .	−$1,000	. . .	−$1,000
1	200	$600	400	0.909	364
2	300	800	500	0.826	413
3	300	800	500	0.751	376
4	400	800	400	0.683	273
4	. . .	200*	200	0.683	137
					$563

*Salvage value.

For the second year, it is $1/(1 + 0.1)^2 = 0.826$, and so on. The present value of the net revenue in each year is obtained by multiplying the net revenue (R) by the present value coefficient for that year. By adding together all present values of the net revenues, we get the net present value of the project (V_0) of $563. Since NPV is positive, the firm should purchase the machine.

Sometimes, complications may arise in applying the net present value rule for investment decisions. First, projects may be interdependent, so that the stream of net cash flows from a project depends on whether other projects are undertaken at the same time. In such a case, the net present value of a group of projects may have to be evaluated together and compared with the net present value of other groups of projects. Second, it may sometimes be difficult to accurately forecast the future stream of net cash flows from a project. Third, the firm may not have the resources and may not be willing or able to borrow to undertake all of the projects that have a positive net present value. The firm should then choose those projects with the highest net present value.

EXAMPLE 16–3

Fields of Education and Higher Lifetime Earnings in the United States

Table 16.4 gives the present value of the higher lifetime earnings with a college degree in various fields in the United States in 2007. Present values were calculated by capitalizing (i.e., finding the present discounted value of) the difference between the higher yearly salaries with a bachelor's degree in the various fields over the average salary of workers with only a high school diploma. The interest rate used to find the present values was 5%. Only the benefits of going to college were included; the earnings foregone or opportunity costs and other costs (tuition, books, and so on) of going to college were not included. To be pointed out is that the higher earnings of the recipients of the bachelor's degree over the earnings of non–college graduates cannot be attributed entirely

TABLE 16.4	Personal Values of Higher Lifetime Earnings with Bachelor's Degree in Various Fields, 2007
Field of Study	**Higher Lifetime Earnings**
Electrical engineering	$690,660
Computer sciences	645,020
Economics	539,640
Finance	512,840
Business	449,120
Political science	289,220
History	285,840
Sociology	227,220
English	222,480

Source: Calculated from data reported in *Salary Survey*, National Association of Colleges and Employers, Fall 2007.

to college education. At least in part, the higher incomes of college graduates may be due to their higher level of intelligence, longer working hours, and more inherited wealth than for non–college graduates. Earnings differentials with and without a college degree declined during the 1970s and increased since 1980.

Sources: J. Bound and G. Johnson, "Changes in the Structure of Wages in the 1980s: An Evaluation of Alternative Explanations," *American Economic Review*, June 1992, pp. 371–392; J. Mincer, "Investment in U.S. Education and Training," National Bureau of Economic Research, *Working Paper No. 4844*, October 1995; C. Goldin and L. F. Katz, "The Race Between Education and Technology: The Evolution of U.S. Educational Wage Differentials, 1890 to 2005," *NBER Working Paper No. 12984*; and College Board, *Education Pays* (Washington, DC: September 2007).

16.4   DETERMINANTS OF THE MARKET RATES OF INTEREST

Default risk The possibility that a loan will not be repaid.

Variability risk The possibility that the return on an investment, such as on a stock, may vary considerably above or below the average.

Until now we have discussed "the" interest rate; however, the rate of interest varies at different times and in different markets. Even at a given point in time and in a specific capital market, there is not a single rate of interest but many. That is, there is a different interest rate on different loans or investments depending on differences in (1) risk, (2) duration of the loan, (3) cost of administering the loan, and (4) tax treatment. We now briefly examine each of these in turn.

The major reason for differences in rates of interest at a given point in time and place is the risk of the loan. In general, the greater the risk, the higher the rate of interest. Two types of risk can be distinguished: default risk and variability risk. **Default risk** refers to the possibility that the loan will not be repaid. If the chance of default is 10%, the lender will usually charge a rate of interest 10% higher than on a loan with no risk of default, such as a government bond. Similarly, loans unsecured by collateral (such as installment credit) usually charge higher rates of interest than loans secured by collateral (such as home mortgages). **Variability risk** refers to the possibility that the yield or return on an investment, such as a stock, may vary considerably above or below the average. Given the usual aversion to risk, investors generally demand a premium or a higher yield for investments whose returns are more uncertain.

The second reason for differences in rates of interest is the duration of the loan. Loans for longer periods of time usually require higher rates of interest than loans for shorter durations. The reason is that the lender has less flexibility or liquidity with loans of longer duration, and so he or she will require a higher rate of interest. It is for this reason that savings deposits offer lower rates of interest than six-month certificates of deposit.[9]

The third reason for differences in rates of interest is the cost of administering the loan. Smaller loans and loans requiring frequent payments (such as installment loans) usually involve greater bookkeeping and service costs per dollar of the loan and, as a result, usually involve a higher interest charge. Finally, the tax treatment of interest and investment income can lead to differences in rates of interest among otherwise comparable loans and investments. For example, state and municipal bonds are exempted from federal income tax, and since investors look at the after-tax return, state and local governments can usually borrow at lower interest rates than corporations.

Thus, at a given point in time and in a given capital market there is a large number of interest rates depending on relative risk, term structure, administration costs, and tax treatment. Yet all of these rates of interest are related. If individuals and firms collectively decide to save less (a leftward shift in the aggregate supply curve of savings), interest rates will rise. Interest rates will also rise if the time preference of consumers shifts in favor of the present or if the net productivity or yield of capital increases. In addition, a rise in short-term rates will lead to higher long-term rates, and vice versa. Furthermore, higher interest rates for comparable instruments in one market than in another market will lead to an outflow of funds from the latter to the former. These flows of funds will reduce (and may eventually eliminate) interest rate differences between the two markets. Specifically, the supply curve of funds will shift to the left (i.e., the supply of funds decreases) and interest rates will rise in the market with lower rates of interest. The opposite occurs in the market with the higher rates of interest, causing interest rates to fall there.

Finally, a distinction must be made between real and nominal or money interest rates. Until this point, we have been discussing the **real rate of interest (r).** This refers to the premium on a unit of a commodity or real consumption income today compared to a unit of the commodity or real consumption income in the future. However, in the everyday usage of the term, the interest rate refers to the nominal or money rate of interest. The **nominal rate of interest (r')** refers to the premium on a unit of a monetary claim today compared to a unit of monetary claim in the future. The nominal rate of interest (r') is affected by the anticipated rate of price inflation (i), while the real rate of interest is not. Thus, the nominal rate of interest equals the real rate of interest plus the anticipated rate of price inflation. That is,

$$r' = r + i \qquad\qquad [16.7]$$

The reason for this is that during the period of the loan, the general price level may rise (i.e., inflation may occur) so that the loan is repaid with dollars of lower purchasing power than the dollars borrowed. Therefore, the nominal rate of interest must be sufficiently high to cover any increase in the price level (or in the price of real claims) during the loan period. It is primarily to avoid this complication (and to deal with the real rate of interest) that we chose to borrow and lend a *commodity* in Sections 16.1 and 16.2.

---

[9] Regulation may also account for part of the difference.

✓ Concept Check
On what does the market interest rate depend?

Real rate of interest (r) The premium on a unit of a commodity or real consumption income today compared to a unit of the commodity or real consumption income in the future.

Nominal rate of interest (r') The real rate of interest plus the anticipated rate of price inflation.

Anyone who borrows money now and repays in money in the future must expect to pay an additional monetary amount to cover any anticipated increase in the monetary price of real claims by the time of repayment. Only if anticipated inflation is zero will $r' = r$. Since some price inflation is always occurring, r' usually exceeds r. For example, if $r' = 11\%$ and $i = 6\%$, then $r = 5\%$. We have concentrated on the real rate of interest throughout most of the chapter because it is the real, and not the nominal, rate of interest that primarily affects incentives to borrow and lend, and to save and invest.

EXAMPLE 16-4

Nominal and Real Interest Rates in the United States: 1990–2006

Table 16.5 shows the nominal annual interest rates on three-month U.S. Treasury bills, the change in the Consumer Price Index, and the real interest rate (the difference between the nominal interest rate and the change in the Consumer Price Index) in the United States from 1990 to 2006. The implicit assumption made here is that the anticipated rate of inflation is equal to the actual rate of inflation. Since the nominal interest rate was greater than the change in the Consumer Price Index (except for 1993 and 2002, when they were equal, and in 2003 and 2004, when they were smaller), the real interest rate was positive. Note that the expectation that the nominal interest rate would move in the same direction as the change in the Consumer Price Index was true only in some years.

TABLE 16.5	Nominal and Real Interest Rates on Three-Month U.S. Treasury Bills: 1990–2006		
Year	Nominal Interest Rate	Change in Consumer Price Index	Real Interest Rate
1990	7.5	5.4	2.1
1991	5.4	4.2	1.2
1992	3.5	3.0	0.5
1993	3.0	3.0	0.0
1994	4.3	2.6	1.7
1995	5.5	2.8	2.7
1996	5.0	3.0	2.0
1997	5.1	2.3	2.8
1998	4.8	1.6	3.2
1999	4.7	2.2	2.5
2000	5.9	3.4	2.5
2001	3.5	2.8	0.7
2002	1.6	1.6	0.0
2003	1.0	2.3	−1.3
2004	1.4	2.7	−1.3
2005	3.2	3.4	0.2
2006	4.7	3.2	1.5

Source: Council of Economic Advisers, *Economic Report of the President* (Washington, DC: U.S. Government Printing Office, 2008), 300, 312.

EXAMPLE 16–5

Investment Risks and Returns in the United States

Table 16.6 shows that riskier assets, such as common stocks or long-term corporate bonds, have provided higher average real rates of returns than more liquid and less risky assets, such as U.S. (three-month) Treasury Bills, in the United States over the period from 1926 to 2006. While corporate bonds can provide higher returns than stocks during some years, over many years, the reverse is usually true. Risk is here measured as the standard deviation of the real return as a percentage of the mean or average real return. Common stocks involve a great deal of variability risk while long-term corporate bonds involve a greater default risk and are less liquid (and therefore provide higher average real returns) than U.S. Treasury Bills. Clearly, risk-averse investors must balance expected return against risk in their investment decisions.

TABLE 16.6	Investment Risks and Inflation-Adjusted Returns in the United States, 1926–2006	
Asset	Real Rate of Return (%)	Risk (Standard Deviation, %)
Common stocks	9.1	20.2
Long-term corporate bonds	3.2	9.6
U.S. Treasury Bills	0.7	4.0

Source: Ibbotson & Associates, *Stocks, Bonds, Bills, and Inflation, 2007 Yearbook* (Chicago, 2007), p. 120.

16.5   THE COST OF CAPITAL

We now examine how a firm estimates the cost of raising capital to invest. This is an essential element of the capital budgeting process. The firm can raise investment funds internally (i.e., from undistributed profits) or externally (i.e., by borrowing and/or from selling stocks). The cost of using internal funds is the opportunity cost or foregone return on these funds outside the firm. The cost of external funds is the lowest rate of return that lenders and stockholders require to lend to or invest their funds in the firm. In this section, we examine how the cost of debt (i.e., the cost of raising capital by borrowing) and the cost of equity capital (i.e., the cost of raising capital by selling stocks) are determined. The estimation of the cost of debt is fairly straightforward. On the other hand, there are at least three methods of estimating the cost of equity capital: the risk-free rate plus premium, the dividend valuation model, and the capital asset pricing model (CAPM). These methods will be examined in turn.

Cost of debt The net (after-tax) interest rate paid by a firm to borrow funds.

Cost of Debt

The **cost of debt** is the return that lenders require to lend their funds to the firm. Since the interest payments made by the firm on borrowed funds are deductible from the firm's taxable income, the *after-tax* cost of borrowed funds to the firm (k_d) is given by the interest paid (r) multiplied by 1 minus the firm's marginal tax rate, t. That is,

$$k_d = r(1 - t) \qquad [16.8]$$

For example, if the firm borrows at a 12.5% interest rate and faces a 40% marginal tax rate on its taxable income, the after-tax cost of debt capital to the firm is

$$k_d = 12.5\%(1 - 0.40) = 7.5\%$$

Cost of Equity Capital: The Risk-Free Rate Plus Premium

As pointed out earlier, the cost of equity capital is the rate of return that stockholders require to invest in the firm. The cost of raising equity capital externally usually exceeds the cost of raising equity capital internally by the flotation costs (i.e., the costs of issuing the stock). For simplicity, we disregard these costs in the following analysis and treat both types of equity capital together. Since dividends paid on stocks (as opposed to the interest paid on bonds) are not deductible as a business expense (i.e., dividends are paid out after corporate taxes have been paid), there is no tax adjustment in determining the equity cost of capital.

One method employed to estimate the cost of equity capital (k_e) is to use the risk-free rate (r_f) plus a risk premium (r_p). That is,

$$k_e = r_f + r_p \qquad [16.9]$$

The risk-free rate (r_f) is usually taken to be the six-month U.S. Treasury bill rate.[10] This is because the obligation to make payments of the interest and principal on government securities is assumed to occur with certainty. The risk premium (r_p) that must be paid in raising equity capital has two components. The first component results because of the greater risk that is involved in investing in a firm's securities (such as bonds) as opposed to investing in federal government securities. The second component is the additional risk resulting from purchasing the common stock rather than the bonds of the firm. Stocks involve a greater risk than bonds because dividends on stocks are paid only after the firm has met its contractual obligations to make interest and principal payments to bondholders. Because dividends vary with the firm's profits, stocks are more risky than bonds, so that their return must include an additional risk premium. If the premiums associated with these two types of risk are labeled p_1 and p_2, we can restate the formula for the cost of equity capital as

$$k_e = r_f + p_1 + p_2 \qquad [16.10]$$

The first type of risk (i.e., p_1) is usually measured by the excess of the rate of interest on the firm's bonds (r) over the rate of return on government bonds (r_f). The additional risk involved in purchasing the firm's stocks rather than bonds (i.e., p_2) is usually taken to be about four percentage points. This is the historical difference between the average yield (dividends plus capital gains) on stocks as opposed to the average yield on bonds

---

[10] Some securities analysts prefer to use instead the long-term government bond rate for r_f.

issued by private companies. For example, if the risk-free rate of return on government securities is 8% and the firm's bonds yield 11%, the total risk premium (r_p) involved in purchasing the firm's stocks rather than government bonds is

$$r_p = p_1 + p_2 = (11\% - 8\%) + 4\% = 3\% + 4\% = 7\%$$

so that the firm's cost of equity capital is

$$k_e = r_f + p_1 + p_2 = 8\% + 3\% + 4\% = 15\%$$

Cost of Equity Capital: The Dividend Valuation Model

Dividend valuation model The method of measuring the equity cost of capital to the firm with the ratio of the dividend per share of the stock to the price of the stock, plus the expected growth rate of dividend payments.

The equity cost of capital to a firm can also be estimated by the **dividend valuation model.** To derive this model, we begin by pointing out that, with perfect information, the value of a share of the common stock of a firm should be equal to the present value of all future dividends expected to be paid on the stock, discounted at the investor's required rate of return (k_e). If the dividend per share (D) paid to stockholders is expected to remain constant over time, the present value of a share of the common stock of the firm (P) is then

$$P = \sum_{t=1}^{\infty} \frac{D}{(1 + k_e)^t} \qquad [16.11]$$

If dividends are assumed to remain constant over time and to be paid indefinitely, equation [16.11] can be rewritten as

$$P = \frac{D}{k_e} \qquad [16.12]$$

If dividends are instead expected to increase over time at the annual rate of g, the price of a share of the common stock of the firm will be greater and is given by

$$P = \frac{D}{k_e - g} \qquad [16.13]$$

Solving equation [16.13] for k_e, we get the following equation to measure the equity cost of capital to the firm:

$$k_e = \frac{D}{P} + g \qquad [16.14]$$

That is, the investor's required rate of return on equity is equal to the ratio of the dividend paid on a share of the common stock of the firm to the price of a share of the stock (the so-called dividend yield) plus the expected growth rate of dividend payments by the firm (g). The value of g is the firm's historic growth rate or the earnings growth forecasts of securities analysts (based on the expected sales, profit margins, and competitive position of the firm) published in *Business Week, Forbes,* and other business publications.

For example, if the firm pays a dividend of $20 per share on common stock that sells for $200 per share and the growth rate of dividend payments is expected to be 5% per year, the cost of equity capital for this firm is

$$k_e = \frac{\$20}{\$200} + 0.05 = 0.10 + 0.05 = 0.15, \text{ or } 15\%$$

Cost of Equity Capital: The Capital Asset Pricing Model (CAPM)

Capital asset pricing model (CAPM) The method of measuring the equity cost of capital as the risk-free rate plus the beta coefficient (β) times the risk premium on the average stock.

Another method commonly used to estimate the equity cost of capital is the **capital asset pricing model (CAPM)**. This model considers not only the risk differential between common stocks and government securities but also the risk differential between the common stock of the firm and the average common stock of all firms, or broad-based market portfolio. The risk differential between common stocks and government securities is measured by ($k_m - r_f$), where k_m is the average return on all common stocks and r_f is the return on government securities.

The risk differential between the common stock of a particular firm and the common stock of all firms is called the **beta coefficient, β**. This is the ratio of the variability in the return of the common stock of the firm to the variability in the average return on the common stocks of all firms. Beta coefficients for individual stocks can be obtained from the *Value Line Investment Survey,* Merrill Lynch, or other brokerage firms.

Beta coefficient (β) The ratio of the variability of the return on the common stock of the firm to the variability of the average return on all stocks.

A beta coefficient of 1 means that the variability in the returns on the common stock of the firm is the same as the variability in the returns on all stocks. Thus, investors holding the stock of the firm face the same risk as holding a broad-based market portfolio of all stocks. A beta coefficient of 2 means that the variability in the returns on (i.e., risk of holding) the stock of the firm is twice that of the average stock. On the other hand, holding a stock with a beta coefficient of 0.5 is half as risky as holding the average stock.

The cost of equity capital to the firm estimated by the capital asset pricing model (CAPM) is then measured by

$$k_e = r_f + \beta(k_m - r_f) \qquad [16.15]$$

✓ Concept Check
How does the capital asset pricing model (CAPM) measure the cost of equity capital?

where k_e is the cost of equity capital to the firm, r_f is the risk-free rate, β is the beta coefficient, and k_m is the average return on the stock of all firms. Thus, CAPM postulates that the cost of equity capital to the firm is equal to the sum of the risk-free rate plus the beta coefficient (β) times the risk premium on the average stock ($k_m - r_f$). Note that multiplying β by ($k_m - r_f$) gives the risk premium on holding the common stock of the particular firm.

For example, suppose that the risk-free rate (r_f) is 8%, the average return on common stocks (k_m) is 15%, and the beta coefficient (β) for the firm is 1. The cost of equity capital to the firm (k_e) is then

$$k_e = 8\% + 1(15\% - 8\%) = 15\%$$

That is, since a beta coefficient of 1 indicates that the stock of this firm is as risky as the average stock of all firms, the equity cost of capital to the firm is 15% (the same as the average return on all stocks). If $\beta = 1.5$ for the firm (so that the risk involved in holding the stock of the firm is 1.5 times larger than the risk on the average stock), the equity cost of capital to the firm would be

$$k_e = 8\% + 1.5(15\% - 8\%) = 18.5\%$$

On the other hand, if $\beta = 0.5$, then

$$k_e = 8\% + 0.5(15\% - 8\%) = 11.5\%$$

In this example and in the examples using the risk-free rate plus premium and the dividend valuation model, the equity cost of capital was found to be the same (15%). This is seldom the case. That is, the different methods of estimating the equity cost of capital to a firm are likely to give somewhat different results. Firms are thus likely to use all three methods and then attempt to reconcile the differences to arrive at an equity cost of capital for the firm.

Weighted Cost of Capital

In general, a firm is likely to raise capital from undistributed profits, by borrowing, and by the sale of stocks, and so the marginal cost of capital to the firm is a weighted average of the cost of raising the various types of capital. Since the interest paid on borrowed funds is tax deductible while the dividends paid on stocks are not, the cost of debt is generally less than the cost of equity capital. The risk involved in raising funds by borrowing, however, is greater than the risk on equity capital because the firm must regularly make payments of the interest and principal on borrowed funds before paying dividends on stocks. Thus, firms do not generally raise funds only by borrowing but also by selling stock (as well as from undistributed profits).

Firms often try to maintain or achieve a particular long-term capital structure of debt to equity. For example, public utility companies may prefer a capital structure involving 60% debt and 40% equity, whereas auto manufacturers may prefer 30% debt and 70% equity. The particular debt-equity ratio that a firm prefers reflects the risk preference of its managers and stockholders and the nature of the firm's business. Public utilities accept the higher risk involved in a higher debt-to-equity ratio because of their more stable flow of earnings than automobile manufacturers. When a firm needs to raise investment capital, it borrows and sells stocks so as to maintain or achieve a desired debt-to-equity ratio.

Composite cost of capital The weighted average of the cost of debt and equity capital to the firm.

The **composite cost of capital** to the firm (k_c) is then a weighted average of the cost of debt capital (k_d) and equity capital (k_e), as given by

$$k_c = w_d k_d + w_e k_e \qquad [16.16]$$

where w_d and w_e are, respectively, the proportion of debt and equity capital in the firm's capital structure. For example, if the (after-tax) cost of debt is 7.5%, the cost of equity capital is 15%, and the firm wants to have a debt-to-equity ratio of 40:60, the composite or weighted marginal cost of capital to the firm is

$$k_c = (0.40)(7.5\%) + (0.60)(15\%) = 3\% + 9\% = 12\%$$

That is, the proportion of debt to equity that the firm seeks to achieve or maintain in the long run is not usually defined for individual projects but for all the investment projects that the firm is considering. Note that the marginal cost of capital eventually rises as the firm raises additional amounts of capital by borrowing and selling stocks because of the higher risk that lenders and investors face as the firm's debt-to-equity ratio increases.

AT THE FRONTIER
Derivatives: Useful but Dangerous

Derivatives Financial instruments or contracts whose values are derived from the price of such underlying financial assets as stocks, bonds, commodities, and currencies.

During the past decade, news about derivatives has been all over the financial and front pages of our newspapers. **Derivatives** are financial instruments or contracts whose value is derived from the price of such underlying financial assets as stocks, bonds, commodities, and currencies. Derivatives are offered by banks and brokerage firms to corporations and investors who wish to protect themselves against such risks as a decrease in the international value of the dollar, an increase in the price of a commodity, or an increase in interest rates. Used properly, derivatives can be a very useful risk-management tool; used without a clear understanding of all their implications, they can be very dangerous and can lead to huge losses. Despite the dangers and risks involved in their use, derivatives have been growing at a very rapid rate during the past decade and are clearly here to stay. The value of the underlying assets on which derivatives are based (called *notional value*) now exceeds $400 trillion (as compared with the $14 trillion of the U.S. gross domestic product, or GDP, in 2007).

Derivatives come in two basic categories: option-type contracts and forward-type contracts. These may be listed on the exchanges or negotiated privately between institutions (i.e., over the counter). *Options* give buyers the right, but not the obligation, to buy (a call) or sell (a put) an asset at a specific price over a given time period. The option price or premium is usually a small percentage of the price of the value of the underlying asset. Although the buyer can never lose more than the premium he or she paid for the option (by not exercising it), the seller's potential losses are unlimited. For example, you can buy a call on GE stock for a specified time, at a specified price, and for a specified premium. If within the specified time the price of the GE stock falls below the specified price, you do not exercise the call option to buy the stock and your losses are limited to the premium that you paid for the call. On the other hand, if the price of GE stock rises above the specified price, you exercise the call and buy the stock and gain the difference between the higher market price of the stock and the agreed call price.

Forward-type contracts, on the other hand, include forwards, futures, and swaps. *Forwards* commit both buyer and seller to trade a fixed amount of a given asset for a specific price at a specific future date. For example, a corporation that has to purchase a given amount of petroleum in three months faces the risk that the price of petroleum may be much higher in three months. The corporation can protect itself (i.e., hedge) this risk by entering today into a contract to purchase the quantity of petroleum that it will need at a price agreed upon today for delivery and payment in three months. In three months, the corporation will get the specified quantity of petroleum by paying the agreed price—whatever the price of petroleum is on that day.

Futures are standardized forward agreements to buy or sell a fixed amount of an asset (currency, bond, stock, or commodity) traded on an exchange. *Swaps* are agreements involving an exchange of streams of payments over time according to terms agreed today. The most common type is an interest rate swap, in which one party holding a fixed-interest rate mortgage and believing that interest rates will fall exchanges it for a flexible exchange rate mortgage owned by another party who believes that interest

Continued . . .

Derivatives: Useful but Dangerous   *Continued*

rates will rise. The first party will then pay the other's flexible rate mortgage in exchange for the second paying the fixed rate mortgage of the first.

Many derivatives are in the form of the simple options, forwards, futures, and swaps discussed above (called "plain vanilla" derivatives). They form the bread and butter of the derivatives market and are used mostly to hedge risks, but provide dealers only thin profit margins. Some of these derivatives, such as currency options and futures, have been used by U.S. and foreign corporations for decades and have been spared criticism. The derivatives that have caught most of the attention and criticism in recent years are the customized, over-the-counter, exotic derivatives whose dazzling growth to over $350 trillion since the late 1980s have provided huge profits for dealers and tremendous risks for users. Examples of exotic derivatives are options that depend on the amount by which one asset will outperform another, or that gamble that the price of oil will not fall below a specified price or that interest rates do rise above a given level. The list of derivatives products is very long and new ones are being created every day.

By allowing users to make big bets with little or no money down (i.e., by providing huge leverage), derivatives became very popular during the 1992–1993 bull market in bonds, when heavy bets were made that interest rates would continue to fall. As long as interest rates did fall, these derivatives provided huge profits for users and fat fees for providers. But when interest rates abruptly reversed course in early 1994, a number of companies that had invested heavily in these exotic derivatives faced huge losses. A fund managed by Orange County, California, lost more than $1.5 billion and was forced to declare bankruptcy. Similar losses by the use of derivatives were incurred by some large European and Asian corporations during the past decade. In September 1998, Long-Term Capital Management (LTCM), the Connecticut-based investment firm, lost $3.6 billion and failed as a result of massive speculative bets gone wrong. Investors in LTCM had little or no information on the fund's investments strategy and no idea on its huge leverage (the ratio of borrowed funds used to the firm's capital). The financial crisis that erupted in the middle of 2007 started in the U.S. subprime (or high-risk) home mortgage loans market and then spread worldwide.

✓ **Concept Check**
What are derivatives? What is their usefulness? Why are they dangerous?

Despite these spectacular failures, there are still few or no disclosure requirements in the United States and abroad on derivatives users. Most derivatives are treated as "off-balance-sheet" items and mentioned in footnotes in companies' financial statements. The systemic danger to which this gives rise is that a party to a derivative transaction may be unable to meet the terms of the transaction and lead to the insolvency of its counterparty (the other party of the derivative transaction), and that this may trigger a domino effect of defaults that could threaten the stability of the entire financial system. The Federal Reserve System and other regulators now face the delicate task of regulating the derivatives market without leading this very lucrative business for many U.S. banks (which are world leaders in this market) to relocate abroad. One proposal is for firms to report their derivatives profits or losses on their earnings statements, rather than carrying them on their books at cost, as they do now.

Source: "The Risk That Won't Go Away," *Fortune*, March 7, 1994, pp. 40–60; "Untangling Derivatives Mess," *Fortune*, March 20, 1995, pp. 51–68; "Hedge Funds Managers Are Back, Profiting in Others' Bad Times," *New York Times*, July 26, 2002, p. C1; "Banks Gone Wild," *New York Times*, November 23, 2007, p. 37; and IMF, *Global Financial Stability Report* (Washington, DC: IMF, 2007).

16.6		EFFECTS OF FOREIGN INVESTMENTS ON THE RECEIVING NATION

Foreign investments reduce the supply of investment funds in the investing nation and increase them in the receiving nation. Foreign investments flow from the nation where the rate of return on investment is lower to the nation where the rate of return is higher. During the 1980s, the United States was the recipient of a large net inflow of foreign investments because of the higher rate of return on investments in the United States than abroad. We can examine the effect of foreign investments on the receiving nation with Figure 16.7. For simplicity, we assume that the rate of interest on borrowed capital is the same as the rate of return on both borrowed and equity capital in the nation.

In Figure 16.7, D is the nation's demand curve for investment funds, while S is the domestic supply curve of investment funds. D and S intersect at point E indicating that, in the absence of foreign investments, $300 billion is invested in the nation at the rate of return (r) of 0.15, or 15%. With $150 billion of foreign investment, the nation's supply curve shifts to the right to S'. The intersection of D and S' defines the new equilibrium point of E', which indicates that total investments in the nation are $400 billion and the rate of return on domestic and foreign investments is 0.10, or 10%. Thus, foreign investments reduced the rate of return on domestic investments from 15% to 10% (and this led to a reduction in the quantity supplied of domestic investments to $250 billion).

The $150 billion foreign investment increases the total output of the receiving nation by $GEE'M$ (about $12.5 billion), of which $GCE'M = $10 billion is paid out to foreign investors as the return on their investment, and $EE'C$ (about $2.5 billion) represents the net benefit or gain to the nation receiving the foreign investments. Some of this net benefit goes to domestic labor because the inflow of foreign investments increases the capital–labor ratio and thus the productivity and wages of domestic labor. Another benefit (not shown in the figure) accruing to the nation receiving the foreign investments is the taxes paid by foreigners on the income (the return on investments) earned in the nation.

In 1985, the United States changed from being a net creditor to being a net debtor nation (i.e., the amount that foreigners lent and invested in the United States began to exceed the amount that the United States lent and invested abroad) for the first time since 1914. Indeed, with a net foreign debt of about $2 trillion in 2000, the United States was by far the most indebted nation in the world. This large debt sparked a lively debate

FIGURE 16.7 **Effects of Foreign Investments on the Receiving Nation** D is the demand curve for and S is the supply curve of investment funds in the nation in the absence of foreign investments. D and S intersect at point E, defining the equilibrium rate of return (r) of 0.15, or 15%, and level of investments of $300 billion. With $150 billion of foreign investments, S shifts to S', defining the new equilibrium point of E', at which total investments in the nation rise to $400 billion ($250 billion domestic and $150 billion foreign) and r falls to 0.10, or 10%. The $150 billion foreign investment increases the total output of the nation by $GEE'M$ (about $12.5 billion), of which $GECE'M = $10 billion is the return on foreign investments and $EE'C$ (about $2.5 billion) is the net gain of the nation.

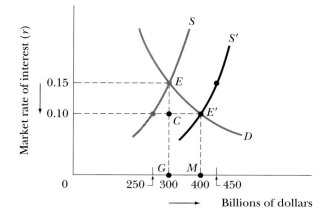

among economists, politicians, and government officials in the United States regarding the benefits, and risks of this recent development.

In terms of benefits, foreign investments allowed the United States to finance about half of its budget deficit without the need for still higher interest rates and more "crowding out" of private investments. To the extent that foreign investments went into directly productive activities and the return on this investment was greater than the interest and dividend payments flowing to foreign investors, this investment was beneficial to the United States.[11] To the extent, however, that foreign investments simply financed larger consumption expenditures in the United States, the interest and dividend payments flowing to foreign investors represent a real burden or drain on future consumption and growth in the United States. Some experts are concerned that a growing share of capital inflows to the United States since 1983 cannot be clearly identified as productive investments, and to that extent they may represent a real burden on the U.S. economy in the future.

There is also the danger that foreigners, for whatever reason, may suddenly withdraw their funds. This would lead to a financial crisis and much higher interest rates in the United States. Some economists and government officials also fear that foreign companies operating in the United States will transfer advanced American technology abroad. They further fear some loss of domestic control over political and economic matters. The irony is that these fears were precisely the complaints usually heard from Canada, smaller European nations, and developing countries with regard to the large American investments in their countries during the 1950s and 1960s. With the great concern often voiced in the United States today about the danger of foreign investments, the tables now seem to have turned.[12]

EXAMPLE 16–6

Fluctuations in the Flow of Foreign Direct Investments to the United States

Table 16.7 shows that the flow of foreign direct investments (FDI) to the United States was $65.9 in 1990. It declined to $15.3 billion 1992 before rising to $321.3 billion in 2000. Afterwards, it declined to $63.8 billion in 2003 and then rose to $180.6 billion in 2006. Foreign direct investments include acquisitions, the formation of new businesses, and the construction of new plants. They do not include the purchase of stocks and bonds.

During the second half of the 1980s, many Americans became concerned that foreigners, particularly the Japanese, were "buying up" America. These fears subsided during the early 1990s, as slow growth and recession made FDI in the United States less attractive to foreigners. With the resumption of rapid growth in the United States since 1993, however, FDI in the United Stated shot up again to much higher levels than during the late 1980s (this time coming mostly from Europe instead of Japan), but with

---

[11] Of course, the United States would have benefitted even more if it had financed its domestic investments entirely through domestic savings. But with inadequate domestic savings, the second best situation was to receive foreign investments and pay the return on investments to foreign investors.

[12] See "A Note on the United States as a Debtor Nation," *Survey of Current Business* (Washington, D.C.: U.S. Government Printing Office, 1985), p. 28.

TABLE 16.7	Foreign Direct Investment Flows to the United States, 1990–2006 (billions of U.S. dollars)			
Year	FDI		Year	FDI
1980	$12.2		1990	$65.9
1981	23.2		1991	25.5
1982	10.8		1992	15.3
1983	8.1		1993	26.2
1984	15.2		1994	49.9
1985	23.1		1995	60.8
1986	39.2		1996	84.5
1987	40.3		1997	103.4
1988	72.7		1998	174.4
1989	71.2		1999	295.0
1990	65.9		2000	281.1

Source: U.S. Department of Commerce, *Survey of Current Business* (Washington, DC: U.S. Government Printing Office, various issues).

the United States doing much better in international competitiveness than in the 1980s (see "At the Frontier" for Chapter 7), the new upsurge in FDI did not cause much concern in the United States. At the same time, the flow of U.S. FDI abroad remained high and reached a peak of $279.1 billion in 2004 and was $235.4 billion in 2006.

16.7   SOME APPLICATIONS OF FINANCIAL MICROECONOMICS

In this section, we discuss some important applications of the theory presented in the chapter. These applications include investment in human capital, the effect of investment in human capital on hours of work, the pricing of exhaustible resources, and the management of nonexhaustible resources. These applications clearly indicate the usefulness and applicability of the theory.

Investment in Human Capital

Investment in human capital Any activity, such as education and training, that increases an individual's productivity.

Investment in human capital is any activity on the part of a worker or potential worker that increases his or her productivity. It refers to expenditures on education, job training, health, migration to areas of better job opportunities, and so on. Like any other investment, investments in human capital involve costs and entail returns. For example, going to college involves explicit and implicit, or opportunity, costs. The explicit costs are tuition, books, fees, and all other out-of-pocket expenses of attending college. The implicit costs are the earnings or opportunities foregone while attending college (the individual could have worked or could have worked more by not attending college). As we have seen in the example in Section 9.1, the implicit costs of attending college are nearly as high as the explicit costs. The returns of attending college take the form of higher lifetime earnings with a college education than without a college education (see Example 16–3).

As with any other investment, we can find the present value of the stream of net cash flows from a college degree. Net cash flows are negative during the college years (because of the explicit and implicit or opportunity costs of attending college) and positive during the working life of the college graduate until retirement. The same is generally true for other investments in human capital. That is, they also lead to a stream of net cash flows and should be undertaken only if their net present value is positive or higher than the present value of other investments (such as the purchasing of a stock). Using this method, it was estimated that the return to a college education was about 10% to 15% per year during the 1950s and 1960s. This was substantially higher than the return on similarly risky investments (such as the purchasing of a stock). During the 1970s, and as a result of the sharp increases in tuition and relatively lower starting salaries, the returns to a college education declined to about 7% per year, but they increased during the 1980s and early 1990s.[13]

These studies, however, face a number of statistical problems. For example, not all expenditures for education represent an investment (as, for example, when a physics student takes a course in Shakespeare). In addition, at least part of the higher earnings of college graduates may be due to their being more intelligent or from working harder than noncollege graduates (see the next section). Nevertheless, there are benefits from a college education that cannot be easily measured. For example, college graduates seem to enjoy their jobs more than noncollege graduates, have happier marriages, and generally suffer less mental illness. In spite of these measurement difficulties, however, the concept of investment in human capital is very important and commonly used. Most differences in labor incomes can be explained by differences in human capital. Juries routinely determine the amount of damages to award injury victims (or their survivors, in cases of fatal accidents) on the basis of the human capital or income lost by the injured party. Developing countries complain about the brain drain or the emigration to rich nations of their young and skilled people (who embody a great deal of human capital), and so on.

Concept Check
What are the returns to college education?

Investment in Human Capital and Hours of Work

People may work more hours as a result of investment in human capital. This can be shown with the aid of Figure 16.8. In Figure 16.8, the movement from left to right on the horizontal axis measures hours of leisure per day. The movement from right to left measures the hours of work. The sum of the hours of leisure and the hours of work always adds up to the 24 hours of the day. The vertical axis measures the daily income of the individual.

We begin by assuming that the individual portrayed in Figure 16.8 has a daily property income of FC ($30). If the hourly wage is $2.50, the individual's budget line is FB (so that the negative of the slope of the budget line gives the wage rate). Before investing in education, the individual maximizes utility or satisfaction at point E, where indifference curve U is tangent to budget line FB. The individual works 8 hours per day and has a daily income of $50 (FC, or $30, from property income plus HE, or $20, from working 8 hours at the wage rate of $2.50 per hour).

---

[13] R. B. Freeman, "The Decline in the Economic Rewards to College Education, *The Review of Economics and Statistics,* February 1977, pp. 18–29; "The Soaring Payoff from Higher Education," *The Margin,* January/February, 1990, p. 6; "The New Math of Higher Education," *Business Week,* March 18, 1996, p. 39; "College Degree Still Pays, But It's Leveling Off," *New York Times,* January 13, 2005, p. C1; and College Board, *Education Pays* (Washington, DC: September 2007).

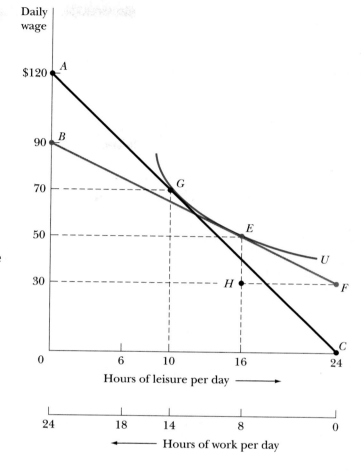

FIGURE 16.8 Education and Hours of Work The individual has a daily property income of $FC = \$30$ and faces budget line FB (with the negative of the slope giving the wage of $2.50 per hour). The individual maximizes utility at point E, where indifference curve U is tangent to FB. The individual works 8 hours and has a daily income of $50 (of which $HE = \$20$ is labor income). Suppose the individual invests all property income in education and as a result earns $5 per hour. The budget line is now CA. The individual maximizes utility at point G, where U is tangent to CA, and works 14 hours for a daily income of $70.

Suppose that now the individual decides to invest all of his or her endowed property income in education (i.e., sacrifice all of his or her nonhuman capital) and that as a result he or she can earn a wage rate of $5 per hour. With education, the budget line of the individual is now CA (see the figure), reflecting zero property income available for consumption and the wage of $5 per hour (the negative of the slope of budget line CA). Assuming that the individual's tastes remain unchanged as a result of the education, the individual will now maximize utility at point G, where indifference curve U is tangent to budget line CA. The individual now works 14 hours per day for a daily income of $70 (all of which is labor income).

Thus, education seems to induce individuals to work more hours (i.e., have fewer leisure hours) and earn higher incomes. Having made the investment in education, the individual will work more hours and earn a higher income to maximize utility. This seems to be confirmed in empirical studies. For example, Lindsay found that physicians work on average 62 hours per week, far more than the average worker.[14] The same seems to be true for other professionals as opposed to nonprofessionals.

---

[14] C. M. Lindsay, "Real Returns to Medical Education," *Journal of Human Resources,* Summer 1982, p. 338. See also "Wages and the Workday," *Economic Inquiry,* spring 2000, p. 15, and "Why High Earners Work Longer Hours," *NBER Reporter,* July 2006, p. 4.

Pricing of Exhaustible Resources

One of the great concerns of modern societies is that the world's resources will become depleted. Resources can generally be classified as exhaustible or nonexhaustible. **Exhaustible resources** are those, such as petroleum and other minerals, that are available in fixed quantities and are nonreplenishable. **Nonexhaustible resources** are those such as fertile land, forests, rivers, and fish, which can last forever if they are properly managed. We first examine the pricing of exhaustible or nonrenewable resources and then look at the pricing of nonexhaustible or renewable resources under proper management.

During the 1970s (and to a large extent as a result of the petroleum crisis), there was great concern that exhaustible resources would soon be depleted. Doomsday models were built that predicted when various exhaustible resources would run out, thereby threatening the living standard and the very future of humanity.[15] Such fears are again being expressed today. Economists, while not entirely shrugging off the danger, were skeptical for the most part. They pointed out that as the price of exhaustible resources tend to rise over time, this would lead to conservation and to the discovery of substitutes. Thus, doomsday models were not to be taken too seriously. Let us see why economists proved to be generally right.

We begin by pointing out that the owner of an exhaustible resource will keep it in the ground and available for future use if the present value of the resource in future use is greater than its current price. For example, suppose that the price of the resource is $100 per unit today, it is expected to be $120 next year, and the market rate of interest is 10% per year. The owner will sell the resource next year, since the present value of a unit of the resource sold next year is $120/(1 + 0.1) = $109.09 and this exceeds its price of $100 today.

In a perfectly competitive market, the net price of the resource (i.e., the price minus the cost of extraction) will rise at a rate equal to the market rate of interest, and this will spread available supplies over time. If the net price of a resource is expected to rise faster than the market rate of interest, more of the resource will be held off the market for future sale. This increases the current price and reduces the future price until the present value of the future net price is equal to the present net price. On the other hand, if the net price of the resource is expected to rise at a slower rate than the market rate of interest, more of the resource will be sold in the present. This will reduce the present price and increase the future price until the present value of the expected future net price equals the present net price. This is shown in Figure 16.9.

In the left panel of the figure, time is measured along the horizontal axis, and the price of the exhaustible resource and its average total cost (assumed to be constant, and thus equal to marginal cost) are measured along the vertical axis. The right panel shows the market demand curve for the resource (input). The net price or benefit to the owners of the resource is given by the difference (*AB* at time zero) between the (gross) price of the resource and the assumed constant cost of extracting it. The owner can obtain these net benefits now or in the future (by leaving the resource in the ground). For the owner of the resource to be indifferent between extracting the resource now or in the future, the net

---

[15] See J. W. Forrester, *World Dynamics* (Cambridge, MA.: Wright-Allen Press, 1971); D. H. Meadows et al., *The Limits to Growth: A Report for the Club of Rome's Project on the Predicament of Mankind* (New York: Universe Books, 1972); M. Mesarovic and E. Pestel, *Mankind at the Turning Point: The Second Report to the Club of Rome* (New York: American Library, 1974); and "Study Warns of Gloomy Future for Resources," *Financial Times*, October 26, 2007, p. 3.

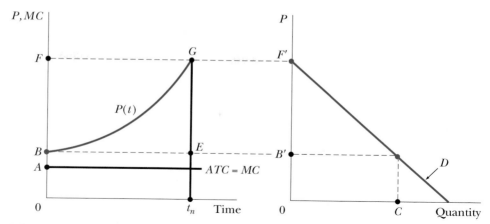

FIGURE 16.9   The Price of Exhaustible Resources   In the left panel, time is measured along the horizontal axis, and the price of the exhaustible resource and its average cost (assumed constant and equal to *MC*) is measured along the vertical axis. The right panel shows the demand curve for the resource. At $P = OB$, the net benefit is AB per unit and the quantity demanded is OC. Over time, the net benefit or net price rises at the same rate as the market rate of interest until at $P = OF$, the supply of the resource is exhausted (point G in the left panel), and the quantity demanded is zero (point F' in the right panel).

Concept Check
How is the price of exhaustible resources measured?

benefit or net price of the resource must appreciate over time at a rate equal to the market rate of interest.

The right panel of Figure 16.9 shows that at the resource (gross) price $P = OB'$, the quantity demanded of the resource is OC. Over time, the net price rises at the same rate as the market rate of interest (from AB to EG in the left panel) until at $P = OF'$ the supply of the resource is exhausted (point G in the left panel) and the quantity demanded of the resource is zero (point F' in the right panel). Thus, in perfectly competitive markets, exhaustion of the resource coincides with zero quantity demanded. If exhaustion occurs before time t_n at $P = OF$, owners of the resource could have sold the resource at a higher price (and net benefit) over time than indicated by line BG. On the other hand, if the resource is not exhausted by t_n at $P = OF$, owners would have gained by selling the resource at a lower price over time.[16] In the real world, the net price of most resources increases at a smaller rate than the market rate of interest (and the net price of many resources actually falls) over time because of new discoveries, technological improvements in extraction, and conservation.

Management of Nonexhaustible Resources

Nonexhaustible or renewable resources such as forests and fish grow naturally over time. Unless the rate of utilization of the resource exceeds its rate of natural growth, the resource will never be depleted.[17] If the renewable resource is trees, the question is when

---

[16] See H. Hotelling, "The Economics of Exhaustible Resources, "*Journal of Political Economy,* April 1931, pp. 137–175.

[17] The term "renewable" is, perhaps, more appropriate than "nonexhaustible" because if the rate of utilization of the resource exceeds its natural growth rate, the resource can be exhausted. For example, if you cut all the trees or catch all the fish now, there will be no trees or fish in the future.

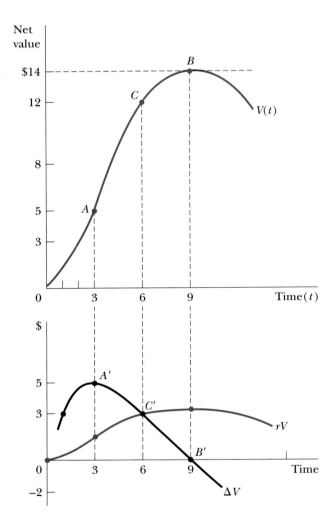

FIGURE 16.10   Optimal Management of a Standing Forest   The top panel shows the net value of the trees if harvested at time t, $V(t)$. The trees should be cut when the growth in the net value of the standing trees (ΔV) is equal to the growth in the net receipts from cutting the trees and investing the proceeds at the market rate of interest (rV). This equilibrium occurs at $t = 6$ when the ΔV, or MV, curve crosses the rV curve (point C' in the bottom panel) and $\Delta V/V = r$.

should the trees be cut? The answer (as you might suspect by now) is that the trees should be allowed to grow as long as the rate of growth in the net value of the trees exceeds the market rate of interest. Cutting the trees when the rate of growth in their net value exceeds the market rate of interest would be equivalent to taking money out of a bank paying a higher rate of interest and depositing the money in another bank that pays a lower rate of interest. We can analyze this situation with the aid of Figure 16.10.

The top panel of Figure 16.10 shows the net value of the trees if harvested at time t. This is given by the $V(t)$ curve. The net value is the total market value of the trees minus the cost of harvesting them. We assume zero maintenance or management costs. The top panel shows that $V(t)$ grows at an increasing rate at first. At time $t = 3$ (point A), diminishing returns begin. $V(t)$ reaches the maximum value of $14 million at $t = 9$ (point B), after which disease, age, and decay set in.

When should the trees be cut? The answer is not at $t = 9$ when $V(t)$ is maximum. This would be the case only if the market rate of interest were zero. With a positive market rate of interest, the correct answer is to cut the trees when the growth in the net value of the standing trees (ΔV) is equal to the growth of the net receipts from cutting the trees and investing the proceeds at the market rate of interest (rV). That is, the trees should be cut when

$$\Delta V = r V \qquad\qquad [16.17]$$

or

$$\Delta V/V = r \qquad\qquad [16.17A]$$

This says that trees should be cut when the *rate* of growth in the value of the standing trees ($\Delta V/V$) equals the market *rate* of interest (r).

In terms of Figure 16.10, the trees should be cut at $t = 6$ when the ΔV curve crosses the rV curve (point C' in the bottom panel). The ΔV curve (in the bottom panel) is the marginal value curve or slope of the $V(t)$ curve in the top panel (i.e., $\Delta V = MV$). The rV curve in the bottom panel is 0.25 or 25% of the $V(t)$ curve, at $r = 25\%$. To the left of point C', MV exceeds rV (i.e., $\Delta V/V > r$) and it pays for the firm to let the trees continue to grow. To the right of point C', MV is smaller than rV (i.e., $\Delta V/V < r$) and it pays for the firm to cut the trees. The optimal choice is to cut the trees at point $t = 6$ (point C', where $MV = rV$). This is the usual marginal rule applicable in all optimization decisions.

SUMMARY

1. Given the consumer's income or endowment for this year and the next, and the rate of interest, we can define the consumer's budget line. The rate of interest is the premium received next year for lending or borrowing one dollar this year. The optimal consumer's choice involves lending or borrowing so as to reach the highest possible indifference curve showing the consumer's time preference between present and future consumption. The wealth of an individual is given by the sum of the present income and the present value of future income. If the rate of interest rises, the borrower will borrow less and the lender will usually lend more. The equilibrium rate of interest is determined at the intersection of the market demand curve for borrowing and the market supply curve for lending.

2. For an isolated individual, optimal saving and investment is given by the point where the production-possibilities curve is tangent to an indifference curve. With saving and investment, and borrowing and lending, the optimal choice of the individual is first to maximize wealth (by reaching the market line that is tangent to the production-possibilities curve) and then to borrow or lend along the market line until the individual reaches the highest indifference curve possible. The equilibrium rate of interest is given by the intersection of (1) the aggregate demand curve for borrowing and the aggregate supply curve of lending, or (2) the aggregate demand curve for investment and the aggregate supply curve of savings.

3. A firm should undertake an investment only if the net present value of the investment is positive. The net present value (NPV) of the investment is the value today from the stream of the net cash flows (positive and negative) from the investment. In choosing between any two projects, the firm will maximize attained wealth by undertaking the project with the highest net present value. The separation theorem refers to the independence of the optimum production decision from the individual's preferences in perfect capital markets.

4. The rate of interest usually varies at different times and in different markets. Even at a given point in time and in a specific capital market, there is not a single rate of interest, but many. That is, there is a different interest rate on loans or investments depending on differences in (1) default and variability risks, (2) duration of the loan, (3) cost of administering the loan, and (4) tax treatment. Interest rates rise if society decides to save less or to borrow and invest more. The nominal rate of interest equals the real rate of interest plus the anticipated rate of price inflation.

5. The cost that a firm incurs for using internal funds is the foregone return on these funds invested outside the firm. The cost of external funds is the rate of return that lenders and stockholders require to lend or invest funds in the firm. The after-tax cost of borrowed funds is given by the interest paid times $(1 - t)$, where t is the firm's marginal tax rate. The cost of equity capital can be measured by (1) the risk-free rate plus a risk premium, (2) the dividend valuation model, and (3) the capital asset pricing model (CAPM). The composite cost of capital is the weighted average of the cost of debt and equity capital.

6. Foreign investments result in a reduction in the rate of return on domestic investments but a net gain for the recipient nation. Labor in a nation receiving foreign investments shares in the gains through higher wages from the higher productivity resulting from an increased capital-labor ratio. The nation also collects taxes on foreign earnings. The United States is now the largest debtor nation in the world. Concern has been voiced on the dangers arising from a sudden withdrawal of foreign investments, technology transfer, and foreign domination. These dangers may be exaggerated.

7. Investment in human capital refers to expenditures on education, job training, health, or migration to areas of better job opportunities that increase the productivity of an individual. Like any other investment, investments in human capital involve costs and entail returns. Education seems to induce people to work more hours. The net price of exhaustible resources tends to rise at the same rate as the market rate of interest, and this spreads the available supply of the resource over time and stimulates the discovery of substitutes. A nonexhaustible resource should be harvested when the growth in its net value equals the market rate of interest.

KEY TERMS

Endowment position	Net present value (*NPV*)	Capital asset pricing model (CAPM)
Rate of interest (*r*)	Separation theorem	Beta coefficient (β)
Wealth	Default risk	Composite cost of capital
Production-possibilities curve	Variability risk	Derivatives
Saving	Real rate of interest (*r*)	Investment in human capital
Investment	Nominal rate of interest (*r′*)	Exhaustible resources
Market line	Cost of debt	Nonexhaustible resources
Capital budgeting	Dividend valuation model	

REVIEW QUESTIONS

1. How much interest must an individual be paid to save part of his or her income this year if his or her time preference is zero? What happens to the individual's satisfaction this year and next if the individual saves part of this year's income and spends it next year? What happens to the individual's combined satisfaction for this year and next if the individual saves part of this year's income and spends it next year?

2. In what way is intertemporal optimum consumer choice analogous or similar to optimum consumer choice at one point in time?

3. Is microeconomic theory concerned primarily with the real or with the nominal interest rate? Why?

4. What is the present discounted value of an inheritance of $10,000 to be paid in two years, if the market rate of interest is 10%?

5. Should you prefer $100 one year from today or $110 two years from today if the market rate of interest is 5% per year? Why?

6. What is the rate of interest or discount if an individual is indifferent between receiving $11,111.11 today or $1,000 at the end of each year in perpetuity?

7. Why is the cost of debt capital usually lower than the cost of equity capital for a firm?

8. What additional risks do the stockholders of a firm face in comparison to holders of government securities?

9. A corporation can sell bonds at an interest rate of 9%, and the interest rate on government securities is 7%. What is the cost of equity capital for this firm?

10. If labor and capital are the only inputs, what are the total gains of labor in Figure 16.7 when the nation receives $100 billion of foreign investments?

11. What are some of the benefits and costs of foreign investments not captured by Figure 16.7? When all benefits and costs are considered, can we still say that foreign investments are beneficial for the receiving nation?

12. Does a nation gain or lose from foreign investments when all benefits and costs from foreign investments are considered?

PROBLEMS

1. Suppose that an individual is endowed with $Y_0 = 7.5$ units of a commodity this year and $Y_1 = 2.75$ units next year. Draw a figure showing that the individual lends 2.5 units of this year's endowment for 2.75 units next year. What is the rate of interest? On the same figure show that the individual lends 3 units for 4.2 units. What would the rate of interest be then?

2. Suppose that an individual is endowed with $Y_0 = 2.5$ units of a commodity this year and $Y_1 = 8.25$ units next year. Draw a figure showing that the individual borrows 2.5 units this year and repays 2.75 units next year. What is the rate of interest? On the same figure, show that the individual borrows 2 units this year and repays 2.80 units next year. What would the rate of interest be then?

3. Assume that (1) the consumer of Problem 2 (call him or her individual B or the borrower) is a different individual from the consumer of Problem 1 (call him or her individual A or the lender), and that (2) both individual A and B have the same tastes or time preference. Draw a figure showing how the equilibrium rate of interest is determined if A and B are the only individuals in the market. What would happen at $r = 40\%$? At $r = 5\%$?

*4. Assume that (1) individuals A and B have identical endowments of a commodity of $Y_0 = 5$ this year and $Y_1 = 6$ next year, and that (2) the optimal choice for individual B is to borrow 2.5 units this year and repay 3 units next year, while the optimal choice for individual A is to lend 2.5 units this year and receive 3 units next year. Draw a figure similar to Figures 16.1 and 16.2 for the above. What is the equilibrium rate of interest if A and B are the only individuals in the market? On the same figure show that at $r = 50\%$, individual B wants to borrow 2 units instead of 2.5 this year and repay 3 units next year, while individual A wants to lend 3 units this year and receive 4.5 units next year. Why is $r = 50\%$ not the equilibrium rate of interest?

*5. a. Why does a lender's supply curve of loans (lending) bend backward at sufficiently high rates of interest?

b. Why is a borrower's demand curve for loans (borrowing) negatively sloped throughout?

6. Draw a figure similar to Figure 16.5 showing that a rise in the rate of interest will reduce the individual's level of investment and borrowing.

7. Starting from Figure 16.5, draw a figure showing that if indifference curve U_5 had been tangent to market line HW_0' to the right of point A, the individual would have been dissaving.

8. Starting from Figure 16.5, draw a figure showing that if indifference curve U_5 had been tangent to market line HW_0' to the left of point H, the individual would have been saving more than he or she invested.

*9. Reestimate the net present value of the project given in Table 16.4 for $r = 5\%$.

*10. A firm expects to earn $200 million after taxes for the current year. The company has a policy of paying out half of its net after-tax income to the holders of the company's 100 million shares of common stock. A share of the common stock of the company currently sells for eight times current earnings. Management and outside analysts expect the growth rate of earnings and dividends for the company to be 7.5% per year. Calculate the cost of equity capital to this firm.

11. A company pays the interest rate of 11% on its bonds, the marginal income tax rate that the firm faces is 40%, the rate on government bonds is 7.5%, the return on the average stock of all firms in the market is 11.55%, the estimated beta coefficient for the common stock of the firm is 2, and the firm wishes to raise 40% of its capital by borrowing. Determine:

a. The cost of debt.

b. The cost of equity capital.

c. The composite cost of capital for this firm.

12. Draw a figure showing the effect of the following on the price of an exhaustible resource.

a. A decrease in the market rate of interest.

b. An increase in the demand for the resource.

---

* = Answer provided at the end of the book.

INTERNET SITE ADDRESSES

Data and analyses of interest rates, savings and investments, and the financial situation in the leading industrial nations are provided in *The Economic Report of the President,* The Federal Reserve Bank of St. Louis, the European Commission (EC), National Bureau of Economic Research (NBER), The Peterson Institute. The Websites are:

http://www.gpoaccess.gov/eop/tables07.html

http://www.stls.frb.org

http://ec.europa.eu/economy_finance/indicators_en.htm

http://www.nber.org

http://www.petersoninstitute.org

Information and data on emerging financial markets are found on the Websites of the Bank for International Settlements (BIS), International Monetary Fund (IMF), and World Bank (WB) at:

http://www.bis.org

http://www.imf.org

http://www.worldbank.org

Financial calculators that can be used to calculate present discounted values can be found at:

http://www.biznizportal.com/calculators/bus10/java/BusinessValuation.html

For the cost of capital analysis for over 300 industries, see the site of the Ibbotson Associates' *Cost of Capital Review* at:

http://valuation.ibbotson.com

The data on foreign direct investments are published by the United Nations in the *World Investment Report* (yearly), the OECD in the *International Investment Statistics Yearbook,* and the Bureau of Economic Analysis on the following Websites:

http://www.unctad.org/Templates/WebFlyer.asp?intItemID=4361&lang=1fs

http://www.unctad.org/Templates/WebFlyer.asp?intItemID=4361&lang=1

http://bea.doc.gov/bea/di1.htm

PART SIX

General Equilibrium, Efficiency, and Public Goods

Part Six (Chapters 17–19) presents the theory of general equilibrium and welfare economics, examines the role of government, and deals with the economics of information. Chapter 17 describes general equilibrium theory and welfare economics. It examines the interdependence or relationship among all products and input markets and shows how the various individual markets (studied in Parts Two through Five) fit together to form an integrated economic system. The chapter also considers questions of equity in the distribution of income. Chapter 18 concentrates on externalities, public goods, and the role of government. It studies why externalities (such as pollution) and the existence of public goods (such as national defense) lead to economic inefficiencies and discusses policies that can be used to overcome these inefficiencies. It also presents the theory of public choice. Finally, Chapter 19 deals with the economics of information. It examines the economics of search and the problems arising from asymmetric information (i.e., the situation where one party to a transaction has more information than another) and moral hazard (i.e., the increased probability of a loss when an economic agent can shift some of its costs to others). As in previous parts of the text, the presentation of theory is reinforced with many real-world examples and important applications, while the *At the Frontier* sections present some new and important developments.

CHAPTER 17

General Equilibrium and Welfare Economics

After Studying This Chapter, You Should Be Able to:

- Know the meaning of partial and general equilibrium analysis and when each is appropriate
- Know the meaning and conditions for general equilibrium in exchange and production
- Understand the meaning and importance of the concept of Pareto optimality
- Understand the relationship between efficiency and equity
- Know how changes in social welfare can be measured

Until this point we have examined the behavior of individual decision-making units (individuals as consumers of commodities and suppliers of inputs, and firms as employers of inputs and producers of commodities) and the workings of individual markets for commodities and inputs under various market structures. Generally missing from our presentation has been an examination of how the various individual pieces fit together to form an integrated economic system.

In this chapter, we take up the topic of interdependence or relationship among the various decision-making units and markets in the economy. This allows us to trace both the effect of a change in any part of the economic system on every other part of the system, and the repercussions from the latter on the former. We begin the chapter by distinguishing between partial equilibrium analysis and general equilibrium analysis and by examining the conditions under which each type of analysis is appropriate. Then, we discuss the conditions required for the economy to be in general equilibrium of exchange, production, and production and exchange simultaneously, and we examine their welfare implications. The numerous examples add realism to the presentation while the *At the Frontier* section examines the hot issue of growing income inequality in the United States today.

17.1   PARTIAL VERSUS GENERAL EQUILIBRIUM ANALYSIS

Partial equilibrium analysis Studies the behavior of individual decision-making units and individual markets, viewed in isolation.

In Parts Two through Five (Chapters 3–16) we conducted **partial equilibrium analysis.** That is, we studied the behavior of individual decision-making units and individual markets *viewed in isolation.* We examined how an individual maximizes satisfaction subject to his or her income constraint (Part Two, Chapters 3–6), how a firm minimizes its costs of production (Part Three, Chapters 7–9) and maximizes profits under various market structures (Part Four, Chapters 10–13), and how the price and employment of each type of input is determined (Part Five, Chapters 14–16). In doing so, we have abstracted from all the interconnections that exist between the market under study and the rest of the economy (the *ceteris paribus* assumption). In short, we have shown how demand and supply in each market determine the equilibrium price and quantity in that market *independent of other markets.*

General equilibrium analysis Studies the interdependence that exists among all markets in the economy.

However, a change in any market has spillover effects on other markets, and the change in these other markets will, in turn, have repercussions or feedback effects on the original market. These effects are studied by **general equilibrium analysis.** That is, general equilibrium analysis studies the **interdependence** or interconnections that exist among all markets and prices in the economy and attempts to give a complete, explicit, and simultaneous answer to the questions of what, how, and for whom to produce. In terms of Section 1.3 (examining the circular flow of economic activity), general equilibrium analysis examines simultaneously the links among all commodity and input markets, rather than studying each market in isolation.

Interdependence The relationship among all markets in the economy such that a change in any of them affects all the others.

For example, a change in the demand and price for new, domestically produced automobiles will immediately affect the demand and price of steel, glass, and rubber (the inputs of automobiles), as well as the demand, wages, and income of auto workers and of the workers in these other industries. The demand and price of gasoline and of public transportation (as well as the wages and income of workers in these industries) are also affected. These affected industries have spillover effects on still other industries, until the entire economic system is more or less involved, and all prices and quantities are affected. This is like throwing a rock in a pond and examining the ripples emanating in every direction until the stability of the entire pond is affected. The size of the ripples declines as they move farther and farther away from the point of impact. Similarly, industries further removed or less related to the automobile industry are less affected than more closely related industries.

What is important is that the effect that a change in the automobile industry has on the rest of the economy will have repercussions (through changes in relative prices and incomes) on the automobile industry itself. This is like the return or feedback effect of the ripples in the pond after reaching the shores. These repercussions or feedback effects are likely to significantly modify the original partial equilibrium conclusions (price and output) reached by analyzing the automobile industry in isolation (see Example 17–1).

When (as in the automobile example) the repercussions or feedback effects from the other industries are significant, partial equilibrium analysis is inappropriate. By measuring only the *impact* effect on price and output, partial equilibrium analysis provides a misleading measure of the total, final effect after all the repercussions or feedback effects from the original change have occurred. On the other hand, if the industry in which the original change occurs is small and the industry has few direct links with the rest of the economy (for example, the U.S. wristwatch industry), then partial equilibrium analysis provides a good first approximation to the results sought.

Concept Check

What is the meaning of partial equilibrium analysis? When is it appropriate?

The logical question is why not use general equilibrium analysis all the time and immediately obtain the total, direct, and indirect results of a change on the industry (in which the change originated) as well as on all the other industries and markets in the economy? The answer is that general equilibrium analysis, dealing with each and all industries in the economy at the same time, is by its very nature difficult, time consuming, and expensive. Happily for the practical economist, partial equilibrium analysis often suffices. In any event, partial equilibrium analysis represents the appropriate point of departure, both for the relaxation of more and more of the *ceteris paribus* or "other things equal" assumptions, and for the inclusion of more and more industries in the analysis, as required.

The first and simplest general equilibrium model was introduced in 1874 by the great French economist, Léon Walras.[1] This model and subsequent general equilibrium models are necessarily mathematical in nature and include one equation for each commodity and input demanded and supplied in the economy, as well as market clearing equations.[2] More recently, economists have extended and refined the general equilibrium model theoretically and proved that under perfect competition, a general equilibrium solution of the model usually exists with all markets *simultaneously* in equilibrium.[3]

EXAMPLE 17–1

Effect of a Reduction in Demand for Domestically Produced Automobiles in the United States

With the sharp increase in the price of imported petroleum from 1973 to 1980, the demand for new, large domestically produced automobiles declined, as from D to D' in panel (a) of Figure 17.1, while the demand for small fuel-efficient, foreign-produced automobiles increased. This reduced the real (i.e., the inflation-adjusted) price and quantity of domestically produced automobiles, as from P to P' and from Q to Q', respectively, in panel (a). This impact effect is what partial equilibrium analysis measures. However, the reduction in the demand for the domestically produced automobiles had spillover effects that disturbed the equilibrium in the steel [panel (b)] industry and other industries that supply inputs to the domestic automobile industry, as well as in the petroleum industry [panel (c)]. The inflation-adjusted price and quantity of steel and other inputs fell, and part of the original increase in the price of gasoline was neutralized. Other industries related to these industries were also affected.

But this is not the end of the story. The demand for workers in the automobile industry [panel (d)] and other affected industries fell, and so did real wages, employment, and incomes. The fall in real incomes reduced the demand, price, and quantity of steaks [panel (e)] and other normal goods purchased. To be sure, the demand for public

---

[1] L. Walras, *Elements of Pure Economics,* translated by William Jaffé (Homewood, IL: Irwin, 1954).
[2] See Section A.16 of the Mathematical Appendix at the end of the text.
[3] K. J. Arrow and G. Debreu, "Existence of an Equilibrium for a Competitive Economy," *Econometrica,* July 1954, pp. 265–290; and L. W. McKenzie, "On the Existence of General Equilibrium for a Competitive Market," *Econometrica,* January 1959, pp. 54–71.

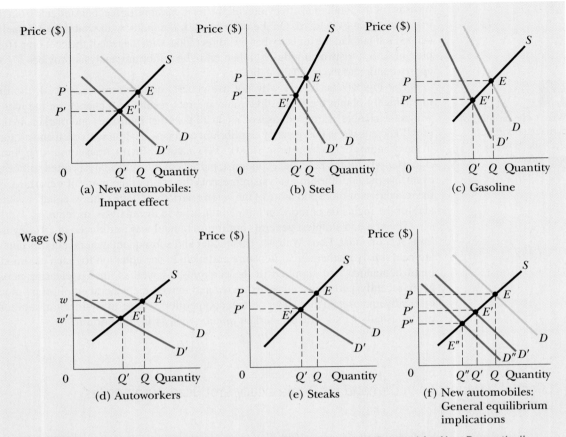

FIGURE 17.1   General Equilibrium Implications of a Reduction in the Demand for New Domestically Produced Automobiles   The impact or partial equilibrium effect of a reduction in the demand for new domestically produced automobiles is to reduce price from P to P' and quantity from Q to Q' [panel (a)]. This reduces the demand for (and price and quantity of) steel [panel (b)] and gasoline [panel (c)], and the demand for (and wages and employment of) workers in the automobile [panel (d)] and other affected industries. This, in turn, has spillover effects on the market for steaks [panel (e)] and other commodities, and feedback effects on the domestic automobile industry itself [panel (f)].

transportation (buses, trains, and drivers and other attendants) and cheaper substitutes for steaks increased, but the net effect of the reduction in the demand for domestically produced cars was to reduce the demand and real income of labor. This, in turn, had feedback effects on the automobile industry, further reducing the demand, the inflation-adjusted price, and the output of domestically produced automobiles [panel (f)]. The same process continued throughout the 1980s and 1990s (long after the petroleum crisis ended), as Japanese automobile exports to and production in the United States displaced more and more domestic production by the big three U.S. automakers.

Panel (f) of Figure 17.1 shows that the feedback effects on the domestic automobile industry were significant. The inflation-adjusted price fell from P to P'' rather than to P', and quantity fell from Q to Q'' instead of falling only to Q'. Thus, partial equilibrium alysis gives only a rough first approximation to the final solution. Note that a first round of spillover and feedback effects (as shown in the above analysis) can be measured by the cross and income elasticities (see Sections 5.3 and 5.4), but these only carry us part of the way. The complete, final effects on the domestic automobile industry and on all other industries can only be measured through full-fledged general equilibrium analysis. This is necessarily mathematical in nature—words and graphs simply fail us.

Sources: "U.S. Giving Up on Making Small Cars," *U.S. News and Worm Report,* December 19, 1983, p. 56; "Auto Industry in U.S. Is Sliding Relentlessly into Japanese Hands," *Wall Street Journal,* February 16, 1990, p. A1; "Detroit Takes the Offensive," *Forbes,* September 28, 1992, pp. 108–112; "American Auto Makers Try to Redefine Their Brands," *Wall Street Journal,* October 30, 1995, p. B1; "Detroit Fights Back," *Forbes,* September 17, 2001, pp. 76–78.; and "Big Three Face New Obstacles in Restructuring," *Wall Street Journal,* January 26, 2007, p. A1.

17.2 GENERAL EQUILIBRIUM OF EXCHANGE AND PRODUCTION

In this section, we examine separately general equilibrium of exchange and of production, and we derive the production-possibilities frontier. In the next section, we examine how both equilibria are achieved *simultaneously* and the conditions for maximum economic efficiency.

General Equilibrium of Exchange

Let us begin by examining general equilibrium of exchange for a very simple economy composed of only two individuals (A and B), two commodities (X and Y), and no production. This allows us to present the general equilibrium of exchange graphically.[4] The general equilibrium of exchange for this simple economy of two individuals, two commodities, and no production was presented earlier in Section 4.5. That analysis is now summarized and extended, and it will be used throughout the rest of the chapter.

Edgeworth box diagram for exchange
A diagram constructed from the indifference curves diagram of two individuals, which can be used to analyze voluntary exchange.

The **Edgeworth box diagram for exchange** of Figure 17.2 is that of Figure 4.8, except that the indifference curves of individual A, convex to origin 0_A, are given by A_1, A_2, and A_3 (rather than by U_1, U_2, and U_3 as in Figure 4.8) and the indifference curves of individual B, convex to origin 0_B, are given by B_1, B_2, and B_3 (rather than by U_1', U_2', and U_3'). The dimensions of the box are given by the total amount of the two commodities ($10X$ and $8Y$) owned by the two individuals together.[5] Any point inside the box indicates how the total amount of the two commodities is distributed between the two individuals. For example, point C indicates that individual A has $3X$ and $6Y$, while individual B has $7X$ and $2Y$, for the combined total of $10X$ and $8Y$ (the dimensions of the box).

Suppose that point C does in fact represent the original distribution of commodities X and Y between individuals A and B. Since at point C, indifference curves A_1 and B_1 intersect, their slope or marginal rate of substitution of commodity X for commodity Y (MRS_{XY}) differs. Starting at point C, individual A is willing to give up $4Y$ to get one additional unit of

---

[4] However, the analysis can be generalized mathematically to more than two individuals and more than two commodities. The graphic presentation in the text follows the well-known article by F. M. Bator, "The Simple Analytics of Welfare Maximization," *American Economic Review,* March 1957, pp. 22–59.

[5] As explained in Section 4.5, the Edgeworth box was obtained by rotating individual B's indifference curves diagram by 180 degrees (so that origin 0_B appears in the top right-hand corner) and superimposing it on individual A's indifference curves diagram (with origin at 0_A) in such a way that the size of the box refers to the combined amount of the X and Y owned by the two individuals together.

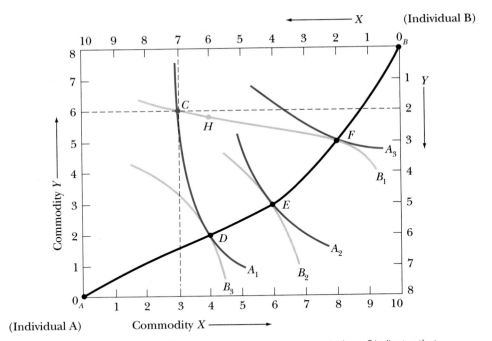

FIGURE 17.2   Edgeworth Box Diagram for Exchange   A point such as C indicates that individual A had 3X and 6Y (viewed from origin O_A), while individual B has 7X and 2Y (viewed from origin O_B) for a total of 10X and 8Y (the dimensions of the box). A's indifference curves (A_1, A_2, and A_3) are convex to O_A, while B's indifference curves (B_1, B_2, and B_3) are convex to O_B. Starting from point C where A_1 and B_1 intersect, individuals A and B can reach points on DEF, where one or both individuals gain. Curve $O_A DEFO_B$ is the contract curve for exchange. It is the locus of tangencies of the indifference curves (at which the MRS_{XY} are equal) for the two individuals and the economy is in general equilibrium of exchange.

X (and move to point D on A_1), while individual B is willing to accept 0.2Y in exchange for one unit of X (and move to point H on B_1).[6] Because A is willing to give up much more Y than necessary to induce B to give up 1X, there is a basis for exchange that will benefit either or both individuals. This is true whenever, as at point C, the MRS_{XY} for the two individuals differs.

For example, starting from point C, if individual A exchanges 4Y for 1X with individual B, A moves from point C to point D along indifference curve A_1, while B moves from point C on B_1 to point D on B_3. Thus, individual B receives all of the gains from exchange while individual A gains or loses nothing (since A remains on A_1). At point D, A_1 and B_3 are tangent, so that their slopes (MRS_{XY}) are equal, and there is no further basis for exchange.[7]

Alternatively, if individual A exchanged 1Y for 5X with individual B, individual A would move from point C on A_1 to point F on A_3, while individual B would move from point C to point F along B_1. Then, A would reap all of the benefits from exchange while B

---

[6] That is, $MRS_{XY} = 4$ for A, and $MRS_{XY} = 0.2$ for B.

[7] At point D, the amount of Y that A is willing to give up for 1X is exactly equal to what B requires to give up 1X. Any further exchange would make either individual worse off than he or she is at point D.

would neither gain nor lose. At point F, MRS_{XY} for A equals MRS_{XY} for B and there is no further basis for exchange. Finally, if A exchanges $3Y$ for $3X$ with B and gets to point E, both individuals gain from exchange since point E is on A_2 and B_2. Thus, starting from point C, which is not on line DEF, both individuals can gain through exchange by getting to a point on line DEF between D and F. The greater A's bargaining strength, the closer the final equilibrium point of exchange will be to point F, and the greater will be the proportion of the total gains from exchange going to individual A (so that less will be left over for individual B).

Contract curve for exchange The locus of tangency points of the indifference curves for two individuals when the economy is in general equilibrium of exchange.

Curve $0_A DEF0_B$ is the **contract curve for exchange.** It is the locus of tangency points of the indifference curves of the two individuals.[8] That is, along the contract curve for exchange, the marginal rate of substitution of commodity X for commodity Y is the same for individuals A and B, and the economy is in general equilibrium of exchange. Thus, for equilibrium,

$$MRS_{XY}^{A} = MRS_{XY}^{B} \qquad [17.1]$$

✓ Concept Check
How is the consumption contract curve derived?

Starting from any point not on the contract curve, both individuals can gain from exchange by getting to a point on the contract curve. *Once on the contract curve, one of the two individuals cannot be made better off without making the other worse off.* For example, a movement from point D (on A_1 and B_3) to point E (on A_2 and B_2) makes individual A better off but individual B worse off. Thus, the consumption contract curve is the locus of general equilibrium of exchange. For an economy composed of many consumers and many commodities, the general equilibrium of exchange occurs where the marginal rate of substitution between every pair of commodities is the same for all consumers consuming both commodities.

General Equilibrium of Production

Now that we have examined general equilibrium in a pure exchange economy with no production, we turn to general equilibrium of production in a simple economy in which no exchange takes place.

To examine general equilibrium of production, we deal with a very simple economy that produces only two commodities (X and Y) with only two inputs, labor (L) and capital (K). We construct an Edgeworth box diagram for production from the *isoquants* for commodities X and Y in a manner completely analogous to the Edgeworth box diagram for exchange of Figure 17.2. This is shown in Figure 17.3.

Edgeworth box diagram for production A diagram constructed from the isoquants diagram of two commodities, which can be used to analyze general equilibrium of production.

The **Edgeworth box diagram for production** shown in Figure 17.3 was obtained by rotating the isoquant diagram for commodity Y by 180 degrees (so that origin 0_Y appears in the top right-hand corner) and superimposing it on the isoquant diagram for commodity X (with origin 0_X) in such a way that the size of the box refers to the total amount of L and K available to the economy ($12L$ and $10K$). Any point inside the box indicates how the total amount of the two inputs is utilized in the production of the two commodities. For example, point R indicates that $3L$ and $8K$ are used in the production of X_1 of commodity X, and the remaining $9L$ and $2K$ are used to produce Y_1 of Y. Three of X's isoquants (convex to origin 0_X) are X_1, X_2, and X_3. Three of Y's isoquants (convex to origin 0_Y) are Y_1, Y_2, and Y_3.

---

[8] Such tangency points are assured because indifference curves are convex and the field is dense (i.e., there is an infinite number of indifference curves).

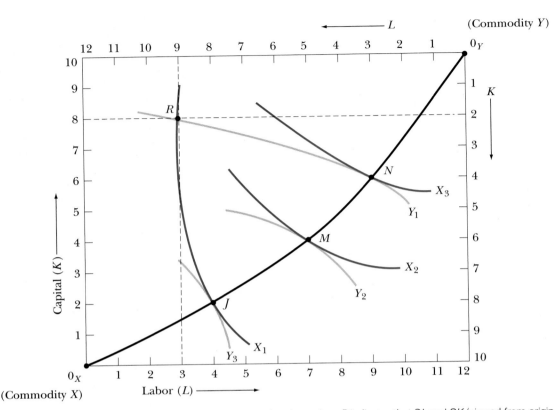

FIGURE 17.3   Edgeworth Box Diagram for Production   A point such as R indicates that $3L$ and $8K$ (viewed from origin O_X) are used to produce X_1 of commodity X, and the remaining $9L$ and $2K$ (viewed from origin O_Y) are used to produce Y_1 of Y. The isoquants for X (X_1, X_2, and X_3) are convex to O_X, while the isoquants of Y (Y_1, Y_2, and Y_3) are convex to O_Y. Starting from point R, where X_1 and Y_1 intersect, the economy can produce more of X, more of Y, or more of both by moving to a point on JMN. Curve $O_X JMNO_Y$ is the contract curve for production. It is the locus of tangencies of the isoquants (at which the $MRTS_{LK}$ are equal) for both commodities, and the economy is in general equilibrium of production.

If this economy was initially at point R, it would not be maximizing its output of commodities X and Y because, at point R, the marginal rate of technical substitution of labor for capital ($MRTS_{LK}$) in the production of X (the absolute slope of X_1) exceeds the $MRTS_{LK}$ in the production of Y (the absolute slope of Y_1).[9] By simply transferring $6K$ from the production of X to the production of Y and $1L$ from the production of Y to the production of X, the economy can move from point R (on X_1 and Y_1) to point J (on X_1 and Y_3) and increase its output of Y without reducing its output of X.

Alternatively, this economy can move from point R to point N (and increase its output of X from X_1 to X_3 without reducing its output of Y_1) by transferring $2K$ from the production of X to the production of Y and $6L$ from Y to X. Or, by transferring $4K$ from the production of X to the production of Y and $4L$ from Y to X, this economy can move from point R (on X_1 and Y_1) to point M (on X_2 and Y_2), and increase its output of both X and Y. At points J, M, and N, an X isoquant is tangent to a Y isoquant so that the $MRTS_{LK}$ in the production of X equals $MRTS_{LK}$ in the production of Y.

---

[9] Review, if necessary, the definition and measurement of the marginal rate of technical substitution in Section 7.4.

Contract curve for production The locus of tangency points of the isoquants for two commodities when the economy is in general equilibrium of production.

✓ Concept Check
How can two firms gain by moving from a point off the production contract curve to a point on it?

Curve $0_X JMN0_Y$ is the **contract curve for production.** It is the locus of tangency points of the isoquants for X and Y at which the marginal rate of technical substitution of labor for capital is the same in the production of X and Y. That is, the economy is in general equilibrium of production when

$$MRTS_{LK}^X = MRTS_{LK}^Y \qquad\qquad [17.2]$$

Thus, by simply transferring some of the given and fixed amounts of available L and K between the production of X and Y, this economy can move from a point not on the contract curve for production to a point on the curve and increase its output of either or both commodities. Once on its production contract curve, the economy can only increase the output of either commodity by reducing the output of the other. For example, by moving from point J (on X_1 and Y_3) to point M (on X_2 and Y_2), the economy increases its output of commodity X (by transferring $3L$ and $2K$ from the production of Y to the production of X), but its output of commodity Y falls. For an economy of many commodities and many inputs, the general equilibrium of production occurs where the marginal rate of technical substitution between any pair of inputs is the same for all commodities and producers using both inputs.

Derivation of the Production-Possibilities Frontier

From the production contract curve, we can derive the corresponding production-possibilities frontier or transformation curve by simply plotting the various combinations of outputs directly. For example, if isoquant X_1 in Figure 17.3 referred to an output of 4 units of commodity X and isoquant Y_3 referred to an output of 13 units of commodity Y, we can go from point J (X_1, Y_3) in Figure 17.3 to point J' ($4X$, $13Y$) in Figure 17.4. Similarly, if isoquant X_2 referred to an output of $10X$ and isoquant Y_2 to an output of $8Y$, we can go from point M (X_2, Y_2) in Figure 17.3 to point M' ($10X$, $8Y$) in Figure 17.4. Finally, if $X_3 = 12X$ and $Y_1 = 4Y$, we can plot point N (X_3, Y_1) from Figure 17.3 as point N' ($12X$, $4Y$) in Figure 17.4. By joining points $J'M'N'$ and other points similarly obtained, we derive the production-possibilities frontier or transformation curve of X for Y, TT, shown in Figure 17.4. Thus, the production-possibilities frontier is obtained by simply mapping or transferring the production contract curve from input space to output space.

The **production-possibilities frontier** or transformation curve shows the various combinations of commodities X and Y that the economy can produce by fully utilizing all of the fixed amounts of labor and capital with the best technology available. Since the production contract curve shows all points of general equilibrium of production, so does the production-possibilities frontier. That is, the production-possibilities frontier shows the maximum amount of either commodity that the economy can produce, given the amount of the other commodity that the economy is producing. For example, given that the economy is producing $10X$, the maximum amount of commodity Y that the economy can produce is $8Y$ (point M' in Figure 17.4), and vice versa.

A point inside the production-possibilities frontier corresponds to a point off the production contract curve and indicates that the economy is not in general equilibrium of production, and it is not utilizing its inputs of labor and capital most efficiently. For example, point R', inside production-possibilities frontier TT in Figure 17.4, corresponds to point R in Figure 17.3, at which isoquant X_1 and Y_1 intersect. By simply reallocating some of the fixed labor and capital available between the production of X and Y, this economy can increase its output of Y only (and move from point R' to point J' in Figure 17.4), it can

Production-possibilities frontier Shows the alternative combinations of commodities that a nation can produce by fully utilizing all of its resources with the best technology available to it.

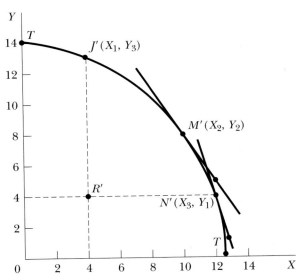

FIGURE 17.4   Production–Possibilities Frontier   The production-possibilities frontier or transformation curve TT is derived by mapping the production contract curve of Figure 17.3 from input to output space. Starting from point R', the economy could increase its output of X (point N'), of Y (point J'), or of both X and Y (point M'). The absolute slope or $MRT_{XY} = 3/2$ at point M' means that $3/2$ of Y must be given up to produce one additional unit of X. MRT_{XY} increases as we move down the frontier. Thus, at point N', $MRT_{XY} = 3$.

✓ Concept Check

How is the production-possibilities frontier derived?

increase the output of X only (and move from point R' to point N'), or it can increase its output of both X and Y (the movement from point R' to point M'). On the other hand, a point outside the production-possibilities frontier cannot be achieved with the available inputs and technology.

Once on the production-possibilities frontier, the output of either commodity can be increased only by reducing the output of the other. For example, starting at point J' ($4X$ and $13Y$) on the production-possibilities frontier in Figure 17.4, the economy can move to point M' and produce $10X$ only by reducing the amount produced of Y by 5 units (i.e., to $8Y$). The amount of commodity Y that the economy must give up, at a particular point on the production-possibilities frontier, so as to release just enough labor and capital to produce one additional unit of commodity X, is called the **marginal rate of transformation of X for Y (MRT_{XY})**. This is given by the absolute value of the slope of the production-possibilities frontier at that point. For example, at point M' on production-possibilities frontier TT in Figure 17.4, $MRT_{XY} = 3/2$ (the absolute value of the slope of the tangent to the production-possibilities frontier at point M').

Marginal rate of transformation of X for Y (MRT_{XY}) The amount of Y that must be given up to release just enough labor and capital to produce one additional unit of X.

The marginal rate of transformation of X for Y is also equal to the ratio of the marginal cost of X to the marginal cost of Y. That is, $MRT_{XY} = MC_X/MC_Y$. For example, at point M', $MRT_{XY} = 3/2$. This means that $3/2$ of Y must be given up to produce one additional unit of X. Thus, $MC_X = 3/2 \, MC_Y$, and $MRT_{XY} = 3/2$. Another way of looking at this is that if $MC_Y = \$10$ and $MC_X = \$15$, this means that to produce one additional unit of X requires 1.5 or $3/2$ more units of labor and capital than to produce one additional unit of Y, so that 3/2 of Y must be given up to produce one additional unit of X. This is exactly what the MRT_{XY} measures. Thus, at point M', $MRT_{XY} = MC_X/MC_Y = 3/2$.

As we move down the production-possibilities frontier (and produce more X and less Y), the MRT_{XY} increases, indicating that more and more Y must be given up to produce each additional unit of X. For example, at point N', the MRT_{XY} or absolute value of the slope of the production-possibilities frontier is 3 (up from 3/2 at point M'). The reason for this is that, as the economy reduces its output of Y (in order to produce more of X), it releases labor and capital in combinations that become less and less suited for the production of more X. Thus, the economy incurs increasing MC_X in terms of Y. It is because of this imperfect input substitutability between the production of X and Y (and rising MC_X in terms of Y) that the production-possibilities frontier is concave to the origin.[10]

GENERAL EQUILIBRIUM OF PRODUCTION AND EXCHANGE AND PARETO OPTIMALITY

In this section, we examine general equilibrium of production and exchange and define the concept of Pareto optimality, which summarizes the marginal conditions for economic efficiency.

Simultaneous General Equilibrium of Production and Exchange

We now can use the production-possibilities frontier and the contract curve for exchange to examine how our very simple economy composed of two individuals (A and B), two commodities (X and Y), and two inputs (L and K) can reach *simultaneous* general equilibrium of production and exchange. This equilibrium is shown in Figure 17.5.

The production-possibilities frontier of Figure 17.5 is that of Figure 17.4, which was derived from the production contract curve of Figure 17.3. Thus, every point on production-possibilities frontier TT is a point of general equilibrium of production. Suppose that this economy produces $10X$ and $8Y$, given by point M' on production-possibilities frontier TT in Figure 17.5.[11] By dropping perpendiculars from point M' to both axes, we can construct in Figure 17.5 the Edgeworth box diagram for exchange between individuals A and B of Figure 17.2. Note that the top right-hand corner of the Edgeworth box diagram for exchange of Figure 17.2 coincides with point M' on production-possibilities frontier TT in Figure 17.5. Given the indifference curves of individuals A and B and the output of $10X$ and $8Y$, we derived contract curve $0_A DEF0_B$ for exchange in Figure 17.2. This curve is reproduced in Figure 17.5. Every point on the contract curve for exchange in Figure 17.5 is a point of general equilibrium of exchange.

Thus, every point on production-possibilities frontier TT in Figure 17.5 is a point of general equilibrium of production, and every point on the contract curve for exchange is a point of general equilibrium of exchange. However, to be *simultaneously* in general equilibrium of production and exchange, the marginal rate of transformation of commodity X for commodity Y in production must be equal to the marginal rate of substitution of commodity X for commodity Y in consumption for individuals A and B. That is,

$$MRT_{XY} = MRS^A_{XY} = MRS^B_{XY} \qquad [17.3]$$

---

[10] If labor and capital were perfectly substitutable in the production of X and Y, MC_X would be constant in terms of Y, and the production-possibilities frontier would be a negatively sloped straight line.
[11] How this particular output level is determined is examined in Section 17.4.

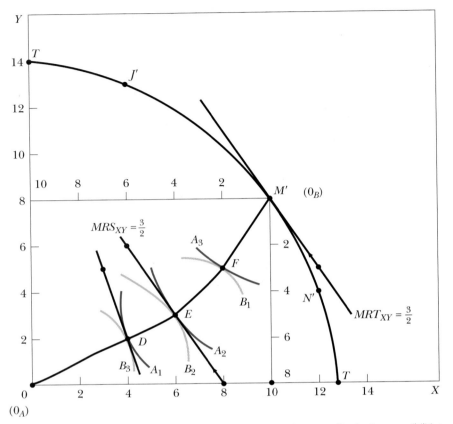

FIGURE 17.5   General Equilibrium of Production and Exchange   Production–possibilities frontier *TT* is that of Figure 17.4. Every point on *TT* is a point of general equilibrium of production. Starting from point M' (10*X*, 8*Y*) on the production–possibilities frontier, we constructed in Figure 17.4 the Edgeworth box diagram for exchange between individuals A and B shown in Figure 17.2. Every point on contract curve $O_A DEFO_B$ is a point of general equilibrium of exchange. Simultaneous general equilibrium of production and exchange is at point *E*, at which $MRT_{XY} = MRS^A_{XY} = MRS^B_{XY} = 3/2$.

✔️ Concept Check

What are the conditions for simultaneous general equilibrium in production and exchange ?

Geometrically, this equation corresponds to the point on the contract curve for exchange at which the common slope of an indifference curve of individual A and individual B equals the slope of production-possibilities frontier *TT* at the point of production. In Figure 17.5, this occurs at point *E*, where

$$MRS^A_{XY} = MRS^B_{XY} = MRT_{XY} = 3/2 \qquad [17.3A]$$

Thus, when producing 10*X* and 8*Y* (point M' on production-possibilities frontier *TT*), this economy is simultaneously in general equilibrium of production and exchange when individual A consumes 6*X* and 3*Y* (point *E* on his or her indifference curve A_2) and individual B consumes the remaining 4*X* and 5*Y* (point *E* on his or her indifference curve B_2).

If condition [17.3] did not hold, the economy would not be simultaneously in general equilibrium of production and exchange. For example, suppose that individuals A and B consumed at point *D* on the contract curve for exchange rather than at point *E* in

Figure 17.5. At point D, the MRS_{XY} (the common absolute value of the slope of indifference curves A_1 and B_3) is 3. This means that individuals A and B are willing (indifferent) to give up $3Y$ to obtain one additional unit of X. Since in production only $3/2 Y$ needs to be given up to produce an additional unit of X, society would have to produce more of X and less of Y to be simultaneously in general equilibrium of production and exchange. That is, if $MRS_{XY} = 3$, this society would not have chosen to produce at point M', but would have produced at point N' ($12X$ and $4Y$), where $MRS_{XY} = MRT_{XY} = 3$.

The opposite is true at point F. That is, at point F, $MRS_{XY} = 1/2$. Since $MRT_{XY} = 3/2$ at point M' (the point of production), more of Y needs to be given up in production to obtain one additional unit of X than individuals A and B are willing to give up in consumption. If this were the case, this society would have chosen to produce at point J' ($4X$ and $13Y$) where $MRS_{XY} = MRT_{XY} = 1/2$, rather than at point M'. Only by consuming at point E will $MRT_{XY} = MRS_{XY}$ for both individuals, and society will be simultaneously in general equilibrium of production and exchange when it produces at point M'.

We conclude the following about this simple economy when it is in general equilibrium of production and exchange: (1) it produces $10X$ and $8Y$ (point M' in Figure 17.5);[12] (2) individual A receives $6X$ and $3Y$, and individual B receives the remaining $4X$ and $5Y$ (point E in Figure 17.5); (3) to produce $10X$, $7L$ and $4K$ are used, while to produce $8Y$, the remaining $5L$ and $6K$ are used (see point M in Figure 17.3).[13]

Marginal Conditions for Economic Efficiency and Pareto Optimality

Economic efficiency The situation in which the marginal rate of transformation in production equals the marginal rate of substitution in consumption.

Pareto optimum The situation in which no reorganization of production or consumption can lead to an increase in the welfare of some without at the same time reducing the welfare of others.

With general equilibrium of production and exchange, **economic efficiency** is maximum and we have **Pareto optimality**.[14] According to this concept, *a distribution of inputs among commodities and of commodities among consumers is Pareto optimal or efficient if no reorganization of production and consumption is possible by which some individuals are made better off (in their own judgment) without making someone else worse off.* Any change that improves the well-being of some individuals without reducing the well-being of others clearly improves the welfare of society as a whole and should be undertaken. This will move society from a Pareto nonoptimal position to Pareto optimum. Once at Pareto optimum, no reorganization of production and exchange is possible that makes someone better off without, at the same time, making someone else worse off. To evaluate such changes requires interpersonal comparisons of utility, which are subjective and controversial.

In a very simple economy of two individuals, two commodities (X and Y), and no production, the contract curve for exchange (along which the MRS_{XY} is the same for both individuals) is the locus of Pareto optimum in exchange and consumption. As we have seen in Section 17.2, a movement from a point off the contract curve to a point on it improves the condition of either or both individuals, with the given quantities of the two commodities. Once on the contract curve, the economy is in general equilibrium or Pareto optimum in exchange, in the sense that either individual can be made better off only by making the other worse off. In an economy of many individuals and many commodities, Pareto optimum in exchange requires that the marginal rate of substitution between any pair of commodities be the same for all individuals consuming both commodities.

[12] As pointed out in footnote 11, we will see how this level of output is determined in Section 17.4.

[13] In Section 17.4, we will also determine the relative price of commodity X (i.e., P_X/P_Y) and the relative price of labor time (i.e., P_L/P_K or w/r) for this simple economy when it is simultaneously in general equilibrium of production and exchange.

[14] Vilfredo Pareto was the great Italian economist of the turn of the century who, in 1909, expressed the condition for maximum economic efficiency, which became known as Pareto optimality. See V. Pareto, *Manual of Political Economy,* translated by William Jaffé (New York: August Kelly, 1971).

✓ Concept Check

What is the relationship
between Pareto
optimality and
economic efficiency?

In a very simple economy of two commodities, two inputs (L and K), and no exchange, the production contract curve (along which the $MRTS_{LK}$ is the same for both commodities) is the locus of Pareto optimum in production. As we have seen in Section 17.2, a movement from a point off the production contract curve to a point on it makes it possible for the economy to produce more of either or both commodities, with the given inputs and technology. Once on the production contract curve, the economy is in general equilibrium or Pareto optimum in production in the sense that the economy can increase the output of either commodity only by reducing the output of the other. In an economy of many commodities and many inputs, Pareto optimum in production requires that the marginal rate of technical substitution between any pair of inputs be the same for all commodities and producers using both inputs.

Finally, Pareto optimum in production and exchange simultaneously in an economy of many inputs, many commodities, and many individuals requires that the marginal rate of transformation in production equals the marginal rate of substitution in consumption for every pair of commodities and for every pair of individuals consuming both commodities. In the case of a very simple economy composed of only two commodities and two individuals (A and B), Pareto optimality in production and consumption requires that

$$MRT_{XY} = MRS_{XY}^A = MRS_{XY}^B$$

This was shown graphically in Figure 17.5 by the point on the contract curve for exchange at which the common slope of an indifference curve of individual A and individual B is equal to the slope of the production frontier at the point of production.

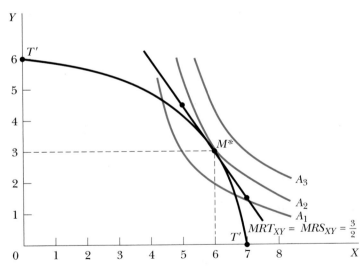

FIGURE 17.6 Efficiency in Production and Exchange in a "Robinson Crusoe" Economy   In a single-person economy, economic efficiency in production and exchange (and maximum social welfare) is achieved at point M^*, at which indifference curve A_2 for individual A (the only individual in society) is tangent to his or her production-possibilities frontier, $T'\,T'$. Output is $6X$ and $3Y$, and $MRT_{XY} = MRS_{XY} = 3/2$.

If we assume that there is only one individual (a Robinson Crusoe) in society, we achieve considerable graphic simplification in showing the point of economic efficiency in production and consumption.[15] This is given by point M^* in Figure 17.6, at which indifference curve A_2 for individual A (the only individual in society) is tangent to his or her production-possibilities frontier, $T'T'$. Any point on $T'T'$ represents a point of efficient production. Given $T'T'$, A_2 is the highest indifference curve that the individual can reach with his or her production-possibilities frontier. At point M^* (the tangency point of A_2 to $T'T'$), output is $6X$ and $3Y$, and $MRT_{XY} = MRS_{XY} = 3/2$. Production and consumption are economically efficient, and society (the individual) maximizes welfare.

17.4	## PERFECT COMPETITION, ECONOMIC EFFICIENCY, AND EQUITY

In this section we show why perfect competition leads to economic efficiency or Pareto optimum, but not necessarily to equity.

Perfect Competition and Economic Efficiency

With perfect competition in all input and commodity markets, the three marginal conditions for economic efficiency or Pareto optimum in production and exchange (Section 17.3) are automatically satisfied. This is the basic argument for perfect competition. We can easily prove that perfect competition leads to economic efficiency.

We have seen in Section 3.5 that a consumer maximizes utility or satisfaction when he or she reaches the highest indifference curve possible with his or her budget line. This occurs where an indifference curve is tangent to the budget line. At the tangency point, the slope of the indifference curve (the MRS_{XY}) is equal to the slope of the budget line (P_X/P_Y). Since P_X and P_Y, and thus P_X/P_Y, are the same for all consumers under perfect competition, the MRS_{XY} is also the same for all consumers consuming both commodities. This is the first marginal condition for economic efficiency or Pareto optimum in exchange. We can now also establish that for the simple economy examined in Section 17.3, $P_X/P_Y = 3/2$ (the absolute value of the slope of the common tangent to indifference curves A_2 and B_2 at point E in Figure 17.5).

We have also seen in Section 8.3 that efficiency in production requires that the $MRTS_{LK}$ (the absolute value of the slope of an isoquant) be equal to P_L/P_K or w/r (the ratio of the input prices given by the absolute value of the slope of the isocost line). Since P_L or w and P_K or r, and thus P_L/P_K or w/r, are the same for all producers under perfect competition, the $MRTS_{LK}$ is also the same for all producers using both inputs. This is the second marginal condition for economic efficiency or Pareto optimum in production. We can now also establish that for the simple economy examined in Section 17.3, P_L/P_K or $w/r = 2/3$ (the absolute value of the common tangent to isoquants X_2 and Y_2 at point M in Figure 17.3).[16]

---

[16] Note that in microeconomic theory, we are only concerned with *relative*, not absolute, input and commodity prices. This means that proportionate changes in (e.g., doubling or halving) all input prices and/or all commodity prices do not change the solution to the general equilibrium model. If we want to get unique absolute (dollar) values for P_X, P_Y, P_L (or w), and P_K (or r), we would have to add a monetary equation, such as Fisher's "equation of exchange" to our model. This is done in a course in macroeconomic theory but is not needed in microeconomics.

[15] Since in this very special case there is no problem of interpersonal comparison of utility, the point of maximum economic efficiency in production and consumption also represents the point of maximum social welfare.

Finally, we have seen in Section 17.3 that $MRT_{XY} = MC_X/MC_Y$, and in Section 9.3 that perfectly competitive firms produce where $MC_X = P_X$ and $MC_Y = P_Y$. Therefore, $MC_X/MC_Y = P_X/P_Y = MRT_{XY}$. Since we have also seen above that under perfect competition $MRT_{XY} = P_X/P_Y$ for all consumers consuming both commodities, we conclude that $MRT_{XY} = MRS_{XY}$ for all consumers consuming both commodities. This is the third marginal condition for economic efficiency and Pareto optimum in production and exchange. Thus, when the simple economy examined in Section 17.3 produces $10X$ and $8Y$ (point M' in Figure 17.5), $MRT_{XY} = MRS_{XY}^A = MRS_{XY}^B = 3/2$. Individual A should then consume $6X$ and $3Y$, and individual B should consume the remaining $4X$ and $5Y$ (point E in Figure 17.5) for the economy to be simultaneously at Pareto optimum in production and exchange.

The output of $10X$ and $8Y$ at point M' in Figure 17.5 is based on a particular distribution of inputs (income) between individuals A and B and on their tastes. A different distribution of income and/or tastes for individuals A and B would lead to a different combination of goods X and Y demanded. This would result in a different P_X/P_Y, different quantities of X and Y produced, and different levels of satisfaction for A and B. For example, suppose that individuals A and B demanded $12X$ and $4Y$ (point N' in Figure 17.5). Then, general equilibrium of production and exchange or Pareto optimality requires that $MRT_{XY} = P_X/P_Y = MRS_{XY}^A = MRS_{XY}^B = 3$ (the absolute slope of TT at point N'). This involves constructing an Edgeworth box diagram from point N' and retracing all the steps of the analysis in Section 17.3. In a purely exchange economy (i.e., one in which there is no production), the equilibrium P_X/P_Y is the one that exactly matches the desired quantity of X and Y that each individual wants to exchange. If B wants more of X for a given amount of Y than A is willing to exchange, then P_X/P_Y will rise until the demand for the quantities of X and Y to be exchanged match. Similarly, if B wants less of X for a given amount of Y than A is willing to exchange, P_X/P_Y will fall until equilibrium is reached.

Efficiency and Equity

Law of the invisible hand The law that postulates that in a free market economy, each individual, by pursuing his or her own selfish interests, also promotes the welfare of society.

First theorem of welfare economics Postulates that equilibrium in competitive markets is Pareto optimum.

Second theorem of welfare economics Postulates that equity in distribution is logically separable from efficiency in allocation.

The fact that perfect competition leads to optimum economic efficiency and Pareto optimum in production and exchange is no small achievement. It proves Adam Smith's famous **law of the invisible hand** stated more than 200 years ago. Smith's law postulates that in a free market economy, each individual by pursuing his or her own selfish interests is led, as if by an *invisible hand,* to promote the well-being of society more than he or she intends or even understands.[17] This law leads to the **first theorem of welfare economics,** which postulates that *an equilibrium produced by competitive markets exhausts all possible gains from exchange,* or that *equilibrium in competitive markets is Pareto optimal.* There is also a **second theorem of welfare economics.** This postulates that *when indifference curves are convex to their origin, every efficient allocation (every point on the contract curve for exchange) is a competitive equilibrium for some initial allocation of goods or distribution of inputs (income).* The significance of the second welfare theorem is that the issue of equity in distribution is logically separable from the issue of efficiency in allocation. This means that whatever the redistribution of income that society wants would lead to the exhaustion of all possible gains from exchange under perfect competition. Pareto optimality does not, therefore, imply equity. Society can use taxes and subsidies to achieve what it considers to be a more equitable distribution of income. These may discourage work, however, and show that there is usually a trade-off between efficiency and equity (see Example 17–5).[18]

---

[17] See A. Smith, *The Wealth of Nations* (Toronto: Random House, 1937), Book IV, Chapter 2, p. 423; and J. Persky, "Adam Smith's Invisible Hand," *Journal of Economic Perspectives,* fall 1989, pp. 195–201.

[18] See A. Okun, *Equality and Efficiency: The Big Tradeoff* (Washington, DC: Brookings Institution, 1975). We will return to questions of equity in Sections 17.6 and 17.7.

Market failures The existence of monopoly, monopsony, price controls, externalities, and public goods that prevent the attainment of economic efficiency or Pareto optimum.

For economic efficiency and Pareto optimum to be reached, there should be no market failure. **Market failures** arise in the presence of imperfect competition, externalities, and public goods. *Externalities* and *public goods* will be examined in the next chapter. Here, we examine why imperfect competition in the product and input markets leads to economic inefficiency and Pareto nonoptimality.

To show that imperfect competition in the product market leads to economic inefficiency and Pareto nonoptimality, remember that in Part Four of the text it was shown that a profit-maximizing firm always produces where marginal revenue (MR) equals marginal cost (MC). If commodity Y is produced in a perfectly competitive market, $P_Y = MR_Y = MC_Y$. On the other hand, if commodity X is produced by a monopolist (or other imperfect competitor), $P_X > MR_X = MC_X$. Then,

$$MRT_{XY} = \frac{MC_X}{MC_Y} = \frac{MR_X}{MR_Y} < \frac{P_X}{P_Y} = MRS_{XY}$$

That is, $MRT_{XY} < MRS_{XY}$, so that the third condition for Pareto optimum and economic efficiency (discussed in Section 17.3) is violated.

To show that imperfect competition in the input market leads to economic inefficiency and Pareto nonoptimality, remember that in Part Five of the text it was shown that a profit-maximizing firm always produces where the marginal revenue product (MRP) of each input equals the marginal resource cost (MRC) for the input. If P is the price of the input, and the input market is perfectly competitive, $MRP = MRC = P$. Otherwise, $MRP = MRC > P$. Now suppose that all markets in the economy are perfectly competitive, except that the firm producing commodity X is a monopsonist in its labor market (i.e., it is the sole employer of labor in its labor market). Therefore, $MRP = MRC > P$ in the production of commodity X, while $MRP = MRC = P$ in the production of Y. That is, $MRTS_{LK}^X > MRTS_{LK}^Y$, so that the first of the conditions for Pareto optimum and economic efficiency (discussed in Section 17.4) is violated.

Finally, note that perfect competition leads to efficiency and Pareto optimum in production and exchange *at a particular point in time*. Over time, tastes, the supply of inputs, and technology change; what is most efficient at one point in time may not be most efficient over time. In short, perfect competition leads to *static, but not necessarily to dynamic, efficiency*. (This was discussed in Section 13.3.)

✓ **Concept Check**
Why does imperfect competition lead to economic inefficiency?

EXAMPLE 17–2

Watering Down Efficiency in the Pricing of Water

In some counties (Los Angeles, for example), the price of water is lower for irrigation than for most other purposes. This reduces economic efficiency because the marginal rate of technical substitution between water and other inputs differs in irrigation than in other uses. For example, suppose that the price of 1,000 cubic feet of water when used for irrigation is equal to the daily wage of an unskilled worker, but when used to wash cars it is twice the daily wage of the unskilled worker. So, a farmer will use water until the marginal rate of technical substitution between water and labor is equal to 1, but a car-washing firm will do so until $MRTS = 2$. Water and labor inputs are then utilized at a point (such as R in Figure 17.3) at which the isoquants intersect off the production contract curve, and production is inefficient. In this case, the farmer will use too much water and too little labor, whereas the car-washing firm will underutilize water and overutilize labor.

If the price of water were the same for both the farmer and the car-washing firm, economic efficiency in production would increase. Each producer would then use water and labor until the *MRTS* between water and labor would be equal to the relative price of these two inputs. The result is that agricultural output declines and car-washing production increases, for a net increase in overall state output, with the given quantity of water and unskilled labor available. With the sharp increase in the demand for water in California as a result of rapid population growth and with the reduced supply due to drought and climate change, the efficient use of scarce water resources became even more important in California since the early 1980s. This has generally meant an increase in the *relative* availability of water for nonirrigation purposes and an increase in the relative price of water in all uses. We will see fewer golf courses in the desert and less cotton and rice grown in California!

Sources: J. Hirschleifer, J. C. DeHaven, and W. J. Milliman, *Water Supply: Economics, Technology, and Policy* (Chicago: University of Chicago Press, 1960); Subcommittee on Water and Power, *Central Valley Project Improvement Act* (Washington, DC: U.S. Government Printing Office, 1992); "California's Water: The Eternal Challenge," *The Economist*, August 27, 2005, p. 28; and J. Brewer, et al; "Water in the West: Prices, Trading, and Contractual Forms," *NBER Working Paper No. 13002*, March 2007; and M. Greenstone, "Tradable Water Rights," *Democracy Journal*, No. 8, Spring 2008, pp. 1–2.

17.5 GENERAL EQUILIBRIUM OF PRODUCTION AND EXCHANGE WITH INTERNATIONAL TRADE

An important example of general equilibrium of production and exchange is provided by international trade, say, between nations A and B. Suppose that nation A is endowed with an abundance of labor (L) relative to capital (K) with respect to nation B, and commodity X is labor intensive (i.e., the L/K ratio in the production of X is greater than in the production of Y). Given the same technology and tastes in the two nations, the cost (in terms of the amount of Y to be given up) of producing an additional unit of X (i.e., $MRT_{XY} = P_X/P_Y$) is lower in nation A than in nation B. We say that nation A has a **comparative advantage** in commodity X and nation B has a comparative advantage in commodity Y.

Comparative advantage The greater *relative* efficiency that an individual, firm, region, or nation has over another in the production of a good or service.

With trade, nation A specializes in the production of commodity X (i.e., it produces more of X than it demands for internal consumption) in order to exchange it for commodity Y from nation B. On the other hand, nation B specializes in the production of commodity Y (i.e., it produces more of Y than it demands for internal consumption) in order to exchange it for commodity X from nation A. With each nation specializing in the production of the commodity of its comparative advantage (nation A in commodity X and B in Y), the combined output of X and Y by the two nations is larger than without specialization. Both nations then share the increased output of X and Y through voluntary exchange (trade), and both are better off than without trade.

As each nation specializes in the production of the commodity of its comparative advantage, it will incur increasing opportunity costs. Specialization in production reaches the equilibrium level when $MRT_{XY} = P_X/P_Y$ is the same in both nations. The two nations are then simultaneously in general equilibrium of production and exchange (trade) when $MRT_{XY} = P_X/P_Y = MRS^A_{XY} = MRS^B_{XY}$.[19]

[19] See D. Salvatore, *International Economics*, 8th ed. (New York: John Wiley & Sons, 2003), Chapter 5.

EXAMPLE 17–3

The Basis of and the Gains from International Trade

We can show general equilibrium of production and exchange and the gains from specialization in production and trade with the aid of Figure 17.7. The production-possibilities frontier is AA for nation A and BB for nation B. The different shapes of the two production-possibilities frontiers result from nation A having a relative abundance of labor and commodity X being the labor-intensive commodity, with nation B having a relative abundance of capital and commodity Y being the capital-intensive commodity. For simplicity, we assume that both technology and tastes are the same in both nations. Suppose that in the absence of trade, nation A is observed to be producing and consuming at point C, while nation B is observed to be at point C'.[20] Since $MRT_{XY} = P_X/P_Y$ (the absolute slope of the production-possibilities frontier) is lower at point C for nation A than at point C' for nation B, nation A has a comparative advantage in commodity X, while nation B has a comparative advantage in commodity Y.

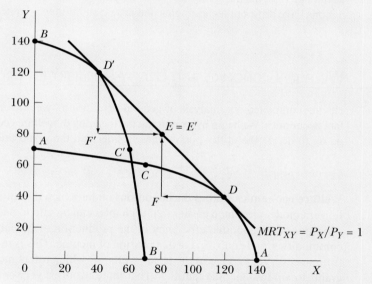

FIGURE 17.7   Graphic Analysis of General Equilibrium with Trade
The production–possibilities frontier is AA for nation A and BB for nation B. In the absence of trade, nation A is at point C and nation B is at point C'. Since $MRT_{XY} = P_X/P_Y$ (the absolute value of the slope of the production–possibilities frontier) is lower at point C than at point C', nation A has a comparative advantage in X while nation B has a comparative advantage in Y. With trade, A produces at point D, exchanges $40X$ for $40Y$ with B, and consumes at $E > C$. Nation B produces at point D', exchanges $40Y$ for $40X$ with A, and consumes at $E' > C'$.

---

[20] This means that $MRT_{XY} = MRS_{XY} = P_X/P_Y$ in each country, so that each country is simultaneously in equilibrium of production and exchange in isolation (i.e., in the absence of trade).

With the opening of trade, nation A specializes in the production of X (moves down its production-possibilities frontier from point C) and incurs increasing opportunity costs in the production of more X (i.e., the $MRT_{XY} = P_X/P_Y$ rises). Nation B specializes in the production of Y (moves up its production-possibilities frontier from point C') and incurs increasing opportunity costs in the production of more Y (i.e., the $MRT_{XY} = P_Y/P_X$ rises, which means that $MRT_{XY} = P_X/P_Y$ falls). Specialization in production proceeds until nation A has reached point D and nation B has reached point D', at which $MRT_{XY} = P_X/P_Y$ is the same in both nations. Nation A might then exchange $40X$ (DF) for $40Y$ (FE) with nation B and reach point E. At point E, nation A consumes $10X$ and $20Y$ more than at point C without trade. With trade, nation B consumes at point E' ($= E$) or $20X$ and $10Y$ more than at point C' without trade. Production and trade is in (general) equilibrium, and both nations gain.

Note that with trade, both nations consume $80X$ and $80Y$ (i.e., point E for nation A coincides with point E' for nation B). This would be true if both nations not only had the same technology and tastes but were also of equal size. These simplifying assumptions were made to simplify the graphic analysis. However, we can show comparative advantage (i.e., the basis for trade) and the gains from trade graphically even if the two nations have different technologies and tastes, and if they are unequal in size.[21]

17.6   WELFARE ECONOMICS AND UTILITY-POSSIBILITIES FRONTIERS

Having completed our analysis of general equilibrium, we now move on to examine welfare economics. We begin by examining the meaning of welfare economics and then we will go on to derive the utility-possibilities frontier and the grand utility-possibilities frontier.

The Meaning of Welfare Economics

Welfare economics
Examines the conditions for economic efficiency in the production of output and in the exchange of commodities and for equity in the distribution of income.

Welfare economics studies the conditions under which the solution to the general equilibrium model presented earlier in this chapter can be said to be optimal. It examines the conditions for economic efficiency in the production of output and in the exchange of commodities, and equity in the distribution of income. This is to be clearly distinguished from the everyday usage of the term "welfare," which refers mostly to government programs to aid low-income families. That topic is only a very small part of what welfare economics covers.

The maximization of society's well-being requires the optimal allocation of inputs among commodities and the optimal allocation of commodities (i.e., distribution of income) among consumers. The conditions for the optimal allocation of inputs among commodities and exchange of commodities among consumers have already been discussed. These are objective criteria devoid of ethical connotations or value judgments. On the other hand, it is impossible to objectively determine the optimal distribution of income. This necessarily requires interpersonal comparisons of utility and value judgments on the relative "deservingness" or merit of various members of society, and different people will inevitably have different opinions.

For example, taxing $100 away from individual A and giving it as a subsidy to individual B will certainly make B better off and A worse off. But who is to say that the society composed of both individuals is better or worse off as a whole? Determining this

---

[21] See D. Salvatore, *International Economics, op. cit.,* Chapter 3.

involves comparing the utility lost by individual A to the utility gained by individual B (i.e., making interpersonal comparison of utility). And even if A has a high income and B has a low income to begin with, different people will have different opinions on whether this increases social welfare, reduces it, or leaves it unchanged. Therefore, no entirely objective or scientific rule can be defined. The difficulty in making interpersonal comparisons of utility is clearly demonstrated in rationing hospital care, discussed in Example 17–4.

EXAMPLE 17–4

"The Painful Prescription: Rationing Hospital Care"

The great difficulty with interpersonal comparison of utility in making social choices is aptly exemplified by the need to ration hospital care. New therapeutic techniques (such as open-heart surgery) and new diagnostic devices (such as CAT scanners) have improved medical care but have greatly added to costs. For example, open-heart surgery costs tens of thousands of dollars and replaces the much cheaper (but some-what less effective) use of drugs in treating patients with heart disease. This development raises difficult choices for society in general, and for physicians and hospitals in particular, as they try to contain the ever-rising costs of medical care. In England, only a handful of patients over the age of 55 with chronic kidney failure are referred for expensive dialysis; the others are simply allowed to die of chronic renal failure. The idea of rationing medical care is generally alien to Americans, accustomed as they are to expect the best care that can be medically provided. Nevertheless, ever-increasing medical costs have inevitably led to rationing in the use of some new and expensive techniques and diagnostic devices.

As pointed out by Fuchs, medical care has always been rationed in the United States and elsewhere, because "no nation is wealthy enough to provide all the care that is technically feasible and desirable...." Therefore, the change is not between "no rationing and rationing, but rather in the way rationing takes place—who does the rationing and who is affected by it." The way hospital care (particularly the use of the more advanced and costly new diagnostic techniques) is to be rationed has given rise to a prolonged national debate in the United States. The introduction of "managed competition" with HMOs (see Example 1–1) during the last decade allows insurance companies to provide consumers with incentives to "price shop" when choosing doctors and hospitals as a way of keeping health-care costs down. The courts need also to redefine negligence so as to limit medical malpractice suits and higher physicians' insurance costs (which are then passed on to consumers in the form of higher costs of medical care). Be that as it may, health-care costs are likely to continue to rise as a proportion of GDP in the United States in the coming years. The same strain is experienced by government-financed health-care services in Canada, Britain, Germany, and Scandinavia, among other countries.

Sources: V. R. Fuchs, "The 'Rationing' of Medical Care," *The New England Journal of Medicine,* December 13, 1984, pp. 1572–1573; H. J. Aaron and W. B. Schwartz, *The Painful Prescription: Rationing Hospital Care* (Washington, D.C.: Brookings Institution, 1984); "How Managed Care Will Allow Market Forces to Solve the Problems," *New York Times,* August 13, 1995, p. 12; M. Feldstein, "The Economics of Health and Health Care: What Have We Learned? What Have I Learned?" *American Economic Review, Papers and Proceedings,* May 1995, pp. 28–31; "Medicine Isn't an Economic-Free Zone," *Wall Street Journal,* June 22, 2001, p. A14; "Canada Health Care Shows Strains," *New York Times,* October 11, 2001, p. 12; and "Beyond Those Health Care Numbers," *New York Times,* December 4, 2007, Sect. IV, p. 4.

Utility-Possibilities Frontier

By assigning utility rankings to the indifference curves of individual A and individual B in Figure 17.5, we can map or transfer the contract curve for exchange of Figure 17.5 from output or commodity space to utility space, and thus derive utility-possibilities frontier $U_{M'}$ $U_{M'}$ in Figure 17.8. Specifically, if indifference curve A_1 in Figure 17.5 refers to 200 units of utility for individual A (i.e., $U_A = 200$ utils) and B_3 refers to $U_B = 600$ utils, we can go from point D (on A_1 and B_3) in commodity space in Figure 17.5 to point D' in utility space in Figure 17.8. Similarly, if A_2 refers to $U_A = 400$ utils and B_2 refers to $U_B = 500$ utils, we can go from point E (on A_2 and B_2) in Figure 17.5 to point E' in Figure 17.8. Finally, if A_3 refers to $U_A = 500$ utils and B_1 refers to $U_B = 200$ utils, we can go from point F (on A_3 and B_1) in Figure 17.5 to point F' in Figure 17.8.[22] By joining points $D'E'F'$ and other points similarly obtained, we derive utility-possibilities frontier $U_{M'}U_{M'}$ in Figure 17.8. Thus, the utility-possibilities frontier is obtained by mapping or transferring the contract curve for exchange from output or commodity space into utility space.

The **utility-possibilities frontier** shows the various combinations of utilities received by individuals A and B (i.e., U_A and U_B) when this simple economy is in general equilibrium or Pareto optimum in exchange. It is the locus of maximum utility for one individual for any given level of utility for the other individual. For example, given that $U_A = 400$ utils, the maximum utility of individual B is $U_B = 500$ utils (point E'). A point such as C in Figure 17.2 (at which indifference curves A_1 and B_1 intersect off exchange contract curve $0_A DEF0_B$) corresponds to point C' inside utility-possibilities frontier $U_{M'}U_{M'}$ in Figure 17.8. By simply redistributing the $10X$ and $8Y$ available to the economy (point M' in Figure 17.5) between individuals A and B, the economy can move from point

> ✓ Concept Check
>
> How is the utility-possibilities frontier derived? What does it show?

Utility-possibilities frontier Shows the various combinations of utilities received by two individuals at which the economy (composed of the two individuals) is in general equilibrium or Pareto optimum in exchange.

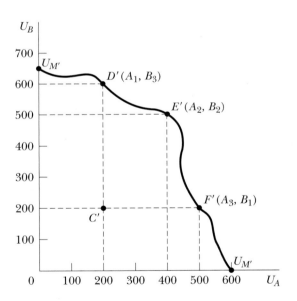

FIGURE 17.8   Utility-Possibilities Frontier   Utility-possibilities frontier $U_{M'}U_{M'}$ shows the various combinations of utilities received by individuals A and B (i.e., U_A and U_B) when the economy composed of individuals A and B is in general equilibrium or Pareto optimum in exchange. The frontier is obtained by mapping exchange contract curve $0_A DEF0_B$ in Figure 17.5 from output or commodity space to utility space. Specifically, if A_1 refers to $U_A = 200$ utils and B_3 to $U_B = 600$ utils, point D in Figure 17.5 can be plotted as point D' in this figure. Point E can be plotted as point E', and point F as F'. By joining points $D'E'F'$, we get utility-possibilities frontier $U_{M'}U_{M'}$.

---

[22] Note that the scale along the horizontal axis refers only to individual A, while the scale along the vertical axis refers only to B. Thus, $U_A = 400$ utils is not necessarily smaller than $U_B = 500$ utils, since no interpersonal comparison of utility is implied. Furthermore, the scale along either axis is ordinal, not cardinal. That is, $U_A = 300$ utils is greater than $U_A = 200$ utils, but not necessarily 1.5 times larger. Note also that utility-possibilities frontier $U_{M'}U_{M'}$, is negatively sloped, but irregularly rather than smoothly shaped.

C' to point D' in Figure 17.8 and increase U_B, or to point F' and increase U_A, or to point E' and increase both U_A and U_B. A point outside the utility-possibilities frontier cannot be reached with the available amounts of commodities X and Y. Of all points of Pareto optimality in exchange along utility-possibilities frontier $U_{M'}U_{M'}$, in Figure 17.8, only point E' (which corresponds to point E in Figure 17.5) is also a point of Pareto optimality in production. That is, at point E', $MRS^A_{XY} = MRS^B_{XY} = MRT_{XY} = P_X/P_Y = 3/2$.

Grand Utility–Possibilities Frontier

We have seen that utility-possibilities frontier $U_{M'},U_{M'}$, in Figure 17.8 (repeated in Figure 17.9) was derived from the contract curve for exchange drawn from point 0 to point M' on the production-possibilities frontier in Figure 17.5. If we pick another point on the production-possibilities frontier of Figure 17.5, say, point N', we can construct another Edgeworth box diagram and get another contract curve for exchange, this one drawn from point 0 to point N' in Figure 17.5. From this different contract curve for exchange (not shown in Figure 17.5), we can derive another utility-possibilities frontier ($U_{N'}U_{N'}$ in Figure 17.9) and obtain another Pareto optimum point in production and exchange (point H' in Figure 17.9). By then joining points E', H', and other points similarly obtained, we can derive grand utility-possibilities frontier $GE'H'G$ in Figure 17.9).[23]

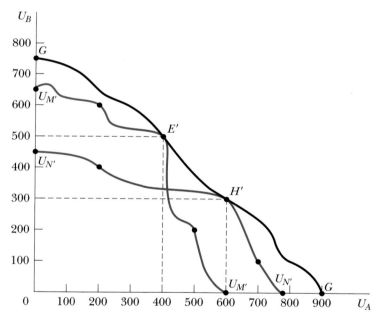

FIGURE 17.9   Grand Utility-Possibilities Frontier   Utility-possibilities frontier $U_{M'}U_{M'}$ is that of Figure 17.8. Utility-possibilities frontier $U_{N'}U_{N'}$ is derived from the contract curve for exchange in the Edgeworth box diagram constructed from point N' on the production-possibilities frontier of Figure 17.5. By joining E', H', and other Pareto optimum points of production and exchange similarly obtained, we get grand utility-possibilities frontier $GE'H'G$.

---

[23] Note that the various utility-possibilities frontiers and the grand utility-possibilities frontier derived from them are negatively sloped but are usually irregularly shaped (as in Figure 17.9).

Grand utility-possibilities frontier
The envelope to utility-possibilities frontiers at Pareto optimum points of production and exchange.

Thus, the **grand utility-possibilities frontier** is the envelope to the utility-possibilities frontiers at Pareto optimum points of production and exchange. The grand utility-possibilities frontier indicates that no reorganization of the production-exchange process is possible that makes someone better off without, at the same time, making someone else worse off. This is as far as objective analysis goes. To determine the Pareto optimum point in production and exchange at which social welfare is maximum, we need a social welfare function. However, since this is based on interpersonal comparisons of utility (which is not allowed), we cannot determine the point of maximum social welfare.

EXAMPLE 17–5
From Welfare to Work—The Success of Welfare Reform in the United States

A 1995 study by Tanner, Moore, and Hartman found that welfare payments provided welfare recipients with higher incomes than they would have received from many entry-level jobs, thus discouraging welfare recipients from finding work. The study measured the combined value of the benefits for a typical welfare family from various programs [such as Aid to Families with Dependent Children (AFDC), food stamps, Medicaid, and housing, nutrition, and energy assistance] and compared it with the income a worker would have to earn to get the same after-tax benefit as under the welfare program.

The study found that in the early 1990s in order to match the value of the welfare benefits, a mother of two children would have to earn as much as $36,000 in Hawaii (the state with the most generous welfare program) and $11,500 in Mississippi (the least generous state). Welfare paid the equivalent of $8 per hour in 40 states, $10 per hour in 17 states, and more than $12 per hour in Hawaii, Alaska, Massachusetts, Connecticut, Washington, D.C., New Work, New Jersey, and Rhode Island. Welfare benefits were even higher in large cities. For example, welfare provided the equivalent of an hourly pretax wage of $14.75 in New York City, $12.45 in Philadelphia, $11.35 in Baltimore, and $10.90 in Detroit. The study also found that welfare paid more than the entry-level salary for a computer programmer in 6 states, more than first-year salary of a teacher in 9 states, more than the average salary of a secretary in 29 states, and more than the salary of a janitor in 47 states. The study concluded that because of generous welfare benefits, welfare recipients were likely to choose welfare over work and become permanently dependent. Indeed, 70% of welfare recipients were found not to be looking for work. It is not difficult to see why: The typical untrained, uneducated welfare mother was not likely to find a job that paid $10 to $12 per hour (more than twice the minimum wage at the time).

All of this changed with the Personal Responsibility and Work Opportunity Reconciliation Act of 1996 (PRWORA), otherwise known as welfare reform. This ended welfare as entitlements, available to all persons who qualified, and required recipients to look for work as a condition for continued assistance. Rather than simply disbursing payments to welfare recipients on demand, the Federal Government provided states with a block of funds to run this portion of the welfare program with the aim of getting welfare recipients off the welfare lists by encouraging them to find jobs. Welfare reform was a stunning success: It cut the number of welfare recipients from 12.2 million in 1996 to 5.8 million in 2000. The reform also led to an increase in the income of poor people, but at a slower rate than the reductions in welfare rolls. The rapidly growing economy helped, but most of the reduction in the number of welfare recipients was due to welfare reform. The proof? During periods of rapid economic expansion in the 1980s and early 1990s, welfare rolls generally increased. Since the welfare reform of 1996, they were cut by more than half. Welfare reform could be improved further by tidying up the food-stamps program, getting rid of the marriage penalty tax for the poor, and expanding the earned-income tax credit for the working poor.

Sources: M. Tanner, S. Moore, and D. Hartman, *The Work vs. Welfare Trade-Off* (Washington, D.C.: Cato Institute, 1995); "Rewriting the Social Contract," *Business Week,* November 20, 1995, pp. 120–134; "From Welfare to Work," *Brookings Review,* fall 1999, pp. 27–30; "America's Great Achievement," *The Economist,* August 25, 2001, pp. 25–27; and "Welfare Reform: Ten Years Later," *New York Times,* August 26, 2006, p. 9.

17.7

SOCIAL POLICY CRITERIA

In this section we examine some very important criteria for measuring changes in social welfare and Arrow's impossibility theorem.

Measuring Changes in Social Welfare

Pareto criterion Postulates that a change increases social welfare if it benefits some members of society without harming anyone.

There are four different criteria to determine whether a particular policy raises social welfare. The first is the **Pareto criterion,** discussed in Section 17.3 and accepted by nearly all economists. According to this criterion, a policy increases social welfare if it benefits some members of society (in their own judgment) without harming anyone. In terms of Figure 17.10, a movement from point C^*, inside grand utility-possibilities frontier GG, to points E', H', or any point between E' and H' (such as point V) on GG, benefits one or both individuals and harms none; thus, it passes the Pareto criterion. In contrast, a movement from point C^* to point Z on GG makes individual B much better off but individual A a little worse off, and so it does not pass the Pareto criterion. Because most policies will benefit some and harm others,[24] the Pareto criterion does not go very far, and it is biased in favor of the status quo.

Compensation principle The amount that gainers from a change could pay losers to fully compensate them for their losses.

Kaldor–Hicks criterion Postulates that a change is an improvement if those who gain from the change can fully compensate the losers and still retain some of the gain.

To overcome this limitation of the Pareto criterion, Kaldor and Hicks introduced the second welfare criterion, which is based on the **compensation principle.**[25] According to the **Kaldor–Hicks criterion,** a change is an improvement if those who gain from the change can fully compensate the losers and still retain some gain. In terms of the movement from point C^* to point Z in Figure 17.10, individual B (the gainer) could fully compensate individual A for his or her loss, so that society could move from point C^* to point E' (instead of from point C^* to Z) on GG and we can determine that social welfare is higher.[26] Yet, this conclusion is not as clear-cut as it may seem.

---

[24] For example, a tax on high-income people to finance aid to low-income families benefits the latter but harms the former. Even the breakup of a monopoly harms someone (the monopolist who loses the source of profits).

[25] N. Kaldor, "Welfare Propositions in Economics and Interpersonal Comparisons of Utility," *Economic Journal,* December 1939, pp. 549–552; and J. R. Hicks, "The Foundations of Welfare Economics," *Economic Journal,* December 1939, pp. 696–712.

[26] One real-world example of actual compensation is given by the trade adjustment assistance provided since 1962 by the Trade Expansion Act for U.S. workers displaced by negotiated tariff reductions. This assistance was justified by the much greater benefits to society as a whole resulting from trade liberalization. See D. Salvatore, *International Economics, op. cit.,* Chapter 9.

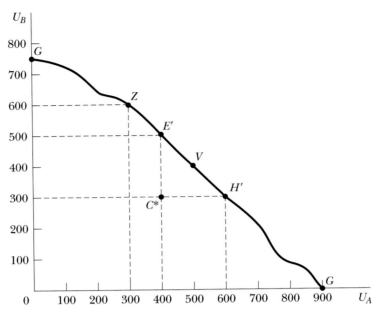

FIGURE 17.10   Measuring Changes in Social Welfare   A movement from point C^* to a point from E' to H' on grand utility-possibilities frontier GG benefits one or both individuals and harms no one. Thus, the movement increases social welfare according to the Pareto criterion. A movement from point C^* to point Z increases social welfare according to the Kaldor–Hicks criterion, since individual B could fully compensate individual A for his or her loss and still retain some gain. However, since this type of reasoning is based on interpersonal comparisons of utility, social welfare need not be higher.

Scitovsky criterion
Postulates that a change is an improvement if it satisfies the Kaldor–Hicks criterion and if, after the change, a movement back to the original position does not satisfy the Kaldor–Hicks criterion.

First, it is possible (though unusual) for the Kaldor–Hicks criterion to indicate that a given policy increases social welfare but also to indicate that, after the change, a movement back to the original position also increases social welfare. This limitation can be overcome with the third or **Scitovsky criterion.**[27] This is a double Kaldor–Hicks test. That is, according to Scitovsky, a change is an improvement if it satisfies the Kaldor–Hicks criterion, and, after the change, a movement back to the original position *does not* satisfy the Kaldor–Hicks criterion.

Another shortcoming of the Kaldor–Hicks criterion is more serious. It arises because the compensation principle measures the welfare changes of the gainers and losers in monetary units. For example, if a policy increases the income of individual B by $100 but lowers the income of individual A by $60, social welfare has increased according to the Kaldor–Hicks criterion (because individual B could transfer $60 of his or her $100 income gain to individual A and retain $40).[28] Since compensation is not actually required, the Kaldor–Hicks criterion is based on the assumption that the gain in utility of

---

[27] T. Scitovsky, "A Note on Welfare Propositions in Economics," *Review of Economics and Statistics,* November 1941, pp. 77–78.
[28] If compensation actually took place (something that is not required by the Kaldor–Hicks criterion), the Pareto criterion would suffice (since individual B is better off and individual A is not harmed), and the Kaldor–Hicks criterion would be superfluous.

Bergson social welfare function A social welfare function based on the explicit value judgments of society.

✓ Concept Check

How can changes in social welfare be measured?

Arrow's impossibility theorem Postulates that a social welfare function cannot be derived by democratic vote to reflect the preferences of all the individuals in society.

individual B (when his or her income rises by $100) is greater than the loss of utility to individual A (when his or her income falls by $60). Yet, this line of reasoning is based on interpersonal comparisons of utility, and social welfare need not be higher.

The only way to overcome this limitation of the Kaldor–Hicks criterion is to squarely face the problem of interpersonal comparison of utility. This leads us to the fourth welfare criterion, which is based on the construction of a **Bergson social welfare function** from the explicit value judgments of society.[29] A particular policy can then be said to increase social welfare if it puts society on a higher social indifference curve. However, as we will see in the next section, a social welfare function is extremely difficult or impossible to construct by democratic vote.

Arrow's Impossibility Theorem

Nobel laureate Kenneth Arrow proved that a social welfare function cannot be derived by democratic vote (i.e., reflect the preferences of all the individuals in society). This proof is known as **Arrow's impossibility theorem**.[30]

Arrow lists the following four conditions that he believes must hold for a social welfare function to reflect individual preferences:

1. Social welfare choices must be transitive. That is, if X is preferred to Y and Y is preferred to Z, then X must be preferred to Z.
2. Social welfare choices must not be responsive in the opposite direction to changes in individual preferences. That is, if choice X moves up in the ranking of one or more individuals and does not move down in the ranking of any other individual, then choice X cannot move down in the social welfare ranking.
3. Social welfare choices cannot be dictated by any one individual inside or outside the society.
4. Social choices must be independent of irrelevant alternatives. For example, if society prefers X to Y and Y to Z, then society must prefer X to Y even in the absence of alternative Z.

Arrow showed that a social welfare function cannot be obtained at by democratic voting without violating at least one of the four conditions. This can easily be proved for the first of the conditions. For example, suppose that Ann, Bob, and Charles (the three individuals in a society) rank alternatives X, Y, and Z as in Table 17.1.

TABLE 17.1 Rankings of Alternatives X, Y, and Z by Ann, Bob, and Charles

Individuals	Alternative		
	X	Y	Z
Ann	1st	2nd	3rd
Bob	3rd	1st	2nd
Charles	2nd	3rd	1st

[29] A. Bergson, "A Reformulation of Certain Aspects of Welfare Economics," *Quarterly Journal of Economics,* February 1938, pp. 310–334.
[30] K. J. Arrow, *Social Choice and Individual Values* (New York: Wiley, 1951).

Consider first the choice between alternatives X and Y. The majority (Ann and Charles) prefers X to Y. Now consider the choice between alternatives Y and Z. The majority (Ann and Bob) prefers Y to Z. It might then be concluded that since the majority prefers X to Y and Y to Z, the society composed of Ann, Bob, and Charles would prefer X to Z. However, from Table 17.1, we see that the majority (Bob and Charles) prefers Z to X. Therefore, the preference of the majority is inconsistent with the preferences of the individuals making up the majority. In short, this society cannot derive a social welfare function by democratic voting even if individual preferences are consistent. This is sometimes referred to as the "voting paradox."

While disturbing, it must be noted that the above conclusion is based on considering only the rank and not the intensity with which various alternatives are preferred. Thus, if half of society *mildly* preferred more space exploration while the other half *strongly* preferred more aid to low-income families instead, the difference in the intensities of these preferences would have to be disregarded in the decision process according to Arrow.

✔ Concept Check
What is Arrow's impossibility theorem? What is its importance?

AT THE FRONTIER
The Hot Issue of Income Inequality in the United States

We have seen in Section 17.2 that once two individuals are on the contract curve for exchange, one of the two individuals cannot be made better off without making the other worse off. Thus, different points on the contract curve refer to different distributions of income between the two individuals. Income inequality has become a hotly debated issue in recent years—especially since the income gap between the rich and poor in the United States is wider than in other industrial countries and has increased somewhat during the past two decades.

The best known summary measure of income inequality is provided by the Lorenz curve and the Gini coefficients. A **Lorenz curve** shows the cumulative percentages of total income (from 0% to 100%) measured along the vertical axis, for various cumulative percentages of the population (also from 0% to 100%) measured along the horizontal axis. The Gini coefficient is calculated from the Lorenz curve as indicated below. An illustration of two Lorenz curves, obtained by plotting the data of Table 17.2, is given in Figure 17.11.

The table and the figure show that the 20% of the families with the lowest income received only 0.9% of the national income before all taxes and transfers to aid low-income families, but 4.8% of national income after all taxes and transfers. The 40% of the families with the lowest income received 8% of total income before taxes and transfers, but 15.5% afterwards, and so on, until 100% of the families received the entire national income. Note that the after-taxes and after-transfers Lorenz curve has a smaller curvature than the before-taxes and before-transfers Lorenz curve, indicating a smaller income inequality after than before taxes and transfers.

If income were equally distributed, the Lorenz curve would coincide with the straight-line diagonal. On the other hand, if one family received the entire income

Lorenz curve A curve showing income inequality by measuring cumulative percentages of total income for various cumulative percentages of the population.

TABLE 17.2	Distribution of Annual Family Income Before and After Taxes and Transfers in the United States in 1993		
		Cumulative Percent of Total Income	
	Cumulative Percent of Families	Before Taxes and Transfers	After Taxes and Transfers
Lowest	20	0.9	4.8
	40	8.0	15.5
	60	22.6	31.6
	80	46.6	55.2
	100	100.0	100.0

Source: U.S. Bureau of the Census, *Current Population Survey* (Washington, DC).

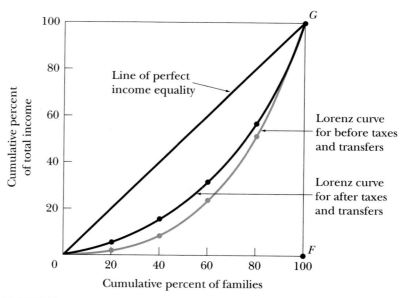

FIGURE 17.11 Lorenz Curves A Lorenz curve gives the cumulative percentages of total income (measured along the vertical axis) for various cumulative percentages of the population or families (measured along the horizontal axis). The after-taxes and after-transfers Lorenz curve has a smaller curvature (or outward bulge from the diagonal) than the before-taxes and before-transfers Lorenz curve, indicating a smaller income inequality after taxes and transfers than before.

Continued . . .

The Hot Issue of Income Inequality in the United States   *Continued*

Gini coefficient A measure of income inequality calculated from the Lorenz curve and ranging from 0 (for perfect equality) to 1 (for perfect inequality).

of the nation, the Lorenz curve would be a right angle (0*FG* in the figure). The **Gini coefficient** is given by the ratio of the area between the Lorenz curve and the straight-line diagonal to the total area of triangle 0*FG*. The Gini coefficient can range from 0 with perfect equality (when the Lorenz curve coincides with the diagonal) to 1 with perfect inequality (when only one family receives all of the income and the Lorenz curve is given by 0*FG*).

For the United States, the Gini coefficient was 0.39 before all taxes and transfers and 0.36 afterwards in 1993, compared with the average of 0.34 for all advanced countries and 0.46 for developing nations. The Gini coefficient (i.e., income inequality) increased in the United States from 0.35 in 1975 and to 0.41 in 2000 (the last year for which this coefficient was available), and it was, on the average, higher than in other advanced countries but lower than in developing countries.

Source: Organization for Economic Cooperation and development (OECD), *Income Distribution in OECD Countries* (Paris: OECD, October 1995); U.S. Bureau of Census, *Measuring the Effect and Benefits of Taxes on Income and Property: 1993, Current Population Report, Series P-60, No. 185RD* (Washington, DC: U.S. Government Printing Office, 1995); F. Campano and D. Salvatore, *Income Distribution* (New York: Oxford University Press, 2006); D. Salvatore, ed., "Income Distribution," Special Issue, *Journal of Policy Modeling*, July/August, 2007; and UN, *Human Development Report 2008* (New York, UN, 2008), pp. 282–284.

17.8   TRADE PROTECTION AND ECONOMIC WELFARE

By increasing commodity prices, trade protection benefits domestic producers and harms domestic consumers (and usually the nation as a whole). However, since producers are few and stand to gain a great deal from protection, they have a strong incentive to lobby the government to adopt protectionist measures. On the other hand, since the losses are diffused among many consumers, each of whom loses very little from the protection, they are not likely to effectively organize to resist protectionist measures. Thus, there is a bias in favor of protectionism. For example, the sugar quota raises individual expenditures on sugar by only a few dollars per person per year in the United States. But with more than 300 million people in the United States, the quota generates nearly $1 billion in rents to the few thousand sugar producers.

In industrial countries, protection is more likely to be provided to labor-intensive industries employing unskilled, low-wage workers who would have great difficulty finding alternative employment if they lost their present jobs. Some empirical support has also been found for the *pressure-group* or *interest-group* theory, which postulates that industries that are highly organized (such as the automobile industry) receive more trade protection than less organized industries. An industry is more likely to be organized if it is composed of only a few firms. Also, industries that produce consumer products generally are able to obtain more protection than industries producing intermediate products used as inputs by other industries, because the latter industries can exercise *countervailing power* (i.e., apply opposing pressure) and block protection (since protection would increase the price of their inputs).

Furthermore, more protection seems to go to geographically decentralized industries that employ large numbers of workers than to industries that operate in only some regions and employ relatively few workers. The large number of workers have strong voting power to elect government officials who support protection for the industry. Decentralization ensures that elected officials from many regions support the trade protection. Another theory suggests that trade policies are biased in favor of maintaining the status quo. That is, it is more likely for an industry to be protected now if it was protected in the past. Governments also seem reluctant to adopt trade policies that result in large changes in the distribution of income, regardless of who gains and who loses. The most highly protected industries in the United States today are the textile and apparel, automobile, and steel. Example 17–6 provides estimates of the effect of removing protection to these industries.

EXAMPLE 17–6

Welfare Effects of Removing U.S. Trade Restrictions

Table 17.3 shows that removing all quantitative restrictions (QRs) on textile and apparel exports to the United States would result in a gain of $11.92 billion for the United States at 1984 prices. Retaining QRs but capturing the rents from foreigners (e.g., by auctioning off export quotas to foreign firms) would result instead in a gain of $6.05 billion for the United States. The gains are smaller for automobiles and much smaller for steel. Removing QRs also leads to employment losses in the industry

TABLE 17.3	Welfare Benefits and Employment Effects of Removing Quantitative Restrictions (QRs) on Export of Textiles, Automobiles, and Steel to the United State		
	Welfare Gain (billions of dollars)	Employment Change in Industry (1,000 worker-years)	Employment Change in Rest of Economy (1,000 worker-years)
Textile and apparel			
Remove QRs	11.92	−157.2	157.2
Capturing rents from foreigners	6.05	−3.1	28.4
Automobiles			
Remove QRs	7.50	−1.2	1.3
Capturing rents from foreigners	7.15	+1.3	37.2
Steel			
Remove QRs	0.86	−20.7	22.3
Capturing rents from foreigners	0.74	−0.1	3.5

Sources: J. de Melo and D. Tarr, A General Equilibrium Analysis of U.S. Foreign Trade Policy (Cambridge, MA: MIT Press, 1992); and H. J. Wall, "Using the Gravity Model to Estimate the Costs of Protection," *Federal Reserve Bank of St. Louis Review,* January/February 1999, pp. 211–244.

losing the QRs, but these employment losses are matched or more than matched by economy-wide employment gains. Removing QRs on all three products leads to a total welfare gain of $20.28 ($11.92 + $7.50 + $0.86) billion for the United States. A more recent study by Wall (1999) found that the benefit removing all forms of trade protection on U.S. imports in 1996 was equal to $112 billion, which represented more than 15 percent of U.S. imports and more 1.9 percent of U.S. GDP in 1996.

SUMMARY

1. Partial equilibrium analysis studies the behavior of individual decision-making units and individual markets, viewed in isolation. General equilibrium analysis studies the interdependence that exists among all markets in the economy. Only when an industry is small and has few direct links with the rest of the economy is partial equilibrium analysis appropriate. The first general equilibrium model was introduced by Walras in 1874. Under perfect competition, a solution to the general equilibrium model usually exists.

2. A simple economy of two individuals (A and B), two commodities (X and Y), and two inputs (L and K) is in general equilibrium of exchange when the economy is on its contract curve for exchange. This is the locus of tangency points of the indifference curves (at which the MRS_{XY} are equal) for the two individuals. The economy is in general equilibrium of production when it is on its production contract curve. This is the locus of the tangency points of the isoquants (at which $MRTS_{LK}$ are equal) for the two commodities. By mapping or transferring the production contract curve from input to output space, we derive the corresponding production-possibilities frontier.

3. For the economy to be simultaneously in general equilibrium of production and exchange, the marginal rate of transformation of X for Y in production must be equal to the marginal rate of substitution of X for Y in consumption for individuals A and B. That is, $MRT_{XY} = MRS^A_{XY} = MRS^B_{XY}$. Geometrically, this corresponds to the point on the contract curve for exchange at which the common slope of the indifference curve of the two individuals equals the slope of the production-possibilities frontier at the point of production. A distribution of inputs among commodities and of commodities among consumers is Pareto optimal or efficient if no reorganization of production and consumption is possible by which some individuals are made better off without making someone else worse off. Thus, the conditions for Pareto optimality are the conditions for general equilibrium of production and exchange.

4. Under perfect competition in all input and output markets, all the conditions for Pareto optimum are automatically satisfied. This is the basic argument in favor of perfect competition and proof of Adam Smith's law of the invisible hand. The first theorem of welfare economics postulates that equilibrium in competitive markets is Pareto optimal. The second theorem of welfare economics postulates that equity in distribution is logically separable from efficiency in allocation. Perfect competition leads to maximum economic efficiency only in the absence of market failures (which arise from imperfect competition, externalities, and public goods). Perfect competition leads to static but not necessarily to dynamic efficiency.

5. Starting from the general equilibrium condition at which $MRT_{XY} = P_X/P_Y = MRS_{XY}$ in each country in the absence of trade, the country with the lower MRT_{XY} or P_X/P_Y

will have a comparative advantage in commodity X. With trade, each nation will specialize in the production of the commodity of its comparative advantage until MRT_{XY} or P_X/P_Y becomes equal in both countries. Then each country will trade until $MRT_{XY} = P_X/P_Y = MRS_{XY}$ so as to be in general equilibrium once again. By specializing in production and trading, each country can consume more of both commodities than it can without trade.

6. Welfare economics studies the conditions under which the solution to the general equilibrium model can be said to the optimal. It examines the conditions for economic efficiency in the production of output and in the exchange of commodities, and for equity in the distribution of income. A utility-possibilities frontier is derived by mapping or transferring a contract curve for exchange from output or commodity space to utility space. It shows the various combinations of utilities received by two individuals at which the economy is in general equilibrium or Pareto optimum in exchange. We can construct an Edgeworth box and contract curve for exchange from each point on the production-possibilities frontier. From each contract curve for exchange, we can then construct the corresponding utility-possibilities frontier and determine on it the point of Pareto optimum in production and exchange. By joining points of Pareto optimality in production and exchange on each utility-possibilities frontier, we can derive the grand utility-possibilities frontier.

7. A change that benefits some but harms others can be evaluated with the Kaldor–Hicks–Scitovsky criterion. However, this is based on the compensation principle which measures the welfare changes of the gainers and the losers in monetary units. The only way to overcome this shortcoming is with a social welfare function. Arrow proved that a social welfare function cannot be derived by democratic vote. This is known as Arrow's impossibility theorem. Income inequality can be measured by the Lorenz curve and the Gini coefficient. These are higher in the United States than in other industrial countries and have increased since 1975.

8. By increasing the commodity price, trade protection benefits producers and harms consumers (and usually the nation as a whole). Protection is more likely to be provided to industries that (1) are labor-intensive and employ unskilled, low-wage workers, (2) are highly organized (such as the automobile industry), (3) produce consumer products rather than intermediate products, and (4) are geographically decentralized.

KEY TERMS

Partial equilibrium analysis	Marginal rate of transformation of X for Y (MRT_{XY})	Welfare economics
General equilibrium analysis	Economic efficiency	Utility-possibilities frontier
Interdependence	Pareto optimality	Grand utility-possibilities frontier
Edgeworth box diagram for exchange	Law of the invisible hand	Pareto criterion
Contract curve for exchange	First theorem of welfare economics	Compensation principle
Edgeworth box diagram for production	Second theorem of welfare economics	Kaldor–Hicks criterion
Contract curve for production	Market failures	Scitovsky criterion
Production-possibilities frontier	Comparative advantage	Bergson social welfare function
		Arrow's impossibility theorem
		Lorenz curve
		Gini coefficient

REVIEW QUESTIONS

1. Are all points on the contract curve for exchange equally desirable from society's point of view? Why?

2. How will an increase in the quantity of labor available to society affect its Edgeworth box diagram for production? What effect will that have on the contract curve for production?

3. How can we show a 10% improvement in technology in the production of commodities X and Y in the Edgeworth diagram and production-possibilities frontier?

4. Why would the economy of Figure 17.5 not be at general equilibrium if production took place at point M' and consumption at point D?

5. If $MRT_{XY} = 3/2$ while $MRS_{XY} = 2$ for individuals A and B, should the economy produce more of X or more of Y to reach equilibrium of production and exchange simultaneously? Why?

6. What makes general equilibrium analysis objective while welfare economics is subjective?

7. Would the Robinson Crusoe of Figure 17.6 maximize utility or welfare by producing and consuming $5X$ and $4.5Y$? Why?

8. What is the relationship between Adam Smith's law of the invisible hand and Pareto optimum?

9. Why do market disequilibria lead to inefficiencies and non-Pareto optimum?

10. Perfect competition is the best form of market organization at one point in time but not over time. True or false? Explain.

11. What is meant by the "voting paradox?" How is this related to Arrow's impossibility theorem?

12. Why is international trade often restricted if it benefits few domestic producers but harms many domestic consumers?

PROBLEMS

1. Starting from a position of general equilibrium in the entire economy, if the supply curve of commodity X falls (i.e., S_X shifts up), examine what happens
   a. in the markets for commodity X, its substitutes, and complements.
   b. in the input markets.
   c. to the distribution of income.

*2. Suppose that the indifference curves of individuals A and B are given by A_1, A_2, A_3, and B_1, B_2, B_3, respectively, in the accompanying table. Suppose also that the total amount of commodities X and Y available to the two individuals together is $10X$ and $10Y$. Draw the Edgeworth box diagram for exchange, and show the contract curve for exchange.

A's Indifference Curves

A_1		A_2		A_3	
X	Y	X	Y	X	Y
3	7	5	6	6	7.5
4	3	6	4	8	6
6	1	8	3	9.5	5.5

B's Indifference Curves

B_1		B_2		B_3	
X	Y	X	Y	X	Y
7	2	6	4	8	4
2	3	4	5	6	6
1	4	3	7	5.5	8

3. For the Edgeworth box diagram of Problem 2 (shown in Appendix B at the end of the text):
   a. Explain how, starting from the point at which A_1 and B_1 intersect, mutually advantageous exchange can take place between individuals A and B.
   b. What is the value of the MRS_{XY} at points E, D, and F?

*4. Suppose that the isoquants for commodities X and Y are given by X_1, X_2, X_3, and Y_1, Y_2, Y_3, respectively, in the following table. Suppose also that a total of $14L$ and $9K$ are available to produce commodities X and Y. Draw the Edgeworth box diagram for exchange and show the production contract curve.

* = Answer provided at end of book.

X's Isoquants

X_1		X_2		X_3	
L	K	L	K	L	K
5	7	8	5	10	7
6	2	9	3	11	5
7	1	11	2	13	4.5

Y's Isoquants

Y_1		Y_2		Y_3	
L	K	L	K	L	K
9	2	7	4	10	4
3	4	5	6	8	7
1	6	4	8	7.5	8.5

5. For the Edgeworth box diagram of Problem 4 (shown in Appendix B at the end of the text):

   a. Explain how, starting from the point at which X_1 and Y_1 intersect, the output of both commodities can be increased by simply reallocating some of the fixed amounts of L and K available between the production of X and Y.

   b. What is the value of the $MRTS_{LK}$ at points M, J, and N?

6. Suppose that in the figure in the answer to Problem 4, $X_1 = 4X$ and $Y_3 = 13Y$, $X_2 = 10X$ and $Y_2 = 9Y$, and $X_3 = 14X$ and $Y_1 = 4Y$. Derive the production-possibilities frontier corresponding to the production contract curve given in the figure in the answer to Problem 4. What does a point inside the production-possibilities frontier indicate? A point outside?

7. a. Find the MRT_{XY} at points J', M', and N' for the production-possibilities frontier of Problem 6.

   b. If $MC_Y = \$100$ at point M', what is MC_X?

   c. Why is the production-possibilities frontier concave to the origin?

   d. When would the production-possibilities frontier be a straight line?

*8. Superimpose the Edgeworth box diagram for exchange of Problem 2 on the production-possibilities frontier of Problem 4 (both shown in Appendix B at the end of the text), and determine the general equilibrium of production and exchange.

9. Explain why the economy portrayed in the answer to Problem 8 would not be simultaneously in general equilibrium of production and exchange at points D and F.

10. Given that the economy of Problem 8 produces at point M' on its production-possibilities frontier, determine

   a. how much of commodities X and Y it produces.

   b. how this output is distributed between individuals A and B.

   c. how much labor (L) and capital (K) are used to produce commodities X and Y.

   d. What questions have been left unanswered in the model?

11. Suppose that the economy represented by the figure in the answer to Problem 8 (shown in Appendix B at the end of the text) grows over time and/or has available a more advanced technology. Explain how this affects the figure and general equilibrium analysis.

*12. Suppose that in the figure in the answer to Problem 8 (see Figure 17c in Appendix B), $A_1 = 100$ utils, $A_2 = 300$ utils, $A_3 = 450$ utils, and $B_1 = 200$ utils, $B_2 = 400$ utils, and $B_3 = 450$ utils.

   a. Derive the utility-possibilities frontier corresponding to contract curve $0_A DEF 0_B$ for exchange in Figure 17c in Appendix B.

   b. Derive the grand utility-possibilities frontier.

INTERNET SITE ADDRESSES

Information and data on the comparative advantage of nations, trade statistics by country and product group, as well as specialization are published by the World Trade Organization (WTO) and the International Trade Administration (ITA) and can be found at:

   http://www.wto.org

   http://www.ita.doc.gov

Data on income inequality and the Gini coefficients are provided by the U.S. Census Bureau and by the United Nations at:

   http://www.census.gov/hhes/income/histinc/h04.html

   http://hdr.undp.org/en/reports/global/hdr2007-2008/

On the efficiency and equity in the allocation of water to different uses in California, see:

   http://www.monolake.org/waterpolicy/outsidebox.htm

The rationing of health care in the United States and in Britain is examined at:

   http://www.globalchange.com/rationin.htm

   http://news.bbc.co.uk/hi/english/health/newsid_249000/249938.stm

CHAPTER 18

Externalities, Public Goods, and the Role of Government

After Studying This Chapter, You Should Be Able to:

- Know the meaning of externalities and public goods and why they lead to economic inefficiencies
- Understand the meaning and importance of the Coase theorem
- Know why the existence of public goods can lead to underinvestment and a free-rider problem
- Understand how government decisions are made and implemented
- Understand why the optimal level of pollution is not zero

In this chapter, we examine why the existence of externalities and public goods leads to economic inefficiencies and to an allocation of inputs and commodities that is not Pareto optimum. We then consider how the government (through regulation, taxes, and subsidies) could attempt to overcome or at least reduce the negative impact of these distortions on economic efficiency. Because these distortions and government attempts to overcome them are fairly common in most societies, the importance of the topics presented in this chapter can hardly be overstated. The "At the Frontier" section examines the shift from equity to efficiency in tax reform in the United States. In this chapter, we also discuss the theory of public choice (i.e., how government decisions are made and implemented) and strategic trade policy (i.e., how comparative advantage can be created by subsidies, trade protection, and other government policies). We conclude by applying the tools of analysis developed in the chapter to the problem of environmental pollution.

18.1   EXTERNALITIES

Externalities Harmful or beneficial side effects borne by those not directly involved in the production or consumption of a commodity.

External costs Harmful side effects borne by those not directly involved in the production or consumption of a commodity.

External benefits Beneficial side effects received by those not directly involved in the production or consumption of a commodity.

External diseconomies of production Uncompensated costs borne by those not directly involved in the production of a commodity.

External diseconomies of consumption Uncompensated costs borne by those not directly involved in the consumption of a commodity.

External economies of production Uncompensated benefits received by those not directly involved in the production of a commodity.

External economies of consumption Uncompensated benefits received by those not directly involved in the consumption of a commodity.

Technical externalities Economies of scale.

In this section, we define externalities and examine why their existence prevents maximum economic efficiency or Pareto optimum, even under perfect competition.

Externalities Defined

In the course of producing and consuming some commodities, harmful or beneficial side effects arise that are borne by firms and people not directly involved in the production or consumption of the commodities. These side effects are called **externalities** because they are felt by economic units (firms and individuals) not directly involved with (i.e., that are external to or outside) the economic units that generate these side effects.[1] Externalities are called **external costs** when they are harmful and **external benefits** when they are beneficial. An example of an external cost is the air pollution that may accompany the production of a commodity. An example of an external benefit is the reduced chance of the spreading of a communicable disease when an individual is inoculated against it.

Externalities are classified into five different types. These are external diseconomies of production, external diseconomies of consumption, external economies of production, external economies of consumption, and technical externalities. Each of these will be examined in turn. **External diseconomies of production** are uncompensated costs imposed on others by the expansion of output by some firms. For example, the increased discharge of waste materials by some firms along a waterway may result in antipollution legislation that increases the cost of disposing of waste materials for all firms in the area. **External diseconomies of consumption** are uncompensated costs imposed on others by the consumption expenditures of some individuals. For example, the riding of a snowmobile by an individual imposes a cost (in the form of noise and smoke) on other individuals who are skiing, hiking, or ice fishing in the area.

On the other hand, **external economies of production** are uncompensated benefits conferred on others by the expansion of output by some firms. An example arises when some firms train more workers to increase output, and some of these workers go to work for other firms (which, therefore, save on training costs). **External economies of consumption** are uncompensated benefits conferred on others by the increased consumption of a commodity by some individual. For example, increased expenditures to maintain his or her lawn by a homeowner increase the value of the neighbor's house. Finally, **technical externalities** arise when declining long-run average costs as output expands lead to monopoly, so that price exceeds marginal cost. Not even regulation to achieve competitive marginal cost pricing is then viable (see Section 13.5).

---

[1] The presentation of this chapter follows F. M. Bator's "The Anatomy of Market Failure," *Quarterly Journal of Economics,* August 1958, pp. 351–379, which was drawn from the work of the great English economist Arthur Cecil Pigou (1877–1959).

Externalities and Market Failure

We have seen in Section 17.4 that perfect competition leads to maximum economic efficiency and Pareto optimum. However, this is true only when private costs equal social costs and when private benefits equal social benefits (i.e., in the absence of externalities). This was implicitly assumed to be the case until now. When externalities are present, the "invisible hand" is led astray and Pareto optimum is not achieved, even under perfect competition. This is shown in Figure 18.1.

We assume that commodity X in Figure 18.1 is produced by a competitive industry. The industry supply curve (S) is the horizontal summation (above minimum average variable costs) of the individual firm's marginal (private) cost curves (i.e., $S = \Sigma MPC$). Given market demand curve D for the commodity, the equilibrium price is \$12 and the equilibrium quantity is 6 million units per time period (given by the intersection of D and S at point E in the figure). Suppose that the production of commodity X involves rising external costs (in the form of air pollution, water pollution, traffic congestion, and so on) that

✓ Concept Check
How do externalities
lead to market failures?

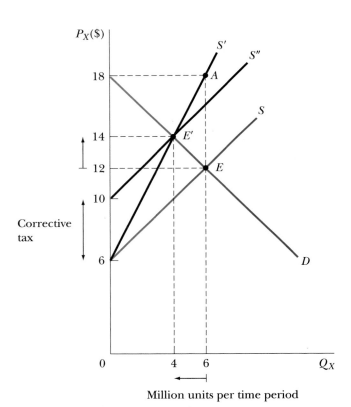

FIGURE 18.1   Competitive Overproduction with External Costs   With perfect competition, $P_X = \$12$ and $Q_X = 6$ million units (given by point E at which D and S intersect). S reflects only marginal private costs, while S' equals marginal private (internal) costs plus marginal external costs. Efficiency and Pareto optimality require that $P_X = \$14$ and $Q_X = 4$ million units (given by point E', at which D and S' intersect). This can be achieved with a \$4 per-unit corrective tax on producers that shifts S to S''.

the firms producing commodity X do not take into account. The industry supply curve that includes both the private and external costs might then be given by S' (see the figure). Curve S' shows that the marginal *social* cost (MSC) of producing 6 million units of commodity X exceeds the marginal private cost (MPC) of \$12 by an amount equal to the marginal external cost (MEC) of \$6 (AE) in the figure).

Thus, efficiency or Pareto optimality requires that $P_X = \$14$ and $Q_X = 4$ million (given by the intersection of D and S' at point E' in the figure). Only then would the commodity price reflect the full social cost of producing it. Starting with S (showing the MPC), this could be achieved with a \$4 per-unit corrective tax on producers of commodity X, which shifts S upward to S'' and defines equilibrium point E' at the intersection of D and S''.[2] As we will see in the next chapter, efficiency and Pareto optimality might also be achieved by the proper specification of property rights. Without any such corrective action, the perfectly competitive industry would charge too low a price and produce too much of commodity X (compare point E with E' in the figure).

Efficiency and Pareto optimality are not achieved whenever private and social costs or benefits differ. With external diseconomies of consumption, consumers do not pay the full marginal social cost of the commodity and consume too much of it. Corrective action would then require a tax on consumers rather than on producers. On the other hand, with external economies of production and consumption, the commodity price exceeds the marginal social cost of the commodity so that production and consumption fall short of the optimum level. Efficiency and Pareto optimum in production and in consumption would then require a subsidy (rather than a tax) on producers and on consumers, respectively (see Problem 5, with the answer at the end of the text). Finally, technical externalities (economies of large-scale production) over a sufficiently large range of outputs lead to the breakdown of competition (natural monopoly). In this case, marginal cost pricing is neither possible nor viable, and Pareto optimum cannot be achieved.

EXAMPLE 18–1

The Case for Government Support for Basic Research

Basic research refers to efforts to discover fundamental relationships in nature, such as natural laws. Often, these cannot be patented and do not have immediate commercial applications. It is also practically impossible for the firm that makes a discovery of this nature to take advantage of the full range of commercial applications that might result from its discovery. Thus, the social benefits from basic research greatly exceed private benefits. As a result, there is likely to be underinvestment in basic research by the private sector. Since technological change and innovations are the most important contributors to growth in modern societies, there is a strong case for government support for basic research. Indeed, past government expenditures in basic research, such as for space

---

[2] However, the marginal external costs created by firms in different areas of the market are likely to be different, so that different corrective per-unit taxes may be required to achieve Pareto optimality. Furthermore, MEC may be constant rather than rising. The corrective tax may also have some unintended side effects that lead to inefficiency (such as the utilization of a less efficient technology).

exploration, laid the foundations of many of today's most productive industries, from aerospace to computers.

The same arguments that apply to firms in a nation apply to nations in the world. That is, the government of a nation may support less than the optimal level of basic research because additions to fundamental knowledge made by a nation can easily be utilized by other nations. For example, until the 1980s, Japan stressed the finding of commercial applications for basic discoveries made by other nations, mostly the United States, rather than doing basic research itself. Primarily to overcome this problem, since 1990 the United States has been supporting generic and precompetitive technologies, such as superconductivity, that could have widespread industrial applications but which take many years to develop and commercialize. Many economists, however, believe that the government has no business picking "winners and losers"; that is, substituting its judgment for that of the market by selecting among technologies and firms may not lead to optimal results (see Example 18–5).

Sources: National Academy of Science, *Basic Research and National Goals* (Washington, D.C.: U.S. Government Printing Office, 1965); The MIT Commission on Industrial Productivity, *Made in America: Regaining the Productive Edge* (Cambridge, MA: The MIT Press, 1989), Chapter 5; "Basic Research Is Losing Out as Companies Stress Results," *New York Times,* October 8, 1996, p. 1; "How to Nurture a High-Technology Culture," *Financial Times,* September 14, 2001, p. 13; C. Wessner, "The Advanced Technology Program: It Works," Issues in Science and Technology, Fall 2001, pp. 59–65; and IEEE-USA, *Federal Support for Basic Research,* (Washington, DC: IEEE-USA, February 16, 2007.

| 18.2 | EXTERNALITIES AND PROPERTY RIGHTS |

Common property
Property, such as air, owned by no one.

We have seen in the previous section that externalities, by driving a wedge between private and social costs or benefits, prevent economic efficiency and Pareto optimality. But why do externalities arise in some cases and not in others? Suppose you own a car. You have a clear property right in the car, and anyone ruining it is liable for damages. The courts will uphold your right to compensation. In this case there are no externalities. Private and social costs are one and the same thing. Compare this with the case of a firm polluting the air. Neither the firm nor the people living next to the firm own the air. That is, the air is **common property.** Since no resident owns the air, no one can sue the firm for damages resulting from the air pollution generated by the firm. The firm imposes an external (i.e., an uncompensated) cost on the individual. These two simple examples clearly demonstrate that externalities arise when property rights are not adequately specified. In the first case, you have a clear property right to the car and there are no externalities. In the second case, no one owns the air and externalities arise. This situation leads to the famous Coase theorem.[3]

Coase theorem
Postulates that when property rights are clearly defined and transaction costs are zero, perfect competition results in the absence of externalities, regardless of how property rights are assigned among the parties involved.

The **Coase theorem** postulates that when property rights are clearly defined, perfect competition results in the internalization of externalities, regardless of how property rights are assigned among the parties (individuals or firms). For example, suppose that a

---

[3] R. R. Coase, "The Problems of Social Cost," *Journal of Law and Economics,* October 1960, pp. 1–44. "A Nobel-Prize Winning Idea, Conceived in the 30's Is a Guide for Net Business," *New York Times,* October 2, 2000, p. C12; and "The Tragedy of the Commons," *Forbes,* September 10, 2001, pp. 61–63.

brewery is located downstream from a paper mill that dumps waste into the stream. Suppose also that in order to filter and purify the water to make beer, the brewery incurs a cost of $1,000 per month, while the paper mill would incur a cost of $400 to dispose of its waste products by other means and not pollute the stream. If the brewery has the property right to clean water, the paper mill will incur the added cost of $400 per month to dispose of its waste without polluting the stream (lest the brewery sue it for damages of $1,000 per month). On the other hand, if the paper mill has the property right to the stream and can freely use it to dump its wastes in it, the brewery will pay the paper mill $400 per month not to pollute the stream (and thus avoid the larger cost of $1,000 to purify the water later).

The cost of avoiding the pollution is *internalized* by the paper mill in the first instance and by the brewery in the second. That is, the $400 cost per month of avoiding the pollution becomes a regular business expense of one party or the other and *no externalities result*. The socially optimal result of **internalizing external costs** and avoiding the pollution at $400 per month, rather than cleaning up afterwards at a cost of $1,000 per month, is achieved regardless of who has the property right to the use of the stream.[4] Thus, externalities are avoided (and economic efficiency and Pareto optimum achieved) under perfect competition, if property rights are clearly defined and transferable. Transaction costs must also be zero.[5]

Transaction costs are the legal, administrative, and informational expenses of drawing up, signing, and enforcing contracts. These expenses are small when the contracting parties are few (as in the above example). When the contracting parties are numerous (as in the case of a firm polluting the air for possibly millions of people in the area), it would be practically impossible or very expensive for the firm to sign a separate contract with each individual affected by the pollution it creates. Contracting costs are then very large, and externalities (and inefficiencies) arise. This is especially true in the case of environmental pollution (see Section 18.7).[6]

Internalizing external costs The process whereby an external cost becomes part of the regular business expense of a firm.

✓ Concept Check
What is the relationship between the Coase theorem and the internalizing of external costs?

EXAMPLE 18–2

Commercial Fishing: Fewer Boats but Exclusive Rights?

As a response to catastrophic overfishing by foreigners during the 1960s, the United States passed the Fisheries Conservation and Management Act of 1976. The act extended the U.S. exclusive economic (fishing) zone from the traditional 3-mile limit to 200 miles and created eight U.S. regional councils dominated by local fishing interests to distribute exclusive rights to the catch. Economists strongly supported the plan to move from public to private ownership as the best method of preventing overfishing

[4] Note that the cost of pollution abatement is minimized rather than entirely eliminated. The only way to completely avoid the cost of pollution is for the paper mill to stop production. But this would result in the greater social cost of the lost production. The above conclusion is also based on the assumption of a zero income effect on the demand curve for the use of the stream regardless of who has the property right of it.
[5] Even if neither the brewery nor the paper mill had a property right to the use of the stream, the conclusion would generally be the same as long as transaction costs are zero. That is, it pays for the brewery to pay the paper mill $400 per month not to pollute. This is equivalent to the paper mill having the right to the use of the stream.
[6] However, the development of class action lawsuits has greatly reduced transaction costs in these cases.

and preserving fisheries for future generations. However, strong disagreement as to who should benefit from the distribution of the rights to the catch (the government, current owners of fishing boats, or fishermen) has so far prevented the privatization plan from being implemented. As a result, the act has only eliminated overfishing by foreigners but not by Americans, so the catches remained well above biologically sustainable levels. Even though a small number of boats could catch the maximum sustainable yield at the lowest possible cost, there remained a strong incentive to overinvest in the industry as long as it was profitable to bring new boats into operation.

Until the year 2000, the attempt to reduce overfishing took the form of sharply reducing the length of the fishing seasons and the size of the catch. For example, off Alaska, the halibut season consisted of only two or three days per year. Since then however, cooperatives began to be created that face annual fishing quotas set by marine biologists to preserve fishing stocks, rather than trip limits on the catch. When fully operational by 2011, this would essentially establish property rights that eliminate overfishing, reduce costs, and increase the efficiency in U.S. fisheries.

Sources: "A Change in Commercial Fishing: Fewer Boats but Exclusive Rights," *New York Times*, April 2, 1991; "Not Enough Fish in the Stormy Sea," *U.S. News & World Report*, August 15, 1994, pp. 55–56; "One Answer to Overfishing: Privatize the Fisheries," *New York Times*, May 11, 1995, p. D2; "Fish Stock Face Global Collapse," *Financial Times*, February 18, 2002, p. 5; and "One Fish, Two Fish, No Fish," *U.S. News & World Report*, August 27, 2007, pp. 50–56.

18.3   PUBLIC GOODS

Public goods
Commodities for which consumption by some individuals does not reduce the amount available to others.

Nonrival consumption
The distinguishing characteristic of a public good whereby its consumption by some individuals does not reduce the amount available to others.

Nonexclusion The situation in which it is impossible or prohibitively expensive to confine the benefit or the consumption of a good to the people paying for it.

We have seen in Section 17.4 that perfect competition leads to maximum economic efficiency and Pareto optimum in the absence of market failures. One type of market failure results from the existence of public goods. In this section, we examine the nature of public goods and their provision.

Nature of Public Goods

If consumption of a commodity by one individual does not reduce the amount available for others, the commodity is a public good. That is, once the good is provided for someone, others can also consume it at no extra cost. Examples of **public goods** are national defense, law enforcement, fire and police protection, and flood control (provided by the government), but also radio and TV broadcasting (which are provided by the private sector in many nations, including the United States).

The distinguishing characteristic of public goods is **nonrival consumption.** For example, when one individual watches a TV program, he or she does not interfere with the reception of others. This is to be contrasted with private goods, which are rival in consumption, in that if an individual consumes a particular quantity of a good, such as apples, these same apples are no longer available for others to consume.

Nonrival consumption must be distinguished from nonexclusion. **Nonexclusion** means that it is impossible or prohibitively expensive to confine the benefits of the consumption of a good (once produced) to selected people (such as only to those paying for it). Whereas nonrival consumption and nonexclusion often go hand in hand, a public good is defined in terms of nonrival consumption only. For example, since national defense and TV broadcasting are nonrival in consumption (i.e., the same amount can be consumed by more than one individual at the same time), they are both public goods. However, national defense also exhibits nonexclusion (i.e., when it is provided for some individuals, others cannot be excluded from also enjoying it), while TV broadcasting can be exclusive (e.g., only paying customers can view cable TV). We will see in the next section that public goods (i.e., goods that are nonrival in consumption) will not be provided in the optimal amount by the private sector under perfect competition, thus requiring government intervention. First, however, we must determine what is the optimal amount of a public good.

Because a given amount of a public good can be consumed by more than one individual at the same time, the aggregate or total amount of a public good is obtained by the vertical (rather than by the horizontal) summation of the demand curves of the various individuals who consume the public good. This is shown in Figure 18.2. In the figure, D_A is the demand curve of Ann and D_B is the demand curve of Bob for public good X. If Ann and Bob are the only two individuals in the market, the aggregate demand curve for good X, D_T, is obtained by the vertical summation of D_A and D_B. The reason for this is that each unit of public good X can be consumed by both individuals at the same time.[7]

Concept Check
What is the relationship between public goods, nonrival consumption, and nonexclusion?

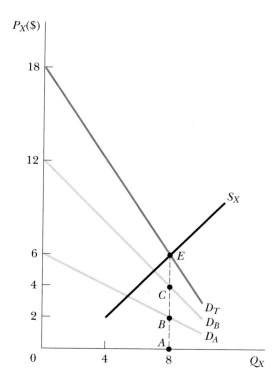

FIGURE 18.2   Optimal Amount of a Public Good   Aggregate demand curve D_T for public good X is obtained by the vertical summation of individual demand curves D_A and D_B. This is because each unit of public good X can be consumed by both individuals at the same time. Given market supply curve S_X, the optimal amount of X is 8 units per time period (given by the intersection of D_T and S_X at point E). At point E, the sum of the individuals' marginal benefits equals the marginal social costs (i.e., $AB + AC = AE$).

---

[7] This is to be contrasted with the *market* demand curve for a private or rival good, which, as we have seen in Section 5.1, is obtained from the *horizontal* summation of the individuals' demand curves (see Problem 10, with the answer at the end of the text).

Given market supply curve S_X for public good X, the optimal amount of X is 8 units per time period (given by the intersection of D_T and S_X at point E in the figure). At point E, the sum of the individuals' marginal benefits or marginal social benefit equals the marginal social cost (i.e., $AB + AC = AE$). Thus, note once again that the marginal principle is at work. The problem is that, in general, less than the optimal amount of public good X will be supplied under perfect competition, and this prevents the attainment of maximum efficiency and Pareto optimum.

EXAMPLE 18–3
The Economics of a Lighthouse and Other Public Goods

A lighthouse is a good example of a public good. Once a lighthouse is built, it can send signals to ships during storms at practically zero extra cost. That is, lighthouse signals are nonrival in consumption. Lighthouse signals are not exclusive, however, as it was originally believed. That is, each user *can* be charged for the service. Indeed, historical research has shown that lighthouses were privately owned in England from 1700 to 1834, and that they must have been doing a good business because their number increased over the period. Lighthouse owners charged ships at dock (according to their tonnage) for their land-demarcation light signals during storms. Usually only one ship at a time was in sight of the lighthouse, and ships were identified by their flag. If a ship had not paid for the service, the light signals were not shown.

The lighthouse provides an example of a public good that is exclusive (so that users can be charged for the service). The same is true for the North Atlantic Treaty Organization (NATO), under which Western European nations and the United States contributed to provide for their mutual protection against past Soviet military threat. A similar public good is education. Entrepreneurs often show great ingenuity in making public goods exclusive. An example is the provision of in-place paying binoculars at Niagara Falls and other scenic sights. Another example is the placing of super-large TV screens in some bars. These and other similar services would not be provided if they were not, or if they could not be made, exclusive (i.e., if consumers could not be charged for them). Other examples of public goods that can be made exclusive are the findings of government-paid basic research and the use of advertising to pay for radio and TV broadcasts. Although any firm can make use of basic-research findings, the specific offshoots or commercial applications of basic research developed by a particular firm can be patented and thus made exclusive.

Sources: Ronald R. Coase, "The Lighthouse in Economics," *Journal of Law and Economics,* October 1974," pp. 357–376; "So, It's a Lighthouse. Now Leave Me alone," *New York Times,* April 18, 2002, p. 1; "Vast Sums for New Discoveries Pose Threat to Basic Science," *New York Times,* May 27, 1990, p. 1; "Do Firms Run Schools Well?" *U.S. News & World Report,* January 8, 1996, pp. 46–49; "Woes for Company Running Schools, *New York Times*, May 14, 2002, p. 1; and "Public vs. Private Schools," *New York Times*, July 19, 2006, p. 20.

Provision of Public Goods

We have seen that the optimal amount of a public good is the amount at which the sum of the marginal benefits of all the individuals consuming the good equals its marginal cost. Graphically, this is given by the point at which the aggregate demand curve for the good (obtained from the vertical summation of the individuals' demand curves) intersects the market supply curve of the good. However, less than this optimal amount of the public good is likely to be supplied by the private sector.

There are two related reasons for this. First, when the public good is nonexclusive (i.e., when those individuals not paying for it cannot be excluded from also consuming it), there is a tendency for each consumer to be a free rider. A **free-rider problem** arises because each consumer believes that the public good will be provided anyway, whether he or she contributes to its payment or not. That is, because there are many people sharing the cost of providing the public good, each individual feels that withdrawing his or her financial support will practically go unnoticed by others and will have little or no effect on the provision of the good. The problem is that since many individuals behave this way (i.e., behave as free riders), less than the optimal amount of the public good will be provided.[8] In general, as the group size increases, the free-rider problem becomes more acute. This problem can be, and generally is, overcome by the government taxing the general public to pay for the public good. A good example of this is national defense.[9] Sometimes governments go to great lengths to induce people to pay their fair share of taxes to provide public goods. For example, at the turn of the century, the government of China retained the right to purchase an individual's house to avoid the owner's incentive to undervalue it for tax purposes.

The second (related) problem cannot be resolved as satisfactorily by government intervention. This arises because each individual has no incentive to accurately reveal his or her preferences or demand for the public good. Therefore, it is practically impossible for the government to know exactly what is the optimal amount of the public good that it should provide or induce the private sector to provide. There is also the problem of possible government inefficiency in providing public goods and in otherwise intervening in the market (see Section 18.5).

Free-rider problem
The problem that arises when an individual does not contribute to the payment of a public good in the belief that it will be provided anyway.

✓ Concept Check
How does the free-rider problem arise in the provision of public goods?

AT THE FRONTIER
Efficiency Versus Equity in the U.S. Tax System

Taxpayers everywhere complain that they pay too much. Contrary to popular belief, however, taxes in the United States are lower than in all other major advanced nations except Japan. Table 18.1 shows that total tax receipts as a percentage of gross domestic product (GDP) were 34.1% in the United States in 2006, compared with an

Continued . . .

---

[8] Note that even a private (rival) good leads to market failure if it is characterized by nonexclusion (i.e., if each individual consuming it cannot be adequately charged for it).

[9] Sometimes a free-rider problem can partially be resolved by the private sector. Examples are educational television stations, tenants' associations, and charitable associations such as the Salvation Army.

Efficiency Versus Equity in the U.S. Tax System   *Continued*

TABLE 18.1 Taxes as a Percentage of GDP in the Leading Advanced Nations in 1990, 2000, and 2006			
Country	1990	2000	2006
Sweden	64.7	60.9	57.6
France	47.1	50.1	51.2
Belgium	45.5	49.1	49.1
Netherlands	49.1	46.1	47.2
Italy	41.5	45.3	45.6
Germany	41.7	46.4	43.9
United Kingdom	40.6	41.5	42.2
Canada	43.0	44.1	40.3
Spain	38.7	38.1	40.3
United States	32.8	35.8	34.1
Japan	33.9	31.4	33.9

Source: OECD Economic Outlook, June 2007, p. 265.

average of over 45.5% in the Euro area. Another difference is that the United States raises most of its revenues from income and profit taxes, while European countries rely mostly on consumption taxes, such as the value-added tax (taxes imposed on the value added at each stage of the production and distribution chain).

Although Europeans pay much higher taxes than Americans, they also get much greater benefits. Europeans have good free medical and nursing home care, nearly free college education, and generous pension and unemployment safety nets. They also have lower crime rates, cleaner streets, state-of-the-art mass transit, less income and wealth inequality, and less social instability, and this makes them more willing to accept higher taxes. In the United States, people do not see such a strong association between taxes and tangible benefits, and so there is a much greater resistance to higher taxes. The very strong welfare state in Europe, where people rely on government for cradle-to-grave care, has its shortcomings, however. For one thing, even with very high taxes, most European nations have big budget deficits and are being forced to scale down welfare benefits. There is also much less labor mobility and much higher rates of unemployment, fewer patents, and much less entrepreneurship than in the United States, and these reduce European international competitiveness and future growth prospects.

Concept Check

Why is there often a conflict between efficiency and equity in taxation?

The recent drive to reduce federal welfare programs and cut taxes represents, to some extent, a fundamental change in the U.S. tax system, from stressing equity and fairness to striving for efficiency and growth. This increased the international competitiveness of the U.S. economy during the past decade, but it is also increased income inequalities, both absolutely and relative to other advanced nations.

Although most people agree that major tax reform is needed in the United States, this is not happening. One proposal for tax reforms is the so-called "fair tax," which would tax consumption (say, with a retail sales tax) rather than income (which discourages economic activity, saving, and investment) and eliminate all exemptions, deductions, exceptions, and special tax provisions. According to its supporters, this would broaden the tax base, significantly reduce tax rates, and improve efficiency. This, however, would require repealing the XVI Amendment (which allows Washington to impose an income tax) and, according to its opponents, would dramatically raise prices of many goods and services. Another tax proposal is the flat tax, which would impose a simple tax rate on personal income and corporate profits, with general exemptions for low-income families. This would greatly stimulate economic activity according to its supporters, but it is a loser on both economic and moral grounds according to its opponents.

Sources: "Gap in Wealth in U.S. Called Widest in West," *New York Times*, April 17, 1995, p. 1; "European Shrug as Taxes Go Up," *New York Times*, February 16, 1995, p. 10; "How Fair Are Our Taxes," *Wall Street Journal*, January 10, 1996, p. A12; D. Altig et al.; "Simulating Fundamental Tax Reforms in the United States," *American Economic Review*, June 2001, pp. 574–595; D. Salvatore, "Relative Taxation and Competitiveness in the European Union: What the European Union Can Learn from the United States," *Journal of Policy Modeling*, May 2002, pp. 401–410; L. J. Kotlikoff, "The Case for the 'Fair Tax,' " *Wall Street Journal*, March 7, 2005, p. A18; "One Simple Rate," *Wall Street Journal*, August 15, 2005, p. A12; "Fair Taxes? Depends What You Mean by 'Fair,'" *New York Times*, July 15, 2007, Sec. IV, p. 4; "Income Tax Foes Regroup," *Wall Street Journal*, August 20, 2007, p. A4; and "The Bag of Tricks Is Almost Empty," *New York Times*, February 10, 2008, p. 9 (Business Section).

18.4   BENEFIT–COST ANALYSIS

Benefit–cost analysis
A procedure for determining the most worthwhile public projects for the government to undertake.

Governments play many roles in modern societies. These roles range from the provision of public goods, to the redistribution of income, the regulation of monopoly, and pollution control. In carrying out these functions, government agencies must constantly decide which projects to implement and which to reject. A useful procedure for determining the most worthwhile projects is **benefit–cost analysis.** This analysis compares the present value of the benefits of a project to the present value of the costs of a project. Government should carry out a project only if the present value of the social benefits from the project exceeds the present value of its social costs (i.e., if the benefit–cost ratio for the project exceeds 1). Often, the government does not have the resources (i.e., cannot raise taxes or borrow sufficiently) to undertake all the projects with a benefit–cost ratio exceeding 1. In such cases, government should rank all possible projects from the highest to the lowest (but exceeding 1) benefit–cost ratio, and starting at the top of the list, it should undertake all projects until its resources are fully utilized.

Although this sounds straightforward, a number of serious difficulties arise in the actual application of benefit–cost analysis, because it is often very difficult to correctly estimate the social benefits and the social costs of a project and to determine the appropriate rate of interest to use to calculate the present value of benefits and costs. First, since the benefits and the costs of most public projects (such as a dam, a highway, a training program, and so on) take place over many years, it is difficult to estimate them correctly so far into the future.

Second, benefits and costs are frequently estimated on the basis of current or projected prices, even though these prices may not reflect the true scarcity value or opportunity cost of the outputs resulting from or the inputs used in the project. For example, commodity prices under imperfectly competitive commodity markets exceed their marginal cost. Similarly, if a project results in the employment of otherwise unemployed labor, the real cost of hiring labor is zero, in spite of the positive wage paid to these workers. In other words, it is the real or opportunity value of the benefits and costs of the project that should be used in benefit–cost analysis. But it may be difficult to estimate them. Real costs may also rise as the project increases the demand for inputs.

Third, some of the benefits and costs of a project may not be quantifiable. For example, while it may be possible to estimate the rise in workers' income resulting from a training program, it is next to impossible to assign a value to their enhanced self-esteem and to their becoming more responsible citizens. Similarly, it is practically impossible to assign a value to the loss of scenery resulting from the construction of a dam. Yet, all of these social benefits and costs should be included in benefit–cost analysis for it to lead to appropriate public investment decisions.

The fourth and perhaps the most serious difficulty with benefit–cost analysis arises in the choice of the proper interest rate to be used to find the present value of the benefits and costs of the project. That is, since the benefits and costs of most projects occur over a number of years, they must be discounted to the present. For this a rate of interest must be used, as discussed in Section 16.3.[10] The question is *which* is the proper interest rate to use? As indicated in Section 16.4, there are a large number of rates of interest in the market (ranging from nearly zero to 40%) depending on the risk, duration, cost of administering, and the tax treatment of the loan. Since the use of resources by the government competes with private use, the interest (discount) rate to be used to find present values should reflect the opportunity cost of funds for a project of similar riskiness, duration, and administrative costs in the private sector. However, because different people may come up with a different rate of interest to use, benefit–cost analysis is usually prepared for a range of interest rates (from a low, to a medium, and a high one) rather than for a single interest rate. The lower the interest rate (or range of interest rates) used, the higher the benefit–cost ratio usually is and the greater the likelihood of the project being undertaken. The reason for this is that the benefits of a project usually arise later or over a longer period of time than its costs.

In spite of the great difficulties inherent in benefit–cost analysis, it is nevertheless a very valuable procedure for organizing our thoughts on the social benefits and the social costs of each project. If nothing else, it forces government officials to make explicit all the assumptions underlying the analysis. Scrutiny of the assumptions has sometimes led to decision reversals. For example, in 1971, the Federal Power Commission (now the Federal Energy Regulatory Commission) approved the construction of a hydroelectric dam on the Snake River, which flows from Oregon to Idaho and forms Hell's Canyon (the deepest in North America). The decision was based on a benefit–cost analysis that ignored some environmental costs. Because these costs were not accounted for, the Supreme Court, on appeal from the secretary of the interior, revoked the order to build the dam pending a new benefit–cost analysis that properly included *all* benefits and costs. Eventually, Congress passed a law prohibiting the construction of the dam.[11]

Although benefit–cost analysis is still more of an art than a science and is somewhat subjective, its usefulness has been proven in a wide variety of projects—water, transportation,

---

[10] In Section 16.3 we showed how to find the present value of a project. For benefit–cost analysis we need to find the present value of the benefits and costs of the project *separately*. The procedure, however, is the same. Note that a positive present value for a project is equivalent to a greater-than-one benefit–cost ratio.

[11] J. V. Krutilla and A. C. Fisher, *The Economics of Natural Environments: Studies in the Valuation of Commodity and Amenity Resources* (Baltimore: Johns Hopkins University Press, 1975), pp. 101–103.

health, education, and recreation. In fact, in 1965, the federal government formally began to introduce benefit–cost analysis for its budgetary procedures under the Planning-Programming-Budgeting System (PPBS). The practice has now spread to state and local governments as well. The process suffered a setback, however, when the Supreme Court ruled in February 2001 in Whitman v. American Trucking Associations Inc. that the EPA must consider only the requirements of public health and safety in setting national air quality standards and may not engage in cost–benefit analysis, as the American Trucking Associations Inc. had argued.[12]

EXAMPLE 18–4
Benefit–Cost Analysis and the SST

In 1971, after a benefit–cost analysis, the development of the supersonic transport plane (SST) was abandoned by the United States. The benefits were simply not large enough to justify the costs. The French and British governments, however, jointly pursued the project and built the Concorde, at a huge cost. Only a handful of such planes was built, and they were operated exclusively by the British and French national airlines in flights between New York and Paris or London from 1976 until it was grounded in 2003. With operating costs more than four times higher than for the Boeing 747, the Concorde must be classified as a clear market failure. Specifically, a one-way seat from New York to London was $6,000, and from New York to Paris it was $5,000, which was more than the roundtrip price from New York and London or Paris on the Boeing 747. This meant that passengers paid more than $1,000 for each hour saved by traveling on the Concorde. Modern people may be hurried today but not that hurried!

British Airways and Air France insisted all along that the Concorde broke even. Even so, the huge development cost of $8 billion was never recouped. And business on the Concorde was not brisk—British Airways and Air France found it increasingly difficult to fill the Concorde. It seems that in their zeal to fly the only supersonic plane, the British and French greatly overestimated the benefits and grossly underestimated the costs of building and running the Concorde in their benefit–cost analysis. This is an example of how imprecise benefit–cost analysis and how costly national pride can sometimes be.

Be that as it may, the Concorde was a marvel of air travel, with no rival in sight. A European project to build the "Concorde 2," with double the capacity of the past Concorde, was scrapped in 1995. Similarly, a 10-year study on the feasibility of building an American supersonic passenger plane by the National Aeronautics and Space Administration and involving Boeing and engine makers General Electric and Pratt & Whitney that cost $1.8 billion was shut down in 1998. Only France and Japan have expressed the intention of trying jointly to develop a supersonic commercial plane. The problem is not technological but economic. Although small supersonic jets are

[12] "E.P.A.'s Right to Set Air Rules Wins Supreme Court Backing," *New York Times,* February 28, 2001, p. 1; and D. Clement, "Cost v. Benefit: Clearing the Air?" *The Region,* Federal Reserve Bank of Minneapolis, December 2001, pp. 19–57.

being developed, there is no possibility at present of building a large supersonic passenger aircraft that could be operated at a profit.

Sources: "The Concorde's Destination," *New York Times*, September 28, 1979, p. 26; "Supersonic on the Back Burner," *The Economist*, March 6, 1999, p. 74; "Concorde Successor Faces Many Hurdles," *Financial Times*, December 12, 2001, p. V; "France and Japan Seek Concorde Alternative," *New York Times*, June 16, 2005, p. C4; and http://www.ubercool.com/2007/06/25/supersonic-travel-reinvented.

18.5   THE THEORY OF PUBLIC CHOICE

In this section we examine the meaning, importance, and policy implications of public-choice theory. Specifically, we explore the process by which government decisions are made and the reasons that these decisions might not increase social welfare.

Meaning and Importance of Public-Choice Theory

Theory of public choice The study of how government decisions are made and implemented.

Government failures Situations where government policies do not reflect the public's interests and reduce rather than increase social welfare.

The **theory of public choice** is the study of how government decisions are made and implemented. It studies how the political process and government *actually* work rather than how they should work, and it recognizes the possibility of **government failures** or situations in which government policies do not reflect the public's interests and reduce rather than increase social welfare. The fact that markets do not operate efficiently does not necessarily mean that government policies will improve the situation; it is always possible that government intervention will make a bad situation worse. The opposite situation is also invalid. That is, the fact that government policies are inefficient does not necessarily mean that private markets can do better. For example, great waste in government defense expenditures does not mean that the provision of national defense can be left to private markets.

The theory of public choice is based on the premise that individuals attempt to further their own personal interests in the political arena just as they seek to further their own economic interests in the marketplace. According to the law of the invisible hand postulated by Adam Smith over two centuries ago, an individual who pursues his or her own selfish economic interests also and at the same time promotes the welfare of society as a whole. This was the basis for favoring and stimulating competition in the marketplace. The theory of public choice seeks to answer the question of whether such an invisible hand mechanism is also at work in the political system. That is, as each individual attempts to further his or her own interests in political activities, is he or she also and at the same time promoting society's welfare?

The Public-Choice Process

The theory of public choice examines how government decisions are made and implemented by analyzing the behavior of individuals within each of four broad groups or participants in the political process. These groups are voters, politicians, special-interest groups, and bureaucrats. Let us examine each in turn.

Voters   The voter in the political process can be regarded as the counterpart of the consumer in the marketplace. Rather than purchasing goods and services for himself or herself in the marketplace, the voter elects government representatives who make and enforce government policies and purchase goods and services for the community as a whole. Other things being equal, voters tend to vote for candidates who favor policies that will further their own individual interests. This is, in fact, the general process by which elected officials are responsive to the electorate.

According to public-choice theorists, however, voters are much less informed about political decisions than about their individual market decisions. This lack of information is often referred to as **rational ignorance.** There are three reasons for ignorance. First, with elected officials empowered to act as the purchasing agents for the community, there is less need for individual voters to be fully informed about public choices. Second, it is generally much more expensive for individuals to gather information about public choices than to become informed about individual market choices. For example, it is much more difficult for an individual to evaluate the full implications of a proposed national health insurance plan than to evaluate the implications of an individual insurance policy. Third, as a single individual, a voter feels—and, indeed, *is*—less influential in and less affected by public choices than by his or her own private market choices.

Politicians   Politicians are the counterpart in the political system of the entrepreneurs or managers of private firms in the market system. Both seek to maximize their personal benefit. While the entrepreneur or manager of a private firm seeks to maximize his or her interest by maximizing the firm's profits, the politician seeks to maximize chances of reelection. In doing so, politicians often respond to the desires of small, well-organized, well-informed, and well-funded special-interest groups. These include associations of farmers, importers, medical doctors, and many others. Faced with rational ignorance on the part of the majority of voters, politicians often support policies that greatly benefit small, vocal interest groups (who can contribute heavily to a candidate's reelection campaign) at the expense of the mostly silent and uninformed majority.

For example, in the early 1980s, U.S. automobile manufacturers were able to greatly increase their profits by having the U.S. government restrict auto imports from Japan (see the example in Section 13.7). The fact that politicians face reelection every few years may also lead politicians to pay undue attention to the short run, even when this leads to more serious long-run problems. For example, public policies are often adopted to reduce the rate of unemployment at election time in November, even though this might lead to higher inflation later. Such policies have led some to postulate the existence of a "political business cycle."

Special-Interest Groups   Perhaps the most maligned of the groups participating in the political process are special-interest groups. These pressure groups or organized lobbies seek to elect politicians who support their cause, and they actively support the passage of laws and regulations that further their interests. For example, for decades the American Medical Association succeeded in limiting admissions to medical schools, thereby increasing doctors' incomes; farmers' associations successfully lobbied the government to provide billions of dollars in subsidies each year; as pointed out earlier, U.S. automakers succeeded in having auto imports from Japan restricted in the early 1980s, thereby greatly increasing their profits. Even though not all lobbies are as successful as those mentioned here, thousands are in operation, and this, according to many, represents the worst aspects of our political system.[13]

Rational ignorance
The condition whereby voters are much less informed about political decisions than about their individual market decisions because of the higher costs of obtaining information and the smaller direct benefits that they obtain from the former than from the latter.

---

[13] In recent years, lobbying in Washington by foreign firms and nations (especially Japan) has increased sharply.

The reason some of these special-interest groups are so influencial is that they are well organized and stand to benefit a great deal when their efforts are successful. Thus, they are very vocal and often can provide millions of dollars in financial support to politicians who advocate their cause. At the same time, most people are usually not aware of the costs (usually small) that they individually face from these laws and regulations. Furthermore, these laws and regulations are invariably rationalized in terms of the national interest. For example, import restrictions on shoes might only increase the price of shoes by $1 per pair while providing millions of dollars in extra profits to the few remaining shoe manufacturers in the nation. Supposedly, these import restrictions are temporary and are essential to give time to American producers to increase efficiency and be able to meet what is regarded as unfair foreign competition.

Bureaucrats   Bureaus are the government agencies that carry out the policies enacted by Congress. They do so by receiving annual lump-sum appropriations to cover the costs of providing the services that they are directed to provide. Bureaus often provide these services under conditions of monopoly (i.e., without any competition from other bureaus or private firms) and so have little incentive to promote internal efficiency. While it is difficult to compare the efficiency of government bureaus and private firms, there have been spectacular cost overruns in many defense projects. For example, the cost of the Lockheed C5A transport plane increased from an estimated $3.4 billion in 1965 to $5.3 billion in 1968.

According to public-choice theory, bureaucrats are not simply passive executors of adopted policies, but seek to influence such policies in order to further their own personal interests. They do so by constantly seeking to increase the scope of the bureau's activities and the amount of funding, even when the raison d'être for the bureau no longer exists. This is because a top bureaucrat's career, income, power, prestige, and promotion are, in general, closely related to the size and growth of the bureau. In essence, the bureau often becomes a separate special-interest group within the government!

Policy Implications of Public-Choice Theory

The above characterization of the political process by public-choice theorists is, perhaps, excessively cynical. Voters elect only politicians who promote their individual interests, and are mostly ignorant and indifferent about most other public choices; politicians only seek to maximize their chances of reelection; special-interest groups only seek special advantages at the expense of the mostly silent and ignorant majority; and bureaucrats only seek to maximize their own interests by promoting the bureau's growth at the expense of efficiency.

Although there is some truth in all of this, we must also point out that many voters are well informed and often unselfish; many politicians have refused to compromise their principles simply to maximize their chances of reelection; many powerful special-interest groups have been unsuccessful in furthering their causes; and many bureaucracies have operated efficiently and sometimes even proposed their own abolition when their function was no longer required. For example, in the past, the majority of U.S. voters consistently voted for and supported most social welfare policies, even though these policies involved a redistribution of income to poor people; President Reagan refused to back away from large defense spending in spite of strong opposition in and out of Congress and the resulting huge budget deficits; the American Medical Association is no longer able to restrict admissions to medical schools as it did over many decades; and the CAB (the Civil Aeronautics Board) proposed its own abolition and is now no longer in existence.

These examples, however, do not necessarily represent contradictions of the theory of public choice. This theory seeks only to identify the forces that must be examined to properly analyze public choices. The theory concludes that while public policies can improve the functioning of the economic system in the presence of market failures, the government itself is subject to systematic forces that can lead to government failures. Public policies could then reduce, rather than increase, social welfare. More importantly, perhaps, the theory of public choice can be used to suggest specific institutional changes and to devise policies that can lead to improvements in public-sector performance.

One way that public-choice theory suggests for improving public-sector performance is to subject government bureaus or agencies to competition whenever feasible. One method of achieving this is by contracting out to private firms as many public services as possible. For example, market evidence suggests that garbage collection and fire protection can be provided more efficiently by private contractors than by public agencies. The same may be true for running school systems and jails.[14] Another method advocated by public-choice theory to promote efficiency in public choices is to allow private firms to compete with government agencies in the provision of services that are not entirely public in nature.[15] For example, families could be given vouchers that they could use for public or private education. Giving parents the option and funding to choose private schools over public schools would stimulate public schools to provide better education and increase efficiency. Still another method of increasing efficiency in government is to encourage interagency competition. While streamlining government operations is likely to eliminate some duplication and waste, it also eliminates competition and incentives for efficient operation. For example, it has been estimated that the cost-effectiveness of the Department of Defense operations declined by one-third following the consolidation of the three branches of the armed forces within the department.

Public-choice theory also suggests at least two ways of reducing the influence of special-interest groups. One option would be to rely more on referenda to decide important political issues. Although the influence of special-interest groups is not entirely eliminated (since they can still spend a great deal of money on influencing the general public through advertisements), reverting from representative to direct democracy in deciding some important issues does overcome the interaction between special-interest groups and politicians. Today, referenda are much more common in European countries than in the United States. Another method of reducing the influence of special-interest groups is to specify the total amount of public funds budgeted for the year and encourage different groups to compete for government funding. Because the total amount of funds is fixed, one group can only gain at the expense of others. Each group is then likely to present its best case for funding while exposing the weaknesses in competitors' funding requests. In the process, a great deal of essential information is made available to government officials, who can therefore allocate funds more effectively. Many policies (such as import restrictions), however, do not involve direct public funding, and so this is not possible.

✓ Concept Check

How does the theory of public choice examine how government decisions are made and implemented?

---

[14] "Hartford Hires Group to Run School System," *New York Times,* October 4, 1994, p. B1; "For Privately Run Prisons, New Evidence of Success," *New York Times,* August 19, 1995, p. 7; M. Haririan and T. A. Bonomo, "Privatization and the Emergence of For-Profit Prisons," Central Business Review, winter 1996, pp. 11–15; "Do Firms Run Schools Well?" *U.S. News & World Report,* January 8, 1996, pp. 46–49; and "Pennsylvania Abandons Plan to Privatize School Offices," *New York Times,* November 21, 2001, p. 14.

[15] See "Public Services Are Found Better if Private Agencies Compete," *New York Times,* April 28, 1988, p. 1.

<table>
<tr><td>18.6</td></tr>
</table>

STRATEGIC TRADE POLICY

Strategic trade policy
The attempt by a nation to create a comparative advantage in some high-tech field through temporary trade protection, subsidies, tax benefits, and cooperative government–industry programs.

One qualified argument in favor of an activist government policy in the international arena is **strategic trade policy.** According to this argument, a nation can create a comparative advantage (through temporary trade protection, subsidies, tax benefits, and cooperative government-industry programs) in such fields as semiconductors, computers, telecommunications, and other industries that are deemed crucial to future growth in the nation. These high-tech industries are subject to high risks, require large-scale production to achieve economies of scale, and give rise to extensive external economies when successful. Strategic trade policy suggests that by encouraging such industries, a nation can reap the resulting large external economies and enhance its future growth prospects. Most nations encourage development in these industries. Indeed, some economists would go so far as to say that a great deal of the post-World War II industrial and technological success of Japan is due to its strategic industrial and trade policies.

Examples of strategic trade and industrial policies can be found in the steel industry in the 1950s and in semiconductors in the 1970s and 1980s in Japan; in the development of the supersonic aircraft, the Concorde, in the 1970s (see Example 18–4); and in the Airbus aircraft in the 1980s in Europe. Semiconductors in Japan are usually given as the textbook case of successful strategic trade and industrial policy. The market for semiconductors (such as computer chips that are used in many products) was dominated by the United States in the 1970s. Starting in the mid-1970s, Japan's powerful Ministry of International Trade and Industry (MITI) targeted the development of this industry by financing research and development, granting tax advantages for investments in the industry, and fostering government-industry cooperation, while protecting the domestic market from foreign (especially U.S.) competition.

These policies are credited for Japan's success in challenging the United States' leading position in the semiconductor market in the mid-1980s. Most economists remain skeptical, however, and attribute Japan's stunning performance in this field primarily to other forces, such as greater educational emphasis on science and mathematics, higher rates of investment, and a willingness to take a long-run view of investments rather than stressing quarterly profits, as in the United States. In steel, the other targeted industry in Japan, the rate of return was lower than the average return for all Japanese industries during the post-war period. In Europe, the Concorde was a technological feat but a commercial disaster, and Airbus Industries would not have survived without continued heavy government subsidies.

While strategic trade policy can theoretically improve the market outcome in oligopolistic markets subject to extensive external economies and increase the nation's growth and welfare, even the originators and popularizers of this theory recognize the serious difficulties in implementing it. First, it is extremely difficult to pick winners (i.e., choose the industries that will provide large external economies in the future) and devise appropriate policies to successfully nurture them. Second, since most leading nations undertake strategic trade policies at the same time, efforts are largely neutralized, so that the potential benefits to each nation may be small. Third, when a country does achieve substantial success with strategic trade policy, this comes at the expense of other countries (i.e., it is a beggar-thy-neighbor policy), and so other countries are likely to retaliate. Faced with all these practical difficulties, even supporters of strategic trade policy grudgingly acknowledge that *free trade is still the best policy, after all.*

✓ Concept Check
What are the uses and dangers of strategic trade and industrial policies?

EXAMPLE 18-5

Strategic Trade and Industrial Policies in the United States

In the early 1980s, the U.S. government drew up a list of 26 generic and critical technologies which it was willing to support in a limited way. Among these were electronic materials, high-performance metals and alloys, flexible computer integrated manufacturing, software, high-performance computing networking, high-definition imaging displays, applied molecular biology, medical technology, aeronautics, and energy technologies. The best example of direct federal support for civilian technology is Semitech. This was an Austin-based consortium of 14 major U.S. semiconductor manufacturers which was established in 1987 with an annual budget of $225 million ($100 million from the government and the rest from the 14 member firms). Its aim was to help develop state-of-the-art manufacturing techniques for computer chips for its members and help firms producing equipment used in the manufacturing of computer chips develop and test more advanced equipment.

By 1991, Semitech claimed that, as a result of its efforts, U.S. computer chip companies had caught up with their Japanese competitors. Since then, Semitech has become entirely private (i.e., it no longer receives U.S. government financial support), and in 1998 it created Semitech International, a wholly owned subsidiary of 12 major U.S. and foreign computer chip companies. It is now (2008) called International Semitech Manufacturing Initiative (ISMI) and has 16 members.

Despite being hailed as a successful model of government-industry cooperation in support of high-tech research and development (R&D) before it was privatized, a recent study found that participating in Semitech led firms to spend less on their own R&D than would have been expected, given the behavior of these firms prior to Semitech and given the behavior of U.S. computer chip firms that did not join Semitech. The study also found that the resurgence of the U.S. computer chip industry after 1987 was due more to the sharp depreciation of the U.S. dollar with respect to the Japanese yen (which made U.S.-made computer chips cheaper than Japanese ones) and the U.S.–Japanese computer chip agreement, which insulated U.S. computer chip firms against Japanese competition, than to Semitech.

Sources: D. Irwin and P. Klenow, "High Tech R & D Subsidies: Estimating the Effect of Semitech," *National Bureau of Economic Research, Working Paper No. 4974*, July 1995; and "When the State Picks Winners," *The Economist*, January 9, 1993, pp. 13–14; C. Wessner, "The Advanced Technology Program: It Works," *Issues in Science and Technology*, Fall 2001, pp. 59–64; and http://ismi.sematech.org.

18.7   GOVERNMENT CONTROL AND REGULATION OF ENVIRONMENTAL POLLUTION

Now we will use the tools of analysis developed in this chapter to analyze environmental pollution and the best way for government to control or regulate it.

Environmental Pollution

We have seen in Section 18.2 that externalities (and inefficiencies) may be eliminated by the clear definition of property rights if the parties involved are not very numerous. Otherwise, transaction costs are too high and externalities persist. This is precisely the case with **environmental pollution,** which refers to air pollution, water pollution, thermal pollution, pollution resulting from garbage disposal, and so on. Environmental pollution has become one of the major political and economic issues in recent decades. Environmental pollution results from and is an example of negative externalities.[16]

Air pollution results mostly from automobile exhaust and smoke from factories and electrical generating plants through the combustion of fossil fuels, which releases particles into the air. While it is difficult to measure precisely the harmful effects of sulfur dioxide, carbon monoxide, and other air pollutants, they are known to cause damage to health (in the form of breathing illnesses and aggravating other diseases, such as circulatory problems) and to property (in the form of higher cleaning bills, and so on). *Water pollution* results from dumping raw (untreated) sewage, chemical waste products from factories and mines, and runoff of pesticides and fertilizers from farms into streams, lakes, and seashores. This reduces the supply of clean water for household uses (drinking, bathing, and so on) and recreational uses (swimming, boating, fishing, and so on). *Thermal pollution* results from the cooling off of electrical power plants and other machinery. This increases water temperature and kills fish. The disposal of garbage such as beer cans, newspapers, cigarette butts, and so on, spoils natural scenery, as do billboards and posters. To this visual pollution must be added noise pollution and many other forms of pollution.

Environmental pollution results whenever the environment is used (abused) as a convenient and cheap dumping ground for all types of waste products. It is convenient and cheap from the private point of view to use the environment in this manner because no one owns property rights to it. As a result, air and water users pay less than the full social cost of using these natural resources, and by so doing they impose serious external costs on society. In short, society produces and consumes too much of products that generate environmental pollution. Since property rights are ambiguous and the parties involved are numerous (often running into the millions), it is impossible and impractical (too costly) to identify and negotiate with individual agents. The external costs of environmental pollution cannot be internalized by the assignment of clear property rights and so government intervention is required. This intervention can take the form of regulation or taxation. However, appropriate corrective action on the part of the government requires knowledge of the exact cost of pollution.

Optimal Pollution Control

If a staunch environmentalist were asked how much environmental pollution society should tolerate, the answer would probably be zero. This would be the wrong answer. The optimal level of pollution is the level at which the marginal social cost of pollution equals the marginal social benefit (in the form of avoiding alternative and more expensive methods of waste disposal). Zero pollution is an ideal situation, but as long as pollution is the inevitable

---

Environmental pollution The lowering of air, water, scenic, and noise qualities of the world around us that results from the dumping of waste products.

---

[16] See "Priority One: Rescue the Environment," *Science,* February 16, 1990, p. 777; M. L. Cropper and W. Oates, "Environmental Economics: A Survey," *Journal of Economic Literature,* June 1992, pp. 675–740; and "Where Money Is No Object," *Forbes,* March 5, 2001, p. 78.

by-product of the production and consumption of commodities that we want, it is silly to advocate zero pollution. Economists advocate optimal pollution control instead. That is, we should be prepared to accept (as inevitable) that amount of pollution which, at the margin, balances the social costs and benefits of pollution. This is shown in Figure 18.3.

In Figure 18.3, the horizontal axis measures the quantity of pollution per year, and the vertical axis measures costs and gains in dollars. The *MC* curve, for example, could measure the value of the marginal loss of fish suffered by fishermen for various amounts of water pollution generated by a firm. The marginal loss (cost) increases with rising amounts of pollution. The *MB* curve would then measure the marginal benefit or saving that the polluting firm receives by being able to freely dump its waste into the water rather than disposing of it by the next-best alternative method (at a positive cost). The *MB* is negatively sloped, indicating declining benefits for the firm for each additional unit of pollution that it discharges into the water.

When the firm does not incur any cost for discharging waste into the water, it will do so until the marginal benefit is zero (point *A* in the figure). That is, as long as the firm saves some cost by discharging its waste into the water, it will do so until the *MB* is zero. However, pollution does impose a cost on society as a whole. The optimal amount of pollution from society's point of view is 8 units, given by the intersection of the *MC* and the *MB* curves at point *E*. Only when pollution is 8 units per year is the marginal benefit to the individual and to society equal to the marginal social cost of pollution. To the left of point *E*, *MB* > *MC* and it pays for society to increase the level of pollution (see the figure). The opposite is true to the right of point *E*. As strange as it may have sounded earlier, we now know that the optimal level of pollution is not zero, but is positive.

 Concept Check
What is the optimal level of pollution?

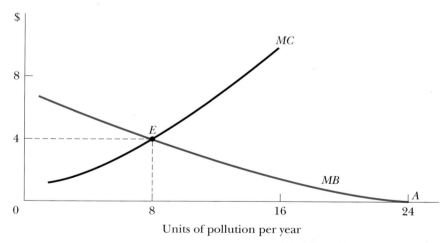

FIGURE 18.3   Optimal Pollution Control   The *MC* curve shows the rising marginal cost or loss to society from increasing amounts of pollution. The *MB* curve shows the declining marginal benefit to the polluter (and to society) by being able to freely dump increasing amounts of waste into the water rather than disposing of it by other costly alternatives. Since the firm does not pay for discharging its waste into the water, it will do so until *MB* = 0 (point *A*). From society's point of view, the optimal level of pollution for the firm is 8 units per year (point *E*, at which *MC* = *MB*).

Direct Regulation and Effluent Fees for Optimal Pollution Control

We have just seen that the optimal level of pollution from society's point of view is not zero, but is given by the level at which the marginal cost of pollution is equal to the private (and social) marginal benefit of disposing of waste by the cheapest method possible. Even though this prescription is theoretically precise, it is often very difficult to actually estimate the marginal social costs and benefits of pollution. Without government intervention, environmental pollution is certainly likely to be excessive (compare point *A* to point *E* in Figure 18.3).

There are generally two ways to achieve the optimal amount of pollution control: direct regulation and effluent fees. By direct regulation, government could legislate that the industry limit pollution to the optimal level (8 units per year in Figure 18.3) or install a particular pollution-abatement device. Alternatively, government could set the **effluent fee** that brings the private cost of pollution equal to its social cost. An effluent fee is a tax that a firm must pay to the government for discharging waste or otherwise polluting. For example, an effluent fee of $4 per unit of waste or pollution per year in Figure 18.3 results in the optimal level of pollution of 8 units per year. That is, an effluent fee of $4 per unit will make the marginal private (and social) cost of pollution equal to its marginal private (and social) benefit.

While direct regulation is sometimes necessary (as in the case of radioactive and other very dangerous waste materials), economists generally prefer effluent fees to achieve optimal pollution control. There are two reasons for this. First, effluent fees generally require less information on the part of the government than direct regulation. Second, and more importantly, effluent fees minimize the cost of optimal pollution control, whereas direct regulation does not. This is because with effluent fees, each polluter will pollute until the marginal benefit of pollution equals the effluent fee. Thus, the optimal amount of pollution is allocated to those firms that benefit the most from polluting. As a result, the social cost of pollution is minimized.

One way to use effluent fees to reduce pollution is by the *sale of pollution rights* by the government. Under such a system, the government determines the amount of pollution that it thinks is socially tolerable (based on the benefits that result from the activities that generate the pollution) and then auctions off licenses to firms that generate pollution up to the specified amount. Pollution costs are thus internalized (i.e., they are considered part of regular production costs) by firms and the allowed amount of pollution is utilized in activities in which it is more valuable (see Example 18–6). Another way to overcome a negative externality is congestion pricing (see Example 18–7).

Effluent fee A tax that a firm must pay for discharging waste or polluting.

✓ Concept Check
Why are effluent fees usually better than regulation for achieving optimal pollution control?

EXAMPLE 18-6

The Market for Dumping Rights

The Clean Air Act of 1990 led to the establishment of a market for dumping rights. In such a market, the Environmental Protection Agency decides how much pollution it wants to allow and then issues marketable rights for that quantity of pollution. Since these dumping rights are marketable (i.e., can be bought and sold by firms), they are likely to be used in those activities in which they are most valuable. For example, suppose that the EPA has imposed specific dumping restrictions on two firms. If the cost of reducing emission by 1 unit is $10,000 for one firm and $50,000 for a second firm, the first firm could sell the right to dump that unit of emission to the second firm for a price between $10,000 and $50,000. The result would be that both firms (and society) would gain without any overall increase in pollution. In fact, the only way that a new firm can build a plant that pollutes the air in an area that does not meet federal air-quality standards is to purchase the right to a specific amount of pollution from an already existing and polluting firm in the area. The EPA can then gradually lower the level of overall pollution over time by reducing the amount of right-to-pollute credits or pollution allowances it issues while allowing each firm to decide to comply with the law by installing antipollution equipment or buying right-to-pollution credits from other firms that have some to spare.

After 1992, when the first right-to-pollute credits were traded, the market grew rapidly, and we now have pollution-rights banks, which act as brokers between firms that want to sell pollution rights and firms that want to purchase them. The concept of marketable pollution rights has also been extended by the so-called "bubble policy." Under this policy, a firm with several plants operating in a single air-pollution area is given a total permissible emission level for all its plants rather than a limit for each one. This allows the firm to concentrate its emission-reduction efforts in plants where it can be done more cheaply. As a result of such a program, electric utilities now emit about 25% fewer tons of sulfur oxide in the atmosphere while producing 41% more electricity and also saving $3 billion. By 2000, the number of generating units participating in the program had risen from 445 to 2,200 and the cap on sulfur emissions was reduced by another 25%. With the quantity demanded of pollution rights far exceeding the quantity supplied, the price of pollution rights skyrocketed from $1,500 in January 1998 to $7,600 in March 1999. Since then, the quantity of pollution rights declined and their price fell to $1,400, because it became cheaper for companies to reduce pollution by installing antipollution equipment than by purchasing pollution rights.

The establishment of a market for pollution permits represents a significant victory for economists (who have been advocating this for many years) and changes the direction of antipollution efforts in the United States for decades to come. In July 2001, a historic accord that set targets for industrialized countries to cut the emission of greenhouse gases that contribute to global warming was signed as part of the implementation of the *Kyoto Protocol* on climate change signed in 1997. The United States refused to sign the agreement, calling its targets arbitrary and too costly for the United States to comply with. The Kyoto Protocol stimulated the development of a market for emissions trading on a global scale. After trading unofficially since 2003, the European Union's carbon-trading program, called the European Emission Trading System (EETS), formally started on January 1, 2005, and it is already valued at billions of dollars annually. The right to release one ton of carbon monoxide into the atmosphere increased from $6 in 2003 to $35 in 2005 in this market. This is the most cost-effective solution to global warming and provides a model on which a future global climate policy can be based. In 2007, the U.S. Congress was considering a national law to replace a growing number of state carbon-emission laws. A tax on carbon emissions will increase the price of using a "dirtier" fuel, such as coal, in favor of cleaner fuels, such as wind power and natural gas. At a UN conference on climate change held in Bali in December 2007, 190 nations (including the United States) signed an agreement to negotiate a new treaty by 2012 to succeed the Kyoto Protocol, which expires in 2012, that would call for the halving of emissions of heat-trapping gases by 2050.

Sources: "A Market Place for Pollution Rights," *U.S. News & World Report*, November 12, 1990, p. 79; "New Rules Harness the Power of Free Markets to Curb Air Pollution," *Wall Street Journal*, April 4, 1992, p. A1; "Cheapest Protection of Nature May Lie in Taxes, Not Laws," *New York Times*, November 24, 1992, p. C1; "How Much Is the Right to Pollute Worth?", *Wall Street Journal*, August 1, 2001, p. A15; "New Limits on Pollution Herald Change in Europe, *New York Times*, January 1, 2005, p. C2; "Europe's Emissions Trading Is a Model for the World," *Financial Times*, June 8, 2006, p. 13; "Climate Wars: Episode Two," *Business Week*, April 23, 2007, pp. 90–92; "The Carbon Calculus," *New York Times*, November 7, 2007, p. H1; "Bali Aims to Share Weight of Emissions Cuts," *Wall Street Journal*, December 12, 2007, p. A3; and "U.N. Effort to Curtail Emissions in Turmoil," *Well Street Journal*, April 12, 2008, p. A1.

EXAMPLE 18–7
Congestion Pricing

Congestion pricing
The charging of different prices at different times of day or based on the degree of congestion.

Every time a driver enters a congested highway or a congested city center he or she slows down the travel speed of all the other drivers (imposes a negative externality on them). Although **congestion pricing**, or the charging of a higher price for a good or service at times of heavy use, is well established for hotels, long-distance telephone service, and air travel, it has been applied only slowly on U.S. roads. Variations of congestion pricing based on charging different prices at different times of day and on the degree of congestion are in effect only on stretches of California Route 91, in Orange County, on Interstate 15 near San Diego, and in Houston, Minneapolis, and Denver—despite the fact that the concept has been known for nearly 40 years (it was introduced by William Vickery, the 1996 Nobel Prize–winning economics professor of Columbia University).

London has had such a congestion-pricing system since 2003 and Stockholm since 2006. Traffic cameras enforce a daily fee of $16 (which can be paid online, by phone, or at gas stations) to drive in central London. This was highly successful and reduced the number vehicles in central London by 10%. Fees for traveling within Stockholm vary according to peak driving time, with higher tolls during rush hours. Fees range from a low of $1.38 from 6:30 to 7:00 AM and 6:00 to 6:30 PM to a high fee of $2.76 from 7:30 to 8:30 AM and 4:00 to 5:30 PM, with fees in between these extremes at other times of day. In 2008, New York's mayor proposed to charge a fee of $8 each time a driver brings his or her car into traffic-congested Manhattan and $21 for a trucks; however, it was rejected. Many other cities throughout the world are now considering congestion pricing.

Congestion pricing is now being considered as a way to encourage airlines to spread their flights more evenly throughout the day, in the pricing of electricity, and even for parking meters. One study estimated that flight delays at New York's airports in 2007 cost passengers nearly \$200 million in lost productivity. Congestion pricing would reduce these delays (i.e., internalize these costs) and lead to more efficient use of scarce resources in a way that is consistent with individual freedom of choice.

Sources: "Stockholm's Syndrome," *Wall Street Journal*, August 29, 2006, p. B1; "What's the Toll? It Depends on the Time of Day," *New York Times*, February 11, 2007, Sect. IV, p. 7; "London Adds to Its Zone for Road Tolls," *New York Times*, February 18, 2007, p. 8; "Study Puts Price Tag on Delays at Airports," *New York Times*, December 2, 2007, p. 41; "\$8 Traffic Fee for Manhattan Fails in Albany," *New York Times*, April 8, 2008, p. 1; and "U.S. Plans Steps to Ease Congestion at Airports," *New York Times*, May 17, 2008, p. B1.

SUMMARY

1. Externalities are harmful or beneficial side effects borne by those not directly involved in the production or consumption of a commodity. Externalities are classified into external economies or diseconomies of production or consumption, and technical externalities. With external diseconomies of production or consumption, the commodity price falls short of the full social cost of the commodity and too much of the commodity is produced or consumed. With external economies of production or consumption, the commodity price exceeds the full social cost of the commodity and too little of the commodity is produced and consumed. Technical externalities may prevent marginal cost pricing.

2. Externalities arise when property rights are not clearly defined and transaction costs are very high. The Coase theorem postulates that when property rights are clearly defined and transaction costs are zero, perfect competition results in the absence of externalities, regardless of how property rights are assigned among the parties involved.

3. Public goods are commodities that are nonrival in consumption. That is, consumption of a public good by some individual does not reduce the amount available for others (at zero marginal cost). Some public goods, such as national defense, exhibit nonexclusion. That is, once the good is produced, it is impossible to confine its use to only those paying for it. Other public goods, such as TV broadcasting, can exhibit exclusion. Because of the free-rider problem, public goods are usually underproduced and underconsumed.

4. Benefit–cost analysis is based on the government calculating the ratio of the present value of all the benefits to the present value of all the costs for each proposed public project. The projects are then ranked from the highest to the lowest in terms of benefit–cost ratios. Government should undertake those projects with the highest benefit–cost ratio (as long as the ratio exceeds 1) and until government resources are fully employed. There are many difficulties in estimating all benefits and costs of a project and in determining the interest rate to use to find the present value of the benefits and costs.

5. According to the theory of public choice, individuals vote for politicians who promote their individual interests; politicians seek to maximize their chances of reelection; special-interest groups seek special advantages for their group; and bureaucrats seek to promote the bureau's growth. The theory postulates that it is possible for government policies to reduce rather than increase social welfare (government failures). It proposes to increase efficiency by increasing competition in public choices and by relying more on referenda to decide important issues.

6. According to strategic trade policy, a nation can create a comparative advantage (through temporary trade protection, subsidies, tax benefits, etc.) in such fields as computers, that can give rise to extensive external economies, and which are deemed crucial to future growth in the nation. However, it is very difficult to determine which industry to promote, and other nations are likely to retaliate.

7. Environmental (air, water, thermal, scenic, and noise) pollution arises because of unclearly defined property rights and too-high transaction costs. The optimal level of pollution from society's point of view is not zero, but is given by the level at which the marginal cost of pollution to society is equal to the private (and social) marginal benefit of disposing of waste by the cheapest method available. Optimal pollution control can be achieved by direct regulation or effluent fees. Although direct regulation is sometimes necessary (as in the case of dangerous waste materials), economists generally prefer effluent fees and the establishment of a market for pollution permits because they are much more efficient.

KEY TERMS

Externalities
External costs
External benefits
External diseconomies of production
External diseconomies
    of consumption
External economies of production
External economies of consumption

Technical externalities
Common property
Coase theorem
Internalizing external costs
Public goods
Nonrival consumption
Nonexclusion
Free-rider problem

Benefit–cost analysis
Theory of public choice
Government failures
Rational ignorance
Strategic trade policy
Environmental pollution
Effluent fee
Congestion pricing

REVIEW QUESTIONS

1. How can typing a report late at night create a negative externality? How can this result in an externality that is mutually harmful?

2. Why is a public-housing project in a high-income neighborhood not likely to satisfy the Pareto optimality criterion?

3. Why does free access to a common resource usually lead to the overuse of the resource?

4. Why, during the Cold War period, did the knowledge that the United States would not have accepted a Soviet invasion of Europe lead to less defense expenditures in Western Europe?

5. What is the basic difference between using a subsidy to induce producers to install antipollution equipment and using a tax on producers who pollute?

6. How does the market demand for a public good differ from the market demand of a private good?

7. Why is it generally more difficult to estimate the benefits and the costs of a public than of a private project?

8. Everyone agrees that large federal budget deficits are bad. Why do budget deficits then persist?

9. What is the unifying concept by which public-choice theory analyzes individual behavior in the political process?

10. What policies does the theory of public choice prescribe (a) in order to increase efficiency in public choices and reduce government failures, and (b) to reduce the influence of special-interest groups?

11. Is there a conflict between the theory of comparative advantage and strategic trade policy?

12. When would direct regulation be better than effluent fees in pollution control?

PROBLEMS

1. Explain why
   a. in a system of private education (i.e., a system in which individuals pay for their own education), there is likely to be underinvestment in education.
   b. the discussion of external economies and diseconomies is in terms of marginal rather than total social costs and benefits.

2. Start with D and S as in Figure 18.1.
   a. Draw D' with the same vertical intercept as D but with twice the absolute value of its slope. Suppose that D' portrays the marginal social benefit of the public consuming various quantities of the commodity.
   b. Does D' indicate the existence of external economies of production or consumption?
   c. What is the marginal external benefit or cost and the marginal social benefit or cost at the competitive equilibrium point?
   d. What is the socially optimal price and consumption of the commodity?

*3. a. Draw a figure showing the corrective tax or subsidy that would induce society to consume the socially optimum amount of the commodity.
   b. What is the total value of the economic gain resulting from the imposition of the corrective tax or subsidy?

4. Start with D and S as in Figure 18.1.
   a. Draw S' with the same vertical intercept as S but with half of its slope. Suppose that S' portrays the marginal *social* costs of supplying various quantities of the commodity.
   b. Does S' indicate the existence of external economies or diseconomies of production or consumption?
   c. What is the marginal external cost or benefit and the marginal social cost at the competitive equilibrium point?
   d. What is the socially optimum price and output of the commodity?

*5. a. Draw a figure showing the corrective tax or subsidy that would induce the industry to produce the socially optimal amount of the commodity.
   b. What is the total value of the economic inefficiency eliminated by the corrective tax or subsidy?

6. Start with D and S as in Figure 18.1.
   a. Draw D' with the same vertical intercept as D but with half the absolute value of its slope. Suppose

that D' portrays the marginal social benefit of the public consuming various quantities of the commodity.
   b. Does D' indicate the existence of external economies or diseconomies of production or consumption?
   c. What is the marginal external benefit or cost and the marginal social benefit or cost at the equilibrium point?
   d. What is the socially optimum price and consumption of the commodity?

7. a. Draw a figure showing the corrective tax or subsidy that would induce the society to consume the socially optimal amount of the commodity.
   b. What is the total value of the economic gain resulting from the imposition of the corrective tax or subsidy?

8. Explain what would be the outcome if the cost of avoiding polluting the stream (with its waste products) by the paper mill of Section 18.2 was $1,200 rather than $400 per month, and property rights to the stream were assigned to the
   a. brewery.
   b. paper mill.
   c. When would the socially optimal solution be reached?

*9. Explain why, in each of the following cases, externalities arise and how they would be avoided or corrected when
   a. one individual owns an oil field next to another oil field owned by another individual.
   b. a firm develops a recreational site (golf, skiing, boating, or the like).

*10. a. Draw a figure showing the market demand curve for good X for Figure 18.2 if good X were a private rather than a public good.
   b. State the condition for the Pareto optimal output of commodity X when X is a private good and when it is a public good.
   c. What is the relationship between public goods and externalities?

11. Three possible solutions were proposed at the time of the severe water shortage experienced by New York City in 1949–1950. These solutions were (1) building a dam that would cost $1,000 per million gallons of water supplied, (2) sealing leaks in water mains, which would cost about $1.60 per million gallons of water gained, or

---

* = Answer provided at end of book.

(3) installing water meters that would cost $160 per million gallons of water saved. The city chose the first project. Was New York's choice the most efficient? If not, why might New York have made this choice?

12. With reference to Figure 18.3, calculate the total social gains by
    a. increasing the level of pollution from 4 to 8 units per year.
    b. reducing pollution from 12 to 8 units per year.

INTERNET SITE ADDRESSES

For externalities, see Chapter 4 at:

http://www.humboldt.edu/~envecon/ppt/423/index.html

For support for basic research in the United States, see:

http://www.ieeeusa.org/policy/positions/basicresearch.pdf

http://www.ti.com/corp/docs/press/company/2004/c04001.shtml

http://www.basicint.org/pubs/subsidy.htm

For law and economics and property rights, see:

http://lawecon.lp.findlaw.com

http://www.indiana.edu/~iascp

Public goods are examined at:

http://en.wikipedia.org/wiki/Public_good

http://www.econlib.org/library/ENC/PublicGoodsandExternalities.html

On efficiency versus equity in tax reform in the United States, see:

http://www.fairtax.org/site/PageServer

http://money.cnn.com/2007/10/25/pf/taxes/rangel_tax_reform/index.htm

http://www.newamerica.net/publications/articles/2007/hopes_for_tax_reform_in_2007_4655

For benefit–cost analysis, see:

http://www.costbenefit.com/index.htm

http://www.humboldt.edu/~envecon/ppt/423/index.html

http://www.ubercool.com/2007/06/25/supersonic-travel-reinvented

For public choice theory, see:

http://en.wikipedia.org/wiki/Public_choice_theory

http://www.econlib.org/library/Enc/PublicChoiceTheory.html

http://perspicuity.net/sd/pub-choice.html

For government support of basic research and R&D in the United States, see:

http://www.ieeeusa.org/policy/positions/basicresearch.pdf

http://www.nsf.gov/statistics/infbrief/nsf04307/

http://www.aaas.org/spp/rd/guitotal.htm

http://ismi.sematech.org/

For U.S. strategic trade and commercial relations, see:

http://www.ustr.gov/Benefits_of_Trade/Section_Index.html

http://pacific.commerce.ubc.ca/spencer/strategic%20trade%20-%20Palgrave.pdf

http://www.keidanren.or.jp/english/policy/2001/029.html

Information on government control and regulation of environmental pollution as well as on the market for dumping rights and tradable permits is found at:

http://www.epa.gov

http://www.environment.tas.gov.au/em_environmental_management_pollution_control_act_1994.html

http://www.env-econ.net/2005/07/free_market_env.html

CHAPTER 19

The Economics of Information

After Studying This Chapter, You Should Be Able to:

- Know the rule as to how long a consumer should search for lower prices
- Know the meaning and importance of asymmetric information and adverse selection
- Understand how the problem of adverse selection can usually be resolved by market signaling
- Understand how moral hazard can arise in the insurance market and how it can be overcome by coinsurance
- Understand the meaning of the principal-agent problem and how it can be resolved by golden parachutes

In this chapter we study the economics of information. This field of study is becoming increasingly important in economics—and deservingly so. The chapter begins by examining the economics of search: search costs, the process of searching for the lowest price, and the informational content of advertising. The chapter goes on to discuss asymmetric information and the market for lemons (i.e., defective products), the insurance market and adverse selection, market signaling, moral hazard, the principal-agent problem, and the efficiency wage theory. The examples and applications of the theory provided in the chapter show the real-world importance and great relevance of the economics of information, while the *At the Frontier* section on the Internet and the information superhighway examines one of the most important and recent forms of the current worldwide information revolution.

THE ECONOMICS OF SEARCH

We begin our study by discussing search costs, outlining the process of searching for the lowest commodity price, and examining the informational content of advertising.[1]

Search Costs

One cost of purchasing a product is the time and money we spend seeking information about the product—what are the properties of the product, what are the alternatives, how good is the product, how safe, how much does the product cost in one store as opposed to another? **Search costs** include the time spent reading ads, telephoning, traveling, inspecting the product, and comparative shopping for the lowest price. Although the most important component of search costs is the time spent learning about the attributes of the product, consumers sometimes also spend money purchasing information to aid them in their search. They might purchase *Consumer Reports* magazine to check on the quality of a product, pay an impartial mechanic to evaluate a used car before deciding on purchasing it, or seek professional help from a financial advisor before making a major investment. In most cases, however, the major cost of search is the time required to learn about the product. Often the government provides a great deal of this information; for example, the government requires mileage disclosures for new automobiles, safety standards for some products, and weather forecasts, all of which greatly reduce uncertainty in the purchasing of many products.

Search costs The time and money spent seeking information about a product.

One of the most important and time-consuming aspects of purchasing a product is comparison shopping for the lowest price. Even when a product is standardized and conditions of sale are identical (i.e., locational convenience, courteousness of service, availability of credit, returns policy, etc.), there will be a dispersion of prices in the absence of perfect information on the part of buyers. Since it takes time and money to gather information, and different consumers place different valuations on their time, some price dispersion will persist in the market even if the product is perfectly standardized and sales conditions are identical.

✓ Concept Check
How long should a consumer search for lower prices?

The general rule is that *a consumer should continue the search for lower prices as long as the marginal benefit from continuing the search exceeds the marginal cost, and until the marginal benefit equals the marginal cost.* The marginal benefit (*MB*) is equal to the degree by which a lower price is found as a result of each additional search times the number of units of the product purchased at the lower price. The marginal cost (*MC*) of continuing the search depends on the value that consumers place on their time (assuming that consumers do not find shopping itself pleasurable). Since the value that consumers place on their time differs for different consumers, the product will be purchased at different prices by different consumers when each consumer behaves according to the *MB* = *MC* rule. Specifically, those consumers forgoing higher wages when searching for lower prices will stop the search before consumers who face lower opportunity costs for their time, and thus will purchase the product at a higher price.[2] On the other hand, with the MC curve of search shifting down because of the Internet, consumers search more now than a decade ago.

---

[1] This discussion draws heavily on George J. Stigler, "The Economics of Information," *Journal of Political Economy,* June 1961, pp. 213–225; and Joseph E. Stiglitz, "The Contributions of the Economics of Information to Twentieth Century Economics," *Quarterly Journal of Economics,* November 2000, pp 1441–1478.

[2] The same general rule applies in searching for a better-quality product. A consumer should continue the search as long as the *MB* exceeds the *MC* and until *MB* = *MC*. The actual application of this rule, however, is usually more difficult than in searching for lower product prices because it is difficult to assign higher monetary values correctly for better-quality products.

Searching for the Lowest Price

At any time, there will be a dispersion of prices in the market even for a homogeneous product. A consumer can accept the price quoted by the first seller of the product he or she approaches, or the consumer can continue the search for lower prices. Unless the consumer knows that the price quoted by the first seller is the lowest price in the market, he or she should continue the search for lower prices as long as the marginal benefit from continuing the search exceeds the marginal cost of additional search. In general, the marginal benefit from searching declines as the time spent searching for lower prices continues. Even if the marginal cost of additional search is constant, a point is reached where $MB = MC$. At that point, the consumer should end the search.

For example, suppose that a consumer wants to purchase a small portable TV of a given brand and knows the prices of different sellers range from $80 to $120. All sellers are identical in location, service, and so on, so that price is the only consideration. Suppose also that sellers are equally divided into five price classifications: Sellers of type I charge a price of $80 for the TV, type II sellers charge $90, type III charge $100, type IV charge $110, and type V charge $120. For a single search, the probability of each price is 1/5, and the expected price is the weighted average of all prices, or $100.[3] The consumer can now purchase the TV at the price of $100, or she can continue the search for lower prices. With each additional search the consumer will find a lower price, until the lowest price of $80 is found. The reduction in price with each search gives the marginal benefit of the search. How many searches the consumer conducts depends on the marginal cost that she faces. The consumer will end the search when the marginal benefit from the search equals the marginal cost.

We can use a simple formula to obtain the approximate lowest price expected with each additional search.[4] This is

$$\text{Expected Price} = \text{Lowest Price} + \frac{\text{Range of Prices}}{\text{Number of Searchers} + 1} \qquad [19.1]$$

For example, the lowest TV price expected from one search is

$$\text{Expected Price} = \$80 + \frac{\$40}{1 + 1} = \$100 \text{ (as found earlier)}$$

The approximate lowest expected price from two searches is $80 + ($40/3) = $93.33.[5] Thus, the approximate marginal benefit from the second search is $100 − $93.33 = $6.67. The lowest expected price with three searches is $80 + ($40/4) = $90, so $MB = $3.33. The lowest expected price with four searches is $80 + ($40/5) = $88, so $MB = $2. The lowest expected price with five searches is $80 + ($40/6) = $86.67, so $MB = $1.33.

Note how the marginal benefit from each additional search declines. $MB = $6.67 for the second search, $3.33 for the third search, $2 for the fourth search, $1.33 for the fifth

---

[3] The expected price is equal to $80(1/5) + $90(1/5) + $100(1/5) + $110(1/5) + $120(1/5) = $16 + $18 + $20 + $22 + $24 = $100.

[4] The formula gives only an approximation of the lowest price found with each additional search, because prices are discrete rather than continuous variables (i.e., market prices are not infinitesimally divisible). Nevertheless, the formula provides a quick method of showing that the marginal benefit (in the form of lower prices) declines with each additional search. To calculate the precise lowest price for the second search, see Problem 1, with the answer at the end of the book.

[5] The *precise* expected price with two searches is $92 and is found with a much longer calculation, as shown in the answer to Problem 1 at the end of the book.

search, and so on. If the marginal cost of each additional search for the consumer is $2, the consumer should, therefore, conduct four searches, because only with the fourth search is the marginal benefit equal to the marginal cost. For fewer searches, $MB > MC$, and it pays for the consumer to continue the search. For more than four searches, $MB < MC$, and it does not pay for the consumer to conduct that many searches. Furthermore, the higher the price of the commodity, and the greater the range of product prices, the more searches a consumer will undertake. The reason for this is that the marginal benefit of each search is then greater (see Problem 3). Finally, note that because consumers face different marginal costs of search, they will end the search at different points and end up paying different prices for the product. This allows different producers to charge different prices. Producers selling the product at a higher price will sell only to those consumers who have less information because they stop searching for lower prices.

Search and Advertising

Even though most advertising contains an important manipulative component, it also provides a great deal of useful information to consumers on the availability of products, their use and properties, the firms selling particular products, retail outlets that carry the product, and product prices. Thus, advertising greatly reduces consumers' search costs. In most cases, it also reduces both price dispersion and average prices. For example, we saw in Section 11.2 that the price of eyeglasses was much higher in New York, which prohibits advertising by optometrists, than in New Jersey, which does not prohibit such advertising. Similarly, the price of an uncontested divorce dropped from $350 to $150 in Phoenix, Arizona, after the Supreme Court allowed advertising for legal services. Clearly, advertising often results in increased competition among sellers and lower product prices, and it provides very useful information to consumers.

In examining the role of advertising, Philip Nelson distinguishes between search goods and experience goods.[6] **Search goods** are those goods whose quality can be evaluated by inspection at the time of purchase. Examples of search goods are fresh fruits and vegetables, apparel, and greeting cards. **Experience goods,** on the other hand, are those which cannot be judged by inspection at the time of purchase but only after using them. Examples of experience goods are automobiles, TV sets, computers, canned foods, and laundry detergents. Some goods, of course, are borderline. For example, the content of a book or magazine can be partially gathered by quick inspection at the bookstore before purchasing it. But its quality can only be fully evaluated after reading it more carefully after the purchase.

Nelson points out that the advertisements of search goods must by necessity contain a large informational content. Any attempt on the part of the seller to misrepresent the product in any way would be easily detected by potential buyers before the purchase and would thus be self-defeating. The situation is different for experience goods, where the buyer cannot determine the true properties of the product before use. Nevertheless, the very fact that a large and established seller is willing to spend a great deal on advertising the product provides indirect support for the seller's claims. After all, a large seller that has been in business for a long time must have enjoyed repeated purchases from other satisfied customers.

In 2005, about $276 billion was spent on advertising in the United States, of which 20.5% was on direct mail, 17.4% in newspapers, 16.4% in broadcast TV, 8.9% on cable

---

✓ Concept Check
In what way does advertising lower consumers' search costs?

Search goods Goods whose quality can be evaluated by inspection at the time of purchase.

Experience goods Goods whose quality can only be judged after using them.

---

[6] P. Nelson, "Advertising as Information," *Journal of Political Economy,* July/August 1974, pp. 729–754.

TV, 7.2% on radio, 5.2% on Yellow Pages, 4.7% on magazines, 2.9% on the Internet, and the rest in other forms of advertising.[7] Newspaper advertising was found to be the most informative, while TV advertising was found to be the least informative among major forms of advertising.[8] Another study found that industries with higher-than-average advertising expenditures relative to sales had lower rates of price increases and higher rates of output increases than the average for 150 major industries.[9] From this, it can be inferred that advertising has a large informational content.

When the cost of gathering information is very high or when use of the product can be dangerous, the government usually steps in to provide the information (as in the case of gas mileage for automobiles) or regulates the use of the product (as in the case of prescription drugs). The spread of information is now growing by leaps and bounds as a result of the phenomenal growth of the Internet (see the "At the Frontier" section). Sometimes the seller announces the lowest possible price at which it will sell a product without bargaining in order to eliminate the need of searching for the lowest price by consumers. An example of this is the recent no-haggling value pricing introduced by General Motors (see Example 19–1).

EXAMPLE 19–1

No-Haggling Value Pricing in Car Buying

During the past decade, General Motors (GM) has been gradually moving toward no-haggling value pricing for some of its cars. Other carmakers have also been experimenting with this policy in the United States. Although some Americans may find it stimulating, most consider the time-honored business of haggling over the price of a new car intimidating and even humiliating. One-price selling was first instituted at GM's Saturn division when it began building cars in 1990. Ford has also started experimenting with one-price selling on a few of its vehicles, and in 2001 Mercedes-Chrysler began to phase in its new N.F.P. (negotiation-free) policy. Although no-haggle pricing in car buying may yet become the rule in the future, as of 2007 only the Saturn division of General Motors had successfully adopted the approach on a large scale. Dealers' great fear of one-price selling is that customers will simply take the offer elsewhere and use it to negotiate a better deal. Advocates of one-price selling respond that dealers can avoid being undercut by combining one-price selling with value pricing and accepting smaller profit margins. They believe that customers are not going to go to other dealers to haggle over $40 or $50 if they know that they are already getting good value for their money.

Although many independent car dealers are retraining their sales force for negotiations-free selling, there is no telling how far this will spread, because most dealers still consider a fixed-price policy heresy. And yet polls indicate that about 65% of

---

[7] U.S. Department of Commerce, *Statistical Abstract of the United States* (Washington, DC: U.S. Government Printing Office, 2007), p. 785.

[8] F. M. Scherer and D. Ross, *Industrial Market Structure and Economic Performance* (Boston: Houghton Mifflin, 1990), p. 572.

[9] E. W. Eckard, "Advertising, Concentration Changes, and Consumer Welfare," *Review of Economics and Statistics,* May 1988, pp. 340–343.

American car buyers say they would rather not haggle over price. Many dealers that have tried no-haggle selling gave it up after being undersold by local competitors. Those that stuck to it, however, say that it saves them money. For example, selling cars by haggling takes an average of 4½ hours as compared with 45 minutes with fixed prices. Not having to advertise the sale of the week also saves dealers on average another $300 per automobile sold. It also requires fewer managers to O.K. a salesman's negotiated price and leads to more loyal customers. With more and more information available and more automobiles sold on the Internet, value pricing or lower prices are in, but some haggling still takes place in most automobile purchases.

Sources: "Buying Without Haggling as Cars Get Fixed Prices," *New York Times,* February 1, 1994, p. 1; "At Car Dealers, a No-Haggle Policy Sets Off a Battle," *New York Times,* August 29, 1999, Sect. 3, p. 4; "The Best Way to Buy a Car," *Wall Street Journal,* November 12, 2001, p. R4; "Motoring Online," *The Economist,* April 2, 2005, pp. 11–12; and "Haggling Starts to Go the Way of the Tail Fin," *Business Week,* October 29, 2007, pp. 71–72.

AT THE FRONTIER
The Internet and the Information Revolution

Internet A collection of thousands of computers, businesses, and millions of people throughout the world linked together in a service called the World Wide Web.

Information superhighway The ability of researchers, firms, and consumers to hook up with libraries, databases, and marketing information through a national high-speed computer network and have at their fingertips a vast amount of information as never before.

Information available to individuals, consumers, and firms is increasing by leaps and bounds as a result of the development of the Internet. The **Internet,** or simply "the Net," is a collection of more than 1 billion computers throughout the world linked together in a service called the World Wide Web (www). In 2007, more than 170 million individuals in the United States and nearly 1 billion people scattered throughout the world were connected through the Web, with hundreds of thousands of new individuals joining each week. In short, the entire globe is very rapidly becoming a single unified **information superhighway** through the Internet. The Internet has been around since the 1960s, but it is only during the last decade that its use has been greatly simplified, which led to massive growth.

This means that individuals, researchers, firms, and consumers could hook up with libraries, databases, and marketing information and have at their fingertips a vast amount of information as never before. Information technology is being applied to fields as diverse as science, manufacturing, finance, and marketing, which is revolutionizing the way business is conducted. An individual can use the Internet to send electronic mail (e-mail) and examine thousands of multimedia documents from anywhere in the world, browse through a firm's catalogue, and be able (in an increasing number of cases) to click on a "buy" button and fill in an electronic order form, including shipping and credit card information.

From 1997 to 2007, worldwide business-to-consumer or retail e-commerce increased from less than $20 billion to nearly $100 billion. More than half of worldwide retail e-commerce is now in the United States, but this is expected to fall below

✓ Concept Check

Why does the creation of the Internet represent an information revolution?

50% in a few years because of its even more rapid growth outside the United States. Many times larger than retail e-commerce are business-to-business (B2B) sales on the Internet. The reasons are that (1) business-to-business spending is far larger than consumer spending and (2) businesses are more willing and able than individuals to use the Internet. Wal-Mart, for one, now conducts all of its business with suppliers over a proprietary B2B network. Nearly half of business-to-business e-commerce is in the computer and electronics industries, while for business-to-consumer e-commerce the largest three categories are travel, PCs, and books. Even though e-commerce accounts for only 15% of global gross domestic product (GDP), it is already having a significant effect on large economic sectors, such as communications, finance, and retailing. For example, trading securities on the Web exceeded nearly one-third of all retail equity trades in the United States in 2007, up from practically zero in 1995.

Producers and sellers have found that online connections with consumers, on the one hand, and corporate customers and suppliers, on the other, have led to a dramatic fall in the cost of doing business, a cut in reaction times, and an expansion of sales reach. For example, while the cost of processing a paper check by banks averages $1.20 and that of processing a credit card payment averages $0.50, the cost of processing an electronic payment is as low a $0.01.

The Internet is not without problems, however. For one thing, even though the Web is making the Internet easier to use and hundreds of companies are developing software to make it easier still, finding what you want in the ocean of information available on the Internet can be maddening slow. Then there is the risk: A file traveling on the Internet could be examined, copied, or altered without the intended recipient's being aware of it. The Internet was simply not designed to ensure secure commerce. For example, in 1995 a hacker, or computer expert, tapped into the Citibank computing system and transferred $10 million to various bank accounts throughout the world. Although this computer fraud was quickly discovered and only $400,000 was actually withdrawn, it vividly points out the danger of doing business on the Internet. Identity theft is also possible via the Internet. All of this can be avoided by encrypting the data (i.e., transmitting the data in code) and then unencrypting it on arrival at the intended recipient. But this still cannot be done easily and conveniently. The Internet also creates problems for publishers, since any copyrighted material can easily be copied and transmitted, thus undermining copyright laws. Furthermore, Internet censorship is spreading rapidly and it is already being practiced by about two dozen countries. It is likely that all these problems will be overcome in time, but at present they present some thorny problems for Internet users.

Sources: "An Information Superhighway," *Business Week*, February 1991, p. 28; "The Internet," *Business Week*, November 14, 1994, pp. 80–88; "Citibank Fraud Case Raises Computer Security Questions," *New York Times*, August 19, 1995, p. 31; "Putting the Internet in Perspective," *Wall Street Journal*, April 16, 1998, p. B12; B. Fraumeni, "E-Commerce: Measurement and Measurement Issues," *American Economic Review*, May 2001, pp. 318–322; D. Lucking-Reiley and D. F. Spulber, "Business-to-Business Electronic Commerce," *Journal of Economic Perspectives*, Winter 2001, pp. 55–68; "Identity Left Unplugged," *Wall Street Journal*, October 9, 2005, p. B1; "Life in a Connected World, *Fortune*, July 10, 2006, pp. 99–100; "The Future of the Web," *MIT Sloan management Review*, Spring 2007, pp. 49–64; and "Web Censorship Spreading Around the World, Report Finds," *Financial Times*, March 15, 2007, p. 1.

| | ASYMMETRIC INFORMATION: THE MARKET FOR LEMONS |
| 19.2 | AND ADVERSE SELECTION |

We now discuss asymmetric information and the market for lemons as well as the problem of adverse selection in the insurance market.

Asymmetric Information and the Market for Lemons

Often one party to a transaction (i.e., the seller or the buyer of a product or service) has more information than the other party regarding the quality of the product or service. This is a case of **asymmetric information.** An example of the problems created by asymmetric information is the market for "lemons" (i.e., defective products, such as used cars, that will require a great deal of costly repairs and are not worth their price), discussed by Ackerlof.[10]

For example, sellers of used cars know exactly the quality of the cars that they are selling while prospective buyers do not. As a result, the market price for used cars will depend on the quality of the average used car available for sale. As such, the owners of "lemons" would then tend to receive a higher price than their cars are worth, while the owners of high-quality used cars would tend to get a lower price than their cars are worth. The owners of high-quality used cars would therefore withdraw their cars from the market, thus lowering the average quality and price of the remaining cars available for sale. Sellers of the now above-average quality cars withdraw their cars from the market, further reducing the quality and price of the remaining used cars offered for sale. The process continues until only the lowest-quality cars are sold in the market at the appropriate very low price. Thus, the end result is that low-quality cars drive high-quality cars out of the market. This is known as **adverse selection.**

The problem of adverse selection that arises from asymmetric information can be overcome or reduced by the acquisition of more information by the party lacking it. For example, in the used-car market, a prospective buyer can have the car evaluated at an independent automotive service center, or the used-car dealer can provide guarantees for the cars they sell. With more information on the quality of used cars, buyers would be willing to pay a higher price for higher-quality cars, and the problem of adverse selection can be reduced. More generally, brand names (such as Bayer aspirin), chain retailers (such as Sears, McDonald's, and Hilton), and professional licensing (of doctors, lawyers, beauticians, etc.) are important methods of ensuring the quality of products and services, and thus reduce the degree of asymmetric information and the resulting problem of adverse selection. Travelers are often willing to pay higher prices for nationally advertised products and services than for competitive local products, because they do not know the quality of local products and services. This is why tourists often pay more for products and services than residents. Sometimes, higher prices are themselves taken as an indication of higher quality.[11]

Asymmetric information The situation where one party to a transaction has more information on the quality of a product or service offered for sale than does the other party.

> ✓ Concept Check
> How does asymmetric information lead to adverse selection?

Adverse selection The situation where low-quality products drive high-quality products out of the market as a result of the existence of asymmetric information between buyers and sellers.

---

[10] G.A. Ackerlof, "The Market for 'Lemons': Qualitative Uncertainty and the Market Mechanism," *Quarterly Journal of Economics,* August 1970, pp. 488–500.

[11] See J. E. Stiglitz, "The Causes and Consequences of the Dependence of Quality on Price," *Journal of Economic Literature,* March 1987, pp. 1–48.

The Insurance Market and Adverse Selection

The problem of adverse selection arises not only in the market for used cars, but in any market characterized by asymmetric information. This is certainly the case for the insurance market. Here, the individual knows much more about the state of her health than an insurance company can ever find out, even with a medical examination. As a result, when an insurance company sets the insurance premium for the average individual (i.e., an individual of average health), unhealthy people are more likely to purchase insurance than healthy people. Because of this adverse selection problem, the insurance company is forced to raise the insurance premium, thus making it even less advantageous for healthy individuals to purchase insurance. This increases even more the proportion of unhealthy people in the pool of insured people, thus requiring still higher insurance premiums. In the end, insurance premiums would have to be so high that even unhealthy people would stop buying insurance. Why buy insurance if the premium is as high as the cost of personally paying for an illness?

The problem of adverse selection arises in the market for any other type of insurance (i.e., for accidents, fire, floods, and so on). In each case, only above-average risk people buy insurance, and this forces insurance companies to raise their premiums. The worsening adverse selection problem can lead to insurance premiums being so high that in the end no one would buy insurance. The same occurs in the market for credit. Since credit card companies and banks must charge the same interest rate to all borrowers, they attract more low- than high-quality borrowers (i.e., more borrowers who either do not repay their debts or repay their debts late). This forces up the interest rate, which increases even more the proportion of low-quality borrowers, until interest rates would have to be so high that it would not pay even for low-quality borrowers to borrow.

Insurance companies try to overcome or reduce the problem of adverse selection by requiring medical checkups, charging different premiums for different age groups and occupations, and offering different rates of coinsurance, amounts of deductibility, length of contracts, and so on. These limit the variation in risk within each group and reduce the problem of adverse selection. Because there will always be some variability in risk within each group, however, the problem of adverse selection cannot be entirely eliminated in this way. The only way to avoid the problem entirely is to provide compulsory insurance to all the people in the group. Individuals facing somewhat lower risks than the group average will then get a slightly worse deal, while individuals facing somewhat higher risks will get a slightly better deal (in relation to the equal premium that each group member must pay). Indeed, this is an argument in favor of universal, government-provided, compulsory health insurance and no-fault auto insurance. On the other hand, credit companies significantly reduce the adverse selection problem that they face by sharing "credit histories" with other credit companies. Although such sharing of credit histories is justifiably attacked as an invasion of privacy, it does allow the credit market to operate and keep interest charges to acceptably low levels.

19.3   MARKET SIGNALING

Market signaling
Signals that convey product quality, good insurance or credit risks, and high productivity.

The problem of adverse selection resulting from asymmetric information can be resolved or greatly reduced by **market signaling**.[12] If sellers of higher-quality products, lower-risk

---

[12] A. M. Spence, *Market Signaling* (Cambridge, MA: Harvard University Press, 1974); and A. M. Spence, "Job Market Signaling," *Quarterly Journal of Economics,* August 1973, pp. 355–379.

individuals, better-quality borrowers, or more productive workers can somehow inform or send signals of their superior quality, lower risk, or greater productivity to potential buyers of the products, insurance companies, credit companies, and employers, then the problem of adverse selection can, for the most part, be overcome. Individuals would then be able to identify high-quality products; insurance and credit companies would be able to distinguish between low and high-risk individuals and firms; and firms would be able to identify higher-productivity workers. As a result, sellers of higher-quality products would be able to sell their products at commensurately higher prices; lower-risk individuals could be charged lower insurance premiums; better-quality borrowers would have more access to credit; and higher-productivity workers could be paid higher wages. Such market signaling can thus overcome the problem of adverse selection.

A firm can signal the higher quality of its products to potential customers by adopting brand names, by offering guarantees and warranties, and by a policy of exchanging defective items. A similar function is performed by franchising (such as McDonald's) and the existence of national retail outlets (such as Sears) that do not produce the goods they sell themselves, but select products from other firms and on which they put their brand name as an assurance of quality. The seller, in effect, is saying "I am so confident of the quality of my products that I am willing to put my name on them and guarantee them." The high rate of product returns and need to service low-quality merchandise would make it too costly for sellers of low-quality products to offer such guarantees and warranties. The acceptance of coinsurance and deductibles by an individual or firm similarly sends a powerful message to insurance companies indicating that they are good risks. The credit history of a potential borrower (indicating that he or she has repaid past debts in full and on time) also sends a strong signal to credit companies that he or she is a good credit risk.

Education serves as a powerful signaling device regarding the productivity of potential employees. That is, higher levels of educational accomplishments (such as years of schooling, degrees awarded, grade-point average achieved, etc.) not only represent an investment in human capital (see Section 16.7) but also serve as a powerful signal to an employer of the greater productivity of a potential employee. After all, the individual had the intelligence and perseverance to complete college. A less intelligent and/or a less motivated person is usually not able to do so, or it might cost her so much more (for example, it may take five or six years rather than four years to get a college degree) as not to pay for her to get a college education even if she could. Thus, a college degree provides a powerful signal that its holder is in general a more productive individual than a person without a degree. Even if education did not in fact increase productivity, it would still serve as an important signal to employers of the greater *innate* ability and higher productivity of a potential employee.[13]

A firm could fire an employee if it subsequently found that the employee's productivity was too low. But this is usually difficult (the firm would have to show due cause) and expensive (the firm might have to give severance pay). In any event, it usually takes a great deal of on-the-job training before the firm can correctly evaluate the productivity of a new employee. Thus, firms are eager to determine as accurately as possible the productivity of a potential employee before he or she is hired. There is empirical evidence to suggest that education does in fact provide such an important signaling device. Liu and Wong found that while firms pay higher *initial* salaries to holders of educational certificates (such as college degrees) than to non–certificate holders, employees' salaries subsequently depend on their

[13] See K. J. Arrow, "Higher Education as a Filter," *Journal of Public Economics,* July 1973, pp. 193–216.

✓ Concept Check
How can market signaling overcome or greatly reduce adverse selection?

actual on-the-job productivity.[14] Thus, the firm relies on the market signal provided by education when it first hires an employee, for lack of a better signaling device, but then relies on actual performance after it has had adequate opportunity to determine the employee's true productivity on the job.

19.4 | THE PROBLEM OF MORAL HAZARD

Moral hazard The increased probability of a loss when an economic agent can shift some of its costs to others.

Another problem that arises in the insurance market is that of **moral hazard.** This refers to the increase in the probability of an illness, fire, or other accident when an individual is insured than when he or she is not. With insurance, the loss from an illness, fire, or other accident is shifted from the individual to the insurance company. Therefore, the individual will take fewer precautions to avoid the illness, fire, or other accident, and when a loss does occur he or she may tend to inflate the amount of the loss. For example, with medical insurance, an individual may spend less on preventive health care (thus increasing the probability of getting ill); and if he or she does become ill, will tend to spend more on treatment than if he or she had no insurance. With auto insurance, an individual may drive more recklessly (thus increasing the probability of a car accident) and then may be likely to exaggerate the injury and inflate the property damage suffered if the driver does get into an accident. Similarly, with fire insurance, a firm may take fewer reasonable precautions (such as the installation of a fire-detector system, thereby increasing the probability of a fire) than in the absence of fire insurance; and then the firm is likely to inflate the property damage suffered if a fire does occur. Indeed, the probability of a fire is high if the property is insured for an amount greater than the real value of the property.

✓ Concept Check
Why does a problem of moral hazard usually arise in the insurance market?

If the problem of moral hazard is not reduced or somehow contained, it could lead to unacceptably high insurance rates and costs and thus defeat the very purpose of insurance. The socially valid purpose of insurance is to share *given* risks of a large loss among many economic units. But if the ability to buy insurance increases total risks and claimed losses, then insurance is no longer efficient and may not even be possible. One method by which insurance companies try to overcome the problem of moral hazard is by specifying the precautions that an individual or firm must take as a condition for buying insurance. For example, the insurance company might require yearly physical checkups as a condition for continuing to provide health insurance to an individual, increase insurance premiums for drivers involved in accidents, and require the installation of a fire detector before providing fire insurance to a firm. By doing this, the insurance company tries to limit the possibility of illness, accident, or fire, and thereby reduce the number and amount of possible claims it will face.

Coinsurance Insurance that covers only a portion of a possible loss.

Another method used by insurance companies to overcome or reduce the problem of moral hazard is **coinsurance.** This refers to insuring only part of the possible loss or value of the property being insured. The idea is that if the individual or firm shares a significant portion of a potential loss with the insurance company, the individual or firm will be more prudent and will take more precautions to avoid losses from illness or accidents. Although we have examined moral hazard in connection with the insurance market, the problem of moral hazard arises whenever an externality is present (i.e., any time an economic agent can shift some of its costs to others). This is clearly shown in Examples 19–2 and 19–3.

✓ Concept Check
How can coinsurance overcome or reduce the problem of moral hazard?

---

[14] P. W. Liu and C. Wong, "Educational Screening by Certificates: An Empirical Test," *Economic Inquiry,* January 1984, pp. 72–83.

EXAMPLE 19-2

Increased Disability Payments Reduce Labor Force Participation

The Social Security program that pays disability benefits to individuals who are able to prove that they are unable to work is a socially useful program. Nevertheless, it may have resulted in a moral hazard problem by encouraging some individuals, who would otherwise be working despite their disability, to withdraw from the job market when receiving disability benefits. For example, an individual who is injured in a non-job-related accident and is unable to walk could train to be an accountant or to hold another sedentary occupation, but that individual may choose instead to remain unemployed and live on disability benefits. There are, of course, many forms of disability that would prevent an individual from doing *any* type of work, but this is not always the case.

Some indirect evidence exists that providing disability benefits since the early 1950s and raising them over time has led to a moral hazard problem. For example, the labor nonparticipation rate for men between the ages of 45 and 54 increased from nearly 4% in 1950 to more than 14% in 1993 at the same time that the Social Security disability-recipiency rate for men in the same age group increased from zero to about 5.3%. The nonparticipation rate refers to the proportion of people in a particular age group who are neither working nor seeking employment because of all causes (disability and other). On the other hand, the Social Security disability-recipiency rate refers to the proportion of people in a particular age group who are neither working nor seeking employment because of a disability.

Providing disability benefits and increasing them over time, thus, seems to have resulted in a moral hazard problem. There are, of course, other reasons besides disability that might have led to the large increase in the nonparticipation rate since the 1950s. However, the sharp and parallel increase in the two rates over time leads to the suspicion that a moral hazard problem was also at work. By providing disincentives for work, U.S. welfare programs also seem to have led to the same situation. In fact, when the welfare reform of 1996 ended welfare as entitlements, available to all persons who qualified, and required recipients to seek work as a condition for continued assistance, the number of people on welfare fell sharply (see Example 17–5).

Sources: Donald O. Parsons, "The Decline in Labor Force Participation," *Journal of Political Economy,* February 1980, pp. 117–134; "Disability Insurance and Male Labor-Force Participation," *Journal of Political Economy,* June 1984, pp. 542–549; Robert Moffitt, "Incentive Effects of the U.S. Welfare System: A Review," *Journal of Economic Literature,* March 1992, pp. 1–61; *U.S. Statistical Abstract* (Washington, D.C.: U.S. Government Printing Office, 2007) p. 357; "U.S. Disability Policy in a Changing World," *Journal of Economic Perspectives*, Winter 2002, pp. 213–224; "Welfare Reforms: Ten Years Later," *New York Times,* August 26, 2006, p. 9; and B. Madrian, "The U.S. Health Care System and labor Markets," *NBER Working Paper No. 11980,* January 2006; and S. Mitra, "The Reservation Wages of Social Security Disability Insurance Beneficiaries," *Social Security Bulletin*, Col. 67 (4), 2008, pp. 89–111.

EXAMPLE 19-3

Medicare and Medicaid and Moral Hazard

Medicare is a government program that covers most of the medical expenses of the elderly, while Medicaid covers practically all medical expenses of the poor. Both programs were enacted in the United States in 1965. While socially useful, Medicare and

Medicaid may lead to a moral hazard problem by encouraging more doctors' visits by the elderly and the poor, resulting in higher prices for medical services for the rest of the population. The effect of Medicare and Medicaid on the price and quantity of medical services consumed by people not covered by either program is analyzed in a simple manner in Figure 19.1. For simplicity, we assume that all medical costs of the elderly and the poor are covered by the programs and all medical services take the form of doctors' visits.

In the figure, D_c is the demand curve of medical services of the elderly and the poor before the subsidy or coverage under Medicare and Medicaid, while D_n is the demand curve of the rest of the population. $D_c + D_n = D_t$. The intersection of D_t and S (point E) defines the equilibrium price of $15 per visit (and a total of 900 million visits) for the to-be covered group and for the noncovered group. At $P = 15, the elderly and the poor purchase 200 million doctors' visits per year, while the rest of the population consumes 700 million per year, for a total of 900 million visits for the entire population.

When the government covers the entire cost of the doctors' visits of the elderly and the poor, their demand curve becomes D_c'. This is vertical at the quantity purchased at zero price. That is, the covered group will demand 400 million visits per year regardless of price. $D_c' + D_n = D_t'$. The intersection of D_t' and S (point E') defines the new equilibrium price of $20 for the noncovered group. The noncovered group now pays a higher price than before ($20 per visit instead of $15) and consumes a smaller quantity of medical services as indicated by D_n (600 million instead of the previous 700 million visits per year). The nonsubsidized group also pays the taxes to pay for the subsidy; the covered group, as well as doctors, receive the benefits. The conclusion of the foregoing analysis has been broadly borne out by the events that followed the adoption of Medicare and Medicaid. In short, Medicare and Medicaid led to a moral hazard problem.

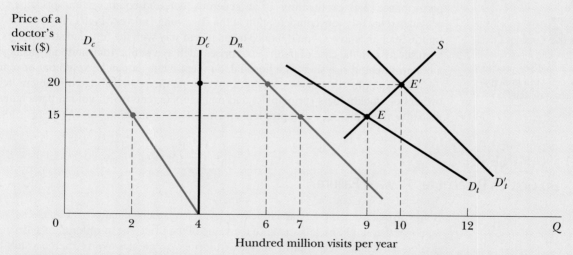

FIGURE 19.1   Medicare and Medicaid and the Price of Medical Services D_c is the demand curve of medical services of the elderly and the poor before the subsidy, while D_n is the demand curve of the rest of the population. $D_c + D_n = D_t$. With D_t and S, $P = $15 (point E). The to-be-covered group purchases 200 million visits and the others 700 million. When the government covers the entire cost of the doctors' visits of the elderly and the poor, their demand curve becomes D_c'. $D_c' + D_n = D_t'$. Then $P = $20 and $Q = 600$ million (point E') for the noncovered group.

| 19.5 | THE PRINCIPAL–AGENT PROBLEM |

Principal-agent problem The fact that the agents (managers and workers) of a firm seek to maximize their own benefits (such as salaries) rather than the total profits or value of the firm, which is the owners' or principals' interest.

✔ Concept Check
How can a principal-agent problem arise in the management of a modern corporation?

Golden parachute A large financial settlement paid out by a firm to its managers if they are forced or choose to leave as a result of a takeover that greatly increases the value of the firm.

✔ Concept Check
How can a golden parachute be used to overcome a principal-agent problem?

A firm's managers act as the *agents* for the owners or stockholders (legally referred to as the *principals*) of the firm. Because of this separation of ownership from control in the modern corporation, a **principal-agent problem** arises.[15] This problem refers to the fact that while the owners of the firm want to maximize the total profits or the present value of the firm, the managers or agents want to maximize their own personal interests, such as their salaries, tenure, influence, and reputation.[16] The principal-agent problem often becomes evident in the case of takeover bids for a firm by another firm. Although the owners or stockholders of the firm may benefit from the takeover if it raises the value of the firm's stock, the managers may oppose it for fear of losing their jobs in the reorganization of the firm that may follow the takeover.

One way of overcoming the principal-agent problem and ensuring that the firm's managers act in the stockholders' interests is by providing managers with **golden parachutes.** These are large financial settlements paid out by a firm to its managers if they are forced out or choose to leave as a result of the firm being taken over. With golden parachutes, the firm is in essence buying the firm managers' approval for the takeover. Even though golden parachutes may cost a firm millions of dollars, they may be more than justified by the sharp increase in the value of the firm that might result from a takeover. Note that a principal-agent problem may also arise in the acquiring firm. Specifically, the agents or managers of a firm may initiate and carry out a takeover bid more for personal gain (in the form of higher salaries, more secure tenure, and the enhanced reputation and prestige in directing the resulting larger corporation) than to further the stockholders' interest. In fact, the managers of the acquiring firm may be carried away by their egos and bid too much for the firm being acquired.

More generally (and independently of takeovers) a firm can overcome the principal-agent problem by offering big bonuses to its top managers based on the firm's long-term performance and profitability or a generous deferred-compensation package, which provides relatively low compensation at the beginning and very high compensation in the future. Such incentives would induce managers to stay with the firm and strive for its long-term success. In the case of public enterprises such as a public-transportation agency, or in a nonprofit enterprise such as a hospital, an inept manager can be voted out or removed.

As Example 19–4 shows, trying to overcome the principal-agent problem between owners or stockholders (principals) and managers (agents) with golden parachutes may not solve the principal-agent problem and may lead to abuses.

EXAMPLE 19–4

Do Golden Parachutes Reward Failure?

Some firms use golden parachutes to overcome their managers' objections to a takeover that might greatly increase the value of the firm. The proliferation and size of golden parachutes has sharply increased during the great wave of mergers that has

---

[15] See E. F. Fama, "Agency Problems of the Theory of the Firm," *Journal of Political Economy,* April 1980, pp. 288–307.
[16] See W. Baumol, *Business Behavior, Value, and Growth* (New York: Harcourt-Brace, 1967); and O. Williamson, *Corporate Control and Business Behavior* (Englewood Cliffs, NJ: Prentice-Hall, 1964).

taken place in the United States since the early 1980s. Some of the largest and most controversial golden parachutes (amounting to a total of nearly $100 million) were set up for ten of Primerica's executives for retiring as a result of its friendly merger with the Commercial Credit Corporation in 1988. These golden parachutes represented 6% of Primerica's $1.7 billion book value and cost stockholders $1.88 a share. Gerald Tsai, Jr., the chairman of Primerica, who arranged the merger, was to receive $19.2 million as severance pay, $8.6 million to defray the excise taxes resulting from the compensation agreement, and several other millions of dollars from Primerica's long-term incentive, life insurance, and retirement benefits program—for an overall total of nearly $30 million!

Even before the final approval of the merger in December 1988, some of Primerica's stockholders filed suit in New York State Supreme Court charging that Primerica's top executives had violated their fiduciary role and had acted in their own interest and against the stockholders' interests; they demanded that the termination agreements for the ten executives be canceled. The lawsuit pointed out that golden parachutes were originally set up in 1985 for six of Primerica's executives to cover only hostile takeovers; they were then extended to ten executives in 1987; and finally they were revised in 1988, three months after Primerica agreed to the merger, to also cover friendly takeovers.

It has been estimated that 15% of the nation's largest corporations offered golden parachutes to its top executives in 1981. This figure rose to 33% in 1985 and to nearly 50% in 1990. Indeed, golden parachutes are no longer confined to the corporation's top executives; they are offered farther and farther down the corporate ladder to middle-level management and sometimes even to all employees. This has resulted in a public outcry and has led the Securities and Exchange Commission to rule that a firm must hold a shareholder vote on its golden parachute plans. Until the early 1990s, corporations typically did not make public their offer of golden parachutes. Not only are they now required to do so, but some companies are even beginning to demand restitution.

The practice of giving golden parachutes, nevertheless, continues. Indeed, after observing huge severance packages given to CEOs who "were let go" in 2000, Dean Foust of *Business Week* (see the reference below) remarked "failure has never looked more lucrative." For example, in August 2000, Proctor & Gamble gave Durk Jager, its just-ousted CEO, a $9.5 million bonus even though he had been at P&G less than one-and-half years and P&G stock had fallen by 50% during his tenure. Also in 2000, Conseco Inc. gave a $49.3 million going-away gift to CEO Stephen Hilbert, who practically bankrupted the company with his ill-fated move into sub-prime lending. Similarly, Mattel gave a parachute package worth nearly $50 million in severance pay to Jill Barard, its departing CEO, and Ford gave Jacques Nasser, its ousted CEO, a compensation package worth $23 million in 2001 even though the company lost $5.5 billion that year. Large-company boards point out, however, that at the point of firing the CEO they usually have limited discretion, if any, in the payouts, due to contractual obligations and other entitlements. Thus, Stanely O'Neil walked away from Merrill Lynch in November 2007 with a $161.5 million package after the company announced a staggering $8.4 billion write-down of securities backed by subprime mortgages, and

Charles Prince left Citigroup soon after, for the same reason, with a $104.7 million exit package.

Sources: "Ten of Primerica Executives' Parachutes Gilded in $98.2 Million Severance Pay," *Wall Street Journal,* November 29, 1988, p. A3; "Primerica Holders File Lawsuit to Halt 'Golden Parachutes'," *Wall Street Journal,* December 2, 1988, p. A9; "Ruling by SEC May Threaten Parachute Plans," *Wall Street Journal,* January 1990, p. A3; "CEO Pay: Nothing Succeeds Like Failure," Business Week, September 11, 2000, p. 46; "When Bosses Get Rich from Selling the Company," *Business Week,* March 30, 1998, p. 33–34; "Golden Parachutes' Emerge in European Deals," *Wall Street Journal,* February 14, 2000, p. A17; "Ex-Ford Chief Receives $23 million in 2001," *New York Times,* April 10, 2002, p. C6; "How Golden Is Their Parachutes?" *Business Week,* November 26, 2007, p 34; and http://dealbook.blogs.nytimes.com/2007/12/05/whos-to-blame-for-big-golden-parachutes.

19.6   THE EFFICIENCY WAGE THEORY

Efficiency wage theory Postulates that firms willingly pay higher-than-equilibrium wages to induce workers to avoid *shirking*, or slacking off on the job.

✓ Concept Check
What is an efficiency wage? Why would a firm pay it?

We have seen in Section 14.5 that in a perfectly competitive labor market, all workers who are willing to work find employment and the equilibrium wage rate reflects (i.e., is equal to) the marginal productivity of labor. In the real world, however, we often observe higher-than-equilibrium wages and a great deal of involuntary unemployment. Why, then, don't firms lower wages?

According to the **efficiency wage theory,** firms willingly pay higher-than-equilibrium wages to induce workers to avoid *shirking,* or slacking off on the job.[17] The theory begins by pointing out that it is difficult or impossible for firms to monitor workers' productivity accurately (thus, firms face a principal-agent problem resulting from asymmetric information). If workers are paid the equilibrium wage, they are likely to shirk, or slack off on the job, because, if fired, they can easily find another, equal-paying job (remember, there is no involuntary unemployment at the equilibrium wage, and in any event it is not easy for a firm to catch a worker shirking). According to the *efficiency* wage theory, by paying a higher-than-equilibrium or efficiency wage, the firm can induce employees to work more productively and not to shirk, because the employees fear losing their high-paying jobs. Even if all firms paid efficiency wages, employees would not shirk and not risk being fired, because it is not easy to find another similarly rewarding job in view of the great deal of unemployment that exists at the efficiency wage.

The efficiency wage theory can be examined graphically with Figure 19.2. In the figure, D_L is the usual negatively sloped demand curve for labor of the firm, and S_L is the supply curve of labor (assumed to be fixed for simplicity) facing the firm. The intersection of D_L and S_L at point E determines the equilibrium wage of $10 per hour and equilibrium number of 600 workers hired by the firm. There are no unemployed workers and this wage is equal to the marginal productivity of labor.

But at this equilibrium wage, workers have an incentive to shirk. To induce workers not to shirk, the firm will have to pay a higher or efficiency wage. The higher the efficiency wage is, the smaller the level of unemployment, because workers can then more easily find another job at the efficiency wage (if fired from the present job because of shirking).

---

[17] See J. L. Yellen, "Efficiency Wage Models of Unemployment," *American Economic Review,* May 1984, pp. 200–205; and J. E. Stiglitz, "The Causes and Consequences of the Dependence of Quality on Price," *Journal of Economic Literature,* March 1987, pp. 1–48.

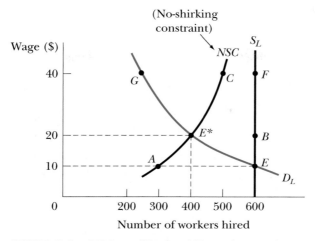

FIGURE 19.2   Efficiency Wage and Unemployment in a Shirking Model D_L and S_L are, respectively, the firm's demand and the supply curve for labor. Their intersection at point E determines the equilibrium wage of $10 per hour at which the firm employs 600 workers and there is no unemployment. Workers, however, have an incentive to shirk at this wage. The no-shirk constraint (NSC) curve is positively sloped and shows that the efficiency or minimum wage that the firm must pay to avoid shirking is higher the smaller the level of unemployment. The no-shirking equilibrium is determined at point E^* where D_L and NSC cross. The efficiency wage is $20 per hour and 200 workers (BE^*) are unemployed.

This is shown by the no-shirking constraint (NSC) curve shown in the figure. The NSC curve shows the minimum wage that workers must be paid for each level of unemployment to avoid shirking. For example, the efficiency wage of $10 requires 300 workers (EA) to be unemployed. With 200 workers (BE^*) unemployed the efficiency wage is $20, and with only 100 workers unemployed (CF) the efficiency wage will have to be $40. Note that the NSC curve is positively sloped (i.e., the efficiency wage is higher the smaller the level of unemployment) and gets closer and closer to the fixed S_L curve but never crosses it (i.e., there will always be some unemployment at the efficiency wage).

In Figure 19.2, the intersection of the D_L and NSC at point E^* determines the *efficiency* wage of $20 per hour. At this wage rate, the firm employs 400 workers and 200 workers are unemployed. The reason that $20 is the equilibrium efficiency wage is that only at this wage is the level of unemployment (BE^*) just enough to avoid shirking. For $10 to be the efficiency wage, 300 workers (EA) would have to be unemployed. But at the wage of $10 there is no unemployment (point E). Thus, *the equilibrium* efficiency wage must be higher. On the other hand, for $40 to be the efficiency wage, only 100 workers (FE) need to be unemployed. But at the wage of $40, 350 workers ($FG$) are unemployed. Thus, the equilibrium efficiency wage must be lower. The efficiency wage is $20 because only at this wage is the number of unemployed workers ($200 = BE^*$) just right for workers not to shirk.

EXAMPLE 19–5

The Efficiency Wage at Ford

One example of the efficiency wage theory is provided by the decision by Henry Ford in January 1914 to reduce the length of the working day from nine to eight hours while increasing the minimum daily wage from $2.34 to $5 for assembly-line workers. What prompted Ford to adopt such a radical (for the time) wage decision was the low productivity and very high turnover of assembly-line workers at Ford's plants under the previous traditional wage system. For example, labor turnover at Ford was 380% in 1912 and nearly 1000% in 1913. This sharply increased costs and reduced profits. The paying of a wage much higher than the going wage by Ford did have the intended effect. Ford was able to attract more productive and loyal workers, absenteeism was cut in half, and productivity increased by more than 50%. In fact, the sharply reduced labor turnover and increased labor productivity was sufficient to actually reduce the cost of producing each automobile. The new wage system was also great publicity, which increased Ford's sales. Lower production costs and higher sales meant higher profits for Ford (Ford's profits rose from $30 million in 1914 to nearly $60 million in 1916). In short, what Ford did in 1914 was to pay the efficiency wage—and it took 70 years for economists to develop the theory to fit the facts!

Sources: J. R. Lee, "So-Called Profit Sharing System in the Ford Plant," *Annals of the American Academy of Political and Social Science,* May 1915, pp. 297–310; D. Raff and L. Summers, "Did Henry Ford Pay Efficiency Wages," *Journal of Labor Economics,* October 1987, pp. S57–S58; G. A. Ackerlof and J. L. Yellen, (eds.), *Efficiency Wage Models of the Labor Market* (New York: Cambridge University Press, 1986; and "What Is the Best Way to Pay Employees?," *MIT Sloan Management Review*, Winter 2007, pp. 8–9.

SUMMARY

1. Search costs refer to the time and money we spend seeking information about a product. The general rule is to continue the search for lower prices, higher quality, and so on until the marginal benefit from the search equals the marginal cost. In most instances, advertising provides a great deal of information and greatly reduces consumers' search costs, especially for search goods. These are goods whose quality can be evaluated by inspection at the time of purchase (as opposed to experience goods, which can only be judged after using them).

2. When one party to a transaction has more information than the other on the quality of the product (i.e., in the case of asymmetric information), the low-quality product, or "lemon," will drive the high-quality product out of the market. One way to overcome or reduce such a problem of adverse selection is for the buyer to get, or the seller to provide, more information on the quality of the product or service. Such is the function of brand names, chain retailers, professional licensing, and guarantees. Insurance companies try to overcome the problem of adverse selection by requiring medical checkups, charging different premiums for different age groups and occupations, and offering different rates of coinsurance, amounts of deductibility, and length of contracts. The only way to avoid the problem entirely is with universal compulsory health insurance. Credit companies reduce the adverse selection process that they face by sharing "credit histories" with other insurance companies.

3. The problem of adverse selection resulting from asymmetric information can also be resolved or greatly reduced by market signaling. Brand names, guarantees, and warranties are used as signals for higher-quality products, for which consumers are willing to pay higher prices. The willingness to accept coinsurance and deductibles signals low-risk individuals to whom insurance companies can charge lower premiums. Credit companies use good credit histories to make more credit available to good-quality borrowers, and firms use educational certificates to identify more-productive potential employees who may then receive higher salaries.

4. The insurance market also faces the problem of moral hazard, or the increase in the probability of an illness, fire, or other accident when an individual is insured than when he or she is not. If not contained, moral hazard could lead to unacceptably high insurance costs. Insurance companies try to overcome the problem of moral hazard by specifying the precautions that an individual or firm must take as a condition of insurance, and by coinsurance (i.e., insuring only part of the possible loss). The problem of moral hazard arises whenever an externality is present (i.e., any time an economic agent can shift some of its costs to others).

5. Because ownership is divorced from control in the modern corporation, a principal-agent problem arises. This refers to the fact that managers seek to maximize their own benefits rather than the owners' or principals' interests, which are to maximize the total profits or value of the firm. The firm may use golden parachutes (large financial payments to managers if they are forced out or choose to leave if the firm is taken over by another firm) to overcome the managers' objections to a takeover bid that sharply increases the value of the firm. The firm may also set up generous deferred-compensation schemes for its managers to reconcile their long-term interests with those of the firm.

6. According to the efficiency wage theory, firms willingly pay higher than equilibrium wages to induce workers to avoid shirking or slacking off on the job. The no-shirk constraint curve is positively sloped and shows that the efficiency or minimum wage that the firm must pay to avoid shirking is higher the smaller the level of unemployment. The equilibrium efficiency wage is given by the intersection of the firm's demand curve for labor and the no-shirking constraint curve.

KEY TERMS

Search costs	Asymmetric information	Principal-agent problem
Search goods	Adverse selection	Golden parachutes
Experience goods	Market signaling	Efficiency wage theory
Internet	Moral hazard	
Information superhighway	Coinsurance	

REVIEW QUESTIONS

1. a. In which market structure was perfect information assumed on the part of all economic agents?

   b. If all consumers have perfect information, can a price dispersion for a given homogeneous product exist in the market if all conditions of the sale are identical? Why?

2. On which do you think consumers spend more time shopping for lower prices, sugar or coffee? Why?

3. Can you explain why the price dispersion for salt is much greater than the price dispersion for sugar?

4. Frozen vegetables are search goods because they are purchased frequently by consumers. True or false? Explain.

5. Most advertising is manipulative and provides very little information to consumers. True or false? Explain.

6. What is the relationship between speculation and the economics of information?

7. a. Adverse selection is the direct result of asymmetric information. True or false? Explain.

   b. How can the problem of adverse selection be overcome?

8. a. How do credit companies reduce the adverse selection problem that they face?

   b. What complaint does this give rise to?

9. a. What problem can arise for the Ford Corporation by providing a 50,000-mile guarantee for its new automobiles sold?

   b. How can Ford reduce this problem?

10. Should education be viewed as an investment in human capital or a market signaling device? Explain.

11. What is the relationship between moral hazard and externalities?

12. What is meant by the efficiency wage? What problem is this intended to solve?

PROBLEMS

*1. Determine the precise expected price for the TV from the second search in the problem discussed in the section on "Searching for the Lowest Price" without the use of equation [19.1].

2. Draw a figure showing the marginal benefit and the marginal cost of each additional search, and show the point of equilibrium for the TV problem using the information given in the text.

*3. a. Suppose that type I sellers charged the price of $60 for the portable TV, type II sellers charged $80, type III sellers charged $100, type IV sellers charged $120, and type V sellers charged $140. Determine the expected lowest price for the TV from one, two, three, four, and five searches.

   b. Determine the marginal benefit from each additional search.

4. Using the data of Problem 3, indicate

   a. How many searches should a consumer undertake if the marginal cost of each additional search is $4?

   b. If it is $2?

   c. How many searches should a consumer undertake if the marginal cost of each additional search is $5.34 and the consumer plans to purchase two TV sets?

5. a. Suppose that type I sellers charged the price of $96 for the portable TV, type II sellers charged $98, type III sellers charged $100, type IV sellers charged $102, and type V sellers charged $104. Determine the expected lowest price for the TV from one, two, three, four, and five searches.

   b. Determine the marginal benefit from each additional search.

   c. How many searches should a consumer undertake if the marginal cost of each additional search is $1.00?

*6. Connect to the Internet from your computer or from any PC and go to http://www.priceline.com. What is Priceline.com?

7. Go to http://www.ebay.com and explain what it is.

*8. Suppose that there are only two types of used cars in the market (high-quality and low-quality), and that all the high-quality cars are identical and all the low-quality cars are identical. With perfect information, the quantity demanded of high-quality used cars is zero at $16,000 and 100,000 at $12,000, while the quantity demanded of low-quality used cars is zero at $8,000 and 100,000 at $4,000. Suppose also that the supply curve for high-quality used cars is horizontal at $12,000, while the supply curve of low-quality used cars is horizontal at $4,000 in the relevant range. Draw a figure showing that with asymmetric information, no high-quality used cars will be sold and 100,000 low-quality used cars will be sold at the price of $4,000 each. Explain the precise sequence of events that leads to this result.

9. Draw another figure similar to the figure in the answer to Problem 8 but with the supply curves of high-quality and low-quality used cars positively sloped rather than horizontal. Assume further that used cars are of many different qualities rather than being simply of high quality and low quality. With reference to the figure, explain the precise sequence of events that leads to only cars of the lowest quality being sold.

10. Explain how franchising signals quality.

11. Suppose that the returns to education are 12% for an intelligent and motivated person but only 8% for a less intelligent and less motivated person (because it takes longer for the latter to get a college degree). Suppose

---

* = Answer provided at end of book.

also that the return on investing in stock is 10% and that such an investment is as risky as getting a college education. Suppose furthermore that getting a college education is viewed as a strictly investment undertaking (i.e., assume that there are no psychological benefits to getting a college education). Explain how a college education can serve as a market signaling device in this case.

12. An insurance company is considering providing fire insurance for $120,000, $100,000, or $80,000 to the owner of a house with a market value of $100,000.

   a. How much insurance is the company likely to sell for the house? Why?

   b. If the probability of a fire is 1 in 1,000, what would be the premium charged by the company?

INTERNET SITE ADDRESSES

For more information on the companies examined in this chapter, see:

   http://www.gm.com

   http://www.ford.com

   http://www.amzon.com

   http://www.barnsandnoble.com

   http://www.priceline.com

   http://www.ebay.com

   http://www.gm.com

For more information on the Internet and e-commerce, see:

   http://en.wikipedia.org/wiki/Internet#Growth

   http://en.wikipedia.org/wiki/Electronic_commerce

   http://www.internetworldstats.com/stats.htm

Asymmetric information is examined at:

   http://www.nobel.se/economics/laureates/2001/ecoadv.pdf

   http://papers.ssrn.com/sol3/papers.cfm?abstract_id=670128

   http://gulzar05.blogspot.com/2007/05/insurance-policies.html

Market signaling is examined at:

   http://www.berkeley.edu/berkeleyan/2001/10/17_asyme.html

   http://en.wikipedia.org/wiki/Signalling_(economics)

   http://www.ncsall.net/?id=667

   http://www.aeaweb.org/joe/signal/

For moral hazard, see:

   http://en.wikipedia.org/wiki/Moral_hazard

   http://www.investopedia.com/terms/m/moralhazard.asp

   http://ingrimayne.com/econ/RiskExclusion/Risk.html

   http://www.questia.com/googleScholar.qst?docId=5000372319

   http://online.wsj.com/article/SB118696170827295489.html

   http://www.americanthinker.com/2007/08/the_moral_hazard_of_regulating.html

   http://www.gladwell.com/2005/2005_08_29_a_hazard.html

For the principal-agent problem, see:

   http://en.wikipedia.org/wiki/Principal-agent_problem

   http://www2.chass.ncsu.edu/garson/pa765/agent.htm

   http://bdm.cqpress.com/chap5/05%20BdM%203e%20WT.ppt#1

   http://economics.about.com/od/economicsglossary/g/principalag.htm

Efficiency wages are discussed at:

   http://en.wikipedia.org/wiki/Efficiency_wages

   http://www.answers.com/topic/efficiency-wages

   http://www.econ.puc-rio.br/pdf/ribeiro.pdf

APPENDIX A

Mathematical Appendix

A.1 INDIFFERENCE CURVES

(Refers to Section 3.2, page 62)

Suppose that a consumer's purchases are limited to commodities X and Y, then

$$U = U(X, Y) \qquad [1A]$$

is a general utility function. Equation [1A] postulates that the utility or satisfaction that the consumer receives is a function of or depends on, the quantity of commodity X and commodity Y that he or she consumes. The more of X and Y the individual consumes, the greater the level of utility or satisfaction that he or she receives.

Using a subscript on u to specify a given level of utility or satisfaction, we can write

$$U_1 = U_1(X, Y) \qquad [2A]$$

This is the general equation for an indifference curve. Equation [2A] postulates that the individual can get U_1 of utility by various combinations of X and Y. Of course, the more of X the individual consumes, the less of Y he or she will have to consume in order to remain on the same indifference curve. Higher subscripts refer to higher indifference curves. Thus, $U_2 > U_1$.

Taking the total differential of equation [1A], we get

$$dU = \frac{\partial U}{\partial X}dX + \frac{\partial U}{\partial Y}dY \qquad [3A]$$

Since a movement along an indifference curve leaves utility unchanged, we set $dU = 0$ and get

$$\frac{\partial U}{\partial X}dX + \frac{\partial U}{\partial Y}dY = 0 \qquad [4A]$$

so that

$$\frac{\partial U}{\partial X}dX = -\frac{\partial U}{\partial Y}dY \qquad [5A]$$

and

$$-\frac{dY}{dX} = \frac{\partial U/\partial X}{\partial U/\partial Y} = \frac{MU_X}{MU_Y} = MRS_{XY} \qquad [6A]$$

Equation [6A] indicates that the negative value of the slope of an indifference curve $(-dY/dX)$ is equal to the ratio of the marginal utility of X to the marginal utility of $Y(MU_X/MU_Y)$, which, in turn, equals the marginal rate of substitution of X for $Y(MRS_{XY})$.

A.2   UTILITY MAXIMIZATION

(Refers to Section 3.5, page 74)

We now wish to maximize utility (i.e., equation [1A]) subject to the budget constraint. The budget constraint of the consumer is

$$P_X X + P_Y Y = I \qquad [7A]$$

where P_X and P_Y are the price of commodity X and commodity Y, respectively, X and Y refer to the quantity X and commodity Y, and I is the consumer's income, which is given and fixed at a particular point in time.

To maximize equation [1A] subject to equation [7A], we form

$$V = U(X, Y) + \lambda(I - P_X X - P_Y Y) \qquad [8A]$$

where λ is the Lagrangian multiplier.

Taking the first partial derivative of V with respect to X and Y and setting them equal to zero gives

$$\frac{\partial V}{\partial X} = \frac{\partial U}{\partial X} - \lambda P_X = 0$$

$$\frac{\partial V}{\partial Y} = \frac{\partial U}{\partial Y} - \lambda P_Y = 0 \qquad [9A]$$

It follows that

$$\frac{\partial U}{\partial X} = \lambda P_X \quad \text{and} \quad \frac{\partial U}{\partial Y} = \lambda P_Y \qquad [10A]$$

Dividing, we get

$$\frac{\partial U / \partial X}{\partial U / \partial Y} = \frac{MU_X}{MU_Y} = MRS_{XY} = \frac{P_X}{P_Y} \qquad [11A]$$

Equation [11A] indicates that the consumer maximizes utility at the point utility at the point where the marginal rate of substitution of X for Y, $(\partial U/\partial X)/(\partial U/\partial Y')$, equals the ratio of the price of X to the price of Y. Graphically, this occurs at the point where the budget line is tangent to the highest indifference curve possible (and their slopes are equal). Equation [11A] is only the first order condition for maximization (and minimization). The second order condition for maximization is that the indifference curves be convex to the origin.

A.3   CONSUMER SURPLUS

(Refers to Section 4.5, page 106)

In Section 4.5, we defined consumer surplus as the difference between what a consumer is willing to pay for a given quantity of a good and what he or she actually pays for it. Graphically, consumer surplus is given by the difference in the area under the demand curve and the area representing the total expenditures of the consumer for the given quantity of the good that he or she purchases.

Starting with $P = g(Q)$, g is the inverse of $Q = f(P)$. For a given price (P_1) and its associated quantity (Q_1),

$$\begin{array}{c} \text{consumer} \\ \text{surplus} \end{array} = \int_0^{Q_1} g(Q)dQ - P_1 Q_1 \qquad [12A]$$

where the integral sign $(\int)$ represents the process of calculating the area under inverse demand function $P = g(Q)$ between zero quantity of the commodity and quantity Q_1, and $P_1 Q_1$ is the total expenditure of the consumer for Q_1 of the commodity.

A.4   SUBSTITUTION AND INCOME EFFECTS

(Refers to Section 4.3, page 97)

The substitution effect of a price change can be measured by a movement along a given indifference curve (so that utility or purchasing power is constant). With a change in the price of commodity X, we have

$$\text{substitution effect} = \frac{\partial X}{\partial P_X} \text{ with constant utility}(U) \qquad [13A]$$

The income effect can be measured by a shift to a different indifference curve (to reflect the change in utility or purchasing power) with prices constant. This is given by the change in the demand for X per dollar increase in income, weighed by the quantity of X purchased. That is,

$$\text{income effect} = X\left(\frac{\partial X}{\partial I}\right) \text{ with constant prices} \qquad [14A]$$

When the price of X falls, the income effect tells us how much the consumer's income should be *reduced* in order to leave his or her purchasing power constant.

Combining the substitution and the income effects we get the Slutsky equation:

$$\frac{\partial X}{\partial P_X} = \frac{\partial X}{\partial P_X} - X\left(\frac{\partial X}{\partial I}\right)$$

$$\text{for constant } U \quad \text{for constant} \quad \quad [15A]$$
$$\text{prices}$$

The first term on the right side gives the substitution effect (shown by a movement along a given indifference curve). The second term gives the income effect (shown by a shift to a different indifference curve but with constant goods prices).

A.5   ELASTICITIES

(Refers to Section 5.2 to 5.4, pages 128–139)

In Chapter 5.2 we defined the *price elasticity of demand*, η, as the percentage change in the quantity demanded of a commodity divided by the percentage change in its price. That is, for $Q = f(P)$,

$$\eta = \frac{\Delta Q/Q}{\Delta P/P} = \frac{\Delta Q}{\Delta P}\frac{P}{Q} \qquad [16A]$$

We also pointed out that since quantity and price move in opposite directions, the value of η is negative. Equation [16A] can be used to measure *are elasticity*. In that case, P and Q refer to the average price and the average quantity, respectively.

As the change in price approaches zero in the limit, we can measure *point elasticity* by

$$\eta = \frac{dQ}{dP}\frac{P}{Q} \qquad [17A]$$

If the demand curve is linear and given by

$$Q = a + bP \qquad [18A]$$

the slope of the demand curve is constant and is given by

$$\frac{dQ}{dP} = \frac{\Delta Q}{\Delta P} = b \qquad [19A]$$

and

$$\eta = b\frac{P}{Q} \qquad [20A]$$

For example, if $b = -2$ and $P/Q = 1$, then $\eta = -2$. Since P/Q is different at every point on the negatively sloped, straight-line demand curve, η varies at every point.

For a curvilinear demand curve of the form

$$Q = aP^b \qquad [21A]$$

$$\frac{dQ}{dP} = abP^{b-1} \qquad [22A]$$

and

$$\eta = abP^{b-1}\frac{P}{Q} = \frac{abP^b}{Q} = b \qquad [23A]$$

since $aP^b = Q$. Thus, equation [21A] is a demand curve with a constant price elasticity equal to the exponent of P (i.e., $\eta = b$). Thus, if $b = -2$, $\eta = -2$ at every point on the demand curve. As pointed out in Chapter 5.2, demand is elastic if $|\eta| > 1$ and inelastic if $|\eta| < 1$.

The *income elasticity of demand*, η_I is defined as the ratio of the relative change in the quantity purchased (Q) to the relative change in income (I), other things remaining constant. That is, for $Q = f(I)$,

$$\eta_I = \frac{dQ}{dI}\frac{I}{Q} \qquad [24A]$$

For the following linear income-demand function

$$Q = a + cI \qquad [25A]$$

where $c > 0$, the derivative of Q with respect to I is

$$\frac{dQ}{dI} = c \qquad [26A]$$

Therefore,

$$\eta_I = c\left(\frac{I}{Q}\right) \qquad [27A]$$

For the following nonlinear income-demand function

$$Q = aI^c \qquad [28A]$$

the derivative of Q with respect to I is

$$\frac{dQ}{dI} = acI^{c-1} \qquad [29A]$$

Therefore,

$$\eta_1 = acI^{c-1}\frac{I}{Q} = \frac{acI^c}{Q} = c \qquad [30A]$$

As pointed out in Chapter 5.3, a commodity is normal if $\eta_I > 0$ and inferior if $\eta_I < 0$. A normal good is luxury if $\eta_I > 1$ and a necessity if η_I is between 0 and 1.

The *cross elasticity of demand* of commodity X for commodity Y, η_{XY}, is defined as the ratio of the relative change in the quantity purchased of commodity X (Q_X) to the relative change in the price of commodity Y (P_Y). That is,

$$\eta_{XY} = \frac{dQ_X/Q_X}{dP_Y/P_Y} = \frac{dQ_X}{dP_Y}\frac{P_Y}{Q_X} \qquad [31A]$$

Consider the following linear demand function for commodity X:

$$Q_X = a + bP_X + cP_Y \qquad [32A]$$

The above function indicates that Q_X depends on P_X and P_Y. The derivative of the function with respect to P_Y is

$$\frac{dQ_X}{dP_Y} = b\frac{dP_X}{dP_Y} + c \qquad [33A]$$

If the P_X remains unchanged when P_Y changes, then

$$\frac{dP_X}{dP_Y} = 0 \quad \text{while} \quad \frac{dQ_X}{dP_Y} = c \qquad [34A]$$

Therefore,

$$\eta_{XY} = c\frac{P_Y}{Q_X} \qquad [35A]$$

As pointed out in Chapter 5.4, commodities X and Y are substitutes if $\eta_{XY} > 0$ and complements if $\eta_{XY} < 0$.

The *price elasticity of supply*, ϵ, is defined as the ratio of the relative change in the quantity supplied of a commodity (Q_s) to the relative change in its price (P). That is, for $Q_s = f(P)$,

$$\epsilon = \frac{dQ_s/Q_s}{dP/P} = \frac{dQ_s}{dP}\frac{P}{Q_s} \qquad [36A]$$

Since the quantity supplied and price move in the same direction (i.e., supply curves are usually positively sloped), ϵ is positive.

For the following linear supply function

$$Q_s = a + bP \qquad [37A]$$

the derivative of Q_s with respect to P is

$$\frac{dQ_s}{dP} = b \qquad [38A]$$

Therefore,

$$\epsilon = b\frac{P}{Q_s} \qquad [39A]$$

Substituting equation [37A] for Q_s into equation [39A], we get

$$\epsilon = \frac{bP}{a + bP} \qquad [40A]$$

Thus, if $a = 0$ (so that the supply curve starts at the origin), $\epsilon = 1$ throughout the supply curve, regardless of the value of its slope (b). If $a > 0$ (so that the supply curve cuts the quantity axis), $\epsilon < 1$ throughout the supply curve. If $a < 0$ (so that the supply curve cuts the price axis), $\epsilon > 1$ throughout. When $a \neq 0$, ϵ varies with price.

A.6   RELATIONSHIP AMONG INCOME ELASTICITIES

(Refers to Sections 5.2 and 5.3, pages 128 and 135)

If a consumer's income increases, say by 10% and the consumption of some commodities increases by less than 10%, the consumption of other commodities must increase by more than 10% for the entire increase in the consumer's income to be fully spent. This leads to the proposition that the income elasticity of demand must be unity, on the average, for all commodities. Assuming, for simplicity, that the entire consumer's income is spent on commodities X and Y, we can restate the above proposition mathematically as

$$K_X\eta_{IX} + K_Y\eta_{IY} \equiv 1 \qquad [41A]$$

where K_X is the proportion of the consumer's income (I) spent on commodity X (i.e., $K_X = P_XX/I$), η_{IX} is the income elasticity of demand for commodity X, K_Y is the proportion of income elasticity of demand for Y.

Starting with the consumer's budget constraint [7A]

$$I = P_XX + P_YY \qquad [7A]$$

we can prove proposition [41A] by differentiating equation [7A] with respect to income, while holding prices constant. This gives

$$\frac{dI}{dI} \equiv 1 \equiv P_X \frac{dX}{dI} + P_Y \frac{dY}{dI} \qquad [42A]$$

If we multiply the first term on the right-hand side by $(X/X)(I/I)$, which equals one, and the second term by $(Y/Y)(I/I)$, which equals one, the value of the expression will not change, and we get

$$1 \equiv P_X \frac{dX}{dI} \frac{X}{X} \frac{I}{I} + P_Y \frac{dY}{dI} \frac{Y}{Y} \frac{I}{I} \qquad [42A']$$

Rearranging equation [42A'], we get

$$\frac{P_x X}{I} \frac{dX}{dI} \frac{I}{X} + \frac{P_Y Y}{I} \frac{dY}{dI} \frac{I}{Y} \equiv 1 \qquad [43A]$$

Since $P_X X/I = K_X$, $(dX/dI)(I/X) = \eta_{IX}$, $P_Y Y/I = K_Y$, and $(dY/dI)(I/Y) = \eta_{IY}$, we have

$$K_X \eta_{IX} + K_Y \eta_{IY} \equiv 1 \qquad [41A]$$

That is, with the K's providing the weights, the weighted average of all income elasticities equals unity. Thus, the income elasticity of demand of a commodity on which the consumer spends a great proportion of his or her income cannot be too different from unity (see Problem 12 in Chapter 5).

A.7   Relationship Among Marginal Revenue, Price, and Elasticity

(Refers to Section 5.6, page 142)

Let P and Q equal the price and the quantity of a commodity, respectively. Then the total revenue of the seller of the commodity (TR) is given by

$$TR = PQ \qquad [44A]$$

and the marginal revenue is

$$MR = \frac{d(TR)}{dQ} = P + Q\frac{dP}{dQ} \qquad [45A]$$

Manipulating expression [45A] mathematically, we get

$$MR = P\left(1 + \frac{Q}{P}\frac{dP}{dQ}\right) = P\left(1 + \frac{1}{\eta}\right) \qquad [46A]$$

where, η is the coefficient of price elasticity of demand. For example, if $P = \$12$ and $\eta = -3$, $MR = \$8$. If $\eta = -\infty$, $P = MR = \$12$.

A.8   Isoquants

(Refers to Sections 7.3 and 7.4, pages 198 and 201)

Suppose that there are two inputs, labor and capital. The

$$Q = Q(L, K) \qquad [47A]$$

is a general production function. Equation [47A] postulates that output (Q) is a function of, or depends on, the quantity of labor (L) and capital (K) used in production. The more L and K are used, the greater is Q.

Using a subscript on Q to specify a given level of output, we can write

$$Q_1 = Q_1(L, K) \qquad [48A]$$

This is the general equation for an isoquant. Equation [48A] postulates that output Q_1 can be produced with various combinations of L and K. The more L is used, the less K will be required to remain on the same isoquant. Higher subscripts refer to higher isoquants. Thus, $Q_2 > Q_1$.

Taking the total differential of equation [47A], we get

$$dQ = \frac{\partial Q}{\partial L}dL + \frac{\partial Q}{\partial K}dK \qquad [49A]$$

Since a movement along an isoquant leaves output unchanged, we set $dQ = 0$ and get

$$\frac{\partial Q}{\partial L}dL + \frac{\partial Q}{\partial K}dK = 0 \qquad [50A]$$

so that

$$\frac{\partial Q}{\partial K}dK = -\frac{\partial Q}{\partial L}dL \qquad [51A]$$

and

$$-\frac{dK}{dL} = \frac{\partial Q/\partial L}{\partial Q/\partial K} = \frac{MP_L}{MP_K} = MRTS_{LK} \qquad [52A]$$

Equation [52A] indicates that the negative value of the slope of an isoquant ($-dK/dL$) is equal to the ratio of the marginal product of L to the marginal product of

$K\ (MP_L/MP_K)$, which, in turn, equals the marginal rate of technical substitution of L for $K\ (MRTS_{LK})$.

A.9   COST MINIMIZATION

(Refers to Section 8.2, page 228)

A firm may wish to minimize the cost of producing a given level of output. The total cost of the firm (TC) is given by

$$TC = wL + rK \qquad [53A]$$

where w is the wage rate of labor and r is the rental price (per unit) of capital. A given level of output $(\overline{Q})$ can be produced with various combinations of L and K:

$$\overline{Q} = \overline{Q}(L, K) \qquad [54A]$$

To minimize equation [53A] subject to equation [54A], we form

$$Z = wL + rK + \lambda^*[\overline{Q} - \overline{Q}(L, K)] \qquad [55A]$$

where λ^* is the Lagrangian multiplier.

Taking the first partial derivative of Z with respect to L and K and setting them equal to zero gives

$$\frac{\partial Z}{\partial L} = w - \lambda^* \frac{\partial Q}{\partial L}$$

and

$$\frac{\partial Z}{\partial K} = r - \lambda^* \frac{\partial Q}{\partial K} \qquad [56A]$$

It follows that

$$w = \lambda^* \frac{\partial Q}{\partial L} \quad \text{and} \quad r = \lambda^* \frac{\partial Q}{\partial K} \qquad [57A]$$

Dividing, we get

$$\frac{w}{r} = \frac{\partial Q/\partial L}{\partial Q/\partial K} = MRTS_{LK} \qquad [58A]$$

Equation [58A] indicates that a firm minimizes the cost of producing a given level of output by hiring labor and capital up to the point where the ratio of the input prices (w/r) equals the ratio of the marginal products of labor and capital, $(\partial Q/\partial L)/(\partial Q/\partial K)$ which equals the marginal rate of technical substitution of labor for capital $(MRTS_{LK})$. Graphically, this occurs at the point where a given isoquant is tangent to an isocost line (and their slopes are equal). Equation [58A]

is only the first order condition for minimization (and maximization). The second order condition for minimization is that the isoquant be convex to the origin.

A.10   PROFIT MAXIMIZATION

(Refers to Section 9.3, page 265)

A firm usually wants to produce the output that maximizes its total profits. Total profits (π) are equal to total revenue (TR) minus total cost (TC). That is,

$$\pi = TR - TC \qquad [59A]$$

where π, TR, and TC are all functions of output (Q).

Taking the first derivative of π with respect to Q and setting it equal to zero gives

$$\frac{d\pi}{dQ} = \frac{d(TR)}{dQ} - \frac{d(TC)}{dQ} = 0 \qquad [60A]$$

so that

$$\frac{d(TR)}{dQ} = \frac{d(TC)}{dQ} \qquad [61A]$$

and

$$MR = MC \qquad [62A]$$

Equation [62A] indicates that in order to maximize profits, a firm must produce where marginal revenue (MR) equals marginal cost (MC).

Furthermore, since for a perfectly competitive firm P is constant and $d(TR)/dQ = MR = P$, the first order condition becomes

$$MR = P = MC \qquad [63A]$$

Equation [61A] is only the first order condition for maximization (and minimization). The second order condition for profit maximization requires that the second derivative of π with respect to Q be negative. That is,

$$\frac{d^2\pi}{dQ^2} = \frac{d^2(TR)}{dQ^2} - \frac{d^2(TC)}{dQ^2} < 0 \qquad [64A]$$

so that

$$\frac{d^2(TR)}{dQ^2} < \frac{d^2(TC)}{dQ^2} \qquad [65A]$$

According to equation [65A], the algebraic value of the slope of the *MC* function must be greater than the algebraic value of the *MR* function. Under perfect competition, *MR* is constant (i.e., the *MR* curve of the firm is horizontal) so that equation [65A] requires that the *MC* curve be rising at the point where *MR = MC* for the firm to maximize its total profits (or minimize its total losses).

Under imperfect competition, $P > MC$ and so the first order condition becomes simply

$$MR = MC \qquad [63B]$$

The second order condition remains [65A], but with *MR* now declining, the second order condition is for the *MC* curve to intersect the *MR* curve from below.

A.11 PRICE DETERMINATION

(Refers to Sections 9.4 and 10.2, pages 271 and 312)

At equilibrium, the quantity demanded of a commodity (Q_d) is equal to the quantity supplied of the commodity (Q_s). That is,

$$Q_d = Q_s \qquad [66A]$$

The demand function can be written as

$$Q_d = a - bP(a, b > 0) \qquad [67A]$$

where *a* is the positive quantity intercept, and $-b$ is the negative of the multiplicative inverse of the slope of the demand curve (so that when *P* rises, Q_d falls). The supply function can take the form of

$$Q_s = -c + dP(c, d > 0) \qquad [68A]$$

where $-c$ refers to the negative quantity intercept (so that the supply curve crosses the price axis at a positive price), and *d* is the positive of the multiplicative inverse of the slope of the supply curve (so that when *P* rises, Q_s also rises).

Setting $Q_d = Q_s$ for equilibrium, we get

$$a - bP = -c + dP \qquad [69A]$$

Solving for *P*, we have

$$\overline{P} = \frac{a+c}{b+d} \qquad [70A]$$

where the bar on *P* refers to the equilibrium price. Since parameters *a, b, c,* and *d* are all positive, $\overline{P}$ is also positive.

To find the equilibrium quantity ($\overline{Q}$) that corresponds to $\overline{P}$, we substitute equation [70A] into equation [67A] or [68A]. Substituting equation [70A] into equation [67A], we get

$$\overline{Q} = a - \frac{b(a+c)}{(b+d)}$$

$$= \frac{a(b+d) - b(a+c)}{b+d} = \frac{ad - bc}{b+d} \qquad [71A]$$

Since the denominator of equation [71A], $(b+d)$, is positive, for $\overline{Q}$ to be positive (and for the model to be economically meaningful) the numerator, $(ad - bc)$, must also be positive. That is, $ad > bc$.

A.12 PRICE DISCRIMINATION

(Refers to Section 10.5, page 326)

A monopolist selling a commodity in two separate markets must decide how much to sell in each market in order to maximize total profits. The total profits of the monopolist (π) are equal to the sum of the total revenue that it receives from selling the commodity in the two markets (i.e., $TR_1 + TR_2$) minus the total cost of producing the total output (*TC*). That is,

$$\pi = TR_1 + TR_2 - TC \qquad [72A]$$

Taking the first partial derivative of π with respect to Q_1 (the quantity sold in the first market) and Q_2 (the quantity sold *in* the second market), and setting them equal to zero, we get

$$\frac{\partial \pi}{\partial Q_1} = \frac{\partial(TR_1)}{\partial Q_1} - \frac{\partial(TC)}{\partial Q_1} = 0,$$

$$\frac{\partial \pi}{\partial Q_2} = \frac{\partial(TR_2)}{\partial Q_2} - \frac{\partial(TC)}{\partial Q_2} = 0 \qquad [73A]$$

or

$$MR_1 = MR_2 = MC \qquad [74A]$$

That is, in order to maximize its total profits, the monopolist must distribute its sales between the two markets in such a way that the marginal revenue is the same in both markets and equal to the common marginal cost. If $MR_1 > MR_2$, the monopolist could increase its total profits by redistributing sales from market 2 to market 1, until $MR_1 = MR_2$.

Equations [73A] and [74A] give the first order condition for profit maximization. The second order condition is given by

$$\frac{\partial^2 \pi}{\partial Q_1^2} < 0 \quad \text{and} \quad \frac{\partial^2 \pi}{\partial Q_2^2} < 0 \qquad [75A]$$

Since we know from equation [46A] that

$$MR = P(1 + 1/\eta) \qquad [46A]$$

profit maximization requires that

$$P_1(1 + 1/\eta_1) = P_2(1 + 1/\eta_2) \qquad [76A]$$

where P_1 and P_2 are the prices in market 1 and market 2, respectively, and η_1 and η_2 are the coefficients of price elasticity of demand in market 1 and market 2. If $|\eta_1| < |\eta_2|$, equation [76A] will hold only if $P_1 > P_2$. That is, in order to maximize total profits the monopolist must sell the commodity at a higher price in the market with the lower price elasticity of demand (see also Figure 9.11). For example, if $\eta_1 = -2$, $\eta_2 = -3$, and $P_2 = \$6$, then $P_1 = \$8$ (so that $MR_1 = MR_2 = \$4$).

A.13   EMPLOYMENT OF INPUTS

(Refers to Section 14.5, page 463)

A firms employs the quantity of inputs that allows it to produce the profit-maximizing level of output. As indicated by equation [59A], total profits (π) are equal to total revenue (TR) minus total cost (TC). Total revenue is given by

$$TR = PQ \qquad [77A]$$

where P is the price of the commodity that the firm - produces and Q is the output, such that $Q = Q(L, K)$. The total cost of the firm was defined by equation [53A]. Thus, the firm employs labor and capital so as to maximize:

$$\pi = PQ(L, K) - (wL + rK) \qquad [78A]$$

When P, w, and r are constant, the firm is a perfect competitor in the product and input markets.

Taking the first partial derivative of π with respect to L and K and setting them equal to zero gives

$$\frac{\partial \pi}{\partial L} = P\frac{\partial Q}{\partial L} - w = 0,$$

$$\frac{\partial \pi}{\partial K} = P\frac{\partial Q}{\partial K} - r = 0 \qquad [79A]$$

It follows that

$$P\frac{\partial Q}{\partial L} = w \quad \text{and} \quad P\frac{\partial Q}{\partial K} = r \qquad [80A]$$

or

$$MRP_L = w \quad \text{and} \quad MRP_K = r \qquad [81A]$$

Equation [81A] indicates that a firm maximizes profits by hiring labor and capital up to the point where the marginal revenue product of labor [$MRP_L = P(\partial Q/\partial L)$] equals the wage rate ($w$) and the marginal revenue product of capital [$MRP_K = P(\partial Q/\partial K)$] equals the rental price of capital (r). Geometrically, this occurs where the MRP_L curve intersects the (horizontal) supply curve of labor and the MRP_K curve intersects the (horizontal) supply curve of rental capital. Equation [81A] is only the first order condition for maximization. The second order condition is that the MRP_L and MRP_K curves be negatively sloped (i.e., that the firm produce in the area of diminishing returns).

A.14   INPUT PRICE, MARGINAL EXPENSE, AND THE PRICE ELASTICITY OF INPUT SUPPLY

(Refers to Sections 15.4 and 15.5, pages 487 and 490)

The total cost (TC) of a firm hiring nly labor is given by

$$TC = wL \qquad [82A]$$

where w is the wage rate and L is the number of workers hired.

If the firm is a monopsonist (i.e., the only employer of labor in the market), it will have to pay higher wages the more labor it wants to hire. That is, the wage rate is a function of or depends on the amount of labor the firm hires (and the amount of labor the firm hires depends on the wage rate).

The firm's marginal resource cost of labor (MRC_L) is then given by

$$MRC_L = \frac{dC}{dL} = w + L\frac{dw}{dL} \qquad [83A]$$

Rearranging equation [83A], we get

$$MRC_L = w\left(1 + \frac{L}{w}\frac{dw}{dL}\right) \qquad [84A]$$

Therefore,

$$MRC_L = w\left(1 + \frac{1}{\epsilon_L}\right) \qquad [85A]$$

where ϵ_L is the price (wage) elasticity of the supply curve of labor. Graphically, this means that the MRC_L curve lies above the (positively sloped) S_L curve (see also Figure 15.3). The same would be true for capital or any other input for which the firm is the only employer in the market.

If the firm were a perfect competitor in the labor market, $\epsilon_L \to \infty$ and $MRC_L = w$ (i.e., the MRC_L curve would coincide with the horizontal S_L curve faced by the firm at the given level of w).

A.15 DERIVATION OF THE FORMULA TO FIND THE PRESENT VALUE OF AN INVESTMENT

(Refers to Section 16.3, page 522)

We have seen in Section 16.3 that the present discounted value (*PDV*) of an investment that yields a constant stream of net cash flows in each future year is given by equation [86A]:

$$PDV = \frac{R}{r} \qquad [86A]$$

where R is the constant net cash flow received the next year and in every subsequent year (i.e., in perpetuity), and r is the rate of interest.

To derive equation [86A], we start with

$$PDV = \frac{R}{(1+r)} + \frac{R}{(1+r)^2} + \cdots \frac{R}{(1+r)^n} \qquad [87A]$$

which is similar to equation [15-6] in Section 15.3.
If we let $1/(1+r) = k$, then

$$PDV = R(k + k^2 + \cdots k^n) \qquad [88A]$$

Multiplying both sides of equation [88A] by k, we get

$$kPDV = R(k^2 + k^3 + \cdots k^{n+1}) \qquad [89A]$$

Subtracting equation [89A] from equation [88A] we have

$$PDV - kPDV = R(k - k^{n+1}) \qquad [90A]$$

From equation [90A], we get

$$PDV = \frac{R(k - k^{n+1})}{1-k} \qquad [91A]$$

Since $k = 1/(1+r)$ is smaller than 1, for n very large, k^{n+1} is very small and can be ignored. Thus, we are left with

$$PDV = R\left(\frac{k}{1-k}\right) \qquad [92A]$$

Substituting $1/(1+r)$ for k into equation [92A], we get

$$PDV = R\left(\frac{\frac{1}{1+r}}{1 - \frac{1}{1+r}}\right)$$

$$= R\left(\frac{\frac{1}{1+r}}{\frac{1+r-1}{1+r}}\right)$$

$$= R\left(\frac{1}{1+r}\right)\left(\frac{1+r}{r}\right)$$

$$= \frac{R}{r} \qquad [93A]$$

A.16   A MODEL OF GENERAL EQUILIBRIUM

(Refers to Section 17.5, page 568)

In this section we outline the Walras-Cassel general equilibrium model.*

Let x_1, x_2, ..., x_n refer to the quantity of the n commodities in the economy, with prices p_1, p_2, ... p_n. Let $r_1, r_2, ... r_m$ refer to the quantity of the m resources or inputs in the economy, with prices v_1, v_2, ... v_m.

The market demand equations for the n commodities can be written as

$$x_1 = f_1(p_1, p_2, \ldots, p_n; v_1, v_2, \ldots, v_m)$$
$$x_2 = f_2(p_1, p_2, \ldots, p_n; v_1, v_2, \ldots, v_m) \qquad \text{[94A]}$$
$$\ldots\ldots\ldots\ldots\ldots\ldots\ldots\ldots\ldots\ldots\ldots\ldots\ldots$$
$$x_n = f_n(p_1, p_2, \ldots p_n; v_1, v_2, \ldots, v_m)$$

The market demand for each commodity is the sum of the demand for the commodity by each consumer and is a function of, or depends on, the prices of all commodities and of all inputs. Input prices affect individuals' incomes and, thus, influence the demand for commodities.

Since in long-run perfectly competitive equilibrium, commodity prices equal their production costs, we have

$$a_{11}v_1 + a_{21}v_2 + \cdots + a_{m1}v_m = p_1$$
$$a_{12}v_1 + a_{22}v_2 + \cdots + a_{m2}v_m = p_2 \qquad \text{[95A]}$$
$$\ldots\ldots\ldots\ldots\ldots\ldots\ldots\ldots\ldots\ldots\ldots\ldots\ldots$$
$$a_{1n}v_1 + a_{2n}v_2 + \cdots + a_{mn}v_m = p_n$$

where a_{11} refers to the quantity of input 1 required to produce one unit of commodity 1. Since v_1 is the price of input 1, $a_{11}v_1$ is then the dollar amount spent on input 1 to produce on unit of commodity 1. On the other hand, a_{21} refers to the quantity of input 2 required to produce one unit of commodity 1, so that $a_{21}v_2$ is the dollar amount spent on input 2 to produce one unit of commodity 1. Finally, a_{m1} is the amount of input m required to produce one unit of commodity 1, and $a_{m1}v_m$ is the expenditure on input m to produce one unit of commodity 1. Therefore, the left-hand side of equation [95A] refers to the total cost of producing one unit of commodity 1. This is equal to the unit price of commodity

1 (p_1). The second equation gives the expenditure on each input to produce one unit of commodity 2, and this is equal input to produce one unit of commodity 2, and this is equal to p_2. The same is true for each of the n commodities. The a'_{ij}s are called input or production coefficients, and they are assumed to be fixed in our simple model.

Setting the total demand for each resource or input (required to produce all commodities) equal to the total supply of the input, we have

$$a_{11}x_1 + a_{12}x_2 + \cdots + a_{1n}X_n = r_1$$
$$a_{21}x_1 + a_{22}X_2 + \cdots + a_{2n}X_n = r_2 \qquad \text{[96A]}$$
$$\ldots\ldots\ldots\ldots\ldots\ldots\ldots\ldots\ldots\ldots\ldots\ldots\ldots$$
$$a_{m1}x_1 + a_{m2}x_2 + \cdots + a_{mn}x_n = r_m$$

where $a_{11}x_1$ is the quantity of resource or input 1 required to produce x_1 units of commodity 1, $a_{12}x_2$ is the quantity of input 1 required to produce x_2 of commodity 2, and $a_{1n}x_n$ is the quantity of input 1 required to produce x_n of commodity n. Thus, the first equation sets the total quantity demanded of input 1 (required to produce x_1, x_2, to x_n) equal to the total supply of resource or input 1 (r_1). Similarly, the second equation sets the total quantity demanded of input 2 used in all commodities to equal the quantity supplied of input 2, and so on for each of the m resources of inputs.

The last step to close the model is to specify the set of equations that relate the supply of each resource or input to prices. This is given by

$$r_1 = g_1(p_1, p_2, \ldots, p_n; v_1, v_2, \ldots, v_m)$$
$$r_2 = g_2(p_1, p_2, \ldots, p_n; v_1, v_2, \ldots, v_m) \qquad \text{[97A]}$$
$$\ldots\ldots\ldots\ldots\ldots\ldots\ldots\ldots\ldots\ldots\ldots\ldots\ldots$$
$$r_m = g_m(p_1, p_2, \ldots, p_n; v_1, v_2, \ldots, v_m)$$

That is, the supply of each resource or input is a function of, or depends on, the price of all inputs (the v'_is) and the price of all commodities (the p'_js). For example, the supply of steel depends on the price of steel, the price of aluminum, the wages of auto workers, and other input prices. The price of steel also depends on the price of automobiles, washing machines, steaks, and other commodity prices. Therefore, a change in

---

* The presentation is adapted from R. Dorfman, P.A. Samuelson, and R.M. Solow, *Linear Programming and Economic Analysis* (New York: McGraw-Hill, 1958), pp. 351–355.

any part of the system affects every other part of the system.

Summing up, in equation [94A] to equation [97A] we have $2n + 2m$ equations and an equal number of unknowns (the x_j's, the p_j's, the v_i's, and the r_i's). However, according to Walras's law, equations [94A] and [97A] have only $n + m - 1$ independent equations, since if all but one of these $n + m$ equations are satisfied, the last one must also be satisfied. However, we can arbitrarily set any commodity price, say, $p_1 = 1$ and express all other prices in terms of p_1 (the *numéraire*). This reduces the number of unknowns in the system by 1, so as to equal the number of independent equations. The system may the have a unique solution (i.e., a set of prices and quantities that simultaneously satisfies all the equations of the model).

Answers to Selected Problems

Chapter 1

1. We study microeconomic theory to understand the economic behavior of individual consumers, resource owners, and business firms; to examine how individual commodity and resource prices are determined; and to understand the conditions for the efficient allocation of consumption and production in a free-enterprise economy. One cannot become an expert in any other field of economics without a thorough understanding of microeconomic theory.

6. a. With a price ceiling, consumers want to purchase more of the commodity than producers are willing to produce. This results in a shortage of the commodity, which leads to rationing and a black market.

    b. With a price floor, consumers want to purchase less of a commodity than producers are willing to produce. This results in a surplus of the commodity.

8. One way to measure the interdependence of the U.S. economy with the rest of the world is to calculate the percentage of U.S. imports and exports in relation to GNP. This percentage increased from about 8% in 1970 to almost 20% in 1996. Thus, U.S. interdependence has increased sharply during the past two decades.

12. a. The positive income aspects of positive analysis refer to such things as the shift in the kinds and quantities of goods and services produced and their effect on employment and incentives to work, on economic growth, and so on. All of these can be objectively measured or estimated.

    b. The normative aspects of income redistribution refer to the value-based disagreement on how much income should be redistributed.

Chapter 2

2. a.

$P(\$)$	8	7	6	5	4	3	2	1	0
QD'	0	10	20	30	40	50	60	70	80

b. See Figure 2a.

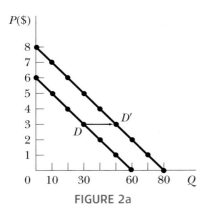

FIGURE 2a

c. D' represents an increase in demand because consumers demand more of the commodity at each and every price.

4. a.

MARKET SUPPLY SCHEDULE, MARKET DEMAND SCHEDULE, AND EQUILIBRIUM

Price	Quantity Supplied	Quantity Demanded	Surplus (+) Deficit (−)	Pressure on Price
$6	60	0	60	Down
5	50	10	40	Down
4	40	20	20	Down
3	30	30	0	Equilibrium
2	20	40	−20	Up
1	10	50	−40	Up
0	0	60	−60	Up

b. See Figure 2b.

9. a. The demand for hamburgers increases, resulting in a higher price and quantity.

b. The supply of hamburgers declines, resulting in an increase in the equilibrium price and a reduction in the equilibrium quantity.

c. The supply of hamburgers increases, lowering the equilibrium price and increasing the quantity purchased.

d. The demand for hamburgers increases, causing the same effect as in part (a).

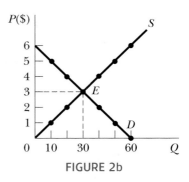

FIGURE 2b

e. A per-unit subsidy is the opposite of a per-unit tax. The per-unit subsidy increases the supply of hamburgers, causing the same effect as in part (c).

12. a. See Figure 2c.

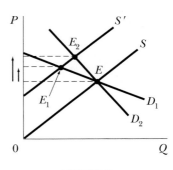

FIGURE 2c

b. See Figure 2d.

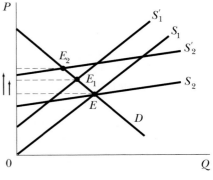

FIGURE 2d

Chapter 3

a. See Figure 3a.

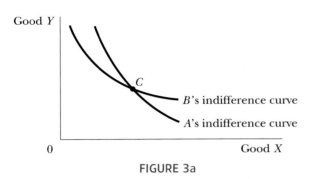

FIGURE 3a

b. Point C is the original equal endowment of good X and good Y of individual A and individual B. Since A prefers X to Y, A's indifference curve is steeper than B's indifference curve. That is, A is willing to give up more of Y for an additional unit of X, and MRS_{XY} for A at point C is greater than for B.

7. a. See Figure 3b.

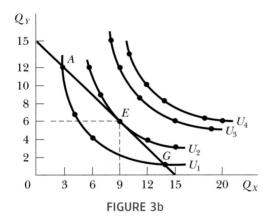

FIGURE 3b

b. The individual maximizes utility at point E, where U_2 is tangent to the budget line, by purchasing $9X$ and $6Y$. To maximize utility, the individual should spend all income in such a way that MRS_{XY} (the absolute slope of the indifference curve) equals P_X/P_Y (the absolute slope of the budget line).

c. Points A and G are on U_1 even though the individual spends all income.

d. The individual does not have sufficient income to reach U_3 and U_4.

9. a. The individual would spend $4 to purchase 4_x and the remaining $3 to purchase $3Y$.

b. $MU_X/P_X = MU_Y/P_Y = 6/\$1$ and $(\$1)(4X) + (\$1)(3Y) = \$7$.

c. The individual would receive 41 utils from consuming $4X$ (the sum of the MU_X up to $4X$) plus 27 utils from purchasing $3Y$ (the sum of the MU_Y up to $3Y$) for a total utility of 68 utils. If the individual spent all $7 on $7X$, he or she would get 49 utils (the sum of all MU_X). If the individual spent all income on $7Y$, he or she would get 38 utils (the sum of all MU_Y).

12. See Figure 3c. The vertical intercepts in the two figures measure the amount of material goods that each couple could enjoy without children. The slope of the budget lines measures the amount of material goods per year that each couple would have to give up per child. The couple portrayed in the top panel is at corner equilibrium A and chooses to have no children. The couple in the bottom panel is in equilibrium at point B by having one child. This couple is willing to give up the amount of material goods indicated on the vertical axis of the graph to have one child.

As the possibility for women to find high-paying jobs has increased in the United States and in other industrial countries since World War II, birth rates have declined because the opportunity costs of having children have increased. High-income people seem to have fewer children but tend to spend more on their education, health, and so on. It seems that high-income people have traded the number of children for a better quality of life for their children.

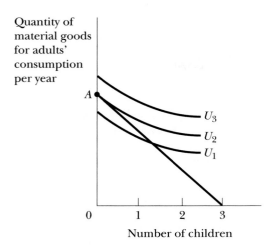

Quantity of
material goods
for adults'
consumption
per year

A

U_3

U_2

U_1

0   1   2   3

Number of children

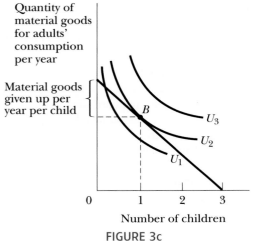

Quantity of
material goods
for adults'
consumption
per year

Material goods
given up per
year per child

B

U_3

U_2

U_1

0   1   2   3

Number of children

FIGURE 3c

Chapter 4

3. a. See Figure 4a.

b. At $P_X = \$0.50$, the consumer maximizes utility
at point G, where U_4 is tangent to budget line 3, by
purchasing 14X. This gives point G' in the bottom
panel. With $P_X = \$1$, the optimum is at point E
where U_2 is tangent to budget line 2 and the consumer purchases 9X. This gives point E' in the bottom panel.

   Finally, with $P_X = \$2$, the consumer is at opti-
mum at point B where U_1 is tangent to budget line

1 by buying 4X. This gives point B' in the bottom
panel. Joining points $G'E'B'$ in the bottom panel
we derive d_X.

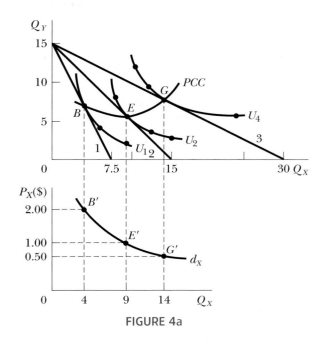

FIGURE 4a

5. See Figure 4b. The sequence in the figure is from A
to B to C.

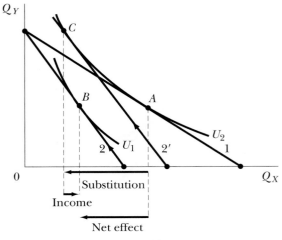

FIGURE 4b

7. In very poor Asian countries, people can purchase little else besides rice. If the price of rice falls, the substitution effect tends to lead people to substitute rice for other goods. However, if rice is an inferior good in these nations, the increase in real income resulting from the decline in the price of rice leads people to purchase less rice. People spend most of their income on rice, so a decline in the price of rice will lead to a relatively large increase in purchasing power, which will allow people to purchase so much more of other goods that they need to purchase less rice.

   That is, it is conceivable that the substitution effect (which leads people to purchase more rice when its price falls) could be overwhelmed by the opposite income effect. The net effect would then be that people purchase less rice when its price falls, so that the demand curve for rice would be positively sloped in these countries. However, there is no proof that this is indeed true.

9. See Figure 4c. The poor family is originally maximizing utility at point A where U_1 is tangent to budget line 1. With the government paying half of the family's food bill, we have budget line 2. With budget line 2, the poor family maximizes utility at point B on U_2. To get to point B, the family spends $2,000 of its income ($FG$). Without the subsidy the family would have to pay $4,000 ($FL$).

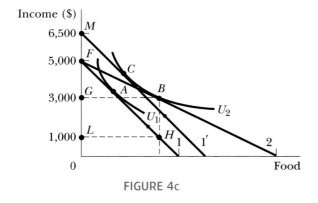

FIGURE 4c

   Thus, the cost of the subsidy to the government is $2,000. The family, however, could reach U_2 at point C with a cash subsidy of $1,500 ($FM$). The government may still prefer to subsidize the

family's food consumption (even if more expensive) if one of its aims is to improve nutrition.

Chapter 5

4. a. When two demand curves are parallel, their slopes $(-\Delta P/\Delta Q)$ and their inverse $(-\Delta Q/\Delta P)$ are the same at every price. However, P/Q (the other component of the price elasticity formula) is smaller (since Q is larger) for the demand curve further to the right at every price. Therefore, the price elasticity of the demand curve further to the right is smaller.

   b. When two demand curves intersect, P/Q is the same for both demand curves at the point of intersection. However, $-\Delta Q/\Delta P$ is larger for the flatter demand curve. Therefore, the flatter demand curve is more elastic at the point where the demand curves intersect.

8. a. In a two-commodity world, both commodities cannot be luxuries because this would imply that a consumer could increase the quantity purchased of both commodities by a percentage larger than the percentage increase in his or her income. This is impossible if the consumer already spent all income on the two commodities before the increase in income (and does not borrow money).

   b. A 10% increase in income results in a 25% increase in the quantity of cars purchased if the income elasticity is 2.5. That is, since $2.5 = \%\Delta Q/10\%$, $(2.5)(10\%) = 25\%$.

10. a. Since $\eta = 0.13$ in the short run and 1.89 in the long run, the demand for electricity is inelastic in the short run and elastic in the long run. With a 10% increase in price, the quantity demanded of electricity will decline by 1.3% in the short run and by 18.9% in the long run.

    b. Since the income elasticity of demand exceeds unity, electricity is a luxury. With a 10% increase in income, consumers would purchase 19.4% more electricity.

    c. Since the cross elasticity of demand between electricity and natural gas is positive, natural gas is a substitute for electricity. However, a 10% increase in the price of natural gas increases electricity consumption by only 8%.

13. a. Since $K_X = 0.75$, K_Y must be 0.25. Thus,

$$(0.75)(0.90) + (0.25)(\eta_{IY}) = 1$$

$$0.25\eta_{IY} = 0.325$$

$$\eta_{IY} = 1.3$$

b. Commodity Y is a luxury, and commodity X is a necessity. For Y to be an inferior good, η_{IY} must be negative. For this to occur, $(0.75)(\eta_{IY})$ must be larger than 1, which means that η must exceed 1.33. Since most goods are normal, the income elasticity of demand of a commodity on which the consumer spends a great proportion of his or her income cannot be much higher than 1.

Chapter 6

1. a. The expected value of investment I is

$$(\$4,000)(0.6) + (\$6,000)(0.4)$$

$$= \$2,400 + \$2,400 = \$4,800$$

The expected value of investment II is

$$(\$3,000)(0.4) + (\$5,000)(0.3) + (\$7,000)(0.3)$$

$$= \$1,200 + \$1,500 + \$2,100 = \$4,800$$

b. The calculation of the standard deviation of each investment is shown in the following table.

c. Since both projects have the same expected value ($4,800) but the standard deviation of investment I is lower than that of investment II, a risk averse individual should choose investment I.

4. a. The expected value of project A is

$$(0.4)(-\$5) + (0.5)(\$35) + (0.1)(\$95)$$

$$= -\$2 + \$17.50 + \$9.50 = \$25$$

The expected value of project B is

$$(0.4)(-\$15) + (0.5)(\$45) + (0.1)(\$135)$$

$$= -\$6 + \$22.50 + \$13.50 = \$30$$

Project B is preferred.

b. The standard deviation is the square root of the variance. The variance of project A is

$$(0.4)(-\$5 - \$25)^2 + (0.5)(\$35 - \$25)^2 + (0.1)(\$95 - \$25)^2$$

$$= (0.4)(-\$30^2) + (0.5)(10^2) + (0.1)(\$70^2)$$

$$= (0.4)(\$900) + (0.5)(\$100) + (0.1)(\$4,900)$$

$$= \$360 + \$50 + \$490 = \$900$$

So the standard deviation of the expected return to Project A is $30. The variance of project B is

$$(0.4)(-\$45^2) + (0.5)(\$15^2) + (0.1)(\$105^2)$$

$$= \$2,025$$

Deviation from Expected Value	Deviation Squared	Probability	Deviation Squares Times Probability
	Investment I		
$4,000 − $4,800 = −$800	$640,000	0.6	$384,000
6,000 − 4,800 = 1,200	1,440,000	0.4	$576,000
	Sum of deviations squared = Variance = $960,000		
	Standard deviation = Square root of variance = $979.80		
	Investment II		
$3,000 − $4,800 = −$1,800	$3,240,000	0.4	$1,296,000
5,000 − 4,800 = 200	40,000	0.3	12,000
7,000 − 4,800 = 2,200	4,840,000	0.3	1,452,500
	Sum of deviations squared = Variance = $2,760,000		
	Standard deviation = Square root of variance = $1,661,000		

So the standard deviation of the expected return to Project A is $45.

(c) The expected value of project A ($25) is lower than the expected value of project B ($30), but the standard deviation of project A ($30) is also lower than the standard deviation of project B ($45). In this case the risk-verse individual should prefer the project with the highest expected value per dollar of standard deviation. This is $25/$30 = 0.83 for project A and $30/$45 = $0.66 for project B. Therefore, the individual should prefer project A.

7. a. Expected value of A = (0.4)($0) + (0.5)($16) + (0.1)($49) = $12.90
Expected value of B = (0.4)($4) + (0.5)($9) + (0.1)($49) = $11.00
Project A is preferred.

(b) Expected utility of A = (0.4)(0 utils) + (0.5)(4 utils) + (0.1)(7 utils) = 2.70 utils
Expected utility of B = (0.4)(2 utils) + (0.5) (3 utils) + (0.1)(7 utils) = 3.0 utils
Project B is preferred.

(c) The individual is risk averse because the utility function of profit increases at a decreasing rate or faces down so that the marginal utility of profit diminishes. Specifically, if profit were $1, the utility of the profit of $1 is the square root of 1, which is 1; if profit were $2, the square root of $2 = 1.41, and if profit were $3, the square root of $3 is 1.732. If you plot profits of $1, $2, and $3 on the horizontal axis of a figure and the expected utility on the vertical axis, you will see that the expected utility of profit curve will be convex or increasing at a decreasing rate, thus making marginal utility diminishing and the individual risk averse.

*12. The U.S. importer can hedge his foreign-exchange risk with a forward purchase of £100,000 for $202,000 at today's three-month forward rate of $2.02/£1. In three months, the importer will pay $202,000 and obtain the £100,000 with which to pay for his imports.
The U.S. importer is usually willing to pay this extra $2,000 as the cost in insuring against having to pay much more in three months if the foreign currency appreciates (i.e., if the dollar depreciates) a great deal.

Chapter 7

7. See Figure 7. The right angle or L-shaped isoquant shows no possibility of substituting one input for the other in production. The straight-line isoquant shows that inputs are perfectly substitutable for each other in production (the $MRTS_{LK}$ is constant). That is, the given level of output could be produced with only labor or only capital.

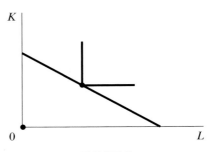

FIGURE 7

8. At 50 mph (point A), traveling the 600 miles requires 12 hours and 16 gallons of gasoline for a total cost of (12)($6) + (16)($1.50) = $96. At 60 mph, the total cost is (10)($6) + (20)($1.50) = $90. At 66.7 mph, the total cost is (9)($6) + (30)($1.50) = $99. Thus, the cost of traveling the 600 miles is minimized at the speed of 60 mph.

10. a. The production function $Q = 10\sqrt{LK}$ exhibits constant returns to scale throughout. For example, when $L = 1$ and $K = 1$, $Q = 10\sqrt{1} = 10$. When $L = 2$ and $K = 2$, $Q = 10\sqrt{4} = 20$. When $L = 3$ and $K = 3$, $Q = 10\sqrt{9} = 30$. With $L = 4$ and $K = 4$, $Q = 10\sqrt{16} = 40$, and so on.

b. The production function exhibits diminishing returns to capital and labor throughout. For example, holding capital constant at $K = 1$ and increasing labor from $L = 1$ to $L = 2$ increases Q from 10 to $10\sqrt{2} = 14.14$. Therefore, the marginal product of labor (MPL) is 4.14. Increasing labor to $L = 3$ results in $Q = 10\sqrt{3} = 17.32$. Thus, MPL declines to 3.18. The law of diminishing returns operates throughout, but MPL always remains positive. The same is true if labor is held constant and capital changes.

11. a. False. As long as returns are diminishing but positive, the student still benefits from additional hours of study.

b. True. If economies of scale were present, larger and more efficient firms would drive smaller and less efficient firms out of business.

Chapter 8

1. a. The explicit costs are $10,000 + $30,000 + $15,000 = $55,000.

    b. The implicit costs are the foregone earnings of $15,000 in the previous occupation.

    c. The total costs are equal to the $55,000 of explicit costs plus the $15,000 of implicit costs, or $70,000. Since the total earnings or revenues are only $65,000, from the economist's point of view, the woman actually lost $5,000 for the year by being in business for herself.

4. a. Since electrical utility companies bring into operation older and less efficient equipment to expand output in the short run to meet peak electricity demand, their short-run marginal costs rise sharply.

    b. New generating equipment would have to be run around the clock, or nearly so, for AFC to be sufficiently low to make ATC lower than for older equipment. To meet only peak demand, older and *fully* depreciated equipment is cheaper.

9. a. The LTC curve would be a positively sloped straight line through the origin when constant returns to scale operate at all levels of output.

    b. The LAC and the LMC curves would coincide and be horizontal at the value of the constant slope of the LTC curve.

    c. Horizontal LAC and LMC curves are consistent with U-shaped $SATC$ curves.

12. a. Rewriting learning curve equation $AC = 1{,}000Q^{-0.3}$ in double log form we get

$$\log(AC) = \log(1{,}000) - 0.3 \log(Q)$$

Substituting the value of 100 for Q into the previous equation we get

$$\log(AC) = \log(1{,}000) - 0.3 \log(100)$$

Substituting 3 for the log of 1,000 and 2 for the log of 100 (obtained by simply entering the numbers 1,000 and 100, respectively, in your calculator and pressing the "log" key), we get

$$\log(AC) = 3 - 0.3(2) = 2.4$$

Thus, AC equals the antilog of 2.4, which equals $251.19 (obtained by imply entering the log of 2.4 in your calculator and pressing the antilog key). The AC for the 100th unit of the product is $251.19.

b. For $Q = 200$, we have

$$\log(AC) = \log(1{,}000) - 0.3 \log(200)$$
$$= 3 - 0.3(2.30103)$$
$$= 3 - 0.69039$$
$$= 2.309691$$

Thus, AC for the 200th unit of the product equals the antilog of 2.309691, which equals $204.03.

c. For $Q = 400$, we have

$$\log(AC) = \log(1{,}000) - 0.3 \log(400)$$
$$= 3 - 0.3(2.60206)$$
$$= 3 - 0.780618$$
$$= 2.219382$$

Thus, AC for the 400th unit of the product equals the antilog of 2.219382, which equals $165.72.

d. Figure 8 shows the figure for the learning curve estimated above.

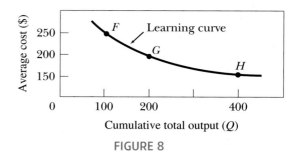

FIGURE 8

Chapter 9

1. a. $QD = QS$

$$4{,}750 - 50P = 1{,}750 + 50P$$
$$3{,}000 = 100P$$
$$P = \$30 \text{ (equilibrium price)}$$

b. See the following table.

MARKET DEMAND AND SUPPLY SCHEDULES

P($)	QD	QS
50	2,250	4,250
40	2,750	3,750
30	3,250	3,250
20	3,750	2,750
10	4,250	2,250

c. See Figure 9a.

d. $P = \$30$.

4. a. See Figure 9b. In Figure 9b, the slope of the *TR* curve refers to the constant price of $10 at which the perfectly competitive firm can sell its output. The *TC* curve indicates total fixed costs of $200 and a constant average variable cost of $5 (the slope of the *TC* curve). This is often the case for many firms for small changes in outputs. The firm breaks even at $Q = 40$ per time period (point *B* in the figure). The firm incurs a loss at smaller outputs and earns a profit at higher output levels. A

figure such as Figure 9b is called a *break-even chart*.

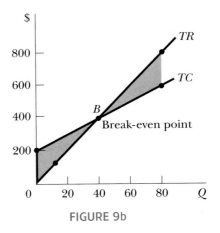

FIGURE 9b

b. An increase in the price of the commodity can be shown by increasing the slope of the *TR* curve; an increase in the total fixed costs of the firm can be shown by an increase in the vertical intercept of the *TC* curve, and an increase in average variable costs by an increase in the slope of the *TC* curve.

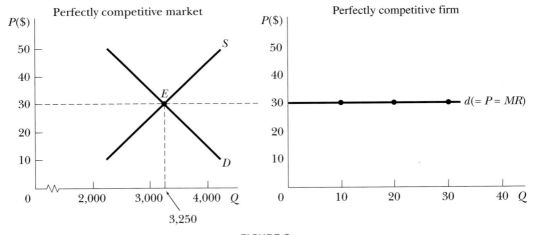

FIGURE 9a

The chart will then show the change in the break-even point of the firm and the profits or losses at other output levels. Thus, the break-even chart is a flexible tool to analyze quickly the effect of changing conditions on the firm.

c. An important shortcoming of break-even charts is that they imply that firms will continue to earn larger and larger profits per time period with greater output levels. From our discussion in Chapter 9, we know that, eventually, the *TC* curve will begin to rise faster than *TR*, and total profits will fall. Thus, break-even charts must be used with caution. Nevertheless, under the appropriate set of circumstances, they can be a useful tool; they are being used extensively today by business executives, government agencies, and nonprofit organizations.

8. See Figure 9c.

10. See Figure 9d. The original long-run equilibrium point is *E* (where *D* crosses *S* and *LS*). If *D* shifts up to *D'*, the equilibrium point is *E'* in the market period (where *D'* and *S* cross), *E''* in the short run (where *D'* and *S'* cross), and *E** in the long run (where *D'* crosses *LS*). Thus, the adjustment to an increase in demand falls entirely on price in the

market period, mostly on price in the short run, and mostly on output in the long run. With a constant-cost industry, long-run adjustment would fall entirely on output.

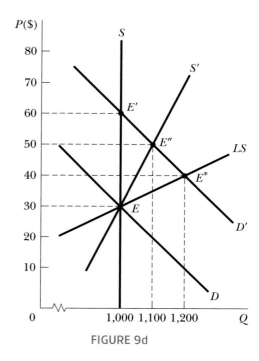

FIGURE 9d

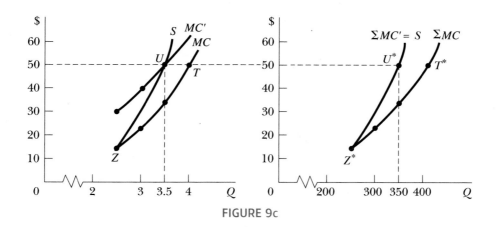

FIGURE 9c

Chapter 10

4. a. See Figure 10a. The best level of output is about $Q = 2$, where the MC curve intersects the MR' curve from below.

  b. Since at $Q = 2$, $P = \$20$ while $ATC = \$30$, the firm incurs a loss of \$10 per unit and \$20 in total. However, since $AVC = \$15$, the monopolist covers \$10 out of its total fixed costs of \$30. Were the monopolist to go out of business, it would incur a total loss equal to its $TFC = \$30$. The shut down point of the monopolist is at $Q = 2.5$, where $P = AVC = \$14$.

7. a. See Figure 10b.

  b. See Figure 10c.

10. With third degree price discrimination, $MR_1 = MR_2$. Also with formula [5–6], $MR_1 = P_1(1 + 1/\eta_1)$ and $MR_2 = P_2(1 + 1/\eta_2)$. Setting MR_1 equal to MR_2, we get

$$P_1(1 + 1/\eta_1) = P_2(1 + 1/\eta_2),$$

so that

$$\frac{P_1}{P_2} = \frac{1 + 1/\eta_2}{1 + 1/\eta_1}$$

and

$$P_1 = \left(\frac{1 + 1/\eta_2}{1 + 1/\eta_1}\right)4.5.$$

Since we were given $P_2 = \$4.50$, we need only to calculate η_1 and η_2 to prove that P_1 should be \$7. By extending D_1 to the horizontal axis and labeling

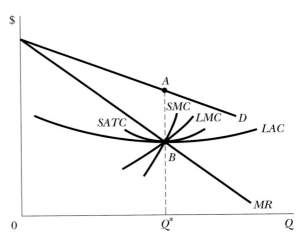

FIGURE 10b

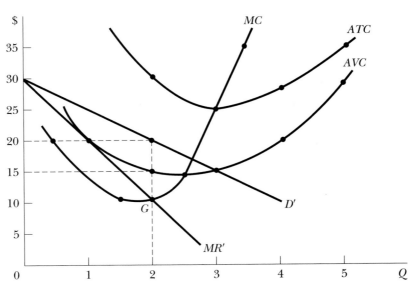

FIGURE 10a

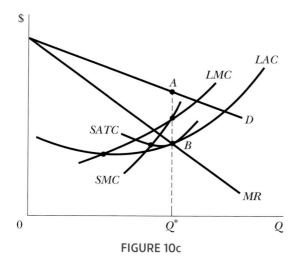

FIGURE 10c

H the intersection point at $Q = 11$ and also labeling *J* the point on the horizontal axis directly below point *A*, we get $\eta_1 = -JH/OJ = -7/4$. Doing the same for D_2, we get $\eta_2 = -3$.

Substituting the η_1, η_2, and P_2 values into the formula for P_1 derived above, we get

$$P_1 = \left(\frac{1 - \frac{1}{3}}{1 - \frac{1}{4/7}} \right) 4.5 = \left(\frac{2/3}{1 - 7/4} \right) 4.5$$

$$= \left(\frac{2/3}{3/7} \right) 4.5 = \left(\frac{2}{3} \right) \left(\frac{7}{3} \right) 4.5 = 7.$$

12. a. See the following table and Figure 10d. The prime indicates the effect of the lump-sum tax of $4.50.

Q	STC	MC	ATC	STC'	ATC'
0	$6	—	—	$10.50	—
1	10	$4	$10	14.50	$14.50
2	12	2	6	16.50	8.25
*3	13.50	1.50	4.50	18	6
4	19	5.50	4.75	23.50	5.88
5	30	11	6	34.50	6.90
6	48	18	8	52.50	8.75

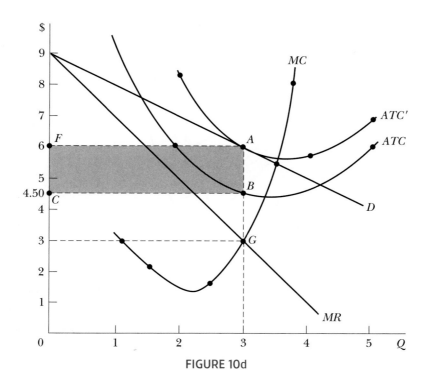

FIGURE 10d

The *STC'* values are obtained by adding $4.50 to the *STC* values.

ATC' = *STC'*/*Q*. Since the lump-sum tax is like a fixed cost, it does not affect *MC*. Thus, the best level of output of the monopolist remains at three units, at which *P* = $6, *ATC'* = $6, and the monopolist breaks even.

b. See the following table and Figure 10e, where the prime indicates the effect of a $2.50 per-unit tax.

Q	STC	MC	ATC	STC'	MC'	ATC'
1	$10	$ 4	$10	$12.50	—	$12.50
2	12	2	6	17	$ 4.50	8.50
3	$13.50	1.50	4.50	21	4	7
4	19	5.50	4.75	29	8	7.25
5	30	$11	6	42.50	$13.50	8.50

The *STC'* values are obtained by adding $2.50 per unit of output to *STC*.

ATC' = *STC'*/*Q*. *MC'* = Δ*STC'*/Δ*Q*. Since a per-unit tax is like a variable cost, both the *ATC* and the *MC* curves shift up to *ATC'* and *MC'*. The new

equilibrium point is 2.5 units, given at point *G'* where the *MC'* curve intersects the *MR* curve from below. At *Q* = 2.5, *P* = $6.50, *ATC'* = $7.50, and the monopolist incurs a loss of $0.50 per unit and $1.25 in total (as opposed to a profit of $4.50 before the per-unit tax). Thus, the monopolist can shift part of the burden of the per-unit tax to consumers.

Chapter 11

2. The more price elastic the demand curve faced by a monopolistically competitive firm when in long-run equilibrium, the closer to the lowest point on its *LAC* curve will the firm be when in long-run equilibrium. Since excess capacity is measured by the distance between the two points, the more elastic the demand curve, the smaller the amount of excess capacity under monopolistic competition.

6. a. See Figure 11a. If the demand curve that the oligopolist faces shifts up by $0.50 but the kink remains at *P* = $8, we get demand curve *d** or *H*B*C**. The marginal revenue curve is then *mr** or *H*K*F*G**. Since the *SMC* curve intersects

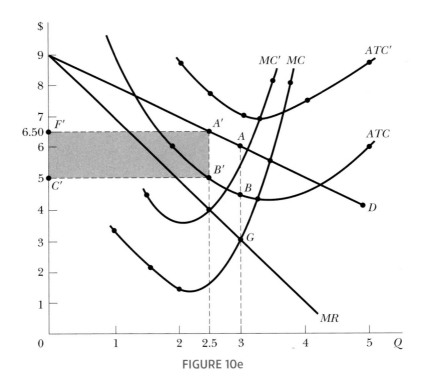

FIGURE 10e

the mr^* curve at point K^*, $Q = 6$ and price remains at $P = \$8$.

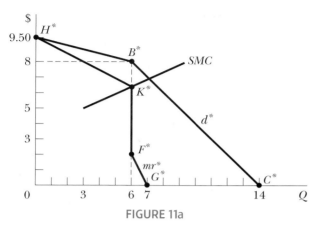

FIGURE 11a

b. See Figure 11b. If the demand curve that the oligopolist faces shifts down by \$0.50 but the kink remains at $P = \$8$, we get demand curve d^{**} or $H^{**}B^{**}C^{**}$. The marginal revenue curve is then mr^{**} or $H^{**}J^{**}J^*G^{**}$. Since the SMC' curve intersects the mr^{**} curve at point J^*, $Q = 2$ and price remains at $P = \$8$.

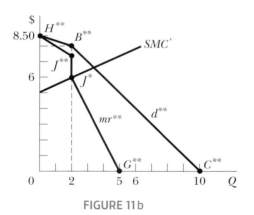

FIGURE 11b

9. a. See Figure 11c. Duopolist 1 (the low-cost duopolist) produces 2 units of the commodity and charges $P = \$8$ (given by point E_1, at which $SMC_1 = mr$, as in Figure 11.6). Duopolist 2 produces 1 unit of the commodity and would like to charge $P = \$10$ (given by point E_2, at which $SMC_2 = mr$). However, since the commodity is homogeneous, duopolist 2 (the high-cost duopolist) is forced to also sell at $P = \$8$ set by low-cost duopolist 1.

b. With $P = \$8$ and $SATC_1 = \$5$ at $Q = 2$, duopolist 1 earns a profit of \$3 per unit and \$6 in total. With $P = \$8$ and $SATC_2 = \$8$ at $Q = 1$, duopolist 2 breaks even. At $P = \$10$ duopolist 2 would have earned a profit of \$2. Thus, only duopolist 1 maximizes profits.

If the high-cost duopolist would go out of business at the profit-maximizing price set by the low-cost duopolist, the latter would probably set a price sufficiently high to allow the high-cost duopolist to remain in the market and avoid possible prosecution under antitrust laws for monopolizing the market. In that case, the low-cost firm would not be maximizing profits.

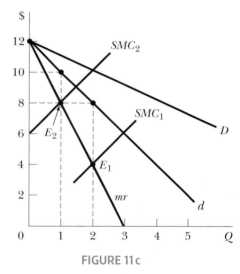

FIGURE 11c

12. a. The markup that the oligopolist should use in pricing its product is

$$m = -1/(\eta + 1)$$

$$= \frac{-1}{(-4 + 1)}$$

$$= \frac{1}{3} \text{ or } 33.33\%.$$

b. Since $AVC = \$10$ and the markup (m) equals 33.33%, the oligopolist should charge

$$P = AVC(1 + m)$$

$$= 10(1 + 0.3333)$$

$$= 10(1.3333)$$

$$= \$13.33$$

Chapter 12

3. a. If firm B produces small cars, firm A will earn a profit of 4 if it produces small cars and have a payoff of -2 (i.e., incurs a loss of 2) if it produces large cars. If firm B produces large cars, firm A will incur a loss of 2 if it also produces small cars and firm A earns a profit of 4 if it produces large cars. Therefore, firm A does not have a dominant strategy.

b. If firm A produces large cars, firm B will earn a profit of 4 if it produces small cars and will have a payoff of -2 (i.e., incur a loss of 2) if it also produces large cars. If firm A produces small cars, firm B will incur a loss of 2 if it also produces small cars and will earn a profit of 4 if it produces large cars. Therefore, firm B does not have a dominant strategy.

c. The optimal strategy is for one firm to produce small cars and the other to produce large cars. In that case, each firm earns a profit of 4. If both firms produce either small cars or large cars, each incurs a loss of 2.

d. In this case we have *two* Nash equilibria: either firm A produces large cars and firm B produces small cars (the top left cell in the payoff matrix), or firm A produces small cars and firm B produces large cars (the bottom right cell in the payoff matrix).

e. A situation such as that indicated in the payoff matrix of this problem might arise if each firm does not have the resources to invest in the plant and equipment necessary to produce both large and small cars, and the demand for either small or large cars is not sufficient to justify the production of small or large cars by both firms. Specifically, if both firms produce the same type of car, the oversupply of that type of car will result in low car prices and losses for both firms.

4. The following table is a hypothetical payoff matrix for Example 2 in Chapter 12.

		OTHER COMPUTER FIRMS	
		No Mail Orders	Mail Orders
Dell	No Mail Orders	0, 1	0, 8
Computers	Mail Orders	6, 2	4, 4

The payoff matrix in this table shows that when other computer companies do not sell computers through mail orders, Dell Computers earns zero profit if it also does not sell through the mail (since Dell was created specifically to sell only through the mail) but earns a profit of 6 if it does. Similarly, when other computer companies do sell through the mail, Dell earns zero profits if it does not sell through the mail and 4 if it does. Thus, Dell's dominant strategy is to sell computers through the mail, regardless of what the other computer companies do.

On the other hand, when Dell does not sell through the mail (i.e., when Dell is not in the market), other computer companies earn a profit of 1 if they do not sell through the mail and 8 if they do (at least that is what they believe). But if Dell is in the market and sells through the mail, other computer companies will earn 2 if they do not accept mail orders and 4 if they do. Thus, the other computer companies do not have a dominant strategy.

With Dell in the market and following its dominant strategy of selling through the mail, however, the other computer companies are also forced to enter the mail-order business. This is the Nash equilibrium.

8. a. Each firm adopts its dominant strategy of cheating (the top left cell) but could do better by cooperating not to cheat (the bottom right cell). Thus, the firms face the prisoners' dilemma.

b. If the payoff in the bottom right cell were changed to (5, 5), the firms would still face the prisoners' dilemma by cheating.

9. The tit-for-tat strategy for the first 5 of an infinite number of games for the payoff matrix of Problem 1, when firm A begins by cooperating but firm B does not cooperate in the next period, is given by the following table:

Period	Firm A	Firm B
1	2	2
2	-1	3
3	1	1
4	3	-1
5	2	2

The preceding table shows that in the first period, firm A sets a high price (i.e., cooperates) and so does firm B (so that each firm earns a profit of 2). If in the second period firm B does not cooperate and sets a low price, while firm A is still cooperating and setting a high price, firm B earns a profit of 3 and firm A incurs a loss of 1. In the third period, firm A retaliates and also sets a low price. As a result, each firm earns a profit of only 1 in period 3. In period 4, firm B cooperates again by setting a high price. With firm A still setting a low price, firm A earns a profit of 3 while firm B incurs a loss of 1. In the fifth period, firm A also cooperates again and sets a high price. Since both firms are now setting a high price, each earns a profit of 2.

Chapter 13

2. In Figure 13a, $P = \$8$ at the best level of output of $Q = 4$ given by point E at which $MR = MC = \$4$, so that $L = (8 - 4)/8 = 0.5$. This value of the Lerner index and the MC curve in Figure 12a is consistent with ATC_1 and ATC_2 and with profits of $3 per unit and $12 in total with ATC_1 and $2 per unit and $8 in total with ATC_2. All that is required is that both the ATC_1 and ATC_2 intersect the MC curve at the lowest points of the former. Thus, a high degree of monopoly power is consistent with high or low profits for the firm.

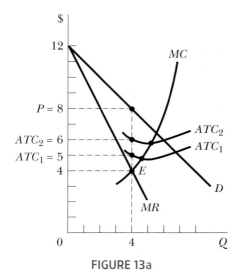

FIGURE 13a

5. In Figure 13b, D is the market demand curve and MC is the positively sloped marginal cost curve faced by the monopolist. The demand curve shows the maximum price that consumers would be willing to pay and the marginal benefit that they would receive for various quantities of the commodity. On the other hand, the MC curve shows the opportunity cost (in terms of the commodities foregone that could have been produced with the same inputs) of producing various quantities of the commodity. The best level of output for the monopolist is Q^* at which $MR = MC$ (point E). The price of the commodity is then P^*. The excess of P^* over MC between outputs Q^* and Q' (shaded triangle P^*EE' in Figure 13b) measures the net social losses of monopoly. Other social losses arise from the rent-seeking activities of the monopolist.

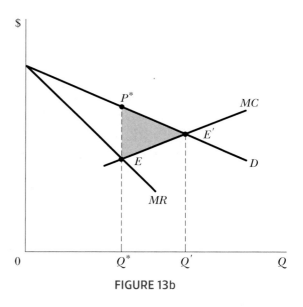

FIGURE 13b

7. In Figure 13c, D and D' are, respectively, the original and new market demand curves. With the new demand curve D' and the unchanged LAC curve, the regulatory commission would set $P' = LAC = \$2$ (point G') and the public-utility company would supply 8 million units of the service per time period (as compared with $P = LAC = \$3$ with $Q = 6$ million units per time period shown by point G on D). In either case, the public-utility company breaks even.

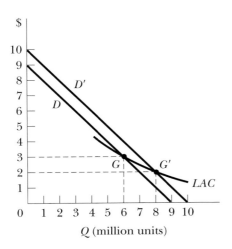

FIGURE 13c

12. a. When substitution in consumption is taken into account with peak-load pricing, the off-peak demand will be higher and the peak demand will be lower as compared with the case where substitution in consumption is not taken into account. This is shown by D_1' and D_2', respectively, in Figure 13d.

b. The gain in shifting from constant pricing to peak-load pricing (shown by the sum of the two shaded triangles in Figure 13d) is smaller when

substitution in consumption is taken into account than when it is not. The reason is that the demand curves differ less with peak-load pricing when substitution in consumption is taken into account than when it is not.

Chapter 14

1. a. $MP_L/w < MP_K/r$. This means that the firm is above the AVC curve at the point where its MC curve intersects its MR curve.

b. The firm is on its AVC cost curve to the right of the point of intersection of its MC and MR curves.

c. $w/MP_L = r/MP_K = MC < MR$. The firm is on its AVC curve to the left of the intersection of its MC and MR curves.

5. a. See Figure 14a. The left panel of Figure 14a shows that the individual maximizes satisfaction at point H (with 16 hours of leisure per day, 8 hours of work, and a daily income of $8) on U_1 with $w = \$1$; at point E (with 14 hours of leisure, 10 hours of work, 8 and an income of $20) on U_2 with $w = \$2$; at point N (with 15 hours of leisure, 9 hours of work, and an income of $27) on U_3 with $w = \$3$; and at point R (with 17 hours of leisure, 7 hours of work, and an income of $28) on U_4 with

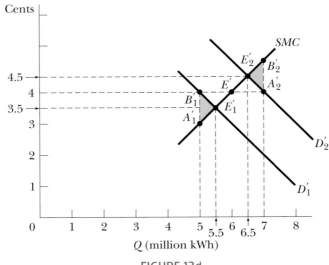

FIGURE 13d

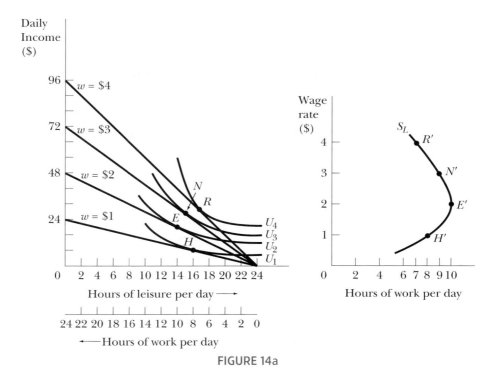

FIGURE 14a

$w = \$4$. Plotting the hours of work per day at various wage rates, we get the individual's supply curve of labor (S_L) in the right panel. Note that S_L bends backward at the wage rate of $2 per hour.

b. An increase in the wage rate, just like an increase in the price of a commodity, leads to a substitution effect and an income effect. The substitution effect leads individuals to substitute work for leisure when the wage rate (the price of leisure) increases. On the other hand, an increase in wages increases the individual's income, and when income rises, the individual demands more of every normal good, including leisure. Thus, the income effect, by itself, leads the individual to demand more leisure and work fewer hours.

Up to $w = \$2$ (point E' on S_L in the right panel of Figure 14a), the substitution effect exceeds the opposite income effect and the individual supplies more hours of work (i.e., S_L is positively sloped). At $w = \$2$, the substitution effect and the opposite income effect are in balance and the individual supplies the same number of hours of work (S_L is vertical). Above $w = \$2$, the substitution effect is smaller than the opposite income effect and the individual works fewer hours (i.e., S_L is negatively sloped or bends backward).

9. See Figure 14b. The movement from point E to point R is the combined substitution and income effects of the wage increase from $2 to $4 (as in Figure 14a). The substitution effect can be isolated by drawing the budget line with slope $w = \$4$ which is tangent to U_2 at point M. The movement along U_2 from point M to point E measures the substitution effect. By itself, it shows that the increase in w leads the individual to reduce leisure time and increase work by 4 hours per day.

The shift from point M on U_2 to point R on U_4 is the income effect of the wage increase. By itself, the income effect leads the individual to increase leisure and reduce work by 7 hours. The net result is that the individual increases leisure (works less) by 3 hours per day (ER).

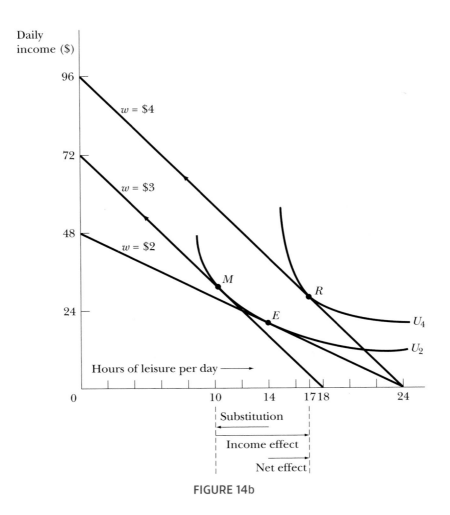

FIGURE 14b

11. See Figure 14c. In Figure 14c, D_T is the total demand for labor and S_T is the total supply of labor in both industries or regions. D_T is obtained from the horizontal summation of D_A and D_B, while S_A is obtained from the horizontal summation of S_A and S_B.

D_T and S_T intersect at point E, defining the equilibrium daily wage of $40 per day (the same as in both panels of Figure 14.6) and the equilibrium employment of labor of 6 million workers—the sum of the workers employed in industry or region A (the left panel in Figure 14.6) and industry or region B (the right panel of Figure 14.6).

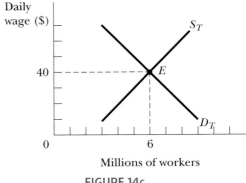

FIGURE 14c

Chapter 15

3. a. See the following table.

L	Q_X	MP_L	P_X	TR_X	MR_X	MRP_L	VMP_L	W
1	12	12	$13	$156	—	—	—	$40
2	22	10	12	264	$10.80	$108	$120	40
3	30	8	11	330	8.25	66	88	40
4	37	7	10	370	5.71	40	70	40
5	43	6	9	387	2.83	17	54	40
6	48	5	8	376	−1.80	−9	40	40

MR_X is obtained by the change in TR_X per unit change in the quantity of the commodity sold. That is, $MR_X = \Delta TR_X/\Delta Q_X = \Delta TR_X/MP_L$. For example, when the firm increases the number of workers it hires from one to two, Q_X rises from 12 to 22 units (i.e., $MP_L = 10$) and TR_X rises from $156 to $264 or by $108. Thus, $MR_X = \$108/10 = \$10.80$. When the firm increases the number of workers it hires from two to three, TR_X increases by $66 and Q_X increases by (i.e., MP_L equal to) eight units. Thus, $MR_X = \$66/8 = \$8.25$, and so on.

$MRP_L = (MP_L)(MR_X)$. For example, when the firm increases the number of workers hired from one to two workers, $MP_L = 10$ and $MR_X = \$10.80$. Thus, $MRP_L = (10)(\$10.80) = \$108$. This is equal to $\Delta TR_X/\Delta L$ or $\$108/1 = \$108$ (as found in the text).

$VMP_L = (MP_L)(P_X)$. For example, when the firm increases the number of workers it hires from one to two, $MP_L = 10$ and $P_X = \$12$, so that the $VMP_L = (10)(\$12) = \$120$.

b. See Figure 15a. If the firm were a perfect competitor in the product market as well as in the labor market, the firm would hire six workers (point E) because only by hiring six workers would $VMP_L = w = \$40$.

Since the firm is a monopolist in the product market but a perfect competitor in the labor market, it hires only four workers (point B) because only by hiring four workers would the $MRP_L = w = \$40$. The difference between the VMP_L and the MRP_L at $L = 4$ ($BC = \$30$ per worker and $120 in total) is the amount of monopolistic exploitation.

9 a. See Figure 15b. The monopsonist's supply curve becomes HMB' and the ME_L curve becomes $HMNRB$. The monopsonist maximizes profits by hiring three

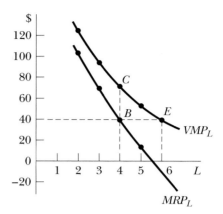

FIGURE 15a

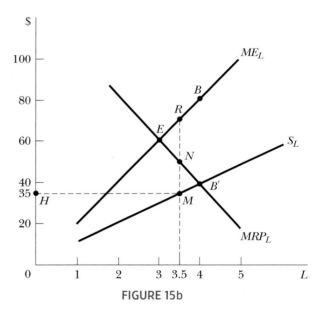

FIGURE 15b

workers on a full time basis and one worker on a half-time basis (given by point N, where the MRP_L curve intersects the vertical segment of the new ME_L curve). Monopsonistic exploitation is NM or $15 per worker.

b. See Figure 15c. The monopsonist's supply curve becomes TNF, and the ME_L curve becomes $TNFG$. The monopsonist maximizes profits by hiring three workers on a full time basis and one worker on a half-time basis (given by point N, where the MRP_L curve intersects the horizontal segment of the new ME_L curve). Now, $MRP_L = w = \$50$ at $L = 3.5$, and the monopsonistic exploitation of labor is zero.

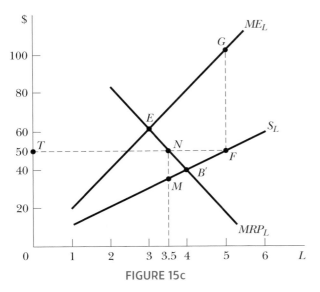

FIGURE 15c

10. See Figure 15d. The union (the monopolist seller of labor time) would like to have 40 workers employed (given by point E, where $MR = MC$) at the daily wage of \$40 (point E' on D_L). The firm (the monopsonist employer of labor) would maximize profits by employing 40 workers (given by point E', where its D_L or MRP_L curve intersects its ME_L curve) at $w = \$20$ (point E on its S_L curve).

Thus, there is agreement between the union and the firm on the number of workers to be employed, but not on the wage. The greater the relative bargaining strength of the union, the closer the wage rate will be to \$40. The greater the relative bargaining strength of the firm, the closer the wage rate will be to \$20. Note that it is not certain that the union will behave entirely as a monopolist (see Section 15.8).

11. See Figure 15e. In the figure, the demand for union labor (D_U) plus the demand for nonunion labor (D_N) gives the total demand for labor (D_T). The intersection of D_T and S_T (the market supply of labor) at point E determines the equilibrium daily wage of \$60 for union and nonunion labor (in the absence of any effect of unions on the wages). At $w = \$60$, 4 million union workers (point E') and 8 million nonunion workers (point E'') are employed.

If unions are now successful in raising union wages from \$60 to \$65, the employment of union labor falls from 4 to 3 million (point A on D_U). The 1 million workers who cannot find union employment will now have to find employment in the nonunion sector. This increases employment in the nonunion sector from 8 to 9 million workers. But 9

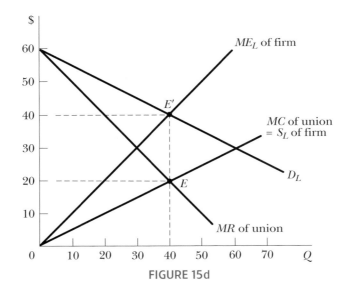

FIGURE 15d

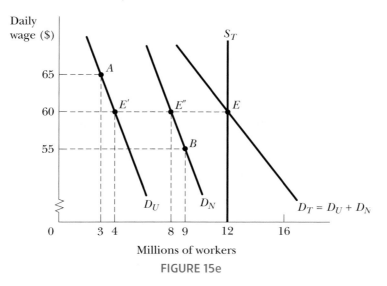

FIGURE 15e

million workers can only be employed in the nonunion sector at $w = \$55$ (point B on D_N).

Thus, when unions increase wages in the unionized sector, employment in the unionized sector falls. More workers must find employment in the nonunionized sector and nonunion wages fall. Thus, what union workers gain comes mostly at the expense of nonunion workers.

Chapter 16

4. See Figure 16a. Starting at point B ($Y_0 = 5$ and $Y_1 = 6$) in the figure, individual B moves to point E (7.5, 3) on indifference curve U_2 by borrowing 2.5 units of the commodity at $r = 20\%$. On the other hand, starting from point A ($Y_0 = 5$ and $Y_1 = 6$) in the figure, individual A moves to point E' (2.5, 9) on indifference curve U_1' by lending 2.5 units of the commodity at $r = 20\%$. Since at $r = 20\%$ desired borrowing equals desired lending, this is the equilibrium rate of interest.

On the other hand, at $r = 50\%$, individual B moves from point B to point E^* on U_1 by borrowing only 2 units of the commodity this year and repaying 3 units next year, while individual A moves from point A to point E'' on U_2' by lending 3 units this year for 4.5 units next year (so that

$r = 50\%$). Since at $r = 50\%$ desired lending exceeds desired borrowing, $r = 50\%$ is higher than the equilibrium rate of interest and r will fall toward 20%.

5. a. The supply curve of loans (lending) is usually positively sloped, indicating that lenders will lend more at higher rates of interest. However, when the interest rate rises, the lender will face a substitution effect and an income or wealth effect (just as a worker does when the wage rate rises). The substitution effect induces the lender to substitute future for present consumption and lend more since the reward for lending has increased.

On the other hand, when the interest rate rises, the lender's wealth rises and he or she will want to consume more both in the present (and lend less) and in the future. Thus, the substitution effect tends to lead the lender to lend more while the wealth effect leads the lender to lend less.

Up to a point, the substitution effect overwhelms the wealth effect and the lender will lend more at higher rates of interest. After a point, however, higher rates of interest will cause the wealth effect to exceed the opposite substitution effect so that the lender will lend less. Thus, at a sufficiently high rate of interest, the lender's supply curve will bend backward (as at r^* in Figure 16b).

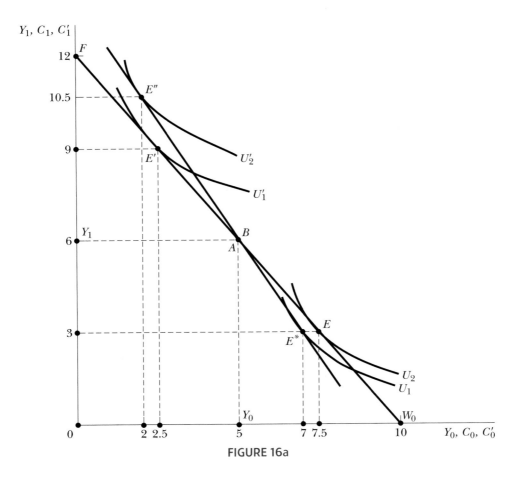

FIGURE 16a

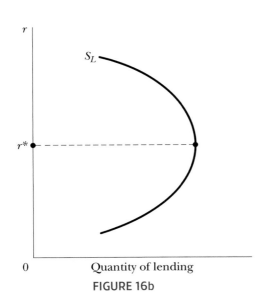

FIGURE 16b

b. For borrowers, both the substitution effect and the wealth effect operate to reduce the amount of desired borrowing when the rate of interest rises, so that the demand curve for borrowing is negatively sloped throughout. The substitution effect reduces the amount of borrowing as the rate of interest rises, because future consumption becomes more expensive in terms of the present consumption to be given up. The wealth effect also tends to reduce the amount of borrowing, because an increase in the rate of interest reduces the borrower's wealth.

9. See the following table. Note that the net present value of the project is higher with $r = 5\%$ than with $r = 10\%$.

BENEFIT–COST ANALYSIS OF AN INVESTMENT PROJECT

End of Year	Invest-ment (year 0) and Cost	Reve-nue	Net Reve-nue	Present Value Coefficient $1/(1+0.05)^n$	Present Value of Net Revenue
0	$1,000	—	-$1,000	—	-$1,000
1	200	$600	400	0.952	381
2	300	800	500	0.907	454
3	300	800	500	0.864	432
4	400	800	400	0.823	329
4	—	200*	200	0.823	165
					$761

*Salvage value

10. The cost of equity capital for this firm (k_e) can be calculated with the dividend valuation model, as follows

$$k_e = D/P + g$$

where D is the amount of the yearly dividend paid per share of the common stock of the firm, P is the price of a share of the common stock of the firm,

and g is the expected annual growth rate of dividend payments.

Since the company pays half of its expected $200 million in net after-tax earnings in dividends and there are 100 million shares of common stock of the firm, the dividend per share is $1. With a share of the common stock of the firm selling for eight times current earnings, the price of a share of the common stock of the firm is $8.

With the expected annual growth of earnings and dividends of the firm of 7.5%, the cost of equity capital for this firm is

$$k_e = \$1/\$8 + 0.075$$
$$= 0.125 + 0.075 = 0.20$$

or 20%.

Chapter 17

2. See Figure 17a. The Edgeworth box diagram of Figure 17a was obtained by rotating individual B's indifference curve diagram by 180 degrees (so that 0_B appears in the top right-hand corner) and

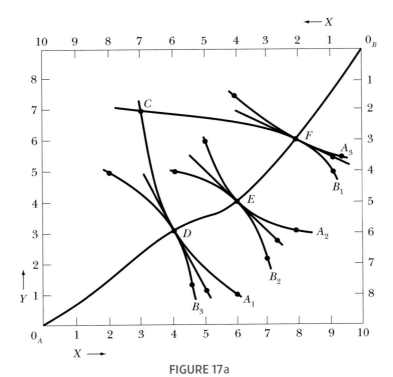

FIGURE 17a

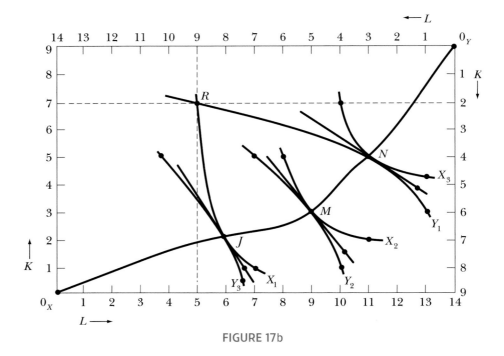

FIGURE 17b

superimposing it on individual A's indifference curve diagram (with origin 0_A) in such a way that the size of the box is $10X$ and $10Y$ (the combined amount of X and Y owned by individuals A and B). The contract curve for exchange is $0_A DEF0_B$ and is given by the tangency points of the indifference curves (at which MRS_{XY} are equal) for the two individuals.

4. See Figure 17b. The Edgeworth box diagram of Figure 17b was obtained by rotating the isoquant diagram for commodity Y by 180 degrees (so that 0_Y appears in the top right-hand corner) and superimposing it on the isoquant diagram for commodity X (with origin 0_X) in such a way that the size of the box is $14L$ and $9K$ (the total amount of L and K available). The production contract curve is $0_X JMN0_Y$ and is given by the tangency points of the isoquants (at which $MRTS_{LK}$ are equal) for commodities X and Y.

8. See Figure 17c. The simple economy portrayed in Figure 17c would be simultaneously in general equilibrium of production and exchange at point E, where

$$MRT_{XY} = MRS^A_{XY} = MRS^B_{XY} = 1$$

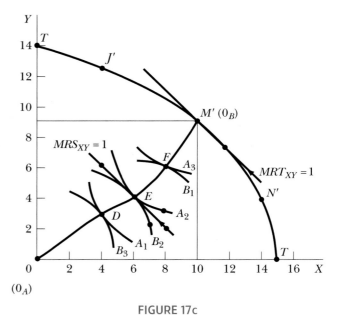

FIGURE 17c

12. a. See Figure 17d. Point D' in Figure 17d corresponds to point D (on A_1 and B_3) in Figure 17a, point E' corresponds to point E (on A_2 and B_2),

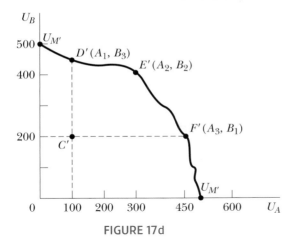

FIGURE 17d

and point F' to point F (on A_3 and B_1). Other points can be similarly obtained. By joining these points, we get utility-possibilities frontier $U_{M'}U_{M'}$. This shows the various combinations of utilities received by individuals A and B at which this economy (composed of individuals A and B) is in general equilibrium and Pareto optimum in exchange. A point outside $U_{M'}U_{M'}$ cannot be reached with the available amount of commodities X and Y.

b. See Figure 17e. Utility-possibilities frontier $U_{M'}U_{M'}$ is that of part (a). Utility-possibilities frontier $U_{N'}U_{N'}$ is derived from the contract curve

for exchange in the Edgeworth box diagram drawn from point N' on the production-possibilities frontier in Figure 17b (not shown in that figure). By joining E', H', and other Pareto optimum points of production and exchange, we get grand utility-possibilities frontier $GE'H'G$ in Figure 17e.

Chapter 18

3. a. See Figure 18a. A corrective tax of $4 per unit imposed on the consumers of commodity X will make D'' the new industry demand curve. With D'', $P_X = \$10$ and $Q_X = 4$ million units per time period (given by the intersection of D'' and S at point E'). This is the socially optimum price and output. Consumers would now pay $P_X = \$10$ plus the $4 tax per unit ($E'B$) or a net $P_X = \$14$ (compared with $P_X = \$12$ under the previous competitive equilibrium at point E).

b. The total value of the economic gain resulting from the imposition of the corrective tax is equal to $6 million (given by area $EE'A$ in the figure). This is the excess of the MSC (shown by supply curve S) over MSB (shown by demand curve D') between $Q_X = 4$ and $Q_X = 6$ million units.

5. a. See Figure 18b. A corrective subsidy of $4 per unit given to producers of commodity X will make S'' the new industry supply curve. With S'', $P_X = \$10$

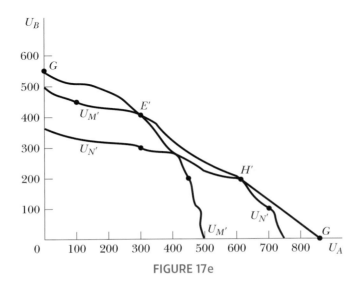

FIGURE 17e

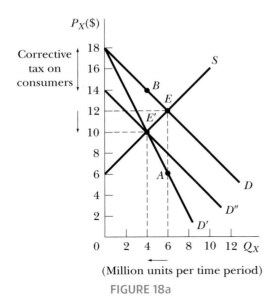

(Million units per time period)

FIGURE 18a

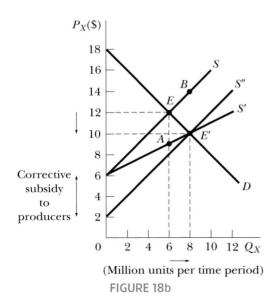

(Million units per time period)

FIGURE 18b

and $Q_X = 8$ million units per time period (given by the intersection of D and S'' at point E'). This is the socially optimum price and output. Producers would now receive $P_X = \$10$ plus the $4 subsidy per unit ($BE'$) for a total of $14 per unit.

b. The total value of the economic inefficiency eliminated by the corrective subsidy is equal to $3 million (given by area $EE'A$ in the figure). This is the excess

of the marginal social value (shown by demand curve D) over the MSC (shown by supply curve S') between $Q_X = 6$ and $Q_X = 8$ million units.

9. a. Each individual will drill more wells and pump oil faster than he or she would if no other oil field were located adjacent to his or hers in order to prevent some of the oil under his or her field to flow to the neighbor's field. The external diseconomies arise because oil is pumped faster than is socially desirable. The external diseconomies can be avoided by merging the two adjacent oil fields under joint ownership, by government regulation, or by taxation.

    b. The development of a recreational site confers external benefits to owners of shops, gasoline stations, and motels in the area. In order to internalize the external benefits, the recreational site developer may also set up and operate establishments that provide these other services near the recreational .site.

10. a. See Figure 18c. Market demand curve D_X ($CFEG$) is obtained by the *horizontal* summation of demand curves D_A and D_B. D_X and S_X intersect at point E and define equilibrium price of $P_X = \$5.50$ and the equilibrium quantity of $Q_X = 7.5$, if the market for commodity X is perfectly competitive. Individual A consumes $1X$, and individual B consumes $6.5X$.

    b. When X is a private good, the condition for Pareto optimal output is $MRT_{XY} = MRS^A_{XY} = MRS^B_{XY}$. That is, at the optimal output level, the marginal benefit that each consumer receives from an additional unit of commodity X equals its marginal cost. That is, $HJ = FR = EV$ in Figure 18c.

       On the other hand, when X is a public good, the condition for the Pareto optimal output is $MRT_{XY} = MRS^A_{XY} + MRS^B_{XY}$. That is, since each consumer can consume the *same* quantity of commodity X when X is a public good, it is the sum of the marginal benefits that each consumer receives from the additional unit of commodity X that must equal its marginal cost (i.e., $AB + AC = AE$ in Figure 18.2).

    c. Public goods that exhibit nonexclusion convey external economies of consumption on free riders (i.e., on the consumers not paying for the public goods).

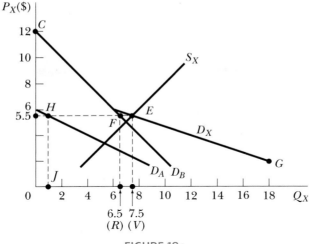

FIGURE 18c

Chapter 19

1. Because there is an equal number of five types of sellers, each price will be encountered one-fifth of the time on the first search.

    If search one yields the price of $120, four-fifths of the time search two will yield a lower price, averaging $95, and so the expected minimum price for search two is

    $$\$120(1/5) + \$95(4/5) = \$24 + \$86$$
    $$= \$100.$$

    If search one yields the price of $110, two-fifths of the time search two will yield a price of $120 or $110 (but in that case the price of $120 on search two would be disregarded), and three-fifths of the time search two will yield a lower price, averaging $90. Thus, the expected minimum price for search two in this case is

    $$\$110(2/5) + \$90(3/5) = \$44 + \$54$$
    $$= \$98.$$

    If search one yields the price of $100, three-fifths of the time search two will yield a price of $100 or higher (but in that case any price higher than $100 on search two would be disregarded), and two-fifths of the time search two will yield a lower

price, averaging $85. Thus, the expected minimum price for search two in this case is

$$\$100(3/5) + \$85(2/5) = \$94.$$

If search one yields the price of $90, four-fifths of the time search two will yield a price of $90 or higher (but in that case any price higher than $90 on search two would be disregarded), and one-fifth of the time search two will yield a price of $80. Thus, the expected minimum price for search two in this case is $90(4/5) + $80(1/5) = $88.

If search one yields the price of $80, the consumer will end the search because $80 is already the lowest price possible.

The expected minimum price for the second search is then the average of the above expected minimum prices for the second search. That is, the *precise* minimum price on the second search is ($100 + $98 + $94 + $88 + $80)/5 = $92 (compared with $93.33 found with the use of formula [19–1] in the text).

3. a. The formula for the lowest expected price for each search is

Expected Price = Lowest Price

$$+ \frac{\text{Range of Prices}}{\text{Number of Searches} + 1}$$

The lowest expected price with one search is

$$\$60 + \frac{\$80}{1+1} = \$100.00.$$

With two searches, the lowest expected price is

$$\$60 + \frac{\$80}{3} = \$86.67.$$

With three searches, the lowest expected price is

$$\$60 + \frac{\$80}{4} = \$80.00.$$

With four searches, the lowest expected price is

$$\$60 + \frac{\$80}{5} = \$76.00.$$

With five searches, the lowest expected price is

$$\$60 + \frac{\$80}{6} = \$73.33.$$

b. The marginal benefit from each search is measured by the reduction in the expected price resulting from the search. Thus, for the second search the marginal benefit (MB) is $\$100 - \$86.67 = \$13.37$.

For the third search, $MB = \$86.67 - \$80.00 = \$6.67$. For the fourth search, $MB = \$80.00 - \$76.00 = \$4.00$. For the fifth search, $MB = \$76.00 - \$73.33 = \$2.67$.

Note that the marginal benefits of each additional search are now twice as large as those found in the text where the range of prices was half what they are in this problem.

6. Priceline is an Internet firm that allows buyers to name their own price for flights, hotel rooms, mortgages, cars, and, most recently, groceries. The only condition is that the buyer be flexible as to seller or brand name. For example, in the purchase of an airline ticket the buyer cannot specify the airline or the time of flight, but has to take what is offered by the carrier that accepts the bid. This allows airlines to sell empty seats without losing their regular customers. As customers gain experience and learn to make more realistic bids, and as Priceline adds more airline and flights to the scheme, more and more bids are likely to be successful (they are now successful less than half of the time).

8. See Figure 19. In the figure, the subscripts H, L, and A refer, respectively, to high quality, low quality,

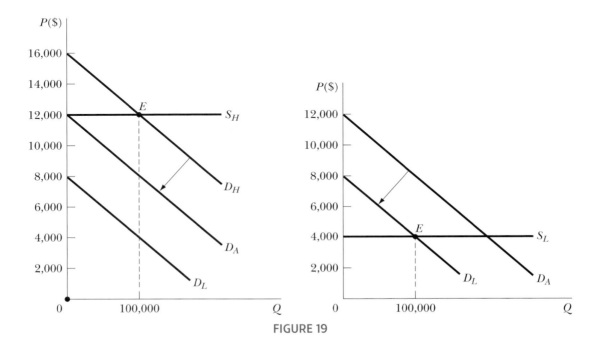

FIGURE 19

and average quality. In the absence of perfect information (i.e., with asymmetric information), the demand for used cars will be the average of the demand curves for the high-quality and the low-quality used cars that would prevail in the market if all potential buyers had perfect information. As a result, the left panel of Figure 19 shows that no high-quality cars will be offered for sale at the price of $12,000.

But with all the high-quality cars withdrawn from the market, only the low-quality cars will be offered for sale. Thus, D_A will fall to D_L in the right panel and only the 100,000 low-quality cars will be sold in the market at $P_L = \$4,000$.

Glossary

Adverse selection The situation where low-quality products drive high-quality products out of the market as a result of the existence of asymmetric information between buyers and sellers.

Alternative or opportunity cost doctrine The doctrine that postulates that the cost to a firm in using any input (whether owned or hired) is what the input could earn in its best alternative use.

Appreciation A decrease in the domestic-currency price of a foreign currency.

Arbitrage The purchase of a commodity or currency where it is cheaper and its sale where it is more expensive.

Arc elasticity of demand The price elasticity of demand between two points on the demand curve; it uses the average price and the average quantity in calculating the percentage change in price and quantity.

Arrow's impossibility theorem The theorem that postulates that a social welfare function cannot be derived by democratic vote to reflect the preferences of all the individuals in society.

Asymmetric information The situation where one party to a transaction has more information on the quality of a product or service offered for sale than does the other party.

Auction The mechanism by which commodities are bought and sold (and their price determined) through a formal bidding process.

Average fixed cost (AFC) Total fixed costs divided by output.

Average product (AP) The total product divided by the quantity of the variable input used.

Average revenue (AR) Total revenue divided by the quantity sold.

Average total cost (ATC) Total costs divided by output. Also equals $AFC + AVC$.

Average variable cost (AVC) Total variable costs divided by output.

Averch–Johnson (A–J) effect The overinvestments or underinvestments in plant and equipment resulting when public utility rates are set too high or too low, respectively.

Bad An item of which less is preferred to more.

Bandwagon effect   The situation where some people demand a commodity because other people purchase it (i.e., in order to "keep up with the Jonesses" or because the commodity becomes more useful the more people buy it).

Barometric firm   An oligopolistic firm that is recognized as a true interpreter or barometer of changes in demand and cost conditions warranting a price change in the industry.

Behavioral economics   The study of how people actually make choices in the real world by drawing on insights from psychology and economics.

Benefit–cost analysis   A procedure for determining the most worthwhile public projects for the government to undertake. It prescribes that government should undertake those projects with the highest benefit-cost ratio, as long as that ratio exceeds 1, and until government resources are fully employed.

Bergson social welfare function   A social welfare function based on the explicit value judgments of society.

Bertrand model   The duopoly model in which each firm assumes that the other will keep its price constant. It leads to the perfectly competitive solution even with only two firms.

Beta coefficient (β)   The ratio of the variability of the return on the common stock of the firm to the variability of the average return on all stocks.

Bilateral monopoly   The case where the monopsonist buyer of a product or input faces the monopolist seller of the product or input.

Brain drain   The migration of highly skilled people from one nation to another. This benefits the receiving nation and harms the nations of emigration.

Break-even point   The point where total revenues equal total costs and profits are zero.

Budget constraint   The limitation on the amount of goods that a consumer can purchase imposed by his or her limited income and the prices of the goods.

Budget line   A line showing the various combinations of two goods that a consumer can purchase by spending all income at the given prices of the two goods.

Bundling   A common form of tying in which the monopolist requires customers buying or leasing one of its products or services also to buy or lease another product or service when customers have different tastes but the monopolist cannot price discriminate.

Capital or investment goods   The machinery, factories, equipment, tools, inventories, irrigation, transportation, and communications networks that can be used to produce goods and services.

Capital asset pricing model (CAPM)   The method of measuring the equity cost of capital as the risk-free rate plus the beta coefficient (β) times the risk premium on the average stock.

Capital budgeting   The ranking of all investment projects from the highest present value to the lowest.

Cardinal utility   The ability to actually provide an index of utility from consuming various amounts of a good or baskets of goods.

Cartel   An organization of suppliers of a commodity aimed at restricting competition and increasing profits.

Centralized cartel   A formal agreement of the suppliers of a commodity that sets the price and allocates output and profits among its members so as to increase joint profits. It can result in the monopoly solution.

Certainty   The situation where there is only one possible outcome to a decision and this outcome is known precisely; risk-free.

Characteristics approach to consumer theory   The theory that postulates that a consumer demands a good because of the characteristics, properties, or attributes of the good, and it is these characteristics that give rise to utility.

Circular flow of economic activity   The flow of resources from households to business firms and the opposite flow of money incomes from business firms to households. Also, the flow of goods and services from business firms to households and the opposite flow of consumption expenditures from households to business firms.

Clayton Act   Prohibits mergers that "substantially lessen competition" or tend to lead to monopoly.

Closed innovation model   The situation where companies generate, develop, and commercialize their own ideas, innovations, or technological breakthoughts.

Coase theorem Postulates that when property rights are clearly defined and transaction costs are zero, perfect competition results in the absence of externalities, regardless of how property rights are assigned among the parties involved.

Cobb–Douglas production function The relationship between inputs and output expressed by $Q = AL^{\alpha}K^{\beta}$, where Q is output, L is labor, K is capital, and A, α, and β are positive parameters estimated from the data.

Coinsurance Insurance that covers only a portion of a possible loss.

Collusion A formal or informal agreement among the suppliers of a commodity to restrict competition.

Common property Property, such as air, owned by no one.

Comparable worth The evaluation of jobs in terms of the knowledge and skills required, working conditions, accountability, and the enforcement of equal pay for comparable jobs, or "comparable worth."

Comparative advantage The greater *relative* efficiency that an individual, firm, region, or nation has over another in the production of a good or service.

Comparative static analysis The analysis of the effect of a change in demand and/or supply on the equilibrium price and output of a commodity.

Compensating wage differentials Wage differences that compensate workers for the nonmonetary differences among jobs.

Compensation principle The amount that gainers from a change could pay losers to fully compensate them for their losses.

Complementary inputs Inputs related to one another in such a way that an increase in the employment of one raises the marginal product of the other.

Complements Two commodities are complements if an increase in the price of one of them leads to less of the other being purchased.

Composite cost of capital The weighted average of the cost of debt and equity capital to the firm.

Computer-aided design (CAD) The process that allows research and development engineers to design a new product or component on a computer screen, quickly experiment with different alternative designs, and test each design's strength and reliability.

Computer-aided manufacturing (CAM) The computer instructions to a network of integrated machine tools to produce a prototype of a new or changed product.

Concentration ratio The percentage of total industry sales of the 4, 8, and 20 largest firms in the industry.

Concept of the margin The central unifying theme in all of microeconomics, according to which the total net benefit is maximized when the marginal benefit is equal to the marginal cost.

Congestion pricing The charging of different prices at different times of day or based on the degree of congestion.

Conscious parallelism The adoption of similar policies by oligopolists in view of their recognized interdependence.

Constant-cost industry An industry with a horizontal long-run supply curve. It results if input prices remain constant as industry output expands.

Constant returns to scale Output changes in the same proportion as inputs.

Constrained utility maximization The process by which the consumer reaches the highest level of satisfaction given his or her income and the prices of goods. This occurs at the tangency of an indifference curve with the budget line.

Consumer equilibrium Constrained utility maximization.

Consumer optimization Constrained utility maximization.

Consumer surplus The difference between what the consumer is willing to pay for a given quantity of a good and what he or she actually pays for it.

Contract curve for exchange The locus of tangency points of the indifference curves (at which the *MRSXY* are equal) for two individuals when the economy is in general equilibrium of exchange.

Contract curve for production The locus of tangency points of the isoquants (at which the *MRTSLK* are equal) for two commodities when the economy is in general equilibrium of production.

Corner solution   Constrained utility maximization with the consumer spending all of his or her income on only one or some goods.

Cost of debt   The net (after-tax) interest rate paid by a firm to borrow funds.

Cost-plus pricing   The setting of a price equal to average cost plus a markup.

Cournot equilibrium   The situation where there is no tendency for each of two duopolists to change the quantity each sells.

Cournot model   The duopoly model in which each firm assumes that the other keeps output constant. With two firms, each will sell one-third of the perfectly competitive output.

Cross elasticity of demand (η_{XY})   The percentage change in the quantity purchased of a commodity divided by the percentage change in the price of another commodity.

Deadweight loss   The excess of the combined loss of consumers' and producers' surplus from a tax.

Decreasing-cost industry   An industry with a negatively sloped long-run supply curve. It results if input prices fall as industry output expands.

Decreasing returns to scale   Output changes by a smaller proportion than inputs.

Default risk   The possibility that a loan will not be repaid.

Depreciation   An increase in the domestic-currency price of a foreign currency.

Deregulation movement   The reduction or elimination of many government regulations since the mid-1970s in order to increase competition and efficiency.

Derivatives   Financial instruments or contracts whose values are derived from the price of such underlying financial assets as stocks, bonds, commodities, and currencies.

Derived demand   The demand for an input that arises from the demand for the final commodities that the input is used in producing.

Differentiated oligopoly   An oligopoly where the product is differentiated.

Differentiated products   Products that are similar but not identical and that satisfy the same basic need.

Diminishing marginal utility of money   The decline in the extra utility received from each dollar increase in income.

Discrimination in employment   The (illegal) unwillingness on the part of employers to hire some group of equally productive workers based on gender, color, religion, or national origin under any circumstances or at the same wage rate.

Diseconomies of scope   The higher costs that a firm can experience when it produces two or more products jointly rather than separate firms producing the products independently.

Disemployment effect   The reduction in the number of workers employed as a result of an increase in the wage rate (as with the imposition of an effective minimum wage).

Diversification   The spreading of risks.

Dividend valuation model   The method of measuring the equity cost of capital to the firm with the ratio of the dividend per share of the stock to the price of the stock, plus the expected growth rate of dividend payments.

Division of labor   The breaking up of a task into a number of smaller, more specialized tasks and assigning each of these tasks to different workers.

Dominant strategy   The optimal strategy for a player no matter what the other player does.

Dumping   International price discrimination, or the sale of a commodity at a lower price abroad than at home.

Duopoly   An oligopoly of two firms.

Economic efficiency   The situation in which the marginal rate of transformation in production equals the marginal rate of substitution in consumption for every pair of commodities and for every pair of individuals consuming both commodities.

Economic growth   The increase in resources, commodities, and incomes, and the improvements in technology over time.

Economic rent That portion of a payment made to the supplier of an input that is in excess of what is necessary to retain the input in its present employment in the long run.

Economic resources Resources that are limited in supply or scarce and thus command a price.

Economics A field of study that deals with the allocation of scarce resources among alternative uses to satisfy human wants.

Economies of scope The lowering of costs that a firm often experiences when it produces two or more products jointly rather than separate firms producing the products independently.

Edgeworth box diagram A diagram constructed from the indifference map diagrams of two individuals, which can be used to analyze voluntary exchange.

Edgeworth box diagram for exchange A diagram constructed from the indifference curves diagram of two individuals, which can be used to analyze voluntary exchange.

Edgeworth box diagram for production A diagram constructed from the isoquants diagram of two commodities, which can be used to analyze general equilibrium of production.

Efficiency The situation where the price of a commodity (which measures the marginal benefit to consumers) equals the marginal cost of producing the commodity.

Efficiency wage theory Postulates that firms willingly pay higher-than-equilibrium wages to induce workers to avoid *shirking,* or slacking off on the job.

Effluent fee A tax that a firm must pay for discharging waste or polluting.

Endowment position The quantity of a commodity that the consumer receives in each year.

Engel curve Shows the amount of a good that a consumer would purchase at various income levels.

Engel's law Postulates that the proportion of total expenditures on food declines as family income rises.

Entrepreneurship The introduction of new technologies and products to exploit perceived profit opportunities.

Environmental pollution The lowering of air, water, scenic, and noise qualities of the world around us that results from the dumping of waste products. It arises because of unclearly defined property rights and too-high transaction costs.

Equilibrium The condition that, once achieved, tends to persist. It occurs when the quantity demanded of a commodity equals the quantity supplied and the market clears.

Equilibrium price The price at which the quantity demanded equals the quantity supplied of a good or service.

Excess capacity The difference between the output indicated by the lowest point on the *LAC* curve and the output actually produced by a monopolistically competitive firm when in long-run equilibrium.

Excess demand The amount by which the quantity demanded of a commodity is larger than the quantity supplied of the commodity at below-equilibrium prices; with a tradable commodity, it gives the quantity demanded of imports of the commodity.

Excess supply The amount by which the quantity supplied of a commodity is larger than the quantity demanded of the commodity at above-equilibrium prices; for a tradable commodity, it gives the quantity supplied of exports of the commodity.

Exchange The trade of one good for another through the medium of money.

Exchange rate The price of a unit of a foreign currency in terms of the domestic currency.

Excise tax A tax on each unit of the commodity.

Exhaustible resources Nonrenewable resour-ces, such as petroleum and other minerals, which are available in fixed quantities and are nonreplenishable.

Expansion path The line joining the origin with the points of tangency of isoquants and isocost lines with input prices held constant. It shows the least-cost input combination to produce various output levels.

Expected income ($\bar{I}$) The probability of one level of income (p) times that income level plus the probability of an alternative income ($1 - p$) times that alternative income level.

Expected utility   The sum of the product of the utility of each possible outcome of a decision or strategy and the probability of its occurrence.

Expected value   The sum of the products of each possible outcome of a decision or strategy and the probability of its occurrence.

Expected value of money   The sum of the product of the amount of money involved from each possible outcome of a decision or strategy and the probability of its occurrence.

Experience goods   Goods whose quality can only be judged after using them.

Experimental economics   The newly developing field of economics that seeks to determine how real markets operate by examining how paid volunteers behave within a simple experimental institutional framework.

Explicit costs   The actual expenditures of the firm to purchase or hire inputs.

External benefits   Beneficial side effects received by those not directly involved in the production or consumption of a commodity.

External costs   Harmful side effects borne by those not directly involved in the production or consumption of a commodity.

External diseconomies of consumption   Uncompensated costs borne by those not directly involved in the consumption of a commodity.

External diseconomies of production   Uncompensated costs borne by those not directly involved in the production of a commodity.

External diseconomy   An upward shift in all firms' per-unit cost curves resulting from an increase in input prices as the industry expands.

External economies of consumption   Uncom-pensated benefits received by those not directly involved in the consumption of a commodity.

External economies of production   Uncom-pensated benefits received by those not directly involved in the production of a commodity.

External economy   A downward shift in all firms' per-unit cost curves resulting from a decline in input prices as the industry expands.

Externalities   Harmful or beneficial side effects borne by those not directly involved in the production or consumption of a commodity.

Firm   An organization that combines and organizes resources for the purpose of producing goods and services for sale at a profit.

First-degree price discrimination   The charging of the highest price for each unit of a commodity that each consumer is willing to pay rather than go without it.

First theorem of welfare economics   Postulates that equilibrium in competitive markets is Pareto optimum.

Fixed inputs   The resources that cannot be varied or can be varied only with excessive cost during the time period under consideration.

Food stamp program   A federal program under which eligible low-income families receive free food stamps to purchase food.

For whom to produce   The way that output is distributed among the members of society.

Foreign-exchange market   The market where national currencies are bought and sold.

Foreign-exchange rate   The price of a unit of a foreign currency in terms of the domestic currency.

Forward contract   An agreement to purchase or sell a specific amount of a foreign currency at a rate specified today for delivery at a specified future date.

Forward or futures transaction   The purchase and sale of a commodity or currency for future delivery at a price agreed upon today.

Forward or futures market   The market where forward transactions take place.

Forward or futures price or rate   The price or rate at which a commodity or currency is bought and sold in the forward market.

Free-enterprise system   The form of market organization where economic decisions are made by individuals and firms.

Free-rider problem   The problem that arises when an individual does not contribute to the payment of a public good, in the belief that it will be provided anyway.

Fringe benefits   Goods and services provided to employees and paid by employers.

Futures contract   A standardized forward contract for predetermined quantities of the currency and selected calendar dates.

Gambler   An individual who is willing to pay a small sum of money in order to have the small probability of a large gain or win; a risk seeker or lover.

Game theory   The theory that examines the choice of optimal strategies in conflict situations.

General equilibrium analysis   Studies the interdependence that exists among all markets in the economy.

Giffen good   An inferior good for which the positive substitution effect is smaller than the negative income effect, so less of the good is purchased when its price falls.

Gini coefficient   A measure of income inequality calculated from the Lorenz curve and ranging from 0 (for perfect equality) to 1 (for perfect inequality).

Globalization of economic activity   The increasing proportion of consumer goods, and parts and components of manufactured goods imported from abroad; the increasing share of domestic production exported; and the rising repercussions of domestic policies on other nations.

Golden parachute   A large financial settlement paid out by a firm to its managers if they are forced or choose to leave as a result of a takeover that greatly increases the value of the firm.

Good   A commodity of which more is preferred to less.

Government failures   Situations where government policies do not reflect the public's interests and reduce rather than increase social welfare.

Grand utility-possibilities frontier   The envelope to utility-possibilities frontiers at Pareto optimum points of production and exchange.

Hedging   The covering of risks arising from changes in future commodity and currency prices.

Herfindahl index   A measure of the degree of monopoly power in an industry, which is given by the sum of the squared values of the market sales shares of all the firms in the industry.

Homogeneous of degree 1   In production, it refers to constant returns to scale.

How to produce   The way resources or inputs are combined to produce the goods and services that consumers want.

Human wants   All the goods, services, and the conditions of life that individuals desire, which provide the driving force for economic activity.

Identification problem   The difficulty sometimes encountered in estimating the market demand or supply curve of a commodity from quantity–price observations.

Implicit costs   The value of the inputs owned and used by the firm; value is imputed from the best alternative use of the inputs.

Import tariff   A per-unit tax on an imported commodity.

Incidence of tax   The relative burden of a tax on buyers and sellers.

Income–consumption curve   The locus of consumer optimum points resulting when only the consumer's income varies.

Income effect   The increase in the quantity purchased of a good resulting only from the increase in real income that accompanies a price decline.

Income elasticity of demand (η_I)   The percentage change in the quantity purchased of a commodity over a specific period of time divided by the percentage change in consumers' income.

Income elasticity of demand for imports   The percentage change in the demand for imports by a nation over a specific period of time divided by the percentage change in the income of the nation.

Income elasticity of demand for exports   The percentage change in the demand for the exports of a nation over a specific period of time divided by the percentage change in the income of other nations.

Income or expenditure index (E)   The ratio of period-1 to base-period money income or expenditures.

Increasing-cost industry   An industry with a positively sloped long-run supply curve. It results if input prices rise as industry output expands.

Increasing returns to scale   Output changes by a larger proportion than inputs.

Indifference curve   The curve showing the various combinations of two commodities that give the consumer equal satisfaction and among which the consumer is indifferent.

Indifference map The entire set of indifference curves reflecting the consumer's tastes and preferences.

Individual's demand curve Shows the quantity that the individual would purchase of a good per unit of time at various alternative prices of the good while keeping everything else constant.

Inferior good A good of which a consumer purchases less with an increase in income.

Information superhighway The ability of researchers, firms, and consumers to hook up with libraries, databases, and marketing information through a national high-speed computer network and have at their fingertips a vast amount of information as never before.

Inputs The resources or factors of production used to produce goods and services.

Insurer An individual who is willing to pay a small sum of money in order to ensure against the small probability of a large loss; a risk averter.

Interdependence The relationship among all markets in the economy such that a change in any of them affects all the others.

Intermediate good The output of a firm or industry that is the input of another firm or industry producing final commodities.

Internalizing external costs The process whereby an external cost becomes part of the regular business expense of a firm.

International economies of scale The lower costs resulting from a firm's integration of its entire system of manufacturing operations around the world.

Internationalization of economic activity The trend toward producing and distributing goods throughout the world.

Internet A collection of thousands of computers, businesses, and millions of people throughout the world linked together in a service called the World Wide Web.

Intraindustry trade International trade in the differentiated products of the same industry or broad product group.

Investment The formation of new capital assets.

Investment in human capital Any activity, such as education and training, that increases an individual's productivity.

Isocost line Shows the various combinations of two inputs that the firm can hire with a given total cost outlay.

Isoquant A curve showing the various combinations of two inputs that can be used to produce a specific level of output.

Kaldor–Hicks criterion Postulates that a change is an improvement if those who gain from the change can fully compensate the losers and still retain some of the gain.

Kinked–demand curve model The model that seeks to explain price rigidity by postulating a demand curve with a kink at the prevailing price.

Labor or human resources The different types of skilled and unskilled workers that can be used in the production of goods and services.

Labor union An organization of workers devoted to increasing the wages and welfare of its members through bargaining with employers.

Land or natural resources The land, its fertility, mineral deposits, and forests that can be used to produce goods and services.

Laspeyres price index (L) The ratio of the cost of purchasing base-period quantities at period-1 prices relative to base-period prices.

Law of demand The inverse price–quantity relationship illustrated by the negative slope of the demand curve.

Law of diminishing marginal utility Each additional unit of a good eventually gives less and less extra utility.

Law of diminishing returns After a point, the marginal product of the variable input declines.

Law of the invisible hand The law stated by Adam Smith over 200 years ago that postulates that in a free market economy, each individual by pursuing his or her own selfish interests is led, as if by an invisible hand, to promote the welfare of society more so than he or she intends or even understands.

Learning curve   The curve showing the decline in average costs with rising cumulative total outputs over time.

Least-cost input combination   The condition where the marginal product per dollar spent on each input is equal. Graphically, it is the point where an isoquant is tangent to an isocost line.

Lerner index   A measure of the degree of a firm's monopoly power, which is given by the ratio of the difference between price and marginal cost to price.

Limit pricing   The charging of a sufficiently low price by existing firms to discourage entry into the industry.

Long run   The time period when all inputs can be varied.

Long-run average cost (*LAC*)   The minimum per-unit cost of producing any level of output when a firm can build any desired scale of plant. It equals long-run total cost divided by output.

Long-run marginal cost (*LMC*)   The change in long-run total costs per unit change in output; the slope of the *LTC* curve.

Long-run total cost (*LTC*)   The minimum total cost of producing various levels of output when a firm can build any desired scale of plant.

Lorenz curve   A curve showing income inequality by measuring cumulative percentages of total income along the vertical axis, for various cumulative percentages of the population (from the lowest to the highest income) measured along the horizontal axis.

Luxury   A commodity with income elasticity of demand greater than 1.

Macroeconomic theory   The study of the total, or *aggregate,* level of output, national income, national employment, consumption, investment, and prices for the economy *viewed as a whole.*

Marginal analysis   The analysis based on the application of the marginal concept according to which net benefits increase as long as the marginal benefit exceeds the marginal cost and until they are equal.

Marginal benefit   The change in the total benefit, or extra benefit, resulting from an economic action.

Marginal cost   The change in the total cost, or extra cost, resulting from an economic action.

Marginal expenditure (*ME*)   The extra expenditure for or cost of hiring an additional unit of an input.

Marginal expenditure on capital (*ME_K*)   The extra expenditure for or cost of hiring an additional unit of capital.

Marginal expenditure on labor (*ME_L*)   The extra expenditure for or cost of hiring an additional unit of labor.

Marginal product (*MP*)   The change in total product per unit change in the variable input used.

Marginal productivity theory   The theory according to which each input is paid a price equal to its marginal productivity.

Marginal rate of substitution (*MRS*)   The amount of a good that a consumer is willing to give up for an additional unit of another good while remaining on the same indifference curve.

Marginal rate of technical substitution (*MRTS*)   The absolute value of the slope of the isoquant. It also equals the ratio of the marginal product of the two inputs.

Marginal rate of transformation of *X* for *Y* (*MRT_XY*)   The amount of *Y* that must be given up to release just enough labor and capital to produce one additional unit of *X*. It is equal to the absolute value of the slope of the production-possibilities frontier and to the ratio of the marginal cost of *X* to the marginal cost of *Y*.

Marginal revenue (*MR*)   The change in total revenue per unit change in the quantity sold.

Marginal revenue product (*MRP*)   The marginal physical product of the input (*MP*) multiplied by the marginal revenue of the commodity (*MR*).

Marginal utility (*MU*)   The extra utility received from consuming one additional unit of a good.

Market   An institutional arrangement under which buyers and sellers can exchange some quantity of a good or service at a mutually agreeable price.

Market demand curve   Shows the quantity demanded of a commodity in the market per time period at various alternative prices of the commodity while holding everything else constant.

Market demand schedule   A table showing the quantity of a commodity that consumers are willing and able to purchase during a given period of time at each price while holding constant all other relevant economic variables on which demand depends.

Market failures   The existence of monopoly, monopsony, price controls, externalities, and public goods that prevent the attainment of economic efficiency or Pareto optimum.

Market line   A line from any point on the production-possibilities curve showing the various amounts of a commodity that the individual can consume in each period by borrowing or lending.

Market period   The time period during which the market supply of a commodity is fixed. Also called the *very short run*.

Market-sharing cartel   An organization of suppliers of a commodity that overtly or tacitly divides the market among its members.

Market signaling   Signals that convey product quality, good insurance or credit risks, and high productivity.

Market supply curve   The graphic representation of the market supply schedule showing the quantity supplied of a commodity per time period at each commodity price, while holding constant all other relevant economic variables on which supply depends.

Market supply schedule   A table showing the quantity supplied of a commodity at each price for a given period of time while holding constant technology, resource prices, and, for agricultural commodities, weather conditions.

Marketing research approaches to demand estimation   The estimation of consumer demand for a product or service by consumer surveys, consumer clinics, or market experiments.

Markup   The percentage over average cost in cost-plus pricing.

Maximum social welfare   The point at which a social indifference curve is tangent to the grand utility-possibilities frontier; also called *constrained bliss*.

Methodology of economics   The proposition that a model is tested by its predictive ability, the consistency of its assumptions, and the logic with which the predictions follow from the assumptions.

Microeconomic theory   The study of the economic behavior of *individual* decision-making units such as individual consumers, resource owners, and business firms, and the operation of individual markets in a free-enterprise economy.

Micromarketing   Narrowing a marketing strategy to the individual store or consumer.

Minimal income maintenance   The transfer or subsidy going to families that have no other income under a negative income-tax program.

Minimum efficient scale (*MES*)   The smallest quantity at which the *LAC* curve reaches its minimum.

Mixed economy   An economy, such as that in the United States, characterized by private enterprise and government actions and regulations.

Mixed strategy   The best strategy for each player in a non–strictly determined game.

Model   Another name for theory, or the set of assumptions from which the result of an event is deduced or predicted.

Monopolistic competition   The form of market organization in which there are many sellers of a differentiated product and entry into or exit from the market is rather easy in the long run.

Monopolistic exploitation   The excess of an input's value of marginal product over its marginal revenue product at the level of utilization of the input.

Monopsonistic competition   The situation where there are many firms hiring a differentiated input.

Monopsonistic exploitation   The excess of the marginal revenue product of an input over the price of the input at the level of utilization of the input.

Monopsony   A single buyer of an input.

Moral hazard   The increased probability of a loss when an economic agent can shift some of its costs to others.

Multiple regression   A statistical technique that allows the economist to disentangle the independent effects of the various determinants of demand so as to identify from the data the average market demand curve for the commodity.

Nash equilibrium   The situation when each player has chosen his or her optimal strategy, *given the strategy chosen by the other player.*

Natural monopoly   The case of declining long-run average costs over a sufficiently large range of outputs so as to leave a single firm supplying the entire market.

Necessity   A commodity with income elasticity of demand between 0 and 1.

Negative income tax (*NIT*)   A type of welfare program involving declining cash transfers to low-income families as the family's earned income rises.

Net present value (*NPV*)   The value today from the stream of net cash flows (positive and negative) from an investment project.

Neuter   A commodity of which an individual is indifferent between having more or less.

Nominal rate of interest (*r′*)   The real rate of interest plus the anticipated rate of price inflation.

Nonclearing markets theory   Theories that seek to explain the persistence of surpluses and shortages in some real-world markets.

Noncompeting groups   Occupations requiring different capacities, skills, education, and training and, therefore, receiving different wages.

Nonexclusion   The situation in which it is impossible or prohibitively expensive to confine the benefit or the consumption of a good (once produced) to selected people (such as only to those paying for it).

Nonexhaustible resources   Renewable resour-ces, such as fertile land, forests, rivers, and fish, which need never be depleted if they are properly managed.

Nonprice competition   Competition based on advertising and product differentiation rather than on price.

Nonrival consumption   The distinguishing characteristic of a public good whereby its consumption by some individuals does not reduce the amount available to others.

Nonzero-sum game   A game where the gains of one player do not come at the expense of or are not equal to the losses of the other player.

Normal good   A good of which the consumer purchases more with an increase in income.

Normative analysis   The study of what *ought* to be or how the basic economic functions *should* be performed. It is based both on positive economics and value judgments.

Oligopoly   The form of market organization in which there are few firms selling either a homogeneous or a differentiated product.

Oligopsony   The form of market organization in which few firms are hiring either a homogeneous or a differentiated input.

Open innovation model   The situation where companies commercialize both their own ideas and innovations as well as the innovations of other firms and deploy external as well as internal, or in-house, pathways to market.

Opportunity cost   What an input could earn in its best alternative use.

Ordinal utility   The rankings of the utility received by an individual from consuming various amounts of a good or various baskets of goods.

Output elasticity of capital   The percentage increase in output resulting from a 1% increase in the quantity of capital used. For the Cobb–Douglas production function, this is given by the exponent of K.

Output elasticity of labor   The percentage increase in output resulting from a 1% increase in the quantity of labor used. For the Cobb–Douglas production function, this is given by the exponent of L.

Overtime pay   The higher hourly wage of many workers for working additional hours after the regular workday.

Paasche price index (*P*)   The ratio of the cost of purchasing period-1 quantities at period-1 prices relative to base-period prices.

Pareto criterion   Postulates that a change increases social welfare if it benefits some members of society (in their own judgment) without harming anyone.

Pareto optimality   The situation in which no reorganization of production and consumption is possible by which some individuals are made better off without making someone else worse off.

Pareto optimum   The situation in which no reorganization of production or consumption can lead to an increase in the welfare of some without at the same time reducing the welfare of others.

Partial equilibrium analysis   Studies the behavior of individual decision-making units and individual markets, viewed in isolation.

Payoff   The outcome or consequence of each combination of strategies by the players in game theory.

Payoff matrix   The table of all the outcomes of the players' strategies.

Peak-load pricing   Refers to the charging of a price equal to short-run marginal cost, both in the peak period, when demand and marginal cost are higher, and in the off-peak period, when both are lower.

Perfectly competitive market   A market where no buyer or seller can affect the price of the product, all units of the product are homogeneous, resources are mobile, and knowledge of the market is perfect.

Planning horizon   The time period when a firm can build any desired scale of plant; the long run.

Players   The decision makers in the theory of games (here, the oligopolistic firm or its managers) whose behavior we are trying to explain and predict.

Point elasticity of demand   The price elasticity of demand at a specific point on the demand curve.

Positive analysis   The study of what *is* or how the economic system performs the basic economic functions. It is entirely statistical in nature and devoid of ethical or value judgments.

Price ceiling   The maximum price allowed for a commodity. If the price ceiling is below the equilibrium price, it leads to a shortage of the commodity.

Price-consumption curve   The locus of consumer optimum points resulting when only the price of a good varies.

Price discrimination   Charging different prices (for different quantities of a commodity or in different markets) that are not justified by cost differences.

Price elasticity of demand (η)   The percentage change in the quantity demanded of a commodity during a specific period of time divided by the percentage change in its price.

Price elasticity of demand for imports   The percentage change in the quantity purchased of imports by a nation divided by the percentage change in their prices.

Price elasticity of demand for exports   The percentage change in the quantity purchased of a nation's exports divided by the percentage change in the price of the nation's exports.

Price elasticity of supply (ϵ)   The percentage change in the quantity supplied of a commodity during a specific period of time divided by the percentage change in its price.

Price floor   A minimum price for a commodity. If the price floor is above the equilibrium price, it leads to a surplus of the commodity.

Price leadership   The form of market collusion in oligopolistic markets whereby the firm that serves as the price leader initiates a price change and the other firms in the industry soon match it.

Price system   The system whereby the organization and coordination of economic activity is determined by commodity and resource prices.

Price theory   Another name for microeconomic theory that stresses the importance of prices in the determination of what goods are produced and in what quantities, the organization of production, and the distribution of output or income.

Principal-agent problem   The fact that the agents (managers and workers) of a firm seek to maximize their own benefits (such as salaries) rather than the total profits or value of the firm, which is the owners' or principals' interest.

Prisoners' dilemma   The situation where each player adopts his or her dominant strategy but could do better by cooperating.

Private costs   The costs incurred by individuals and firms.

Probability   The chance or odds that an event will occur.

Probability distribution   The list of all possible outcomes of a decision or strategy and the probability attached to each.

Producer surplus   The excess of the market price of the commodity over the marginal cost of production.

Product group   The sellers of a differentiated product.

Product cycle model   The introduction of new products by firms in an advanced nation, which are then copied and produced by firms in lower-wage countries.

Product innovation   The introduction of new or improved products.

Process innovation   The introduction of new or improved production processes.

Production   The transformation of resources or inputs into outputs of goods and services.

Production function   The unique relationship between inputs and outputs represented by a table, graph, or equation showing the maximum output of a commodity that can be produced per period of time with each set of inputs.

Production-possibilities frontier or transformation curve   Shows the alternative combinations of commodities that a nation can produce by fully utilizing all of its resources with the best technology available to it.

Product variation   Differences in some of the characteristics of differentiated products.

Public goods   Commodities for which consumption by some individuals does not reduce the amount available to others. That is, once the good is provided for someone, others can consume it at no additional cost.

Pure monopoly   The form of market organization in which there is a single seller of a commodity for which there are no close substitutes.

Pure oligopoly   An oligopoly in which the product of the firms in the industry is homogeneous.

Quasi-rent   The return or payment to inputs that are fixed in the short run (i.e., $TR - TVC$).

Rate of interest (r)   The premium received in one year for lending one dollar this year.

Rational consumer   An individual who seeks to maximize utility or satisfaction in spending his or her income.

Rational ignorance   The condition whereby voters are much less informed about political decisions than about their individual market decisions because of the higher costs of obtaining information and the smaller direct benefits that they obtain from the former than from the latter.

Rationing   Quantitative restrictions imposed by the government on the amount of a good that an individual can purchase per unit of time.

Rationing over time   The allocation of a given amount of a commodity over time.

Reaction function   A formula that shows how a duopolist reacts to the other duopolist's action.

Real rate of interest (r)   The premium on a unit of a commodity or real consumption income today compared to a unit of the commodity or real consumption income in the future.

Relative price   The price of one good in terms of that of another.

Repeated games   Prisoners' dilemma games of more than one move.

Ridge lines   The lines that separate the relevant (i.e., the negatively sloped) from the irrelevant (or the positively sloped) portions of the isoquants.

Risk   The situation where there is more than one possible outcome to a decision and the probability of each possible outcome is known or can be estimated.

Risk averter   An individual for whom the marginal utility of money diminishes; he or she would not accept a fair bet.

Risk neutral   An individual for whom the marginal utility of money is constant; he or she is indifferent to a fair bet.

Risk premium   The maximum amount that a risk-averse individual would be willing to pay to avoid a risk.

Risk–return indifference curve   A curve showing the various risk–return combinations among which a manager or investor is indifferent.

Risk seeker or lover   An individual for whom the marginal utility of money increases; he or she would accept a fair bet and even some unfair bets.

Saddle point   The solution or outcome of a strictly determined game.

Saving   Refraining from present consumption.

Scitovsky criterion   Postulates that a change is an improvement if it satisfies the Kaldor–Hicks criterion and if, after the change, a movement back to the original position does not satisfy the Kaldor–Hicks criterion.

Search costs   The time and money spent seeking information about a product.

Search goods   Goods whose quality can be evaluated by inspection at the time of purchase.

Second-degree price discrimination   Charging a lower price for each additional batch or block of the commodity.

Second theorem of welfare economics   Postulates that equity in distribution is logically separable from efficiency in allocation.

Selling expenses   Expenditures (such as advertising) that the firm incurs to induce consumers to purchase more of its product.

Separation theorem   The independence of the optimum investment decision from the individual's preferences.

Sherman Antitrust Act   Prohibits all contracts and combinations in restraint of trade and all attempts to monopolize the market.

Shortage   The excess quantity demanded of a commodity at lower than equilibrium prices.

Short run   The time period when at least one input is fixed.

Shutdown point   The output level at which price equals average variable cost and losses equal total fixed costs, whether the firm produces or not. Also, the lowest point on the AVC curve, at which $MC = AVC$.

Snob effect   The situation where some people demand a smaller quantity of a commodity as more people consume it in order to be different and exclusive.

Social costs   The costs incurred by society as a whole.

Specialization   The use of labor and other resources to perform those tasks in which each resource is most efficient.

Speculator   An individual or firm that buys a commodity or currency when it expects the price to rise, and sells the commodity or currency if it expects the price to fall.

Spot market   The market where spot transactions take place.

Spot price or rate   The price or rate of a commodity or currency in the spot market.

Spot transaction   The purchase and sale of a commodity or currency for immediate delivery and payment.

Stackelberg model   The extension of the Cournot model in which one duopolist knows how the other behaves and, by using this information, earns higher profits than in the Cournot solution, at the expense of the other duopolist.

Standard deviation (sd)   A measure of the dispersion of possible outcomes from the expected value of a distribution; the square root of the variance.

Strategies   The potential choices that can be made by the players (firms) in the theory of games.

Strategic move   A player's strategy of constraining his or her own behavior to make a threat credible so as to gain a competitive advantage.

Strategic trade policy   The attempt by a nation to create a comparative advantage in some high-tech field through temporary trade protection, subsidies, tax benefits, and cooperative government–industry programs.

Substitutes   Two commodities are substitutes if an increase in the price of one of them leads to more of the other being purchased.

Substitution effect   The increase in the quantity demanded of a good when its price falls, resulting only from the relative price decline and independent of the change in real income.

Surplus   The excess quantity supplied of a commodity at higher than equilibrium prices.

Technical externalities   Economies of scale.

Technological progress   Refers to the development of new and better production techniques to make a given, improved, or entirely new product.

Theory of contestable markets   The theory that postulates that even if an industry has only one or a few firms, it would still operate as if it were perfectly competitive if entry into the industry is absolutely free and if exit is entirely costless.

Theory of public choice   The study of how government decisions are made and implemented.

Theory of revealed preference   The theory that postulates that a consumer's indifference curve can be derived from the consumer's market behavior and without any need to inquire directly into his or her preferences.

Third-degree price discrimination   Charging a higher price for a commodity in the one market of two that has the less elastic demand in such a way as to equalize the *MR* of the last unit of the commodity sold in the two markets.

Tit-for-tat   The best strategy in repeated prisoners' dilemma games, which postulates, "Do to your opponent what he or she has just done to you."

Time budget line   A line showing the various combinations of two goods that an individual can obtain with his or her available time.

Total costs (*TC*)   *TFC* plus *TVC*.

Total fixed costs (*TFC*)   The total obligations of a firm per time period for all fixed inputs.

Total product (*TP*)   Total output.

Total revenue (*TR*)   The price of a commodity times the quantity sold of the commodity.

Total utility (*TU*)   The aggregate amount of satisfaction received from consuming various amounts of a good or baskets of goods.

Total variable costs (*TVC*)   The total obligations of a firm per time period for all the variable inputs the firm uses.

Transfer pricing   The determination of the price of intermediate products sold by one semiautonomous division of a firm to another semiautonomous division of the same enterprise.

Two-part tariff   The pricing practice whereby a monopolist maximizes its total profits by charging a usage fee or price equal to its marginal cost and an initial or membership fee equal to the entire consumer surplus.

Tying   The requirement that a consumer who buys or leases a monopolist's product also puchase another product needed in the use of the first.

Uncertainty   The situation where there is more than one possible outcome to a decision and the probability of each specific outcome is not known or even meaningful.

Unemployment gap   The excess in the quantity supplied over the quantity demanded of labor at above-equilibrium wages.

Util   The arbitrary unit of measure of utility.

Utility   The ability of a good to satisfy a want.

Utility-possibilities frontier   Shows the various combinations of utilities received by two individuals at which the economy (composed of the two individuals) is in general equilibrium or Pareto optimum in exchange.

Value of the marginal product (*VMP*)   The marginal (physical) product of the input (*MP*) multiplied by the commodity price (*P*).

Variability risk   The possibility that the return on an investment, such as on a stock, may vary considerably above or below the average.

Variable inputs   The resources that can be varied easily and on short notice during the time period under consideration.

Veblen effect   The situation in which some people purchase more of certain commodities the more expensive they are; also called *conspicuous consumption*.

Virtual corporation   A temporary network of independent companies coming together, with each contributing its core technology to take quickly advantage of fast-changing opportunities.

Voluntary export restraints (VER)   The situation in which an importing country induces another nation to reduce its exports of a commodity "voluntarily" under the threat of higher all-around trade restrictions.

Water–diamond paradox   The question of why water, which is essential to life, is so cheap while diamonds, which are not essential, are so expensive.

Wealth   The individual's income this year plus the present value of future income.

Welfare economics   Examines the conditions for economic efficiency in the production of output and in the exchange of commodities and for equity in the distribution of income.

What to produce   Which goods and services a society chooses to produce and in what quantities.

Winner's curse   The overbidding or the paying of a price higher than the true (but unknown) value of an asset by the highest bidder at an auction.

Zero-sum game   A game where the gains of one player equal the losses of the other (so that total gains plus total losses sum to zero).

NAME INDEX

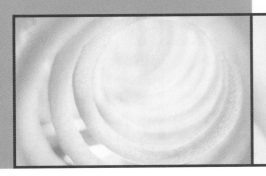

SUBJECT INDEX